Fundamentals of Abnormal Psychology

ninth edition

RONALD J. COMER | JONATHAN S. COMER

Princeton University   Florida International University

worth publishers
Macmillan Learning
New York

Senior Vice President, Content Strategy: Charles Linsmeier
Program Director, Social Sciences: Shani Fisher
Executive Program Manager: Matt Wright
Senior Development Editor: Mimi Melek
Assistant Editor: Un Hye Kim
Senior Marketing Manager: Clay Bolton
Marketing Assistant: Chelsea Simens
Director of Media Editorial & Assessment, Social Sciences: Noel Hohnstine
Media Editor: Stefani Wallace
Media Project Manager: Eve Conte
Director, Content Management Enhancement: Tracey Kuehn
Senior Managing Editor: Lisa Kinne
Senior Content Project Manager: Martha Emry
Senior Workflow Project Supervisor: Susan Wein
Photo Editor: Jennifer Atkins
Permissions Manager: Jennifer MacMillan
Permissions Associate: Michael McCarty
Director of Design, Content Management: Diana Blume
Design Services Manager: Natasha A.S. Wolfe
Cover Design: John Callahan
Text Design and Infographics: Charles Yuen
Layout Designer: Paul Lacy
Art Manager: Matthew McAdams
Composition: Lumina Datamatics, Inc.
Printing and Binding: LSC Communications
Cover: Lucille Clerc/Illustration (USA) Inc.

Library of Congress Control Number: 2018951322

ISBN-13: 978-1-319-12669-8
ISBN-10: 1-319-12669-3

Printed in the United States of America

1 2 3 4 5 6 22 21 20 19 18

Worth Publishers
One New York Plaza
Suite 4500
New York, NY 10004-1562
www.macmillanlearning.com

LHB Photo / Alamy

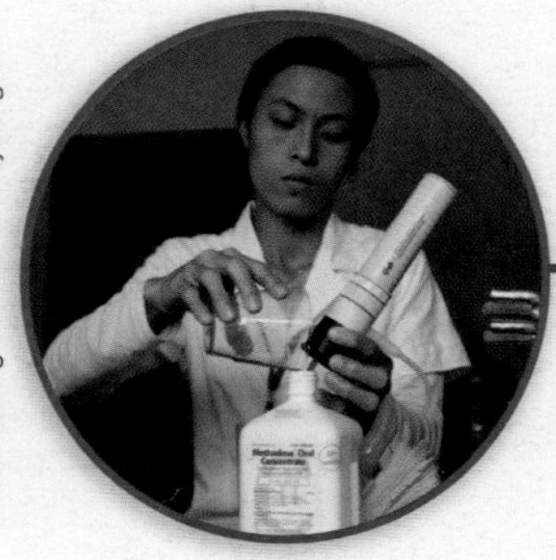
Chau Doan/LightRocket via Getty Images

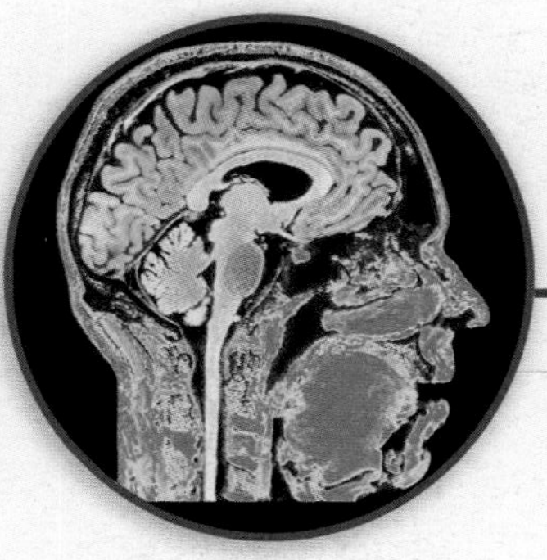
Du Cane Medical Imaging LTD./Science Photo Library/Getty Images

AP Photo/Jeff Chiu

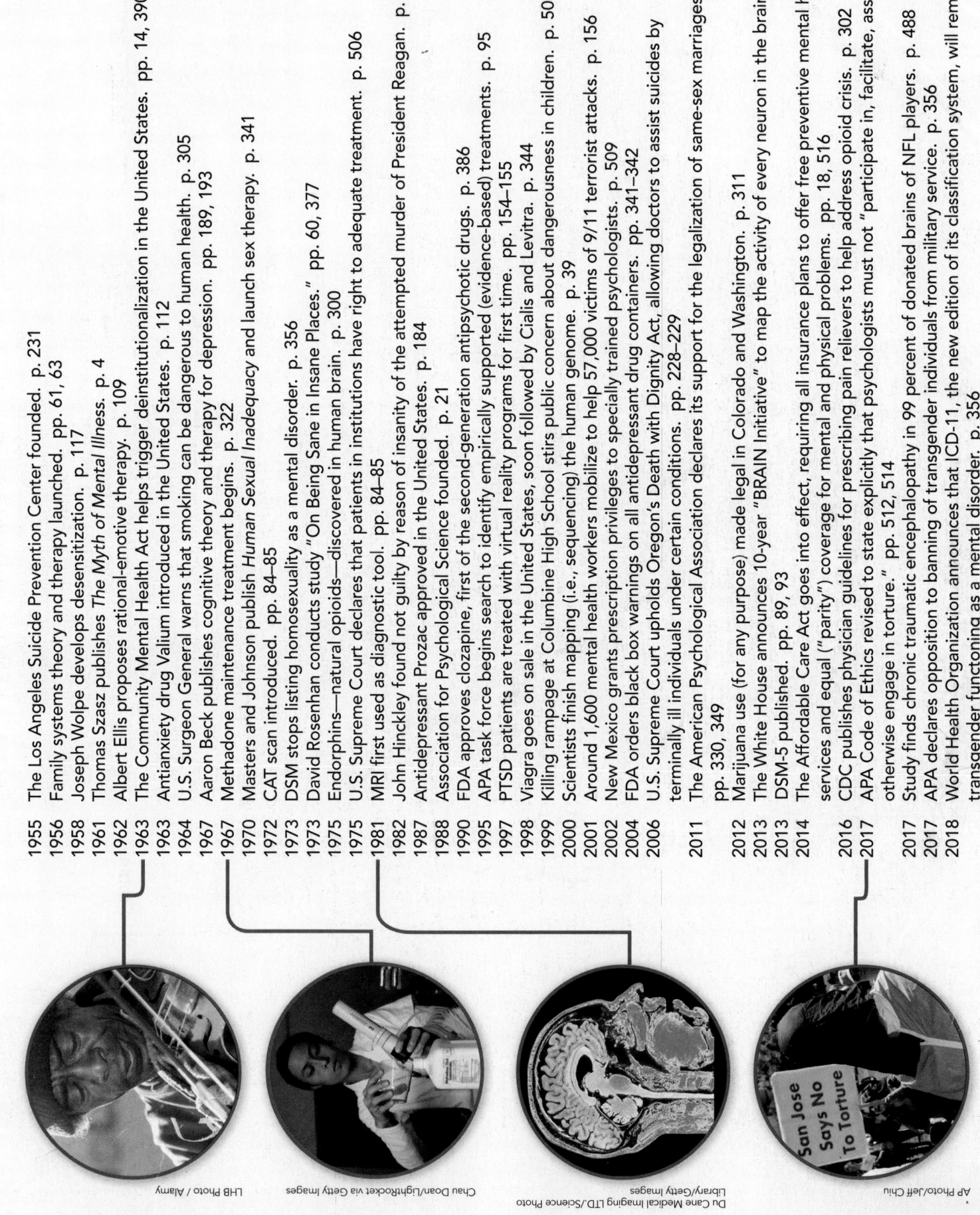

1955 The Los Angeles Suicide Prevention Center founded. p. 231
1956 Family systems theory and therapy launched. pp. 61, 63
1958 Joseph Wolpe develops desensitization. p. 117
1961 Thomas Szasz publishes *The Myth of Mental Illness*. p. 4
1962 Albert Ellis proposes rational-emotive therapy. p. 109
1963 The Community Mental Health Act helps trigger deinstitutionalization in the United States. pp. 14, 390
1963 Antianxiety drug Valium introduced in the United States. p. 112
1964 U.S. Surgeon General warns that smoking can be dangerous to human health. p. 305
1967 Aaron Beck publishes cognitive theory and therapy for depression. pp. 189, 193
1967 Methadone maintenance treatment begins. p. 322
1970 Masters and Johnson publish *Human Sexual Inadequacy* and launch sex therapy. p. 341
1972 CAT scan introduced. pp. 84–85
1973 DSM stops listing homosexuality as a mental disorder. p. 356
1973 David Rosenhan conducts study "On Being Sane in Insane Places." pp. 60, 377
1975 Endorphins—natural opioids—discovered in human brain. p. 300
1975 U.S. Supreme Court declares that patients in institutions have right to adequate treatment. p. 506
1981 MRI first used as diagnostic tool. pp. 84–85
1982 John Hinckley found not guilty by reason of insanity of the attempted murder of President Reagan. p. 497
1987 Antidepressant Prozac approved in the United States. p. 184
1988 Association for Psychological Science founded. p. 21
1990 FDA approves clozapine, first of the second-generation antipsychotic drugs. p. 386
1995 APA task force begins search to identify empirically supported (evidence-based) treatments. p. 95
1997 PTSD patients are treated with virtual reality programs for first time. pp. 154–155
1998 Viagra goes on sale in the United States, soon followed by Cialis and Levitra. p. 344
1999 Killing rampage at Columbine High School stirs public concern about dangerousness in children. p. 505
2000 Scientists finish mapping (i.e., sequencing) the human genome. p. 39
2001 Around 1,600 mental health workers mobilize to help 57,000 victims of 9/11 terrorist attacks. p. 156
2002 New Mexico grants prescription privileges to specially trained psychologists. p. 509
2004 FDA orders black box warnings on all antidepressant drug containers. pp. 341–342
2006 U.S. Supreme Court upholds Oregon's Death with Dignity Act, allowing doctors to assist suicides by terminally ill individuals under certain conditions. pp. 228–229
2011 The American Psychological Association declares its support for the legalization of same-sex marriages. pp. 330, 349
2012 Marijuana use (for any purpose) made legal in Colorado and Washington. p. 311
2013 The White House announces 10-year "BRAIN Initiative" to map the activity of every neuron in the brain. p. 37
2013 DSM-5 published. pp. 89, 93
2014 The Affordable Care Act goes into effect, requiring all insurance plans to offer free preventive mental health services and equal ("parity") coverage for mental and physical problems. pp. 18, 516
2016 CDC publishes physician guidelines for prescribing pain relievers to help address opioid crisis. p. 302
2017 APA Code of Ethics revised to state explicitly that psychologists must not "participate in, facilitate, assist, or otherwise engage in torture." pp. 512, 514
2017 Study finds chronic traumatic encephalopathy in 99 percent of donated brains of NFL players. p. 488
2017 APA declares opposition to banning of transgender individuals from military service. p. 356
2018 World Health Organization announces that ICD-11, the new edition of its classification system, will remove transgender functoning as a mental disorder. p. 356

With boundless love and appreciation,
to Marlene Comer and Jami Furr,
who fill our lives with love and joy.

About the Authors

Denise Applewhite

Courtesy Jon Comer

RONALD J. COMER has been a professor in Princeton University's Department of Psychology for the past 44 years, serving also as director of Clinical Psychology Studies and as chair of the university's Institutional Review Board. He has recently transitioned to emeritus status at the university. He has received the President's Award for Distinguished Teaching at Princeton, where his various courses in abnormal psychology have been among the university's most popular.

Professor Comer is also Clinical Associate Professor of Family Medicine and Community Health at Rutgers Robert Wood Johnson Medical School. He is a practicing clinical psychologist and a consultant to Eden Autism Services and to hospitals and family practice residency programs throughout New Jersey.

In addition to writing the textbooks *Fundamentals of Abnormal Psychology* (ninth edition), *Abnormal Psychology* (tenth edition), *Psychology Around Us* (second edition), and *Case Studies in Abnormal Psychology* (second edition), Professor Comer has published a range of journal articles and produced numerous widely used educational video programs, including *The Higher Education Video Library Series, The Video Anthology for Abnormal Psychology, Video Segments in Neuroscience, Introduction to Psychology Video Clipboard,* and *Developmental Psychology Video Clipboard.*

Professor Comer was an undergraduate at the University of Pennsylvania and a graduate student at Clark University. He currently lives in Lawrenceville, New Jersey, with his wife Marlene. From there he can keep a close eye on the often-frustrating Philadelphia sports teams with whom he grew up.

JONATHAN S. COMER is a professor of psychology at Florida International University, where he also directs the Mental Health Interventions and Technology (MINT) Program. He is President of the Society of Clinical Psychology (Division 12 of the American Psychological Association) and a leader in the field of clinical child and adolescent psychology. The author of 130 scientific papers and chapters, he has received career awards from the American Psychological Association, the Association for Psychological Science, and the Association for Behavioral and Cognitive Therapies for his research on innovative treatment methods, childhood anxiety and disruptive behaviors, and the impact of traumatic stress, disasters, and terrorism on children. His current work also focuses on ties between psychopathology, neurocircuitry, and the intergenerational transmission of psychological problems.

In addition to *Fundamentals of Abnormal Psychology* (ninth edition), Professor Comer has authored *Abnormal Psychology* (tenth edition) and *Childhood Disorders* (second edition) and edited *The Oxford Handbook of Research Strategies for Clinical Psychology*, among other books. He serves as Associate Editor of the journal *Behavior Therapy* and is on the Board of Directors of the Society of Clinical Child and Adolescent Psychology. He is a Fellow of the American Psychological Association, the Society of Clinical Psychology, and the Society for Child and Family Policy and Practice. He is also a practicing clinical psychologist.

Professor Comer was an undergraduate at the University of Rochester and a graduate student at Temple University. He currently lives in South Florida with his wife Jami and their children Delia and Emmett. He loves music—both playing and listening—and enjoys keeping an eye on the often-frustrating Philadelphia sports teams that his father taught him to love/hate.

Brief Contents

Abnormal Psychology in Science and Clinical Practice

Problems of Anxiety and Mood

Problems of the Mind and Body

Problems of Psychosis

Life-Span Problems

Conclusion

Contents

Preface

Ron Comer

I thought it was cute when my 13-year-old son Jon sometimes sat in on my 400-student Abnormal Psychology lectures at Princeton, interesting when he took his first psychology course at the University of Rochester, amusing when his undergraduate abnormal psychology course used my textbook, troubling when he autographed copies of the book for his classmates, surprising when he decided to major in psychology, and very satisfying when he entered the clinical psychology graduate program at Temple University. However, what Jon has accomplished professionally from that point forward has been nothing short of mind-boggling to me, and I am not easily mind-boggled.

He has become one of today's most productive and influential researchers, a leader in the clinical field, a magnificent teacher, and a deeply caring and wise clinician. Little of this has to do with me and everything to do with his intellectual gifts and remarkable work ethic, and the giants in the field who have mentored him over the years—particularly Dave Barlow, Phil Kendall, Dante Cicchetti, Bill Pelham, Anne Marie Albano, and Mark Olfson. Nevertheless, I'll take it.

At some point during Jon's flourishing career at Boston University and now Florida International University, an unstated question began to emerge: Should he join me as co-author on my abnormal psychology textbooks *Fundamentals of Abnormal Psychology* and *Abnormal Psychology*? I had never entertained the possibility of having a co-author during my 35 years of writing these textbooks; and anyway, I believed Jon was too busy making his mark on the field, receiving multiple career awards from the American Psychological Association and other organizations, being elected President of the APA's Society of Clinical Psychology, writing over 130 scientific papers, and the like. But, as the saying goes, "If you want to make God laugh, tell Him your future plans." Lo and behold, Jon and I are now co-authors of these books.

Ultimately, the decision to ask Jon to join me in this endeavor was a natural one. As textbook authors grow older, publishers seek out possible co-authors (for reasons that shall go unstated in order to protect my fragile ego and growing sense of mortality). It was clear to me that the ideal co-author would have to be a highly accomplished researcher and writer who would complement my particular areas of expertise and bring special knowledge in such areas as the developmental psychopathology perspective, technology-driven and novel treatment interventions, cognitive-behavioral approaches, brain circuitry, and more. And it was obvious that Jon was that person. Moreover, Jon was receiving offers from various publishing companies to author their abnormal psychology textbooks, and the notion of having a Comer textbook competing with another Comer textbook was simply too much for me to bear (did I mention my fragile ego?). And, of course, personally, the possibility of collaborating with someone whom I respect deeply and love greatly was too alluring to pass up. Thus, with the current editions of *Fundamentals of Abnormal Psychology* and *Abnormal Psychology*, Jon and I have begun a new journey, from which, we hope and believe, readers will learn much and profit greatly.

Jon Comer

Roughly two decades ago, I entered the University of Rochester with the intention of studying music. But I soon realized that, despite my continuing love of music, the study of clinical psychology fascinated me most. Two pivotal undergraduate experiences brought the clinical field to life for me and prompted me to realize that work in this area should eventually be at the center of my professional life.

The first experience was taking a psychology course with (and later working in the laboratory of) Dante Cicchetti, the contagiously passionate researcher and professor who introduced me to developmental psychopathology—his "neurons-to-neighborhoods" perspective that focuses on how dynamic interactions among psychological, biological, and sociocultural factors unfold across time to produce both normal and abnormal human functioning. I was excited by the power of this comprehensive perspective to explain individual differences, embrace interacting causal factors, and meaningfully inform prevention and treatment interventions. To this day, the developmental psychopathology perspective explicitly guides much of my research and thinking.

The second influential undergraduate experience was the power of a unique textbook. In the fall of my sophomore year, I enrolled in an abnormal psychology course and found a familiar name on the syllabus: "Comer". . . as in "the required text for this course is Ronald Comer's *Abnormal Psychology* (Second Edition)." At the time I did not have a particularly deep understanding of my father's work. I knew he worked very hard writing this book and that a great many colleges and universities had adopted it, but I had never sat down to read more than a few paragraphs here or there. But now, his book, cover-to-cover, was on my list of required readings.

As I read through the chapters for class, I became captivated by the book's engaging writing style, empathic descriptions of people with psychological disorders, blend of clinical research and practice, and strategic incorporation of current events and popular culture. I was also struck by how the book translated complex ideas into highly readable and easy to digest material. The book managed to present clinical psychology as a vibrant and evolving science, with many of the biggest answers still ahead. I was hooked; this was the field for me.

I recognize that it may seem like I was biased to be so favorably disposed toward this particular textbook, given the family connection. However, I would actually suggest the opposite—I was in my late teens at the time, and I must confess that I was not exactly looking to give my father copious credit for much during those years.

Over the past 20 years, from my time as a young undergraduate to my current academic and professional roles, I have been continually reminded that I am far from alone in my experiences with this extraordinary text. Countless individuals, from college freshmen to many of the field's senior leaders, have approached me to tell me what a special experience they have had with my father's textbook—whether as a student, as an instructor, or (like myself) as both.

When the opportunity arose to join *Fundamentals of Abnormal Psychology* and *Abnormal Psychology* as a co-author, it was a no-brainer for me. It has been a privilege to bring my particular background and areas of expertise to help expand these already outstanding books. For example, together my father and I have worked to incorporate the increasingly influential developmental psychopathology perspective throughout the books, along with a contemporary emphasis on biopsychosocial accounts of abnormality. As an instructor in psychology, I have always taken seriously my role as an ambassador for this field, someone who can introduce a captivating field to students, excite them about it, and provide them with insights that can influence their continued intellectual and professional development. Co-authoring the new editions of *Fundamentals of Abnormal Psychology* and *Abnormal Psychology* has provided me with a special opportunity to expand this ambassadorship and to reach a greater number of students than I could have previously imagined. I am very appreciative.

On a more personal note, the greatest joy of undertaking this project has been to do so under the mentorship of my father, Ronald Comer—a peerless educator and writer who has helped teach and cultivate so many individuals over the years. Working with him has given me a coveted front row seat to learn from the "master" about how to best communicate the complexities of the field and how to respectfully portray mental dysfunction and human suffering, all with his unique blend of empathy, dignity, and humor. He has mentored me on this project—as he has throughout so many experiences of my life—with great wisdom, common sense, patience, selflessness, and love. This field has no shortage of individuals who feel fortunate to have been touched by his inimitable gifts. But no one more so than me.

Ron & Jon Comer Between *Fundamentals of Abnormal Psychology* and *Abnormal Psychology*, the current textbook represents the nineteenth edition of one or the other of the books. This textbook journey has been a labor of love, but also one in which each edition is accompanied by an enormous amount of work and ridiculous pressure, not to mention countless sleepless nights. We mention these labors not only because we are world-class whiners but also to emphasize that we approach each edition as a totally new undertaking rather than as a superficial update of past editions. Our goal is to make each edition fresh by approaching our content coverage and pedagogical offerings as if we were writing a completely new book. As a result, each edition includes cutting-edge content reflecting new developments in the field, as well as in the world around us, delivered to readers via innovative and enlightening pedagogical techniques.

With this in mind, and with the addition of Jon's areas of expertise, we have added much new material and many exciting new features for this edition of *Fundamentals of Abnormal Psychology*—while at the same time retaining the successful themes, material, and techniques that have been embraced enthusiastically by past students and instructors. The result is, we believe, a book that will excite readers and speak to them and their times. We have tried to convey our passion for the field of abnormal psychology, and we have built on the generous feedback of our colleagues in this undertaking—the students and professors who have used this textbook over the years.

New and Expanded Features

This edition of *Fundamentals of Abnormal Psychology* reflects the many changes that have occurred over the past several years in the fields of abnormal psychology, education, and publishing, and in the world. Accordingly, we have introduced a number of new features and changes to the current edition.

•NEW• **Developmental Psychopathology Perspective** The *developmental psychopathology perspective* is introduced and applied throughout the book (for example, pages 68–69, 135–136, 151–152, and 317–318). This cutting-edge perspective—the clinical field's leading integrative perspective—uses a developmental framework to bring together the explanations and treatments of the various models, explaining how biological, psychological, and sociocultural factors may intersect and interact at key points throughout the life span to help produce both normal and abnormal functioning. Over the course of our discussions, readers will also come to appreciate that developmental factors are typically at work in both adult and child psychopathology. They will also come to recognize this perspective's principles of *prevention, resilience, equifinality*, and *multifinality*.

•NEW• **Brain Circuitry** *Brain circuits* are now at the center of the textbook's biological discussions of anxiety, posttraumatic stress, depressive, personality, and other disorders (for example, pages 38, 111, 125, 132, 149, 180, and 316–317). Over the past decade, researchers have made striking discoveries about brain circuits—networks of brain structures whose interconnectivity produces distinct behaviors, cognitions, and emotions. We discuss the particular kinds of brain circuit dysfunction that contribute to each of the psychological disorders. At the same time, we clarify how genetic factors, neurotransmitter activity, brain anatomy, and immune functioning interface with the operation of the brain circuits to produce psychological dysfunction.

•NEW• **The Cognitive-Behavioral Model: Merging the Behavioral and Cognitive Perspectives** We now merge behavioral and cognitive explanations and treatments into a cohesive and nuanced *cognitive-behavioral model*, consistent with today's most prominent point of view. Previous editions presented behavioral and cognitive discussions separately to help readers understand the important distinctions between behavior-focused and cognition-focused principles and research. This edition's more integrated presentations of the cognitive-behavioral model enable readers to better appreciate why today's cognitive-behavioral theorists and practitioners include both behavioral and cognitive principles in their work and the complementary and interactive nature of behavioral and cognitive principles.

In addition, in this edition of *Fundamentals of Abnormal Psychology* we further expand our coverage of "new wave" cognitive-behavioral theories and therapies, including *mindfulness-based* interventions and *Acceptance and Commitment Therapy* (ACT) (for example, pages 53–54, 110, 195, and 389).

•NEW• "Trending" Boxes Throughout this edition, we present *Trending* boxes in addition to the *PsychWatch* boxes and *MindTech* boxes featured in previous editions. Whereas *PsychWatch* boxes explore important topics in the field and *MindTech* boxes give special attention to provocative technological issues, the *Trending* boxes focus on particularly hot topics that are trending, or current, in abnormal psychology. New *Trending* boxes include the following:

- Separation Anxiety Disorder, Not Just For Kids Anymore (Chapter 4)
- Internet Horrors: Live-Streaming of Suicides (Chapter 7)
- Shame on Body Shamers (Chapter 9)
- The Opioid Crisis (Chapter 10)
- Mass Murders: Where Does Such Violence Come From? (Chapter 13)
- Damaging the Brain: CTE and Football (Chapter 15)
- Doctor Do No Harm: Enhanced Interrogation (Chapter 16)

•NEW• Additional InfoCentrals Our previous edition introduced a feature called **InfoCentrals**—numerous lively, full-page infographics on important topics in the field. Given the very positive reader response to these stimulating visual data offerings, we have included them again in this edition—updating all of them, substantially changing some, and adding a number of totally new ones. Brand-new InfoCentrals include the following:

- DSM: The Bigger Picture (Chapter 3, page 93)
- Fear (Chapter 4, page 114)
- Exercise and Dietary Supplements (Chapter 6, page 182)
- The Dark Triad (Chapter 13, page 429)

•NEW• Additional and Expanded Topic Coverage Over the past several years, a number of topics in abnormal psychology have received special attention. In this edition, we have provided new or expanded sections on these topics, including *the impact of changing health care laws* (pages 18, 516); *transgender issues* (pages 356–360); *PTSD and the #MeToo movement* (page 145); *social media–based research* (pages 31, 122); *mass murders* (page 408); *resilience and the Parkland, Florida, school shootings* (page 151); *terrorism and mental health* (pages 145–146, 514); *cognitive processing therapy* (page 154); *prolonged exposure therapy* (page 154); *exercise and mental health* (page 182); *the interpersonal theory of suicide* (pages 223–224); *the implicit association test for suicidal risk* (page 234); *teenage eating habits* (page 280); *body shaming* (page 288); *motivational interviewing* (page 283); *the opioid crisis* (page 302); *addiction to prescription pain relievers* (pages 301–302); *community naloxone treatments for drug overdoses* (page 321); *recreational cannabis laws* (pages 311–312); *contingency management treatment* (page 320); *erotomanic delusions* (page 370); *disorders among the offspring of older fathers* (pages 205, 389); *cognitive remediation for schizophrenia* (page 387); *mental health courts* (page 392); *mentalization* (pages 413–414); *selective mutism* (pages 439–440); *parent management training* (page 446); *joint attention* (page 456); *biomarkers for Alzheimer's disease* (page 486); *chronic traumatic encephalopathy* (page 488); *outpatient civil commitment* (pages 500, 504); and *psychologists and enhanced interrogations* (page 514).

•NEW• Additional Focus on Technology In this edition we have expanded the previous edition's focus on the psychological impact of technology and the use of new technology in treatment. In text discussions, *MindTech* boxes, photographs, and figures throughout the book, we examine many additional technology topics such as telemental health (pages 20, 517–518), Internet social media–based research (page 31), videoconferencing and parent-management training (page 446), and live streaming of suicides (page 216).

•NEW• Case Material Over the years, one of the hallmarks of *Fundamentals of Abnormal Psychology* has been the inclusion of numerous and culturally diverse clinical examples that bring theoretical and clinical issues to life. In our continuing quest for relevance to the reader and to today's world, we have replaced or revised many of the clinical examples in this edition (for example, pages 349–350, 410, 415, and 423).

•NEW• Additional Critical Thought Questions *Critical thought questions* have long been a stimulating feature of *Fundamentals of Abnormal Psychology*. These questions pop up within the text narrative, asking students to pause at precisely the right moment and think critically about the material they have just read. We have added a number of new such questions throughout this edition.

•NEW• Additional "Hashtags" This edition retains a fun and thought-provoking feature that has been very popular among students and professors over the years—reader-friendly *Hashtags* (#), previously called *Between the Lines*. Hashtags consist of surprising facts, current events, historical notes, interesting lists, and quotes that are strategically placed in the book's margins. Numerous new *Hashtags* have been added to this edition.

•NEW• Thorough Update In this edition we present the most current theories, research, and events, and include more than 2,000 new references from the years 2017–2019, as well as numerous new photos, tables, and figures.

•EXPANDED COVERAGE• Prevention and Mental Health Promotion In accord with the clinical field's growing emphasis on prevention, positive psychology, and psychological wellness, we have increased the textbook's attention to these important approaches (for example, pages 16, 70, and 492).

•EXPANDED COVERAGE• Multicultural Issues Consistent with the field's continuing appreciation of the impact of ethnicity, race, gender, gender identity, and other cultural factors on psychological functioning, this edition further expands its coverage of the *multicultural perspective* and includes additional multicultural material and research throughout the text (for example, pages 66–67, 281–282, 427–428, and 453–454). Even a quick look through the pages of this textbook will reveal that it truly reflects the diversity of our society and of the field of abnormal psychology.

Continuing Strengths

As we noted earlier, in this edition we have also retained the themes, material, and techniques that have worked successfully for and been embraced enthusiastically by past readers.

Breadth and Balance The field's many theories, studies, disorders, and treatments are presented completely and accurately. All major models—psychological, biological, and sociocultural—receive objective, balanced, up-to-date coverage, without bias toward any single approach.

Integration of Models Discussions throughout the text help students better understand where and how the various models work together and how they differ.

Empathy The subject of abnormal psychology is people—very often people in great pain. We have tried therefore to write always with empathy and to impart this awareness to students.

Pervasive Coverage of Treatment Discussions of treatment are presented throughout the book. In addition to a complete overview of treatment in the opening chapters, each of the pathology chapters includes a full discussion of relevant treatment approaches.

Rich Case Material As we mentioned earlier, the textbook features hundreds of culturally diverse clinical examples to bring theoretical and clinical issues to life.

DSM-5 This edition continues to include discussions of DSM-5 throughout the book, highlighting the classification system's flaws as well as its utility. In addition to weaving DSM-5 categories, criteria, and information into the narrative of each chapter, we regularly provide a reader-friendly pedagogical feature called *Dx Checklist* to help students fully grasp DSM-5 and related diagnostic tools (for example, pages 89–93, 102, 120, 187, and 248).

Margin Glossary Hundreds of key words are defined in the margins of pages on which the words appear. In addition, a traditional glossary is featured at the back of the book.

Focus on Critical Thinking The textbook provides various tools for thinking critically about abnormal psychology. As we mentioned earlier, for example, "critical thought" questions appear at carefully selected locations within the text discussion, asking readers to stop and think critically about the material they have just read.

Striking Photos and Stimulating Illustrations Once again, the textbook features a wide range of truly stunning photographs, diagrams, graphs, and anatomical figures that bring to life the discussions of various concepts, disorders, and treatments. The carefully chosen photos range from historical to today's world to pop culture. They do more than just illustrate topics: they touch and move readers and enhance understanding.

Adaptability Chapters are self-contained, so they can be assigned in any order that makes sense to the professor.

Supplements

We are delighted by the enthusiastic responses of both professors and students to the supplements that have accompanied *Fundamentals of Abnormal Psychology* over the years. This edition offers those supplements once again, revised and enhanced, and adds a number of exciting new ones.

For Professors

Worth Video Collection for *Abnormal Psychology 2.0* *Produced and edited by Ronald J. Comer, Princeton University, and Gregory P. Comer, Princeton Academic Resources. Faculty Guide included.* This incomparable video package offers more than 125 clips on different kinds of clinical events, psychopathologies, and treatments. More than 50 new videos have been added to this edition on current topics such as the national opioid crisis, the impact of body shaming, mindfulness-based interventions, transgender issues, borderline personality disorder, dialectical behavior therapy, cell phone addiction, gaming addiction, acceptance and commitment therapy, binge-eating disorder, training police for mental health interventions, mental health courts, and CTE and football. These cutting-edge videos are available on LaunchPad and on the *Video Collection for Abnormal Psychology 2.0* flash drive. The package is accompanied by a guide that fully describes each video clip, so that professors can make informed decisions about the use of the segments in lectures.

Instructor's Resource Manual *by Jeffrey B. Henriques, University of Wisconsin–Madison and Laurie A. Frost.* This comprehensive guide, revised by an experienced instructor and a clinician, ties together the ancillary package for professors and teaching assistants. The manual includes detailed chapter outlines, lists of principal learning objectives, ideas for lectures, discussion launchers, classroom activities, extra credit projects, and DSM criteria for each of the disorders discussed in the text. It also offers strategies for using the accompanying media, including the video collection. Finally, it includes a comprehensive set of valuable materials that can be obtained from outside sources—items such as relevant feature films, documentaries, teaching references, and Internet sites related to abnormal psychology.

Lecture Slides These slides focus on key concepts and themes from the text and can be used as is or customized to fit a professor's needs.

iClicker Classroom Response System This is a versatile polling system developed by educators for educators that makes class time more efficient and interactive. iClicker allows you to ask questions and instantly record your students' responses, take attendance, and gauge students' understanding and opinions. A set of iClicker Questions for each chapter is available online and in LaunchPad.

Image Slides and Tables These slides, featuring all chapter photos, illustrations, and tables, can be used as is or customized to fit a professor's needs.

Chapter Figures and Photos This collection gives professors access to all of the photographs, illustrations, and alt text from *Fundamentals of Abnormal Psychology,* Ninth Edition.

Assessment Tools

Computerized Test Bank powered by Diploma, includes a full assortment of test items. Each chapter features over 200 questions to test students at several levels of Bloom's taxonomy. All the questions are tagged to the outcomes recommended in the 2013 *APA Guidelines for the Undergraduate Psychology Major,* Bloom's level, the book page, the chapter section, and the learning objective from the Instructor's Resource Manual. The Diploma Test Bank files also provide tools for converting the Test Bank into a variety of useful formats as well as Blackboard- and WebCT-formatted versions of the Test Bank for *Fundamentals of Abnormal Psychology,* Ninth Edition.

For Students

***Case Studies In Abnormal Psychology*, Second Edition,** *by Ethan E. Gorenstein, Behavioral Medicine Program, New York–Presbyterian Columbia Hospital, and Ronald J. Comer, Princeton University.* This edition of our popular case study book provides 20 case histories, each going beyond diagnoses to describe the individual's history and symptoms, theories behind treatment, a specific treatment plan, and the actual treatment conducted. The casebook also provides three cases without diagnoses or treatment so that students can identify disorders and suggest appropriate therapies. Wonderful case material for somatic symptom disorder, hoarding disorder, and gender dysphoria has been added by Danae Hudson and Brooke Whisenhunt, professors at Missouri State University.

LaunchPad with LearningCurve Quizzing—*Multimedia to Support Teaching and Learning* *Available at www.launchpadworks.com*

A comprehensive Web resource for teaching and learning psychology, LaunchPad combines Worth Publishers' award-winning media with an innovative platform for easy navigation. For students, it is the ultimate online study guide, with rich interactive tutorials, videos, an e-book, and the LearningCurve adaptive quizzing system. For instructors, LaunchPad is a full-course space where class documents can be posted, quizzes can be easily assigned and graded, and students' progress can be assessed and recorded. Whether you are looking for the most effective study tools or a robust platform for an online course, LaunchPad is a powerful way to enhance your class.

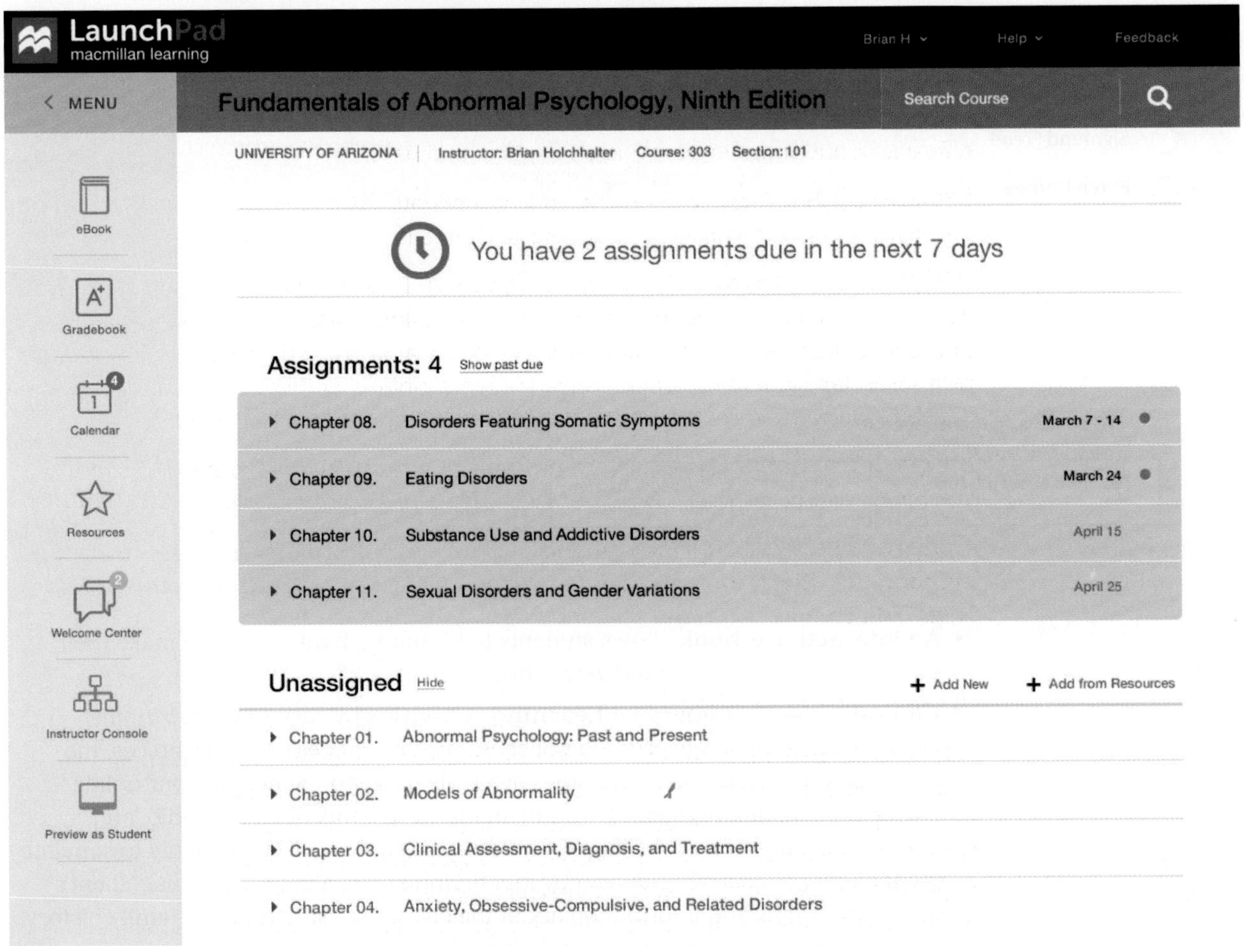

LaunchPad to accompany *Fundamentals of Abnormal Psychology,* Ninth Edition, can be previewed at www.launchpadworks.com. *Fundamentals of Abnormal Psychology,* Ninth Edition, and LaunchPad can be ordered together with:

ISBN-10: 1-319-25126-9
ISBN-13: 978-1-319-25126-0

LaunchPad for *Fundamentals of Abnormal Psychology,* Ninth Edition, includes the following resources:

- The **LearningCurve** quizzing system was designed based on the latest findings from learning and memory research. It combines adaptive question selection, immediate and valuable feedback, and a game-like interface to engage students in a learning experience that is unique to each student. Each LearningCurve quiz is fully integrated with other resources in LaunchPad through the Personalized

Study Plan, so students will be able to review the material with Worth's extensive library of videos and activities. And state-of-the-art question-analysis reports allow instructors to track the progress of individual students as well as that of their class as a whole.

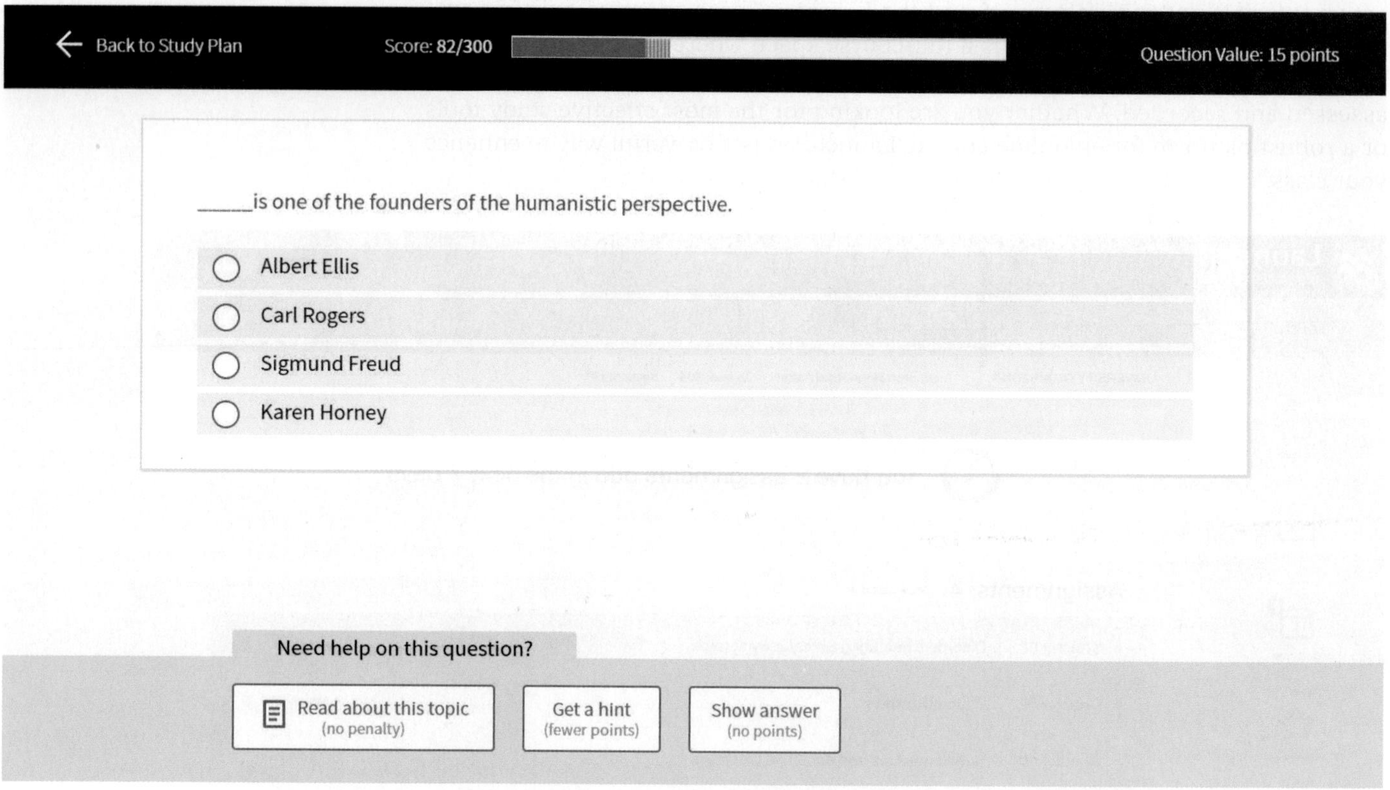

- An **interactive e-book** allows students to highlight, bookmark, and make their own notes, just as they would with a printed textbook.
- ***Clinical Choices* Immersive Learning Activities** by *Taryn Myers, Virginia Wesleyan University*. This edition polishes and streamlines Clinical Choices, the well-received interactive case studies available through LaunchPad, our online course-management system. Through an immersive mix of video, audio, and assessment, each of the 11 Clinical Choices case studies allows students to simulate the thought process of a clinician by identifying and evaluating a virtual "client's" symptoms, gathering information about the client's life situation and family history, determining a diagnosis, and formulating a treatment plan.
- ***Abnormal Psychology Video Activities***, *by Ronald J. Comer, Princeton University; Jonathan S. Comer, Florida International University; and Taryn Myers, Virginia Wesleyan*. These intriguing video cases run 3 to 7 minutes each and focus on people affected by disorders discussed in the text. Students first view a video case and then answer a series of thought-provoking questions.
- **Research Exercises** in each chapter help stimulate critical thinking skills. Students are asked to consider real research, make connections among ideas, and analyze arguments and the evidence on which they are based.

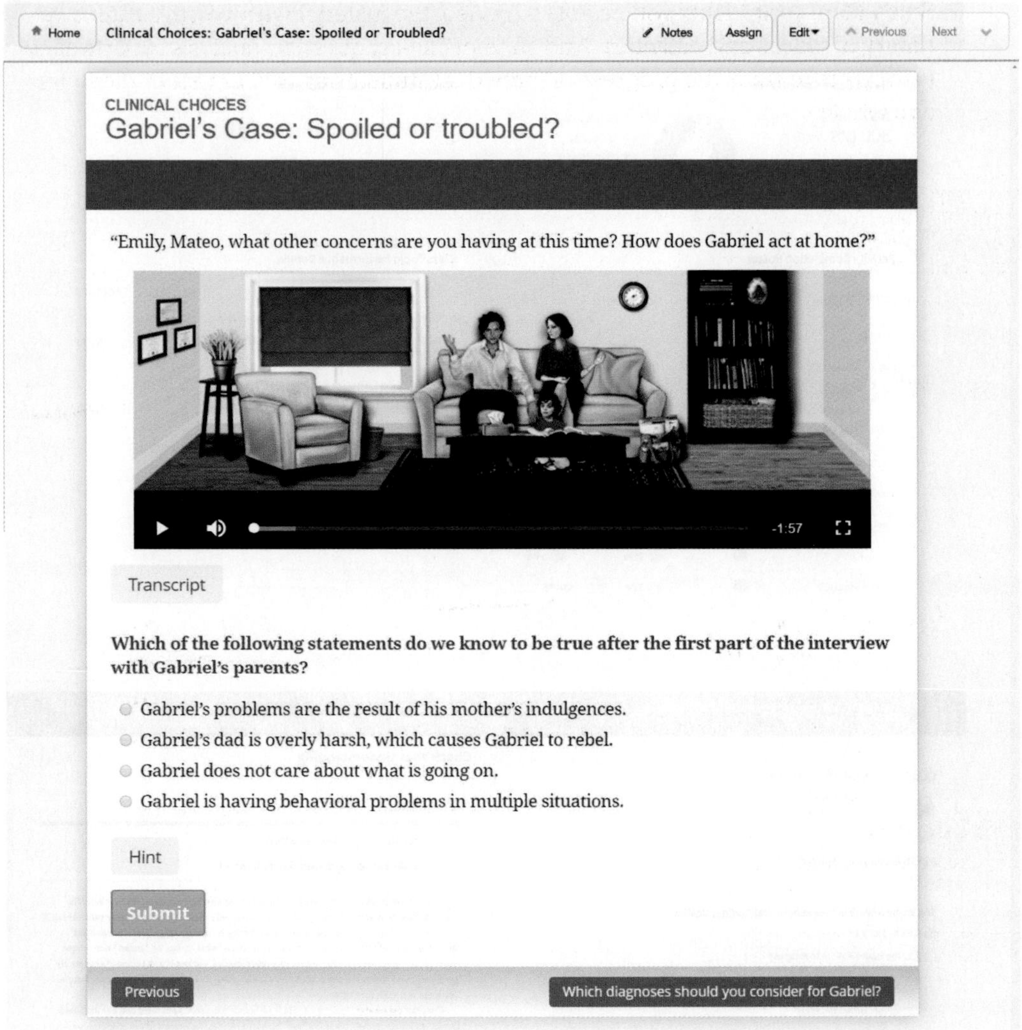

- **Deep integration** is available between LaunchPad products and Blackboard, Brightspace by Desire2Learn, Canvas, and Moodle. These deep integrations offer educators single sign-on and Gradebook sync, now with auto-refresh. Also, these best-in-class integrations offer deep linking to all Macmillan digital content at the chapter and asset level, giving professors ultimate flexibility and customization capability within their learning management system.

Achieve

•NEW• Achieve Read & Practice with LearningCurve Quizzing—Achieve Read & Practice is the marriage of Worth's LearningCurve adaptive quizzing and our mobile, accessible e-book in one easy-to-use and affordable product.

With Achieve Read & Practice, instructors can arrange and assign chapters and sections from the e-book in any sequence they prefer, assign the readings to their class, and track student performance.

Assignments come with LearningCurve quizzes offering individualized and adaptive question sets, immediate feedback, and e-book references for correct and incorrect answers. If students struggle with a particular topic, they are encouraged to reread the material and check their understanding by answering a few short additional questions before being given the option to quiz themselves again.

The Read & Practice Gradebook provides analytics for student performance individually and for the whole class, by chapter, section, and topic, helping instructors prepare for class and one-on-one discussions.

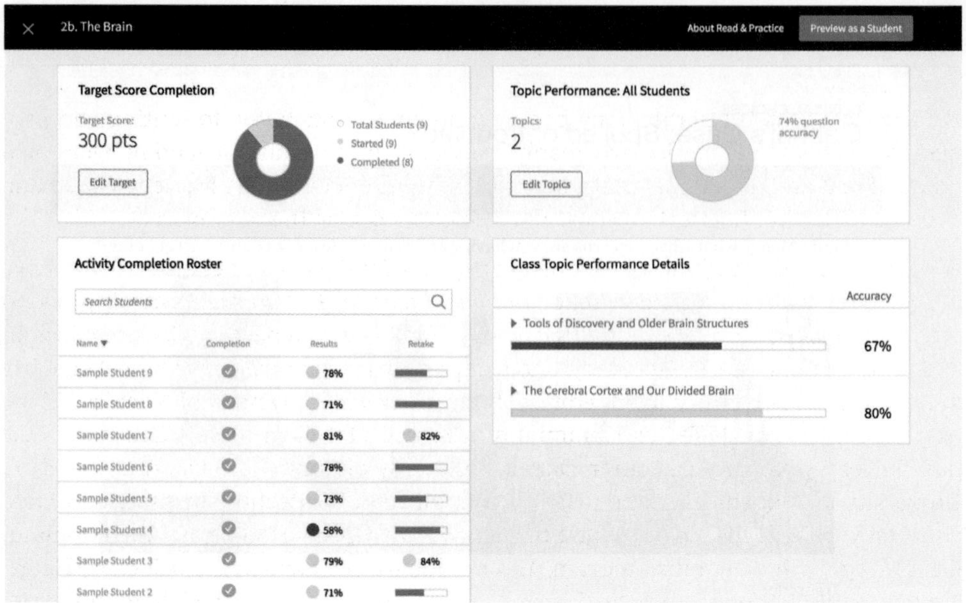

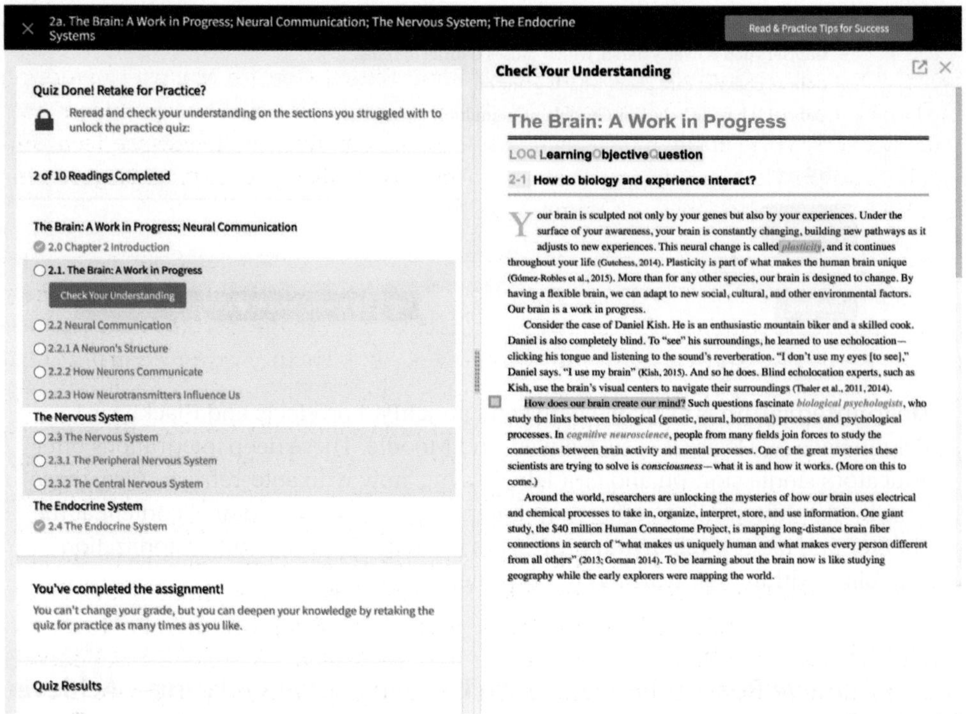

Fundamentals of Abnormal Psychology and Read & Practice can be ordered together with

ISBN-10: 1-319-25132-3
ISBN-13: 978-1-319-25132-1

The Loose-leaf Edition of *Fundamentals of Abnormal Psychology* and Read & Practice can be ordered together with

ISBN-10: 1-319-25130-7
ISBN-13: 978-1-319-25130-7

Acknowledgments

We are very grateful to the many people who have contributed to writing and producing this book. We particularly thank Gregory Comer for his outstanding work on a range of text and digital materials. In addition, we are indebted to Marlene Glissmann and Jean Erler for their fast, furious, and fantastic work on the references.

We are indebted greatly to those outstanding academicians and clinicians who have provided feedback on this new edition of *Fundamentals of Abnormal Psychology,* along with that of its partner, *Abnormal Psychology,* and have commented with great insight and wisdom on its clarity, accuracy, and completeness. Their collective knowledge has in large part shaped the current edition: Seth A. Brown, University of Northern Iowa; Andrea Cartwright, Jefferson Community & Technical College; Gisele Casanova, Purdue University Northwest; Lauren Dattilo, University of South Carolina; Andrea Glenn, University of Alabama; Amanda Haliburton, Virginia Polytechnic Institute and State University; Jacqueline Heath, Ohio State University; Robert Hoople, Ivy Tech Community College of Indiana; Rick Ingram, The University of Kentucky; Joni Jecklin, Heartland Community College; Kristin Juarez, Cochise College; Julia Kim-Cohen, University of Illinois–Chicago; Terese Landry, Houston Community College; Vance Maloney, Taylor University; Donna Marie McElroy, Atlantic Cape Community College; Jane-Marie McKinney, Gordon State College; Alejandro Morales, California State Polytechnic University, Pomona; Justin Peer, University of Michigan–Dearborn; Christopher Schulte, Coastal Carolina Community College; Jerome Short, George Mason University; LaTishia Smith, Ivy Tech Community College of Indiana; Caroline Stanley, Bridgewater State University; Helen Taylor, Bellevue College; Sandra Terneus, Tennessee Tech University; Joseph Vielbig, Arizona Western College; BJ Wallace, Albright College; Shannon Williams, Prince George's Community College.

Earlier we also received valuable feedback from academicians and clinicians who reviewed portions of the previous editions of *Fundamentals of Abnormal Psychology* and *Abnormal Psychology.* Certainly their collective knowledge has also helped shape this new edition, and we gratefully acknowledge their important contributions: Christopher Adams, Fitchburg State University; Dave W. Alfano, Community College of Rhode Island; Jeffrey Armstrong, Northampton Community College; Alisa Aston, University of North Florida; Kent G. Bailey, Virginia Commonwealth University; Stephanie Baralecki, Chestnut Hill College; Sonja Barcus, Rochester College; Wendy Bartkus, Albright College; Marna S. Barnett, Indiana University of Pennsylvania; Jennifer Bennett, University of New Mexico; Jillian Bennett, University of Massachusetts Boston; Otto A. Berliner, Alfred State College; Allan Berman, University of Rhode Island; Douglas Bernstein, University of Toronto Mississauga; Sarah Bing, University of Maryland Eastern Shore; Greg Bolich, Cleveland Community College; Stephen Brasel, Moody Bible Institute; Conrad Brombach, Christian Brothers University; Barbara Brown, Georgia Perimeter College; Christine Browning, Victory University; Gregory M. Buchanan, Beloit College; Jeffrey A. Buchanan, Minnesota State University, Mankato; Laura Burlingame-Lee, Colorado State University; Loretta Butehorn, Boston College; Glenn M. Callaghan, San José State University; E. Allen Campbell, University of St. Francis; Julie Carboni, San Jose Christian College and National University; David N. Carpenter, Southwest Texas University; Marc Celentana, The College of New Jersey; Edward Chang, University of Michigan; Daniel Chazin, Rutgers University; Sarah Cirese, College of Marin; June Madsen Clausen, University of San Francisco; Victor B. Cline, University of Utah; E. M. Coles, Simon Fraser University; Michael Connor, California State University, Long Beach; Frederick L. Coolidge, University of Colorado, Colorado Springs; Patrick J. Courtney, Central Ohio Technical College; Charles Cummings,

Asheville Buncombe Technical Community College; Dennis Curtis, Metropolitan Community College; Timothy K. Daugherty, Missouri State University; Megan Davies, NOVA, Woodbridge Campus; Pernella Deams, Grambling State University; Lauren Doninger, Gateway Community College; Pernella Deams, Grambling State University; Mary Dosier, University of Delaware; S. Wayne Duncan, University of Washington, Seattle; Anne Duran, California State University, Bakersfield; Morris N. Eagle, York University; Miriam Ehrenberg, John Jay College of Criminal Justice; Jon Elhai, University of Toledo; Frederick Ernst, University of Texas, Pan American; Daniella K. C. Errett, Pennsylvania Highlands Community College; Carlos A. Escoto, Eastern Connecticut State University; William Everist, Pima Community College; Jennifer Fiebig, Loyola University Chicago; David M. Fresco, Kent State University; Anne Fisher, University of Southern Florida; William E. Flack Jr., Bucknell University; John Forsyth, State University of New York, Albany; Alan Fridlund, University of California, Santa Barbara; Stan Friedman, Southwest Texas State University; Dale Fryxell, Chaminade University; Lawrence L. Galant, Gaston College; Kathryn E. Gallagher, Georgia State University; Rosemarie B. Gilbert, Brevard Community College; Karla Gingerich, Colorado State University; Nicholas Greco, College of Lake County; Jane Halonen, James Madison University; James Hansell, University of Michigan; David Harder, Tufts University; Morton G. Harmatz, University of Massachusetts; Jinni A. Harrigan, California State University, Fullerton; Jumi Hayaki, College of the Holy Cross; RaNae Healy, GateWay Community College; Anthony Hermann, Kalamazoo College; Paul Hewitt, University of British Columbia; Abby Hill, Trinity International University; Tony Hoffman, University of California, Santa Cruz; Art Hohmuth, The College of New Jersey; Art Houser, Fort Scott Community College; Danae Hudson, Missouri State University; William G. Iacono, University of Minnesota; Jessica Goodwin Jolly, Gloucester County College; Ashleigh E. Jones, University of Illinois at Urbana-Champaign; Ricki E. Kantrowitz, Westfield State University; Barbara Kennedy, Brevard Community College; Lynn M. Kernen, Hunter College; Audrey Kim, University of California, Santa Cruz; Guadalupe Vasquez King, Milwaukee Area Technical College; Tricia Z. King, Georgia State University; Bernard Kleinman, University of Missouri, Kansas City; Craig Knapp, College of St. Joseph; Futoshi Kobayashi, Northern State University; Alan G. Krasnoff, University of Missouri, St. Louis; Sally Kuhlenschmidt, Western Kentucky University; Robert D. Langston, University of Texas, Austin; Kimberlyn Leary, University of Michigan; Harvey R. Lerner, Kaiser-Permanente Medical Group; Arnold D. LeUnes, Texas A&M University; Michael P. Levin, Kenyon College; Barbara Lewis, University of West Florida; Paul Lewis, Bethel College; Mary Margaret Livingston, Louisiana Technical University; Karsten Look, Columbus State Community College; Joseph LoPiccolo, University of Missouri, Columbia; L. E. Lowenstein, Southern England Psychological Services; Gregory Mallis, University of Indianapolis; Jerald J. Marshall, University of Central Florida; Toby Marx, Union County College; Janet R. Matthews, Loyola University; Robert J. McCaffrey, State University of New York, Albany; Rosemary McCullough, Ave Maria University; F. Dudley McGlynn, Auburn University; Tara McKee, Hamilton College; Lily D. McNair, University of Georgia; Mary W. Meagher, Texas A&M University; Dorothy Mercer, Eastern Kentucky University; Michele Metcalf, Coconino Community College; Joni L. Mihura, University of Toledo; Andrea Miller, Georgia Southwestern State University; Antoinette Miller, Clayton State University; Regina Miranda, Hunter College; John Mitchell, Lycoming College; Robin Mogul, Queens University; Linda M. Montgomery, University of Texas, Permian Basin; Jeri Morris, Roosevelt University; Karen Mottarella, University of Central Florida; Maria Moya, College of Southern Nevada; Karla Klein Murdock, University of Massachusetts, Boston; Taryn Myers, Virginia Wesleyan University; Sandy Naumann, Delaware Technical Community College; David Nelson, Sam Houston State University; Hansjörg Neth, Rensselaer Polytechnic Institute; Paul Neunuebel, Sam Houston State University; Ryan Newell, Oklahoma Christian

University; Katherine M. Nicolai, Rockhurst University; Susan A. Nolan, Seton Hall University; Fabian Novello, Purdue University; Edward O'Brien, Marywood University; Ryan O'Loughlin, Nazareth College; Mary Ann M. Pagaduan, American Osteopathic Association; Crystal Park, University of Connecticut; Dominic J. Parrott, Georgia State University; Daniel Paulson, Carthage College; Paul A. Payne, University of Cincinnati; Mary Pelton-Cooper, Northern Michigan University; David V. Perkins, Ball State University; Julie C. Piercy, Central Virginia Community College; Lloyd R. Pilkington, Midlands Technical College; Harold A. Pincus, chair, DSM-IV, University of Pittsburgh, Western Psychiatric Institute and Clinic; Chris Piotrowski, University of West Florida; Debbie Podwika, Kankakee Community College; Ginger Pope, South Piedmont Community College; Norman Poppel, Middlesex County College; David E. Powley, University of Mobile; Laura A. Rabin, Brooklyn College; Max W. Rardin, University of Wyoming, Laramie; Lynn P. Rehm, University of Houston; Leslie A. Rescorla, Bryn Mawr College; R. W. Rieber, John Jay College, CUNY; Lisa Riley, Southwest Wisconsin Technical College; Esther Rothblum, University of Vermont; Vic Ryan, University of Colorado, Boulder; Randall Salekin, Florida International University; Edie Sample, Metropolitan Community College; Jackie Sample, Central Ohio Technical College; A. A. Sappington, University of Alabama, Birmingham; Martha Sauter, McLennan Community College; Laura Scaletta, Niagara County Community College; Ty Schepis, Texas State University; Elizabeth Seebach, Saint Mary's University of Minnesota; George W. Shardlow, City College of San Francisco; Shalini Sharma, Manchester Community College; Roberta S. Sherman, Bloomington Center for Counseling and Human Development; Wendy E. Shields, University of Montana; Sandra T. Sigmon, University of Maine, Orono; Susan J. Simonian, College of Charleston; Janet A. Simons, Central Iowa Psychological Services; Jay R. Skidmore, Utah State University; Rachel Sligar, James Madison University; Katrina Smith, Polk Community College; Robert Sommer, University of California, Davis; Jason S. Spiegelman, Community College of Baltimore County; John M. Spores, Purdue University, South Central; Caroline Stanley, Wilmington College; Wayne Stein, Brevard Community College; Arnit Steinberg, Tel Aviv University; David Steitz, Nazareth College; B. D. Stillion, Clayton College & State University; Deborah Stipp, Ivy Tech Community College; Joanne H. Stohs, California State University, Fullerton; Jaine Strauss, Macalester College; Mitchell Sudolsky, University of Texas, Austin; John Suler, Rider University; Sandra Todaro, Bossier Parish Community College; Terry Trepper, Purdue University Calumet; Thomas A. Tutko, San José State University; Maggie VandeVelde, Grand Rapids Community College; Arthur D. VanDeventer, Thomas Nelson Community College; Jennifer Vaughn, Metropolitan Community College; Norris D. Vestre, Arizona State University; Jamie Walter, Roosevelt University; Steve Wampler, Southwestern Community College; Eleanor M. Webber, Johnson State College; Lance L. Weinmann, Canyon College; Doug Wessel, Black Hills State University; Laura Westen, Emory University; Brook Whisenhunt, Missouri State University; Joseph L. White, University of California, Irvine; Justin Williams, Georgia State University; Amy C. Willis, Veterans Administration Medical Center, Washington, DC; James M. Wood, University of Texas, El Paso; Lisa Wood, University of Puget Sound; Lucinda E. Woodward, Indiana University Southeast; Kim Wright, Trine University; David Yells, Utah Valley State College; Jessica Yokely, University of Pittsburgh; Carlos Zalaquett, University of South Florida; and Anthony M. Zoccolillo, Rutgers University.

We would also like to thank a group of talented professors who provided valuable feedback that shaped the development of our exciting immersive learning activities, Clinical Choices: David Berg, Community College of Philadelphia; Seth Brown, University of Northern Iowa; Julia Buckner, Louisiana State University; Robin Campbell, Eastern Florida State University; Christopher J. Dyszelski, Madison Area Technical College; Paul Deal, Missouri State University; Urminda Firlan, Kalamazoo Valley Community

College; Roy Fish, Zane State College; Julie Hanauer, Suffolk County Community College; Stephanie Brooke Hindman, Greenville Technical College; Sally Kuhlenschmidt, Western Kentucky University; Alejandro Morales, California State Polytechnic University, Pomona; Erica Musser, Florida International University; Garth Neufeld, Highline Community College; Kruti Patel, Ohio University; and Jeremy Pettit, Florida International University.

A special thank you to the authors of the book's supplements package for doing splendid jobs with their respective supplements: Jeffrey B. Henriques, University of Wisconsin–Madison and Laurie A. Frost (*Instructor's Resource Manual*); Taryn Myers, Virginia Wesleyan University (*Clinical Choices*); Joy Crawford, Green River Community College (*Practice Quizzes*). And thank you to the contributors from previous editions: Ann Brandt-Williams, Glendale Community College; Elaine Cassel, Marymount University and Lord Fairfax Community College; Danae L. Hudson, Missouri State University; John Schulte, Cape Fear Community College and University of North Carolina; and Brooke L. Whisenhunt, Missouri State University.

We also extend our deep appreciation to the core team of professionals at Worth Publishers and W. H. Freeman and Company who have worked with us almost every day for the past year to produce this edition: Un Hye Kim, assistant editor; Mimi Melek, senior development editor; Martha Emry, senior content project manager; Paul Lacy, layout designer; and Jennifer Atkins, photo editor and video researcher. It is accurate to say that these members of the core team were our co-authors and co-teachers in this enterprise, and we are in their debt.

We also thank the following individuals, each of whom made significant contributions to the writing and production of this textbook: Chuck Linsmeier, senior vice president, content strategy; Matt Wright, executive program manager; Jennifer MacMillan, permissions manager; Susan Wein, senior workflow project supervisor; Shani Fisher, program director, social sciences; Tracey Kuehn, director of content management enhancement; Diana Blume, director of design; Blake Logan, designer; John Callahan, cover designer; Natasha Wolfe, design services manager; Matthew McAdams, art manager; Chuck Yuen, book and InfoCentral designer; Lucille Clerc, cover and chapter-opener artist; Stefani Wallace, media editor; Noel Hohnstine, director of media editorial & assessment, social sciences; Michael McCarty, permissions associate; Arthur Johnson, text permissions researcher; Christine Buese, media permissions manager; Hillary Newman, director of rights and permissions; Lisa Kinne, senior managing editor; Jean Erler, copyeditor and references editor; William LaDue, proofreader; and Sherri Dietrich, indexer.

And, of course, not to be overlooked are the superb professionals at Worth Publishers who continuously work with great passion, skill, and judgment to bring our books to the attention of professors across the world: Kate Nurre, executive marketing manager; Clay Bolton, senior marketing manager; Chelsea Simens, marketing assistant; Greg David, senior vice president, Macmillan Learning sales; and the company's wonderful sales representatives. Thank you so much.

Two remaining notes. First, as you can imagine, we have found it more than a little exciting to work together on this monumental project. But beyond our personal delight, we believe that our co-authorship brings a valuable blend to the textbook. More than father and son, we are psychology professors and clinicians at very different points in our lives and careers, with different areas of expertise and accomplishment, and, at times, different sensibilities. Bridging such differences in the writing of this book has enabled us to grow enormously—both professionally and personally. We hope that our collaboration has, likewise, resulted in a special textbook for our readers.

Finally, both in terms of our textbooks and more generally, we are very aware of just how fortunate we are. We feel profoundly privileged to be able to work with so many interesting and stimulating students during this important and exciting stage of their lives. Similarly, we are grateful beyond words for our dear friends and for our extraordinary family, particularly our magnificent wives Marlene and Jami (Marlene is also Jon's mom); our wonderful son/brother, Greg, and daughter-/sister-in-law, Emily; Jon's loving parents-in-law, Jim and Mindy Furr; and the lights of our lives, Delia (age 7) and Emmett (age 5).

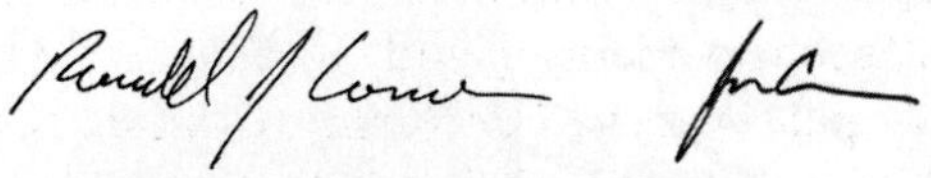

Ronald J. Comer   Jonathan S. Comer

January, 2019

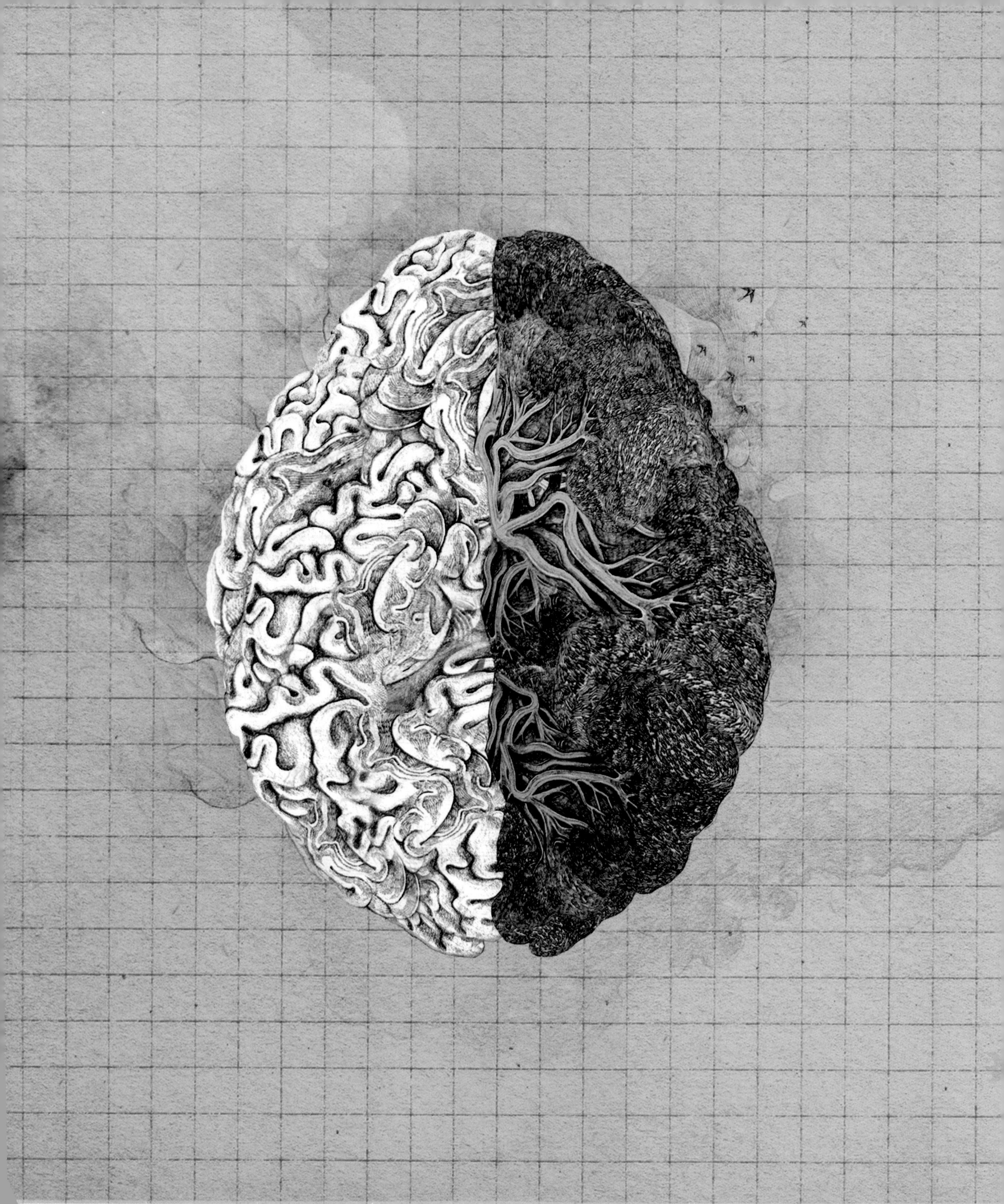

CHAPTER

1

Abnormal Psychology: Past and Present

Johanne cries herself to sleep every night. She is certain that the future holds nothing but misery. Indeed, this is the only thing she does feel certain about. "I'm going to suffer and suffer and suffer, and my daughters will suffer as well. We're doomed. The world is ugly. I hate every moment of my life." She has great trouble sleeping. She is afraid to close her eyes. When she does, the hopelessness of her life—and the ugly future that awaits her daughters—becomes all the clearer to her. When she drifts off to sleep, her dreams are nightmares filled with terrible images—bodies, decay, death, destruction.

Some mornings Johanne even has trouble getting out of bed. The thought of facing another day overwhelms her. She wishes that she and her daughters were dead. "Get it over with. We'd all be better off." She feels paralyzed by her depression and anxiety, overwhelmed by her sense of hopelessness, and filled with fears of becoming ill, too tired to move, too negative to try anymore. On such mornings, she huddles her daughters close to her and remains all day in the cramped tent she shares with her daughters. She feels she has been deserted by the world and left to rot. She is both furious at life and afraid of it at the same time.

During the past year Alberto has been hearing mysterious voices that tell him to quit his job, leave his family, and prepare for the coming invasion. These voices have brought tremendous confusion and emotional turmoil to Alberto's life. He believes that they come from beings in distant parts of the universe who are somehow wired to him. Although it gives him a sense of purpose and specialness to be the chosen target of their communications, the voices also make him tense and anxious. He does all he can to warn others of the coming apocalypse. In accordance with instructions from the voices, he identifies online articles that seem to be filled with foreboding signs, and he posts comments that plead with other readers to recognize the articles' underlying messages. Similarly, he posts long, rambling YouTube videos that describe the invasion to come. The online comments and feedback that he receives typically ridicule and mock him. If he rejects the voices' instructions and stops his online commentary and videos, then the voices insult and threaten him and turn his days into a waking nightmare.

Alberto has put himself on a sparse diet as protection against the possibility that his enemies may be contaminating his food. He has found a quiet apartment far from his old haunts, where he has laid in a good stock of arms and ammunition. After witnessing the abrupt and troubling changes in his behavior and watching his ranting and rambling videos, his family and friends have tried to reach out to Alberto, to understand his problems, and to dissuade him from the disturbing course he is taking. Every day, however, he retreats further into his world of mysterious voices and imagined dangers.

Most of us would probably consider Johanne's and Alberto's emotions, thoughts, and behaviors psychologically abnormal. They are the result of a state sometimes called *psychopathology, maladjustment, emotional disturbance,* or *mental illness* (see **PsychWatch** on the next page). These terms have been applied to the many problems that seem closely tied to the human brain or mind. Psychological abnormality affects the famous and the unknown, the rich and the poor. Celebrities, writers, politicians, and other public figures of the present and the past have struggled with

TOPIC OVERVIEW

PSYCHWATCH

Verbal Debuts

We use words like "abnormal" and "mental disorder" so often that it is easy to forget that there was a time not that long ago when these terms did not exist. When did these and similar words (including slang terms) make their debut in print as expressions of psychological dysfunction? The *Oxford English Dictionary* offers the following dates.

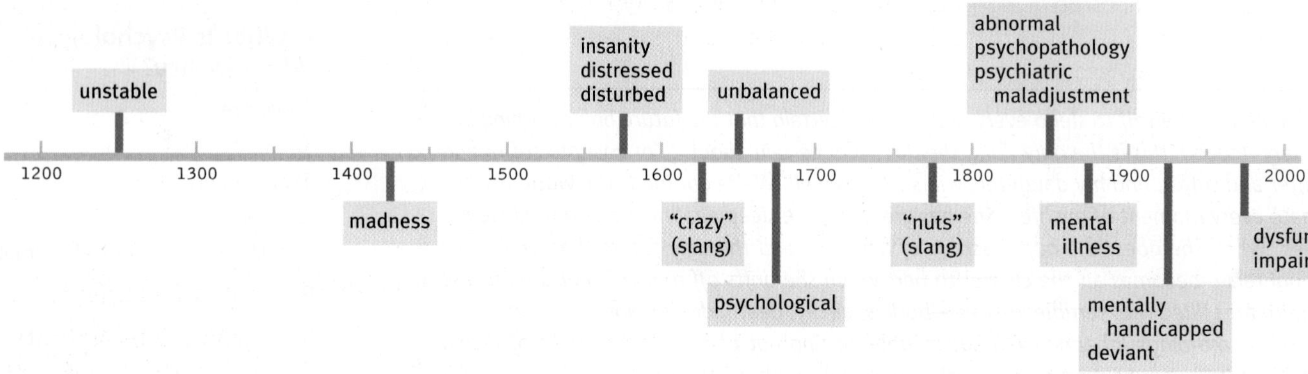

it. Psychological problems can bring great suffering, but they can also be the source of inspiration and energy.

Because they are so common and so personal, these problems capture the interest of us all. Hundreds of novels, plays, films, and television programs have explored what many people see as the dark side of human nature, and self-help books flood the market. Mental health experts are popular guests on both television and radio, and some even have their own shows, Web sites, and blogs.

> Why do actors who portray characters with psychological disorders tend to receive more awards for their performances?

The field devoted to the scientific study of the problems we find so fascinating is usually called **abnormal psychology.** As in any science, workers in this field, called *clinical scientists,* gather information systematically so that they can describe, predict, and explain the phenomena they study. The knowledge that they acquire is then used by *clinical practitioners,* whose role is to detect, assess, and treat abnormal patterns of functioning.

Eric Lafforgue/Art in All of Us/Getty Images

Deviance and abnormality This woman, like others from certain tribes in Myanmar (Burma), has permanently tattooed her entire face with an elaborate pattern of black lines, a tradition that began centuries ago to repel invaders and discourage kidnappings. In Western society, total facial disfigurement of this kind would break norms and might be considered abnormal.

What Is Psychological Abnormality?

Although their general goals are similar to those of other scientific professionals, clinical scientists and practitioners face problems that make their work especially difficult. One of the most troubling is that psychological abnormality is very hard to define. Consider once again Johanne and Alberto. Why are we so ready to call their responses abnormal?

While many definitions of abnormality have been proposed over the years, none has won total acceptance (Bergner & Bunford, 2017, 2014). Still, most of the definitions have certain features in common, often called "the four Ds": deviance, distress, dysfunction, and danger. That is, patterns of psychological abnormality are typically *deviant* (different, extreme, unusual, perhaps even bizarre), *distressing* (unpleasant and upsetting to the person), *dysfunctional* (interfering with the person's ability to conduct daily activities in a constructive way), and possibly *dangerous.* This definition offers a useful starting point from which to explore the phenomena of psychological abnormality. As you will see, however, it has key limitations.

AP Photo/Katsumi Kasahara

Changing times Prior to this century, a woman's love for race car driving might have been considered strange, perhaps even abnormal. Then recently retired Danica Patrick (right) became one of America's finest race car drivers. The size difference between her first-place trophy at the 2008 Indy Japan 300 auto race and that of second-place male driver Hélio Castroneves symbolizes just how far women have come in this sport.

Deviance

Abnormal psychological functioning is *deviant,* but deviant from what? Johanne's and Alberto's behaviors, thoughts, and emotions are different from those that are considered normal in our place and time. We do not expect people to cry themselves to sleep each night, hate the world, wish themselves dead, or obey voices that no one else hears.

In short, abnormal behavior, thoughts, and emotions are those that differ markedly from a society's ideas about proper functioning. Each society establishes **norms**—stated and unstated rules for proper conduct. Behavior that breaks legal norms is considered to be criminal. Behavior, thoughts, and emotions that break norms of psychological functioning are called abnormal.

Judgments about what constitutes abnormality vary from society to society. A society's norms grow from its particular **culture**—its history, values, institutions, habits, skills, technology, and arts. A society that values competition and assertiveness may accept aggressive behavior, whereas one that emphasizes cooperation and gentleness may consider aggressive behavior unacceptable and even abnormal. A society's values may also change over time, causing its views of what is psychologically abnormal to change as well. In Western society, for example, a woman seeking the power of running a major corporation or indeed of leading the country would have been considered inappropriate and even delusional a hundred years ago. Today the same behavior is valued.

Judgments of abnormality depend on *specific circumstances* as well as on cultural norms. What if, for example, we were to learn that Johanne is a citizen of Haiti and that her desperate unhappiness began in the days, weeks, and months following the massive earthquake that struck her country, already the poorest country in the Western hemisphere, on January 12, 2010? The quake, one of the worst natural disasters in history, killed 250,000 Haitians and left 1.5 million homeless. Half of Haiti's homes and buildings were immediately turned into rubble, and its electricity and other forms of power disappeared. Tent cities replaced homes for most people (Dube et al., 2018).

In the weeks and months that followed the earthquake, Johanne came to accept that she wouldn't get all of the help she needed and that she might never again see the friends and neighbors who had once given her life so much meaning. As she and her daughters moved from one temporary tent or hut to another throughout the country, always at risk of developing serious diseases, she gradually gave up all hope that her life would ever return to normal. In this light, Johanne's reactions do not seem quite so inappropriate. If anything is abnormal here, it is her situation. Many human experiences produce intense reactions—financial ruin, large-scale catastrophes and disasters, rape, child abuse, war, terminal illness, chronic pain (Compean & Hamner, 2019; Scott et al., 2018). Is there an "appropriate" way to react to such things? Should we ever call reactions to such experiences abnormal?

Distress

Even functioning that is considered unusual does not necessarily qualify as abnormal. According to many clinical theorists, behavior, ideas, or emotions usually have to cause *distress* before they can be labeled abnormal. Consider the Ice Breakers, a group of people in Michigan who go swimming in lakes throughout the state every weekend from November through February. The colder the weather, the better they like it. One man, a member of the group for 17 years, says he loves the challenge of human against nature. A 37-year-old lawyer believes that the weekly shock is good for her health. "It cleanses me," she says. "It perks me up and gives me strength." Certainly these people

abnormal psychology The scientific study of abnormal behavior undertaken to describe, predict, explain, and change abnormal patterns of functioning.

norms A society's stated and unstated rules for proper conduct.

culture A people's common history, values, institutions, habits, skills, technology, and arts.

Daniel Zuchnik/Getty Images

Context is key A couple dressed as Supergirl and Superman stop and point upward as they cross a street in New York City. Their appearance and behavior might suggest psychological dysfunction were it not for the fact that they are attendees at a 2016 Comic-Con, one of the many popular conventions held across the country to showcase comic books, graphic novels, and the like.

are different from most of us, but is their behavior abnormal? Far from experiencing distress, they feel energized and challenged. Their positive feelings must cause us to hesitate before we decide that they are functioning abnormally.

Should we conclude, then, that feelings of distress must always be present before a person's functioning can be considered abnormal? Not necessarily. Some people who function abnormally maintain a positive frame of mind. Consider once again Alberto, the young man who hears mysterious voices. What if he enjoyed listening to the voices, felt honored to be chosen, loved sending out warnings on the Internet, and looked forward to saving the world? Shouldn't we still regard his functioning as abnormal?

Dysfunction

Abnormal behavior tends to be *dysfunctional;* that is, it interferes with daily functioning. It so upsets, distracts, or confuses people that they cannot care for themselves properly, participate in ordinary social interactions, or work productively. Alberto, for example, has quit his job, left his family, and prepared to withdraw from the productive life he once led. Because our society holds that it is important to carry out daily activities in an effective manner, Alberto's behavior is likely to be regarded as abnormal and undesirable. In contrast, the Ice Breakers, who continue to perform well in their jobs and enjoy fulfilling relationships, would probably be considered simply unusual.

Danger

Perhaps the ultimate psychological dysfunction is behavior that becomes *dangerous* to oneself or others. Individuals whose behavior is consistently careless, hostile, or confused may be placing themselves or those around them at risk. Alberto, for example, seems to be endangering both himself, with his diet, and others, with his buildup of arms and ammunition.

Although danger is often cited as a feature of abnormal psychological functioning, research suggests that it is actually the exception rather than the rule (Taylor, 2018; Bonnet et al., 2017). Most people struggling with anxiety, depression, and even bizarre thinking pose no immediate danger to themselves or to anyone else.

The Elusive Nature of Abnormality

Efforts to define psychological abnormality typically raise as many questions as they answer. Ultimately, a society selects general criteria for defining abnormality and then uses those criteria to judge particular cases. One clinical theorist, Thomas Szasz (1920–2012), placed such emphasis on society's role that he found the whole concept of mental illness to be invalid, a *myth* of sorts (Szasz, 2011, 1963, 1960). According to Szasz, the deviations that society calls abnormal are simply "problems in living," not signs of something wrong within the person.

Even if we assume that psychological abnormality is a valid concept and that it can indeed be defined, we may be unable to apply our definition consistently. If a behavior—excessive use of alcohol among college students, say—is familiar enough, the society may fail to recognize that it is deviant, distressful, dysfunctional, and dangerous. Thousands of college students throughout the United States are so dependent on alcohol that it interferes with their personal and academic lives, causes them great discomfort, jeopardizes their health, and often endangers them and the people around them (Martin & Chaney, 2018; Testa & Cleveland, 2017). Yet their problem often goes

#TheirWords

"I can calculate the motion of heavenly bodies but not the madness of people."

Sir Isaac Newton

What behaviors fit the criteria of deviant, distressful, dysfunctional, or dangerous but would not be considered abnormal by most people?

unnoticed and undiagnosed. Alcohol is so much a part of the college subculture that it is easy to overlook drinking behavior that has become abnormal.

Conversely, a society may have trouble separating an abnormality that requires intervention from an *eccentricity,* an unusual pattern with which others have no right to interfere. From time to time we see or hear about people who behave in ways we consider strange, such as a man who lives alone with two dozen cats and rarely talks to other people. The behavior of such people is deviant, and it may well be distressful and dysfunctional, yet many professionals think of it as eccentric rather than abnormal (see ***PsychWatch***).

In short, while we may agree to define psychological abnormalities as patterns of functioning that are deviant, distressful, dysfunctional, and sometimes dangerous, we should be clear that these criteria are often vague and subjective. In turn, few of the current categories of abnormality that you will meet in this book are as clear-cut as they may seem, and most continue to be debated by clinicians.

PSYCHWATCH

Marching to a Different Drummer: Eccentrics

- Writer **James Joyce** always carried a tiny pair of lady's bloomers, which he waved in the air to show approval.
- **Benjamin Franklin** took "air baths" for his health, sitting naked in front of an open window.
- **Alexander Graham Bell** covered the windows of his house to keep out the rays of the full moon. He also tried to teach his dog how to talk.
- Writer **D. H. Lawrence** enjoyed removing his clothes and climbing mulberry trees.

These famous persons have been called eccentrics. The dictionary defines an *eccentric* as a person who deviates from common behavior patterns or displays odd or whimsical behavior. But how can we separate a psychologically healthy person who has unusual habits from a person whose oddness is a symptom of psychopathology? Little research has been done on eccentrics, but a few studies offer some insights (Weeks, 2015; Neuman, 2013; Weeks & James, 1995).

Researcher David Weeks (2015) studied 1,000 eccentrics and estimated that as many as 1 in 5,000 persons may be "classic, full-time eccentrics." Weeks pinpointed 15 characteristics common to the eccentrics in his study: *nonconformity, creativity, strong curiosity, idealism, extreme interests and hobbies, lifelong awareness of being different, high intelligence, outspokenness, noncompetitiveness, unusual eating and living habits, disinterest in others' opinions or company, mischievous sense of humor, nonmarriage, eldest or only child,* and *poor spelling skills.*

Weeks suggests that eccentrics do not typically suffer from mental disorders. Whereas the unusual behavior of persons with mental disorders is thrust upon them and usually causes them suffering, eccentricity is chosen freely and provides pleasure. In short, "Eccentrics know they're different and glory in it" (Weeks & James, 1995, p. 14). Similarly, the thought processes of eccentrics are not severely disrupted and do not leave these persons dysfunctional. In fact, Weeks found that eccentrics in his study actually had fewer emotional problems than individuals in the general population. Perhaps being an "original" is good for mental health.

AP Photo/Thanh Nien

Eccentric, but not abnormal Tran Van Hay holds his hair—more than 20 feet in length—around his body, as if it were a cobra. When he died in 2010, he had not had a haircut for 50 years and had washed his hair only a few times. The Vietnamese man otherwise lived and worked as a respected and productive herbalist who cared for many people in need. He just liked his hair on the long side—longer than any other person on earth.

9... SUMMING UP

WHAT IS PSYCHOLOGICAL ABNORMALITY? Abnormal functioning is generally considered to be deviant, distressful, dysfunctional, and dangerous. Because behavior must also be considered in the context in which it occurs, however, the concept of abnormality depends on the norms and values of the society in question.

What Is Treatment?

Once clinicians decide that a person is indeed suffering from some form of psychological abnormality, they seek to treat it. **Treatment,** or **therapy,** is a procedure designed to change abnormal behavior into more normal behavior; it, too, requires careful definition. For clinical scientists, the problem is closely related to defining abnormality. Consider the case of Bill:

February: *He cannot leave the house; Bill knows that for a fact. Home is the only place where he feels safe—safe from humiliation, danger, even ruin. If he were to go to work, his coworkers would somehow reveal their contempt for him. A pointed remark, a quizzical look—that's all it would take for him to get the message. If he were to go shopping at the store, before long everyone would be staring at him. Surely others would see his dark mood and thoughts; he wouldn't be able to hide them. He dare not even go for a walk alone in the woods—his heart would probably start racing again, bringing him to his knees and leaving him breathless, incoherent, and unable to get home. No, he's much better off staying in his room, trying to get through another evening of this curse called life. Thank goodness for the Internet. Were it not for his reading of news sites and blog posts and online forums, he would, he knows, be cut off from the world altogether.*

July: *Bill's life revolves around his circle of friends: Bob and Jack, whom he knows from the office, where he was recently promoted to director of customer relations, and Frank and Tim, his weekend tennis partners. The gang meets for dinner every week at someone's house, and they chat about life, politics, and their jobs. Particularly special in Bill's life is Janice. They go to movies, restaurants, and shows together. She thinks Bill's just terrific, and Bill finds himself beaming whenever she's around. Bill looks forward to work each day and to his one-on-one dealings with customers. He is taking part in many activities and relationships and more fully enjoying life.*

Courtesy Adam Ortiz

Therapy . . . not At age 11, Ciro Ortiz set up a "therapy" office each week on a New York City subway platform. Calling himself the Emotional Advice Kid, he talked to people of all ages with various kinds of psychological issues, charging 2 dollars for a five-minute session. Ciro's advice may have been therapeutic for many persons, but it was not therapy. The discussions lacked, for example, a "trained healer" and a series of systematic contacts between healer and sufferer.

Bill's thoughts, feelings, and behavior interfered with all aspects of his life in February. Yet most of his symptoms had disappeared by July. All sorts of factors may have contributed to Bill's improvement—advice from friends and family members, a new job or vacation, perhaps a big change in his diet or exercise regimen. Any or all of these things may have been useful to Bill, but they could not be considered treatment or therapy. Those terms are usually reserved for special, systematic procedures for helping people overcome their psychological difficulties. According to a pioneering clinical theorist, Jerome Frank, all forms of therapy have three essential features:

1. A *sufferer* who seeks relief from the healer.
2. A trained, socially accepted *healer,* whose expertise is accepted by the sufferer and his or her social group.
3. A *series of contacts* between the healer and the sufferer, through which the healer . . . tries to produce certain changes in the sufferer's emotional state, attitudes, and behavior.

(Frank, 1973, pp. 2–3)

Despite this seemingly straightforward definition, clinical treatment is surrounded by conflict and, at times, confusion. Some clinicians view abnormality as an illness and so consider therapy a procedure that helps *cure* the illness. Others see abnormality as a problem in living and therapists as *teachers* of more functional behavior and thought. Clinicians even differ on what to call the person who receives therapy: those who see abnormality as an illness speak of the "patient," while those who view it as a problem in living refer to the "client." Because both terms are so common, this book will use them interchangeably.

Despite their differences, most clinicians do agree that large numbers of people need therapy of one kind or another. Later you will encounter evidence that therapy is indeed often helpful.

treatment A systematic procedure designed to change abnormal behavior into more normal behavior. Also called *therapy*.

trephination An ancient operation in which a stone instrument was used to cut away a circular section of the skull to treat abnormal behavior.

...SUMMING UP

WHAT IS TREATMENT? Therapy is a systematic process for helping people overcome their psychological difficulties. It typically requires a patient, a therapist, and a series of therapeutic contacts.

How Was Abnormality Viewed and Treated in the Past?

In any given year, as many as 30 percent of the adults and 19 percent of the children and adolescents in the United States display serious psychological disturbances and are in need of clinical treatment (Williams et al., 2018; Kessler et al., 2015, 2012, 2009; Merikangas et al., 2013). The rates in other countries are similarly high. It is tempting to conclude that something about the modern world is responsible for these many emotional problems—perhaps rapid technological change, resultant losses of employment, the threat of terrorism, or a decline in religious, family, or other support systems (Elhai et al., 2017). But, as we shall see in the following sections, every society, past and present, has witnessed psychological abnormality.

Ancient Views and Treatments

Historians who have examined the unearthed bones, artwork, and other remnants of ancient societies have concluded that these societies probably regarded abnormal behavior as the work of evil spirits. People in prehistoric societies apparently believed that all events around and within them resulted from the actions of magical, sometimes sinister, beings who controlled the world. In particular, they viewed the human body and mind as a battleground between external forces of good and evil. Abnormal behavior was typically interpreted as a victory by evil spirits, and the cure for such behavior was to force the demons from a victim's body.

This supernatural view of abnormality may have begun as far back as the Stone Age, a half-million years ago. Some skulls from that period recovered in Europe and South America show evidence of an operation called **trephination,** in which a stone instrument, or *trephine,* was used to cut away a circular section of the skull (Verano, 2017; Wang, 2017). Some historians have concluded that this early operation was performed as a treatment for severe abnormal behavior—either hallucinations, in which people saw or heard things not actually present, or melancholia, characterized

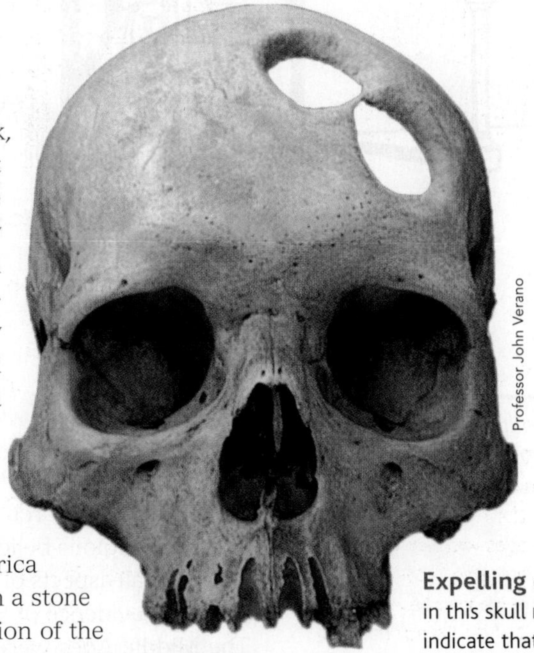

Professor John Verano

Expelling evil spirits The two holes in this skull recovered from ancient times indicate that the person underwent trephination, possibly for the purpose of releasing evil spirits and curing mental dysfunction.

humors According to the Greeks and Romans, bodily chemicals that influence mental and physical functioning.

asylum A type of institution that first became popular in the sixteenth century to provide care for persons with mental disorders. Most asylums became virtual prisons.

by extreme sadness and immobility. The purpose of opening the skull was to release the evil spirits that were supposedly causing the problem (Selling, 1940).

Later societies also explained abnormal behavior by pointing to possession by demons. Egyptian, Chinese, and Hebrew writings all account for psychological deviance this way, and the Bible describes how an evil spirit from the Lord affected King Saul and how David feigned madness to convince his enemies that he was visited by divine forces.

The treatment for abnormality in these early societies was often *exorcism.* The idea was to coax the evil spirits to leave or to make the person's body an uncomfortable place in which to live. A *shaman,* or priest, might recite prayers, plead with the evil spirits, insult the spirits, perform magic, make loud noises, or have the person drink bitter potions. If these techniques failed, the shaman performed a more extreme form of exorcism, such as whipping or starving the person.

What demonological explanations or treatments, besides exorcism, are still around today, and why do they persist?

Greek and Roman Views and Treatments

In the years from roughly 500 B.C. to 500 A.D., when the Greek and Roman civilizations thrived, philosophers and physicians often offered different explanations and treatments for abnormal behaviors. Hippocrates (460–377 B.C.), often called the father of modern medicine, taught that illnesses had *natural* causes. He saw abnormal behavior as a disease arising from internal physical problems. Specifically, he believed that some form of brain pathology was the culprit and that it resulted—like all other forms of disease, in his view—from an imbalance of four fluids, or **humors,** that flowed through the body: *yellow bile, black bile, blood,* and *phlegm* (Smith & Smith, 2016). An excess of yellow bile, for example, caused *mania,* a state of frenzied activity; an excess of black bile was the source of *melancholia,* a condition marked by unshakable sadness.

To treat psychological dysfunction, Hippocrates sought to correct the underlying physical pathology. He believed, for instance, that the excess of black bile underlying melancholia could be reduced by a quiet life, a diet of vegetables, temperance, exercise, celibacy, and even bleeding. Hippocrates' focus on internal causes for abnormal behavior was shared by the great Greek philosophers Plato (427–347 B.C.) and Aristotle (384–322 B.C.) and by influential Greek and Roman physicians.

"Just tell me about the new continent. I don't give a damn what you've discovered about yourself."

Europe in the Middle Ages: Demonology Returns

The enlightened views of Greek and Roman physicians and scholars were not enough to shake ordinary people's belief in demons. And with the decline of Rome, demonological views and practices became popular once again. A growing distrust of science spread throughout Europe.

From 500 to 1350 A.D., the period known as the Middle Ages, the power of the clergy increased greatly throughout Europe. In those days the church rejected scientific forms of investigation, and it controlled all education. Religious beliefs, which were highly superstitious and demonological, came to dominate all aspects of life. Deviant behavior, particularly psychological abnormality, was seen as evidence of Satan's influence.

The Middle Ages were a time of great stress and anxiety—of war, urban uprisings, and plagues. People blamed the devil for these troubles and feared being possessed by him (Ruys, 2017; Sluhovsky, 2017, 2011). Abnormal behavior apparently increased greatly during this period. In addition, there were outbreaks of *mass madness,* in which large numbers of people apparently shared absurd false beliefs and imagined sights or sounds. In one such disorder, *tarantism* (also known as *Saint Vitus' dance*), groups of people would suddenly start to jump, dance, and go into convulsions (Lanska, 2018; Corral-Corral & Corral-Corral, 2016). All were convinced that they had been bitten and possessed by a wolf spider, now called a tarantula, and they sought to cure their disorder by performing a dance called a tarantella. In another form of mass madness, *lycanthropy*, people thought they were possessed by wolves or other animals. They acted wolflike and imagined that fur was growing all over their bodies.

Not surprisingly, some of the earlier demonological treatments for psychological abnormality reemerged during the Middle Ages. Once again the key to the cure was to rid the person's body of the devil that possessed it. Exorcisms were revived, and clergymen, who generally were in charge of treatment during this period, would plead, chant, or pray to the devil or evil spirit (Sluhovsky, 2017, 2011). If these techniques did not work, they had others to try, some amounting to torture.

It was not until the Middle Ages drew to a close that demonology and its methods began to lose favor. Towns throughout Europe grew into cities, and government officials gained more power and took over nonreligious activities. Among their other responsibilities, they began to run hospitals and direct the care of people suffering from mental disorders. Medical views of abnormality gained favor once again, and many people with psychological disturbances received treatment in medical hospitals, such as the Trinity Hospital in England (Allderidge, 1979).

Bettmann/Getty Images

Bewitched or bewildered? A great fear of witchcraft swept Europe beginning in the 1300s and extending through the "enlightened" Renaissance. Tens of thousands of people, mostly women, were thought to have made a pact with the devil. Some appear to have had mental disorders, which caused them to act strangely (Zilboorg & Henry, 1941). This woman is being "dunked" repeatedly until she confesses to witchery.

The Renaissance and the Rise of Asylums

During the early part of the Renaissance, a period of flourishing cultural and scientific activity from about 1400 to 1700, demonological views of abnormality continued to decline. German physician Johann Weyer (1515–1588), the first physician to specialize in mental illness, believed that the mind was as susceptible to sickness as the body was. He is now considered the founder of the modern study of psychopathology.

The care of people with mental disorders continued to improve in this atmosphere. In England, such individuals might be kept at home while their families were aided financially by the local parish. Across Europe, religious shrines were devoted to the humane and loving treatment of people with mental disorders. Perhaps the best known of these shrines was at Gheel in Belgium. Beginning in the fifteenth century, people came to Gheel from all over the world for psychic healing. Local residents welcomed these pilgrims into their homes, and many stayed on to form the world's first "colony" of mental patients. Gheel was the forerunner of today's *community mental health programs* (Goldstein, 2016; Aring, 1975, 1974). Many patients still live in foster homes there, interacting with other residents, until they recover.

Unfortunately, these improvements in care began to fade by the mid-sixteenth century. Government officials discovered that private homes and community residences could house only a small percentage of those with severe mental disorders and that medical hospitals were too few and too small. More and more, they converted hospitals and monasteries into **asylums,** institutions whose primary purpose was to care for people with mental illness. These institutions were begun with the intention that they would provide good care (Philo & Andrews, 2016; Kazano, 2012). Once the asylums started to overflow, however, they became virtual prisons where patients were held in filthy conditions and treated with unspeakable cruelty.

#

#DoctorShakespeare

Writing during the Renaissance, Shakespeare speculated on the nature and causes of abnormal behavior in 20 of his 38 plays and in many of his sonnets.

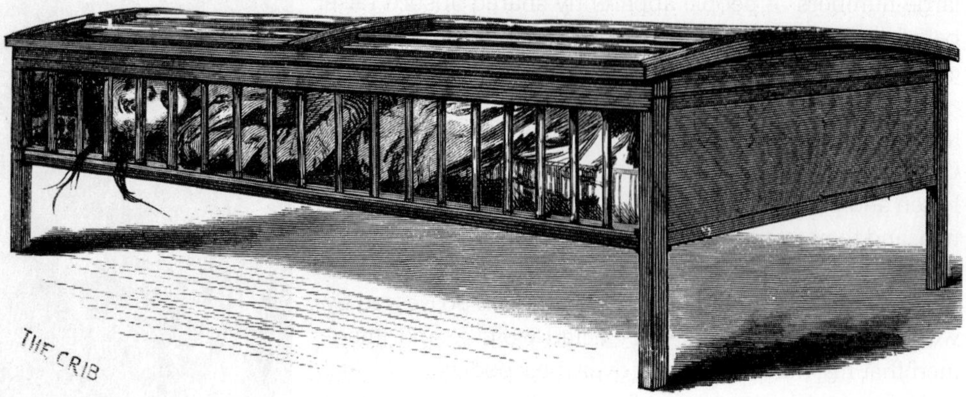

Bettmann/Getty Images

The "crib" Outrageous devices and techniques, such as the "crib," were used in asylums, and some continued to be used even during the reforms of the nineteenth century.

In 1547, for example, Bethlehem Hospital was given to the city of London by Henry VIII for the sole purpose of confining the mentally ill. In this asylum, patients bound in chains cried out for all to hear. The hospital even became a popular tourist attraction; people were eager to pay to look at the howling and gibbering inmates. The hospital's name, pronounced "Bedlam" by the local people, has come to mean a chaotic uproar (Arie, 2016; Selling, 1940).

The Nineteenth Century: Reform and Moral Treatment

As 1800 approached, the treatment of people with mental disorders began to improve once again. Historians usually point to La Bicêtre, an asylum in Paris for male patients, as the first site of asylum reform. In 1793, during the French Revolution, Philippe Pinel (1745–1826) was named the chief physician there. He argued that the patients were sick people whose illnesses should be treated with sympathy and kindness rather than chains and beatings (Sushma & Tavaragi, 2016; Pelletier & Davidson, 2015). He allowed them to move freely about the hospital grounds; replaced the dark dungeons with sunny, airy rooms; and offered support and advice. Pinel's approach proved remarkably successful. Many patients who had been shut away for decades improved greatly over a short period of time and were released. Pinel later brought similar reforms to a mental hospital in Paris for female patients, La Salpetrière.

Meanwhile, an English Quaker named William Tuke (1732–1819) was bringing similar reforms to northern England. In 1796 he founded the York Retreat, a rural estate where about 30 mental patients lived as guests in quiet country houses and were treated with a combination of rest, talk, prayer, and manual work (Rollin & Reynolds, 2018; Kibria & Metcalfe, 2016).

#MythBuster

Although it is popularly believed that a full moon is regularly accompanied by significant increases in crime, strange and abnormal behaviors, and admissions to mental hospitals, decades of research have failed to support this notion (Chaput et al., 2016; Bakalar, 2013; McLay et al., 2006).

The Spread of Moral Treatment The methods of Pinel and Tuke, called **moral treatment** because they emphasized moral guidance and humane and respectful techniques, caught on throughout Europe and the United States. Patients with psychological problems were increasingly perceived as potentially productive human beings who deserved individual care, including discussions of their problems, useful activities, work, companionship, and quiet.

The person most responsible for the early spread of moral treatment in the United States was Benjamin Rush (1745–1813), an eminent physician at Pennsylvania Hospital who is now considered the father of American psychiatry. Limiting his practice to mental illness, Rush developed humane approaches to treatment (Brown, 2018; Hopkins, 2014). For example, he required that the hospital hire intelligent and sensitive attendants to work closely with patients, reading and talking to them and taking them on regular walks. He also suggested that it would be therapeutic for doctors to give small gifts to their patients now and then.

Rush's work was influential, but it was a Boston schoolteacher named Dorothea Dix (1802–1887) who made humane care a public and political concern in the United States. From 1841 to 1881, Dix went from state legislature to state legislature and to Congress, speaking of the horrors she had observed at asylums and calling for reform. Dix's campaign led to new laws and greater government funding to improve the treatment of people with mental disorders (Stamberg, 2017; Kazano, 2012). Each state was made responsible for developing effective public mental hospitals, or **state hospitals,** all of which were intended to offer moral treatment. Similar hospitals were established throughout Europe.

Dance in a Madhouse, 1917 (litho)/Bellows, George Wesley (1882–1925)/ San Diego Museum of Art, USA/Bridgeman Images

Dance in a madhouse A popular feature of moral treatment was the "lunatic ball." Hospital officials would bring patients together to dance and enjoy themselves. One such ball is shown in this painting, *Dance in a Madhouse*, by George Bellows.

The Decline of Moral Treatment By the 1850s, a number of mental hospitals throughout Europe and America reported success using moral approaches. By the end of that century, however, several factors led to a reversal of the moral treatment movement (Bartlett, 2017; Shepherd, 2016). One factor was the speed with which the movement had spread. As mental hospitals multiplied, severe money and staffing shortages developed, recovery rates declined, and overcrowding in the hospitals became a major problem. Another factor was the assumption behind moral treatment that all patients could be cured if treated with humanity and dignity. For some, this was indeed sufficient. Others, however, needed more effective treatments than any that had yet been developed. An additional factor contributing to the decline of moral treatment was the emergence of a new wave of prejudice against people with mental disorders. The public came to view them as strange and dangerous. Moreover, many of the patients entering public mental hospitals in the United States in the late nineteenth century were poor foreign immigrants, whom the public had little interest in helping.

By the early years of the twentieth century, the moral treatment movement had ground to a halt in both the United States and Europe. Public mental hospitals were providing only custodial care and ineffective medical treatments, and they were becoming more overcrowded every year. Long-term hospitalization became the rule once again.

The Early Twentieth Century: The Somatogenic and Psychogenic Perspectives

As the moral movement was declining in the late 1800s, two opposing perspectives emerged and began to compete for the attention of clinicians: the **somatogenic perspective,** the view that abnormal psychological functioning has physical causes, and the **psychogenic perspective,** the view that the chief causes of abnormal functioning are psychological. These perspectives came into full bloom during the twentieth century.

The Somatogenic Perspective The somatogenic perspective has at least a 2,400-year history—remember Hippocrates' view that abnormal behavior resulted from brain disease and an imbalance of humors? Not until the late nineteenth century, however, did this perspective make a triumphant return and begin to gain wide acceptance.

Two factors were responsible for this rebirth. One was the work of a distinguished German researcher, Emil Kraepelin (1856–1926). In 1883, Kraepelin published an influential textbook arguing that physical factors, such as fatigue, are responsible for mental dysfunction. In addition, as you will see in Chapter 4, he developed the first modern system for classifying abnormal behaviors, listing their physical causes and discussing their expected course (Kendler & Engstrom, 2018; Hoff, 2015).

moral treatment A nineteenth-century approach to treating people with mental dysfunction that emphasized moral guidance and humane and respectful treatment.

state hospitals State-run public mental institutions in the United States.

somatogenic perspective The view that abnormal functioning has physical causes.

psychogenic perspective The view that the chief causes of abnormal functioning are psychological.

The more things change . . . Two patients lie on a table in their cage-like ward at a modern-day mental hospital in Bekasi, Indonesia, while other patients live with a similar lack of privacy, activity, and sanitation in the wire-walled units behind them. Despite the passage of Indonesia's Mental Health Law in 2014, many patients still wind up living under conditions reminiscent of those that existed in some state hospitals throughout the United States well into the twentieth century.

New biological discoveries also triggered the rise of the somatogenic perspective. One of the most important discoveries was that an organic disease, *syphilis,* led to *general paresis,* an irreversible disorder with both mental symptoms such as delusions of grandeur and physical ones like paralysis (Kragh, 2017). In 1897, the German neurologist Richard von Krafft-Ebing (1840–1902) injected matter from syphilis sores into patients suffering from general paresis and found that none of the patients developed symptoms of syphilis. Their immunity could have been caused only by an earlier case of syphilis. Since all of his patients with general paresis were now immune to syphilis, Krafft-Ebing theorized that syphilis had been the cause of their general paresis. The work of Kraepelin and the new understanding of general paresis led many researchers and practitioners to suspect that physical factors were responsible for many mental disorders, perhaps all of them.

Despite the general optimism, biological approaches yielded mostly disappointing results throughout the first half of the twentieth century. Although many medical treatments were developed for patients in mental hospitals during that time, most of the techniques failed to work. Physicians tried tooth extraction, tonsillectomy, hydrotherapy (alternating hot and cold baths), and lobotomy, a surgical cutting of certain nerve fibers in the brain. Even worse, biological views and claims led, in some circles, to proposals for immoral solutions such as *eugenic sterilization,* the elimination (through medical or other means) of the ability of individuals to reproduce (see **Table 1-1**). Not until the 1950s, when a number of effective medications were finally discovered, did the somatogenic perspective truly begin to pay off for patients.

TABLE: 1-1

Eugenics and Mental Disorders

Year	Event
1896	Connecticut became the first state in the United States to prohibit persons with mental disorders from marrying.
1896–1933	Every state in the United States passed a law prohibiting marriage by persons with mental disorders.
1907	Indiana became the first state to pass a bill calling for people with mental disorders, as well as criminals and other "defectives," to undergo sterilization.
1927	The U.S. Supreme Court ruled that eugenic sterilization was constitutional.
1907–1945	Approximately 45,000 Americans were sterilized under eugenic sterilization laws; 21,000 of them were patients in state mental hospitals.
1929–1932	Denmark, Norway, Sweden, Finland, and Iceland passed eugenic sterilization laws.
1933	Germany passed a eugenic sterilization law, under which 375,000 people were sterilized by 1940.
1940	Nazi Germany began to use "proper gases" to kill people with mental disorders; 70,000 or more people were killed in less than two years.

Information from: Lombardo, 2017; Stern, 2016; Fischer, 2012; Whitaker, 2002.

The Psychogenic Perspective The late 1800s also saw the emergence of the psychogenic perspective, the view that the chief causes of abnormal functioning are often psychological. This view, too, had a long history, but it did not gain much of a following until studies of *hypnotism* demonstrated its potential.

Hypnotism is a procedure in which a person is placed in a trancelike mental state during which he or she becomes extremely suggestible. It was used to help treat psychological disorders as far back as 1778, when an Austrian physician named Friedrich Anton Mesmer (1734–1815) established a clinic in Paris. His patients suffered from *hysterical disorders,* mysterious bodily ailments that had no apparent physical basis. Mesmer had his patients sit in a darkened room filled with music; then he appeared, dressed in a colorful costume, and touched the troubled area of each patient's body with a special rod. A surprising number of patients seemed to be helped by this treatment, called *mesmerism* (Deeley, 2017; Ellis, 2015). Their pain, numbness, or paralysis disappeared. Several scientists believed that Mesmer was inducing a trancelike state in his patients and that this state was causing their symptoms to disappear. The treatment was so controversial, however, that eventually Mesmer was banished from Paris.

psychoanalysis Either the theory or the treatment of abnormal mental functioning that emphasizes unconscious psychological forces as the cause of psychopathology.

It was not until years after Mesmer died that many researchers had the courage to investigate his procedure, later called *hypnotism* (from *hypnos,* the Greek word for "sleep"), and its effects on hysterical disorders. The experiments of two physicians practicing in the city of Nancy in France, Hippolyte-Marie Bernheim (1840–1919) and Ambroise-Auguste Liébault (1823–1904), showed that hysterical disorders could actually be induced in otherwise normal people while they were under the influence of hypnosis. That is, the physicians could make normal people experience deafness, paralysis, blindness, or numbness by means of hypnotic suggestion—and they could remove these artificial symptoms by the same means. Thus they established that a *mental* process—hypnotic suggestion—could both cause and cure even a physical dysfunction. Leading scientists concluded that hysterical disorders were largely psychological in origin, and the psychogenic perspective rose in popularity.

Among those who studied the effects of hypnotism on hysterical disorders was Josef Breuer (1842–1925) of Vienna. Breuer, a physician, discovered that his patients sometimes awoke free of hysterical symptoms after speaking candidly under hypnosis about past upsetting events. During the 1890s, Breuer was joined in his work by another Viennese physician, Sigmund Freud (1856–1939). As you will see in Chapter 3, Freud's work eventually led him to develop the theory of **psychoanalysis,** which holds that many forms of abnormal and normal psychological functioning are psychogenic. In particular, Freud believed that *unconscious* psychological processes are at the root of such functioning.

AP/Oscar Sosa

Hypnotism update Hypnotism, the procedure that opened the door for the psychogenic perspective, continues to influence many areas of modern life, including psychotherapy, entertainment, and law enforcement. Here, a forensic clinician uses hypnosis to help a witness recall the details of a crime. Recent research has clarified, however, that hypnotic procedures are as capable of creating false memories as they are of uncovering real memories.

Freud also developed the *technique* of psychoanalysis, a form of discussion in which clinicians help troubled people gain insight into their unconscious psychological processes. He believed that such insight, even without hypnotic procedures, would help the patients overcome their psychological problems. Freud and his followers offered psychoanalytic treatment to patients in their offices for sessions of approximately an hour—a format now known as *outpatient therapy.* By the early twentieth century, psychoanalytic theory and treatment were widely accepted throughout the Western world.

9... SUMMING UP

HOW WAS ABNORMALITY VIEWED AND TREATED IN THE PAST? The history of psychological disorders stretches back to ancient times. Prehistoric societies apparently viewed abnormal behavior as the work of evil spirits. There is evidence that Stone Age cultures used trephination to treat abnormal behavior. People of early societies also sought to drive out evil spirits by exorcism.

(continued on the next page)

#

#OddName

Doctors who treated people with mental disorders in the 18th century were called "mad-doctors."

Physicians of the Greek and Roman empires offered more enlightened explanations of mental disorders. Hippocrates believed that abnormal behavior was caused by an imbalance of the four bodily fluids, or humors.

In the Middle Ages, Europeans returned to demonological explanations of abnormal behavior. The clergy was very influential and held that mental disorders were the work of the devil. As the Middle Ages drew to a close, such explanations and treatments began to decline, and care of people with mental disorders continued to improve during the early part of the Renaissance. Certain religious shrines became dedicated to the humane treatment of such individuals. By the middle of the sixteenth century, however, persons with mental disorders were being warehoused in asylums.

Care of those with mental disorders started to improve again in the nineteenth century. In Paris, Philippe Pinel started the movement toward moral treatment. In the United States, Dorothea Dix spearheaded a movement to ensure legal rights and protection for people with mental disorders and to establish state hospitals for their care. However, the moral treatment movement disintegrated by the late nineteenth century, and mental hospitals again became warehouses where inmates received minimal care.

The turn of the twentieth century saw the return of the somatogenic perspective and the rise of the psychogenic perspective. Sigmund Freud's psychogenic approach, psychoanalysis, eventually gained wide acceptance and influenced future generations of clinicians.

Recent Decades and Current Trends

It would hardly be accurate to say that we now live in a period of great enlightenment about or dependable treatment of mental disorders. In fact, surveys have found that 43 percent of respondents believe that people bring mental disorders on themselves, 31 percent consider such disorders to be a sign of personal weakness, and 35 percent believe the disorders are caused by sinful behavior (Roper, 2017; NMHA, 1999). Nevertheless, there have been major changes over the past 60 years in the ways clinicians understand and treat abnormal functioning. There are more theories and types of treatment, more research studies, more information, and—perhaps because of those increases—more disagreements about abnormal functioning today than at any time in the past.

LHB Photo/Alamy

From Juilliard to the streets Nathaniel Ayers, subject of the book and movie *The Soloist*, plays his violin on the streets of Los Angeles while living as a homeless person in 2005. Once a promising musical student at the Juilliard School in New York, Ayers developed schizophrenia and eventually found himself without treatment and without a home. Tens of thousands of people with severe mental disorders are currently homeless.

How Are People with Severe Disturbances Cared For?

In the 1950s, researchers discovered a number of new **psychotropic medications**—drugs that primarily affect the brain and reduce many symptoms of mental dysfunction. They included the first *antipsychotic drugs,* which correct extremely confused and distorted thinking; *antidepressant drugs,* which lift the mood of depressed people; and *antianxiety drugs,* which reduce tension and worry.

When given these drugs, many patients who had spent years in mental hospitals began to show signs of improvement. Hospital administrators, encouraged by these results and pressured by a growing public outcry over the terrible conditions in public mental hospitals, began to discharge patients almost immediately.

Since the discovery of these medications, mental health professionals in most of the developed nations of the world have followed a policy of **deinstitutionalization,** releasing hundreds of thousands of patients from public mental hospitals. On any given day in 1955, close to 600,000 people were confined in public mental institutions across the United States (see **Figure 1-1**). Today the daily patient population in the same kinds of hospitals is around 42,000 (Amadeo, 2017; Smith & Milazzo-Sayre, 2014). In addition,

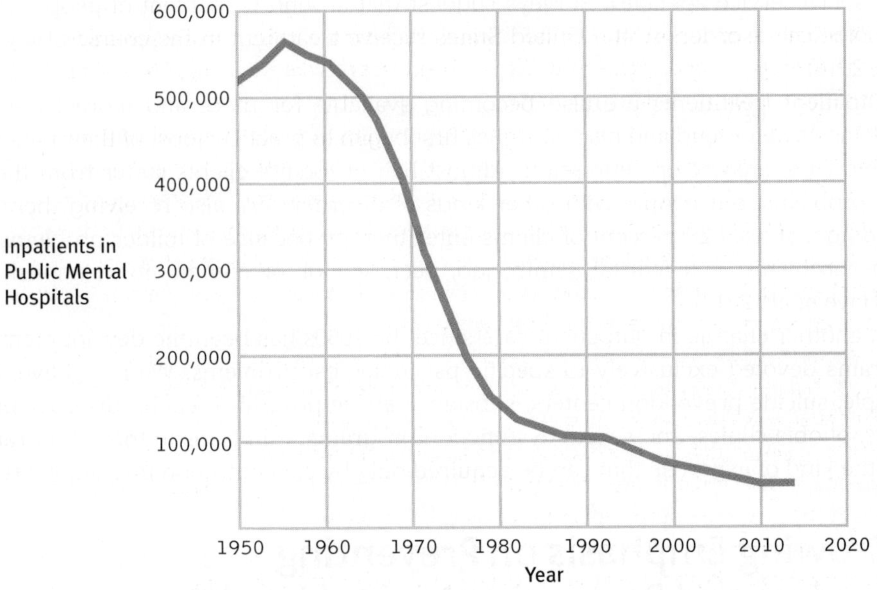

FIGURE 1-1

The Impact of Deinstitutionalization

The number of patients (around 42,000) now hospitalized in public mental hospitals in the United States is a small fraction of the number hospitalized in 1955. (Information from: Amadeo, 2017; Smith & Milazzo-Sayre, 2014; Torrey, 2001; Lang, 1999.)

some 58,000 people receive treatment in *private* psychiatric hospitals, care that is paid for by the patients themselves and/or their insurance companies. On average, the private facilities offer more pleasant surroundings and more favorable staff–patient ratios than the public ones.

Without question, outpatient care has now become the primary mode of treatment for people with severe psychological disturbances as well as for those with more moderate problems. When severely disturbed people do need institutionalization these days, they are usually hospitalized for a short period of time. Ideally, they are then provided with outpatient psychotherapy and medication in community programs and residences (Stein et al., 2015).

Chapters 2 and 12 will look more closely at this current emphasis on community care for people with severe psychological disturbances—a philosophy called the *community mental health approach.* The approach has been helpful for many patients, but too few community programs are available to address current needs in the United States (NIMH, 2017; Dixon & Schwarz, 2014). As a result, hundreds of thousands of persons with severe disturbances fail to make lasting recoveries, and they shuttle back and forth between the mental hospital and the community. After release from the hospital, they at best receive minimal care and often wind up living in decrepit rooming houses or on the streets. Around 140,000 people with such disturbances are homeless on any given day; another 440,000 are inmates of jails and prisons (Allison et al., 2017; NAMI, 2016). Their abandonment is truly a national disgrace.

How Are People with Less Severe Disturbances Treated?

The treatment picture for people with moderate psychological disturbances has been more positive than that for people with severe disorders. Since the 1950s, outpatient care has continued to be the preferred mode of treatment for them, and the number and types of facilities that offer such care have expanded to meet the need.

Before the 1950s, almost all outpatient care took the form of **private psychotherapy,** in which individuals meet with a self-employed therapist for counseling services. Since the 1950s, most health insurance plans have expanded coverage to include private psychotherapy, so that it is now also widely available to people of all incomes. Today, outpatient therapy is also offered in a number of less expensive settings, such as community mental health centers, crisis intervention centers, family service centers, and

psychotropic medications Drugs that mainly affect the brain and reduce many symptoms of mental dysfunction.

deinstitutionalization The practice, begun in the 1960s, of releasing hundreds of thousands of patients from public mental hospitals.

private psychotherapy An arrangement in which a person directly pays a therapist for counseling services.

prevention Interventions aimed at deterring mental disorders before they can develop.

positive psychology The study and enhancement of positive feelings, traits, and abilities.

multicultural psychology The field that examines the impact of culture, race, ethnicity, and gender on behaviors and thoughts, and focuses on how such factors may influence the origin, nature, and treatment of abnormal behavior.

other social service agencies. Surveys suggest that around 60 percent of people with psychological disorders in the United States receive treatment in the course of a year (APA, 2016).

Outpatient treatments are also becoming available for more and more kinds of problems. When Freud and his colleagues first began to practice, most of their patients suffered from anxiety or depression. Almost half of today's clients suffer from those same problems, but people with other kinds of disorders are also receiving therapy. In addition, at least 20 percent of clients enter therapy because of milder problems in living—problems with marital, family, job, peer, school, or community relationships (Ten Have et al., 2013).

Yet another change in outpatient care since the 1950s has been the development of programs devoted exclusively to specific psychological problems. We now have, for example, suicide prevention centers, substance abuse programs, eating disorder programs, phobia clinics, and sexual dysfunction programs. Clinicians in these programs have the kind of expertise that can be acquired only by concentration in a single area.

A Growing Emphasis on Preventing Disorders and Promoting Mental Health

Although the community mental health approach has often failed to address the needs of people with severe disorders, it has given rise to an important principle of mental health care—**prevention** (Mendelson & Eaton, 2018). Rather than wait for psychological disorders to occur, many of today's community programs try to correct the social conditions that underlie psychological problems (poverty or violence in the community, for example) and to help individuals who are at risk for developing emotional problems (for example, teenage mothers or the children of people with severe psychological disorders). As you will see later, community prevention programs are not always successful, but they have grown in number, offering great promise as the ultimate form of intervention.

Prevention programs have been further energized in the past few decades by the field of psychology's ever-growing interest in **positive psychology** (Yaden, Eichstaedt, & Medaglia, 2018; Seligman & Fowler, 2011). Positive psychology is the study and promotion of positive feelings such as optimism and happiness, positive traits like hard work and wisdom, and group-directed virtues, including altruism and tolerance (see ***InfoCentral***).

Why do you think it has taken psychologists so long to start studying positive behaviors?

While researchers study and learn more about positive psychology in the laboratory, clinical practitioners with this orientation are teaching people coping skills that may help to protect them from stress and adversity and encouraging them to become more involved in personally meaningful activities and relationships—thus helping to prevent mental disorders (Sergeant & Mongrain, 2014).

AP Photo/Matthew S. Gunby

Positive psychology in action Often, positive psychology and multicultural psychology work together. Here, for example, two young girls come together as one at the end of a "slave reconciliation" walk by 400 people in Maryland. The walk was intended to promote racial understanding and to help Americans overcome the lasting psychological effects of slavery.

Multicultural Psychology

We are, without question, a society of multiple cultures, races, and languages. Members of racial and ethnic minority groups in the United States collectively make up 39 percent of the population, a percentage that is expected to grow to more than 50 percent by the year 2044 (KFF, 2016; U.S. Census Bureau, 2015). This change is due in part to shifts in immigration trends and also to higher birth rates among minority groups in the United States (NVSR, 2016, 2010).

In response to this growing diversity, an area of study called **multicultural psychology** has emerged. Multicultural psychologists seek to understand how culture, race, ethnicity, gender, and similar factors affect behavior and thought and how people of different cultures, races, and genders may differ psychologically (Alegría et al., 2018,

HAPPINESS

Positive psychology is the study of positive feelings, traits, and abilities. A better understanding of constructive functioning enables clinicians to better promote psychological wellness. **Happiness** is the positive psychology topic currently receiving the most attention.

Many, but far from all, people are happy. In fact, only **one-third** of adults declare themselves "very happy." Let's take a look at some of today's leading facts, figures, and notions about happiness.

WHO Is "Very Happy?"

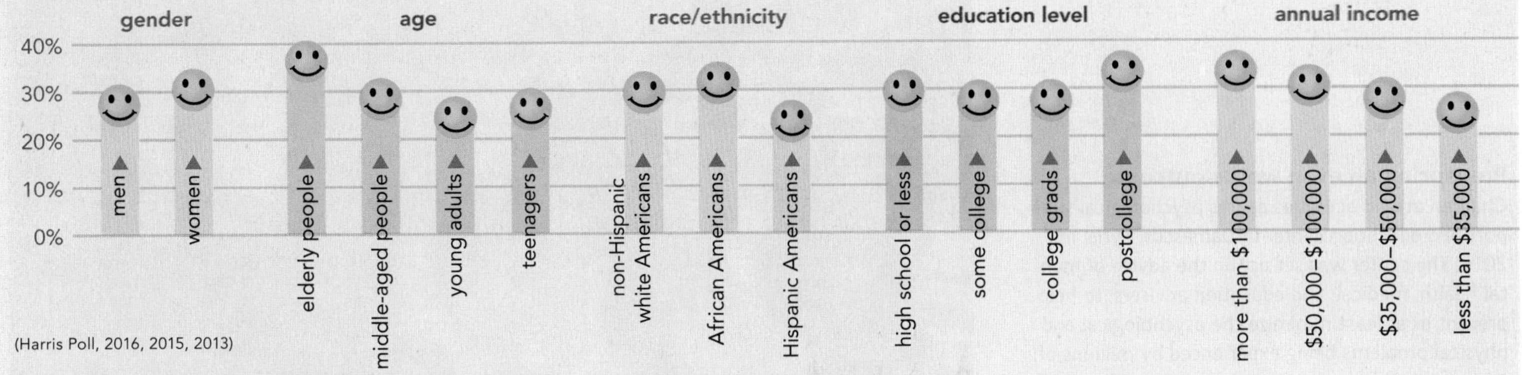

(Harris Poll, 2016, 2015, 2013)

Happiness Building Blocks

Are people born with a happy disposition? Or do their surroundings and life circumstances make them more or less happy? Researchers of this **nature-versus-nurture** question have learned that both sets of factors **interact** to determine one's degree of happiness. But the factors have different degrees of impact.

(Joseph, 2015; Brooks, 2013)

Who Tends to Be *Happier*?

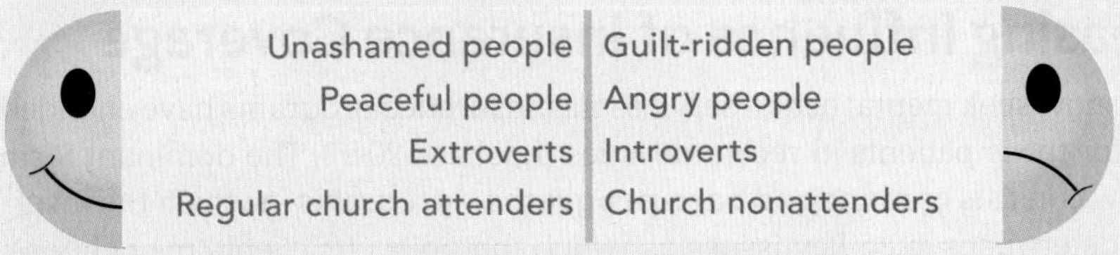

Unashamed people
Peaceful people
Extroverts
Regular church attenders
Guilt-ridden people
Angry people
Introverts
Church nonattenders

(Harris Poll, 2016, 2015; Brooks, 2013; DePaulo, 2013; *The Economist*, 2010)

The Pursuit of Happiness

People tend to pursue a happy life. For some, that means pursuit of a **pleasant life**—filled with as many pleasures as possible. Others pursue an **engaging life**, characterized by satisfaction in work, parenting, love, and leisure. Still others pursue a **meaningful life**—recognizing and using their strengths in the service of others. (Seligman, 2012, 2002)

WHAT Do Happy People Do?

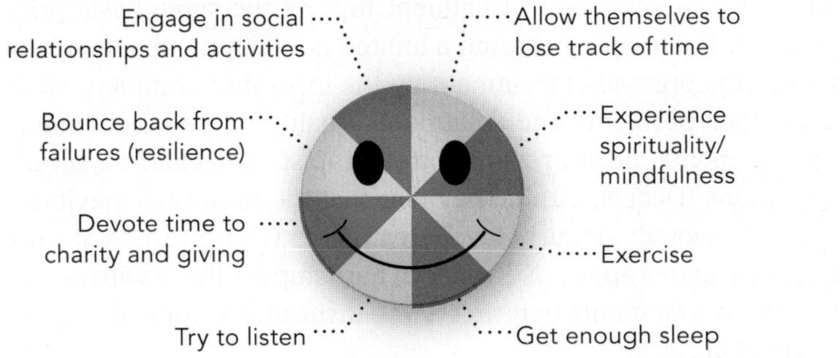

(Harris Poll, 2016, 2015; Bratskeir, 2013)

Non-online Social Contact and Happiness

The more social contact, the happier we are—up to a point!

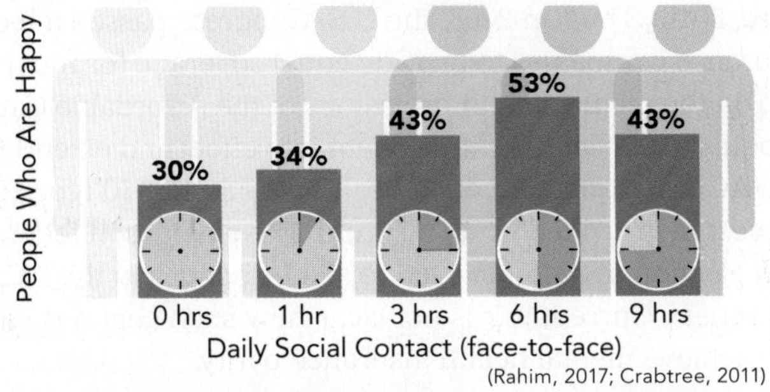

(Rahim, 2017; Crabtree, 2011)

Work and Happiness

Certain jobs have a higher percentage of happy people than others.

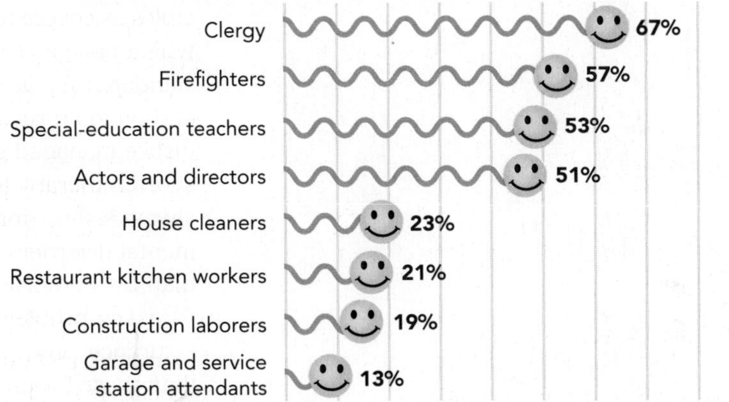

(MyPlan, 2016; Mann, 2009; Smith, 2007)

Marriage and Happiness

Married people are, on average, a bit happier than people with a different marital status.

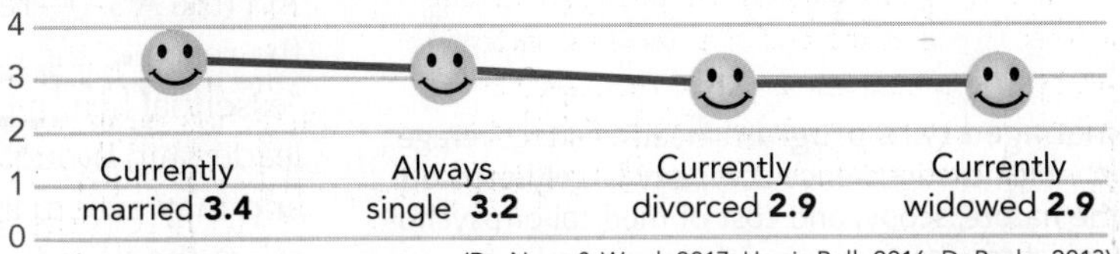

(De Neve & Ward, 2017; Harris Poll, 2016: DePaulo, 2013)

Anadolu Agency/Getty Images

Preventing an even worse outcome
Children attend activities at this psychological support and education center in Damascus, Syria, in 2016. The center was set up, on the advice of mental health, medical, and education advisers, to help prevent or at least minimize the psychological and physical problems being experienced by millions of Syrian children caught up in the ongoing horrors of the country's civil war.

2016, 2013, 2010). As you will see throughout this book, the field of multicultural psychology has begun to have a powerful effect on our understanding and treatment of abnormal behavior.

The Increasing Influence of Insurance Coverage

So many people now seek mental health services that insurance programs have changed their coverage for these patients in recent decades (Iglehart, 2016). The dominant form of insurance now consists of **managed care programs**—programs in which the insurance company determines such key issues as which therapists its clients may choose, the cost of sessions, and the number of sessions for which a client may be reimbursed (Xiang et al., 2018; Bowers, Owen, & Heller, 2016).

Managed care coverage for mental health treatment follows the same basic principles as coverage for medical treatment, including a limited pool of practitioners from which patients can choose, preapproval of treatment by the insurance company, strict standards for judging whether problems and treatments qualify for reimbursement, and ongoing reviews. In the mental health realm, both therapists and clients typically dislike managed care programs (Decker, 2016). They fear that the programs inevitably shorten therapy (often for the worse), unfairly favor treatments whose results are not always lasting (for example, drug therapy), pose a special hardship for those with severe mental disorders, and result in treatments determined by insurance companies rather than by therapists (Bowers et al., 2016).

A key problem with insurance coverage—both managed care and other kinds of insurance programs—is that reimbursements for mental disorders tend to be lower than those for physical disorders. This places persons with psychological difficulties at a distinct disadvantage (McGuire, 2016). Thus, in 2008, the U.S. Congress passed a federal *parity* law that directed insurance companies to provide equal coverage for mental and physical problems, and in 2014 the mental health provisions of the Affordable Care Act (the ACA)—referred to colloquially as "Obamacare"—went into effect and extended the reach of the earlier law. The ACA designated mental health care as 1 of 10 types of "essential health benefits" that *must* be provided by all insurers. The changes in federal leadership brought about by the election of 2016 have led to some changes in the ACA and may eventually result in its repeal. Currently, it is not clear how such changes will affect the decade-long efforts to achieve mental health insurance parity.

managed care program Health care coverage in which the insurance company largely controls the nature, scope, and cost of medical or psychological services.

What Are Today's Leading Theories and Professions?

One of the most important developments in the clinical field has been the growth of numerous theoretical perspectives that now coexist in the field. Before the 1950s, the *psychoanalytic* perspective, with its emphasis on unconscious psychological problems as the cause of abnormal behavior, was dominant. Since then, additional influential perspectives have emerged, particularly the *biological, cognitive-behavioral, humanistic-existential, sociocultural,* and *developmental psychopathology* schools of thought. At present, no single viewpoint dominates the clinical field as the psychoanalytic perspective once did. In fact, the perspectives often conflict and compete with one another.

In addition, a variety of professionals now offer help to people with psychological problems. Before the 1950s, psychotherapy was offered only by *psychiatrists,* physicians who complete three to four additional years of training after medical school (a *residency*) in the treatment of abnormal mental functioning. After World War II, however, with millions of soldiers returning home to countries throughout North America and Europe, the demand for mental health services expanded so rapidly that other professional groups had to step in to fill the need.

Among those other groups are *clinical psychologists*—professionals who earn a doctorate in clinical psychology by completing four to five years of graduate training in abnormal functioning and its treatment as well as a one-year internship in a mental health setting. Psychotherapy and related services are also provided by *counseling psychologists, educational and school psychologists, psychiatric nurses, marriage therapists, family therapists,* and—the largest group—*clinical social workers* (see **Table 1-2**). Each of these specialties has its own graduate training program. Theoretically, each conducts therapy in a distinctive way, but in reality clinicians from the various specialties often use similar techniques.

A related development in the study and treatment of mental disorders since World War II has been the growth of effective research. *Clinical researchers* have tried to determine which concepts best explain and predict abnormal behavior, which treatments are most effective, and what kinds of changes in clinical theory or practice may be required. Well-trained clinical researchers conduct studies in universities, medical schools, laboratories, mental hospitals, mental health centers, and other clinical settings throughout the world. Their work has produced important discoveries and has changed many of our ideas about abnormal psychological functioning.

#FilmPsych

"My philosophy is if you worry, you suffer twice." (*Fantastic Beasts and Where to Find Them,* 2016)

"I suffer from short-term memory loss." (*Finding Dory,* 2016)

"Fear of death is illogical." (*Star Trek Beyond,* 2016)

"She wore the gloves all the time, so I just thought, maybe she has a thing about dirt." (*Frozen,* 2013)

"I just want to be perfect." (*Black Swan,* 2010)

"Take baby steps." (*What About Bob?,* 1991)

"I love the smell of napalm in the morning." (*Apocalypse Now,* 1979)

"Snakes. Why'd it have to be snakes?" (*Raiders of the Lost Ark,* 1981)

"Are you talkin' to me?" (*Taxi Driver,* 1976)

"Mother's not herself today." (*Psycho,* 1960)

Technology and Mental Health

The breathtaking rate of technological change that characterizes today's world has begun to have significant effects—both positive and negative—on the mental health field, and it will undoubtedly affect the field even more in the coming years.

Our digital world provides new triggers for abnormal behavior (Turkle, 2017, 2015; Cottle, 2016). As you'll see in Chapter 10, for example, many individuals who grapple

TABLE: 1-2

Profiles of Mental Health Professionals in the United States

	Degree	Began to Practice	Current Number	Average Annual Salary	Percent Female
Psychiatrists	MD, DO	1840s	49,000	$194,000	35%
Psychologists	PhD, PsyD, EdD	Late 1940s	188,000	$73,000	67%
Social workers	MSW, DSW	Early 1950s	649,000	$46,000	84%
Counselors	Various	Early 1950s	570,000	$45,000	71%

Information from: BLS, 2017, 2016; DPE, 2016; Salary.com, 2016; APA, 2015; Block, 2015; Pallardy, 2015.

"Looks like another case of someone over forty trying to understand Snapchat."

with gambling disorder have found the ready availability of Internet gambling to be all too inviting. Similarly, the Internet, texting, and social media have become convenient tools for those who wish to stalk or bully others, express sexual exhibitionism, or pursue pedophilic desires. Likewise, some clinicians believe that violent video games may contribute to the development of antisocial behavior. And, in the opinion of many clinicians, constant texting, tweeting, and Internet browsing may become an addictive behavior or may help lead to shorter attention spans.

A number of clinicians also worry that social networking can contribute to psychological dysfunction in certain cases. On the positive side, research indicates that, on average, social media users are particularly likely to maintain close relationships, receive social support, be trusting, and lead active lives (Hu et al., 2017; ACOG, 2016). But, on the negative side, there is research suggesting that social networking sites may increase peer pressure and social anxiety in some adolescents (Hanna et al., 2017; Houston, 2016). The sites may, for example, cause some people to develop fears that others in their network will exclude them socially. Similarly, such sites may facilitate shy or socially anxious people's withdrawal from valuable face-to-face relationships.

In addition, the face of clinical treatment is constantly changing in our fast-moving digital world. For example, **telemental health,** the use of various technologies to deliver mental health services without the therapist being physically present, is growing by leaps and bounds (Carpenter et al., 2018; Comer et al., 2017). As you'll see in Chapter 2, telemental health takes such forms as long-distance therapy between clients and therapists using videoconferencing, therapy offered by computer programs, and Internet-based support groups. And literally thousands of smartphone apps are devoted to relaxing people, cheering them up, giving them feel-good advice, helping them track their shifting moods and thoughts, or otherwise improving their psychological states.

Similarly, countless Web sites offer mental health information. Unfortunately, along with this wealth of online information comes an enormous amount of misinformation about psychological problems and their treatments, offered by persons and sites that are far from knowledgeable. And there are numerous antitreatment Web sites that try to guide people away from seeking help for their psychological problems. In later chapters, for example, you will read about pro-anorexia and pro-suicide Web sites and their dangerous influences. Clearly, the impact of technological change presents difficult challenges for clinicians and researchers alike.

#GenderShift

28% Percentage of psychologists in 1978 who were female

74% Percentage of current psychology graduate students who are female

(NCES, 2016; APA, 2015, 2014; Cynkar, 2007)

...SUMMING UP

RECENT DECADES AND CURRENT TRENDS In the 1950s, researchers discovered a number of new psychotropic medications. Their success contributed to a policy of deinstitutionalization, under which hundreds of thousands of patients were released from public mental hospitals. In addition, outpatient treatment has become the primary approach for most people with mental disorders, both mild and severe; prevention programs are growing in number and influence; the field of multicultural psychology has begun to influence how clinicians view and treat abnormality; and insurance coverage is having a significant impact on the way treatment is conducted.

It is also the case that a variety of perspectives and professionals have come to operate in the field of abnormal psychology, and many well-trained clinical researchers now investigate the field's theories and treatments. And finally, the remarkable technological advances of recent times have also affected the mental health field.

What Do Clinical Researchers Do?

Research is the key to accuracy in all fields of study; it is particularly important in abnormal psychology because a wrong belief in this field can lead to great suffering. At the same time, clinical researchers, also called clinical scientists, face certain challenges that make their work very difficult. They must, for example, figure out how to measure such elusive concepts as private thoughts, mood changes, and human potential. They must consider the different cultural backgrounds, races, and genders of the people they choose to study. And they must always ensure that the rights of their research participants, both human and animal, are not violated. Let us examine the leading methods used by today's researchers.

Clinical researchers try to discover broad laws, or principles, of abnormal psychological functioning. They search for a general, or *nomothetic,* understanding of the nature, causes, and treatments of abnormality. To gain such broad insights, clinical researchers, like scientists in other fields, use the **scientific method**—that is, they collect and evaluate information through careful observations. These observations in turn enable them to pinpoint and explain relationships between *variables.*

Simply stated, a variable is any characteristic or event that can vary, whether from time to time, from place to place, or from person to person. Age, sex, and race are human variables. So are eye color, occupation, and social status. Clinical researchers are interested in variables such as childhood upsets, present life experiences, moods, social functioning, and responses to treatment. They try to determine whether two or more such variables change together and whether a change in one variable causes a change in another. Will the death of a parent cause a child to become depressed? If so, will a given treatment reduce that depression?

Such questions cannot be answered by logic alone because scientists, like all human beings, frequently make errors in thinking. Thus, clinical researchers must depend mainly on three methods of investigation: the *case study,* which typically is focused on one individual, and the *correlational method* and *experimental method,* approaches that are usually used to gather information about many individuals. Each is best suited to certain kinds of circumstances and questions. Together, these methods enable scientists to form and test **hypotheses,** or hunches, that certain variables are related in certain ways—and to draw broad conclusions as to why. More properly, a hypothesis is a tentative explanation offered to provide a basis for an investigation.

telemental health The use of digital technologies to deliver mental health services without the therapist being physically present.

scientific method The process of systematically gathering and evaluating information, through careful observations, to understand a phenomenon.

hypothesis A hunch or prediction that certain variables are related in certain ways.

case study A detailed account of a person's life and psychological problems.

The Case Study

A **case study** is a detailed description of a person's life and psychological problems. It describes the person's history, present circumstances, and symptoms. It may also include speculation about why the problems developed, and it may describe the person's treatment (Tight, 2017). As you will see in Chapter 5, one of the field's best-known case studies, called *The Three Faces of Eve,* describes a woman with three alternating personalities, each having a distinct set of memories, preferences, and personal habits (Thigpen & Cleckley, 1957).

Most clinicians take notes and keep records in the course of treating their patients, and some further organize such notes into a formal case study to be shared with other professionals. The clues offered by a case study may help a clinician better understand or treat the person under discussion. In addition, case studies may play nomothetic roles that go far beyond the individual clinical case.

How Are Case Studies Helpful? Case studies are useful to researchers in many ways (Gerring, 2017; Tight, 2017). They can, for example, be a

The Genains One of the most celebrated case studies in abnormal psychology is a study of identical quadruplets dubbed the "Genain" sisters by researchers (after the Greek term for "dire birth"). All of the sisters developed schizophrenia in their twenties.

J.B. Handelsman The New Yorker Collection/The Cartoon Bank

"I'm a social scientist, Michael. That means I can't explain electricity or anything like that, but if you ever want to know about people I'm your man."

source of *new ideas* about behavior and "open the way for discoveries" (Bolgar, 1965). Sigmund Freud's theory of psychoanalysis was based mainly on the patients he saw in private practice. In addition, a case study may offer *tentative support* for a theory. Freud used case studies in this way as well, regarding them as evidence for the accuracy of his ideas. Conversely, case studies may serve to *challenge a theory's assumptions.*

Case studies may also show the value of *new therapeutic techniques.* And finally, case studies may offer opportunities to study *unusual problems* that do not occur often enough to permit a large number of observations. Investigators of disorders such as *dissociative identity disorder,* the multiple personality pattern on display in *The Three Faces of Eve,* once relied entirely on case studies for information.

What Are the Limitations of Case Studies? Case studies also have limitations (Gerring, 2017; Tight, 2017). First, they are reported by *biased observers,* that is, by therapists who have a personal stake in seeing their treatments succeed. These therapists must choose what to include in a case study, and their choices may at times be self-serving. Second, case studies rely on *subjective evidence.* Is a client's problem really caused by the events that the therapist or client says are responsible? After all, those are only a fraction of the events that may be contributing to the situation. Finally, case studies provide *little basis for generalization.* Even if we agree that Little Hans developed a dread of horses because he was terrified of castration and feared his father, how can we be confident that other people's phobias are rooted in the same kinds of causes? Events or treatments that seem important in one case may be of no help at all in efforts to understand or treat others.

Why do case studies and other anecdotal offerings influence people so much, often more than systematic research does?

The limitations of the case study are largely addressed by two other methods of investigation: the *correlational method* and the *experimental method.* These methods do not offer the rich detail that makes case studies so interesting, but they do help investigators draw broad conclusions about abnormality in the population at large. Thus most clinical investigators prefer these methods over the case study.

Three features of the correlational and experimental methods enable clinical investigators to gain general, or nomothetic, insights: (1) The researchers typically observe many individuals. (2) The researchers apply procedures uniformly and can thus repeat, or *replicate,* their investigations. (3) The researchers use *statistical tests* to analyze the results of their studies and determine whether broad conclusions are justified.

The Correlational Method

Correlation is the degree to which events or characteristics vary with each other. The **correlational method** is a research procedure used to determine this "co-relationship" between variables (Salkind, 2017). This method can be used, for example, to answer the question, "Is there a correlation between the amount of stress in people's lives and the degree of depression they experience?" That is, as people keep experiencing stressful events, are they increasingly likely to become depressed?

To test this question, researchers have collected life stress scores (for example, the number of threatening events experienced during a certain period of time) and depression scores (for example, scores on a depression survey) from individuals and have correlated these scores. The people who are chosen for a study are its subjects, or *participants,* the term preferred by today's investigators. Typically, investigators have found

correlation The degree to which events or characteristics vary along with each other.

correlational method A research procedure used to determine how much events or characteristics vary along with each other.

Bill Pugliano/Getty Images

Stress and depression At a 2016 prayer service in Flint, Michigan, a woman holds a sign that conveys the desperate predicament faced by her and thousands of other victims in the wake of the city's water contamination crisis. Studies find that the stress produced by this and similar community catastrophes has been accompanied by depression and other psychological symptoms in many residents (Goodnough & Atkinson, 2016).

that life stress and depression variables do indeed increase or decrease together (Yang et al., 2017; Hammen, 2016). That is, the greater someone's life stress score, the higher his or her score on the depression scale. When variables change the same way, their correlation is said to have a positive *direction* and is referred to as a *positive correlation*. Alternatively, correlations can have a negative rather than a positive direction. In a *negative correlation,* the value of one variable increases as the value of the other variable decreases. Researchers have found, for example, a negative correlation between depression and activity level. The greater one's depression, the lower the number of one's activities.

There is yet a third possible outcome for a correlational study. The variables under study may be *unrelated,* meaning that there is no consistent relationship between them. As the measures of one variable increase, those of the other variable sometimes increase and sometimes decrease. Studies have found that depression and intelligence are unrelated, for example.

In addition to knowing the direction of a correlation, researchers need to know its *magnitude,* or strength. That is, how closely do the two variables correspond? Does one *always* vary along with the other, or is their relationship less exact? When two variables are found to vary together very closely in person after person, the correlation is said to be high, or strong.

The direction and magnitude of a correlation are often calculated numerically and expressed by a statistical term called the *correlation coefficient.* The correlation coefficient can vary from +1.00, which indicates a perfect positive correlation between two variables, down to −1.00, which represents a perfect negative correlation. The *sign* of the coefficient (+ or −) signifies the direction of the correlation; the *number* represents its magnitude. The closer the correlation is to .00, the weaker, or lower in magnitude, it is. Thus correlations of +.75 and −.75 are of equal magnitude and equally strong, whereas a correlation of +.25 is weaker than either.

Everyone's behavior is changeable, and many human responses can be measured only approximately. Most correlations found in psychological research, therefore, fall short of perfect positive or negative correlation. For example, studies of life stress and depression have found correlations as high as +.53 (Krishnan, 2017; Miller et al., 1976). Although hardly perfect, a correlation of this magnitude is considered large in psychological research.

#

#WEIRDParticipants

Nearly 70 percent of psychology studies use college students as participants. These participants are often described by the acronym WEIRD, because they are overwhelmingly from societies that are Western, Educated, Industrialized, Rich, and Democratic (Robson, 2017; Henrich et al., 2010).

Imaginechina via AP Images

Twins, correlation, and inheritance These healthy twin sisters are participating in a twin cultural festival at Honglingjin Park in Beijing, China. Correlational studies of many pairs of twins have suggested a link between genetic factors and certain psychological disorders. Identical twins (who have identical genes) display a higher correlation for some disorders than do fraternal twins (whose genetic makeup is not identical).

When Can Correlations Be Trusted? Scientists must decide whether the correlation they find in a given sample of participants accurately reflects a real correlation in the general population. Could the observed correlation have occurred by mere chance? They can test their conclusions with a statistical analysis of their data, using principles of probability (Salkind, 2017). In essence, they ask how likely it is that the study's particular findings have occurred by chance. If the statistical analysis indicates that chance is unlikely to account for the correlation they found, researchers may conclude that their findings reflect a real correlation in the general population.

What Are the Merits of the Correlational Method? The correlational method has certain advantages over the case study (see **Table 1-3**). Because researchers measure their variables, observe many participants, and apply statistical analyses, they are in a better position to generalize their correlations to people beyond the ones they have studied. Furthermore, researchers can easily repeat correlational studies using new samples of participants to check the results of earlier studies.

Can you think of other correlations in life that are interpreted mistakenly as causal?

Although correlations allow researchers to describe the relationship between two variables, they do not *explain* the relationship. When we look at the positive correlation found in many life stress studies, we may be tempted to conclude that increases in recent life stress cause people to feel more depressed. In fact, however, the two variables may be correlated for any one of three reasons: (1) Life stress may cause depression. (2) Depression may cause people to experience more life stress (for example, a depressive approach to life may cause

TABLE: 1-3

Relative Strengths and Weaknesses of Research Methods

	Provides Individual Information	Provides General Information	Provides Causal Information	Statistical Analysis Possible	Replicable
Case study	Yes	No	No	No	No
Correlational method	No	Yes	No	Yes	Yes
Experimental method	No	Yes	Yes	Yes	Yes

people to perform poorly at work or may interfere with social relationships). (3) Depression and life stress may each be caused by a third variable, such as financial problems (Yazdi et al., 2018; Gutman & Nemeroff, 2011).

Although correlations say nothing about causation, they can still be of great use to clinicians. Clinicians know, for example, that suicide attempts increase as people become more depressed. Thus, when they work with severely depressed clients, they stay on the lookout for signs of suicidal thinking. Perhaps depression directly causes suicidal behavior, or perhaps a third variable, such as a sense of hopelessness, causes both depression and suicidal thoughts. Whatever the cause, just knowing that there is a correlation may enable clinicians to take certain measures (such as hospitalization) to help save lives.

Of course, in other instances, clinicians do need to know whether one variable causes another. Do parents' marital conflicts cause their children to be more anxious? Does job dissatisfaction lead to feelings of depression? Will a given treatment help people to cope more effectively in life? Questions about causality call for the experimental method.

experiment A research procedure in which a variable is manipulated and the effect of the manipulation on another variable is observed.

independent variable The variable in an experiment that is manipulated to determine whether it has an effect on another variable.

dependent variable The variable in an experiment that is expected to change as the independent variable is manipulated.

confound In an experiment, a variable other than the independent variable that is also acting on the dependent variable.

control group In an experiment, a group of participants who are not exposed to the independent variable.

The Experimental Method

An **experiment** is a research procedure in which a variable is manipulated and the manipulation's effect on another variable is observed (Leavy, 2017). The manipulated variable is called the **independent variable** and the variable being observed is called the **dependent variable.**

To examine the experimental method more fully, let's consider a question that is often asked by clinicians (Priday et al., 2017): "Does a particular therapy relieve the symptoms of a particular disorder?" Because this question is about a causal relationship, it can be answered only by an experiment. That is, experimenters must give the therapy in question to people who are suffering from a disorder and then observe whether they improve. Here the therapy is the independent variable, and psychological improvement is the dependent variable.

As with correlational studies, investigators who conduct experiments must do a statistical analysis on their data and find out how likely it is that the observed improvement is due to chance (Salkind, 2017). Again, if that likelihood is very low, the improvement is considered to be statistically significant, and the experimenter may conclude with some confidence that it is due to the independent variable.

If the true cause of changes in the dependent variable cannot be separated from other possible causes, then an experiment gives very little information. Thus, experimenters must try to eliminate all **confounds** from their studies—variables other than the independent variable that may also be affecting the dependent variable. When there are confounds in an experiment, they, rather than the independent variable, may be causing the observed change.

For example, situational variables, such as the location of the therapy office (say, a quiet country setting, as opposed to a busy city street) or soothing background music in the office, may have a therapeutic effect on participants in a therapy study. Or perhaps the participants are unusually motivated or have high expectations that the therapy will work, factors that thus account for their improvement. To guard against confounds, researchers should include three important features in their experiments—a *control group, random assignment,* and a *masked design* (Comer & Bry, 2018).

The Control Group A **control group** is a group of research participants who are not exposed to the independent variable under investigation but whose experience is similar to that of the experimental group, the participants who are exposed to the independent variable. By comparing the two groups, an experimenter can better determine the effect of the independent variable.

Is animal companionship an effective intervention? A ring-tailed lemur sits on the shoulder of an individual at Serengeti Park near Hodenhagen, Germany. It's part of a monthly program called "Psychiatric Animal Days" based on the premise that animals—even lemurs—have a calming effect on people. More than 400 kinds of intervention are currently used for psychological problems. An experimental design is needed to determine whether this or any other form of treatment causes clients to improve.

Holger Hollemann/picture-alliance/dpa/AP Images

experimental group In an experiment, the participants who are exposed to the independent variable under investigation.

random assignment A selection procedure that ensures that participants are randomly placed either in the control group or in the experimental group.

masked design An experiment in which participants do not know whether they are in the experimental or the control condition. Previously called a *blind design*.

quasi-experimental design A research design that fails to include key elements of a "pure" experiment and/or intermixes elements of both experimental and correlational studies. Also called a *mixed design*.

matched design A research design that matches the experimental participants with control participants who are similar on key characteristics.

To study the effectiveness of a particular therapy, for example, experimenters typically divide participants into two groups. The **experimental group** may come into an office and receive the therapy for an hour, while the control group may simply come into the office for an hour. If the experimenters find later that the people in the experimental group improve more than the people in the control group, they may conclude that the therapy was effective, above and beyond the effects of time, the office setting, and any other confounds. To guard against confounds, experimenters try to provide all participants, both control and experimental, with experiences that are identical in every way—except for the independent variable.

Random Assignment Researchers must also watch out for differences in the makeup of the experimental and control groups since those differences may also confound a study's results. In a therapy study, for example, the experimenter may unintentionally put wealthier participants in the experimental group and poorer ones in the control group. This difference, rather than their therapy, may be the cause of the greater improvement later found among the experimental participants. To reduce the effects of preexisting differences, experimenters typically use **random assignment.** This is the general term for any selection procedure that ensures that every participant in the experiment is as likely to be placed in one group as the other (Comer & Bry, 2018). Researchers might, for example, assign people to groups by flipping a coin or picking names out of a hat.

Masked Design A final confound problem is *bias*. Participants may bias an experiment's results by trying to please or help the experimenter. In a therapy experiment, for example, if those participants who receive the treatment know the purpose of the study and which group they are in, they might actually work harder to feel better or fulfill the experimenter's expectations. If so, *subject*, or *participant*, bias rather than therapy could be causing their improvement.

Why might sugar pills or other kinds of placebo treatments help some people feel better?

To avoid this bias, experimenters can prevent participants from finding out which group they are in. This experimental strategy is called a **masked design** (previously termed a *blind design*) because the individuals are kept unaware of their assigned group. In a therapy study, for example, control participants could be given a *placebo* (Latin for "I shall please"), something that looks or tastes like real therapy but has none of its key ingredients. This "imitation" therapy is called *placebo therapy*. If the experimental (true therapy) participants improve more than the control (placebo therapy) participants, experimenters have more confidence that the true therapy has caused their improvement.

An experiment may also be confounded by *experimenter bias*—that is, experimenters may have expectations that they unintentionally transmit to the participants in their

Peter Mueller The New Yorker Collection/The Cartoon Bank

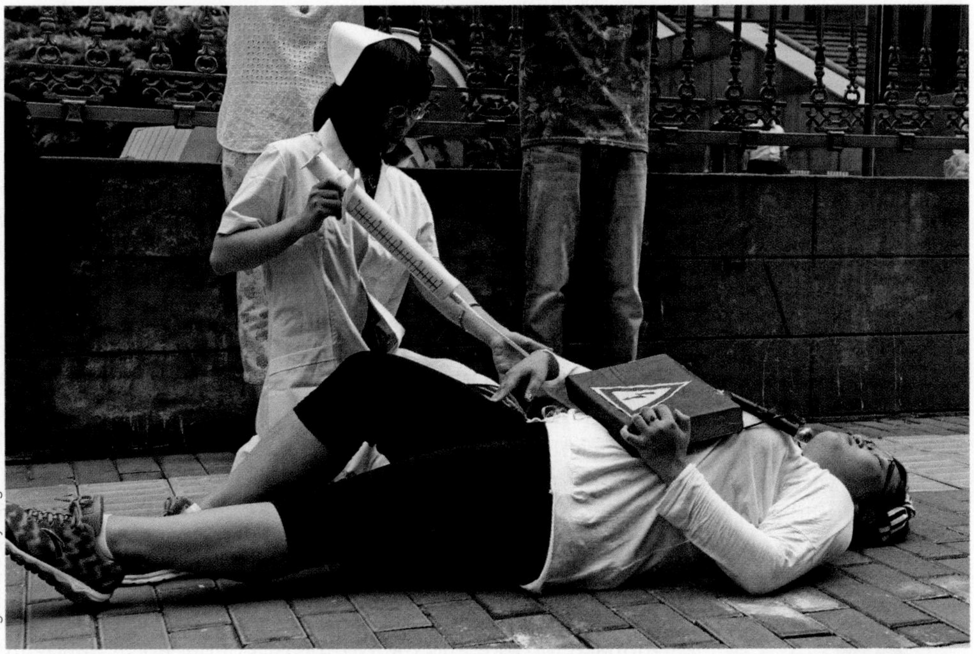

Greg Baker/Getty Images

Flawed studies, gigantic impact Outside a court hearing in Beijing on *conversion*, or *reparative, therapy*, an LGBTQ activist protests by pretending to inject a patient with a giant syringe. Conversion therapy, a now widely discredited psychological treatment to help gay persons change their sexual orientation, was positively received in a number of clinical circles after its development in the late 1990s. However, in 2012, Robert Spitzer, one of the world's most respected psychiatric researchers, offered a public apology to the gay community, saying that his and other influential research studies that had seemed to support the effectiveness of conversion therapy were fatally flawed and morally wrong.

studies. In a drug therapy study, for example, the experimenter might smile and act confident while providing real medications to the experimental participants but frown and appear hesitant while offering placebo drugs to the control participants. This kind of bias is sometimes referred to as the *Rosenthal effect,* after the psychologist who first identified it (Rosenthal, 1966). Experimenters can eliminate their own bias by arranging to be unaware themselves. In a drug therapy study, for example, an aide could make sure that the real medication and the placebo drug look identical. The experimenter could then administer treatment without knowing which participants were receiving true medications and which were receiving false medications. While either the participants or the experimenter may be kept unaware in an experiment, it is best that both be unaware—a research strategy called a *double-masked design*. In fact, most medication experiments now use double-masked designs to test promising drugs (Kim et al., 2017).

Alternative Research Designs

Clinical scientists must often settle for research designs that are less than ideal. These alternative designs are often called **quasi-experimental designs,** or **mixed designs**—designs that fail to include key elements of a "pure" experiment or intermix elements of both experimental and correlational studies (Leavy, 2017; Salkind, 2017). Such variations include the *matched design, natural experiment, analogue experiment, single-subject experiment, longitudinal study,* and *epidemiological study*.

In **matched designs,** investigators do not randomly assign participants to control and experimental groups, but instead make use of groups that already exist in the world at large. Consider, for example, research into the effects of child abuse. Because it would be unethical for investigators of this issue to actually abuse a randomly chosen group of children, they must instead compare children who already have a history of abuse with children who do not. To make this comparison as valid as possible, the researchers match the experimental participants (abused children) with control participants (non-abused children) who are similar in age, sex, race, number of children in the family, type of neighborhood, or other characteristics (Jacobsen, 2016). When the data from studies using this kind of design show that abused children are typically sadder and have lower self-esteem than matched control participants who have not been abused, the investigators can conclude with some confidence that abuse is causing the differences (Greger et al., 2016; Jaschek et al., 2016).

#

#EthicallyChallenged

Symptom-Exacerbation Studies In some studies, patients are given drugs to intensify their symptoms so that researchers may learn more about the biology of their disorder.

Medication-Withdrawal Studies In some studies, researchers prematurely stop medications for patients who have been symptom-free for a while, hoping to learn more about when patients can be taken off particular medications.

In **natural experiments,** nature itself manipulates the independent variable, while the experimenter observes the effects. Natural experiments must be used for studying the psychological effects of unusual and unpredictable events, such as floods, earthquakes, plane crashes, and fires. Because the participants in these studies are selected by an accident of fate rather than by the investigators' design, natural experiments are in fact quasi-experiments.

On December 26, 2004, an earthquake occurred beneath the Indian Ocean off the coast of Sumatra, Indonesia. The earthquake triggered a series of massive tsunamis that flooded the ocean's coastal communities, killed more than 225,000 people, injured over half a million, and left millions of survivors homeless, particularly in Indonesia, Sri Lanka, India, and Thailand. Within months of this disaster, researchers conducted natural experiments in which they collected data from hundreds of survivors and from control groups of people who lived in areas not directly affected by the tsunamis. The disaster survivors scored significantly higher on anxiety and depression measures (dependent variables) than the controls did. The survivors also experienced more sleep problems, feelings of detachment, arousal, difficulties concentrating, startle responses, and guilt feelings than the controls did (Adeback et al., 2018; Hussain et al., 2016). Over the past several years, other natural experiments have focused on survivors of the 2010 Haitian earthquake, Japan's massive earthquake in 2011, and the Northeast's Superstorm Sandy in 2012, as well as the devastating hurricanes in Houston, Florida, and Puerto Rico in 2017 and the raging wildfires that swept through parts of California in 2017 and 2018. These studies have also revealed lingering psychological symptoms among survivors of those disasters (Li et al., 2018; Usami et al., 2016).

Mikel Roberts/Getty Images

Similar enough? Celebrity chimpanzee Cheetah, age 59, does some painting along with her friend and trainer. Chimps and human beings share more than 90 percent of their genetic material, but their brains and bodies are very different, as are their perceptions and experiences. Thus, abnormal-like behavior produced in animal analogue experiments may differ from the human abnormality under study.

Researchers often run **analogue experiments.** Here they induce laboratory participants to behave in ways that seem to resemble real-life abnormal behavior and then conduct experiments on the participants in the hope of shedding light on the real-life abnormality. For example, as you'll see in Chapter 6, investigator Martin Seligman, in a classic body of work, has produced depression-like symptoms in laboratory participants—both animals and humans—by repeatedly exposing them to negative events (shocks, loud noises, task failures) over which they have no control. In these "learned helplessness" analogue studies, the participants seem to give up, lose their initiative, and become sad—suggesting to some clinicians that human depression itself may indeed be caused by loss of control over the events in one's life.

Scientists often use a **single-subject experimental design** when they do not have the luxury of experimenting on many participants (Comer & Bry, 2018; Lane et al., 2017). They may, for example, be investigating a disorder so rare that few participants are available. In designs of this kind, a single participant is observed both before and after the manipulation of an independent variable.

For example, using a particular single-subject design, called an *ABAB,* or *reversal, design,* one researcher sought to determine whether the systematic use of rewards would reduce a teenage boy's habit of disrupting his special education class with loud talk (Deitz, 1977). He rewarded the boy, who suffered from intellectual disability (previously called mental retardation), with extra teacher time whenever he went 55 minutes without interrupting the class more than three times. In condition A, the student was observed prior to receiving any reward, and he was found to disrupt the class frequently with loud talk. In condition B, the boy was given a series of teacher reward sessions (introduction of the independent variable); as expected, his loud talk decreased dramatically. Next, the rewards from the teacher were stopped (condition A again), and the student's loud talk increased once again. Apparently, the independent variable had indeed been the cause of the improvement. To be still more confident about this

Yuri_Arcurs/Getty Images

Life is a longitudinal study Photos of this same individual at different points in his life underscore the logic behind longitudinal studies. Just as this person's eyes, nose, and overall smile at the age of 5 seem to predict similar facial features at the ages of 35 and 55, so too might an individual's early temperament, sociability, or other psychological features sometimes predict adult characteristics. In some longitudinal studies, clinical researchers have found that a number of children who seem to be at particular risk for psychological disorders do indeed develop such disorders at later stages of their lives.

conclusion, the researcher had the teacher apply reward sessions yet again (condition B again). Once again the student's behavior improved.

Yet another alternative research design is the **longitudinal study,** in which investigators observe the same individuals on many occasions over a long period of time (Bryman, 2016). In several such studies, investigators have observed the progress over the years of normally functioning children whose mothers or fathers suffered from schizophrenia (Hameed & Lewis, 2016; Rasic et al., 2014). The researchers have found, among other things, that the children of the parents with the most severe cases of schizophrenia were particularly likely to develop a psychological disorder and to commit crimes at later points in their development.

As with some of the other quasi-experiments, researchers cannot directly manipulate the independent variable or randomly assign participants to conditions in a longitudinal study, and so they cannot definitively pinpoint causes. However, because longitudinal studies report the order of events, they do provide compelling clues about which events are more likely to be causes and which are more likely to be consequences.

Finally, researchers may conduct **epidemiological studies** to reveal how often a problem, such as a particular psychological disorder, occurs in a particular population. More specifically, they determine the incidence and prevalence of the problem (Jacobsen, 2016). *Incidence* is the number of new cases that emerge in a population during a given period of time. *Prevalence* is the total number of cases in the population during a given period; prevalence includes both existing and new cases.

Over the past 45 years, clinical researchers throughout the United States have worked on one of the largest epidemiological studies of mental disorders ever conducted, called the Epidemiologic Catchment Area Study (Cottler et al., 2016; Ramsey et al., 2013). They have interviewed more than 20,000 people in five cities to determine the prevalence of many psychological disorders in the United States and the treatment programs used. Two other large-scale epidemiological studies in the United States, the National Comorbidity Survey and the National Comorbidity Survey Replication, have questioned almost 15,000 individuals (Kelly & Mezuk, 2017; Kessler et al., 2014, 2012). Findings from these broad-population studies have been further compared with epidemiological studies of specific populations, such as Hispanic Americans and Asian Americans, or with epidemiological studies conducted in other countries, to see how rates of mental disorders and treatment programs vary from population to population and from country to country (Nobles et al., 2016).

Such epidemiological comparisons have helped researchers identify groups at risk for particular disorders. Women, it turns out, have a higher rate of anxiety disorders and depression than men, while men have a higher rate of alcoholism than women. Elderly people have a higher rate of suicide than young people. Hispanic Americans experience posttraumatic stress disorder more than other racial and ethnic groups in the United States. And persons in Western countries have higher rates of eating disorders than those in non-Western ones.

natural experiment An experiment in which nature, rather than an experimenter, manipulates an independent variable.

analogue experiment A research method in which the experimenter produces abnormal-like behavior in laboratory participants and then conducts experiments on the participants.

single-subject experimental design A research method in which a single participant is observed and measured both before and after the manipulation of an independent variable.

longitudinal study A study that observes the same participants on many occasions over a long period of time.

epidemiological study A study that measures the incidence and prevalence of a problem, such as a disorder, in a given population.

Institutional Review Board (IRB) An ethics committee in a research facility that is empowered to protect the rights and safety of human research participants.

What Are the Limits of Clinical Investigations?

We began this section by noting that clinical scientists look for general laws that will help them understand, treat, and prevent psychological disorders. As we have seen, however, circumstances can interfere with their progress.

Each method of investigation that we have observed addresses some of the problems involved in studying human behavior, but no one approach overcomes them all. Thus it is best to view each research method as part of a team of approaches that together may shed light on abnormal human functioning. When more than one method has been used to investigate a disorder, it is important to ask whether all the results seem to point in the same direction. If they do, clinical scientists are probably making progress toward understanding and treating that disorder. Conversely, if the various methods seem to produce conflicting results, the scientists must admit that knowledge in that particular area is still limited.

Protecting Human Participants

Human research participants have needs and rights that must be respected (see ***MindTech***). In fact, researchers' primary obligation is to avoid harming the human participants in their studies—physically or psychologically.

The vast majority of researchers are conscientious about fulfilling this obligation. They try to conduct studies that test their hypotheses and further scientific knowledge in a safe and respectful way (Leavy, 2017; Salkind, 2017). But there have been some notable exceptions to this over the years, particularly three infamous studies conducted in the mid-twentieth century. Partly because of such exceptions, the government and the institutions in which research is conducted now take careful measures to ensure that the safety and rights of human research participants are properly protected.

Who, beyond researchers themselves, might directly watch over the rights and safety of human participants? For the past several decades, that responsibility has been given to **Institutional Review Boards,** or **IRBs.** Each research facility has an IRB—a committee of five or more members who review and monitor every study conducted at that institution, starting when the studies are first proposed (Parker, 2016). The institution may be a university, medical school, psychiatric or medical hospital, private research facility, mental health center, or the like. If research is conducted there, the institution must have an IRB, and that IRB has the responsibility and power to require changes in a proposed study as a condition of approval. If acceptable changes are not made by the researcher, then the IRB can disapprove the study altogether. Similarly, if over the course of the study, the safety or rights of the participants are placed in jeopardy, the IRB must intervene and can even stop the study if necessary. These powers are granted to IRBs (or similar ethics committees) by nations around the world. In the United States, for example, IRBs are empowered by two agencies of the federal government—the Office for Human Research Protections and the Food and Drug Administration.

Might outside restrictions on research interfere with necessary investigations and thus limit potential gains for human beings?

It turns out that protecting the rights and safety of human research participants is a complex undertaking. Thus, IRBs often are forced to conduct a kind of risk-benefit analysis in their reviews. They may, for example, approve a study that poses minimal or slight risks to participants if that "acceptable" level of risk is offset by the study's potential benefits to society. In general, IRBs try to ensure that each study grants the following rights to its participants:

- The participants enlist voluntarily.
- Before enlisting, the participants are adequately informed about what the study entails ("informed consent").

A national disgrace In a 1997 White House ceremony, President Bill Clinton offers an official apology to 94-year-old Herman Shaw and other African American men whose syphilis went untreated by government doctors and researchers in the Tuskegee Syphilis Study, a research undertaking conducted from 1932 to 1972, prior to the emergence of Institutional Review Boards. In this infamous study, 399 participants were not informed that they had the disease, and they continued to go untreated even after it was discovered that penicillin is an effective intervention for syphilis.

Stephen Jaffe/AFP/Getty Images

MINDTECH

The Use and Misuse of Social Media

Over the past several years, more and more researchers have been turning to social networks for their studies. One study, for example, demonstrates the power and potential of using social media data (Kosinski et al., 2016, 2013). In this investigation, 58,000 Facebook subscribers allowed the researchers access to their list of "likes," and the subscribers further filled out online personality tests. The study found that information about a participant's likes could predict with some accuracy his or her personality traits, level of happiness, use of addictive substances, and level of intelligence, among other variables.

What a great resource, right? Not so fast. The study above did indeed ask subscribers whether they were willing to participate. However, in a number of other such studies, social media users do not know that their posted data is being examined and tested. Here, the researchers assert that because posted information is already publicly available, users need not be informed that their data is under examination—a view that has produced enormous debate.

An area that has raised additional ethical concerns involves the direct and secret *manipulation* of social media users by researchers—an approach illustrated in a study conducted by a team of researchers from both Facebook and academia (Kramer et al., 2014). The investigators wanted to determine whether the content of news feeds on Facebook influences the moods of its users. Without the users knowing it, the researchers reduced the number of positive news feed posts seen by around 350,000 users and reduced the number of negative posts seen by another 350,000 users over a one-week period. As a result, the moods of the former users became slightly (but significantly) more negative than those of the latter users, as measured by the number of negative and positive words posted by the users themselves in their Facebook status updates over the course of that same week.

This study immediately triggered a flood of criticism (Golder et al., 2017; Flick, 2016). One concern was that the users in the study were unaware of and did not give consent for their participation. Critics holding this view were unimpressed with the claim that signing on to Facebook's lengthy and small-print user agreement represents a sufficient form of informed consent for this or similar social

Dominic Lipinski/Press Association via AP Images

media studies. Another concern was that, by inducing more negative moods, the researchers in this study might have been feeding into the clinical depressions of some negative news feed users.

Can an argument be made that ethical standards for studies using the Internet and social media should be different from those applied to other kinds of research?

A core problem for all social media studies is that most social media sites do not really have policies prohibiting researchers from studying subscribers or subscriber profiles without clear permission. While the technology-driven questions of what's public and what's private are under debate, it is probably best that posters follow a new version of that most sacred rule of consumerism—"poster beware."

- The participants can end their participation in the study at any time.
- The benefits of the study outweigh its costs/risks.
- The participants are protected from physical and psychological harm.
- The participants have access to information about the study.
- The participants' privacy is protected by principles such as confidentiality or anonymity.

Unfortunately, even with IRBs on the job, these rights can be in jeopardy. Consider, for example, the right of informed consent. To help ensure that participants understand what they are getting into when they enlist for a study, IRBs typically require that the individuals read and sign an "informed consent form" that spells out everything they need to know. But how clear are such forms? Not very, according to some investigations (Perrault & Nazione, 2016; Mathew & McGrath, 2002).

It turns out that most such forms—the very forms deemed acceptable by IRBs—are too long and/or are written at an advanced college level, making them incomprehensible to a large percentage of participants. In fact, fewer than half of all participants may fully understand the informed consent forms they are signing. Still other investigations

Raveendran/AFP/Getty Images

Making a point The rights of animal subjects must also be considered. Here, with his body painted as a monkey, an activist from the organization PETA (People for the Ethical Treatment of Animals) sits in a cage to protest the use of animals in research at a medical science institute in India.

indicate that only around 10 percent of human participants carefully read the informed consent forms before signing them, and only 30 percent ask questions of the researchers during the informed consent phase of the studies (CISCRP, 2013).

In short, the IRB system is flawed, much like the research undertakings it oversees. One reason for this is that ethical principles are subtle notions that do not always translate into simple guidelines. Another reason is that ethical decisions—whether by IRB members or by researchers—are subject to differences in perspective, interpretation, decision-making style, and the like. Despite such problems, most observers agree that the creation and work of IRBs have helped improve the rights and safety of human research participants over the years.

...SUMMING UP

WHAT DO CLINICAL RESEARCHERS DO? Researchers use the scientific method to uncover nomothetic principles of abnormal psychological functioning. They attempt to identify and examine relationships between variables and depend primarily on three methods of investigation: the case study, the correlational method, and the experimental method.

A case study is a detailed account of a person's life and psychological problems. Correlational studies are used to systematically observe the degree to which events or characteristics vary together. This method allows researchers to draw broad conclusions about abnormality in the population at large. In experiments, researchers manipulate suspected causes to see whether expected effects will result. This method enables researchers to determine the causes of various conditions or events.

Clinical scientists must often settle for alternative research designs that are less than ideal, called quasi-experimental designs, or mixed designs. These include the matched design, natural experiment, analogue experiment, single-subject experiment, longitudinal study, and epidemiological study.

Each research facility has an Institutional Review Board (IRB) that has the power and responsibility to protect the rights and safety of human participants in all studies conducted at that facility. Members of the IRB review each study during the planning stages and can require changes in the proposed study before granting approval for the undertaking. Among the important participant rights that the IRB protects is the right of informed consent, an acceptable risk/benefit balance, and privacy (confidentiality or anonymity).

Moving Forward

Since ancient times, people have tried to explain, treat, and study abnormal behavior. By examining the responses of past societies to such behaviors, we can better understand the roots of our present views and treatments. In addition, a look backward helps us appreciate just how far we have come.

At the same time, we must recognize the many problems in abnormal psychology today. The field has yet to agree on one definition of abnormality. It is currently made up of conflicting schools of thought and treatment whose members are often unimpressed by the claims and accomplishments of the others. Clinical practice is carried out by a variety of professionals trained in different ways. And current research methods each have flaws that limit our knowledge and use of clinical information.

As you travel through the topics in this book, keep in mind the field's current strengths and weaknesses, the progress that has been made, and the journey that lies ahead. Perhaps the most important lesson to be learned from our look at the history of this field is that our current understanding of abnormal behavior represents a work in progress—with some of the most important insights, investigations, and changes yet to come.

#

#TheirWords

"I became insane, with long intervals of horrible sanity."

Edgar Allen Poe

... Key Terms

abnormal psychology, p. 2
deviance, p. 3
norms, p. 3
culture, p. 3
distress, p. 3
dysfunction, p. 4
danger, p. 4
treatment, p. 6
trephination, p. 7
humors, p. 8
asylum, p. 9
moral treatment, p. 10
state hospitals, p. 11
somatogenic perspective, p. 11
psychogenic perspective, p. 11
psychoanalysis, p. 13
psychotropic medications, p. 14
deinstitutionalization, p. 14
private psychotherapy, p. 15
prevention, p. 16
positive psychology, p. 16
multicultural psychology, p. 16
managed care program, p. 18
telemental health, p. 20
scientific method, p. 21
hypothesis, p. 21
case study, p. 21
correlation, p. 22
correlational method, p. 22
experiment, p. 25
independent variable, p. 25
dependent variable, p. 25
confound, p. 25
control group, p. 25
experimental group, p. 26
random assignment, p. 26
masked design, p. 26
placebo therapy, p 26
quasi-experimental design, p. 27
matched design, p. 27
natural experiment, p. 28
analogue experiment, p. 28
single-subject experimental design, p. 28
longitudinal study, p. 29
epidemiological study, p. 29
prevalence, p. 29
Institutional Review Board (IRB), p. 30
informed consent, p. 30

... Quick Quiz

1. What features are common to abnormal psychological functioning? *pp. 2–4*
2. Name two forms of past treatments that reflect a demonological view of abnormal behavior. *pp. 7–9*
3. Give examples of the somatogenic view of psychological abnormality from Hippocrates, the Renaissance, the nineteenth century, and the twentieth century. *pp. 8–12*
4. Describe the role of hypnotism and hysterical disorders in the development of the psychogenic view. *pp. 12–13*
5. How did Sigmund Freud come to develop the theory and technique of psychoanalysis? *p. 13*
6. Describe the major changes that have occurred since the 1950s in the understanding and treatment of psychological abnormality. *pp. 14–20*
7. What are the advantages and disadvantages of the case study, correlational method, and experimental method? *pp. 21–30*
8. What techniques do researchers include in experiments to guard against the influence of confounds? *pp. 25–27*
9. Describe six alternative research designs often used by investigators. *pp. 27–29*
10. What are Institutional Review Boards, and what are their responsibilities and goals? *pp. 30–32*

Visit ***LaunchPad***
to access the e-Book, Clinical Choices, videos, activities, and LearningCurve, as well as study aids including flashcards, FAQs, and research exercises.

LaunchPad

CHAPTER

2

Models of Abnormality

TOPIC OVERVIEW

Philip Berman, a 25-year-old single unemployed former copy editor for a large publishing house . . . had been hospitalized after a suicide attempt in which he deeply gashed his wrist with a razor blade. He described [to the therapist] how he had sat on the bathroom floor and watched the blood drip into the bathtub for some time before he [contacted] his father at work for help. He and his father went to the hospital emergency room to have the gash stitched, but he convinced himself and the hospital physician that he did not need hospitalization. The next day when his father suggested he needed help, he knocked his dinner to the floor and angrily stormed to his room. When he was calm again, he allowed his father to take him back to the hospital.

The immediate precipitant for his suicide attempt was that he had run into one of his former girlfriends with her new boyfriend. The patient stated that they had a drink together, but all the while he was with them he could not help thinking that "they were dying to run off and jump in bed." He experienced jealous rage, got up from the table, and walked out of the restaurant. He began to think about how he could "pay her back."

Mr. Berman had felt frequently depressed for brief periods during the previous several years. He was especially critical of himself for his limited social life and his inability to have managed to have sexual intercourse with a woman even once in his life. As he related this to the therapist, he lifted his eyes from the floor and with a sarcastic smirk said, "I'm a 25-year-old virgin. Go ahead, you can laugh now." He has had several girlfriends to date, whom he described as very attractive, but who he said had lost interest in him. On further questioning, however, it became apparent that Mr. Berman soon became very critical of them and demanded that they always meet his every need, often to their own detriment. The women then found the relationship very unrewarding and would soon find someone else.

During the past two years Mr. Berman had seen three psychiatrists briefly, one of whom had given him a drug, the name of which he could not remember, but that had precipitated some sort of unusual reaction for which he had to stay in a hospital overnight. . . . Concerning his hospitalization, the patient said that "It was a dump," that the staff refused to listen to what he had to say or to respond to his needs, and that they, in fact, treated all the patients "sadistically." The referring doctor corroborated that Mr. Berman was a difficult patient who demanded that he be treated as special, and yet was hostile to most staff members throughout his stay. After one angry exchange with an aide, he left the hospital without [permission], and subsequently signed out against medical advice.

Mr. Berman is one of two children of a middle-class family. His father is 55 years old and employed in a managerial position for an insurance company. He perceives his father as weak and ineffectual, completely dominated by the patient's overbearing and cruel mother. He states that he hates his mother with "a passion I can barely control." He claims that his mother used to call him names like "pervert" . . . when he was growing up, and that in an argument she once "kicked me in the balls." Together, he sees his parents as rich, powerful, and selfish, and, in turn, thinks that they see him as lazy, irresponsible, and a behavior problem. When his parents called the therapist to discuss their son's treatment, they stated that his problem began with the birth of his younger brother, Arnold, when Philip was 10 years old. After Arnold's birth Philip apparently became [a disagreeable] child who cursed a lot and was difficult to discipline. Philip recalls this period only vaguely. He reports that his mother once was hospitalized for depression, but that now "she doesn't believe in psychiatry."

Mr. Berman had graduated from college with average grades. Since graduating he had worked at three different publishing houses, but at none of them for more than one year. He always found some justification for quitting. He usually sat around his house doing very little for two or three months after quitting a job, until his parents prodded him into getting a new one. He described innumerable interactions in his life with teachers, friends, and employers in which he felt offended or unfairly treated . . . and frequent arguments that left him feeling bitter . . . and [he] spent most of his time alone, "bored." He was unable to commit himself to any person, he held no strong convictions, and he felt no allegiance to any group.

The patient appeared as a very thin, bearded . . . young man with pale skin who maintained little eye contact with the therapist and who had an air of angry bitterness about him. Although he complained of depression, he denied other symptoms of the depressive syndrome. He seemed preoccupied with his rage at his parents, and seemed particularly invested in conveying a despicable image of himself. . . .

(Spitzer et al., 1983, pp. 59–61)

Philip Berman is clearly a troubled person, but how did he come to be that way? How do we explain and correct his many problems? To answer these questions, we must first look at the wide range of complaints we are trying to understand: Philip's depression and anger, his social failures, his lack of employment, his distrust of those around him, and the problems within his family. Then we must sort through all kinds of potential causes—internal and external, biological and interpersonal, past and present.

Although we may not realize it, we all use theoretical frameworks as we read about Philip. Over the course of our lives, each of us has developed a perspective that helps us make sense of the things other people say and do. In science, the perspectives used to explain events are known as **models,** or **paradigms.** Each model spells out the scientist's basic assumptions, gives order to the field under study, and sets guidelines for its investigation (Kuhn, 1962). It influences what the investigators observe as well as the questions they ask, the information they seek, and how they interpret this information. To understand how a clinician explains or treats a specific set of symptoms, such as Philip's, we must know his or her preferred model of abnormal functioning.

AP Photo/Bloomington Herald-Times, Jeremy Hogan

A fascinating subject The human brain increasingly has captured the attention not only of neuroscientists but also the public at large. Here an eighth-grade student holds and examines a brain ever so carefully during a visit to the psychology department at Indiana University.

Until relatively recently, clinical scientists of a given place and time tended to agree on a single model of abnormality—a model greatly influenced by the beliefs of their culture. The *demonological model* that was used to explain abnormal functioning during the Middle Ages, for example, borrowed heavily from medieval society's concerns with religion, superstition, and warfare. Medieval practitioners would have seen the devil's guiding hand in Philip Berman's efforts to commit suicide and his feelings of depression, rage, jealousy, and hatred. Similarly, their treatments for him—from prayers to whippings—would have sought to drive foreign spirits from his body.

Today several models are used to explain and treat abnormal functioning. This variety has resulted both from shifts in values and beliefs over the past half-century and from improvements in clinical research. At one end of the spectrum is the *biological model,* which sees physical processes as key to human behavior. In the middle are three models that focus on more psychological and personal aspects of human functioning: The *psychodynamic model* looks at people's unconscious internal processes and conflicts; the *cognitive-behavioral model* emphasizes behavior, the ways in which it is learned, and the thinking that underlies behavior; and the *humanistic-existential model* stresses the role of values and choices. At the far end of the spectrum is the *sociocultural model,* which looks to social and cultural forces as the keys to human functioning. This model includes the *family-social perspective,* which focuses on an individual's family and social interactions, and the *multicultural perspective,* which emphasizes an individual's culture and the shared beliefs, values, and history of that culture.

Given their different assumptions and principles, the models are sometimes in conflict. Those who exclusively follow one perspective often scoff at the "naïve" interpretations, investigations, and treatment efforts of the others. Yet none of the models is complete in itself. Each focuses mainly on one aspect of human functioning, and none can explain all aspects of abnormality. ■

The Biological Model

Philip Berman is a biological being. His thoughts and feelings are the results of biochemical and bioelectrical processes throughout his brain and body. Proponents of the *biological model* believe that a full understanding of Philip's thoughts, emotions, and behavior must therefore include an understanding of their biological basis. Not surprisingly, then, they believe that the most effective treatments for Philip's problems will be biological ones.

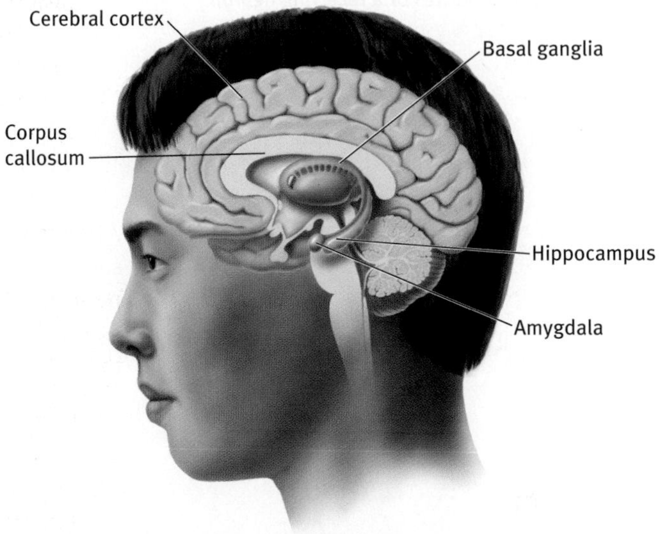

FIGURE 2-1

The Cerebrum

Some psychological disorders can be traced to abnormal functioning of neurons in the cerebrum, which includes brain structures such as the cerebral cortex, corpus callosum, basal ganglia, hippocampus, and amygdala.

How Do Biological Theorists Explain Abnormal Behavior?

Adopting a medical perspective, biological theorists view abnormal behavior as an illness brought about by malfunctioning parts of the organism. Typically, they point to problems in brain anatomy, brain chemistry, and/or brain circuitry as the cause of such behavior.

Brain Anatomy and Abnormal Behavior The brain is made up of approximately 86 billion nerve cells, called **neurons,** and thousands of billions of support cells, called *glia* (from the Greek word for "glue") (Jernigan & Stiles, 2017). Within the brain large groups of neurons form distinct regions, or *brain structures.* Toward the top of the brain, for example, is a cluster of structures, collectively referred to as the *cerebrum,* which includes the *cortex, corpus callosum, basal ganglia, hippocampus,* and *amygdala* (see Figure 2-1). The neurons in each of these brain structures help control important functions. The basal ganglia, for example, plays a crucial role in planning and producing movement, and the amygdala plays a key role in emotional memory. Clinical researchers have sometimes linked particular psychological disorders to problems in specific structures of the brain. One such disorder is *Huntington's disease,* a disorder marked by involuntary body movements, violent emotional outbursts, memory loss, suicidal thinking, and absurd beliefs. This disease has been linked in part to a loss of cells in the basal ganglia and cortex.

Brain Chemistry and Abnormal Behavior Biological researchers have also learned that psychological disorders can be related to problems in the transmission of messages from neuron to neuron. Information is communicated throughout the brain in the form of electrical impulses that travel from one neuron to one or more others. An impulse is first received by a neuron's *dendrites,* antenna-like extensions located at one end of the neuron. From there it travels down the neuron's *axon,* a long fiber extending from the neuron's body. Finally, it is transmitted through the *nerve ending* at the end of the axon to the dendrites of other neurons (see Figure 2-2). Each neuron has multiple dendrites and a single axon. But that axon can be very long indeed, often extending all the way from one structure of the brain to another.

How do messages get from the nerve ending of one neuron to the dendrites of another? After all, the neurons do not actually touch each other. A tiny space, called the **synapse,** separates one neuron from the next, and the message must somehow move across that space. When an electrical impulse reaches a neuron's ending, the nerve ending is stimulated to release a chemical, called a **neurotransmitter,** that travels across the synaptic space to **receptors** on the dendrites of the neighboring neurons.

model A set of assumptions and concepts that help scientists explain and interpret observations. Also called a *paradigm.*

neuron A nerve cell.

synapse The tiny space between the nerve ending of one neuron and the dendrite of another.

neurotransmitter A chemical that, released by one neuron, crosses the synaptic space to be received at receptors on the dendrites of neighboring neurons.

receptor A site on a neuron that receives a neurotransmitter.

FIGURE 2-2

A Neuron Communicating Information

A message in the form of an electrical impulse travels down the sending neuron's axon to its nerve ending, where neurotransmitters are released and carry the message across the synaptic space to the dendrites of a receiving neuron.

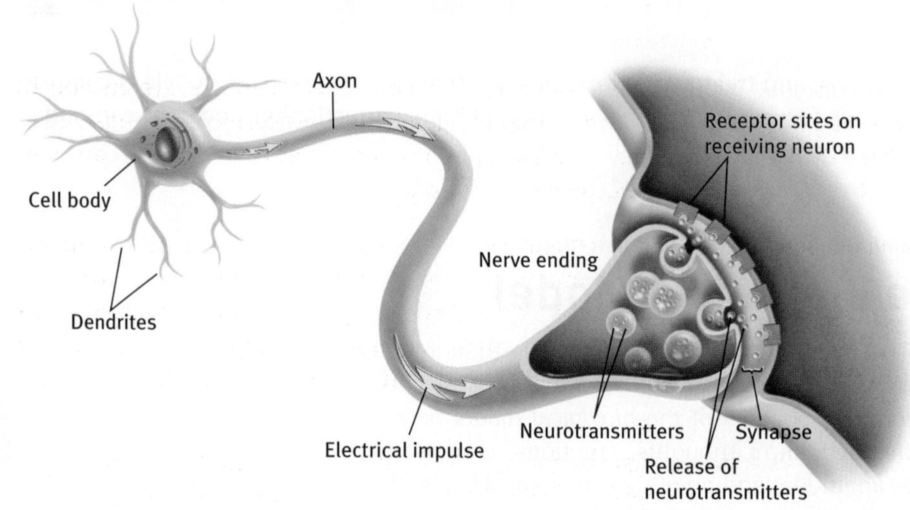

After binding to the receiving neuron's receptors, some neurotransmitters give a message to receiving neurons to "fire," that is, to trigger their own electrical impulse. Other neurotransmitters carry an inhibitory message; they tell receiving neurons to stop all firing. As you can see, neurotransmitters play a key role in moving information through the brain.

Researchers have identified dozens of neurotransmitters in the brain, and they have learned that each neuron uses only certain kinds. Studies indicate that abnormal activity by certain neurotransmitters is sometimes tied to mental disorders. Depression, for example, has been linked in part to low activity of the neurotransmitters *serotonin* and *norepinephrine*. Perhaps low serotonin activity is at play in Philip Berman's pattern of depression and rage.

In addition to focusing on neurons and neurotransmitters, researchers have learned that mental disorders are sometimes related to abnormal chemical activity in the body's *endocrine system*. Endocrine glands, located throughout the body, work along with neurons to control such vital activities as growth, reproduction, sexual activity, heart rate, body temperature, and responses to stress. The glands release chemicals called **hormones** into the bloodstream, and these chemicals then propel body organs into action. During times of stress, for example, the *adrenal glands*, located on top of the kidneys, secrete the hormone *cortisol* to help the body deal with the stress. Abnormal secretions of this chemical have been tied to anxiety and depression.

Brain Circuitry and Abnormal Behavior Over the past decade, researchers have increasingly focused on **brain circuits** as the key to psychological disorders rather than on dysfunction within a single brain structure or by a single brain chemical. A brain circuit is a network of particular brain structures that work together, triggering each other into action to produce a distinct behavioral, cognitive, or emotional reaction. How do the structures of a given circuit work together? The answer, as you might anticipate by now, is through their neurons. The long axons of the neurons from one structure bundle together and extend across the brain to communicate with the neurons of another structure, setting up a fiber pathway between the structures. The structures and neurotransmitters that make up a given brain circuit are, as you read above, important individually, but research indicates that it is usually most informative to look at the operation of the entire circuit, including its interconnecting fiber pathways, to fully understand human functioning. Proper *interconnectivity* (communication) among the structures of a circuit tends to result in healthy psychological functioning, whereas flawed interconnectivity may lead to abnormal functioning.

One of the brain's most important circuits is the "fear circuit." As you will see in Chapter 4, this circuit consists of a number of specific structures (including the amygdala and prefrontal cortex) whose interconnecting fiber pathways enable the structures to trigger each other into action and to produce our everyday fear reactions. Studies suggest that this circuit functions improperly (that is, displays flawed interconnectivity)

hormones The chemicals released by endocrine glands into the bloodstream.

brain circuit A network of particular brain structures that work together, triggering each other into action to produce a distinct kind of behavioral, cognitive, or emotional reaction.

genes Chromosome segments that control the characteristics and traits we inherit.

in people suffering from anxiety disorders (Williams, 2017). Perhaps dysfunction by Philip Berman's fear circuit is contributing to his repeated concerns that things will go badly and that other people will have low opinions and negative motives toward him, concerns that keep triggering his depression and anger.

Sources of Biological Abnormalities Why might the brain structures, neurotransmitters, or brain circuits of some people function differently from the norm? As you will see throughout the textbook, a wide range of factors can play a role—from prenatal events to brain injuries, viral infections, environmental experiences, and stress. Two factors that have received particular attention in the biological model are *genetics* and *evolution*.

GENETICS AND ABNORMAL BEHAVIOR Each cell in the human brain and body contains 23 pairs of *chromosomes*, with each chromosome in a pair inherited from one of the person's parents. Every chromosome contains numerous **genes**—segments that control the characteristics and traits a person inherits. Altogether, each cell contains around 20,000 genes (Dunham, 2018). Scientists have known for years that genes help determine such physical characteristics as hair color, height, and eyesight. Genes can make people more prone to heart disease, cancer, or diabetes, and perhaps to possessing artistic or musical skill. Studies suggest that inheritance also can play a part in certain mental disorders.

In most instances, several or more genes combine to help produce our actions and reactions, both functional and dysfunctional. The precise contributions of various genes or gene combinations to mental disorders have become clearer in recent years, thanks in part to the completion of the *Human Genome Project* in 2000, a major undertaking in which scientists used the tools of molecular biology to *map*, or *sequence*, all of the genes in the human body.

EVOLUTION AND ABNORMAL BEHAVIOR Genes that contribute to mental disorders are typically viewed as unfortunate occurrences—almost mistakes of inheritance. The responsible gene may be a *mutation*, an abnormal form of the appropriate gene that emerges by accident. Or the problematic gene may be inherited by an individual after it has initially entered his or her family line as a mutation. According to some theorists, however, many of the genes that contribute to abnormal functioning are actually the result of normal *evolutionary* principles (Ram, Liberman, & Feldman, 2018; Fábrega, 2010).

#

#TheirWords

"Help! I'm being held prisoner by my heredity and environment."

Dennis Allen

Etienne Oliveau/Getty Images

More than coincidence? Identical twins Mike and Bob Bryan, shown here returning a shot during a semifinal tennis match at the 2016 China Open, have had storied careers. Ranked as the world's top doubles tennis players, they have won multiple Olympic medals representing the United States. Studies of twins suggest that some aspects of behavior and personality are influenced by genetic factors. Many identical twins, like the Bryans, have similar tastes, behave similarly, and make similar life choices. Some even develop similar abnormal behaviors.

psychotropic medications Drugs that primarily affect the brain and reduce many symptoms of mental dysfunction.

brain stimulation Interventions that directly or indirectly stimulate the brain in order to bring about psychological improvement.

electroconvulsive therapy (ECT) A biological treatment in which a brain seizure is triggered when an electric current passes through electrodes attached to the patient's forehead.

In general, evolutionary theorists argue that human reactions and the genes responsible for them have survived over the course of time because they have helped individuals to thrive and adapt. Ancestors who had the ability to run fast, for example, or the craftiness to hide were most able to escape their enemies and to reproduce. Thus, the genes responsible for effective walking, running, or problem solving were particularly likely to be passed on from generation to generation to the present day.

Similarly, say evolutionary theorists, the capacity to experience fear was, and in many instances still is, adaptive. Fear alerted our ancestors to dangers, threats, and losses so that persons could avoid or escape potential problems. People who were particularly sensitive to danger—those with greater fear responses—were more likely to survive catastrophes, battles, and the like and to reproduce and pass on their fear genes. Of course, in today's world, pressures are more numerous and often more subtle than they were in the past, condemning many individuals with such genes to a near-endless stream of fear and arousal. That is, the very genes that helped their ancestors to survive and reproduce might now leave these individuals particularly prone to fear reactions, anxiety disorders, or related psychological patterns.

The evolutionary perspective is controversial in the clinical field and has been rejected by many theorists. Imprecise and at times impossible to research, scientists often find such explanations unacceptable.

Biological Treatments

Biological practitioners look for certain kinds of clues when they treat people who are behaving abnormally. Does the person's family have a history of that behavior, and hence a possible genetic predisposition to it? (Philip Berman's case history mentions that his mother was once hospitalized for depression.) Is the behavior produced by events that could have had a physiological effect? (Philip was having a drink when he flew into a jealous rage at the restaurant.) Once the clinicians have pinpointed physical sources of dysfunction, they are in a better position to choose a biological course of treatment. The three leading kinds of biological treatments used today are *drug therapy, brain stimulation,* and *psychosurgery*. Drug therapy is by far the most common of these approaches.

In the 1950s, researchers discovered several effective **psychotropic medications,** drugs that mainly affect emotions and thought processes. These drugs have greatly changed the outlook for a number of mental disorders and today are used widely, either alone or with other forms of therapy (see ***Trending***). However, the psychotropic drug revolution has also produced some major problems. Many people believe, for example, that the drugs are overused. Moreover, while drugs are effective in many cases, they do not help everyone.

What might the popularity of psychotropic drugs suggest about coping styles and problem-solving skills in our society?

Four major psychotropic drug groups are used in therapy. *Antianxiety drugs,* also called *minor tranquilizers* or *anxiolytics,* help reduce tension and anxiety. *Antidepressant drugs* help improve the functioning of people with depression and certain other disorders. *Antibipolar drugs,* also called *mood stabilizers,* help steady the moods of those with a bipolar disorder, a condition marked by mood swings from mania to depression. And *antipsychotic drugs* help reduce the confusion, hallucinations, and delusions that often accompany *psychosis,* a loss of contact with reality found in schizophrenia and other disorders.

Psychotropic drugs, like all medications, reach the marketplace only after systematic research and review. It takes an average of 12 years and hundreds of millions of dollars for a pharmaceutical company in the United States to bring a newly identified chemical compound to market. Along the way, the drug is vigorously tested in study after study—first on animals and then on humans—to determine its efficacy, safety, dosage, and side effects, until finally it receives approval by the U.S. Food and Drug Administration. Only 3 percent of newly discovered chemical compounds make it to animal testing,

...TRENDING

TV Drug Ads Come Under Attack

"Ask your doctor about Abilify." "There is no need to suffer any longer." Anyone who watches television or browses the Internet is familiar with phrases such as these. They are at the heart of *direct-to-consumer (DTC)* drug advertising—advertisements in which pharmaceutical companies appeal directly to consumers, coaxing them to ask their physicians to prescribe particular drugs for them. The United States and New Zealand are the only developed countries in the world that allow such advertising. Around 80 percent of American adults have seen these ads, and at least 30 percent ask their doctors about the specific medications they see advertised (ProCon, 2016; Hausman, 2008). Half of today's leading DTC-advertised medications are *psychotropic* drugs such as antibipolar and antipsychotic drugs (Brown, 2017; Bulik, 2017).

DTC ads have flooded the airwaves since 1997 when the U.S. Food and Drug Administration (FDA) relaxed its restrictions for drug advertising on television, ruling that DTC ads must simply recommend that consumers speak with a doctor about the drug, mention the drug's important risks, and indicate where consumers can get further information about it—often a Web site or phone number (Chesnes & Jin, 2016; FDA, 2016, 2015). Such ads have received relatively little criticism over the past two decades, but this climate of tolerance is now changing. A number of consumer groups and even the American Medical Association (AMA) are now calling for a ban on such advertising, saying that the ads often contribute to economic hardships, patient misinformation, and less-than-optimal treatment (Kuzucan, Doshi, & Zito, 2017; AMA, 2015).

First, the economic concerns. Altogether, pharmaceutical companies spend $5.2 billion a year on American television and some online advertising, an amount that keeps growing (Lazarus, 2017; Campbell, 2016). This leads to higher drug prices, at a time when prescription drug costs and insurance premiums are already skyrocketing, increasing by close to 5 percent each year. Moreover, the DTC ads typically promote newer and more expensive drugs, inflating the demand for such drugs even when older, generic, and cheaper drugs might be equally or more appropriate (Campbell, 2016; AMA, 2015).

DTC ads also may adversely affect patient awareness and clinical treatment (Aikin et al., 2017). Three-quarters of surveyed doctors believe that most of the ads overemphasize a drug's benefits while leaving out key negative information (ProCon, 2016). Similarly, 80 percent of doctors believe DTC ads help patients better understand the benefits of a drug, but only 40 percent of them believe that patients understand the possible risks of a drug after seeing the ad (Kiernicki & Helme, 2017; FDA, 2016, 2015). Small wonder that many patients believe their mental or physical health will be put in jeopardy if they do not take advertised drugs (Campbell, 2016).

Despite these problems, doctors often feel pressured to prescribe DTC-advertised drugs, even in cases in which the drugs are not appropriate for patients (Brown, 2017; FDA, 2015). Over half of patient requests for such drugs are granted by doctors. This has apparently contributed to an overuse of psychotropic and other drugs.

So why do DTC ads continue to rise in number? One reason is that this form of advertising has its supporters. The FDA, for example, believes that the ads may indeed serve a public service, protecting consumers—although imperfectly—by directly educating them about drugs that are available in the marketplace (FDA, 2016, 2015). Many doctors also believe that DTC ads get patients more involved in their mental and physical health care, and a number report that they now have better discussions with their patients about treatment options as a result of DTC advertising. Finally, not to be overlooked are the profits that DTC advertising helps generate for pharmaceutical companies. The average number of prescriptions written for DTC-advertised new drugs are a whopping nine times greater than those written for new drugs that do not have DTC ads (ProCon, 2016).

only 2 percent of animal-tested compounds reach human testing, and only 21 percent of human-tested drugs are eventually approved (FDA, 2018, 2016, 2014).

As the name implies, a second form of biological treatment, **brain stimulation,** refers to interventions that directly or indirectly stimulate certain areas of the brain. The oldest (and most controversial) such approach, used primarily on severely depressed people, is **electroconvulsive therapy (ECT).** Two electrodes are attached to a patient's forehead, and an electrical current of 65 to 140 volts is passed briefly through the brain. The current causes a brain seizure that lasts up to a few minutes. After seven to nine

#FDAApproval

1954	Thorazine (antipsychotic drug)
1955	Ritalin (ADHD drug)
1958	MAO inhibitors (antidepressant drugs)
1960	Librium (antianxiety drug)
1961	Elavil (antidepressant drug)
1963	Valium (antianxiety drug)
1970	Lithium (mood stabilizer/antibipolar drug)
1987	Prozac (antidepressant drug)
1998	Viagra (erectile disorder drug)

ECT sessions, spaced two or three days apart, many patients feel considerably less depressed. This treatment is used on tens of thousands of persons annually, particularly those whose depression fails to respond to other treatments (Hermida et al., 2018).

As you will see in Chapter 6, several other brain stimulation techniques have increasingly been used over the past decade, particularly in cases of depression. In one, *transcranial magnetic stimulation* (*TMS*), an electromagnetic coil is placed on or above a person's head, sending a current into certain areas of his or her brain. In another such technique, *vagus nerve stimulation* (*VNS*), a pulse generator is implanted in a person's neck, helping to stimulate his or her vagus nerve, a long nerve that extends from the brain down through the neck and on to the abdomen. The stimulated vagus nerve then delivers electrical signals to the brain. In a third technique, called *deep brain stimulation*, electrodes are implanted in specific areas of a person's brain and connected to a battery ("pacemaker") in his or her chest. The pacemaker proceeds to power the electrodes, sending a steady stream of low-voltage electricity to the targeted brain areas. As with ECT, research suggests that each of these newer brain stimulation techniques is able to improve the psychological functioning of many people whose depressive or related disorders have been unresponsive to other forms of treatment (Bari et al., 2018; Luber et al., 2017).

A third kind of biological treatment is **psychosurgery,** brain surgery for mental disorders. It has roots as far back as trephining, the prehistoric practice of chipping a hole in the skull of a person who behaved strangely. Modern procedures are derived from a notorious technique developed in the late 1930s by a Portuguese neuropsychiatrist, António Egas Moniz. In that procedure, known as a *lobotomy,* a surgeon would cut the connections between the brain's frontal lobes and the lower regions of the brain. Today's psychosurgery procedures are much more precise than the lobotomies of the past (Bari et al., 2018). Even so, they are typically used only after certain severe disorders have continued for years without responding to any other treatment. It is worth noting that deep brain stimulation, one of the interventions described above, is also a psychosurgery procedure inasmuch as it involves making small incisions in a person's skull in order to implant electrodes in a targeted brain area.

Assessing the Biological Model

Today the biological model enjoys considerable respect. Biological research constantly produces valuable new information, and biological treatments often bring great relief when other approaches have failed. At the same time, this model has its shortcomings. Some of its proponents seem to expect that all human behavior can be explained in biological terms and treated with biological methods. This view can limit rather than enhance our understanding of abnormal functioning. Our mental life is an interplay of biological and nonbiological factors, and it is important to understand that interplay rather than to focus on biological variables alone.

Another shortcoming is that several of today's biological treatments are capable of producing significant undesirable effects. Certain antipsychotic drugs, for example, may produce movement problems such as severe shaking, bizarre-looking contractions of the face and body, and extreme restlessness. Clearly such costs must be addressed and weighed against the drug's benefits.

#TheirWords

"Mental illness is so much more complicated than any pill that any mortal could invent."

Elizabeth Wurtzel, *Prozac Nation*

...SUMMING UP

THE BIOLOGICAL MODEL Biological theorists look at biological factors to explain abnormal behavior, pointing in particular to problematic brain structures, chemicals, and circuits. Such abnormalities are sometimes the result of genetic inheritance or normal evolution. Biological therapists use chemical and physical methods to help people overcome their psychological problems. The leading methods are drug therapy, brain stimulation, and psychosurgery.

The Psychodynamic Model

The psychodynamic model is the oldest and most famous of the modern psychological models. Psychodynamic theorists believe that a person's behavior, whether normal or abnormal, is determined largely by underlying psychological forces of which he or she is not consciously aware. These internal forces are described as *dynamic*—that is, they interact with one another—and their interaction gives rise to behavior, thoughts, and emotions. Abnormal symptoms are viewed as the result of conflicts between these forces.

Psychodynamic theorists would view Philip Berman as a person in conflict. They would want to explore his past experiences because, in their view, psychological conflicts are tied to early relationships and to traumatic experiences that occurred during childhood. Psychodynamic theories rest on the *deterministic* assumption that no symptom or behavior is "accidental": all behavior is determined by past experiences. Thus Philip's hatred for his mother, his memories of her as cruel and overbearing, the apparent weakness of his father, and the birth of a younger brother when Philip was 10 may all be important to the understanding of his current problems.

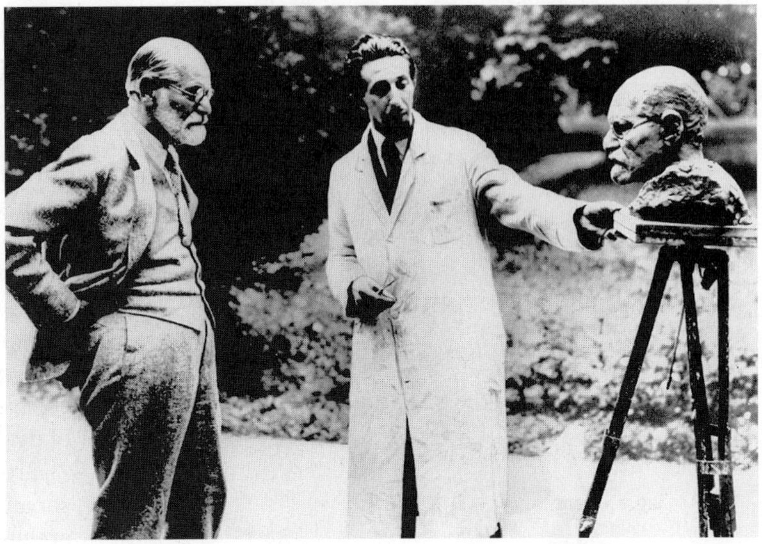

AP Photo

Freud takes a closer look at Freud Sigmund Freud, founder of psychoanalytic theory and therapy, contemplates a sculptured bust of himself in 1931 at his village home in Potzlein, near Vienna. As Freud and the bust go eyeball to eyeball, one can only imagine what conclusions each is drawing about the other.

The psychodynamic model was first formulated by Viennese neurologist Sigmund Freud (1856–1939) at the turn of the twentieth century. After studying hypnosis, Freud developed the theory of *psychoanalysis* to explain both normal and abnormal psychological functioning as well as a corresponding method of treatment, a conversational approach also called psychoanalysis. During the early 1900s, Freud and several of his colleagues in the Vienna Psychoanalytic Society—including Carl Gustav Jung (1875–1961)—became the most influential clinical theorists in the Western world.

How Did Freud Explain Normal and Abnormal Functioning?

Freud believed that three central forces shape the personality—instinctual needs, rational thinking, and moral standards. All of these forces, he believed, operate at the *unconscious level,* unavailable to immediate awareness; he further believed these forces to be dynamic, or interactive. Freud called the forces the *id,* the *ego,* and the *superego.*

The Id Freud used the term **id** to denote instinctual needs, drives, and impulses. The id operates in accordance with the *pleasure principle;* that is, it always seeks gratification. Freud also believed that all id instincts tend to be sexual, noting that from the very earliest stages of life a child's pleasure is obtained from nursing, defecating, masturbating, or engaging in other activities that he considered to have sexual ties. He further suggested that a person's *libido,* or sexual energy, fuels the id.

The Ego During our early years we come to recognize that our environment will not meet every instinctual need. Our mother, for example, is not always available to do our bidding. A part of the id separates off and becomes the **ego.** Like the id, the ego unconsciously seeks gratification, but it does so in accordance with the *reality principle,* the knowledge we acquire through experience that it can be unacceptable to express our id impulses outright. The ego, employing reason, guides us to know when we can and cannot express those impulses.

The ego develops basic strategies, called **ego defense mechanisms,** to control unacceptable id impulses and avoid or reduce the anxiety they arouse. The most basic defense mechanism, *repression,* prevents unacceptable impulses from ever reaching

psychosurgery Brain surgery for mental disorders.

id According to Freud, the psychological force that produces instinctual needs, drives, and impulses.

ego According to Freud, the psychological force that employs reason and operates in accordance with the reality principle.

ego defense mechanisms According to psychoanalytic theory, strategies developed by the ego to control unacceptable id impulses and to avoid or reduce the anxiety they arouse.

Pat Byrnes/The New Yorker Collection/The Cartoon Bank

"I'm doing a lot better now that I'm back in denial."

consciousness. There are many other ego defense mechanisms, and each of us tends to favor some over others (see **Table 2-1**).

The Superego The **superego** is the personality force that operates by the *morality principle,* a sense of what is right and what is wrong. As we learn from our parents that many of our id impulses are unacceptable, we unconsciously adopt our parents' values. Judging ourselves by their standards, we feel good when we uphold their values; conversely, when we go against them, we feel guilty. In short, we develop a *conscience.*

According to Freud, these three parts of the personality—the id, the ego, and the superego—are often in some degree of conflict. A healthy personality is one in which an effective working relationship, an acceptable compromise, has formed among the three forces. If the id, ego, and superego are in excessive conflict, the person's behavior may show signs of dysfunction.

Freudians would therefore view Philip Berman as someone whose personality forces have a poor working relationship. His ego and superego are unable to control his id impulses, which lead him repeatedly to act in impulsive and often dangerous ways—suicide gestures, jealous rages, job resignations, outbursts of temper, frequent arguments.

Developmental Stages Freud proposed that at each stage of development, from infancy to maturity, new events challenge individuals and require adjustments in their id, ego, and superego. If the adjustments are successful, they lead to personal growth. If not, the person may become **fixated,** or stuck, at an early stage of development. Then all subsequent development suffers, and the individual may well be headed for abnormal functioning in the future. Because parents are the key figures during the early years of life, they are often seen as the cause of improper development.

Freud named each stage of development after the body area that he considered most important to the child at that time. For example, he referred to the first 18 months of life as the *oral stage.* During this stage, children fear that the mother who feeds and comforts them will disappear. Children whose mothers consistently fail to gratify their oral

TABLE: 2-1

The Defense Never Rests

Defense Mechanism	Operation	Example
Repression	Person avoids anxiety by simply not allowing painful or dangerous thoughts to become conscious.	An executive's desire to run amok and attack his boss and colleagues at a board meeting is denied access to his awareness.
Denial	Person simply refuses to acknowledge the existence of an external source of anxiety.	You are not prepared for tomorrow's final exam, but you tell yourself that it's not actually an important exam and that there's no good reason not to go to a movie tonight.
Projection	Person attributes his or her own unacceptable impulses, motives, or desires to other individuals.	The executive who repressed his destructive desires may project his anger onto his boss and claim that it is actually the boss who is hostile.
Rationalization	Person creates a socially acceptable reason for an action that actually reflects unacceptable motives.	A student explains away poor grades by citing the importance of the "total experience" of going to college and claiming that too much emphasis on grades would actually interfere with a well-rounded education.
Displacement	Person displaces hostility away from a dangerous object and onto a safer substitute.	After a perfect parking spot is taken by a person who cuts in front of your car, you release your pent-up anger by starting an argument with your roommate later.
Intellectualization	Person represses emotional reactions in favor of overly logical response to a problem.	A woman who has been beaten and raped gives a detached, methodical description of the effects that such attacks may have on victims.
Regression	Person retreats from an upsetting conflict to an early developmental stage in which no one is expected to behave maturely or responsibly.	A boy who cannot cope with the anger he feels toward his rejecting mother regresses to infantile behavior, soiling his clothes and no longer taking care of his basic needs.

Lucasfilm Ltd./20th Century Fox/Photofest

"Luke . . . I am your father." This lightsaber fight between Luke Skywalker and Darth Vader highlights the most famous, and contentious, father–son relationship in movie history. According to Sigmund Freud, however, all fathers and sons have significant tensions and conflicts that they must work through, even in the absence of the special pressures faced by Luke and his father in the *Star Wars* series.

needs may become fixated at the oral stage and display an "oral character" throughout their lives, one marked by extreme dependence or extreme mistrust. Such persons are particularly prone to develop depression. As you will see in later chapters, Freud linked fixations at the other stages of development—*anal* (18 months to 3 years of age), *phallic* (3 to 5 years), *latency* (5 to 12 years), and *genital* (12 years to adulthood)—to yet other kinds of psychological dysfunction.

How Do Other Psychodynamic Explanations Differ from Freud's?

Personal and professional differences between Freud and his colleagues led to a split in the Vienna Psychoanalytic Society early in the twentieth century. Carl Jung and others developed new theories. Although the new theories departed from Freud's ideas in important ways, each held on to Freud's belief that human functioning is shaped by dynamic (interacting) psychological forces. Thus all such theories, including Freud's, are referred to as *psychodynamic*.

Two of today's most influential psychodynamic theories are self theory and object relations theory. *Self theorists* emphasize the role of the *self*—the unified personality. They believe that the basic human motive is to strengthen the wholeness of the self (Corey, 2017; Kohut, 2001, 1977). *Object relations theorists*, on the other hand, propose that people are motivated mainly by a need to have relationships with others and that severe problems in the relationships between children and their caregivers may lead to abnormal development (Kernberg, 2018, 2005, 1997; Rankin, 2017).

Psychodynamic Therapies

Psychodynamic therapies range from Freudian psychoanalysis to modern therapies based on self theory or object relations theory. Psychodynamic therapists seek to uncover past traumas and the inner conflicts that have resulted from them (Safran, Kriss, & Foley, 2019). They try to help clients resolve, or settle, those conflicts and to resume personal development.

According to most psychodynamic therapists, therapists must subtly guide therapy discussions so that the patients discover their underlying problems for themselves. To aid in the process, the therapists rely on such techniques as *free association, therapist interpretation, catharsis,* and *working through*.

superego According to Freud, the psychological force that represents a person's values and ideals.

fixation According to Freud, a condition in which the id, ego, or superego do not mature properly and are frozen at an early stage of development.

free association A psychodynamic technique in which the patient describes any thought, feeling, or image that comes to mind, even if it seems unimportant.

resistance An unconscious refusal to participate fully in therapy.

transference According to psychodynamic theorists, the redirection toward the psychotherapist of feelings associated with important figures in a patient's life, now or in the past.

dream A series of ideas and images that form during sleep.

catharsis The reliving of past repressed feelings in order to settle internal conflicts and overcome problems.

working through The psychoanalytic process of facing conflicts, reinterpreting feelings, and overcoming one's problems.

Free Association In psychodynamic therapies, the patient is responsible for starting and leading each discussion. The therapist tells the patient to describe any thought, feeling, or image that comes to mind, even if it seems unimportant. This practice is known as **free association.** The therapist expects that the patient's associations will eventually uncover unconscious events. In the following excerpts from a famous psychodynamic case, notice how free association helps a woman to discover threatening impulses and conflicts within herself:

Patient: *So I started walking, and walking, and decided to go behind the museum and walk through [New York's] Central Park. . . . I saw a park bench next to a clump of bushes and sat down. There was a rustle behind me and I got frightened. I thought of men concealing themselves in the bushes. I thought of the sex perverts I read about in Central Park. I wondered if there was someone behind me exposing himself. The idea is repulsive, but exciting too. I think of father now and feel excited. . . . . There is something about this pushing in my mind. I don't know what it is, like on the border of my memory.* (Pause)

Therapist: *Mm-hmm.* (Pause) *On the border of your memory?*

Patient: (The patient breathes rapidly and seems to be under great tension.) *As a little girl, I slept with my father. I get a funny feeling. I get a funny feeling over my skin, tingly-like. It's a strange feeling, like a blindness, like not seeing something. My mind blurs and spreads over anything I look at. I've had this feeling off and on since I walked in the park.*

(Wolberg, 2005, 1967, p. 662)

Therapist Interpretation Psychodynamic therapists listen carefully as patients talk, looking for clues, drawing tentative conclusions, and sharing interpretations when they think the patient is ready to hear them. Interpretations of three phenomena are particularly important—*resistance, transference,* and *dreams.*

Patients are showing **resistance,** an unconscious refusal to participate fully in therapy, when they suddenly cannot free associate or when they change a subject to avoid a painful discussion. They demonstrate **transference** when they act and feel toward the therapist as they did or do toward important persons in their lives, especially their parents, siblings, and spouses. Consider again the woman who walked in Central Park. As she continues talking, the therapist helps her to explore her transference:

Patient: *I get so excited by what is happening here. I feel I'm being held back by needing to be nice. . . . The worst thing would be that you wouldn't like me. You wouldn't speak to me friendly. . . you'd feel you can't treat me and discharge me from treatment. . . .*

Therapist: *Where do you think these attitudes come from?*

Patient: *When I was nine years old, I read a lot about great men in history. I'd quote them and be dramatic. I'd want a sword at my side; I'd dress like an Indian. Mother would scold me. Don't frown, don't talk so much. Sit on your hands, over and over again. I did all kinds of things. I was a naughty child. She told me I'd be hurt. Then at fourteen I fell off a horse and broke my back. I had to be in bed. Mother told me on the day I went riding not to . . . I went against her will and suffered an accident that changed my life, a fractured back. Her attitude was, "I told you so."*

(Wolberg, 2005, 1967, p. 662)

Finally, many psychodynamic therapists try to help patients interpret their **dreams** (Altszyler et al., 2017) (see **Table 2-2**). Freud (1924) called dreams the "royal road to the unconscious." He believed that repression and other defense mechanisms operate less

#FreudFacts

Freud's fee for one session of therapy was $20.

For almost 40 years, Freud treated patients 10 hours per day, 5 or 6 days per week.

Freud was nominated for the Nobel Prize in 12 different years, but never won.

(Grohol, 2015; Hess, 2009; Gay, 2006, 1999)

> Why do you think most people try to interpret and make sense of their own dreams? Are such interpretations of value?

completely during sleep, and that dreams, if correctly interpreted, can reveal unconscious instincts, needs, and wishes. Freud identified two kinds of dream content—manifest and latent. *Manifest content* is the consciously remembered dream; *latent content* is its symbolic meaning. To interpret a dream, therapists must translate its manifest content into its latent content.

Catharsis Insight must be an emotional as well as an intellectual process. Psychodynamic therapists believe that patients must experience **catharsis,** a reliving of past repressed feelings, if they are to settle internal conflicts and overcome their problems.

Working Through A single episode of interpretation and catharsis will not change the way a person functions. The patient and therapist must examine the same issues over and over in the course of many sessions, each time with greater clarity. This process, called **working through,** usually takes a long time, often years.

Current Trends in Psychodynamic Therapy The past 40 years have witnessed significant changes in the way many psychodynamic therapists conduct sessions. An increased demand for focused, time-limited psychotherapies has resulted in efforts to make psychodynamic therapy more efficient and affordable. Two current psychodynamic approaches that illustrate this trend are *short-term psychodynamic therapies* and *relational psychoanalytic therapy.*

SHORT-TERM PSYCHODYNAMIC THERAPIES In several short versions of psychodynamic therapy, patients choose a single problem—a *dynamic focus*—to work on, such as difficulty getting along with other people (Levenson, 2017). The therapist and patient focus on this problem throughout the treatment and work only on the psychodynamic issues that relate to it (such as unresolved oral needs). Only a limited number of studies have tested the effectiveness of these short-term psychodynamic therapies, but their findings do suggest that the approaches are sometimes quite helpful to patients (Town et al., 2017).

RELATIONAL PSYCHOANALYTIC THERAPY Whereas Freud believed that psychodynamic therapists should take on the role of a neutral, distant expert during a treatment session, a contemporary school of psychodynamic therapy referred to as *relational*

"Look! I'm having enough trouble right now without your bringing up the past."

Frank Modell/The New Yorker Collection/The Cartoon Bank

TABLE: 2-2

Percent of Research Participants Who Have Had Common Dreams

	Men	Women
Being chased or pursued, not injured	78%	83%
Sexual experiences	85	73
Falling	73	74
Schools, teachers, studying	57	71
Arriving too late, e.g., for a train	55	62
Trying to do something repeatedly	55	53
Flying or soaring through the air	58	44
Failing an examination	37	48
Being physically attacked	40	44
Being frozen with fright	32	44

Information from: Cherry, 2018; Robert & Zadra, 2014; Copley, 2008; Kantrowitz & Springen, 2004.

psychoanalytic therapy argues that therapists are key figures in the lives of patients—figures whose reactions and beliefs should be included in the therapy process (Corey, 2017). Thus, a key principle of relational therapy is that therapists should also disclose things about themselves, particularly their own reactions to patients, and try to establish more equal relationships with patients.

Assessing the Psychodynamic Model

Freud and his followers have helped change the way abnormal functioning is understood. Largely because of their work, a wide range of theorists today look for answers outside of biological processes. Psychodynamic theorists have also helped us to understand that abnormal functioning may be rooted in the same processes as normal functioning. Psychological conflict is a common experience; it leads to abnormal functioning only if the conflict becomes excessive.

What are some of the ways that Freud's theories have affected literature, film and television, philosophy, child rearing, and education in Western society?

Freud and his many followers have also had a monumental impact on treatment. They were the first to apply theory systematically to treatment. They were also the first to demonstrate the potential of psychological, as opposed to biological, treatment, and their ideas have served as starting points for many other psychological treatments.

At the same time, the psychodynamic model has its shortcomings. Its concepts are hard to research (Safran et al., 2019). Because processes such as id drives, ego defenses, and fixation are abstract and supposedly operate at an unconscious level, there is no way of knowing for certain if they are occurring. Not surprisingly, then, psychodynamic explanations and treatments have received relatively limited research support over the years, and psychodynamic theorists rely largely on evidence from individual case studies. Nevertheless, recent research evidence suggests that long-term psychodynamic therapy may be helpful for many persons with long-term complex disorders (Berman, 2017; Werbart et al., 2017), and 18 percent of today's clinical psychologists identify themselves as psychodynamic therapists (Prochaska & Norcross, 2018).

9... SUMMING UP

THE PSYCHODYNAMIC MODEL Psychodynamic theorists believe that an individual's behavior, whether normal or abnormal, is determined by underlying psychological forces. They consider psychological conflicts to be rooted in early parent–child relationships and traumatic experiences. The psychodynamic model was formulated by Sigmund Freud, who said that three dynamic forces—the id, ego, and superego—interact to produce thought, feeling, and behavior. Other psychodynamic theories are self theory and object relations theory.

Psychodynamic therapists help people uncover past traumas and the inner conflicts that have resulted from them. They use a number of techniques, including free association and interpretations of psychological phenomena such as resistance, transference, and dreams. The leading contemporary psychodynamic approaches include short-term psychodynamic therapies and relational psychoanalytic therapy.

conditioning A simple form of learning.

classical conditioning A process of learning by temporal association in which two events that repeatedly occur close together in time become fused in a person's mind and produce the same response.

modeling A process of learning in which an individual acquires responses by observing and imitating others.

operant conditioning A process of learning in which individuals come to behave in certain ways as a result of experiencing consequences of one kind or another whenever they perform the behavior.

The Cognitive-Behavioral Model

The cognitive-behavioral model of abnormality focuses on the behaviors people display and the thoughts they have. The model is also interested in the interplay between behaviors and thoughts—how behavior affects thinking and how thinking affects behavior. In addition, the model is concerned with the impact the behavior–cognition interplay often has on feelings and emotions.

Whereas the psychodynamic model had its beginnings in the clinical work of physicians, the cognitive-behavioral model began in laboratories where psychology researchers had been studying *behaviors*, the responses an organism makes to its environment, since the late 1800s. Such researchers believed that behaviors can be external (going to work, say) or internal (having a feeling), and they ran experiments on **conditioning,** simple forms of learning, in order to better understand how behaviors are acquired. In these experiments, researchers would manipulate *stimuli* and *rewards,* then observe how such manipulations affect the behaviors of animal and human subjects.

During the 1950s, a number of clinicians, frustrated with what they viewed as the vagueness and slowness of the psychodynamic model, began to explain and treat psychological abnormality by applying principles derived from those laboratory conditioning studies. Consistent with the laboratory studies, the clinicians viewed severe human anxiety, depression, and the like as maladaptive behaviors, and they focused their work on how such behaviors might be learned and changed.

A decade or so later, yet other clinicians came to believe that a focus on behaviors alone, while moving in the right direction, was too simplistic, that behavioral conditioning principles failed to account fully for the complexity of human functioning and dysfunction. They recognized that human beings also engage in *cognitive processes,* such as anticipating or interpreting—ways of thinking that until then had been largely ignored in the behavior-focused explanations and therapies. These clinicians developed cognitive-behavioral theories of abnormality that took both behaviors and cognitive processes into account, and cognitive-behavioral therapies that sought to change both counterproductive behaviors and dysfunctional ways of thinking (Kodal et al., 2018; Craske, 2017).

Some of today's theorists and therapists still focus exclusively on the behavioral aspects of abnormal functioning, while others focus only on cognitive processes. However, most clinicians with such orientations include *both* behavioral and cognitive principles in their work. To best appreciate the cognitive-behavioral model, let us look first at its behavioral dimension and then its cognitive dimension.

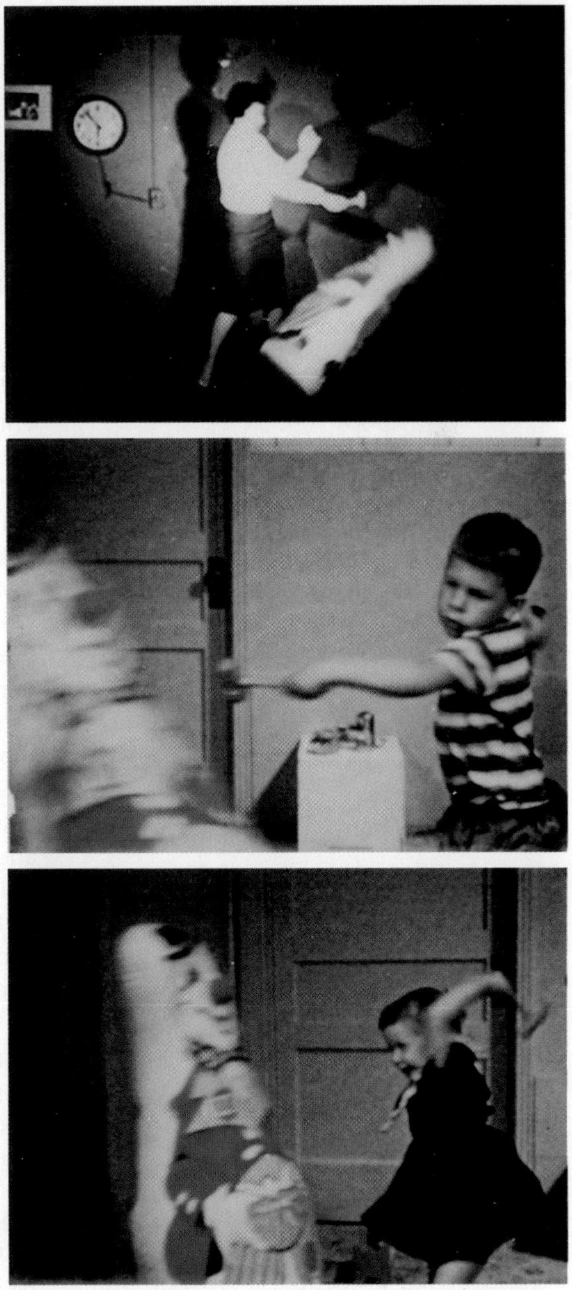

A. Bandura, Stanford University

See and do Modeling may account for some forms of abnormal behavior. A well-known study by Albert Bandura and his colleagues (1963) demonstrated that children learned to abuse a doll by observing an adult hit it. Children who had not been exposed to the adult model did not mistreat the doll.

The Behavioral Dimension

Many learned behaviors help people to cope with daily challenges and to lead happy, productive lives. However, abnormal behaviors also can be learned. Philip Berman, for example, might be viewed as a man who has received improper training: he has learned behaviors that offend others and get him into various kinds of trouble.

Theorists have identified several forms of conditioning, and each may produce abnormal behavior as well as normal behavior. In **classical conditioning,** for example, people learn to respond to one stimulus the same way they respond to another as a result of the two stimuli repeatedly occurring together close in time. If, say, a physician wears a white lab coat whenever she gives painful allergy shots to a little boy, the child may learn to fear not only injection needles, but also white lab coats. Many phobias are acquired by classical conditioning, as you will see in Chapter 4. In **modeling,** another form of conditioning, individuals learn responses simply by observing other individuals and then repeating their behaviors. Phobias can also be acquired by modeling. If a little girl observes her father become frightened whenever a dog crosses his path, she herself may develop a phobic fear of dogs.

In a third form of conditioning, **operant conditioning,** individuals learn to behave in certain ways as a result of experiencing consequences of one kind or another—*reinforcements* (for example, *rewards*) or *punishments*—whenever they perform the behavior (Skinner, 1958, 1957). Research suggests that a number of abnormal behaviors may be acquired by operant conditioning (Held-Poschardt et al, 2018; Calarco, 2016). Some children, for example, learn to display extremely aggressive behaviors when

The Washington Post/Getty Images

Conditioning for entertainment and profit
Animals can be taught a wide assortment of tricks by using the principles of conditioning—but at what cost? Here an Asian elephant performs one called "the living statue" as she acknowledges the crowd at a circus in Virginia. In recent years the public has become alarmed at the training procedures used on circus animals, leading some circuses to remove elephants from their shows. This in turn has led to declining ticket sales and contributed to the closing of several circuses, including the famous Ringling Brothers and Barnum & Bailey Circus.

their parents or peers consistently surrender to their threats or demands or shower them with extra attention when they act out. In addition, a number of people learn to abuse alcohol because initially such behaviors bring feelings of calm, comfort, or pleasure.

In treatment, behavior-focused therapists seek to replace a person's problematic behaviors with more appropriate ones, applying the principles of operant conditioning, classical conditioning, or modeling (Antony, 2019; Foa et al., 2018). When treating extremely aggressive children, for example, the therapists may guide parents to change the reinforcers they have been unintentionally providing for their children's behaviors. The parents may be taught to systematically reinforce polite and appropriate behaviors by their children by providing the children with displays of extra attention or special privileges. In addition, the parents may be taught to systematically punish highly aggressive behaviors by withdrawing attention and withholding privileges in the aftermath of such behaviors (Cornacchio et al., 2017; Elkins et al., 2017).

The Cognitive Dimension

Philip Berman, like the rest of us, has *cognitive* abilities—special intellectual capacities to think, remember, and anticipate. These abilities can help him accomplish a great deal in life. Yet they can also work against him. As he thinks about his experiences, Philip may misinterpret them in ways that lead to poor decisions, maladaptive responses, and painful emotions.

In the 1960s two clinicians, Albert Ellis (1962) and Aaron Beck (1967), proposed that we can best explain and treat abnormal functioning, not only by looking at behaviors, but also by focusing on cognitions. Ellis and Beck claimed that clinicians must ask questions about the assumptions and attitudes that color a client's perceptions, the thoughts running through that person's mind, and the conclusions to which the assumptions and thoughts are leading.

According to these and other cognition-focused theorists, abnormal functioning can result from several kinds of cognitive problems. Some people may make *assumptions* and adopt *attitudes* that are disturbing and inaccurate (Beck & Weishaar, 2019; Ellis & Ellis, 2019). Philip Berman, for example, often seems to assume that his past history has locked him into his present situation. He believes that he was victimized by his parents and that he is now forever doomed by his past. He approaches all new experiences and relationships with expectations of failure and disaster.

Illogical thinking processes are another source of abnormal functioning, according to cognition-focused theorists. Beck has found that depressed people consistently think in illogical ways and keep arriving at self-defeating conclusions (Beck & Weishaar, 2019). They may, for example, *overgeneralize*—draw broad negative conclusions on the basis of single insignificant events. One depressed student couldn't remember the date of Columbus' third voyage to America while she was in history class. Overgeneralizing, she spent the rest of the day in despair over her wide-ranging ignorance.

In treatment, cognition-focused therapists use several strategies to help people with psychological disorders adopt new, more functional ways of thinking. In an influential approach developed by Beck, the therapists guide depressed clients to identify and challenge any negative thoughts, biased interpretations, and errors in logic that dominate their thinking and contribute to their disorder. The therapists also guide the clients to try out new ways of thinking in their daily lives. As you will see in Chapter 6, depressed people treated with Beck's approach improve much more than those who receive no treatment (Beck & Weishaar, 2019).

#TheirWords

"We cannot solve our problems with the same thinking we used when we created them."

Albert Einstein

In the excerpt that follows, a Beck-like therapist guides a depressed 26-year-old graduate student to see the link between her interpretations and her feelings and to begin questioning the accuracy of those interpretations:

> Patient: *I get depressed when things go wrong. Like when I fail a test.*
> Therapist: *How can failing a test make you depressed?*
> Patient: *Well, if I fail I'll never get into law school.*
> Therapist: *So failing the test means a lot to you. But if failing a test could drive people into clinical depression, wouldn't you expect everyone who failed the test to have a depression? . . . Did everyone who failed get depressed enough to require treatment?*
> Patient: *No, but it depends on how important the test was to the person.*
> Therapist: *Right, and who decides the importance?*
> Patient: *I do.*
> Therapist: *And so, what we have to examine is your way of viewing the test (or the way that you think about the test) and how it affects your chances of getting into law school. Do you agree?*
> Patient: *Right. . . .*
> Therapist: *Now what did failing mean?*
> Patient: (Tearful) *That I couldn't get into law school.*
> Therapist: *And what does that mean to you?*
> Patient: *That I'm just not smart enough.*
> Therapist: *Anything else?*
> Patient: *That I can never be happy . . .*
> Therapist: *So it is the meaning of failing a test that makes you very unhappy. In fact, believing that you can never be happy is a powerful factor in producing unhappiness. So, you get yourself into a trap—by definition, failure to get into law school equals "I can never be happy."*
>
> *(Beck et al., 1979, pp. 145–146)*

social anxiety disorder A psychological disorder in which people fear social situations.

The Cognitive-Behavioral Interplay

As you read earlier, most of today's cognitive-behavioral theorists and therapists interweave both behavioral and cognitive elements in their explanations and treatments for psychological disorders. Let's look, for example, at the cognitive-behavioral approach to social anxiety disorder, a problem that you will be reading more about in Chapter 4.

People with **social anxiety disorder** have severe anxiety about social situations in which they may face scrutiny by other people. They worry that they will function poorly in front of others and will wind up feeling humiliated. Thus they may avoid speaking in public, reject social opportunities, and limit their lives in numerous ways.

Cognitive-behavioral theorists contend that people with this disorder hold a group of social beliefs and expectations that consistently work against them (Hofmann, 2018; Thurston et al., 2017; Heimberg et al., 2010). These include:

- Holding unrealistically high social standards and so believing that they must perform perfectly in social situations.
- Viewing themselves as unattractive social beings.
- Viewing themselves as socially unskilled and inadequate.
- Believing they are always in danger of behaving incompetently in social situations.
- Believing that inept behaviors in social situations will inevitably lead to terrible consequences.

Overrun by such beliefs and expectations, people with social anxiety disorder find that their anxiety levels increase as soon as they enter into a social situation. In turn, say

#SocialDistress

For most people, silence becomes awkward after about four seconds (Pear, 2013).

exposure therapy A behavior-focused intervention in which fearful people are repeatedly exposed to the objects or situations they dread.

cognitive-behavioral theorists, the individuals learn to regularly perform "avoidance" and "safety" behaviors (Mesri et al., 2017; Moscovitch et al., 2013). Avoidance behaviors include, for example, talking only to people they already know well at gatherings or parties, or avoiding social gatherings altogether. Safety behaviors include wearing makeup to cover up blushing. Such behaviors are reinforced by eliminating or reducing the individuals' feelings of anxiety and the number of unpleasant events they encounter.

To undo this cycle of problematic beliefs and behaviors, cognitive-behavioral therapists combine several techniques, including **exposure therapy,** a behavior-focused intervention in which fearful people are repeatedly exposed to the objects or situations they dread (Thurston et al., 2017). In cases of social anxiety disorder, the therapists encourage clients to immerse themselves in various dreaded social situations and to remain there until their fears subside. Usually the exposure is gradual. Then, back in therapy, the clinicians and clients reexamine and challenge the individuals' maladaptive beliefs and expectations in light of the recent social encounters.

In the following discussion, a cognitive-behavioral therapist works with a socially anxious client who fears he will be rejected if he speaks up at gatherings. The therapy discussion is taking place after the man has done a homework assignment in which he was asked to identify his negative social expectations and force himself to say anything he had on his mind in social situations, no matter how stupid it might seem to him:

After two weeks of this assignment, the patient came into his next session of therapy and reported: "I did what you told me to do. . . . [Every] time, just as you said, I found myself retreating from people, I said to myself: 'Now, even though you can't see it, there must be some sentences. What are they?' And I finally found them. And there were many of them! And they all seemed to say the same thing."

"What thing?"

"That I, uh, was going to be rejected. . . . [If] I related to them I was going to be rejected. And wouldn't that be perfectly awful if I was to be rejected." . . .

"And did you do the second part of the homework assignment?"

"The forcing myself to speak up and express myself?"

"Yes, that part."

"That was worse. That was really hard. Much harder than I thought it would be. But I did it."

"And?"

"Oh, not bad at all. I spoke up several times; more than I've ever done before. Some people were very surprised." . . .

"And how did you feel after expressing yourself like that?"

"Remarkable! . . . I felt, uh, just remarkable—good, that is. . . . But it was so hard. I almost didn't make it. And a couple of other times during the week I had to force myself again. But I did. And I was glad!"

(Ellis, 1962, pp. 202–203)

In cognitive-behavioral approaches of this kind, clients come to adopt more accurate social beliefs, engage in more social situations, and experience less fear during, and in anticipation of, social encounters. Avoidance and safety behaviors drop away while social approach behaviors are reinforced by opening the door to the joy and enrichment of social encounters. Studies show that such approaches do indeed help many individuals to overcome social anxiety disorder (Gregory & Peters, 2017; Heimberg & Magee, 2014).

Assessing the Cognitive-Behavioral Model

The cognitive-behavioral model has become a powerful force in the clinical field. Various cognitive and behavioral theories have been proposed over the years, and many treatment techniques have been developed. As you can see in **Figure 2-3,** nearly half of today's clinical psychologists report that their approach is cognitive and/or behavioral (Prochaska & Norcross, 2018).

#TheirWords

"The greatest discovery of my generation is that human beings can alter their lives by altering their attitudes of mind."

William James (1842–1910)

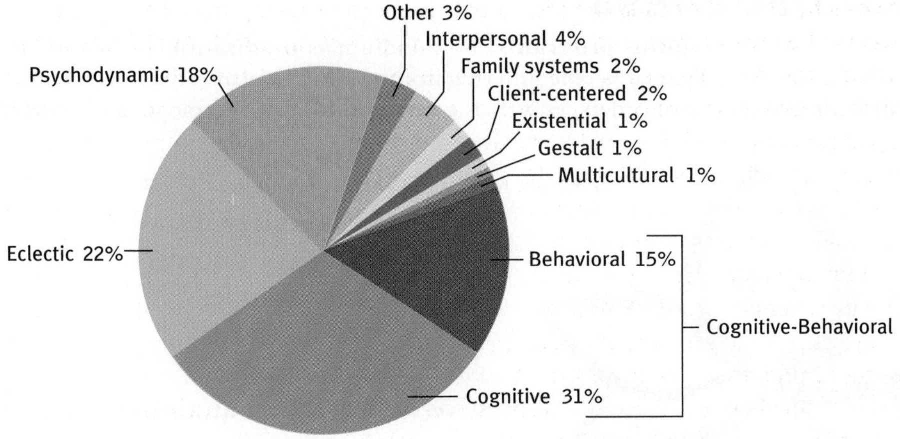

FIGURE 2-3

Theoretical Orientations of Today's Clinical Psychologists

In surveys, 22 percent of clinical psychologists labeled their approach as "eclectic," 46 percent considered their model "cognitive" and/or "behavioral," and 18 percent called their orientation "psychodynamic." (Information from: Prochaska & Norcross, 2018.)

One reason for the appeal of the cognitive-behavioral model is that it can be tested in the laboratory, whereas psychodynamic theories generally cannot. Many of the model's basic concepts—stimulus, response, reward, attitude, and interpretation—can be observed or, at least, measured. Moreover, investigators have found that people with psychological disorders often display the kinds of reactions, assumptions, and errors in thinking that cognitive-behavioral theorists would predict (Kube et al., 2018).

Yet another reason for the popularity of this model is the impressive research performance of cognitive-behavioral therapies. Both in the laboratory and real life, they have proved very helpful to many people with anxiety disorders, depression, sexual dysfunction, intellectual disability, and yet other problems (Reavell et al., 2018; Dobson & Dobson, 2017).

At the same time, the cognitive-behavioral model has drawbacks. First, although maladaptive behaviors and disturbed cognitive processes are found in many forms of abnormality, their precise role has yet to be determined. The problematic behaviors and cognitions seen in psychologically troubled people could well be a result rather than a cause of their difficulties. Second, although cognitive-behavioral therapies are clearly of help to many people, they do not help everyone. Research indicates, in fact, that it is not always possible for clients to rid themselves fully of their negative thoughts and biased interpretations (Sharf, 2015).

In response to such limitations, a new group of therapies, sometimes called the *new wave of cognitive-behavioral therapies,* has emerged in recent years. These new approaches, including the increasingly used *acceptance and commitment therapy* (*ACT*), help clients to *accept* many of their problematic thoughts rather than judge them, act on them, or try fruitlessly to change them (Gonzalez-Fernandez et al., 2018; Hayes, 2016). The hope is that by recognizing such thoughts for what they are—just thoughts—clients will eventually be able to let them pass through their awareness without being particularly troubled by them.

As you will see in Chapter 4, ACT and similar therapies often employ *mindfulness-based* techniques to help clients achieve such acceptance. These techniques borrow heavily from a form of meditation called *mindfulness meditation,* which teaches individuals to pay attention to the thoughts and feelings that are flowing through their minds during meditation and to accept such thoughts in a nonjudgmental way (see ***InfoCentral*** on the next page). Research suggests that ACT and other mindfulness-based approaches are often quite helpful in the treatment of anxiety and depression, among other problems (Walsh, 2019; Gonzalez-Fernandez et al., 2018).

A final drawback of the cognitive-behavioral model is that it is narrow in certain ways. Although behavior and cognition obviously

Bruce Eric Kaplan/The New Yorker Collection/The Cartoon Bank

"Don't take that tone of thought with me."

MINDFULNESS

Over the past decade, **mindfulness** has become one of the most common terms in psychology. Mindfulness involves being in the present moment, intentionally and nonjudgmentally. **Mindfulness training programs** use mindfulness **meditation** techniques to help treat people suffering from pain, anxiety disorders, and depressive disorders, as well as a variety of other psychological disorders.

MINDFULNESS TRAINING PROGRAMS

- Have the goal of achieving a state of intentional, nonjudgmental attention on the present.

attention to **body** sensations

attention to **breathing** sensations

attention to **wandering** and busy **thoughts**

simple **yoga**

homework **assignments** (practice and **journal** keeping)

8 weeks of instruction

(Ackerman, 2017; Creswell, 2017; Winston, 2016; Noonan, 2014; Russell, 2014)

- Help treat other disorders, including:

pain conditions

PTSD and other **stress** disorders

depressive disorders

asthma

substance use disorders

borderline personality disorder

(Creswell, 2017; Schmidtman et al., 2017; Barnes et al., 2016; Soler et al., 2016; Wieczner, 2016)

- Help reduce the anxiety found in . . .

generalized **anxiety** disorder

social **anxiety** disorder

panic disorder

test **anxiety**

illness **anxiety**

depressive disorder with **anxious** distress

(Creswell, 2017; Hoge et al., 2017; Dundas et al., 2016; Kim et al., 2016; Surawy et al., 2015)

Number of mindfulness apps **1,000**

Number of medical schools in North America that teach mindfulness **>120**

Why Do People Seek Out Mindfulness?

"Cell phones, texting, social networking, e-mailing, etc., easily distract me from what I'm doing."

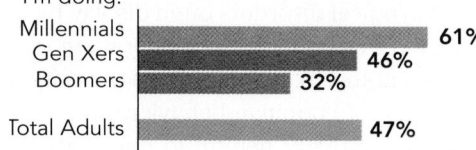

Millennials	61%
Gen Xers	46%
Boomers	32%
Total Adults	47%

(Gray, 2017; Palley, 2014)

Estimated amount that U.S. adults spend on mindfulness programs each year **as much as $8 billion**

Percentage of the U.S. population that practice mindfulness meditation techniques **10%**

Percentage of employers who offer mindfulness training **33%**

(NIH, 2016; Weiczner, 2016; Brewer, 2014; Marchand, 2014; Noonan, 2014; Pickert, 2014)

MINDFUL LIFE STRATEGIES

(Ackerman, 2017; Noonan, 2014; Russell, 2014)

Employ conscious awareness each morning—notice how you feel before starting the day. • Slow yourself down throughout the day. • Do nothing for at least 5 minutes each day. • Practice mindful breathing for 5 to 30 minutes throughout the day, especially before important tasks. • Inhale and exhale deeply and focus on your breath. • Take regular breaks from sitting at your desk. • Unplug from technology periodically throughout the day. • Eat lunch slowly, savoring every bite and body sensation. • Choose an object in your environment and observe it carefully for 60 seconds. • Take a slow 10-minute walk, synchronizing your breathing with your steps. • At the end of the day, reflect about the day, without judgment.

RESEARCH-SUPPORTED EFFECTS OF MINDFULNESS

Mindfulness appears to

- improve control over anxiety and related emotions
- promote more peaceful sleep
- improve functioning of the autonomic nervous system
- decrease rumination and other negative thinking
- improve occupational functioning
- lower stress
- improve decision-making under stress
- heighten attention
- improve working memory and verbal reasoning
- improve functioning of the immune system
- increase enjoyment and experience of music
- decrease feelings of loneliness among elderly people

(Creswell, 2017; Hoge et al., 2017; Tang & Bruya, 2017; Schmidtman et al., 2017; Noonan, 2014) are key dimensions in life, they are still only two aspects of human functioning. Shouldn't explanations of human functioning also consider broader issues, such as how people approach life, what value they extract from it, and how they deal with the question of life's meaning? This is the position of the humanistic-existential model.

...SUMMING UP

THE COGNITIVE-BEHAVIORAL MODEL Proponents of the cognitive-behavioral model focus on maladaptive behaviors and cognitions to explain and treat psychological disorders. Most such proponents include *both* the behavioral and cognitive dimensions in their work.

On the behavioral side, the proponents hold that three types of conditioning—classical conditioning, modeling, and operant conditioning—account for behavior, whether normal or dysfunctional, and they treat people who display problematic behaviors by replacing such behaviors with more appropriate ones, using techniques based on the principles of conditioning. On the cognitive side, the model's proponents point to cognitive problems, like maladaptive assumptions and illogical thinking processes, to explain abnormal functioning; and they treat dysfunctional people by helping them recognize, challenge, and change their problematic ways of thinking.

In addition to the traditional cognitive-behavioral approaches, a new wave of cognitive-behavioral therapies, such as acceptance and commitment therapy (ACT), try to teach clients to be mindful of and accept many of their problematic thoughts.

The Humanistic-Existential Model

Philip Berman is more than the sum of his psychological conflicts, learned behaviors, or cognitions. Being human, he also has the ability to pursue philosophical goals such as self-awareness, strong values, a sense of meaning in life, and freedom of choice. According to humanistic and existential theorists, Philip's problems can be understood only in the light of such complex goals. Humanistic and existential theorists are often grouped together—in an approach known as the *humanistic-existential model*—because of their common focus on these broader dimensions of human existence. At the same time, there are important differences between them.

Humanists, the more optimistic of the two groups, believe that human beings are born with a natural tendency to be friendly, cooperative, and constructive. People, these theorists propose, are driven to **self-actualize**—that is, to fulfill their potential for goodness and growth. They can do so, however, only if they honestly recognize and accept their weaknesses as well as their strengths and establish satisfying personal values to live by. Humanists further suggest that self-actualization leads naturally to a concern for the welfare of others and to behavior that is loving, courageous, spontaneous, and independent (Maslow, 1970).

Existentialists agree that human beings must have an accurate awareness of themselves and live meaningful—they say "authentic"—lives in order to be psychologically well adjusted. These theorists do not believe, however, that people are naturally inclined to live positively. They believe that from birth we have total freedom, either to face up to our existence and give meaning to our lives or to shrink from that responsibility. Those who choose to "hide" from responsibility and choice will view themselves as helpless and may live empty, inauthentic, and dysfunctional lives as a result.

The humanistic and existential views of abnormality both date back to the 1940s. At that time Carl Rogers (1902–1987), often considered the pioneer of the humanistic perspective, developed **client-centered therapy,** a warm and supportive approach that contrasted sharply with the psychodynamic techniques of the day. He also proposed a theory of personality that paid little attention to irrational instincts and conflicts.

#

#WanderingThoughts

Your mind wanders almost one-half of the time on average (Killingsworth, 2013; Killingsworth & Gilbert, 2010).

self-actualization The humanistic process by which people fulfill their potential for goodness and growth.

client-centered therapy The humanistic therapy developed by Carl Rogers in which clinicians try to help clients by conveying acceptance, accurate empathy, and genuineness.

The existential view of personality and abnormality appeared during this same period. Many of its principles came from the ideas of nineteenth-century European existential philosophers who held that human beings are constantly defining and so giving meaning to their existence through their actions (Schneider & Krug, 2017; Cooper, 2016).

The humanistic and existential theories, and their uplifting implications, were extremely popular during the 1960s and 1970s, years of considerable soul-searching and social upheaval in Western society. They have since lost some of their popularity, but they continue to influence the ideas and work of many clinicians. In particular, humanistic principles are apparent throughout positive psychology (the study and enhancement of positive feelings, traits, abilities, and selfless virtues), an area of psychology that, as you read in Chapter 1, has gained much momentum in recent years (see page 16).

Rick Eglinton/Getty Images

Actualizing the self Humanists suggest that self-actualized people show concern for others, among other positive qualities. Many work as volunteers. For example, as part of the Free Hugs Project, a worldwide campaign, volunteers offer hugs to passersby who look like they could use a quick dose of comfort.

Rogers' Humanistic Theory and Therapy

According to Carl Rogers, the road to dysfunction begins in infancy (Raskin, Rogers, & Witty, 2019; Rogers, 1987, 1951). We all have a basic need to receive *positive regard* from the important people in our lives (primarily our parents). Those who receive *unconditional* (nonjudgmental) *positive regard* early in life are likely to develop *unconditional self-regard*. That is, they come to recognize their worth as persons, even while recognizing that they are not perfect. Such people are in a good position to actualize their positive potential.

Unfortunately, some children repeatedly are made to feel that they are not worthy of positive regard. As a result, they acquire *conditions of worth*, standards that tell them they are lovable and acceptable only when they conform to certain guidelines. To maintain positive self-regard, these people have to look at themselves very selectively, denying or distorting thoughts and actions that do not measure up to their conditions of worth. They thus acquire a distorted view of themselves and their experiences. They do not know what they are truly feeling, what they genuinely need, or what values and goals would be meaningful for them. Problems in functioning are then inevitable.

Rogers might view Philip Berman as a man who has gone astray. Rather than striving to fulfill his positive human potential, he drifts from job to job and relationship to relationship. In every interaction he is defending himself, trying to interpret events in ways he can live with, usually blaming his problems on other people. Nevertheless, his basic negative self-image continually reveals itself. Rogers would probably link this problem to the critical ways Philip was treated by his mother throughout his childhood.

Clinicians who practice Rogers' client-centered therapy try to create a supportive climate in which clients feel able to look at themselves honestly and acceptingly (Raskin et al., 2019). The therapist must display three important qualities throughout the therapy—*unconditional positive regard* (full and warm acceptance for the client), *accurate empathy* (skillful listening and restating), and *genuineness* (sincere communication). In the following classic case, the therapist uses all these qualities to move the client toward greater self-awareness:

Client:	*Yes, I know I shouldn't worry about it, but I do. Lots of things—money, people, clothes. In classes I feel that everyone's just waiting for a chance to jump on me. . . . When I meet somebody I wonder what he's actually thinking of me. Then later on I wonder how I match up to what he's come to think of me.*
Therapist:	*You feel that you're pretty responsive to the opinions of other people.*
Client:	*Yes, but it's things that shouldn't worry me.*
Therapist:	*You feel that it's the sort of thing that shouldn't be upsetting, but they do get you pretty much worried anyway.*

Client:	*Just some of them. Most of those things do worry me because they're true. The ones I told you, that is. But there are lots of little things that aren't true. . . . Things just seem to be piling up, piling up inside of me. . . . It's a feeling that things were crowding up and they were going to burst.*
Therapist:	*You feel that it's a sort of oppression with some frustration and that things are just unmanageable.*
Client:	*In a way, but some things just seem illogical. I'm afraid I'm not very clear here but that's the way it comes.*
Therapist:	*That's all right. You say just what you think.*

(Snyder, 1947, pp. 2–24)

gestalt therapy The humanistic therapy developed by Fritz Perls in which clinicians actively move clients toward self-recognition and self-acceptance by using techniques such as role playing and self-discovery exercises.

In such an atmosphere, clients are expected to feel accepted by their therapists. They then may be able to look at themselves with honesty and acceptance. They begin to value their own emotions, thoughts, and behaviors, and so they are freed from the insecurities and doubts that prevent self-actualization.

Client-centered therapy has not fared very well in research (Prochaska & Norcross, 2018, 2013). Although some studies show that participants who receive this therapy improve more than control participants, many other studies have failed to find any such advantage. All the same, Rogers' therapy has had a positive influence on clinical practice (Raskin et al., 2019). It was one of the first major alternatives to psychodynamic therapy, and it helped open up the clinical field to new approaches. Rogers also helped pave the way for *psychologists* to practice psychotherapy, which had previously been considered the exclusive territory of psychiatrists. And his commitment to clinical research helped promote the systematic study of treatment. Approximately 2 percent of today's clinical psychologists, 1 percent of social workers, and 3 percent of counseling psychologists report that they employ the client-centered approach (Prochaska & Norcross, 2018).

Gestalt Theory and Therapy

Gestalt therapy, another humanistic approach, was developed in the 1950s by a charismatic clinician named Frederick (Fritz) Perls (1893–1970). Gestalt therapists, like client-centered therapists, guide their clients toward self-recognition and self-acceptance (Yontef & Jacobs, 2019). But unlike client-centered therapists, they try to achieve this goal by challenging and even frustrating the clients, demanding that they stay in the *here and now* during therapy discussions, and pushing them to embrace their real emotions.

For example, gestalt therapists often use the technique of *role playing,* instructing clients to act out various roles. A person may be told to be another person, an object, an alternative self, or even a part of the body. The gestalt version of role playing can become intense, as individuals are encouraged to express emotions fully. Many cry out, scream, kick, or pound. Through this experience they may come to "own" (accept) feelings that previously made them uncomfortable.

Approximately 1 percent of clinical psychologists and other kinds of clinicians describe themselves as gestalt therapists

Beating the blues Gestalt therapists often guide clients to express their needs and feelings in their full intensity by banging on pillows, crying out, kicking, or pounding things. Building on these techniques, a new approach, *drum therapy,* teaches clients, such as this woman, how to beat drums in order to help release traumatic memories, change beliefs, and feel more liberated.

(Prochaska & Norcross, 2018). Because they believe that subjective experiences and self-awareness cannot be measured objectively, proponents of gestalt therapy have not often performed controlled research on this approach (Yontef & Jacobs, 2019).

Spiritual Views and Interventions

For most of the twentieth century, clinical scientists viewed religion as a negative—or at best neutral—factor in mental health. In the early 1900s, for example, Freud argued that religious beliefs were defense mechanisms, "born from man's need to make his helplessness tolerable" (1961, p. 23). This negative view of religion now seems to be ending, however. During the past decade, many articles and books linking spiritual issues to clinical treatment have been published, and the ethical codes of psychologists, psychiatrists, and counselors have each concluded that religion is a type of diversity that mental health professionals must respect (APA, 2017, 2010).

Researchers have learned that spirituality does, in fact, often correlate with psychological health. In particular, studies have examined the mental health of people who are devout and who view God as warm, caring, helpful, and dependable. Repeatedly, these individuals are found to be less lonely, pessimistic, depressed, or anxious than people without any religious beliefs or those who view God as cold and unresponsive (Kucharska, 2017; Steffen, Masters, & Baldwin, 2017). Such people also seem to cope better with major life stressors—from illness to war—and to attempt suicide less often. In addition, they are less likely to abuse drugs.

What various explanations might account for the correlation between spirituality and mental health?

Do such correlations indicate that spirituality helps *produce* greater mental health? Not necessarily. As you'll recall from Chapter 1, correlations do not indicate causation. It may be, for example, that a sense of optimism leads to more spirituality, and that, independently, optimism contributes to greater mental health. Whatever the proper interpretation, many therapists now make a point of including spiritual issues when they treat religious clients, and some further encourage clients to use their spiritual resources to help them cope with current stressors (Barnett, 2018; McClintock, Lau, & Miller, 2016). Similarly, a number of religious institutions offer counseling services to their members.

AP Photo/John Amis

Spirituality and science A few years ago, Tibetan spiritual leader the Dalai Lama (right) met with professor of psychiatry Zindel Segal (left) and other mental health researchers at a conference examining possible ties between science, mental health, and spirituality.

Existential Theories and Therapy

Like humanists, existentialists believe that psychological dysfunction is caused by self-deception; existentialists, however, are talking about a kind of self-deception in which people hide from life's responsibilities and fail to recognize that it is up to them to give meaning to their lives. According to existentialists, many people become overwhelmed by the pressures of present-day society and so look to others for explanations, guidance, and authority. They overlook their personal freedom of choice and avoid responsibility for their lives and decisions (Yalom & Josselson, 2019; Cooper, 2016). Such people are left with empty, inauthentic lives. Their dominant emotions are anxiety, frustration, boredom, alienation, and depression.

Existentialists might view Philip Berman as a man who feels overwhelmed by the forces of society. He sees his parents as "rich, powerful, and selfish," and he perceives teachers, acquaintances, and employers as being oppressive. He fails to appreciate his choices in life and his own capacity for finding meaning and direction. Quitting becomes a habit with him—he leaves job after job, ends every romantic relationship, and flees difficult situations.

In **existential therapy,** people are encouraged to accept responsibility for their lives and for their problems. Therapists try to help clients recognize their freedom so that they may choose a different course and live with greater meaning (Yalom & Josselson, 2019; Schneider & Krug, 2017). The precise techniques used in existential therapy vary from clinician to clinician. At the same time, most existential therapists place great emphasis on the *relationship* between therapist and client and try to create an atmosphere of honesty, hard work, and shared learning and growth.

existential therapy A therapy that encourages clients to accept responsibility for their lives and to live with greater meaning and value.

Patient:	*I don't know why I keep coming here. All I do is tell you the same thing over and over. I'm not getting anywhere.*
Doctor:	*I'm getting tired of hearing the same thing over and over, too.*
Patient:	*Maybe I'll stop coming.*
Doctor:	*It's certainly your choice.*
Patient:	*What do you think I should do?*
Doctor:	*What do you want to do?*
Patient:	*I want to get better.*
Doctor:	*I don't blame you.*
Patient:	*If you think I should stay, ok, I will.*
Doctor:	*You want me to tell you to stay?*
Patient:	*You know what's best; you're the doctor.*
Doctor:	*Do I act like a doctor?*

(Keen, 1970, p. 200)

Existential therapists do not believe that experimental methods can adequately test the effectiveness of their treatments. To them, research dehumanizes individuals by reducing them to test measures. Not surprisingly, then, little controlled research has been devoted to the effectiveness of this approach (Yalom & Josselson, 2019; Schneider & Krug, 2017). Nevertheless, around 1 percent of today's clinical psychologists use an approach that is primarily existential (Prochaska & Norcross, 2018).

Assessing the Humanistic-Existential Model

The humanistic-existential model appeals to many people in and out of the clinical field. In recognizing the special challenges of human existence, humanistic and existential theorists tap into an aspect of psychological life that typically is missing from the other models. Moreover, the factors that they say are essential to effective functioning—self-acceptance, personal values, personal meaning, and personal choice—are certainly lacking in many people with psychological disturbances.

The optimistic tone of the humanistic-existential model is also an attraction. Such optimism meshes quite well with the goals and principles of *positive psychology* (see page 16) (Rashid & Seligman, 2019). Theorists who follow the principles of the humanistic-existential model offer great hope when they assert that, despite past and present events, we can make our own choices, determine our own destiny, and accomplish much. Still another attractive feature of the model is its emphasis on health. Unlike clinicians from some of the other models who see individuals as patients with psychological illnesses, humanists and existentialists view them simply as people who have yet to fulfill their potential.

At the same time, the humanistic-existential focus on abstract issues of human fulfillment gives rise to a major problem from a scientific point of view: these issues are difficult to research. In fact, with the notable exception of Rogers, who tried to investigate his clinical methods carefully, humanists and existentialists have traditionally rejected the use of empirical research. This anti-research position is now beginning to change among some humanistic and existential researchers—a change that may lead to important insights about the merits of this model in the coming years (Vos & Vitali, 2018; Schneider & Krug, 2017).

#CharitableActs

83%	Percentage of adult Americans who make charitable contributions each year
32%	Percentage of charitable donations contributed to religious organizations
68%	Percentage of donations directed to education, human services, health, and the arts
27%	Percentage of adult Americans who do volunteer work each year

(Information from: NPT, 2017; Gallup, 2013)

...SUMMING UP

THE HUMANISTIC-EXISTENTIAL MODEL The humanistic-existential model focuses on the human need to successfully deal with philosophical issues such as self-awareness, values, meaning, and choice.

Humanists believe that people are driven to self-actualize. When this drive is interfered with, abnormal behavior may result. One group of humanistic therapists, client-centered therapists, tries to create a very supportive therapy climate in which people can look at themselves honestly and acceptingly, thus opening the door to self-actualization. Another group, gestalt therapists, uses more active techniques to help people recognize and accept their needs. Recently, the role of religion as an important factor in mental health and in treatment has caught the attention of researchers and clinicians.

According to existentialists, abnormal behavior results from hiding from life's responsibilities. Existential therapists encourage people to accept responsibility for their lives, recognize their freedom to choose a different course, and choose to live with greater meaning.

#TheirWords

"I've learned that people will forget what you said, people will forget what you did, but people will never forget how you made them feel."

Maya Angelou

The Sociocultural Model: Family-Social and Multicultural Perspectives

Philip Berman is also a social and cultural being. He is surrounded by people and by institutions, he is a member of a family and a cultural group, he participates in social relationships, and he holds cultural values. Such forces are always operating upon Philip, setting rules and expectations that guide or pressure him, helping to shape his behaviors, thoughts, and emotions.

According to the *sociocultural model,* abnormal behavior is best understood in light of the broad forces that influence an individual. What are the norms of the individual's society and culture? What roles does the person play in the social environment? What kind of family structure or cultural background is the person a part of? And how do other people view and react to him or her? In fact, the sociocultural model is composed of two major perspectives—the *family-social perspective* and the *multicultural perspective.*

How Do Family-Social Theorists Explain Abnormal Functioning?

Proponents of the family-social perspective argue that clinical theorists should concentrate on those broad forces that operate *directly* on an individual as he or she moves through life—that is, family relationships, social interactions, and community events. They believe that such forces help account for both normal and abnormal behavior, and they pay particular attention to three kinds of factors: *social labels and roles, social networks,* and *family structure and communication.*

Social Labels and Roles Abnormal functioning can be influenced greatly by the labels and roles assigned to troubled people (Ruscio, 2015). When people stray from the norms of their society, the society calls them deviant and, in many cases, "mentally ill." Such labels tend to stick. Moreover, when people are viewed in particular ways, reacted to as "crazy," and perhaps even encouraged to act sick, they gradually learn to accept and play the assigned social role. Ultimately the label seems appropriate.

A famous study called "On Being Sane in Insane Places" by clinical investigator David Rosenhan (1973) supports this position. Eight normal people, actually colleagues of Rosenhan, presented themselves at various mental hospitals, falsely complaining that they had been hearing voices say the words "empty," "hollow," and "thud." On the basis of this complaint alone, each was diagnosed as having schizophrenia and admitted.

family systems theory A theory that views the family as a system of interacting parts whose interactions exhibit consistent patterns and unstated rules.

Moreover, the pseudopatients had a hard time convincing others that they were well once they had been given the diagnostic label. Their hospitalizations ranged from 7 to 52 days, even though they behaved normally and stopped reporting symptoms as soon as they were admitted. In addition, the label "schizophrenia" kept influencing the way the staff viewed and dealt with them. For example, one pseudopatient who paced the corridor out of boredom was, in clinical notes, described as "nervous." Overall, the pseudopatients came to feel powerless, invisible, and bored.

David Sipress/The New Yorker Collection/The Cartoon Bank

"We broke up, Stuart—don't you read your e-mail?"

Social Connections and Supports Family-social theorists are also concerned with the social environments in which people operate, including their social and professional relationships. How well do they communicate with others? What kind of signals do they send to or receive from others? Researchers have often found ties between deficient social connections and psychological dysfunction (Teo et al., 2019; Hsiao, Chang, & Gean, 2018). They have observed, for example, that people who are isolated and lack social support or intimacy in their lives are more likely to become depressed when under stress and to remain depressed longer than are people with supportive spouses or warm friendships.

Some clinical theorists believe that people who are unwilling or unable to communicate and develop relationships in their everyday lives will, alternatively, find adequate social contacts online, using social networking platforms like Facebook or Instagram. Although this may be true for some such individuals, research suggests that people's online relationships tend to parallel their offline relationships. Several studies of college students, for example, have found that students who are self-disclosing and have many friends on Facebook also are particularly social offline, while those who reveal less about themselves and initiate fewer relationships on Facebook are less willing to communicate with other people offline (Dunbar, 2016; Sheldon, 2008).

Family Structure and Communication Of course, one of the important social networks for an individual is his or her family. According to **family systems theory,** the family is a system of interacting parts—the family members—who interact with one another in consistent ways and follow rules unique to each family (Goldenberg &

Richard Cartwright/ABC via Getty Images

Today's TV families Unlike television viewers during the twentieth century, when problem-free families ruled the airwaves, today's viewers prefer more complex and occasionally dysfunctional families, like the Johnsons, whose trials and tribulations, including dealing with racial-cultural dilemmas, are on display in ABC's popular series *Black-ish*.

group therapy A therapy format in which a group of people with similar problems meet together with a therapist to work on those problems.

self-help group A group made up of people with similar problems who help and support one another without the direct leadership of a clinician. Also called a *mutual help group*.

family therapy A therapy format in which the therapist meets with all members of a family and helps them to change in therapeutic ways.

Stanton, 2019). Family systems theorists believe that the *structure* and *communication* patterns of some families actually force individual members to behave in a way that otherwise seems abnormal. If the members were to behave normally, they would severely strain the family's usual manner of operation and would actually increase their own and their family's turmoil.

Family systems theory holds that certain family systems are particularly likely to produce abnormal functioning in individual members (Lindblom et al., 2017). Some families, for example, have an *enmeshed* structure in which the members are grossly overinvolved in one another's activities, thoughts, and feelings. Children from this kind of family may have great difficulty becoming independent in life. Some families display *disengagement,* which is marked by very rigid boundaries between the members. Children from these families may find it hard to function in a group or to give or request support.

Philip Berman's angry and impulsive personal style might be seen as the product of a disturbed family structure. According to family systems theorists, the whole family—Philip's mother, father, and brother, and Philip himself—relate in such a way as to maintain Philip's behavior. Family theorists might be particularly interested in the conflict between Philip's mother and father and the imbalance between their parental roles. They might see Philip's behavior as both a reaction to and stimulus for his parents' behaviors. With Philip acting out the role of the misbehaving child, or scapegoat, his parents may have little need or time to question their own relationship.

Family systems theorists would also seek to clarify the precise nature of Philip's relationship with each parent. Is he enmeshed with his mother and/or disengaged from his father? They would look too at the rules governing the sibling relationship in the family, the relationship between Philip's parents and brother, and the nature of parent–child relationships in previous generations of the family.

Creative group work *Psychodrama*, developed by psychiatrist Jacob Moreno in 1921, is one of the oldest forms of group treatment. Its group members act out their emotions, past or present situations, social interactions, and the like—often in creative ways and sometimes on a stage. Although not as widely conducted as conventional group therapy, this format is still offered in a number of locations, such as this psychodrama group in Pignan, France.

Kasia Wandycz/Paris Match via Getty Images

Family-Social Treatments

The family-social perspective has helped spur the growth of several treatment approaches, including *group, family,* and *couple therapy,* and *community treatment.* Therapists of any orientation may work with clients in these various formats, applying the techniques and principles of their preferred models (see ***MindTech***). However, more and more of the clinicians who use these formats believe that psychological problems emerge in family and social settings and are best treated in such settings, and they include special sociocultural strategies in their work.

Group Therapy Thousands of therapists specialize in **group therapy,** a format in which a therapist meets with a group of clients who have similar problems. Typically, members of a therapy group meet together with a therapist and discuss the problems of one or more of the people in the group. Together they develop important insights, build social skills, strengthen feelings of self-worth, and share useful information or advice (Brown, 2017). Many groups are created with particular client populations in mind; for example, there are groups for people with alcoholism, for those who are physically handicapped, and for people who are divorced, abused, or bereaved.

Research suggests that group therapy is of help to many clients, often as helpful as individual therapy (Mergl et al., 2018; Law et al., 2016). The group format also has been used for purposes that are educational rather than therapeutic, such as "consciousness raising" and spiritual inspiration.

MINDTECH

Have Your Avatar Call My Avatar

The sociocultural model holds that abnormal behavior is best understood and treated in a social context. Thus, as part of the movement toward technology-enhanced interventions, a growing number of clinicians are particularly interested in using *avatars*—three-dimensional graphical representations of the clients and/or other key persons in their lives—in their treatment programs (Alderson-Day & Jones. 2018; Craig et al., 2018, 2016).

Guia Besana/Anzenberger/Redux

As you will see in Chapters 4 and 5, the use of 3D computer graphics to simulate real-world objects and situations, called *virtual reality therapy*, has become a popular technique for treating people with phobias, traumatic memories, and other disorders. In such cases, the technique enables clients to be exposed—through computer simulation—to the objects and memories they dread, thus helping them to confront their fears head-on.

On the other hand, avatar therapy, one version of virtual reality therapy, seeks primarily to immerse clients in digitalized social situations—situations in which they interact with avatars as a bridge toward social improvement.

In one form of avatar-centered therapy, users are guided by computer software programs to interact with on-screen virtual therapist figures who ask questions such as "What kinds of things do you dislike about yourself?" The virtual therapist may also nod sympathetically when the users offer self-criticisms and may reinforce certain user statements with smiles or encouraging words (Rehm et al., 2016; Reamer, 2013).

In another use of avatars, clients are guided by their real-life therapists to enter virtual environments on their computers, acquire virtual bodies, and interact with animated figures who resemble their parents, bosses, friends, or enemies—in situations that feel very real (Allen, Jameson, & Myers, 2017; Myers et al., 2016). In one highly publicized case, for example, a woman with social anxiety and agoraphobia—a fear of leaving the house—was guided by her therapist to adopt an avatar and enter into a virtual world of other avatars, a journey that eventually enabled her to venture outside into the real world and into relationships with other persons (Smith, 2008).

Not surprisingly, given its social focus, avatar therapy is used most often to help individuals suffering from problems such as social anxiety, loneliness, interpersonal deficits, and hallucinations that hinder normal interactions (Allen et al., 2017; Falconer et al., 2017). These applications are often quite helpful according to research (Craig et al., 2018; Leff et al., 2014, 2013).

A format similar to group therapy is the **self-help group** (or **mutual-help group**). Here people who have similar problems (for example, bereavement, substance abuse, illness, unemployment, or divorce) come together to help and support one another without the direct leadership of a professional clinician (Bond, Wright, & Bacon, 2017). According to estimates, there are now between 500,000 and 3 million such groups in the United States alone, attended each year by as many as 3 to 4 percent of the population (Ahmadi, 2016). In addition, an ever-growing number of self-help chat groups have emerged on the Internet.

Why might group therapy actually be more helpful to some people with psychological problems than individual therapy?

Family Therapy **Family therapy** was first introduced in the 1950s. A therapist meets with all members of a family, points out problem behaviors and interactions, and helps

#ShiftingValues

59%	Percentage of adults who say their families have fewer family dinners than when they were growing up
10	Average number of weekly hours today's fathers spend doing housework, compared with 4 hours a half century ago
18	Average number of weekly hours today's mothers spend doing housework, compared with 32 hours a half century ago

(Information from: Pew Research Center, 2015, 2013; Harris Interactive, 2013)

the whole family to change its ways (Goldenberg & Stanton, 2019). Here, the entire family is viewed as the unit under treatment, even if only one of the members receives a clinical diagnosis. The following is a typical interaction between family members and a therapist:

> *Tommy sat motionless in a chair gazing out the window. He was fourteen and a bit small for his age. . . . Sissy was eleven. She was sitting on the couch between her Mom and Dad with a smile on her face. Across from them sat Ms. Fargo, the family therapist.*
>
> *Ms. Fargo spoke. "Could you be a little more specific about the changes you have seen in Tommy and when they came about?"*
>
> *Mrs. Davis answered first. "Well, I guess it was about two years ago. Tommy started getting in fights at school. When we talked to him at home he said it was none of our business. He became moody and disobedient. He wouldn't do anything that we wanted him to. He began to act mean to his sister and even hit her."*
>
> *"What about the fights at school?" Ms. Fargo asked.*
>
> *This time it was Mr. Davis who spoke first. "Ginny was more worried about them than I was. I used to fight a lot when I was in school and I think it is normal. . . . But I was very respectful to my parents, especially my Dad. If I ever got out of line he would smack me one."*
>
> *"Have you ever had to hit Tommy?" Ms. Fargo inquired softly.*
>
> *"Sure, a couple of times, but it didn't seem to do any good."*
>
> *All at once Tommy seemed to be paying attention, his eyes riveted on his father. "Yeah, he hit me a lot, for no reason at all!"*
>
> *"Now, that's not true, Thomas." Mrs. Davis has a scolding expression on her face. "If you behaved yourself a little better you wouldn't get hit. Ms. Fargo, I can't say that I am in favor of the hitting, but I understand sometimes how frustrating it may be for Bob."*
>
> *"You don't know how frustrating it is for me, honey." Bob seemed upset. . . .*
>
> *Ginny gave him a hard stare . . . "I could use some support from you [too]. You think . . . I will do everything. . . . Well, I am not about to do that anymore." . . . [She] began to cry. "I just don't know what to do anymore. Things just seem so hopeless. Why can't people be nice in this family anymore? I don't think I am asking too much, am I?"*
>
> *Ms. Fargo . . . looked at each person briefly and was sure to make eye contact. "There seems to be a lot going on . . . I think we are going to need to understand a lot of things to see why this is happening."*
>
> *(Sheras & Worchel, 1979, pp. 108–110)*

Family therapists may follow any of the major theoretical models, but many of them adopt the principles of *family systems theory*. Today 2 percent of all clinical psychologists, 4 percent of counseling psychologists, and 14 percent of social workers identify themselves mainly as *family systems therapists* (Prochaska & Norcross, 2018).

As you read earlier, family systems theory holds that each family has its own rules, structure, and communication patterns that shape the individual members' behavior. Thus, family systems therapists often try to change the family power structure, the roles each person plays, and the relationships between members. They may also try to help members recognize and change harmful patterns of communication (Corey, 2017; Minuchin, 2007, 1987, 1974).

Family therapy is often helpful to individuals, although research has not yet clarified how helpful (Goldenberg & Stanton, 2019). Some studies have found that as many as 65 percent of individuals treated with family approaches improve, while other studies suggest much lower success rates. Nor has any one type of family therapy emerged as consistently more helpful than the others (Lebow, 2017).

couple therapy A therapy format in which the therapist works with two people who share a long-term relationship. Also called *marital therapy*.

community mental health treatment A treatment approach that emphasizes community care.

Couple Therapy In **couple therapy**, or **marital therapy**, the therapist works with two individuals who are in a long-term relationship. Often, they are husband and wife, but the couple need not be married or even living together. Like family therapy, couple therapy often focuses on the structure and communication patterns in the relationship

(Baucom et al., 2018, 2015, 2010; Lebow, 2017). A couple approach may also be used when a child's psychological problems are traced to problems in the parents' relationship.

Although some degree of conflict exists in any long-term relationship, many couples in our society have serious marital discord. The divorce rate in Canada, the United States, and Europe is now close to 50 percent of the marriage rate. Many couples who live together without marrying apparently have similar levels of difficulty (Martins et al., 2014).

Couple therapy, like family and group therapy, may follow the principles of any of the major therapy orientations. *Cognitive-behavioral couple therapy,* for example, uses many techniques from the cognitive and behavioral perspectives (Epstein & Zheng, 2017). Therapists help spouses recognize and change problem behaviors largely by teaching specific problem-solving and communication skills. A broader, more sociocultural version, called *integrative behavioral couple therapy,* further helps partners accept behaviors that they cannot change and embrace the whole relationship nevertheless (Christensen & Doss, 2017). Partners are asked to see such behaviors as an understandable result of basic differences between them.

Couples treated by couple therapy seem to show greater improvement in their relationships than couples with similar problems who do not receive treatment, but no one form of couple therapy stands out as superior to others (Christensen et al., 2016, 2014, 2010). Although marital functioning improved in two-thirds of treated couples by the end of therapy, fewer than half of those who are treated achieve "distress-free" or "happy" relationships. One-fourth of all treated couples eventually separate or divorce.

Community Treatment **Community mental health treatment** programs allow clients, particularly those with severe psychological difficulties, to receive treatment in familiar social surroundings as they try to recover. Such community-based treatments, including *community day programs* and *residential services,* seem to be of special value to people with severe mental disorders (Schroeder, 2018). A number of other countries have launched such programs over the past several decades.

As you read in Chapter 1, a key principle of community treatment is *prevention*. This involves clinicians actively reaching out to clients rather than waiting for them to seek treatment. Research suggests that such efforts are often very successful (Mendelson & Eaton, 2018; Koh, 2017). Community workers recognize three types of prevention, which they call *primary, secondary,* and *tertiary.*

Primary prevention consists of efforts to improve community attitudes and policies. Its goal is to prevent psychological disorders altogether. Community workers may, for example, consult with a local school board, offer public workshops on stress reduction, or construct Web sites on how to cope effectively.

Secondary prevention consists of identifying and treating psychological disorders in the early stages, before they become serious. Community workers may work with teachers, ministers, or police to help them recognize the early signs of psychological dysfunction and teach them how to help people find treatment. Similarly, hundreds of mental health Web sites provide this same kind of information to family members, teachers, and the like.

The goal of *tertiary prevention* is to provide effective treatment as soon as it is needed so that moderate or severe disorders do not become long-term problems. Community agencies across the United States successfully offer tertiary care for millions of people with moderate psychological problems but, as you read in Chapter 1, they often fail to provide the services needed by hundreds of thousands with severe disturbances (NIMH, 2017). One of the reasons for this failure is lack of funding, an issue that you will read about in later chapters.

NYPD
November 27, 2012 ·
Jennifer Foster of Florence, AZ was visiting Times Square with her husband Nov. 14 when they saw a shoeless man asking for change… See More

Reaching out On a freezing night in 2012, New York City police officer Lawrence DiPrimo bought a pair of socks and shoes for a homeless man he had come across, then knelt down and gently put them on the man's feet. Unbeknownst to the officer, his humane act was photographed by a passerby and was viewed online by millions of people. Although DiPrimo's behavior came from the heart, it reflected the key principles of community mental health, including reaching out to the needy in the community with kindness and understanding, which may help prevent mental health problems.

An unacceptable difference Dressed in traditional American Indian clothing, a high school student from the Mescalero Apache Reservation in New Mexico testifies before Congress on "The Preventable Epidemic: Youth Suicides and the Urgent Need for Mental Health Care Resources in Indian Country."

How Do Multicultural Theorists Explain Abnormal Functioning?

Culture refers to the set of values, attitudes, beliefs, history, and behaviors shared by a group of people and communicated from one generation to the next (Matsumoto & Juang, 2016). We are, without question, a society of multiple cultures. Indeed, by the year 2044, members of racial and ethnic minority groups in the United States will collectively outnumber non-Hispanic white Americans (Frey, 2018; U.S. Census Bureau, 2015).

Partly in response to this growing diversity, the **multicultural,** or **culturally diverse, perspective** has emerged (Comas-Díaz, 2019). Multicultural psychologists seek to understand how culture, race, ethnicity, gender, and similar factors affect behavior and thought and how people of different cultures, races, and genders differ psychologically (Alegría et al., 2018, 2016, 2014). Today's multicultural view is different from past—less enlightened—cultural perspectives: it does not imply that members of racial, ethnic, and other minority groups are in some way inferior or culturally deprived in comparison with a majority population. Rather, the model holds that an individual's behavior, whether normal or abnormal, is best understood when examined in the light of that individual's unique cultural context, from the values of that culture to the special external pressures faced by members of the culture.

The groups in the United States that have received the most attention from multicultural researchers are ethnic and racial minority groups (African American, Hispanic American, American Indian, and Asian American groups) and groups such as economically disadvantaged persons, LGBTQ individuals, and women (although women are not a minority group numbers-wise). Each of these groups is subjected to special pressures in American society that may contribute to feelings of stress and, in some cases, to abnormal functioning. Researchers have learned, for example, that psychological abnormality, especially severe psychological abnormality, is indeed more common among poorer people than among wealthier people (APA, 2018; Sareen et al., 2011) (see **Figure 2-4**). Perhaps the pressures of poverty explain this relationship.

FIGURE 2-4

Poverty and Mental Health

Surveys in the United States find that people with low annual incomes (below $20,000) have a greater risk of experiencing mental disorders than do those with higher incomes (above $70,000). For example, 10 percent of low-income people have persistent symptoms of anxiety, compared with 6 percent of higher-income people. (Information from: APA, 2018; CDC, 2015; Sareen et al., 2011.)

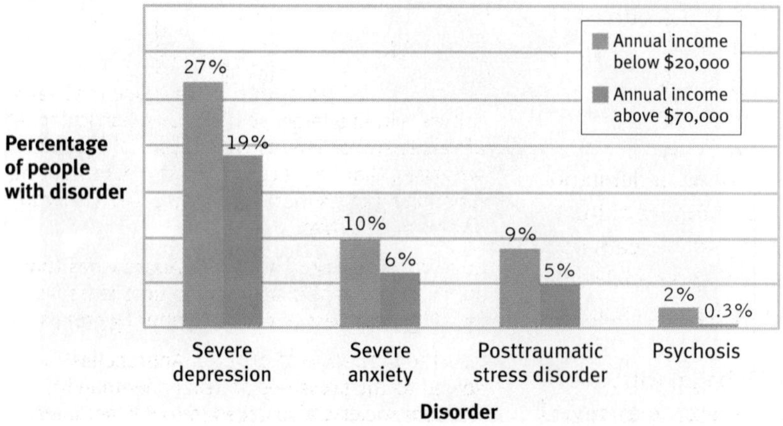

Of course, membership in these various groups overlaps. Many members of minority groups, for example, also live in poverty. The higher rates of crime, unemployment, overcrowding, and homelessness; the inferior medical care; and the limited educational opportunities typically available to poor people may place great stress on many members of such minority groups (APA, 2018; Joshi et al., 2016).

Multicultural researchers have also noted that the prejudice and discrimination faced by many minority groups may contribute to various forms of abnormal functioning (Yoon, Coburn, & Spence, 2018). Women in Western society receive diagnoses of anxiety disorders and of depression at least twice as often as men (MHA, 2018). Similarly, African Americans, Hispanic Americans, and American Indians are more likely than non-Hispanic white Americans to experience serious psychological distress (APA, 2018; HHS, 2009). American Indians also have exceptionally high alcoholism and suicide rates (AFSP, 2018; NSDUH, 2016). Although many factors may combine to produce these differences, prejudice based on race and sexual orientation, and the problems such prejudice poses, may contribute to abnormal patterns of tension, unhappiness, and low self-esteem.

Multicultural Treatments

Studies conducted throughout the world have found that members of ethnic and racial minority groups tend to show less improvement in clinical treatment, make less use of mental health services, and stop therapy sooner than members of majority groups (Alegría et al., 2018, 2016, 2014).

A number of studies suggest that two features of treatment can increase a therapist's effectiveness with minority clients: (1) greater sensitivity to cultural issues and (2) inclusion of cultural morals and models in treatment, especially in therapies for children and adolescents (Comas-Díaz, 2019; Chu et al., 2016). Given such findings, some clinicians have developed **culture-sensitive therapies,** approaches that are designed to help address the unique issues faced by members of cultural minority groups. Therapies geared to the pressures of being female, called **gender-sensitive,** or **feminist, therapies,** follow similar principles (Corey, 2017; Vasquez & Vasquez, 2016).

AP Photo/Ali Burafi

Community mental health: Argentine style Staff members and patients from Borda Neuropsychiatric Hospital in Buenos Aires set up a laptop and begin broadcasting on the popular radio station Radio La Colifata (*colifa* is slang for "crazy one"). The station was started more than 20 years ago to help patients pursue therapeutic activities and reach out to the community.

Culture-sensitive approaches typically include the following elements:

1. Special cultural instruction for therapists in their graduate training program
2. The therapist's awareness of a client's cultural values
3. The therapist's awareness of the stress, prejudices, and stereotypes to which minority clients are exposed
4. The therapist's awareness of the hardships faced by the children of immigrants
5. Helping clients recognize the impact of both their own culture and the dominant culture on their self-views and behaviors
6. Helping clients identify and express suppressed anger and pain
7. Helping clients achieve a bicultural balance that feels right for them
8. Helping clients raise their self-esteem—a sense of self-worth that has often been damaged by generations of negative messages

Assessing the Sociocultural Model

The family-social and multicultural perspectives have added greatly to the understanding and treatment of abnormal functioning. Today most clinicians take family, cultural, social, and societal issues into account, factors that were overlooked just 35 years ago. In addition, clinicians have become more aware of the impact of clinical and social roles. Finally, the treatment formats offered by the sociocultural model sometimes succeed where traditional approaches have failed.

At the same time, the sociocultural model has certain problems. To begin with, sociocultural research findings are often difficult to interpret. Indeed, research may reveal

multicultural perspective The view that each culture within a larger society has a particular set of values and beliefs, as well as special external pressures, that help account for the behavior and functioning of its members. Also called *culturally diverse perspective.*

culture-sensitive therapies Approaches that are designed to help address the unique issues faced by members of cultural minority groups.

gender-sensitive therapies Approaches geared to the pressures of being a woman in Western society. Also called *feminist therapies.*

#

#FamilyRestructuring

9%	Percentage of U.S. children living with only one parent in 1960
27%	Percentage of U.S. children living with only one parent today

(U.S. Census Bureau, 2016)

a relationship between certain family or cultural factors and a particular disorder, yet fail to establish that they are its *cause*. Studies show a link between family conflict and schizophrenia, for example, but that finding does not necessarily mean that family dysfunction causes schizophrenia. It is equally possible that family functioning is disrupted by the tension and conflict created by the psychotic behavior of a family member.

Another limitation of the sociocultural model is its inability to predict abnormality in specific individuals. If, for example, social conditions such as prejudice and discrimination are key causes of anxiety and depression, why do only some of the people subjected to such forces experience psychological disorders? Are still other factors necessary for the development of the disorders?

Given these limitations, most clinicians view the family-social and multicultural explanations as operating in conjunction with the biological or psychological explanations. They agree that family, social, and cultural factors may create a climate favorable to the development of certain disorders. They believe, however, that biological or psychological conditions—or both—must also be present for the disorders to evolve.

...SUMMING UP

THE SOCIOCULTURAL MODEL One sociocultural perspective, the family-social perspective looks outward to three kinds of factors: social labels and roles, social connections and supports, and the family system. Practitioners from this perspective may practice group, family, or couple therapy, or community treatment.

The multicultural perspective, another sociocultural perspective, holds that an individual's behavior, whether normal or abnormal, is best understood when examined in the light of his or her unique cultural context, including the values of that culture and the special pressures faced by members of that culture. Practitioners of this perspective may provide culture-sensitive therapies.

Integrating the Models: The Developmental Psychopathology Perspective

Today's leading models vary widely (see **Table 2-3**), and none of the models has proved consistently superior. Each helps us appreciate a key aspect of human functioning, and each has important strengths as well as serious limitations.

Despite all their differences, the conclusions and techniques of the various models are often compatible. And, indeed, many clinicians now favor explanations of abnormal behavior that consider more than one kind of cause at a time. These explanations state that abnormality results from the interaction of genetic, biological, emotional, behavioral, cognitive, social, cultural, and societal influences. In a similar quest for integration, many therapists now combine treatment techniques from several models (Norcross & Beutler, 2019). In fact, 22 percent of today's clinical psychologists, 31 percent of counseling psychologists, and 26 percent of social workers describe their approach as "eclectic" or "integrative" (Prochaska & Norcross, 2018). Studies confirm that clinical problems often respond better to combined approaches than to any one therapy alone.

One of today's most influential integrative views is the **developmental psychopathology** perspective. As its name implies, this perspective uses a *developmental* framework to understand how variables and principles from the various models may collectively account for human functioning—both adaptive and maladaptive functioning (Cicchetti, 2018, 2016; Halperin, 2017). As such, the perspective pays particular attention to the *timing* of influential variables. The emergence of particular events,

developmental psychopathology A perspective that uses a developmental framework to understand how variables and principles from the various models may collectively account for human functioning.

equifinality The principle that a number of different developmental pathways can lead to the same psychological disorder.

experiences, or biological factors—from neurons to neighborhoods—can continue to have enormous impact on later functioning if they occur at vulnerable points in a person's life. Moreover, the critical question for developmental psychopathologists is not *which* single factor is the cause of an individual's current psychological problems, but rather when, how, in what context, and to what degree the multiple factors in his or her life interact with one another. In Philip Berman's case, for example, when did his brother's birth occur, what was going on in Philip's life at that point in time, how did his mother's depression affect her parenting skills, did his childhood experiences teach him how to cope effectively with stress, and were his social systems during childhood, college, and adulthood supportive or did they intensify his difficulties?

What are the factors that developmental psychopathologists look at collectively when seeking to understand a person's abnormal functioning? As noted above, they draw from each of the clinical field's major models. They draw from the biological model, for example, by determining how certain genetic and brain factors have set the stage for the individual's important environmental experiences (Barker, 2018; Halperin, 2017). They extract from the psychodynamic model by considering how earlier events in a person's life—including parent–child relationships—have stifled subsequent development (Moreno, 2018; Chambers, 2017). They employ principles from the cognitive-behavioral model by determining how the individual's maladaptive behaviors have been reinforced over the years and how he or she has interpreted and processed life experiences (Hankin et al., 2016). In addition, developmental psychopathologists draw from the humanistic-existential model by considering the person's competencies, uniqueness, and resilience, even in the face of overwhelming life stress (Hornor, 2017; Burt et al., 2016). And finally, they embrace the sociocultural model's emphasis on the influence of social context and culture—both present and past—on the individual's functioning (Shulman & Scharf, 2018; Pianta, 2016).

The developmental psychopathology perspective contends that various developmental routes, or *pathways*, can lead to dysfunction. In fact, two key principles—*equifinality* and *multifinality*—are at the center of the perspective. According to the principle of **equifinality,** a number of different developmental pathways can lead to the same psychological disorder. Consider, for example, two teenage boys with conduct disorder, a disorder that you'll be reading about in Chapter 14. Both boys may display the characteristic symptoms of this disorder, such as stealing, skipping school, lying, and breaking into cars. However, for one of the boys, factors such as unfavorable genes,

#

#TheirWords

"Even a minor event in the life of a child is an event of that child's world and thus a world event."

Gaston Bachelard, French philosopher

TABLE: 2-3

Comparing the Models

	Biological	Psychodynamic	Cognitive-Behavioral	Humanistic	Existential	Family-Social	Multicultural
Cause of dysfunction	Biological malfunction	Underlying conflicts	Maladaptive thinking and learning	Self-deceit	Avoidance of responsibility	Family or social stress	External pressures or cultural conflicts
Research support	Strong	Modest	Strong	Weak	Weak	Moderate	Moderate
Consumer designation	Patient	Patient	Client	Patient or client	Patient or client	Client	Client
Therapist role	Doctor	Interpreter	Collaborator/teacher	Observer	Collaborator	Family/social facilitator	Cultural advocate/teacher
Key therapy technique	Biological intervention	Free association and interpretation	Reasoning and conditioning	Reflection	Varied	Family/social intervention	Culture-sensitive intervention
Therapy goal	Biological repair	Broad psychological change	Functional thoughts and behaviors	Self-actualization	Authentic life	Effective family or social system	Cultural awareness and comfort

High-flying equifinality The principle of *equifinality*—the notion that people can arrive at the same end point through different developmental pathways—has been observed in the physical realm as well as the psychological realm. Consider Neil Douglas and Robert Stirling, two men born to different parents, inheriting different genes, experiencing different childhoods, and raised in different cities. When the two strangers took a plane flight in 2015, they each were flabbergasted to see that the passenger seated next to them was their "spitting image"—same red hair and beard, head shape, eyes, teeth, smile, and more. They immediately took this selfie, and the photo went viral.

poor parenting, and a limited cognitive capacity for empathy may have interacted to foster the development of conduct disorder. In contrast, the other boy with the disorder may not have any genetic vulnerabilities, may have been raised by highly attentive parents, and may actually demonstrate a high capacity for empathy. His serious conduct problems may have resulted instead from the interaction of long-term feelings of depression, low self-esteem, strong needs for peer approval, and affiliations with peers who typically engage in delinquent activities.

According to the principle of **multifinality** (the flipside of equifinality), persons who have experienced a number of similar developmental variables (for example, comparable biological predispositions, family structures, schools, and neighborhoods) may nevertheless react to comparable current situations in very different ways or have different clinical outcomes. Consider two women who lose their jobs suddenly. Despite their similar developmental variables, one woman may react to this loss with devastation and spiral toward depression, while the other may view the job loss as an opportunity for reinvention and enthusiastically seek out a wide range of new employment opportunities. Why this enormous difference in the reactions of the two individuals? Perhaps their developmental histories or current circumstances do in fact differ in undetected ways. The latter woman may, for example, have experienced uniquely challenging events while growing up that fostered a strong sense of resilience, or she may currently have greater financial savings to help her weather a period of unemployment.

Given their emphasis on timing and development to explain psychological disorders, it is not surprising that developmental psychopathologists focus more on the timing of treatment than on specific treatment techniques. For example, they tend to prioritize prevention and early intervention for vulnerable persons over treatment for individuals who have already developed severe disorders (Beelmann et al., 2018; Toth et al., 2016). Further, consistent with the perspective's special emphasis on context and sociocultural influences, developmental psychopathologists echo the call of community mental health advocates for community-wide interventions, commonly targeting entire schools or neighborhoods, as opposed to individual treatment formats. Indeed, developmental psychopathologists often play prominent roles in social policy, seeking changes in societal factors that negatively influence development, such as poverty, community violence, and social inequalities.

Given the rise of integrative perspectives and combination treatments, our examinations of abnormal behavior throughout this book will take two directions. As various disorders are presented, we will look at how today's models explain and treat each disorder, and how well those explanations and treatments are supported by research. Just as important, however, we will also be observing how the explanations and treatments may build upon one another, and we will examine current efforts toward integration of the models, including the efforts of developmental psychopathologists.

9... SUMMING UP

INTEGRATING THE MODELS Many theorists now favor explanations for abnormal behavior that consider more than one kind of cause, and many therapists combine treatment techniques from several models. An influential integrative view, the developmental psychopathology perspective, uses a developmental framework to understand how variables and principles from the various models may collectively account for human functioning—both adaptive and maladaptive functioning. Two principles at the center of this perspective are equifinality and multifinality.

multifinality The principle that persons with a similar developmental history may nevertheless react to similar current situations in very different ways.

... Key Terms

model, p. 36
neuron, p. 37
synapse, p. 37
neurotransmitter, p. 37
receptors, p. 37
endocrine system, p. 38
hormone, p. 38
brain circuit, p. 38
genes, p. 39
psychotropic medication, p. 40
brain stimulation, p. 41
electroconvulsive therapy (ECT), p. 41
psychosurgery, p. 42
unconscious, p. 43
id, p. 43
ego, p. 43
ego defense mechanism, p. 43
superego, p. 44
fixation, p. 44
object relations theory, p. 45
free association, p. 46
resistance, p. 46
transference, p. 46
dream, p. 46
catharsis, p. 47
working through, p. 47
short-term psychodynamic therapies, p. 47
relational psychoanalytic therapy, p. 47
conditioning, p. 49
classical conditioning, p. 49
modeling, p. 49
operant conditioning, p. 49
social anxiety disorder, p. 51
exposure therapy, p. 52
self-actualization, p. 55
client-centered therapy, p. 55
gestalt therapy, p. 57
existential therapy, p. 58
family systems theory, p. 61
group therapy, p. 62
self-help group, p. 63
family therapy, p. 63
couple therapy, p. 64
community mental health treatment, p. 65
multicultural perspective, p. 66
culture-sensitive therapy, p. 67
gender-sensitive therapy, p. 67
developmental psychopathology, p. 68
equifinality, p. 69
multifinality, p. 70

... Quick Quiz

1. What are brain structures, neurotransmitters, and brain circuits? Describe the biological treatments for psychological disorders. *pp. 37–42*
2. Identify the models associated with learned responses (*p. 49*), values (*p. 55*), responsibility (*p. 58*), spirituality (*p. 58*), underlying conflicts (*p. 43*), and maladaptive assumptions (*p. 50*).
3. Identify the treatments that use unconditional positive regard (*p. 56*), free association (*p. 46*), exposure (*p. 52*), mindfulness meditation (*p. 53*), and dream interpretation (*p. 46*).
4. What are the key principles of the psychodynamic (*pp. 43–45*), cognitive-behavioral (*pp. 48–51*), humanistic-existential (*pp. 55–59*), and sociocultural models (*pp. 60–67*)?
5. According to psychodynamic theorists, what roles do the id, ego, and superego play in the development of both normal and abnormal behavior? What are the key techniques used by psychodynamic therapists? *pp. 43–48*
6. What forms of conditioning do cognitive-behavioral practitioners focus on in their explanations and treatments of abnormal behaviors? What kinds of cognitive dysfunctions can contribute to abnormal behavior, and which treatment approaches are used to address such dysfunctions? *pp. 49–52*
7. How do humanistic theories and therapies differ from existential ones? *pp. 55–59*
8. How might social labels and roles, social connections, family factors, and culture relate to psychological functioning? *pp. 60–62, 66–67*
9. What are the key features of culture-sensitive therapy, group therapy, family therapy, couple therapy, and community treatment? How effective are these various approaches? *pp. 62–67*
10. What are the key principles of the developmental psychopathology perspective? How does this perspective integrate the variables and principles found in the various models of psychological abnormality? *pp. 68–70*

Key Terms

model, p. 36
neuron, p. 37
synapse, p. 37
neurotransmitter, p. 37
receptors, p. 37
endocrine system, p. 38
hormone, p. 38
brain circuit, p. 38
genes, p. 39
psychotropic medication, p. 40
brain stimulation, p. 41
electroconvulsive therapy (ECT), p. 41
psychosurgery, p. 42
unconscious, p. 43
id, p. 43
ego, p. 43
ego defense mechanism, p. 43
superego, p. 44
fixation, p. 44
object relations theory, p. 45
free association, p. 46
resistance, p. 46
transference, p. 46
dream, p. 46
catharsis, p. 47
working through, p. 47
short-term psychodynamic therapies, p. 47
relational psychoanalytic therapy, p. 47
conditioning, p. 49
classical conditioning, p. 49
modeling, p. 49
operant conditioning, p. 49
social anxiety disorder, p. 51
exposure therapy, p. 52
self-actualization, p. 55
client-centered therapy, p. 55
gestalt therapy, p. 57
existential therapy, p. 58
family systems theory, p. 61
group therapy, p. 62
self-help group, p. 63
family therapy, p. 63
couple therapy, p. 64
community mental health treatment, p. 65
multicultural perspective, p. 66
culture-sensitive therapy, p. 67
gender-sensitive therapy, p. 67
developmental psychopathology, p. 68
equifinality, p. 69
multifinality, p. 70

Quick Quiz

1. What are brain structures, neurotransmitters, and brain circuits? Describe the biological treatments for psychological disorders. *pp. 37–42*
2. Identify the models associated with learned responses (*p. 49*), values (*p. 55*), responsibility (*p. 58*), spirituality (*p. 58*), underlying conflicts (*p. 43*), and maladaptive assumptions (*p. 50*).
3. Identify the treatments that use unconditional positive regard (*p. 56*), free association (*p. 46*), exposure (*p. 52*), mindfulness meditation (*p. 53*), and dream interpretation (*p. 46*).
4. What are the key principles of the psychodynamic (*pp. 43–45*), cognitive-behavioral (*pp. 48–51*), humanistic-existential (*pp. 55–59*), and sociocultural models (*pp. 60–67*)?
5. According to psychodynamic theorists, what roles do the id, ego, and superego play in the development of both normal and abnormal behavior? What are the key techniques used by psychodynamic therapists? *pp. 43–48*
6. What forms of conditioning do cognitive-behavioral practitioners focus on in their explanations and treatments of abnormal behaviors? What kinds of cognitive dysfunctions can contribute to abnormal behavior, and which treatment approaches are used to address such dysfunctions? *pp. 49–52*
7. How do humanistic theories and therapies differ from existential ones? *pp. 55–59*
8. How might social labels and roles, social connections, family factors, and culture relate to psychological functioning? *pp. 60–62, 66–67*
9. What are the key features of culture-sensitive therapy, group therapy, family therapy, couple therapy, and community treatment? How effective are these various approaches? *pp. 62–67*
10. What are the key principles of the developmental psychopathology perspective? How does this perspective integrate the variables and principles found in the various models of psychological abnormality? *pp. 68–70*

CHAPTER 3

Clinical Assessment, Diagnosis, and Treatment

TOPIC OVERVIEW

Franco started seeing a therapist at the urging of his friend Jesse. It had been almost four months since Franco broke up with his girlfriend, and he still seemed unable to pull himself together. He had totally stopped playing sports and attending concerts, things he normally did on a regular basis. When he finally returned Jesse's calls, he mentioned several serious and avoidable mistakes that he had made at work recently, but he barely seemed to care. He also confided to his friend that he felt very tired and was unable to touch his food. Jesse suspected that Franco was clinically depressed, but, then again, he was not a therapist.

Feelings of despondency led Franco to make an appointment with a therapist at a local counseling center. His clinician's first step was to learn as much as possible about Franco and his disturbance: Who is he, what is his life like, and what are his symptoms? The answers might help to reveal the causes and probable course of his present dysfunction and suggest what kinds of strategies would be most likely to help him. Treatment could then be tailored to Franco's needs and particular pattern of abnormal functioning.

In Chapters 1 and 2 you read about how researchers in abnormal psychology build a general understanding of abnormal functioning. Clinical practitioners apply this broad information in their work, but their main focus when faced with new clients is to gather **idiographic,** or individual, information about them. To help a client overcome problems, clinicians must fully understand the client and his or her particular difficulties. To gather such individual information, clinicians use the procedures of *assessment* and *diagnosis*. Then they are in a position to offer *treatment*. ■

Clinical Assessment: How and Why Does the Client Behave Abnormally?

Assessment is simply the collecting of relevant information in an effort to reach a conclusion. It goes on in every realm of life. We make assessments when we decide what cereal to buy or which presidential candidate to vote for. College admissions officers, who have to select the "best" of the students applying to their college, depend on academic records, recommendations, achievement test scores, interviews, and application forms to help them decide. Employers, who have to predict which applicants are most likely to be effective workers, collect information from résumés, interviews, references, and perhaps on-the-job observations.

Clinical assessment is used to determine whether, how, and why a person is behaving abnormally and how that person may be helped. It also enables clinicians to evaluate people's progress after they have been in treatment for a while and decide whether the treatment should be changed. The hundreds of clinical assessment techniques and tools that have been developed fall into three categories: *clinical interviews, tests,* and *observations*. To be useful, these tools must be *standardized* and must have clear *reliability* and *validity*.

▲ Lucille Clerc/Illustration (USA) Inc.

idiographic information Information about a particular individual, as opposed to a larger population.

assessment The process of collecting and interpreting relevant information about a client or research participant.

standardization The process in which a test is administered to a large group of people whose performance then serves as a standard or norm against which any individual's score can be measured.

reliability A measure of the consistency of test or research results.

validity A measure of the accuracy of a test's or study's results.

Characteristics of Assessment Tools

All clinicians must follow the same procedures when they use a particular type of assessment tool. To **standardize** such a tool is to set up common steps to be followed whenever it is administered. Similarly, clinicians must standardize the way they interpret the results of an assessment tool in order to be able to understand what a particular score means. They may standardize the scores of a test, for example, by first administering it to a group of research participants whose performance will then serve as a common standard, or norm, against which later individual scores can be measured. The group that initially takes the test must be typical of the larger population for whom the test is intended. If an aggressiveness test meant for the public at large were standardized on a group of Marines, for example, the resulting "norm" might turn out to be misleadingly high.

Reliability refers to the *consistency* of assessment measures. A good assessment tool will always yield similar results in the same situation (Blanchard et al., 2017). An assessment tool has high *test–retest reliability,* one kind of reliability, if it yields similar results every time it is given to the same people. If a woman's responses on a particular test indicate that she is generally a heavy drinker, the test should produce a similar result when she takes it again a week later. To measure test–retest reliability, participants are tested on two occasions and the two scores are correlated (Tenke et al., 2017). The higher the correlation (see Chapter 1), the greater the test's reliability.

How reliable and valid are the tests you take in school? What about the tests you see online?

An assessment tool shows high *interrater* (or *interjudge*) *reliability,* another kind of reliability, if different judges independently agree on how to score and interpret it. True–false and multiple-choice tests yield consistent scores no matter who evaluates them, but other tests require that the evaluator make a judgment. Consider a test that requires the person to draw a copy of a picture, which a judge then rates for accuracy. Different judges may give different ratings to the same drawing.

Finally, an assessment tool must have **validity:** it must *accurately* measure what it is supposed to measure. Suppose a weight scale reads 12 pounds every time a 10-pound bag of sugar is placed on it. Although the scale is reliable because its readings are consistent, those readings are not valid, or accurate.

Joe Murphy/Getty Images

Reliable assessment? Former National Basketball Association stars Magic Johnson, Shaquille O'Neal, Tracy McGrady, Dikembe Mutombo, and George Gervin served as judges at the 2016 All-Star slam dunk contest. Assigning a relatively wide range of scores after each dunk, they displayed low interrater reliability.

A given assessment tool may appear to be valid simply because it makes sense and seems reasonable. However, this sort of validity, called *face validity,* does not by itself mean that the instrument is trustworthy. A test for depression, for example, might include questions about how often a person cries. Because it makes sense that depressed people would cry, these test questions have face validity. It turns out, however, that many people cry a great deal for reasons other than depression, and some extremely depressed people do not cry at all. Thus an assessment tool should not be used unless it has high *predictive validity* or *concurrent validity* (Duan et al., 2018).

Predictive validity is a tool's ability to predict future characteristics or behavior. Let's say that a test has been developed to identify elementary schoolchildren who are likely to take up cigarette smoking in high school. The test gathers information about the children's parents—their personal characteristics, smoking habits, and attitudes toward smoking—and on that basis identifies high-risk children. To establish the test's predictive validity, investigators could administer it to a group of elementary school students, wait until they were in high school, and then check to see which children actually did become smokers.

Concurrent validity is the degree to which the measures gathered from one tool agree with the measures gathered from other assessment techniques. Participants' scores on a new test designed to measure anxiety, for example, should correlate highly with their scores on other anxiety tests or with their behavior during clinical interviews.

Before any assessment technique can be fully useful, it must meet the requirements of standardization, reliability, and validity. No matter how insightful or clever a technique may be, clinicians cannot profitably use its results if those results are uninterpretable, inconsistent, or inaccurate. Unfortunately, more than a few clinical assessment tools fall short, suggesting that at least some clinical assessments, too, miss their mark.

Imaginechina via AP Images

Seeking the right stuff During China's annual military recruitment period, young men sit in front of computers to undergo a series of psychological tests. The tests are used by the country's armed forces to help assess the psychological stability, coping skills, intellect, and leadership potential of each enlistee.

Clinical Interviews

Most of us feel instinctively that the best way to get to know people is to meet with them face-to-face. Under these circumstances, we can see them react to what we do and say, observe as well as listen as they answer, and generally get a sense of who they are. A *clinical interview* is just such a face-to-face encounter (Sommers-Flanagan & Sommers-Flanagan, 2017). If during a clinical interview a man looks as happy as can be while describing his sadness over the recent death of his mother, the clinician may suspect that the man actually has conflicting emotions about this loss.

Conducting the Interview The interview is often the first contact between client and clinician. Clinicians use it to collect detailed information about the person's problems and feelings, lifestyle and relationships, and other personal history. They may also ask about the person's expectations of therapy and motives for seeking it. The clinician who worked with Franco began with a face-to-face interview:

Franco arrived for his appointment in gray sweatpants and a T-shirt. His stubble suggested that he had not shaved, and the many food stains on his shirt indicated he had not washed it for quite some time. Franco spoke without emotion. He slouched into the chair, sending signals that he did not want to be there.

When pressed, he talked about his two-year relationship with Maria, who, at 25, was 13 years younger than he was. Franco had believed that he had met his future wife, but Maria's domineering mother was unhappy about the age difference and kept telling her daughter

(continued on the next page)

mental status exam A set of interview questions and observations designed to reveal the degree and nature of a client's abnormal functioning.

clinical test A device for gathering information about a few aspects of a person's psychological functioning from which broader information about the person can be inferred.

projective test A test consisting of ambiguous material that people interpret or respond to.

that she could find someone better. Franco wanted Maria to stand up to her mother and to move in with him, but this was not easy for her to do. Believing that Maria's mother had too much influence over her and frustrated that she would not commit to him, he had broken up with Maria during a fight. He soon realized that he had acted impulsively, but Maria refused to take him back.

When asked about his childhood, Franco described his father's death in a gruesome car crash on his way to pick up 12-year-old Franco from soccer practice. Initially, his father had told Franco that he could not come get him from practice, but Franco "threw a tantrum" and his father agreed to rearrange his schedule. Franco believed himself responsible for his father's death.

Franco stated that, over the years, his mother had encouraged this feeling of self-blame by complaining that she had been forced to "give up her life" to raise Franco alone. She was always nasty to Franco and nasty to every woman he later dated. She even predicted that Franco would "die alone."

Franco described being very unhappy throughout his school years. He hated school and felt less smart than the other kids. On occasion, a teacher's critique—meant as encouragement—left him unable to do his homework for days, and his grades suffered. He truly believed he was stupid. Similarly, later in life, he interpreted his rise to a position as bank manager as due entirely to hard work. "I know I'm not as smart as the others there."

Franco explained that since the breakup with Maria, he had experienced more unhappiness than ever before. He often spent all night watching television. At the same time, he could barely pay attention to what was happening on the screen. He said that some days he actually forgot to eat. He had no wish to see his friends. At work, the days blurred into one another, distinguished only by a growing number of reprimands from his bank supervisors. He attributed these work problems to his basic lack of ability. His supervisors had simply figured out that he had not been good enough for the job all along.

Beyond gathering basic background data of this kind, clinical interviewers give special attention to those topics they consider most important (Sommers-Flanagan & Sommers-Flanagan, 2017; Miller, 2015). Psychodynamic interviewers try to learn about the person's needs and memories of past events and relationships. Cognitive-behavioral interviewers try to identify information about the stimuli that trigger responses, consequences of the responses, and/or assumptions and interpretations that influence the person. Humanistic clinicians ask about the person's self-evaluation, self-concept, and values. Biological clinicians look for signs of biochemical or brain dysfunction. And sociocultural interviewers ask about the family, social, and cultural environments.

Interviews can be either unstructured or structured. In an *unstructured interview,* the clinician asks mostly open-ended questions, perhaps as simple as "Would you tell me about yourself?" The lack of structure allows the interviewer to follow leads and explore relevant topics that could not have been anticipated before the interview.

In a *structured interview,* clinicians ask prepared—mostly specific—questions. Sometimes they use a published *interview schedule*—a standard set of questions designed for all interviews. Many structured interviews include a **mental status exam,** a set of questions and observations that systematically evaluate the client's awareness, orientation with regard to time and place, attention span, memory, judgment and insight, thought content and processes, mood, and appearance (Palsetia et al., 2018; Sommers-Flanagan & Sommers-Flanagan, 2017). A structured format ensures that clinicians will cover the same kinds of important issues in all of their interviews and enables them to compare the responses of different individuals.

Although most clinical interviews have both unstructured and structured portions (Lee et al., 2017), many clinicians favor one kind over the other. Unstructured interviews typically appeal to psychodynamic and humanistic clinicians, while structured formats are widely used by cognitive-behavioral clinicians, who need to pinpoint behaviors or thinking processes that may underlie abnormal function.

#

#EmploymentScreening

Around 60 percent of companies use social networking sites to help screen job candidates. Why? To see whether candidates present themselves professionally (65%), are good fits for the company's culture (51%), are qualified (45%), and/or are well rounded (35%) (CareerBuilder, 2017, 2012).

What Are the Limitations of Clinical Interviews? Although interviews often produce valuable information about people, there are limits to what they can accomplish. One problem is that they sometimes lack validity, or accuracy (Sommers-Flanagan & Sommers-Flanagan, 2017). Individuals may intentionally mislead in order to present themselves in a positive light or to avoid discussing embarrassing topics. Or people may be unable to give an accurate report in their interviews. Individuals who suffer from depression, for example, take a negative view of themselves and may describe themselves as poor workers or inadequate parents when that isn't the case at all.

Interviewers too may make mistakes in judgments that slant the information they gather (Kiger, 2017; Groth-Marnat & Wright, 2016). They usually rely too heavily on first impressions, for example, and give too much weight to unfavorable information about a client. Interviewer biases, including gender, race, and age biases, may also influence the interviewers' interpretations of what a client says.

Interviews, particularly unstructured ones, may also lack reliability (Young, Bell, & Fristad, 2016). People respond differently to different interviewers, providing, for example, less information to a cold interviewer than to a warm and supportive one (Quas et al., 2007). Similarly, a clinician's race, gender, age, and appearance may influence a client's responses (Davis et al., 2010).

Because different clinicians can obtain different answers and draw different conclusions even when they ask the same questions of the same person, some researchers believe that interviewing should be discarded as a tool of clinical assessment. As you'll see, however, the two other kinds of clinical assessment methods also have serious limitations.

#PopTerm

Online disinhibition effect refers to the tendency of people to show less restraint when on the Internet (Suler, 2016, 2004; Sitt, 2013).

Clinical Tests

Clinical tests are devices for gathering information about a few aspects of a person's psychological functioning from which broader information about the person can be inferred. On the surface, it may look easy to design an effective test. Web sites, for example, regularly present new tests that supposedly tell us about our personalities, relationships, sex lives, reactions to stress, or ability to succeed. Such tests might sound convincing, but most of them lack reliability, validity, and standardization. That is, they do not yield consistent, accurate information or reveal where we stand in comparison with others.

More than 1,000 clinical tests are currently in use around the world (EBSCO, 2018). Clinicians use six kinds most often: *projective tests, personality inventories, response inventories, psychophysiological tests, neurological and neuropsychological tests,* and *intelligence tests.*

D. Bayes/Lebrecht Music & Arts/Alamy

D. Bayes/Lebrecht Music & Arts/Alamy

The art of assessment Clinicians often view works of art as informal projective tests in which artists reveal their conflicts and mental stability. The sometimes bizarre cat portraits by early-twentieth-century artist Louis Wain, for example, have been interpreted as reflections of the psychosis with which he struggled for many years.

Projective Tests **Projective tests** require that clients interpret vague stimuli, such as inkblots or ambiguous pictures, or follow open-ended instructions such as "Draw a person." Theoretically, when clues and instructions are so general, people will "project" aspects of their personality into the task. Projective tests are used primarily by psychodynamic clinicians to help assess the unconscious drives and conflicts they believe to be at the root of abnormal functioning (Fournier, 2018). The most widely used projective tests are the *Rorschach test,* the *Thematic Apperception Test, sentence-completion tests,* and *drawings.*

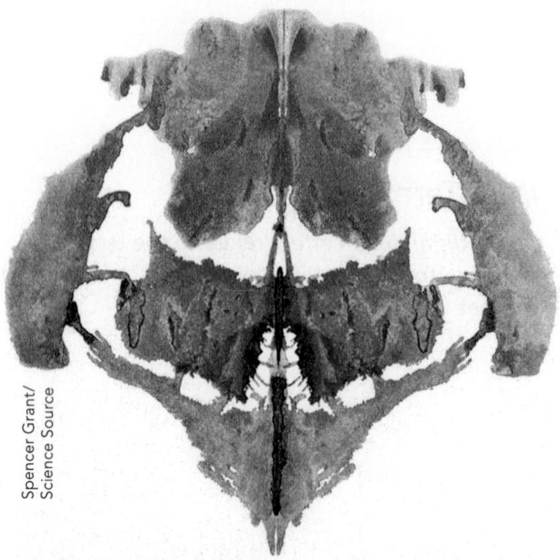

Spencer Grant/ Science Source

FIGURE 3-1

An Inkblot Similar to Those Used in the Rorschach Test

RORSCHACH TEST In 1911 Hermann Rorschach, a Swiss psychiatrist, experimented with the use of inkblots in his clinical work. He made thousands of blots by dropping ink on paper and then folding the paper in half to create a symmetrical but wholly accidental design, such as the one shown in **Figure 3-1.** Rorschach found that everyone saw images in these blots. In addition, the images a viewer saw seemed to correspond in important ways with his or her psychological condition. People diagnosed with schizophrenia, for example, tended to see images that differed from those described by people experiencing depression.

Rorschach selected 10 inkblots and published them in 1921 with instructions for their use in assessment (see ***MindTech***). This set was called the *Rorschach Psychodynamic Inkblot Test.* Rorschach died just 8 months later, at the age of 37, but his work was continued by others, and his inkblots took their place among the most widely used projective tests of the twentieth century.

Despite its limitations, just about everyone has heard of the Rorschach. Why do you think it is so famous and popular?

Clinicians administer the "Rorschach," as it is commonly called, by presenting one inkblot card at a time and asking respondents what they see, what the inkblot seems to be, or what it reminds them of. In the early years, Rorschach testers paid special attention to the themes and images that the inkblots brought to mind (Choca & Rossini, 2018). Testers now also pay attention to the style of the responses: Do the clients view the design as a whole or see specific details? Do they focus on the blots or on the white spaces between them?

MINDTECH

Psychology's WikiLeaks?

In 2009, an emergency room physician posted the images of all 10 Rorschach cards, along with common responses to each card, on Wikipedia, the online encyclopedia. The publisher of the test, Hogrefe Publishing, immediately threatened to take Wikipedia to court, saying that the encyclopedia's willingness to post the images was "unbelievably reckless" (Cohen, 2009). However, no legal actions took place, and to this day, the 10 cards remain on Wikipedia for the entire world to see.

Will & Deni McIntyre/Getty Images

Since the initial Wikipedia posting, many psychologists have criticized the site's actions, arguing that the Rorschach test responses of patients who have previously seen the test on Wikipedia cannot be trusted (White, 2017). In support of their concerns, one study found that reading the Wikipedia Rorschach test article did indeed help many individuals perform more positively on the test itself (Schultz & Brabender, 2012). These clinical concerns are consistent with the long-standing positions of the British, Canadian, and American Psychological Associations, who hold that nonprofessional publications of psychological test answers are wrong and potentially harmful to patients.

Still other critics point out that the free online publication of the Rorschach cards jeopardizes the usefulness of thousands of published studies—studies that have tried to link patients' Rorschach responses to particular psychological disorders (White, 2017; Plante, 2016). These studies were conducted on first-time inkblot observers, not on people who had already viewed the cards online.

Despite these criticisms, the number of online sites posting images of the Rorschach cards has increased steadily since the first Wikipedia presentation (Plante, 2016). Why? One reason is that the whole controversy brought to light a fact that relatively few had been aware of previously: The copyright for the test actually ran out in the 1990s in a number of countries, including Switzerland and the United States (White, 2017; Adamowicz, 2016). According to copyright laws, because more than 70 years have passed since the author's death and/or because the test was first published before 1923, the Rorschach images are in the *public domain.* This means that, legally, anyone can use or publicly display the cards. Of course, this legal distinction does not put to rest the important ethical and professional concerns that surround this controversy.

THEMATIC APPERCEPTION TEST The Thematic Apperception Test (TAT) is a pictorial projective test (Cramer, 2017; Morgan & Murray, 1935). People who take the TAT are commonly shown 30 cards with black-and-white pictures of individuals in vague situations and are asked to make up a dramatic story about each card. They must tell what is happening in the picture, what led up to it, what the characters are feeling and thinking, and what the outcome of the situation will be.

Clinicians who use the TAT believe that people always identify with one of the characters on each card. The stories are thought to reflect the individuals' own circumstances, needs, and emotions. For example, a female client seems to be revealing her own feelings when telling this story about a TAT picture similar to the image shown in **Figure 3-2**:

> *This is a woman who has been quite troubled by memories of a mother she was resentful toward. She has feelings of sorrow for the way she treated her mother, her memories of her mother plague her. These feelings seem to be increasing as she grows older and sees her children treating her the same way that she treated her mother.*
>
> *(Aiken, 1985, p. 372)*

carterdayne/Getty Images

FIGURE 3-2

A Picture Similar to One Used in the Thematic Apperception Test

SENTENCE-COMPLETION TEST In the sentence-completion test, first developed in the 1920s (Payne, 1928), the test-taker completes a series of unfinished sentences, such as "I wish . . ." or "My father . . ." The test is considered a good springboard for discussion and a quick and easy way to pinpoint topics to explore (Weiner & Greene, 2017).

DRAWINGS On the assumption that a drawing tells us something about its creator, clinicians often ask clients to draw human figures and talk about them (Weiner & Greene, 2017). Evaluations of these drawings are based on the details and shape of the drawing, the solidity of the pencil line, the location of the drawing on the paper, the size of the figures, the features of the figures, the use of background, and the comments made by the respondent during the drawing task. In the *Draw-a-Person (DAP) test,* the most popular of the drawing tests, individuals are first told to draw "a person" and then are instructed to draw a person of the other sex.

WHAT ARE THE MERITS OF PROJECTIVE TESTS? Until the 1950s, projective tests were the most commonly used method for assessing personality. In recent years, however, clinicians and researchers have relied on them largely to gain "supplementary" insights. One reason for this shift is that practitioners who follow the newer models have less use for the tests than psychodynamic clinicians do. Even more important, the tests have not consistently shown much reliability or validity (Weiner & Greene, 2017; Mihura et al., 2016).

In reliability studies, different clinicians have tended to score the same person's projective test quite differently. Similarly, in validity studies, when clinicians try to describe a client's personality and feelings on the basis of responses to projective tests, their conclusions often fail to match the self-report of the client, the view of the psychotherapist, or the picture gathered from an extensive case history (Bornstein, 2007).

Another validity problem is that projective tests are sometimes biased against minority ethnic groups (see **Table 3-1** on page 81). For example, people are supposed to identify with the characters in the TAT when they make up stories about them, yet no members of minority groups are represented in the TAT pictures. In response to this problem, some clinicians have developed other TAT-like tests with African American or Hispanic figures (Costantino et al., 2014, 2007).

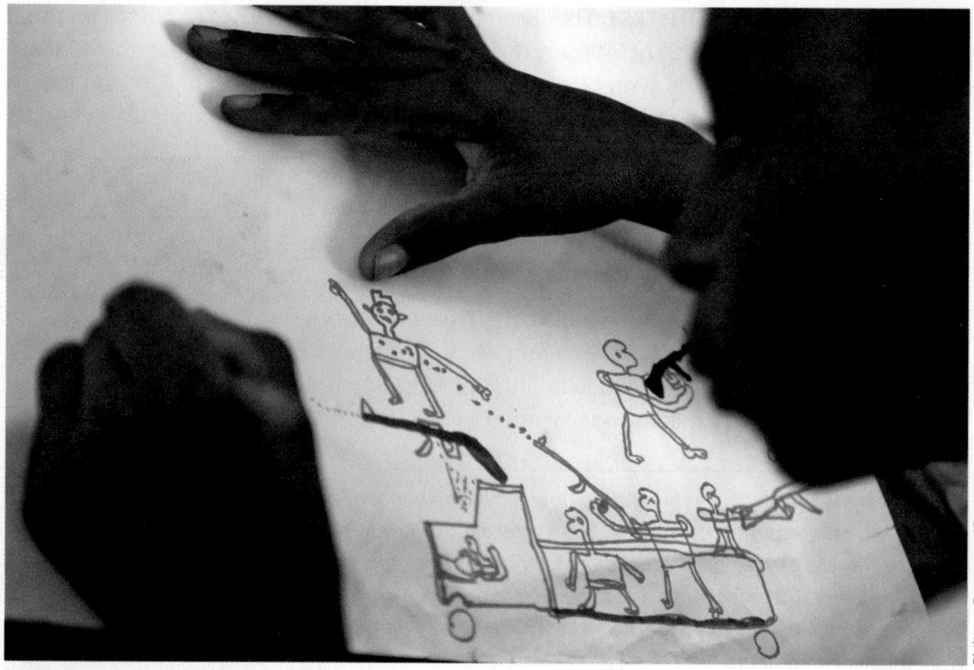

Drawing test Drawing tests are commonly used to assess the psychological functioning of children. As part of a therapy program administered by UNICEF, this young Nigerian refugee draws an attack scene. The program is provided in Baga Sola, a town in western Chad that welcomes people who have fled extremist groups in northeastern Nigeria.

Personality Inventories An alternative way to collect information about individuals is to ask them to assess themselves. Respondents to a **personality inventory** answer a wide range of questions about their behavior, beliefs, and feelings. In the typical personality inventory, individuals indicate whether each of a long list of statements applies to them. Clinicians then use the responses to draw conclusions about the person's personality and psychological functioning.

By far the most widely used personality inventory is the *Minnesota Multiphasic Personality Inventory* (*MMPI*). Two adult versions are available—the original test, published in 1945, and the *MMPI-2*, a 1989 revision that was itself revised in 2001. There is also an alternative and streamlined version of the inventory called the *MMPI-2-Restructured Form* and a special version of the test for adolescents, the *MMPI-A* (Weiner & Greene, 2017; Handel, 2016).

The MMPI consists of more than 500 self-statements, to be labeled "true," "false," or "cannot say." The statements cover issues ranging from physical concerns to mood, sexual behaviors, and social activities. Altogether the statements make up 10 clinical scales, on each of which an individual can score from 0 to 120. When people score above 70 on a scale, their functioning on that scale is considered deviant. When the 10 scale scores are considered side by side, a pattern called a *profile* takes shape, indicating the person's general personality. The 10 scales on the MMPI measure the following:

Hypochondriasis Items showing abnormal concern with bodily functions ("I have chest pains several times a week.")

Depression Items showing extreme pessimism and hopelessness ("I often feel hopeless about the future.")

Hysteria Items suggesting that the person may use physical or mental symptoms as a way of unconsciously avoiding conflicts and responsibilities ("My heart frequently pounds so hard I can feel it.")

Psychopathic deviate Items showing a repeated and gross disregard for social customs and an emotional shallowness ("My activities and interests are often criticized by others.")

Masculinity–femininity Items that are thought to separate male and female respondents ("I like to arrange flowers.")

personality inventory A test, designed to measure broad personality characteristics, consisting of statements about behaviors, beliefs, and feelings that people evaluate as either characteristic or uncharacteristic of them.

Paranoia Items that show abnormal suspiciousness and delusions of grandeur or persecution ("There are evil people trying to influence my mind.")

Psychasthenia Items that show obsessions, compulsions, abnormal fears, and guilt and indecisiveness ("I save nearly everything I buy, even after I have no use for it.")

Schizophrenia Items that show bizarre or unusual thoughts or behavior ("Things around me do not seem real.")

Hypomania Items that show emotional excitement, overactivity, and flight of ideas ("At times I feel very 'high' or very 'low' for no apparent reason.")

Social introversion Items that show shyness, little interest in people, and insecurity ("I am easily embarrassed.")

The MMPI and other personality inventories have several advantages over projective tests (Weiner & Greene, 2017). Because they are computerized or paper-and-pencil tests, they do not take much time to administer, and they are objectively scored. Most of them are standardized, so one person's scores can be compared with those of many others. Moreover, they often display greater test–retest reliability than projective tests. For example, people who take the MMPI a second time after a period of less than two weeks receive approximately the same scores (Graham, 2011, 2006).

Personality inventories also appear to have more validity, or accuracy, than projective tests (McCord, 2018; Moultrie & Engel, 2017). However, they can hardly be considered *highly* valid. When clinicians have used these tests alone, they have not regularly been able to judge a respondent's personality accurately (Braxton et al., 2007). One problem is that the personality traits that the tests seek to measure cannot be examined directly. How can we fully know a person's character, emotions, and needs from self-reports alone?

TABLE: 3-1

Multicultural Hot Spots in Assessment and Diagnosis

Cultural Hot Spot	Effect on Assessment or Diagnosis
Immigrant Client	**Dominant-Culture Assessor**
Homeland culture may differ from current country's dominant culture	May misread culture-bound reactions as pathology
May have left homeland to escape war or oppression	May overlook client's vulnerability to posttraumatic stress
May have weak support systems in this country	May overlook client's heightened vulnerability to stressors
Lifestyle (wealth and occupation) in this country may fall below lifestyle in homeland	May overlook client's sense of loss and frustrations
May refuse or be unable to learn dominant language	May misunderstand client's assessment responses, or may overlook or misdiagnose client's symptoms
Ethnic-Minority Client	**Dominant-Culture Assessor**
May reject or distrust members of dominant culture, including assessor	May experience little rapport with client, or may misinterpret client's distrust as pathology
May be uncomfortable with dominant culture's values (e.g., assertiveness, confrontation) and so find it difficult to apply clinician's recommendations	May view client as unmotivated
May manifest stress in culture-bound ways (e.g., somatic symptoms such as stomachaches)	May misinterpret symptom patterns
May hold cultural beliefs that seem strange to dominant culture (e.g., belief in communication with the dead)	May misinterpret cultural responses as pathology (e.g., a delusion)
May be uncomfortable during assessment	May overlook and feed into client's discomfort
Mere cultural differences may seem to be pathological symptoms	May be unknowledgeable or biased about ethnic-minority culture
May become tense and anxious	May nonverbally convey own discomfort to ethnic-minority client

Information from: Borden, 2017; Franklin, 2017; Dana, 2015; Rose et al., 2011; Bhattacharya et al., 2010; Westermeyer, 2004, 2001, 1993; López & Guarnaccia, 2005, 2000; Kirmayer, 2003, 2002, 2001.

Peter Steiner/The New Yorker Collection/The Cartoon Bank

"We're going to run some tests: blood work, a cat-scan, and the S.A.T.'s."

Another problem is that despite the use of more diverse standardization groups by the MMPI-2 designers, this and other personality tests continue to have certain cultural limitations. Responses that indicate a psychological disorder in one culture may be normal responses in another (Weiner & Greene, 2017; Dana, 2005, 2000). In Puerto Rico, for example, where it is common to practice spiritualism, it would be normal to answer "true" to the MMPI item "Evil spirits possess me at times." In other populations, that response could indicate psychopathology (Rogler, 1989).

Despite such limits in validity, personality inventories continue to be popular. Research indicates that they can help clinicians learn about people's personal styles and disorders as long as they are used in combination with interviews or other assessment tools.

Response Inventories Like personality inventories, **response inventories** ask people to provide detailed information about themselves, but these tests focus on one specific area of functioning (Sleboda & Sokolowska, 2017). For example, one such test may measure affect (emotion), another social skills, and still another cognitive processes. Clinicians can use the inventories to determine the role such factors play in a person's disorder.

Affective inventories measure the severity of such emotions as anxiety, depression, and anger. In one of the most widely used affective inventories, the Beck Depression Inventory, people rate their level of sadness and its effect on their functioning. For *social skills inventories,* used particularly by behavioral and family-social clinicians, respondents indicate how they would react in a variety of social situations. *Cognitive inventories* reveal a person's typical thoughts and assumptions and can help uncover counterproductive patterns of thinking.

Both the number of response inventories and the number of clinicians who use them have increased steadily in the past 35 years. At the same time, however, these inventories have major limitations. With the notable exceptions of the Beck Depression Inventory and a few others, many of the tests have not been subjected to careful standardization, reliability, and validity procedures (Englbrecht et al., 2017). Often they are created as a need arises, without being tested for accuracy and consistency.

Psychophysiological Tests Clinicians may also use **psychophysiological tests,** which measure physiological responses as possible indicators of psychological problems. This practice began three decades ago, after several studies suggested that states of anxiety are regularly accompanied by physiological changes, particularly increases in heart rate, body temperature, blood pressure, skin reactions (*galvanic skin response*), and muscle contractions. The measuring of physiological changes has since played a key role in the assessment of certain psychological disorders.

One psychophysiological test is the *polygraph,* popularly known as a *lie detector* (Amsel, 2017; Rosky, 2016, 2013). Electrodes attached to various parts of a person's body detect changes in breathing, perspiration, and heart rate while the person answers questions. The clinician observes these functions while the person answers "yes" to *control questions*—questions whose answers are known to be yes, such as "Are both your parents alive?" Then the clinician observes the same physiological functions while the person answers *test questions,* such as "Did you commit this robbery?" If breathing, perspiration, and heart rate suddenly increase, the person is suspected of lying.

Like other kinds of clinical tests, psychophysiological tests have their drawbacks (Elliott & Völlm, 2016). Many require expensive equipment that must be carefully tuned and maintained. In addition, psychophysiological measurements can be inaccurate and

response inventories Tests designed to measure a person's responses in one specific area of functioning, such as affect, social skills, or cognitive processes.

psychophysiological test A test that measures physical responses (such as heart rate and muscle tension) as possible indicators of psychological problems.

unreliable (see ***Trending***). The laboratory equipment itself—elaborate and sometimes frightening—may arouse a participant's nervous system and thus change his or her physical responses. Physiological responses may also change when they are measured repeatedly in a single session. Galvanic skin responses, for example, often decrease during repeated testing.

...TRENDING

The Truth, the Whole Truth, and Nothing but the Truth

In movies, criminals being grilled by the police reveal their guilt by sweating, shaking, cursing, or twitching. When they are hooked up to a *polygraph* (a lie detector), the needles bounce all over the paper. This image has been with us since World War I, when some clinicians developed the theory that people who are telling lies display systemic changes in their breathing, perspiration, and heart rate (Marston, 1917).

The danger of relying on polygraph tests is that they do not work as well as we would like (Ben-Shakhar & Bar, 2019; Rosky, 2016, 2015, 2013). Research indicates that at least 1 out of 10 truths, or as many as 1 out of 4 truths, are, on average, called lies in polygraph testing (Wen, 2016; Grubin, 2010; MacLaren, 2001). Imagine how many innocent people might be convicted of crimes if polygraph findings were taken as valid evidence in criminal trials.

Given such findings, polygraphs are less trusted and less popular today than they once were. For example, few courts now admit results from such tests as evidence of criminal guilt (Balmer, 2018; Vogel & Baran, 2016). Nevertheless, the FBI and other law enforcement agencies use them extensively in criminal investigations; parole boards and probation offices routinely administer them to help decide whether to release convicted offenders; and their use may actually be on the increase in public-sector hiring, such as for police officers (CDPS, 2018; Vicianova, 2015; Meijer & Verschuere, 2010).

Given the polygraph's flawed performance, researchers have been looking for other ways to detect lies over the past 15 years. The most promising alternative seems to be brain scanning. Some MRI studies have found that when participants deny clear truths, certain parts of their brain—particularly regions within the *prefrontal, anterior cingulate,* and *parietal cortex*—become more active than when they are confirming such truths (Mongilio, 2017; Wood, 2016).

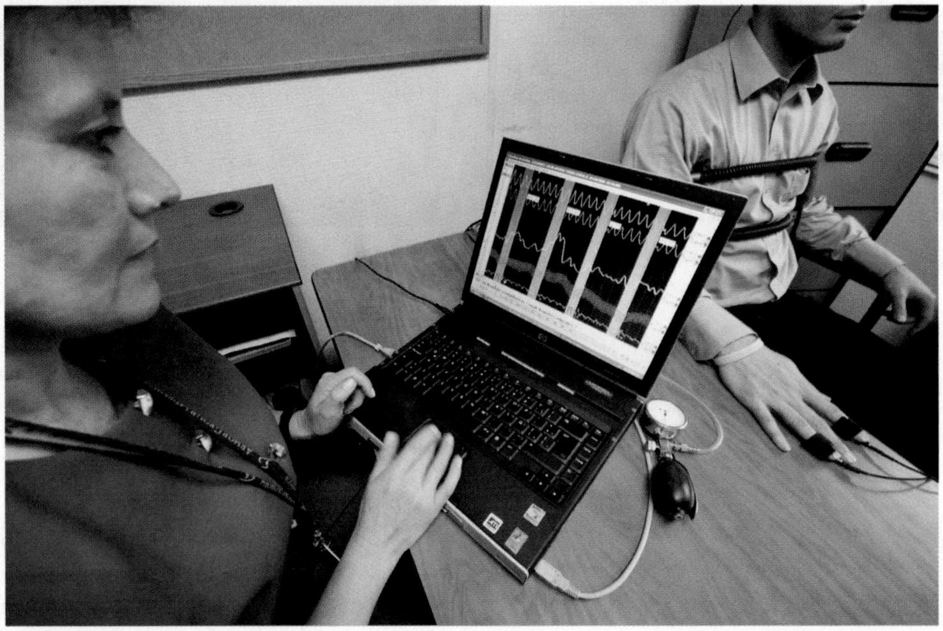

Guy Bell/Alamy

All the rage A security administrator conducts a polygraph exam in Bogota, Colombia. Despite evidence that these tests are often invalid, they are widely used by businesses in Colombia, where deception by employees has become a major problem.

In general, MRI studies have yielded better lie-detection rates than have polygraph studies, but the procedures and degree of accuracy have varied from study to study. Moreover, like polygraph testing, scanning procedures can produce *false positives*. That is, the brain regions under study may also become more active when an individual is experiencing intense anxiety or related emotions. Thus some anxious truth-tellers may be viewed as lying in the MRI procedures.

These questions and limitations have been partly addressed in a study at the University of Pennsylvania (Langleben et al., 2016). Participants were instructed to secretly write down one of six numbers and to then deny, while being evaluated by a polygraph and later by an MRI, the correctness of each number. That is, in each session, they were lying about their selected number and telling the truth about the other five numbers.

Although both tools were far from perfect in detecting the particular number that each participant was lying about, the MRI conclusions were 24 percent more accurate than the polygraph conclusions. Moreover, the accuracy of lie detection rose to 100 percent in cases in which the MRI and polygraph agreed on which number was being concealed, suggesting to some theorists that the two techniques should be used jointly in real-life applications. We will not know for some time whether MRI testing or combined MRI-polygraph testing will eventually gain traction in the judicial, law enforcement, security, or employment realms. But the implications of the study already have some researchers quite excited—and some ethicists very worried.

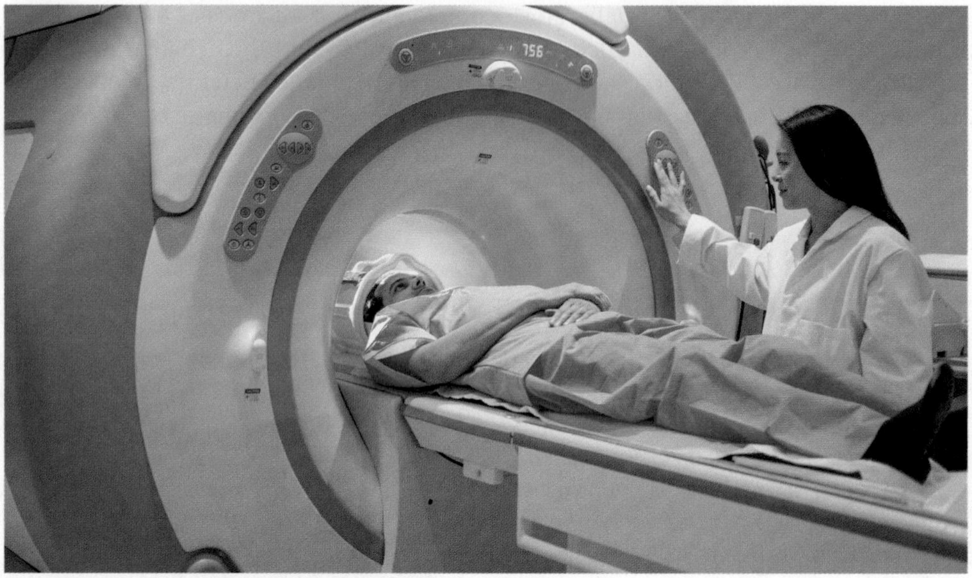

(a) MRI

Variations in scanning A doctor prepares a patient for an MRI procedure (a). Today's most widely used neuroimaging techniques each produce pictures of the living brain. Opposite, an MRI scan (b) shows the image of a normal functioning brain; a CT scan (c) reveals a mass of blood within the brain; and a PET scan (d) shows which areas of the brain are active (those colored in red, orange, and yellow) when an individual is being stimulated.

Neurological and Neuropsychological Tests Some problems in personality or behavior are caused primarily by damage to the brain or by changes in brain activity. Head injuries, brain tumors, brain malfunctions, alcoholism, infections, and other disorders can all cause such impairment. If a psychological dysfunction is to be treated effectively, it is important to know whether its primary cause is a physical abnormality in the brain.

A number of techniques may help pinpoint brain abnormalities. Some procedures, such as brain surgery, biopsy, and X ray, have been used for many years. More recently, scientists have developed a number of **neurological tests,** which are designed to measure brain structure and activity directly. One neurological test is the *electroencephalogram (EEG),* which records *brain waves,* the electrical activity that takes place within the brain as a result of neurons firing. In an EEG, electrodes placed on the scalp send brain-wave impulses to a machine that records them.

Other neurological tests actually take "pictures" of brain structure or brain activity. These tests, called **neuroimaging,** or **brain scanning, techniques,** include *computerized axial tomography (CT scan* or *CAT scan),* in which X rays of the brain's structure

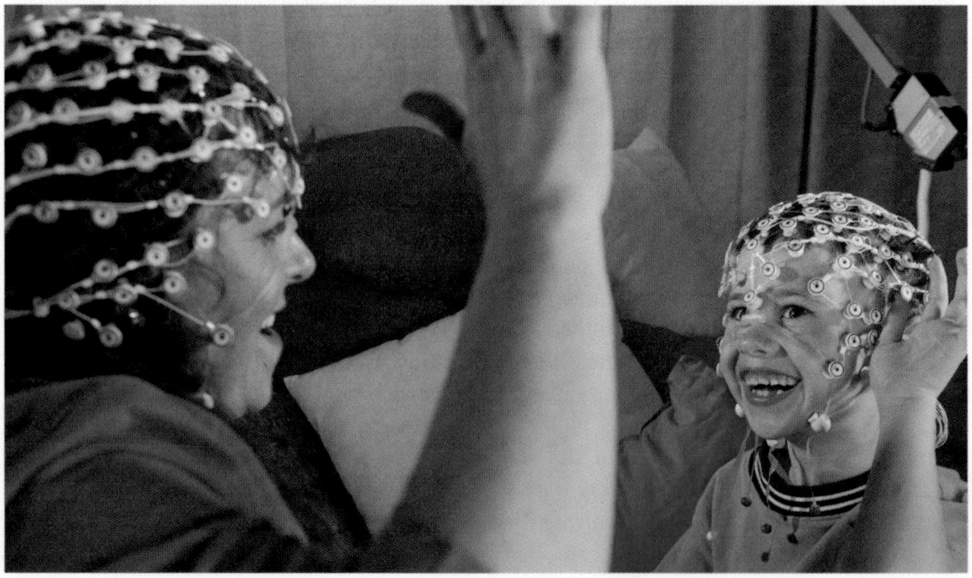

Family EEG As part of a study conducted at York University in Toronto, a mother and her 5-year-old autistic child play, socialize, and share tasks while wearing nets containing EEG sensors. The electrodes attached to their scalps help measure their brain waves, and these measurements are later compared to those derived from other mothers and their non-autistic children during similar interactions.

Du Cane Medical Imaging LTD./Science Photo Library/Getty Images

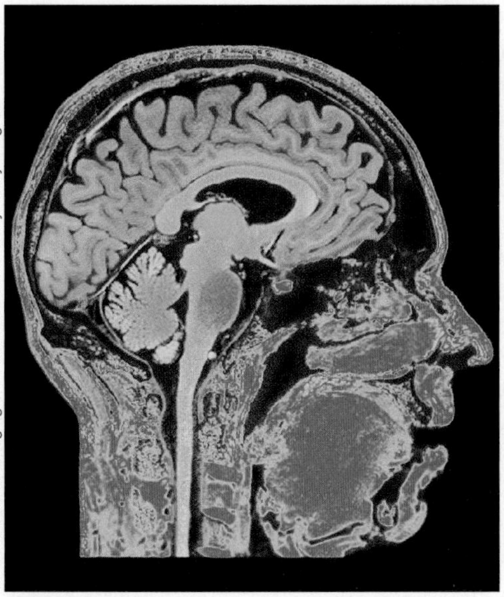

(b) MRI scan

Lester V. Bergman/Getty Images

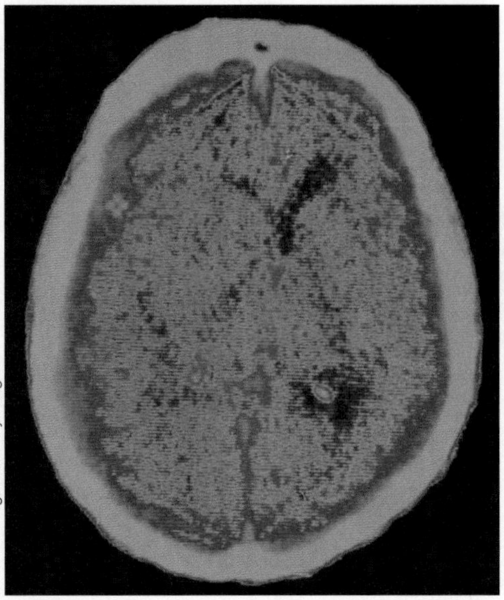

(c) CT scan

National Institute on Aging/NIH/Science Source

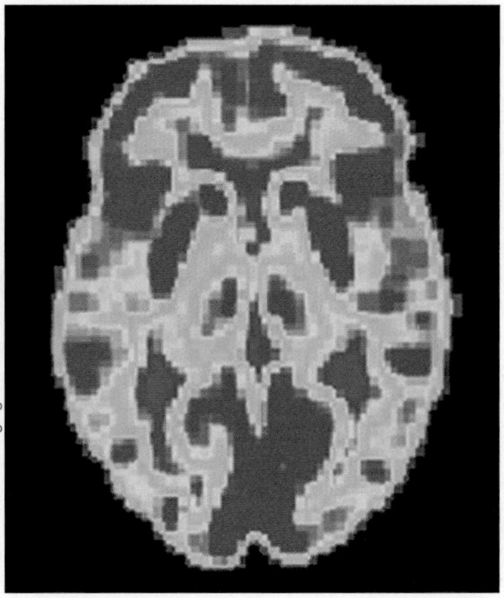

(d) PET scan

are taken at different angles and combined; *positron emission tomography* (*PET scan*), a computer-produced motion picture of chemical activity throughout the brain; and *magnetic resonance imaging* (*MRI*), a procedure that uses the magnetic property of certain hydrogen atoms in the brain to create a detailed picture of the brain's structure.

One version of the MRI, *functional magnetic resonance imaging* (*fMRI*), converts MRI pictures of brain structures into detailed pictures of neuron activity, thus offering a picture of the *functioning* brain. Partly because fMRI-produced images of brain functioning are so much clearer than PET scan images, the fMRI has generated enormous enthusiasm among brain researchers since it was first developed in 1990.

Though widely used, these techniques are sometimes unable to detect subtle brain abnormalities. Clinicians have therefore developed less direct but sometimes more revealing **neuropsychological tests** that measure cognitive, perceptual, and motor performances on certain tasks; clinicians interpret abnormal performances as an indicator of underlying brain problems (Daugherty et al., 2017). Brain damage is especially likely to affect visual perception, memory, and visual-motor coordination, so neuropsychological tests focus particularly on these areas. The famous *Bender Visual-Motor Gestalt Test,* for example, consists of nine cards, each displaying a simple geometrical design. Patients look at the designs one at a time and copy each one onto a piece of paper. Later they try to redraw the designs from memory. Notable errors in accuracy by individuals older than 12 are thought to reflect organic brain impairment. Clinicians often use a *battery,* or series, of neuropsychological tests, each targeting a specific skill area (Hamo, Abramovitch, & Zohar, 2018; Reitan & Wolfson, 2005, 1996).

Intelligence Tests An early definition of intelligence described it as "the capacity to judge well, to reason well, and to comprehend well" (Binet & Simon, 1916, p. 192). Because intelligence is an *inferred* quality rather than a specific physical process, it can be measured only indirectly. In 1905, French psychologist Alfred Binet and his associate Théodore Simon produced an **intelligence test** consisting of a series of tasks requiring people to use various verbal and nonverbal skills. The general score derived from this and later intelligence tests is termed an **intelligence quotient (IQ).** There are now more than 100 different intelligence tests available. As you will see in Chapter 14, intelligence tests play a key role in the diagnosis of intellectual disability and they can also help clinicians identify other problems (Bram, 2017; Keyes et al., 2017).

Intelligence tests are among the most carefully produced of all clinical tests (Bowden et al., 2011). Because they have been standardized on large groups of people, clinicians

neurological test A test that directly measures brain structure or activity.

neuroimaging techniques Neurological tests that provide images of brain structure or activity, such as CT scans, PET scans, and MRIs. Also called *brain scanning*.

neuropsychological test A test that detects brain impairment by measuring a person's cognitive, perceptual, and motor performances.

intelligence test A test designed to measure a person's intellectual ability.

intelligence quotient (IQ) An overall score derived from intelligence tests.

have a good idea how each individual's score compares with the performance of the population at large. These tests have also shown very high reliability: people who repeat the same IQ test years later receive approximately the same score. Finally, the major IQ tests appear to have fairly high validity: children's IQ scores often correlate with their performance in school, for example.

How might IQ scores be misused by school officials, parents, or other individuals? Why is society preoccupied with these scores?

Nevertheless, intelligence tests have some key shortcomings. Factors that have nothing to do with intelligence, such as low motivation or high anxiety, can greatly influence test performance (Groth-Marnat & Wright, 2016). In addition, IQ tests may contain cultural biases in their language or tasks that place people of one background at an advantage over those of another background (Shuttleworth-Edwards, 2016). Similarly, members of some minority groups may have little experience with this kind of test, or they may be uncomfortable with test examiners of a majority ethnic background. Either way, their performances may suffer.

Clinical Observations

In addition to interviewing and testing people, clinicians may systematically observe their behavior. In one technique, called *naturalistic observation,* clinicians observe clients in their everyday environments. In another, *analog observation,* they observe them in an artificial setting, such as a clinical office or laboratory. Finally, in *self-monitoring,* clients are instructed to observe themselves.

Naturalistic and Analog Observations Naturalistic clinical observations usually take place in homes, schools, institutions such as hospitals and prisons, or community settings. Most of them focus on parent–child, sibling–sibling, or teacher–child interactions and on fearful, aggressive, or disruptive behavior (Moens et al., 2018; Wang & Repetti, 2016). Often such observations are made by *participant observers*—key people in the client's environment—and reported to the clinician.

When naturalistic observations are not practical, clinicians may resort to analog observations, often aided by special equipment such as a video camera or one-way mirror. Analog observations often have focused on children interacting with their parents, married couples attempting to settle a disagreement, speech-anxious people giving a speech, and phobic people approaching an object they find frightening.

Although much can be learned from actually witnessing behavior, clinical observations have certain disadvantages. For one thing, they are not always reliable. It is

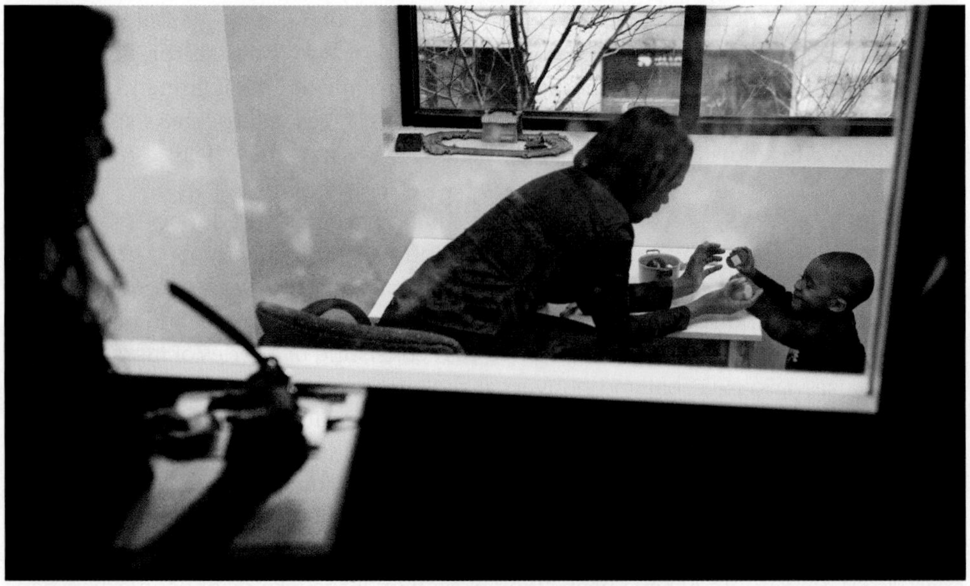

The Washington Post/Getty Images

Observation plus Using a one-way mirror, a clinical observer views a client interacting with her child during a play session. In addition, with the aid of a microphone and ear bug device, the clinician can coach the client and offer real-time parenting suggestions, a procedure commonly known as parent–child interaction therapy (PCIT).

possible for various clinicians who observe the same person to focus on different aspects of behavior, assess the person differently, and arrive at different conclusions (Meersand, 2011). Careful training of observers and the use of observer checklists can help reduce this problem.

Similarly, observers may make errors that affect the validity, or accuracy, of their observations (Wilson et al., 2010). The observer may suffer from *overload* and be unable to see or record all of the important behaviors and events. Or the observer may experience *observer drift,* a steady decline in accuracy as a result of fatigue or of a gradual unintentional change in the standards used when an observation continues for a long period of time. Another possible problem is *observer bias*—the observer's judgments may be influenced by information and expectations he or she already has about the person (Mahtani et al., 2018).

A client's *reactivity* may also limit the validity of clinical observations; that is, his or her behavior may be affected by the very presence of the observer (Antal et al., 2015). If schoolchildren are aware that someone special is watching them, for example, they may change their usual classroom behavior, perhaps in the hope of creating a good impression.

Finally, clinical observations may lack *cross-situational validity.* A child who behaves aggressively in school is not necessarily aggressive at home or with friends after school. Because behavior is often specific to particular situations, observations in one setting cannot always be applied to other settings (Kagan, 2007).

Self-Monitoring As you saw earlier, personality and response inventories are tests in which individuals report their own behaviors, feelings, or cognitions. In a related assessment procedure, *self-monitoring,* people observe themselves and carefully record the frequency of certain behaviors, feelings, or thoughts as they occur over time. How frequently, for instance, does a drug user have an urge for drugs or a headache sufferer have a headache? Self-monitoring is especially useful in assessing behavior that occurs so infrequently that it is unlikely to be seen during other kinds of observations. It is also useful for behaviors that occur so frequently that any other method of observing them in detail would be impossible—for example, smoking, drinking, or other drug use. Finally, self-monitoring may be the only way to observe and measure private thoughts or perceptions. Increasingly, people in treatment are recording such private experiences on smartphone apps as they are occurring—observations that can be sent immediately to their therapists or collectively reported in their treatment sessions (Sperry & Kwapil, 2017; Rickard et al., 2016).

Like all other clinical assessment procedures, however, self-monitoring has drawbacks (Schat et al., 2017; Huh et al., 2013). Here too validity is often a problem. People do not always manage or try to record their observations accurately. Furthermore, when people monitor themselves, they may change their behaviors unintentionally. Smokers, for example, often smoke fewer cigarettes than usual when they are monitoring themselves, and teachers give more positive and fewer negative comments to their students.

…SUMMING UP

CLINICAL ASSESSMENT Clinical practitioners are interested primarily in gathering individual information about each client. They seek an understanding of the specific nature and origins of a client's problems through clinical assessment.

To be useful, assessment tools must be standardized, reliable, and valid. Most clinical assessment methods fall into three general categories: clinical interviews, tests, and observations. A clinical interview may be either unstructured or structured. Types of clinical tests include projective, personality, response, psychophysiological, neurological, neuropsychological, and intelligence tests. Types of observation include naturalistic observation, analog observation, or self-monitoring.

#TheirWords

"You can observe a lot just by watching."
Yogi Berra, baseball great

#EarlyBeginnings

Because of his love for sketching inkblots all the time, Hermann Rorschach's young schoolmates gave him the nickname Klex, a variant of the German Klecks, which means "inkblot" (Cacioppo & Freberg, 2016; Schwartz, 1993).

diagnosis A determination that a person's problems reflect a particular disorder.

syndrome A cluster of symptoms that usually occur together.

classification system A list of disorders, along with descriptions of symptoms and guidelines for making appropriate diagnoses.

Diagnosis: Does the Client's Syndrome Match a Known Disorder?

Clinicians use the information from interviews, tests, and observations to construct an integrated picture of the factors that are causing and maintaining a client's disturbance, a construction sometimes known as a *clinical picture* (Sommers-Flanagan & Sommers-Flanagan, 2017). The clinical picture also may be influenced to a degree by the clinician's theoretical orientation (Grohol, 2016; Garb, 2010, 2006). The psychologist who worked with Franco held a cognitive-behavioral view of abnormality and so produced a picture that emphasized modeling and reinforcement principles and Franco's expectations, assumptions, and interpretations:

Franco's mother had reinforced his feelings of insecurity and his belief that he was unintelligent and inferior. When teachers tried to encourage and push Franco, his mother actually called him "an idiot." Although he was the only one in his family to attend college and did well there, she told him he was too inadequate to succeed in the world. When he received a B in a college algebra course, his mother told him, "You'll never have money." She once told him, "You're just like your father, dumb as a post," and railed against, "the dumb men I got stuck with."

As a child Franco had watched his parents argue. Between his mother's self-serving complaints and his father's rants about his backbreaking work to provide for his family, Franco had decided that life would be unpleasant. He believed it was natural for couples to argue and blame each other. Using his parents as models, Franco believed that when he was displeased with a girlfriend—Maria or a prior girlfriend—he should yell at her. At the same time, he was confused that several of his girlfriends had complained about his temper.

He took the termination of his relationship with Maria as proof that he was "stupid." He felt foolish to have broken up with her. He interpreted his behavior and the breakup as proof that he would never be loved and that he would never find happiness. In his mind, all he had to look forward to from here on out was a lifetime of problematic relationships, fights, and getting fired from lesser and lesser jobs. This hopelessness fed his feelings of depression and also made it hard for him to try to make himself feel better.

With the assessment data and clinical picture in hand, clinicians are ready to make a **diagnosis** (from the Greek word for "a discrimination")—that is, a determination that a person's psychological problems constitute a particular disorder. When clinicians decide, through diagnosis, that a client's pattern of dysfunction reflects a particular disorder, they are saying that the pattern is basically the same as one that has been displayed by many other people, has been investigated in a variety of studies, and perhaps has responded to particular forms of treatment. They can then apply what is generally known about the disorder to the particular individual they are trying to help. They can, for example, better predict the future course of the person's problem and the treatments that are likely to be helpful.

Classification Systems

The principle behind diagnosis is straightforward. When certain symptoms occur together regularly—a cluster of symptoms is called a **syndrome**—and follow a particular course, clinicians agree that those symptoms make up a particular mental disorder. If people display this particular pattern of symptoms, diagnosticians assign them to that diagnostic category. A list of such categories, or disorders, with descriptions of the symptoms and guidelines for assigning individuals to the categories, is known as a **classification system.**

#NervousBreakdown?

The term "nervous breakdown" is used by laypersons, not clinicians. Most people use it to refer to a sudden psychological disturbance that incapacitates a person, perhaps requiring hospitalization. Some people use the term simply to connote the onset of any psychological disorder (Hall-Flavin, 2016; Padwa, 1996).

In 1883, Emil Kraepelin developed the first modern classification system for abnormal behavior (see Chapter 1). His categories formed the foundation for the *Diagnostic and Statistical Manual of Mental Disorders* (*DSM*), the classification system currently written by the American Psychiatric Association (APA, 2013). The DSM is the most widely used classification system in North America. The content of the DSM has been changed significantly over time. The current edition, called *DSM-5*, was published in 2013. It features a number of changes from the previous editions. Most other countries rely primarily on a system called the *International Classification of Diseases* (*ICD*), developed by the World Health Organization, which lists both medical and psychological disorders. The current edition of this system is called ICD-10. A new edition, ICD-11, is scheduled to go into effect in 2022.

Why do you think many clinicians prefer the label "person with schizophrenia" over "schizophrenic person"?

Although there are some differences between the disorders listed in the DSM and ICD and in their descriptions of criteria for various disorders (the DSM's descriptions are more detailed), the numerical codes used by DSM-5 for all disorders match those used by the ICD-10—a matching that produces uniformity when clinicians fill out insurance reimbursement forms.

DSM-5

DSM-5 lists more than 500 mental disorders (see **Figure 3-3**). Each entry describes the criteria for diagnosing the disorder and the key clinical features of the disorder. The system also describes features that are often but not always related to the disorder. The classification system is further accompanied by background information such as research findings; age, culture, or gender trends; and each disorder's prevalence, risk, course, complications, predisposing factors, and family patterns.

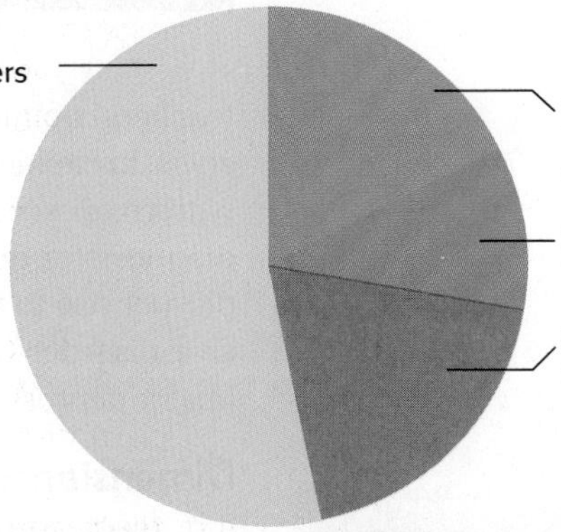

FIGURE 3-3

How Many People in the United States Qualify for a DSM Diagnosis During Their Lives?

Almost half, according to some surveys. Some people even experience two or more different disorders, which is known as comorbidity. (Information from: APA, 2017; Greenberg, 2011; Kessler et al., 2005.)

DSM-5 requires clinicians to provide both categorical and dimensional information as part of a proper diagnosis. *Categorical information* refers to the name of the distinct category (disorder) indicated by the client's symptoms. *Dimensional information* is a rating of how severe a client's symptoms are and how dysfunctional the client is across various dimensions of personality and behavior.

Categorical Information

First, the clinician must decide whether the person is displaying one of the hundreds of psychological disorders listed in the manual. Some of the most frequently diagnosed disorders are the anxiety disorders and depressive disorders.

ANXIETY DISORDERS People with anxiety disorders may experience general feelings of anxiety and worry (*generalized anxiety disorder*); fears of specific situations, objects, or activities (*phobias*); anxiety about social situations (*social anxiety disorder*); repeated outbreaks of panic (*panic disorder*); or anxiety about being separated from one's parents or from other key individuals (*separation anxiety disorder*).

DEPRESSIVE DISORDERS People with depressive disorders may experience an episode of extreme sadness and related symptoms (*major depressive disorder*), persistent and chronic sadness (*persistent depressive disorder*), or severe premenstrual sadness and related symptoms (*premenstrual dysphoric disorder*).

Although people may receive just one diagnosis from the DSM-5 list, they often receive more than one. Franco would likely receive a diagnosis of *major depressive disorder*. In addition, let's suppose the clinician judged that Franco's worries about his

Elizabeth Eckert, Middletown, NY. Courtesy Tracy DeMichiel

The power of labeling When looking at this late-nineteenth-century photograph of a baseball team at the State Homeopathic Asylum for the Insane in Middletown, New York, most observers assume that the players are patients. As a result, they tend to "see" depression or confusion in the players' faces and posture. In fact, the players are members of the asylum staff, some of whom even sought their jobs for the express purpose of playing for the hospital team.

teachers' opinions of him and his later concerns that supervisors at work would discover his inadequate skills were really but two examples of a much broader, persistent pattern of excessive worry, concern, and avoidance. He might then receive an additional diagnosis of *generalized anxiety disorder.* Alternatively, if Franco's anxiety symptoms did not rise to the level of generalized anxiety disorder, his diagnosis of major depressive disorder might simply specify that he is experiencing some features of anxiety (*major depressive disorder with anxious distress*).

Dimensional Information In addition to deciding what disorder a client is displaying, diagnosticians assess the current severity of the client's disorder—that is, how extensive are the symptoms and how much do they impair the client's functioning? For each disorder, the framers of DSM-5 have suggested various rating scales for evaluating the severity of the disorder (APA, 2013). Using a depression rating scale, for example, Franco's therapist might assign a severity rating of *moderate* to the young man's depression, meaning his symptoms are quite frequent and disabling but not as extreme and incapacitating as those found in the most severe cases of depression. DSM-5 is the first edition of the DSM to consistently seek both categorical and dimensional information as equally important parts of the diagnosis, rather than categorical information alone.

Additional Information Clinicians also may include other useful information when making a diagnosis. They may, for example, indicate special psychosocial problems the client has. Franco's recent breakup with his girlfriend might be noted as *relationship distress.* Altogether, Franco might receive the following diagnosis:

> **Diagnosis: Major depressive disorder with anxious distress**
>
> *Severity:* Moderate
>
> *Additional information:* Relationship distress

Each diagnosis also has a numerical code that clinicians must state—a code listed in ICD-10, the current edition of the international classification system mentioned earlier. Thus if Franco were assigned the DSM-5 diagnosis indicated above, his clinician would also state a numerical code of *F32.1*—the code corresponding to *major depressive disorder, moderate severity.*

#

#TheirWords

"The boundary of psychiatry keeps expanding; the realm of normal is shrinking. . . . As chairman of the DSM-IV Task Force, I must take partial responsibility for diagnostic inflation."

Allen Frances, 2013
Chair of the DSM-IV Task Force

Is DSM-5 an Effective Classification System?

A classification system, like an assessment method, is judged by its reliability and validity. Here *reliability* means that different clinicians are likely to agree on the diagnosis when they use the system to diagnose the same client. Early versions of the DSM were, at best, moderately reliable (Blashfield et al., 2014). In the early 1960s, for example, four clinicians, each relying on DSM-I, the first edition of the DSM, independently interviewed 153 patients (Beck et al., 1962). Only 54 percent of their diagnoses were in agreement. Because all four clinicians were experienced diagnosticians, their failure to agree suggested deficiencies in the classification system.

The framers of DSM-5 followed certain procedures in their development of the new manual to help ensure that DSM-5 would have greater reliability than the previous DSMs (APA, 2013). For example, they conducted extensive reviews of research to pinpoint which categories in past DSMs had been too vague and unreliable. In addition, they gathered input from a wide range of experienced clinicians and researchers. They then developed a number of new diagnostic criteria and categories, expecting that the new criteria and categories would be reliable. Although some studies have indeed found enhanced reliability in DSM-5, others have not (Aggarwal, 2017; Wakefield, 2015).

Why are the reliability findings less than stellar? Critics point to faulty procedures used in the development of DSM-5. They suggest, for example, that the framers failed to run a sufficient number of *field studies* to test the merits of the new criteria and categories. In turn, DSM-5 may have retained several of the reliability problems found in past editions of the DSM.

The *validity* of a classification system is the accuracy of the information that its diagnostic categories provide. Categories are of most use to clinicians when they demonstrate *predictive validity*—that is, when they help predict future symptoms or events. A common symptom of major depressive disorder is either insomnia or excessive sleep. When clinicians give Franco a diagnosis of major depressive disorder, they expect that he may eventually develop sleep problems even if none are present now. In addition, they expect him to respond to treatments that are effective for other depressed persons. The more often such predictions are accurate, the greater a category's predictive validity.

DSM-5's framers tried to also ensure the validity of this edition by conducting extensive reviews of research and consulting with numerous clinical advisors. As a result,

"Correct me if I'm wrong, but hasn't the fine line between sanity and madness gotten finer?"

#

#BandPsychNames

- Alcoholics Unanimous
- Widespread Panic
- Madness
- Obsession
- Bad Brains
- Fear Factory
- Mood Elevator
- Neurosis
- 10,000 Maniacs
- Grupo Mania
- The Insane Clown Posse
- Unsane

according to several studies, its criteria and categories do appear to have stronger validity than those of the earlier versions of the DSM, but other research clarifies that the manual's validity is still less than desirable (La Greca, Danzi, & Chan, 2017; Frances, 2016, 2015; Stinchfield et al., 2016). Among other validity issues, some of DSM-5's criteria and categories may reflect gender or racial bias.

Actually, one important organization has already concluded that the validity of DSM-5 is lacking and is acting accordingly. The National Institute of Mental Health (NIMH), the world's largest funding agency for mental health research, no longer gives financial support to clinical studies that rely exclusively on DSM-5 criteria. And, more generally, the agency has developed its own neuroscience-focused classification tool, called the *Research Domain Criteria (RDoC)*, that it expects will eventually be the primary classification guide used by researchers (NIMH, 2018).

#TheirWords

"I spent 13 years at NIMH really pushing on the neuroscience and genetics of mental disorders, and when I look back on that I realize that while I think I succeeded at getting lots of really cool papers published by cool scientists at fairly large costs—I think $20 billion—I don't think we moved the needle in reducing suicide, reducing hospitalizations, improving recovery for the tens of millions of people who have mental illness. I hold myself accountable for that."

Tom Insel, 2017
Director of the National Institute of Mental Health (2002–2015)

Call for Change

The effort to produce DSM-5 took more than a decade. After years of preliminary work by a DSM-5 task force and numerous work groups, whose goal was to develop a DSM that addressed the limitations of previous DSM editions, the new diagnostic and classification system was published in 2013. The categories and criteria of DSM-5 are featured throughout this textbook (APA, 2013).

DSM-5 has raised concerns among many clinical practitioners and researchers (see ***InfoCentral***). In addition to the possible reliability and validity limitations described above, critics worry that some of its changes in criteria and categories are ill-advised and can, on occasion, lead to problems for clients. The DSM-5 changes that have raised the most concern include the following:

- It calls for a diagnosis of "major depressive disorder" for some recently bereaved people (see Chapter 6).
- It adds a new category, "premenstrual dysphoric disorder" (see Chapter 6).
- It adds a new category, "somatic symptom disorder," that can be assigned to people who are overly anxious about serious medical problems (see Chapter 8).
- It combines the patterns of substance dependence and substance abuse (patterns that may each require different treatments) into a single category, "substance use disorder" (see Chapter 10).
- It groups the category "gambling disorder" as an addictive disorder alongside the substance use disorders (see Chapter 10).
- It combines all forms of autism into a single category, "autism spectrum disorder," thus eliminating the past category of "Asperger's syndrome" (see Chapter 14).
- It adds a new category, "mild neurocognitive disorder," that could be misapplied to normal age-related forgetfulness (see Chapter 15).

Can Diagnosis and Labeling Cause Harm?

Even with trustworthy assessment data and reliable and valid classification categories, clinicians will sometimes arrive at a wrong conclusion (Norman et al., 2017). Like all human beings, clinicians are flawed information processors. Studies show that they are overly influenced by information gathered early in the assessment process. In addition, they may pay too much attention to certain sources of information, such as a parent's report about a child, and too little to others, such as the child's point of view. Finally, their judgments can be distorted by any number of personal biases—gender, age, race, and socioeconomic status, to name just a few. Given the limitations of assessment tools, assessors, and classification systems, it is small wonder that studies sometimes uncover shocking errors in diagnosis, especially in hospitals (Liese & Reis, 2016; Schildkrout, 2016).

#StigmaContinues

33%	Percentage of Americans who would not seek counseling for fear of being labeled "mentally ill"
51%	Percentage of Americans who would hesitate to see a psychotherapist if a diagnosis were required

(Roper, 2017; Opinion Research Corporation, 2011, 2004)

DSM: THE BIGGER PICTURE

The Diagnostic and Statistical Manual of Mental Disorders (DSM) is the most widely used classification system in North America. It is actually a work in progress. DSM-5, the 947-page current edition, is but the latest version of this system, which has undergone many changes over the past seven decades. The DSM also faces competition from other diagnostic systems around the world.

Competitors

Both within North America and around the world, the **DSM** faces competition from two other diagnostic systems—the **International Classification of Disorders (ICD)** and **Research Domain Criteria (RDoC)**.

	DSM	ICD	RDoC
Producer	APA	WHO*	NIMH**
Disorders	Psychological	Psychological/ medical	Psychological
Criteria	Detailed	Brief	Neuro/ biological
Application	Practice/research	Practice/research	Research
Area of use	North America	Worldwide	United States

* World Health Organization ** National Institute of Mental Health

Just a Generation Ago . . .

Many of the disorders listed in the DSM are very familiar, giving the impression that they have been recognized forever. But many of the disorders and/or their labels are relatively new.

Just a generation ago, the DSM did not include:

- Bulimia nervosa
- Autistic disorder
- PTSD
- Panic disorder
- Narcissistic personality disorder
- Borderline personality disorder

Just a generation ago, the DSM had different names for certain disorders:

Past	Present
Mental retardation	Intellectual disability (page 460)
Manic-depressive disorder	Bipolar disorder (page 201)
Multiple personality disorder	Dissociative identity disorder (page 160)
Dementia	Neurocognitive disorder (page 480)
Hypochondriasis	Illness anxiety disorder (page 248)

Top DSM-5 Concerns

Many of the DSM-5 changes have raised concerns. Several have been particularly controversial in some clinical circles.

People with a **serious medical disease**, such as cancer, may also receive a psychiatric diagnosis of somatic symptom disorder if they are "excessively" distressed.

People experiencing **normal grief reactions** may receive a psychiatric diagnosis of depression if they are "excessively" distressed.

Many **behaviors pursued excessively**, such as sex, Internet use, and shopping, may eventually be considered behavioral addictions.

People with **normal age-related forgetfulness** may receive a psychiatric diagnosis of mild neurocognitive disorder.

The DSM Timeline

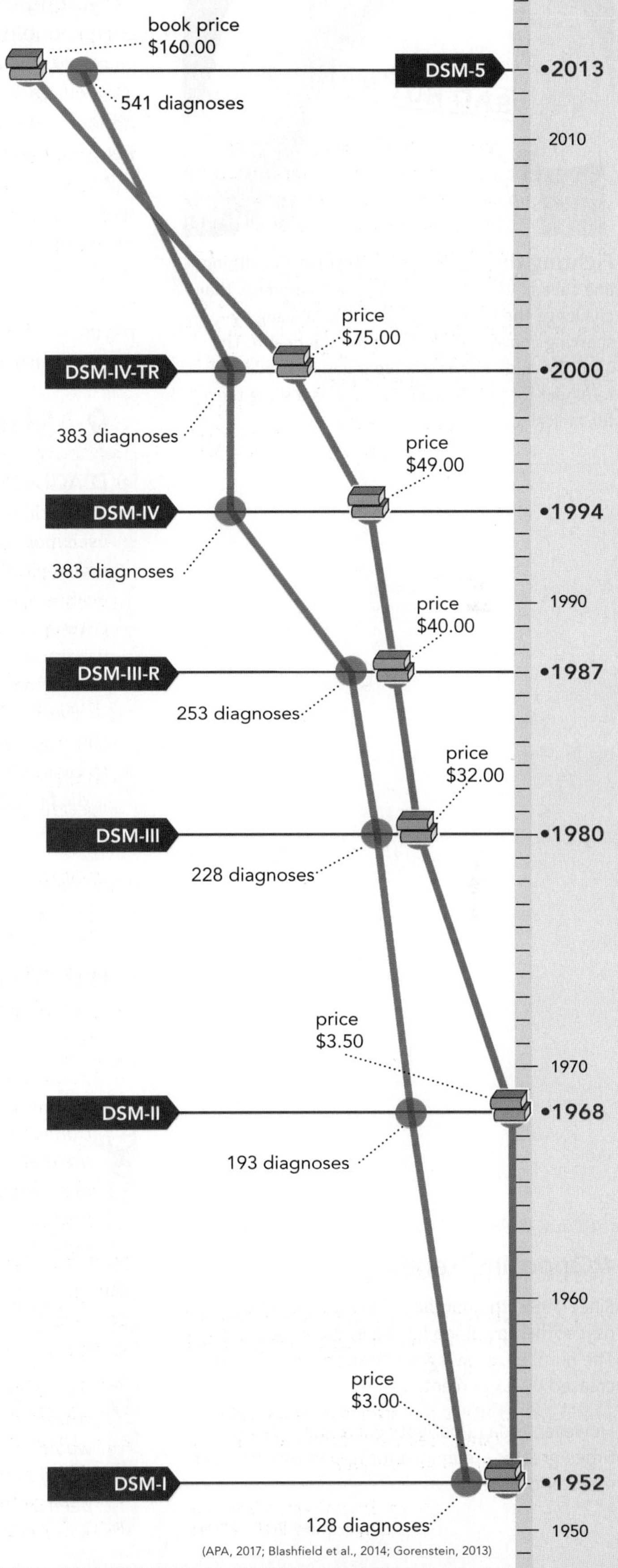

(APA, 2017; Blashfield et al., 2014; Gorenstein, 2013)

Maya Sherwood Photography/REX/Shutterstock

Fighting the stigma of labeling A clothing line called "Wear Your Label" offers garments that challenge the stigma of psychiatric labeling by sparking conversations about mental health. The "Sad But Rad" T-shirt is a big seller. (A heads-up/reminder for people over 30: "rad" is a slang term for radical, cool, and/or wonderful.)

Beyond the potential for misdiagnosis, the very act of classifying people can lead to unintended results. As you read in Chapter 2, for example, many family-social theorists believe that diagnostic labels can become self-fulfilling prophecies. When people are diagnosed as mentally disturbed, they may be perceived that way and reacted to correspondingly. If others expect them to take on a sick role, they may begin to consider themselves sick as well and act that way. Furthermore, our society attaches a stigma to abnormality (Corrigan et al., 2017). People labeled mentally ill may find it difficult to get a job, especially a position of responsibility, or to be welcomed into social relationships. Once a label has been applied, it may stick for a long time.

Why are medical diagnoses usually valued, while the use of psychological diagnoses is often criticized?

Because of these problems, some clinicians would like to do away with diagnoses. Others disagree. They believe we must simply work to increase what is known about psychological disorders and improve diagnostic techniques. They hold that classification and diagnosis are critical to understanding and treating people in distress.

9... SUMMING UP

DIAGNOSIS After collecting assessment information, clinicians form a clinical picture and decide on a diagnosis. The diagnosis is chosen from a classification system. The system used most widely in North America is the Diagnostic and Statistical Manual of Mental Disorders (DSM). The most recent version of the DSM, known as DSM-5, lists more than 500 disorders. DSM-5 contains numerous additions and changes to the diagnostic categories, criteria, and organization that were found in past editions of the DSM. The reliability and validity of this revised diagnostic and classification system are currently receiving clinical review and, in some circles, criticism.

Even with trustworthy assessment data and reliable and valid classification categories, clinicians will not always arrive at the correct conclusion. They are human and so fall prey to various biases, misconceptions, and expectations. Another problem related to diagnosis is the prejudice that labels arouse, which may be damaging to the person who is diagnosed.

Treatment: How Might the Client Be Helped?

Over the course of 10 months, Franco was treated for depression and related symptoms. He improved considerably during that time, as the following report describes:

During therapy, Franco's debilitating depression relented. Increasingly, he came to appreciate that his mother's accusations against him—and his self-accusations—were not accurate. He also started to consider the possibility that Maria's reluctance to commit to him had been more about where she was in her life than a sign that he was a terrible or inadequate person. Eventually, Maria and Franco talked again, although they did not renew their relationship. Franco felt better realizing that she did not hate him. She even told him that her mother had said some kind things about him after their breakup.

Franco also managed to straighten out his problems at work. He explained his recent difficulties to his immediate supervisor at the bank and committed himself to improving his recent performance. His supervisor, with whom he had been friendly before his recent struggles, said she was glad that he was communicating openly, and emphasized that he would be given the opportunity to improve his performance. He was surprised to hear how highly he had been regarded over the years, although as she put it, "Why would you have been promoted otherwise?"

#OpposingTrends

Since 1998, the number of patients receiving psychotherapy alone has fallen by 34 percent. The number receiving medication alone has increased by 23 percent.

However, today's patients express a three-times-greater preference for psychotherapy over medications.

(Gaudiano, 2013)

> *Over the course of therapy, Franco also forced himself to spend more time having fun with his friends. He found his mood on the upswing as a result of these re-established relationships. In addition, he began dating a woman he met through Jesse. He often considered the lessons he learned in treatment, trying to handle this new relationship in ways different from the destructive patterns of his past.*

empirically supported treatment Therapy that has received clear research support for a particular disorder and has corresponding treatment guidelines. Also known as *evidence-based treatment.*

Clearly, treatment helped Franco, and by its conclusion he was a happier, more functional person than the man who had first sought help 10 months earlier. But how did his therapist decide on the treatment program that proved to be so helpful?

Treatment Decisions

Franco's therapist began, like all therapists, with assessment information and diagnostic decisions. Knowing the specific details and background of Franco's problem (idiographic data) and combining this individual information with broad information about the nature and treatment of depression, the clinician arrived at a treatment plan for him.

Yet therapists may be influenced by additional factors when they make treatment decisions. Their treatment plans typically reflect their theoretical orientations and how they have learned to conduct therapy (Wedding & Corsini, 2019). As therapists apply a favored model in case after case, they become more and more familiar with its principles and treatment techniques and tend to use them in work with still other clients.

Current research may also play a role. Most clinicians say that they value research as a guide to practice (Gyani et al., 2015; Beutler et al., 1995). However, not all of them actually read research articles, so they cannot be directly influenced by them (Holt et al., 2015; Stewart & Chambless, 2007). In fact, according to surveys, therapists gather much of their information about the latest developments in the field from colleagues, professional newsletters, workshops, conferences, Web sites, books, and the like (Farrell & Shaw, 2018; Corrie & Callanan, 2001). Unfortunately, the accuracy and usefulness of these sources vary widely.

To help clinicians become more familiar with and apply research findings, there is an influential movement in North America, the United Kingdom, and elsewhere toward **empirically supported,** or **evidence-based, treatment** (Wiltsey-Stirman & Comer, 2019; Stamm et al., 2018). Proponents of this movement have formed task forces that

AP Photo/Michael Dwyer

Raising public awareness Believing that more public awareness about stress and psychological disorders will lead to better assessment and treatment, Boston's Logan International Airport displays an art exhibit of enormous posters, featuring dozens of people—from ordinary to famous—who have experienced such disorders.

rapprochement movement A movement to identify a set of common factors, or common strategies, that run through all successful therapies.

seek to identify which therapies have received clear research support for each disorder, to propose corresponding treatment guidelines, and to spread such information to clinicians. The movement has gained considerable momentum over the past few decades.

The Effectiveness of Treatment

Altogether, more than 400 forms of therapy are currently practiced in the clinical field (Zarbo et al., 2015). Naturally, the most important question to ask about each of them is whether it does what it is supposed to do. Does a particular treatment really help people overcome their psychological problems? On the surface, the question may seem simple. In fact, it is one of the most difficult questions for clinical researchers to answer.

The first problem is how to *define* "success." If, as Franco's therapist implies, he still has much progress to make at the conclusion of therapy, should his recovery be considered successful? The second problem is how to *measure* improvement (Lambert, 2015, 2010). Should researchers give equal weight to the reports of clients, friends, relatives, therapists, and teachers? Should they use rating scales, inventories, therapy insights, observations, or some other measure?

Perhaps the biggest problem in determining the effectiveness of treatment is the *variety* and *complexity* of the treatments currently in use. People differ in their problems, personal styles, and motivations for therapy. Therapists differ in skill, experience, orientation, and personality. And therapies differ in theory, format, and setting. Because an individual's progress is influenced by all these factors and more, the findings of a particular study will not always apply to other clients and therapists (see **Figure 3-4**).

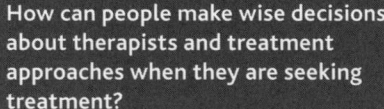

How can people make wise decisions about therapists and treatment approaches when they are seeking treatment?

Proper research procedures address some of these problems. By using control groups, random assignment, matched research participants, and the like, clinicians can draw certain conclusions about various therapies. Even in studies that are well designed, however, the variety and complexity of treatment limit the conclusions that can be reached (Kazdin, 2017, 2015).

Despite these issues and difficulties, the job of evaluating therapies must be done, and clinical researchers have plowed ahead with it. Investigators have, in fact, conducted thousands of *therapy outcome studies,* studies that measure and compare the effects of various treatments. The studies typically ask one of three questions: (1) Is therapy *in general* effective? (2) Are *particular* therapies generally effective? (3) Are *particular* therapies effective for *particular* problems?

Is Therapy Generally Effective? Studies suggest that therapy often is more helpful than no treatment or than placebos. A pioneering review examined 375 controlled studies, covering a total of almost 25,000 people seen in a wide assortment of therapies (Smith, Glass, & Miller, 1980; Smith & Glass, 1977). The reviewers combined the findings

FIGURE 3-4

What Factors Contribute to Therapy Outcomes?

According to research, a client's progress in therapy relates only partly to the specific strategies used by his or her therapist. In fact, factors such as the client's expectations, the client–therapist relationship, and concurrent events in the client's life may collectively have the most influence on the outcome of treatment. (Information from: De Nadai et al., 2017; McClintock et al., 2017; Davidson & Chan, 2014; Norcross & Lambert, 2011; Cooper, 2008.)

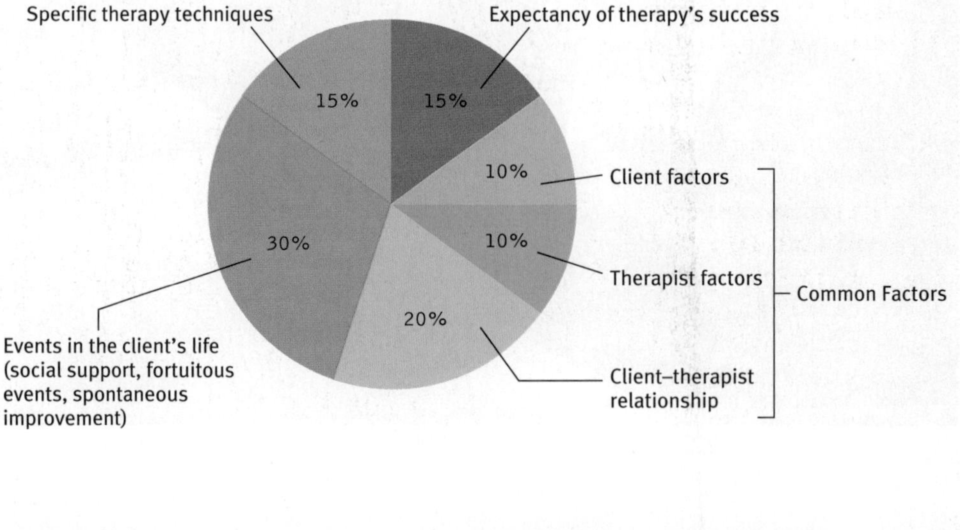

of these studies by using a special statistical technique called *meta-analysis.* According to this analysis, the average person who received treatment was better off than 75 percent of the untreated persons. Other meta-analyses have found similar relationships between treatment and improvement (Sharf, 2015).

Some clinicians have concerned themselves with an important related question: Can therapy be harmful? A number of studies suggest that 5 to 10 percent of patients actually seem to get worse because of therapy (Lambert, 2015, 2010; Lambert et al., 1986). Their symptoms may become more intense, or they may develop new ones, such as a sense of failure, guilt, reduced self-concept, or hopelessness, because of their inability to profit from therapy.

Are Particular Therapies Generally Effective? The studies you have read about so far have lumped all therapies together to consider their general effectiveness. Many researchers, however, consider it wrong to treat all therapies alike. Some critics suggest that these studies are operating under a *uniformity myth*—a false belief that all therapies are equivalent despite differences in the therapists' training, experience, theoretical orientations, and personalities (Heppner et al., 2016; Kiesler, 1995, 1966).

Thus, an alternative approach examines the effectiveness of *particular* therapies. Most research of this kind shows each of the major forms of therapy to be superior to no treatment or to placebo treatment (Prochaska & Norcross, 2018). A number of other studies have compared particular therapies with one another and found that no one form of therapy generally stands out over all others (Luborsky et al., 2006, 2002, 1975).

If different kinds of therapy have similar successes, might they have something in common? People in the **rapprochement movement** have tried to identify a set of *common factors,* or *common strategies,* that may run through all effective therapies, regardless of the clinicians' particular orientations (Yang & Zhang, 2017). Surveys of highly successful therapists suggest, for example, that most give feedback to clients, help clients focus on their own thoughts and behavior, pay attention to the way they and their clients are interacting, and try to promote self-mastery in their clients. In short, effective therapists of any type may practice more similarly than they preach.

Are Particular Therapies Effective for Particular Problems? People with different disorders may respond differently to the various forms of therapy (Norcross et al., 2017; Norcross & Beutler, 2014). In an oft-quoted statement, influential clinical theorist

Harley L. Schwadron/The New Yorker Collection/The Cartoon Bank

"Batman is getting more press than me."

#MovieClinicians

Dr. Fletcher (*Split,* 2017)

Dr. Aurelius (*The Hunger Games: Mockingjay, Part 2,* 2015)

Dr. Banks (*Side Effects,* 2013)

Dr. Patel (*The Silver Linings Playbook,* 2012)

Dr. Cawley (*Shutter Island,* 2010)

Dr. Steele (*Changeling,* 2008)

Dr. Rosen (*A Beautiful Mind,* 2001)

Dr. Crowe (*The Sixth Sense,* 1999)

Dr. Sobel (*Analyze This,* 1999)

Dr. Maguire (*Good Will Hunting,* 1997)

Dr. Lecter (*The Silence of the Lambs,* 1991)

Dr. Marvin (*What About Bob?,* 1991)

Dr. Sayer (*Awakenings,* 1990)

Dr. Berger (*Ordinary People,* 1980)

psychopharmacologist A psychiatrist who primarily prescribes medications.

Gordon Paul said a half-century ago that the most appropriate question regarding the effectiveness of therapy may be *"What* specific treatment, by *whom,* is most effective for *this* individual with *that* specific problem, and under *which* set of circumstances?" (Paul, 1967, p. 111). Researchers have investigated how effective particular therapies are at treating particular disorders, and they often have found sizable differences among the various therapies. Cognitive-behavioral therapies, for example, appear to be the most effective of all in treating phobias (Antony, 2019; Grohol, 2016), whereas drug therapy seems to be the single most effective treatment for schizophrenia (Joshi et al., 2018; Andrade, 2016).

As you read previously, studies also show that some clinical problems may respond better to *combined* approaches (Kamenov et al., 2017; Norcross & Beutler, 2014). Drug therapy is sometimes combined with certain forms of psychotherapy, for example, to treat depression. In fact, it is now common for clients to be seen by two therapists—one of them a **psychopharmacologist,** a psychiatrist who primarily prescribes medications, and the other a psychologist, social worker, or other therapist who conducts psychotherapy. Obviously, knowledge of how particular therapies fare with particular disorders can help therapists and clients alike make better decisions about treatment. We will keep returning to this issue as we examine the various disorders throughout the book.

9... SUMMING UP

TREATMENT The treatment decisions of therapists may be influenced by assessment information, the diagnosis, the clinician's theoretical orientation and familiarity with research, and the state of knowledge in the field. Determining the effectiveness of treatment is difficult. Nevertheless, therapy outcome studies have led to three general conclusions: (1) people in therapy are usually better off than people with similar problems who receive no treatment; (2) the various therapies do not appear to differ dramatically in their general effectiveness; and (3) certain therapies or combinations of therapies do appear to be more effective than others for certain disorders. Some therapists currently advocate empirically supported treatment—the active identification, promotion, and teaching of those interventions that have received clear research support.

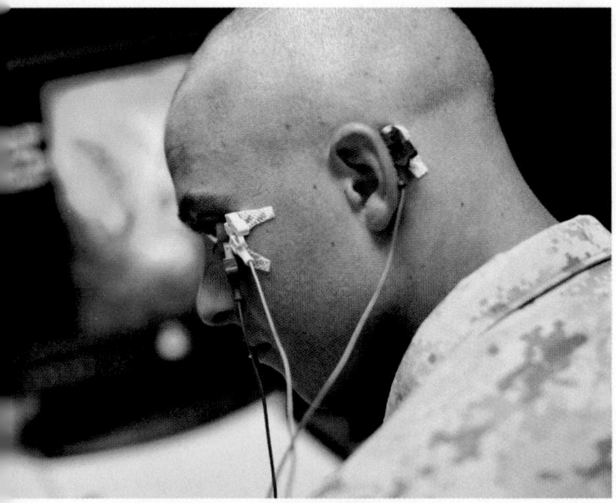

AP Photo/Jae C. Hong

Blink of the eye Before entering combat duty, this Marine takes an eyeblink test—a psychophysiological test in which sensors are attached to the eyelid and other parts of the face. The test tries to detect physical indicators of tension and anxiety and to predict which Marines might be particularly susceptible to posttraumatic stress disorder.

What Lies Ahead for Clinical Assessment?

It is clear from this chapter that proper diagnoses and effective treatments rest on the shoulders of accurate clinical assessment. Correspondingly, before the 1950s, assessment tools were a highly regarded part of clinical practice. However, as research in the 1960s and 1970s began to reveal that a number of the tools were inaccurate or inconsistent, many clinicians abandoned systematic assessment. Today, respect for assessment is on the rise once again. One reason for this renewal of interest is the drive by researchers for more rigorous tests to help them select appropriate participants for clinical studies. Still another factor is the growing belief in the field that brain-scanning techniques may soon offer assessment information about a wide range of psychological disorders. Along with heightened respect for assessment has come increased research in this area.

Ironically, just as clinicians and researchers are rediscovering systematic assessment, rising costs and economic factors may be conspiring to discourage the use of assessment tools. As you read in Chapter 1, insurance parity and treatment coverage, including assessment coverage, for people with psychological problems had been improving during the twenty-first century as a result of federal parity laws and the Affordable Care Act (see page 18). However, with new federal leadership and different health care priorities now unfolding, many experts fear that clinical assessment will receive only limited insurance support in the future. Which forces will ultimately have a stronger influence on clinical assessment—promising research or economic pressure? Only time will tell.

Key Terms

idiographic information, p. 73
assessment, p. 73
standardization, p. 74
reliability, p. 74
validity, p. 74
clinical interview, p. 75
mental status exam, p. 76
clinical test, p. 77
projective test, p. 77
Rorschach test, p. 78
Thematic Apperception Test (TAT), p. 79
personality inventory, p. 80
Minnesota Multiphasic Personality Inventory (MMPI), p. 80
response inventories, p. 82
psychophysiological test, p. 82
neurological test, p. 84
EEG, p. 84
neuroimaging techniques, p. 84
CT scan, p. 84
PET scan, p. 85
MRI, p. 85
fMRI, p. 85
neuropsychological test, p. 85
battery, p. 85
intelligence test, p. 85
intelligence quotient (IQ), p. 85
naturalistic observation, p. 86
analog observation, p. 86
self-monitoring, p. 87
diagnosis, p. 88
syndrome, p. 88
classification system, p. 88
DSM-5, p. 89
categorical information, p. 89
dimensional information, p. 90
empirically supported treatment, p. 95
therapy outcome study, p. 96
rapprochement movement, p. 97
common factors, p. 97
psychopharmacologist, p. 98

Quick Quiz

1. What forms of reliability and validity should clinical assessment tools display? *pp. 74–75*
2. What are the strengths and weaknesses of structured and unstructured interviews? *pp. 76–77*
3. List and describe today's leading projective tests. *pp. 77–79*
4. What are the key features of the MMPI? *pp. 80–81*
5. What are the strengths and weaknesses of projective tests (*p. 79*), personality inventories (*pp. 81–82*), and other kinds of clinical tests (*pp. 82–86*)?
6. How do clinicians determine whether psychological problems are linked to brain damage? *pp. 84–85*
7. Describe the ways in which clinicians may make observations of clients' behaviors. *pp. 86–87*
8. What is the purpose of clinical diagnoses? *p. 88*
9. Describe DSM-5. What problems may accompany the use of classification systems and the process of clinical diagnosis? *pp. 89–94*
10. According to therapy outcome studies, how effective is therapy? *pp. 96–98*

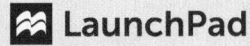

CHAPTER 4

Anxiety, Obsessive-Compulsive, and Related Disorders

TOPIC OVERVIEW

Tomas, a 25-year-old Web designer, was afraid that he was "losing his mind." He had always been a worrier. He worried about his health, his girlfriend, his work, his social life, his future, his finances, and so on. Would his best friend get angry at him? Was his girlfriend tiring of him? Was he investing his money wisely? Were his clients pleased with his work? But, lately, those worries had increased to an unbearable level. He was becoming consumed with the notion that something terrible was about to happen to him. Within an hour's time, he might have intense concerns about going broke, developing cancer, losing one of his parents, offending his friends, and more. He was certain that disaster awaited him at every turn. No amount of reassurance, from himself or from others, brought relief for very long.

He started therapy with Dr. Adena Morven, a clinical psychologist. Dr. Morven immediately noticed how disturbed Tomas appeared. He looked tense and frightened and could not sit comfortably in his chair; he kept tapping his feet and jumped when he heard traffic noise from outside the office building. He kept sighing throughout the visit, fidgeting and shifting his position, and he appeared breathless while telling Dr. Morven about his difficulties.

Tomas described his frequent inability to concentrate to the therapist. When designing client Web sites, he would lose his train of thought. Less than 5 minutes into a project, he'd forget much of his overall strategy. During conversations, he would begin a sentence and then forget the point he was about to make. TV watching had become impossible. He found it difficult to concentrate on anything for more than 5 minutes; his mind kept drifting away from the task at hand.

To say the least, he was worried about all of this. "I'm worried about being so worried," he told Dr. Morven, almost laughing at his own remark. At this point, Tomas expected the worst whenever he began a conversation, task, plan, or outing. If an event or interaction did in fact start to go awry, he would find himself overwhelmed with uncomfortable feelings—his heart would beat faster, his breathing would increase, and he'd sweat profusely. On some occasions, he thought he was actually having a heart attack—at the ripe old age of 25.

Typically, such physical reactions lasted but a matter of seconds. However, those few seconds felt like an eternity to Tomas. He acknowledged coming back down to earth after those feelings subsided—but, for him, "back down to earth" meant back to worrying and then worrying some more.

Dr. Morven empathized with Tomas about how upsetting this all must be. She asked him why he had decided to come into therapy now—as opposed to last year, last month, or last week. Tomas was able to pinpoint several things. First, all the worrying and anxiety seemed to be on the increase. Second, he was finding it hard to sleep. His nights were filled with tossing and turning—and, of course, more worrying. Third, he suspected that all of his worrying, physical symptoms, and lack of sleep were bad for his health. Wouldn't they eventually lead to a major medical problem of some kind? And finally, his constant anxiety had begun to interfere with his life. Although his girlfriend and other acquaintances did not seem to realize how much he was suffering, he was growing weary of covering it all up. He found himself turning down social invitations and work opportunities more and more. He had even quit his once-beloved weekly poker game. Not that staying home helped in any real way. He wondered how much longer he could go on this way.

fear The central nervous system's physiological and emotional response to a serious threat to one's well-being.

anxiety The central nervous system's physiological and emotional response to a vague sense of threat or danger.

generalized anxiety disorder A disorder marked by persistent and excessive feelings of anxiety and worry about numerous events and activities.

You don't need to be as troubled as Tomas to experience fear and anxiety. Think about a time when your breathing quickened, your muscles tensed, and your heart pounded with a sudden sense of dread. Was it when your car almost skidded off the road in the rain? When your professor announced a pop quiz? What about when the person you were in love with went out with someone else, or your boss suggested that your job performance ought to improve? Any time you face what seems to be a serious threat to your well-being, you may react with the state of immediate alarm known as **fear.** Sometimes you cannot pinpoint a specific cause for your alarm, but still you feel tense and edgy, as if you expect something unpleasant to happen. The vague sense of being in danger is usually called **anxiety,** and it has the same features—the same increases in breathing, muscular tension, perspiration, and so forth—as fear.

Although everyday experiences of fear and anxiety are not pleasant, they often are useful. They prepare us for action—for "fight or flight"—when danger threatens. They may lead us to drive more cautiously in a storm, keep up with our reading assignments, treat our friends more sensitively, and work harder at our jobs. Unfortunately, some people suffer such disabling fear and anxiety that they cannot lead normal lives. Their discomfort is too severe or too frequent, lasts too long, or is triggered too easily. These people are said to have an *anxiety disorder* or a related kind of disorder.

If fear is so unpleasant, why do many people seek out the feelings of fear brought about by amusement park rides, scary movies, bungee jumping, and the like?

Anxiety disorders are the most common mental disorders in the United States. In any given year around 18 percent of the adult population suffer from one or another of the anxiety disorders identified by DSM-5, while close to 29 percent of all people develop one of the disorders at some point in their lives (NAMI, 2017; Kessler et al., 2012, 2010, 2009). Around 37 percent of these individuals receive treatment (NIMH, 2017; Wang et al., 2005). Surveys suggest that non-Hispanic white Americans are more likely than African, Hispanic, or Asian Americans to develop an anxiety disorder during their lifetime (NIMH, 2017; Hofmann & Hinton, 2014). The cause of this racial-ethnic difference is not well understood.

People with *generalized anxiety disorder* experience general and persistent feelings of worry and anxiety. People with *specific phobias* have a persistent and irrational fear of a particular object, activity, or situation. People with *agoraphobia* fear traveling to public places such as stores or movie theaters. Those with *social anxiety disorder* are intensely afraid of social or performance situations in which they may become embarrassed. And people with *panic disorder* have recurrent attacks of terror. Most individuals with one anxiety disorder suffer from a second one as well (Baldwin, 2018; Greist, 2018). Tomas, for example, has the excessive worry found in generalized anxiety disorder and the repeated attacks of terror that mark panic disorder. In addition, many of those with an anxiety disorder also experience depression (Chen et al., 2019; Salcedo, 2018).

Anxiety also plays a major role in a different group of problems, called *obsessive-compulsive and related disorders.* People with these disorders feel overrun by recurrent thoughts that cause anxiety or by the need to perform certain repetitive actions to reduce anxiety. Because anxiety is so prominent in these disorders, they will be examined in this chapter along with the anxiety disorders. ■

Generalized Anxiety Disorder

People with **generalized anxiety disorder** experience excessive anxiety under most circumstances and worry about practically anything. In fact, their problem is sometimes described as *free-floating anxiety.* Like the young Web designer Tomas, they typically feel restless, keyed up, or on edge; tire easily; have difficulty concentrating; suffer from muscle tension; and have sleep problems (see **Table 4-1**). The symptoms last at least 6 months (APA, 2013) and lead to a reduced quality of life. Nevertheless, many people with the disorder are able, although with some difficulty, to carry on social relationships and job activities.

TABLE: 4-1

Dx Checklist

Generalized Anxiety Disorder
1. For 6 months or more, person experiences disproportionate, uncontrollable, and ongoing anxiety and worry about multiple matters.
2. The symptoms include at least three of the following: edginess, fatigue, poor concentration, irritability, muscle tension, sleep problems.
3. Significant distress or impairment.

Information from: APA, 2013.

Generalized anxiety disorder is common in Western society. Surveys suggest that as many as 4 percent of the U.S. population have the symptoms of this disorder in any given year, a rate that holds across Canada, Britain, and other Western countries (NIMH, 2017; Watterson et al., 2017; Kessler et al., 2012, 2010). Altogether, around 6 percent of all people develop generalized anxiety disorder sometime during their lives. It may emerge at any age (see ***Trending*** on the next page). Women diagnosed with this disorder outnumber men 2 to 1. Non-Hispanic white Americans are more likely than members of minority groups to develop the disorder (Budhwani, Hearld, & Chavez-Yenter, 2015). Around 43 percent of people who have generalized anxiety disorder receive treatment for it (NIMH, 2017; Wang et al., 2005).

A variety of explanations and treatments have been proposed for this disorder. Let's look at the views and approaches offered by the sociocultural, psychodynamic, humanistic, cognitive-behavioral, and biological models.

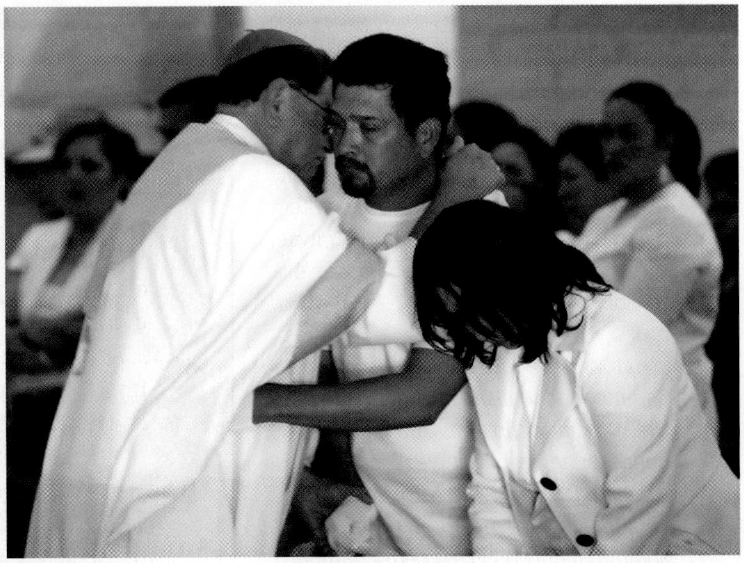

AP Photo/The Monterey County Herald, Orville Myers

The role of society Bishop Richard Garcia hugs the father of a 6-year-old child who was killed by a stray bullet fired by gang members outside his house. People who live in dangerous environments experience greater anxiety and have a higher rate of generalized anxiety disorder than those who live in other settings.

The Sociocultural Perspective: Societal and Multicultural Factors

According to sociocultural theorists, generalized anxiety disorder is most likely to develop in people who are faced with ongoing societal conditions that are dangerous. Studies have found that people in highly threatening environments are indeed more likely to develop the general feelings of tension, anxiety, and fatigue and the sleep disturbances found in this disorder (Comer et al., 2016). For example, there are higher rates of generalized anxiety disorder and similar syndromes among people who live in crime-ridden or hostile neighborhoods and among people living near nuclear power plants, especially ones that have had radiation accidents in the past (Cerdá et al., 2017; Rubens et al., 2018).

One of the most powerful forms of societal stress is poverty. People without financial means are likely to live in rundown communities with high crime rates, have fewer educational and job opportunities, and run a greater risk for health problems (Vittana, 2018; West, 2016). As sociocultural theorists would predict, such people also have a higher rate of generalized anxiety disorder (Delgadillo et al., 2016). Across North America, the rate is almost twice as high among people with low incomes as among those with higher incomes (Watterson et al., 2017; Sareen et al., 2011). As wages decrease, the rate of generalized anxiety disorder steadily increases (see **Table 4-2**).

It appears that race and ethnicity can affect the precise picture of generalized anxiety disorder (NIMH, 2017). For example, researchers have noted that the disorder often takes on a pattern called *nervios* ("nerves"), or *ataques de nervios*, for Hispanic individuals in both the United States and Latin America (Vazquez et al., 2017). People with *nervios* experience enormous emotional distress, so-called brain aches marked by poor concentration and nervousness, reactions like irritability and tearfulness, and physical symptoms such as headaches, stomachaches, trembling, and heat in the chest rising into the head.

Although poverty and various societal pressures may help create a climate in which generalized anxiety disorder is more likely to develop, sociocultural variables are not the only factors at work. After all, most people in

TABLE: 4-2

Looking at Demographics

Prevalence of Anxiety Disorders and Obsessive-Compulsive Disorder (Compared with Rate in Total Population)

	Female	Low-Income	Elderly
Generalized anxiety disorder	Higher	Higher	Higher
Specific phobias	Higher	Higher	Lower
Agoraphobia	Higher	Higher	Higher
Social anxiety disorder	Higher	Higher	Lower
Panic disorder	Higher	Higher	Lower
Obsessive-compulsive disorder	Same	Higher	Lower

Information from: McCabe, 2018; Watterson et al., 2017; de Jonge et al., 2016; Remes et al., 2016; Polo et al., 2011; Sareen et al., 2011; Hopko et al., 2008; Schultz et al., 2008.

...TRENDING

Separation Anxiety Disorder, Not Just For Kids Anymore

Individuals with *separation anxiety disorder* feel extreme anxiety, often panic, whenever they are separated from home or from key people in their lives. Jonah's symptoms began when he was 4 years old:

> *Jonah, age 4, began crying as soon as his parents tried to place him in the car for the 30-minute trip to his grandparents' house for an overnight weekend there. He screamed, "I only want to be here with you! If you make me go, I'll never see you again! What if you like it better without me? What if you die?" He cried all the way to his grandparents' house. At their door, Jonah hugged his mother as though he would never let her go. During the next several months, Jonah became hysterical every time his parents tried to get him to leave the house for a play date or journey elsewhere.*
>
> *Five months later, Jonah began kindergarten. That first day lasted all of two hours. The principal called, asking Jonah's mother to come get the child. Though sympathetic, the principal explained that Jonah's nonstop crying was affecting all the other children. "Perhaps tomorrow Jonah will have a better day," he said. But the next day, Jonah's reaction was the same. And the next day. And the next day.*

Steve Stoner/Fort Morgan Times/AP Photo

Oh, that first day! The first day of kindergarten is overwhelming for this child and perhaps also for his mother. Such reactions to the beginning of school are common. But for some individuals, separations from attachment figures repeatedly bring on severe and disabling anxiety reactions that may impair their lives.

Like Jonah, children with separation anxiety disorder have great trouble traveling away from their family, and they often refuse to visit friends' houses, go on errands, or attend camp or school. Many cannot stay alone in a room and cling to their parents around the house. Some also have temper tantrums, cry, or plead to keep their parents from leaving them. The children may fear that they will get lost when separated from their parents or that the parents will meet with an accident or illness. As long as the children are near their parents, they may function quite normally. At the first hint of separation, however, the dramatic pattern of symptoms may be set in motion.

For years, clinicians believed that separation anxiety disorder is developed *only* by children or adolescents. But in 2013 DSM-5 determined that the disorder can also occur in adulthood, particularly after adults have experienced traumas such as the death of a spouse or child, a relationship break-up, separation caused by military service, or the like (Gesi et al., 2017; APA, 2013). Such individuals may become consumed with concern about the health, safety, or well-being of a significant other—their spouse, a surviving child, or another important person in their life. They may constantly and excessively try to be with the other individual, check on the other's whereabouts, protect the other person, and restrict the person's activities and travels. Their extreme anxiety and invasive demands cause them severe distress and can greatly damage their social and occupational lives (Gesi et al., 2017).

Given this new perspective, DSM-5 now categorizes separation anxiety disorder as one kind of anxiety disorder rather than as a unique childhood disorder (APA, 2013). It states that symptoms must persist for at least 6 months for adults to receive a diagnosis, compared to 4 weeks for children. Applying DSM-5's criteria, studies find that as many as 2 percent of all adults have the disorder in addition to 4 percent of all children (Schneier et al., 2017; Baldwin et al., 2016).

This new categorization is controversial (Gesi et al., 2017). Although most clinicians agree that certain adults do indeed manifest the loss-triggered symptoms described above, many of them believe that the adult syndrome may be qualitatively different from the one displayed by Jonah and other such children. These critics believe that adults who now receive a diagnosis of separation anxiety disorder may actually be suffering from another disorder, such as posttraumatic stress disorder (see Chapter 5), or an extended case of bereavement (see Chapter 6). Researchers are currently trying to sort out this controversy, but in the meantime the term "for children only" cannot be applied to this debilitating pattern.

poor or dangerous environments do not develop this disorder. Even if sociocultural factors play a broad role, theorists still must explain why some people develop the disorder and others do not. The psychodynamic, humanistic-existential, cognitive-behavioral, and biological schools of thought have all tried to explain why and have offered corresponding treatments.

The Psychodynamic Perspective

Sigmund Freud (1933, 1917) believed that all children experience some degree of anxiety as part of growing up and that all use ego defense mechanisms to help control such anxiety (see pages 43–45). However, some children have particularly high levels of anxiety, or their defense mechanisms are particularly inadequate, and these individuals may develop generalized anxiety disorder.

Psychodynamic Explanations: When Childhood Anxiety Goes Unresolved

According to Freud, early developmental experiences may produce an unusually high level of anxiety in certain children. Say that a boy is spanked every time he cries for milk as an infant, messes his pants as a 2-year-old, and explores his genitals as a toddler. He may eventually come to believe that his various id impulses are very dangerous, and he may feel overwhelming anxiety whenever he has such impulses, setting the stage for generalized anxiety disorder.

Alternatively, a child's ego defense mechanisms may be too weak to cope with even normal levels of anxiety. Overprotected children, shielded by their parents from all frustrations and threats, have little opportunity to develop effective defense mechanisms. When they face the pressures of adult life, their defense mechanisms may be too weak to cope with the resulting anxieties.

Today's psychodynamic theorists often disagree with specific aspects of Freud's explanation for generalized anxiety disorder. Most continue to believe, however, that the disorder can be traced to inadequacies in the early relationships between children and their parents (Sharf, 2015). Researchers have tested the psychodynamic explanations in various ways. In one strategy, they have tried to show that people with generalized anxiety disorder are particularly likely to use defense mechanisms. For example, a classic investigation examined the early therapy transcripts of patients with this diagnosis and found that the patients often reacted defensively. When asked by therapists to discuss upsetting experiences, they would quickly forget (*repress*) what they had just been talking about, change the direction of the discussion, or deny having negative feelings (Luborsky, 1973).

In another line of research, investigators have studied people who as children suffered extreme punishment for id impulses. As psychodynamic theorists would predict, these people have higher levels of anxiety later in life (Parisette-Sparks & Kreitler, 2017; Wang, Wang, & Liu, 2016). In addition, several studies have supported the psychodynamic position that extreme protectiveness by parents may often lead to high levels of anxiety in their children (Howard et al., 2016; Manfredi et al., 2011).

#

#InsecureAdults?

Children may cling to blankets or cuddly toys to feel more secure. Adults, too, may hug a beloved object in order to relax: 1 in 5 women and 1 in 20 men admit to sleeping with a stuffed animal on a regular basis (Kanner, 1995).

Alex Gregory/The New Yorker Collection/The Cartoon Bank

"Since my mother was rarely home, I guess I blame my nanny."

#

#FearFilmFranchises

1. *Alien* (7 films)
2. *Saw* (7 films)
3. *Jaws* (4 films)
4. *Paranormal Activity* (6 films)
5. *Friday the 13th* (12 films)
6. *A Nightmare on Elm Street* (9 films)
7. *Scream* (4 films)
8. *The Conjuring* (3 films)
9. *Halloween* (10 films)
10. *The Exorcist* (5 films)

(Information from: Thompson, 2016)

Although these studies are consistent with psychodynamic explanations, some scientists question whether they show what they claim to show. When people have difficulty talking about upsetting events early in therapy, for example, they are not necessarily repressing those events. They may be focusing purposely on the positive aspects of their lives, or they may be too embarrassed to share personal negative events until they develop trust in the therapist.

Psychodynamic Therapies Psychodynamic therapists use the same general techniques to treat all psychological problems: *free association* and the therapist's interpretations of *transference, resistance*, and *dreams. Freudian psychodynamic therapists* use these methods to help clients with generalized anxiety disorder become less afraid of their id impulses and more successful in controlling them. Other psychodynamic therapists, particularly *object relations therapists,* use them to help anxious patients identify and settle the childhood relationship problems that continue to produce anxiety in adulthood (Mullin et al., 2017).

Controlled studies have typically found psychodynamic treatments to be of only modest help to persons with generalized anxiety disorder (Craske, 2018). An exception to this trend is *short-term psychodynamic therapy* (see Chapter 2), which has in some cases significantly reduced the levels of anxiety, worry, and social difficulty of patients with this disorder (Glasofer, 2017).

The Humanistic Perspective

Humanistic theorists propose that generalized anxiety disorder, like other psychological disorders, arises when people stop looking at themselves honestly and acceptingly. Repeated denials of their true thoughts, emotions, and behavior make these people extremely anxious and unable to fulfill their potential as human beings.

The humanistic view of why people develop this disorder is best illustrated by Carl Rogers' explanation. As you saw in Chapter 2, Rogers believed that children who fail to receive *unconditional positive regard* from others may become overly critical of themselves and develop harsh self-standards, what Rogers called *conditions of worth*. They try to meet these standards by repeatedly distorting and denying their true thoughts and experiences. Despite such efforts, however, threatening self-judgments keep breaking through and causing them intense anxiety. This onslaught of anxiety sets the stage for generalized anxiety disorder or some other form of psychological dysfunction.

Practitioners of Rogers' treatment approach, **client-centered therapy** (also called *person-centered therapy*), try to show unconditional positive regard for their clients and to empathize with them. The therapists hope that an atmosphere of genuine acceptance and caring will help clients feel secure enough to recognize their true needs, thoughts, and emotions. When clients eventually are honest and comfortable with themselves, their anxiety or other symptoms will subside. In the following excerpt, Rogers describes the progress made by a client with anxiety and related symptoms:

> *Therapy was an experiencing of her self, in all its aspects, in a safe relationship . . . the experiencing of self as having a capacity for wholeness . . . a self that cared about others. This last followed . . . the realization that the therapist cared, that it really mattered to him how therapy turned out for her, that he really valued her. . . . She gradually became aware of the fact that . . . there was nothing fundamentally bad, but rather, at heart she was positive and sound.*
>
> *(Rogers, 1954, pp. 261–264)*

Despite such optimistic case reports, controlled studies have failed to offer strong support for this approach. Although research does suggest that client-centered therapy is usually more helpful to anxious clients than no treatment, the approach is only sometimes superior to placebo therapy (Prochaska & Norcross, 2018). In addition, researchers

Walt Disney Studios Motion Pictures/Photofest

Animated anxiety In the animated film *Inside Out*, a young girl's five basic emotions (Fear, Joy, Sadness, Disgust, and Anger) come to life and guide her every behavior. More than a few clinicians note that the emotional figure named Fear (left) personifies the core symptoms of generalized anxiety disorder. Like people with this disorder, he is always looking for potential catastrophes and evaluating possible dangers—a mindset that leads to continuous worrying and tension.

have found, at best, only limited support for Rogers' explanation of generalized anxiety disorder and other forms of abnormal behavior. Nor have other humanistic theories and treatment received much research support.

The Cognitive-Behavioral Perspective

As you read in Chapter 2, followers of the cognitive-behavioral model suggest that psychological disorders are often caused by problematic behaviors and dysfunctional ways of thinking. Thus, their explanations and treatments focus on the nature of such behaviors and thoughts, how they are acquired, and how they influence feelings and emotions. Although cognitive-behavioral explanations and treatments center most often on *both* behavioral and cognitive dimensions of a given disorder, sometimes they focus primarily on one of these dimensions; such is the case with regard to generalized anxiety disorder, where many proponents of this model concentrate largely on the cognitive dimension of the disorder.

Maladaptive Assumptions Initially, cognitive-behavioral theorists suggested that generalized anxiety disorder is primarily caused by *maladaptive assumptions,* a notion that continues to be influential. Albert Ellis, for example, proposed that many people are guided by irrational beliefs that lead them to act and react in inappropriate ways (Ellis & Ellis, 2019; Ellis, 2016, 1962). Ellis called these **basic irrational assumptions,** and he claimed that people with generalized anxiety disorder often hold the following ones:

> "It is a dire necessity for an adult human being to be loved or approved of by virtually every significant other person in his community."
>
> "It is awful and catastrophic when things are not the way one would very much like them to be."
>
> "If something is or may be dangerous or fearsome, one should be terribly concerned about it and should keep dwelling on the possibility of its occurring."
>
> "One should be thoroughly competent, adequate, and achieving in all possible respects if one is to consider oneself worthwhile."
>
> (Ellis, 1962)

When people who make these assumptions are faced with a stressful event, such as an exam or a first date, they are likely to interpret it as dangerous, to overreact, and to feel fear. As they apply the assumptions to more and more events, they may begin to develop generalized anxiety disorder.

client-centered therapy The humanistic therapy developed by Carl Rogers in which clinicians try to help clients by being accepting, empathizing accurately, and conveying genuineness. Also known as *person-centered therapy.*

basic irrational assumptions The inaccurate and inappropriate beliefs held by people with various psychological problems, according to Albert Ellis.

Similarly, theorist Aaron Beck argued that people with generalized anxiety disorder constantly hold silent assumptions (for example, "A situation or a person is unsafe until proven to be safe" or "It is always best to assume the worst") that imply they are in imminent danger (Clark, 2018; Clark & Beck, 2012, 2010). Since the time of Ellis' and Beck's initial proposals, researchers have repeatedly found that people with generalized anxiety disorder do indeed hold maladaptive assumptions, particularly about dangerousness, and are, in turn, overattentive to potentially threatening stimuli (Craske, 2018; Goodwin, Yiend, & Hirsch, 2017).

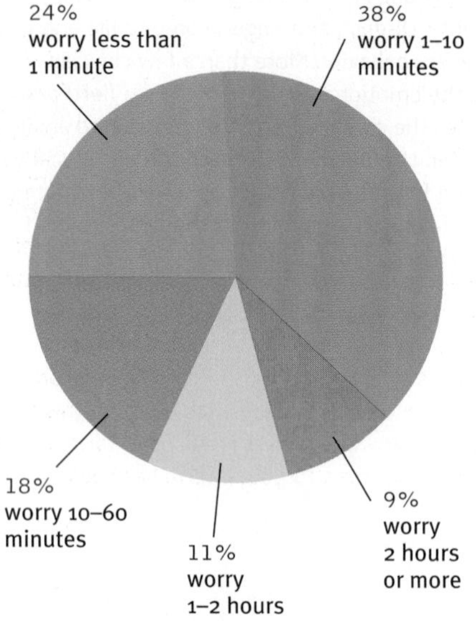

FIGURE 4-1

How Long Do Your Worries Last?

In one survey, 62 percent of college students said they spend less than 10 minutes at a time worrying about something. In contrast, 20 percent worry for more than an hour. (Information from: Tallis, 2015, 2014; Tallis et al., 1994.)

Newer Cognitive-Behavioral Explanations In recent years, several additional cognitive-behavioral explanations for generalized anxiety disorder have emerged. Each of them builds on the work of Ellis and Beck and their emphasis on danger.

The *metacognitive theory,* developed by the researcher Adrian Wells suggests that people with generalized anxiety disorder implicitly hold both positive and negative beliefs about worrying (Capobianco, Morrison, & Wells, 2018; Wells, 2014, 2011, 2005). On the positive side, they believe that worrying is a useful way of appraising and coping with threats in life. And so they look for and examine all possible signs of danger—that is, they worry constantly (see **Figure 4-1**).

Why might many people believe, at least implicitly, that worrying is useful—even necessary—for problems to work out?

At the same time, Wells argues, people with generalized anxiety disorder also hold negative beliefs about worrying, and these negative attitudes are the ones that open the door to the disorder. Because society teaches them that worrying is a bad thing, they come to believe that their repeated worrying is in fact harmful (mentally and physically) and uncontrollable. Now they further worry about the fact that they always seem to be worrying (so-called *meta-worries*). Their meta-worries may include concerns that they are "going crazy" with worry, making themselves ill with worry, or losing out in life because of worrying. The net effect of all this worrying: generalized anxiety disorder.

This explanation has received considerable research support. Studies indicate, for example, that people who generally hold both positive and negative beliefs about worrying are particularly prone to developing generalized anxiety disorder and that repeated metaworrying is a powerful predictor of developing the disorder (Baldwin, 2018; Wells, 2014, 2011, 2005).

According to another more recent explanation for generalized anxiety disorder, the *intolerance of uncertainty theory,* certain individuals cannot tolerate the knowledge that negative events *may* occur, even if the possibility of occurrence is very small. Inasmuch as life is filled with uncertain events, these individuals worry constantly that such events are about to occur. Such intolerance and worrying leave them highly vulnerable to the development of generalized anxiety disorder (Koerner, Meija, & Kusec, 2017; Dugas et al., 2012, 2010, 2004). Think of when you meet someone you're attracted to and how you then feel prior to texting or calling this person for the first time—or how you feel while you're waiting for the individual to contact you for the first time. The worry that you experience in such instances—the sense of unbearable uncertainty over the possibility of an unacceptable negative outcome—is, according to this theory, how people with generalized anxiety disorder feel all the time.

Proponents of this theory believe that people with generalized anxiety disorder keep worrying and worrying in their efforts to find "correct" solutions for various situations in their lives and to restore certainty to the situations. However, because they can never really be sure that a given solution is a correct one, they are always left to grapple with intolerable levels of uncertainty, triggering new rounds of worrying and new efforts to find correct solutions. Like the metacognitive theory of worry, considerable research supports this theory. Studies have found, for example, that people with generalized anxiety disorder display higher levels of intolerance of uncertainty than people with normal degrees of anxiety (Koerner et al., 2017; Dugas et al., 2012, 2004). Research also

rational-emotive therapy A cognitive therapy developed by Albert Ellis that helps clients identify and change the irrational assumptions and thinking that help cause their psychological disorder.

suggests that intolerance of uncertainty develops in early childhood and can be passed on from parents to children (Osmanağaoğlu et al., 2018; Sanchez et al., 2017, 2016).

Finally, a third relatively recent explanation for generalized anxiety disorder, the *avoidance theory*, developed by researcher Thomas Borkovec, suggests that people with this disorder have greater bodily arousal (higher heart rate, perspiration, respiration) than other people and that worrying actually serves to *reduce* this arousal, perhaps by distracting the individuals from their unpleasant physical feelings (Baldwin, 2018; Borkovec, Alcaine, & Behar, 2004). In short, the avoidance theory holds that people with generalized anxiety disorder worry repeatedly in order to reduce or avoid uncomfortable states of bodily arousal. When, for example, they find themselves in an uncomfortable job situation or social relationship, they implicitly choose to worry about losing their job or losing a friend rather than having to stew in a state of intense negative arousal.

Productions/REX/Shutterstock

Fearful delights Many people enjoy the feeling of fear as long as it occurs under controlled circumstances, as when they are safely watching the tension grow in the hugely popular series of *Paranormal Activity* movies. These six films are among the most profitable ever made. In this scene from the first film, the lead character Katie tries to escape a supernatural presence in her house.

Borkovec's explanation has also been supported by numerous studies. Research reveals that people with generalized anxiety disorder experience particularly fast and intense bodily reactions, find such reactions overwhelming, worry more than other people upon becoming aroused, and successfully reduce their arousal whenever they worry (Owens et al., 2017; Hirsch et al., 2012).

Cognitive-Behavioral Therapies

Two kinds of cognitive-behavioral approaches are used in cases of generalized anxiety disorder. In one, based on the pioneering work of Ellis and Beck, therapists help clients change the maladaptive assumptions that characterize their disorder (Meichenbaum, 2017). In the other, "new-wave" cognitive-behavioral therapists (see page 53) help clients understand the special role that worrying may play in their disorder, modify their views about worrying, and change their behavioral reactions to such unnerving concerns.

CHANGING MALADAPTIVE ASSUMPTIONS Therapists using Ellis' technique of **rational-emotive therapy** point out the irrational assumptions held by clients, suggest more appropriate assumptions, and assign homework that gives the clients practice at challenging old assumptions and applying new ones (Ellis & Ellis, 2019; Ellis, 2016). Studies suggest that this and similar approaches bring at least modest relief to those suffering from generalized anxiety (Clark, 2018; Kishita & Laidlaw, 2017). Ellis' approach is illustrated in the following discussion between him and an anxious client who fears failure and disapproval at work, especially over a testing procedure that she has developed for her company:

Client: *I'm so distraught these days that I can hardly concentrate on anything for more than a minute or two at a time. My mind just keeps wandering to that damn testing procedure I devised, and that they've put so much money into; and whether it's going to work well or be just a waste of all that time and money. . . .*

Ellis: *Point one is that you must admit that you are telling yourself something to start your worrying going, and you must begin to look, and I mean really look, for the specific nonsense with which you keep reindoctrinating yourself. . . . The false statement is: "If, because my testing procedure doesn't work and I am functioning inefficiently on my job, my co-workers do not want me or approve of me, then I shall be a worthless person." . . .*

Client: *But if I want to do what my firm also wants me to do, and I am useless to them, aren't I also useless to me?*

(continued on the next page)

#DelayedDiagnosis

It is estimated that 45 percent of clients in treatment for generalized anxiety disorder had suffered from its symptoms for 2 or more years before being diagnosed correctly (Bandelow & Michaelis, 2015).

family pedigree study A research design in which investigators determine how many and which relatives of a person with a disorder have the same disorder.

benzodiazepines The most common group of antianxiety drugs, which includes Valium and Xanax.

gamma-aminobutyric acid (GABA) A neurotransmitter whose low activity in the brain's fear circuit has been linked to anxiety.

brain circuits Networks of brain structures that work together, triggering each other into action.

sedative-hypnotic drugs Drugs that calm people at lower doses and help them fall asleep at higher doses.

> Ellis: *No—not unless you think you are. You are frustrated, of course, if you want to set up a good testing procedure and you can't. But need you be desperately unhappy because you are frustrated? And need you deem yourself completely unworthwhile because you can't do one of the main things you want to do in life?*
>
> *(Ellis, 1962, pp. 160–165)*

BREAKING DOWN WORRYING Alternatively, some of today's new-wave cognitive-behavioral therapists specifically guide clients with generalized anxiety disorder to recognize and change their dysfunctional use of worrying (Craske & Bystritsky, 2017; Topper et al., 2017). They begin by educating the clients about the role of worrying in their disorder and have them observe their bodily arousal and cognitive responses across various life situations. In turn, the clients come to appreciate the triggers of their worrying, their misconceptions about worrying, and their misguided efforts to control their lives by worrying. As their insights grow, clients are expected to see the world as less threatening (and thus less arousing), try out more constructive ways of dealing with arousal, and worry less about the fact that they worry so much. Research indicates that a concentrated focus on worrying is indeed a helpful addition to the traditional cognitive-behavioral treatment for generalized anxiety disorder.

Treating individuals with generalized anxiety disorder by helping them to recognize their inclination to worry is similar to another cognitive-behavioral approach that has gained popularity in recent years. The approach, *mindfulness-based cognitive-behavioral therapy,* which you read about in Chapter 3, was brought into the mainstream by psychologist Steven Hayes and his colleagues as part of their broader treatment approach called *acceptance and commitment therapy* (Hayes, 2016). Here therapists help clients to become aware of their streams of thoughts, including their worries, as they are occurring and to *accept* such thoughts as mere events of the mind. By accepting their worries rather than trying to eliminate them, the clients are expected to be less upset by them and less influenced by them in their behaviors and life decisions. This is indeed what happens for many clients with generalized anxiety disorder when they receive this and related forms of treatment (Hoge et al., 2018; Kishita & Laidlaw, 2017).

Mindfulness-based therapy has also been applied to a range of other psychological problems, such as depression, posttraumatic stress disorder, personality disorders, and substance use disorders, often with promising results (Segal, 2017; Hayes, 2016). As we observed in Chapter 2, this cognitive-behavioral approach borrows heavily from a form of meditation called *mindfulness meditation,* which teaches people to pay attention to the thoughts and feelings that flow through their mind during meditation and to accept such thoughts in a nonjudgmental way.

The Biological Perspective

Biological theorists believe that generalized anxiety disorder is caused chiefly by biological factors. For years this claim was supported primarily by **family pedigree studies,** in which researchers determine how many and which relatives of a person with a disorder have the same disorder. If biological tendencies toward generalized anxiety disorder are inherited, people who are biologically related should have similar probabilities of developing this disorder. Studies have in fact found that biological relatives of persons with generalized anxiety disorder are more likely than nonrelatives to have the disorder also (Havinga et al., 2017; Schienle et al., 2011). Approximately 15 percent of the relatives of people with the disorder display it themselves—a much higher prevalence rate than that found in the general population. And the closer the relative (an identical twin, for example), the greater the likelihood that he or she will also have the disorder.

#

#MostGoogledSymptoms

1. Infection symptoms
2. Measles symptoms
3. Gastritis symptoms
4. **Anxiety symptoms**
5. Heat stroke symptoms

(Drain, 2016)

Biological Explanations In recent decades, important discoveries by brain researchers have offered clearer evidence that generalized anxiety disorder is related to biological factors (Shinba, 2017). One of the first such discoveries was made in the 1950s, when investigators determined that **benzodiazepines,** the family of drugs that includes *alprazolam* (Xanax), *lorazepam* (Ativan), and *diazepam* (Valium), provide relief from anxiety. At first, no one understood why benzodiazepines reduce anxiety. Eventually, however, researchers were able to pinpoint the exact neurons in the brain to which benzodiazepines travel (Mohler & Okada, 1977). Apparently certain neurons have receptors that receive the benzodiazepines, just as a lock receives a key.

University of Wisconsin Primate Library, Madison

Do monkeys experience anxiety? Clinical researchers must be careful in interpreting the reactions of animal subjects. This infant monkey was considered "fearful" after being separated from its mother. But perhaps it was feeling depressed or experiencing arousal that does not correspond to either fear or depression.

Investigators then discovered that these benzodiazepine receptors ordinarily receive **gamma-aminobutyric acid (GABA),** a common neurotransmitter in the brain (Müller et al., 2017). As you read in Chapter 2, neurotransmitters are chemicals that carry messages from one neuron to another. GABA carries *inhibitory* messages: when GABA is received at a receptor, it causes the neuron to stop firing. Initially, researchers believed that GABA activity throughout the brain must be deficient in people with generalized anxiety disorder (Salari, Bakhtiari, & Homberg, 2015; Bremner & Charney, 2010). However, research conducted in this century indicates that the biological basis of generalized anxiety disorder is more complicated than the disturbed activity of this single neurotransmitter.

Investigators now know that our everyday fear reactions—like most other emotional, behavioral, and cognitive reactions—are tied to **brain circuits,** networks of brain structures that work together, triggering each other into action. As you read in Chapter 2, in a given brain circuit, the long axons of the neurons from one structure bundle together, extend across the brain, and use neurotransmitters to communicate with the neurons of another structure—thus setting up interconnecting fiber pathways between the structures (see pages 38–39). The particular circuit that produces and manages fear reactions, often called the "fear circuit," includes such brain structures as the *prefrontal cortex, anterior cingulate cortex, insula,* and *amygdala,* a small almond-shaped brain structure that usually starts the emotional ball rolling (see **Figure 4-2**).

Studies reveal that the fear circuit is excessively active (that is, *hyperactive*) in people with generalized anxiety disorder, producing experiences of fear and worry that are excessive in number and duration (Weber-Goericke & Muehlhan, 2019; Williams, 2017). In turn, many theorists have concluded that such fear circuit hyperactivity is responsible for the development of the disorder (Mohlman et al., 2017; Duval et al., 2015). GABA is one of the important neurotransmitters at work in this circuit (particularly in the amygdala), so low GABA activity could indeed help produce excessive communications between the structures in this circuit and, as initially suggested, contribute to the development of generalized anxiety disorder. At the same time, improper functioning by various neurons, structures, interconnections, or other neurotransmitters throughout the fear circuit can also lead to broad circuit hyperactivity and contribute to the development of generalized anxiety disorder (Yao et al., 2017).

FIGURE 4-2

The Biology of Anxiety

The circuit in the brain that helps produce anxiety reactions includes structures such as the amygdala, prefrontal cortex, anterior cingulate cortex, and insula (not visible from this view of the brain).

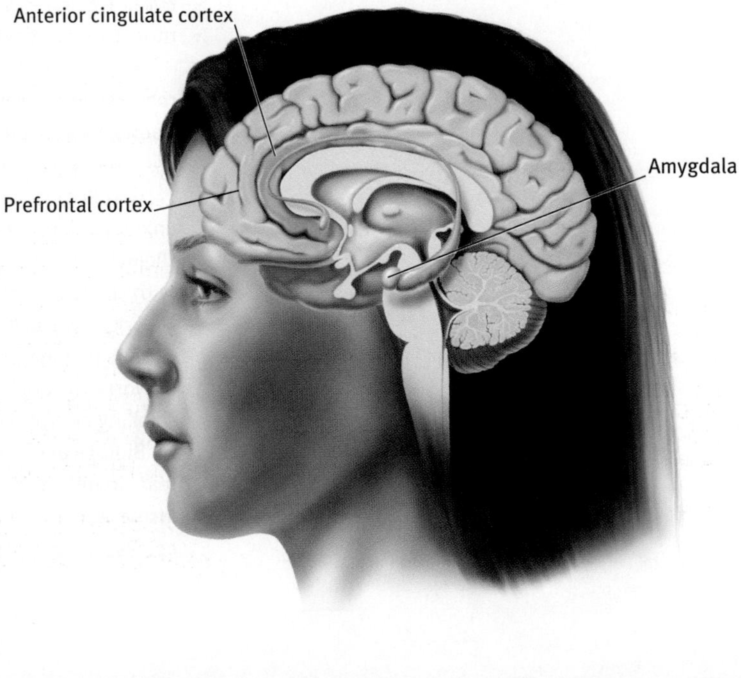

Drug Therapies After their discovery in the 1950s, benzodiazepines were marketed as **sedative-hypnotic drugs**—drugs that calm people in low doses and help them fall asleep in higher doses. The benzodiazepines seemed less addictive than previous sedative-hypnotic medications, such as *barbiturates,* and they appeared to produce less tiredness. Thus, these newly discovered drugs were quickly embraced by both doctors and patients, and many new ones were developed to help alleviate anxiety (see **Table 4-3** on the next page).

As you have read, researchers eventually learned that benzodiazepines reduce anxiety by traveling to receptor sites in the brain circuit—particularly in the amygdala—that ordinarily receive the neurotransmitter GABA. Apparently, when benzodiazepines bind to these neuron receptor sites, they increase the ability of GABA itself to bind to the sites and to stop neurons from firing, thus helping to improve the overall functioning of the fear circuit and, in turn, reducing an individual's excessive levels of anxiety (Bystritsky, 2018; Muller et al., 2017).

Studies indicate that as many as 60 percent of people with generalized anxiety disorder experience at least some improvement when they take benzodiazepines, compared to 40 percent of similar individuals who take placebo drugs (Bystritsky, 2018; Islam et al., 2014). However, clinicians have come to realize that these drugs pose significant problems. First, the effects of the medications are short-lived. When they are stopped, anxiety returns as strong as ever. Second, people who take benzodiazepines in large doses for an extended time can become physically dependent on them. Third, the drugs can produce undesirable effects such as drowsiness, lack of coordination, memory loss, depression, and aggressive behavior. Finally, the drugs mix badly with certain other drugs or substances. If, for example, people on benzodiazepines drink even small amounts of alcohol, their breathing can slow down dangerously (Bystritsky, 2018).

Why are antianxiety drugs so popular in today's world? Does their popularity say something about our society?

Thus over the past two decades, other kinds of drugs have become more widely prescribed for people with generalized anxiety disorder. The treatment of choice is now *antidepressant* medications, drugs that are usually used to lift the moods of depressed persons. Like benzodiazepines, these drugs bring at least some relief to 60 percent of the people with generalized anxiety disorder who take them (Bystritsky, 2018). As you will see in Chapter 6, antidepressant drugs often increase the activity of the neurotransmitters *serotonin* and *norepinephrine*. These two neurotransmitters are prominent in certain parts of the fear circuit (LeDoux & Pine, 2016; Bukalo, Pinard, & Holmes, 2014). The antidepressant drugs may help relieve anxiety by improving the functioning of the fear circuit in these areas.

Finally, *antipsychotic* medications, drugs commonly given to people with schizophrenia and other forms of psychosis, are also helpful to some individuals with generalized anxiety disorder (Bystritsky, 2018). These drugs may help relieve anxiety by altering the activity of *dopamine*, yet another neurotransmitter of importance in certain parts of the fear circuit (Bukalo et al., 2014).

TABLE: 4-3

Common Benzodiazepine Drugs

Generic Name	Trade Name
Alprazolam	Xanax
Chlordiazepoxide	Librium
Clonazepam	Klonopin
Clorazepate	Tranxene
Diazepam	Valium
Estazolam	ProSom
Lorazepam	Ativan
Midazolam	Versed
Oxazepam	Serax

9... SUMMING UP

GENERALIZED ANXIETY DISORDER People with generalized anxiety disorder experience excessive anxiety and worry about a wide range of events and activities. According to the sociocultural view, societal dangers, economic stress, or related racial and cultural pressures may create a climate in which cases of generalized anxiety disorder are more likely to develop.

In the original psychodynamic explanation, Freud said that generalized anxiety disorder may develop when anxiety is excessive and defense mechanisms break down and function poorly. Psychodynamic therapists use free association, interpretation, and related psychodynamic techniques to help people overcome this problem.

Carl Rogers, the leading humanistic theorist, believed that people with generalized anxiety disorder fail to receive unconditional positive regard from significant others during their childhood and so become overly critical of themselves. He treated such individuals with client-centered therapy.

Cognitive-behavioral theorists believe that generalized anxiety disorder is caused by various maladaptive assumptions and/or inaccurate beliefs about the power and value of worrying. Cognitive-behavioral therapists help their clients change their maladaptive thinking and/or dysfunctional uses of worrying.

Biological theorists hold that generalized anxiety disorder results from a hyperactive fear circuit, a brain circuit that includes the prefrontal cortex, anterior cingulate cortex, insula, and amygdala. Common biological treatments are antidepressant drugs, benzodiazepines, and antipsychotic drugs.

Phobias

A **phobia** is a persistent and unreasonable fear of a particular object, activity, or situation. People with a phobia (from the Greek word for "fear") become fearful if they even think about the object or situation they dread, but they usually remain comfortable as long as they avoid it or thoughts about it.

We all have our areas of special fear, and it is normal for some things to upset us more than other things (see ***InfoCentral*** on the next page). How do such common fears differ from phobias? DSM-5 indicates that a phobia is more intense and persistent and the desire to avoid the object or situation is stronger (APA, 2013). People with phobias often feel so much distress that their fears may interfere dramatically with their lives.

Most phobias technically fall under the category of *specific phobias,* DSM-5's label for an intense and persistent fear of a specific object or situation. In addition, there is a broader kind of phobia called *agoraphobia,* a fear of venturing into public places or situations in which escape might be difficult if one were to become panicky or incapacitated.

phobia A persistent and unreasonable fear of a particular object, activity, or situation.

specific phobia A severe and persistent fear of a specific object or situation.

Specific Phobias

A **specific phobia** is a persistent fear of a specific object or situation (see **Table 4-4**). When sufferers are exposed to the object or situation, they typically experience immediate fear. Common specific phobias are intense fears of specific animals or insects, heights, enclosed spaces, thunderstorms, and blood. Here Andrew talks about his phobic fear of flying:

> *We got on board, and then there was the take-off. There it was again, that horrible feeling as we gathered speed. It was creeping over me again, that old feeling of panic. I kept seeing everyone as puppets, all strapped to their seats with no control over their destinies, me included. Every time the plane did a variation of speed or route, my heart would leap and I would hurriedly ask what was happening. When the plane started to lose height, I was terrified that we were about to crash.*
>
> *(Melville, 1978, p. 59)*

Each year as many as 10 percent of all people in the United States have the symptoms of a specific phobia (McCabe, 2018; Bandelow & Michaelis, 2015; Kessler et al., 2012). Almost 14 percent of individuals develop such phobias at some point during their lives, and many people have more than one at a time. Women with the disorder outnumber men by at least 2 to 1.

TABLE: 4-4

Dx Checklist

Specific Phobia
1. Marked, persistent, and disproportionate fear of a particular object or situation; usually lasting at least 6 months.
2. Exposure to the object or situation produces immediate fear.
3. Avoidance of the feared situation.
4. Significant distress or impairment.

Information from: APA 2013.

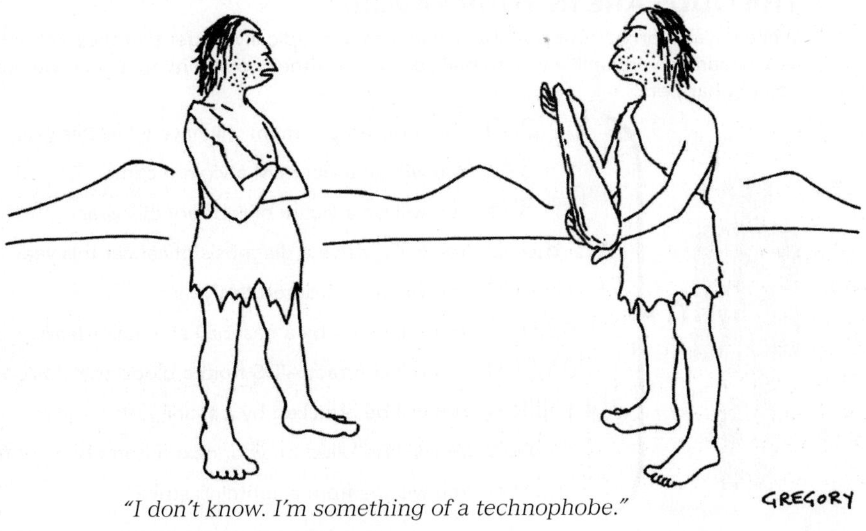

"I don't know. I'm something of a technophobe."

Alex Gregory/The New Yorker Collection/The Cartoon Bank

FEAR

Fear is a normal part of life. Like all emotions, it can be good or bad. On the positive side, fear can alert us to danger, help us behave constructively, and guide us to make wise decisions. Up to a point it can be stimulating and even fun. On the negative side, fear can be excessive and inappropriate and contribute to phobias and other anxiety disorders.

CROSSING THE LINE

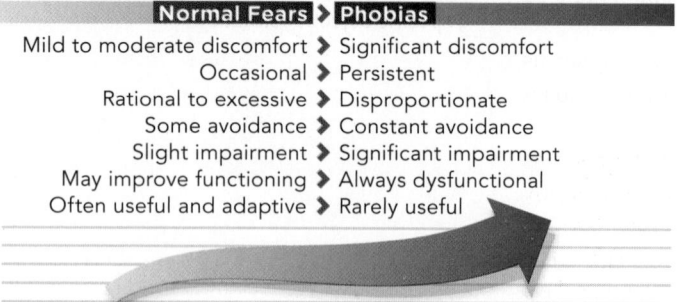

Normal Fears	Phobias
Mild to moderate discomfort	Significant discomfort
Occasional	Persistent
Rational to excessive	Disproportionate
Some avoidance	Constant avoidance
Slight impairment	Significant impairment
May improve functioning	Always dysfunctional
Often useful and adaptive	Rarely useful

FEARS HELP US TO:

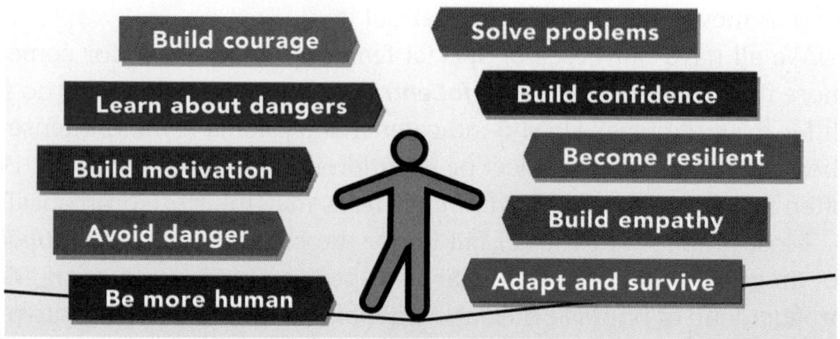

(Sam, 2016)

HOW TO CONQUER OUR FEARS

Clinicians have developed special techniques — such as exposure-based treatments — to help people overcome pathological fear. However, there are a number of things people can do on their own to help reduce their problematic everyday fears. Some of these things are but minor-league versions of exposure therapy and other clinical treatments.

- Perform increasingly frightening acts
- Employ simple deep breathing
- Exercise
- Participate in relaxing activities (e.g., listen to music)
- Challenge scary thoughts with evidence
- Gradually and repeatedly face the fear
- Recall past fears you have resolved
- Don't let unreasonable fears guide your decisions or behaviors

(Smith et al., 2017)

BIGGEST FEARS IN TODAY'S WORLD

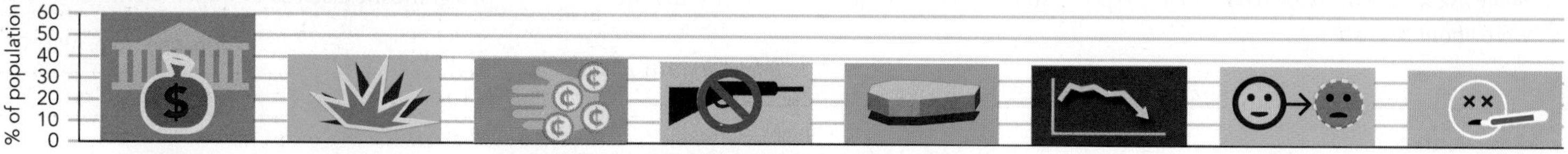

	% of population
Corruption of government officials	60.6%
Terrorist attacks	41%
Not having enough money for the future	39.9%
Government regulations of firearms and ammunition	38.5%
Death of loved ones	38.1%
Economic or financial collapse	37.5%
Identity theft	37.1%
Serious illness of loved ones	35.9%

(Bowerman, 2016)

BIGGEST EXISTENTIAL FEARS

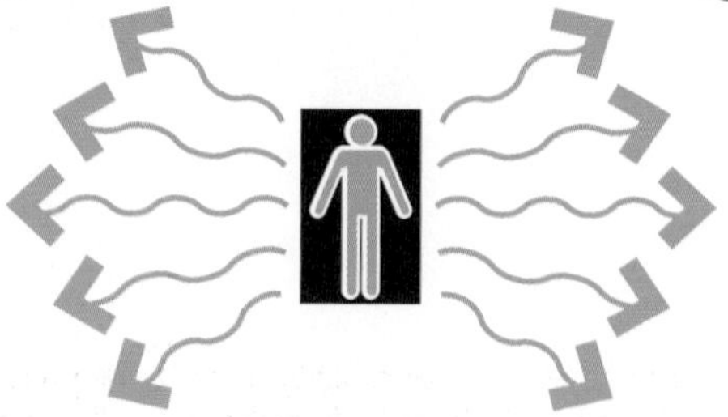

- Failure
- Death
- Rejection
- Ridicule
- Misery
- Disappointment
- Pain
- The unknown
- Loss of freedom
- Inadequacy
- Being judged
- Change
- Loneliness
- Uncertainty
- Separation
- Being unimportant
- Deprivation

(McGauran, 2016; Wisehart, 2015)

THE ODDS ARE IN YOUR FAVOR!

While we all worry about possible calamities, we typically forget that they are unlikely — sometimes very unlikely — to happen. What is the probability that what we fear will actually happen?

1 in	
200	Your house/apartment will have a fire this year
322	You will be a victim of a violent crime
885	You will be a victim of robbery this year
8,000	You will receive a diagnosis of cancer this year
20,000	You will be murdered this year
42,000	You will be hit by a baseball at a major-league game
286,000	You will contract AIDS from a blood transfusion
4 million	You will be attacked by a shark
4 million	You will be killed on your next automobile outing
10 million	You will die from a lightning strike

(FBI, 2017, 2014; Glovin, 2014; CDC, 2013; Quillian & Pager, 2010; Britt, 2005)

The impact of a specific phobia on a person's life depends on what arouses the fear (McCabe, 2018). People whose phobias center on dogs, insects, or water will keep encountering the objects they dread. Their efforts to avoid them must be elaborate and may greatly restrict their activities. Urban residents with snake phobias have a much easier time. At most, 32 percent of people with a specific phobia seek treatment (McCabe, 2018; NIMH, 2017). Most individuals with the disorder try instead to avoid the objects they fear.

Agoraphobia

People with **agoraphobia** are afraid of being in public places or situations in which escape might be difficult or help unavailable, should they experience panic or become incapacitated (APA, 2013) (see **Table 4-5**). This is a pervasive and complex phobia. Around 1.7 percent of the population experience agoraphobia in any given year; around 2.6 percent display it at some point in their lives. The disorder also is twice as common among women as men and among poor people as wealthy people (Bandelow & Michaelis, 2015; Kessler et al., 2012; Sareen et al., 2011). Around 46 percent of those with agoraphobia receive treatment for it (NIMH, 2017).

It is typical of people with agoraphobia to avoid entering crowded streets or stores, driving in parking lots or on bridges, and traveling on public transportation or in airplanes. If they venture out of the house at all, it is usually only in the company of close relatives or friends. Some insist that family members or friends stay with them at home, but even at home and in the company of others they may continue to feel anxious.

In many cases the intensity of the agoraphobia fluctuates. In severe cases, people become virtual prisoners in their own homes. Their social life dwindles and they cannot hold a job. People with agoraphobia may also become depressed, sometimes as a result of the severe limitations that their disorder places on their lives (McCabe, 2018).

Many people with agoraphobia do, in fact, have extreme and sudden explosions of fear, called *panic attacks,* when they enter public places, a problem that may have first set the stage for their development of agoraphobia. Such individuals may receive two diagnoses—agoraphobia and *panic disorder,* an anxiety disorder that you will read about later in this chapter—because their difficulties extend considerably beyond an excessive fear of venturing away from home into public places (APA, 2013).

TABLE: 4-5

Dx Checklist

Agoraphobia
1. Pronounced, disproportionate, or repeated fear about being in at least two of the following situations: • Public transportation (e.g., auto or plane travel) • Parking lots, bridges, or other open spaces • Shops, theaters, or other confined places • Lines or crowds • Away from home unaccompanied
2. Fear of such agoraphobic situations derives from a concern that it would be hard to escape or get help if panic, embarrassment, or disabling symptoms were to occur.
3. Avoidance of the agoraphobic situations.
4. Symptoms usually continue for at least 6 months.
5. Significant distress or impairment.

Information from: APA, 2013.

What Causes Phobias?

Each of the models offers explanations for phobias. Those offered by *cognitive-behavioral* theorists have received the most research support. Focusing primarily on the behavioral dimension of this disorder, they believe that people with phobias first learn to fear certain objects, situations, or events through conditioning (McCabe, 2018). Once the fears are acquired, the individuals avoid the dreaded object or situation, permitting the fears to become all the more entrenched.

How Are Fears Learned? Many cognitive-behavioral theorists propose **classical conditioning** as a common way of acquiring phobic reactions. Here, two events that occur close together in time become strongly associated in a person's mind, and the person then reacts similarly to both of them. If one event triggers a fear response, the other may also.

In the 1920s, a clinician described the case of a young woman who apparently acquired a specific phobia of running water through classical conditioning (Bagby, 1922). When she was 7 years old she went on a picnic with her mother and aunt and ran off by herself into the woods after lunch. While she was climbing over some large

agoraphobia An anxiety disorder in which a person is afraid to be in public situations from which escape might be difficult or help unavailable if panic-like or embarrassing symptoms were to occur.

classical conditioning A process of learning in which two events that repeatedly occur close together in time become tied together in a person's mind and so produce the same response.

Phobias, not Although these young women cling tightly to each other, frozen with fear as they try to walk across a bridge, they are not displaying abnormal fear or a phobia. A closer look reveals that the bridge, which stands 600 feet high and spans 1000 feet, has a glass floor, the first of its kind in China. Almost all visitors to this new tourist destination initially experience the same emotional reaction—overwhelming and near-paralyzing fear.

rocks, her feet became caught between two rocks. The harder she tried to free herself, the more trapped she became. No one heard her screams, and she grew more and more terrified. In the language of behaviorists, the entrapment was eliciting a fear response.

Entrapment → Fear response

As she struggled to free her feet, the girl heard a waterfall nearby. The sound of the running water became linked in her mind to her terrifying battle with the rocks, and she developed a fear of running water as well.

Running water → Fear response

Eventually the aunt found the screaming child, freed her from the rocks, and comforted her, but the psychological damage had been done. From that day forward, the girl was terrified of running water. For years family members had to hold her down to bathe her. When she traveled on a train, friends had to cover the windows so that she would not have to look at any streams. The young woman had apparently acquired a specific phobia through classical conditioning.

In conditioning terms, the entrapment was an *unconditioned stimulus* (*US*) that understandably elicited an *unconditioned response* (*UR*) of fear. The running water represented a *conditioned stimulus* (*CS*), a formerly neutral stimulus that became associated with entrapment in the child's mind and came also to elicit a fear reaction. The newly acquired fear was a *conditioned response* (*CR*).

US: Entrapment → R: Fear

CS: Running water → R: Fear

Another way of acquiring a fear reaction is through **modeling,** that is, through observation and imitation (Bandura & Rosenthal, 1966). A person may observe that others are afraid of certain objects or events and develop fears of the same things. Consider a young boy whose mother is afraid of illness, doctors, and hospitals. If she frequently expresses those fears, before long the boy himself may fear illness, doctors, and hospitals.

Why should one or a few upsetting experiences or observations develop into a long-term phobia? Shouldn't the trapped girl see later that running water will bring her no harm? Shouldn't the boy see later that illnesses are temporary and doctors and hospitals helpful? Cognitive-behavioral theorists believe that after acquiring a fear response, people try to *avoid* what they fear. They do not get close to the dreaded objects often enough to learn that the objects are really quite harmless.

How Have Cognitive-Behavioral Explanations Fared in Research? Some laboratory studies have found that animals and humans can indeed be taught to fear objects through classical conditioning (Miller, 1948; Mowrer, 1947, 1939). In one famous report, psychologists John B. Watson and Rosalie Rayner (1920) described how they taught a baby boy called Little Albert to fear white rats. For weeks Albert was allowed to play with a white rat and appeared to enjoy doing so. One time when Albert reached for the rat, however, the experimenter struck a steel bar with a hammer, making a very loud noise that frightened Albert. The next several times that Albert reached for the rat, the experimenter again made the loud noise. Albert acquired a fear and avoidance response to the rat.

What concerns might today's human-participant research review boards raise about the study on Little Albert?

Research has also supported the cognitive-behavioral position that fears can be acquired through modeling. In a pioneering study, for example, psychologists Albert

modeling A process of learning in which a person observes and then imitates others. Also, a therapy approach based on the same principle.

preparedness A predisposition to develop certain fears.

exposure treatment Treatment in which persons are exposed to the objects or situations they dread.

systematic desensitization An exposure treatment that uses relaxation training and a fear hierarchy to help clients with phobias react calmly to the objects or situations they dread.

Bandura and Theodore Rosenthal (1966) had human research participants observe a person apparently being shocked by electricity whenever a buzzer sounded. The victim was actually the experimenter's accomplice—in research terminology, a *confederate*—who pretended to feel pain by twitching and yelling whenever the buzzer was turned on. After the unsuspecting participants had observed several such episodes, they themselves had a fear reaction whenever they heard the buzzer. Similarly, some studies on children with real-life fears and phobias have found that modeling played a key role in the acquisition of such problems (Reynolds et al., 2017).

Although these studies support cognitive-behavioral explanations of phobias, other research has called those explanations into question (McCabe, 2018). Several laboratory studies with children and adults have failed to condition fear reactions. In addition, although many case studies have traced phobias to incidents of classical conditioning or modeling, quite a few fail to do so. So, although it appears that a phobia *can* be acquired by classical conditioning or modeling, researchers have not established that the disorder is *ordinarily* acquired in this way.

A Behavioral-Evolutionary Explanation Some phobias are much more common than others. Phobic reactions to animals, heights, and darkness are more common than phobic reactions to meat, grass, and houses. Theorists often account for these differences by proposing that human beings, as a species, have a predisposition to develop certain fears (McCabe, 2018; McNally, 2016). This idea is referred to as **preparedness** because human beings, theoretically, are "prepared" to acquire some phobias and not others. The following case makes the point:

> *A four-year-old girl was playing in the park. Thinking that she saw a snake, she ran to her parents' car and jumped inside, slamming the door behind her. Unfortunately, the girl's hand was caught by the closing car door, the results of which were severe pain and several visits to the doctor. Before this, she may have been afraid of snakes, but not phobic. After this experience, a phobia developed, not of cars or car doors, but of snakes. The snake phobia persisted into adulthood, at which time she sought treatment from me.*
>
> *(Marks, 1977, p. 192)*

Courtesy Ko Kobayakawa

BFF Is a mouse's fear of cats a conditioned reaction or genetically hardwired? Scientists at Tokyo University used genetic engineering to switch off this rodent's instinct to cower at the smell or presence of cats. But mouse beware! The cat has not been genetically engineered correspondingly.

Where might such predispositions to fear come from? According to some theorists, the predispositions have been transmitted genetically through an evolutionary process. Among our ancestors, the ones who more readily acquired fears of animals, darkness, heights, and the like were more likely to survive long enough to reproduce and to pass on their fear inclinations to their offspring (McNally, 2016; Ohman & Mineka, 2003).

How Are Phobias Treated?

Every theoretical model has its own approach to treating phobias, but the cognitive-behavioral approach is more widely used and, according to research, more successful than the rest, particularly for specific phobias. Here again, practitioners of the model focus primarily on the behavioral dimension of phobias.

Treatments for Specific Phobias Specific phobias were among the first anxiety disorders to be treated successfully. The major cognitive-behavioral approach to treating them is **exposure treatment,** an approach in which people are exposed to the objects or situations they dread (McCabe & Swinson, 2017). There are actually a number of different exposure techniques. Three of the oldest, and most famous, are *systematic desensitization, flooding,* and *modeling.*

People treated by **systematic desensitization,** an exposure technique developed by Joseph Wolpe (1987, 1969), learn to relax while gradually facing the objects or situations they fear. Since relaxation and fear are incompatible, the new relaxation response

Boris Horvat/Getty Images

The world of exposure At a treatment program in France, this man undergoes exposure therapy to help him overcome acrophobia, a severe fear of heights. Wearing a virtual reality headset, he feels as if he is approaching a vast, deep canyon. Virtual reality techniques have greatly expanded the kinds of exposure available to clients receiving treatment for various anxiety disorders or OCD.

is thought to substitute for the fear response. Desensitization therapists first offer *relaxation training* to clients, teaching them how to bring on a state of deep muscle relaxation at will. In addition, the therapists help clients create a *fear hierarchy,* a list of feared objects or situations, ordered from mildly to extremely upsetting.

Then clients learn how to pair relaxation with the objects or situations they fear. While the client is in a state of relaxation, the therapist has the client face the event at the bottom of his or her hierarchy. This may be an actual confrontation, a process called *in vivo desensitization.* A person who fears heights, for example, may stand on a chair or climb a stepladder. Or the confrontation may be imagined, a process called *covert desensitization.* In this case, the person imagines the frightening event while the therapist describes it. The client moves through the entire list, pairing his or her relaxation responses with each feared item. Because the first item is only mildly frightening, it is usually only a short while before the person is able to relax totally in its presence. Over the course of several sessions, clients move up the ladder of their fears until they reach and overcome the one that frightens them most of all.

Another exposure treatment for specific phobias is **flooding.** Therapists who use flooding believe that people will stop fearing things when they are exposed to them repeatedly and made to see that they are actually quite harmless. Clients are forced to face their feared objects or situations without relaxation training and without a gradual buildup. The flooding procedure, like desensitization, can be either in vivo or covert.

When flooding therapists guide clients in imagining feared objects or situations, they often exaggerate the description so that the clients experience intense emotional arousal. In the case of a woman with a snake phobia, the therapist had her imagine the following scene, among others:

> *Close your eyes again. Picture the snake out in front of you, now make yourself pick it up. Reach down, pick it up, put it in your lap, feel it wiggling around in your lap, leave your hand on it, put your hand out and feel it wiggling around. Kind of explore its body with your fingers and hand. You don't like to do it, make yourself do it. Make yourself do it. Really grab onto the snake. Squeeze it a little bit, feel it. Feel it kind of start to wind around your hand. Let it. Leave your hand there, feel it touching your hand and winding around it, curling around your wrist.*
>
> *(Hogan, 1968, p. 423)*

In another exposure technique, *modeling,* it is the therapist who confronts the feared object or situation while the fearful person observes (Bandura, 2011, 1977, 1971; Bandura et al., 1977). The therapist acts as a model to demonstrate that the person's fear is groundless. After several sessions many clients are able to approach the objects or situations calmly. In one version of modeling, *participant modeling,* the client is actively encouraged to join in with the therapist.

Clinical researchers have repeatedly found that these and other exposure treatments help people with specific phobias. Around 70 percent of phobic patients show significant improvement after receiving exposure treatment (McCabe & Swinson, 2017; Ryan et al., 2017). The key to greater success in all forms of exposure treatment appears to be *actual* contact with the feared object or situation. That is, in vivo exposure tends to be more effective than covert exposure. It is also worth noting that a growing number of cognitive-behavioral therapists are using *virtual reality*—3D computer graphics that

flooding An exposure treatment for phobias in which clients are exposed repeatedly and intensively to a feared object and made to see that it is actually harmless.

simulate real-world objects and situations—as an exposure tool, and are having considerable success with this approach (Costa et al., 2018). As you'll see in Chapter 5, the exposures provided by this computer tool are so intense that they often are as powerful as real-life exposures.

Treatments for Agoraphobia For years clinicians made little impact on agoraphobia, the fear of leaving one's home and entering public places. However, approaches have now been developed that enable many people with agoraphobia to venture out with less anxiety. These new approaches do not always bring as much relief to sufferers as the highly successful treatments for specific phobias, but they do offer considerable relief to many people.

Cognitive-behavioral therapists have again led the way, this time by developing a variety of exposure approaches for agoraphobia (Gloster et al., 2017, 2015, 2014; Klan, Jasper, & Hiller, 2017). The therapists typically help clients to venture farther and farther from their homes and to gradually enter outside places, one step at a time. Sometimes the clinicians use support, reasoning, and coaxing to get clients to confront the outside world. They also use more precise exposure methods, such as those described in the following case study:

Ocean/Corbis

Recovering lost revenues Several amusement parks offer behavioral programs to help prospective customers overcome their fears of roller coasters and other horror rides. After "treatment," some clients are able to ride the rails with the best of them. For others, it's back to the relative calm of the Ferris wheel.

[Lenita] was a young woman who, shortly after she married, found herself unable to leave home. Even walking a few yards from her front door terrified her. . . .

It is not surprising . . . that this young woman found herself unable to function independently after leaving home to marry. Her inability to leave her new home was reinforced by an increasing dependence on her husband and by the solicitous overconcern of her mother, who was more and more frequently called in to stay with her. . . . Since she was cut off from her friends and from so much enjoyment in the outside world, depression added to her misery. . . .

[After several years of worsening symptoms, Lenita was admitted to our psychiatric hospital.] To measure [her] improvement, we laid out a mile-long course from the hospital to downtown, marked at about 25-yard intervals. Before beginning [treatment], we asked the patient to walk as far as she could along the course. Each time she balked at the front door of the hospital. Then the first phase of [treatment] began: we held two sessions each day in which the patient was praised for staying out of the hospital for a longer and longer time. The reinforcement schedule was simple. If the patient stayed outside for 20 seconds on one trial and then on the next attempt stayed out for 30 seconds, she was praised enthusiastically. Now, however, the criterion for praise was raised—without the patient's knowledge—to 25 seconds. If she met the criterion she was again praised, and the time was increased again. If she did not stay out long enough, the therapist simply ignored her performance. To gain the therapist's attention, which she valued, she had to stay out longer each time.

This she did, until she was able to stay out for almost half an hour. But was she walking farther each time? Not at all. She was simply circling around in the front drive of the hospital, keeping the "safe place" in sight at all times. We therefore changed the reinforcement to reflect the distance walked. Now she began to walk farther and farther each time. Supported by this simple therapeutic procedure, the patient was progressively able to increase her self-confidence. . . .

Praise was then thinned out, but slowly, and the patient was encouraged to walk anywhere she pleased. Five years later, she [is] still perfectly well. We might assume that the benefits of being more independent maintained the gains and compensated for the loss of praise from the therapist.

(Agras, 1985, pp. 77–80)

#WrongSuffix?

In 2012, the Associated Press banned its reporters from using the increasingly popular suffix "-phobia" when describing people who are intolerant of particular groups of individuals. The news organization's reason was that such uses of the suffix—for example, "homophobia," "xenophobia," "Islamophobia," and "transphobia"—inaccurately ascribes a mental disability to prejudiced people, suggesting a knowledge the reporters (and society) do not have (Hess, 2016).

Exposure therapy for people with agoraphobia often includes additional features—particularly the use of support groups and home-based self-help programs—to motivate

social anxiety disorder A severe and persistent fear of social or performance situations in which embarrassment may occur.

clients to work hard at their treatment. In the *support group* approach, a small number of people with agoraphobia go out together for exposure sessions that last for several hours. The group members support and encourage one another, and eventually coax one another to move away from the safety of the group and perform exposure tasks on their own. In the *home-based self-help programs,* clinicians give clients and their families detailed instructions for carrying out exposure treatments themselves.

Around 70 percent of agoraphobic clients who receive exposure treatment find it easier to enter public places, and the improvement persists for years (Gloster et al., 2017, 2015, 2014; Craske & Barlow, 2014). Unfortunately, these improvements are often partial rather than complete, and as many as half of successfully treated clients have relapses, although these people readily recapture previous gains if they are treated again. Those whose agoraphobia is accompanied by a panic disorder seem to benefit less than others from exposure therapy alone (Craske, 2017). We shall take a closer look at this group when we investigate treatments for panic disorder.

... SUMMING UP

PHOBIAS A phobia is a severe, persistent, and unreasonable fear of a particular object, activity, or situation. The two main categories of phobias are specific phobias and agoraphobia. Cognitive-behavioral theorists believe that phobias are often learned from the environment through classical conditioning or modeling and maintained by avoidance behaviors.

Specific phobias have been treated most successfully with exposure techniques, cognitive-behavioral approaches in which people confront the objects they fear. The exposures may be gradual and relaxed (desensitization), intense (flooding), or observed (modeling). Agoraphobia is also treated effectively by exposure therapy.

Social Anxiety Disorder

Many people are uncomfortable when interacting with others or talking or performing in front of others. A number of entertainers and sports figures, from the singer Adele to the actor Johnny Depp, have described episodes of significant anxiety before performing. Social fears of this kind certainly are unpleasant, but usually the people who have them manage to function adequately.

People with **social anxiety disorder,** by contrast, have severe, persistent, and irrational anxiety about social or performance situations in which they may face scrutiny by others and possibly feel embarrassment (APA, 2013) (see **Table 4-6**). The social anxiety may be narrow, such as a fear of talking in public or eating in front of others, or it may be broad, such as a general fear of functioning poorly in front of others. In both forms, people repeatedly judge themselves as performing less competently than they actually do (see ***MindTech*** on page 122).

Why do so many professional performers seem prone to performance anxiety? Might their repeated exposure to audiences have a therapeutic effect?

Social anxiety disorder can interfere greatly with one's life (Schneier, 2017). A person who cannot interact with others or speak in public may fail to carry out important responsibilities. One who cannot eat in public may reject meal invitations and other social offerings. Since many people with this disorder keep their fears secret, their social reluctance is often misinterpreted as snobbery, lack of interest, or hostility.

Surveys reveal that 8 percent of people in the United States and other Western countries (around 60 percent of them female) experience social anxiety disorder in any given year (see **Table 4-7**). Around 13 percent develop this disorder at some point in their lives (NIMH, 2017; Bandelow & Michaelis, 2015; Kessler et al., 2012). Poor people

TABLE: 4-6

Dx Checklist

Social Anxiety Disorder
1. Pronounced, disproportionate, and repeated anxiety about social situation(s) in which the individual could be exposed to possible scrutiny by others; typically lasting 6 months or more.
2. Fear of being negatively evaluated by or offensive to others.
3. Exposure to the social situation almost always produces anxiety.
4. Avoidance of feared situations.
5. Significant distress or impairment.

Information from: APA, 2013.

are 50 percent more likely than wealthier people to have social anxiety disorder (Sareen et al., 2011). Non-Hispanic white Americans are more likely to experience this problem than African, Hispanic, or Asian Americans (Hofmann & Hinton, 2014). It tends to begin in late childhood or adolescence and may continue into adulthood (Schneier, 2017). Around 40 percent of individuals with social anxiety disorder are currently in treatment (NIMH, 2017).

Graham Denholm/Getty Images

Much harder than it looks World-renowned singer Adele performs in front of 60,000 people at a stadium in Melbourne, Australia, during her "Adele Live 2017" concert tour. When the gifted artist mesmerizes her fans in such venues, it is hard to believe that she has struggled for years with severe performance anxiety and related panic attacks, particularly when singing before large crowds.

What Causes Social Anxiety Disorder?

The leading explanation for social anxiety disorder has been proposed by cognitive-behavioral theorists (Hofmann, 2018; Heimberg et al, 2010). The explanation features an interplay of both cognitive and behavioral factors. As you read in Chapter 2, cognitive-behavioral theorists start with the contention that people with this disorder hold a group of dysfunctional beliefs and expectations regarding the social realm. These can include:

- Holding unrealistically high social standards and so believing that they must perform perfectly in social situations.
- Believing they are unattractive social beings.
- Believing they are socially unskilled and inadequate.
- Believing they are always in danger of behaving incompetently in social situations.
- Believing that inept behaviors in social situations will inevitably lead to terrible consequences.
- Believing they have no control over the feelings of anxiety that emerge in social situations.

Cognitive-behavioral theorists hold that, because of these beliefs, people with social anxiety disorder keep anticipating that social disasters will occur, overestimate how poorly things go in their social interactions, and dread most social situations (Hofmann, 2018; Gavric et al., 2017). Moreover, they learn to perform "avoidance" and "safety" behaviors to help prevent or reduce such disasters (Mesri et al., 2017). Avoidance behaviors include, for example, avoiding parties or avoiding interactions with new coworkers or acquaintances. Safety behaviors include wearing makeup to cover up blushing or gloves to hide shaking hands. Behaviors of this kind are reinforced by reducing feelings of anxiety and the number of awkward encounters.

Researchers have found that people with social anxiety disorder do indeed manifest the beliefs, expectations, interpretations, feelings, and behaviors listed above (Parsons et al., 2017; Thurston et al., 2017). These dysfunctional cognitions and behaviors have

TABLE: 4-7

Profile of Anxiety Disorders and Obsessive-Compulsive Disorder

	One-Year Prevalence	Female to Male Ratio	Typical Age at Onset	Prevalence Among Close Relatives	Percentage Receiving Clinical Treatment Currently
Generalized anxiety disorder	4.0%	2:1	0–35 years	Elevated	43%
Specific phobia	10.0%	2:1	Variable	Elevated	32%
Agoraphobia	1.7%	2:1	15–35 years	Elevated	46%
Social anxiety disorder	8.0%	3:2	10–20 years	Elevated	40%
Panic disorder	3.1%	5:2	15–35 years	Elevated	59%
Obsessive-compulsive disorder	1.0%–2.0%	1:1	4–25 years	Elevated	40%

Information from: McCabe, 2018; Roy-Byrne, 2018; NIMH, 2017; Watterson et al., 2017; Remes et al., 2016; Roy-Byrne, 2016; Simpson, 2016; Bandelow & Michaelis, 2015; Phillips, 2015; Kessler et al., 2010, 2005, 1999, 1994; Ritter et al., 2010; Wang et al., 2005.

MINDTECH

Social Media Jitters

In recent years, researchers have learned that the use of computers and mobile devices can unintentionally produce various forms of anxiety, including social and generalized anxiety (Gao et al., 2018; Golbeck, 2016).

The biggest culprit here seems to be spending too much time on social media such as Facebook, Instagram, or Snapchat. Although frequenting social network sites helps many people feel supported and included (Hu et al., 2017), for others, the visits seem to produce significant insecurities and fears (Levula, Harré, & Wilson, 2018). Surveys suggest, for example, that more than one-third of social networkers develop a fear that others will post or use information or photos of them without their permission (Smith, 2014; Szalavitz, 2013). In addition, a fourth of all users feel a constant pressure to disclose too much personal information on their social networks, and a number feel intense pressure to post material that will be popular and get numerous comments and "likes." More than a few users also worry that they will discover posts about social activities from which they were excluded.

One study found that a third of users feel distinctly worse after visiting their social network—more anxious, more envious, and more dissatisfied with their lives (Krasnova et al., 2013). These feelings are particularly triggered when users observe vacation photos of other users, read birthday greetings received by other users, and see how many "likes" or comments others receive for their postings or photos. Such experiences seem to lead some users to worry that they are less desirable, less interesting, or less capable than most other social media users (Eckler, Kalyango, & Paasch, 2017; Hanna et al., 2017).

Can you think of other negative feelings that might be triggered by social networking?

Cultura RM/Alamy

Of course, as noted earlier, many of today's users do feel more positive about their social network visits. But even these people may have some social network–induced anxiety and tension. Around two-thirds, for example, are truly afraid that they will miss something if they don't check their social networks constantly—a phenomenon known as FOMO ("fear of missing out") (Wolniewicz et al., 2018).

Social networking is not the only digital source of anxiety. Studies show that excessive cell phone use often results in high levels of anxiety and tension (Richardson, Hussain, & Griffiths, 2018; Lepp et al., 2014; Archer, 2013). Why? Some theorists speculate that frequent phone users feel obligated to stay in touch with friends, another version of FOMO. Others believe that the rise in anxiety among heavy cell phone users is really the result of other cell phone effects, such as poorer performance in school or a reduction in positive time spent alone and self-reflecting. Whatever the explanation, two-thirds of cell phone users report feeling "panicked" when they misplace or lose their phones, even for a few minutes. Many experience "nomophobia" (no-mobile-phone-phobia), a pop term for the rush of fear that people have when they realize that they are disconnected from the world, friends, and family (Dasgupta et al., 2017).

been tied to factors such as genetic predispositions, trait tendencies, biological abnormalities, traumatic childhood experiences, and overprotective parent–child interactions (Young et al., 2019; Schneier, 2017).

Treatments for Social Anxiety Disorder

Only in recent decades have clinicians been able to treat social anxiety disorder successfully. Their success is due in part to the growing recognition that the disorder has two distinct features that may feed upon each other: (1) sufferers have overwhelming social fears, and (2) they often lack skill at starting conversations, communicating their needs, or meeting the needs of others. Armed with this insight, clinicians now treat social anxiety disorder by trying to reduce social fears or by providing training in social skills, or both.

How Can Social Fears Be Reduced? Medication often helps alleviate social fears (Stein, 2018; Curtiss et al., 2017). Such fears are reduced to some degree in 55 percent of patients who take either benzodiazepines or antidepressant drugs, compared to 24 percent of similar patients who take placebo drugs. It appears that these medications bring about relief by improving functioning in the brain's fear circuit, which tends to be hyperactive for people with social anxiety disorder, just as it is in cases of generalized anxiety disorder (Schneier, 2017; Brühl et al., 2014).

At the same time, cognitive-behavioral therapy has proved to be at least as effective as medication at reducing social fears, and people helped by this approach seem less likely to relapse than those treated with medications alone (Gregory & Peters, 2017; Thurston et al., 2017). This finding suggests to some clinicians that this form of therapy should always be featured in the treatment of social fears, either alone or in combination with medication.

To undo the cycle of problematic social beliefs and behaviors described earlier, cognitive-behavioral therapists combine both behavioral and cognitive techniques. On the behavioral side, they conduct *exposure therapy,* the intervention so effective with phobias. The therapists encourage clients to expose themselves to their dreaded social situations and to remain in these situations as their fears subside. Usually the exposure is gradual, and it often includes homework assignments. On the cognitive side, the clinicians and clients have systematic therapy discussions in which the clients are guided to reexamine and challenge their maladaptive beliefs and expectations, given the less-than-dire outcomes of their social exposures.

How Can Social Skills Be Improved? In **social skills training,** also conducted by cognitive-behavioral therapists, several techniques are combined. The therapists usually *model* appropriate social behaviors for clients and encourage the individuals to try them out. The clients then *role-play* with the therapists, *rehearsing* their new behaviors until they become more effective. Throughout the process, therapists provide frank *feedback* and *reinforce* (praise) the clients for effective performances.

Reinforcement from other people with similar social difficulties is often more powerful than reinforcement from a therapist alone. Thus in *social skills training groups* and *assertiveness training groups,* members try out and rehearse new social behaviors with other group members. Such groups also provide guidance on what is socially appropriate. According to research, social skills training, in both individual and group formats, has helped many people perform better in social situations (Probst et al., 2017; Beidel et al., 2014).

social skills training A therapy approach that helps people learn or improve social skills and assertiveness through role-playing and rehearsing of desirable behaviors.

panic attacks Periodic, short bouts of panic that occur suddenly, reach a peak within minutes, and gradually pass.

#TheirWords

"There are two types of speakers. Those who get nervous and those who are liars."

Mark Twain

...SUMMING UP

SOCIAL ANXIETY DISORDER People with social anxiety disorder experience severe and persistent anxiety about social or performance situations in which they may be scrutinized by others or be embarrassed. Cognitive-behavioral theorists believe that the disorder is particularly likely to develop among people who hold certain dysfunctional social beliefs and expectations and who learn to perform corresponding avoidance and safety behaviors.

Therapists who treat social anxiety disorder try to reduce social fears by drug therapy and/or cognitive-behavioral therapy (including exposure techniques). They may also try to improve social skills by social skills training.

Panic Disorder

Sometimes an anxiety reaction takes the form of a smothering, nightmarish panic in which people lose control of their behavior and, in fact, are practically unaware of what they are doing. Anyone can react with panic when a real threat looms up suddenly. Some people, however, experience **panic attacks**—periodic, short bouts of panic that occur suddenly, reach a peak within minutes, and gradually pass (APA, 2013).

#TheirWords

"Neither a man nor a crowd nor a nation can be trusted to act humanely or to think sanely under the influence of a great fear."

Bertrand Russell

The attacks feature at least four of the following symptoms of panic: palpitations of the heart, tingling in the hands or feet, shortness of breath, sweating, hot and cold flashes, trembling, chest pains, choking sensations, faintness, dizziness, and a feeling of unreality (APA, 2013). Small wonder that during a panic attack many people fear they will die, go crazy, or lose control.

My first panic attack happened when I was traveling for spring break with my mom. . . . [W]hile I was driving . . . , a random thought entered my head, . . . and BOOM—it was like my body . . . had been waiting for an invitation and jumped me right in to a full-blown panic attack. I felt huge waves of warm adrenaline surging across my chest and back, my hands were shaking, and I felt scared that I was losing control—whatever that meant. "I've got to pull over," I said. . . . Catching my breath, a part of me knew I had experienced a panic attack, but was still utterly bewildered at why it happened and how quickly it came on, taking over body and mind. . . . If you've never had a panic attack before, it feels as scary as if someone jumped out from a dark alley and put a gun to your head, leaving you pleading for your life. You would do whatever it took to get away and fast. . . . It's so intense that in the height of panic, the survival instinct kicks in and it seems like a toss-up whether you'll make it out alive or with your mental faculties in place. . . .

(LeCroy & Holschuh, 2012)

Approximately one-third of all people have one or more panic attacks at some point in their lives (Roy-Byrne, 2018). Some people, however, have panic attacks repeatedly and unexpectedly and without apparent reason. They may be suffering from **panic disorder.** In addition to the panic attacks, people who are diagnosed with panic disorder experience dysfunctional changes in their thinking or behavior as a result of the attacks (see **Table 4-8**). They may, for example, worry persistently about having additional attacks, have concerns about what such attacks mean ("Am I losing my mind?"), or plan their lives around the possibility of future attacks (APA, 2013).

Around 3.1 percent of all people in the United States suffer from panic disorder in a given year; more than 5 percent develop it at some point in their lives (Roy-Byrne, 2018; Bandelow & Michaelis, 2015; Kessler et al., 2012). The disorder tends to develop in late adolescence or early adulthood and is at least twice as common among women as among men. Poor people are 50 percent more likely than wealthier people to experience panic disorder (de Jonge et al., 2016). Surveys indicate that 59 percent of those with this disorder in the United States are currently in treatment (NIMH, 2017; Wang et al., 2005).

The prevalence of panic disorder is higher among non-Hispanic white Americans than among racial-ethnic minority groups in the United States (Hofmann & Hinton, 2014). The actual features of panic attacks may also differ among these groups (Barrera et al., 2010). For example, Asian Americans appear more likely than non-Hispanic white Americans to experience dizziness, unsteadiness, and choking, while African Americans seem less likely to have those particular symptoms.

As you read earlier, panic disorder is often accompanied by agoraphobia, the broad phobia in which people are afraid to travel to public places where escape might be difficult should they have panic symptoms or become incapacitated. In such cases, the panic disorder typically sets the stage for the development of agoraphobia. That is, after experiencing multiple unpredictable panic attacks, a person becomes increasingly fearful of having new attacks in public places.

TABLE: 4-8

Dx Checklist

Panic Disorder

1. Unforeseen panic attacks occur repeatedly.
2. One or more of the attacks precedes either of the following symptoms:
   (a) At least a month of continual concern about having additional attacks
   (b) At least a month of dysfunctional behavior changes associated with the attacks (for example, avoiding new experiences)

Information from: APA, 2013.

The Biological Perspective

Over the past half-century, researchers have learned that panic disorder has biological underpinnings and can respond to biological treatments. Researchers began their journey in the 1960s, when they discovered that the symptoms of this disorder were sometimes alleviated by *antidepressant drugs,* specifically those antidepressant drugs that increase the activity of the neurotransmitter *norepinephrine* throughout the brain (Klein, 1964; Klein & Fink, 1962).

panic disorder An anxiety disorder marked by recurrent and unpredictable panic attacks.

locus coeruleus A small area of the brain that seems to be active in the regulation of emotions. Many of its neurons use norepinephrine.

What Biological Factors Contribute to Panic Disorder? To understand the biology of panic disorder, researchers worked backward from their understanding of the antidepressant drugs that seemed to reduce its symptoms. Given that the drugs were so helpful in eliminating panic attacks, the researchers began to suspect that panic disorder might be caused in the first place by abnormal norepinephrine activity.

Several studies produced evidence that norepinephrine activity is indeed irregular in people who suffer from panic attacks. For example, the **locus coeruleus** is a brain area rich in neurons that use norepinephrine, and serves as a kind of "on-off" switch for many norepinephrine-using neurons throughout the brain (Hedaya, 2011). When this area is electrically stimulated in monkeys, the monkeys have a panic-like reaction, suggesting that panic reactions may be related to irregularities in norepinephrine activity in the locus coeruleus (Redmond, 1981, 1979, 1977). Similarly, in another line of research, scientists were able to produce panic attacks in human beings by injecting them with chemicals known to disturb the activity of norepinephrine (Bourin et al., 1995; Charney et al., 1990, 1987).

Based on these findings, biological theorists initially reasoned that panic attacks might be caused by abnormal activity of norepinephrine in the locus coeruleus. However, once again, more recent research suggests that the root of panic attacks is more complicated than a single neurotransmitter or a single brain structure. It turns out that panic reactions are produced by a brain circuit consisting of structures such as the *amygdala, hippocampus, ventromedial nucleus of the hypothalamus, central gray matter,* and *locus coeruleus* (Roy-Byrne, 2018; Henn, 2013; Etkin, 2010) (see **Figure 4-3**). When a person confronts a frightening object or situation, the amygdala is stimulated. In turn, the amygdala stimulates the other brain structures in the circuit, temporarily setting into motion an "alarm and escape" response (increased heart rate, respiration, blood pressure, and the like) that is very similar to a panic reaction (Gray & McNaughton, 1996). Most of today's researchers believe that this circuit—often called the "panic circuit"—tends to be hyperactive in people who suffer from panic disorder (Roy-Byrne, 2018).

Some of the brain structures and neurotransmitters in the panic circuit overlap with those in the fear circuit discussed earlier; for example, the amygdala is a part of each circuit. However, the panic circuit seems to be more extensive than the fear circuit, suggesting to some researchers that panic responses are more complex reactions than fear responses (Roy-Byrne, 2018).

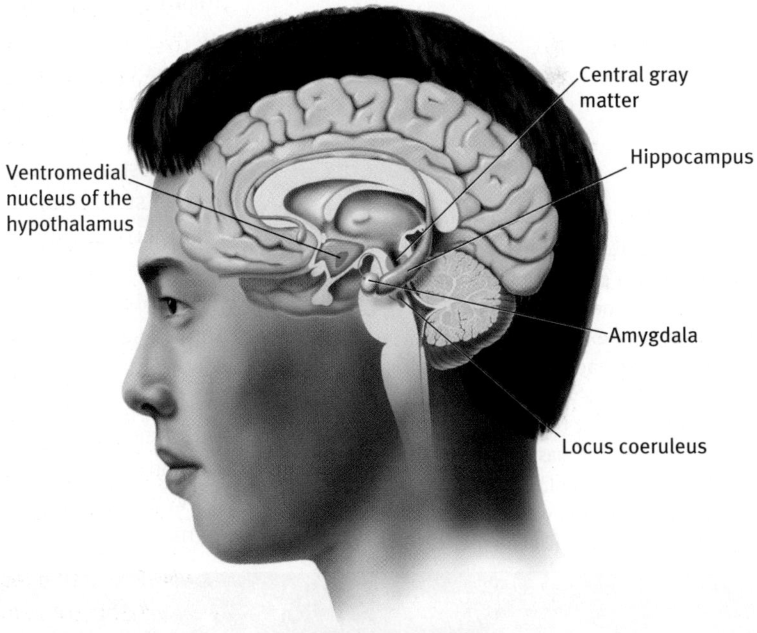

FIGURE 4-3

The Biology of Panic

The circuit in the brain that helps produce panic reactions includes structures such as the amygdala, hippocampus, ventromedial nucleus of the hypothalamus, central gray matter, and locus coeruleus.

Why might some people have hyperactive panic circuits and be prone to the development of panic disorder? One possibility is that a predisposition to develop such abnormalities is inherited. Once again, if a genetic factor is at work, close relatives should have higher rates of panic disorder than more distant relatives. Studies do find that among identical twins (twins who share all their genes), if one twin has panic disorder, the other twin has the same disorder in 31 percent of cases (Roy-Byrne, 2018; Tsuang et al., 2004; Kendler et al., 1995, 1993). Among fraternal twins (who share only some of their genes), if one twin has panic disorder, the other twin has the same disorder in, at most, only 11 percent of cases.

Drug Therapies Ever since researchers discovered in 1962 that certain antidepressant drugs could prevent or reduce panic attacks, studies across the world have repeatedly confirmed this initial observation. Various antidepressant drugs bring at least some improvement to more than two-thirds of patients who have panic disorder, and the

biological challenge test A procedure used to produce panic in participants or clients by having them exercise vigorously or perform some other potentially panic-inducing task in the presence of a researcher or therapist.

anxiety sensitivity A tendency to focus on one's bodily sensations, assess them illogically, and interpret them as harmful.

improvement can last indefinitely, as long as the drugs are continued (Roy-Byrne, 2017; Cuijpers et al., 2014). These antidepressant drugs appear to prevent or reduce panic attacks by increasing the activity of the neurotransmitters *serotonin* and *norepinephrine* in the locus coeruleus and other parts of the panic circuit, thus helping to correct the circuit's tendency to be hyperactive (Gerez et al., 2016; Duval et al., 2015). Researchers have also discovered that *alprazolam* (Xanax) and other powerful benzodiazepine drugs can be effective in many cases of panic disorder, although they are used less often than antidepressants because of their potential for producing physical dependence and other risks. These various antidepressant drugs and benzodiazepines also seem to be helpful in cases of panic disorder accompanied by agoraphobia.

The Cognitive-Behavioral Perspective

Cognitive-behavioral theorists argue that biological factors are but one part of the cause of panic attacks. In their view, full panic reactions are experienced only by people who further *misinterpret* the physiological events that are taking place within their bodies. Cognitive-behavioral treatments are aimed at correcting such misinterpretations.

The Cognitive-Behavioral Explanation: Misinterpreting Bodily Sensations

Cognitive-behavioral theorists believe that panic-prone people may be very sensitive to certain bodily sensations; when they unexpectedly experience such sensations, they misinterpret them as signs of a medical catastrophe (Craske, 2017; Gloster et al., 2017, 2014). Rather than understanding the probable cause of their sensations as "something I ate" or "a fight with the boss," those prone to panic grow increasingly upset about losing control, fear the worst, lose all perspective, and rapidly plunge into panic. For example, many people with panic disorder seem to "overbreathe," or hyperventilate, in stressful situations. The abnormal breathing makes them think that they are in danger of suffocation, so they panic. They further develop the belief that these and other "dangerous" sensations may return at any time and so set themselves up for future panic attacks.

In **biological challenge tests,** researchers produce hyperventilation or other biological sensations by administering drugs or by instructing clinical research participants to breathe, exercise, or simply think in certain ways. As you might expect, participants with panic disorder experience greater upset during these tests than participants without the disorder, particularly when they believe that their bodily sensations are dangerous or out of control (Leibold et al., 2017).

Why might some people be prone to such misinterpretations? One possibility is that panic-prone individuals actually experience more frequent or intense bodily sensations than other people do. Indeed, the kinds of sensations that are most often misinterpreted in panic disorders seem to be carbon dioxide increases in the blood, shifts in blood pressure, and rises in heart rate, bodily events that are controlled in part by the brain's panic circuit—and, as you'll recall, the panic circuit is overactive in people with panic disorder (Lieberman et al., 2017). Another possibility, supported by some research, is that panic-prone people have had more trauma-filled events over the course of their lives than other persons, leading to higher expectations of catastrophe (Asselmann et al., 2018; De Cort et al., 2017). Whatever the precise cause of such misinterpretations may be, once they take hold, they increasingly guide behaviors and choices in life. Panic-prone individuals may, for example, learn to display avoidance and safety behaviors that help control their bodily sensations. They may repeatedly hold onto people or objects to avoid feeling faint, or they may move slowly or sit still much of the time to avoid upsetting increases in heart rate (Craske, 2017).

"It came out of nowhere" All Star Kevin Love tries to make a pass during this National Basketball Association game on November 5, 2017. Later in the game, Love experienced a panic attack—his first ever—and had to leave for hospital tests and evaluation. The Cleveland Cavaliers player has since written about the attack, "It came out of nowhere. . . . But it was real—as real as a broken hand or a sprained ankle. Since that day, almost everything about the way I think about my mental health has changed" (Ducharme, 2018).

AP Photo/Tony Dejak, File

Given such misinterpretations, it is not surprising that panic-prone individuals generally have a high degree of what is called **anxiety sensitivity;** that is, they focus on their bodily sensations much of the time, are unable to assess them logically, and interpret them as potentially harmful. Studies have found that people who scored high on anxiety-sensitivity surveys are up to five times more likely than other people to develop panic disorder (Hawks et al., 2011; Maller & Reiss, 1992). Other studies have found that individuals with panic disorder typically earn higher anxiety-sensitivity scores than other persons do (Kim et al., 2017).

Cognitive-Behavioral Therapy Cognitive-behavioral therapists use a combination of techniques to correct people's misinterpretations of their bodily sensations (Craske, 2017). First, they educate clients about the general nature of panic attacks, the actual causes of bodily sensations, and the tendency of the clients to misinterpret their sensations. Next, they teach the clients to apply more accurate interpretations during stressful situations, thus short-circuiting the panic sequence at an early point. The therapists may also teach the clients ways to cope better with anxiety—for example, by using relaxation and breathing techniques—and to distract themselves from their sensations, perhaps by striking up a conversation with someone.

In addition, cognitive-behavioral therapists often use biological challenge procedures to induce panic sensations so that clients can apply their new interpretations and skills under watchful supervision (Gloster et al., 2017, 2014). Individuals whose attacks typically are triggered by a rapid heart rate, for example, may be instructed to jump up and down for several minutes or to run up a flight of stairs. They can then practice interpreting the resulting sensations appropriately, without dwelling on them.

"Weekends I like to be able to panic without having all the distractions."

According to research, cognitive-behavioral treatment often helps people with panic disorder (Craske, 2017; Cuijpers et al., 2016). In studies across the world, at least two-thirds of participants who receive this treatment have become free of panic, compared with only 13 percent of control participants. Cognitive-behavioral therapy has proved to be at least as helpful as antidepressant drugs or benzodiazepines in the treatment of panic disorder, sometimes even more so (Roy-Byrne & Craske, 2017). In view of the effectiveness of both cognitive-behavioral and drug treatments, many clinicians have tried, with some success, to combine them (Choi, Lee, & Cho, 2017). Similarly, research suggests that cognitive-behavioral therapy, drug therapy, or a combination of these approaches are helpful to those individuals who display both panic disorder and agoraphobia (Craske, 2017; Roy-Byrne, 2017).

... SUMMING UP

PANIC DISORDER Panic attacks are periodic, discrete bouts of panic that occur suddenly. Sufferers of panic disorder experience panic attacks repeatedly and unexpectedly and without apparent reason. Panic disorder may be accompanied by agoraphobia in some cases, leading to two diagnoses.

Many biological theorists believe that panic disorder is caused by a hyperactive panic circuit, a brain circuit that includes structures such as the amygdala, hippocampus, ventromedial nucleus of the hypothalamus, central gray matter, and locus coeruleus. Biological therapists use certain antidepressant drugs or benzodiazepines to treat people with this disorder.

Cognitive-behavioral theorists suggest that panic-prone people become preoccupied with some of their bodily sensations and misinterpret them as signs of medical catastrophe. In turn, they have panic attacks, learn to display avoidance and safety behaviors that help control their bodily sensations, and in some cases develop panic disorder. Cognitive-behavioral therapists teach clients to interpret their physical sensations more accurately and to cope better with anxiety.

Obsessive-Compulsive Disorder

Obsessions are persistent thoughts, ideas, impulses, or images that seem to invade a person's consciousness. **Compulsions** are repetitive and rigid behaviors or mental acts that people feel they must perform in order to prevent or reduce anxiety. As **Figure 4-4** indicates, minor obsessions and compulsions are familiar to almost everyone. You may find yourself filled with thoughts about an upcoming performance or exam or keep wondering whether you forgot to turn off the stove or lock the door. You may feel better when you avoid stepping on cracks, turn away from black cats, or arrange your closet in a particular manner. Repetitive thoughts or behaviors of this kind, however, are hardly a reflection of abnormality.

According to DSM-5, a diagnosis of **obsessive-compulsive disorder** is called for when obsessions or compulsions feel excessive or unreasonable, cause great distress, take up much time, and interfere with daily functions (see **Table 4-9**). Although obsessive-compulsive disorder is not classified as an anxiety disorder in DSM-5, anxiety does play a major role in this pattern. The obsessions cause intense anxiety, while the compulsions are aimed at preventing or reducing anxiety. In addition, anxiety rises if a person tries to resist his or her obsessions or compulsions.

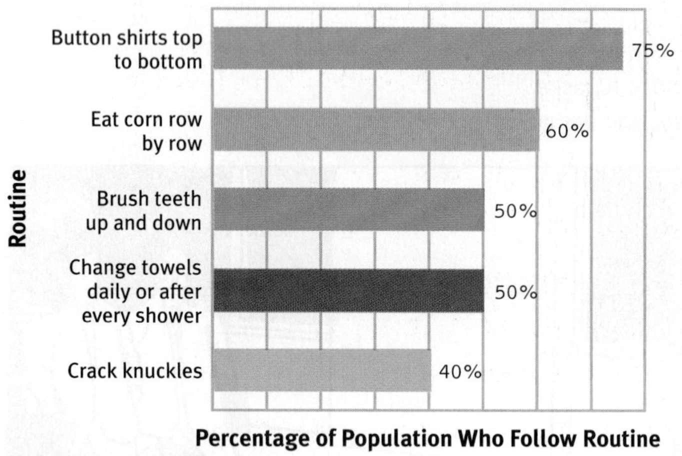

FIGURE 4-4

Normal Routines

Most people find it comforting to follow set routines when they carry out everyday activities, and, in fact, 40 percent become irritated if they must depart from their routines. (Information from: Kanner, 2005, 1998, 1995.)

An individual with this disorder observed: "I can't get to sleep unless I am sure everything in the house is in its proper place so that when I get up in the morning, the house is organized. I work like mad to set everything straight before I go to bed, but, when I get up in the morning, I can think of a thousand things that I ought to do. . . . I can't stand to know something needs doing and I haven't done it" (McNeil, 1967, pp. 26–28). Research indicates that several additional disorders are closely related to obsessive-compulsive disorder in their features, causes, and treatment responsiveness, and so, as you will soon see, DSM-5 has grouped them together with obsessive-compulsive disorder.

Between 1 and 2 percent of the people in the United States and other countries throughout the world suffer from obsessive-compulsive disorder in any given year (Simpson, 2017; Kessler et al., 2012). As many as 3 percent develop the disorder at some point during their lives. It is equally common in men and women and among people of different races and ethnic groups. The disorder usually begins by childhood or young adulthood (Chou et al., 2017) and typically persists for many years, although its symptoms and their severity may fluctuate over time. It is estimated that 40 percent of people with obsessive-compulsive disorder seek treatment, many for an extended period (Phillips, 2015; Patel et al., 2014).

What Are the Features of Obsessions and Compulsions?

Obsessive thoughts feel both intrusive and foreign to the people who experience them. Attempts to ignore or resist these thoughts may arouse even more anxiety, and before long they come back more strongly than ever. People with obsessions typically are quite aware that their thoughts are excessive.

Certain basic themes run through the thoughts of most people troubled by obsessive thinking (Schwartzman et al., 2017; Simpson, 2017). The most common theme appears to be dirt or contamination. Other common ones are violence and aggression, orderliness, religion, and sexuality. The prevalence of such themes may vary from culture to culture (McIngvale et al., 2017). Religious obsessions, for example, seem to be more common in cultures or countries with strict moral codes and religious values.

TABLE: 4-9

Dx Checklist

Obsessive-Compulsive Disorder
1. Occurrence of repeated obsessions, compulsions, or both.
2. The obsessions or compulsions take up considerable time.
3. Significant distress or impairment.

Information from: APA, 2013.

Compulsions are similar to obsessions in many ways. For example, although compulsive behaviors are technically under voluntary control, the people who feel they must do them have little sense of choice in the matter. Most of these individuals recognize that their behavior is unreasonable, but they believe at the same time something terrible will happen if they don't perform the compulsions. After performing a compulsive act, they usually feel less anxious for a short while. For some people the compulsive acts develop into detailed *rituals*. They must go through the ritual in exactly the same way every time, according to certain rules.

Like obsessions, compulsions take various forms. *Cleaning compulsions* are very common. People with these compulsions feel compelled to keep cleaning themselves, their clothing, or their homes. The cleaning may follow ritualistic rules and be repeated dozens or hundreds of times a day. People with *checking compulsions* check the same items over and over—door locks, gas taps, important papers—to make sure that all is as it should be. Another common compulsion is the constant effort to seek *order* or *balance*. People with this compulsion keep placing certain items (clothing, books, foods) in perfect order in accordance with strict rules. *Touching, verbal,* and *counting* compulsions are also common.

Although some people with obsessive-compulsive disorder experience obsessions only or compulsions only, most experience both. In fact, compulsive acts are often a response to obsessive thoughts. One study found that in most cases, compulsions seemed to represent a *yielding* to obsessive doubts, ideas, or urges (Akhtar et al., 1975). A woman who keeps doubting that her house is secure may yield to that obsessive doubt by repeatedly checking locks and gas jets, or a man who obsessively fears contamination may yield to that fear by performing cleaning rituals. The study also found that compulsions sometimes serve to help *control* obsessions. A teenager describes how she tried to control her obsessive fears of contamination by performing counting and verbal rituals:

Patient: *If I heard the word, like, something that had to do with germs or disease, it would be considered something bad, and so I had things that would go through my mind that were sort of like "cross that out and it'll make it okay" to hear that word.*

Interviewer: *What sort of things?*

Patient: *Like numbers or words that seemed to be sort of like a protector.*

Interviewer: *What numbers and what words were they?*

Patient: *It started out to be the number 3 and multiples of 3 and then words like "soap and water," something like that; and then the multiples of 3 got really high, and they'd end up to be 124 or something like that. It got real bad then.*

(Spitzer et al., 1981, p. 137)

Obsessive-compulsive disorder was once among the least understood of the psychological disorders. In recent decades, however, researchers have begun to learn more about it. The most influential explanations and treatments come from the psychodynamic, cognitive-behavioral, and biological models.

The Psychodynamic Perspective

As you have seen, psychodynamic theorists believe that an anxiety disorder develops when children come to fear their own id impulses and use ego defense mechanisms to lessen the resulting anxiety. What distinguishes obsessive-compulsive disorder from other anxiety disorders, in their view, is that here the battle between anxiety-provoking id impulses and anxiety-reducing defense mechanisms is not buried in the unconscious but is played out in overt thoughts and actions. The id impulses usually take the form

obsession A persistent thought, idea, impulse, or image that is experienced repeatedly, feels intrusive, and causes anxiety.

compulsion A repetitive and rigid behavior or mental act that a person feels driven to perform in order to prevent or reduce anxiety.

obsessive-compulsive disorder A disorder in which a person has recurrent obsessions, compulsions, or both.

Jim Spellman/Getty Images

Personal knowledge The HBO hit series *Girls* (2012–2017) followed the struggles of Hannah Horvath and her friends as they navigated their twenties, "one mistake at a time." The show's creator and star, Lena Dunham, says that Hannah's difficulties often were inspired by her own real-life experiences, including her childhood battle with OCD and anxiety.

neutralizing A person's attempt to eliminate unwanted thoughts by thinking or behaving in ways that put matters right internally, making up for the unacceptable thoughts.

exposure and response prevention A cognitive-behavioral technique used to treat obsessive-compulsive disorder that exposes a client to anxiety-arousing thoughts or situations and then prevents the client from performing his or her compulsive acts. Also called *exposure and ritual prevention*.

of obsessive thoughts, and the ego defenses appear as counterthoughts or compulsive actions. A woman who keeps imagining her mother lying broken and bleeding, for example, may counter those thoughts with repeated safety checks throughout the house.

Sigmund Freud traced obsessive-compulsive disorder to the *anal stage* of development (occurring at about 2 years of age). He proposed that during this stage some children experience intense rage and shame as a result of negative toilet-training experiences. Other psychodynamic theorists have argued instead that such early rage reactions are rooted in feelings of insecurity (Erikson, 1963; Sullivan, 1953; Horney, 1937). Either way, these children repeatedly feel the need to express their strong aggressive id impulses while at the same time knowing they should try to restrain and control the impulses. If this conflict between the id and ego continues, it may eventually blossom into obsessive-compulsive disorder. Overall, research has not clearly supported the psychodynamic explanation (Goodman, 2017; Busch et al., 2010).

When treating patients with obsessive-compulsive disorder, psychodynamic therapists try to help the individuals uncover and overcome their underlying conflicts and defenses, using the customary techniques of free association and therapist interpretation. Research has offered little evidence, however, that a traditional psychodynamic approach is of much help (Goodman, 2017; Fonagy, 2015). Thus some psychodynamic therapists now prefer to treat these patients with short-term psychodynamic therapies, which, as you saw in Chapter 2, are more direct and action-oriented than the classical techniques.

The Cognitive-Behavioral Perspective

Cognitive-behavioral theorists begin their explanation of obsessive-compulsive disorder by pointing out that everyone has repetitive, unwanted, and intrusive thoughts. Anyone might have thoughts of harming others or being contaminated by germs, for example, but most people dismiss or ignore them with ease. Those who develop this disorder, however, typically blame themselves for such thoughts and expect that somehow terrible things will happen (Salkovskis et al., 2017, 2003; Salkovskis, 1999, 1985). To avoid such negative outcomes, they try to **neutralize** the thoughts—thinking or behaving in ways meant to put matters right or to make amends.

Neutralizing acts might include requesting special reassurance from others, deliberately thinking "good" thoughts, washing one's hands, or checking for possible sources of danger. When a neutralizing effort brings about a temporary reduction in discomfort, it is reinforced and will likely be repeated (Goodman, 2017). Eventually the neutralizing thought or act is used so often that it becomes, by definition, an obsession or compulsion. At the same time, the individual becomes more and more convinced that his or her unpleasant intrusive thoughts are dangerous. As the person's fear of such thoughts increases, the thoughts begin to occur more frequently and they, too, become obsessions.

In support of this explanation, studies have found that people with obsessive-compulsive disorder have intrusive thoughts more often than other people, resort to more elaborate neutralizing strategies, and experience reductions in anxiety after using neutralizing techniques (Salkovskis et al., 2017, 2003; Jacob et al., 2014).

Although everyone sometimes has undesired thoughts, only some people develop obsessive-compulsive disorder. Why do these individuals find such normal thoughts so disturbing to begin with? Researchers have found that this population tends (1) to have exceptionally high standards of conduct and morality; (2) to believe that intrusive negative thoughts are equivalent to actions and capable

Bruce Eric Kaplan/The New Yorker Collection/The Cartoon Bank

"Gretel, I don't like living in this culture of fear."

of causing harm, a point of view called *thought-action fusion;* and (3) to believe that they should have perfect control over all of their thoughts and behaviors in life (Schwartzman et al., 2017; Simpson, 2017).

Cognitive-behavioral therapists use a combination of techniques to treat clients with obsessive-compulsive disorder. They begin by educating the clients, pointing out how misinterpretations of unwanted thoughts, an excessive sense of responsibility, and neutralizing acts have helped to produce and maintain their symptoms. The therapists then guide the clients to identify and challenge their distorted cognitions. Increasingly, the clients come to appreciate that their obsessive thoughts are inaccurate occurrences rather than valid and dangerous cognitions for which they are responsible. Correspondingly, they recognize their compulsive acts as unnecessary.

Bill Pugliano/Getty Images

Getting down and dirty In one *exposure and response prevention* assignment, clients with cleaning compulsions might be instructed to do heavy-duty gardening and then resist washing their hands or taking a shower. They may never go so far as to participate in and enjoy mud wrestling, like these delightfully filthy individuals at the annual Mud Day event in Westland, Michigan, but you get the point.

With such gains in hand, the clients become willing to subject themselves to the rigors of a distinctly behavioral technique called **exposure and response prevention** (or **exposure and ritual prevention**). In this technique, the clients are repeatedly exposed to objects or situations that produce anxiety, obsessive fears, and compulsive behaviors, but they are told to *resist* performing the behaviors they usually feel so bound to perform. Because people find it very difficult to resist such behaviors, the therapists may set an example first.

Have you ever tried an informal version of exposure and response prevention in order to stop behaving in certain ways?

In recent years, therapists who conduct exposure and response prevention have often used videoconferencing to go beyond the office and deliver specific instructions to clients directly in their home settings where compulsions cause the most problems (Comer et al., 2017). At the very least, a number of therapists compose exposure-and-response-prevention exercises that clients must carry out in the form of homework (Gellatly et al., 2017; Franklin & Foa, 2014), such as these assignments given to a woman with a cleaning compulsion:

- Do not mop the floor of your bathroom for a week. After this, clean it within three minutes, using an ordinary mop. Use this mop for other chores as well without cleaning it.
- Buy a fluffy mohair sweater and wear it for a week. When taking it off at night do not remove the bits of fluff. Do not clean your house for a week.
- You have to keep shoes on. Do not clean the house for a week.
- Drop a cookie on the contaminated floor, pick the cookie up and eat it.
- Leave the sheets and blankets on the floor and then put them on the beds. Do not change these for a week.

(Emmelkamp, 1982, pp. 299–300)

Eventually this woman was able to set up a reasonable routine for cleaning herself and her house.

Techniques of this kind often help reduce the number and impact of obsessions and compulsions (Lenhard et al., 2017; Liu et al., 2017). Overall, between 50 and 70 percent of clients with obsessive-compulsive disorder have been found to improve considerably with cognitive-behavioral therapy, improvements that often continue indefinitely (Abramowitz, 2017). The effectiveness of this approach suggests that people with the disorder are like the superstitious man in the old joke who keeps snapping his fingers to keep elephants away. When someone points out, "But there aren't any elephants

#

#LosingBattle

People who try to avoid all contamination and rid themselves and their world of all germs are fighting a losing battle. While talking, the average person sprays 300 microscopic saliva droplets per minute, or 2.5 per word.

around here," the man replies, "See? It works!" One review concludes, "With hindsight, it is possible to see that the [obsessive-compulsive] individual has been snapping his fingers, and unless he stops (response prevention) and takes a look around at the same time (exposure), he isn't going to learn much of value about elephants" (Berk & Efran, 1983, p. 546).

The Biological Perspective

In recent years, researchers have uncovered direct evidence that biological factors play a key role in obsessive-compulsive disorder. For example, some genetic studies have identified gene abnormalities that characterize individuals with this disorder (Grünblatt et al., 2018). In addition, using brain scan procedures, researchers have identified a brain circuit that helps regulate our primitive impulses such as sexual desires, aggressive instincts, and needs to excrete (Simpson, 2017; Parmar & Sarkar, 2016; Tang et al., 2016). The circuit, which brings such impulses to our attention and leads us to act on or disregard them, includes brain structures such as the *orbitofrontal cortex* (just above each eye), *cingulate cortex, striatum* (including the *caudate nucleus* and *putamen*, two other structures at the back of the striatum), and *thalamus* (see **Figure 4-5**). Among the most important neurotransmitters at work in this circuit are *serotonin, glutamate,* and *dopamine* (Gerez et al., 2016).

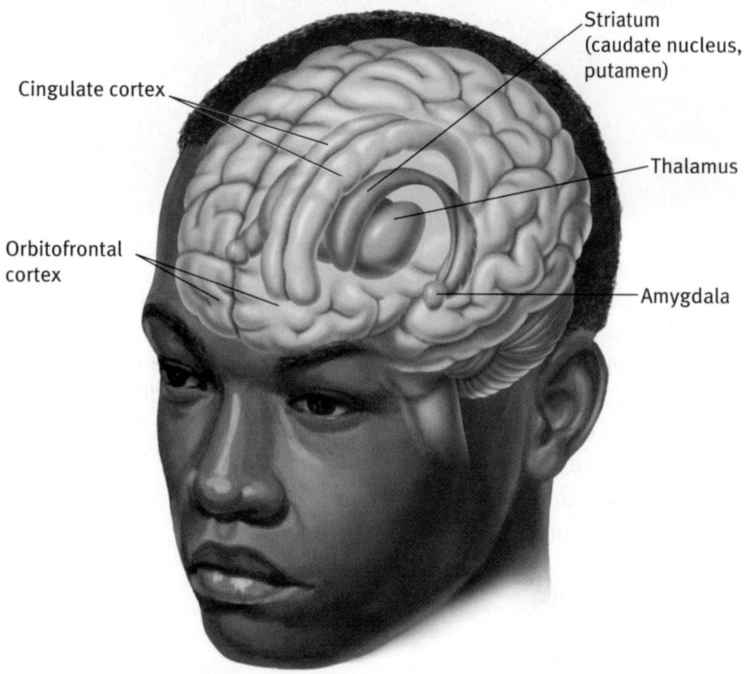

FIGURE 4-5

The Biology of Obsessive-Compulsive Disorder

The brain circuit that has been linked to obsessive-compulsive disorder includes structures such as the orbitofrontal cortex, cingulate cortex, striatum, thalamus, and amygdala.

Studies indicate that this circuit, called the *cortico-striato-thalamo-cortical circuit,* is hyperactive in people with obsessive-compulsive disorder, making it difficult for them to turn off or dismiss their various impulses, needs, and related thoughts (Frydman et al., 2016). After most people use the bathroom, for example, they have concerns about contamination and they act accordingly by washing their hands. When they perform this behavior, their brain circuit calms their contamination concerns and cleanliness needs. In contrast, because the cortico-striato-thalamo-cortical circuit of people with obsessive-compulsive disorder is hyperactive, these individuals may continue to experience contamination concerns and need to perform cleaning actions—again and again and again.

As you just read, brain scan studies have provided evidence that the cortico-striato-thalamo-cortical circuit is hyperactive in people with obsessive-compulsive disorder. In addition, medical scientists have observed for years that obsessive-compulsive symptoms often arise or subside after the orbitofrontal cortex, striatum, or other structures in the circuit are damaged by accident, illness, or surgical procedures (Simpson, 2017; Hofer et al., 2013).

By far, the most widely used biological treatment for obsessive-compulsive disorder is *antidepressant drugs,* particularly ones that specifically increase activity of the neurotransmitter serotonin. Numerous studies have found that such drugs bring improvement to between 50 and 60 percent of those with obsessive-compulsive disorder. Their obsessions and compulsions do not usually disappear totally, but on average they are cut almost in half (Simpson, 2017; Bareggi et al., 2004; DeVeaugh-Geiss et al., 1992).

Given the effectiveness of serotonin-enhancing antidepressant drugs in treating obsessive-compulsive disorder, theorists initially reasoned that the disorder must be caused primarily by low serotonin activity throughout the entire brain. However, most of today's researchers believe instead that the drugs bring improvement by increasing the activity of serotonin within the cortico-striato-thalamo-cortical circuit, thus helping to correct the circuit's tendency to be hyperactive. Consistent with this notion, studies have found that the structures in the circuit interconnect more appropriately after individuals with obsessive-compulsive disorder respond successfully to antidepressant treatment (Tang et al., 2016).

While many clients with obsessive-compulsive disorder receive *either* cognitive-behavioral therapy or antidepressant drug therapy, a growing number are now being treated by a combination of those interventions. According to research, such combinations often yield higher levels of symptom reduction and bring relief to more clients than do each of the approaches alone—improvements that may continue for years (Abramowitz, 2017).

Obsessive-Compulsive-Related Disorders

Some people perform particular patterns of repetitive and excessive behavior that greatly disrupt their lives. Among the most common such patterns are hoarding, hair-pulling, skin-picking, and appearance-checking. DSM-5 has created the group name **obsessive-compulsive-related disorders** and assigned these four patterns to that group: *hoarding disorder, trichotillomania (hair-pulling disorder), excoriation (skin-picking) disorder,* and *body dysmorphic disorder.* Collectively, these disorders are displayed by at least 5 percent of all people (Mataix-Cols & de la Cruz, 2017; Phillips, 2016).

People who display **hoarding disorder** feel that they must save items, and they become very distressed if they try to discard them (APA, 2013). These feelings make it difficult for them to part with possessions, resulting in an extraordinary accumulation of items that clutter their lives and living areas. This pattern causes the individuals significant distress and may greatly impair their personal, social, or occupational functioning (Mathes et al., 2017). It is common for them to wind up with numerous useless and valueless items, from junk mail to broken objects to unused clothes. Parts of their homes may become inaccessible because of the clutter. For example, sofas, kitchen appliances, or beds may be unusable. In addition, the pattern often results in fire hazards, unhealthful sanitation conditions, or other dangers.

People with **trichotillomania,** also known as **hair-pulling disorder,** repeatedly pull out hair from their scalp, eyebrows, eyelashes, or other parts of the body (APA, 2013). The disorder usually centers on just one or two of these body sites, most often the scalp. Typically, those with the disorder pull one hair at a time. It is common for anxiety or stress to trigger or accompany the hair-pulling behavior (Grant et al., 2017). Some sufferers follow specific rituals as they pull their hair, including pulling until the

obsessive-compulsive-related disorders Disorders in which obsessive-like concerns drive people to repeatedly and excessively perform certain abnormal patterns of behavior.

hoarding disorder A disorder in which individuals feel compelled to save items and become very distressed if they try to discard them, resulting in an excessive accumulation of items.

trichotillomania A disorder in which people repeatedly pull out hair from their scalp, eyebrows, eyelashes, or other parts of the body. Also called *hair-pulling disorder.*

A messy aftermath This man prepares to clean out his mother's home after her death. This is not an easy task—emotionally or physically—under the best of circumstances, but it is particularly difficult in this instance: his mother had suffered from hoarding disorder.

Kazuhiro Nogi/AFP/Getty Images

Cultural rituals Rituals do not necessarily reflect compulsions. Indeed, cultural and religious rituals often give meaning and comfort to their practitioners. Here Buddhist monks splash water over themselves during their annual winter prayers at a temple in Tokyo. This cleansing ritual is performed to pray for good luck.

hair feels "just right" and selecting certain types of hairs for pulling (Alexander et al., 2017; Starcevic, 2015). Because of the distress, impairment, or embarrassment caused by this behavior, the individuals often try to reduce or stop the hair-pulling. The term "trichotillomania" is derived from the Greek for "frenzied hair-pulling."

People with **excoriation (skin-picking) disorder** keep picking at their skin, resulting in significant sores or wounds (APA, 2013). Like those with hair-pulling disorder, they often try to reduce or stop the behavior. Most sufferers pick with their fingers and center their picking on one area, most often the face (Grant & Chamberlain, 2017; Grant et al., 2015, 2012). Other common areas of focus include the arms, legs, lips, scalp, chest, and extremities such as fingernails and cuticles. The behavior is typically triggered or accompanied by anxiety or stress (Park & Koo, 2017; Torales, Barrios, & Villalba, 2017).

People with **body dysmorphic disorder** become preoccupied with the belief that they have a particular defect or flaw in their physical appearance. Actually, the perceived defect or flaw is imagined or greatly exaggerated in the person's mind (APA, 2013). Such beliefs drive the individuals to repeatedly check themselves in the mirror, groom themselves, pick at the perceived flaw, compare themselves with others, seek reassurance, or perform other, similar behaviors. Here too, those with the problem experience significant distress or impairment.

Body dysmorphic disorder is the obsessive-compulsive-related disorder that has received the most study to date. Researchers have found that, most often, individuals with this problem focus on wrinkles; spots on the skin; excessive facial hair; swelling of the face; or a misshapen nose, mouth, jaw, or eyebrow (Phillips, 2017, 2016). Some worry about the appearance of their feet, hands, breasts, penis, or other body parts. Still others, like the woman described here, are concerned about bad odors coming from sweat, breath, genitals, or the rectum.

A woman of 35 had for 16 years been worried that her sweat smelled terrible. . . . For fear that she smelled, for 5 years she had not gone out anywhere except when accompanied by her husband or mother. She had not spoken to her neighbors for 3 years. . . . She avoided cinemas, dances, shops, cafes, and private homes. . . . Her husband was not allowed to invite any friends home; she constantly sought reassurance from him about her smell. . . . Her husband bought all her new clothes as she was afraid to try on clothes in front of shop assistants. She used vast quantities of deodorant and always bathed and changed her clothes before going out, up to 4 times daily.

(Marks, 1987, p. 371)

Of course, it is common in our society to worry about appearance (see **Figure 4-6**). Many teenagers and young adults worry about acne, for instance. The concerns of people with body dysmorphic disorder, however, are extreme. Sufferers may severely limit contact with other people, be unable to look others in the eye, or go to great lengths to conceal their "defects"—say, always wearing sunglasses to cover their supposedly misshapen eyes. As many as half of people with the disorder seek plastic surgery or dermatology treatment, and often they feel worse rather than better afterward (Bouman et al., 2017; Phillips, 2017). A large number are housebound, 80 percent have suicidal thoughts, and as many as 25 percent may attempt suicide at some point in their lives (Phillips, 2016).

#

#LookingGood

42 percent of facial plastic surgeons report that many of their patients seek cosmetic procedures in order to look better in selfies, Instagram, Snapchat, and Facebook Live, and other social media (AAFPRS, 2017).

As with the other obsessive-compulsive-related disorders, theorists typically account for body dysmorphic disorder by using the same kinds of explanations, both psychological and biological, that have been applied to obsessive-compulsive disorder. Similarly, clinicians typically treat clients with this disorder by applying the kinds of treatment used with obsessive-compulsive disorder, particularly antidepressant drugs and cognitive-behavioral therapy (Krebs et al., 2017; Phillips, 2017, 2016).

In an early study, for example, 17 clients with this disorder were treated with exposure and response prevention (Neziroglu et al., 2004, 1996). Over the course of 4 weeks, the clients were repeatedly reminded of their perceived physical defects and, at the same time, prevented from doing anything to help reduce their discomfort (such as checking their appearance). By the end of treatment, these individuals were less concerned with their "defects" and spent less time checking their body parts and avoiding social interactions.

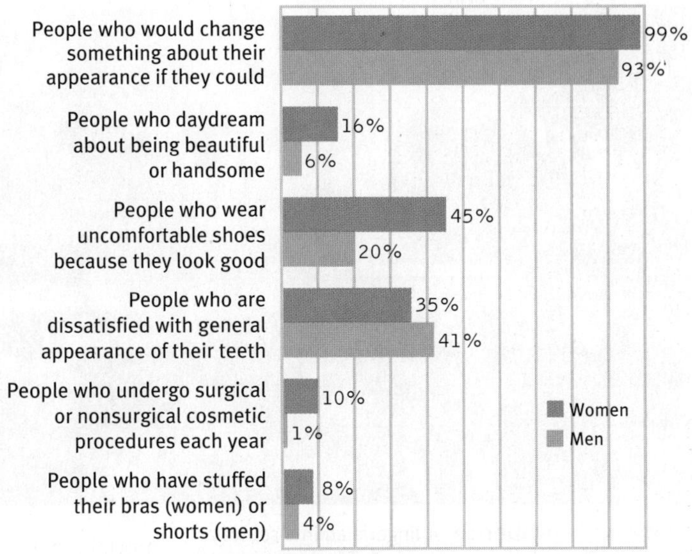

FIGURE 4-6

"Mirror, Mirror, on the Wall . . ."

People with body dysmorphic disorder are not the only ones who have concerns about their appearance. Surveys find that in our appearance-conscious society, large percentages of people regularly think about and try to change the way they look. (Information from: ASPS, 2017; Samorodnitzky-Naveh et al., 2007; Noonan, 2003; Kimball, 1993; Poretz & Sinrod, 1991; Weiss, 1991; Simmon, 1990.)

...SUMMING UP

OBSESSIVE-COMPULSIVE DISORDER People with obsessive-compulsive disorder are beset by obsessions, perform compulsions, or both. According to the psychodynamic view, this disorder arises out of a battle between id impulses and ego defense mechanisms. In contrast, cognitive-behavioral theorists believe that the disorder grows from a normal human tendency to have unwanted and unpleasant thoughts. The efforts of some people to understand, eliminate, or avoid such thoughts actually lead to obsessions and compulsions. Cognitive-behavioral therapists first help clients correct their misinterpretations of the unwanted thoughts, then conduct exposure and response prevention.

Biological researchers have tied obsessive-compulsive disorder to a hyperactive brain circuit featuring such brain structures as the orbitofrontal cortex, cingulate cortex, striatum, and thalamus. Antidepressant drugs that raise serotonin activity are a useful form of treatment. In addition to obsessive-compulsive disorder, DSM-5 lists a group of obsessive-compulsive-related disorders, disorders in which obsessive-like concerns drive individuals to repeatedly and excessively perform specific patterns of behavior that greatly disrupt their lives. This group consists of hoarding disorder, trichotillomania, excoriation (skin-picking) disorder, and body dysmorphic disorder.

Integrating the Models: The Developmental Psychopathology Perspective

While reading through this chapter, you may have noticed that certain findings and principles from each of the models seem compatible, and you may have wondered whether the explanations offered by the models could sometimes be combined to provide a fuller understanding of the various anxiety, obsessive-compulsive, and obsessive-compulsive-related disorders. A number of clinical theorists have asked the same question and have looked for ways to integrate the variables cited by the models. As you read in Chapter 2, one of today's most influential integrative views is the *developmental psychopathology* perspective. This perspective focuses on the *intersection* and *context* of important factors at key points of *time* throughout an individual's life span (Moreno, 2018; Eme, 2017; Cicchetti, 2016).

excoriation disorder A disorder in which people repeatedly pick at their skin, resulting in significant sores or wounds. Also called *skin-picking disorder.*

body dysmorphic disorder A disorder in which individuals become preoccupied with the belief that they have certain defects or flaws in their physical appearance. Such defects or flaws are imagined or greatly exaggerated.

Mark Henley/Panos

Worldwide influence A lingerie ad in a subway station in Shanghai, China, displays a woman in a push-up bra. As West meets East, Asian women have been bombarded by ads encouraging them to make Western-like changes to their various body parts. Perhaps not so coincidentally, cases of body dysmorphic disorder among Asians are becoming more and more similar to those among Westerners.

What are the factors that developmental psychopathologists look at when seeking to understand the development of anxiety-related disorders? Drawing from the biological model, they have been interested in the growing number of studies that link particular genetic variations to hyperactive fear circuits and, in turn, to inhibited—that is, fearful—temperaments in certain infants and toddlers (Buzzell et al., 2017; Johnson et al., 2016; Fox et al., 2015). From the earliest days of life, such children show a withdrawn, isolated, and cautious pattern known as *behavioral inhibition*. They are wary of new objects, people, and environments, and always seem on guard against potential threats. Research indicates that this inhibited temperament often endures throughout a person's life and places some individuals at heightened risk for the development of anxiety-related disorders (Abulizi et al., 2017; Buzzell et al., 2017).

Drawing from the cognitive-behavioral and psychodynamic models, developmental psychopathologists have also been interested in research findings that highlight the important role of *parenting styles* (Moreno, 2018; Hankin et al., 2016). Investigations indicate that as children grow, *overprotective parenting*—in which parents rush in too quickly to prevent or rescue their children from experiencing distress—denies them opportunities to learn how to manage distress by themselves and to build a strong sense of self-confidence. If children already have a biological vulnerability and an inhibited temperament, exposure to overprotective parenting can help promote repeated eruptions of anxiety, setting the stage for lifelong anxiety.

Finally, drawing from the sociocultural model, developmental psychopathologists have also been interested in research showing that life stress, poverty, school difficulties, family disharmony, peer pressure, and community danger can heighten the likelihood of developing anxiety-related disorders. Indeed, a growing number of studies suggest that, in many cases, some such factors must be present for these disorders to emerge, in addition to any unfavorable biological factors, temperament, or parenting experiences the individual may have (Eme, 2017; Pianta, 2016).

While the developmental psychopathology perspective helps us appreciate that the principles of the various models may often be combined to better account for anxiety-related disorders, it also highlights that the models have not typically addressed important questions about the *development* of these disorders. Precisely *how* and *when*, for example, do the variables from each of the models interact to produce the disorders? A growing body of research suggests that the various key factors—from biological to temperament to parenting to life events—may have greater or lesser impact at different points of development (Moreno, 2018; Eme, 2017; Cicchetti, 2016). The early settling in of a fearful temperament, for example, may place a lid on the later impact of positive life events. Conversely, effective parenting may reduce the impact of an unfavorable biological predisposition or of later negative life events. Clearly, in order for anxiety-related disorders to be more fully understood and effectively treated, these important developmental issues need to be clarified.

CLINICAL CHOICES

Now that you've read about anxiety, obsessive-compulsive, and related disorders, try the interactive case study for this chapter. See if you are able to identify Priya's symptoms and suggest a diagnosis based on her symptoms. What kind of treatment would be most effective for Priya? Go to **LaunchPad** to access ***Clinical Choices***.

...SUMMING UP

INTEGRATING THE MODELS To explain anxiety-related disorders, proponents of the developmental psychopathology perspective examine how key factors emerge and intersect at points throughout an individual's life span. The factors of interest to them include genetic factors, a hyperactive fear circuit in the brain, an inhibited temperament, parenting style, maladaptive thinking, avoidance behaviors, life stress, and negative social factors.

... Key Terms

fear, p. 102
anxiety, p. 102
generalized anxiety disorder, p. 102
unconditional positive regard, p. 106
client-centered therapy, p.106
basic irrational assumptions, p. 107
metacognitive theory, p. 108
rational-emotive therapy, p. 109
mindfulness-based cognitive-behavioral therapy, p. 110
family pedigree studies, p. 110
benzodiazepines, p. 111
gamma-aminobutyric acid (GABA), p. 111
brain circuit, p. 111
fear circuit, p. 111
sedative-hypnotic drugs, p. 111
phobia, p. 113
specific phobia, p. 113
agoraphobia, p. 115
classical conditioning, p. 115
modeling, p. 116
preparedness, p. 117
exposure treatment, p. 117
systematic desensitization, p. 117
flooding, p. 118
social anxiety disorder, p. 120
social skills training, p. 123
panic attacks, p. 123
panic disorder, p. 124
norepinephrine, p. 125
locus coeruleus, p. 125
panic circuit, p. 125
biological challenge test, p. 126
anxiety sensitivity, p. 127
obsession, p. 128
compulsion, p. 128
obsessive-compulsive disorder, p. 128
neutralizing, p. 130
exposure and response prevention, p. 131
cortico-striato-thalamo-cortical circuit, p. 132
serotonin, p. 132
obsessive-compulsive-related disorders, p. 133
hoarding disorder, p. 133
trichotillomania, p. 133
excoriation disorder, p. 134
body dysmorphic disorder, p. 134
developmental psychopathology, p. 135
behavioral inhibition, p. 136
overprotective parenting, p. 136

... Quick Quiz

1. What are the key principles in the sociocultural, psychodynamic, humanistic, cognitive-behavioral, and biological explanations of generalized anxiety disorder? *pp. 103–111*
2. How effective have treatments been for generalized anxiety disorder? *pp. 106–112*
3. Define and compare specific phobias and agoraphobia. How do cognitive-behavioral theorists explain phobias? *pp. 113–116*
4. Describe the three exposure techniques used to treat specific phobias. *pp. 117–118*
5. What are the various components of social anxiety disorder, and how is this disorder treated? *pp. 120–123*
6. How do biological and cognitive-behavioral clinicians explain and treat panic disorder? *pp. 124–127*
7. Which factors do psychodynamic, cognitive-behavioral, and biological theorists believe are at work in obsessive-compulsive disorder? *pp. 129–132*
8. Describe and compare the effectiveness of exposure and response prevention and antidepressant medications as treatments for obsessive-compulsive disorder. *pp. 131–133*
9. Describe the four obsessive-compulsive-related disorders. *pp. 133–135*
10. How do developmental psychopathology theorists integrate the findings and principles from the various models to explain anxiety, obsessive-compulsive, and obsessive-compulsive-related disorders? *pp. 135–136*

Visit ***LaunchPad***
to access the e-Book, Clinical Choices, videos, activities, and LearningCurve, as well as study aids including flashcards, FAQs, and research exercises.

LaunchPad

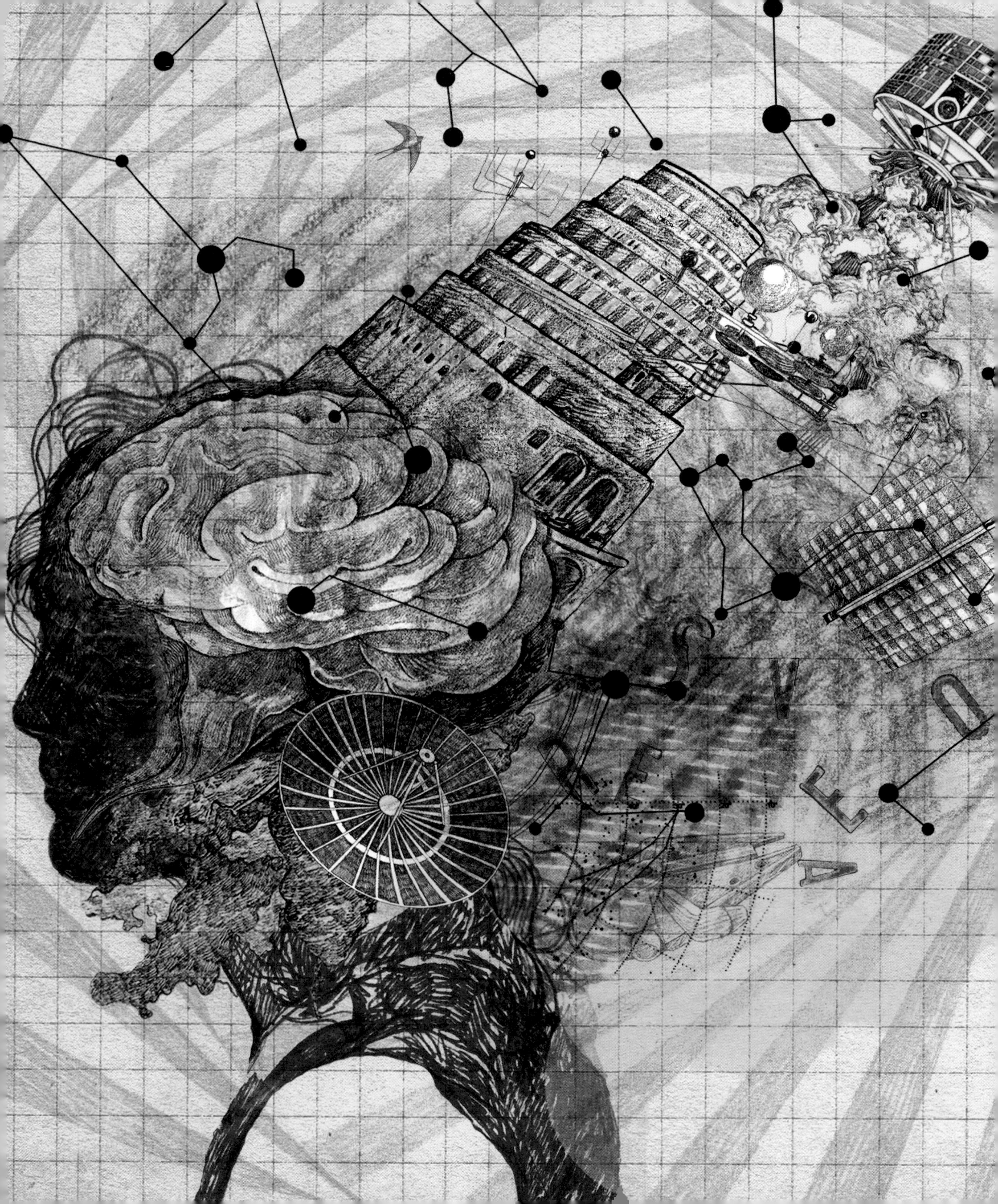

CHAPTER

5

Disorders of Trauma and Stress

TOPIC OVERVIEW

Specialist Latrell Robinson, a 25-year-old single African American man, was an activated National Guardsman [serving in the Iraq war]. He [had been] a full-time college student and competitive athlete raised by a single mother in public housing. . . . Initially trained in transportation, he was called to active duty and retrained as a military policeman to serve with his unit in Baghdad. He described enjoying the high intensity of his deployment and [became] recognized by others as an informal leader because of his aggressiveness and self-confidence. He [had] numerous [combat] exposures while performing convoy escort and security details [and he came] under small arms fire on several occasions, witnessing dead and injured civilians and Iraqi soldiers and on occasion feeling powerless when forced to detour or take evasive action. He began to develop increasing mistrust of the [Iraq] environment as the situation "on the street" seemed to deteriorate. He often felt that he and his fellow soldiers were placed in harm's way needlessly.

On a routine convoy mission [in 2003], serving as driver for the lead HUMVEE, his vehicle was struck by an Improvised Explosive Device showering him with shrapnel in his neck, arm, and leg. Another member of his vehicle was even more seriously injured. . . . He was evacuated to the Combat Support Hospital (CSH) where he was treated and returned to duty . . . after several days despite requiring crutches and suffering chronic pain from retained shrapnel in his neck. He began to become angry at his command and doctors for keeping him in [Iraq] while he was unable to perform his duties effectively. He began to develop insomnia, hypervigilance, and a startle response. His initial dreams of the event became more intense and frequent and he suffered intrusive thoughts and flashbacks of the attack. He began to withdraw from his friends and suffered anhedonia, feeling detached from others, and he feared his future would be cut short. He was referred to a psychiatrist at the CSH. . . .

After two months of unsuccessful rehabilitation for his battle injuries and worsening depressive and anxiety symptoms, he was evacuated to a . . . military medical center [in the United States]. . . . He was screened for psychiatric symptoms and was referred for outpatient evaluation and management. He met . . . criteria for acute PTSD and was offered medication management, supportive therapy, and group therapy. . . . He was ambivalent about taking passes or convalescent leave to his home because of fears of being "different, irritated, or aggressive" around his family or girlfriend. After three months at the military service center, he was [deactivated from service and] referred to his local VA Hospital to receive follow-up care.

(National Center for PTSD, 2008)

During the horror of combat, soldiers often become highly anxious and depressed, confused and disoriented, even physically ill. Moreover, for many, like Latrell, these and related reactions to extraordinary stress or trauma continue well beyond the combat experience itself.

Of course, it is not just combat soldiers who are affected by stress. Nor does stress have to rise to the level of combat trauma to have a profound effect on psychological and physical functioning. Stress comes in all sizes and shapes, and we are all greatly affected by it.

We feel some degree of stress whenever we are faced with demands or opportunities that require us to change in some manner. The state of stress has two components: a *stressor,* the event that creates the demands, and a *stress response,* the person's reactions to the demands. The stressors of life may include annoying everyday hassles, such as rush-hour traffic; turning-point events, such as college graduation or marriage; long-term problems, such as poverty or poor health; or traumatic events, such as major accidents, assaults, tornadoes, or military combat. Our response to such stressors is influenced by the way we *judge* both the events and our capacity to react to them in an effective way (Blaxton & Bergeman, 2017; Lazarus & Folkman, 1984). People who sense that they have the ability and the resources to cope are more likely to take stressors in stride and to respond well.

When we view a stressor as threatening, a natural reaction is arousal and a sense of fear—a response frequently discussed in Chapter 4. Stress reactions, and the sense of fear they produce, are often at play in psychological disorders. People who experience a large number of stressful events are particularly vulnerable to the onset of the anxiety disorders that you read about in Chapter 4 (Furr et al., 2018). Similarly, increases in stress have been linked to the onset of depression, schizophrenia, sexual dysfunctions, and other psychological problems.

Extraordinary stress and trauma play an even more central role in certain psychological disorders. In these disorders, the reactions to stress become severe and debilitating, linger for a long period of time, and may make it impossible for the individual to live a normal life. Under the heading "Trauma- and Stressor-Related Disorders," DSM-5 lists several disorders in which trauma and extraordinary stress trigger a range of significant stress symptoms, including heightened arousal, anxiety and mood problems, memory and orientation difficulties, and behavioral disturbances. Two of these disorders, *acute stress disorder* and *posttraumatic stress disorder,* are discussed in this chapter. In addition, DSM-5 lists the "dissociative disorders," a group of disorders also triggered by traumatic events, in which the primary symptoms are severe memory and orientation problems. These disorders are also examined in this chapter.

To fully understand these various stress-related disorders, it is important to appreciate the precise nature of stress and how the brain and body typically react to stress. Thus let's first discuss stress and arousal, then move on to discussions of acute and posttraumatic stress disorders and the dissociative disorders.

Peio Hernandez/EPA/Newscom

Jon Dimis/AP Photo

Different strokes for different folks Some people are exhilarated by the opportunity to chase bulls through the streets of Pamplona, Spain, during the annual "running of the bulls." Others are terrified by such a prospect and prefer instead to engage tamer animals, such as ostriches, during the "running of the ostriches" fiesta in Irurzun, Spain.

Stress and Arousal: The Fight-or-Flight Response

The features of arousal are set in motion by the brain structure called the *hypothalamus.* When our brain interprets a situation as dangerous, neurotransmitters in the hypothalamus are released, triggering the firing of neurons throughout the brain and the release of chemicals throughout the body. Actually, the hypothalamus activates two important systems—the *autonomic nervous system* and the *endocrine system.* The **autonomic nervous system (ANS)** is the extensive network of nerve fibers that connect the *central nervous system* (the brain and spinal cord) to all the other organs of the body. These fibers help control the *involuntary* activities of the organs—breathing, heartbeat, blood pressure, perspiration, and the like (see **Figure 5-1**). The **endocrine system** is the network of *glands* located throughout the body. (As you read in Chapter 2, glands release *hormones* into the bloodstream and on to the various body organs.) The ANS and the endocrine system often overlap in their responsibilities. There are two brain–body pathways, or routes, by which these systems produce arousal—the *sympathetic nervous system* pathway and the *hypothalamic-pituitary-adrenal* pathway.

When we face a dangerous situation, the hypothalamus first excites the **sympathetic nervous system,** a group of ANS fibers that work to quicken our heartbeat and produce the other changes that we come to experience as fear or anxiety. These nerves may stimulate the organs of the body directly—for example, they may directly stimulate the heart and increase heart rate. The nerves may also influence the organs indirectly, by stimulating the *adrenal glands* (glands located on top of the kidneys), particularly an area of these glands called the *adrenal medulla*. When the adrenal medulla is stimulated, the chemicals *epinephrine* (*adrenaline*) and *norepinephrine* (*noradrenaline*) are released. You have already seen that these chemicals are important neurotransmitters when they operate in the brain (see page 38). When released from the adrenal medulla, however, they act as hormones and travel through the bloodstream to various organs and muscles, further producing arousal.

When the perceived danger passes, a second group of autonomic nervous system fibers, called the **parasympathetic nervous system,** helps return our heartbeat and other body processes to normal. Together the sympathetic and parasympathetic nervous systems help control our arousal reactions.

autonomic nervous system (ANS) The network of nerve fibers that connect the central nervous system to all the other organs of the body.

endocrine system The system of glands located throughout the body that help control important activities such as growth and sexual activity.

sympathetic nervous system The nerve fibers of the autonomic nervous system that quicken the heartbeat and produce other changes experienced as arousal.

parasympathetic nervous system The nerve fibers of the autonomic nervous system that help return bodily processes to normal.

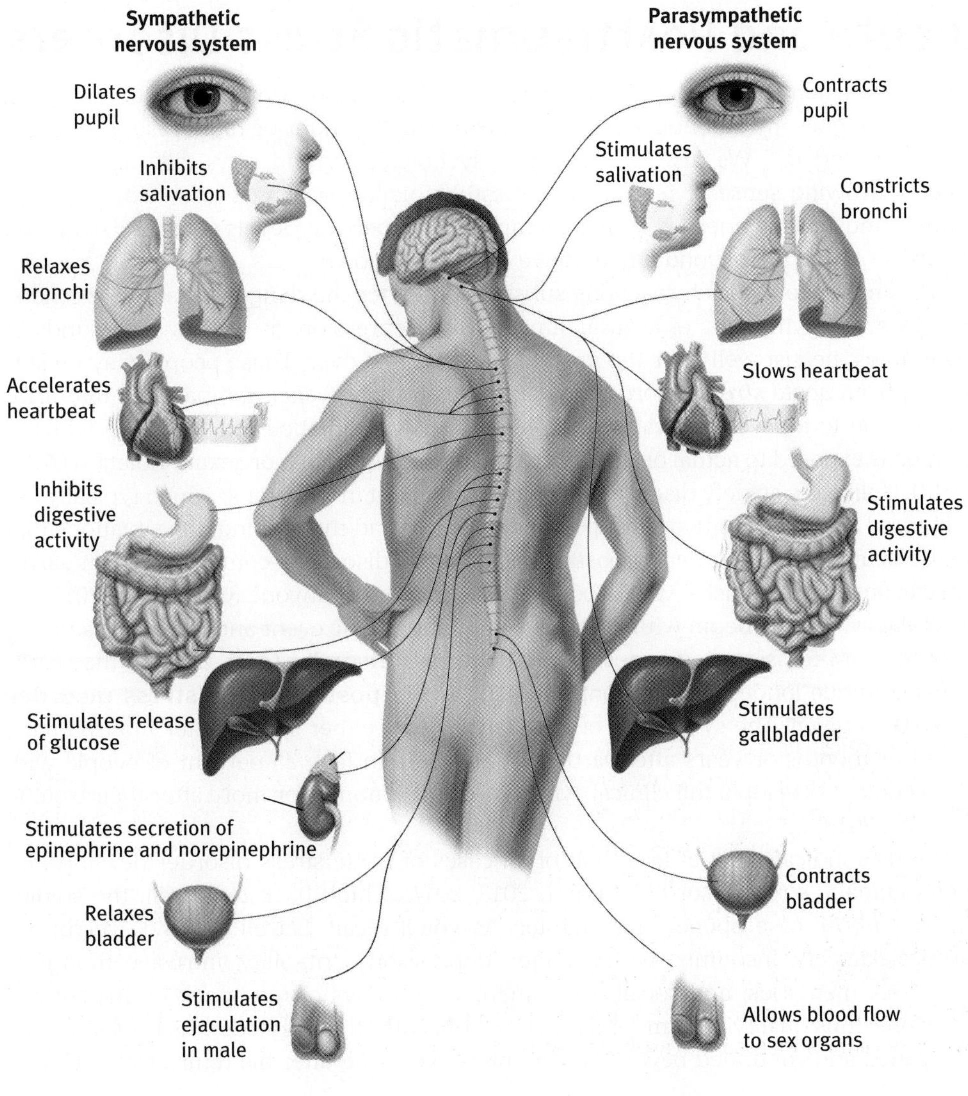

FIGURE 5-1

The Autonomic Nervous System (ANS)

When the sympathetic division of the ANS is activated, it stimulates some organs and inhibits others. The result is a state of general arousal. In contrast, activation of the parasympathetic division leads to an overall calming effect.

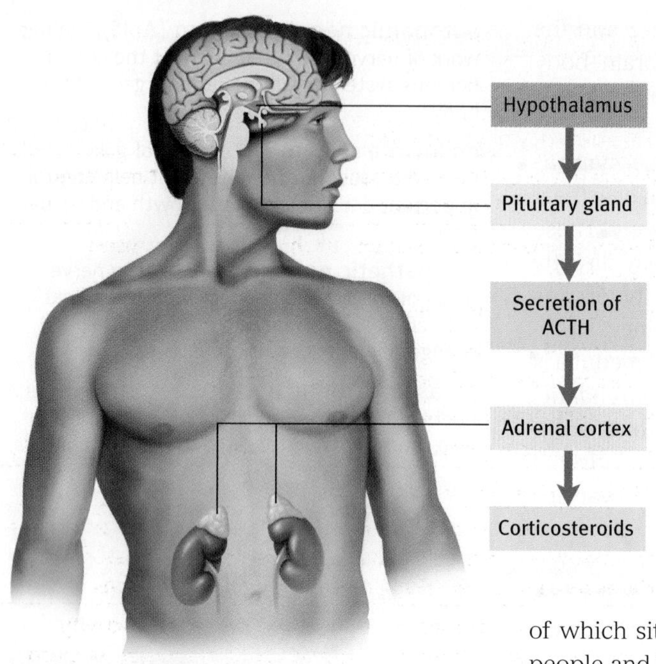

FIGURE 5-2

The Endocrine System: The HPA Pathway

When a person perceives a stressor, the hypothalamus activates the pituitary gland to secrete the adrenocorticotropic hormone, or ACTH, which stimulates the adrenal cortex. The adrenal cortex releases stress hormones called corticosteroids that act on other body organs to trigger arousal and fear reactions.

The second brain–body pathway by which arousal is produced is the **hypothalamic-pituitary-adrenal (HPA) pathway** (see **Figure 5-2**). When we are faced by stressors, the hypothalamus also signals the *pituitary gland,* which lies nearby, to secrete the *adrenocorticotropic hormone* (*ACTH*), sometimes called the body's "major stress hormone." ACTH, in turn, stimulates the outer layer of the adrenal glands, an area called the *adrenal cortex,* triggering the release of a group of stress hormones called **corticosteroids,** including the hormone *cortisol.* These corticosteroids travel to various body organs, where they further produce arousal reactions (Donohoue, 2017; Jacoby et al., 2016).

The reactions on display in these two pathways are collectively referred to as the *fight-or-flight* response, precisely because they arouse our body and prepare us for a response to danger. Each person has a particular pattern of autonomic and endocrine functioning and so has a particular way of experiencing arousal when he or she confronts stressors. Some people, for example, react with relatively little tension even in the face of significant threats, while others react with considerable tension even when they encounter minimal threats. People also differ in their sense of which situations are threatening. Flying in an airplane may arouse terror in some people and boredom in others.

Acute and Posttraumatic Stress Disorders

Of course when we actually confront stressful situations, we do not think to ourselves, "Oh, there goes my autonomic nervous system," or "My fight-or-flight response seems to be kicking in." We just feel aroused psychologically and physically and experience a growing sense of fear. If the stressful situation is perceived as extraordinary and/or unusually dangerous, we may temporarily experience levels of arousal, fear, and depression that are beyond anything we have ever known.

For most people, such reactions subside soon after the danger passes. For others, however, the symptoms of arousal, anxiety, and depression, as well as other kinds of symptoms, persist well after the upsetting situation is over. These people may be suffering from *acute stress disorder* or *posttraumatic stress disorder,* patterns that arise in reaction to a psychologically traumatic event. A traumatic event is one in which a person is exposed to actual or threatened death, serious injury, or sexual violation (APA, 2013). Unlike the anxiety disorders that you read about in Chapter 4, which typically are triggered by situations that most people would not find threatening, the situations that cause acute stress disorder or posttraumatic stress disorder—combat, rape, an earthquake, an airplane crash—would be traumatic for almost anyone (Chou et al., 2017).

If the symptoms begin within 4 weeks of the traumatic event and last for less than a month, DSM-5 assigns a diagnosis of **acute stress disorder** (APA, 2013). If the symptoms continue longer than a month, a diagnosis of **posttraumatic stress disorder (PTSD)** is given. The symptoms of PTSD may begin either shortly after the traumatic event or months or years afterward (see **Table 5-1**). In fact, 25 percent of people with PTSD do not develop a full clinical syndrome until 6 months or more after their trauma (Sareen, 2018).

Studies indicate that at least half of all cases of acute stress disorder develop into posttraumatic stress disorder (Bryant, 2018, 2017). Think back to Latrell, the soldier in Iraq whose case opened this chapter. As you'll recall, Latrell became overrun by arousal, anxiety, insomnia, worry, anger, depression, irritability, intrusive thoughts, flashback memories, and social detachment within days of the attack on his convoy mission—thus qualifying him for a diagnosis of acute stress disorder. As his symptoms worsened and continued beyond one month—even long after his return to the United

hypothalamic-pituitary-adrenal (HPA) pathway One route by which the brain and body produce arousal.

corticosteroids Hormones, including cortisol, released by the adrenal glands at times of stress.

acute stress disorder A disorder in which a person experiences fear and related symptoms soon after a trauma but for less than a month.

posttraumatic stress disorder (PTSD) A disorder in which a person experiences fear and related symptoms long after a traumatic event.

States—this diagnosis became PTSD. Aside from the differences in onset and duration, the symptoms of acute stress disorder and PTSD are almost identical:

INCREASED AROUSAL, NEGATIVE EMOTIONS, AND GUILT People may feel excessively alert (hyperalertness), be easily startled, have trouble concentrating, and develop sleep problems. They may display anxiety, anger, or depression, and feel extreme guilt because they survived the traumatic event while others did not (Norman et al., 2018). Some also feel guilty about what they may have had to do to survive.

REEXPERIENCING THE TRAUMATIC EVENT People may be battered by recurring thoughts, memories, dreams, or nightmares connected to the event (Walton et al., 2017). A few relive the event so vividly in their minds (flashbacks) that they think it is actually happening again.

AVOIDANCE People usually avoid activities that remind them of the traumatic event and try to avoid related thoughts, feelings, or conversations.

REDUCED RESPONSIVENESS AND DISSOCIATION People with these disorders may feel detached from other people, be unresponsive to external stimuli, and lose interest in activities that once brought enjoyment. Many endure symptoms of *dissociation,* or psychological separation: that is, they feel dazed, have trouble remembering things, experience *depersonalization* (feeling that their conscious state or body is unreal), or have a sense of *derealization* (feeling that the environment is unreal or strange).

You can see these symptoms in the recollections of a Vietnam combat veteran years after he returned home:

> *I can't get the memories out of my mind! The images come flooding back in vivid detail, triggered by the most inconsequential things, like a door slamming or the smell of stir-fried pork. Last night I went to bed, was having a good sleep for a change. Then in the early morning a storm-front passed through and there was a bolt of crackling thunder. I awoke instantly, frozen in fear. I am right back in Vietnam, in the middle of the monsoon season at my guard post. I am sure I'll get hit in the next volley and convinced I will die. My hands are freezing, yet sweat pours from my entire body. I feel each hair on the back of my neck standing on end. I can't catch my breath and my heart is pounding. I smell a damp sulfur smell.*
>
> *(Davis, 1992)*

Clinicians have come to appreciate that people who experience symptoms of dissociation and unresponsiveness as part of their stress syndrome tend to be more impaired and distressed than other sufferers (Hansen, Ross, & Armour, 2017). This pattern is particularly common among PTSD victims whose traumas involved military combat, sexual abuse, or other forms of physical abuse, especially repeated abuse or childhood abuse.

An acute or posttraumatic stress disorder can occur at any age, even in childhood (Furr et al., 2018). Surveys indicate that 3.5 to 6 percent of people in North America have one of the stress disorders in any given year; 7 to 12 percent suffer from one of them during their lifetimes (Sareen, 2018; Kessler et al., 2012). Around half of these individuals seek treatment, but relatively few do so when they first develop the disorder (NIMH, 2017; Wang et al., 2005). Approximately 20 percent attempt suicide (Cunningham et al., 2019). People with these stress disorders often develop other psychological disorders as well, such as depressive, anxiety, or substance use disorders (Dworkin et al., 2018). They also have an increased risk of developing physical ailments such as bronchitis, asthma, heart disease, and liver disease (Sareen, 2018; La Greca, Comer, & Lai, 2016).

TABLE: 5-1

Dx Checklist

Posttraumatic Stress Disorder
1. Person is exposed to a traumatic event—death or threatened death, severe injury, or sexual violation.
2. Person experiences at least one of the following intrusive symptoms: • Repeated, uncontrolled, and distressing memories • Repeated and upsetting trauma-linked dreams • Dissociative experiences such as flashbacks • Significant upset when exposed to trauma-linked cues • Pronounced physical reactions when reminded of the event(s)
3. Person continually avoids trauma-linked stimuli.
4. Person experiences negative changes in trauma-linked cognitions and moods, such as being unable to remember key features of the event(s) or experiencing repeated negative emotions.
5. Person displays conspicuous changes in arousal or reactivity, such as excessive alertness, extreme startle responses, or sleep disturbances.
6. Person experiences significant distress or impairment, with symptoms lasting more than a month.

Information from: APA, 2013.

Craig F. Walker/Getty Images

Lingering impact More than four decades after the Vietnam War, over a quarter million veterans of that war are still suffering from PTSD. Until his death in 2016, one such veteran was King Charsa Bakari Kamau. He is seen here playing the piano at a mall in Denver, Colorado, an avocation that he considered to be his best therapy.

People with low incomes are twice as likely as people with higher incomes to experience stress disorders (Sareen, 2018; Sareen et al., 2011). Women are more likely than men to develop one of these disorders: around 20 percent of women who are exposed to a severe trauma may develop one, compared with 8 percent of men (Perrin et al., 2014; Russo & Tartaro, 2008). Similarly, Hispanic Americans, African Americans, and American Indians are more likely than non-Hispanic white Americans to develop a stress disorder after confronting a severe trauma (Tull, 2017; Ghafoori et al., 2013). The reason for this racial-ethnic difference is not clear.

What Triggers Acute and Posttraumatic Stress Disorders?

Any traumatic event can trigger a stress disorder; however, some are particularly likely to do so (Sareen, 2018). Among the most common are combat, disasters, and abuse and victimization.

Combat For years clinicians have recognized that many soldiers develop symptoms of severe anxiety and depression *during* combat. It was called "shell shock" during World War I and "combat fatigue" during World War II and the Korean War (Figley, 1978). Not until after the Vietnam War, however, did clinicians learn that a great many soldiers also experience serious psychological symptoms *after* combat (Ruzek et al., 2011).

By the late 1970s, it became apparent that many Vietnam combat veterans were still experiencing war-related psychological difficulties. We now know that as many as 29 percent of all Vietnam veterans, male and female, suffered an acute or posttraumatic stress disorder, while another 22 percent have had at least some stress symptoms (Hermes, Hoff, & Rosenheck, 2014; Krippner & Paulson, 2006). In fact, 10 percent of the veterans of that war still deal with posttraumatic stress symptoms, including flashbacks, night terrors, nightmares, and persistent images and thoughts (Gradus, 2017; Marmar et al., 2015).

A similar pattern has unfolded among the nearly 2.7 million veterans of the wars in Afghanistan and Iraq (Stevelink et al., 2018; Vasterling et al., 2016; Ruzek et al., 2011). Around 20 percent of the individuals deployed to those wars have so far reported symptoms of PTSD. Among those directly exposed to prolonged periods of combat-related stress, the percentage with PTSD is higher still.

Disasters and Accidents Acute and posttraumatic stress disorders may also follow natural and accidental disasters such as earthquakes, floods, tornadoes, fires, airplane crashes, and serious car accidents (see **Table 5-2**). Researchers have found, for example, unusually high rates of PTSD among the survivors of 2005's Hurricane Katrina, 2010's BP Gulf Coast oil spill, and the devastating hurricanes that struck Puerto Rico, Florida, and Texas in 2017 (Dickerson, 2017; Brown et al., 2016). In fact, because they occur more often, civilian traumas have been the trigger of stress disorders at least 10 times as often as combat traumas (Bremner, 2002). Studies have found that between 12 and 40 percent of people involved in traffic accidents—adult or child—may develop PTSD within a year of the accident (Sareen, 2018; Noll-Hussong et al., 2013).

Victimization People who have been abused or victimized often have stress symptoms that linger. Research suggests that over one-third of all victims of physical or sexual assault develop PTSD (Sareen, 2018; Koss et al., 2011). As many as half of all people directly exposed to terrorism or torture may develop the disorder (Comer et al., 2018; Basoglu et al., 2001).

TABLE: 5-2

Worst Natural Disasters of the Past 110 Years

Disaster	Year	Location	Number Killed
Flood	1931	Huang River, China	3,700,000
Tsunami	2004	South Asia	280,000
Earthquake	1976	Tangshan, China	255,000
Heat wave	2003	Europe	35,000
Volcano	1985	Nevado del Ruiz, Colombia	23,000
Hurricane	1998	(Mitch) Central America	18,277
Landslide	1970	Yungay, Peru	17,500
Avalanche	1916	Italian Alps	10,000
Blizzard	1972	Iran	4,000
Tornado	1989	Saturia, Bangladesh	1,300

Information from: Statista, 2018; Infogalactic, 2016; USGS, 2011; Ash, 2001.

SEXUAL ASSAULT A common form of victimization in our society today is sexual assault (see ***InfoCentral*** on page 147). **Rape** is forced sexual intercourse or another sexual act committed against a nonconsenting person or intercourse between an adult and an underage person. In the United States, approximately 96,000 cases of rape or attempted rape are reported to the police each year (FBI, 2017). Most experts believe that these are but a fraction of the actual number of rapes and rape attempts, given the reluctance of many victims to report their sexual assaults. Most rapists are men, and most victims are women. Around one in six women is raped at some time during her life. Approximately 71 percent of the victims are raped by acquaintances, intimates, or relatives (BJS, 2017, 2016, 2013).

David McNew/Getty Images

The power of disclosure These demonstrators participate in a #MeToo Survivors March in Los Angeles, California. As part of the #MeToo movement, which began in 2017 after a series of high-profile revelations of sexual assault and harassment, women around the world have spoken out about their sexual victimization experiences—a wave of disclosures that has raised public awareness, provided support and empathy to millions of victims, and led to calls for change in our society's laws, workplace policies, and social norms. According to research, disclosure—in written or verbal form—often enhances a person's recovery from traumatic experiences and can help prevent the onset of PTSD.

The rates of rape differ among racial-ethnic groups. Around 27 percent of American Indian women and 22 percent of African American women have been raped at some point in their lives, compared with 19 percent of non-Hispanic white American women, 15 percent of Hispanic American women, and 12 percent of Asian American women (BJS, 2017; Black et al., 2011).

The psychological impact of rape on a victim is immediate and may last a long time (Bates, 2017; Koss et al., 2015, 2011, 2008). Rape victims typically experience enormous distress during the week after the assault. Stress continues to rise for the next 3 weeks, maintains a peak level for another month or so, and then starts to improve. In one study, 94 percent of rape victims fully qualified for a clinical diagnosis of acute stress disorder when they were observed around 12 days after the assault (Rothbaum et al., 1992). Although some rape victims improve psychologically within three or four months, for many others, the profound effects of their assault persist for up to 18 months or longer. Victims typically continue to have higher-than-average levels of anxiety, suspiciousness, depression, self-esteem problems, self-blame, flashbacks, sleep problems, and sexual dysfunction (Bates, 2017; Remes et al., 2016).

How might physicians, police, the courts, and other agents better meet the psychological needs of rape victims?

Female victims of rape and other crimes also are much more likely than other women to suffer serious long-term health problems (Bates, 2017; Koss & Heslet, 1992). Interviews with 390 women revealed that such victims had poorer physical well-being for at least five years after the crime and made twice as many visits to physicians.

Ongoing victimization and abuse in the family—specifically child and spouse abuse—may also lead to psychological stress disorders (Mills, Hill, & Johnson, 2018; Ng et al., 2018). Because these forms of abuse may occur over the long term and violate family trust, many victims develop other symptoms and disorders as well.

TERRORISM People who are victims of *terrorism* or who live under the threat of terrorism often experience posttraumatic stress symptoms (Comer et al., 2018, 2016; Glad et al., 2017). Unfortunately, this source of traumatic stress is on the rise in our society. The terrorist events of September 11, 2001, have left a lasting mark on the United States and the rest of the world. Hijacked airplanes crashed into and brought down the World Trade Center in New York City and partially destroyed the Pentagon in Washington, DC, killing thousands of victims and rescue workers and forcing thousands more to desperately run, crawl, and even dig their way to safety. A number of studies have indicated that in the aftermath of that fateful day, many individuals developed immediate and long-term psychological effects, ranging from brief stress reactions, such as shock, fear, and anger, to enduring psychological disorders, such as PTSD (Comer et al., 2018; Ruggero et al., 2013).

rape Forced sexual intercourse or another sexual act committed against a nonconsenting person or intercourse between an adult and an underage person.

Loic Venance/Getty Images

Je suis Charlie In 2015, terrorists conducted a three-day killing spree in Paris, including the murder of 12 employees of the weekly satirical newspaper *Charlie Hebdo*. Using the slogan *Je suis Charlie* ("I am Charlie"), close to 4 million people joined rallies around France, voicing their support for free speech and their resolve against terrorism. This terrorist attack, like others, led to a significant rise in the rate of PTSD across France (Ben-Ezra et al., 2015).

Follow-up studies suggest that many such individuals continue to struggle with terrorism-related stress reactions (Tucker et al., 2018; Adams & Boscarino, 2005). Indeed, even years after the attacks, 42 percent of all adults in the United States and 70 percent of all New York adults report high terrorism fears; 23 percent of all adults in the United States report feeling less safe in their homes; 15 percent of all U.S. adults report drinking more alcohol than they did prior to the attacks; and 9 percent of New York adults display PTSD, compared with the national annual prevalence of 3.5 percent. Studies of subsequent acts of terrorism, such as the 2004 commuter train bombings in Madrid, the 2013 Boston Marathon bombing, the 2016 Bastille Day truck attack in Nice, France, and the 2017 Ariana Grande concert bombing in Manchester, United Kingdom, tell a similar story (Comer et al., 2018, 2014; Goodwin et al., 2017).

An ever-growing phenomenon in the United States and across the world are *mass shootings*—sometimes in the name of terrorism, sometimes not—at schools and other public places, such as the 2017 killings of 58 concertgoers in Las Vegas, Nevada, and the 2018 killings of 17 individuals at the Marjory Stoneman Douglas High School in Parkland, Florida (see page 408). Here again, studies suggest that many survivors of these shootings develop shooting-related stress disorders (Godlasky, 2018; Bekker, 2017).

TORTURE Torture refers to the use of "brutal, degrading, and disorienting strategies in order to reduce victims to a state of utter helplessness" (Okawa & Hauss, 2007). Often, it is done on the orders of a government or another authority to force persons to yield information or make a confession (Dando, 2017). As you will see in Chapter 16, the question of the morality of torturing prisoners who are considered suspects in the "war on terror" has been the subject of much discussion over the past decade.

People from all walks of life are subjected to torture worldwide—from suspected terrorists to student activists and members of religious, ethnic, and cultural minority groups. The techniques used on them may include *physical torture* (beatings, waterboarding, electrocution), *psychological torture* (threats of death, mock executions, verbal abuse, degradation), *sexual torture* (rape, violence to the genitals, sexual humiliation), or *torture through deprivation* (sleep, sensory, social, nutritional, medical, or hygiene deprivation). Torture victims often experience physical ailments as a result of their ordeal, from scarring and fractures to neurological problems and chronic pain. It also appears that between 30 and 50 percent of torture victims develop PTSD (Ibrahim & Hassan, 2017; Taylor et al., 2013).

torture The use of brutal, degrading, and disorienting strategies to reduce victims to a state of utter helplessness.

SEXUAL ASSAULT

People who are **sexually assaulted** have been forced to engage in a sexual act against their will. According to most definitions, people who are **raped** have been forced into sexual intercourse or other forms of sexual penetration. Rape victims often experience **rape trauma syndrome (RTS),** a pattern of problematic physical and psychological symptoms. RTS is actually a form of PTSD. Approximately **one-third** of rape victims develop PTSD.

THE PSYCHOLOGICAL EFFECTS OF RAPE

suicidal thoughts
attempted **suicide**
vulnerability to develop **psychological disorders**
feelings of self-blame and **betrayal**
flashbacks
panic attacks
sleep problems
memory problems

Rape victims are more likely to:

3 X suffer from depression
4 X contemplate suicide
6 X suffer from PTSD
13 X abuse alcohol
26 X abuse drugs

(CMSAC, 2017; RAINN, 2016, 2009; Adams, 2013)

WHO ARE THE VICTIMS?

Gender

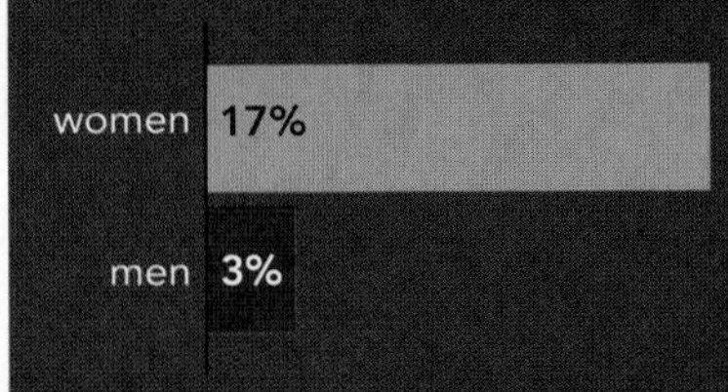

Age

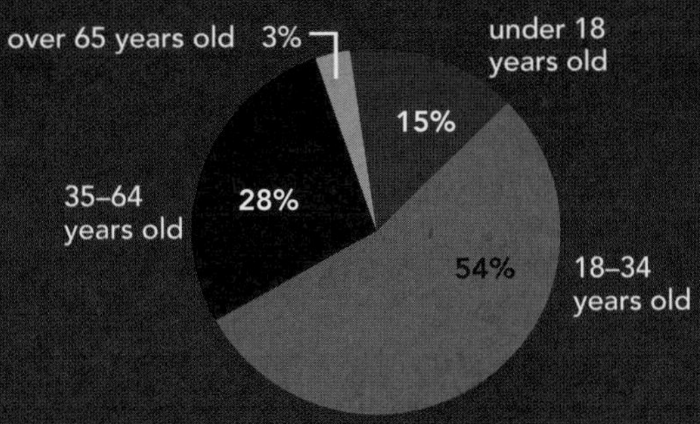

(Bates, 2017; RAINN, 2016, 2009)

Who commits rape?

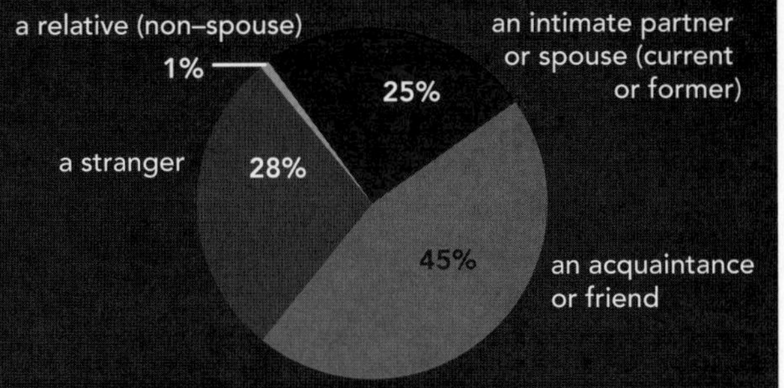

(BJS, 2017, 2016, 2013; RAINN, 2016; Adams, 2013)

SEXUAL ASSAULT ON COLLEGE CAMPUSES

In 2014, the White House pressured colleges to develop better guidelines to address the problem of sexual assaults on campus. It also encouraged all students and university staff to sign the **"It's On Us"** pledge, which makes everyone on campus responsible for preventing and intervening in sexual assaults. That initiative has now grown into a nationwide campaign, called "It's On Us," that uses social media platforms to increase awareness about sexual assault on campus.

IT'S ON US

I pledge:

To RECOGNIZE that non-consensual sex is sexual assault.

To IDENTIFY situations in which sexual assault may occur.

To INTERVENE in situations where consent has not or cannot be given.

To CREATE an environment in which sexual assault is unacceptable and survivors are supported.

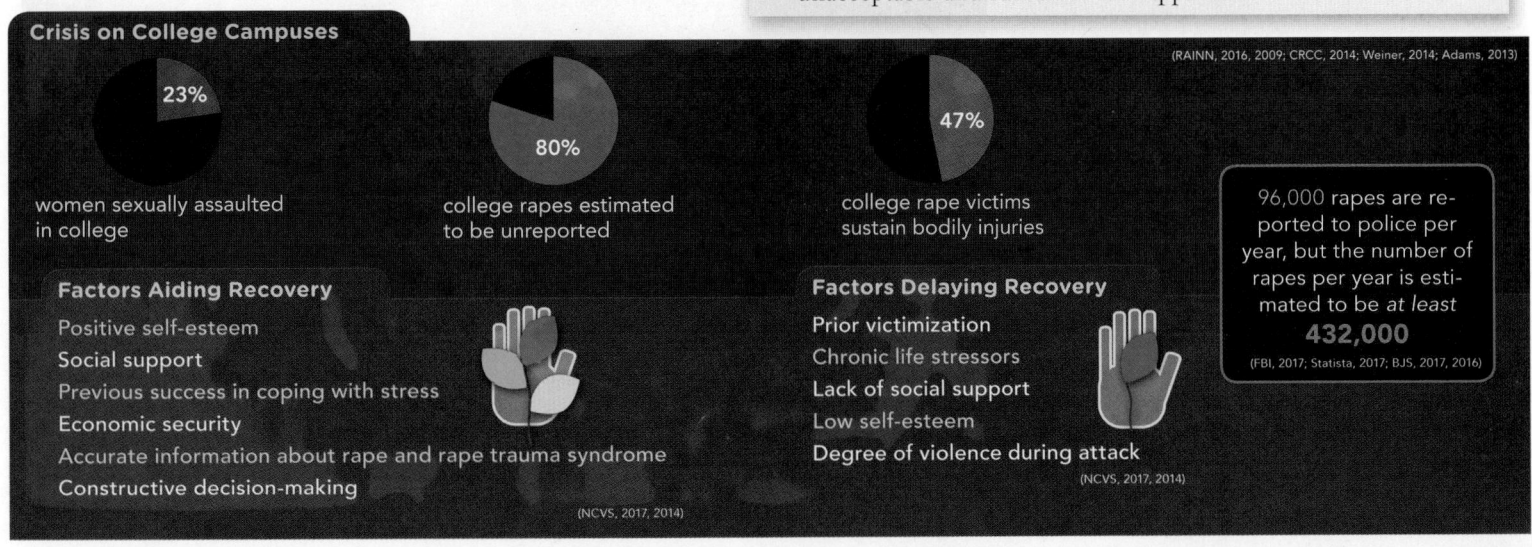

Crisis on College Campuses

(RAINN, 2016, 2009; CRCC, 2014; Weiner, 2014; Adams, 2013)

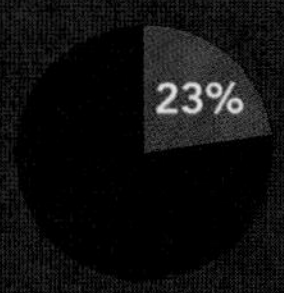

women sexually assaulted in college

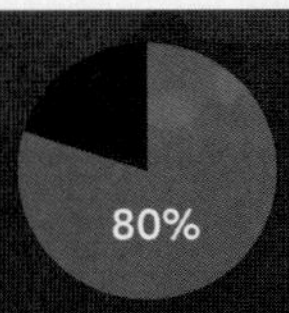

college rapes estimated to be unreported

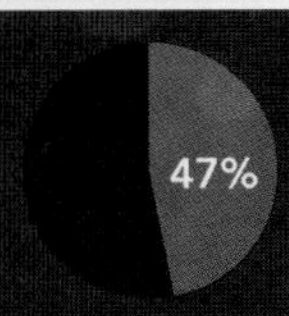

college rape victims sustain bodily injuries

96,000 rapes are reported to police per year, but the number of rapes per year is estimated to be *at least* **432,000**

(FBI, 2017; Statista, 2017; BJS, 2017, 2016)

Factors Aiding Recovery

- Positive self-esteem
- Social support
- Previous success in coping with stress
- Economic security
- Accurate information about rape and rape trauma syndrome
- Constructive decision-making

(NCVS, 2017, 2014)

Factors Delaying Recovery

- Prior victimization
- Chronic life stressors
- Lack of social support
- Low self-esteem
- Degree of violence during attack

(NCVS, 2017, 2014)

#CommonEvent

More than 60% of adults have experienced a traumatic event at least once in their lives (NCPTSD, 2016; Sidran Institute, 2016).

Why Do People Develop Acute and Posttraumatic Stress Disorders?

Clearly, extraordinary trauma can cause a stress disorder. The stressful event alone, however, may not be the entire explanation. Anyone who experiences an unusual trauma will be affected by it, but only some people develop a stress disorder. To understand the development of these disorders more fully, researchers have looked at *biological factors, childhood experiences, personal styles, social support systems,* and the *severity and nature of the traumas.* Our discussions in this section will center on PTSD because that is the stress disorder that is most researched.

Biological Factors Investigators have linked posttraumatic stress disorder to several biological factors. The ones that have received the most attention are the brain–body *stress pathways,* the brain's *stress circuit,* and *inherited predispositions.*

THE BRAIN–BODY STRESS PATHWAYS As you'll recall, when we are stressed, the brain's hypothalamus activates two stress pathways throughout the brain and body—the sympathetic nervous system pathway and the hypothalamic-pituitary-adrenal (HPA) pathway (see pages 141–142). These pathways react to stress by producing a general state of arousal, the former through nerve cell firing and the latter through releasing hormones into the bloodstream.

While everyone reacts to traumatic events with increased arousal throughout these two pathways, research suggests that people who develop PTSD react with especially heightened arousal in the pathways (Dayan, Rauchs, & Guillery-Girard, 2017; Ross et al., 2017). There is evidence that, even prior to confronting a severe trauma, such individuals' pathways are overly reactive to modest stressors, thus setting up a predisposition to develop PTSD. There is also evidence that *after* confrontation with a severe trauma, those brain–body pathways become even more overly reactive (Lehrner & Yehuda, 2018; Rasmusson & Shalev, 2014). Small wonder that researchers have found abnormal activity of the hormone *cortisol* and the neurotransmitter/hormone *norepinephrine*—major players in the two pathways—in the urine, blood, and saliva of combat soldiers, rape victims, concentration camp survivors, and survivors of other severe stresses (Tull et al., 2018; Gola et al., 2012). In short, once PTSD sets in, an individual's brain–body pathways are characterized by still greater overreactivity in the

AP Photo/M. Spencer Green

Candidates for dysfunction A stock trader reacts with exhaustion, worry, and disbelief after a particularly bad—stock-plummeting—day. Business difficulties, such as the trader's, are among the most common triggers of *adjustment disorder,* a DSM-5 disorder characterized by excessive and extended feelings of anxiety, depressed mood, or antisocial behavior in response to life stressors. The symptoms of an adjustment disorder are not as severe as those in PTSD or in anxiety disorders, but they do cause individuals considerable stress and may interfere with their job, schoolwork, or social life.

Omar Havana/Getty Images

Helpers at risk Emergency rescue workers and volunteers frantically carry a victim from the ruins of an earthquake in Kathmandu, Nepal. Studies reveal that those who are called on to help people during disasters, accidents, and other life-and-death situations may themselves be at high risk for developing acute and/or posttraumatic stress disorders (Luftman et al., 2017).

face of stress, and this persistent overreactivity may lock in brain and body dysfunction and the continuing symptoms of PTSD.

THE BRAIN'S STRESS CIRCUIT Researchers believe that the chronic overreactivity of the two stress pathways may help bring about dysfunction in a distinct brain circuit, sometimes called the brain's *stress circuit*. As you have seen in earlier chapters, emotional, behavioral, and cognitive reactions of various kinds are tied to brain circuits—networks of brain structures that communicate and trigger each other into action. Dysfunction in one such circuit, the stress circuit, apparently contributes to the symptoms of PTSD. The brain's stress circuit includes such structures as the *amygdala, prefrontal cortex, anterior cingulate cortex, insula*, and *hippocampus*, among others (Sheynin & Liberzon, 2017; Pedersen, 2016). Given the close relationship between arousal, fear, and anxiety, it is not surprising that several of the structures in this circuit are also parts of the brain's fear and panic circuits that help produce anxiety disorders. But in the case of PTSD, the problematic activity and interconnections of these structures differ from those found in anxiety disorders.

INHERITED PREDISPOSITION Researchers also believe that certain individuals inherit a tendency for overly reactive brain–body stress pathways and a dysfunctional brain stress circuit. In turn, such individuals may have a susceptibility to PTSD. Genetic studies have located several genes that might be involved in this inherited susceptibility (Sheerin et al., 2017; Young, 2017). Similarly, family pedigree research supports the notion of an inherited susceptibility. Studies conducted on thousands of pairs of twins who have served in the military find that if one twin develops posttraumatic stress symptoms after combat, an identical twin is more likely than a fraternal twin to develop the same problem (Koenen et al., 2003; True & Lyons, 1999).

In related work, researchers have found that people suffering from PTSD are more likely to transmit relevant biological abnormalities to their children (Cook et al., 2018; Yehuda et al., 2015). In one study, for example, investigators examined the cortisol levels of women who had been pregnant during the September 11, 2001, terrorist attack and had developed PTSD in its aftermath (Yehuda & Bierer, 2007). Not only did these women have higher-than-average cortisol levels, but their babies born after the attacks also displayed higher cortisol levels, suggesting that the babies inherited a predisposition to develop PTSD.

#TopStressors

1. Personal finances
2. Job pressure
3. The economy
4. Relationships
5. Health

(Information from: APA, 2015)

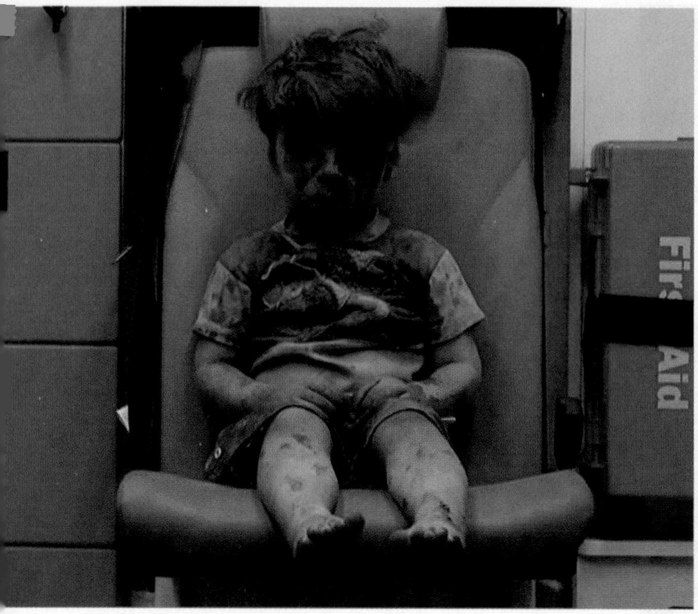

Aleppo Media Center via AP

Children too In this famous and heart-wrenching photo, a bloodied and disoriented 5-year-old child named Omran Daqneesh sits in an ambulance covered with dirt and dust after being pulled from the rubble of a building destroyed by an airstrike in Aleppo, Syria. After confronting horrific traumas, especially repeated ones, children too may develop PTSD, leading clinicians to worry greatly about the mental health of children caught in the middle of Syria's civil war.

Childhood Experiences Other researchers agree that certain individuals have overly reactive stress pathways and a dysfunctional stress circuit that predispose them to develop PTSD. However, they believe that such a predisposition may be acquired during childhood rather than inherited at birth (Ross et al., 2017). In support of this notion, a number of studies have found that young children who are chronically neglected or abused or otherwise traumatized develop overly reactive stress pathways and a dysfunctional brain stress circuit that carry into later life (Lee, Coe, & Ryff, 2017; Zannas & West, 2014). Apparently, their unfortunate childhood experiences actually play a role in reprogramming their brain and body stress responses.

Do the vivid images children see regularly on the Web, on TV, and in video games make them more vulnerable to later developing psychological stress disorders or less vulnerable?

Consistent with these findings, researchers have also found that certain childhood experiences increase a person's risk for later PTSD. People whose childhoods were marked by poverty appear more likely to develop the disorder in the face of later trauma (Lee et al., 2017). So do people whose childhoods included an assault, abuse, or a catastrophe; multiple traumas; parental separation or divorce; or living with family members suffering from psychological disorders (Carroll et al., 2017; Hyland et al., 2017).

Personal Styles Research suggests that people with certain personalities, attitudes, and coping styles are particularly likely to develop posttraumatic stress disorder (Ning, Guan, & Liu, 2017). For example, a classic study conducted after the monster 1989 storm, Hurricane Hugo, revealed that children who had been highly anxious before the storm were more likely than other children to develop severe stress reactions (Hardin et al., 2002). Research has also found that people who generally view life's negative events as beyond their control tend to develop more severe stress symptoms after sexual abuse or other kinds of traumatic events than people who feel that they have more control over their lives (Catanesi et al., 2013; Bremner, 2002). Similarly, people who generally find it difficult to derive anything positive from unpleasant situations adjust more poorly after traumatic events than other people (Kunst, 2011).

Conversely, it has been found that people with a *resilient* style of personality are *less* likely than other individuals to develop PTSD after encountering traumatic events (Thompson et al., 2018; Ross et al., 2017). The term "resilient" has been applied to people who adapt well and cope effectively in the face of life adversity. Although there is evidence that genetic factors may help determine one's level of *resilience,* studies also find that young children who are regularly exposed to *manageable* stress often develop heightened resilience, a gain that may continue throughout childhood and adulthood. Not surprisingly, studies also find that the brain–body stress pathways and brain stress circuits of resilient persons tend to operate better than those of other people (Meng et al., 2018).

Social Support Systems People whose social and family support systems are weak are also more likely to develop posttraumatic stress disorder after a traumatic event (Sareen, 2018). Rape victims who feel loved, cared for, valued, and accepted by their friends and relatives recover from their ordeal more successfully. So do those treated with dignity and respect by the criminal justice system (AAMFT, 2018; Patterson, 2011). In contrast, clinical reports have suggested that poor social support contributes to the development of PTSD in some combat veterans (Schumm et al., 2014).

The Severity and Nature of the Trauma As you might expect, the severity and nature of the traumatic event a person encounters help determine whether the individual will develop a stress disorder. Some events may override a favorable biological foundation, nurturing childhood, positive attitudes, and/or social support (Conrad et al., 2017). One early study examined 253 Vietnam War prisoners five years after their release. Some 23 percent qualified for a clinical diagnosis of PTSD, though all had been evaluated as well adjusted before their imprisonment (Ursano et al., 1981).

Generally, the more severe or prolonged the trauma and the more direct one's exposure to it, the greater the likelihood of developing a stress disorder (Hyland et al., 2017; Ursano et al., 2003). Mutilation, severe physical injury, or sexual assault in particular seem to increase the risk of stress disorders, as does witnessing the injury or death of other people. In addition, people who experience intentionally inflicted traumas are more likely to develop a stress disorder than persons who encounter unintentional traumas (Sareen, 2018).

There is also growing evidence that encounters with multiple or recurring traumas can lead to a particularly severe pattern called *complex PTSD* (Hyland et al., 2017; Jakob et al., 2017). Persons with complex PTSD experience virtually all of the symptoms mentioned throughout this chapter along with profound disturbances in their emotional control, self-concept, and relationships.

Putting the Factors Together Most of today's stress theorists believe that the various factors we have been looking at work together to help produce posttraumatic stress disorder (Ross et al., 2017). The *developmental psychopathology* perspective, which has received considerable research support in the realm of PTSD, provides one of the most influential explanations of how this might occur (Cicchetti, 2018, 2016; Meyer et al., 2017).

As you'll recall from Chapters 2 and 4, theorists from this perspective focus on the *intersection* and *context* of important variables at key *points of time* throughout an individual's life span. In the case of PTSD, they suggest that certain people have a biological predisposition—either inherited or acquired—for overreactivity in their brain–body stress pathways (that is, the sympathetic nervous system pathway and the hypothalamic-pituitary-adrenal pathway) and for dysfunction in their brain's stress circuit. This predisposition sets the stage for, but does not guarantee, the later development of PTSD. If, however, these individuals encounter extreme stressors throughout their childhood, their stress pathways may become still more overreactive and their brain's stress circuit may become more dysfunctional, and their risk of later developing PTSD may continue to grow. This risk may increase still further if, over the course of their lives, the individuals acquire poor coping mechanisms, develop problematic personal styles, and/or have weak social supports. When they confront extraordinary traumas in life, such individuals will be particularly vulnerable to the development of PTSD.

#GenderDifference

Many researchers believe that women's higher rates of posttraumatic stress disorder are tied to the types of violent traumas they experience—namely, interpersonal assaults such as rape or sexual abuse (Sareen, 2018; USDVA, 2015; Street et al., 2011).

Rhona Wise/Getty Images

Empowerment and resilience One week after 17 students and teachers were killed in a 2018 mass shooting at Marjory Stoneman Douglas High School in Parkland, Florida, thousands of nearby south Florida students streamed out of their classrooms and staged this rally on the grounds of the stricken high school, demanding improvements in school safety and stricter gun-control laws. A month later, more than a million students nationwide followed suit in the "National School Walkout." Beyond the validity and importance of these protests, clinical theorists believe that the qualities of empowerment and resilience demonstrated by the students—particularly those who directly experienced the school shooting trauma—has helped protect some of them from developing posttraumatic stress disorder.

#

#StressfulOutcome

20%	Percentage of people who report they have no one to support them during stress
29%	Percentage of people who report feeling more stress this year than last year
41%	Percentage of married people who say stress has caused them to yell at their spouse during the past month

(Information from: APA, 2017, 2015)

It is important to note that in the developmental psychopathology perspective, the relationship between the contributing factors is often a two-way street. For example, while overreactive stress pathways can contribute to poor coping during childhood and beyond, it is also the case that a childhood filled with experiences of *manageable* stress can, as we saw earlier, improve the functioning of the stress pathways, facilitate better coping skills, and help build a resilient personal style, thus reducing the risk of later developing PTSD (Southwick & Charney, 2012).

According to developmental psychopathologists, the *timing* of stressors and traumas over the course of development has a profound influence on whether an individual will develop PTSD (Moreno, 2018; Bremner, 2016). For example, extreme stressors in childhood disrupt and alter newly developing brain–body stress pathways and brain stress circuits, increasing the likelihood that those pathways and circuits will operate poorly over the course of life. Thus experiences of intense stress early in life are particularly likely to set the stage for PTSD should an individual eventually confront extraordinary traumas. At the same time, each stage of development ushers in new psychological and biological challenges, so extreme stressors at any point across the life span can increase a person's vulnerability to PTSD.

The consequence of all this, according to the developmental psychopathology perspective, is that one person born with, say, overreactive stress pathways may eventually develop PTSD when confronted by an extraordinary trauma, whereas another person born with similar predisposing stress pathways may not develop PTSD in the face of such trauma. It all depends on the presence, timing, and intersections of the various factors we have been discussing. As you'll recall from Chapter 2, this is the principle of *multifinality,* the notion that persons with similar beginnings may wind up at very different end points (Cicchetti, 2018, 2016). Conversely, two persons—one born with overreactive stress pathways and the other with pathways that react to stressors more appropriately—may both develop PTSD when eventually confronted by an extraordinary trauma. In such cases, the person born with favorable stress pathways might nonetheless come to develop overreactive pathways as a result of aversive childhood experiences, inadequate social supports, and other such factors. This principle is known as *equifinality,* the notion that different developmental pathways may lead to the same end point (Cicchetti, 2018, 2016).

Sergey Ponomarev/The New York Times/Redux

End of a journey? Not necessarily, at least in the psychological realm. This small boat filled with migrants comes ashore at Lesbos, a pastoral Greek island through which a half million refugees—mostly from Syria—have passed on their way to countries throughout Europe. The rate of PTSD among refugees can be as high as 56 percent in some areas of the world, particularly for those who were tortured in their homeland or whose travels were perilous. Thus a small team of clinicians in Lesbos work full-time to help reduce the stress-related symptoms of refugees during their short stay on the island (Yaser et al., 2016).

ZUMA Press, Inc./Alamy

Standing down To help prevent, reduce, or treat combat-related PTSD, the U.S. military and other organizations now offer stress- and trauma-release exercises for soldiers and ex-soldiers to perform. Here relaxation training and yoga are taught to veterans during the 2013 Veteran Stand Down hosted by Goodwill Southern California.

How Do Clinicians Treat Acute and Posttraumatic Stress Disorders?

Treatment can be very important for people who have been overwhelmed by traumatic events. Overall, one-third of all cases of posttraumatic stress disorder improve within 12 months. The remainder of cases may persist for years, and, indeed, one-third of people with PTSD do not achieve normal functioning even after many years (Sareen, 2018; Byers et al., 2014).

Today's treatment procedures for troubled survivors often vary from trauma to trauma. Was it combat, an act of terrorism, sexual molestation, or a major accident? Yet all the programs share basic goals: they try to help survivors put an end to their stress reactions, gain perspective on their painful experiences, and return to constructive living (Rothbaum, 2017; Brown et al., 2016). Programs for combat veterans who suffer from PTSD illustrate how these issues may be addressed.

Treatment for Combat Veterans Therapists have used a variety of techniques to help reduce veterans' posttraumatic symptoms. Among the most common are *antidepressant drug therapy, cognitive-behavioral therapy, couple or family therapy,* and *group therapy.* Commonly, the approaches are combined, as no one of them successfully reduces all the symptoms (Rothbaum, 2017).

ANTIDEPRESSANT DRUGS Antidepressant drugs are widely used for veterans with PTSD (Stein, 2017). Typically, these medications are more helpful for the PTSD symptoms of increased arousal and negative emotions, and less helpful for the recurrent negative memories, dissociations, and avoidance behaviors that also characterize the disorder. Around half of PTSD patients who take antidepressant drugs experience some symptom reductions. Other psychotropic drugs do not fare as well in PTSD research and are prescribed less often (Stein, 2017).

COGNITIVE-BEHAVIORAL THERAPY Cognitive-behavioral therapy has proved to be of considerable help to many veterans with PTSD, bringing significant overall improvement to half or more of those who receive such treatment (Rothbaum, 2017; Shou et al., 2017). On the cognitive side, the therapists guide the veterans to examine and change the dysfunctional attitudes and styles of interpretation they have developed as a result of their traumatic experiences. Over the course of such examinations and efforts, often

#

#SmellingStress

Stress is odorless. The bacteria that feed off of our sweat are what give our bodies an odor during very stressful events.

#GenderImpact

51% Percentage of U.S. women who often lie awake at night due to stress

32% Percentage of U.S. men who often lie awake at night due to stress

(Information from: APA, 2017, 2015)

called *cognitive processing therapy* when applied in cases of PTSD, the veterans learn to deal with difficult memories and feelings, come to accept what they have done and experienced, become less judgmental of themselves, and begin to trust other people once again (Holliday et al., 2017). Increasingly, a number of cognitive-behavioral therapists are adding mindfulness-based techniques (see page 53) to further help the clients become more accepting and less judgmental of their recurring thoughts, feelings, and memories. Research indicates that such mindfulness techniques produce some additional improvements (Rothbaum, 2017).

On the behavioral side, cognitive-behavioral therapists typically apply *exposure* techniques when treating veterans with PTSD. These techniques have been quite successful at reducing specific symptoms and, in turn, bringing about improvements in overall adjustment (Cooper et al., 2017; Korte et al., 2017). In fact, some studies indicate that exposure may be the single most helpful intervention for people with PTSD (Haagen et al., 2015).

During exposure therapy, veterans with PTSD are guided to confront trauma-related—usually combat-related—objects, events, and situations that continue to cause them extreme upset and anxiety. Their exposures may be imagined or in vivo. Of course, it is technically impossible, not to mention unethical, to expose veterans with PTSD to actual combat experiences, so many of today's exposure treatments rely on the vivid, multisensory images produced by virtual reality procedures (Maples-Keller et al., 2017) (see ***MindTech***).

Perhaps the most widely applied exposure technique in cases of PTSD is **prolonged exposure** (Foa et al., 2018; Acierno et al., 2017). Here therapists direct clients to confront not only trauma-related objects and situations but also their painful memories of traumatic experiences—memories they have been actively avoiding (Mahoney, Karatzias, & Hutton, 2019). The clients repeatedly recall and describe the memories in great detail for extended periods of time, holding on to them until becoming less aroused, anxious, and upset by them. Here a therapist conducting prolonged exposure typically offers instructions to a client with PTSD:

> *Up to this point . . . you have been making great progress and have been experiencing the decrease in anxiety that we expect to see. Today we are going to do the exposure a little differently. . . . I will ask you to tell me . . . what the most distressing or upsetting parts of this memory are for you now. And then . . . I will ask you to focus the revisiting and recounting on each of these "hot spots," one at a time. We will pick one to begin with and you will repeat that one part of the memory over and over just by itself, focusing in closely and describing what happened in great detail, as if in slow motion, including what you felt, saw, heard, and thought. We will repeat it as many times as necessary to "wear it out" or bring about a big decrease in your [discomfort] level. When that part seems to have been sufficiently processed, we will move to the next one.*
>
> *(Foa et al., 2007, pp. 100–101)*

Over the course of prolonged exposure, the clients are expected to remember more and more details of their traumas, experience less distress during such memories, become less fearful of the memories, and indeed display fewer symptoms of PTSD. Research suggests that for clients who can stay with such intense memory exercises (many cannot), prolonged exposure is even more helpful than more gradual exposure interventions (Foa et al., 2018).

Another popular form of exposure therapy is **eye movement desensitization and reprocessing (EMDR),** in which clients move their eyes in a rhythmic manner from side to side while flooding their minds with images of the objects and situations they ordinarily try to avoid. Although this approach has a number of skeptics, case studies and some controlled studies suggest that the treatment can sometimes be helpful to people with PTSD (Rothbaum, 2017; Shapiro & Forrest, 2016). Many theorists argue that

prolonged exposure A treatment approach in which clients confront not only trauma-related objects and situations but also their painful memories of traumatic experiences.

eye movement desensitization and reprocessing (EMDR) An exposure treatment in which clients move their eyes in a rhythmic manner from side to side while flooding their minds with images of objects and situations they ordinarily avoid.

MINDTECH

Virtual Reality Therapy: Better than the Real Thing?

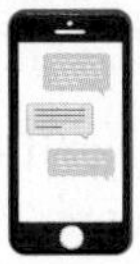

For years, exposure-based treatment for PTSD for combat veterans was less than optimal. Unable to revisit real-life battle settings, veterans had to imagine rifle fire, bomb explosions, dead bodies, and/or other traumatic stimuli for their treatment.

All that changed a decade ago, when "virtual" exposure to combat conditions became available for veterans with PTSD. The Office of Naval Research funded the development of "Virtual Iraq," a war simulation treatment game (McIlvaine, 2011). This game was able to produce sights and sounds that seemed every bit as real and produced as much—or more—alarm as real battle conditions. The use of virtual reality as an exposure technique has since become a standard in PTSD treatment.

In *virtual reality therapy,* PTSD clients use wraparound goggles and joysticks to navigate their way through a computer-generated military convoy, battle, or bomb attack in a landscape that looks like Iraq, Afghanistan, or other war zones. The therapist controls the intensity of the horrifying sights, terrifying sounds, and awful smells of combat, triggering very real feelings of fear or panic in the client. Exposures to these stimuli are applied by the therapist in either gradual steps or abruptly.

Study after study has suggested that virtual reality therapy is extremely helpful for combat veterans with PTSD, more so than covert exposure therapy (Maples-Keller et al., 2017). In addition, the improvements produced by this intervention appear to last for extended periods, perhaps indefinitely. Small wonder that virtual reality therapy is now also becoming common in the treatment of other anxiety disorders and phobias, including social anxiety disorder and fears of heights, flying, and closed spaces (Bouchard et al., 2017).

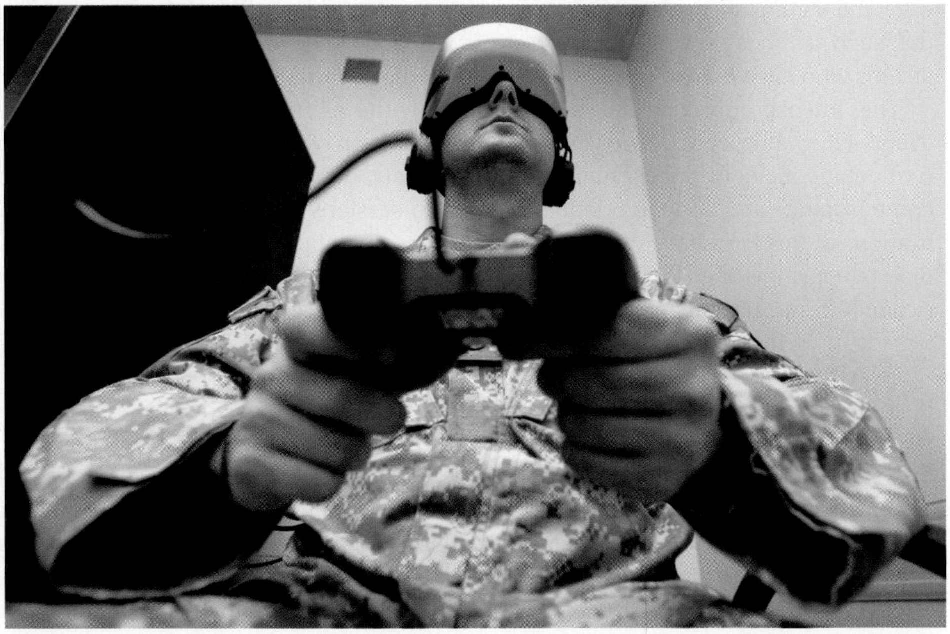

AP Photo/Ted S. Warren

"Virtual" exposure An ex-soldier's headset and video game–type controller take him back to a battle scene in Iraq.

it is the exposure feature of EMDR, rather than the eye movement per se, that accounts for its success as a treatment (Lamprecht et al., 2004).

COUPLE AND FAMILY THERAPY Veterans with PTSD may be further helped in couple therapy or family therapy formats (Rothbaum, 2017; Vogt et al., 2017, 2011). The symptoms of PTSD are particularly apparent to spouses and other family members, who may be directly affected by the client's anxieties, depressed mood, or angry outbursts (Freytes et al., 2017). With the help and support of their family members, clients may come to examine their impact on others, learn to communicate better, and improve their problem-solving skills (Sareen, 2018).

GROUP THERAPY In group therapy sessions, called *rap groups* when initiated during the 1980s, veterans meet with others like themselves to share experiences and feelings (particularly guilt and rage), develop insights, and give mutual support (Levi et al., 2017; Ellis et al., 2014). Today hundreds of small *Veterans Outreach Centers* across the country, as well as treatment programs in Veterans Administration hospitals and mental health clinics, provide group treatment (Finley et al., 2017). These agencies also offer individual therapy, counseling for spouses and children, family therapy, and aid in seeking jobs, education, and benefits. Clinical reports suggest that such programs offer a necessary, sometimes life-saving, treatment opportunity.

psychological debriefing A form of crisis intervention in which victims are helped to talk about their feelings and reactions to traumatic incidents. Also called *critical incident stress debriefing*.

dissociative disorders Disorders marked by major changes in memory that do not have clear physical causes.

memory The faculty for recalling past events and past learning.

dissociative amnesia A disorder marked by an inability to recall important personal events and information.

Psychological Debriefing People who are traumatized by disasters, victimization, or accidents profit from many of the same treatments that are used to help survivors of combat (Rothbaum, 2017). In addition, because their traumas occur in their own community, where mental health resources are close at hand, they may, according to many clinicians, further benefit from immediate community interventions.

One of the leading such approaches is called **psychological debriefing,** or **critical incident stress debriefing,** an intervention applied widely over the past 30 years. Psychological debriefing is a form of crisis intervention that has victims of trauma talk extensively about their feelings and reactions within days of the critical incident (Tarquinio et al., 2016; Mitchell, 2003, 1983). The clinicians then clarify to the victims that their reactions are normal responses to a terrible event, offer stress management tips, and in some cases, refer the victims to professionals for long-term counseling. Based on the assumption that such sessions prevent or reduce stress reactions, they are often provided to trauma victims who have not yet displayed any symptoms at all, as well as to those who have.

This intense approach has been applied in the aftermath of countless traumatic events (Tarquinio et al., 2016; Pfefferbaum, Newman, & Nelson, 2014). Indeed, when a traumatic incident affects numerous individuals, debriefing-trained counselors may come from far and wide to conduct debriefing sessions with the victims. Large mobilizations of this kind have offered free emergency mental health services at the sites of disasters such as the 2001 World Trade Center attack, the 2005 floods caused by Hurricane Katrina, and the mass killings of 49 persons at Pulse, a gay nightclub in Orlando, Florida, in 2016 and of 58 individuals at a concert in Las Vegas, Nevada, in 2017.

Over the years, personal testimonials for rapid mobilization programs have often been favorable (Healy & Tyrrell, 2013; Watson & Shalev, 2005). However, research conducted over the past decade has called into question the effectiveness of this kind of intervention (Tarquinio et al., 2016; USDVA, 2016). In fact, some clinicians believe that the early intervention programs may encourage victims to dwell too long on the traumatic events they have experienced. And a number worry that early disaster counseling may unintentionally "suggest" problems to certain victims, thus helping to produce stress disorders (USDVA, 2016; McNally, 2004). Thus, although many mental health professionals continue to believe in psychological debriefing programs, the current clinical climate is moving away from the ready application of this approach.

9... SUMMING UP

ACUTE AND POSTTRAUMATIC STRESS DISORDERS When we appraise a stressor as threatening, we often experience a stress response consisting of arousal and a sense of fear. The features of arousal are set in motion by the hypothalamus, a brain structure that activates two different pathways—the sympathetic nervous system pathway and the hypothalamic-pituitary-adrenal pathway.

People with acute stress disorder or posttraumatic stress disorder react with arousal, anxiety, and other stress symptoms long after a traumatic event, including reexperiencing the traumatic event, avoiding related events, being markedly less responsive than normal, and feeling guilt. Traumatic events may include combat experiences, disasters, or episodes of victimization.

In attempting to explain why certain people develop a psychological stress disorder, researchers have focused on biological factors (particularly, overly reactive brain–body stress pathways, a dysfunctional brain stress circuit, and an inherited predisposition), childhood experiences, personal styles, social support systems, and the severity and nature of traumatic events, as well as on how these factors may work together to produce such a disorder. Techniques used to treat the stress disorders include antidepressant drugs, cognitive-behavioral therapy (including exposure techniques), family therapy, and group therapy. Critical incident stress debriefing initially appeared helpful after large-scale disasters; however, recent studies have raised questions about the usefulness of this intervention.

#

#TheirWords

"Reality is the leading cause of stress among those in touch with it."

Lily Tomlin

Dissociative Disorders

As you have just read, a number of people with acute and posttraumatic stress disorders have symptoms of dissociation along with their other symptoms. They may, for example, feel dazed, have trouble remembering things, or have a sense of depersonalization or derealization. Symptoms of this kind are also on display in **dissociative disorders,** another group of disorders triggered by traumatic events. The memory difficulties and other dissociative symptoms found in these disorders are particularly intense, extensive, and disruptive. Moreover, in such disorders, dissociative reactions are the main or only symptoms. People with dissociative disorders do not typically have the significant arousal, negative emotions, sleep difficulties, and other problems that characterize acute and posttraumatic stress disorders. Nor are there clear physical factors at work in dissociative disorders.

Barcroft/Getty Images

Managing without memory Andy Wray developed dissociative amnesia after witnessing several horrific deaths in his work as a policeman. His disorder is marked by *continuous forgetting.* Every few days, many of his new memories disappear, leaving him unable to recognize friends, relatives, and events in any detail. To help him get on with his life, he uses countless notebooks and reminder cards like the ones he is looking at here.

Most of us experience a sense of wholeness and continuity as we interact with the world. We perceive ourselves as being more than a collection of isolated sensory experiences, feelings, and behaviors. In other words, we have an *identity,* a sense of who we are and where we fit in our environment. **Memory** is a key to this sense of identity, the link between our past, present, and future. Without a memory, we would always be starting over; with it, our life and our identity move forward. In dissociative disorders, one part of a person's memory or identity becomes *dissociated,* or separated, from other parts of his or her memory or identity.

There are several kinds of dissociative disorders. People with *dissociative amnesia* are unable to recall important personal events and information. People with *dissociative identity disorder,* once known as *multiple personality disorder,* have two or more separate identities that may not always be aware of each other's memories, thoughts, feelings, and behavior. And people with *depersonalization-derealization disorder* feel as though they have become detached from their own mental processes or bodies or are observing themselves from the outside.

Several famous books and movies have portrayed dissociative disorders. Two classics are *The Three Faces of Eve* and *Sybil,* each about a woman who developed multiple personalities after having been subject to traumatic events in childhood. The topic is so fascinating that most television drama series seem to include at least one case of dissociation every season, creating the impression that the disorders are very common. Many clinicians, however, believe that they are rare.

TABLE: 5-3

Dx Checklist

Dissociative Amnesia
1. Person cannot recall important life-related information, typically traumatic or stressful information. The memory problem is more than simple forgetting.
2. Significant distress or impairment.
3. The symptoms are not caused by a substance or medical condition.
Dissociative Identity Disorder
1. Person experiences a disruption to his or her identity, as reflected by at least two separate personality states or experiences of possession.
2. Person repeatedly experiences memory gaps regarding daily events, key personal information, or traumatic events, beyond ordinary forgetting.
3. Significant distress or impairment.
4. The symptoms are not caused by a substance or medical condition.

Information from: APA, 2013.

Dissociative Amnesia

People with **dissociative amnesia** are unable to recall important information, usually of a stressful nature, about their lives (APA, 2013). The loss of memory is much more extensive than normal forgetting and is not caused by physical factors such as a blow to the head (see **Table 5-3**). Typically, an episode of amnesia is directly triggered by a traumatic or upsetting event (Odagaki, 2017).

Dissociative amnesia may be *localized, selective, generalized,* or *continuous.* In *localized amnesia,* the most common type of dissociative amnesia, a person loses all memory of events that took place within a limited period of time, almost always beginning with some very disturbing occurrence. A soldier, for example, may awaken a week after a horrific combat battle and be unable to recall the battle or any of the events surrounding it. She may remember everything that happened up to the battle, and may recall everything that has occurred over the

#FrequentlyForgotten

- Online passwords
- Where cell phone was left
- Where keys were left
- Where remote control was left
- Phone numbers
- Names
- Dream content
- Birthdays/anniversaries

past several days, but the events in between remain a total blank. The forgotten period is called the *amnestic episode*. During an amnestic episode, people may appear confused; in some cases they wander about aimlessly. They are already experiencing memory difficulties but seem unaware of them.

People with *selective amnesia*, the second most common form of dissociative amnesia, remember some, but not all, events that took place during a period of time. If the combat soldier mentioned in the previous paragraph had selective amnesia, she might remember certain interactions or conversations that occurred during the battle, but not more disturbing events such as the death of a friend or the screams of enemy soldiers.

Why do many people question the authenticity of people who seem to lose their memories at times of severe stress?

In some cases the loss of memory extends back to times long before the upsetting period. In addition to forgetting battle-linked events, the soldier may not remember events that occurred earlier in her life. In this case, she would have what is called *generalized amnesia*. In extreme cases, she might not even recognize relatives and friends.

In the forms of dissociative amnesia just discussed, the period affected by the amnesia has an end. In *continuous amnesia*, however, forgetting continues into the present. The soldier might forget new and ongoing experiences as well as what happened before and during the battle.

These various forms of dissociative amnesia are similar in that the amnesia interferes mostly with a person's memory of personal material. Memory for abstract or encyclopedic information usually remains. People with dissociative amnesia are as likely as anyone else to know the name of the president of the United States and how to read or drive a car.

Studies suggest that at least 2 percent of all adults experience dissociative amnesia in a given year (Loewenstein, 2018). Many cases seem to begin during serious threats to health and safety, as in wartime and natural disasters. Like the soldier in the earlier examples, combat veterans often report memory gaps of hours or days, and some forget personal information, such as their name and address (Guina et al., 2018; Bremner, 2016, 2002).

Childhood abuse, particularly child sexual abuse, can also trigger dissociative amnesia (Hébert et al., 2018); indeed, in the 1990s there were many reports in which adults claimed to recall long-forgotten experiences of childhood abuse (see ***PsychWatch***). In addition, dissociative amnesia may occur under more ordinary circumstances, such as

David Becker/Getty Images

An additional risk Three concertgoers desperately run for cover during the 2017 mass shooting at an outdoor country music festival in Las Vegas, Nevada, a horrific incident that left 58 people dead and 546 injured. People who experience severe threats to their health and safety—as in natural and human-produced disasters—are particularly vulnerable to amnesia and other dissociative reactions. In the aftermath of mass shootings, for example, survivors may forget specific details of their ordeal, personal information, or even their identities.

PSYCHWATCH

Repressed Childhood Memories or False Memory Syndrome?

Throughout the 1990s, reports of repressed childhood memory of abuse attracted much public attention. Adults with this type of dissociative amnesia seemed to recover buried memories of sexual and physical abuse from their childhood. A woman might claim, for example, that her father had sexually molested her repeatedly between the ages of 5 and 7. Or a young man might remember that a family friend had made sexual advances on several occasions when he was very young. Often the repressed memories surfaced during therapy for another problem.

Although the number of such claims has declined dramatically in recent years, clinicians remain divided on this issue (Andrews & Brewin, 2017; McNally, 2017). Some believe that recovered memories are just what they appear to be—horrible memories of abuse that have been buried for years in the person's mind (MacIntosh, Fletcher, & Collin-Vézina, 2016). Other clinicians—the majority—believe that the memories are actually illusions, false images created by a mind that is confused. Opponents of the repressed memory concept hold that the details of childhood sexual abuse are often remembered all too well, not completely wiped from memory. They also point out that memory in general is often flawed. Moreover, false memories of various kinds can be created in the laboratory by tapping into research participants' imaginations (McNally, 2017; Volz et al., 2017).

If the alleged recovery of childhood memories is not what it appears to be, what is it? According to opponents of the concept, it may be a powerful case of suggestibility (McNally, 2017; Loftus, 2003, 2001). These theorists hold that the attention paid to the phenomenon by both clinicians and the public leads some therapists to make the diagnosis without sufficient evidence. Moreover, certain therapists use special memory recovery techniques, including hypnosis and regression therapy. Perhaps some clients respond to the techniques by unknowingly forming false memories of abuse (McNally, 2017; McNally & Garaerts, 2009).

Of course, repressed memories of childhood sexual abuse do not emerge only in clinical settings. Some individuals come forward on their own (MacIntosh et al., 2016). Opponents of the repressed memory concept explain these cases by pointing to various books, Web sites, and television shows that seem to validate the phenomenon of repressed memories of childhood abuse (Haaken & Reavey, 2010; Loftus, 1993). Still other opponents believe that some individuals are simply more prone than others to experience false memories—either of childhood abuse or of other kinds of events (McNally, 2017; McNally et al., 2005).

It is important to recognize that the theorists who question the recovery of repressed childhood memories do not in any way deny the problem of child sexual abuse. In fact, proponents and opponents alike are greatly concerned that the public may take this debate to mean that clinicians have doubts about the scope of the problem of child sexual abuse. Unfortunately, that problem is all too real and all too common.

Bettmann/Getty Images

Early recall These siblings, all born on the same day in different years, have very different reactions to their cakes at a 1958 birthday party. But how do they each remember that party today? Research suggests that our memories of early childhood may be influenced by the reminiscences of family members, our dreams, television and movie plots, and our present self-image.

the sudden loss of a loved one through rejection or death, or extreme guilt over certain actions (for example, an extramarital affair) (Guina et al., 2018).

The personal impact of dissociative amnesia depends on how much is forgotten. Obviously, an amnestic episode of two years is more of a problem than one of two hours. Similarly, an amnestic episode during which a person's life changes in major ways causes more difficulties than one that is quiet.

An extreme version of dissociative amnesia is called **dissociative fugue.** Here persons not only forget their personal identities and details of their past lives but also flee to an entirely different location. Some people travel a short distance and make few social contacts in the new setting (Harrison et al., 2017; APA, 2013). Their fugue may be brief—a matter of hours or days—and end suddenly. In other cases, however, the person may travel far from home, take a new name, and establish a new identity,

dissociative fugue A form of dissociative amnesia in which a person travels to a new location and may assume a new identity, simultaneously forgetting his or her past.

new relationships, and even a new line of work. Such people may also display new personality characteristics; often they are more outgoing. This pattern is seen in the century-old case of the Reverend Ansel Bourne, whose last name was the inspiration for Jason Bourne, the memory-deprived secret agent in the modern-day Bourne books and movies.

On January 17, 1887, [the Reverend Ansel Bourne, of Greene, R.I.] drew 551 dollars from a bank in Providence with which to pay for a certain lot of land in Greene, paid certain bills, and got into a Pawtucket horsecar. This is the last incident which he remembers. He did not return home that day, and nothing was heard of him for two months. He was published in the papers as missing, and foul play being suspected, the police sought in vain his whereabouts. On the morning of March 14th, however, at Norristown, Pennsylvania, a man calling himself A. I. Brown who had rented a small shop six weeks previously, stocked it with stationery, confectionery, fruit and small articles, and carried on his quiet trade without seeming to any one unnatural or eccentric, woke up in a fright and called in the people of the house to tell him where he was. He said that his name was Ansel Bourne, that he was entirely ignorant of Norristown, that he knew nothing of shop keeping, and that the last thing he remembered—it seemed only yesterday—was drawing the money from the bank, etc. in Providence. . . . He was very weak, having lost apparently over twenty pounds of flesh during his escapade, and had such a horror of the idea of the candy-store that he refused to set foot in it again.

(James, 1890, pp. 391–393)

AP Photo/Peter Cosgrove

Lost and found Cheryl Ann Barnes is helped off a plane by her grandmother and stepmother upon arrival in Florida in 1996. The 17-year-old high school honor student had disappeared from her Florida home and was found one month later in a New York City hospital listed as Jane Doe, apparently suffering from a dissociative fugue.

Fugues tend to end abruptly. In some cases, as with Reverend Bourne, the person "awakens" in a strange place, surrounded by unfamiliar faces, and wonders how he or she got there. In other cases, the lack of personal history may arouse suspicion. Perhaps a traffic accident or legal problem leads police to discover the false identity; at other times friends search for and find the missing person. When people are found before their state of fugue has ended, therapists may find it necessary to ask them many questions about the details of their lives, repeatedly remind them who they are, and even begin psychotherapy before they recover their memories (Harrison et al., 2017; Igwe, 2013). As these people recover their past, some forget the events of the fugue period.

The majority of people who go through a dissociative fugue regain most or all of their memories and never have a recurrence. Since fugues are usually brief and totally reversible, those who have experienced them tend to have few aftereffects. People who have been away for months or years, however, often do have trouble adjusting to the changes that took place during their flight. In addition, some people commit illegal or violent acts in their fugue state and later must face the consequences.

Dissociative Identity Disorder

Dissociative identity disorder is both dramatic and disabling, as we see in the case of Luisa:

Luisa was first brought in for treatment after she was found walking in circles by the side of the road in a suburban neighborhood near Denver. Agitated, malnourished, and dirty, this 30-year-old woman told police that her name was Franny and that she was a 15-year-old who was running away from her home in Telluride. At first, the police officers suspected she was giving a false identity to avoid prosecution for prostitution or drug possession, but there really was no evidence for either crime when she was found.

Once it became apparent that she fully believed what she was saying, the woman, who carried no identification of any kind, was transferred to a psychiatric hospital for observation. By the time she met with a therapist, she was no longer a young child speaking rapidly about a terrible family situation. She was now calling herself Luisa, and she spoke in slow, measured, and sad tones—eloquent but often confused.

Luisa described how she had been sexually abused for years by her stepfather, starting when she was six. She said she had run away from home at the age of 15 and had not spoken since to either her mother or stepfather. She claimed that, although she had spent considerable time living on the streets over the years, she was currently living with her boyfriend, Tim, in a small apartment. However, when pressed, she was unable to say what Tim did for a living, nor could she provide his address or last name. Thus she remained in treatment.

Over the course of treatment, as her therapist continued to probe for details of her unhappy childhood and sexual abuse, Luisa became more and more agitated, until finally, she actually transformed back into 15-year-old Franny during one session. Her therapist wrote in his notes, "Her entire physical presence transformed itself suddenly and almost violently. Her face, previously relaxed and even flat, became tense and scrunched up, and her entire body hunched over. She moved her chair back almost two feet and repeatedly flinched from me if I even gestured in her direction. Her voice became high-pitched, clipped, and fast, spitting out words, and her vocabulary became limited, to that which a child would display. She seemed to be a different person in every way possible."

Over the following several sessions, Luisa's therapist wound up meeting still other personalities. One was Miss Johnson, a strict school principal who claimed to have taught Luisa when she was younger. Another was Roger—homeless, tough, and threatening—who made it clear that he was in charge of Luisa and the other personalities. In addition there was Sarah, aged 55 and divorced, and Lilly, aged 24, a math genius and accountant who seemed to appear whenever Luisa needed to deal with money or complex mathematical issues.

A person with **dissociative identity disorder,** known in the past as *multiple personality disorder,* develops two or more distinct personalities, often called **subpersonalities,** or **alternate personalities,** each with a unique set of memories, behaviors, thoughts, and emotions (see again Table 5-3). At any given time, one of the subpersonalities takes center stage and dominates the person's functioning. Usually one subpersonality, called the *primary,* or *host,* personality, appears more often than the others.

The transition from one subpersonality to another, called *switching,* is usually sudden and may be dramatic. Luisa, for example, twisted her face and hunched her shoulders and body forward violently. Switching is usually triggered by a stressful event, although clinicians can also bring about the change with hypnotic suggestion.

Cases of dissociative identity disorder were first reported almost three centuries ago (Rieber, 2006, 2002). Many clinicians consider the disorder to be rare, but some reports suggest that it may be more common than was once thought (Foote, 2018; Dorahy et al., 2014). Most cases are first diagnosed in late adolescence or early adulthood, but more often than not, the symptoms actually began in early childhood after episodes of trauma or abuse (often sexual abuse) (Foote, 2018). Women receive this diagnosis at least three times as often as men.

Why might women be more likely than men to receive a diagnosis of dissociative identity disorder?

How Do Subpersonalities Interact? How subpersonalities relate to or recall one another varies from case to case (Morton, 2018, 2017; Ellenberger, 1970). Generally, however, there are three kinds of relationships. In *mutually amnesic relationships,* the subpersonalities have no awareness of one another. Conversely, in *mutually cognizant patterns,* each subpersonality is well aware of the rest. They may hear one another's voices and even talk among themselves. Some are on good terms, while others do not get along at all.

In *one-way amnesic relationships,* the most common relationship pattern, some subpersonalities are aware of others, but the awareness is not mutual. Those who are aware, called *coconscious subpersonalities,* are "quiet observers" who watch the actions and thoughts of the other subpersonalities but do not interact with them. Sometimes while another subpersonality is present, the coconscious personality makes itself known through indirect means, such as auditory hallucinations (perhaps a voice giving

#

#AssessmentDelay

People with dissociative identity disorder do not receive that diagnosis until they have been in therapy for an average of seven years (Foote, 2018).

dissociative identity disorder A dissociative disorder in which a person develops two or more distinct personalities. Also known as *multiple personality disorder.*

subpersonalities The two or more distinct personalities found in individuals suffering with dissociative identity disorder. Also known as *alternate personalities.*

#MemoryMovies

Split (2017)

Finding Dory (2016)

The Bourne series (2012, 2007, 2004, 2002)

Total Recall (2012, 1990)

Black Swan (2010)

Shutter Island (2010)

The Hangover (2009)

Spider-Man 3 (2007)

Eternal Sunshine of the Spotless Mind (2004)

The Manchurian Candidate (2004, 1962)

Finding Nemo (2003)

Memento (2000)

commands) or "automatic writing" (the current personality may find itself writing down words over which it has no control).

Investigators used to believe that most cases of dissociative identity disorder involved two or three subpersonalities. Studies now suggest, however, that the average number of subpersonalities per patient is much higher—15 for women and 8 for men (Foote, 2018; APA, 2000). In fact, there have been cases in which 100 or more subpersonalities were observed. Often the subpersonalities emerge in groups of 2 or 3 at a time.

In the case of "Eve White," made famous in the book and movie *The Three Faces of Eve*, a woman had three subpersonalities—Eve White, Eve Black, and Jane (Thigpen & Cleckley, 1957). Eve White, the primary personality, was quiet and serious; Eve Black was carefree and mischievous; and Jane was mature and intelligent. According to the book, these three subpersonalities eventually merged into Evelyn, a stable personality who was really an integration of the other three.

The book was mistaken, however; this was not to be the end of Eve's dissociation. In an autobiography 20 years later, she revealed that altogether 22 subpersonalities had come forth during her life, including 9 subpersonalities after Evelyn. Usually they appeared in groups of three, and so the authors of *The Three Faces of Eve* apparently never knew about her previous or subsequent subpersonalities. She later overcame her disorder, achieving a single, stable identity, and was known as Chris Sizemore for four decades until her death in 2016 (Weber, 2016; Sizemore, 1991).

How Do Subpersonalities Differ? As in Chris Sizemore's case, subpersonalities often exhibit dramatically different characteristics. They may also have their own names and different *identifying features, abilities and preferences,* and even *physiological responses.*

IDENTIFYING FEATURES The subpersonalities may differ in features as basic as age, gender, race, and family history, as in the case of Sybil Dorsett, whose disorder is described in the famous novel *Sybil* (Schreiber, 1973). According to the novel, Sybil displayed 17 subpersonalities, all with different identifying features. They included adults, a teenager, and even a baby. One subpersonality, Vicky, saw herself as attractive and blonde, while another, Peggy Lou, believed herself to be "a pixie with a pug nose." Yet another, Mary, was plump with dark hair, and Vanessa was a tall, thin redhead. (It is

Michael Maslin/The New Yorker Collection/The Cartoon Bank

"Would it surprise you to learn, Felix, that we're already married?"

worth noting that the accuracy of the real-life case on which this novel was based has been challenged in recent years.)

ABILITIES AND PREFERENCES Although memories of abstract or encyclopedic information are not usually affected in dissociative amnesia, they are often disturbed in dissociative identity disorder. It is not uncommon for the different subpersonalities to have different abilities: one may be able to drive, speak a foreign language, or play a musical instrument, while the others cannot (Foote, 2018; Coons & Bowman, 2001). Their handwriting can also differ. In addition, the subpersonalities usually have different tastes in food, friends, music, and literature. Chris Sizemore ("Eve") later pointed out, "If I had learned to sew as one personality and then tried to sew as another, I couldn't do it. Driving a car was the same. Some of my personalities couldn't drive" (Sizemore & Pitillo, 1977, p. 4).

What verdict is appropriate for accused criminals who experience dissociative identity disorder and whose crimes are committed by one of their subpersonalities?

PHYSIOLOGICAL RESPONSES Researchers have discovered that subpersonalities may have physiological differences, such as differences in blood pressure levels and allergies (Spiegel, 2009; Putnam et al., 1990). A pioneering study looked at the brain activities of different subpersonalities by measuring their *evoked potentials*—that is, brain-response patterns recorded on an electroencephalograph (Putnam, 1984). The brain pattern a person produces in response to a specific stimulus (such as a flashing light) is usually unique and consistent. However, when an evoked potential test was administered to four subpersonalities of each of 10 people with dissociative identity disorder, the results were dramatic. The brain-activity pattern of each subpersonality was unique, showing the kinds of variations usually found in totally different people. A number of other studies conducted over the past two decades have yielded similar findings (Boysen & VanBergen, 2014).

How Common Is Dissociative Identity Disorder? As you have seen, dissociative identity disorder has traditionally been thought of as rare. Some researchers even argue that many or all cases are *iatrogenic*—that is, unintentionally produced by practitioners (Foote, 2018). They believe that therapists create this disorder by subtly suggesting the existence of other personalities during therapy or by explicitly asking a patient to produce different personalities while under hypnosis. In addition, they believe, a therapist who is looking for multiple personalities may reinforce these patterns by displaying greater interest when a patient displays symptoms of dissociation.

These arguments seem to be supported by the fact that many cases of dissociative identity disorder first come to attention while the person is already in treatment for a less serious problem. But such is not true of all cases; many people seek treatment because they have noticed time lapses throughout their lives or because relatives and friends have observed their subpersonalities (Foote, 2018; Putnam, 2006, 2000).

The number of people diagnosed with dissociative identity disorder increased dramatically in the 1980s and 1990s, only to decrease again in the twenty-first century (Foote, 2018; Paris, 2012). Notwithstanding this decline, thousands of cases have now been diagnosed in the United States and Canada alone and some clinical theorists estimate that around 1 percent of the population in the United States and other Western countries displays the disorder (Foote, 2018). On the other side of the coin, many clinicians continue to question the legitimacy of this category.

#

#TreatingSybil

Recent reports, including claims by several colleagues who worked closely with the author of *Sybil* and with Sybil's real-life therapist, suggest that Shirley Mason (the person on whom Sybil was based) was highly hypnotizable, extremely suggestible, and anxious to please her therapist, and that her disorder was in fact induced largely by hypnosis, sodium pentothal, and therapist suggestion (Carey, 2017; Nathan, 2011; Rieber, 2002, 1999).

How Do Theorists Explain Dissociative Amnesia and Dissociative Identity Disorder?

A variety of theories have been proposed to explain dissociative amnesia and dissociative identity disorder. Older explanations, such as that offered by psychodynamic theorists, have not received much investigation (Merenda, 2008). However, newer viewpoints, which highlight such factors as *state-dependent learning* and *self-hypnosis,* have captured the interest of clinical scientists.

state-dependent learning Learning that becomes associated with the conditions under which it occurred, so that it is best remembered under the same conditions.

The Psychodynamic View Psychodynamic theorists believe that these dissociative disorders are caused by *repression,* the most basic ego defense mechanism: people fight off anxiety by unconsciously preventing painful memories, thoughts, or impulses from reaching awareness. Everyone uses repression to a degree (see ***PsychWatch***), but people with dissociative amnesia and dissociative identity disorder are thought to repress their memories excessively (Snyder, 2018; Henderson, 2010).

In the psychodynamic view, dissociative amnesia is a *single episode* of massive repression. A person unconsciously blocks the memory of an extremely upsetting event to avoid the pain of facing it (Foote, 2018; Kikuchi et al., 2010). Repressing may be his or her only protection from overwhelming anxiety.

In contrast, dissociative identity disorder is thought to result from a *lifetime* of excessive repression (Snyder, 2018; Howell, 2011). Psychodynamic theorists believe that this continuous use of repression is motivated by traumatic childhood events, particularly abusive parenting (Foote, 2018; Blass, 2015). Children who experience such traumas may come to fear the dangerous world they live in and take flight from it by pretending to be another person who is looking on safely from afar. Abused children may also come to fear the impulses that they believe are the reasons for their excessive punishments. Whenever they experience "bad" thoughts or impulses, they unconsciously try to disown and deny them by assigning them to other personalities.

Support for the psychodynamic explanation of dissociative identity disorder comes from a variety of studies, largely case studies, which report such brutal childhood

PSYCHWATCH

Peculiarities of Memory

Usually memory problems must interfere greatly with a person's functioning before they are considered a sign of a disorder. Peculiarities of memory, on the other hand, fill our daily lives. Memory investigators have identified a number of these peculiarities—some familiar, some useful, some problematic, but none abnormal.

Barcroft/Getty Images

Memory for music Eight-year-old blind pianist Ying-Shan Tseng performs at a concert in South Africa. The young artist can breeze through complex concertos by Tchaikovsky, Mozart, and others from memory—a skill beyond the reach of most accomplished pianists.

- **Absentmindedness** Often we fail to register information because our thoughts are focusing on other things. If we haven't absorbed the information in the first place, it is no surprise that later we can't recall it.
- **Déjà vu** Almost all of us have at some time had the strange sensation of recognizing a scene that we happen upon for the first time. We feel sure we have been there before.
- **Jamais vu** Sometimes we have the opposite experience: a situation or scene that is part of our daily life seems suddenly unfamiliar. "I knew it was my car, but I felt as if I'd never seen it before."
- **The tip-of-the-tongue phenomenon** To have something on the tip of the tongue is an acute "feeling of knowing": we are unable to recall some piece of information, but we know that we know it.
- **Eidetic images** Some people have such vivid visual afterimages that they can describe a picture in detail after looking at it just once. The images may be memories of pictures, events, fantasies, or dreams.
- **Memory while under anesthesia** Some surgical patients continue to understand language while they are under anesthesia and may later recall what was said by others during the surgical procedure.
- **Memory for music** Even as a small child, Mozart could memorize and reproduce a piece of music after having heard it only once. In a similar vein, many musicians can mentally hear whole pieces of music, so they can rehearse anywhere, far from their instruments.
- **Visual memory** Most people recall visual information better than other kinds of information: they easily can bring to their mind the appearance of places, objects, faces, or the pages of a book. They almost never forget a face, yet they may well forget the name attached to it. Other people have stronger verbal memories: they remember sounds or words particularly well, and the memories that come to their minds are often puns or rhymes.

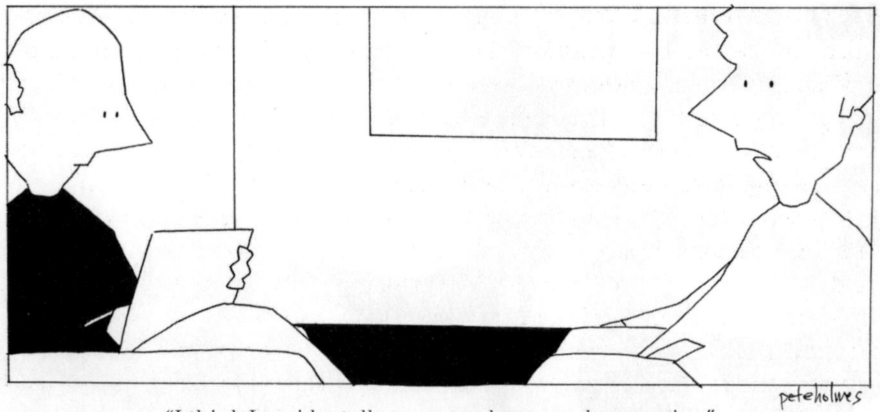

Pete Holmes/The New Yorker Collection/The Cartoon Bank

"I think I accidentally repressed my good memories."

experiences as beatings, cuttings, burnings with cigarettes, imprisonment in closets, rape, and extensive verbal abuse (Foote, 2018; Ross & Ness, 2010). Yet some individuals with this disorder do not seem to have experiences of abuse in their background (Ross, 2018). For example, Chris Sizemore, the subject of *The Three Faces of Eve,* reported that her disorder first emerged during her preschool years after she witnessed two deaths and a horrifying accident within a three-month period.

State-Dependent Learning: A Cognitive-Behavioral View If people learn something when they are in a particular situation or state of mind, they are likely to remember it best when they are again in that same condition. If they are given a learning task while under the influence of alcohol, for example, their later recall of the information may be strongest under the influence of alcohol. Similarly, if they smoke cigarettes while learning, they may later have better recall when they are again smoking.

Might it be possible to use the principles of state-dependent learning to produce better results in school or at work?

This link between state and recall is called **state-dependent learning.** It was initially observed in animals who learned things during experiments while under the influence of certain drugs (Radulovic et al., 2017; Overton, 1966, 1964). Research with human participants later showed that state-dependent learning can be associated with mood states as well: material learned during a happy mood is recalled best when the participant is again happy, and sad-state learning is recalled best during sad states (Xie & Zhang, 2018; Bower, 1981) (see **Figure 5-3**).

What causes state-dependent learning? One possibility is that *arousal* levels are an important part of learning and memory. That is, a particular level of arousal will have a set of remembered events, thoughts, and skills attached to it. When a situation produces that particular level of arousal, the person is more likely to recall the memories linked to it.

Although people remember certain events better in some arousal states than in others, most can recall events under a variety of states. However, some theorists suggest, people who are prone to develop dissociative disorders have state-to-memory links that are unusually rigid and narrow (Miller, 2017; Barlow, 2011). Each of their thoughts, memories, and skills may be tied *exclusively* to a particular state of arousal, so they recall a given event only when they experience an arousal state almost identical to the state in which the memory was first acquired. When such people are calm, for example, they may forget what happened during stressful times, thus laying the groundwork for dissociative amnesia. Similarly, in dissociative identity disorder, different arousal levels may produce entirely different groups of memories, thoughts, and abilities—that is, different subpersonalities. This could explain why personality transitions in dissociative identity disorder tend to be sudden and stress-related.

FIGURE 5-3

State-Dependent Learning

In one study, participants who learned a list of words while in a hypnotically induced happy state remembered the words better if they were in a happy mood when tested later than if they were in a sad mood. Conversely, participants who learned the words when in a sad mood recalled them better if they were sad during testing than if they were happy. (Information from: Bower, 1981.)

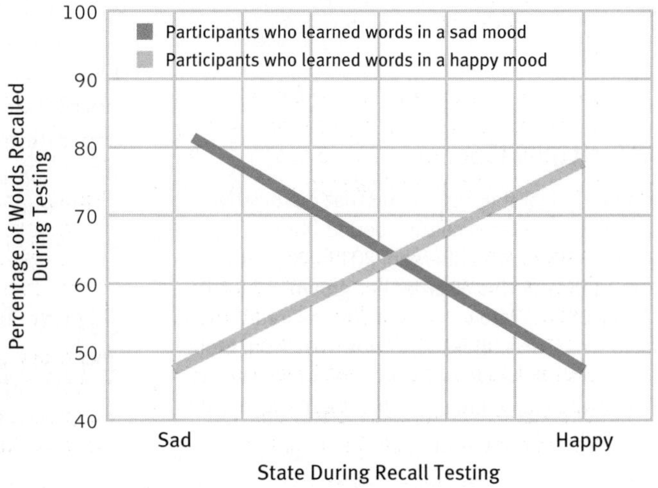

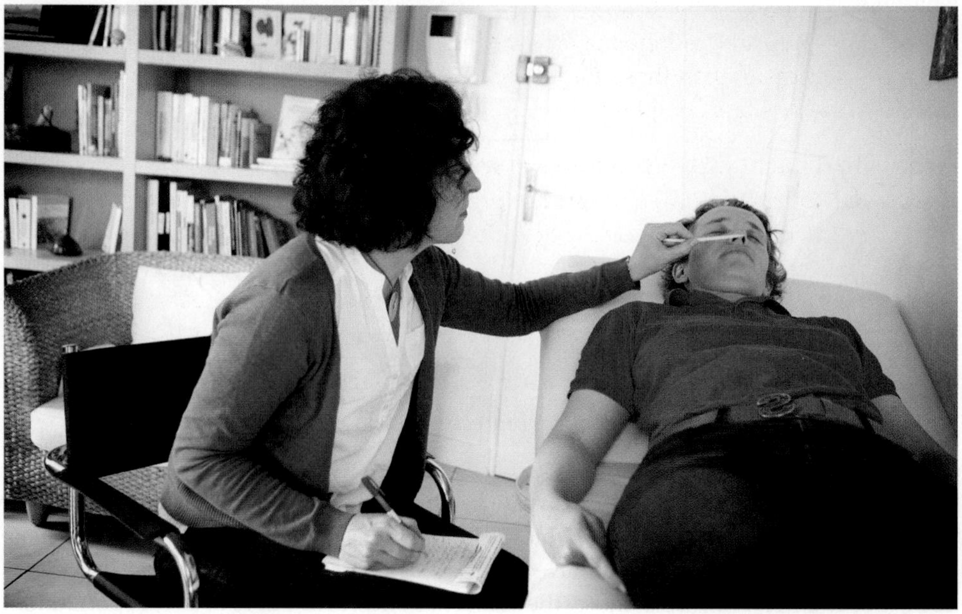

Sensory memories Sensory stimuli often trigger important memories. Thus some clinicians practice *olfactotherapy,* a method that uses the smells and vibrations of essential oils to help elicit memories from clients.

Self-Hypnosis As you first saw in Chapter 1, people who are *hypnotized* enter a sleeplike state in which they become very suggestible. While in this state, they can behave, perceive, and think in ways that would ordinarily seem impossible. They may, for example, become temporarily blind, deaf, or insensitive to pain. Hypnosis can also help people remember events that occurred and were forgotten years ago, a capability used by many psychotherapists. Conversely, it can make people forget facts, events, and even their personal identities—an effect called *hypnotic amnesia*.

The parallels between hypnotic amnesia and the dissociative disorders we have been examining are striking (Foote, 2018; van der Kruijs et al., 2014). Both are conditions in which people forget certain material for a period of time yet later remember it. And in both, the people forget without any insight into why they are forgetting or any awareness that something is being forgotten. These parallels have led some theorists to conclude that dissociative disorders may be a form of **self-hypnosis** in which people hypnotize themselves to forget unpleasant events (Brenner, 2018; Dell, 2010). Dissociative amnesia may develop, for example, in people who, consciously or unconsciously, hypnotize themselves into forgetting horrifying experiences that have recently taken place in their lives. If the self-induced amnesia covers all memories of a person's past and identity, that person may undergo a dissociative fugue.

The self-hypnosis theory might also be used to explain dissociative identity disorder (Brenner, 2018; Wood, 2016). On the basis of several investigations, some theorists believe that this disorder often begins between the ages of 4 and 6, a time when children are generally very suggestible and excellent hypnotic subjects (Lyons, 2015; Kohen & Olness, 2011). These theorists argue that some children who experience abuse or other horrifying events manage to escape their threatening world by self-hypnosis, mentally separating themselves from their bodies and fulfilling their wish to become some other person or persons (Foote, 2018). One patient with multiple personalities observed, "I was in a trance often [during my childhood]. There was a little place where I could sit, close my eyes and imagine, until I felt very relaxed just like hypnosis" (Bliss, 1980, p. 1392).

#CulturalTies

Some clinical theorists argue that dissociative identity disorder is culture-bound (Kim et al., 2016; Boysen & VanBergen, 2013). While the prevalence of this disorder has grown in North America, it is rare or nonexistent in Great Britain, Sweden, Russia, India, and Southeast Asia. Moreover, within the United States the prevalence is particularly low among Hispanic Americans and Asian Americans.

How Are Dissociative Amnesia and Dissociative Identity Disorder Treated?

As you have seen, people with dissociative amnesia often recover on their own. Only sometimes do their memory problems linger and require treatment. In contrast, people with dissociative identity disorder usually require treatment to regain their lost memories and develop an integrated personality. Treatments for dissociative amnesia tend to be more successful than those for dissociative identity disorder, probably because the former pattern is less complex.

self-hypnosis The process of hypnotizing oneself, sometimes for the purpose of forgetting unpleasant events.

hypnotic therapy A treatment in which the patient undergoes hypnosis and is then guided to recall forgotten events or perform other therapeutic activities. Also known as *hypnotherapy*.

How Do Therapists Help People with Dissociative Amnesia? The leading treatments for dissociative amnesia are *psychodynamic therapy*, *hypnotic therapy*, and *drug therapy*, although support for these interventions comes largely from case studies rather than controlled investigations (Gentile, Dillon, & Gillig, 2013). Psychodynamic therapists guide patients to search their unconscious in the hope of bringing forgotten experiences back to consciousness (Howell, 2011). The focus of psychodynamic therapy seems particularly well suited to the needs of people with dissociative amnesia. After all, the patients need to recover lost memories, and the general approach of psychodynamic therapists is to try to uncover memories—as well as other psychological processes—that have been repressed. Thus many theorists, including some who do not ordinarily favor psychodynamic approaches, believe that psychodynamic therapy may be the most appropriate treatment for dissociative amnesia.

Another common treatment for dissociative amnesia is **hypnotic therapy**, or **hypnotherapy.** Therapists hypnotize patients and then guide them to recall their forgotten events (Brenner, 2018; Rathbone et al., 2014). Given the possibility that dissociative amnesia may be a form of self-hypnosis, hypnotherapy may be a particularly useful intervention. It has been applied both alone and in combination with other approaches (Colletti et al., 2010).

Sometimes injections of barbiturates such as *sodium amobarbital* (Amytal) or *sodium pentobarbital* (Pentothal) have been used to help patients with dissociative amnesia regain their lost memories. These drugs are often called "truth serums," but actually their effect is to calm people and free their inhibitions, thus helping them to recall anxiety-producing events. These drugs do not always work, however, and if used at all, they are likely to be combined with other treatment approaches.

How Do Therapists Help People with Dissociative Identity Disorder? Unlike victims of dissociative amnesia, people with dissociative identity disorder do not typically recover without treatment. Treatment for this pattern is complex and difficult, much like the disorder itself. Therapists usually try to help the clients (1) recognize fully the nature of their disorder, (2) recover the gaps in their memory, and (3) integrate their subpersonalities into one functional personality (Ross, 2018; Bressert, 2017).

Erin Painter/Midland Daily News/AP Photo

Hypnotic recall Northwood University students react while under hypnosis to the suggestion of being on a beach in Hawaii and needing suntan lotion. Many clinicians use hypnotic procedures to help clients recall past events, but research reveals that such procedures often create false memories.

fusion The final merging of two or more subpersonalities in dissociative identity disorder.

depersonalization-derealization disorder A dissociative disorder marked by the presence of persistent and recurrent episodes of depersonalization, derealization, or both.

RECOGNIZING THE DISORDER Once a diagnosis of dissociative identity disorder is made, therapists typically try to bond with the primary personality and with each of the subpersonalities (Meganck, 2017; Howell, 2011). As bonds are formed, therapists try to educate patients and help them to recognize fully the nature of their disorder. Some therapists actually introduce the subpersonalities to one another, by hypnosis, for example, or by having patients look at videos of their other personalities (Ross, 2018; Howell, 2011). A number of therapists have also found that group therapy helps to educate patients (Fine & Madden, 2000). In addition, family therapy may be used to help educate spouses and children about the disorder and to gather helpful information about the patient (Kluft, 2001, 2000).

RECOVERING MEMORIES To help patients recover the missing pieces of their past, therapists typically use the same approaches applied in dissociative amnesia, including psychodynamic therapy, hypnotherapy, and drug treatment (Brenner, 2018; Brand, Loewenstein, & Spiegel, 2014). These techniques work slowly for patients with dissociative identity disorder, however, as some subpersonalities may keep denying experiences that the others recall. One of the subpersonalities may even assume a "protector" role to prevent the primary personality from suffering the pain of recollecting traumatic experiences (Chefetz, 2017).

INTEGRATING THE SUBPERSONALITIES The final goal of therapy is to merge the different subpersonalities into a single, integrated identity. Integration is a continuous process that occurs throughout treatment until patients "own" all of their behaviors, emotions, sensations, and knowledge. **Fusion** is the final merging of two or more subpersonalities. Many patients distrust this final treatment goal, and their subpersonalities may see integration as a form of death (Howell, 2011; Kluft, 2001, 1991). Therapists have used a range of approaches to help merge subpersonalities, including psychodynamic, supportive, cognitive-behavioral, and drug therapies (Ross, 2018; Cronin et al., 2014).

Once the subpersonalities are integrated, further therapy is typically needed to maintain the complete personality and to teach social and coping skills that may help prevent later dissociations. In case reports, some therapists note high success rates (Ross, 2018; Brand et al., 2014), but others find that patients continue to resist full integration. A few therapists have in fact questioned the need for full integration.

Depersonalization-Derealization Disorder

#

#TheirWords

"I was trying to daydream, but my mind kept wandering."

Steven Wright, comedian

As you read earlier, DSM-5 categorizes **depersonalization-derealization disorder** as a dissociative disorder, even though it is not characterized by the memory difficulties found in the other dissociative disorders. Its central symptoms are persistent and recurrent episodes of *depersonalization* (the sense that one's own mental functioning or body are unreal or detached) and/or *derealization* (the sense that one's surroundings are unreal or detached).

> *A 24-year-old graduate student . . . had begun to doubt his own reality. He felt he was living in a dream in which he saw himself from without, and did not feel connected to his body or his thoughts. When he saw himself through his own eyes, he perceived his body parts as distorted—his hands and feet seemed quite large. As he walked across campus, he often felt the people he saw might be robots. . . .*
>
> *[By] his second session, he . . . had begun to perceive [his girlfriend] in a distorted manner. He . . . hesitated before returning, because he wondered whether his therapist was really alive.*
>
> *(Kluft, 1988, p. 580)*

Like this graduate student, people experiencing depersonalization feel as though they have become separated from their body and are observing themselves from outside. Occasionally their mind seems to be floating a few feet above them—a sensation known as *doubling*. Their body parts feel foreign to them, their hands and feet smaller or bigger than usual. Many sufferers describe their emotional state as "mechanical," "dreamlike," or "dizzy." Throughout the whole experience, however, they are aware that their perceptions are distorted, and in that sense they remain in contact with reality. In some cases this sense of unreality also extends to other sensory experiences and behavior. People may, for example, have distortions in their sense of touch or smell or their judgments of time or space, or they may feel that they have lost control over their speech or actions.

In contrast to depersonalization, derealization is characterized by feeling that the external world is unreal and strange. Objects may seem to change shape or size; other people may seem removed, mechanical, or even dead. The graduate student, for example, saw other people as robots, perceived his girlfriend in a distorted manner, and hesitated to return for a second session of therapy because he wondered whether his therapist was really alive.

Depersonalization and derealization experiences by themselves do not indicate a depersonalization-derealization disorder. Transient depersonalization or derealization reactions are fairly common (Simeon, 2017; Michal, 2011). One-third of all people say that on occasion they have felt as though they were watching themselves in a movie. Similarly, one-third of individuals who confront a life-threatening danger experience feelings of depersonalization or derealization (van Duijl et al., 2010). People sometimes have feelings of depersonalization after practicing meditation or after traveling to new places. Young children may also experience depersonalization from time to time as they are developing their capacity for self-awareness. In most such cases, the affected people are able to compensate for the distortion and continue to function with reasonable effectiveness until the temporary episode eventually ends.

If you have ever experienced feelings of depersonalization or derealization, how did you explain them at the time?

Daniel Morel/Reuters/Alamy

Religious dissociations As part of religious or cultural practices, many people voluntarily enter into trances that are similar to the symptoms found in dissociative identity disorder and depersonalization-derealization disorder. Here, voodoo followers sing and flail about in trances inside a sacred pool at a temple in Souvenance, Haiti.

The symptoms of depersonalization-derealization disorder, in contrast, are persistent or recurrent, cause considerable distress, and may impair social relationships and job performance (Simeon, 2017; Gentile et al., 2014). The disorder is experienced by around 2 percent of the population, most often adolescents and young adults, hardly ever in people over 40. It usually comes on suddenly and may be triggered by extreme fatigue, physical pain, intense stress, or recovery from substance abuse. Survivors of traumatic experiences or people caught in life-threatening situations, such as hostages or kidnap victims, seem to be particularly vulnerable to this disorder. The disorder tends to be long-lasting; the symptoms may improve and even disappear for a time, only to return or intensify during times of severe stress. Like the graduate student in our case discussion, many sufferers fear that they are losing their minds and become preoccupied with worry about their symptoms. Few theories have been offered to explain depersonalization-derealization disorder. Several different forms of psychotherapy have been applied in cases of this disorder, but there have been almost no studies that test the efficacy of these approaches (Simeon, 2017).

9... SUMMING UP

DISSOCIATIVE DISORDERS People with dissociative disorders experience major changes in memory and identity that are not caused by clear physical factors—changes that often emerge after a traumatic event. Typically, one part of the memory or identity

(continued on the next page)

#TheirWords

"There are lots of people who mistake their imagination for their memory."

Josh Billings

is dissociated, or separated, from the other parts. People with dissociative amnesia are unable to recall important personal information or past events in their lives. Those with dissociative fugue, an extreme form of dissociative amnesia, not only fail to remember personal information but also flee to a different location and may establish a new identity. In another dissociative disorder, dissociative identity disorder, a person develops two or more distinct subpersonalities.

Dissociative amnesia and dissociative identity disorder are not well understood. Among the processes that have been cited to explain them are extreme repression, state-dependent learning, and self-hypnosis.

Dissociative amnesia may end on its own or may require treatment. Dissociative identity disorder typically requires treatment. Approaches commonly used to help people with dissociative amnesia recover their lost memories are psychodynamic therapy, hypnotic therapy, and sodium amobarbital or sodium pentobarbital. Therapists who treat people with dissociative identity disorder use the same approaches and also try to help the clients recognize the nature and scope of their disorder, recover the gaps in their memory, and integrate their subpersonalities into one functional personality.

People with yet another kind of dissociative disorder, depersonalization-derealization disorder, feel as though they are detached from their own mental processes or body and are observing themselves from the outside, or feel as though the people or objects around them are unreal or detached.

Getting a Handle on Trauma and Stress

The concepts of trauma and stress have been prominent in the field of abnormal psychology since its early days when, for example, Sigmund Freud proposed that most forms of psychopathology begin with traumatic losses or events. But why and how do trauma and stress translate into psychopathology? The answer to that question has, in fact, eluded clinical theorists and researchers—until recent times. Researchers now better understand the relationship between trauma, stress, and psychological dysfunction—viewing it as a complex and unfolding interaction of many variables, including biological factors, childhood experiences, personal styles, and social supports. Similarly, clinicians are now developing more effective treatment programs for people with acute and posttraumatic stress disorders—programs that *combine* biological, cognitive-behavioral, family, and group interventions.

Insights and treatments for the dissociative disorders, the other group of trauma-triggered disorders discussed in this chapter, have not moved as quickly. However, the field's focus on these disorders has surged during the past two decades—partly because of intense clinical interest in the memory abnormalities on display in posttraumatic stress reactions and in physically rooted disorders such as Alzheimer's disease.

Amidst the rapid developments in the realms of trauma and stress lies a cautionary tale. When problems are studied heavily, it is common for the public, as well as some researchers and clinicians, to draw conclusions that may be too bold. For example, many people—perhaps too many—are now receiving diagnoses of posttraumatic stress disorder, partly because the symptoms of PTSD are many and because PTSD has received so much attention. Similarly, some of today's clinicians worry that the resurging interest in dissociative disorders may be creating a false impression of their prevalence. We shall see such potential problems again when we look at other forms of pathology that are currently receiving great focus, such as bipolar disorder among children and attention-deficit/hyperactivity disorder. The line between enlightenment and overenthusiasm is often thin.

CLINICAL CHOICES

Now that you've read about disorders of trauma and stress, try the interactive case study for this chapter. See if you are able to identify Michelle's symptoms and suggest a diagnosis based on her symptoms. What kind of treatment would be most effective for Michelle? Go to **LaunchPad** to access *Clinical Choices*.

... Key Terms

stressor, p. 139
hypothalamus, p. 140
autonomic nervous system (ANS), p. 140
endocrine system, p. 140
sympathetic nervous system, p. 141
parasympathetic nervous system, p. 141
hypothalamic-pituitary-adrenal (HPA) pathway, p. 142
corticosteroids, p. 142
acute stress disorder, p. 142
posttraumatic stress disorder (PTSD), p. 142
rape, p. 145
terrorism, p. 145
torture, p. 146
stress circuit, p. 149
resilience, p. 150
complex PTSD, p. 151
developmental psychopathology, p. 151
cognitive processing therapy, p. 154
prolonged exposure, p. 154
eye movement desensitization and reprocessing (EMDR), p. 154
psychological debriefing, p. 156
dissociative disorders, p. 157
memory, p. 157
dissociative amnesia, p. 157
amnestic episode, p. 158
dissociative fugue, p. 159
dissociative identity disorder, p. 161
subpersonalities, p. 161
iatrogenic, p. 163
repression, p. 164
state-dependent learning, p. 165
self-hypnosis, p. 166
hypnotic therapy, p. 167
fusion, p. 168
depersonalization-derealization disorder, p. 168

... Quick Quiz

1. What factors determine how people react to stressors in life? *pp. 139–142*
2. What factors help influence whether persons will develop acute and posttraumatic stress disorders after experiencing a traumatic event? How does the developmental psychopathology perspective integrate these factors to explain the onset of posttraumatic stress disorder? *pp. 148–152*
3. What treatment approaches have been used with people suffering from acute or posttraumatic stress disorder? *pp. 153–156*
4. List and describe the different dissociative disorders. *pp. 157–169*
5. What are the various patterns of dissociative amnesia? What is dissociative fugue? *pp. 157–160*
6. What are the different kinds of relationships that the subpersonalities may have in dissociative identity disorder? *pp. 161–162*
7. Describe the psychodynamic, state-dependent learning, and self-hypnosis explanations of dissociative amnesia and dissociative identity disorder. How well is each explanation supported by research? *pp. 164–166*
8. What approaches have been used to treat dissociative amnesia? *p. 167*
9. What are the key features of treatment for dissociative identity disorder? Is treatment successful? *pp. 167–168*
10. Define and describe depersonalization-derealization disorder. How well is this problem understood? *pp. 168–169*

INITIAL

CHAPTER

6

Depressive and Bipolar Disorders

TOPIC OVERVIEW

The first conscious thought that all was not well with me came . . . when I was twenty-two. I had been living in Los Angeles for two years, working various temp jobs while trying to establish myself as a writer and performance artist. Out of nowhere and for no apparent reason—or so it seemed—I started feeling strong sensations of grief. I don't remember the step-by-step progression of the illness. What I can recall is that my life disintegrated; first, into a strange and terrifying space of sadness and then, into a cobweb of fatigue. I gradually lost my ability to function. It would take me hours to get up out of bed, get bathed, put clothes on. By the time I was fully dressed, it was well into the afternoon. . . .

After a while I stopped showing up at my temp job, stopped going out altogether, and locked myself in my home. It was over three weeks before I felt well enough to leave. During that time, I cut myself off from everything and everyone. Days would go by before I bathed. I did not have enough energy to clean up myself or my home. There was a trail of undergarments and other articles of clothing that ran from the living room to the bedroom to the bathroom of my tiny apartment. Dishes with decaying food covered every counter and tabletop in the place. Even watching TV or talking on the phone required too much concentration. . . . All I could do was take to my pallet of blankets and coats positioned on the living room floor and wait for whatever I was going through to pass. And it did. Slowly. . . .

. . . Deep down, I knew that something had gone wrong with me, in me. But what could I do? Stunned and defenseless, the only thing I felt I could do was move on. I assured myself that my mind and the behaviors it provoked were well within my control. In the future I would just have to be extremely aware. I would make sure that what happened did not happen again. But it did. Again and again, no matter how aware, responsible, or in control I tried to be. . . .

Each wave of the depression cost me something dear. I lost my job because the temp agencies where I was registered could no longer tolerate my lengthy absences. Unable to pay rent, I lost my apartment and ended up having to rent a small room in a boarding house. I lost my friends. Most of them found it too troublesome to deal with my sudden moodiness and passivity so they stopped calling and coming around.

(Danquah, 1998)

Most people's moods come and go. Their feelings of elation or sadness are understandable reactions to daily events and do not affect their lives greatly. However, the moods of certain people last a long time. As in the case of Meri Nana-Ama Danquah, a performance artist and poet who described her disorder above, their moods color all of their interactions with the world and even interfere with normal functioning. Such people struggle in particular with depression, mania, or both. **Depression** is a low, sad state in which life seems dark and its challenges overwhelming. **Mania,** the opposite of depression, is a state of breathless euphoria, or at least frenzied energy, in which people may have an exaggerated belief that the world is theirs for the taking.

Mood problems of these kinds are at the center of two groups of disorders—depressive disorders and bipolar disorders (APA, 2013). These groups are examined in this chapter. People with **depressive disorders** suffer only from depression, a pattern called **unipolar depression.** They have no history of mania and return to a normal or

depression A low, sad state marked by significant levels of sadness, lack of energy, low self-worth, guilt, or related symptoms.

mania A state or episode of euphoria or frenzied activity in which people may have an exaggerated belief that the world is theirs for the taking.

depressive disorders The group of disorders marked by unipolar depression.

unipolar depression Depression without a history of mania.

bipolar disorder A disorder marked by alternating or intermixed periods of mania and depression.

nearly normal mood when their depression lifts. In contrast, those with **bipolar disorders** have periods of mania that alternate with periods of depression.

Mood problems have always captured people's interest, in part because so many famous people have suffered from them. The Bible speaks of the severe depressions of Nebuchadnezzar, Saul, and Moses. Queen Victoria of England and Abraham Lincoln seem to have experienced recurring depressions. Mood difficulties also have plagued writers Ernest Hemingway and Sylvia Plath, comedian Jim Carrey, and musical performers Bruce Springsteen and Beyoncé. Their problems have been shared by millions. ■

Unipolar Depression: The Depressive Disorders

Whenever we feel particularly unhappy, we are likely to describe ourselves as "depressed." In all likelihood, we are merely responding to sad events, fatigue, or unhappy thoughts. This loose use of the term confuses a perfectly normal mood swing with a clinical syndrome. All of us experience dejection from time to time, but only some experience a depressive disorder. Depressive disorders bring severe and long-lasting psychological pain that may intensify as time goes by. Those who suffer from such disorders may lose their will to carry out the simplest of life's activities; some even lose their will to live.

Almost every day we have ups and downs in mood. How can we distinguish the everyday blues from clinical depression?

How Common Is Unipolar Depression?

Around 8 percent of adults in the United States suffer from a severe unipolar pattern of depression in any given year, while as many as 5 percent suffer from mild forms (Krishnan, 2017; Kessler et al., 2012, 2010). Around 20 percent of all adults experience an episode of severe unipolar depression at some point in their lives. These prevalence rates are similar in Canada, England, France, and many other countries. Moreover, the rate of depression—mild or severe—is higher among poor people than wealthier people (Wood, 2017; Sareen et al., 2011).

Women are at least twice as likely as men to have episodes of severe unipolar depression (WHO, 2017). As many as 26 percent of women have an episode at some time in their lives, compared with 12 percent of men. As you will see in Chapter 14, among children the prevalence of unipolar depression is similar for girls and boys.

An episode of severe depression can occur at any point throughout the life span. The average age of onset is 19 years, with the peak age being late adolescence or early adulthood (Weissman et al., 2016). In any given year, the rate of severe depression is twice as high among adults under 65 years of age as among those 65 years and older (Krishnan, 2017).

Approximately 85 percent of people with unipolar depression, including severe depression, recover within 6 months, some without treatment. More than half of those who recover from severe depression have at least one other episode later in their lives (Coryell, 2018; Simon & Ciechanowski, 2017).

Dear diary,
Sorry to bother you again.
LOW SELF-ESTEEM

Mike Twohy/The New Yorker Collection/The Cartoon Bank

What Are the Symptoms of Depression?

The picture of depression may vary from person to person. Earlier you saw how Meri's profound sadness, fatigue, and cognitive deterioration brought her job and social life to a standstill. Some depressed people have symptoms that are less severe. They manage to function, although their depression typically robs them of much effectiveness or pleasure.

As the case of Meri indicates, depression has many symptoms other than sadness. The symptoms, which often exacerbate one another, span five areas of functioning: emotional, motivational, behavioral, cognitive, and physical.

Emotional Symptoms Most people who are depressed feel sad and dejected. They describe themselves as feeling "miserable," "empty," and "humiliated." They tend to lose their sense of humor, report getting little pleasure from anything, and in some cases display *anhedonia*, an inability to experience any pleasure at all. A number also experience anxiety, anger, or agitation (Chen et al., 2019). Terrie Williams, author of *Black Pain*, a book about depression in African Americans, describes the agony she went through each morning as her depression was unfolding:

> *Nights I could handle. I fell asleep easily, and sleep allowed me to forget. But my mornings were unmanageable. To wake up each morning was to remember once again that the world by which I defined myself was no more. Soon after opening my eyes, the crying bouts would start and I'd sit alone for hours, weeping and mourning my losses.*
>
> *(Williams, 2008, p. 9)*

Motivational Symptoms Depressed people typically lose the desire to pursue their usual activities. Almost all report a lack of drive, initiative, and spontaneity. They may have to force themselves to go to work, talk with friends, eat meals, or have sex. Terrie describes her social withdrawal during a depressive episode:

> *I woke up one morning with a knot of fear in my stomach so crippling that I couldn't face light, much less day, and so intense that I stayed in bed for three days with the shades drawn and the lights out.*
>
> *Three days. Three days not answering the phone. Three days not checking my e-mail. I was disconnected completely from the outside world, and I didn't care.*
>
> *(Williams, 2008, p. xxiv)*

Suicide represents the ultimate escape from life's challenges. As you will see in Chapter 7, many depressed people become uninterested in life or wish to die; others wish they could kill themselves, and some actually do. It has been estimated that between 6 and 15 percent of people who suffer from severe depression die by suicide (Holmes, 2018; Alridge, 2012).

Behavioral Symptoms Depressed people are usually less active and less productive. They spend more time alone and may stay in bed for long periods. One man recalls, "My eyes would open at the crack of dawn, but getting out of bed was impossible. I just stayed there, and stayed there, and stayed there some more, virtually paralyzed, knowing that a day filled with misery awaited me." Depressed people may also move, and even speak, more slowly (Liu et al., 2019).

Cognitive Symptoms Depressed people hold extremely negative views of themselves. They consider themselves inadequate, undesirable, inferior, perhaps even evil (Scheffers et al., 2019; Dinger et al., 2017). They also blame themselves for nearly every unfortunate event, even things that have nothing to do with them, and they rarely credit themselves for positive achievements.

Another cognitive symptom of depression is pessimism. Sufferers are usually convinced that nothing will ever improve, and they feel helpless to change any aspect of their lives. Because they expect the worst, they are likely to procrastinate. Their sense of hopelessness and helplessness makes them especially vulnerable to suicidal thinking (Lyness, 2016).

Tim Mosenfelder/Getty Images

"Idk what peace feels like" A few months after this 2016 concert performance in New Orleans, the hugely successful rap artist and actor Kid Cudi revealed on his Facebook page that he had entered an inpatient program to receive treatment for depression and suicidal urges. He wrote to his fans, "My anxiety and depression have ruled my life for as long as I can remember . . . Idk what peace feels like." He returned to performing a month later.

major depressive disorder A severe pattern of depression that is disabling and not caused by such factors as drugs or a general medical condition.

persistent depressive disorder A chronic form of unipolar depression marked by ongoing and repeated symptoms of either major or mild depression.

premenstrual dysphoric disorder A disorder marked by repeated episodes of significant depression and related symptoms during the week before menstruation.

People with depression frequently complain that their intellectual ability is very poor (Beblo et al., 2017). They feel confused, unable to remember things, easily distracted, and unable to solve even the smallest problems. In laboratory studies, depressed people do perform somewhat, but not extremely, more poorly than nondepressed people on tasks of memory, attention, and reasoning (Baune et al., 2018; Bowler et al., 2018). It may be, however, that these difficulties sometimes reflect motivational problems rather than cognitive ones.

Physical Symptoms People who are depressed frequently have such physical ailments as headaches, indigestion, constipation, dizzy spells, and general pain (Taycan, Özdemi, & Erdogan, 2017). In fact, many depressions are misdiagnosed as medical problems at first (Tse, González, & Jenkins, 2018). Disturbances in appetite and sleep are particularly common (Chang et al., 2017). Most depressed people eat less, sleep less, and feel more fatigued than they did prior to the disorder. Some, however, eat and sleep excessively.

Diagnosing Unipolar Depression

According to DSM-5, a *major depressive episode* is a period of two or more weeks marked by at least five symptoms of depression, including sad mood and/or loss of pleasure (see **Table 6-1**). In extreme cases, the episode may include psychotic symptoms, ones marked by a loss of contact with reality, such as *delusions*—bizarre ideas without foundation—or *hallucinations*—perceptions of things that are not actually present. A depressed man with psychotic symptoms may imagine that he cannot eat "because my intestines are deteriorating and will soon stop working," or he may believe that he sees his dead wife.

DSM-5 lists several types of depressive disorders. People who go through a major depressive episode without having any history of mania receive a diagnosis of **major depressive disorder** (APA, 2013) (see Table 6-1 again). The disorder may be additionally further described as *seasonal* if it changes with the seasons (for example, if the depression recurs each winter), *catatonic* if it is marked by either immobility or excessive activity, *peripartum* if it occurs during pregnancy or within four weeks of giving birth (see ***PsychWatch*** on page 179), or *melancholic* if the person is almost totally unaffected by pleasurable events.

People whose unipolar depression is chronic receive a diagnosis of **persistent depressive disorder** (see Table 6-1 again). Some people with this chronic disorder have repeated major depressive episodes, a pattern technically called *persistent*

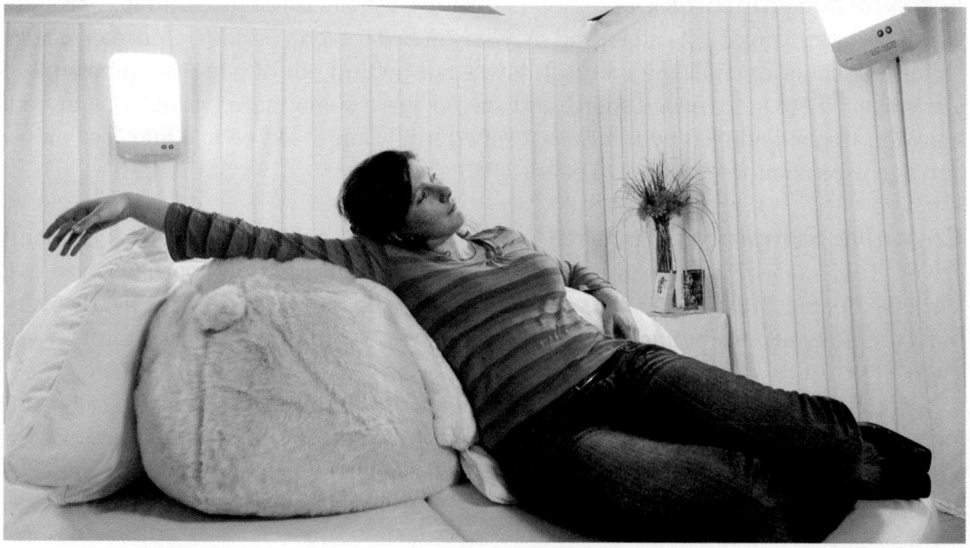

SSPL/Getty Images

Lighting up depression This visitor to the Science Museum in London makes herself comfortable in the Light Lounge, a white enclosure containing four light boxes, where people can relax on a sofa and experience "light therapy" to help beat the winter blues and prevent seasonal recurrences of depression. Winter depression has been linked to the decrease in the amount of light people are exposed to at that time of year and to an accompanying shift in secretions of the hormone *melatonin*.

depressive disorder with major depressive episodes. Others have less severe and less disabling symptoms, a pattern technically called *persistent depressive disorder with dysthymic syndrome*.

A third type of depressive disorder is **premenstrual dysphoric disorder**, a diagnosis given to certain women who repeatedly have clinically significant depressive and related symptoms during the week before menstruation. The inclusion of this pattern in DSM-5 is controversial. Many clinicians believe that the category is sexist and "pathologizes" severe cases of *premenstrual syndrome* (*PMS*), premenstrual discomforts that are common and normal among women.

Yet another kind of depressive disorder, *disruptive mood dysregulation disorder*, is characterized by a combination of persistent depressive symptoms and recurrent outbursts of severe temper. This disorder emerges during mid-childhood or adolescence and so is discussed in Chapter 14.

TABLE: 6-1

Dx Checklist

Major Depressive Episode
1. For a 2-week period, person displays an increase in depressed mood for the majority of each day and/or a decrease in enjoyment or interest across most activities for the majority of each day.
2. For the same 2 weeks, person also experiences at least 3 or 4 of the following symptoms: • Considerable weight change or appetite change • Daily insomnia or hypersomnia • Daily agitation or decrease in motor activity • Daily fatigue or lethargy • Daily feelings of worthlessness or excessive guilt • Daily reduction in concentration or decisiveness • Repeated focus on death or suicide, a suicide plan, or a suicide attempt.
3. Significant distress or impairment.
Major Depressive Disorder
1. Presence of a major depressive episode
2. No pattern of mania or hypomania
Persistent Depressive Disorder
1. Person experiences the symptoms of major or mild depression for at least 2 years.
2. During the 2-year period, symptoms not absent for more than 2 months at a time.
3. No history of mania or hypomania.
4. Significant distress or impairment.

Information from: APA, 2013.

Stress and Unipolar Depression

Episodes of unipolar depression often seem to be triggered by stressful events in an individual's life (Krishnan, 2017; Shin et al., 2017). In fact, researchers have found that 80 percent of all severe episodes occur within a month or two of a significant negative event (Hammen, 2016). Stressful life events also precede other psychological disorders, but depressed people report more such events than anybody else.

Some clinicians consider it important to distinguish a *reactive* (*exogenous*) *depression*, which follows clear-cut stressful events, from an *endogenous depression*, which seems to be a response to internal factors. But can one ever know for certain whether a depression is reactive or not? Even if stressful events occurred before the onset of depression, that depression may not be reactive. The events could actually be a coincidence. Thus, today's clinicians usually concentrate on recognizing both the situational and the internal aspects of any given case of unipolar depression.

Why do you think stressful events or periods in life might trigger depressed feelings and other negative emotions?

The Biological Model of Unipolar Depression

Medical researchers have been aware for years that certain diseases and drugs produce mood changes. Could unipolar depression itself have biological causes? Studies of genetic factors, biochemical factors, brain circuits, and the immune system suggest that often it does.

Genetic Factors Three kinds of research—family pedigree, twin, and gene studies—suggest that some people inherit a predisposition to unipolar depression. *Family pedigree studies* select people with unipolar depression, examine their relatives, and see whether depression also afflicts other members of the family. If a predisposition to unipolar depression is inherited, the relatives should have a higher rate of depression than the population at large. Researchers have in fact found that as many as 30 percent of those relatives are depressed (see **Table 6-2** on the next page), compared with fewer than 10 percent of the general population (Levinson & Nichols, 2014).

If a predisposition to unipolar depression is inherited, you might also expect to find a particularly large number of cases among the close relatives of depressed persons. *Twin studies* have supported this expectation. When an identical twin has unipolar depression, there is a 38 percent chance that the other twin has already had or will eventually have the same disorder. In contrast, when a fraternal twin has unipolar depression, the other twin has only a 20 percent chance of having the disorder (Krishnan, 2017; McGuffin et al., 1996).

Finally, today's scientists have at their disposal techniques from the field of molecular biology to help them directly identify genes and determine whether certain gene

TALE: 6-2

Comparing Depressive and Bipolar Disorders

	One-Year Prevalence (Percent)	Female-to-Male Ratio	Typical Age at Onset (Years)	Prevalence Among First-Degree Relatives	Percentage Receiving Treatment Currently
Major depressive disorder	8.0	2:1	18–29	Elevated	50
Persistent depressive disorder (with dysthymic syndrome)	1.5–5.0	Between 3:2 and 2:1	10–25	Elevated	62
Bipolar I disorder	1.6	1:1	15–44	Elevated	49
Bipolar II disorder	1.0	1:1	15–44	Elevated	49
Cyclothymic disorder	0.4	1:1	15–25	Elevated	Unknown

Information from: Bressart, 2018; Stovall, 2018; Krishnan, 2017; NIMH, 2017; WHO, 2017; Stovall, 2016; Weissman et al., 2016; Kessler et al., 2012, 2010; Wang et al., 2005.

#WorldCount

More than 300 million people suffer from depression worldwide (WHO, 2017).

abnormalities are related to depression. Using such techniques, researchers have found evidence that unipolar depression may be tied to genes on chromosomes 1, 3, 4, 6, 9, 10, 11, 12, 13, 14, 17, 18, 20, 21, 22, and X (Naoi et al., 2018; Wang et al., 2018). For example, a number of researchers have found that people who are depressed often have an abnormality of their *5-HTT* gene, a gene located on chromosome 17 that is responsible for the activity of the neurotransmitter serotonin. As you will read in the next section, low activity of serotonin in certain regions of the brain is closely tied to depression.

Biochemical Factors Low activity of two neurotransmitter chemicals, **norepinephrine** and **serotonin**, has been strongly linked to unipolar depression. In the 1950s, several pieces of evidence began to point to this relationship. First, medical researchers discovered that certain medications for high blood pressure often caused depression (Ayd, 1956). As it turned out, some of these medications lowered norepinephrine activity and others lowered serotonin. A second piece of evidence was the discovery of the first truly effective antidepressant drugs. Although these drugs were discovered by accident, researchers soon learned that while the drugs were relieving depression, they also were bringing about increases in norepinephrine and/or serotonin activity.

For years it was thought that low activity of *either* norepinephrine or serotonin directly produce depression, but theorists now believe that their relationship to depression is more complicated (Krishnan, 2017). Research indicates that interactions between serotonin and norepinephrine activity, or between them and other kinds of neurotransmitters in the brain, are more influential than the operation of any one neurotransmitter alone. In addition, as you will read shortly, a number of studies suggest that the activity of these neurotransmitters may either reflect or help produce dysfunction of a depression-related circuit in the brain, dysfunction that may itself be a key to the development of depression.

Biological researchers have also learned that another group of chemicals—the body's *hormones*—are linked to depression. As you read in Chapter 5, whenever we confront stressors in life, our brain triggers two stress pathways of the brain and body into action. One of those pathways, the *hypothalamic-pituitary-adrenal* (*HPA*) pathway, ultimately brings about the release of hormones at various locations throughout the body, and those hormones spur assorted body organs into action, causing us to temporarily experience a heightened state of arousal (see page 142). You may recall that the HPA pathway of people with posttraumatic stress disorder and certain anxiety disorders consistently *overreacts* when those individuals confront stressors. Research indicates that the HPA pathway of people with depression is also overly reactive in the face of stress, causing excessive releases of *cortisol* and related hormones at times of stress (Geerlings

norepinephrine A neurotransmitter whose abnormal activity is linked to depression and panic disorder.

serotonin A neurotransmitter whose abnormal activity is linked to depression, obsessive-compulsive disorder, and eating disorders.

PSYCHWATCH

Sadness at the Happiest of Times

Women usually expect the birth of a child to be a happy experience. But for at least 10 percent of new mothers, the weeks and months after childbirth bring clinical depression (Kendig et al., 2017; Ko et al., 2017). Peripartum depression, popularly called postpartum depression, typically begins within four weeks after the birth of a child; many cases actually begin during pregnancy (APA, 2013). This disorder is far more severe than simple "baby blues." It is also different from other postpartum syndromes such as postpartum psychosis, a problem that is examined in Chapter 12.

Lucas Oleniuk/Getty Images

Fending off postpartum depression Spin instructor Anouk Malavoy works out at a quads gym with her baby. Malavoy has written columns for the *Toronto Star* about the role exercise can play in helping some women prevent or combat postpartum depression.

The "baby blues" are so common—as many as 80 percent of women experience them—that most researchers consider them normal. As new mothers try to cope with the wakeful nights, rattled emotions, and other stresses that accompany the arrival of a new baby, they may have crying spells, fatigue, anxiety, insomnia, and sadness (Lewis et al., 2018; Enatescu et al., 2014). These symptoms usually disappear within days or weeks (Viguera, 2016).

In postpartum depression, however, depressive symptoms continue and may last up to a year or more. The symptoms include extreme sadness, despair, tearfulness, insomnia, anxiety, intrusive thoughts, compulsions, panic attacks, feelings of inability to cope, and suicidal thoughts (Shi et al., 2018). The mother–infant relationship and the psychological and physical health of the child may suffer as a result (Jacques et al., 2019; Weissman, 2018). Women who have an episode of postpartum depression have a 25 to 50 percent chance of developing it again with a subsequent birth (Kendig et al., 2017).

Many clinicians believe that the hormonal changes accompanying childbirth trigger postpartum depression. All women go through a kind of hormone "withdrawal" after delivery, as estrogen and progesterone levels, which rise as much as 50 times above normal during pregnancy, now drop sharply to levels far below normal (Horowitz et al., 2005, 1995). Perhaps some women are particularly influenced by these dramatic hormone changes (Viguera, 2016; Mehta et al., 2014). Other theorists suggest that some women may have a genetic predisposition to postpartum depression (McEvoy, 2017). A woman with a family history of mood disorders appears to be at high risk, even if she herself has not previously had a mood disorder (Kendig et al., 2017; Viguera, 2016).

At the same time, psychological and sociocultural factors may play important roles in the disorder. The birth of a baby brings enormous psychological and social change. A woman typically faces changes in her marital relationship, daily routines, and social roles. Sleep and relaxation are likely to decrease, and financial pressures may increase. Perhaps she feels the added stress of giving up a career or of trying to maintain one. This pileup of stress may heighten the risk of depression (Viguera, 2016; Kendall-Tackett, 2010). Mothers whose infants are sick or temperamentally "difficult" may be under yet additional pressure (Badr, 2018).

Fortunately, treatment can make a big difference for most women with postpartum depression. Self-help support groups have proved extremely helpful for many women who have or who are at risk for postpartum depression (Ashford et al., 2017; Viguera, 2017). In addition, many respond well to the same approaches that are applied to other forms of depression—antidepressant medications, cognitive-behavioral therapy, interpersonal psychotherapy, or a combination of these approaches (Viguera, 2017; Kim et al., 2014).

However, many women who would benefit from treatment do not seek help because they feel ashamed about being sad at a time that is supposed to be joyous, and they are concerned about being judged harshly (Bina & Glasser, 2017; Kendig et al., 2017). For them, and for the spouses and family members close to them, a large dose of education is in order. Even positive events, such as the birth of a child, can be stressful if they also bring major change to one's life. Recognizing and addressing such feelings are in everyone's best interest.

& Gerritsen, 2017). This relationship is not all that surprising, given that stressful events so often seem to trigger depression. Once again, it is possible that the HPA overreactivity and heightened hormone activity found in depressed people either reflects or helps produce dysfunction in a *depression-related circuit* in the brain, the biological focus that we turn to next.

Brain Circuits As you have read in previous chapters, biological researchers have determined that emotional reactions of various kinds are tied to brain *circuits*—networks of brain structures that work together, triggering each other into action and producing a particular kind of emotional or behavioral reaction. A brain circuit whose dysfunction contributes to unipolar depression has begun to emerge (Schmitgen et al., 2019; Newman et al., 2017). An array of brain-imaging studies point to several brain structures that are likely members of this depression-related brain circuit, including the *prefrontal cortex, hippocampus, amygdala,* and *subgenual cingulate* (also called *Brodmann Area 25*), among other structures (see **Figure 6-1**). You may notice that several of the structures in this circuit are also members of the brain circuits that contribute to certain anxiety disorders and PTSD. However, the subgenual cingulate, a subregion of the brain's anterior cingulate cortex, is distinctly part of the depression-related circuit. Indeed, some theorists believe that dysfunction by this particular structure may be the single most important contributor to depression.

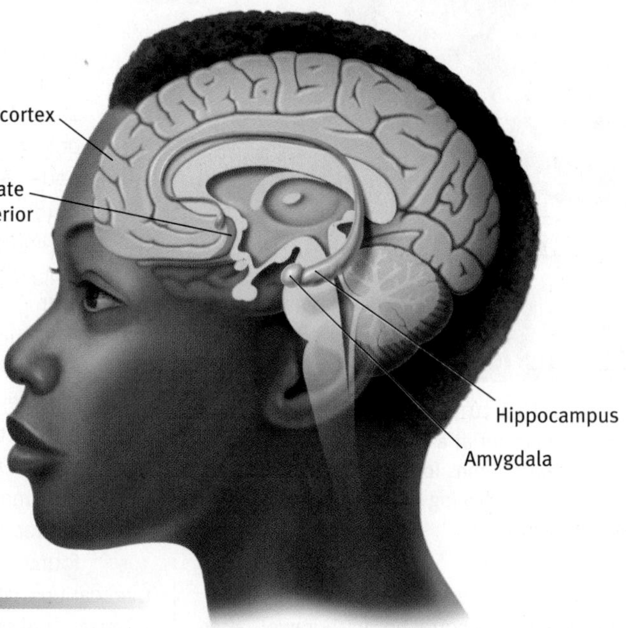

FIGURE 6-1

The Biology of Depression

Researchers believe that the brain circuit involved in unipolar depression includes the prefrontal cortex, hippocampus, amygdala, and subgenual cingulate, among other structures.

Unlike some of the other brain circuits we have discussed, dysfunctions of this depression-related brain circuit cannot be characterized in general terms, as, for example, a "hyperactive" or "underactive" circuit. But there are many indications that the circuit does operate abnormally in persons with depression. Research suggests, for example, that among depressed people, activity and blood flow are unusually low in certain parts and unusually high in other parts of the prefrontal cortex; the hippocampus is undersized and its production of new neurons is low; activity and blood flow are high in the amygdala; the subgenual cingulate is particularly small and active; and communication between these various structures, called *interconnectivity,* is often problematic (Walsh et al., 2019; Newman et al., 2017; Pizzagalli, 2017).

Studies indicate that under usual circumstances the neurotransmitters serotonin and norepinephrine are both plentiful and active in this brain circuit. It appears, however, that, among depressed people, the activity of serotonin and norepinephrine in this circuit is distinctly lower than among other people (Avraham et al., 2017; James et al., 2017). This is not surprising, considering all the research that we observed earlier linking depression to generally low activity by these neurotransmitters. The abnormal activity of these neurotransmitters in this brain circuit might be the result of dysfunction within or between the circuit's various structures, *or,* alternatively, the cause of such circuit dysfunction. At this point researchers do not know which is the case.

The Immune System As you will see in Chapter 8, the *immune system* is the body's network of activities and body cells that fight off bacteria, viruses, and other foreign invaders. When people are under intense stress for a while, their immune systems may become dysregulated, leading to slower functioning of important white blood cells called *lymphocytes* and to increased production of *C-reactive protein* (*CRP*), a protein that spreads throughout the body and causes inflammation and various illnesses (see pages 256–257). There is a growing belief among some researchers that immune system dysregulation of this kind helps produce depression (Anderson, 2018; Faugere et al., 2018).

MAO inhibitor An antidepressant drug that prevents the action of the enzyme monoamine oxidase.

What Are the Biological Treatments for Unipolar Depression? Usually biological treatment means *antidepressant drugs* or popular alternatives such as herbal supplements (see ***InfoCentral*** on the next page), but for people whose depression does not respond to medications, psychotherapy, or the like, it sometimes means *brain stimulation*.

"This next one is a sad little blues tune about love and pain that I wrote before I started taking Celexa."

ANTIDEPRESSANT DRUGS Two kinds of drugs discovered in the 1950s reduce the symptoms of depression: *monoamine oxidase* (*MAO*) *inhibitors* and *tricyclics*. Over the years, these drugs have been joined by a third group, the *second-generation antidepressants* (see **Table 6-3**).

The effectiveness of **MAO inhibitors** as a treatment for unipolar depression was discovered accidentally. Physicians noted that *iproniazid*, a drug being tested on patients with tuberculosis, had an interesting effect: it seemed to make the patients happier (Sandler, 1990). It was found to have the same effect on depressed patients (Kline, 1958; Loomer, Saunders, & Kline, 1957). What this and several related drugs had in common biochemically was that they slowed the body's production of the enzyme *monoamine oxidase* (*MAO*). Thus they were called MAO inhibitors.

Normally, brain supplies of the enzyme MAO break down, or degrade, the neurotransmitters serotonin and norepinephrine. MAO inhibitors block MAO from carrying out this activity and thereby stop the destruction of serotonin and norepinephrine (Naoi et al., 2018). The result is a rise in the activity levels of these neurotransmitters, and, in turn, a reduction of depressive symptoms. Approximately half of depressed patients who take MAO inhibitors are helped by them (Hirsch & Birnbaum, 2017; Ciraulo et al., 2011). There is, however, a potential danger with regard to these drugs. When people who take MAO inhibitors eat foods containing the chemical *tyramine*—including such common foods as cheeses, bananas, and certain wines—their blood pressure rises dangerously. Thus people on these drugs must stick to a rigid diet.

TABLE: 6-3

Some Drugs That Reduce Unipolar Depression

Monoamine Oxidase Inhibitors		Tricyclics		Second-Generation Antidepressants	
Generic Name	*Trade Name*	Generic Name	*Trade Name*	Generic Name	*Trade Name*
Iscarboxazid	*Marplan*	Imipramine	*Tofranil*	Trazodone	*Desyrel*
Phenelzine	*Nardil*	Amitriptyline	*Elavil*	Fluoxetine	*Prozac*
Tranylcypromine	*Parnate*	Doxepin	*Sinequan; Silenor*	Sertraline	*Zoloft*
Selegiline	*Eldepryl*	Trimipramine	*Surmontil*	Paroxetine	*Paxil*
		Desipramine	*Norpramin*	Venlafaxine	*Effexor*
		Nortriptyline	*Aventil; Pamelor*	Bupropion	*Wellbutrin*
		Protriptyline	*Vivactil*	Citalopram	*Celexa*
		Clomipramine	*Anafranil*	Escitalopram	*Lexapro*
		Amoxapine	*Asendin*	Duloxetine	*Cymbalta*
		Mirtazapine	*Remeron*	Desvenlafaxine	*Pristiq*
				Atomoxetine	*Strattera*

EXERCISE AND DIETARY SUPPLEMENTS

"Complementary and Alternative Medicine (CAM)" is the popular term for interventions that fall outside of conventional Western treatments. Two of the most common CAM interventions are **physical exercise** and **dietary supplements** (also known as **nutraceuticals**). Depression is the psychological problem for which these approaches are used most often, and research indicates that each can indeed help improve the moods of modestly or moderately depressed people, particularly when integrated with psychotherapy or medication, rather than applied alone (Jabr, 2017; Remick et al., 2017; Schuch et al., 2017).

EXERCISE ALLEVIATES DEPRESSION BY . . .

- Triggering positive changes in depression-related brain circuits, brain-body stress pathways, and neurotransmitter activity
- Increasing self-esteem
- Improving immune functioning
- Raising self-confidence
- Producing social interactions
- Improving cognitive functioning
- Improving sleep
- Distracting from unhappy thoughts

(Busch et al., 2017; Davenport, 2017; Hallgren et al., 2017; Jabr, 2017; Levine, 2017; Sadeghi et al., 2017; Sharma et al., 2006)

TOP EXERCISES FOR DEPRESSION

The most commonly recommended exercises for depression are *aerobic*—exercises that increase oxygen intake and raise heart rate. All aerobic exercises are equally helpful for depression (Jabr, 2017; Levine, 2017).

(Busch et al., 2017; Levine, 2017; Overdorf et al., 2016; Sharma et al., 2006)

EXERCISE VS. LEADING TREATMENTS

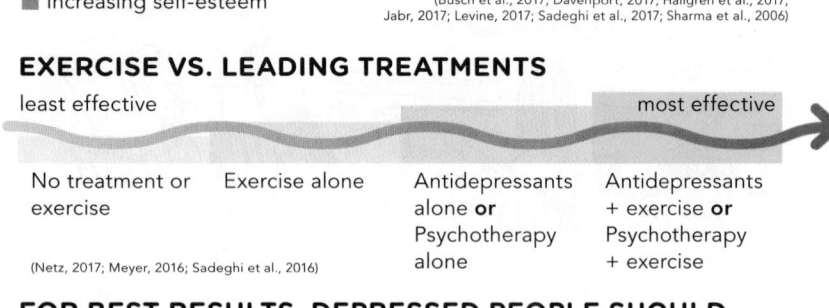

No treatment or exercise	Exercise alone	Antidepressants alone **or** Psychotherapy alone	Antidepressants + exercise **or** Psychotherapy + exercise

(Netz, 2017; Meyer, 2016; Sadeghi et al., 2016)

FOR BEST RESULTS, DEPRESSED PEOPLE SHOULD EXERCISE . . .

- At least 5 days per week
- At least 30 minutes per day
- With moderate or high intensity
- With a buddy or group
- Guided by a trainer
- In collaboration with their clinician

(Hallgren et al., 2017; Jain, 2017; Levine, 2017; Remick et al., 2017; Thompson, 2017; Overdorf et al., 2016; Stubbs et al., 2016)

WHY DEPRESSED PEOPLE DON'T EXERCISE

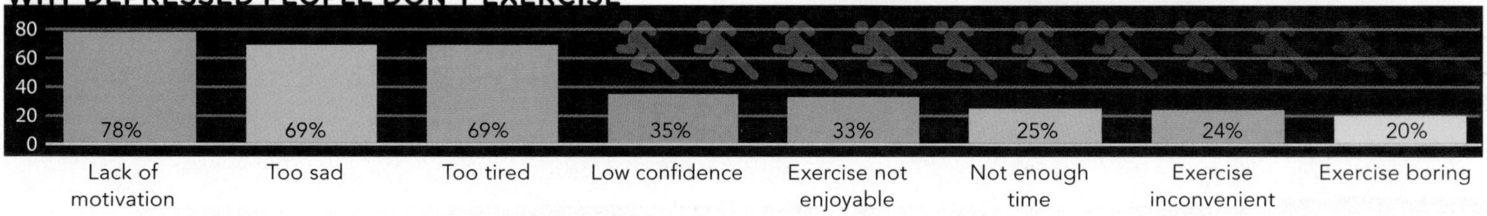

(Busch et al., 2017)

POPULAR NUTRACEUTICALS FOR DEPRESSION

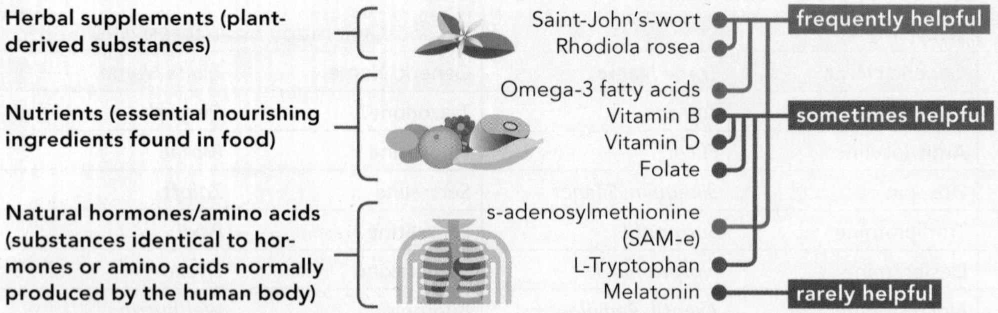

(Lee & Bae, 2017; PMH, 2017; Qureshi & Al-Bedah, 2013; Howland, 2012; Lakhan & Vieira, 2008)

Depressed people take nutraceuticals because . . .

- They are not helped by conventional treatments
- They developed major side effects to antidepressant drugs
- They cannot afford conventional treatments
- They dislike modern medications
- They prefer more natural treatments

(Jain, 2017; Qureshi & Al-Bedah, 2013)

NUTRACEUTICAL USE IS . . .

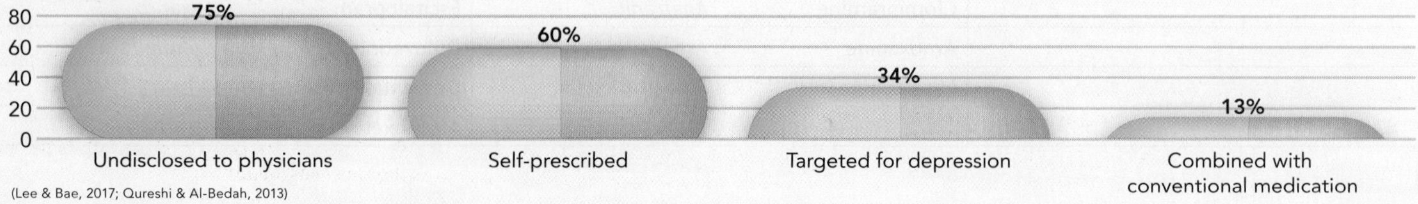

(Lee & Bae, 2017; Qureshi & Al-Bedah, 2013)

The discovery of **tricyclics** in the 1950s was also accidental. Researchers who were looking for a new drug to combat schizophrenia ran some tests on a drug called *imipramine* (Kuhn, 1958). They discovered that imipramine was of no help in cases of schizophrenia, but it did relieve unipolar depression in many people. The new drug (trade name Tofranil) and related ones became known as tricyclic antidepressants because they all share a three-ring molecular structure.

tricyclic An antidepressant drug such as imipramine that has three rings in its molecular structure.

In hundreds of studies, depressed patients taking tricyclics have improved significantly more than similar patients taking placebos, although the drugs must be taken for at least 10 days before such improvements take hold (Hirsch & Birnbaum, 2017). Around 50 to 60 percent of patients who take tricyclics are helped by them (Simon & Ciechanowski, 2017). If, however, recovered individuals stop taking the drugs immediately after obtaining relief, they run a high risk of relapsing. As many as half of recovered patients who discontinue the drugs in this way relapse within a year (Jarrett & Vittengl, 2016). As a result, most clinicians now keep patients on antidepressant drugs for at least five months after being free of depressive symptoms, an extension called "continuation therapy" or "maintenance therapy." Research indicates that this approach decreases the individuals' chances of relapse (Jarrett & Vittengl, 2016).

Most researchers have concluded that one of the ways in which tricyclics are able to reduce depression is by acting on the *neurotransmitter "reuptake" mechanisms* of key neurons (Hirsch & Birnbaum, 2017). Remember from Chapter 2 that brain messages are carried from a "sending" neuron across the synaptic space to a receiving neuron by a neurotransmitter, the chemical released from the end of the sending neuron. However, there is a complication in this process. While the sending neuron releases the neurotransmitter, a pumplike mechanism in the neuron's ending immediately starts to reabsorb it in a process called *reuptake*. The purpose of this reuptake process is to limit how long the neurotransmitter remains in the synaptic space and to prevent it from overstimulating the receiving neuron. Unfortunately, reuptake does not always progress properly. In particular, the reuptake mechanisms for depressed people are *too vigorous* in neurons that use either serotonin or norepinephrine—cutting off the activity of those neurotransmitters in their synaptic spaces too soon, preventing messages from reaching the receiving neurons, and helping to produce the symptoms of their disorder. Tricyclics inhibit (that is, *block*) this overly vigorous reuptake process, allowing serotonin and norepinephrine to remain in their synapses longer, thus increasing their stimulation of receiving neurons (see **Figure 6-2**).

Recent studies suggest that, for many depressed people, once these reuptake processes are corrected, serotonin and norepinephrine activity becomes smoother and

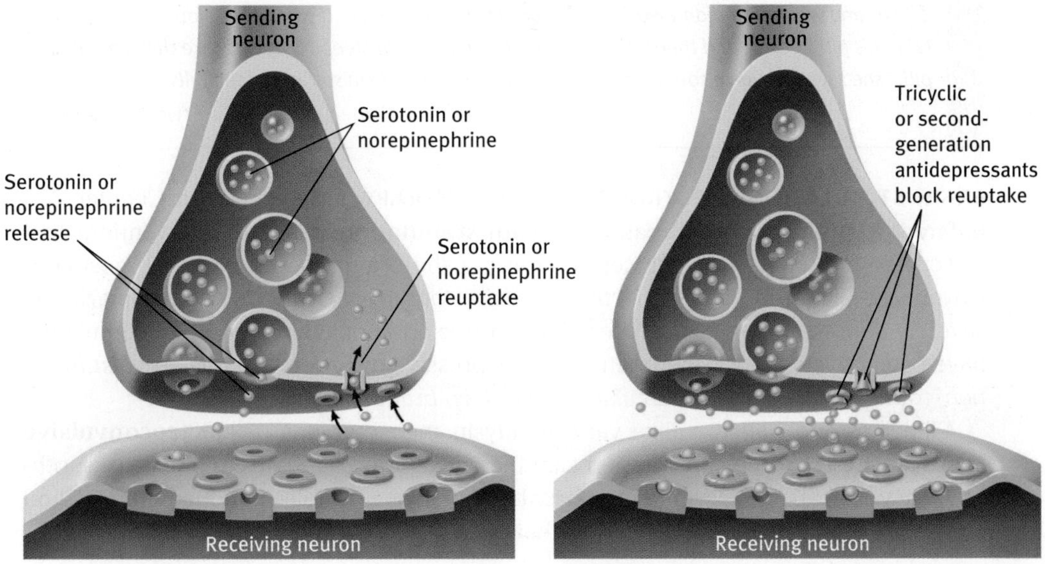

FIGURE 6-2

Reuptake and Antidepressants

(Left) Soon after a neuron releases neurotransmitters such as norepinephrine or serotonin into its synaptic space, it activates a pumplike reuptake mechanism to reabsorb excess neurotransmitters. In depression, however, this reuptake process is too active, removing too many neurotransmitters before they can bind to a receiving neuron. (Right) Tricyclic and most second-generation antidepressant drugs block the reuptake process, enabling norepinephrine or serotonin to remain in the synapse longer and bind to the receiving neuron.

Topham/The Image Works

Flower power *Hypericum perforatum*, known as *Saint-John's-wort*, is a low, wild-growing shrub, not an antidepressant drug. It is currently among the hottest-selling products in health stores, with studies indicating that it can be quite helpful in cases of mild or moderate depression.

more appropriate throughout their depression-related brain circuit (Rolls, 2017). Correspondingly, the interconnections between the structures in that circuit become more orderly and functional (James et al., 2017). With such biological corrections in place, depression subsides for many patients.

A third group of effective antidepressant drugs, structurally different from the MAO inhibitors and tricyclics, has been developed over the past three decades. Most of these second-generation antidepressants are called **selective serotonin reuptake inhibitors (SSRIs)** because they increase serotonin activity specifically, without affecting norepinephrine or other neurotransmitters. The SSRIs include *fluoxetine* (trade name Prozac), *sertraline* (Zoloft), and *escitalopram* (Lexapro). Other second-generation antidepressants are *selective norepinephrine reuptake inhibitors* (such as *atomoxetine*, or Strattera), which increase norepinephrine activity only, and *serotonin-norepinephrine reuptake inhibitors* (such as *venlafaxine*, or Effexor), which increase both serotonin and norepinephrine activity.

In effectiveness and speed of action, the second-generation antidepressant drugs are on a par with the tricyclics, yet their sales have skyrocketed (Hirsch & Birnbaum, 2017; Simon, 2017). Because they primarily affect one or at most two neurotransmitters, they do not produce as many undesired effects as MAO inhibitors or tricyclics. At the same time, these relatively newer antidepressants can produce significant side effects of their own. Some people gain weight, feel drowsy, or have a reduced sex drive, for example (Simon & Ciechanowski, 2017).

If antidepressant drugs are effective, why do many people seek out herbal supplements, such as Saint-John's-wort or melatonin, for depression?

As popular as the antidepressants are, it is important to recognize that they do not work for everyone. As you have read, even the most successful of them *fails* to help at least 40 percent of clients with depression. In fact, a number of recent reviews have raised the strong possibility that the failure rate is higher still (Deacon & Spielmans, 2017; Turner et al., 2008). How are clients who do not respond to antidepressant drugs treated currently? Researchers have noted that, all too often, their psychiatrists or family physicians simply prescribe alternative antidepressants or antidepressant mixtures—one after another—without directing the clients to psychotherapy or counseling of some kind (Rush, 2018). Melissa, a depressed woman for whom psychotropic drug treatment has failed to work over many years, reflects on this issue:

> *[S]he spoke, in a wistful manner, of how she wished her treatment could have been different. "I do wonder what might have happened if [at age 16] I could have just talked to someone, and they could have helped me learn about what I could do on my own to be a healthy person. . . . Instead, it was you have this problem with your neurotransmitters, and so here, take this pill Zoloft, and when that didn't work, it was take this pill Prozac, and when that didn't work, it was take this pill Effexor, and then when I started having trouble sleeping, it was take this sleeping pill," she says, her voice sounding more wistful than ever. "I am so tired of the pills."*
>
> *(Whitaker, 2010)*

BRAIN STIMULATION: ELECTROCONVULSIVE THERAPY As you read in Chapter 2, a different form of biological treatment, **brain stimulation,** refers to interventions that directly or indirectly stimulate certain areas of the brain. The oldest—and most controversial—such approach is *electroconvulsive therapy* (*ECT*). It is used primarily on severely depressed people. In recent years, three additional kinds of brain stimulation have been developed for the treatment of depressive disorders—*vagus nerve stimulation, transcranial magnetic stimulation,* and *deep brain stimulation*.

Clinicians and patients alike vary greatly in their opinions of **electroconvulsive therapy (ECT).** Some consider it a safe biological approach with minimal risks; others believe it to be an extreme measure that can cause troublesome memory loss and even neurological damage. Despite the heat of this controversy, ECT is used frequently,

selective serotonin reuptake inhibitors (SSRIs) A group of second-generation antidepressant drugs that increase serotonin activity specifically, without affecting other neurotransmitters.

brain stimulation Biological treatments that directly or indirectly stimulate certain areas of the brain.

electroconvulsive therapy (ECT) A treatment for depression in which electrodes attached to a patient's head send an electrical current through the brain, causing a convulsion.

vagus nerve stimulation A treatment for depression in which an implanted pulse generator sends regular electrical signals to a person's vagus nerve; the nerve then stimulates the brain.

largely because it can be a very effective and fast-acting intervention for unipolar depression.

In an ECT procedure, two electrodes are attached to the patient's head, and 65 to 140 volts of electricity are passed through the brain for half a second or less. This results in a *brain seizure* that lasts from 15 to 70 seconds (Kellner, 2018). After 6 to 12 such treatments, spaced over 2 to 4 weeks, most patients feel less depressed (van Dierman et al., 2018).

The discovery that electric shock can be therapeutic was made by accident. In the 1930s, clinical researchers mistakenly came to believe that brain seizures, or the *convulsions* (severe body spasms) that accompany them, could cure schizophrenia and other psychotic disorders. One early technique was to give patients the drug *metrazol*. Another was to give them large doses of insulin (*insulin coma therapy*). These procedures produced the desired brain seizures, but each was quite dangerous and sometimes even caused death. Finally, an Italian psychiatrist named Ugo Cerletti discovered that he could produce seizures more safely by applying electric currents to a patient's head.

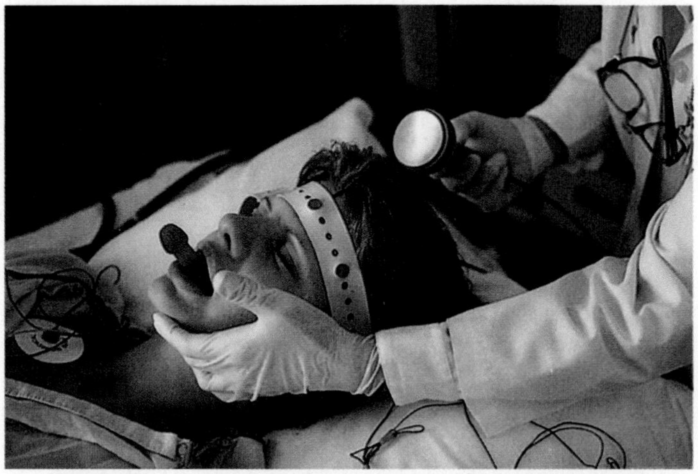

Will McIntyre/Science Source

ECT today The techniques for administering ECT have changed significantly since the treatment's early days. Today, patients are given drugs to help them sleep, muscle relaxants to prevent severe jerks of the body and broken bones, and oxygen to guard against brain damage.

ECT soon became popular and was tried out on a wide range of psychological problems, as new techniques so often are. Its effectiveness with severe depression in particular became apparent (Rothschild, 2017). In the early years of ECT, broken bones and dislocations of the jaw or shoulders sometimes resulted from patients' severe convulsions. Today's practitioners avoid these problems by giving patients strong *muscle relaxants* to minimize convulsions. They also use *anesthetics* (*barbiturates*) to put patients to sleep during the procedure, reducing their terror.

Patients who receive ECT typically have difficulty remembering some events, most often events that took place immediately before and after their treatments (Kellner, 2018; Martin et al., 2015). In most cases, this memory loss clears up within a few months (Bodnar et al., 2016), but some patients are left with gaps in more distant memory, and this form of amnesia can be permanent (Hanna et al., 2009; Wang, 2007).

ECT is clearly effective in treating unipolar depression, although it has been difficult to determine why it works so well (Wang et al., 2018). Studies find that between 50 and 80 percent of ECT patients improve (Kellner, 2018; Perugi et al., 2011). The approach is particularly effective when patients follow up the initial cluster of sessions with continuation, or maintenance, therapy—either ongoing antidepressant medications or periodic ECT sessions (Kellner, 2018). ECT also seems to be quite effective in severe cases of depression that include delusions (Rothschild, 2017).

OTHER FORMS OF BRAIN STIMULATION Over the past decade, three additional kinds of brain stimulation have been developed for the treatment of depressive disorders—*vagus nerve stimulation, transcranial magnetic stimulation,* and *deep brain stimulation*.

The vagus nerve, the longest nerve in the human body, runs from the brain stem through the neck down the chest and on to the abdomen. A number of years ago, a group of depression researchers suspected that they might be able to stimulate the brain by electrically stimulating the vagus nerve. They were hoping to mimic the positive effects of ECT without producing the undesired effects or trauma associated with ECT. Their efforts gave birth to a new treatment for depression—**vagus nerve stimulation.**

As you read in Chapter 2, in this procedure a surgeon implants a small device called a *pulse generator* under the skin of the chest. The surgeon then guides a wire, which extends from the pulse generator, up to the neck and attaches it to the vagus nerve (see **Figure 6-3**). Electrical signals travel from the pulse generator through the wire to the vagus nerve. The stimulated vagus nerve then delivers electrical signals to the brain. The pulse generator is typically programmed to provide 30 seconds of stimulation to the vagus nerve (and, in turn, the brain) every five minutes.

#MedicalBonding

50%	Stroke victims who experience clinical depression
30%	Cancer patients who experience depression
20%	Heart attack victims who become depressed
18%	People with diabetes who are depressed

(Caruso et al., 2018; NCI, 2017; Williams & Nieuwsma, 2016; Udesky, 2014; Kerber et al., 2011)

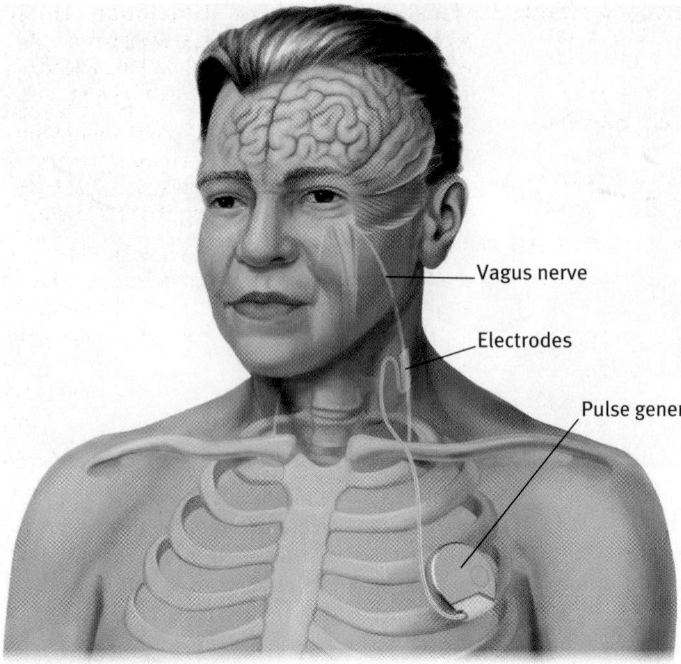

FIGURE 6-3

Vagus Nerve Stimulation

In the procedure called vagus nerve stimulation, an implanted pulse generator sends electrical signals to the vagus nerve, which then delivers electrical signals to the brain. This stimulation of the brain helps reduce depression in many patients.

Research has found that vagus nerve stimulation can bring significant relief (Aaronson et al., 2017). In fact, studies find that a substantial number of severely depressed people who have not responded to any other form of treatment may improve significantly when treated with this procedure (Holtzheimer, 2018; Howland, 2014).

Transcranial magnetic stimulation (TMS) is another technique that is being used to try to stimulate the brain without subjecting depressed patients to the undesired effects or trauma of ECT. In this procedure, the clinician places an electromagnetic coil on or above the patient's head. The coil sends a current into the prefrontal cortex. As you'll remember, some parts of the prefrontal cortex of depressed people are underactive. TMS appears to increase neuron activity in that structure, and, in turn, may improve functioning throughout the rest of the brain's depression-related circuit (Holtzheimer, 2017). A number of studies have found that the procedure reduces depression when it is administered daily for 4 to 6 weeks (Iimori et al., 2019; van den Noort, 2018).

As you have read, around a decade ago, researchers linked depression to high activity in the subgenual cingulate, a key member of the depression-related brain circuit. This finding led neurologist Helen Mayberg and her colleagues (2005) to administer an experimental treatment called **deep brain stimulation (DBS)** to six severely depressed patients who had previously been unresponsive to all other forms of treatment. The Mayberg team drilled two tiny holes into the patient's skull and implanted electrodes in the subgenual cingulate. The electrodes were connected to a battery, or "pacemaker," that was implanted in the patient's chest (for men) or stomach (for women). The pacemaker powered the electrodes, sending a steady stream of low-voltage electricity to the brain structure. Mayberg's expectation was that this repeated stimulation would reduce activity in the structure to a normal level and help "recalibrate" the depression-related brain circuit.

In the initial study of DBS, four of the six severely depressed patients became almost depression-free within a matter of months (Mayberg et al., 2005). Subsequent research with other severely depressed individuals has also yielded promising findings (Holtzheimer, 2018; Riva-Posse et al., 2018). Understandably, this work has produced

Florence Low/Sacramento Bee/MCT via Getty Images

Stimulating the brain In this version of transcranial magnetic stimulation, a woman wears headgear that contains an electromagnetic coil. The coil sends currents into and stimulates her brain.

considerable enthusiasm in the clinical field, but it is important to recognize that research on DBS is still in its early stages.

The Psychological Models of Unipolar Depression

The psychological models that have been most widely applied to unipolar depression are the psychodynamic and cognitive-behavioral models. The psychodynamic model has not been strongly supported by research, but the cognitive-behavioral model has received considerable support and has gained a large following.

The Psychodynamic Model Sigmund Freud (1917) and his student Karl Abraham (1916, 1911) developed the first psychodynamic explanation and treatment for depression. Their emphasis on dependence and loss continues to influence today's psychodynamic clinicians.

PSYCHODYNAMIC EXPLANATIONS Freud and Abraham began by noting the similarity between clinical depression and grief in people who lose loved ones: constant weeping, loss of appetite, difficulty sleeping, loss of pleasure in life, and general withdrawal. According to the theorists, a series of unconscious processes is set in motion when a loved one dies. Unable to accept the loss, mourners at first regress to the *oral stage* of development, the period of total dependency when infants cannot distinguish themselves from their parents. By regressing to this stage, the mourners merge their own identity with that of the person they have lost, and so symbolically regain the lost person. They direct all their feelings for the loved one, including sadness and anger, toward themselves. For most mourners, this reaction, called *introjection,* is temporary. However, for some—particularly those whose various dependency needs were improperly met during infancy and early childhood—grief worsens over time, and they develop clinical depression (Gipps, 2017; Bemporad, 1992).

Of course, many people become depressed without losing a loved one. To explain why, Freud proposed the concept of **symbolic,** or **imagined, loss,** in which a person equates other kinds of events with the loss of a loved one. A college student may, for example, experience failure in a calculus course as the loss of her parents, believing that they love her only when she excels academically.

Although many psychodynamic theorists have parted company with Freud and Abraham's theory of depression, it continues to influence current psychodynamic thinking (Gabbard & DeJean, 2018; Gipps, 2017). For example, *object relations theorists* (the psychodynamic theorists who emphasize relationships) propose that depression results when people's relationships—especially their early relationships—leave them feeling unsafe, insecure, and dependent on others.

The following description by the therapist of a depressed middle-aged woman illustrates the psychodynamic concepts of dependence, loss of a loved one, symbolic loss, and introjection:

Marie Carls . . . had always felt very attached to her mother. . . . She always tried to placate her volcanic [emotions], to please her in every possible way. . . .

After marriage [to Julius], she continued her pattern of submission and compliance. Before her marriage she had difficulty in complying with a volcanic mother, and after her marriage she almost automatically assumed a submissive role. . . .

[W]hen she was thirty years old . . . [Marie] and her husband invited Ignatius, who was single, to come and live with them. Ignatius and [Marie] soon discovered that they had an attraction for each other. They both tried to fight that feeling; but when Julius had to go to another city for a few days, the so-called infatuation became much more than that. There were a few physical contacts. . . . There was an intense spiritual affinity. . . . A few months later everybody had to leave the city. . . . Nothing was done to maintain contact. Two years later . . . Marie heard that Ignatius had married. She felt terribly alone and despondent. . . .

(continued on the next page)

transcranial magnetic stimulation (TMS) A treatment in which an electromagnetic coil, which is placed on or above a patient's head, sends a current into the individual's brain.

deep brain stimulation (DBS) A treatment for depression in which a pacemaker powers electrodes that have been implanted in subgenual cingulate, thus stimulating that brain area.

symbolic loss According to Freudian theory, the loss of a valued object (for example, a loss of employment) that is unconsciously interpreted as the loss of a loved one. Also called *imagined loss.*

#ControversialChange

In past editions of the DSM, people who lose a loved one were excluded from receiving a diagnosis of *major depressive disorder* during the first 2 months of their bereavement. However, according to DSM-5, newly bereaved people can qualify for this diagnosis if their depressive symptoms are severe enough. Critics fear that many people undergoing a normal grief reaction may now receive an incorrect diagnosis of major depressive disorder.

Spencer Platt/Getty Images

Early loss The young daughter of a female police officer killed during the September 11, 2001, terrorist attack on the World Trade Center in New York City, stands onstage holding her father's hand while the names of attack victims are read during ceremonies at Ground Zero marking the fifth anniversary of the event. Research has found that people who lose their parents as children have an increased likelihood of experiencing depression as adults.

> *Her suffering had become more acute as she [came to believe] that old age was approaching and she had lost all her chances. Ignatius remained as the memory of lost opportunities. . . . Her life of compliance and obedience had not permitted her to reach her goal. . . . When she became aware of these ideas, she felt even more depressed. . . . She felt that everything she had built in her life was false or based on a false premise.*
>
> *(Arieti & Bemporad, 1978, pp. 275–284)*

Studies have offered general support for the psychodynamic idea that major losses, especially ones suffered early in life, may set the stage for later depression (Cheong et al., 2017; Krishnan, 2017). When, for example, a diagnostic survey was administered to thousands of adults in one study, the individuals whose fathers had died during their childhood scored higher on depression (Jacobs & Bovasso, 2009). Related research supports the psychodynamic idea that people whose childhood needs were poorly met are particularly likely to become depressed after experiencing loss (Conradi et al., 2018; Paterniti et al., 2017). At the same time, research does not indicate that loss or problematic early relationships are always at the core of depression. In fact, it is estimated that less than 10 percent of all people who have major losses in life actually become depressed (Hammen, 2016; Sandler et al., 2008). Moreover, research into the loss-depression link has yielded inconsistent findings. Though some studies find evidence of a relationship between childhood loss and later depression, others do not.

WHAT ARE THE PSYCHODYNAMIC TREATMENTS FOR UNIPOLAR DEPRESSION? Because they believe that unipolar depression results from unconscious grief over real or imagined losses, compounded by excessive dependence on other people, psychodynamic therapists seek to help clients bring these underlying issues to consciousness and work them through (Ribeiro, Ribeiro, & von Doellinger, 2018; Busch et al., 2004). Using the arsenal of basic psychodynamic procedures, they encourage the depressed client to associate freely during therapy; suggest interpretations of the client's associations, dreams, and displays of resistance and transference; and help the person review past events and feelings. Free association, for example, helped one man recall the early experiences of loss that, according to his therapist, had set the stage for his depression:

> *Among his earliest memories, possibly the earliest of all, was the recollection of being wheeled in his baby cart under the elevated train structure and left there alone. Another memory that recurred vividly during the analysis was of an operation around the age of five. He was anesthetized and his mother left him with the doctor. He recalled how he had kicked and screamed, raging at her for leaving him.*
>
> *(Lorand, 1968, pp. 325–326)*

Despite case reports of such successes as this, researchers have found that long-term psychodynamic therapy is only occasionally helpful in cases of unipolar depression (Prochaska & Norcross, 2018). Two features of the approach may help limit its effectiveness. First, depressed clients may be too passive and feel too weary to join fully in the subtle therapy discussions. And second, they may become discouraged and end treatment too early when this long-term approach is unable to provide the quick relief that they desperately seek. Short-term psychodynamic therapies have performed better than the longer-term approaches, especially when they are combined with psychotropic medications (Goodyer et al., 2017; Fonagy, 2015).

The Cognitive-Behavioral Model As with other kinds of psychological disorders, cognitive-behavioral theories contend that unipolar depression results from a combination of problematic behaviors and dysfunctional ways of thinking. These theories fall into three groups: explanations that focus mostly on the behavioral realm, those that give primary attention to negative thinking, and ones that feature a complex interplay between cognitive and behavioral factors.

THE BEHAVIORAL DIMENSION Clinical researcher Peter Lewinsohn was one of the first theorists to link depression to significant changes in the number of rewards and punishments people receive in their lives (Lewinsohn et al., 1990, 1984). He suggested that the positive rewards in life dwindle for some people, leading them to perform fewer and fewer constructive behaviors. The rewards of campus life, for example, disappear when a young woman graduates from college and takes a job; and an aging baseball player loses the rewards of high salary and adulation when his skills deteriorate. Although many people manage to fill their lives with other forms of gratification, some become particularly disheartened. The positive features of their lives decrease even more, and the decline in rewards leads them to perform still fewer constructive behaviors. In this manner, they spiral toward depression.

In a number of studies, researchers have found that the number of rewards people receive in life is indeed related to the presence or absence of depression. Not only do depressed participants typically report fewer positive rewards than nondepressed participants, but when their rewards begin to increase, their mood improves as well (Chan et al., 2017; Nyström et al., 2017). Similarly, other investigations have found a strong relationship between positive life events and feelings of life satisfaction and happiness (He et al., 2019; Sotgiu, 2016).

Lewinsohn and other theorists have further proposed that *social* rewards are particularly important in the downward spiral of depression (Werner-Seidler et al., 2017; Martell et al., 2013). This claim has been supported by research showing that depressed persons receive fewer social rewards than nondepressed persons and that as their mood improves, their social rewards increase (see ***MindTech*** on the next page). Although depressed people are sometimes the victims of social circumstances, it may also be that their dark mood and flat behaviors help produce a decline in social rewards (Hodgetts et al., 2017; Hammen, 2016).

Patrick Smith/Getty Images

When the applause stops The reduction in rewards brought about by retirement may place athletes and other high achievers at risk for depression unless they find new sources of gratification. Standing in front of photos of his great moments as an NFL quarterback, Terry Bradshaw waves to a crowd of 71,000 fans at the 50th Super Bowl. Bradshaw, now a successful football analyst on FOX NFL Sunday, has struggled with depression throughout much of his adult life, but he went through particularly intense episodes in the years following his 1984 retirement from the game.

NEGATIVE THINKING Aaron Beck believes that negative thinking lies at the heart of depression (Beck & Weishaar, 2019; Beck, 2016, 2002, 1967). According to Beck, *maladaptive attitudes*, a *cognitive triad*, *errors in thinking*, and *automatic thoughts* combine to produce unipolar depression.

Beck believes that some people develop *maladaptive attitudes* as children, such as "My general worth is tied to every task I perform" or "If I fail, others will feel repelled by me." The attitudes result from their own experiences and the judgments of the people around them. Many failures are inevitable in a full, active life, so such attitudes are inaccurate and set the stage for all kinds of negative thoughts and reactions. Beck suggests that later in these people's lives, upsetting situations may trigger an extended round of negative thinking. That thinking typically takes three forms, which he calls the **cognitive triad:** the individuals repeatedly interpret (1) their *experiences*, (2) *themselves*, and (3) their *futures* in negative ways that lead them to feel depressed. The cognitive triad is at work in the thinking of this depressed person:

> *I can't bear it. I can't stand the humiliating fact that I'm the only woman in the world who can't take care of her family, take her place as a real wife and mother, and be respected in her community. When I speak to my young son Billy, I know I can't let him down, but I feel so ill-equipped to take care of him; that's what frightens me. I don't know what to do or where to turn; the whole thing is too overwhelming. . . . I must be a laughing stock. It's more than I can do to go out and meet people and have the fact pointed out to me so clearly.*
>
> *(Fieve, 1975)*

cognitive triad The three forms of negative thinking that Aaron Beck theorizes lead people to feel depressed. The triad consists of a negative view of one's experiences, oneself, and the future.

MINDTECH

Texting: A Relationship Buster?

Texting has now become the leading way that most people communicate with others (Coyne, Padilla-Walker, & Holmgren, 2018; Burke, 2016; Pew Research Center, 2015). The average 18- to 24-year-old, for example, sends and receives a total of 128 texts each day. In fact, surveys suggest that people often fail to fully attend to their current activities in order to juggle their text conversations. Some clinicians worry that excessive texting may damage our relationships—relationships with the people we are texting and relationships with those we are ignoring while texting.

Based on her studies, MIT professor Sherry Turkle (2017, 2015, 2013) has concluded that communicating primarily via text does indeed affect relationships negatively. Many of her participants reported, "I'd rather text than talk." Turkle concludes from her research that people often use texting as a crutch to avoid direct communication and possible confrontations. Her participants said that texting saves valuable time over face-to-face conversations, but, Turkle concludes, "People who feel they are too busy to have conversations in person are not making the important emotional connections they otherwise would."

In related work, researcher Karla Klein Murdock (2013) interviewed 83 college freshmen about their daily texting habits, along with their levels of social and personal stress, sleep patterns, and happiness. She found that hastily written texts (which is to say, most texts) often lend themselves to misunderstandings between senders and receivers—misunderstandings that can quickly spin out of control. Murdock also noted that many participants in her study felt the need to constantly keep up with ongoing text conversations, interrupting their in-person conversations—thus inviting damage to those relationships as well. Small wonder that the participants who averaged the most daily texts were more likely than other participants to report more stress, unhappiness, anxiety, and sleeping problems. Murdock believes that in many such cases, the negative effects of texting on the participants' personal relationships are leading to broader feelings of stress and unhappiness.

Luis Acosta/Getty Images

Can you think of ways in which texting might sometimes be helpful to relationships and communications?

None of this suggests that texting per se is a detriment to social or personal happiness. Rather, it seems to be the exclusive and excessive use of it that is the problem. Although half of all young adults say that text conversations are just as meaningful as other avenues of communication (Burke, 2016), it just may be that truly important discussions are better served by in-person, or at least phone, conversations.

According to Beck, depressed people also make *errors in their thinking*. In one common error of logic, they draw arbitrary inferences—negative conclusions based on little evidence. A man walking through the park, for example, passes a woman who is looking at nearby flowers and concludes, "She's avoiding looking at me." Similarly, depressed people often minimize the significance of positive experiences or magnify that of negative ones. A college student receives an A on a difficult English exam, for example, but concludes that the grade reflects the professor's generosity rather than her own ability (minimization). Later in the week the same student must miss an English class and is convinced that she will be unable to keep up the rest of the semester (magnification).

Finally, depressed people have *automatic thoughts*, a steady train of unpleasant thoughts that keep suggesting to them that they are inadequate and that their situation is hopeless. Beck labels these thoughts "automatic" because they seem to just happen, as if by reflex. In the course of only a few hours, depressed people may be visited by hundreds of such thoughts: "I'm worthless. . . . I'll never amount to anything . . . I let everyone down. . . . Everyone hates me. . . . My responsibilities are overwhelming. . . . I've failed as a parent . . . I'm stupid. . . . Everything is difficult for me. . . . Things will never change."

Many studies have produced evidence in support of Beck's explanation (Krishnan, 2017). Several of them confirm that depressed people hold maladaptive attitudes and that the more of these maladaptive attitudes they hold, the more depressed they tend to be (Brouwer et al., 2019; Beck, 2016). A number of studies have found the cognitive triad at work in depressed people (Oltean et al., 2018). And still others have supported Beck's claims about errors of logic (Özdel et al., 2014).

Finally, research has supported Beck's notion that automatic thoughts are tied to depression (Riley, Lee, & Safren, 2017; Wang et al., 2016). In several classic studies, for example, nondepressed participants who were tricked into reading negative automatic-thought-like statements about themselves became increasingly depressed (Bates et al., 1999; Strickland et al., 1975). In a related line of research, it has been found that people who generally make *ruminative responses* during their depressed moods—that is, repeatedly dwell mentally on their mood without acting to change it—feel dejection longer and are more likely to develop clinical depression later in life than people who avoid such ruminations (Liu et al., 2017; Watkins & Nolen-Hoeksema, 2014).

LEARNED HELPLESSNESS: A COGNITIVE-BEHAVIORAL INTERPLAY According to psychologist Martin Seligman (1975), feelings of helplessness are at the center of depression. Since the mid-1960s Seligman has been developing the **learned helplessness** theory of depression (Maier & Seligman, 2016). It holds that people become depressed when they think (1) that they no longer have control over the reinforcements (the rewards and punishments) in their lives, and (2) that they themselves are responsible for this helpless state. Feelings of helplessness fill this account of a young woman's depression:

> *Mary was 25 years old and had just begun her senior year in college. . . . Asked to recount how her life had been going recently, Mary began to weep. Sobbing, she said that for the last year or so she felt she was losing control of her life and that recent stresses (starting school again, friction with her boyfriend) had left her feeling worthless and frightened. Because of a gradual deterioration in her vision, she was now forced to wear glasses all day. "The glasses make me look terrible," she said, and "I don't look people in the eye much any more." Also, to her dismay, Mary had gained 20 pounds in the past year. She viewed herself as overweight and unattractive. At times she was convinced that with enough money to buy contact lenses and enough time to exercise she could cast off her depression; at other times she believed nothing would help. . . . Mary saw her life deteriorating in other spheres, as well. She felt overwhelmed by schoolwork and, for the first time in her life, was on academic probation. . . . In addition to her dissatisfaction with her appearance and her fears about her academic future, Mary complained of a lack of friends. Her social network consisted solely of her boyfriend, with whom she was living. Although there were times she experienced this relationship as almost unbearably frustrating, she felt helpless to change it and was pessimistic about its permanence.*
>
> *(Spitzer et al., 1983, pp. 122–123)*

Seligman's theory first began to take shape when he was working with laboratory dogs. In one procedure, he strapped dogs into an apparatus called a hammock, in which they received shocks periodically no matter what they did. The next day each dog was placed in a *shuttle box*, a box divided in half by a barrier over which the animal could jump to reach the other side (see **Figure 6-4**). Seligman applied shocks to the dogs in the box, expecting that they, like other dogs in this situation, would soon learn to escape by jumping over the barrier. However, most of these dogs failed to learn anything in the shuttle box. After a flurry of activity, they simply "lay down and quietly whined" and accepted the shock.

#

#TheirWords

"No one can make you feel inferior without your consent."

Eleanor Roosevelt

learned helplessness The perception, based on past experiences, that one has no control over the reinforcements in one's life.

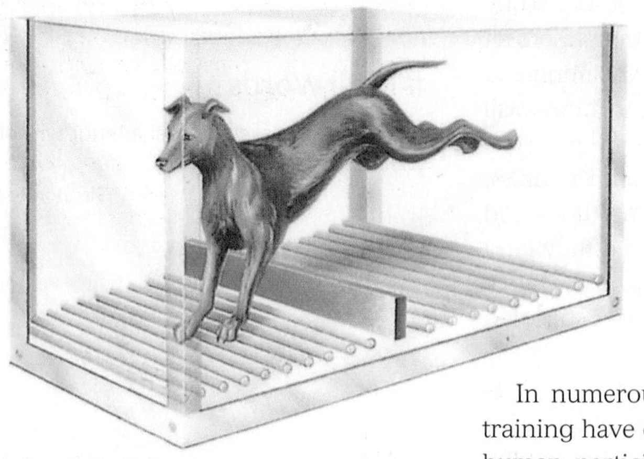

FIGURE 6-4

Jumping to Safety

Experimental animals learn to escape or avoid shocks that are administered on one side of a shuttle box by jumping to the other (safe) side.

Seligman decided that while receiving inescapable shocks in the hammock the day before, the dogs had learned that they had no control over unpleasant events (shocks) in their lives. That is, they had learned that they were helpless to do anything to change negative situations. Thus, when later they were placed in a new situation (the shuttle box) where they could in fact control their fate, they continued to believe that they were generally helpless. Seligman noted that the effects of learned helplessness greatly resemble the symptoms of human depression, and he proposed that people in fact become depressed after developing a general belief that they have no control over reinforcements in their lives.

In numerous human and animal studies, participants who undergo helplessness training have displayed reactions similar to depressive symptoms. When, for example, human participants are exposed to uncontrollable negative events, they later score higher than other individuals on a depressive mood scale. Similarly, helplessness-trained animal subjects lose interest in sexual and social activities—a common symptom of human depression (Smith et al., 2017; Zhou et al., 2017).

The learned helplessness explanation of depression has been revised somewhat over the past several decades. According to one modified version of the theory, the *attribution-helplessness theory,* when people view events as beyond their control, they ask themselves why this is so (Rubenstein et al., 2016; Abramson et al., 2002, 1989, 1978). If they attribute their present lack of control to some *internal* cause that is both *global* and *stable* ("I am inadequate at everything and I always will be"), they may well feel helpless to prevent future negative outcomes and they may experience depression. If they make other kinds of attributions, they are unlikely to have this reaction.

Consider a college student whose girlfriend breaks up with him. If he attributes this loss of control to an internal cause that is both global and stable—"It's my fault [internal], I ruin everything I touch [global], and I always will [stable]"—he then has reason to expect similar losses of control in the future and may generally experience a sense of helplessness. According to the learned helplessness view, he is a prime candidate for depression. If the student had instead attributed the breakup to causes that were more *specific* ("The way I've behaved the past couple of weeks blew this relationship"), *unstable* ("I don't know what got into me—I don't usually act like that"), or *external* ("She never did know what she wanted"), he might not expect to lose control again and would probably not experience helplessness and depression. Hundreds of studies have supported the relationship between styles of attribution, helplessness, and depression (O'Sullivan et al., 2018; Rotenberg et al., 2012).

Some theorists have refined the helplessness model yet again in recent years. They suggest that attributions are likely to cause depression only when they further produce a sense of *hopelessness* in a person (Liu et al., 2015; Abramson et al., 2002, 1989). By taking this factor into consideration, clinicians are often able to predict depression with still greater precision.

Although the learned helplessness theory of unipolar depression has been very influential, it too has imperfections. For example, much of the learned helplessness research relies on animal subjects. It is impossible to know whether the animals' symptoms do in fact reflect the clinical depression found in humans (Kim et al., 2017). In addition, the attributional feature of the theory raises difficult questions. What about the dogs and rats who learn helplessness? Can animals make attributions, even implicitly?

COGNITIVE-BEHAVIORAL THERAPY Cognitive-behavioral therapists combine behavioral and cognitive techniques to help clients suffering from depression. On the behavioral side, they seek to get the clients moving again—to engage in and enjoy more activities. On the cognitive side, they guide the clients to think in more adaptive, less negative ways. A variety of approaches have been developed to help bring about these changes. Two of the leading ones are *behavioral activation* and *Beck's cognitive therapy.*

#

#DarkestColor

In Western society, *black* is often the color of choice in describing depression. British Prime Minister Winston Churchill called his recurrent episodes a "black dog always waiting to bare its teeth." American novelist Ernest Hemingway referred to his bouts as "black-assed" days. And the Rolling Stones sing about depressive thinking: "I see a red door and I want to paint it black."

In **behavioral activation,** therapists work systematically to increase the number of constructive and rewarding activities and events in a client's life. The approach builds on the work of Peter Lewinsohn, the theorist who, as you'll recall, ties mood to the rewards one experiences in life. There are three key components to the approach. The therapists (1) reintroduce depressed clients to pleasurable events and activities, (2) consistently reward nondepressive behaviors and withhold rewards for depressive behaviors, and (3) help clients improve their social skills (Martin & Oliver, 2018; Moshier & Otto, 2017).

First, the therapist selects activities that the client considers pleasurable, such as going shopping or taking photos, and encourages the person to set up a weekly schedule for engaging in them. Studies have shown that adding positive activities to a person's life can indeed lead to a better mood. Second, while reintroducing pleasurable events into a client's life, the therapist makes sure that the person's various behaviors are reinforced correctly. Behavioral activation theorists argue that when people become depressed, their negative behaviors—crying, ruminating, complaining, or self-depreciation—keep others at a distance, reducing chances for rewarding experiences and interactions (Hammen, 2016). To change this pattern, therapists guide clients to monitor their negative behaviors and to try new, more positive ones (Farchione, Boswell, & Willner, 2017; Martell et al., 2010). Dozens of smartphone apps are now available to help clients accurately record the negative and positive activities they perform in life and the mood changes that result, making behavioral activation a more precise approach than it once was (Dahne et al., 2017; Huguet et al., 2016). Finally, behavior activation therapists train clients in effective social skills (Farmer & Chapman, 2015). In group therapy programs, for example, members may work together to improve eye contact, facial expression, posture, and other behaviors that send social messages.

Can you think of other uses, advantages, and disadvantages that might result from the growing use of mood-tracking apps?

Behavioral activation techniques seem to be of only limited help when they are the sole feature of treatment, particularly if the severity of depression is more than modest (Chan et al., 2017; Dimidjian et al., 2014). But when they are combined with cognitive techniques, they are, as you'll see next, often quite helpful (Moshier & Otto, 2017).

To help depressed clients overcome their negative thinking, Aaron Beck has developed a treatment approach that he calls **cognitive therapy.** He uses this label because

behavioral activation A therapy for depression in which the therapist works systematically to increase the number of constructive and pleasurable activities and events in a client's life.

cognitive therapy A therapy developed by Aaron Beck that helps people identify and change the maladaptive assumptions and ways of thinking that help cause their psychological disorders.

China Photos/Getty Images

Reintroducing pleasure Following the principles of *behavioral activation,* depressed patients at the Zhongshan Mental Hospital in China are encouraged to weed a garden. Behavioral activation therapists systematically guide clients to increase the number of pleasurable activities in their lives, particularly activities that brought them joy (in this case, gardening) prior to their disorders.

Ward Sutton/The New Yorker Collection/The Cartoon Bank

"Let's try focusing on your posts that do receive comments."

the approach focuses largely on guiding clients to recognize and change negative cognitive processes that he believes underlie depression (Beck & Weishaar, 2019; Beck, 2016). However, as you will note, the approach also includes several behavioral techniques such as those we have just examined. The approach follows four phases and usually requires fewer than 20 sessions.

PHASE 1: Increasing activities and elevating mood Using behavioral techniques to set the stage for the cognitive dimensions of treatment, therapists first encourage clients to become more active and confident. Clients spend time during each session preparing a detailed schedule of hourly activities for the coming week. As they become more active from week to week, their mood is expected to improve.

PHASE 2: Challenging automatic thoughts Once people are more active and feeling some emotional relief, therapists begin to educate them about their negative automatic thoughts. The individuals are instructed to recognize and record automatic thoughts as they occur and to bring their lists to each session. Here again, clients may use smartphone apps to accurately identify and document such thoughts as they arise in their daily lives (Huguet et al., 2016). The therapist and client then test the reality behind the thoughts, often concluding that they are groundless.

PHASE 3: Identifying negative thinking and biases As people begin to recognize the flaws in their automatic thoughts, the therapists show them how illogical thinking processes are contributing to these thoughts. The therapists also guide clients to recognize that almost all their interpretations of events have a negative bias and to change that style of interpretation.

PHASE 4: Changing primary attitudes Therapists help clients change the maladaptive attitudes that set the stage for their depression in the first place. As part of the process, therapists often encourage clients to test their attitudes, as in the following therapy discussion:

Therapist:	*On what do you base this belief that you can't be happy without a man?*
Patient:	*I was really depressed for a year and a half when I didn't have a man.*
Therapist:	*Is there another reason why you were depressed?*
Patient:	*As we discussed, I was looking at everything in a distorted way. But I still don't know if I could be happy if no one was interested in me.*
Therapist:	*I don't know either. Is there a way we could find out?*
Patient:	*Well, as an experiment, I could not go out on dates for a while and see how I feel.*
Therapist:	*I think that's a good idea. Although it has its flaws, the experimental method is still the best way currently available to discover the facts. You're fortunate in being able to run this type of experiment. Now, for the first time in your adult life you aren't attached to a man. If you find you can be happy without a man, this will greatly strengthen you and also make your future relationships all the better.*

(Beck et al., 1979, pp. 253–254)

Over the past several decades, numerous studies have shown that cognitive-behavioral approaches help with unipolar depression. Depressed adults who receive these therapies improve much more than those who receive placebos or no treatment at all (Forand et al., 2018; Young et al., 2014). Around 50 to 60 percent show significant improvement in or elimination of their symptoms.

It is worth noting that a growing number of today's cognitive-behavioral therapists do not agree with the proposition that individuals must fully discard their negative cognitions in order to overcome depression. These therapists, the new-wave cognitive-behavioral therapists about whom you read in Chapters 2 and 4, including those who practice *acceptance and commitment therapy* (ACT), use mindfulness training and other cognitive-behavioral techniques to help depressed clients recognize and accept their negative cognitions simply as streams of thinking that flow through their minds, rather than as valuable guides for behavior and decisions. As clients increasingly accept their negative thoughts for what they are, they may better work around those thoughts as they navigate their way through life. Research suggests that approaches of this kind are particularly useful as ongoing procedures that help prevent recurrences of depression once individuals recover from an episode (Segal, 2017; Twohig & Levin, 2017).

#TheirWords

"Don't cry because it's over, smile because it happened."

Dr. Seuss

The Sociocultural Model of Unipolar Depression

Sociocultural theorists propose that unipolar depression is strongly influenced by the social context that surrounds people. Their belief is supported by the finding, discussed earlier, that depression is often triggered by outside stressors (Krishnan, 2017). Once again, there are two kinds of sociocultural views—the *family-social perspective* and the *multicultural perspective.*

The Family-Social Perspective Earlier you read that some cognitive-behavioral theorists believe that a decline in social rewards is particularly important in the development of depression. This view is also consistent with the family-social perspective.

The connection between declining social rewards and depression is a two-way street (Hammen, 2016). On the one hand, researchers have found that depressed people often display weak social skills and communicate poorly. They seek repeated reassurances from others, and they typically speak more slowly and quietly than nondepressed people, pause longer between words, and take longer to respond to others. Such social deficits make other people uncomfortable and may cause them to avoid the depressed individuals. As a result, the social contacts and rewards of depressed people decrease, and, as they participate in fewer and fewer social interactions, their social skills deteriorate still further.

Why might problems in the social arena—for example, social loss, social ties, and social rewards—be particularly tied to depression?

Consistent with these findings, depression has been tied repeatedly to the unavailability of social support such as that found in a happy marriage (Cao et al., 2017; Krishnan, 2017). Research indicates that people in troubled marriages are 25 times more likely to have a depressive disorder than people in untroubled marriages (Keitner, 2017).

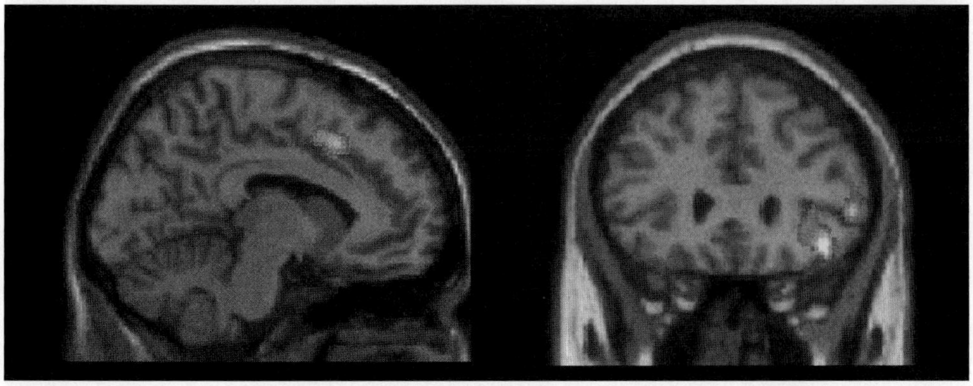

Matthew D. Lieberman

Social exclusion, depression, and the brain In a widely used research design called *cyberball,* a participant lies in an fMRI scanner and is told (falsely) that he or she is playing a game of cyber catch with two players in other rooms. As the other players increasingly exclude the participant from the three-way catch, the fMRI records what parts of his or her brain are being affected. As shown in these brain scans, subregions of the anterior cingulate cortex (left) and the prefrontal cortex (right), key structures in the depression-related brain circuit, become active during this lab-induced social exclusion, just as they do in cases of clinical depression.

interpersonal psychotherapy (IPT) A treatment for unipolar depression that is based on the belief that clarifying and changing one's interpersonal problems helps lead to recovery.

couple therapy A therapy format in which the therapist works with two people who share a long-term relationship.

In some cases, the spouse's depression may contribute to marital discord or divorce, but often the interpersonal conflicts and low social support found in troubled relationships seem to lead to depression (Williams & Nieuwsma, 2018).

Researchers have also found that people whose lives are characterized by weak social supports, isolation, and lack of intimacy are particularly likely to become depressed and to remain depressed longer than other people (Liang et al., 2019; Levula et al., 2018; Werner-Seidler et al., 2017). For example, some highly publicized studies conducted in England several decades ago showed that women who had three or more young children, lacked a close confidante, and had no outside employment were more likely than other women to become depressed after going through stressful events (Brown, 2002; Brown & Harris, 1978).

Family-Social Treatments Therapists who use family and social approaches to treat depression help clients change how they deal with the close relationships in their lives. The most effective family-social approaches are *interpersonal psychotherapy* and *couple therapy*.

INTERPERSONAL PSYCHOTHERAPY Developed by clinical researchers Gerald Klerman and Myrna Weissman, **interpersonal psychotherapy (IPT)** holds that any of four interpersonal problem areas may lead to depression and must be addressed: interpersonal loss, interpersonal role dispute, interpersonal role transition, and interpersonal deficits (Swartz, 2018, 2017; Pu et al., 2017). Over the course of around 20 sessions, IPT therapists address these areas.

First, depressed people may, as psychodynamic theorists suggest, be having a grief reaction over an important *interpersonal loss,* the loss of a loved one. In such cases, IPT therapists encourage clients to explore their relationship with the lost person and express any feelings of anger they may discover. Eventually clients develop new ways of remembering the lost person and also look for new relationships.

Second, depressed people may find themselves in the midst of an *interpersonal role dispute*. Role disputes occur when two people have different expectations of their relationship and of the role each should play. IPT therapists help clients examine whatever role disputes they may be involved in and then develop ways of resolving them.

Depressed people may also be going through an *interpersonal role transition,* brought about by major life changes such as divorce or the birth of a child. They may

AP Photo/Ariana Cubillos

Is laughter the best medicine? A man laughs during a session of laughter therapy in a public plaza in South America. He is one of many who attended this open session of laughter therapy, a relatively new group treatment being offered around the world, based on the belief that laughing at least 15 minutes each day drives away depression and other ills.

feel overwhelmed by the role changes that accompany the life change. In such cases, IPT therapists help them develop the social supports and skills the new roles require.

Finally, some depressed people display *interpersonal deficits,* such as extreme shyness or social awkwardness, that prevent them from having intimate relationships. IPT therapists may help such clients recognize their deficits and teach them social skills and assertiveness in order to improve their social effectiveness. In the following discussion, the therapist encourages a depressed man to recognize the effect his behavior has on others:

Client: (After a long pause with eyes downcast, a sad facial expression, and slumped posture) *People always make fun of me. I guess I'm just the type of guy who really was meant to be a loner, damn it.* (Deep sigh)

Therapist: *Could you do that again for me?*

Client: *What?*

Therapist: *The sigh, only a bit deeper.*

Client: *Why?* (Pause) *Okay, but I don't see what . . . okay.* (Client sighs again and smiles)

Therapist: *Well, that time you smiled, but mostly when you sigh and look so sad I get the feeling that I better leave you alone in your misery, that I should walk on eggshells and not get too chummy or I might hurt you even more.*

Client: (A bit of anger in his voice) *Well, excuse me! I was only trying to tell you how I felt.*

Therapist: *I know you felt miserable, but I also got the message that you wanted to keep me at a distance, that I had no way to reach you.*

Client: (Slowly) *I feel like a loner, I feel that even you don't care about me—making fun of me.*

Therapist: *I wonder if other folks need to pass this test, too?*

(Beier & Young, 1984, p. 270)

Studies suggest that IPT and related interpersonal treatments for depression have a success rate similar to that of cognitive-behavioral therapy (Zhou et al., 2017). That is, symptoms almost totally disappear in 50 to 60 percent of clients who receive treatment. Not surprisingly, IPT is considered especially useful for depressed people who are struggling with social conflicts or undergoing changes in their careers or social roles (Ravitz, Watson, & Grigoriadis, 2013).

COUPLE THERAPY As you have read, depression can result from marital discord, and recovery from depression is often slower for people who do not receive support from their spouse (Keitner, 2017). In fact, as many as half of all depressed clients may be in a dysfunctional relationship. Thus it is not surprising that many cases of depression have been treated by **couple therapy,** the approach in which a therapist works with two people who share a long-term relationship.

Therapists who offer *integrative behavioral couples therapy* combine cognitive-behavioral and sociocultural techniques to teach couples specific communication and problem-solving skills, guide them to recognize that their problematic interactions often reflect basic differences between them, and steer them to become more accepting and supportive of each other (see Chapter 2). When the depressed person's spousal relationship is filled with conflict, this approach and similar ones may be as effective as—or even more effective than—individual cognitive-behavioral therapy, interpersonal psychotherapy, or drug therapy in helping to reduce depression (Keitner, 2017; Lebow et al., 2012).

The Multicultural Perspective Two kinds of relationships have captured the interest of multicultural theorists: (1) links between *gender and depression,* and (2) ties between *cultural and ethnic background and depression.* In the case of gender, a strong relationship has been found, but a clear explanation for that relationship has yet to

#SeriousOversight

Family physicians, internists, and pediatricians fail to detect depression in at least 50 percent of their depressed patients (Lyness, 2017; Mitchell et al., 2011).

#WaningConfidants

Intimate social contact has been declining over the past 30 years. When research participants were asked in 1985 how many confidants they turned to for discussion of important matters, most answered 3. Today, the most common response to the same question is 2 or less (GSS, 2016; Bryner, 2011; McPherson et al., 2006).

emerge. The clinical field is still sorting out whether and what ties exist between cultural factors and depression.

GENDER AND DEPRESSION As you have read, there is a strong link between gender and depression. Women in places as far apart as France, Sweden, Lebanon, New Zealand, and the United States are at least twice as likely as men to receive a diagnosis of unipolar depression. Why the huge difference between the sexes? A variety of theories have been offered and studied (Assari, 2017; Hammen, 2016; Nolen-Hoeksema, 2012, 2002, 1990).

The *artifact theory* holds that women and men are equally prone to depression but that clinicians often fail to detect depression in men. Perhaps depressed women display more emotional symptoms, such as sadness and crying, which are easily diagnosed, while depressed men mask their depression behind traditionally "masculine" symptoms such as anger. Although this is a popular explanation, research indicates that women are actually no more willing or able than men to identify their depressive symptoms and to seek treatment.

The *hormone explanation* holds that hormone changes trigger depression in many women, particularly during puberty, pregnancy, and menopause. Research suggests, however, that the social and life events that accompany these developmental milestones are also profound and may account for experiences of depression as well as, or better than, hormone shifts. Hormone explanations have also been criticized as sexist, since they imply that a woman's normal biology is flawed.

The *life stress theory* suggests that women in our society are subject to more stress than men. On average they face more poverty, more menial jobs, less adequate housing, and more discrimination than men—all factors that have been linked to depression. And in many homes, women bear a disproportionate share of responsibility for child care and housework.

The *body dissatisfaction explanation* states that females in Western society are taught, almost from birth, but particularly during adolescence, to seek a low body weight and slender body shape—goals that are unreasonable, unhealthy, and often unattainable. As you'll read in Chapter 9, research finds that, as adolescence unfolds, girls do become more and more dissatisfied with their weight and body and, on average, display an increased rate of depression. However, it is not clear that eating and weight concerns actually cause depression; they may instead be the result of depression.

The *lack-of-control theory,* which draws on the learned helplessness research, proposes that women may be more prone to depression because they feel less control than men over their lives. It has been found that victimization of any kind, from discrimination to burglary to rape, often produces a sense of helplessness and increases the symptoms of depression—and women in our society are, on average, more likely than men to be victims across various domains (BJS, 2017, 2016).

A final explanation for the gender differences found in depression is the *rumination theory.* As you read earlier, rumination is related to depression. Research reveals that women are more likely than men to ruminate when their mood darkens, perhaps making them more vulnerable to the onset of clinical depression.

Each of these explanations for the gender difference in unipolar depression offers food for thought. Each has gathered just enough supporting evidence to make it interesting and just enough evidence to the contrary to raise questions about its usefulness. Thus, at present, the gender difference in depression remains one of the most talked-about but least understood phenomena in the clinical field.

CULTURAL BACKGROUND AND DEPRESSION Depression is a worldwide phenomenon, and certain symptoms of this disorder seem to be constant across all countries.

A dance metaphor Many theorists believe that the reason for the large gender difference in depression rates is that, on average, women face more stressors, discrimination, unattainable body ideals, and victimization than men. A popular description for this gender disadvantage is that women must "dance backwards and in high heels"—a term that has its origins in the dance team of Ginger Rogers and Fred Astaire, iconic partners in 10 popular movies in the 1930s. Although they were both remarkably talented, Astaire's acclaim and professional success ultimately exceeded that of Rogers, who had, after all, done everything Astaire did, but "backwards and in high heels."

A landmark study of four countries—Canada, Switzerland, Iran, and Japan—found that the great majority of depressed people in these very different countries reported symptoms of sadness, joylessness, tension, lack of energy, loss of interest, loss of ability to concentrate, ideas of insufficiency, and thoughts of suicide (WHO, 2017; Matsumoto & Juang, 2016). Beyond such core symptoms, however, research suggests that the precise picture of depression varies from country to country (Shafi & Shafi, 2014; Kok et al., 2012). Depressed people in non-Western countries—China and Nigeria, for example—are more likely to be troubled by physical symptoms such as fatigue, weakness, sleep disturbances, and weight loss. Depression in those countries is less often marked by cognitive symptoms such as self-blame, low self-esteem, and guilt.

David South/Alamy

Non-Western depression Depressed people in non-Western countries tend to have fewer cognitive symptoms, such as self-blame, and more physical symptoms, such as fatigue, weakness, and sleep disturbances.

Within the United States, researchers have found few differences in the symptoms of depression among members of different ethnic or racial groups. Nor have they found significant differences in the *overall* rates of depression between such minority groups. On the other hand, research reveals that there are often striking differences between ethnic/racial groups in the *recurrence* of depression. Hispanic Americans and African Americans are 50 percent more likely than non-Hispanic white Americans to have recurrent episodes of depression (Krishnan, 2017). Why this difference? Around 54 percent of depressed non-Hispanic white Americans receive treatment for their disorders (medication and/or psychotherapy), compared with 34 percent of depressed Hispanic Americans and 40 percent of depressed African Americans (González et al., 2010). It may be that minority groups in the United States are more vulnerable to repeated experiences of depression partly because many of their members have more limited treatment opportunities when they are depressed.

Research has also revealed that depression is distributed unevenly within some minority groups. This is not totally surprising, given that each minority group itself consists of people of varied backgrounds and cultural values. For example, depression is more common among Hispanic and African Americans born in the United States than among Hispanic and African American immigrants (González et al., 2010; Miranda et al., 2005). Moreover, within the Hispanic American population, Puerto Ricans have a higher rate of depression than do Mexican Americans or Cuban Americans.

Multicultural Treatments In Chapter 2, you read that *culture-sensitive therapies* are designed to address the unique issues faced by members of cultural minority groups (Comas-Díaz, 2019; Chu et al., 2016). For such approaches, therapists typically have special cultural training and a heightened awareness of their clients' cultural values and the culture-related stressors, prejudices, and stereotypes that their clients face. They make an effort to help clients develop a comfortable (for them) bicultural balance and to recognize the impact of their own culture and the dominant culture on their views of themselves and on their behaviors.

Do you think culture-sensitive therapies might be more useful for some kinds of disorders than for others? Why or why not?

In the treatment of unipolar depression, culture-sensitive approaches increasingly are being combined with traditional forms of psychotherapy to help minority clients overcome their disorders (Aguilera et al., 2017, 2010; Chu et al., 2016). A number of today's therapists, for example, offer cognitive-behavioral therapy for depressed minority clients while also focusing on the clients' economic pressures, minority identity, and related cultural issues. A range of studies indicate that Hispanic American, African American, American Indian, and Asian American clients are more likely to overcome their depressive disorders when a culture-sensitive focus is added to the form of psychotherapy that they are otherwise receiving (Aguilera et al., 2017, 2010; Chowdhary et al., 2014).

Integrating the Models: The Developmental Psychopathology Perspective

#FathersToo

At least 8% of new fathers may also experience some degree of postpartum depression (Cameron et al., 2017). Research indicates that, as in cases of a mother's postpartum depression, this syndrome can affect a child's psychological development (Gentile & Fusco, 2017; Koh et al., 2014).

As with their explanations of other psychological disorders, proponents of the developmental psychopathology perspective contend that unipolar depression is caused by a combination of the factors we have been examining throughout this chapter. Moreover, they believe that the factors unfold and intersect in a developmental sequence, with early negative factors generally setting the stage for later negative factors and ultimately for depression, but with later positive factors sometimes able to offset the lingering impact of early negative factors. Developmental psychopathology explanations of unipolar depression have received considerable research support (Meng et al., 2018; Lieberman & Chu, 2016).

Consistent with biological findings, developmental psychopathologists believe that the road to unipolar depression often begins with a genetically inherited predisposition—a predisposition that is characterized by low activity of key neurotransmitters (serotonin and norepinephrine) in key brain structures, an overly reactive HPA stress pathway (see pages 178–179), and a dysfunctional depression-related brain circuit (Newman et al., 2017; Bagot et al., 2016). Researchers from this perspective have found that such biological predispositions will most likely result in later depression if the individual is *also* subjected to significant losses or other traumas early in life and/or inadequate parenting, such as parenting that is disrupted, depressive in style, inconsistent, or rejecting (Dittrich et al., 2018; Wang et al., 2018). Still other studies indicate that this combination of biological and childhood factors often leads to a low self-concept, a temperament marked by guilt, a negative style of thinking, general feelings of helplessness, and interpersonal dependence—variables that are themselves each linked to depression (Reinfjell et al., 2016; Lau et al., 2014). According to developmental psychopathologists, individuals who travel through this unfavorable developmental sequence are particularly likely to become depressed when they experience stress in adult life, especially interpersonal stress (Hammen, 2016; Morris et al., 2014).

However, this precise sequence of intersecting factors is not the only avenue to later depression. Developmental psychopathology studies indicate, for example, that individuals who experience severe childhood traumas or inadequate parenting often develop depression when they later encounter life stress, even if they have no genetic predisposition for the disorder (Nishikawa et al., 2018; Mullins et al., 2016). Such findings are apparently related to the two-way relationship that exists between many of these factors. Research has found, for example, that exposure to severe traumas at key points early in life may negatively alter a child's HPA stress pathway and depression-related brain circuit, even if the pathway and circuit had previously been functioning properly (Palagini et al., 2019; Hammen, 2016).

At the same time, the developmental psychopathology perspective is not all gloom and doom. The presence of negative developmental factors does not inevitably produce a march toward depression. Studies have found, for example, that individuals who experience *moderate* and *manageable* adversities throughout their childhood often develop resilience and become better able to withstand the depressive effects of life stress in adulthood (Meng et al., 2018; Oldehinkel et al., 2014). One study even found that participants who had repeatedly experienced moderate adversities throughout their lives were less likely to become depressed in the face of significant life stress than were participants who had faced little or no adversity in their lives (Seery, Homan, & Silver, 2010).

"Katia, I know that with the right combination of therapy and medication I could have a committed relationship with you."

9... SUMMING UP

UNIPOLAR DEPRESSION People with unipolar depression suffer from depression only. The symptoms of depression span five areas of functioning: emotional, motivational, behavioral, cognitive, and physical. Women are at least twice as likely as men to experience severe unipolar depression.

According to the biological view, low activity of two neurotransmitters, norepinephrine and serotonin, are linked to depression. Hormonal factors, the result of an HPA stress pathway that is overly reactive to stress, may also be at work. Research has also tied depression to abnormalities in a circuit of brain structures, including the prefrontal cortex, hippocampus, amygdala, and subgenual cingulate. Most biological treatments for unipolar depression consist of antidepressant drugs, but several brain stimulation techniques are also used.

According to the psychodynamic view, certain people who experience real or imagined losses may regress to an earlier stage of development, fuse with the person they have lost, and eventually become depressed. Psychodynamic therapists try to help depressed persons recognize and work through their losses and excessive dependence on others.

The cognitive-behavioral view features explanations of depression that are primarily behavioral, primarily cognitive, or a combination of behavioral and cognitive principles. On the behavioral side, the model says that when people experience a large reduction in their positive rewards in life, they become more and more likely to become depressed. On the cognitive side, Beck's theory of negative thinking holds that maladaptive attitudes, the cognitive triad, errors in thinking, and automatic thoughts help produce unipolar depression. Also, according to Seligman's learned helplessness theory, people become depressed when they believe that they have lost control over the reinforcements in their lives and when they attribute this loss to causes that are internal, global, and stable. Cognitive-behavioral therapists reintroduce clients to pleasurable events, reinforce nondepressive behaviors, teach interpersonal skills, and further help the clients change their dysfunctional cognitions.

Sociocultural theories propose that unipolar depression is influenced by social and cultural factors. Family-social theorists point, for example, to a low level of social support. Correspondingly, interpersonal psychotherapy and couple therapy are often helpful in cases of depression. Multicultural theories have noted that the character and prevalence of depression may vary by gender and culture, an issue that culture-sensitive therapies for depression seek to address.

The developmental psychopathology perspective contends that unipolar depression is caused by a combination of the factors cited by the various models and that these factors unfold and intersect in a developmental sequence.

Roberto Panucci/Getty Images

Born to run "The Boss," Bruce Springsteen, performs at a sold-out concert while his image is projected on a mega-screen behind him. In his 2016 memoir, *Born to Run,* Springsteen detailed his long history of depression, describing one episode as "a freight train bearing down . . . running quickly out of track."

Bipolar Disorders

People with a bipolar disorder experience both the lows of depression and the highs of mania. Many describe their lives as an emotional roller coaster, as they shift back and forth between extreme moods. A number of sufferers become suicidal. Approximately 10 to 15 percent of them eventually end their own lives, usually out of a sense of hopelessness (Suppes, 2018). Their roller coaster ride also has a dramatic impact on relatives and friends.

What Are the Symptoms of Mania?

Unlike people sunk in the gloom of depression, those in a state of mania typically experience dramatic and inappropriate rises in mood. The symptoms of mania span the same areas of functioning—*emotional, motivational, behavioral, cognitive,* and *physical*—as those of depression, but mania affects those areas in an opposite way.

#

#FrenziedMasterpiece

George Frideric Handel wrote his *Messiah* in less than a month during a manic episode (Roesch, 1991).

"Sometimes Mommy cries" Lawyer and social worker Loran Kundra reads and laughs with her daughters at their home in Pennsylvania. Kundra, who has bipolar disorder, is co-founder of a program called *Child and Family Connections*, which helps parents with psychological disorders effectively discuss their disorders with their children. During a depressive episode, Kundra found herself explaining to her daughter, "Sometimes Mommy cries and gets upset just the way that you cry and get upset"—an exchange that spurred her to reach out to other persons with similar parenting issues.

A person in the throes of mania has active, powerful emotions in search of an outlet. The mood of euphoric joy and well-being is out of all proportion to the actual happenings in the person's life. Not every person with mania is a picture of happiness, however. Some instead become very irritable and angry, especially when others get in the way of their exaggerated ambitions.

In the motivational realm, people with mania seem to want constant excitement, involvement, and companionship. They enthusiastically seek out new friends and old, new interests and old, and have little awareness that their social style is overwhelming, domineering, and excessive.

The behavior of people with mania is usually very active. They move quickly, as though there were not enough time to do everything they want to do. They may talk rapidly and loudly, their conversations filled with jokes and efforts to be clever or, conversely, with complaints and verbal outbursts. Flamboyance is not uncommon: dressing in flashy clothes, giving large sums of money to strangers, or even getting involved in dangerous activities.

In the cognitive realm, people with mania usually show poor judgment and planning, as if they feel too good or move too fast to consider possible pitfalls. Filled with optimism, they rarely listen when others try to slow them down, interrupt their buying sprees, or prevent them from investing money unwisely. They may also hold an inflated opinion of themselves, and sometimes their self-esteem approaches grandiosity. During severe episodes of mania, some have trouble remaining coherent or in touch with reality.

Finally, in the physical realm, people with mania feel remarkably energetic. They typically get little sleep yet feel and act wide awake (Suppes, 2018). Even if they miss a night or two of sleep, their energy level may remain high.

#

#WrongCall

Around 70 percent of people with a bipolar disorder are initially misdiagnosed by a physician or psychologist (Statistic Brain, 2018).

Diagnosing Bipolar Disorders

People are considered to be in a full *manic episode* when for at least one week they display an abnormally high or irritable mood, increased activity or energy, and at least three other symptoms of mania (see **Table 6-4**). The episode may even include psychotic features such as delusions or hallucinations. When the symptoms of mania are less severe (causing little impairment), the person is said to be having a *hypomanic episode*.

DSM-5 distinguishes two kinds of bipolar disorders—bipolar I and bipolar II. People with **bipolar I disorder** have full manic and major depressive episodes. Most of them experience an *alternation* of the episodes; for example, weeks of mania followed by a period of wellness, followed in turn by an episode of depression. Some, however, have *mixed* features, in which they display both manic and depressive symptoms within the same episode—for example, having racing thoughts amidst feelings of extreme sadness. In **bipolar II disorder,** hypomanic—that is, mildly manic—episodes alternate with major depressive episodes over the course of time. Some people with this pattern accomplish huge amounts of work during their mild manic periods (see ***PsychWatch*** on the next page).

bipolar I disorder A type of bipolar disorder marked by full manic and major depressive episodes.

bipolar II disorder A type of bipolar disorder marked by mildly manic (hypomanic) episodes and major depressive episodes.

Without treatment, the mood episodes tend to recur for people with either type of bipolar disorder. If a person has four or more episodes within a one-year period, his or her disorder is considered to be *rapid cycling.* A woman describes her rapid cycling in the following excerpt, taken from a journal article she wrote anonymously several years ago.

> *My mood may swing from one part of the day to another. I may wake up low at 10 am, but be high and excitable by 3 pm. I may not sleep for more than 2 hours one night, being full of creative energy, but by midday be so fatigued it is an effort to breathe.*
>
> *If my elevated states last more than a few days, my spending can become uncontrollable . . . I will sometimes drive faster than usual, need less sleep and can concentrate well, making quick and accurate decisions. At these times I can also be sociable, talkative and fun, focused at times, distracted at others. If this state of elevation continues I often find that feelings of violence and irritability towards those I love will start to creep in. . . .*
>
> *My thoughts speed up. . . . I frequently want to be able to achieve several tasks at the same moment. . . . Physically my energy levels can seem limitless. The body moves smoothly, there is little or no fatigue. I can go mountain biking all day when I feel like this and if my mood stays elevated not a muscle is sore or stiff the next day. But it doesn't last, my elevated phases are short . . . [T]he shift into severe depression or a mixed mood state occurs sometimes within minutes or hours, often within days and will last weeks often without a period of normality. . . .*
>
> *Initially my thoughts become disjointed and start slithering all over the place. . . . I start to believe that others are commenting adversely on my appearance or behaviour. . . . My sleep will be poor and interrupted by bad dreams. . . . The world appears bleak . . . I become repelled by the proximity of people . . . I will be overwhelmed by the slightest tasks, even imagined tasks. . . . Physically there is immense fatigue: my muscles scream with pain. . . Food becomes totally uninteresting. . . .*
>
> *I start to feel trapped, that the only escape is death. . . . I become passionate about one subject only at these times of deep and intense fear, despair and rage: suicide. . . . I have made close attempts on my life . . . over the last few years. . . .*
>
> *Then inexplicably, my mood will shift again. The fatigue drops from my limbs like shedding a dead weight, my thinking returns to normal, the light takes on an intense clarity, flowers smell sweet and my mouth curves to smile at my children, my husband and I are laughing again. Sometimes it's for only a day but I am myself again, the person that I was a frightening memory. I have survived another bout of this dreaded disorder. . . .*
>
> (*Anonymous, 2006*)

Surveys from around the world indicate that between 1 and 2.6 percent of all adults are suffering from a bipolar disorder at any given time (NIMH, 2017; Kessler et al., 2012). As many as 4 percent experience one of the bipolar disorders at some time in their life. The bipolar disorders are equally common in women and men, but they are more common among people with low incomes than those with higher incomes (Bressert, 2018; Sareen et al., 2011). Onset usually occurs between the ages of 15 and 44 years (Stovall, 2018). In most untreated cases, the manic and depressive episodes eventually subside, only to recur at a later time.

TABLE: 6-4

Dx Checklist

Manic Episode
1. For 1 week or more, person displays a continually abnormal, inflated, unrestrained, or irritable mood as well as continually heightened energy or activity, for most of every day.
2. Person also experiences at least three of the following symptoms: • Grandiosity or overblown self-esteem • Reduced sleep need • Increased talkativeness, or drive to continue talking • Rapidly shifting ideas or the sense that one's thoughts are moving very fast • Attention pulled in many directions • Heightened activity or agitated movements • Excessive pursuit of risky and potentially problematic activities.
3. Significant distress or impairment.
Bipolar I Disorder
1. Occurrence of a manic episode.
2. Hypomanic or major depressive episodes may precede or follow the manic episode.
Bipolar II Disorder
1. Presence or history of major depressive episode(s).
2. Presence or history of hypomanic episode(s).
3. No history of a manic episode.

Information from: APA, 2013.

PSYCHWATCH

Abnormality and Creativity: A Delicate Balance

The ancient Greeks believed that various forms of "divine madness" inspired creative acts, from poetry to performance (Ludwig, 1995). Even today many people expect "creative geniuses" to be psychologically disturbed. A popular image of the artist includes a glass of liquor, a cigarette, and a tormented expression. Classic examples include writer William Faulkner, who suffered from alcoholism and received electroconvulsive therapy for depression; poet Sylvia Plath, who was depressed for most of her life and eventually died by suicide at age 31; and ballet dancer Vaslav Nijinsky, who suffered from schizophrenia and spent many years in institutions. In fact, a number of studies indicate that artists and writers are somewhat more likely than others to suffer from certain mental disorders, particularly bipolar disorders (Vellante et al., 2018; Collingwood, 2016).

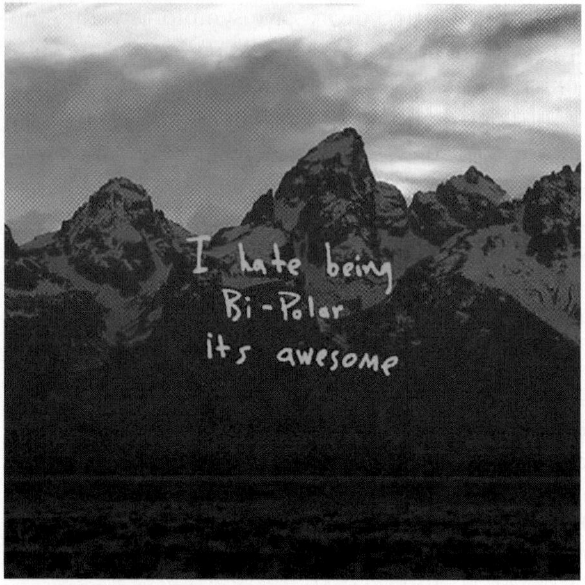

Kanye's "superpower" Based on his unusual behaviors, proclamations, and emotional displays, fans and the media have long speculated about the mental state of Kanye West, one of the twenty-first century's most acclaimed musicians. In "*Ye*," his 2018 album, West acknowledged having psychological difficulties and hinted at a diagnosis of bipolar disorder—on the album cover (shown here), in the album's lyrics, and during promotional interviews. Indeed, he suggested that his bipolar functioning enhances his creativity and serves as a kind of "superpower" in his endeavors.

Why might creative people be prone to such psychological disorders? Some may be predisposed to such disorders long before they begin their artistic careers (Vellante et al., 2018; Simonton, 2010). Indeed, creative people often have a family history of psychological problems (Kyaga et al., 2013, 2011). A number also have experienced intense psychological trauma during childhood. English writer Virginia Woolf, for example, endured sexual abuse as a child.

A second explanation for the link between creativity and psychological disorders is that the creative professions offer a welcome climate for those with psychological disturbances. In the worlds of poetry, painting, and acting, for example, emotional expression, unusual thinking, and/or personal turmoil are valued as sources of inspiration and success (Collingwood, 2016; Galvez et al., 2011).

Much remains to be learned about the relationship between emotional turmoil and creativity, but work in this area has already clarified two important points. First, psychological disturbance is hardly a requirement for creativity. Most "creative geniuses" are, in fact, psychologically stable and happy throughout their entire lives (Rothenberg, 2015; Kaufman, 2013). Second, mild psychological disturbances relate to creative achievement much more strongly than severe disturbances do (Collingwood, 2016; Galvez et al., 2011). For example, nineteenth-century composer Robert Schumann produced 27 works during one hypomanic year but next to nothing during years when he was severely depressed and suicidal (Jamison, 1995).

Some artists worry that their creativity would disappear if their psychological suffering were to stop. In fact, however, research suggests that successful treatment for severe psychological disorders more often than not improves the creative process (Rothenberg, 2015; Ludwig, 1995). Romantic notions aside, severe mental dysfunction has little redeeming value, in the arts or anywhere else.

Some people have numerous periods of hypomanic symptoms and *mild* depressive symptoms, a pattern that is called **cyclothymic disorder** in DSM-5. The symptoms of this milder form of bipolar disorder continue for two or more years, interrupted occasionally by normal moods that may last for only days or weeks. This disorder, like bipolar I and bipolar II disorders, usually begins in adolescence or early adulthood and is equally common among women and men. At least 0.4 percent of the population develops cyclothymic disorder. In some cases, the milder symptoms eventually blossom into a bipolar I or II disorder (Zeschel et al., 2015).

What Causes Bipolar Disorders?

Throughout the first half of the twentieth century, the search for the cause of bipolar disorders made little progress. More recently, biological research has produced some promising clues. The biological insights have come from research into *neurotransmitter activity, ion activity, brain structure,* and *genetic factors.*

cyclothymic disorder A disorder marked by numerous periods of hypomanic symptoms and mild depressive symptoms.

Neurotransmitters Could *overactivity* of norepinephrine be related to mania? This was the expectation of clinicians back in the 1960s after investigators first found a relationship between low norepinephrine activity and unipolar depression (Schildkraut, 1965). And indeed, some studies did find the norepinephrine activity of people with mania to be higher than that of depressed or control participants (Post et al., 1980, 1978).

Because serotonin activity often parallels norepinephrine activity in unipolar depression, theorists at first expected that mania would also be related to high serotonin activity, but no such relationship has been found. Instead, research suggests that mania, like depression, may be linked to *low* serotonin activity (Nikolaus, Müller, & Hautzel, 2017; Nugent et al., 2013). Perhaps low activity of serotonin opens the door to a mood disorder and *permits* the activity of norepinephrine (or perhaps other neurotransmitters) to define the particular form the disorder will take. That is, low serotonin activity accompanied by low norepinephrine activity may lead to depression; low serotonin activity accompanied by high norepinephrine activity may lead to mania.

Don Emmert/AFP/Getty Images

Speaking out A few months after this New Year's Eve performance in Times Square on December 31, 2017, singer and songwriter Mariah Carey revealed that she is being treated for bipolar disorder, a diagnosis she first received almost two decades ago (Cagle, 2018). Carey says that after years of living "in constant fear someone would expose me . . . , I knew it was time to finally share my story." The superstar's public acknowledgment and positive outlook have received enormous praise from mental health advocacy groups.

Ion Activity While neurotransmitters play a significant role in the communication *between* neurons, *ions* seem to play a critical role in relaying messages *within* a neuron. That is, ions help transmit messages down the neuron's axon to the nerve endings. Positively charged *sodium ions* (Na^+) sit on both sides of a neuron's cell membrane. When the neuron is at *rest*, more sodium ions sit outside the membrane. When the neuron receives an incoming message at its receptor sites, pores in the cell membrane open, allowing the sodium ions to flow to the inside of the membrane, thus increasing the positive charge inside the neuron. This starts a wave of electrical activity that travels down the length of the neuron and results in its "firing."

If messages are to be relayed effectively down the axon, the ions must be able to travel easily between the outside and the inside of the neural membrane. Some studies suggest that, among bipolar individuals, irregularities in the transport of these ions may cause neurons to fire too easily (resulting in mania) or to stubbornly resist firing (resulting in depression) (Gottschalk et al., 2017).

Brain Structure Brain imaging and postmortem studies have identified a number of abnormal brain structures in people with bipolar disorders (Ivleva et al., 2017; Eker et al., 2014). For example, the hippocampus, basal ganglia, and cerebellum of these people tend to be smaller than those of other people; they have lower amounts of gray matter in the brain; and their raphe nuclei, striatum, amygdala, and prefrontal cortex have some structural abnormalities (Dusi et al., 2019; Sun et al., 2018; Janicak, 2017). It is not clear what role such abnormalities play in bipolar disorders. Some researchers believe that they collectively reflect dysfunction throughout a bipolar-related brain circuit (Gong et al., 2019). It may also be that they are related to the brain's depression-related circuit that you read about earlier (see page 180).

Genetic Factors Many theorists believe that people inherit a biological predisposition to develop bipolar disorders (Stovall, 2018). Family pedigree studies support this idea. Identical twins of those with a bipolar disorder have a 40 to 70 percent likelihood of developing the same disorder, and fraternal twins, siblings, and other close relatives of such persons have a 5 to 10 percent likelihood, compared with the 1 to 2.6 percent prevalence rate in the general population.

Researchers have also used techniques from *molecular biology* to more directly examine possible genetic factors in large families. Their work has linked bipolar disorders to genes on chromosomes 1, 4, 6, 10, 11, 12, 13, 15, 18, 20, 21, and 22 (Charney et al., 2017; Bigdeli et al., 2013). Such wide-ranging findings suggest that a number of genetic abnormalities probably combine to help bring about bipolar disorders.

#

#HigherRisk

"The risk of developing bipolar disorder is 6 times higher for children of older men (over 45 years when their children were born) than children of young men (20–24 years). Why? One theory is that, as men age, they produce increased genetic mutations during the manufacture of sperm cells (Stovall, 2018; Chudal et al., 2014).

Alexander Joe/Getty Images

While the world observed In this 2013 photo, then-President Barack Obama delivers a speech next to a sign language interpreter (right) at a memorial service for the late Nelson Mandela, former president of South Africa. However, the interpreter's signs were gibberish and unintelligible, alarming and confusing people around the world. The interpreter later explained that he had been hearing voices and seeing angels during the speech, symptoms caused by his struggle with bipolar disorder and/or schizophrenia.

What Are the Treatments for Bipolar Disorders?

Until the latter part of the twentieth century, people with bipolar disorders were destined to spend their lives on an emotional roller coaster. Psychotherapists reported almost no success, and early antidepressant drugs were of limited help. In fact, the drugs sometimes triggered a manic episode (Stovall, 2018).

Lithium and Other Mood Stabilizers This gloomy picture changed dramatically in 1970 when the FDA approved the use of **lithium,** a silvery-white element found in various simple mineral salts throughout the natural world, as a treatment for bipolar disorder. Additional **mood stabilizing,** or **antibipolar, drugs** have since been developed, including *carbamazepine* (Tegretol), *valproate* (Depakote), and certain antipsychotic drugs, and several of them are now used more widely than lithium, either because they produce fewer undesired effects or because they are even more effective than lithium.

Nevertheless, it was lithium that first brought hope to those suffering from bipolar disorder. In her widely read memoir, *An Unquiet Mind,* psychiatric researcher Kay Redfield Jamison describes how lithium, combined with psychotherapy, enabled her to overcome bipolar disorder:

> *I took [lithium] faithfully and found that life was a much stabler and more predictable place than I had ever reckoned. My moods were still intense and my temperament rather quick to the boil, but I could make plans with far more certainty and the periods of absolute blackness were fewer and less extreme. . . .*
>
> *At this point in my existence, I cannot imagine leading a normal life without both taking lithium and having had the benefits of psychotherapy. Lithium prevents my seductive but disastrous highs, diminishes my depressions, clears out the wool and webbing from my disordered thinking, slows me down, gentles me out, keeps me from ruining my career and relationships, keeps me out of a hospital, alive, and makes psychotherapy possible. [At the same time], ineffably, psychotherapy heals. It makes some sense of the confusion, reins in the terrifying thoughts and feelings, returns some control and hope and possibility of learning from it all. . . . No pill can help me deal with the problem of not wanting to take pills; likewise, no amount of psychotherapy alone can prevent my manias and depressions. I need both. . . .*
>
> (Jamison, 1995)

lithium A metallic element that occurs in nature as a mineral salt and is an effective treatment for bipolar disorders.

mood stabilizing drugs Psychotropic drugs that help stabilize the moods of people suffering from bipolar disorder. Also known as *antibipolar drugs*.

All manner of research has attested to the effectiveness of lithium and other mood stabilizers, such as, for example, in treating *manic* episodes (Stovall, 2018). More than 60 percent of patients with mania improve on these medications. In addition, most such patients have fewer new episodes as long as they continue taking the medications (Malhi et al., 2013). One study found that the risk of relapse is 28 times higher if patients stop taking a mood stabilizer (Suppes et al., 1991). These findings suggest that the mood stabilizers are also prophylactic drugs, ones that actually help prevent symptoms from developing. Thus, today's clinicians usually continue patients on some level of a mood stabilizing drug even after their manic episodes subside (Post, 2017).

In the limited body of research that has been done on this subject, the mood stabilizers also seem to help those with bipolar disorder overcome their *depressive* episodes, though to a lesser degree than they help with their manic episodes (Stovall, 2018; Malhi et al., 2013). Given the drugs' less powerful impact on depressive episodes, many clinicians use a combination of mood stabilizers and antidepressant drugs to treat bipolar depression, although research suggests that antidepressants may trigger manic episodes in some patients (Stovall, 2018).

Rick Rowell/ABC via Getty Images

Powerful plot device In the popular soap opera *General Hospital,* actor Maurice Bernard plays Sonny Corinthos (left), a mob kingpin who is mercurial, impulsive, and unpredictable, to the delight of viewers. One of the show's key features is the character's bipolar disorder, which greatly affects his behaviors, decisions, and relationships. Interestingly, Bernard himself has bipolar disorder, a diagnosis he first received at the age of 22.

Researchers do not fully understand how mood stabilizing drugs reduce the symptoms of bipolar disorder (Janicak, 2017). One possibility is that the drugs change synaptic activity in neurons, but in a way different from that of antidepressant drugs. The firing of a neuron actually consists of several phases that ensue at lightning speed. When the neurotransmitter binds to a receptor on the receiving neuron, a series of changes occur *within* the receiving neuron to set the stage for firing. The substances in the neuron that carry out those changes are often called *second messengers* because they relay the original message from the receptor site to the firing mechanism of the neuron. (The neurotransmitter itself is considered the *first messenger.*) Whereas antidepressant drugs affect a neuron's initial reception of neurotransmitters, mood stabilizers appear to affect a neuron's second messengers.

In a similar vein, it has been found that lithium and other mood stabilizing drugs also increase the production of a protein called *brain-derived neurotrophic factor* (*BDNF*) and other proteins within certain neurons whose job it is to prevent cell death. The drugs may increase the health and functioning of those cells and thus reduce bipolar symptoms (Malhi et al., 2013; Gray et al., 2003).

Finally, it may be that lithium and other mood stabilizers reduce bipolar symptoms by improving the functioning of or communications between key structures in the brain (Altinay, Karne, & Anand, 2018). In support of this possibility, it has been found that lithium actually increases the size of the hippocampus and the amount of gray matter in bipolar patients (Sun et al., 2018; Janicak, 2017). Recall that bipolar individuals have a smaller hippocampus and lower amount of gray matter than other people, among other abnormalities.

Adjunctive Psychotherapy As Jamison stated in her memoir, psychotherapy alone is rarely helpful for persons with bipolar disorders. At the same time, clinicians have learned that mood stabilizing drugs alone are not always sufficient either. Thirty percent or more of patients with these disorders may not respond to lithium or a related drug, may not receive the proper dose, or may relapse while taking it. In addition, individuals stop taking mood stabilizers on their own because they are bothered by the drugs' unwanted effects, feel too well to recognize the need for the drugs, miss the euphoria felt during manic episodes, or worry about becoming less productive when they take the drugs (Vieta & Colom, 2017).

In view of these problems, many clinicians now use individual, group, or family therapy as an *adjunct* to mood stabilizing drugs (Chu et al., 2018; Post, 2017). Most often, therapists use these formats to emphasize the importance of continuing to take

#

#IrresistableWriting

Hypergraphia is a compulsive need to write. People with this rare problem write constantly, not only filling up notebooks or computer screens but also feverishly finding unusual writing surfaces, including their own skin. The problem has been linked to bipolar disorders, temporal lobe epilepsy, and schizophrenia. Famous sufferers include prolific author Fyodor Dostoyevski and painter Vincent van Gogh.

medications; to improve social skills and relationships that may be affected by bipolar episodes; to educate patients and families about bipolar disorders; to help patients solve the family, school, and occupational problems caused by their disorder; and to help prevent patients from attempting suicide. Studies have found that such adjunctive therapy at least doubles the likelihood that bipolar individuals will continue to take their medications properly, and it helps reduce hospitalizations, improve social functioning, and increase patients' ability to obtain and hold a job (Vieta & Colom, 2017; Culver & Pratchett, 2010).

#TheirWords

"You cannot outrun insanity, anymore than you can outrun your own shadow."

—Alyssa Reyans, *Letters from a Bipolar Mother*

...SUMMING UP

BIPOLAR DISORDERS In bipolar disorders, episodes of mania alternate or intermix with episodes of depression. These disorders are much less common than unipolar depression. They may take the form of bipolar I, bipolar II, or cyclothymic disorder.

Mania may be related to improper neurotransmitter activity, improper transport of ions, or abnormalities in key brain structures. Genetic studies suggest that people may inherit a predisposition to these biological abnormalities. Lithium and other mood stabilizing drugs have proved to be effective in the treatment of bipolar disorders. Patients tend to fare better when mood stabilizing and/or other psychotropic drugs are combined with adjunctive psychotherapy.

Making Sense of All That Is Known

During the past 50 years, researchers have made significant gains in the understanding and treatment of depressive and bipolar disorders. These are now among the most treatable of all psychological disorders. The choice of treatment for bipolar disorders is narrow and simple: drug therapy, perhaps accompanied by psychotherapy, is the single most successful approach. The picture for unipolar depression is more varied and complex, although no less promising. Cognitive-behavioral, interpersonal, couple, drug, and brain stimulation treatments can each be helpful.

Several factors have been tied closely to unipolar depression, including biological abnormalities, a reduction in positive reinforcements, negative ways of thinking, a perception of helplessness, and life stress and other sociocultural influences. Indeed, more contributing factors have been associated with unipolar depression than with most other psychological disorders. Developmental psychopathology theorists and researchers have done an admirable and promising job of trying to put these various factors together; it is still not entirely clear, however, how all of these factors relate to unipolar depression.

As with unipolar depression, clinicians and researchers have learned much about bipolar disorders during the past 50 years. But bipolar disorders appear to be best explained by a focus on *one* kind of variable—biological factors. The evidence suggests that biological abnormalities, perhaps inherited and perhaps triggered by life stress, cause bipolar disorders. Whatever roles other factors may play, the primary one appears to lie in this realm.

There is no question that investigations into depressive and bipolar disorders have been fruitful and enlightening. And it is more than reasonable to expect that important research findings will continue to unfold in the years ahead. Now that clinical researchers have gathered so many important pieces of the puzzle, they must put the pieces together into a still more meaningful picture that will suggest even better ways to predict, prevent, and treat these disorders.

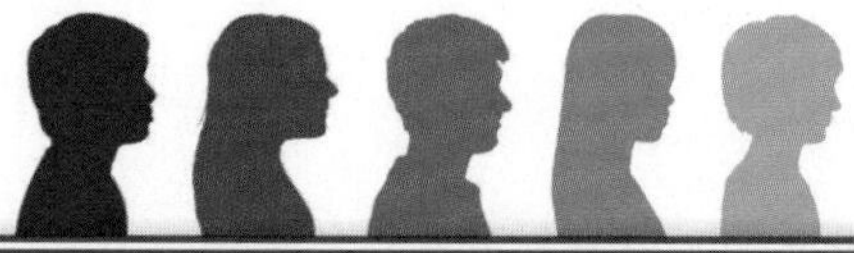

CLINICAL CHOICES

Now that you've read about disorders of mood, try the interactive case study for this chapter. See if you are able to identify John's symptoms and suggest a diagnosis based on his symptoms. What kind of treatment would be most effective for John? Go to **LaunchPad** to access ***Clinical Choices***.

night, he knew he was just fooling himself with such notions. He kept sinking, withdrew from others, and felt increasingly hopeless.

Six months after losing his job, Dave began to consider ending his life. The pain was too great, the humiliation unending. He hated the present and dreaded the future. Throughout February he went back and forth. On some days he was sure he wanted to die. On other days, an enjoyable evening or uplifting conversation might change his mind temporarily. On a Monday late in February he heard about a job possibility, and the anticipation of the next day's interview seemed to lift his spirits. But Tuesday's interview did not go well. He knew there'd be no job offer. He went home, took a recently purchased gun from his locked desk drawer, and shot himself.

Demaine *never truly recovered from his mother's death. He was only seven years old and unprepared for such a loss. His father sent him to live with his grandparents for a time, to a new school with new kids and a new way of life. In Demaine's mind, all these changes were for the worse. He missed the joy and laughter of the past. He missed his home, his father, and his friends. Most of all he missed his mother.*

He did not really understand her death. His father said that she was in heaven now, at peace, happy. Demaine's unhappiness and loneliness continued day after day and he began to put things together in his own way. He believed he would be happy again if he could join his mother. He felt she was waiting for him, waiting for him to come to her. The thoughts seemed so right to him; they brought him comfort and hope. One evening, shortly after saying good night to his grandparents, Demaine climbed out of bed, went up the stairs to the roof of their apartment house, and jumped to his death. In his mind he was joining his mother in heaven.

Tya *and Noah had met on a speed date. On a lark, Tya and a friend had registered at the speed date event, figuring, "What's the worst thing that can happen?" On the night of the big event, Tya talked to dozens of guys, none of whom appealed to her—except for Noah! He was quirky. He was witty. And he seemed as turned off by the whole speed date thing as she was. His was the only name that she put on her list. As it turned out, he also put her name down on his list, and a week later each of them received an email with contact information about the other. A flurry of email exchanges followed, and before long, they were going together. She marveled at her luck. She had beaten the odds. She had had a successful speed date experience.*

It was Tya's first serious relationship; it became her whole life. Thus she was truly shocked and devastated when, on the one-year anniversary of their speed date, Noah told her that he no longer loved her and was leaving her for someone else.

As the weeks went by, Tya was filled with two competing feelings—depression and anger. Several times she texted or called Noah, begged him to reconsider, and pleaded for a chance to win him back. At the same time, she hated him for putting her through such misery.

Tya's friends became more and more worried about her. At first they sympathized with her pain, assuming it would soon lift. But as time went on, her depression and anger worsened, and Tya began to act strangely. Always a bit of a drinker, she started to drink heavily and to mix her drinks with various kinds of drugs.

One night Tya went into her bathroom, reached for a bottle of sleeping pills, and swallowed a handful of them. She wanted to make her pain go away, and she wanted Noah to know just how much pain he had caused her. She continued swallowing pill after pill, crying and swearing as she gulped them down. When she began to feel drowsy, she decided to call her close friend Dedra. She was not sure why she was calling, perhaps to say good-bye, to explain her actions, or to make sure that Noah was told; or perhaps to be talked out of it. Dedra pleaded and reasoned with her and tried to motivate her to live. Tya was trying to listen, but she became less and less coherent. Dedra hung up the phone and quickly called Tya's neighbor and the police. When reached by her neighbor, Tya was already in a coma. Seven hours later, while her friends and family waited for news in the hospital lounge, Tya died.

While Tya seemed to have mixed feelings about her death, Dave was clear in his wish to die. Whereas Demaine viewed death as a trip to heaven, Dave saw it as an end to his existence. Such differences can be important in efforts to understand and treat suicidal persons. Accordingly, Shneidman distinguished four kinds of people who intentionally end their lives: the *death seeker, death initiator, death ignorer,* and *death darer.*

#

#StunningComparison1

More people die by suicide (42,773) than by motor vehicle crashes (33,736) in the United States each year (CDC, 2017; Heron, 2016).

#

#StunningComparison2

More people die by suicide (42,773) than by homicide (15,809) in the United States each year (CDC, 2017; Heron, 2016).

NurPhoto/NurPhoto via Getty Images

Death darers? A teenager jumps from one high rooftop to another, performing flips and other creative moves along the way, all part of the extremely dangerous "sport" called Parkour, or Freerunning. Are practitioners of this increasingly popular activity searching for new challenges or highs, as many of them claim, or are some actually death darers?

Death seekers clearly intend to end their lives at the time they attempt suicide. This singleness of purpose may last only a short time. It can change to confusion the very next hour or day, and then return again in short order. Dave, the middle-aged investment counselor, was a death seeker. He had many misgivings about suicide and was ambivalent about it for weeks, but on Tuesday night he was a death seeker—clear in his desire to die and acting in a manner that virtually guaranteed a fatal outcome.

Death initiators also clearly intend to end their lives, but they act out of a belief that the process of death is already under way and that they are simply hastening the process. Some expect that they will die in a matter of days or weeks. Many suicides among the elderly and very sick fall into this category. Robust novelist Ernest Hemingway was profoundly concerned about his failing body as he approached his sixty-second birthday—a concern that some observers believe was at the center of his suicide.

Death ignorers do not believe that their self-inflicted death will mean the end of their existence. They believe they are trading their present lives for a better or happier existence. Many child suicides, like Demaine, fall into this category, as do those of adult believers in a hereafter who kill themselves to reach another form of life. In 1997, for example, the world was shocked to learn that 39 members of an unusual cult named Heaven's Gate had died by suicide at an expensive house outside San Diego. It turned out that these members had acted out of the belief that their deaths would free their spirits and enable them to ascend to a "higher kingdom."

How should clinicians decide whether to hospitalize a person who is considering suicide or even one who has made an attempt?

Death darers experience mixed feelings, or ambivalence, about their intent to die, even at the moment of their attempt, and they show this ambivalence in the act itself. Although to some degree they wish to die, and they often do die, their risk-taking behavior does not guarantee death. The person who plays Russian roulette—that is, pulls the trigger of a revolver randomly loaded with one bullet—is a death darer. Tya might be considered a death darer. Although her unhappiness and anger were great, she was not sure that she wanted to die. Even while taking pills, she called her friend, reported her actions, and listened to her friend's pleas.

When people play *indirect, covert, partial,* or *unconscious* roles in their own deaths, Shneidman (2001, 1993, 1981) classified them in a suicide-like category called **subintentional deaths.** Traditionally, clinicians have cited drug, alcohol, or tobacco use, recurrent physical fighting, and medication mismanagement as behaviors that may contribute to subintentional deaths. In recent years, another behavioral pattern, *self-injury* or *self-mutilation,* has been added to this list—for example, cutting or burning oneself or banging one's head. Although this pattern is not officially classified as a mental disorder, the framers of DSM-5 have proposed that a category called *nonsuicidal self-injury* be studied for possible inclusion in future revisions of DSM-5.

Self-injurious behavior is more common than previously recognized, particularly among teenagers and young adults, and it may be on the increase (Cipriano, Cella, & Cotrufo, 2017). Studies suggest that 17 percent of all adolescents try to injure themselves at least once (Brown & Plener, 2017). It appears that the behavior becomes addictive in nature. The pain brought on by self-injury seems to offer some relief from tension or other kinds of emotional suffering, the behavior serves as a temporary distraction from problems, and the scars that result may document the person's distress (Skodol, 2017). More generally, self-injury may help a person deal with chronic feelings of emptiness,

#

#SteadyRise

The rate of suicide in the United States has gone up year by year throughout the twenty-first century. Today's rate is 28 percent higher than the rate in the year 2000 (CDC, 2017).

boredom, and identity confusion. Although self-injury and the other risky behaviors mentioned earlier may indeed represent an indirect attempt at suicide (Burke et al., 2018), the true intent behind them is unclear, so, for the most part, these behaviors are not included in the discussions of this chapter.

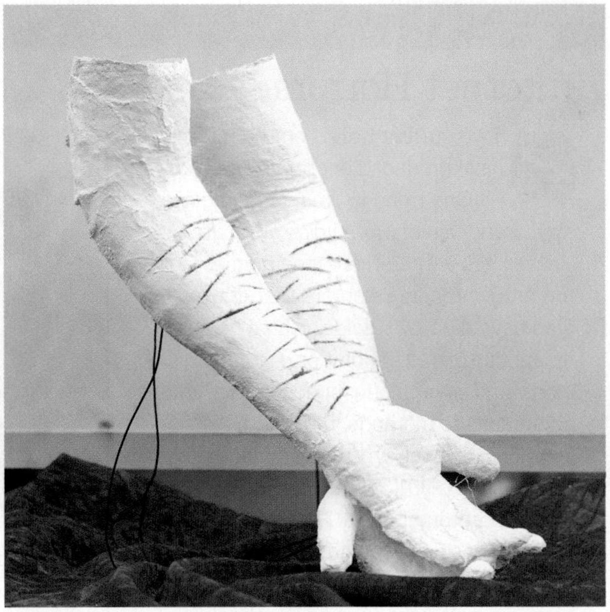
AAron Ontiveroz/Getty Images

Creative expression At least 17 percent of teenagers and young adults purposely injure themselves, particularly by skin cutting (MHA, 2017). Thus, Olivia Stewart, a high school student in Colorado, chose mental illness as the topic for her senior project and produced this remarkable sculpture on self-mutilation. Stewart, whose project also featured art representations of other psychological disorders, hopes that her work will help increase education and public awareness regarding mental disorders.

How Is Suicide Studied?

Suicide researchers face a major obstacle: the people they study are no longer alive. How can investigators draw accurate conclusions about the intentions, feelings, and circumstances of those who can no longer explain their actions? Two research methods attempt to deal with this problem, each with only partial success.

One strategy is **retrospective analysis,** a kind of psychological autopsy in which clinicians and researchers piece together data from the suicide victim's past (Nock et al., 2017; Riblet et al., 2017). Relatives, friends, therapists, or physicians may remember past statements, conversations, and behaviors that shed light on a suicide. Retrospective information may also be provided by the suicide notes that some victims leave behind. However, such sources of information are not always available or reliable (Stack & Rockett, 2018). Many suicide victims do not leave notes. Moreover, a grieving, perhaps guilt-ridden relative or a distraught therapist may be incapable of objective recollections or simply reluctant to discuss an act that is so stigmatizing in our society (Fouet, 2017).

Because of these limitations, many researchers also use a second strategy—*studying people who survive their suicide attempts*. It is estimated that there are 12 nonfatal suicide attempts for every fatal suicide (AFSP, 2018). However, it may be that people who survive suicide attempts differ in important ways from those who do not. Many of them may not really have wanted to die, for example. Nevertheless, suicide researchers have found it useful to study survivors of suicide attempts, and this chapter shall consider those who attempt suicide and those who complete suicide as more or less alike.

Patterns and Statistics

Suicide happens within a larger social setting (see ***Trending*** on the next page), and researchers have gathered many statistics regarding the social contexts in which such deaths take place. They have found, for example, that suicide rates vary from country to country (WHO, 2017). Sri Lanka, Guyana, South Korea, Lithuania, and Angola have very high rates—more than 20 suicides annually per 100,000 persons; conversely, Egypt, Mexico, Greece, and Indonesia have relatively low rates, fewer than 5 per 100,000. Falling in between are England (7.4), China (8.5), Germany (9.1), Canada (10.4), the United States (12.6), and Russia (17.9).

Religious affiliation and beliefs may help account for these national differences (Hsieh, 2017). For example, countries that are largely Catholic, Jewish, or Muslim tend to have low suicide rates. Perhaps in these countries, strict prohibitions against suicide or a strong religious tradition deter many people from attempting suicide. Yet there are exceptions to this tentative rule. Poland, a largely Roman Catholic country, has a suicide rate of 18.5 suicides per 100,000 persons, one of the higher suicide rates in the world (WHO, 2017).

What factors besides religious affiliation and beliefs might help account for national variations in suicide rates?

Research is beginning to suggest that religious doctrine may not help prevent suicide as much as the degree of an individual's *devoutness*. Regardless of their particular persuasion, very religious people seem less likely to die by suicide (Kralovec et al., 2018).

The suicide rates of men and women also differ. Three times as many women *attempt* suicide as men, yet men die from their attempts at more than three times the rate of women (AFSP, 2018). Although various explanations have been proposed for

subintentional death A death in which the victim plays an indirect, hidden, partial, or unconscious role.

retrospective analysis A psychological autopsy in which clinicians piece together information about a person's suicide from the person's past.

...TRENDING

Internet Horrors

Two current trends on the Internet have produced enormous concern.

One trend is the increasing availability and use of *pro-suicide Web sites.* These sites vary in their specific messages, but many of them celebrate former users who have died by suicide, others help set up appointments for joint or partner suicides, and several offer specific instructions about suicide methods, prospective suicide locations, and the writing of suicide notes (Miguel et al., 2017; Minkkinen et al., 2017, 2016; Thornton et al., 2017).

The sites have spread across the Internet—on Web forums and chat groups; on social networks such as Facebook, Instagram, Tumblr, and Live Journal; and on video platforms such as YouTube and Vimeo (Miguel et al., 2017). According to one study, 7.5 percent of teenagers seek out information about suicide on the Internet (Mars et al., 2015). While most such individuals access sites offering support, help, or constructive advice, more than a third of them further access sites that provide information on how to hurt or kill oneself.

A second trend of great concern is the live-streaming of suicides. On January 22, 2017, a 14-year-old girl named Nakia Venant hanged herself in her Florida bathroom while live-streaming the act on Facebook (see photo). Nakia had a long history of significant behavioral problems, as well as a background of being physically abused and rejected. She had been in and out of numerous foster care homes for the previous eight years (Barnes, 2017; Miller & Burch, 2017). Just months before her suicide, the teen had texted her biological mother seeking to return home, but such a return never took place.

Although precise numbers are not yet available, live-streaming of suicides is clearly on the rise (Reidenberg, 2017).

A tragic end On January 22, 2017, 14-year-old Nakia Venant broadcast her suicide on Facebook while sending and receiving texts—one of at least three suicides that were live-streamed in the United States that same month.

Indeed, Nakia was the third person in the United States to broadcast her suicide on social media that same month (Bever, 2017). Public suicides are not new, but they have never before been able to reach so many viewers. Clinicians do not really know why certain people attempt suicide online. Some propose that, in addition to being in great psychological pain, the individuals may be trying to display their pain to others, memorialize their death, or solicit interventions by others (Bever, 2017).

Worried about the increase in broadcast suicides and the possible risk of copycat deaths, Facebook has recently taken steps to help prevent both live-streamed and other forms of suicides. First, it has updated tools to make it easier for users to alert Facebook about suicide and self-harm postings that may come their way (O'Brien, 2017; Schuster, 2016). Upon receiving such alerts, Facebook offers immediate guidance and resources to the concerned friends or acquaintances, for example, providing them with tips on how to talk with a suicidal friend or how to contact a mental health professional through a lifeline. In cases of live-streaming, Facebook also tries to help the streamers directly (Harris, 2017). The screens of the streamers are partially blocked by a message that says, "Someone thinks you might need extra support right now and asked us to help." In turn, the streamer can contact a suicide helpline, view tips from Facebook, and/or text a friend directly from their window (Harris, 2017).

Facebook also now makes it possible for troubled individuals to immediately chat with a trained counselor from the National Suicide Prevention Lifeline, Crisis Text Line, and other crisis support organizations through its *Facebook Messenger* platform (Guynn, 2017). In addition, the social networking service is currently testing the use of pattern recognition software to help identify self-harm and suicide warning signals in user posts and comments. The network's community monitor team then acts proactively by reaching out to the posters and beyond (Harris, 2017). Certainly, such efforts by Facebook and other social networking services regarding suicidal posters and live-streamers are very welcome indeed.

this gender difference, a popular one points to the different methods used by men and women (Anestis & Houtsma, 2018). Men tend to use more violent methods, such as shooting, stabbing, or hanging themselves, whereas women use less violent methods, such as drug overdose. Guns are used in 62 percent of the male suicides in the United States, compared with 37 percent of the female suicides (Schreiber & Culpepper, 2018; CDC, 2014).

Suicide is also related to social environment and marital status. Studies suggest that at least half of individuals who carry out suicide are socially isolated and have few or no close personal friends, although they may be active on social network sites (Berman, 2018; Maris, 2001). In a related vein, research has revealed that never-married and divorced persons have a higher suicide rate than married or cohabitating individuals (Schreiber & Culpepper, 2018).

Finally, in the United States at least, suicide rates seem to vary according to race and ethnicity (see **Figure 7-1**). The overall suicide rate of non-Hispanic white Americans is more than twice as high as that of African Americans, Hispanic Americans, and Asian Americans (AFSP, 2018; CDC, 2016). A major exception to this pattern is the suicide rate of American Indians, which is higher than that of non-Hispanic white Americans. Although the extreme poverty of many American Indians may partly explain their high suicide rate, studies show that factors such as alcohol use, modeling, and the availability of guns may also play a role (Dillard et al., 2017; Lanier, 2010).

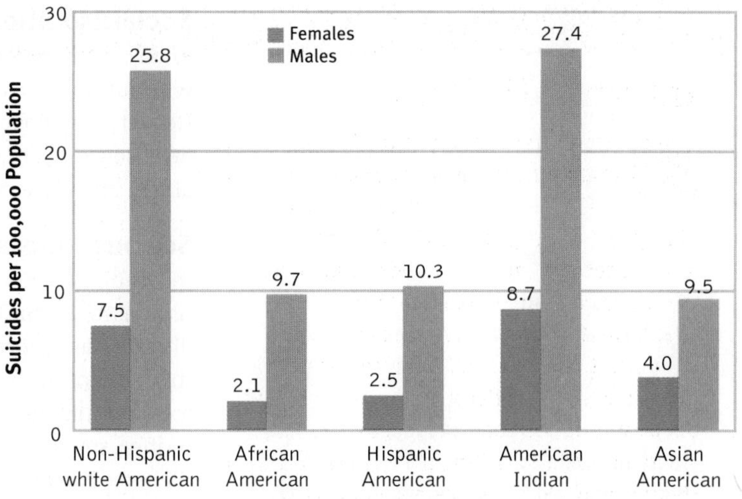

FIGURE 7-1

Suicide, Race, and Gender

In the United States, American Indians have the highest suicide rates among both males and females. (Information from: AFSP, 2018, 2017; CDC, 2016, 2014, 2010; SPRC, 2013.)

...SUMMING UP

WHAT IS SUICIDE? Suicide is a self-inflicted death in which a person makes an intentional, direct, and conscious effort to end his or her life. Four kinds of people who intentionally end their lives have been distinguished: the death seeker, the death initiator, the death ignorer, and the death darer.

Two major strategies are used in the study of suicide: retrospective analysis and the study of people who survive suicide attempts. Suicide rates vary from country to country. One reason for that seems to be cultural differences in religious affiliation, beliefs, and degree of devoutness. Suicide rates also vary according to race, gender, and marital status.

What Triggers a Suicide?

Suicidal acts may be connected to recent events or current conditions in a person's life. Although such factors may not be the basic motivation for the suicide, they can precipitate it. Common triggering factors include *stressful events, mood and thought changes, alcohol and other drug use, mental disorders,* and *modeling.*

Stressful Events and Situations

Researchers have counted more stressful events in the recent lives of suicide attempters than in the lives of nonattempters (Buchman-Schmitt et al., 2017; McFeeters et al., 2015). One stressor that has been consistently linked to suicide is combat stress. Research indicates that combat veterans from various wars are more than twice as likely to die by suicide as nonveterans (Nock et al., 2017, 2014, 2013). At the beginning of this chapter, for example, you read about a young man who killed himself upon returning to civilian life, after experiencing the enormous stressors of combat in Iraq.

The stressors that help lead to suicide do not need to be as horrific as those tied to combat. Common forms of *immediate stress* seen in cases of suicide are the loss of a loved one through death, divorce, or rejection; loss of a job; significant financial loss; and stress caused by hurricanes, earthquakes, or other natural disasters, even among very young children (Cawley et al., 2019; Kerr et al., 2017; Fujiwara et al., 2017). People may also attempt suicide in response to *long-term* rather than recent stress. Four such stressors are particularly common—social isolation, serious illness, an abusive environment, and occupational stress.

#FatalAccess

The rate of gun-related suicide is 11 times higher in the United States than in all other industrialized countries.

People who die by suicide are at least twice as likely to have a gun in their house as people who survive their suicide attempts.

Suicide rates increase 4 to 10 times among teenagers who live in a house with a gun.

(Anestis & Houtsma, 2018; Schreiber & Culpepper, 2018; Kennebeck & Bonin, 2017)

Social Isolation As you saw in the cases of Dave, Demaine, and Tya, people from loving families or supportive social systems may carry out suicide. However, those without such social supports are particularly vulnerable to suicidal thinking and actions. Researchers have found a heightened risk for suicidal behavior among those who feel little sense of "belongingness," believe that they have limited or no social support, live alone, and have ongoing conflicts with other people (Schreiber & Culpepper, 2018).

Serious Illness People whose illnesses cause them great pain or severe disability may attempt suicide, believing that death is unavoidable and imminent (Schneider & Shenassa, 2008). They may also believe that the suffering and problems caused by their illnesses are more than they can endure. Studies suggest that as many as one-third of those who die by suicide have been in poor physical health during the months prior to their suicidal acts (Schreiber & Culpepper, 2018). Illnesses that have been linked to higher suicide rates include cancer, heart disease, chronic lung disease, stroke, and diabetes mellitus (Bartoli et al., 2017; Conti et al., 2017; Zhang et al., 2017).

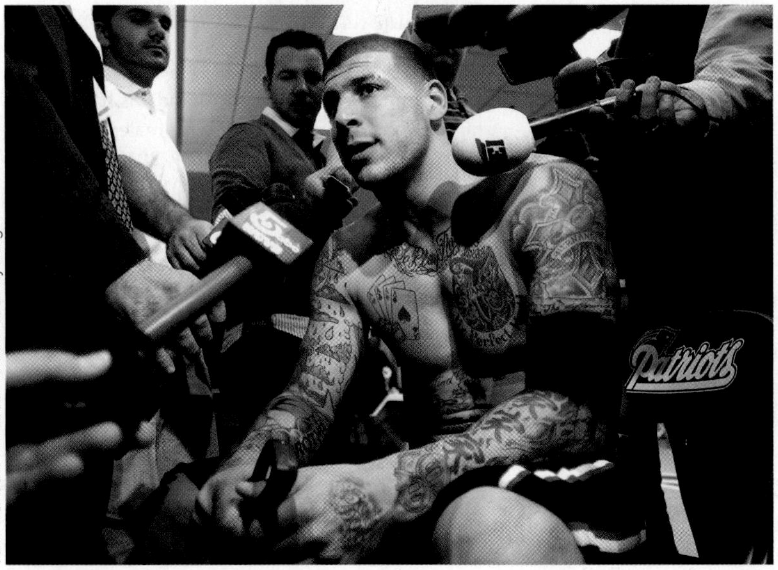

John Tlumacki/The Boston Globe via Getty Images

Famous prison suicide In 2015, Aaron Hernandez, a star tight end in the National Football League, was convicted of first-degree murder and sentenced to life in prison without parole for the 2013 killing of an acquaintance. Hernandez, shown here at a locker room press interview during his playing days, killed himself by hanging at a Massachusetts prison in 2017, just days after being acquitted of two additional killings. Around 11 percent of all prison deaths are due to suicide (BJS, 2018, 2016).

Abusive or Repressive Environment Victims of an abusive or repressive environment from which they have little or no hope of escape sometimes pursue suicide. For example, some prisoners of war, inmates of concentration camps, abused spouses, abused children, and prison inmates try to end their lives (Vadini et al., 2018; Ayhan et al., 2017). Like those who have serious illnesses, these people may feel that they can endure no more suffering and believe that there is no hope for improvement in their condition.

Occupational Stress Some jobs create feelings of tension or dissatisfaction that may trigger suicide attempts. Studies have revealed higher suicide rates among people working in unskilled occupations. For persons in skilled occupations, research has found relatively high rates for psychiatrists and psychologists, physicians, nurses, dentists, lawyers, police officers, firefighters, emergency workers, and farmers (Mckew, 2017; Witt et al., 2017). Such correlations do not necessarily mean that occupational pressures directly cause suicidal actions. Perhaps unskilled workers are responding to financial insecurity rather than job stress when they attempt suicide. Similarly, rather than reacting to the emotional strain of their work, suicidal psychiatrists and psychologists may have long-standing emotional problems that stimulated their career interest in the first place.

Mood and Thought Changes

Many suicide attempts are preceded by a change in mood. The change may not be severe enough to warrant a diagnosis of a mental disorder, but it does represent a significant shift from the person's past mood. The most common change is an increase in sadness (James et al., 2017). Also common are increases in feelings of anxiety, tension, frustration, anger, or shame (Hill et al., 2018; Reisch et al., 2010).

Suicide attempts may also be preceded by shifts in patterns of thinking. People may become preoccupied with their problems, lose perspective, and see suicide as the only effective solution to their difficulties (Schreiber & Culpepper, 2018). They often develop a sense of **hopelessness**—a pessimistic belief that their present circumstances, problems, or mood will never change (Sun et al., 2018). Some clinicians believe that a feeling of hopelessness is the single most likely indicator of suicidal intent.

Many people who attempt suicide fall victim to **dichotomous thinking,** viewing problems and solutions in rigid either/or terms (Shneidman, 2005, 2001, 1993). Indeed,

Shneidman said that the "four-letter word" in suicide is "only," as in "suicide was the *only* thing I could do" (Maris, 2001). In the following statement a woman who survived her leap from a building describes her dichotomous thinking at the time. She saw death as the only alternative to her pain:

> *I was so desperate. I felt, my God, I couldn't face this thing. Everything was like a terrible whirlpool of confusion. And I thought to myself: There's only one thing to do. I just have to lose consciousness. That's the only way to get away from it. The only way to lose consciousness, I thought, was to jump off something good and high. . . .*
>
> *(Shneidman, 1987, p. 56)*

Alcohol and Other Drug Use

Studies indicate that as many as 70 percent of the people who attempt suicide drink alcohol just before they do so (Choi et al., 2018; McCloud et al., 2004). Autopsies reveal that about one-quarter of these people are legally intoxicated (Schreiber & Culpepper, 2018; Flavin et al., 1990). Moreover, the more intoxicated suicide attempters are, the more lethal their chosen suicide method (Park et al., 2017). It may be that the use of alcohol lowers a person's inhibitions, reduces his or her fears of suicide, releases underlying aggressive feelings, or impairs judgment and problem-solving ability. Research shows that the use of other kinds of drugs may have a similar tie to suicide, particularly in teenagers and young adults (Beckman et al., 2019).

Mental Disorders

Although people who attempt suicide may be troubled or anxious, they do not necessarily have a psychological disorder. Nevertheless, the vast majority of all suicide attempters do have such a disorder (Schreiber & Culpepper, 2018; Nock et al., 2017, 2013). Research suggests that as many as 70 percent of all suicide attempters had been experiencing severe *depression* (unipolar or bipolar), 20 percent *chronic alcoholism,* and 10 percent *schizophrenia*. Correspondingly, as many as 25 percent of people with each of these disorders try to kill themselves. People who are both depressed and substance-dependent seem particularly prone to suicidal impulses (Harford et al., 2018; Bohnert et al., 2017). It is also the case that many people with borderline personality disorder, a broad pattern that you will read about in Chapter 13, try to harm themselves or make suicidal gestures as part of their disorder (Soloff & Chiappetta, 2018).

As you saw in Chapter 6, people with major depressive disorder often have suicidal thoughts. Even when depressed people begin showing improvements in mood, they may remain at high risk for suicide. In fact, among those who are severely depressed, the risk of suicide may actually increase as their mood improves and they have more energy to act on their suicidal wishes. Severe depression also may play a key role in suicide attempts made by those with serious physical illnesses (Cheung & Sundram, 2017).

A number of the people who drink alcohol or use drugs just before a suicide attempt actually have a long history of abusing such substances (Beckman et al., 2019; Mukamal, 2018; Agrawal et al., 2017). The basis for the link between substance use disorders and suicide is not clear. Perhaps the tragic lifestyle of many persons with these disorders or their sense of being hopelessly trapped by a substance leads to suicidal thinking. Alternatively, a third factor—psychological pain, for instance, or desperation—may cause both substance abuse and suicidal thinking.

Research indicates that suicides by people with schizophrenia and other disorders featuring psychosis usually reflect feelings of demoralization, a sense of being entrapped by their disorder, and fears of further mental deterioration (Owen et al., 2018). Many young and unemployed people with schizophrenia who have had relapses

Kevin Winter/Getty Images

Acting happy Fans of megastar, comedian, and actor Robin Williams were shocked when he killed himself by hanging in 2014. Close friends reported that Williams had been battling depression and the early stages of Parkinson's disease for some time—a painful emotional state that he managed to conceal from the public with his joyful performances. Williams' autopsy also revealed a type of neurocognitive disorder called Lewy body disease.

hopelessness A pessimistic belief that one's present circumstances, problems, or mood will never change.

dichotomous thinking Viewing problems and solutions in rigid either/or terms.

over several years come to believe that the disorder will forever disrupt their lives. Still others seem to be disheartened by their substandard living conditions.

Modeling: The Contagion of Suicide

It is not unusual for people, particularly teenagers, to attempt suicide after observing or reading about someone else who has done so (Vitelli, 2016). Perhaps they have been struggling with major problems and the other person's suicide seems to reveal a possible solution, or perhaps they have been thinking about suicide and the other person's suicide seems to give them permission or finally persuades them to act. Either way, one suicidal act apparently serves as a *model* for another. Suicides by family members and friends, those by celebrities, and suicides by coworkers or colleagues are particularly common triggers.

Family Members and Friends A recent suicide by a family member or friend increases the likelihood that a person will attempt suicide (Campos, Holden, & Santos, 2018; Ali et al., 2011). Of course, the death of a family member or friend, especially when self-inflicted, is a life-changing event, and suicidal thoughts or attempts may be tied largely to that trauma or sense of loss. Indeed, such losses typically have a lifelong impact on surviving relatives and friends, including a heightened risk of suicide that can continue for years (Schreiber & Culpepper, 2018). However, even when researchers factor out these issues, they find increases in the risk of suicide among the relatives and friends of people who recently committed suicide. This additional risk factor is often called the *social contagion effect*.

MR1805/Getty Images

Far from a game The *Blue Whale Game*, or *Blue Whale Challenge*, is an Internet "game" that is currently stirring great public concern. The challenge is comprised of daily tasks that participants are assigned by administrators, culminating, on the 50th day, with an instruction to kill oneself. It is estimated that dozens of teenagers across the world have died by suicide playing the game, whose name is derived from the behavior of whales that strand themselves on beaches and die.

Celebrities Research suggests that suicides by entertainers, political figures, and other well-known people are regularly followed by unusual increases in the number of suicides across the nation. Studies on this issue have found, for example, that the national suicide rate rose around 19 percent during the weeks after the 2014 suicide of comedian Robin Williams and the 1963 suicide of actress Marilyn Monroe (Fink, Santaella-Tenorio, & Keyes, 2018; Phillips, 1974).

Some clinicians argue that more responsible reporting could reduce the impact of celebrity or other highly publicized suicides (Fink et al., 2018; Sullivan et al., 2015). A careful approach to reporting was seen in the media's coverage of the suicide of Kurt Cobain. MTV's repeated theme on the evening of the suicide was "Don't do it!" In fact, thousands of young people called MTV and other radio and television stations in the hours after Cobain's death, upset, frightened, and in some cases suicidal. Some of the stations responded by posting the phone numbers of suicide prevention centers, presenting interviews with suicide experts, and offering counseling services and advice directly to callers. Perhaps because of such efforts, the usual rate of suicide both in Seattle, where Cobain lived, and elsewhere held steady during the weeks that followed (Colburn, 1996).

Coworkers and Colleagues The word-of-mouth publicity that attends suicides in a school, workplace, or small community may trigger suicide attempts. The suicide of a recruit at a U.S. Navy training school, for example, was followed within 2 weeks by another and also by an attempted suicide at the school. To head off what threatened to become a suicide epidemic, the school began a program of staff education on suicide and group therapy sessions for recruits who had been close to the suicide victims (Grigg, 1988). Today, a number of schools, for individuals of all ages, put into action programs of this kind after a student dies by suicide (AFSP, 2018; Joshi et al., 2015). Such postsuicide programs are often referred to by clinicians as *postvention*.

Jeffrey Mayer/Getty Images

AP Photo/Katy Winn

Parallel journeys In 1994 rock star Kurt Cobain (left), leader of the grunge band Nirvana, shot himself to death at age 27, shaking millions of young fans to their core. In 2017, rock star Chris Cornell (right), a contemporary of Cobain's and lead singer in the grunge band Soundgarden, hanged himself at age 52. Cornell's suicide, occurring 23 years after Cobain's, stunned and disheartened many of the same (now middle-aged) fans.

... SUMMING UP

WHAT TRIGGERS A SUICIDE? Many suicidal acts are triggered by the current events or conditions in a person's life. The acts may be triggered by recent stressors, such as loss of a loved one and job loss, or long-term stressors, such as serious illness, an abusive environment, and job stress. They may also be preceded by changes in mood or thought, particularly increases in one's sense of hopelessness. In addition, the use of alcohol or other kinds of substances, mental disorders, or news of another's suicide may precede suicide attempts.

What Are the Underlying Causes of Suicide?

Most people faced with difficult situations never try to kill themselves. In an effort to understand why some people are more prone to suicide than others, theorists have proposed more fundamental explanations for self-destructive actions than the immediate triggers considered in the previous section. The leading theories come from the psychodynamic, sociocultural, and biological models. Some of these hypotheses have, however, received limited research support and fail to address the full range of suicidal acts. Thus the clinical field currently lacks a satisfactory understanding of suicide.

The Psychodynamic View

Many psychodynamic theorists believe that suicide results from depression and from anger at others that is redirected toward oneself. To make this point, the influential psychiatrist Karl Menninger called suicide "murder in the 180th degree."

As you read in Chapter 6, Freud (1917) and Abraham (1916, 1911) proposed that when people experience the real or symbolic loss of a loved one, they come to "introject" the lost person; that is, they unconsciously incorporate the person into their own identity and feel toward themselves as they had felt toward the other. For a short while, negative feelings toward the lost loved one are experienced as self-hatred. Anger toward

#

#DealBreaker

If clients state an intention to kill themselves, therapists may break the doctor–patient confidentiality agreement that usually governs treatment discussions (Middleman & Olson, 2017).

#AdditionalPunishment

Up through the nineteenth century, the bodies of suicide victims in France and England were sometimes dragged through the streets on a frame, head downward, the way criminals were dragged to their executions (Wertheimer, 2001; Fay, 1995).

the loved one may turn into intense anger against oneself and finally into depression. Suicide is thought to be an extreme expression of this self-hatred and self-punishment (Campbell & Hale, 2017).

In support of Freud's view, researchers have often found a relationship between childhood losses—real or symbolic—and later suicidal behaviors (Burrell, Mehlum, & Qin, 2018). A classic study of 200 family histories, for example, found that early parental loss was much more common among suicide attempters (48 percent) than among nonsuicidal individuals (24 percent) (Adam, Bouckoms, & Streiner, 1982). Common forms of loss were death of the father and divorce or separation of the parents. Similarly, a study of 343 depressed individuals found that those who had felt rejected or neglected as children by their parents were more likely than other people to attempt suicide as adults (Ehnvall et al., 2008).

Late in his career, Freud proposed that human beings have a basic "death instinct." He called this instinct *Thanatos* and said that it opposes the "life instinct." According to Freud, while most people learn to redirect their death instinct by aiming it toward others, suicidal people, caught in a web of self-anger, direct it squarely toward themselves.

Sociological findings are consistent with this explanation of suicide. National suicide rates have been found to drop in times of war (Osman & Parnell, 2015; Maris, 2001), when, one could argue, people are encouraged to direct their self-destructive energy against "the enemy." In addition, in many parts of the world, societies with high rates of homicide tend to have low rates of suicide, and vice versa (Bills & Li, 2005).

By the end of his career, Freud himself expressed dissatisfaction with his theory of suicide. Other psychodynamic theorists have also challenged his ideas over the years, yet themes of loss and self-directed aggression generally remain at the center of most psychodynamic explanations (Campbell & Hale, 2017).

In the service of others According to Emile Durkheim, people who intentionally sacrifice their lives for others are committing altruistic suicide. In the 2016 movie *Rogue One*, renegade Jyn Erso leads a small band of Rebel volunteers on a "suicide mission" to capture the schematic diagram of the Death Star, a powerful superweapon capable of destroying planets. Jyn and her group successfully capture and transmit the diagram back to the Rebel command ship, setting in motion the destruction of the Death Star and the saving of the galaxy, but all of them die in the process—as they knew they would.

Walt Disney Studios Motion Pictures/Photofest

Durkheim's Sociocultural View

Toward the end of the nineteenth century, Emile Durkheim (1897), a sociologist, developed a broad theory of suicidal behavior. Today this theory is still influential and is often supported by research (Osman & Parnell, 2015; Fernquist, 2007). According to Durkheim, the probability of suicide is determined by how attached a person is to such social groups as the family, religious institutions, and community. The more thoroughly a person belongs, the lower the risk of suicide. Conversely, people who have poor relationships with their society are at higher risk of killing themselves. He defined several categories of suicide, including *egoistic, altruistic,* and *anomic* suicide.

Why might towns and countries in past times have been inclined to punish both those who attempted suicide and their relatives?

Egoistic suicides are carried out by people over whom society has little or no control. These people are not concerned with the norms or rules of society, nor are they integrated into the social fabric. According to Durkheim, this kind of suicide is more likely in people who are isolated, alienated, and nonreligious. The larger the number of such people living in a society, the higher that society's suicide rate.

Altruistic suicides, in contrast, are undertaken by people who are so well integrated into the social structure that they intentionally sacrifice their lives for its well-being. Soldiers who threw themselves on top of a live grenade to save others, Japanese kamikaze pilots who crashed their planes into enemy ships during World War II, and Buddhist monks and nuns who protested the Vietnam War by setting themselves on fire may have been undertaking altruistic suicide. According to Durkheim, societies that encourage people to sacrifice themselves for others and to preserve their own honor (as East Asian societies do) are likely to have higher suicide rates.

Anomic suicides, another category proposed by Durkheim, are those pursued by people whose social environment fails to provide stable structures, such as family and religion, to support and give meaning to life. Such a societal condition, called *anomie* (literally, "without law"), leaves people without a sense of belonging. Unlike egoistic suicide, which is the act of a person who rejects the structures of a society, anomic suicide is the act of a person who has been let down by a disorganized, inadequate, often decaying society.

Durkheim argued that when societies go through periods of anomie, their suicide rates increase. Historical trends support this claim. Periods of economic depression may bring about some degree of anomie in a country, and national suicide rates tend to rise during such times (Kerr et al., 2017). Periods of population change and increased immigration, too, tend to bring about a state of anomie, and again suicide rates rise (Kposowa et al., 2008).

A major change in a person's immediate surroundings, rather than general societal problems, can also lead to anomic suicide. People who suddenly inherit a great deal of money, for example, may go through a period of anomie as their relationships with social, economic, and occupational structures are changed. Thus Durkheim predicted that societies with more opportunities for changes in individual wealth or status would have higher suicide rates; this prediction is also supported by research (Cutright & Fernquist, 2001).

Thaier Al-Sudani/Reuters

Altruistic suicide? A clay sculpture of a suicide bomber is displayed at a Baghdad art gallery. Some sociologists believe that the acts of such bombers fit Durkheim's definition of altruistic suicide, arguing that the bombers believe they are sacrificing their lives for the well-being of their society. Other theorists, however, point out that many such bombers seem indifferent to the innocent lives they are destroying and categorize the bombers instead as mass murderers motivated by hatred rather than by feelings of altruism (Lankford, 2013; Humphrey, 2006).

Although today's sociocultural theorists do not always embrace Durkheim's particular ideas, most agree that interpersonal variables, social structure, and cultural stress often play major roles in suicide. The recent work of researcher Thomas Joiner, which is discussed in the following section, is a case in point.

The Interpersonal View

For more than a decade, clinical researcher Thomas Joiner and his colleagues have been developing the **interpersonal theory of suicide** (Joiner et al., 2017; Joiner, 2009, 2005). This view, also called the *interpersonal-psychological theory*, asserts that people will be inclined to pursue suicide if they hold two key interpersonal beliefs—*perceived burdensomeness* and *thwarted belongingness*—and, at the same time, have a psychological *capability* to carry out suicide, a capability that they have acquired from life experiences. The theory does not dismiss the importance of the other factors you have been reading about throughout this chapter. However, says the Joiner research team, without the further presence of perceived burdensomeness, thwarted belongingness, and acquired capability, those factors are not likely to result in self-inflicted death (Rogers et al., 2017).

According to this theory, people with perceived burdensomeness believe that their existence places a heavy and permanent burden on their family, friends, and even society. This belief—typically inaccurate—may produce the notion that "my death would be worth more than my life to my family and friends" (Silva et al., 2017; Joiner, 2009).

People with thwarted belongingness feel isolated and alienated from others—not an integral part of a family or social network. Their sense of social disconnect may be overstated or it may be accurate, but, either way, it *feels* enduring, unchangeable, and confining.

Research indicates that people who experience *both* of these interpersonal perceptions are inclined to develop a *desire* for suicide (Buckner et al., 2017; Ma et al., 2016). However, studies also indicate that such individuals are unlikely to attempt suicide unless they further possess the third variable cited by the theory—the psychological capability to inflict lethal harm on themselves (Ribeiro & Joiner, 2009).

interpersonal theory of suicide A theory that asserts that people with perceived burdensomeness, thwarted belongingness, and a psychological capability to carry out suicide are the most likely to attempt suicide. Also called *interpersonal-psychological theory*.

#

#HeightenedRisk

Some studies find that birthdays are associated with a greater risk of suicide. People are significantly more likely to complete suicide on their birthday (Stickley et al., 2016).

According to Joiner, we all have a basic motive to live and preserve ourselves—a motive that weakens for certain people as a result of their repeated exposure to painful or frightening life experiences, like abuse, trauma, severe illness, or the like. Given such recurrent experiences, these individuals may develop a heightened tolerance for pain and a fearlessness about death (Rogers et al., 2017; Joiner, 2009). In Joiner's terms, they acquire a psychological capability for suicidal acts.

Studies conducted across a range of populations—from adolescents to the elderly—reveal that people with a combination of perceived burdensomeness, thwarted belongingness, and acquired suicide capability are significantly more likely to attempt suicide than people without these characteristics (Rogers et al., 2017; Horton et al., 2016).

Although this trio of factors has certainly been linked to civilian suicides, the theory's ability to help account for military suicides, which are twice as prevalent as civilian suicides, has stirred particular interest among clinical researchers (Monteith et al., 2018; Nock et al., 2017). Studies have revealed that many soldiers and veterans, perhaps due in part to the nature and impact of military training and combat, eventually develop feelings that they are a hardship on their families (perceived burdensomeness), have difficulty integrating into civilian life (thwarted belongingness), and grow accustomed to violence (acquired suicide capability) (Lusk et al., 2015). Correspondingly, studies have found that such individuals often develop suicidal thoughts (Silva et al., 2017).

The Biological View

For years, biological researchers have repeatedly found higher rates of suicide among the parents and close relatives of suicidal people than among those of nonsuicidal people (Wang et al., 2017). Such findings may suggest that genetic, and so biological, factors are at work.

Suicide sometimes runs in families. How might clinicians and researchers explain such family patterns?

Laboratory studies also offer more direct support for a biological view of suicide. One promising line of research focuses on *serotonin*. The activity level of this neurotransmitter has often been found to be low in people who complete suicide (Fanelli & Serretti, 2019; Kennebeck & Bonin, 2017). At first glance, this finding may seem to tell us only that depressed people often attempt suicide. After all, depression is itself related to low serotonin activity and to dysfunction of the depression-related brain circuit. On the other hand, there is evidence of low serotonin activity and brain-circuit dysfunction even among suicidal people who have no history of depression (Mann & Currier, 2007). That is, low serotonin activity and brain-circuit dysfunction also seem to play a role in suicide separate from depression.

Is aggression the key? Biological theorists believe that heightened feelings of aggression and impulsivity, produced by low serotonin activity and poor brain-circuit functioning, are key factors in suicide. In 2007, professional wrestling champion Chris Benoit (right) killed his wife and son and then hanged himself, a tragedy that seemed consistent with this theory. In addition, toxicology reports found steroids, drugs known to help cause aggression and impulsivity, in Benoit's body.

J. Shearer/Getty Images

How might such serotonin and brain-circuit abnormalities directly increase the likelihood of suicidal behavior? One possibility is that they contribute to aggressive and impulsive behaviors (Huang et al., 2017; Rizzi & Marras, 2017). It has been found, for example, that aggressive and impulsive men (including those who commit arson and murder) display lower serotonin activity and poorer brain-circuit functioning than do other men (Mann & Currier, 2007; Oquendo et al., 2006, 2004). Such findings suggest that low serotonin activity and brain-circuit dysfunction help produce aggressive feelings and impulsive behavior. In people who are clinically depressed, these biological abnormalities may lead to aggressive tendencies that cause them to be particularly vulnerable to suicidal thoughts and acts. Even in the absence of a depressive disorder, however, people with low serotonin activity and a dysfunctional brain circuit may develop such aggressive feelings that they, too, are dangerous to themselves or to others.

?... SUMMING UP

WHAT ARE THE UNDERLYING CAUSES OF SUICIDE? The leading explanations for suicide come from the psychodynamic, sociocultural, and biological models. Psychodynamic theorists believe that suicide usually results from depression and self-directed anger. Emile Durkheim's sociocultural theory defines three categories of suicide, based on the person's relationship with society: egoistic, altruistic, and anomic suicides. A more recent theory, the interpersonal theory, asserts that people with perceived burdensomeness, thwarted belongingness, and a psychological capability to carry out suicide are more likely to attempt suicide. And biological theorists suggest that low serotonin activity and abnormalities in the depression-related brain circuit contribute to suicide.

Is Suicide Linked to Age?

Although people of all ages may try to kill themselves, the likelihood of dying by suicide steadily increases with age up through middle age, then decreases during the early stages of old age, and then increases again beginning at age 75 (see **Figure 7-2**). Currently, 2 of every 100,000 people under 15 years of age in the United States kills himself or herself each year, compared with 11 of every 100,000 people between 15 and 24 years old, 16 of every 100,000 people between 25 and 44 years old, 20 of every 100,000 between 45 and 64 years old, 16 of every 100,000 between 65 and 74, and 21 of every 100,000 people over age 75 (AFSP, 2018; CDC, 2016). The exceptional rate of suicide among those who are middle-aged is a relatively recent phenomenon and is not fully understood (Schreiber & Culpepper, 2018).

Clinicians have paid particular attention to self-destructive behavior in three age groups: *children*, *adolescents*, and the *elderly*. Although the features and theories of suicide discussed throughout this chapter apply to all age groups, each group faces unique problems that may play key roles in the suicidal acts of its members.

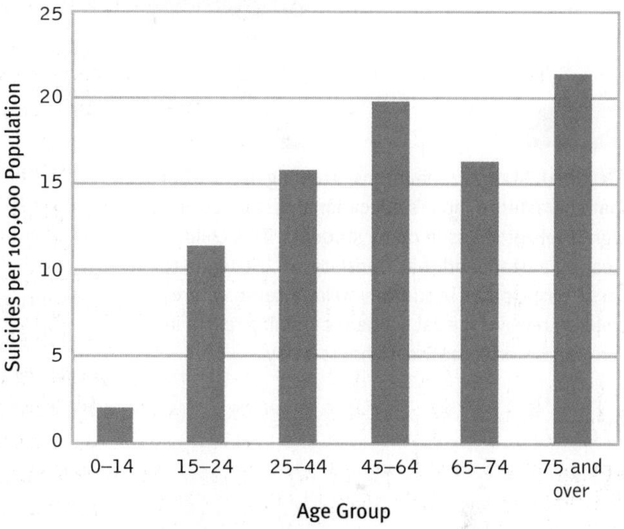

FIGURE 7-2

Suicide and Age

In the United States, suicide rates keep rising through middle age, then fall during the first decade of old age, then rise again among people over the age of 74. (Information from: AFSP, 2018, 2017; CDC, 2016.)

Children

Suicide is infrequent among children, although it has been increasing over the past several decades (Schreiber & Culpepper, 2018). For children under 11 years of age, one out of every million individuals kill themselves. That rate rises to two per 100,000 among children aged 11 to 14 years and, as you will see shortly, 8 per 100,000 among teens aged 15 to 19 years (Kennebeck & Bonin, 2017; CDC, 2016). In addition, it has been estimated that 1 of every 100 children tries to harm himself or herself, and many thousands of children are hospitalized each year for deliberately self-destructive acts, such as stabbing, cutting, burning, or shooting themselves; overdosing; or jumping from high places (Fortune & Hawton, 2007).

Researchers have found that suicide attempts by the very young are commonly preceded by such behavioral patterns as running away from home; accident-proneness; aggressive acting out; temper tantrums; self-criticism; social withdrawal and loneliness; extreme sensitivity to criticism by others; low tolerance of frustration; sleep problems; dark fantasies, daydreams, or hallucinations; marked personality change; and overwhelming interest in death and suicide (Soole et al., 2015; Wong et al., 2011). Further, studies have linked child suicides to the recent or anticipated loss of a loved one, family stress and a parent's unemployment, abuse by parents, victimization by peers (for example, bullying), and a clinical level of depression (Kennebeck & Bonin, 2017; van Geel, Vedder, & Tanilon, 2014).

Kaku Kurita/Getty Images

Student stress The intense training and testing that characterize Japan's educational system produce high levels of stress in many students. This child, wearing a headband that translates to "Struggle to Pass," participates in summer *juku*, a camp where children receive special academic training, extra lessons, and exam practice 11 hours a day.

Most people find it hard to believe that children fully comprehend the meaning of a suicidal act. They argue that because a child's thinking is so limited, children who attempt suicide fall into Shneidman's category of "death ignorers," like Demaine, who sought to join his mother in heaven (Kennebeck & Bonin, 2017). Many child suicides, however, appear to be based on a clear understanding of death and on a clear wish to die (Pfeffer, 2003). In addition, interviews with schoolchildren have revealed that between 6 and 33 percent have thought about suicide (Riesch et al., 2008; Culp, Clyman, & Culp, 1995).

Adolescents

> *Dear Mom, Dad, and everyone else,*
>
> *I'm sorry for what I've done, but I loved you all and I always will, for eternity. Please, please, please don't blame it on yourselves. It was all my fault and not yours or anyone else's. If I didn't do this now, I would have done it later anyway. We all die some day, I just died sooner.*
>
> *Love,*
> *John*
>
> *(Berman, 1986)*

The suicide of John, age 17, was not an unusual occurrence. Suicidal actions become much more common after the age of 13 than at any earlier age. Each year, according to official records, 8 of every 100,000 teenagers (age 14 to 18) in the United States end their lives (Kennebeck & Bonin, 2017; Nock et al., 2013). In addition, at least 12 percent of teenagers have persistent suicidal thoughts and 4 to 8 percent make suicide attempts. Because fatal illnesses are uncommon among the young, suicide has become the second leading cause of death in this age group, after accidents (CDC, 2017). Around 19 percent of all adolescent deaths are the result of suicide (Heron, 2016).

About half of teenage suicides, like those of people in other age groups, have been tied to clinical depression, low self-esteem, and feelings of hopelessness, but many teenagers who try to kill themselves also appear to struggle with anger and impulsiveness or to have serious alcohol or drug problems (Schreiber & Culpepper, 2018; Kennebeck & Bonin, 2017). Some also have deficiencies in their ability to sort out and solve problems.

Teenagers who consider or attempt suicide are often under great stress (Steele et al., 2018; Stewart et al., 2018). They may be dealing with long-term pressures such as poor (or missing) relationships with parents, family conflict, inadequate peer relationships, social isolation, or repeated bullying. Indeed, suicide attempts are at least twice as common among teenage victims of bullying as among other teenagers. Alternatively, their actions also may be triggered by more immediate stress, such as a parent's unemployment or medical illness, financial setbacks for the family, or a social loss such as a breakup with a boyfriend or girlfriend. Stress at school seems to be a particularly common problem for teenagers who attempt suicide. Some have trouble keeping up at school, while others may be high achievers who feel pressured to be perfect and to stay at the top of the class.

One group under particular stress are LGBTQ teenagers (lesbian, gay, bisexual, transgender, and questioning). In addition to possible sexual or gender doubts and concerns, they often experience abuse, prejudice, stigmatization, and victimization by peers, including bullying, in their lives. Studies indicate that they are three times more likely than other teenagers to have suicidal thoughts and to attempt suicide (Forcier & Olson-Kennedy, 2017).

Some theorists believe that the period of adolescence itself produces a stressful climate in which suicidal actions are more likely. Adolescence is a period of rapid growth that is often marked by conflicts, depressed feelings, tensions, and difficulties at home

#LimitedHelp

More than 55 percent of teens who attempt suicide received some form of therapy before the onset of their suicidal behavior, but it failed to prevent their later actions (Nock et al., 2013).

and school. Adolescents tend to react to events more sensitively, angrily, dramatically, and impulsively than individuals in other age groups; thus the likelihood of their engaging in suicidal acts during times of stress is higher (Greening et al., 2008). Finally, the suggestibility of adolescents and their eagerness to imitate others, including others who attempt suicide, may set the stage for suicidal action (Kennebeck & Bonin, 2017). One study found that adolescents exposed to suicide by an acquaintance or relative within the past year were more likely to attempt suicide than adolescents without a personal exposure of this kind (Swanson & Colman, 2013). It is believed that recent suicides by individuals on social networking sites—including individuals never met in person—may also raise the likelihood of attempted suicide by many young users (Briggs, Slater, & Bowley, 2017).

Teen Suicides: Attempts Versus Completions Far more teenagers attempt suicide than actually kill themselves—most experts believe that the ratio is at least 100 to 1, and in fact estimates range as high as 200 to 1 (Schreiber & Culpepper, 2018; Kennebeck & Bonin, 2017). In contrast, the ratio is thought to be 4 to 1 among the elderly (AFSP, 2018). The unusually large number of unsuccessful teenage suicides may mean that adolescents are less certain than middle-age and elderly people who make such attempts. While some do indeed wish to die, many may simply want to make others understand how desperate they are, or they may want to get help or teach others a lesson (Apter & Wasserman, 2007). Up to half of teenagers who make a suicide attempt try again in the future, and as many as 14 percent eventually die by suicide (Horwitz, Czyz, & King, 2014; Wong et al., 2008).

Why is the rate of suicide attempts so high among teenagers (as well as among young adults)? Several explanations, most pointing to societal factors, have been proposed. First, as the number and proportion of teenagers and young adults in the general population have risen, the competition for jobs, college positions, and academic and athletic honors has intensified for them, leading increasingly to shattered dreams and ambitions (Kim & Cho, 2017; Holinger & Offer, 1993, 1991, 1982). Other explanations point to weakening ties in the family (which may produce feelings of alienation and rejection in many of today's young people) and to the easy availability of alcohol and other drugs, and the pressure to use them, among teenagers and young adults (Kennebeck & Bonin, 2017; Cutler et al., 2001).

The mass media coverage of suicides by teenagers and young adults may also contribute to the high rate of suicide attempts among the young (Shain & AAP Committee on Adolescence, 2016). The detailed descriptions of teenage suicide that the media and the arts often offer may serve as models for young people who are contemplating suicide (Gould et al., 2014).

Teen Suicides: Multicultural Issues Teenage suicide rates vary by race and ethnicity in the United States. Around 9 of every 100,000 non-Hispanic white American teenagers die by suicide each year, compared with 5 of every 100,000 African American

Beth Dubber/©Netflix/courtesy Everett Collection

13 Reasons Why Few TV series have produced the stir caused by *13 Reasons Why*, a Netflix drama wildly popular among teenagers. The show depicts young Hannah Baker who fatally cuts her wrists after experiencing a number of traumatic events, each brought on by a different classmate. After Hannah's suicide, those classmates receive a package of tapes from her—an audio diary—describing the 13 reasons she killed herself. On the plus side, the show has raised awareness about teenage suicide and helped generate peer-to-peer and parent–child discussions about this topic. On the negative side, many clinicians and educators worry that the show depicts suicide too graphically, inadvertently normalizes it, and may trigger acts of self-destruction and self-harm by some viewers.

#TwitterAlert

Numerous tweeters express suicidality on Twitter. All suicide-related tweets should be taken seriously, but research has found that those with a higher word count, greater use of first-person pronouns, and more references to death may be of particular concern (O'Dea et al., 2018).

AP Photo/Michael Albans

Continuing trend The rate of suicide among American Indians is much higher than the national average. Here a memorial is held for a young suicide victim at a middle school on the Fort Peck Indian Reservation in Poplar, Montana.

teens and 5 of every 100,000 Hispanic American teens (CDC, 2016; Goldston et al., 2008). At the same time, the rates of these three groups are becoming closer (Schreiber & Culpepper, 2018). This closing trend may reflect increasingly similar pressures on young African, Hispanic, and non-Hispanic white Americans—competition for grades and college opportunities, for example, is now intense for all three groups. The growing suicide rates for young African and Hispanic Americans may also be linked to their rising unemployment, the many pressures of inner-city life, and the indignation many feel over racial inequities and discrimination in our society (Kennebeck & Bonin, 2017). Studies further indicate that 5.7 of every 100,000 Asian American teens now end their lives each year.

The highest teenage suicide rate of all is displayed by American Indians. Currently, around 18 of every 100,000 American Indian teenagers die by suicide each year, double the rate of non-Hispanic white American teenagers and triple that of other minority teenagers (CDC, 2016). Clinical theorists attribute this extraordinarily high rate to factors such as the extreme poverty faced by most American Indian teens, their limited educational and employment opportunities, their particularly high rate of alcohol abuse, and the geographical isolation of those who live on reservations (SAMHSA, 2018; Dillard et al., 2017). In addition, it appears that certain American Indian reservations have extreme suicide rates—called *cluster suicides*—and that teenagers who live in such communities are unusually likely to be exposed to suicide, to have their lives disrupted, to observe suicidal models, and to be at risk for suicide contagion (SAMHSA, 2017).

The Elderly

More than 16 of every 100,000 people between the ages of 65 and 74 years in the United States kill themselves, a rate that rises to 21.4 per 100,000 among people over the age of 74 years, as you read earlier (AFSP, 2018; CDC, 2016). Elderly people account for over 18 percent of all suicides in the United States, yet they comprise only 15 percent of the total population (NVSR, 2016; U.S. Census Bureau, 2016).

Many factors contribute to this high suicide rate. As people grow older, all too often they become ill, lose close friends and relatives, lose control over their lives, and lose status in our society (Steele et al., 2018). Such experiences may result in feelings of hopelessness, loneliness, depression, "burdensomeness," or inevitability among aged persons and so increase the likelihood that they will attempt suicide (Steele et al., 2018; Kim et al., 2014). One study found that two-thirds of particularly elderly individuals (those over 80 years old) who died by suicide had been hospitalized for medical reasons within 2 years preceding the suicide (Erlangsen et al., 2005), and another found a heightened rate of vascular or respiratory illnesses among elderly people who attempted suicide (Levy et al., 2011). Still other research has shown that the suicide rate of elderly people who have recently lost a spouse is particularly high (Schreiber & Culpepper, 2018).

Why do people often view the suicides of elderly or chronically sick people as less tragic than those of young or healthy people?

Elderly people are typically more determined than younger people in their decision to die and give fewer warnings, so their success rate is much higher (Dennis & Brown, 2011). As you read earlier, an estimated one of every four elderly persons who attempts suicide succeeds. Given the determination of aged persons and their physical decline, some people argue that older persons who want to die are clear in their thinking and should be allowed to carry out their wishes (Emanuel, 2017) (see ***InfoCentral***). However, clinical depression appears to play an important role in as many as 60 percent of suicides by the elderly, suggesting that more elderly people who are suicidal should be

#TheirWords

"What an amount of good nature and humor it takes to endure the gruesome business of growing old."

Sigmund Freud, 1937

THE RIGHT TO DIE BY SUICIDE

In ancient Greece, citizens with a grave illness or mental anguish could obtain official permission from the Senate to take their own lives. In contrast, most Western countries have traditionally discouraged suicide, based on their belief in the "sanctity of life." Today, however, a person's "**right to die by suicide**" is receiving more and more support from the public, particularly in connection with ending great pain and terminal illness (Quill & Battin, 2018; Braverman et al., 2017).

WHO SUPPORTS THE RIGHT OF TERMINALLY ILL PATIENTS TO DIE BY SUICIDE?

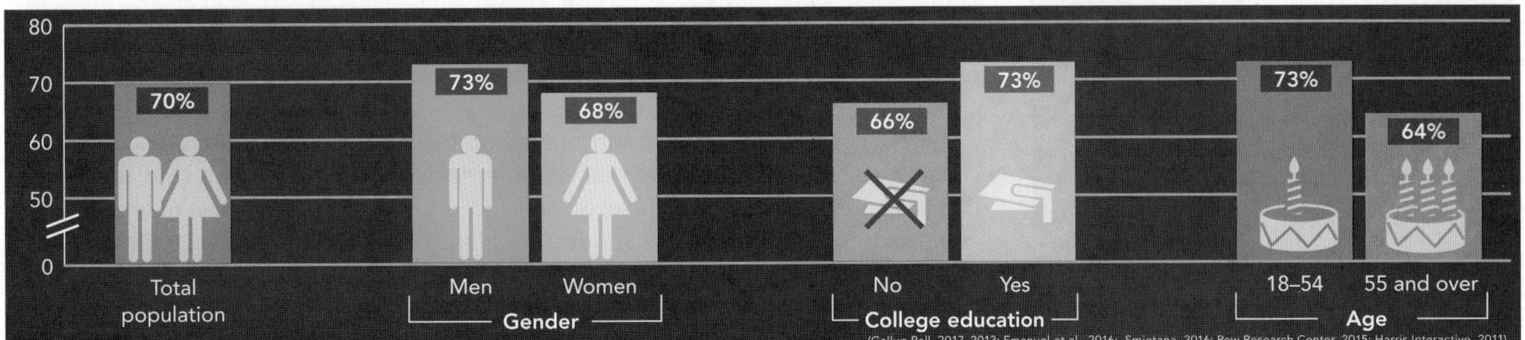

(Gallup Poll, 2017, 2013; Emanuel et al., 2016; Smietana, 2016; Pew Research Center, 2015; Harris Interactive, 2011)

EUTHANASIA AND PHYSICIAN-ASSISTED SUICIDE

Euthanasia, also called "mercy killing," is the practice of killing someone who is terminally sick or badly injured to stop the suffering. Euthanasia is not necessarily initiated by the patient. **Physician-assisted suicide** is a particular form of euthanasia, in which a physician helps a patient to end his or her life in response to the patient's request.

Should physicians provide indirect or direct assistance?

Physicians may *advise* patients about how to end their life (indirect assistance) or may *actually end* a patient's life (direct assistance). Many people who support physician-assisted suicide remain uncomfortable with the prospect of a doctor directly inducing a patient's death.

Around 57 percent of U.S. physicians believe that physician-assisted suicide should be available to terminally ill patients (Lowes, 2016). At the same time, fewer than 20 percent of all U.S. physicians have received requests for such assistance and fewer than 5 percent have ever provided it (Emanuel et al., 2016).

Should doctors be allowed to *advise* or *directly end* the lives of patients?

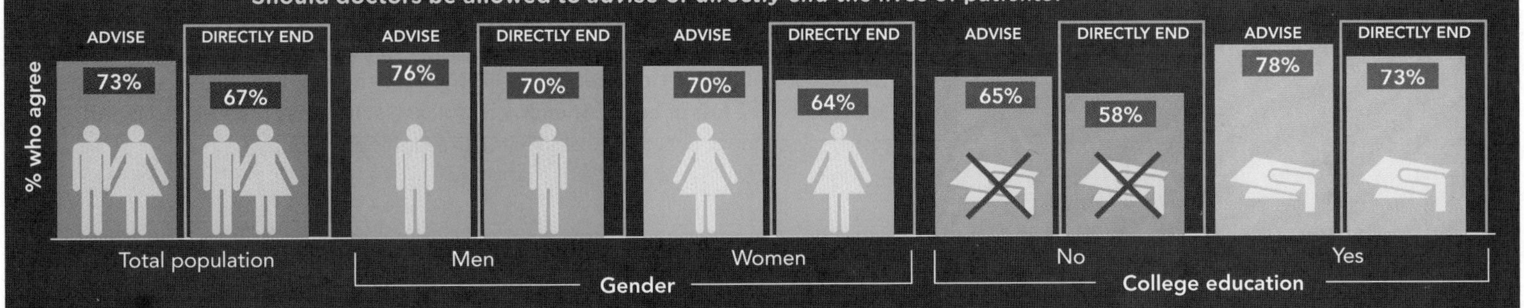

(Gallup Poll, 2017, 2013; Emanuel et al., 2016; Smietana, 2016; Pew Research Center, 2015; Harris Interactive, 2011)

WHERE IS EUTHANASIA AND PHYSICIAN-ASSISTED SUICIDE LEGAL?

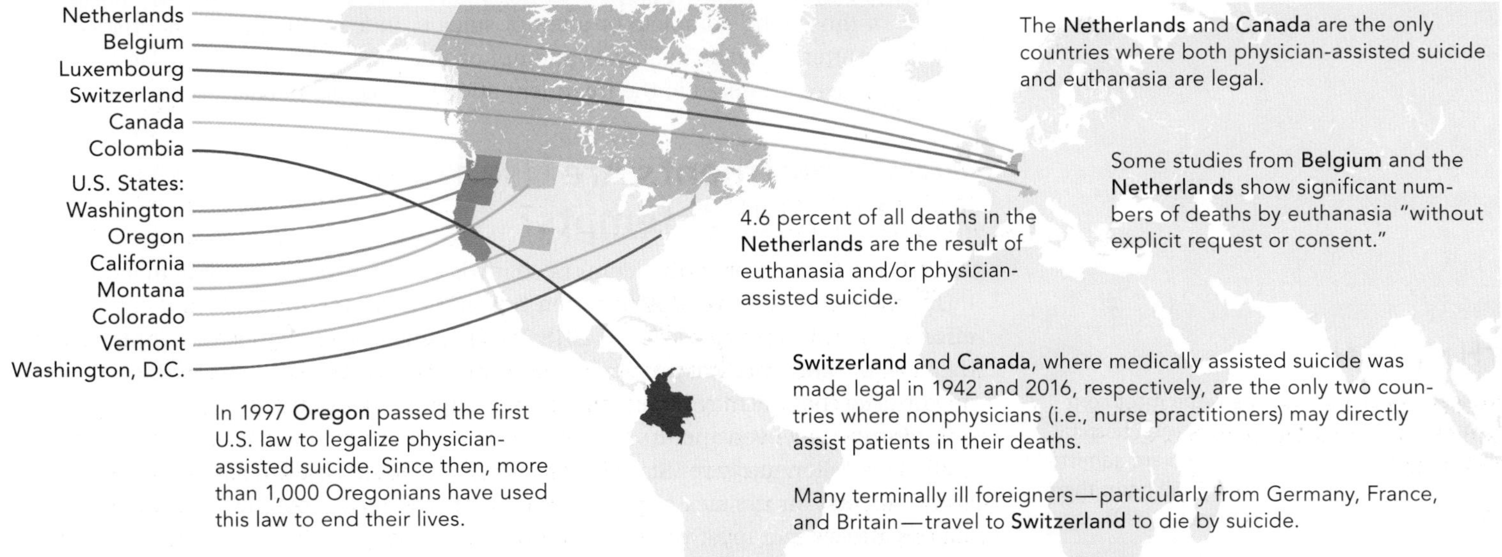

The **Netherlands** and **Canada** are the only countries where both physician-assisted suicide and euthanasia are legal.

Some studies from **Belgium** and the **Netherlands** show significant numbers of deaths by euthanasia "without explicit request or consent."

4.6 percent of all deaths in the **Netherlands** are the result of euthanasia and/or physician-assisted suicide.

Switzerland and **Canada**, where medically assisted suicide was made legal in 1942 and 2016, respectively, are the only two countries where nonphysicians (i.e., nurse practitioners) may directly assist patients in their deaths.

Many terminally ill foreigners—particularly from Germany, France, and Britain—travel to **Switzerland** to die by suicide.

In 1997 **Oregon** passed the first U.S. law to legalize physician-assisted suicide. Since then, more than 1,000 Oregonians have used this law to end their lives.

(Quill & Battin, 2018; Emanuel, 2017; Emanuel et al., 2016; Onwuteaka-Philipsen et al., 2012; Schadenberg, 2012; Thomasson, 2012)

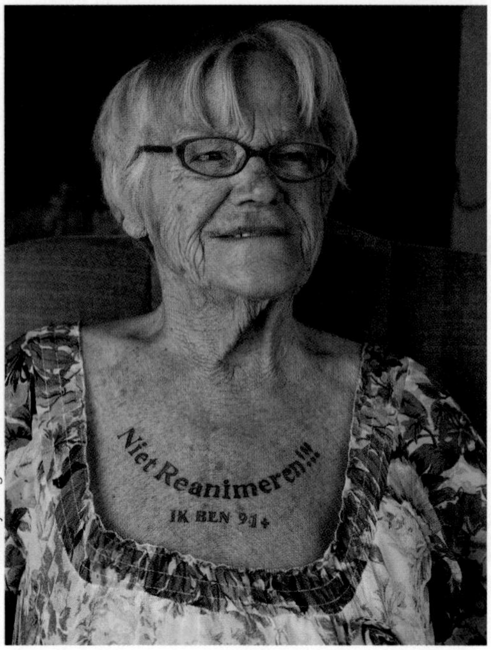

Michel Porro/Getty Images

A right to die? Although she has not tried to end her life, Nel Bolten, a resident of the Netherlands, recently brought attention to the right-to-die debate when she had her chest tattooed with these words (which mean "Do not resuscitate. I am 91 plus"). The Dutch health minister has confirmed that the tattoo is a legally binding declaration in that country, where euthanasia and physician-assisted suicide are permitted.

receiving treatment for their depressive disorders (Kiosses et al., 2017; Draper, 2014). In fact, research suggests that treating depression in older persons helps reduce their risk of suicide markedly.

The suicide rate among the elderly in the United States is lower in some minority groups (Heron, 2016). Although American Indians have the highest overall suicide rate, for example, the rate among elderly American Indians is relatively low. The aged are held in high esteem by American Indians and are looked to for the wisdom and experience they have acquired over the years, and this may help account for their low suicide rate. Such high regard is in sharp contrast to the loss of status often experienced by elderly non-Hispanic white Americans.

Similarly, the suicide rate is only one-quarter as high among elderly African Americans as among elderly non-Hispanic white Americans (CDC, 2016). One reason for this low suicide rate may be the pressures faced by African Americans, of whom it has been said: "only the strongest survive" (Seiden, 1981). Those who reach an advanced age often have overcome significant adversity, and many feel proud of what they have accomplished. Because reaching old age is not in itself a significant achievement for non-Hispanic white Americans, their attitude toward aging may be more negative. Another possible explanation is that aged African Americans have managed to overcome or reduce the feelings of indignation that prompt many suicides in younger African Americans.

...SUMMING UP

IS SUICIDE LINKED TO AGE? The likelihood of suicide varies with age. It is uncommon among children, although it has been rising in that group during the past several decades. Adolescent suicide has been linked to clinical depression, anger, impulsiveness, major stress, and adolescent life itself. Suicide attempts by this age group are numerous. The rate of suicide among American Indian teens is twice as high as that among non-Hispanic white American teens and three times as high as those of African, Hispanic, and Asian American teens.

In Western societies, the elderly are more likely to end their lives than people in most other age groups. The loss of health, friends, control, and status may produce feelings of hopelessness, loneliness, depression, or inevitability in this age group.

Treatment and Suicide

Treatment of suicidal people falls into two major categories: *treatment after suicide has been attempted* and *suicide prevention*. Treatment may also be beneficial to relatives and friends of those who complete or attempt suicide. Indeed, their feelings of loss, guilt, and anger after a suicide fatality or attempt can be intense (Fouet, 2017). However, the discussion here is limited to the treatment afforded suicidal people themselves.

What Treatments Are Used After Suicide Attempts?

After a suicide attempt, most victims need medical care. Close to one-half million people in the United States are admitted to a hospital each year for injuries resulting from efforts to harm themselves (AFSP, 2018, 2014). Some are left with severe injuries, brain damage, or other medical problems. Once the physical damage is treated, psychotherapy or drug therapy may begin, on either an inpatient or outpatient basis.

Unfortunately, even after trying to kill themselves, many suicidal people fail to receive systematic follow-up care (Stanley et al., 2015). In some cases, health care professionals are at fault for the lack of follow-up care. In others, the person who has attempted suicide refuses therapy (Spirito et al., 2011).

#

#HospitalAlert

Suicidal behavior or thinking is the most common reason for admission to a mental hospital. Around two-thirds of patients who are admitted have aroused concern that they will harm themselves (Miret et al., 2011; Jacobson, 1999).

The goals of therapy for those who have attempted suicide are to keep the individuals alive, reduce their psychological pain, help them achieve a nonsuicidal state of mind, provide them with hope, and guide them to develop better ways of handling stress (Sun et al., 2018). Studies indicate that people who receive therapy after their suicide attempts have a lower risk of future suicide attempts and deaths than do attempters who do not receive such therapy (Schreiber & Culpepper, 2018; Kennebeck & Bonin, 2017). Various therapies have been employed, including drug, psychodynamic, cognitive-behavioral, group, and family therapies.

Research indicates that cognitive-behavioral therapy may be particularly helpful (Asarnow et al., 2017; Mewton & Andrews, 2016). When clients are suicidal, this approach focuses largely on identifying and changing the painful thoughts, sense of hopelessness, dichotomous thinking, poor coping skills, weak problem-solving abilities, and other cognitive and behavioral features that characterize suicidal people. Applying the principles of *mindfulness-based* cognitive-behavioral therapy (see pages 53 and 110), the therapists may also guide the clients to *accept* many of the negative thoughts that keep streaming through their minds rather than try to eliminate them. Acceptance of this kind is expected to increase the clients' tolerance of psychological distress. All such treatment features are particularly prominent in a new-wave cognitive-behavioral approach called *dialectical behavior therapy* (*DBT*), which is being used increasingly in cases of suicidal thinking and attempts. You will be reading about DBT in Chapter 13, Personality Disorders.

Lawrence Migdale/Pix

The power of respect Elderly people are held in high esteem in many traditional societies because of the store of knowledge they have accumulated. Perhaps not so coincidentally, suicides among the elderly seem to be less common in these cultures than in those of many industrialized nations.

What Is Suicide Prevention?

During the past half-century, emphasis around the world has shifted from suicide treatment to suicide prevention. In some respects this change is most appropriate: the last opportunity to keep many potential suicide victims alive comes before their first attempt.

The first **suicide prevention program** in the United States was founded in Los Angeles in 1955; the first in England, called the *Samaritans,* was started in 1953. There are now hundreds of suicide prevention centers in the United States and England. In addition, many of today's mental health centers, hospital emergency rooms, pastoral counseling centers, and poison control centers include suicide prevention programs among their services.

There are also hundreds of *suicide hotlines,* 24-hour-a-day telephone services, in the United States. Callers reach a counselor, typically a *paraprofessional*—a person trained in counseling but without a formal degree—who provides services under the supervision of a mental health professional.

Suicide prevention programs and hotlines respond to suicidal people as individuals *in crisis*—that is, under great stress, unable to cope, feeling threatened or hurt, and interpreting their situations as unchangeable. Thus the programs offer **crisis intervention:** they try to help suicidal people see their situations more accurately, make better decisions, act more constructively, and overcome their crises. Because crises can occur at any time, the centers advertise their hotlines and also welcome people who walk in without appointments. A growing number of centers also offer their services through modalities such as text messaging and Internet chat (Predmore et al., 2017; Nauert, 2016).

One nonprofit service, the Crisis Text Line, has been offering text counseling since 2013, in partnership with a number of hotlines across the United States (Greenberg, 2018; Lublin, 2014). In the first half year of operation, it exchanged nearly a million texts with 19,000 teenagers, with only minimal advertising, and by 2017 it had processed a

suicide prevention program A program that tries to identify people who are at risk of killing themselves and to offer them crisis intervention.

crisis intervention A treatment approach that tries to help people in a psychological crisis to view their situation more accurately, make better decisions, act more constructively, and overcome the crisis.

total of 28 million texts. As you read earlier, Facebook and Google now link suicidal users or friends and relatives of suicidal persons to this service (Guynn, 2017).

What limitations or problems might result from attempts to prevent suicides by the use of texting?

Some prevention centers and hotlines reach out to particular suicidal populations. The *Trevor Lifeline,* for example, is a nationwide, around-the-clock hotline available for LGBTQ teenagers who are thinking about suicide. This hotline is one of several services offered by the *Trevor Project,* a wide-reaching organization dedicated to providing support, guidance, and information and to promoting acceptance of LGBTQ teens.

Today, suicide prevention takes place not only at prevention centers and hotlines but also in therapists' offices. A number of guidelines have been developed to help therapists effectively uncover, assess, prevent, and treat suicidal thinking and behavior in their daily work (de Beurs et al., 2015).

Although specific techniques vary from therapist to therapist and from prevention center to prevention center, the approach developed originally by the Los Angeles Suicide Prevention Center continues to reflect the goals and techniques of many clinicians and organizations. During the initial contact at the center, the counselor has several tasks:

Working with suicide After persuading this man to not jump to his death, California Highway Patrol officers help him back over a rail of the Golden Gate Bridge. Police departments across the world typically provide special crisis intervention training so that officers can develop the skills to help suicidal individuals.

John Storey/San Francisco Chronicle/Polaris

Establish a Positive Relationship As callers must trust counselors in order to confide in them and follow their suggestions, counselors try to set a positive and comfortable tone for the discussion. They convey that they are listening, understanding, interested, nonjudgmental, and available.

Understand and Clarify the Problem Counselors first try to understand the full scope of the caller's crisis and then help the person see the crisis in clear and constructive terms. In particular, they try to help callers see the central issues and the transient nature of their crises and recognize the alternatives to suicide.

Assess Suicide Potential Crisis workers at the Los Angeles Suicide Prevention Center fill out a questionnaire, often called a *lethality scale,* to estimate the caller's potential for suicide. It helps them determine the degree of stress the caller is under, the caller's relevant personality characteristics, how detailed the suicide plan is, the severity of symptoms, and the coping resources available to the caller.

Assess and Mobilize the Caller's Resources Although they may view themselves as ineffectual, helpless, and alone, people who are suicidal usually have many strengths and resources, including relatives and friends. It is the counselor's job to recognize, point out, and activate those resources.

Formulate a Plan Together the crisis worker and caller develop a plan of action. In essence, they are agreeing on a way out of the crisis, an alternative to suicidal action. Most plans include a series of follow-up counseling sessions over the next few days or weeks, either in person at the center or by phone. Each plan also requires the caller to take certain actions and make certain changes in his or her personal life. Counselors usually negotiate a *no-suicide contract* with the caller—a promise not to attempt suicide, or at least a promise to reestablish contact if the caller again considers suicide. Although such contracts are popular, their effectiveness has been called into question in recent years (Schreiber & Culpepper, 2018). In addition, if callers are in the midst of a suicide attempt, counselors try to find out their whereabouts and get medical help to them immediately.

Although crisis intervention may be sufficient treatment for some suicidal people, longer-term therapy is needed for most. If a crisis intervention center does not offer this kind of therapy, its counselors will refer the clients elsewhere.

Yet another way to help prevent suicide may be to reduce the public's access to particularly lethal and common means of suicide through measures such as gun control, safer medications, better bridge barriers, and car emission controls (Sinyor et al., 2019;

Kevin Mazur/Getty Images for NARAS

Life-saving performance In a powerful moment at the 2018 Grammy Awards, rapper Logic (center) performs his song "1-800-273-8255," flanked by singer-songwriters Khalid and Alessia Cara and joined onstage by individuals personally affected by suicide. The title of the song is the phone number of the National Suicide Prevention Lifeline. Help-seeking phone calls and Web site visits to the suicide prevention organization tripled during the hours following this performance. Similarly, the organization had previously experienced a 50 percent increase in calls after Logic performed the song at the MTV Video Music Awards, and it had received the second-most calls in its history the day the song was released.

Anestis & Houtsma, 2018; Zalsman et al., 2016). In the 1990s, for example, Canada passed a law restricting the availability of and access to certain firearms. Since then, there has been a decrease in firearm suicides across the country.

Do Suicide Prevention Programs Work?

It is difficult for researchers to measure the effectiveness of suicide prevention programs. There are many kinds of programs, each with its own procedures and each serving populations that vary in number, age, and the like. Communities with high suicide risk factors, such as a high elderly population or economic problems, may continue to have higher suicide rates than other communities regardless of the effectiveness of their local prevention centers.

Do suicide prevention centers reduce the number of suicides in a community? Clinical researchers do not know (Sanburn, 2013). Studies comparing local suicide rates before and after the establishment of community prevention centers have yielded different findings. Some find a decline in a community's suicide rates, others no change, and still others an increase (De Leo & Evans, 2004; Leenaars & Lester, 2004). Of course, even an increase may represent a positive impact, if it is lower than the larger society's overall increase in suicidal behavior.

Do suicidal people contact prevention centers? Apparently only a small percentage do (Sanburn, 2013). On the other hand, prevention programs do seem to reduce the number of suicides among those high-risk people who do call. One famous study identified 8,000 high-risk individuals who contacted the Los Angeles Suicide Prevention Center (Farberow & Litman, 1970). Approximately 2 percent of these callers later killed themselves, compared with the 6 percent suicide rate usually found in similar high-risk groups. Clearly, centers need to be more visible and available to people who are thinking of suicide. The growing number of advertisements and announcements on the Web, television, radio, and billboards indicate movement in this direction.

A key difficulty for suicide prevention programs is that they depend on accurate assessments of suicide risk, and accurate assessments are elusive (Nock et al., 2018). People who are suicidal do not necessarily recognize, admit to, or talk about their true feelings in discussions with professionals. With this in mind, some researchers are working to develop tools of suicide assessment that rely less on verbal self-reports and more on nonverbal behaviors, psychophysiological measures, brain scans, and the like.

#

#RecentRockSuicides

Chester Bennington, singer/songwriter (2017)

Chris Cornell, singer/songwriter/musician (2017)

Bob Welch, guitarist/singer/songwriter (2012)

Ronnie Montrose, guitarist (2012)

Mark Linkous, singer/songwriter/musician (2010)

Vic Chesnutt, singer/songwriter (2009)

Johnny Lee Jackson, rapper (2008)

Brad Delp, singer (2007)

Vince Welnick, keyboardist (2006)

One alternative assessment approach is the *Self-Injury Implicit Association Test*, developed by researcher Matthew Nock. Rather than asking people if they plan to attempt suicide, this cognitive test simply instructs them to pair various suicide-related words (for example, "dead," "lifeless," "suicide") with words that are personally relevant ("I," "myself," "mine") and with words that are not personally relevant ("they," "them," "other"). It turns out that individuals who are inclined to attempt suicide pair the suicide-related words with personally relevant words much more quickly than with nonpersonally relevant words. In a number of studies, this test has detected and predicted past and future suicide behavior more accurately than traditional self-report assessment scales (Barnes et al., 2017; Glenn et al., 2017). Needless to say, this promising approach to assessment has captured the attention of many suicide researchers and clinicians.

Why might some schools be reluctant to offer suicide education programs, especially if they have never experienced a suicide attempt by one of their students?

While the field awaits more accurate assessment tools and more effective interventions, many theorists believe that public education about suicide is the ultimate form of prevention—and a number of *suicide education programs* have emerged. Most of these programs take place in schools and concentrate on students and their teachers (SAMHSA, 2017; Zalsman et al., 2016). There are also a growing number of online sites that provide education about suicide—targeting troubled persons, their family members, and friends. These offerings agree with the following statement by Shneidman:

> *The primary prevention of suicide lies in education. The route is through teaching one another and . . . the public that suicide can happen to anyone, that there are verbal and behavioral clues that can be looked for . . . and that help is available. . . .*
>
> *In the last analysis, the prevention of suicide is everybody's business.*
>
> *(Shneidman, 1985, p. 238)*

... SUMMING UP

TREATMENT AND SUICIDE Treatment may follow a suicide attempt. When it does, therapists try to help the person achieve a nonsuicidal state of mind and develop better ways of handling stress and solving problems.

Over the past half-century, emphasis has shifted to suicide prevention. Suicide prevention programs include 24-hour-a-day hotlines and walk-in centers staffed largely by paraprofessionals. Many of today's centers also offer services through text messaging and Internet chat. During their initial contact with a suicidal person, counselors try to establish a positive relationship, understand and clarify the problem, assess the potential for suicide, assess and mobilize the caller's resources, and formulate a plan for overcoming the crisis. Beyond such crisis intervention, most suicidal people also need longer-term therapy. In a still broader attempt at prevention, suicide education programs for the public are on the increase.

Psychological and Biological Insights Lag Behind

Once a mysterious and hidden problem, hardly acknowledged by the public and barely investigated by professionals, suicide today is the focus of much attention. During the past 50 years in particular, investigators have learned a great deal about this life-or-death problem.

In contrast to most other problems covered in this textbook, suicide has received much more examination from the sociocultural model than from any other. Sociocultural theorists have, for example, highlighted the importance of societal change and stress, national and religious affiliation, marital status, gender, race, and the mass

#TheirWords

"I am extremely thankful that I did not take my own life."

Michael Phelps, 2018, decorated Olympic swimmer, discussing his struggles with depression media. The insights and information gathered by psychological and biological researchers have been more limited.

Although sociocultural factors certainly shed light on the general background and triggers of suicide, they typically leave us unable to predict that a given person will attempt suicide. Clinicians do not yet fully understand why some people kill themselves while others in similar circumstances manage to find better ways of addressing their problems. Psychological and biological insights must catch up to the sociocultural insights if clinicians are truly to explain and understand suicide.

At the same time, the growth in the amount of research on suicide offers great promise. And perhaps most promising of all, clinicians are now enlisting the public in the fight against this problem. They are calling for broader public education about suicide—for programs aimed at both young and old. It is reasonable to expect that the current commitment will lead to a better understanding of suicide and to more successful interventions. Such goals are of importance to everyone. Although suicide itself is typically a lonely and desperate act, the impact of such acts is very broad indeed.

...Key Terms

parasuicide, p. 212
suicidal behavior disorder, p. 212
suicide, p. 212
death seeker, p. 214
death initiator, p. 214
death ignorer, p. 214
death darer, p. 214
subintentional death, p. 214
nonsuicidal self injury, p. 214
retrospective analysis, p. 215
hopelessness, p. 218
dichotomous thinking, p. 218
postvention, p. 220
Thanatos, p. 222
egoistic suicide, p. 222
altruistic suicide, p. 222
anomic suicide, p. 223
interpersonal theory of suicide, p. 223
serotonin, p. 224
brain-circuit dysfunction, p. 224
suicide prevention program, p. 231
suicide hotline, p. 231
paraprofessional, p. 231
crisis intervention, p. 231
Self-Injury Implicit Association Test, p. 234
suicide education program, p. 234

...Quick Quiz

1. Define suicide and subintentional death. Describe four different kinds of people who attempt suicide. What is nonsuicidal self-injury? *pp. 212–215*
2. What techniques do researchers use to study suicide? *p. 215*
3. How do statistics on suicide vary according to country, religion, gender, marital status, and race? *pp. 215–217*
4. What kinds of immediate and long-term stressors have been linked to suicide? *pp. 217–218*
5. What other conditions or events may help trigger suicidal acts? *pp. 218–220*
6. How do psychodynamic, sociocultural (including work by Emile Durkheim and Thomas Joiner), and biological theorists explain suicide, and how well supported are their theories? *pp. 221–224*
7. Compare the risk, rate, and causes of suicide among children, adolescents, and elderly persons. *pp. 225–230*
8. How do theorists explain the high rate of suicide attempts by adolescents and young adults? *p. 227*
9. Describe the nature and goals of treatment given to people after they have attempted suicide. Do such people often receive this treatment? *pp. 230–231*
10. Describe the principles of suicide prevention programs. What procedures are used by counselors in these programs? How effective are the programs? *pp. 231–234*

Visit ***LaunchPad***
to access the e-Book, Clinical Choices, videos, activities, and LearningCurve, as well as study aids including flashcards, FAQs, and research exercises.

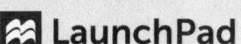

LaunchPad

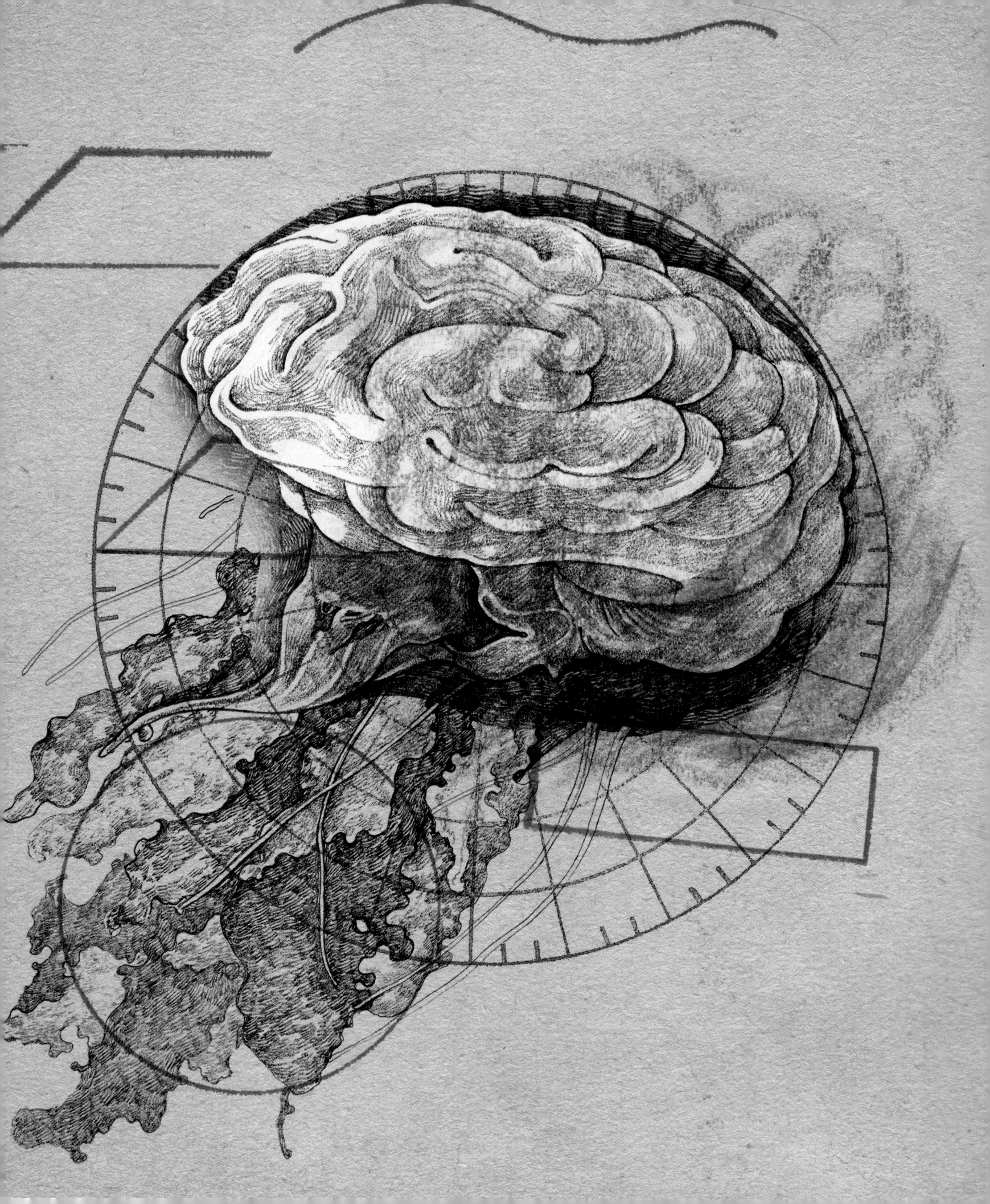

CHAPTER 8

Disorders Featuring Somatic Symptoms

It was Wednesday. The big day. Midterms in history and physics back to back, beginning at 11:30, and an oral presentation in psych at 3:30. Jarell had been preparing for, and dreading, this day for weeks, calling it "D-Day" to his friends. He had been up until 3:30 A.M. the night before, studying, trying to nail everything down. It seemed like he had fallen asleep only minutes ago, yet here it was 9:30 A.M. and the killer day was under way.

As soon as he woke, Jarell felt a tight pain grip his stomach. He also noticed buzzing in his ears, a lightheadedness, and even aches throughout his body. He wasn't surprised, given the day he was about to face. One test might bring a few butterflies of anxiety; two and a presentation were probably good for a platoon of dragonflies.

As he tried to get going, however, Jarell began to suspect that this was more than butterflies. His stomach pain soon turned to spasms, and his lightheadedness became outright dizziness. He could barely make it to the bathroom without falling. Thoughts of breakfast made him nauseous. He knew he couldn't keep anything down.

Jarell began to worry, even panic. This was hardly the best way to face what was in store for him today. He tried to shake it off, but the symptoms stayed. Finally, his roommate convinced him that he had better go to a doctor. At 10:30, just an hour before the first exam, he entered the big brick building called "Student Health." He felt embarrassed, like a wimp, but what could he do? Persevering and taking two tests under these conditions wouldn't prove anything—except maybe that he was foolish.

Psychological factors may contribute to somatic, or bodily, illnesses in a variety of ways. The physician who sees Jarell has some possibilities to sort out. Jarell could be *faking* his pain and dizziness to avoid taking some tough tests. Alternatively, he may be *imagining* his illness, that is, faking to himself. Or he could be *overreacting* to his pain and dizziness. Then again, his physical symptoms could be both real and significant, yet triggered by *stress:* whenever he feels extreme pressure, such as a person can feel before an important test, Jarell's gastric juices may become more active and irritate his intestines, and his blood pressure may rise and cause him to become dizzy. Finally, he may be coming down with the flu. Even this "purely medical" problem, however, could be linked to psychological factors. Perhaps weeks of constant worry about the exams and presentation have weakened Jarell's body so that he was not able to fight off the flu virus. Whatever the diagnosis, Jarell's state of mind is affecting his body. The physician's view of the role played by psychological factors will in turn affect the treatment Jarell receives.

You have observed throughout the book that psychological disorders frequently have physical causes. Dysfunctional brain circuits and abnormal neurotransmitter activity, for example, contribute to generalized anxiety disorder, panic disorder, and posttraumatic stress disorder. Is it surprising, then, that bodily illnesses may have psychological causes? Today's clinicians recognize the wisdom of Socrates' assertion made many centuries ago: "You should not treat body without soul."

The idea that psychological factors may contribute to somatic illnesses has ancient roots, yet it had few proponents before the twentieth century. It was particularly unpopular during the Renaissance, when medicine began to be a physical science and scientists became committed to the pursuit of objective "fact" (Conti, 2014). At that time, the

Bruce Eric Kaplan/The New Yorker Collection/TheCartoon Bank

"My back is fine. My mind went out."

mind was considered the territory of priests and philosophers, not of physicians and scientists. By the seventeenth century, the French philosopher René Descartes went so far as to claim that the mind, or soul, is totally separate from the body—a position called *mind-body dualism.* Over the course of the twentieth century, however, numerous studies convinced medical and clinical researchers that psychological factors such as stress, worry, and perhaps even unconscious needs can contribute in major ways to bodily illness.

DSM-5 lists a number of psychological disorders in which bodily symptoms or concerns are the primary features of the disorders. These include *factitious disorder,* in which patients intentionally produce or feign physical symptoms; *conversion disorder,* which is characterized by medically unexplained physical symptoms that affect voluntary motor or sensory functioning; *somatic symptom disorder,* in which people become disproportionately concerned, distressed, and disrupted by bodily symptoms; *illness anxiety disorder,* in which people who are anxious about their health become preoccupied with the notion that they are seriously ill despite the absence of bodily symptoms; and *psychological factors affecting other medical conditions,* disorders in which psychological factors adversely affect a person's general medical condition. ■

Factitious Disorder

Like Jarell, people who become physically sick usually go to a physician. Sometimes, however, the physician cannot find a medical cause for the problem and may suspect that other factors are involved. Perhaps the patient is *malingering*—intentionally feigning illness to achieve some external gain, such as financial compensation or time off from work.

Alternatively, a patient may intentionally produce or feign physical symptoms from a wish to be a patient; that is, the motivation for assuming the sick role may be the role itself (Irwin & Bursch, 2018). Physicians would then decide that the patient is manifesting **factitious disorder** (see **Table 8-1**). Consider, for example, the symptoms of Adia, a patient with bacteremia—presence of bacteria in the blood, which can, if not corrected, lead to the life-threatening condition called sepsis. As you will see, the medical team's handling of Adia's right to privacy raises ethical issues, but the case itself illustrates the features of factitious disorder.

[Adia] was referred to [the medical center] for evaluation of recurrent urinary tract infections and bacteremia. . . . She also had a skin disorder with blisters. An extensive workup showed . . . a completely normal genitourinary tract. . . .

Based on [Adia's unexplained] symptoms . . . , one of the several doctors on this case suspected that the patient was inducing her own illness, and he decided to secretly search her personal possessions. . . .

While the patient was having an x-ray, her room was searched. Her purse contained a Petri dish with growing bacterial colonies, as well as needles, a syringe, and a tourniquet. The . . . Petri dish [was] replaced. Later that day, the patient was asked whether she might be harming herself by injection [of bacteria into her body]. She denied this, saying that she wanted to get better. Still later that day, the doctor told the patient that he knew she had some incriminating items in her purse. She then opened her purse so the doctor could see inside, and the items were apparently no longer present. To prove her point, the patient

factitious disorder A disorder in which a person feigns or induces physical symptoms, typically for the purpose of assuming the role of a sick person.

turned her purse upside down. At that point, one needle and a syringe fell out, which she had apparently overlooked when she returned from her x-ray and suspected that someone had searched her purse. The patient was upset about the room search but not visibly angry. She readily agreed to see a psychiatrist but continued to deny self-injection.

The next day, the patient tearfully confessed that she had had bacteriological materials in her purse, but she said she used them only to aspirate and culture some blisters on her skin. She still denied self-injection with bacteria and said she wanted the doctors to "keep looking for the cause of my problems."

(Savino & Fordtran, 2006, pp. 201–202)

Factitious disorder is known popularly as *Munchausen syndrome,* a label derived from the exploits of Baron von Münchhausen, an eighteenth-century cavalry officer who journeyed from tavern to tavern in Europe telling fantastical tales about his supposed military adventures (Ayoub, 2010). People with factitious disorder often go to extremes to create the appearance of illness (APA, 2013). Many give themselves medications secretly. Some, like the woman just described, inject drugs to cause bleeding, infections, or other problems (Yates & Feldman, 2017). Still others use laxatives to produce chronic diarrhea. High fevers are especially easy to create. In studies of patients with a prolonged mysterious fever, 9 percent were eventually diagnosed with factitious disorder (Irwin & Bursch, 2018).

People with factitious disorder often research their supposed ailments and are impressively knowledgeable about medicine. Many eagerly undergo painful testing or treatment, even surgery. When confronted with evidence that their symptoms are factitious, they typically deny the charges and leave the hospital; they may enter another hospital the same day.

Clinical researchers have had a hard time determining the prevalence of factitious disorder, since patients with the disorder hide the true nature of their problem (Kapfhammer, 2017). Overall, the pattern appears to be more common in women than men. Men, however, may more often have severe cases. The disorder usually begins during early adulthood.

Factitious disorder seems to be particularly common among people who (1) received extensive treatment for a medical problem as children, (2) carry a grudge against the medical profession, or (3) have worked as a nurse, laboratory technician, or medical aide (Yates & Feldman, 2017). A number have poor social support, few enduring social relationships, and little family life (Irwin & Bursch, 2018; McDermott et al., 2012).

The precise causes of factitious disorder are not understood, although clinical reports have pointed to factors such as depression, unsupportive parental relationships during childhood, and extreme needs for attention and/or social support that are not otherwise available (Irwin & Bursch, 2018). Nor have clinicians been able to develop dependably effective treatments for this disorder.

Psychotherapists and medical practitioners often report feelings of annoyance or anger toward people with factitious disorder, feeling that these people are, at the very least, wasting their time (Jafferany et al., 2018; Weis et al., 2016). Yet people with the disorder feel they have no control over the problem, and they often experience great distress.

In a related pattern, *factitious disorder imposed on another,* known popularly as *Munchausen syndrome by proxy,* parents or caretakers make up or produce physical illnesses in their children, leading in some cases to repeated painful diagnostic tests, medication, and surgery (Roesler & Jenny, 2018) (see **Table 8-1** again). If the children are removed from their parents and placed in the care of others, their symptoms disappear (see ***PsychWatch*** on the next page).

#SeekingRelief

Research suggests that 17 percent of patients under the care of family physicians display physical symptoms that have no apparent physical cause (Greenberg, 2016).

TABLE: 8-1

Dx Checklist

Factitious Disorder Imposed on Self
1. False creation of physical psychological symptoms, or deceptive production of injury or disease, even without external rewards for such ailments.
2. Presentation of oneself as ill, damaged, or hurt.
Factitious Disorder Imposed on Another
1. False creation of physical or psychological symptoms, or deceptive production of injury or disease, in another person, even without external rewards for such ailments.
2. Presentation of another person (victim) as ill, damaged, or hurt.

Information from: APA, 2013.

PSYCHWATCH

Munchausen Syndrome by Proxy

Tanya, a mere 8 years old, had been hospitalized 127 times over the past five years and undergone 28 different medical procedures—from removal of her spleen to exploratory surgery of her intestines. Two months ago, her mother was arrested, charged with child endangerment. When Tanya's grandmother gently tried to talk to the girl about her mother's arrest (or, as she put it, "Mommy's going away"), Tanya was upset and confused.

"I miss Mommy so much. She's the best person in the world. She spent all her time with me in the hospital. They say Mommy was making me feel bad, putting bad stuff in my tube. But there's no way Mommy made me feel that bad."

Convalescent, 1867, by Frank Holl

Cases like Tanya's have horrified the public and called attention to *Munchausen syndrome by proxy.* This form of factitious disorder is caused by a caregiver who uses various techniques to induce symptoms in a child—giving the child drugs, tampering with medications, contaminating a feeding tube, or even smothering the child, for example (Roesler & Jenny, 2018; Akin et al., 2016). The illness can take almost any form, but the most common symptoms are bleeding, seizures, asthma, comas, diarrhea, vomiting, "accidental" poisonings, infections, fevers, and sudden infant death syndrome (Wittkowski et al., 2017).

Between 6 and 30 percent of the victims of Munchausen syndrome by proxy die as a result of their symptoms, and 8 percent of those who survive are permanently disfigured or physically impaired (Braham et al., 2017; Ayoub, 2006). Psychological, educational, and physical development are also affected (Bass & Glaser, 2014).

The syndrome is very hard to diagnose and may be more common than clinicians once thought (Roesler & Jenny, 2018). The parent (usually the mother) seems to be so devoted and caring that others sympathize with and admire her. Yet the physical problems disappear when the child and parent are separated. In many cases, siblings of the sick child are also victimized (Braham et al., 2017).

Should society treat or punish those parents who produce Munchausen syndrome by proxy in their children?

What kind of parent carefully inflicts pain and illness on her own child? The typical Munchausen mother is emotionally needy: she craves the attention and praise she receives for her devoted care of her sick child (Anderson, Feldman, & Bryce, 2018; Ashraf & Thevasagayam, 2014). She may have little social support outside the medical system. Often the mothers have a medical background of some kind—perhaps having worked formerly in a doctor's office (Yates & Bass, 2017). A number have medically unexplained physical problems of their own (Roesler & Jenny, 2018). Typically, they deny their actions, even in the face of clear evidence, and initially may refuse to undergo therapy.

Law enforcement authorities approach Munchausen syndrome by proxy as a crime—a carefully planned form of child abuse (Irwin & Bursch, 2018). They almost always require that the child be separated from the mother (Koetting, 2015; Ayoub, 2010, 2006). At the same time, a parent who resorts to such actions is seriously disturbed and greatly in need of clinical help. In the majority of cases, particularly those that are of moderate or modest severity, treatment makes it possible for the parent to be reintegrated into the family (Roesler & Jenny, 2018). Currently, clinical researchers and practitioners are working to develop still clearer insights and more effective treatments for such parents and their young victims.

9... SUMMING UP

FACTITIOUS DISORDER People with factitious disorder feign or induce physical disorders, typically for the purpose of assuming the role of a sick person. In a related pattern, factitious disorder imposed on another, a parent fabricates or induces a physical illness in his or her child.

Conversion Disorder and Somatic Symptom Disorder

When a bodily ailment has an excessive and disproportionate impact on the person, has no apparent medical cause, or is inconsistent with known medical diseases, physicians may suspect a *conversion disorder* or a *somatic symptom disorder*. Consider the plight of Brian:

conversion disorder A disorder in which bodily symptoms affect voluntary motor and sensory functions, but the symptoms are inconsistent with known medical diseases.

Brian was spending Saturday sailing with his wife, Helen. The water was rough but well within what they considered safe limits. They were having a wonderful time and really didn't notice that the sky was getting darker, the wind blowing harder, and the sailboat becoming more difficult to control. After a few hours of sailing, they found themselves far from shore in the middle of a powerful and dangerous storm.

The storm intensified very quickly. Brian had trouble controlling the sailboat amidst the high winds and wild waves. He and Helen tried to put on the safety jackets they had neglected to wear earlier, but the boat turned over before they were finished. Brian, the better swimmer of the two, was able to swim back to the overturned sailboat, grab the side, and hold on for dear life, but Helen simply could not overcome the rough waves and reach the boat. As Brian watched in horror and disbelief, his wife disappeared from view.

After a time, the storm began to lose its strength. Brian managed to right the sailboat and sail back to shore. Finally he reached safety, but the personal consequences of this storm were just beginning. The next days were filled with pain and further horror: the Coast Guard finding Helen's body . . . texts, e-mails, and conversations with family members and friends . . . self-blame . . . grief . . . and more. Compounding this horror, the accident had left Brian with a severe physical impairment—he could not walk properly. He first noticed this terrible impairment when he sailed the boat back to shore, right after the accident. As he tried to run from the sailboat to get help, he could hardly make his legs work. By the time he reached the nearby beach restaurant, all he could do was crawl. Two patrons had to lift him to a chair, and after he told his story and the authorities were alerted, he had to be taken to a hospital.

At first Brian and the hospital physician assumed that he must have been hurt during the accident. One by one, however, the hospital tests revealed nothing—no broken bones, no spinal damage, nothing. Nothing that could explain such severe impairment.

By the following morning, the weakness in his legs had become near paralysis. Because the physicians could not pin down the nature of his injuries, they decided to keep his activities to a minimum. He was not allowed to talk long with the police. To his deep regret, he was not even permitted to attend Helen's funeral.

The mystery deepened over the following days and weeks. As Brian's paralysis continued, he became more and more withdrawn, unable to see more than a few friends and family members and unable to take care of the many unpleasant tasks attached to Helen's death. He could not bring himself to return to work or get on with his life. Texting, e-mailing, and phone conversations slowly came to a halt. At most, he was able to go online and surf the Internet. Almost from the beginning, Brian's paralysis had left him self-absorbed and drained of emotion, unable to look back and unable to move forward.

Conversion Disorder

Eventually, Brian received a diagnosis of **conversion disorder** (see **Table 8-2**). People with this disorder display physical symptoms that affect voluntary motor or sensory functioning, but the symptoms are inconsistent with known medical diseases (APA, 2013). In short, they have neurological-like symptoms—for example, paralysis, blindness, or loss of feeling—that have no neurological basis.

TABLE: 8-2

Dx Checklist

Conversion Disorder
1. Presence of at least one symptom or deficit that affects voluntary or sensory function.
2. Symptoms are found to be inconsistent with known neurological or medical disease.
3. Significant distress or impairment.

Information from: APA, 2013.

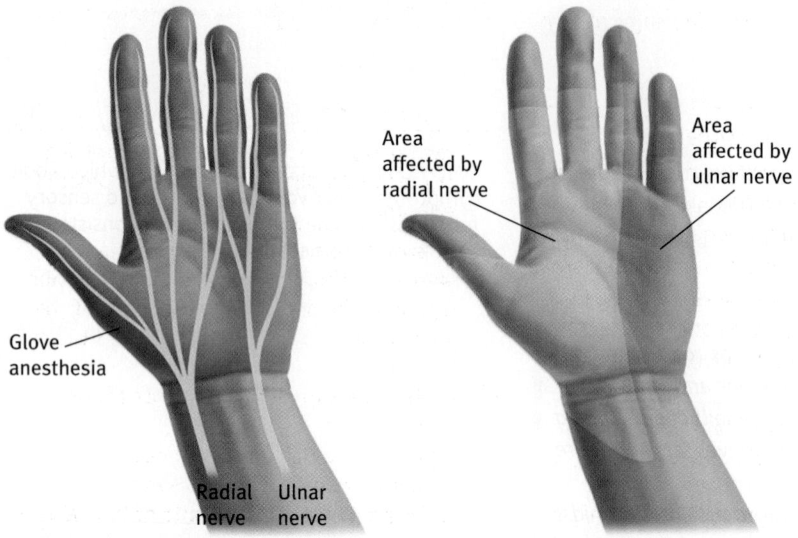

FIGURE 8-1

Glove Anesthesia

In this conversion symptom (left figure) the entire hand, extending from the fingertips to the wrist, becomes numb. Actual physical damage (right figure) to the ulnar nerve, in contrast, causes anesthesia in the ring finger and little finger and beyond the wrist partway up the arm; damage to the radial nerve causes loss of feeling only in parts of the ring, middle, and index fingers and the thumb and partway up the arm. (Information from: Gray, 1959.)

Conversion disorder often is hard, even for physicians, to distinguish from a genuine medical problem (Redinger et al., 2018; Tsui, Deptula, & Yuan, 2017). In fact, it is always possible that a diagnosis of conversion disorder is a mistake and that the patient's problem has an undetected neurological or other medical cause (Stone & Sharpe, 2018, 2017). Because conversion disorders are so similar to "genuine" medical ailments, physicians sometimes rely on oddities in the patient's medical picture to help distinguish the two (Tsui et al., 2017). The symptoms of a conversion disorder may, for example, be at odds with the way the nervous system is known to work. In a conversion symptom called *glove anesthesia,* numbness begins sharply at the wrist and extends evenly right to the fingertips. As **Figure 8-1** shows, real neurological damage is rarely as abrupt or evenly spread out.

The physical effects of a conversion disorder may also differ from those of the corresponding medical problem (Stone & Sharpe, 2018, 2017). For example, when paralysis from the waist down, or paraplegia, is caused by damage to the spinal cord, a person's leg muscles may *atrophy,* or waste away, unless physical therapy is applied. The muscles of people whose paralysis is the result of a conversion disorder, in contrast, do not usually atrophy. Perhaps those with a conversion disorder exercise their muscles without being aware that they are doing so. Similarly, people with conversion blindness have fewer accidents than people who are organically blind, an indication that they have at least some vision even if they are unaware of it.

Unlike people with factitious disorder, those with conversion disorder do not consciously want or purposely produce their symptoms. Like Brian, they almost always believe that their problems are genuinely medical. This pattern is called "conversion" disorder because clinical theorists used to believe that individuals with the disorder are converting psychological needs or conflicts into their neurological-like symptoms (Ding & Kanaan, 2017). Although some theorists still believe that conversion is at work in the disorder, others prefer alternative kinds of explanations, as you'll see later.

Conversion disorder usually begins between late childhood and young adulthood; it is diagnosed at least twice as often in women as in men (Raj et al., 2014). It often appears suddenly, at times of extreme stress. In some, but far from all, cases, conversion disorder lasts a matter of weeks (Stone & Sharpe, 2018, 2017). Some research suggests that people who develop the disorder tend to be generally suggestible (see ***MindTech*** on page 245); many are highly susceptible to hypnotic procedures, for example (Tsui et al., 2017). It is thought to be a rare problem, occurring in at most 5 of every 1,000 persons (Stone & Sharpe, 2018, 2017).

Somatic Symptom Disorder

People with **somatic symptom disorder** become excessively distressed, concerned, and anxious about bodily symptoms that they are experiencing, and their lives are greatly disrupted by those symptoms (APA, 2013) (see **Table 8-3**). The symptoms last longer but are less dramatic than those found in conversion disorder. In some cases, the somatic symptoms have no known cause; in others, the cause can be identified. Either way, the person's concerns are disproportionate to the seriousness of the bodily problems.

Two patterns of somatic symptom disorder have received particular attention. In one, sometimes called a *somatization pattern,* the individual experiences a large and varied number of bodily symptoms. In the other, called a *predominant pain pattern,* the person's primary bodily problem is the experience of pain.

somatic symptom disorder A disorder in which people become excessively distressed, concerned, and anxious about bodily symptoms they are experiencing, and their lives are disproportionately disrupted by the symptoms.

Somatization Pattern Sheila baffled medical specialists with the wide range of her symptoms:

> *Sheila reported having abdominal pain since age 17, necessitating exploratory surgery that yielded no specific diagnosis. She had several pregnancies, each with severe nausea, vomiting, and abdominal pain; she ultimately had a hysterectomy for a "tipped uterus." Since age 40 she had experienced dizziness and "blackouts," which she eventually was told might be multiple sclerosis or a brain tumor. She continued to be bedridden for extended periods of time, with weakness, blurred vision, and difficulty urinating. At age 43 she was worked up for a hiatal hernia because of complaints of bloating and intolerance of a variety of foods. She also had additional hospitalizations for neurological, hypertensive, and renal workups, all of which failed to reveal a definitive diagnosis.*
>
> *(Spitzer et al., 1994, 1981, pp. 185, 260)*

Like Sheila, people with a somatization pattern of somatic symptom disorder experience many long-lasting physical ailments—ailments that typically have little or no physical basis. This pattern, first described by Pierre Briquet in 1859, is also known as *Briquet's syndrome*. A sufferer's ailments often include pain symptoms (such as headaches or chest pain), gastrointestinal symptoms (such as nausea or diarrhea), sexual symptoms (such as erectile or menstrual difficulties), and neurological-type symptoms (such as double vision or paralysis).

People with a somatization pattern usually go from doctor to doctor in search of relief. They often describe their many symptoms in dramatic and exaggerated terms. Most also feel anxious and depressed (Witthöft, Gropalis, & Weck, 2018; Walentynowicz et al., 2017). The pattern typically lasts for many years, fluctuating over time but rarely disappearing completely without therapy (Greenberg, 2016; Abbey, 2005).

As many as 4 percent of all people in the United States may experience a somatization pattern in any given year, women much more commonly than men (Greenberg, 2016). The pattern often runs in families; as many as 20 percent of the close female relatives of women with the pattern also develop it. It usually begins between adolescence and young adulthood.

Predominant Pain Pattern If the primary feature of somatic symptom disorder is pain, the person is said to have a predominant pain pattern. Patients with conversion disorder or another pattern of somatic symptom disorder may also experience pain, but it is the key symptom in this pattern. The source of the pain may be known or unknown. Either way, the concerns and disruption produced by the pain are disproportionate to its severity and seriousness.

Although the precise prevalence has not been determined, this pattern appears to be fairly common (Witthöft et al., 2018; Cozzi et al., 2017). It may begin at any age, and women seem more likely than men to experience it. Often it develops after an accident or during an illness that has caused genuine pain, after which the pain takes on a life of its own. For example, Laura, a 36-year-old woman, reported pains that went far beyond the usual symptoms of her tubercular disease called sarcoidosis:

> *Before the operation I would have little joint pains, nothing that really bothered me that much. After the operation I was having severe pains in my chest and in my ribs, and those were the type of problems I'd been having after the operation, that I didn't have before. . . . I'd go to an emergency room at night, 11:00, 12:00, 1:00 or so. I'd take the medicine, and the next day it stopped hurting, and I'd go back again. In the meantime this is when I went to the other doctors, to complain about the same thing, to find out what was wrong; and they could never find out what was wrong with me either. . . .*

(continued on the next page)

TABLE: 8-3

Dx Checklist

Somatic Symptom Disorder
1. Person experiences at least one upsetting or repeatedly disruptive physical (somatic) symptom.
2. Person experiences an unreasonable number of thoughts, feelings, and behavior regarding the nature or implications of the physical symptoms, including one of the following: (a) Repeated, excessive thoughts about their seriousness. (b) Continual high anxiety about their nature or health implications. (c) Disproportionate amounts of time and energy spent on the symptoms or their health implications.
3. Physical symptoms usually continue to some degree for more than 6 months.

Information from: APA, 2013.

#AdditionalPain

32%	Percentage of low-income people with chronic knee or leg pain
19%	Percentage of high-income people with chronic knee or leg pain

(Information from: Anson, 2017; Brown, 2012)

#

#DiagnosticConfusion

In the past, whiplash was regularly misdiagnosed as a psychologically caused condition.

> *... At certain points when I go out or my husband and I go out, we have to leave early because I start hurting. . . . A lot of times I just won't do things because my chest is hurting for one reason or another. . . . Two months ago when the doctor checked me and another doctor looked at the x-rays, he said he didn't see any signs of the sarcoid then and that they were doing a study now, on blood and various things, to see if it was connected to sarcoid. . . .*
>
> *(Green, 1985, pp. 60–63)*

What Causes Conversion and Somatic Symptom Disorders?

For many years, conversion and somatic symptom disorders were referred to as *hysterical* disorders. This label was meant to convey the prevailing belief that excessive and uncontrolled emotions underlie the bodily symptoms found in these disorders.

Work by Ambroise-Auguste Liébault and Hippolyte Bernheim in the late nineteenth century helped foster the notion that such psychological factors were at the root of hysterical disorders. These researchers founded the Nancy School in Paris for the study and treatment of mental disorders. There they were able to produce hysterical symptoms in normal people—deafness, paralysis, blindness, and numbness—by hypnotic suggestion, and they could remove the symptoms by the same means (see Chapter 1). If hypnotic suggestion could both produce and reverse physical dysfunctions, they concluded, hysterical disorders might themselves be caused by psychological processes.

Today's leading explanations for conversion and somatic symptom disorders come from the psychodynamic, cognitive-behavioral, and multicultural models. None has received much research support, however, and the disorders are still poorly understood (Levenson, 2018; Stone & Sharpe, 2017).

The Psychodynamic View As you read in Chapter 1, Freud's theory of psychoanalysis began with his efforts to explain hysterical symptoms. Indeed, he was one of the few clinicians of his day to treat patients with these symptoms seriously, as people with genuine problems. After studying hypnosis in Paris, Freud became interested in the work of an older physician, Josef Breuer (1842–1925). Breuer had successfully used hypnosis to treat a woman he called Anna O., who suffered from hysterical deafness, disorganized speech, and paralysis (Ellenberger, 1972). On the basis of this and similar cases, Freud (1894) came to believe that hysterical disorders represented a *conversion* of underlying emotional conflicts into physical symptoms and concerns (Ding & Kanaan, 2017).

Electra complex goes awry Freud argued that a hysterical disorder may result when parents overreact to their daughter's early displays of affection for her father, by repeatedly punishing her, for example. The child may go on to exhibit sexual repression in adulthood and convert sexual feelings into physical ailments.

Hero Images/Getty Images

Observing that most of his patients with hysterical disorders were women, Freud centered his explanation of such disorders on the needs of girls during their *phallic stage* (ages 3 through 5). At that time in life, he believed, all girls develop a pattern of desires called the *Electra complex:* each girl experiences sexual feelings for her father and at the same time recognizes that she must compete with her mother for his affection. However, aware of her mother's more powerful position and of cultural taboos, the child typically represses her sexual feelings and rejects these early desires for her father.

Freud believed that if a child's parents overreact to her sexual feelings—with strong punishments, for example—the Electra conflict will be unresolved and the child may reexperience sexual anxiety throughout

MINDTECH

Can Social Media Spread "Mass Hysteria"?

In Chapter 1, you read about outbreaks during the Middle Ages of *mass madness,* also called *mass hysteria* or *mass psychogenic illness,* in which large numbers of people would share psychological or physical maladies that had no apparent cause (see pages 8–9). Periodic outbreaks of mysterious illnesses are not a thing of the past. In fact, the number of such cases currently seems to be on the increase (Loharikar et al., 2018; Boissoneault, 2017). Most of today's clinicians consider these outbreaks to be a form of conversion disorder.

New Zealand sociologist Robert Bartholemew (2014) has been studying mass psychogenic illnesses that date back over 400 years, and he argues that social media is a major factor in the current increase. One notable 2011 outbreak in Le Roy, New York, demonstrates the suggestive role played by social media (Goldstein & Hall, 2015; Vitelli, 2013). A local high school student began having facial spasms. After several weeks, others started having similar symptoms, and eventually 18 girls from the high school were affected. Apparently, a number of these teenagers began to show symptoms after they saw a YouTube video featuring a girl from a nearby town who had significant tics. Doctors eventually concluded that this was an example of mass psychogenic illness.

An unusual aspect of the Le Roy case that further points to the likely role of social media is that in addition to the 18 high school girls, a 36-year-old woman with no connection to the teenage girls also began having the same symptoms during the same period of time (NBC, 2012). She stated that she first saw the facts of the case on a Facebook post.

This case mirrors others in recent years, such as an outbreak of hiccups and vocal tics in 2013 among teenagers in Danvers, Massachusetts, and the case of 400 garment workers in a Bangladesh factory who had severe gastrointestinal symptoms for which there was ultimately no physical explanation (Boissoneault, 2017; Vitelli, 2013). In these and other cases, the symptoms seemed to be spread, at least in part, by social media exposure.

Bartholomew (2014) believes that due to the power of social media, future outbreaks may be more numerous, wide ranging, and severe than any yet recorded. He observes that in the distant past "the local priests, who were . . . summoned to [treat mass psychogenic illnesses], faced a daunting task . . . but they were fortunate in one regard: they did not have to contend with mobile phones, Twitter, and Facebook."

Sergei Bobylev/TASS via Getty Images

Modern mass hysteria? A "flash mob" gathers around a security officer at Moscow's International Airport, waving their hands and arms. Some theorists believe that these increasingly common gatherings of numerous people are a form of mass hysteria—especially those flash mobs that are sudden, unplanned, and characterized by chaotic dance moves and flailing limbs.

her life. Whenever events trigger sexual feelings, she may feel an unconscious need to hide them from both herself and others. Freud concluded that some women hide their sexual feelings by unconsciously converting them into physical symptoms and concerns.

Most of today's psychodynamic theorists take issue with parts of Freud's explanation of conversion and somatic symptom disorders, but they continue to believe that sufferers of the disorders have unconscious conflicts carried forth from childhood that arouse anxiety, and that they convert this anxiety into "more tolerable" physical symptoms (Levenson, 2018).

Psychodynamic theorists propose that two mechanisms are at work in these disorders—primary gain and secondary gain. People derive *primary gain* when their

"Try falling down and scraping your knee. Then you can talk to me about pain."

bodily symptoms keep their internal conflicts out of awareness. During an argument, for example, a man who has underlying fears about expressing anger may develop a conversion paralysis of the arm, thus preventing his feelings of rage from reaching consciousness. People derive *secondary gain* when their bodily symptoms further enable them to avoid unpleasant activities or to receive sympathy from others. When, for example, a conversion paralysis allows a soldier to avoid combat duty or conversion blindness prevents the breakup of a relationship, secondary gain may be at work. Similarly, the conversion paralysis of Brian, the man who lost his wife in the boating accident, seemed to help him avoid many painful duties after the accident, such as attending her funeral and returning to work.

The Cognitive-Behavioral View Cognitive-behavioral theorists point to rewards and communication skills to help explain conversion and somatic symptom disorders. Regarding *rewards*, they propose that the physical symptoms of these disorders yield important benefits to sufferers (see **Table 8-4**). Perhaps the symptoms remove the individuals from an unpleasant relationship or perhaps the symptoms bring attention from other people (Levenson, 2018; Witthöft et al., 2018). In response to such rewards, the sufferers learn to display the bodily symptoms more and more prominently. The theorists also hold that people who are familiar with an illness will more readily adopt its physical symptoms. In fact, studies find that many sufferers develop their bodily symptoms after they or their close relatives or friends have had similar medical problems (Stone & Sharpe, 2018, 2017).

Clearly, this focus on the role of rewards is similar to the psychodynamic notion of secondary gain. The key difference is that psychodynamic theorists view the gains as indeed secondary—that is, as gains that come only after underlying conflicts produce the disorders. Cognitive-behavioral theorists view them as the primary cause of the development of the disorders.

Like the psychodynamic explanation, the reward explanation of conversion and somatic symptom disorders has received little research support. Even clinical case reports only occasionally support this position. In many cases the pain and upset that surround the disorders seem to outweigh any rewards the symptoms might bring.

In the *communication* realm, some cognitive-behavioral theorists propose that conversion and somatic symptom disorders are forms of self-expression, providing a means for people to reveal emotions that would otherwise be difficult for them to convey (Levenson, 2018). Like their psychodynamic colleagues, these theorists hold that the emotions of people with the disorders are being converted into physical symptoms. They suggest, however, that the purpose of the conversion is not to defend against anxiety but to communicate extreme feelings—anger, fear, depression, guilt, jealousy—in a "physical language" that is familiar and comfortable for the person with the disorder.

According to this view, people who find it particularly hard to recognize or express their emotions are candidates for conversion and somatic symptom disorders (Erkic et al., 2018). So are those who "know" the language of physical symptoms through firsthand experience with a genuine physical ailment. Because children are less able to express their emotions verbally, they are particularly likely to develop physical symptoms as a form of communication (Cozzi et al., 2017; Shaw et al., 2010). Like the other explanations, this cognitive-behavioral view has not been widely tested or supported by research.

TABLE: 8-4

Disorders That Have Somatic Symptoms

Disorders	Voluntary Control of Symptoms?	Symptoms Linked to Psychosocial Factor?	An Apparent Goal?
Malingering	Yes	Maybe	Yes
Factitious disorder	Yes	Yes	No*
Conversion disorder	No	Yes	Maybe
Somatic symptom disorders	No	Yes	Maybe
Illness anxiety disorder	No	Yes	No
Psychophysiological disorder	No	Yes	No
Physical illness	No	Maybe	No

*Except for medical attention.

The Multicultural View Most Western clinicians believe that it is inappropriate to produce or focus excessively on somatic symptoms in response to personal distress. That is, in part, why conversion and somatic symptom disorders are included in DSM-5. Some theorists believe, however, that this position reflects a Western bias—a bias that sees somatic reactions as an *inferior* way of dealing with emotions (Krupić et al., 2019; Bagayogo, Interian, & Escobar, 2013; Moldavsky, 2004).

In fact, the transformation of personal distress into somatic complaints is the norm in many non-Western cultures (Calzada et al., 2017). In such cultures, the formation of such complaints is viewed as a socially and medically correct—and less stigmatizing—reaction to life's stressors. Studies have found very high rates of stress-caused bodily symptoms in non-Western medical settings throughout the world, including those in China, Japan, and Arab countries (Löwe & Gerloff, 2018; Matsumoto & Juang, 2016). People throughout Latin America seem to display the most somatic reactions (Escobar, 2004, 1995). Even within the United States, Hispanic Americans display more somatic reactions in the face of stress than do other populations (Calzada et al., 2017).

The lesson to be learned from such multicultural findings is not that somatic reactions to stress are superior to psychological ones or vice versa, but rather, once again, that both bodily and psychological reactions to life events are often influenced by one's culture. Overlooking this point can lead to knee-jerk mislabels or misdiagnoses.

How Are Conversion and Somatic Symptom Disorders Treated?

People with conversion and somatic symptom disorders usually seek psychotherapy only as a last resort. They believe that their problems are completely medical and at first reject all suggestions to the contrary. When a physician tells them that their symptoms or concerns have a psychological dimension, they often go to another physician. Eventually, however, many patients with these disorders do consent to psychotherapy, psychotropic drug therapy, or both.

Many therapists focus on the *causes* of these disorders (the trauma or anxiety tied to the physical symptoms) and apply insight, exposure, and drug therapies. Psychodynamic therapists, for example, try to help those with somatic symptoms become conscious of and resolve their underlying fears, thus eliminating the need to convert anxiety into physical symptoms (Stone & Sharpe, 2018; Kaplan, 2016). Alternatively, cognitive-behavioral therapists use exposure treatments. They expose clients to features of the horrific events that first triggered their physical symptoms, expecting that the clients will become less anxious over the course of repeated exposures and more able to face those upsetting events directly rather than through physical channels (Newby et al., 2018; Tsui et al., 2017). And biological therapists most often use antidepressant drugs to help reduce anxiety and depression in patients with these disorders (Levenson, 2018; Kurlansik & Maffei, 2016).

AP Photo/Lefteris Pitarakis

Mind over matter The opposite of conversion and somatic symptom disorders are instances in which people "ignore" pain or other physical symptoms. Here a London performance artist smiles comfortably at onlookers while her skin is being pierced with sharp hooks that help suspend her from the ceiling above. Her action was part of a protest to end shark finning—the practice of cutting off a shark's fin and throwing its still-living body back into the sea.

Other therapists try to address the *physical symptoms* of these disorders rather than the causes, using techniques such as education, reinforcement, and cognitive restructuring (Stone & Sharpe, 2018). Those who employ *education* explain the disorder to patients, while also offering emotional support and hope that the physical symptoms may soon disappear. Therapists who take a *reinforcement* approach arrange for the removal of rewards for a client's "sickness" symptoms and an increase of rewards for healthy behaviors. And those who offer *cognitive restructuring* guide clients to think differently about the nature and causes of physical symptoms and illness (Levenson, 2018). Researchers have not fully evaluated the effects of these approaches on conversion and somatic symptom disorders; several studies, however, have found them to be useful interventions (Stone & Sharpe, 2018; 2017; Tsui et al., 2017). It is also the case that antidepressant medications sometimes help alleviate the physical symptoms of people with these disorders in addition to reducing their feelings of anxiety and depression.

#DiagnosticControversy

Even people whose physical symptoms are caused by significant medical problems may qualify for a diagnosis of *somatic symptom disorder* if they are *overly* anxious or upset by their medical problems. Critics worry that many patients who are understandably upset by having cancer, heart disease, or other serious diseases may incorrectly receive a diagnosis of somatic symptom disorder (Barsky, 2016).

... SUMMING UP

CONVERSION AND SOMATIC SYMPTOM DISORDERS Conversion disorder involves bodily symptoms that affect voluntary motor and sensory functions, but the symptoms are inconsistent with known medical diseases. In somatic symptom disorder, people become excessively distressed, concerned, and anxious about bodily symptoms that they are experiencing, and their lives are greatly and disproportionately disrupted by the symptoms.

Freud developed the initial psychodynamic view of conversion and somatic symptom disorders, proposing that the disorders represent a conversion of underlying emotional conflicts into physical symptoms. According to cognitive-behavioral theorists, the physical symptoms of these disorders bring rewards to the sufferer, and such reinforcement helps maintain the symptoms. Some cognitive-behavioral theorists further propose that the disorders are forms of communication and that people express their emotions through their physical symptoms. Treatments for these disorders include insight, exposure, and drug therapies and may include techniques such as education, reinforcement, or cognitive restructuring.

Illness Anxiety Disorder

People with **illness anxiety disorder,** previously known as *hypochondriasis,* are chronically anxious about their health and are convinced that they have or are developing a serious medical illness, despite the absence of somatic symptoms (see **Table 8-5**). They repeatedly check their body for signs of illness and misinterpret various bodily events as signs of serious medical problems. Typically the events are merely normal bodily changes, such as occasional coughing, sores, or sweating. Those with illness anxiety disorder persist in such misinterpretations no matter what friends, relatives, and physicians say. Some such people recognize that their concerns are excessive, but many do not.

#StrangeCoincidence?

On February 17, 1673, French actor-playwright Molière collapsed onstage and died while performing in *Le Malade Imaginaire* (*The Hypochondriac*).

Although illness anxiety disorder can begin at any age, it starts most often in early adulthood, among men and women in equal numbers. Between 1 and 5 percent of all people experience the disorder (Weck et al., 2015; Abramowitz & Braddock, 2011). Their symptoms tend to rise and fall over the years. Physicians report seeing many cases. As many as 5 percent of all patients seen by primary care physicians may display the disorder (Levenson, 2018; Dimsdale et al., 2011).

Theorists typically explain illness anxiety disorder much as they explain anxiety-related disorders (see Chapter 4). Cognitive-behavioral theorists, for example, believe

TABLE: 8-5

Dx Checklist

Illness Anxiety Disorder
1. Person is preoccupied with thoughts about having or getting a significant illness. In reality, person has no or, at most, mild somatic symptoms.
2. Person has easily triggered high anxiety about health.
3. Person displays unduly high number of health-related behaviors (e.g., keeps focusing on body) or dysfunctional health-avoidance behaviors (e.g., avoids doctors).
4. Person's concerns continue to some degree for at least 6 months.

Information from: APA, 2013.

(1) that the illness fears are acquired through classical conditioning or modeling, and (2) that people with the disorder are so sensitive to and threatened by bodily cues that they come to misinterpret them (Levenson, 2018; Marshall et al., 2007).

People with illness anxiety disorder usually receive the kinds of treatments that are used to treat obsessive-compulsive disorder (see pages 130–133). Studies reveal, for example, that clients with the disorder often improve considerably when given the same *antidepressant drugs* that are helpful in cases of obsessive-compulsive disorder. Many clients also improve when treated with the cognitive-behavioral approach of *exposure and response prevention*. The therapists repeatedly point out bodily variations to the clients while, at the same time, preventing them from seeking their usual medical attention. In addition, the cognitive-behavioral therapists guide the clients to identify, challenge, and change their beliefs about illness that are helping to maintain their disorder (Levenson, 2018; Newby et al., 2018).

9... SUMMING UP

ILLNESS ANXIETY DISORDER People with illness anxiety disorder are chronically anxious about and preoccupied with the notion that they have or are developing a serious medical illness, despite the absence of substantial somatic symptoms. Theorists explain this disorder much as they do anxiety disorders. Treatment includes drug and cognitive-behavioral approaches originally developed for obsessive-compulsive disorder.

Psychophysiological Disorders: Psychological Factors Affecting Other Medical Conditions

About 90 years ago, clinicians identified a group of physical illnesses that seemed to be caused or worsened by an *interaction* of biological, psychological, and sociocultural factors (Bott, 1928). Early editions of the DSM labeled these illnesses **psychophysiological,** or **psychosomatic, disorders,** but DSM-5 labels them as **psychological factors affecting other medical conditions** (see **Table 8-6**). The more familiar term "psychophysiological" will be used in this chapter.

It is important to recognize that significant medical symptoms and conditions are involved in psychophysiological disorders and that the disorders often result in serious physical damage (APA, 2013). They are different from the factitious, conversion, and illness anxiety disorders that are accounted for primarily by psychological factors.

Traditional Psychophysiological Disorders

Before the 1970s, clinicians believed that only a limited number of illnesses were psychophysiological. The best known and most common of these disorders were ulcers, asthma, insomnia, chronic headaches, high blood pressure, and coronary heart disease. Recent research, however, has shown that many other physical illnesses—including bacterial and viral infections—may also be caused by an interaction of psychosocial and physical factors. Let's look first at the traditional psychophysiological disorders and then at the illnesses that are newer to this category.

Ulcers are lesions (holes) that form in the wall of the stomach or of the duodenum, resulting in burning sensations or pain in the stomach, occasional vomiting, and stomach bleeding. More than 25 million people in the United States have ulcers at some point during their lives, and ulcers cause an estimated 6,500 deaths each year (Vakil, 2017, 2015; Pizzorno, Murray, & Joiner-Bey, 2016; Simon, 2013). Ulcers often are caused

illness anxiety disorder A disorder in which people are chronically anxious about and preoccupied with the notion that they have or are developing a serious medical illness, despite the absence of somatic symptoms.

psychophysiological disorders Disorders in which biological, psychological, and sociocultural factors interact to cause or worsen a physical illness. Also known as *psychological factors affecting other medical conditions*.

ulcer A lesion that forms in the wall of the stomach or of the duodenum.

TABLE: 8-6

Dx Checklist

Psychological Factors Affecting Other Medical Conditions

1. The presence of a medical condition.
2. Psychological factors negatively affect the medical condition by:
   - Affecting the course of the medical condition.
   - Providing obstacles for the treatment of the medical condition.
   - Posing new health risks.
   - Triggering or worsening the medical condition.

Information from: APA, 2013.

FIGURE 8-2

What Do People Do to Relieve Stress?

According to surveys, most of us go on the Internet, watch television, read, or listen to music. Tweeting is on the rise. (Information from: BLS, 2016; Pew Research Center, 2016, 2011, 2010; Wagstaff, 2015; IWS, 2011; MHA, 2008; NPD Group, 2008.)

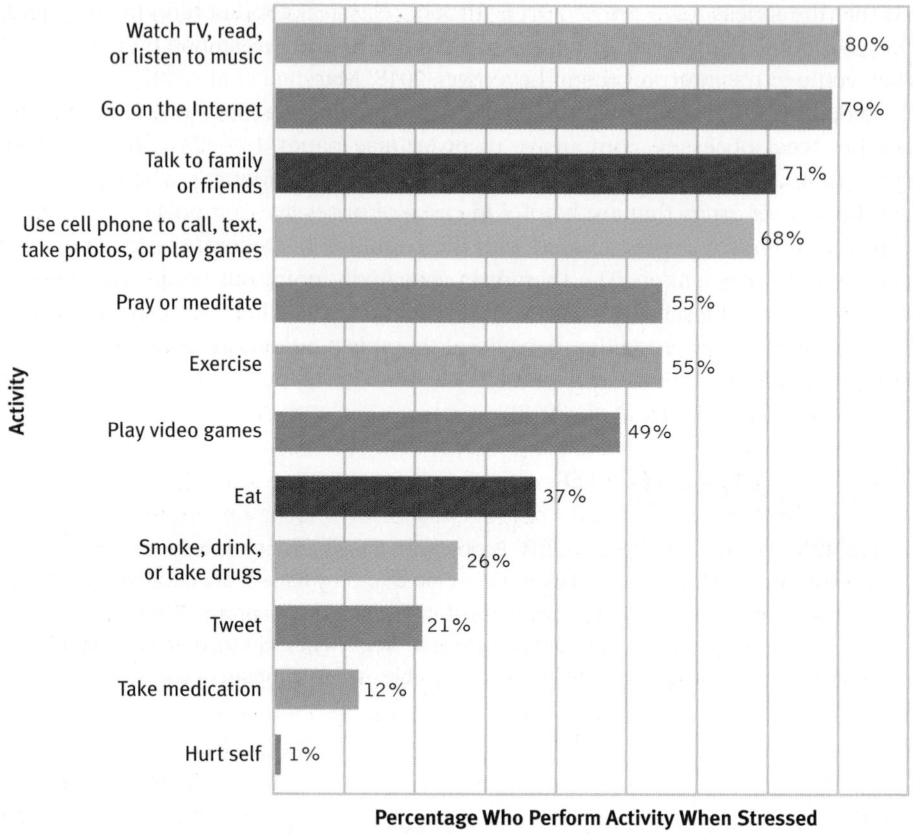

by an interaction of stress factors, such as environmental pressure or intense feelings of anger or anxiety (see **Figure 8-2**), and physiological factors, such as the bacteria *H. pylori* (Lanas & Chan, 2017).

Asthma causes the body's airways (the trachea and bronchi) to narrow periodically, making it hard for air to pass to and from the lungs. The resulting symptoms are shortness of breath, wheezing, coughing, and a terrifying choking sensation. Some 235 million people in the world—25 million in the United States alone—currently suffer from asthma (CDC, 2017; WHO, 2017), and most were children or young teenagers at the time of the first attack. Seventy percent of all cases appear to be caused by an interaction of stress factors, such as environmental pressures or anxiety, and physiological factors, such as allergies to specific substances, a slow-acting sympathetic nervous system, or a weakened respiratory system (WHO, 2018; Fanta, 2017).

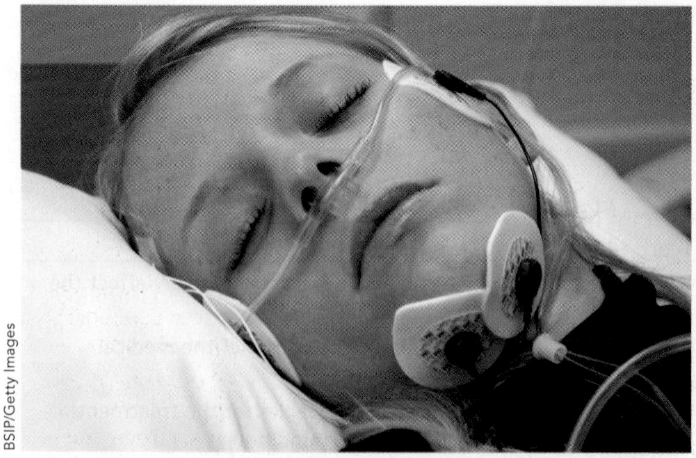

Studying sleep Clinicians use special techniques to assess sleep disorders. This woman is undergoing a *polysomnographic* examination, a procedure that measures physiological activity during sleep, including measurements of brain, eye, lung, and heart activity.

Insomnia, difficulty falling asleep or maintaining sleep, plagues 30 percent of the population each year (ASA, 2017). Although many of us have temporary bouts of insomnia that last a few nights or so, a large number of people—10 percent of the population—have insomnia that lasts months or years (see ***InfoCentral*** on page 252). Chronic insomniacs feel as though they are almost constantly awake. They often are very sleepy during the day and may have difficulty functioning. Their problem may be caused by a combination of psychosocial factors, such as high levels of anxiety or depression, and physiological problems, such as an overactive arousal system or certain medical ailments (Bonnet & Arand, 2018, 2017).

Chronic headaches are frequent intense aches of the head or neck that are not caused by another physical disorder. There are two major types. **Muscle contraction,** or **tension, headaches** are marked by pain at the back or front of the head or the back of the neck. These occur when the muscles surrounding the skull tighten, narrowing the blood vessels. Approximately 45 million Americans suffer from such headaches (Burch, Rizzoli, & Loder, 2018; CDC, 2015, 2010).

Migraine headaches are extremely severe, often nearly paralyzing, headaches that are located on one side of the head and are sometimes accompanied by dizziness, nausea, or vomiting. Migraine headaches are thought by some medical theorists to develop in two phases: (1) blood vessels in the brain narrow so that the flow of blood to parts of the brain is reduced, and (2) the same blood vessels later expand so that blood flows through them rapidly, stimulating many neuron endings and causing pain. Twenty-three million people in the United States suffer from migraines.

Research suggests that chronic headaches are caused by an interaction of stress factors, such as environmental pressures or general feelings of helplessness, anger, anxiety, or depression, and physiological factors, such as abnormal activity of the neurotransmitter serotonin, vascular problems, or muscle weakness (Cutrer & Bajwa, 2017; Taylor, 2017).

Hypertension is a state of chronic high blood pressure. That is, the blood pumped through the body's arteries by the heart produces too much pressure against the artery walls. Hypertension has few outward signs, but it interferes with the proper functioning of the entire cardiovascular system, greatly increasing the likelihood of stroke, heart disease, and kidney problems. It is estimated that 77 million people in the United States have hypertension, thousands die directly from it annually, and millions more perish because of illnesses caused by it (Basile & Bloch, 2018; CDC, 2018, 2017, 2011). Around 10 percent of all cases are caused by physiological abnormalities alone; the rest result from a combination of psychological and physiological factors and are called *essential hypertension*. Some of the leading psychosocial causes of essential hypertension are constant stress, environmental danger, and general feelings of anger or depression. Physiological factors include obesity, smoking, poor kidney function, and an unusually high proportion of the gluey protein *collagen* in a person's blood vessels (Basile & Bloch, 2018).

Coronary heart disease is caused by a blocking of the *coronary arteries*, the blood vessels that surround the heart and are responsible for carrying oxygen to the heart muscle. The term actually refers to several problems, including blockage of the coronary arteries and *myocardial infarction* (a "heart attack"). In the United States, more than 16 million people currently have some form of coronary heart disease. It is the leading cause of death for both men and women, accounting for 17 million deaths around the world each year, 600,000 of them in the United States—around one-third of all deaths (CDC, 2017; Wilson & Douglas, 2017). Approximately half of all middle-aged men and one-third of middle-aged women develop coronary heart disease at some point in their lives. The majority of all cases of this disease are related to an interaction of psychosocial factors, such as job stress or high levels of anger or depression, and physiological factors, such as high cholesterol, obesity, hypertension, smoking, or lack of exercise (Tofler, 2018; Wilson & Douglas, 2017).

What Factors Contribute to Psychophysiological Disorders? Over the years, clinicians have identified a number of variables that may generally contribute to the development of psychophysiological disorders. The variables can be grouped as biological, psychological, and sociocultural factors, respectively.

BIOLOGICAL FACTORS You saw in Chapter 5 that one way the brain activates body organs is through the operation of the *autonomic nervous system* (*ANS*), the network of nerve fibers that connect the central nervous system to the body's organs. Defects

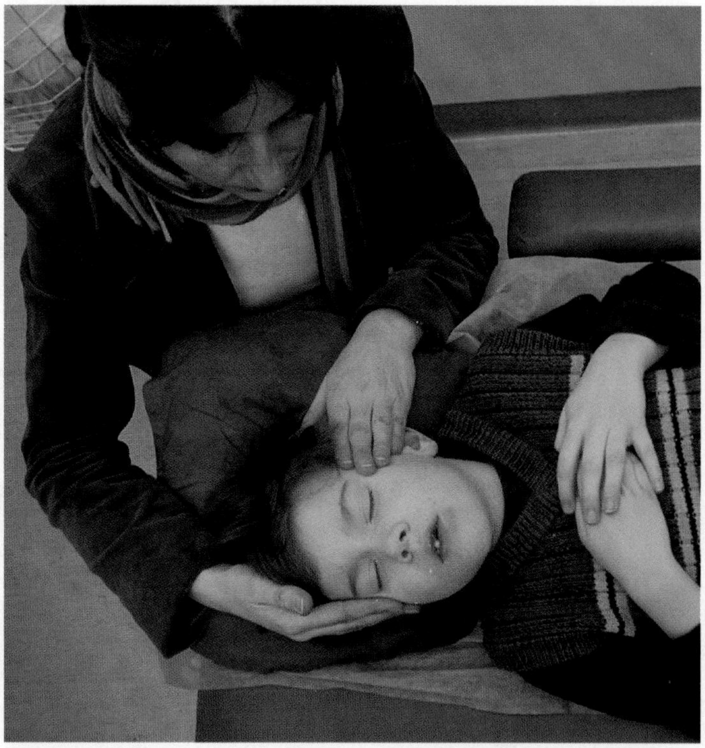

Rob Schoenbaum/Polaris

More than head pain Migraine headaches produce much more pain and a wider range of symptoms than most other kinds of headaches. Here, at a program in Stockholm, Sweden, a mother massages the head of her young son, who suffers from migraines. Systematic massaging is partially helpful to him during particularly severe episodes.

asthma A disease marked by narrowing of the trachea and bronchi, resulting in shortness of breath, wheezing, coughing, and a choking sensation.

insomnia Difficulty falling or staying asleep.

muscle contraction headache A headache caused by a narrowing of muscles surrounding the skull. Also known as *tension headache*.

migraine headache A very severe headache that occurs on one side of the head, often preceded by a warning sensation and sometimes accompanied by dizziness, nausea, or vomiting.

hypertension Chronic high blood pressure.

coronary heart disease Illness of the heart caused by a blockage in the coronary arteries.

SLEEP AND SLEEP DISORDERS

Sleep is a naturally recurring state that features altered consciousness, suspension of voluntary bodily functions, muscle relaxation, and reduced perception of environmental stimuli. Researchers have acquired much data about the stages, cycles, brain waves, and mechanics of sleep, but they do not fully understand its precise purpose. We do know, however, that humans and other animals need sleep to survive and function properly.

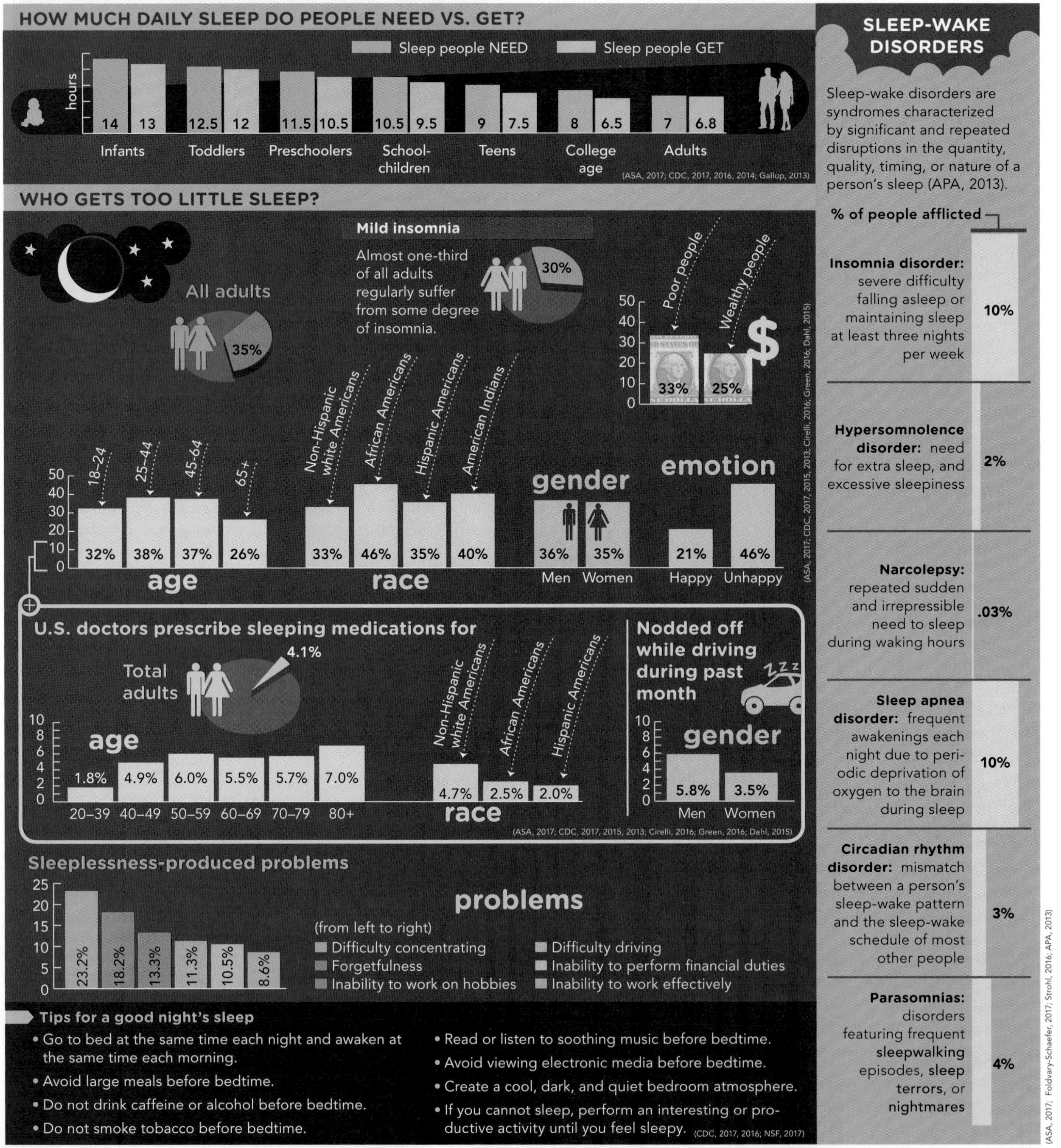

in this system are believed to contribute to the development of psychophysiological disorders (Ackland et al., 2016; Lundberg, 2011). If one's ANS is stimulated too easily, for example, it may overreact to situations that most people find only mildly stressful, eventually damaging certain organs and causing a psychophysiological disorder. Other more specific biological problems may also contribute to psychophysiological disorders. A person with a weak gastrointestinal system, for example, may be a prime candidate for an ulcer, whereas someone with a weak respiratory system may develop asthma readily.

In a related vein, people may display favored biological reactions that raise their chances of developing psychophysiological disorders. Some individuals perspire in response to stress, others develop stomachaches, and still others have a rise in blood pressure. Research has indicated, for example, that some people are particularly likely to have temporary rises in blood pressure when stressed (Yuenyongchaiwat, 2017; Lundberg, 2011). It may be that they are prone to develop hypertension.

Type A personality style A personality pattern characterized by hostility, cynicism, drivenness, impatience, competitiveness, and ambition.

Type B personality style A personality pattern in which a person is more relaxed, less aggressive, and less concerned about time.

PSYCHOLOGICAL FACTORS According to many theorists, certain needs, attitudes, emotions, or coping styles may cause people to overreact repeatedly to stressors, and so increase their chances of developing psychophysiological disorders. Researchers have found, for example, that men with a *repressive coping style* (a reluctance to express discomfort, anger, or hostility) tend to have a particularly sharp rise in blood pressure and heart rate when they are stressed (Howard, Myers, & Hughes, 2017).

Another personality style that may contribute to psychophysiological disorders is the **Type A personality style,** an idea introduced a half-century ago by two cardiologists, Meyer Friedman and Ray Rosenman (1959). People with this style are said to be consistently angry, cynical, driven, impatient, competitive, and ambitious. They interact with the world in a way that, according to Friedman and Rosenman, produces continual stress and often leads to coronary heart disease. People with a **Type B personality style,** by contrast, are thought to be more relaxed, less aggressive, and less concerned about time and thus are less likely to develop cardiovascular deterioration.

Which jobs in our society might be particularly stressful and traumatizing? Might certain lifestyles be more stressful than others?

The link between the Type A personality style and coronary heart disease has been supported by many studies. In one well-known investigation of more than 3,000 people, Friedman and Rosenman (1974) separated healthy men in their forties and fifties into Type A and Type B categories and then followed their health over the next eight years. More than twice as many Type A men developed coronary heart disease. Later studies found that Type A functioning correlates similarly with heart disease in women (Haynes et al., 1980).

Recent studies indicate that the link between the Type A personality style and heart disease may not be as strong as the earlier studies suggested. These studies do suggest, however, that several of the characteristics that supposedly make up the Type A style, particularly *hostility, competitiveness,* and *time urgency,* may indeed be strongly related to heart disease (Tofler, 2018; Jennings et al., 2017).

Walt Disney Pictures/Photofest

Type B sea turtle Most people have a clear picture of a Type A personality, but they have difficulty spotting a Type B personality. They need look no farther than Crush, the ever so relaxed and laid-back sea turtle in the animation films *Finding Nemo* and *Finding Dory*. Crush always goes with the flow and surfs the seas at his own comfortable pace.

SOCIOCULTURAL FACTORS: THE MULTICULTURAL PERSPECTIVE Adverse social conditions may set the stage for psychophysiological disorders. Such conditions produce ongoing stressors that trigger and interact with the biological and personality factors just discussed. One of society's most negative social conditions, for example, is poverty. In study after study, it has been found that impoverished people have more psychophysiological disorders, poorer health in general, and poorer health outcomes than wealthier people (Robinson-Papp et al., 2017; Singh & Siahpush, 2014). One obvious reason for this relationship is that poor people typically experience higher rates of crime, unemployment, overcrowding, and other negative stressors than wealthier people. In addition, they typically receive inferior medical care.

The relationship between race and psychophysiological and other health problems is complicated. On the one hand, as one might expect from the economic trends just discussed, African Americans have more health problems than do non-Hispanic white Americans. African Americans have, for example, higher rates of high blood pressure, high cholesterol, diabetes, and asthma (CDC, 2017, 2016, 2014). They are also more likely to die of heart disease and stroke. Certainly, economic factors may help explain this racial difference. Many African Americans live in poverty, and those who do often must contend with the high rates of crime and unemployment that can contribute to poor health (Greer et al., 2014).

Research further suggests that the high rate of psychophysiological and other medical disorders among African Americans probably extends beyond economic factors. Consider, for example, the finding that 44 percent of African Americans have high blood pressure, compared with 33 percent of non-Hispanic white Americans (CDC, 2018, 2016, 2011). Although this difference may be explained in part by the dangerous environments in which many African Americans live and the unsatisfying jobs at which many must work (Marden et al., 2016), other factors may also be operating (Muntner et al., 2017). A physiological predisposition among African Americans may, for example, increase their risk of developing high blood pressure. Or it may be that repeated experiences of racial discrimination constitute special stressors that help raise the blood pressure of African Americans (see **Figure 8-3**). Studies have found, for example, that the more discrimination people experience over a 1-year period, the greater their daily rise in blood pressure, and the more discrimination African Americans experience over the course of their lives, the more likely they are to have high blood pressure in middle age and old age (Colen et al., 2018; Beatty Moody et al., 2016; Dolezsar et al., 2014).

Looking at the health picture of African Americans, one might expect to find a similar trend among Hispanic Americans. After all, a high percentage of Hispanic Americans also live in poverty, are exposed to discrimination, are affected by high rates of crime and unemployment, and receive inferior medical care (U.S. Census Bureau, 2016, 2010; BLS, 2015). However, despite such disadvantages, the health of Hispanic Americans is, on average, at least as good and often better than that of both non-Hispanic white Americans and African Americans (CDC, 2017, 2016, 2015). For example, Hispanic Americans have lower rates of high blood pressure and asthma and live longer than non-Hispanic white Americans and African Americans do.

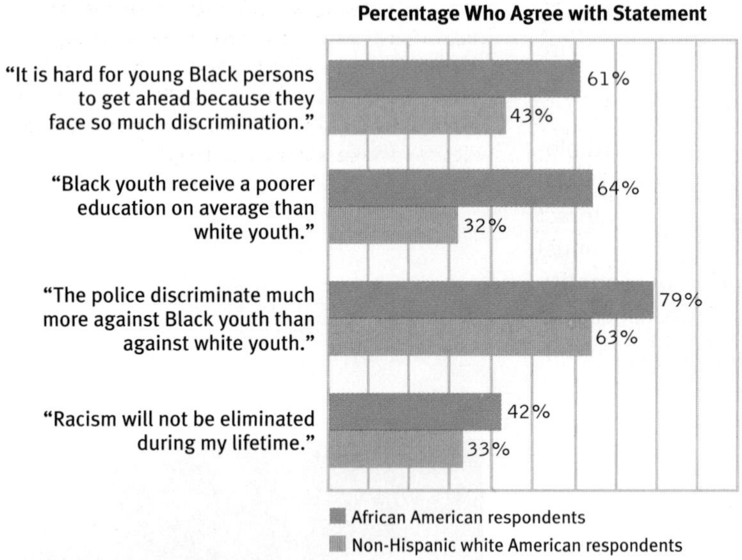

Percentage Who Agree with Statement
"It is hard for young Black persons to get ahead because they face so much discrimination."
61%
43%
"Black youth receive a poorer education on average than white youth."
64%
32%
"The police discriminate much more against Black youth than against white youth."
79%
63%
"Racism will not be eliminated during my lifetime."
42%
33%
African American respondents
Non-Hispanic white American respondents

FIGURE 8-3

How Much Discrimination Do Racial Minority Teenagers Face?

It depends on who's being asked the question. In surveys of teenagers and young adults, African American respondents were more likely than non-Hispanic white American respondents to recognize that African American teens experience various forms of discrimination. (Information from: Black Youth Project, 2018, 2016, 2011; OA, 2017.)

The relatively positive health picture for Hispanic Americans in the face of clear economic disadvantage has been referred to in the clinical field as the "Hispanic Health Paradox." Generally, researchers are puzzled by this pattern, but a few explanations have been offered (Erving, 2017; Giuntella, 2016). It may be, for example, that the strong emphasis on social relationships, family support, and religiousness that often characterize Hispanic American cultures increase health resilience among their members. Or Hispanic Americans may have a physiological predisposition that improves their likelihood of having better health outcomes.

New Psychophysiological Disorders

Clearly, biological, psychological, and sociocultural factors combine to produce psychophysiological disorders. In fact, the interaction of such factors is now considered the *rule* of bodily functioning, not the exception (Levenson, 2018). As the years have passed, more and more illnesses have been added to the list of traditional psychophysiological disorders and researchers have found many links between psychosocial stress and a wide range of physical illnesses. Let's look at how these links were established and then at *psychoneuroimmunology,* the area of study that ties stress and illness to the body's immune system.

Are Physical Illnesses Related to Stress? Back in 1967 two researchers, Thomas Holmes and Richard Rahe, developed the *Social Readjustment Rating Scale,* which assigns numerical values to the stresses that most people experience at some time in their lives (see **Table 8-7**). Answers given by a large sample of participants indicated that the most stressful event on the scale is the death of a spouse, which receives a score of 100 *life change units* (*LCUs*). Lower on the scale is retirement (45 LCUs), and still lower is a minor violation of the law (11 LCUs). This scale gave researchers a yardstick for measuring the total amount of stress a person faces over a period of time. If, for example, in the course of a year a woman started a new business (39 LCUs), sent her son off to college (29 LCUs), moved to a new house (20 LCUs), and had a close friend die (37 LCUs), her stress score for the year would be 125 LCUs, a considerable amount of stress for such a period of time.

Lionel Hahn/Sipa USA via AP Images

The ultimate body–mind connection? Psychologists have studied the relationship between psychological trauma and immediate death—called the *sudden death*, or *"giving-up,"* phenomenon. In 2017, movie legend Debbie Reynolds (right) died just one day after the death of her daughter, actress Carrie Fisher (left). According to Reynolds's son, "She literally said 'I want to be with Carrie' and closed her eyes and went to sleep."

With this scale in hand, Holmes and Rahe (1989, 1967) examined the relationship between life stress and the onset of illness. They found that the LCU scores of sick people during the year before they fell ill were much higher than those of healthy people. If a person's life changes totaled more than 300 LCUs over the course of a year, he or she was particularly likely to develop serious health problems.

Why are marriage, moving to a new house, and other positive events also included on stress scales?

Using the Social Readjustment Rating Scale or similar scales, studies have since linked stresses of various kinds to a wide range of physical conditions, from trench mouth and upper respiratory infections to cancer (Jager, 2018; Harkness & Monroe, 2016; Baum et al., 2011). Overall, the greater the amount of life stress, the greater the likelihood of illness. Researchers even have found a relationship between traumatic stress and death. Widows and widowers, for example, display an increased risk of death during their period of bereavement (King et al., 2017).

TABLE: 8-7

Most Stressful Life Events

Adults: Social Readjustment Rating Scale*	Students: Undergraduate Stress Questionnaire†
1. Death of spouse	1. Death (family member or friend)
2. Divorce	2. Had a lot of tests
3. Marital separation	3. It's finals week
4. Jail term	4. Applying to graduate school
5. Death of close family member	5. Victim of a crime
6. Personal injury or illness	6. Assignments in all classes due the same day
7. Marriage	7. Breaking up with boy/girlfriend
8. Fired at work	8. Found out boy/girlfriend cheated on you
9. Marital reconciliation	9. Lots of deadlines to meet
10. Retirement	10. Property stolen
11. Change in health of family member	11. You have a hard upcoming week
12. Pregnancy	12. Went into a test unprepared

*Full scale has 43 items.

(Reprinted from *Journal of Psychosomatic Research*, Vol. 11, Holmes, T. H., & Rahe, R. H., The Social Readjustment Rating Scale, 213–218, Copyright 1967, with permission from Elsevier.)

†Full scale has 83 items.

(Information from: Crandall, C. S., Preisler, J. J., & Aussprung, J. (1992). Measuring life event stress in the lives of college students: The Undergraduate Stress Questionnaire (USQ). *Journal of Behavioral Medicine*, 15(6), 627–662.)

psychoneuroimmunology The study of the connections between stress, the body's immune system, and illness.

immune system The body's network of activities and cells that identify and destroy antigens and cancer cells.

antigen A foreign invader of the body, such as a bacterium or virus.

lymphocytes White blood cells that circulate through the lymph system and bloodstream, helping the body identify and destroy antigens and cancer cells.

One shortcoming of Holmes and Rahe's Social Readjustment Rating Scale is that it does not take into consideration the particular life stress reactions of specific populations. For example, in their development of the scale, the researchers sampled non-Hispanic white Americans predominantly. Few of the respondents were African Americans or Hispanic Americans. But since their ongoing life experiences often differ in key ways, might not members of minority groups and non-Hispanic white Americans differ in their stress reactions to various kinds of life events? Research indicates that indeed they do (Oates, 2016). One recent study found, for example, that African American and Hispanic American teachers perceived and reacted to occupational stressors (for example, heavy workload and administrator pressure) very differently than did non-Hispanic white American teachers (Rauscher & Wilson, 2017).

Finally, college students may face stressors that are different from those listed in the Social Readjustment Rating Scale. Instead of having marital difficulties, being fired, or applying for a job, a college student may have trouble with a roommate, fail a course, or apply to graduate school. When researchers use special scales to measure life events in this population, they find the expected relationships between stressful events and illness (Kaya et al., 2017; Amirkhan et al., 2015) (see **Table 8-7** again).

Psychoneuroimmunology How do stressful events result in a viral or bacterial infection? Researchers in an area of study called **psychoneuroimmunology** seek to answer this question by uncovering the links between psychosocial stress, the immune system, and health. The **immune system** is the body's network of activities and cells that identify and destroy **antigens**—foreign invaders, such as bacteria, viruses, fungi, and parasites—and cancer cells. Among the most important cells in this system are billions of **lymphocytes,** white blood cells that circulate through the lymph system and the bloodstream. When stimulated by antigens, lymphocytes spring into action to help the body overcome the invaders.

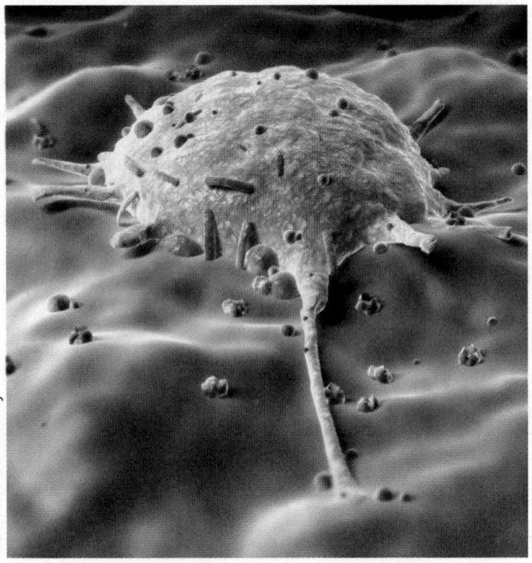

MedicalRF.com/Alamy

First line of defense How do lymphocytes meet up with invading antigens? The lymphocytes are first alerted by *macrophages,* big white blood cells in the immune system that recognize an antigen, engulf it, break it down, and hand off its dissected parts to the lymphocytes. Here a macrophage stretches its long "arms" (pseudopods) to detect and capture the suspected antigens.

One group of lymphocytes, called *helper T-cells,* identifies antigens and then multiplies and triggers the production of other kinds of immune cells. Another group, *natural killer T-cells,* seeks out and destroys body cells that have already been infected by viruses, thus helping to stop the spread of a viral infection. A third group of lymphocytes, *B-cells,* produces *antibodies,* protein molecules that recognize and bind to antigens, mark them for destruction, and prevent them from causing infection (Leem & Deane, 2019).

Researchers now believe that stress can interfere with the activity of lymphocytes and other parts of the immune system, slowing them down and thus increasing a person's susceptibility to viral and bacterial infections (Levenson, 2018; Peters et al., 2017). In a landmark study, investigator Roger Bartrop and his colleagues (1977) in New South Wales, Australia, compared the immune systems of 26 people whose spouses had died 8 weeks earlier with those of 26 matched control group participants whose spouses had not died. Blood samples revealed that lymphocyte functioning was much lower in the bereaved people than in the controls. Still other studies have shown poor immune functioning in people who are exposed to long-term stress (Gao et al., 2018). For example, researchers have found poorer immune functioning among those who provide ongoing care for a relative with Alzheimer's disease (Allen et al., 2017).

These studies seem to be telling a remarkable story. During periods when healthy people happened to have unusual levels of stress, they remained healthy on the surface, but their stressors apparently slowed their immune systems so that they became susceptible to illness. If stress affects our capacity to fight off illness, it is no wonder that researchers have repeatedly found a relationship between life stress and illnesses of various kinds. But why and when does stress interfere with the immune system? Several factors influence whether stress will result in a slowdown of the system, including *biochemical activity, behavioral changes, personality style,* and *degree of social support.*

BIOCHEMICAL ACTIVITY As you'll recall from Chapter 5, there are two biological stress pathways by which stressors produce arousal throughout the brain and body (see pages 141–142). One is the *sympathetic nervous system*, which, among its many actions, triggers the release of the neurotransmitter *norepinephrine*. It turns out that in addition to its role in producing arousal, an extended release of norepinephrine can influence the immune system adversely. Research indicates that if stress continues for too long a period, norepinephrine eventually travels to receptors on certain lymphocytes and gives them an *inhibitory message* to stop their activity, thus slowing down immune functioning (Bucsek et al., 2018; Takenaka et al., 2016).

Recall also that the other biological stress pathway is the *hypothalamic-pituitary-adrenal* (*HPA*) pathway, which, among its various actions, triggers the release of *cortisol* and other stress hormones. Apparently, in addition to producing bodily arousal, an extended release of cortisol and other stress hormones can contribute to poorer immune system functioning. As in the case of norepinephrine, if stress continues for too long, the stress hormones travel to receptor sites located on certain lymphocytes and give an inhibitory message, again causing a slowdown of the activity of the lymphocytes (Ciliberti et al., 2017; Huo et al., 2017).

Research has further indicated that another action of norepinephrine and the various stress hormones is to trigger an increase in the production of *cytokines*, proteins that bind to receptors throughout the body. At moderate levels of stress, the cytokines, another key player in the immune system, help combat infection. But as stress continues and more norepinephrine and stress hormones are released, the growing production and spread of cytokines lead to *chronic inflammation* throughout the body, contributing at times to heart disease, stroke, and other illnesses (Huo et al., 2017).

BEHAVIORAL CHANGES Stress may set in motion a series of behavioral changes that indirectly affect the immune system. Some people under stress may, for example, become anxious or depressed, perhaps even develop an anxiety or depressive disorder. As a result, they may sleep badly, eat poorly, exercise less, or smoke or drink more—behaviors known to slow down the immune system (Levenson, 2018).

PERSONALITY STYLE According to research, people who generally respond to life stress with optimism, constructive coping, and resilience—that is, people who welcome challenges and are willing to take control in their daily encounters—experience better immune system functioning and are better prepared to fight off illness (Pandey &

#MaritalStress

During and after marital spats, women typically release more stress hormones than men, and so have poorer immune functioning (Martire et al., 2018; Jaremka et al., 2013; Gouin et al., 2009; Kiecolt-Glaser et al., 1996).

Win McNamee/Getty Images

Religious protection? In this famous photo of a 2015 prayer vigil, church congregants hold up pictures of 9 Bible study participants who had been shot and killed two days earlier at the Emanuel African Methodist Episcopal Church in Charleston, South Carolina. Some relatives of the victims later talked directly to the mass murderer, telling him they forgave him and were praying for him. Research indicates that people with strong institutional, religious, and social ties often recover more readily and more healthfully from the effects of traumatic events.

Helen H. Richardson/The Denver Post via Getty Images

The power of support Cancer survivors clasp hands at the Susan G. Komen "Race for the Cure," a 5K run held annually throughout the world, with millions of participants. The run, begun almost 30 years ago, not only raises awareness about cancer, it helps survivors support and encourage one another—applying research findings that social support can help facilitate recovery from various illnesses.

Shrivastava, 2017). Some studies have found, for example, that people with "hardy" or resilient personal styles remain healthy after stressful events, while those whose personalities are less hardy seem more susceptible to illness (Rolin et al., 2018). Researchers have even discovered that men with a general sense of hopelessness die at above-average rates from heart disease and critical illnesses (Orwelius et al., 2017; Kangelaris et al., 2010). Similarly, a growing body of research suggests that people who are spiritual tend to be healthier than people without spiritual beliefs, and a few studies have linked spirituality to better immune system functioning (Brooks et al., 2018; Roth et al., 2016).

In related work, researchers have found a relationship between certain personality characteristics and a person's ability to cope effectively with cancer. They have found, for example, that patients with certain forms of cancer who display a helpless coping style and who cannot easily express their feelings, particularly anger, tend to have a poorer quality of life in the face of their disease than patients who do express their emotions (You et al., 2018; Kim, Nho, & Nam, 2017). A few investigators have even suggested a relationship between personality and cancer *outcome*, but this claim has not been supported clearly by research (Pillay et al., 2014; Urcuyo et al., 2005).

SOCIAL SUPPORT Finally, people who have few social supports and feel lonely tend to have poorer immune functioning in the face of stress than people who do not feel lonely (Russo, 2018; Pandey & Shrivastava, 2017). In a pioneering study, medical students were given the *UCLA Loneliness Scale* and then divided into "high" and "low" loneliness groups (Kiecolt-Glaser et al., 1984). The high-loneliness group showed lower lymphocyte responses during a final exam period.

Other studies have found that social support and affiliation may actually help protect people from stress, poor immune system functioning, and subsequent illness, or help speed up recovery from illness or surgery (Levenson, 2018; Hicks, 2014). Similarly, some studies have suggested that patients with certain forms of cancer who receive social support in their personal lives or supportive therapy often have better immune system functioning and more successful recoveries than patients without such supports (Imm et al., 2017; Hulett et al., 2015).

...SUMMING UP

PSYCHOPHYSIOLOGICAL DISORDERS Psychological factors affecting other medical conditions, known commonly as psychophysiological disorders, are those in which biological, psychosocial, and sociocultural factors interact to cause or worsen a physical problem. Factors linked to these disorders are biological factors, such as defects in the autonomic nervous system or particular organs; psychological factors, such as particular needs, attitudes, or personality styles; and sociocultural factors, such as aversive social conditions and cultural pressures.

For years, clinical researchers singled out a limited number of physical illnesses as psychophysiological, such as ulcers and hypertension. Recently many other psychophysiological disorders have been identified. Indeed, scientists have linked many physical illnesses to stress and have developed a new area of study called psychoneuroimmunology. Stress can slow lymphocyte activity, thereby interfering with the immune system's ability to protect against illness during times of stress. Factors that seem to affect immune functioning include norepinephrine and cortisol activity, behavioral changes, personality style, and social support.

#

#TheirWords

"I would rather have anything wrong with my body than something wrong with my head."

Sylvia Plath, *The Bell Jar*

Psychological Treatments for Physical Disorders

As clinicians have discovered that stress and related psychological and sociocultural factors may contribute to physical disorders, they have applied psychological treatments to more and more medical problems. The most common of these interventions are relaxation training, biofeedback, meditation, hypnosis, cognitive interventions, support groups, and therapies to increase awareness and expression of emotions. The field of treatment that combines psychological and physical approaches to treat or prevent medical problems is known as **behavioral medicine.**

behavioral medicine A field that combines psychological and physical interventions to treat or prevent medical problems.

relaxation training A treatment procedure that teaches clients to relax at will so they can calm themselves in stressful situations.

biofeedback A technique in which a client is given information about physiological reactions as they occur and learns to control the reactions voluntarily.

Relaxation Training

As you saw in Chapter 4, therapists sometimes teach clients to relax their muscles at will. The notion behind such **relaxation training** is that physical relaxation will lead to a state of psychological relaxation. In one version, therapists teach clients to identify individual muscle groups, tense them, release the tension, and ultimately relax the whole body. With continued practice, they can bring on a state of deep muscle relaxation. Given that relaxation training is useful in the treatment of phobias and other anxiety disorders, clinicians believe that it can also help prevent or treat medical illnesses that are related to stress.

Although doctors now prescribe psychological interventions for a range of medical problems, many patients resist such treatments. Why?

Relaxation training, often in combination with medication, has been widely used in the treatment of high blood pressure (Aalami et al., 2016). It has also been of some help in treating somatic symptom disorder, headaches, insomnia, asthma, diabetes, pain, certain vascular diseases, and the undesirable effects of certain cancer treatments (Martin, 2018; Simkin & Klein, 2018; Ernst, 2017).

Biofeedback

In **biofeedback,** therapists use electrical signals from the body to train people to control physiological processes such as heart rate or muscle tension. Clients are connected

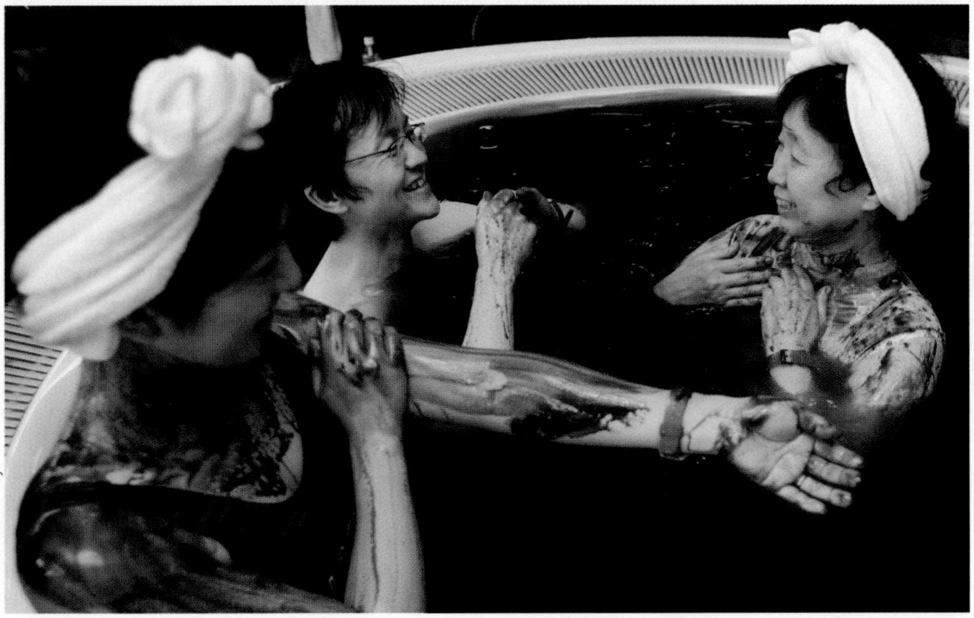

AP Photo/Itsuo Inouye

Relaxing—and delicious! New stress-relief programs, techniques, and products are constantly being introduced to the marketplace. These three individuals, for example, are able to unwind and relax in a chocolate spa at the Hakone Yunessun spa resort in Japan.

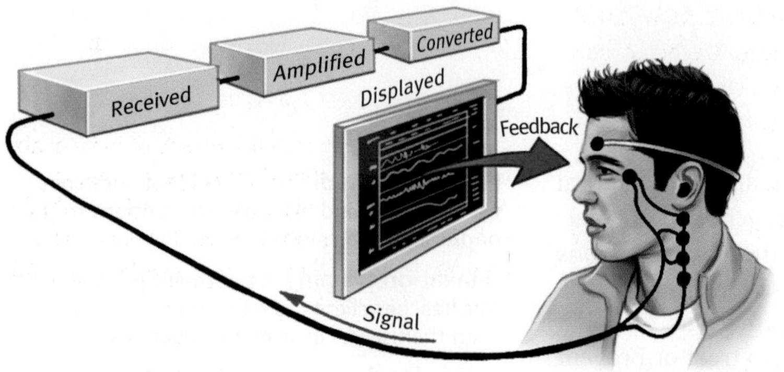

FIGURE 8-4

Biofeedback at Work

This biofeedback system records tension in the forehead muscles of a person with severe headaches. The system receives, amplifies, converts, and displays information about the tension, allowing the client to "observe" it and to try to reduce his tension responses.

to a monitor that gives them continuous information about their bodily activities. By attending to the signals from the monitor, they may gradually learn to control even seemingly involuntary physiological processes.

The most widely applied method of biofeedback uses a device called an *electromyograph* (*EMG*), which provides feedback about the level of muscular tension in the body. Electrodes are attached to the client's muscles—usually the forehead muscles—where they detect the minute electrical activity that accompanies muscle tension (see **Figure 8-4**). The device then converts the electric energy, or *potentials,* coming from the muscles into an image, such as lines on a screen, or into a tone whose pitch changes along with changes in muscle tension. Thus clients "see" or "hear" when their muscles are becoming more or less tense. Through repeated trial and error, the individuals become skilled at voluntarily reducing muscle tension.

In a classic study, EMG feedback was used to treat 16 patients who had facial pain caused in part by tension in their jaw muscles (Dohrmann & Laskin, 1978). Changes in the pitch and volume of the tone indicate changes in muscle tension. After "listening" to EMG feedback repeatedly, the 16 patients in this study learned how to relax their jaw muscles at will and later reported that they had less facial pain.

EMG feedback has also been used successfully in the treatment of headaches and muscular disabilities caused by strokes or accidents. Still other forms of biofeedback training have been of some help in the treatment of heartbeat irregularities, asthma, high blood pressure, stuttering, and pain (Garza & Schwedt, 2018; Tofler, 2018).

Meditation

Although meditation has been practiced since ancient times, Western health care professionals have only recently become aware of its effectiveness in relieving physical distress. *Meditation* is a technique of turning one's concentration inward, achieving a slightly changed state of consciousness, and temporarily ignoring all stressors. Typically, meditators go to a quiet place, assume a comfortable posture, utter or think a particular sound (called a *mantra*) to help focus their attention, and allow their mind to turn away from all outside thoughts and concerns. Many people who meditate regularly report feeling more peaceful, engaged, and creative (Basso et al., 2019). Meditation has been used to help manage pain and to treat high blood pressure, heart problems, asthma, skin disorders, diabetes, insomnia, and even viral infections (Bonnet & Arand, 2018; Park & Han, 2017; Tofler, 2017).

One form of meditation that has been used in particular by patients suffering from severe pain is *mindfulness meditation* (Gu, Hou, & Fang, 2018; Anheyer et al., 2017). Here, as you read in Chapters 2 and 4, mindfulness meditators pay attention to the feelings, thoughts, and sensations that are flowing through their mind during meditation, but they do so with detachment and objectivity and, most importantly, without judgment. By just being mindful but not judgmental of their feelings and thoughts, including feelings of pain, they are less inclined to label them, fixate on them, or react negatively to them.

#FunnyRemedy

After watching a humorous video, research participants who laughed at the video showed decreases in stress and improvements in natural killer cell activity (Radcliff, 2017; Bennett, 1998).

Hypnosis

As you saw in Chapter 1, people who undergo *hypnosis* are guided by a hypnotist into a sleeplike, suggestible state during which they can be directed to act in unusual ways, feel unusual sensations, remember seemingly forgotten events, or forget remembered events. With training, some people are even able to induce their own hypnotic state (*self-hypnosis*). Hypnosis is now used as an aid to psychotherapy and to help treat many physical conditions.

Hypnosis seems to be particularly helpful in the control of pain (Simkin & Klein, 2018; Strada & Portenoy, 2018). A breakthrough case study described a patient who underwent dental surgery under hypnotic suggestion: after a hypnotic state was induced, the dentist suggested to the patient that he was in a pleasant and relaxed setting listening to a friend describe his own success at undergoing similar dental surgery under hypnosis. The dentist then proceeded to perform a successful 25-minute operation (Gheorghiu & Orleanu, 1982). Although only some people are able to go through surgery while anesthetized by hypnosis alone, hypnosis combined with chemical forms of anesthesia is apparently helpful to many patients. Beyond its use in the control of pain, hypnosis has been used successfully to help treat such problems as skin diseases, asthma, insomnia, high blood pressure, warts, and other forms of infection (Sawni & Breuner, 2017; Becker, 2015).

#GoodViewTherapy

According to one hospital's records of individuals who underwent gallbladder surgery, those in rooms with a good view from their window had shorter hospitalizations and needed fewer pain medications than those in rooms without a good view (Ulrich, 1984).

Cognitive-Behavioral Interventions

People with physical ailments have sometimes been taught new attitudes or cognitive responses toward their ailments as part of treatment (Sandler et al., 2017). For example, an approach called *self-instruction training,* or *stress inoculation training,* has helped patients cope with severe pain (Meichenbaum, 2017, 1993, 1975). In this training, therapists teach people to identify and eventually rid themselves of unpleasant thoughts that keep emerging during pain episodes (so-called *negative self-statements,* such as "Oh no, I can't take this pain") and to replace them with *coping self-statements* instead (for example, "When pain comes, just pause; keep focusing on what you have to do").

Support Groups and Emotion Expression

If anxiety, depression, anger, and the like contribute to a person's physical ills, interventions to reduce these negative emotions should help reduce the ills. Thus it is not surprising that some medically ill people have profited from support groups, including online support groups, and from therapies that guide them to become more aware of and express their emotions and needs (Gabbe et al., 2017; Cacioppo et al., 2016). Research suggests that the discussion, or even the writing down, of past and present emotions or upsets may help improve a person's health, just as it may help one's psychological functioning (Krupnick et al., 2017; Smyth & Pennebaker, 2001). In one

© Li Muyi /Color China Photos/ZUMA Press

AP Photo/Jerry Lai

Student stress-busters: East and West
According to research, frequent testing is the second-most-stressful life event for high school and college students. To reduce such stress, college applicants from Beijing give one another head massages in preparation for China's college entrance exams (left). In the meantime, students at a dorm at Northwestern University in the United States try to blow off steam by performing "primal screams" during their final exam period (right).

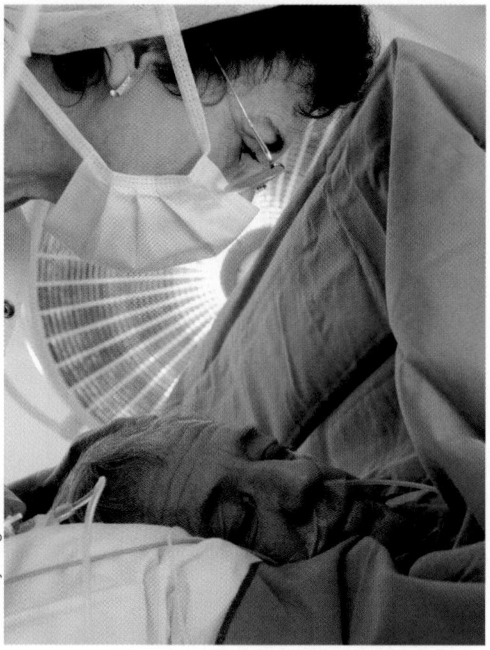

BSIP/Getty Images

The hypnotic way An anesthesiologist hypnotizes a patient undergoing major surgery at the University Hospital Center of Liege in Belgium. Many surgeries at the hospital are conducted using a combination of hypnosis and a local anesthetic rather than general anesthesia.

study, asthma and arthritis patients who wrote down their thoughts and feelings about stressful events for a handful of days showed lasting improvements in their conditions. Similarly, stress-related writing was found to be beneficial for patients with either HIV or cancer.

Combination Approaches

Studies have found that the various psychological interventions for physical problems tend to be equally effective (Sawni & Breuner, 2017). Relaxation and biofeedback training, for example, are equally helpful (and more helpful than placebos) in the treatment of high blood pressure, headaches, and asthma. Psychological interventions are, in fact, often most helpful when they are combined with other psychological interventions and with medical treatments (Strada & Portenoy, 2018; Sandler et al., 2017). In a classic study, ulcer patients who were given relaxation, self-instruction, and assertiveness training along with medication were found to be less anxious and more comfortable, to have fewer symptoms, and to have a better long-term outcome than patients who received medication only (Brooks & Richardson, 1980). Combination interventions have also been helpful in changing Type A patterns and in reducing the risk of coronary heart disease among people who display Type A kinds of behavior (Burg, 2017; Burke & Riley, 2010).

Clearly, the treatment picture for physical illnesses has been changing dramatically. While medical treatments continue to dominate, today's medical practitioners are traveling a course far removed from that of their counterparts in centuries past.

...SUMMING UP

PSYCHOLOGICAL TREATMENTS FOR PHYSICAL DISORDERS Behavioral medicine combines psychological and physical interventions to treat or prevent medical problems. Psychological approaches such as relaxation training, biofeedback training, meditation, hypnosis, cognitive-behavioral techniques, support groups, and therapies that heighten the awareness and expression of emotions and needs are increasingly being included in the treatment of various medical problems.

Expanding the Boundaries of Abnormal Psychology

Once considered outside the field of abnormal psychology, bodily ailments and physical illnesses are now seen as problems that fall squarely within its boundaries. Just as physical factors have long been recognized as playing a role in abnormal mental functioning, psychological conditions are now considered important contributors to abnormal physical functioning. In fact, many of today's clinicians believe that psychological and sociocultural factors contribute to some degree to the onset and course of virtually all physical ailments.

The number of studies devoted to this relationship has risen steadily during the past 40 years. What researchers once saw as a vague connection between stress and physical illness is now understood as a complex interaction of many variables. Such factors as life changes, a person's particular psychological state, social support, biochemical activity, and slowing of the immune system are all recognized as contributors to disorders once considered purely physical.

One of the most exciting aspects of these recent developments is the field's growing emphasis on the *interrelationship* of the social environment,

CLINICAL CHOICES

Now that you've read about disorders featuring somatic symptoms, try the interactive case study for this chapter. See if you are able to identify Joanne's symptoms and suggest a diagnosis based on her symptoms. What kind of treatment would be most effective for Joanne? Go to **LaunchPad** to access ***Clinical Choices***.

the brain, and the rest of the body. Researchers have observed repeatedly that mental disorders are often best understood and treated when sociocultural, psychological, and biological factors are all taken into consideration. They now know that this interaction also helps explain medical problems. We are reminded that the brain is part of the body and that both are part of a social context. For better and for worse, the three are intertwined.

...Key Terms

mind-body dualism, p. 238
malingering, p. 238
factitious disorder, p. 238
Munchausen syndrome, p. 239
Munchausen syndrome by proxy, p. 239
conversion disorder, p. 241
somatic symptom disorder, p. 242
Electra complex, p. 244
primary gain, p. 245
secondary gain, p. 246
illness anxiety disorder, p. 248
psychophysiological disorder, p. 249
psychological factors affecting other medical conditions, p. 249
ulcer, p. 249
asthma, p. 250
insomnia, p. 250
muscle contraction headaches, p. 250
migraine headaches, p. 251
hypertension, p. 251
coronary heart disease, p. 251
Type A personality style, p. 253
Type B personality style, p. 253
Social Readjustment Rating Scale, p. 255
psychoneuroimmunology, p. 256
immune system, p. 256
antigen, p. 256
lymphocyte, p. 256
cytokines, p. 257
behavioral medicine, p. 259
relaxation training, p. 259
biofeedback, p. 259
electromyograph, p. 260
meditation, p. 260
hypnosis, p. 260
self-instruction training, p. 261

...Quick Quiz

1. What are the symptoms of factitious disorder, conversion disorder, and somatic symptom disorder? *pp. 238–244*
2. How do practitioners distinguish conversion disorder from a "genuine" medical problem? What are two different patterns of somatic symptom disorder? *pp. 242–244*
3. What are the leading explanations and treatments for conversion and somatic symptom disorder? How well does research support them? *pp. 244–248*
4. What are the symptoms, causes, and treatments of illness anxiety disorder? *pp. 248–249*
5. What are the specific causes of ulcers, asthma, insomnia, headaches, hypertension, and coronary heart disease? *pp. 249–251*
6. What kinds of biological, psychological, and sociocultural factors appear to contribute to psychophysiological disorders? *pp. 251–254*
7. What kind of relationship has been found between life stress and physical illnesses? What scale has helped researchers investigate this relationship? *pp. 254–256*
8. Describe the connection between stress, the immune system, and physical illness. Explain the specific roles played by various types of lymphocytes. *p. 256*
9. Discuss how immune system functioning at times of stress may be affected by a person's biochemical activity, behavioral changes, personality style, and social support. *pp. 256–258*
10. What psychological treatments have been used to help treat physical illnesses? To which specific illnesses has each been applied? *pp. 259–262*

Visit ***LaunchPad***
to access the e-Book, Clinical Choices, videos, activities, and LearningCurve, as well as study aids including flashcards, FAQs, and research exercises.
LaunchPad

65
70cm

CHAPTER

9

Eating Disorders

Shani, age 15: While I was learning to resist the temptation of hunger, I walked into the kitchen when no one was around, took a slice of bread out the packet, toasted it, spread butter on it, took a deep breath and bit. Guilty. I spat it in the trash and tossed the rest of it in and walked away. Seconds later I longed for the toast, walked back to the trash, popped open the lid and sifted around in the debris. I found it and contemplated, for minutes, whether to eat it. I brought it close to my nose and inhaled the smell of melted butter. Guilty. Guilty for trashing it. Guilty for craving it. Guilty for tasting it. I threw it back in the trash and walked away. No is no, I told myself. No is no.

. . . And no matter how hard I would try to always have The Perfect Day in terms of my food, I would feel the guilt every second of every day . . . It was my desire to escape the guilt that perpetuated my compulsion to starve.

In time I formulated a more precise list of "can" and "can't" in my head that dictated what I was allowed or forbidden to consume. . . . It became my way of life. My manual. My blueprint. But more than that, it gave me false reassurance that my life was under control. I was managing everything because I had this list in front of me telling me what—and what not—to do. . . .

In the beginning, starving was hard work. It was not innate. Day by day I was slowly lured into another world, a world that was . . . as rewarding as it was challenging. . . .

That summer, despite the fact that I had lost a lot of weight, my mother agreed to let me go to summer camp with my fifteen-year-old peers, after I swore to her that I would eat. I broke that promise as soon as I got there. . . . At breakfast time when all the teens raced into the dining hall to grab cereal boxes and bread loaves and jelly tins and peanut butter jars, I sat alone cocooned in my fear. I fingered the plastic packet of a loaf of white sliced bread, took out a piece and tore off a corner, like I was marking a page in a book, onto which I dabbed a blob of peanut butter and jelly the size of a Q-tip. That was my breakfast. Every day. For three weeks.

I tried to get to the showers when everyone else was at the beach so nobody would see me. I heard girls behind me whispering, "That's the girl I told you about that looks so disgusting." Someone invariably walked in on me showering and covered her mouth with her hand like I was a dead body. I wished I could disappear into the drain like my hair that was falling out in chunks. . . .

[Upon returning to school] I was labeled the "concentration camp victim." On my return, over the months everyone watched my body shrink as though it were being vacuum packed in slow motion. . . . At my lowest weight my hipbones protruded like knuckle bones under my dress and I had to minimize the increments of the belt holes until there was so much extra belt material dangling down that I did away with the belt completely. My shoes were too big for my feet; my ankles were so thin that I wore three pairs of socks at a time and still my shoes would slide off my heels. And my panties were so baggy I secured them with safety pins on the sides so they wouldn't fall down. . . .

On the home front things were worse than ever. . . I locked my door and forbade anyone from entering. Even so, my mother and I had screaming matches every day, with her trying to convince me that "your body needs food as fuel" and me retaliating with "I'm not hungry." . . .

TOPIC OVERVIEW

> *For nine months my mother stood by, forbidden to interfere, while I starved myself. She had no idea what was going on, nor did I. . . . She watched me transform from an innocent, soft, kind, loving girl into a reclusive, vicious, aggressive, defiant teenager. . . . And there was nothing she could say or do to stop me. . . .*
>
> *(Raviv, 2010)*

It has not always done so, but Western society today equates thinness with health and beauty. In fact, in the United States thinness has become a national obsession. Most of us are as preoccupied with how much we eat as with the taste and nutritional value of our food. Thus it is not surprising that during the past three decades we have also witnessed an increase in two eating disorders that have at their core a morbid fear of gaining weight. Sufferers of *anorexia nervosa,* like Shani, are convinced that they need to be extremely thin, and they lose so much weight that they may starve themselves to death. People with *bulimia nervosa* go on frequent eating binges, during which they uncontrollably consume large quantities of food, and then force themselves to vomit or take other extreme steps to keep from gaining weight. A third eating disorder, *binge-eating disorder,* in which people frequently go on eating binges but do not force themselves to vomit or engage in other such behaviors, also is on the rise. People with binge-eating disorder do not fear weight gain to the same degree as those with anorexia nervosa and bulimia nervosa, but they do have many of the other features found in those disorders (NIMH, 2017).

The news media have published many reports about eating disorders. One reason for the surge in public interest is the frightening medical consequences that can result from the disorders. The public first became aware of such consequences in 1983 when Karen Carpenter died from medical problems related to anorexia. Carpenter, the 32-year-old lead singer of the soft-rock brother-and-sister duo called the Carpenters, had been enormously successful and was admired by many as a wholesome and healthy model to young women everywhere. Another reason for the current concern is the disproportionate prevalence of anorexia nervosa and bulimia nervosa among adolescent girls and young women (Keel, 2018; NIMH, 2017).

#EarlyPublication

The first diet book was published in England, in the mid-1800s (Herman, 2015).

Anorexia Nervosa

Shani, 15 years old and in the ninth grade, displays many symptoms of **anorexia nervosa** (APA, 2013). She purposely maintains a significantly low body weight, intensely fears becoming overweight, has a distorted view of her weight and shape, and is excessively influenced by her weight and shape in her self-evaluations (see **Table 9-1**).

Like Shani, at least half of the people with anorexia nervosa reduce their weight by restricting their intake of food, a pattern called *restricting-type anorexia nervosa*. First they tend to cut out sweets and fattening snacks; then, increasingly, they eliminate other foods. Eventually people with this kind of anorexia nervosa show almost no variability in diet. Others, however, lose weight by forcing themselves to vomit after meals or by abusing laxatives or diuretics, and they may even engage in eating binges, a pattern called *binge-eating/purging-type anorexia nervosa*, which you will read about in more detail in the section on bulimia nervosa.

Between 75 and 90 percent of all cases of anorexia nervosa occur in females (NIMH, 2017). Although the disorder can appear at any age, the peak age of onset is between 14 and 20 years. Between 0.6 and 4.0 percent of all females in Western countries develop the disorder in their lifetime, and many more display at least some of its symptoms (NIMH, 2017; Forman, 2017). It seems to be on the increase in North America, Europe, and Japan.

TABLE: 9-1

Dx Checklist

Anorexia Nervosa
1. Individual purposely takes in too little nourishment, resulting in body weight that is very low and below that of other people of similar age and gender.
2. Individual is very fearful of gaining weight, or repeatedly seeks to prevent weight gain despite low body weight.
3. Individual has a distorted body perception, places inappropriate emphasis on weight or shape in judgments of herself or himself, or fails to appreciate the serious implications of her or his low weight.

Information from: APA, 2013.

Typically the disorder begins after a person who is slightly overweight or of normal weight has been on a diet (NEDA, 2018; APA, 2015). The escalation toward anorexia nervosa may follow a stressful event such as separation of parents, a move away from home, or an experience of personal failure. Although most people with the disorder recover, as many as 6 percent of them become so seriously ill that they die, usually from medical problems brought about by starvation, or from suicide (Mehler, 2017). The suicide rate among people with anorexia nervosa is five times the rate found in the general population (Klein & Attia, 2017).

The Clinical Picture

Becoming thin is the key goal for people with anorexia nervosa, but *fear* provides their motivation. People with this disorder are afraid of becoming obese, of giving in to their growing desire to eat, and more generally of losing control over the size and shape of their bodies. In addition, despite their focus on thinness and the severe restrictions they may place on their food intake, people with anorexia are *preoccupied with food*. They may spend considerable time thinking and even reading about food and planning their limited meals (Ekern, 2018; Klein & Attia, 2017). Many report that their dreams are filled with images of food and eating.

This preoccupation with food may in fact be a result of food deprivation rather than its cause. In a famous "starvation study" conducted in the late 1940s, 36 normal-weight conscientious objectors were put on a semistarvation diet for six months (Keys et al., 1950). Like people with anorexia nervosa, the volunteers became preoccupied with food and eating. They spent hours each day planning their small meals, talked more about food than about any other topic, studied cookbooks and recipes, mixed food in odd combinations, and dawdled over their meals. Many also had vivid dreams about food.

Wallace Kirkland/Getty Images

Laboratory starvation Thirty-six conscientious objectors who were put on a semistarvation diet for six months developed many of the symptoms seen in anorexia nervosa and bulimia nervosa (Keys et al., 1950).

Persons with anorexia nervosa also *think in distorted ways*. They usually have a low opinion of their body shape, for example, and consider themselves unattractive (Klein & Attia, 2017). In addition, they are likely to overestimate their actual proportions. While most women in Western society overestimate their body size, the estimates of those with anorexia nervosa are particularly high. In one of her classic books on eating disorders, Hilde Bruch, a pioneer in this field, recalled the self-perceptions of a 23-year-old patient:

> *I look in a full-length mirror at least four or five times daily and I really cannot see myself as too thin. Sometimes after several days of strict dieting, I feel that my shape is tolerable, but most of the time, odd as it may seem, I look in the mirror and believe that I am too fat.*
>
> *(Bruch, 1973)*

This tendency to overestimate body size has been tested in the laboratory (Klein & Attia, 2017). In a popular assessment technique, research participants look at a photograph of themselves through an adjustable lens. They are asked to adjust the lens until the image that they see matches their actual body size. The image can be made to vary from 20 percent thinner to 20 percent larger than actual appearance. In one study, more than half of the individuals with anorexia nervosa overestimated their body size, stopping the lens when the image was larger than they actually were.

The distorted thinking of anorexia nervosa also takes the form of certain maladaptive attitudes and misperceptions (Grzelak et al., 2017). Sufferers tend to hold such beliefs as "I must be perfect in every way"; "I will become a better person if I deprive myself"; and "I can avoid guilt by not eating."

People with anorexia nervosa also have certain *psychological problems,* such as depression, anxiety, low self-esteem, and insomnia or other sleep disturbances (Klein

anorexia nervosa A disorder marked by the pursuit of extreme thinness and by extreme weight loss.

& Attia, 2017). A number grapple with substance abuse. And many display obsessive-compulsive patterns. They may set rigid rules for food preparation or even cut food into specific shapes. Broader obsessive-compulsive patterns are common as well. Many, for example, exercise compulsively, prioritizing exercise over most other activities in their lives. In some research, people with anorexia nervosa and others with obsessive-compulsive disorder score equally high for obsessiveness and compulsiveness. Finally, persons with anorexia nervosa tend to be perfectionistic, a characteristic that typically precedes the onset of the disorder.

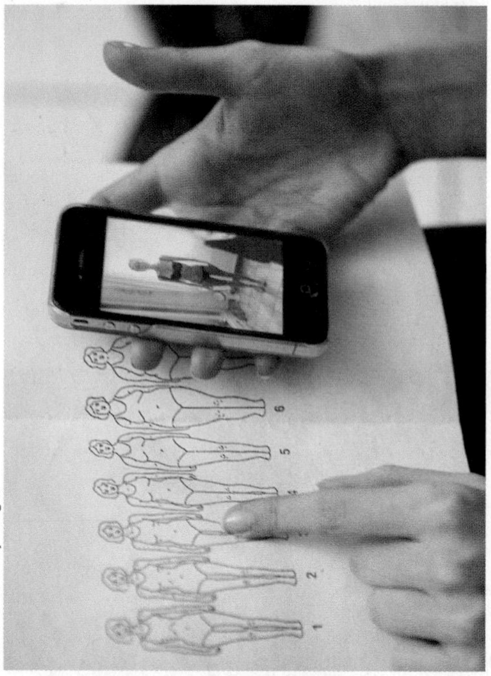

BSIP/UIG via Getty Images

Seeing is deceiving In one assessment and research technique, people look at drawings of bodies, ranging from very thin to obese, then select the silhouette they believe represents their own body size. Individuals with anorexia nervosa typically pick the wrong body size even if they hold photos of themselves during the task.

Medical Problems

The starvation habits of anorexia nervosa cause medical problems (Lawson & Miller, 2017; Mehler, 2017). Women develop **amenorrhea,** the absence of menstrual cycles. Other problems include lowered body temperature, low blood pressure, body swelling, reduced bone mineral density, and slow heart rate. Metabolic and electrolyte imbalances also may occur and can lead to death by heart failure or circulatory collapse. The poor nutrition of people with anorexia nervosa may also cause skin to become rough, dry, and cracked; nails to become brittle; and hands and feet to be cold and blue. Some people lose hair from the scalp, and some grow *lanugo* (the fine, silky hair that covers some newborns) on their trunk, extremities, and face. Shani, the young woman whose self-description opened this chapter, recalls how her body deteriorated as her disorder was progressing: "Nobody knew that I was always cold no matter how many layers I wore, that my hair came out in thick wads whenever I wet it or washed it, that I stopped menstruating, [and] that my hipbones hurt to lie on my stomach and my coccyx hurt to sit on the floor" (Raviv, 2010).

...SUMMING UP

ANOREXIA NERVOSA Rates of eating disorders have increased dramatically as thinness has become a national obsession. People with anorexia nervosa pursue extreme thinness and lose dangerous amounts of weight. They may follow a pattern of restricting-type anorexia nervosa or binge-eating/purging-type anorexia nervosa. The central features of anorexia nervosa are a drive for thinness, intense fear of weight gain, and disturbed body perception and other cognitive disturbances. People with this disorder develop various medical problems, particularly amenorrhea. As many as 90 percent of all cases of anorexia nervosa occur among females.

Bulimia Nervosa

People with **bulimia nervosa**—a disorder also known as **binge-purge syndrome**—engage in repeated episodes of uncontrollable overeating, or **binges.** A binge episode takes place over a limited period of time, often two hours, during which the person eats much more food than most people would eat during a similar time span (APA, 2013). In addition, people with this disorder repeatedly perform inappropriate *compensatory behaviors,* such as forcing themselves to vomit; misusing laxatives, diuretics, or enemas; fasting; or exercising excessively (see **Table 9-2**). Lindsey, a woman who has since recovered from bulimia nervosa, describes a morning during her disorder:

> *Today I am going to be really good and that means eating certain predetermined portions of food and not taking one more bite than I think I am allowed. I am very careful to see that I don't take more than Doug does. I judge by his body. I can feel the tension building. I wish Doug would hurry up and leave so I can get going!*

amenorrhea The absence of menstrual cycles.

bulimia nervosa A disorder marked by frequent eating binges followed by forced vomiting or other extreme compensatory behaviors to avoid gaining weight. Also known as *binge-purge syndrome.*

binge An episode of uncontrollable eating during which a person ingests a very large quantity of food.

As soon as he shuts the door, I try to get involved with one of the myriad of responsibilities on the list. I hate them all! I just want to crawl into a hole. I don't want to do anything. I'd rather eat. I am alone, I am nervous, I am no good, I always do everything wrong anyway, I am not in control, I can't make it through the day, I just know it. It has been the same for so long.

I remember the starchy cereal I ate for breakfast. I am into the bathroom and onto the scale. It measures the same, but I don't want to stay the same! I want to be thinner! I look in the mirror, I think my thighs are ugly and deformed looking. I see a lumpy, clumsy, pear-shaped wimp. There is always something wrong with what I see. I feel frustrated trapped in this body and I don't know what to do about it.

I float to the refrigerator knowing exactly what is there. I begin with last night's brownies. I always begin with the sweets. At first I try to make it look like nothing is missing, but my appetite is huge and I resolve to make another batch of brownies. I know there is half of a bag of cookies in the bathroom, thrown out the night before, and I polish them off immediately. I take some milk so my vomiting will be smoother. I like the full feeling I get after downing a big glass. I get out six pieces of bread and toast one side in the broiler, turn them over and load them with patties of butter and put them under the broiler again till they are bubbling. I take all six pieces on a plate to the television and go back for a bowl of cereal and a banana to have along with them. Before the last toast is finished, I am already preparing the next batch of six more pieces. Maybe another brownie or five, and a couple of large bowlfuls of ice cream, yogurt or cottage cheese. My stomach is stretched into a huge ball below my ribcage. I know I'll have to go into the bathroom soon, but I want to postpone it. I am in never-never land. I am waiting, feeling the pressure, pacing the floor in and out of the rooms. Time is passing. Time is passing. It is getting to be time.

I wander aimlessly through each of the rooms again tidying, making the whole house neat and put back together. I finally make the turn into the bathroom. I brace my feet, pull my hair back and stick my finger down my throat, stroking twice, and get up a huge pile of food. Three times, four and another pile of food. I can see everything come back. I am glad to see those brownies because they are SO fattening. The rhythm of the emptying is broken and my head is beginning to hurt. I stand up feeling dizzy, empty and weak. The whole episode has taken about an hour.

(Hall & Cohn, 2010, p. 1)

Like anorexia nervosa, bulimia nervosa usually occurs in females, again in 75 to 90 percent of the cases (NIMH, 2017; Forman, 2017). It begins in adolescence or young adulthood (most often between 15 and 20 years of age) and often lasts for years, with periodic letup. The weight of people with bulimia nervosa usually stays within a normal range, although it may fluctuate markedly within that range. Some people with this disorder, however, become seriously underweight and may eventually qualify for a diagnosis of anorexia nervosa instead (see **Figure 9-1**).

TABLE: 9-2

Dx Checklist

Bulimia Nervosa
1. Repeated binge-eating episodes.
2. Repeated performance of ill-advised compensatory behaviors (e.g., forced vomiting) to prevent weight gain.
3. Symptoms take place at least weekly for a period of 3 months.
4. Inappropriate influence of weight and shape on appraisal of oneself.

Information from: APA, 2013.

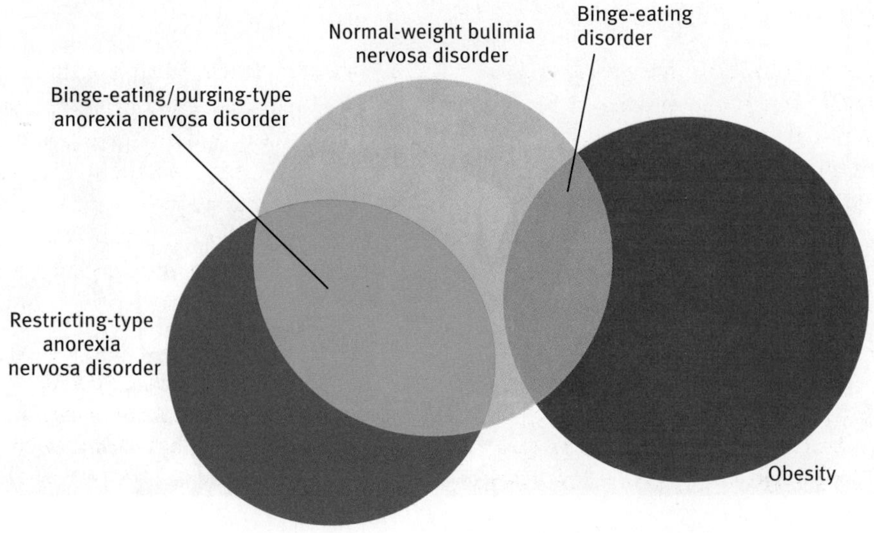

FIGURE 9-1

Overlapping Patterns of Eating Disorders

Some people with anorexia nervosa binge and purge their way to weight loss, and some obese people binge eat. However, most people with bulimia nervosa are not obese, and most overweight people do not binge eat.

TABLE: 9-3

Comparing the Eating Disorders

	One-Year Prevalence	Percentage Who Are Female	Typical Age at Onset	Percentage Who Receive Treatment	Successful Long-Term Recovery After Treatment
Anorexia nervosa	0.6–4.0%	75–90%	14–20 years	34%	75%
Bulimia nervosa	0.5–5.0%	75–90%	15–20 years	43%	75%
Binge-eating disorder	2.0–7.0%	64–70%	22–30 years	44%	60%

Information from: Ekern, 2018, 2014; Mitchell, 2018; Crow, 2017; Engel et al., 2017; Forman, 2017; Klein & Attia, 2017; NIMH, 2017; Sysko & Devlin, 2017.

#

#DietBusiness

Americans spend $68 billion each year on weight-reduction foods, products, and services. The vast majority of that amount is spent on diet foods (LaRosa, 2018; Fooducate, 2016).

Many teenagers and young adults go on occasional eating binges or experiment with vomiting or laxatives after they hear about these behaviors from their friends or the media. Indeed, according to global studies, 25 to 50 percent of all students report periodic binge eating or self-induced vomiting (Ekern, 2018). Only some of these individuals, however, qualify for a diagnosis of bulimia nervosa. Surveys in several Western countries suggest that between 0.5 and 5.0 percent of women develop the full syndrome (Engel, Steffen, & Mitchell, 2017; NIMH, 2017) (see **Table 9-3**). Among college students the rate seems to be particularly high (Jacobson, 2018; Zerbe, 2008).

Binges

People with bulimia nervosa may have between 1 and 30 binge episodes per week (Fairburn et al., 2015, 2008). In most cases, they carry out the binges in secret. The person eats massive amounts of food very rapidly, with minimal chewing—usually sweet, high-calorie foods with a soft texture, such as ice cream, cookies, doughnuts, and sandwiches. The food is hardly tasted or thought about. Binge eaters consume an average of 2,000 to 3,400 calories during an episode (Engel et al., 2017). Some individuals consume as many as 10,000 calories.

Curtis Means/NBC NewsWire/Getty Images

Eating for sport Many people go on occasional eating binges. In fact, sometimes binges are officially endorsed, as you see in this photo from the annual Nathan's Famous International Hot Dog Eating Contest in Brooklyn's Coney Island, New York. However, people are considered to have an eating disorder only when the binges recur, the pattern endures, and the issues of weight or shape dominate self-evaluation.

Binges are usually preceded by feelings of great tension. The person feels irritable, "unreal," and powerless to control an overwhelming need to eat "forbidden" foods. During the binge, the person feels unable to stop eating (APA, 2013). Although the binge itself may be experienced as pleasurable in the sense that it relieves the unbearable tension the individual has been experiencing, it is followed by feelings of extreme self-blame, shame, guilt, and depression, as well as fears of gaining weight and being discovered (Engel et al., 2017).

Compensatory Behaviors

After a binge, people with bulimia nervosa try to compensate for and undo its effects. Many resort to vomiting, for example. But vomiting actually fails to prevent the absorption of half of the calories consumed during a binge. Furthermore, because repeated vomiting affects one's general ability to feel satiated, it leads to greater hunger and more frequent and intense binges. Similarly, the use of laxatives or diuretics largely fails to undo the caloric effects of bingeing (Mitchell, 2018).

Vomiting and other compensatory behaviors may temporarily relieve the uncomfortable physical feelings of fullness or reduce the feelings of anxiety and self-disgust attached to binge eating (Stewart & Williamson, 2008). Over time, however, a cycle develops in which purging allows more bingeing, and bingeing necessitates more purging (Mitchell, 2018). The cycle eventually causes people with the disorder to feel powerless and disgusted with themselves (Engel et al., 2017). Most recognize fully that they have an eating disorder. Lindsey, the woman we met earlier, recalls how the pattern of binge eating, purging, and self-disgust took hold while she was a teenager in boarding school.

Can you think of other areas of life besides eating and food in which people sometimes binge and purge?

Every bite that went into my mouth was a naughty and selfish indulgence, and I became more and more disgusted with myself. . . .

The first time I stuck my fingers down my throat was during the last week of school. I saw a girl come out of the bathroom with her face all red and her eyes puffy. She had always talked about her weight and how she should be dieting even though her body was really shapely. I knew instantly what she had just done and I had to try it. . . .

I began with breakfasts which were served buffet-style on the main floor of the dorm. I learned which foods I could eat that would come back up easily. When I woke in the morning, I had to make the decision whether to stuff myself for half an hour and throw up before class, or whether to try and make it through the whole day without overeating. . . . I always thought people noticed when I took huge portions at mealtimes, but I figured they assumed that because I was an athlete, I burned it off. . . . Once a binge was under way, I did not stop until my stomach looked pregnant and I felt like I could not swallow one more time.

That year was the first of my nine years of obsessive eating and throwing up. . . . I didn't want to tell anyone what I was doing, and I didn't want to stop. . . . [Though] being in love or other distractions occasionally lessened the cravings, I always returned to the food.

(Hall & Cohn, 2010, p. 55)

As with anorexia nervosa, a bulimic pattern typically begins during or after a period of intense dieting, often one that has been successful and earned praise from family members and friends (APA, 2015). Studies of both animals and humans have found that normal research participants placed on very strict diets also develop a tendency to binge (Pankevich et al., 2010). Some of the participants in the conscientious objector "starvation study," for example, later binged when they were allowed to return to regular eating, and a number of them continued to be hungry even after large meals (Keys et al., 1950).

#RoyalBulimia

During her three years as queen of England, Anne Boleyn, King Henry VIII's second wife, displayed a habit, first observed during her coronation banquet, of vomiting during meals. In fact, she assigned a lady-in-waiting the task of holding up a sheet when the queen looked likely to vomit (Shaw, 2004).

binge-eating disorder A disorder marked by frequent binges without extreme compensatory acts.

Bulimia Nervosa Versus Anorexia Nervosa

Bulimia nervosa is similar to anorexia nervosa in many ways. Both disorders typically begin after a period of dieting by people who are fearful of becoming obese; driven to become thin; preoccupied with food, weight, and appearance; and struggling with depression, anxiety, obsessiveness, and the need to be perfect (Engel et al., 2017; Klein & Attia, 2017). People with either of the disorders have a heightened risk of suicide attempts and fatalities. Substance abuse may accompany either disorder, perhaps beginning with the excessive use of diet pills. People with either disorder believe that they weigh too much and look too heavy regardless of their actual weight or appearance (see ***InfoCentral*** on the next page). And both disorders are marked by disturbed attitudes toward eating.

Yet the two disorders also differ in important ways. Although people with either disorder worry about the opinions of others, those with bulimia nervosa tend to be more concerned about pleasing others, being attractive to others, and having intimate relationships (Zerbe, 2017, 2010, 2008). They also tend to be more sexually experienced and active than people with anorexia nervosa (Gonidakis et al., 2015). Particularly troublesome, they are more likely to have long histories of mood swings, become easily frustrated or bored, and have trouble coping effectively or controlling their impulses and strong emotions (Engel et al., 2017). More than one-third of those with bulimia nervosa display the characteristics of a personality disorder, particularly borderline or avoidant personality disorder, which you will be looking at more closely in Chapter 13.

Another difference is the nature of the medical complications that accompany the two disorders (Forman, 2017; Mitchell & Zunker, 2017). Only half of women with bulimia nervosa are amenorrheic or have very irregular menstrual periods, compared with almost all of those with anorexia nervosa. On the other hand, repeated vomiting bathes teeth and gums in hydrochloric acid, leading some women with bulimia nervosa to have serious dental problems, such as breakdown of enamel and even loss of teeth. Moreover, frequent vomiting or chronic diarrhea (from the use of laxatives) can cause a host of serious medical problems, including dangerous potassium deficiencies, which may lead to weakness, intestinal disorders, kidney disease, or heart damage.

...SUMMING UP

BULIMIA NERVOSA People with bulimia nervosa go on frequent eating binges and then force themselves to vomit or perform other inappropriate compensatory behaviors. The binges are often in response to increasing tension and are followed by feelings of guilt and self-blame. Compensatory behavior is at first reinforced by the temporary relief from uncomfortable feelings of fullness or the reduction of feelings of anxiety, self-disgust, and loss of control attached to bingeing. Over time, however, sufferers generally feel disgusted with themselves, depressed, and guilty. As many as 90 percent of all cases of bulimia nervosa occur among females.

Binge-Eating Disorder

Like those with bulimia nervosa, people with **binge-eating disorder** engage in repeated eating binges during which they feel no control over their eating (APA, 2013). However, they do *not* perform inappropriate compensatory behavior (see **Table 9-4**). As a result of their frequent binges, around half of people with binge-eating disorder become overweight or even obese (Forman, 2017; Sysko & Devlin, 2017).

Binge-eating disorder was first identified 60 years ago as a pattern common among many overweight people (Stunkard, 1959). It is important to recognize, however, that

TABLE: 9-4

Dx Checklist

Binge-Eating Disorder
1. Recurrent binge-eating episodes.
2. Binge-eating episodes include at least three of these features: • Unusually fast eating • Absence of hunger • Uncomfortable fullness • Secret eating due to sense of shame • Subsequent feelings of self-disgust, depression, or severe guilt.
3. Significant distress.
4. Binge-eating episodes take place at least weekly over the course of 3 months.
5. Absence of excessive compensatory behaviors.

Information from: APA, 2013.

BODY DISSATISFACTION

People who evaluate their weight and shape negatively are experiencing **body dissatisfaction**. Around 73% of all girls and women are dissatisfied with their bodies, compared with 56% of all boys and men (Ross, 2018; Pop, 2016; Swami et al., 2016). The vast majority of dissatisfied females believe they are overweight; in contrast, half of dissatisfied males consider themselves overweight and half consider themselves underweight. The factors most closely tied to body dissatisfaction are perfectionism and unrealistic expectations. Body dissatisfaction is the single most powerful contributor to dieting and to the development of eating disorders.

BODY DISSATISFACTION CORRELATES WITH...

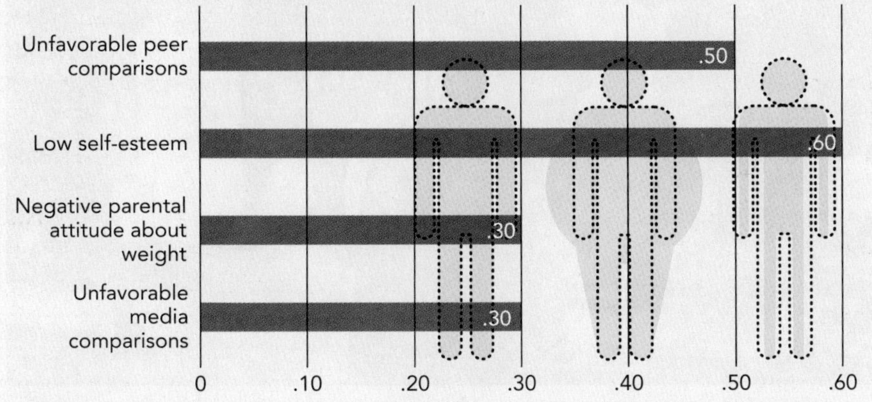

(Fardouly et al., 2017; Swami et al., 2016; Van Vonderen & Kinnally, 2012)

PEOPLE WITH HIGH BODY DISSATISFACTION ARE MORE PRONE TO...

- Eating disorders
- Depressive disorders
- Anxiety disorders
- Body dysmorphic disorder
- Problems in interpersonal relationships
- Difficulties at work

(Griffiths et al., 2017; Frederick et al., 2016; Marques et al., 2012; Dyl et al., 2006; Ohring et al., 2002)

ADULTS AND BODY DISSATISFACTION

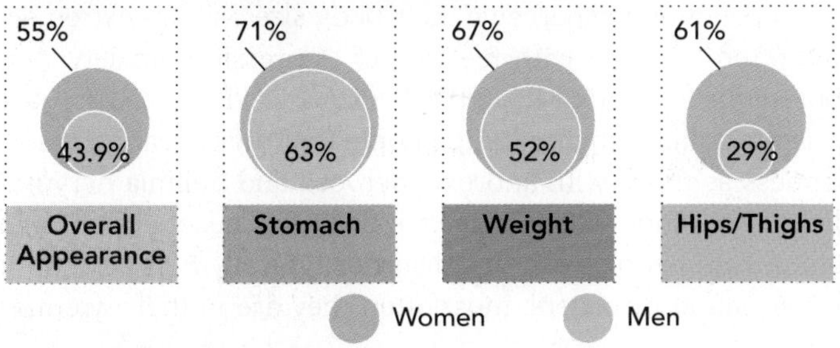

(Frederick et al., 2016; Weinshenker, 2014; Garner, 1997)

NEGATIVE BODY THOUGHTS

97% of women have at least one negative thought about their bodies each day.

On average, a woman has **13** negative body thoughts each day.

Examples of negative body thoughts:

"I hate my thighs, my stomach, and my arms."

"I look disgusting."

"I'm obese. All the pretty girls are size 2."

(Brodeur, 2016; Dreisbach, 2011)

ADOLESCENTS AND BODY DISSATISFACTION

Females of all ages tend to be dissatisfied with their bodies, but the biggest leap in dissatisfaction occurs when girls transition from early to mid-adolescence.

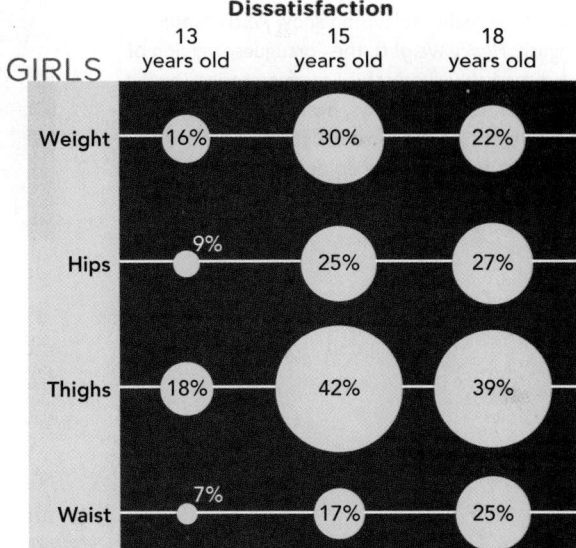

Dissatisfaction

GIRLS

	13 years old	15 years old	18 years old
Weight	16%	30%	22%
Hips	9%	25%	27%
Thighs	18%	42%	39%
Waist	7%	17%	25%

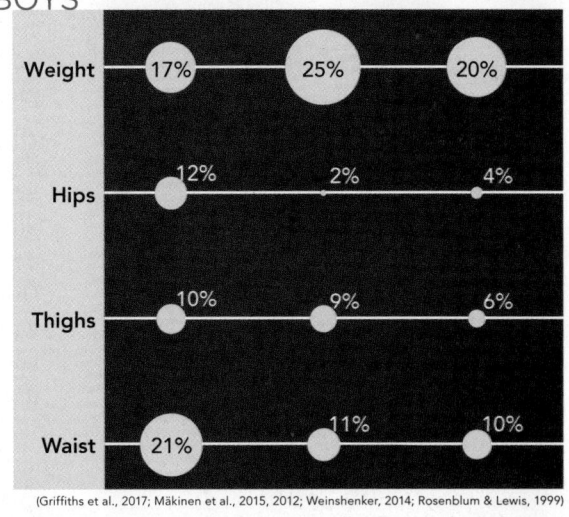

BOYS

	13 years old	15 years old	18 years old
Weight	17%	25%	20%
Hips	12%	2%	4%
Thighs	10%	9%	6%
Waist	21%	11%	10%

(Griffiths et al., 2017; Mäkinen et al., 2015, 2012; Weinshenker, 2014; Rosenblum & Lewis, 1999)

SOCIAL MEDIA AND BODY DISSATISFACTION

- The more time teenage girls spend on social media, the higher their body dissatisfaction.
- Most teens say that social network sites hurt their body confidence.

(Griffiths et al., 2018; Makwana et al., 2018; Dove, 2016; Kim & Chock, 2015)

Cityfiles/Polaris

"The Biggest Loser" phenomenon These men participate in a group exercise program as part of the reality television show *Peso Pesado* (English: *Heavy Weight*), the Portuguese version of the remarkably successful American series *The Biggest Loser*. In these shows, overweight contestants compete to lose the most weight for cash prizes. Most overweight people do not display binge-eating disorder, but most people with the disorder are overweight.

most overweight people do not engage in repeated binges; their weight results from frequent overeating and/or a combination of biological, psychological, and sociocultural factors (ANAD, 2018, 2014).

Between 2 and 7 percent of the population have binge-eating disorder (NEDA, 2018; NIMH, 2017; Brownley et al., 2015). As with the other eating disorders, women with this disorder outnumber men; at least 64 percent of sufferers are female (Forman, 2017; NIMH, 2017). In addition, the binges that characterize this pattern are similar to those seen in bulimia nervosa, particularly the amount of food eaten and the sense of loss of control experienced by individuals during the binge. Moreover, like people with bulimia nervosa or anorexia nervosa, those with binge-eating disorder typically are preoccupied with food, weight, and appearance; tend to base their evaluation of themselves largely on their weight and shape; often misperceive their body size and are extremely dissatisfied with their body; often struggle with feelings of depression, anxiety, and perfectionism; and may abuse substances (NIMH, 2017; Sysko & Devlin, 2017). On the other hand, although they aspire to limit their eating, people with binge-eating disorder are not as driven to thinness as those with anorexia nervosa and bulimia nervosa. Unlike the other eating disorders, binge-eating disorder does not necessarily begin with efforts at extreme dieting. And people with this disorder typically first develop it later than those with the other eating disorders; most often they are in their twenties (Forman, 2017; NIMH, 2017).

9... SUMMING UP

BINGE-EATING DISORDER People with binge-eating disorder have frequent binge-eating episodes in which they feel no control over their eating, but they do not display inappropriate compensatory behaviors. Although most overweight people do not have binge-eating disorder, half of those with binge-eating disorder become overweight. Between 2 and 7 percent of the population have binge-eating disorder.

Like sufferers of anorexia nervosa and bulimia nervosa, people with binge-eating disorder tend to be preoccupied with food, misperceive their body size, experience body dissatisfaction, and struggle with negative emotions. Unlike anorexia nervosa and bulimia nervosa, most cases of this disorder begin after the age of 20.

#

#ClimateControl

Women in warmer climates (where more revealing clothing is worn) have lower weight, engage in more binge eating and purging, and have more body image concerns than women in cooler climates (Delgado, 2018; Paulk et al., 2014; Sloan, 2002).

What Causes Eating Disorders?

Most of today's theorists and researchers use a *multidimensional risk perspective* to explain eating disorders. That is, they identify several key factors that place a person at risk for these disorders (Stice & Desjardins, 2018; Stice et al., 2017). Generally, the more of these factors that are present, the more likely it is that a person will develop an eating disorder. The multidimensional risk perspective for eating disorders is not as specific as the developmental psychopathology perspective, but it does share many principles with the latter perspective. That is, it too contends that the risk factors for eating disorders unfold over the course of development, that interactions between these factors are key, and that different risk factors and combinations of factors may lead to the same eating disorders (Stice & Desjardins, 2018; Stice et al., 2017).

As you will see, most of the risk factors that have been cited and investigated center on anorexia nervosa and bulimia nervosa. Binge-eating disorder, formally identified as a clinical syndrome more recently, is only now being broadly investigated. The factors that are also at work in this "newer" disorder will probably become clear in the coming years.

Barcroft Media via Getty Images

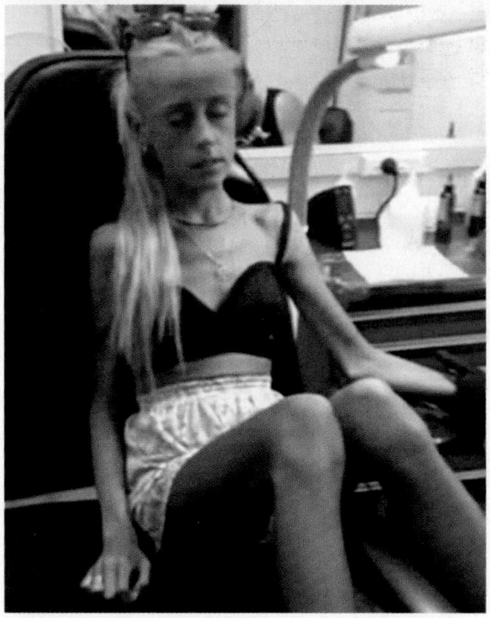

Barcroft Media via Getty Images

Downward spiral Aspiring to look like a Victoria's Secret model, Australian teenager Christie Swadling transformed from a healthy-weight individual into a 70-pound hospital patient suffering from anorexia nervosa in 2015. Now recovered, she speaks out on social media about the dangers of disordered eating.

Psychodynamic Factors: Ego Deficiencies

Hilde Bruch, a pioneer in the study and treatment of eating disorders, was mentioned earlier in this chapter. Bruch developed a largely psychodynamic theory of the disorders. She argued that disturbed mother–child interactions lead to serious *ego deficiencies* in the child (including a poor sense of independence and control) and to severe *perceptual disturbances* that jointly help produce disordered eating (Treasure & Cardi, 2017; Bruch, 2001, 1991, 1962).

According to Bruch, parents may respond to their children either effectively or ineffectively. *Effective parents* accurately attend to their children's biological and emotional needs, giving them food when they are crying from hunger and comfort when they are crying out of fear. *Ineffective parents,* by contrast, fail to attend to their children's needs, deciding that their children are hungry, cold, or tired without correctly interpreting the children's actual condition. They may feed their children when their children are anxious rather than hungry, or comfort them when they are tired rather than anxious. Children who receive such parenting may grow up confused and unaware of their own internal needs, not knowing for themselves when they are hungry or full and unable to identify their own emotions.

Because they cannot rely on internal signals, these children turn instead to external guides, such as their parents. They seem to be "model children," but they fail to develop genuine self-reliance and to "experience themselves as not being in control of their behavior, needs, and impulses, as not owning their own bodies" (Bruch, 1973, p. 55). Adolescence increases their basic desire to establish independence, yet they feel unable to do so. To overcome their sense of helplessness, they seek excessive control over their body size and shape and over their eating habits. Helen, an 18-year-old patient of Bruch's, described such needs and efforts:

> *There is a peculiar contradiction—everybody thinks you're doing so well and everybody thinks you're great, but your real problem is that you think that you are not good enough. You are afraid of not living up to what you think you are expected to do. You have one great fear, namely that of being ordinary, or average, or common—just not good enough. This peculiar dieting begins with such anxiety. You want to prove that you have control, that you can do it. The peculiar part of it is that it makes you feel good about yourself, makes you feel "I can accomplish something." It makes you feel "I can do something nobody else can do."*
>
> *(Bruch, 1978, p. 128)*

David Sipress/The New Yorker Collection/ www.thecartoonbank.com

"What do you eat for anxiety?"

Clinical reports and research have provided some support for Bruch's theory (Treasure & Cardi, 2017; Holtom-Viesel & Allan, 2014). Clinicians have observed that the parents of teenagers with eating disorders do tend to define their children's needs rather than allow the children to define their own needs (Ihle et al., 2005). When Bruch interviewed the mothers of 51 children with anorexia nervosa, many proudly recalled that they had always "anticipated" their young child's needs, never permitting the child to "feel hungry" (Bruch, 1973).

Research has also supported Bruch's belief that people with eating disorders perceive internal cues, including emotional cues, inaccurately (Treasure & Cardi, 2017). When research participants with an eating disorder are anxious or upset, for example, many of them mistakenly think they are also hungry, and they respond as they might respond to hunger—by eating. And finally, studies support Bruch's argument that people with eating disorders rely excessively on the opinions, wishes, and views of others (Treasure & Cardi, 2017) (see ***MindTech***).

Cognitive-Behavioral Factors

If you look closely at Bruch's explanation of eating disorders, you'll see that it contains several *cognitive-behavioral* ideas. She held, for example, that as a result of ineffective parenting, people with eating disorders improperly label their internal sensations and needs, generally feel little control over their lives, and in turn, want to have excessive levels of control over their body size, shape, and eating habits. According to cognitive-behavioral theorists, these deficiencies contribute to a broad cognitive distortion that lies at the center of disordered eating, namely, people with anorexia nervosa and bulimia nervosa judge themselves—often exclusively—based on their shape and weight and their ability to control them (Mitchell, 2018; Fairburn et al., 2015, 2008). This "core pathology," say cognitive-behavioral theorists, contributes to all other aspects of the disorders, including the repeated efforts to lose weight and the preoccupation with shape, weight, and eating.

As you saw earlier in the chapter, research indicates that people with eating disorders do indeed display such cognitive deficiencies (Klein & Attia, 2017). Although studies have not clarified that the deficiencies are the *cause* of eating disorders, many cognitive-behavioral therapists proceed from this assumption and center their treatment for the disorders on correcting the clients' cognitive distortions and their accompanying behaviors. As you'll soon see, cognitive-behavioral therapies are among the most widely used of all treatments for eating disorders (Mitchell, 2018; Fairburn et al., 2015, 2008).

Depression

Many people with eating disorders, particularly those with bulimia nervosa, have symptoms of depression (Klein & Attia, 2017). This finding has led some theorists to suggest that depressive disorders help set the stage for eating disorders.

Their claim is supported by four kinds of evidence. First, many more people with an eating disorder qualify for a clinical diagnosis of major depressive disorder than do people in the general population. Second, the close relatives of people with eating disorders seem to have a higher rate of depressive disorders than do close relatives of people without such disorders. Third, as you will soon see, the depression-related brain circuit of many people with eating disorders shows abnormalities that are similar to those of people with depression. And finally, people with eating disorders are sometimes helped by the same antidepressant drugs that reduce depression. Of course, although such

#TheirWords

"To be born woman is to know—Although they do not talk of it at school—Women must labour to be beautiful."

W. B. Yeats, 1904

MINDTECH

Dark Sites of the Internet

Mental health practitioners and researchers try to combat psychological disorders—in person, in journals and books, and online. Unfortunately, today there are also other—more negative—forces that run counter to the work of these professionals. Among the most common are so-called *dark sites* of the Internet—sites with the goal of promoting behaviors that the clinical community, and most of society, consider abnormal and destructive. *Pro-anorexia sites* are a prime example of this phenomenon.

By conservative estimates, there are at least 600 pro-anorexia Internet sites, with names such as "Dying to Be Thin" and "Starving for Perfection" (Yom-Tov, 2018, 2016). These sites are commonly called *pro-Ana* sites, using a girl named Ana as the personification of this eating disorder. Some of the sites view anorexia nervosa (and bulimia nervosa) as lifestyles rather than psychological disorders; others present themselves as nonjudgmental sites for people with anorexic symptoms. Either way, the sites are enormously popular and appear to outnumber "pro-recovery" Web sites.

Besides promoting eating disorders, might there be other ways in which pro-Ana sites are potentially harmful to regular visitors?

Many users of the sites exchange tips on how they can starve themselves and disguise their weight loss from family, friends, and doctors (Boepple & Thompson, 2016; Griffiths et al., 2015). The sites also offer support and feedback about starvation diets. Many offer mottos, emotional messages, and photos and videos of extremely thin actresses and models as "thinspiration."

As with the pro-suicide Web sites you read about in Chapter 7, the pro-Ana movement and its messages appear across the Internet—for example, on Web forums and chat groups; social networks such as Facebook, Tumblr, and LiveJournal; and video platforms such as YouTube and Vimeo (Branley & Covey, 2017). Most social networks try to seek out and delete pro-Ana material and groups. A few years ago, for example, Instagram banned hashtags that glorify self-harm and threatened to disable those accounts. However, despite such efforts, the sites—and their pro-Ana messages—continue to flourish.

Research suggests that, on average, regular visitors to the sites experience a rise in body dissatisfaction and depression, increase their dieting behavior, display more disordered eating, and attempt more self-harm as a result of their many visits (Yom-Tov et al., 2018, 2016; Rodgers et al., 2016). This worries professionals and parents alike.

Many people are concerned that pro-Ana sites place vulnerable people at great risk, and they have called for more active efforts to ban the sites. Others argue, however, that despite their potential dangers, the sites represent basic freedoms that should not be violated—freedom of speech, for example, and perhaps even the freedom to do oneself harm.

Jean Claude Moshetti/REA/Redux

findings suggest that depression may help cause eating disorders, other explanations are possible. For example, the pressure and pain of having an eating disorder may *cause* depression.

Biological Factors

Biological theorists suspect that certain genes may leave some people particularly susceptible to eating disorders (Mayhew et al., 2018; Bulik, Kleiman, & Yilmaz, 2016). Consistent with this idea, relatives of people with eating disorders are up to six times more likely than other people to develop the disorders themselves. Moreover, if one identical twin has anorexia nervosa, the other twin also develops the disorder in as many as

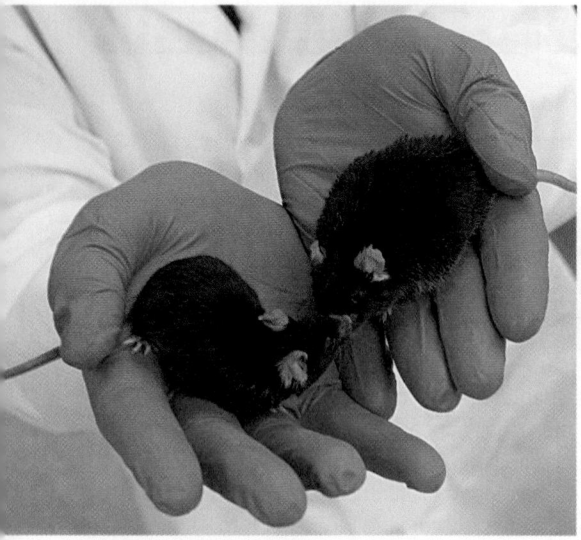

Laboratory obesity Biological theorists believe that certain genes leave some individuals particularly susceptible to eating disorders. To help support this view, researchers have created mutant ("knockout") mice—mice without certain genes. The mouse on the left is missing a gene that helps produce obesity, and it is thin. In contrast, the mouse on the right, which retains that gene, is obese.

70 percent of cases; in contrast, the rate for fraternal twins, who are genetically less similar, is 20 percent. Similarly, in the case of bulimia nervosa, identical twins display a concordance rate of 23 percent, compared with a rate of 9 percent among fraternal twins (Kendler et al., 2018, 1995, 1991; Thornton, Mazzeo, & Bulik, 2011).

One factor that has captured the attention of biological investigators is the possible role of dysfunctional *brain circuits* in people with eating disorders (Monteleone et al., 2018). As you have read throughout this book, a brain circuit is a network of particular brain structures that work together, triggering each other into action to produce a distinct kind of behavioral, cognitive, or emotional reaction (see pages 38–39). Research suggests that each of the circuits linked to generalized anxiety, obsessive-compulsive, and depressive disorders also acts dysfunctionally to some degree in people with eating disorders (Donnelly et al., 2018; Foerde et al., 2015; Frank et al., 2013). For example, among individuals with eating disorders, the *insula* (a structure in the anxiety-related circuit) is abnormally large and active, the *orbitofrontal cortex* (a structure in the obsessive-compulsive-related circuit) is uncommonly large, the *striatum* (another structure in the obsessive-compulsive-related circuit) is hyperactive, and the *prefrontal cortex* (a structure in the anxiety-related, obsessive-compulsive-related, *and* depression-related circuits) is unusually small. Similarly, the activity levels of serotonin, dopamine, and glutamate (key neurotransmitters in the anxiety-related, obsessive-compulsive-related, and depression-related circuits) are abnormal in people with eating disorders (Godlewska et al., 2017).

Given such findings, some researchers believe that dysfunction across or within those various brain circuits collectively help cause eating disorders. However, at this early stage of research, it is just as possible that the dysfunctions in those circuits are actually the *result* of eating disorders (Forman, 2017). Alternatively, the observed circuit dysfunctions may simply reflect the fact that many people with eating disorders also suffer from anxiety, obsessive-compulsive, and/or depressive disorders (Engel et al., 2017; Klein & Attia, 2017).

Finally, a number of biological theorists focus their explanation of eating disorders on one part of the brain in particular, the **hypothalamus,** a structure that regulates many bodily functions (Gao et al., 2017; Tandon et al., 2017). Researchers have located two separate areas in the hypothalamus that help control eating. One, the **lateral hypothalamus (LH),** produces hunger when it is activated. When the LH of a laboratory animal is stimulated electrically, the animal eats, even if it has been fed recently. In contrast, another area, the **ventromedial hypothalamus (VMH),** reduces hunger when it is activated. When the VMH is electrically stimulated, laboratory animals stop eating.

These areas of the hypothalamus and related brain structures are apparently activated by chemicals from the brain and body, depending on whether the person is eating or fasting. One such brain chemical is the natural appetite suppressant *glucagon-like peptide-1* (*GLP-1*) (Harada et al., 2017; Dossat et al., 2014). When one team of researchers collected and injected GLP-1 into the brains of rats, the chemical traveled to receptors in the hypothalamus and caused the rats to reduce their food intake almost entirely even though they had not eaten for 24 hours. Conversely, when "full" rats were injected with a substance that blocked the reception of GLP-1 in the hypothalamus, they more than doubled their food intake.

Some researchers believe that the hypothalamus, related brain structures, and chemicals such as GLP-1, working together, comprise a "weight thermostat" in the body, which is responsible for keeping an individual at a particular weight level called the **weight set point.** Genetic inheritance and early eating practices seem to determine each person's weight set point (Yu, 2017; Chhabra et al., 2016). When a person's weight falls below his or her particular set point, the LH and certain other brain areas are activated and seek to restore the lost weight by producing hunger and lowering the body's *metabolic rate,* the rate at which the body expends energy. When a person's weight rises above his or her set point, the VMH and certain other brain areas are activated, and they try to remove the excess weight by reducing hunger and increasing the body's metabolic rate.

hypothalamus A brain structure that helps regulate various bodily functions, including eating and hunger.

lateral hypothalamus (LH) A brain region that produces hunger when activated.

ventromedial hypothalamus (VMH) A brain region that depresses hunger when activated.

weight set point The weight level that a person is predisposed to maintain, controlled in part by the hypothalamus.

According to the weight set point theory, when people diet and fall to a weight below their weight set point, their brain starts trying to restore the lost weight. Hypothalamic and related brain activity produce a preoccupation with food and a desire to binge. They also trigger bodily changes that make it harder to lose weight and easier to gain weight, however little is eaten (Yu, 2017; Chhabra et al., 2016). Once the brain and body begin conspiring to raise weight in this way, dieters actually enter into a battle against themselves. Some people apparently manage to shut down the inner "thermostat" and control their eating almost completely. These people move toward restricting-type anorexia nervosa. For others, the battle spirals toward a binge-purge or binge-only pattern. Although the weight set point explanation has received considerable debate in the clinical field, it continues to be accepted by many theorists and practitioners.

#TheirWords

"Nothing tastes as good as skinny feels."
Kate Moss, model

Societal Pressures

Eating disorders are more common in Western countries than in other parts of the world. Thus, many theorists believe that Western standards of female attractiveness are partly responsible for the emergence of the disorders (Forman, 2017; MacNeill & Best, 2015). Western standards of female beauty have changed throughout history, with a noticeable shift in preference toward a thin female frame over the past 60 years or so. For example, some "pioneering" studies conducted throughout the second half of the twentieth century tracked the weight, bust, and hip measurements of *Playboy* magazine centerfold models and Miss America Pageant contestants and found a steady year-by-year decrease in those measurements that has continued into the current century (Gilbert et al., 2005; Garner et al., 1980).

How might you explain the finding that eating disorders tend to be less common in cultures that restrict a woman's freedom to make decisions about her life?

Because thinness is especially valued in the subcultures of performers, fashion models, and certain athletes, members of these groups are likely to be particularly concerned and/or criticized about their weight. For example, after undergoing an inpatient treatment program for eating disorders, the popular singer and rapper Kesha wrote, "The music industry has set unrealistic expectations for what a body is supposed to look like, and I started becoming overly critical of my own body because of that" (Sebert, 2014).

Studies have found that performers, models, and athletes are indeed more prone than others to anorexia nervosa and bulimia nervosa (Forman, 2017). In fact, many famous young women from these fields have publicly acknowledged grossly disordered eating patterns over the years. Surveys of athletes at colleges around the United States reveal that more than 9 percent of female college athletes suffer from an eating disorder and at least another 33 percent display eating behaviors that put them at risk for such disorders (Ekern, 2018; Van Durme et al., 2012). By some estimates, a full 20 percent of gymnasts may have an eating disorder.

Paul J. Kolnik

Dangerous professions Certain occupations—fashion modeling, dancing, acting, and sports—place a premium on thinness, thus putting their professionals at particular risk for eating disorders. In a recent autobiography, *Dancing Throughout*, famous ballet artist Jenifer Ringer (performing here in the ballet *The Nutcracker*) described her struggles with eating disorders, both prior to and during her successful career as a principal dancer with the New York City Ballet.

Attitudes toward thinness may also help explain economic differences in the rates of eating disorders. In the past, women in the upper socioeconomic classes expressed more concern about thinness and dieting than women of the lower socioeconomic classes (Margo, 1985). Correspondingly, anorexia nervosa and bulimia nervosa were more common among women higher on the socioeconomic scale (Foreyt et al., 1996; Rosen et al., 1991). In recent years, however, dieting and a preoccupation with thinness have increased to some degree in all socioeconomic classes, as has the prevalence of these eating disorders (Javier, Moore, & Belgrave, 2016).

Western society not only glorifies thinness but also creates a climate of prejudice against overweight people (Brewis, SturtzSreetharan, & Wutich, 2018.). Whereas slurs based on ethnicity, race, and gender are considered unacceptable, cruel jokes about obesity are standard fare on the Web and television and in movies, books, and magazines. Research indicates that the prejudice against obese people is deep-rooted (Grilo et al., 2005). Prospective parents who were shown pictures of a chubby child and a

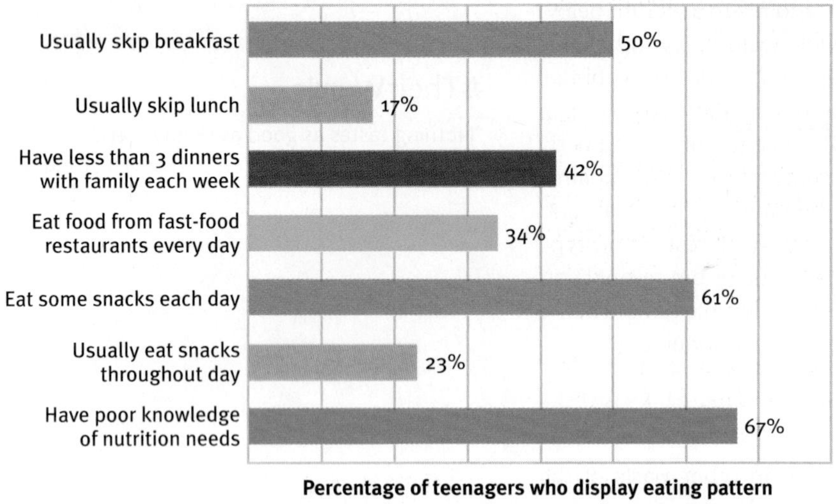

FIGURE 9-2

What Does Teenage Eating Look Like?

Teenage eating habits are not particularly healthful in general and are, in fact, poor for many teens, according to research. Small wonder that the majority of adolescents fail to meet dietary recommendations for nutrient intake. (Information from: Demory-Luce & Motil, 2018; Lehman, 2016; CDC, 2015; Johnson, 2011; Sebastian et al., 2010.)

medium-weight or thin child rated the former as less friendly, energetic, intelligent, and desirable than the latter. In another study, preschool children who were given a choice between a chubby and a thin rag doll chose the thin one, although they could not say why. Thus it is small wonder that the number of children under 12 years who develop a full eating disorder is growing, especially among girls (Ekern, 2018; NIMH, 2017).

Given these trends, it is not totally surprising that one survey of 248 adolescent girls directly tied eating disorders and body dissatisfaction to social networking, Internet activity, and television browsing (Latzer, Katz, & Spivak, 2011). The survey found that the respondents who spent more time on Facebook were more likely to display eating disorders, have negative body image, eat in dysfunctional ways, and want to diet (see **Figure 9-2**). Those who spent more time on fashion and music Web sites and those who viewed more gossip- and leisure-related television programs showed similar tendencies.

Family Environment

Families may play an important role in the development and maintenance of eating disorders (Cerniglia et al., 2017). Research suggests that as many as half of the families of people with anorexia nervosa or bulimia nervosa have a long history of emphasizing thinness, physical appearance, and dieting. In fact, the mothers in these families are more likely to diet themselves and to be generally perfectionistic than are the mothers in other families (Zerbe, 2017, 2008; Woodside et al., 2002). Tina, a 16-year-old, describes her view of the roots of her eating disorder:

> *When I was a kid, say 6 or 7, my Mom and I would go to the drugstore all the time. She was heavy and bought all kinds of books and magazines on how to lose weight. Whenever we talked, like after I got home from school, it was almost always about dieting and how to lose weight. . . . I [went] on diets with my Mom, to keep her company. . . . My eating disorder is my Mom's therapy. . . . We've stopped talking about diets since I got anorexia, and now I don't know what we can talk about.*
>
> *(Zerbe, 2008, pp. 20–21)*

Abnormal interactions and forms of communication within a family may also set the stage for an eating disorder (Cerniglia et al., 2017). Family systems theorists argue that the families of people who develop eating disorders are often dysfunctional to begin with and that the eating disorder of one member is a reflection of the larger problem. Influential family theorist Salvador Minuchin, for example, believed that an **enmeshed family pattern** often leads to eating disorders (Minuchin et al., 2017, 2006).

In an enmeshed system, family members are overinvolved in each other's affairs and overconcerned with the details of each other's lives. On the positive side, enmeshed families can be affectionate and loyal. On the negative side, they can be clingy and foster dependency. Parents are too involved in the lives of their children, allowing little room for individuality and independence. Minuchin argued that adolescence poses a special problem for these families. The teenager's normal push for independence threatens the family's apparent harmony and closeness. In response, the family may subtly force the child to take on a "sick" role—to develop an eating disorder or some other illness. The child's disorder enables the family to maintain its appearance of harmony. A sick child needs her family, and family members can rally to protect her. Although some studies have supported such family systems explanations (Cerniglia et al., 2017), they have

enmeshed family pattern A family system in which members are overinvolved with each other's affairs and overly concerned about each other's welfare.

failed to show that particular family patterns consistently set the stage for the development of eating disorders.

Multicultural Factors: Racial and Ethnic Differences

In 1995 there was a popular movie titled *Clueless* in which Cher and Dionne, wealthy teenage friends of different races, had similar tastes, beliefs, and values about everything from boys to schoolwork. In particular, they had the same kinds of eating habits and beauty ideals, and they were even similar in weight and physical form. But did the story of these young women reflect the realities of non-Hispanic white American and African American females in our society?

In the early 1990s, the answer to this question appeared to be a resounding no. Most studies conducted up to the time of *Clueless* indicated that the eating behaviors, values, and goals of young African American women were considerably healthier than those of young non-Hispanic white American women (Lovejoy, 2001; Cash & Henry, 1995; Parker et al., 1995). A widely publicized 1995 study at the University of Arizona, for example, found that the eating behaviors and attitudes of young African American women were more positive than those of young non-Hispanic white American women. It found, specifically, that "only" 70 percent of the African American respondents were dissatisfied with their weight and body shape, compared with nearly 90 percent of the non-Hispanic white American teens.

Are girls and women in Western society destined to struggle with at least some issues of eating and appearance?

The study also suggested that non-Hispanic white American and African American adolescent girls had different ideals of beauty. The former teens, asked to define the "perfect girl," described a girl of 5′7″ weighing between 100 and 110 pounds—proportions that mirror those of so-called supermodels. Attaining a perfect weight, many said, was the key to being happy and popular. In contrast, the African American respondents emphasized personality traits over physical characteristics. They defined the "perfect" African American girl as smart, fun, easy to talk to, not conceited, and funny; she did not necessarily need to be "pretty," as long as she was well groomed. The body dimensions the African American teens described were more attainable for the typical girl; they favored fuller hips, for example. Moreover, the African American respondents were less likely than the non-Hispanic white American respondents to diet for extended periods.

Unfortunately, research conducted over the past two decades suggests that body image concerns, dysfunctional eating patterns, and anorexia nervosa and bulimia nervosa are on the rise among young African American women as well as among women of other minority groups (Rodgers et al., 2017; Starr & Kreipe, 2014; Gilbert, 2011). For example, in a frequently cited survey conducted by *Essence*, a popular magazine geared toward African Americans, 65 percent of African American respondents reported dieting, 39 percent said that food controlled their lives, 19 percent avoided eating when hungry, 17 percent used laxatives, and 4 percent vomited to lose weight.

The shift in the eating behaviors and eating problems of African American women appears to be partly related to their *acculturation* (Rittenhouse, 2016; Ford, 2000). One study compared African American women at a predominately non-Hispanic white American university with those at a predominately African American university. Those at the former school had significantly higher depression scores, and those scores were positively correlated with eating problems.

Still other studies indicate that Hispanic American female adolescents and young adults engage in disordered eating behaviors (particularly bingeing behavior) and express body dissatisfaction at rates about equal to those of non-Hispanic white American women (Perez, Ohrt, & Hoek, 2016; Cachelin et al., 2006). Moreover, those who consider themselves more oriented to non-Hispanic white American culture have particularly high rates of anorexia nervosa and bulimia nervosa. These eating disorders also appear to be on the increase among young Asian American women and young women in several Asian countries (Thomas, Lee, & Becker, 2016; Pike et al., 2013).

Chris Moore/Catwalking/Getty Images

Embracing diversity? The Western ideal of extreme thinness remains the standard for fashion models, regardless of their nationality or cultural background. Psychologists worry that the success of supermodels such as Ethiopia's Liya Kebede (above) and Sudan's Alek Wek may contribute to thinner body ideals and more eating disorders in their African countries.

Not for women only A growing number of today's men are developing eating disorders. Some of them aspire to a very lean body shape and develop anorexia nervosa or bulimia nervosa. Singer Zayn Malik (left) has acknowledged falling into this pattern when he was a member of the boy band One Direction. Other men want the ultramuscular look displayed by bodybuilders (right) and may develop an eating disorder called *muscle dysmorphia*. These individuals inaccurately consider themselves to be scrawny and small and keep striving for a "perfect" body through excessive weight lifting and abuse of steroids.

Multicultural Factors: Gender Differences

Males account for only 10 percent of all people with anorexia nervosa and bulimia nervosa. The reasons for this striking gender difference are not entirely clear, but Western society's double standard for attractiveness is, at the very least, one reason. Our society's emphasis on a thin appearance is clearly aimed at women much more than men, and some theorists believe that this difference has made women much more inclined to diet and more prone to eating disorders. Surveys of college men have, for example, found that the majority select "muscular, strong and broad shoulders" to describe the ideal male body and "thin, slim, slightly underweight" to describe the ideal female body (Mayo & George, 2014).

A second reason for the different rates of anorexia nervosa and bulimia nervosa between men and women may be the different methods of weight loss favored by the two genders. According to some clinical observations and studies, men are more likely to use exercise to lose weight, whereas women more often diet (Thackray et al., 2016). And, as you have read, dieting often precedes the onset of these eating disorders.

Why do some men develop anorexia nervosa or bulimia nervosa? In a number of cases, the disorder is linked to the *requirements and pressures of a job or sport* (Cottrell & Williams, 2016; Braun, 1996). According to one study, 37 percent of men with these eating disorders had jobs or played sports for which weight control was important, compared with 13 percent of women with such disorders. The highest rates of male eating disorders have been found among jockeys, wrestlers, distance runners, body builders, and swimmers.

For other men who develop anorexia nervosa or bulimia nervosa, *body image* appears to be a key factor, just as it is in women (Lavender et al., 2017; Mayo & George, 2014). Many report that they want a "lean, toned, thin" shape similar to the ideal female body, rather than the muscular, broad-shouldered shape of the typical male ideal.

Still other men seem to be caught up in a different kind of eating disorder, called *reverse anorexia nervosa* or *muscle dysmorphia*. Men with this disorder are very muscular but still see themselves as scrawny and small and therefore continue to strive for a "perfect" body through extreme measures such as excessive weight lifting or the abuse of steroids (Lavender et al., 2017). People with muscle dysmorphia typically feel shame about their bodies, and many have a history of depression, anxiety, and self-destructive compulsive behavior. About one-third of them also engage in related dysfunctional behaviors such as binge eating.

Why do you think that the prevalence of eating disorders among men has been on the increase in recent years?

9... SUMMING UP

WHAT CAUSES EATING DISORDERS? Most theorists now use a multidimensional risk perspective to explain eating disorders and to identify several key contributing factors. Principal among these are ego deficiencies; cognitive-behavioral factors; depression; biological factors such as dysfunctional brain circuits, problematic activity of the hypothalamus, and disturbances of the body's weight set point; society's emphasis on thinness and bias against obesity; family environment; racial and ethnic differences; and gender differences.

How Are Eating Disorders Treated?

Today's treatments for eating disorders have two goals. The first is to correct the dangerous eating pattern as quickly as possible. The second is to address the broader psychological and situational factors that have led to and maintain the eating problem. Family and friends can also play an important role in helping to overcome the disorder.

Treatments for Anorexia Nervosa

Around one-third of those with anorexia nervosa receive treatment (NIMH, 2017). The immediate aims of treatment for anorexia nervosa are to help people regain their lost weight, recover from malnourishment, and eat normally again (Mehler, 2017). Therapists must then help them to make psychological and perhaps family changes to lock in those gains.

How Are Proper Weight and Normal Eating Restored? A variety of treatment methods are used to help patients with anorexia nervosa gain weight quickly and return to health within weeks, a phase of treatment called *nutritional rehabilitation* (Peebles et al., 2017). In the past, treatment almost always took place in a hospital, but now it is often offered in day hospitals or outpatient settings.

In life-threatening cases, clinicians may need to force *tube and intravenous feedings* on a patient who refuses to eat (Rocks et al., 2014). Unfortunately, this use of force may cause the client to distrust the clinician. In contrast, clinicians using behavioral weight-restoration approaches offer *rewards* whenever patients eat properly or gain weight and offer no rewards when they eat improperly or fail to gain weight.

Perhaps the most popular nutritional rehabilitation approach is a combination of supportive nursing care, nutritional counseling, and a relatively high-calorie diet (Steinglass, 2016). Here nurses and other staff members *gradually* increase a patient's diet over the course of several weeks, to more than 3,000 calories a day (Zerbe, 2017, 2010, 2008). The nurses educate patients about the program, track their progress, provide encouragement, and help them appreciate that their weight gain is under control and will not lead to obesity. In some programs, the nurses also use **motivational interviewing**, an intervention that uses a mixture of empathy and inquiring review to help motivate clients to recognize they have a serious eating problem and commit to making constructive choices and behavior changes (Pike, 2017). Studies find that patients in nutritional rehabilitation programs usually gain the necessary weight over 8 to 12 weeks.

How Are Lasting Changes Achieved? Clinical researchers have found that people with anorexia nervosa must overcome their underlying psychological problems in order to create lasting improvement. Therapists typically use a combination of education, psychotherapy, and family therapy to help reach this broader goal (Knatz et al., 2015). Psychotropic drugs, particularly antipsychotic drugs, are sometimes used when patients do not respond to the other forms of treatments, but research has found that such medications are typically of limited benefit (Walsh, 2018).

COGNITIVE-BEHAVIORAL THERAPY A combination of cognitive and behavioral interventions are included in most treatment programs for anorexia nervosa. Such techniques are designed to help clients appreciate and alter the behaviors and thought processes that help keep their restrictive eating going (Pike, 2017). On the behavioral side, clients are typically required to monitor (perhaps by keeping a diary) their feelings, hunger levels, and food intake and the ties between these variables. On the cognitive side, they are taught to identify their "core pathology"—the deep-seated belief that they should in fact be judged by their shape and weight and by their ability to control these physical characteristics. The clients may also be taught alternative ways of coping with stress and of solving problems.

Jeff Kravitz/Getty Images

A dangerous trip back When actress and model Zoe Kravitz agreed to play an anorexic woman in the movie *The Road Within*, she believed her past history with eating disorders would be an asset. However, Kravitz reported that dieting down to 90 pounds for the movie "triggered some old stuff," and she had difficulty calling an end to the new weight loss (Takeda, 2015).

motivational interviewing A treatment that uses empathy and inquiring review to help motivate clients to recognize they have a serious psychological problem and commit to making constructive choices and behavior changes.

#TheirWords

"Girls should be encouraged to take an interest in their appearance when they are very young."

Ladies' Home Journal, 1940

The therapists who provide cognitive-behavioral therapy are particularly careful to help patients with anorexia nervosa recognize their need for independence and teach them more appropriate ways to exercise control (Pike, 2017). The therapists may also teach them to better identify and trust their internal sensations and feelings. In the following session, a therapist tries to help a 15-year-old client recognize and share her feelings:

Patient: *I don't talk about my feelings; I never did.*

Therapist: *Do you think I'll respond like others?*

Patient: *What do you mean?*

Therapist: *I think you may be afraid that I won't pay close attention to what you feel inside, or that I'll tell you not to feel the way you do—that it's foolish to feel frightened, to feel fat, to doubt yourself, considering how well you do in school, how you're appreciated by teachers, how pretty you are.*

Patient: (Looking somewhat tense and agitated) *Well, I was always told to be polite and respect other people, just like a stupid, faceless doll.* (Affecting a vacant, doll-like pose)

Therapist: *Do I give you the impression that it would be disrespectful for you to share your feelings, whatever they may be?*

Patient: *Not really; I don't know.*

Therapist: *I can't, and won't, tell you that this is easy for you to do. . . . But I can promise you that you are free to speak your mind, and that I won't turn away.*

(Strober & Yager, 1985, pp. 368–369)

#FamilyTeasing

Adolescents teased about their weight by family members are twice as likely as nonteased teens to become overweight within five years and 1.5 times more likely to become binge eaters and use extreme weight control measures (Saltzman & Liechty, 2016; Neumark-Sztainer et al., 2007).

Finally, cognitive-behavioral therapists seek to help clients with anorexia nervosa change their attitudes about eating and weight (Pike, 2017; Fairburn et al., 2015, 2008) (see **Table 9-5**). The therapists may guide the clients to identify, challenge, and change maladaptive assumptions, such as "I must always be perfect" or "My weight and shape determine my value." They may also educate the clients about the body distortions typical of anorexia nervosa and help them see that their own assessments of their size are incorrect. Even if a client never learns to judge her body shape accurately, she may at least reach a point where she says, "I know that a key feature of anorexia nervosa is a misperception of my own size, so I can expect to feel fat regardless of my actual size."

TABLE: 9-5

Sample Items from the Eating Disorder Inventory

For each item, decide if the item is true about you ALWAYS (A), USUALLY (U), OFTEN (O), SOMETIMES (S), RARELY (R), or NEVER (N). Circle the letter that corresponds to your rating.

A	U	O	S	R	N	I eat when I am upset.
A	U	O	S	R	N	I stuff myself with food.
A	U	O	S	R	N	I think about dieting.
A	U	O	S	R	N	I think that my thighs are too large.
A	U	O	S	R	N	I feel extremely guilty after overeating.
A	U	O	S	R	N	I am terrified of gaining weight.
A	U	O	S	R	N	I get confused as to whether or not I am hungry.
A	U	O	S	R	N	I have the thought of trying to vomit in order to lose weight.
A	U	O	S	R	N	I think my buttocks are too large.
A	U	O	S	R	N	I eat or drink in secrecy.

Information from: Clausen et al., 2011; Garner, 2005; Garner, Olmsted, & Polivy, 2004, 1991, 1984.

According to research, cognitive-behavioral techniques are often very effective in cases of anorexia nervosa, more effective than psychodynamic therapies, psychoeducation, or supportive therapy alone (Pike, 2017). The approach helps many individuals to restore their weight, overcome their fear of becoming overweight, develop greater self-esteem, correct their body distortions and dissatisfaction, adopt more accurate and adaptive eating attitudes, acquire more appropriate eating and exercise habits, and develop better problem-solving skills. The treatment is most successful at preventing relapses when it continues for at least a year beyond a patient's recovery—the *maintenance* therapy strategy that you read about in Chapter 6 (see pages 183 and 185). At the same time, studies further suggest that the cognitive-behavioral approach brings the best results when it is supplemented by other approaches. In particular, family therapy is often included in treatment.

Bruce Eric Kaplan/The New Yorker Collection/The Cartoon Bank

"You can't keep comparing yourself to those skinny little aliens you see in movies."

CHANGING FAMILY INTERACTIONS Family therapy can be an invaluable part of treatment for anorexia nervosa, particularly for children and adolescents with the disorder (Pike, 2017). As in other family therapy situations, the therapist meets with the family as a whole, points out troublesome family patterns, and helps the members make appropriate changes. In particular, family therapists may try to help the person with anorexia nervosa separate her feelings and needs from those of other members of her family. Although the role of family in the development of anorexia nervosa is not yet clear, research strongly suggests that family therapy (or at least parent counseling) can be helpful in the treatment of this disorder (Richards et al., 2018).

Mother:	*I think I know what [Susan] is going through: all the doubt and insecurity of growing up and establishing her own identity.* (Turning to the patient, with tears) *If you just place trust in yourself, with the support of those around you who care, everything will turn out for the better.*
Therapist:	*Are you making yourself available to her? Should she turn to you, rely on you for guidance and emotional support?*
Mother:	*Well, that's what parents are for.*
Therapist:	(Turning to patient) *What do you think?*
Susan:	(To mother) *I can't keep depending on you, Mom, or everyone else. That's what I've been doing, and it gave me anorexia. . . .*
Therapist:	*Do you think your mom would prefer that there be no secrets between her and the kids—an open door, so to speak?*
Older sister:	*Sometimes I do.*
Therapist:	(To patient and younger sister) *How about you two?*
Susan:	*Yeah. Sometimes it's like whatever I feel, she has to feel.*
Younger sister:	*Yeah.*

(Strober & Yager, 1985, pp. 381–382)

What Is the Aftermath of Anorexia Nervosa? The use of combined treatment approaches, with cognitive-behavioral therapy typically at the center, has greatly improved the outlook for people with anorexia nervosa, although the road to recovery can be difficult. The course and outcome of this disorder vary from person to person, but researchers have noted certain trends.

On the positive side, weight is often quickly restored once treatment for the disorder begins, and treatment gains may continue for years. As many as 75 percent of patients continue to show improvement—either full or partial—when they are interviewed several years or more after their initial recovery (Klein & Attia, 2017; Isomaa & Isomaa, 2014).

#

#FashionDownsizing

In 1968, the average fashion model was 8 percent thinner than the typical woman. In 2016, models were 32 percent thinner (Firger, 2016; Tashakova, 2011).

Reuters/Stefano Rellandini

The beginning of a movement An early effort at responsible advertising regarding body shape and eating disorders occurred back in 2007 when the Nolita clothing brand launched a major ad campaign against excessive thinness. One of the brand's billboards featured an emaciated naked woman appearing beneath the words "No Anorexia." The billboard model Isabelle Caro died in 2010 of complications from anorexia nervosa.

Another positive note is that most females with anorexia nervosa menstruate again when they regain their weight, and other medical improvements follow (Mehler, 2016). Also encouraging is that the death rate from anorexia nervosa seems to be falling. Earlier diagnosis and safer and faster weight-restoration techniques may account for this trend. Deaths that do occur are usually caused by suicide, starvation, infection, gastrointestinal problems, or electrolyte imbalance (Mehler, 2017).

On the negative side, as many as 25 percent of persons with anorexia nervosa remain seriously troubled for years (Klein & Attia, 2017; Isomaa & Isomaa, 2014). Furthermore, recovery, when it does occur, is not always permanent. At least one-third of recovered patients have recurrences of anorexic behavior, usually triggered by new stresses, such as marriage, pregnancy, or a major relocation (Stice et al., 2017, 2013; Fennig et al., 2002). Even years later, many who have recovered continue to express concerns about their weight and appearance (Klein & Attia, 2017). Some still restrict their diets to a degree, feel anxiety when they eat with other people, or hold some distorted ideas about food, eating, and weight (Isomaa & Isomaa, 2014; Fairburn et al., 2008).

About half of those who have suffered from anorexia nervosa continue to have certain psychological problems—particularly depression, obsessiveness, and social anxiety—years after treatment. Such problems are particularly common in those who had not reached a fully normal weight by the end of treatment (Steinglass, 2016).

Why might some people who recover from anorexia nervosa and bulimia nervosa remain vulnerable to relapse even after recovery?

The more weight persons have lost and the more time that passes before they enter treatment, the poorer the recovery rate (Klein & Attia, 2017; Zerwas et al., 2013). People who had psychological or sexual problems before the onset of the disorder tend to have a poorer recovery rate than those without such a history. People whose family or interpersonal relationships are troubled have less positive treatment outcomes. Younger sufferers seem to have a better recovery rate than older patients.

Treatments for Bulimia Nervosa

Around 43 percent of those with bulimia nervosa receive treatment (NIMH, 2017). Treatment programs for the disorder are often offered in eating disorder clinics. Such programs offer (1) nutritional rehabilitation, which, for bulimia nervosa, means helping clients to eliminate their binge-purge patterns and establish good eating habits, and (2) a combination of therapies aimed at eliminating the underlying causes of bulimic patterns (Mitchell, 2018; Crow, 2017; Fairburn & Cooper, 2014). The programs emphasize education as much as therapy. Cognitive-behavioral therapy is particularly helpful in cases of bulimia nervosa—perhaps even more helpful than in cases of anorexia nervosa. And antidepressant drug therapy, which is of limited help to people with anorexia nervosa, appears to be quite effective in many cases of bulimia nervosa.

Cognitive-Behavioral Therapy When treating clients with bulimia nervosa, cognitive-behavioral therapists employ many of the same techniques that they use to help treat people with anorexia nervosa. However, they tailor the techniques to the unique features of bulimia (for example, bingeing and purging) and to the specific beliefs at work in bulimia nervosa (Mitchell, 2018).

The therapists often instruct clients with bulimia nervosa to keep diaries of their eating behavior, changes in sensations of hunger and fullness, and the ebb and flow of other feelings (Mitchell, 2018). This helps the clients to observe their eating patterns more objectively and recognize the emotions and situations that trigger their desire to binge. Smartphone apps have been particularly useful in keeping track of such changes throughout the day.

One team of researchers studied the effectiveness of an online version of the diary technique (Shapiro et al., 2010). They had 31 clients with bulimia nervosa, each an outpatient in a 12-week cognitive-behavioral therapy program, send nightly texts to their therapists, reporting on their bingeing and purging urges and episodes. The clients received feedback messages, including reinforcement and encouragement for the treatment goals they had been able to reach that day. The clinical researchers reported that by the end of therapy, the clients showed significant decreases in binges, purges, other bulimic symptoms, and feelings of depression.

Cognitive-behavioral therapists may also use the behavioral technique of *exposure and response prevention* to help break the binge-purge cycle. As you read in Chapter 4, this approach consists of exposing people to situations that would ordinarily raise anxiety and then preventing them from performing their usual compulsive responses until they learn that the situations are actually harmless and their compulsive acts unnecessary. For bulimia nervosa, the therapists require clients to eat particular kinds and amounts of food and then prevent them from vomiting to show that eating can be a harmless and even constructive activity that needs no undoing (Mitchell, 2018; Agras, Fitzsimmons-Craft, & Wilfley, 2017). Typically the therapist sits with the client while the client eats the forbidden foods and stays until the urge to purge has passed. Studies find that this treatment often helps reduce eating-related anxieties, bingeing, and vomiting.

Beyond such behavioral techniques, a primary focus of cognitive-behavioral therapists is to help clients with bulimia nervosa recognize and change their maladaptive attitudes toward food, eating, weight, and shape. The therapists typically teach the clients to identify and challenge the negative thoughts that regularly precede their urge to binge—I have no self-control; I might as well give up; I look fat. They may also guide clients to recognize, question, and eventually change their perfectionistic standards, sense of helplessness, and low self-concept (see ***Trending*** on the next page). Cognitive-behavioral approaches help as many as 75 percent of patients stop or reduce bingeing and purging (Mitchell, 2018; Poulsen et al., 2014).

Other Forms of Psychotherapy Because of its effectiveness in the treatment of bulimia nervosa, cognitive-behavioral therapy is often tried first, before other therapies are considered. If clients do not respond to it, other approaches with promising but less impressive track records may then be tried (Mitchell, 2018; Crow, 2017). A common alternative is *interpersonal psychotherapy,* the treatment that is used to help improve interpersonal functioning (Gomez Penedo et al., 2018). *Psychodynamic therapy* has also been used in cases of bulimia nervosa, but only a few research studies have tested and supported its effectiveness (Thompson-Brenner, 2016; Tasca et al., 2014). The various

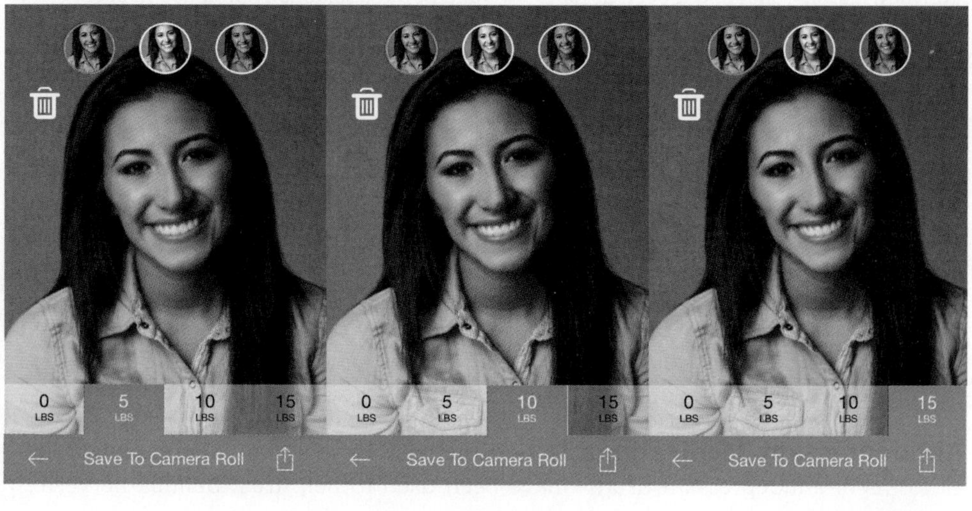

Medavia/ZUMA Press/Newscom

It was only a matter of time A new app hit the marketplace a few years ago enabling users to "doctor" their selfies before posting them. Like the woman in this app demonstration, a user's appearance can, through facial recognition software, be made to look lighter by 5 pounds (left), 10 pounds (center), or 15 pounds (right). Critics worry that the app, whose sales have boomed, is likely to further fuel body dissatisfaction and eating disorders.

#CelebrityEatingDisorders

- Kesha, singer
- Demi Lovato, singer
- Zane Malik, singer
- Zosia Mamet, actress
- Alanis Morissette, singer
- Ashlee Simpson, singer
- Adam Rippon, figure skater
- Zoe Kravitz, actress
- Kate Winslet, actress
- Lady Gaga, singer/songwriter
- Mary-Kate Olsen, actress
- Kelly Clarkson, singer
- Jessica Alba, actress
- Elton John, singer
- Ashley Rickards, actress
- Fiona Apple, singer
- Princess Diana, British royalty
- Kate Beckinsale, actress

...TRENDING

Shame on Body Shamers

"What happened to . . . ? Did she eat all her back-up singers?" Thousands of cruel tweets like this one about a popular singer's weight appear on social media every day. They are examples of body shaming, the practice of criticizing people publicly for being overweight, or, less frequently, underweight.

Body shaming itself is not new. It has been around since the mid-nineteenth century (Herman, 2015). What is new is the current and ever-increasing volume of this practice. Our world of tweets, social networking, blogging, provocative Web sites, opinionated talk shows, and the like has provided numerous platforms for cruel comments, including ones about people's appearance (Green & Lankford, 2017). As one eating disorder expert has said, "We are learning the language of body shaming from the mass media culture" (Mysko, 2016).

Of course, the body shaming of celebrities receives the most attention, but widely read comments of that kind have opened the door to an onslaught of body shaming in smaller circles and in everyday life. A recent survey revealed that a staggering 94 percent of today's teenage girls and 64 percent of teenage boys have been body shamed in one form or another (Miller, 2016).

Body shaming can bring great personal pain to the victims of such comments (Chomet, 2018; Webb et al., 2016). In addition, the practice appears to be contributing, along with other factors, to an increase in body dissatisfaction and disordered eating throughout our society, especially among women (Kolata, 2016).

The good news is that a counter-trend is currently also taking place across society—growing concern and anger by millions of people, including clinicians and educators, over the unacceptability and harmful impact of these forms of communication, along with a determination to fight back. In the legal arena, criminal charges have been brought against body shamers whose actions have been particularly ugly, invasive of privacy, and/or damaging (Feuer, 2016).

Perhaps the most important development in the fight against body shaming is that hundreds of influential celebrities are now calling out the perpetrators. Over the past year, for example, in response to negative tweets or posts about their bodies, celebrities have posted self-affirming messages such as the following:

"I will never conform to your skinny standards."
—Reality TV star Kim Kardashian

"I am not a woman whose self-worth comes from her chest size."
—Actress Kristen Bell

"I am so proud of what my body has done for me."
—Actress Gabourey Sidibe

"I'm healthy and happy, and if you're hating on my weight, you obviously aren't."
—Singer Demi Lovato

"[Body shaming] lets you know something's wrong with our culture and we all need to work together to change it."
—Comedian Amy Schumer

"People . . . body shame me because . . . I'm not good enough for their standards. . . . But at the end of the day I'm good enough for me."
—Model Ashley Graham

"I love being happy with me."
—Singer and actress Selena Gomez

These are but a small fraction of the countershaming messages being posted by celebrities every day. Hopefully, the self-acceptance, independent thinking, and body satisfaction contained in such responses will come to influence readers more than the body-shaming messages themselves.

Timothy A. Clary/AFP/Getty Images

Responding to shamers As Lady Gaga was giving a universally acclaimed half-time performance at the 2017 Super Bowl (above), many viewers took to social media to criticize her for daring to wear a crop-top and displaying the "flab" on her stomach. In an Instagram post, the superstar responded, "I'm proud of my body and you [i.e., all people] should be proud of yours too. No matter who you are or what you do."

forms of psychotherapy—cognitive-behavioral, interpersonal, and psychodynamic—are often supplemented by family therapy (Mitchell, 2018).

Cognitive-behavioral, interpersonal, and psychodynamic therapy may each be offered in either an individual or a group therapy format, including self-help groups. Research suggests that group formats are at least somewhat helpful for as many as 75 percent of people with bulimia nervosa (Mitchell, 2018; Valbak, 2001).

Antidepressant Medications During the past 15 years, antidepressant drugs—all forms of antidepressant drugs—have been used to help treat bulimia nervosa. In

Catherine Wylie/Press Association via AP Images

i-Images/Polaris

Battling ad campaigns In 2015, the weight loss company Protein World released an ad in London featuring a thin, bikini-clad model asking, "Are You Beach Body Ready?" The ad (left) quickly produced a wave of protests by critics who believed that it implied other body shapes were inferior. In fact, the plus-size fashion brand *Simply Be* countered with an ad campaign featuring a larger-sized model (right) asserting, "Every Body Is Beach Body Ready." The controversial Protein World ad is now banned in England.

contrast to people with anorexia nervosa, those with bulimia nervosa are often helped considerably by these drugs (Crow, 2017; Starr & Kreipe, 2014). According to research, the drugs help as many as 40 percent of patients, reducing their binges by an average of 67 percent and vomiting by 56 percent. Once again, drug therapy seems to work best in combination with other forms of therapy, particularly cognitive-behavioral therapy. Alternatively, some therapists wait to see whether cognitive-behavioral therapy or another form of psychotherapy is effective before trying antidepressants (Agras et al., 2017). Studies suggest that psychotherapy is more effective than antidepressant drugs, but that a combination of the two is more effective than either form of treatment alone (Crow, 2017).

What Is the Aftermath of Bulimia Nervosa? Left untreated, bulimia nervosa can last for years, sometimes improving temporarily but then returning. Treatment, however, produces immediate, significant improvement in approximately 40 percent of clients: they stop or greatly reduce their bingeing and purging, eat properly, and maintain a normal weight (Mitchell, 2018; Isomaa & Isomaa, 2014). Another 40 percent show a moderate response—at least some decrease in binge eating and purging. Follow-up studies, conducted years after treatment, suggest that around 75 percent of people with bulimia nervosa have recovered, either fully or partially (Engel et al., 2017).

Relapse can be a problem even among people who respond successfully to treatment (Engel et al., 2017). As with anorexia nervosa, relapses are usually triggered by a new life stress, such as an upcoming exam, a job change, marriage, or divorce (Liu, 2007). One study found that 28 percent of those who had recovered from bulimia nervosa relapsed within six months (Olmsted et al., 2015). Relapse is more likely among people who had longer histories of bulimia nervosa before treatment, had vomited more frequently during their disorder, continued to vomit at the end of treatment, had histories of substance abuse, and continue to be lonely or to distrust others after treatment (Engel et al., 2017; Vall & Wade, 2015).

Treatments for Binge-Eating Disorder

Approximately 44 percent of people with binge-eating disorder receive treatment (NIMH, 2017). Given the key role of binges in both this disorder (bingeing without purging) and bulimia, today's treatments for binge-eating disorder are often similar to those for bulimia nervosa. In particular, cognitive-behavioral therapy, other forms of psychotherapy, and in some cases, antidepressant medications are provided to help reduce or eliminate the binge-eating patterns and to change disturbed thinking such as being overly concerned with weight and shape (Sysko & Devlin, 2017; Fischer et al., 2014). According to research, psychotherapy is generally more helpful than antidepressants.

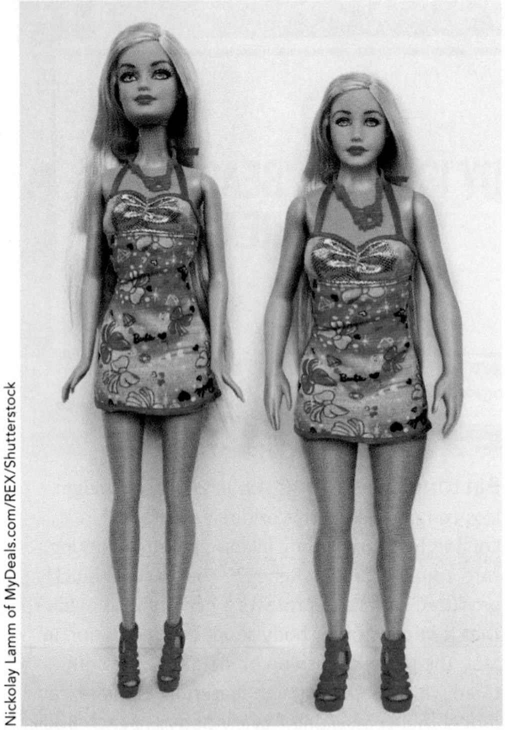
Nickolay Lamm of MyDeals.com/REX/Shutterstock

"Normal Barbie" For years, the ultra-slim measurements of the Barbie doll have introduced young girls to an unattainable ideal. Hoping to show instead that "average is beautiful," artist Nickolay Lamm has designed a Normal Barbie (right), using the CDC measurements of the average 19-year-old woman. Normal Barbie turns out to be shorter, curvier, and bustier than the classic doll.

Evidence indicates that these kinds of interventions are indeed often effective, at least in the short run. As many as 60 percent of clients no longer fit the criteria for binge-eating disorder by the end of treatment (Sysko & Devlin, 2017). Many of these early gains may continue for years. However, only around one-third of the recovered individuals showed total improvement in those follow-up studies. As with the other eating disorders, many of those who initially recover from binge-eating disorder continue to have a relatively high risk of relapse (ANAD, 2018, 2014; Sysko & Devlin, 2017).

Of course, many people with binge-eating disorder also are overweight, a problem that requires additional kinds of intervention. Their weight problems are often resistant to long-term improvement, even if regular binge eating is reduced or eliminated (Sysko & Devlin, 2017; Grilo et al., 2014). In one follow-up study of hospitalized patients with severe symptoms of binge-eating disorder, 36 percent of those who had been treated were still significantly overweight 12 years after hospitalization (Fichter et al., 2008).

9... SUMMING UP

HOW ARE EATING DISORDERS TREATED? The first step in treating anorexia nervosa is to help patients regain weight and return to health, a part of treatment called nutritional rehabilitation. The second step is to deal with the underlying psychological and family problems, often using a combination of education, cognitive-behavioral approaches, and family therapy. As many as 75 percent of people who are successfully treated for anorexia nervosa continue to show full or partial improvements years later. However, some of them relapse along the way.

Treatments for bulimia nervosa focus first on stopping the binge-purge pattern (nutritional rehabilitation) and then on addressing the underlying causes of the disorder. Often several treatment strategies are combined, including education, psychotherapy (particularly cognitive-behavioral therapy), and, in some cases, antidepressant medications. As many as 75 percent of those who receive treatment eventually improve either fully or partially. While relapse can be a problem, treatment leads to lasting improvements in psychological and social functioning for many people. Similar treatments are used to help people with binge-eating disorder. These individuals, however, may also require interventions to address their excessive weight.

Prevention of Eating Disorders: Wave of the Future

Clearly, eating disorders are profoundly destructive. Moreover, the various treatments for these disorders, while improving greatly in recent years, do not bring about a full recovery (or, in some instances, any recovery) for many people with these disorders. Thus, some clinical theorists believe that researchers must invest more work into the development of programs that *prevent* the onset of eating disorders.

One of today's promising prevention programs is called *Body Project*, a program developed and expanded by psychologists Eric Stice and Carolyn Black Becker and their colleagues (Becker et al., 2017; Stice et al., 2017, 2015, 2013). Keeping in mind the key factors that predispose people to the development of eating disorders, Body Project offers a total of four weekly group sessions for high school and college-age women. In these sessions, group members are guided through a range of intense verbal, written, role-playing, and behavioral exercises that critique Western society's ultra-thin ideal. The participants also engage in body acceptance exercises, eating and related activities that run counter to the ultra-thin ideal, motivation enhancement techniques, skill-building training, and social support exercises.

CLINICAL CHOICES

Now that you've read about eating disorders, try the interactive case study for this chapter. See if you are able to identify Jenny's symptoms and suggest a diagnosis based on her symptoms. What kind of treatment would be most effective for Jenny? Go to **LaunchPad** to access ***Clinical Choices.***

Although early in its development, the Body Project prevention program has performed well in research (Stice et al., 2017, 2015). In comparison to other young women who received education-only prevention programs or no prevention programs at all, participants in Body Project develop fewer eating disorders, hold more realistic and healthful appearance ideals, display fewer maladaptive eating attitudes and behaviors, have greater body satisfaction, and experience more positive emotions in follow-up studies conducted a year or more after the program.

Clearly, this program is promising and important. Whether in the form of Body Project or other such undertakings, prevention programs address a critical need in the clinical field's commitment to overcome eating disorders and are likely to increase in the years to come.

... Key Terms

anorexia nervosa, p. 266
restricting-type anorexia nervosa, p. 266
amenorrhea, p. 268
bulimia nervosa, p. 268
binge, p. 268
compensatory behavior, p. 271
binge-eating disorder, p. 272
multidimensional risk perspective, p. 275
effective parents, p. 275
brain circuits, p. 278
hypothalamus, p. 278
lateral hypothalamus (LH), p. 278
ventromedial hypothalamus (VMH), p. 278
glucagon-like peptide-1 (GLP-1), p. 278
weight set point, p. 278
enmeshed family pattern, p. 280
nutritional rehabilitation, p. 283
motivational interviewing, p. 283
prevention, p. 290
Body Project, p. 290

... Quick Quiz

1. What are the symptoms and main features of anorexia nervosa and bulimia nervosa? How are people with anorexia nervosa similar to those with bulimia nervosa? How are they different? *pp. 266–272*
2. What are the symptoms and main features of binge-eating disorder? How is this disorder different from bulimia nervosa? *pp. 272, 274*
3. According to Hilde Bruch, how might parents' failure to attend appropriately to their baby's internal needs and emotions contribute to the later development of an eating disorder? *pp. 275–276*
4. How might a person's brain circuits, hypothalamus, and weight set point contribute to the development of an eating disorder? *pp. 277–279*
5. What evidence suggests that sociocultural pressures and factors may set the stage for eating disorders? *pp. 279–282*
6. When clinicians treat people with anorexia nervosa, what are their short-term and long-term goals? What approaches do they use to accomplish them? *pp. 283–285*
7. How well do people with anorexia nervosa recover from their disorder? What factors affect a person's recovery? What risks and problems may linger after recovery? *pp. 285–286*
8. What are the key goals and approaches used in the treatment of bulimia nervosa, and how successful are they? What factors affect a person's recovery? What risks and problems may linger after recovery? *pp. 286–289*
9. How are treatments for binge-eating disorder similar to and different from treatments for bulimia nervosa? *pp. 289–290*
10. What are some of the key features of eating disorder prevention programs such as Body Project? *pp. 290–291*

CHAPTER

10

Substance Use and Addictive Disorders

TOPIC OVERVIEW

"I am Duncan. I am an alcoholic." The audience settled deeper into their chairs at these familiar words. Another chronicle of death and rebirth would shortly begin [at] Alcoholics Anonymous. . . .

"I must have been just past my 15th birthday when I had that first drink that everybody talks about. And like so many of them . . . it was like a miracle. With a little beer in my gut, the world was transformed. I wasn't a weakling anymore, I could lick almost anybody on the block. And girls? Well, you can imagine how a couple of beers made me feel like I could have any girl I wanted. . . .

"Though it's obvious to me now that my drinking even then, in high school, and after I got to college, was a problem, I didn't think so at the time. After all, everybody was drinking and getting drunk and acting stupid, and I didn't really think I was different. . . . I guess the fact that I hadn't really had any blackouts and that I could go for days without having to drink reassured me that things hadn't gotten out of control. And that's the way it went, until I found myself drinking even more—and more often—and suffering more from my drinking, along about my third year of college. . . .

"My roommate, a friend from high school, started bugging me about my drinking. It wasn't even that I'd have to sleep it off the whole next day and miss class, it was that he had begun to hear other friends talking about me, about the fool I'd made of myself at parties. He saw how shaky I was the morning after, and he saw how different I was when I'd been drinking a lot—almost out of my head was the way he put it. And he could count the bottles that I'd leave around the room, and he knew what the drinking and carousing was doing to my grades. . . . [P]artly because I really cared about my roommate and didn't want to lose him as a friend, I did cut down on my drinking by half or more. I only drank on weekends—and then only at night. . . . And that got me through the rest of college and, actually, through law school as well. . . .

"Shortly after getting my law degree, I married my first wife, and . . . for the first time since I started, my drinking was no problem at all. I would go for weeks at a time without touching a drop. . . .

"My marriage started to go bad after our second son, our third child, was born. I was very much career- and success-oriented, and I had little time to spend at home with my family. . . . My traveling had increased a lot, there were stimulating people on those trips, and, let's face it, there were some pretty exciting women available, too. So home got to be little else but a nagging, boring wife and children I wasn't very interested in. My drinking had gotten bad again, too, with being on the road so much, having to do a lot of entertaining at lunch when I wasn't away, and trying to soften the hassles at home. I guess I was putting down close to a gallon of very good scotch a week, with one thing or another.

"And as that went on, the drinking began to affect both my marriage and my career. With enough booze in me and under the pressures of guilt over my failure to carry out my responsibilities to my wife and children, I sometimes got kind of rough physically with them. I would break furniture, throw things around, then rush out and drive off in the car. I had a couple of wrecks, lost my license for two years because of one of them. Worst of all was when I tried to stop. By then I was totally hooked, so every time I tried to stop drinking, I'd experience withdrawal in all its horrors . . . with the vomiting and the 'shakes' and being unable to sit still or to lie down. And that would go on for days at a time. . . .

#FamilyVictims

More than 10 percent of children live with a parent with alcohol problems (NIAAA, 2018).

Then, about four years ago, with my life in ruins, my wife given up on me and the kids with her, out of a job, and way down on my luck, [Alcoholics Anonymous] and I found each other. . . . I've been dry now for a little over two years, and with luck and support, I may stay sober. . . ."

(Spitzer et al., 1983, pp. 87–89)

Human beings enjoy a remarkable variety of foods and drinks. Every substance on earth probably has been tried by someone, somewhere, at some time. We also have discovered substances that have interesting effects—both medical and pleasurable—on our brains and the rest of our bodies. We may swallow an aspirin to quiet a headache, an antibiotic to fight an infection, or a tranquilizer to calm us down. We may drink coffee to get going in the morning or wine to relax with friends. We may smoke cigarettes to soothe our nerves. However, many of the substances we consume can harm us or disrupt our behavior or mood. The misuse of such substances has become one of society's biggest problems; it has been estimated that the cost of substance misuse is $740 billion each year in the United States alone (NIDA, 2017).

Not only are numerous substances available in our society, new ones are introduced almost every day. Some are harvested from nature, others derived from natural substances, and still others produced in the laboratory. Some, such as antianxiety drugs, require a physician's prescription for legal use. Others, such as alcohol and nicotine, are legally available to adults. Still others, such as heroin, are illegal under all circumstances. In 1962, only 4 million people in the United States had ever used marijuana, cocaine, heroin, or another illegal substance; today the number has climbed to 131 million (SAMHSA, 2018). In fact, 27 million people have used illegal substances within the past month. A quarter of all teenagers have used an illegal substance.

A *drug* is defined as any substance other than food that affects our bodies or minds. It need not be a medicine or be illegal. The term "substance" is now frequently used in place of "drug," in part because many people fail to see that such substances as alcohol, tobacco, and caffeine are drugs, too. When a person ingests a substance—whether it be alcohol, cocaine, marijuana, or some form of medication—trillions of powerful molecules surge through the bloodstream and into the brain. Once there, the molecules set off a series of biochemical events that disturb the normal operation of the brain and body. Not surprisingly, then, substance misuse may lead to various kinds of abnormal functioning.

Substances may cause *temporary* changes in behavior, emotion, or thought; this cluster of changes is called **substance intoxication** in DSM-5. As Duncan found out, for example, an excessive amount of alcohol may lead to *alcohol intoxication,* a temporary state of poor judgment, mood changes, irritability, slurred speech, and poor coordination. Similarly, drugs such as LSD may produce *hallucinogen intoxication,* sometimes called *hallucinosis,* which consists largely of perceptual distortions and hallucinations.

Some substances can also lead to *long-term* problems. People who regularly ingest them may develop **substance use disorders,** patterns of maladaptive behaviors and reactions brought about by the repeated use of substances (APA, 2013). People with a substance use disorder may come to crave a particular substance and rely on it excessively, resulting in damage to their family and social relationships, poor functioning at work, and/or danger to themselves or others (see **Table 10-1**). In many cases, people with such a disorder also become physically dependent on the substance, developing a *tolerance* for it and experiencing *withdrawal* reactions. When people develop **tolerance,** they need increasing doses of the substance to produce the desired effect. **Withdrawal** reactions consist of unpleasant and sometimes dangerous symptoms—cramps, anxiety attacks, sweating, nausea—that occur when the person suddenly stops taking or cuts back on the substance. Duncan, who described his problems to fellow members at an Alcoholics Anonymous meeting, was caught in a form of substance use disorder called

TABLE: 10-1

Dx Checklist

Substance Use Disorder
1. Individual displays a maladaptive pattern of substance use leading to significant impairment or distress.
2. Presence of at least 2 of the following substance-produced symptoms within a 1-year period: • Substance is often taken in larger amounts • Unsuccessful efforts to reduce or control substance use • Much time spent trying to obtain, use, or recover from effects of substance • Failure to fulfill major role obligations • Continued use despite persistent interpersonal problems • Reduction of important activities • Continued use in dangerous situations • Continued use despite worsening of physical or psychological problems • Craving for substance • Tolerance effects • Withdrawal reactions.

Information from: APA, 2013.

alcohol use disorder. When he was a college student and later a lawyer, alcohol damaged his family, social, academic, and work life. He also built up a tolerance for alcohol over time and had withdrawal symptoms such as vomiting and shaking when he tried to stop using it.

In any given year, 7.8 percent of all teens and adults in the United States, around 21 million people, have a substance use disorder (SAMHSA, 2018). American Indians have the highest rate of substance use disorders in the United States (11.6 percent), while Asian Americans have the lowest (3.8 percent). Non-Hispanic white Americans, Hispanic Americans, and African Americans have rates between 7 and 8.2 percent (SAMHSA, 2018) (see **Figure 10-1**). Only 18 percent of all those with substance use disorders receive treatment from a mental health professional.

The substances people misuse fall into several categories: *depressants, stimulants, hallucinogens,* and *cannabis.* In this chapter you will read about some of the most problematic substances and the abnormal patterns they may produce. In addition, at the end of the chapter, you'll read about *gambling disorder,* a problem that DSM-5 lists as an additional addictive disorder. By listing this behavioral pattern alongside the substance use disorders, DSM-5 is suggesting that this problem has addictive-like symptoms and causes that share more than a passing similarity to those at work in substance use disorders. ■

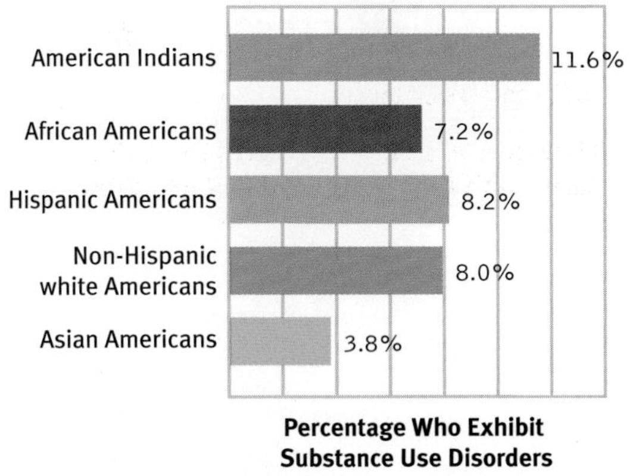

FIGURE 10-1

How Do Racial/Ethnic Groups Differ in Substance Use Disorders?

In the United States, American Indians are more likely than members of other ethnic or cultural groups to have substance use disorders. (Information from: SAMHSA, 2018.)

Depressants

Depressants slow the activity of the central nervous system. They reduce tension and inhibitions and may interfere with a person's judgment, motor activity, and concentration. The three most widely used groups of depressants are *alcohol, sedative-hypnotic drugs,* and *opioids.*

Alcohol

The World Health Organization estimates that 2 billion people worldwide consume **alcohol.** In the United States more than half of all residents at least from time to time drink beverages that contain alcohol (SAMHSA, 2018). Purchases of beer, wine, and liquor amount to tens of billions of dollars each year in the United States alone.

When people consume five or more drinks on a single occasion, it is called a *binge drinking* episode. Twenty-five percent of people in the United States over the age of 11, most of them male, binge drink each month (SAMHSA, 2018). Around 6.5 percent of people over 11 years of age binge drink at least five times each month. They are considered heavy drinkers. Among heavy drinkers, males outnumber females by at least 2 to 1.

All alcoholic beverages contain *ethyl alcohol,* a chemical that is quickly absorbed into the blood through the lining of the stomach and the intestine. The ethyl alcohol immediately begins to take effect as it is carried in the bloodstream to the central nervous system (the brain and spinal cord), where it acts to depress, or slow, functioning by binding to various neurons. One important group of neurons to which ethyl alcohol binds are those that normally receive the neurotransmitter GABA. As you saw in Chapter 4, GABA carries an *inhibitory* message—a message to stop firing—when it is received at certain neurons. When alcohol binds to receptors on those neurons, it apparently helps GABA to shut down the neurons, thus helping to relax the drinker (Farokhnia et al., 2018; Nace, 2011, 2005).

At first ethyl alcohol depresses the areas of the brain that control judgment and inhibition; people become looser, more talkative, and often more friendly. As their inner control breaks down, they may feel relaxed, confident, and happy. When more alcohol is absorbed, it slows down additional areas in the central nervous system, leaving drinkers

substance intoxication A cluster of temporary undesirable behavioral or psychological changes that develop during or shortly after the ingestion of a substance.

substance use disorder A pattern of long-term maladaptive behaviors and reactions brought about by repeated use of a substance.

tolerance The brain and body's need for ever-larger doses of a drug to produce earlier effects.

withdrawal Unpleasant, sometimes dangerous reactions that may occur when people who use a drug regularly stop taking it or reduce the dosage.

alcohol Any beverage containing ethyl alcohol, including beer, wine, and liquor.

less able to make sound judgments, their speech less careful and less coherent, and their memory weaker. Many people become highly emotional and perhaps loud and aggressive.

Motor difficulties increase as a person continues drinking, and reaction times slow. People may be unsteady when they stand or walk and clumsy in performing even simple activities. They may drop things, bump into doors and furniture, and misjudge distances. Their vision becomes blurred, particularly their peripheral, or side, vision, and they have trouble hearing. As a result, people who have drunk too much alcohol may have great difficulty driving or solving simple problems.

The extent of the effect of ethyl alcohol is determined by its *concentration*, or proportion, in the blood. Thus, a given amount of alcohol has less effect on a large person than on a small one. Gender also affects the concentration of alcohol in the blood. Women have less of the stomach enzyme *alcohol dehydrogenase*, which breaks down alcohol in the stomach before it enters the blood. So women become more intoxicated than men on equal doses of alcohol, and women may be at greater risk for physical and psychological damage from alcohol than men who drink similar quantities of it (Mukamal, 2018).

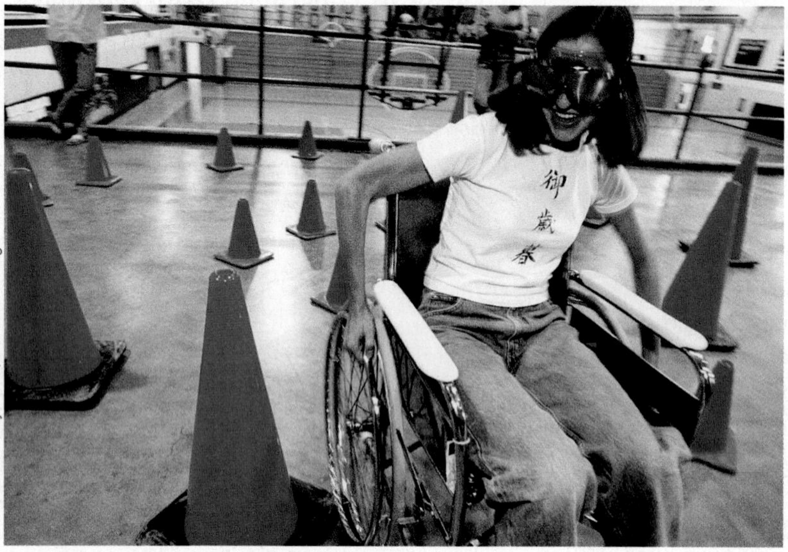

AP Photo/The Daily Times, Marc F. Henning

Simulating alcohol's effects A 16-year-old student weaves her way through an obstacle course while wearing a pair of goggles that produce alcohol-like impairment. The exercise is part of a DUI-prevention program at her New Mexico high school, designed to give students hands-on experience with alcohol's effects on vision and balance.

Levels of impairment are closely related to the concentration of ethyl alcohol in the blood. When the alcohol concentration reaches 0.06 percent of the blood volume, a person usually feels relaxed and comfortable. By the time it reaches 0.09 percent, however, the drinker crosses the line into intoxication. If the level goes as high as 0.55 percent, the drinker will likely die. Most people lose consciousness before they can drink enough to reach this level; nevertheless, more than 1,000 people in the United States die each year from too high a blood alcohol level (Mukamal, 2018; Hart & Ksir, 2017).

The effects of alcohol subside only when the alcohol concentration in the blood declines. Most of the alcohol is broken down, or *metabolized*, by the liver into carbon dioxide and water, which can be exhaled and excreted. The average rate of this metabolism is 25 percent of an ounce per hour, but different people's livers work at different speeds; thus rates of "sobering up" vary. Despite popular belief, only time and metabolism can make a person sober. Drinking black coffee, splashing cold water on one's face, or "pulling oneself together" cannot hurry the process.

Alcohol Use Disorder Though legal, alcohol is actually one of the most dangerous of recreational drugs, and its reach extends across the life span. In fact, around 23 percent of middle school students admit to some alcohol use, while 33 percent of high school seniors drink alcohol each month (most to the point of intoxication) and 1.3 percent report drinking every day (Johnston et al., 2017). Alcohol misuse is also a major problem on college campuses (see ***PsychWatch***).

Surveys indicate that over a one-year period, 5.9 percent of all people over 11 years of age in the United States display *alcohol use disorder*, known in popular terms as *alcoholism* (SAMHSA, 2018). For teenagers specifically, the rate is 2.5 percent. Men with this disorder outnumber women by 2 to 1.

The current prevalence of alcoholism is around 6.1 percent for non-Hispanic white Americans, 6.4 percent for Hispanic Americans, and 4.9 percent for African Americans (SAMHSA, 2018). American Indians, particularly men, tend to display a higher rate of alcohol use disorder than any of these groups. Overall, 9.7 percent of them experience the disorder, although specific prevalence rates differ widely across the various American Indian reservation communities. Generally, Asians in the United States and elsewhere have a lower rate of alcoholism (3.2 percent) than do people from other cultures. As many as half of these individuals have a deficiency of alcohol dehydrogenase, the

PSYCHWATCH

College Binge Drinking: An Extracurricular Crisis

Drinking large amounts of alcohol in a short time, or *binge drinking*, is a serious problem on college campuses, as well as in many other settings. Studies show that 38 percent of college students binge drink at least once each month, one-third of them six times or more per month (SAMHSA, 2018; NIAAA, 2017). In many circles, alcohol use is an accepted part of college life, but consider some of the following statistics:

- Alcohol-related arrests account for 83 percent of all campus arrests.
- More than half of all sexual assaults on college campuses involve the heavy consumption of alcohol.
- Alcohol is a factor in at least 25 percent of academic problems and 28 percent of all instances of dropping out of college.
- Approximately 700,000 students each year are physically or emotionally traumatized or assaulted by a student drinker.
- Half of college students say "drinking to get drunk" is an important reason for drinking.
- Binge drinking often has a lingering effect on mood, memory, brain functioning, and heart functioning.
- Binge drinking is tied to 4,300 deaths among college-age persons every year.
- The number of female binge drinkers among college students has increased 31 percent over the past decade.

(CDC, 2018, 2017, 2016; NIAAA, 2017; Nourse et al., 2017; NCASA, 2007; Abbey, 2002)

© Andrew Lichtenstein/Sygma via Getty Images

Testing the limits College binge drinking, which involves behaviors similar to that shown here, has led to a number of deaths in recent years.

These findings have led some educators to describe binge drinking as "the number one public health hazard" for full-time college students, and many researchers and clinicians have turned their attention to it. Studies have collectively surveyed more than 100,000 students at college campuses around the United States (CDC, 2018, 2017; Greene & Maggs, 2017; NIAAA, 2017). Among other useful information, the surveys have found that the students most likely to binge drink are those who live in fraternity or sorority houses, pursue a party-centered lifestyle, and engage in high-risk behaviors such as substance misuse. The surveys have also suggested that students who are binge drinkers in high school are more likely to binge drink in college.

Efforts to change such patterns have begun. For example, many universities now provide substance-free dorms. Studies indicate that the rate of binge drinking by residents in these college housing facilities is half the rate displayed by students who live in a fraternity or sorority house (Lippy & DeGue, 2016; Wechsler et al., 2002). This and other current research efforts are promising. However, most people in the clinical field agree that much more work is needed to help us fully understand, prevent, and treat what has become a major societal problem.

chemical responsible for breaking down alcohol, so they react quite negatively to even a modest intake of alcohol. Such reactions in turn help prevent extended use (Chang, Hsiao, & Chen, 2017).

CLINICAL PICTURE Generally speaking, people with alcohol use disorder drink large amounts regularly and rely on it to enable them to do things that would otherwise make them anxious. Eventually the drinking interferes with their social behavior and ability to think and work. They may have frequent arguments with family members or friends, miss work repeatedly, and even lose their jobs. MRI scans of chronic heavy drinkers have revealed damage in various structures of their brains and, correspondingly, impairments in their memory, speed of thinking, attention skills, and balance (Tetrault & O'Connor, 2017).

#EndangeredAthletes

College athletes (both male and female) are more likely to drink, drink heavily, and binge drink than college students who are not athletes (Taylor et al., 2017; Burnsed, 2014).

Individually, people's patterns of alcoholism vary. Some drink large amounts of alcohol every day and keep drinking until intoxicated. Others go on periodic binges of heavy drinking that can last weeks or months. They may remain intoxicated for days and later be unable to remember anything about the period. Still others may limit their excessive drinking to weekends, evenings, or both.

TOLERANCE AND WITHDRAWAL For many people, alcohol use disorder includes the symptoms of tolerance and withdrawal reactions (Pace, 2017; Tetrault & O'Connor, 2017). As their bodies build up a tolerance for alcohol, they need to drink ever larger amounts to feel its effects. In addition, they have withdrawal symptoms when they stop drinking. Within hours their hands, tongue, and eyelids begin to shake; they feel weak and nauseated; they sweat and vomit; their heart beats rapidly; and their blood pressure rises. They may also become anxious, depressed, unable to sleep, or irritable (APA, 2013).

A small percentage of people with alcohol use disorder go through a particularly dramatic withdrawal reaction called **delirium tremens ("the DTs").** It consists of terrifying visual hallucinations that begin within three days after they stop or reduce their drinking. Some people see small, frightening animals chasing or crawling on them or objects dancing about in front of their eyes. Like most other alcohol withdrawal symptoms, the DTs usually run their course in 2 to 3 days. However, people who have severe withdrawal reactions such as this may also have seizures, lose consciousness, suffer a stroke, or even die. Today certain medical procedures can help prevent or reduce such extreme reactions.

What Are the Personal and Social Impacts of Alcoholism? Alcoholism destroys millions of families, social relationships, and careers (Mukamal, 2018). Medical treatment, lost productivity, and losses due to deaths from alcoholism cost society many billions of dollars annually. The disorder also plays a role in more than one-third of all suicides, homicides, assaults, rapes, and accidental deaths, including 29 percent of all fatal automobile accidents in the United States (CDC, 2017; Gifford et al., 2010). Altogether, intoxicated drivers are responsible for more than 10,000 deaths each year. Around 10 percent of all adults have driven while intoxicated at least once in the past year (SAMHSA, 2018). Although this is a frightening number, it represents a significant drop since 2002 when 14 percent of adults had driven in an intoxicated state.

Substance misuse and sports fans A problem that has received growing attention in recent years is excessive drinking by fans at sports events. While two soccer players were jumping for a high ball at this playoff game in Athens, Greece, fans—many of them intoxicated—ripped out plastic seats, threw flares on the field, and hurled coins and rocks at the players.

AP Photo/Aris Messinis

Alcoholism has serious effects on the 30 million children of people with this disorder. Home life for these children is likely to include much conflict and perhaps sexual or other forms of abuse. In turn, the children themselves have higher rates of psychological problems (Thapa, Selya, & Jonk, 2017; Gold, 2016). Many have low self-esteem, poor communication skills, poor sociability, and marital problems.

Long-term excessive drinking can also seriously damage a person's physical health (Mukamal, 2018; Gramlich, Tandon, & Rahman, 2017). It so overworks the liver that people may develop an irreversible condition called *cirrhosis,* in which the liver becomes scarred and dysfunctional. Cirrhosis accounts for more than 38,000 deaths each year (CDC, 2017). Alcohol use disorder may also damage the heart and lower the immune system's ability to fight off cancer, bacterial infections, and AIDS.

Long-term excessive drinking also causes major nutritional problems. Alcohol makes people feel full and lowers their desire for food, yet it has no nutritional value. As a result, chronic drinkers become malnourished, weak, and prone to disease. Their vitamin and mineral deficiencies may also cause problems. An alcohol-related deficiency of vitamin B1 (thiamine), for example, may lead to *Korsakoff's syndrome,* a disease marked by extreme confusion, memory loss, and other neurological symptoms (Mukamal, 2018; Gramlich et al., 2017). People with Korsakoff's syndrome cannot remember the past or learn new information and may make up for their memory losses by *confabulating*—reciting made-up events to fill in the gaps.

Women who drink during pregnancy place their fetuses at risk (Chang, 2018; Popova et al., 2017). Excessive alcohol use during pregnancy may cause a baby to be born with **fetal alcohol syndrome,** a pattern of abnormalities that can include intellectual disability, hyperactivity, head and face deformities, heart defects, and slow growth (Weitzman & Rojmahamongkol, 2018). It has been estimated that in the overall population, around 1 of every 1,000 babies is born with this syndrome (CDC, 2017). The rate may increase to as many as 67 of every 1,000 babies of women who are problem drinkers (Popova et al., 2017). If all alcohol-related birth defects (known as *fetal alcohol spectrum disorder*) are counted, the rate becomes 80 to 200 such births per 1,000 heavy-drinking women. In addition, heavy drinking early in pregnancy often leads to a miscarriage. According to surveys, 9.3 percent of pregnant American women have drunk alcohol during the past month and 4.6 percent of pregnant women have had binge drinking episodes (SAMHSA, 2018).

If alcohol is highly addictive and capable of causing so many psychological, physical, social, and personal problems, why does it remain legal in most countries?

Sedative-Hypnotic Drugs

Sedative-hypnotic drugs, also called **anxiolytic** (meaning "anxiety-reducing") **drugs,** produce feelings of relaxation and drowsiness. At low dosages, the drugs have a calming or sedative effect. At higher dosages, they are sleep inducers, or hypnotics. For the first half of the twentieth century, a group of drugs called **barbiturates** were the most widely prescribed sedative-hypnotic drugs. Although still prescribed by some physicians, these drugs have been largely replaced by **benzodiazepines,** which are generally safer and less likely to lead to intoxication, tolerance effects, and withdrawal reactions.

As Chapter 4 noted, benzodiazepines, developed in the 1950s, are the most popular sedative-hypnotic drugs available. Xanax, Ativan, and Valium are just three of the dozens of these compounds in clinical use. Altogether, 130 million prescriptions are written annually for benzodiazepines (Soyka, 2017; Bachhuber et al., 2016). Like alcohol and barbiturates, they calm people by binding to receptors on the neurons that receive GABA and by increasing GABA's activity at those neurons (Tietze & Fuchs, 2017). Benzodiazepines relieve anxiety without making people as drowsy as other kinds of sedative-hypnotics. They are also less likely to slow a person's breathing, so they are less likely to cause death in the event of an overdose.

When benzodiazepines were first discovered, they seemed so safe and effective that physicians prescribed them generously, and their use spread. Eventually it became clear that in high enough doses the drugs can cause intoxication and lead to *sedative-hypnotic use disorder,* a pattern marked by craving for the drugs, tolerance effects, and withdrawal reactions (Greller & Gupta, 2017; Park, 2017). Over a one-year period, 0.4 percent of all adults in the United States display this disorder (SAMHSA, 2018).

Opioids

Opioids include opium, which is taken from the sap of the opium poppy; drugs derived from opium, such as heroin, morphine, and codeine; and similar *synthetic* (laboratory-blended) drugs. **Opium** itself has been in use

delirium tremens (DTs) A dramatic alcohol withdrawal reaction that consists of confusion, clouded consciousness, and visual hallucinations.

fetal alcohol syndrome A cluster of problems in a child, including irregularities in the head and face and intellectual deficits, caused by excessive alcohol intake during pregnancy.

sedative-hypnotic drug A drug used in low doses to reduce anxiety and in higher doses to help people sleep. Also called an *anxiolytic drug.*

barbiturates Addictive sedative-hypnotic drugs that reduce anxiety and help people sleep.

benzodiazepines The most common group of antianxiety drugs; includes Xanax.

opioid Opium, drugs derived from opium, and similar synthetic drugs.

opium A highly addictive substance made from the sap of the opium poppy.

Purer blend Heroin, derived from poppies such as this one in a poppy field in southern Afghanistan, is purer and stronger today than it was three decades ago (65 percent pure versus 5 percent pure).

Stringer /EPA/Newscom

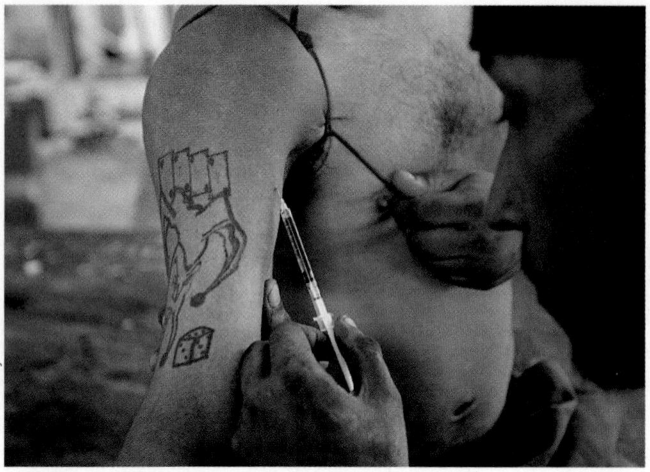

Injecting heroin Opioids may be taken by mouth, inhaled, snorted, injected just beneath the surface of the skin, or injected intravenously. Here, one addict injects another with heroin inside one of the many so-called shooting galleries where addicts gather in downtown San Juan, Puerto Rico.

for thousands of years. In the past it was used widely in the treatment of medical disorders because of its ability to reduce both physical and emotional pain. Eventually, however, physicians discovered that the drug was addictive.

In 1804 a new substance, **morphine,** was derived from opium. Named after Morpheus, the Greek god of sleep, this drug relieved pain even better than opium did and initially was considered safe. However, wide use of the drug eventually revealed that it, too, could lead to addiction. During the United States Civil War, so many wounded soldiers received morphine injections that morphine addiction became known as "soldiers' disease."

In 1898, morphine was converted into yet another new pain reliever, **heroin.** For several years heroin was viewed as a wonder drug and was used as a cough medicine and for other medical purposes. Eventually, however, physicians learned that heroin is even more addictive than the other opioids. By 1917, the U.S. Congress had concluded that all drugs derived from opium were addictive, and it passed a law making opioids illegal except for medical purposes.

Can you think of other substances or activities that, like opioids, can be helpful in controlled portions but dangerous when used excessively or uncontrollably?

Still other drugs have been derived from opium, and, as noted above, synthetic opioids such as *methadone* have also been developed. These various opioid drugs are also known collectively as *narcotics*. Each drug has a different strength, speed of action, and tolerance level. Morphine, *codeine*, and *oxycodone* (the key ingredient in OxyContin and Percocet) are medical opioids usually prescribed to relieve pain. In contrast to these opioids, heroin is illegal in the United States in all circumstances.

Most opioids are smoked, inhaled, snorted, injected, or, as in the case of many pain relievers, swallowed in pill or liquid form. In injections, the opioid may be deposited just beneath the skin ("skin-popping"), deep into a muscle, or directly into a vein ("mainlining"). An injection quickly brings on a *rush*—a spasm of warmth and ecstasy that is sometimes compared with orgasm. The brief spasm is followed by several hours of a pleasant feeling called a *high* or *nod*. During a high, the drug user feels relaxed, happy, and unconcerned about food, sex, or other bodily needs.

Opioids create these effects by depressing the central nervous system, particularly the centers that help control emotion. The drugs attach to brain receptor sites that ordinarily receive **endorphins**—neurotransmitters that help relieve pain and reduce emotional tension (Stolbach & Hoffman, 2018). When neurons at these receptor sites receive opioids, they produce pleasurable and calming feelings just as they would do if they were receiving endorphins. In addition to reducing pain and tension, opioids cause nausea, narrowing of the pupils ("pinpoint pupils"), and constipation—bodily reactions that can also be brought about by releases of endorphins in the brain.

Opioid Use Disorder Heroin use exemplifies the kinds of problems posed by opioids. After taking heroin repeatedly for just a few weeks, users may develop *opioid use disorder*. Their heroin use interferes significantly with their social and occupational functioning, and their lives center around the drug. They may also build a tolerance for heroin and experience a withdrawal reaction when they stop taking it (Sevarino, 2017; Strain, 2017). At first the withdrawal symptoms are anxiety, restlessness, sweating, and rapid breathing; later they include severe twitching, aches, fever, vomiting, diarrhea, loss of appetite, high blood pressure, and weight loss of up to 15 pounds (due to loss of bodily fluids). These symptoms usually peak by the third day, gradually subside, and disappear by the eighth day. A person in heroin withdrawal can either wait out the symptoms or end withdrawal by taking the drug again.

Such people soon need heroin just to avoid going into withdrawal, and they must continually increase their doses in order to achieve even that relief. The temporary high

morphine A highly addictive substance derived from opium that is particularly effective in relieving pain.

heroin One of the most addictive substances derived from opium.

endorphins Neurotransmitters that help relieve pain and reduce emotional tension. They are sometimes referred to as the body's own opioids.

becomes less intense and less important. Heroin users may spend much of their time planning their next dose, in many cases turning to criminal activities, such as theft and prostitution, to support the expensive "habit" (Hart & Ksir, 2017).

Surveys suggest that more than 1 percent of adults in the United States, a total of 2.6 million people, display an opioid use disorder within a given year (SAMHSA, 2018). Among teenagers specifically, the prevalence may be even higher (Johnston et al., 2017). Most of these persons (80 percent) are addicted to pain-reliever opioids, prescription drugs such as oxycodone (see **Figure 10-2**). Around 20 percent of those with opioid use disorder are addicted to heroin. The rate of opioid dependence dropped considerably during the 1980s, rose in the early 1990s, fell in the late 1990s, and now is high once again. Indeed, the accelerated increase of this rate over the past several years—including the increase among teenagers—and the growing number of deaths caused by opioid overdoses have many clinicians referring to it as an epidemic (see ***Trending*** on the next page). According to some studies, the mortality rate of persons with untreated opioid use disorder is 63 times the rate of other persons (Strain, 2017).

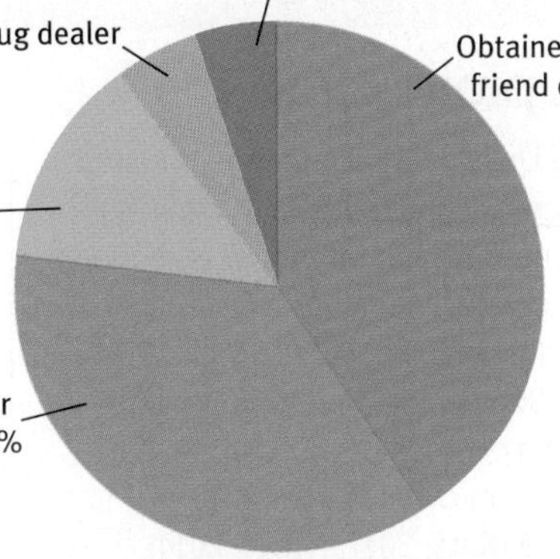

FIGURE 10-2

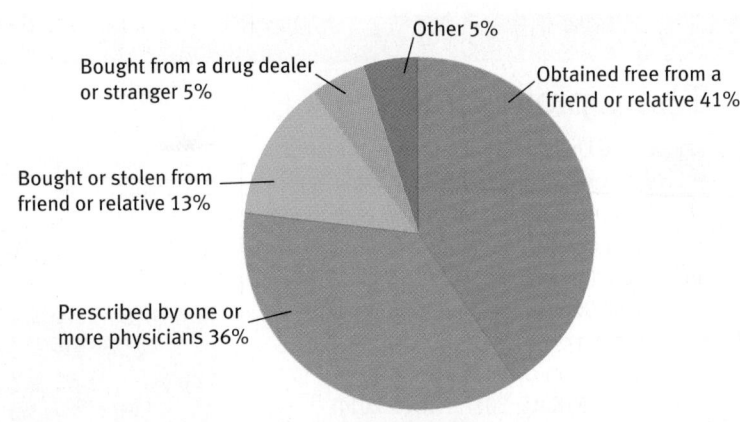

Where Do People Obtain Painkillers for Nonmedical Use?

More than 40 percent get the drugs from friends or relatives and 36 percent obtain them from doctors. Only 5 percent buy them from drug dealers. (Information from: SAMHSA, 2018.)

What Are the Dangers of Opioid Use? The most immediate danger of opioid use is an overdose, which closes down the respiratory center in the brain, almost paralyzing breathing and in many cases causing death (Coffin, 2017; Stolbach & Hoffman, 2017). Death is particularly likely during sleep, when a person is unable to fight this effect by consciously working to breathe. People who resume heroin or pain reliever use after having avoided it for some time often make the fatal mistake of taking the same dose they had built up to before. Because their bodies have been without such opioids for some time, however, they can no longer tolerate this high level. There has been a 400 percent increase in the number of deaths caused by opioid overdoses in the past decade (CDC, 2017). Currently, approximately 20,000 people in the United States die from pain reliever overdoses each year, 15,000 from heroin overdoses, and 8,000 from overdoses of other opioids (Moberg, 2018; Coffin, 2017). These numbers represent two-thirds of all drug overdose deaths.

Heroin users run other risks as well. Drug dealers often mix heroin with a cheaper drug or even a deadly substance such as cyanide or battery acid. In addition, dirty

Mark Ralston/AFP/Getty Images

Deadly effects In 2016 music giant Prince died at the age of 57 from an overdose of the opioid drug *fentanyl*, an extremely powerful prescription pain reliever. Immediately after his death, fans started leaving messages outside his residential compound in Minnesota, including this one with apt lyrics from Prince's song "Let's Go Crazy."

...TRENDING

The Opioid Crisis

The United States is in the midst of an opioid epidemic—a staggering increase in the number of addictions and overdose deaths related to painkillers and heroin (Stevens et al., 2018; CDC 2017). In 2016, 62,000 people died from various kinds of drug overdoses; by comparison, 16,000 died from overdoses in 2010 and 4,000 in 1999 (Katz, 2017; NIDA, 2014). Two-thirds of all such drug deaths involve opioids. The last drug epidemic of this magnitude was the crack epidemic of the 1980s, which witnessed a comparable number of annual deaths if one calculates both overdoses and crack-related homicides (Regier, 2016).

How did the current opioid epidemic emerge? Several factors have contributed. First is the painkiller factor (Becker & Starrels, 2018; Piper et al., 2018). Back in the 1990s, the number of Americans diagnosed with some form of chronic pain rose to one hundred million (a third of the population), leading to increased prescriptions of several powerful pain medications such as Percocet, Vicodin, and Oxycontin—drugs more powerful than morphine or heroin (CDC, 2017). These medications soon became overprescribed, despite the good intentions of physicians, and between 1991 and 2011, the number of U.S prescriptions for painkillers tripled to 219 million per year (Trotter Davis et al., 2017; Voon, Karamouzian, & Kerr, 2017). Many patients developed a painkiller use disorder, and, as word about the opioid impact of these drugs spread, the illicit acquisition and use of prescription painkillers rose as well.

While the use of painkillers was increasing between 1991 and 2011, so was their potency, as pharmaceutical companies sought to develop more effective and powerful painkillers. One of the most powerful pain relief drugs is *fentanyl,* which is 50 to 100 times more powerful than morphine, 20 to 35 times more powerful than heroin, and, correspondingly, more dangerous than either (Phalen et al., 2018; Caldwell, 2017). Given its potency, rapid onset, and short duration, fentanyl became a very popular street drug. Illegal—and, thus, uncontrolled—manufacture of this drug escalated correspondingly (CDC, 2017; Beletsky & Davis, 2017). Fentanyl is by far the painkiller most commonly linked to overdose deaths. (The 2016 death of the iconic musical performer Prince was caused by a fentanyl overdose.)

John Moore/Getty Images

"Fed Up!" At the National Mall in Washington, D.C., this man and thousands of other activists and family members rally for federal funding to help end the opioid epidemic. The rally was organized by Fed Up!, a coalition that is working for an end to the epidemic of opioid addictions and overdoses.

A second and related factor in the opioid explosion is the rising availability of heroin. As painkiller prescriptions were tripling between 1991 and 2011, foreign drug cartels recognized the growing thirst of the United States population for opioids, and, in turn, they flooded the United States marketplace with heroin (CRS, 2016; Nolan & Amico, 2016). This increased heroin availability led, in turn, to lower heroin prices, easier acquisition, and greater heroin use.

Since 2011, the increased affordability, availability, and potency of opioid drugs have produced a still greater demand for opioids—both illicitly acquired painkillers and heroin—that has resulted in the current opioid epidemic. As the head of the CDC observed, "America is awash in opioids" (Frieden, 2016). Moreover, heroin and painkillers are not necessarily competing with each other in the U.S. marketplace. Rather, they are often combined or intermixed for users—a phenomenon that has multiplied their dangers exponentially. Fentanyl-laced heroin is, for example, now common on the streets (Perry, 2017). Users who think they are taking heroin at their usual dose often are taking the much more powerful fentanyl—a misperception that can readily lead to their death. Similarly, illegal manufacturers of painkillers often make the pain drugs look identical—although their potencies differ significantly. As one U.S. attorney stated, purposeful disguises of this kind represent "an overdose waiting to happen" (STAT, 2016).

The opioid epidemic is currently being fought on all fronts: federal and state legislatures have, for example, passed laws calling for more funding to fight the opioid epidemic, greater efforts to combat international opioid trafficking, more coordination between the states, more monitoring of doctors' prescription practices, more accountability from pharmaceutical companies, and better funding of opioid treatment programs (Kolodny & Frieden, 2018; CDC, 2017). In addition, the clinical field is devoting a greater portion of its professionals and resources to the prevention and treatment of opioid use disorders. These efforts seem to be making an impact in some realms. For example, the number of prescriptions of opioid painkillers dropped 10.2 percent in 2017 (Herper, 2018). Thus authorities and clinicians are hopeful that the epidemic will soon recede, but how soon and how much it will recede are far from clear at the present time (Piper et al., 2018; Stevens et al., 2018).

needles and other unsterilized equipment spread infections such as AIDS, hepatitis C, and skin abscesses (Strain, 2017). In some areas of the United States, the HIV infection rate among active heroin users is reported to be as high as 60 percent.

cocaine An addictive stimulant obtained from the coca plant. It is the most powerful natural stimulant known.

...SUMMING UP

SUBSTANCE MISUSE AND DEPRESSANTS Repeated and excessive use can lead to substance use disorders. Many people with such disorders also develop a tolerance for the substance in question and/or have unpleasant withdrawal symptoms when they abstain from it.

Depressants are substances that slow the activity of the central nervous system. Repeated and excessive use of these substances can lead to problems such as alcohol use disorder, sedative-hypnotic use disorder, or opioid use disorder. Alcohol intoxication occurs when the concentration of alcohol in the bloodstream reaches 0.09 percent. Among other actions, alcohol increases the activity of the neurotransmitter GABA at key sites in the brain. The sedative-hypnotic drugs, which produce feelings of relaxation and drowsiness, include barbiturates and benzodiazepines. These drugs also increase the activity of GABA. Opioids include opium and drugs derived from it, such as morphine and heroin, as well as laboratory-made opioids. Opioids reduce tension and pain and cause other reactions. They operate by binding to neurons that ordinarily receive endorphins.

Stimulants

Stimulants are substances that increase the activity of the central nervous system, resulting in increased blood pressure and heart rate, more alertness, and sped-up behavior and thinking. Among the most troublesome stimulants are *cocaine* and *amphetamines,* whose effects on people are very similar. When users report different effects, it is often because they have ingested different amounts of the drugs. Two other widely used and legal stimulants are *caffeine* and *nicotine* (see ***InfoCentral*** on page 305).

Cocaine

Cocaine—the central active ingredient of the coca plant, found in South America—is the most powerful natural stimulant now known (Nelson & Odujebe, 2017). The drug was first separated from the plant in 1865. Native people of South America, however, have chewed the leaves of the plant since prehistoric times for the energy and alertness the drug offers. Processed cocaine (*hydrochloride powder*) is an odorless, white, fluffy powder. For recreational use, it is most often snorted so that it is absorbed through the mucous membrane of the nose. Some users prefer the more powerful effects of injecting cocaine intravenously or smoking it in a pipe or cigarette.

For years people believed that cocaine posed few problems aside from intoxication and, on occasion, temporary psychosis (see **Table 10-2**). Only later did researchers come to appreciate its many dangers (Gorelick, 2017). Their insights came after society witnessed a dramatic surge in the drug's popularity and in problems related to its use. In the early 1960s, an estimated 10,000 people in the United States had tried cocaine. Today 39 million people have tried it, and 1.9 million—most of them teenagers or young adults—are using it currently (SAMHSA, 2018).

Cocaine brings on a euphoric rush of well-being and confidence. Given a high enough dose, this rush can be almost orgasmic, like the one produced by heroin. At first cocaine stimulates the higher centers of the central nervous system, making users feel excited, energetic,

Smoking crack Crack, a powerful form of free-base cocaine, is produced by boiling cocaine down into crystalline balls and is smoked with a crack pipe.

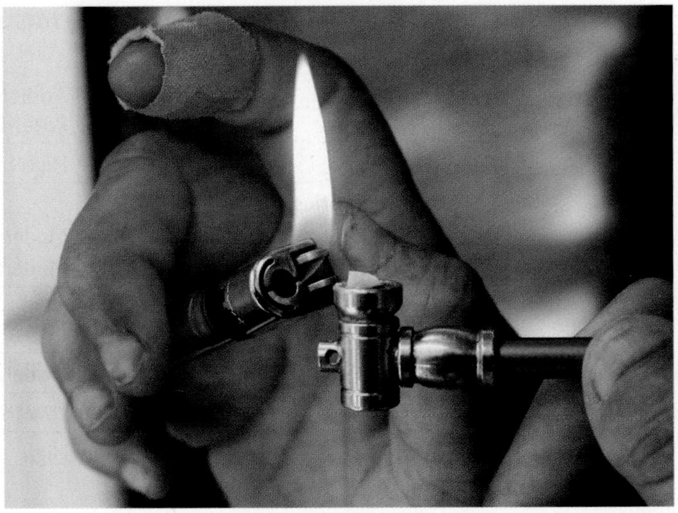

freebasing A technique for ingesting cocaine in which the pure cocaine basic alkaloid is chemically separated from processed cocaine, vaporized by heat from a flame, and inhaled with a pipe.

crack A powerful, ready-to-smoke freebase cocaine.

talkative, and even euphoric. As more is taken, it stimulates other centers of the central nervous system, producing a faster pulse, higher blood pressure, faster and deeper breathing, and further arousal and wakefulness.

Cocaine apparently produces these effects largely by increasing supplies of the neurotransmitter *dopamine* at key neurons throughout the brain (Gorelick, 2017). Excessive amounts of dopamine travel to receiving neurons throughout the central nervous system and overstimulate them. Cocaine appears to also increase the activity of the neurotransmitters *norepinephrine* and *serotonin* in some areas of the brain.

High doses of the drug produce *cocaine intoxication,* whose symptoms are poor muscle coordination, grandiosity, bad judgment, anger, aggression, compulsive behavior, anxiety, and confusion (Nelson & Odujebe, 2017). Some people have hallucinations, delusions, or both, a condition called *cocaine-induced psychosis.*

> *A young man described how, after free-basing, he went to his closet to get his clothes, but his suit asked him, "What do you want?" Afraid, he walked toward the door, which told him, "Get back!" Retreating, he then heard the sofa say, "If you sit on me, I'll kick your ass." With a sense of impending doom, intense anxiety, and momentary panic, the young man ran to the hospital where he received help.*
>
> *(Allen, 1985, pp. 19–20)*

As the stimulant effects of cocaine subside, the user goes through a depression-like letdown, popularly called *crashing,* a pattern that may also include headaches, dizziness, and fainting (Gorelick, 2017). For occasional users, the aftereffects usually disappear within 24 hours, but they may last longer for people who have taken a particularly high dose. These people may sink into a stupor, deep sleep, or, in some cases, coma.

Ingesting Cocaine In the past, cocaine use and impact were limited by the drug's high cost. Moreover, cocaine was usually snorted, a form of ingestion that has less powerful effects than either smoking or injection (AAC, 2018; Haile, 2012). Since 1984, however, the availability of newer, more powerful, and sometimes cheaper forms of cocaine has produced an enormous increase in the use of the drug. For example, many people now ingest cocaine by **freebasing,** a technique in which the pure cocaine basic alkaloid is chemically separated, or "freed," from processed cocaine, vaporized by heat from a flame, and inhaled through a pipe.

Millions more people use **crack,** a powerful form of freebase cocaine that has been boiled down into crystalline balls. It is smoked with a special pipe and makes a

TABLE: 10-2

Risks and Consequences of Drug Misuse

	Potential Intoxication	Addiction Potential	Risk of Organ Damage or Death	Risk of Severe Social or Economic Consequences	Risk of Severe or Long-Lasting Mental & Behavioral Change
Opioids	High	High	Moderate	High	Low to moderate
Sedative-Hypnotics					
Barbiturates	Moderate	Moderate to high	Moderate to high	Moderate to high	Low
Benzodiazepines	Moderate	Moderate	Low	Low	Low
Stimulants (cocaine, amphetamines)	High	High	Moderate	Low to moderate	Moderate to high
Alcohol	High	Moderate	High	High	High
Cannabis	High	Low to moderate	Low	Low to moderate	Low
Mixed drugs	High	High	High	High	High

Information from: Mukamal, 2018; Hart & Ksir, 2017; APA, 2013.

SMOKING, TOBACCO, AND NICOTINE

Around **24%** percent of all Americans over the age of 11 regularly smoke tobacco—a total of **63 million** people (NSDUH, 2017).

Similarly, **20%** of the world population over 11 smoke regularly—a total of **1.1 billion** people (WHO, 2017).

WHO SMOKES REGULARLY IN THE UNITED STATES?

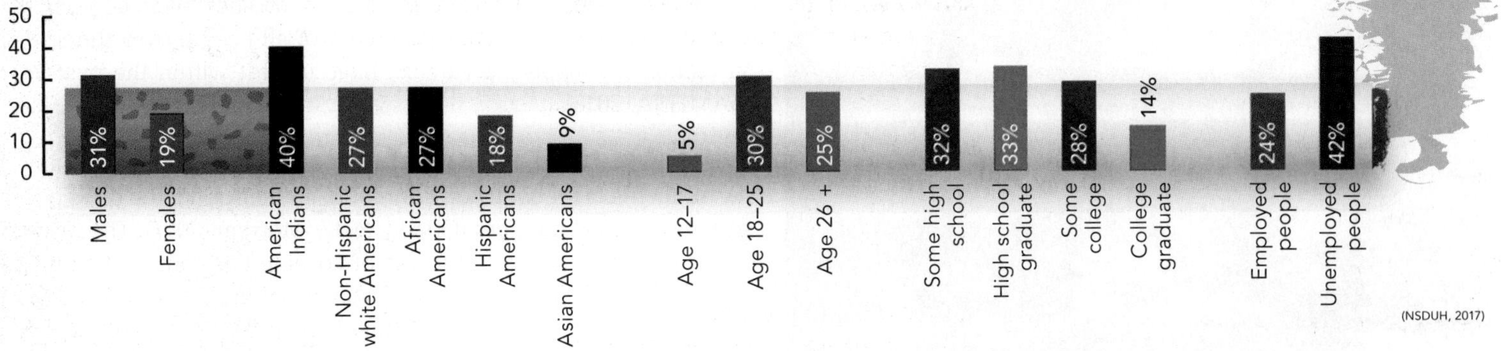

(NSDUH, 2017)

SMOKING AND HEALTH

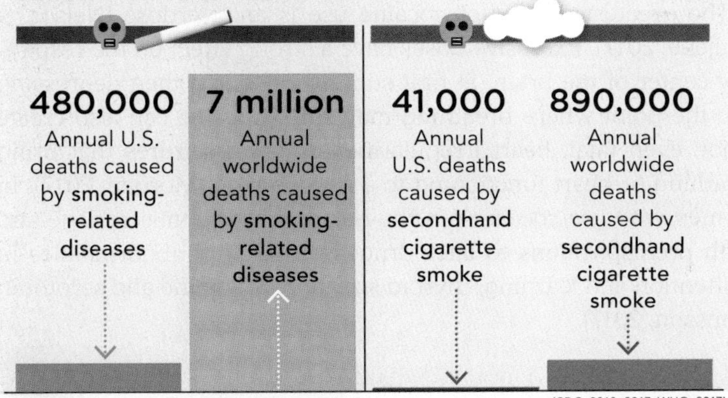

(CDC, 2018, 2017; WHO, 2017)

WHY DO PEOPLE CONTINUE TO SMOKE?

As many as 75% of smokers keep smoking because they are addicted to **nicotine**, the active substance in tobacco (WHO, 2017, 2014). Nicotine is a stimulant of the central nervous system that acts on the same neurotransmitters and reward centers in the brain as amphetamines and cocaine. It is as addictive as those drugs and heroin. Smokers addicted to nicotine are said to have **tobacco use disorder** (APA, 2013).

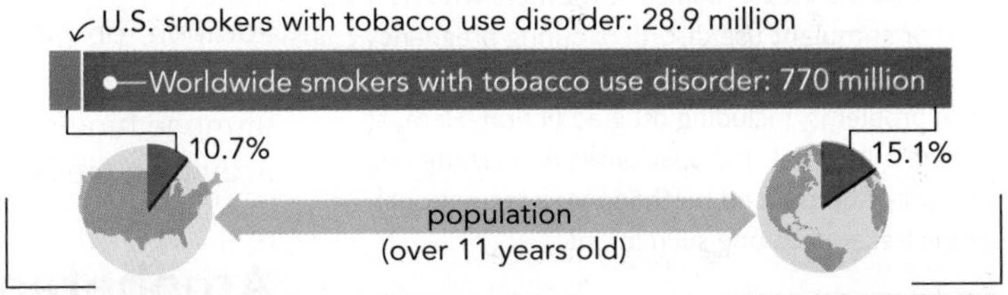

(NSDUH, 2017; WHO, 2017, 2014)

QUITTING SMOKING

More and more smokers try to quit each year. One reason is that many studies have identified the severe health dangers smoking poses. Another is the outstanding job that health agencies have done spreading the word about these dangers. With the declining acceptability of smoking, a market for products and techniques to help people kick the habit has emerged.

Getting the Message

Teens who believe that smoking is harmful

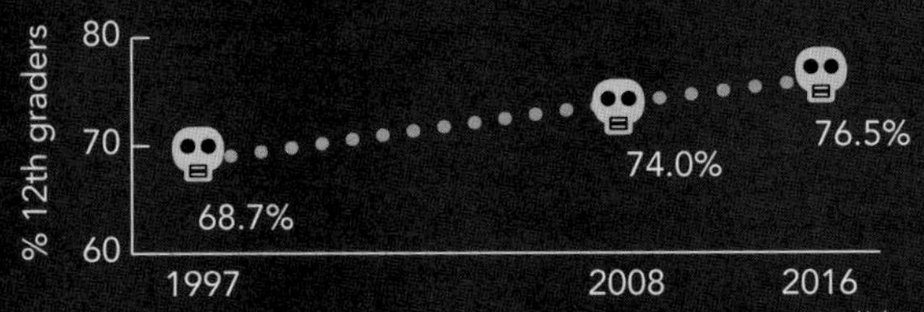

(Johnston et al., 2017)

Common Aids for Quitting

- **NICOTINE GUM**—Releases nicotine when chewed
- **NICOTINE PATCH**—Releases nicotine through the skin
- **NICOTINE LOZENGES**—Dissolves in the mouth and releases nicotine
- **NASAL SPRAY**—Delivers aerosol nicotine into the nostrils
- **PSYCHOTROPIC DRUGS (VARENICLINE, BUPROPION, AND NORTRIPTYLINE)**—Reduce craving for nicotine
- **SELF-HELP GROUPS**—Offer psychological support
- **BEHAVIORAL COUNSELING**—Teaches alternative behaviors

(CDC, 2018, 2017; Park, 2018; Rigotti, 2018, 2017)

Trying to Stop

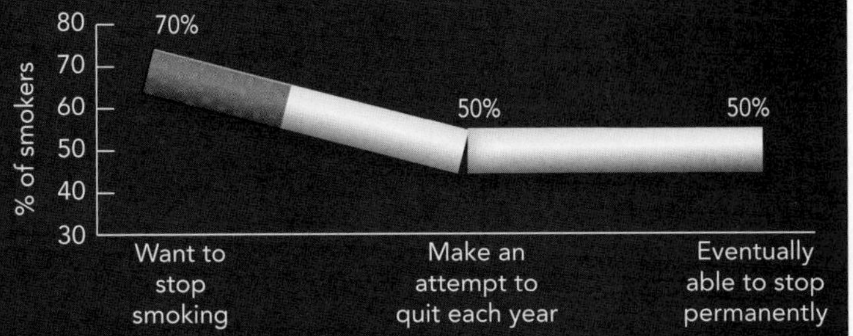

(CDC, 2018, 2017, 2014; Rigotti, 2018, 2017; NSDUH, 2017, 2013)

E-Cigarettes: Battery-Operated Electronic Vaping

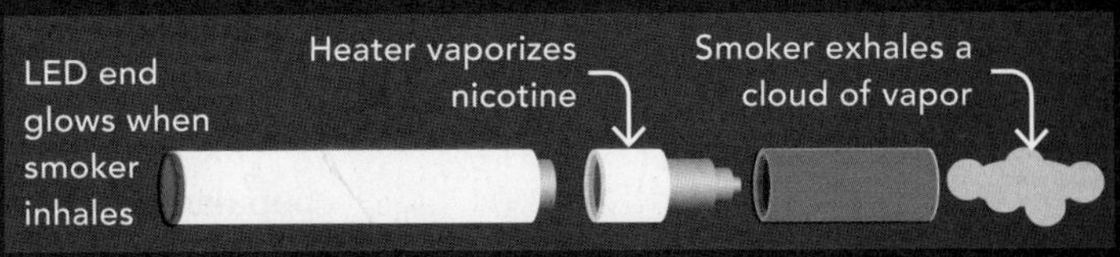

Tobacco Cigarette	vs.	E-Cigarette
Smoked by 24% of U.S. adults		Smoked by 4% of U.S. adults
Smoke poses biggest danger		No actual burning or smoke
Very addictive		Addiction depends on nicotine level
$117 billion annual U.S. revenues		$600 million annual U.S. revenues

(CDC, 2018, 2017; Rigotti & Kalkhoran, 2018, 2017; Maloney & Chaudhuri, 2017; CSP, 2017; Griffin, 2014)

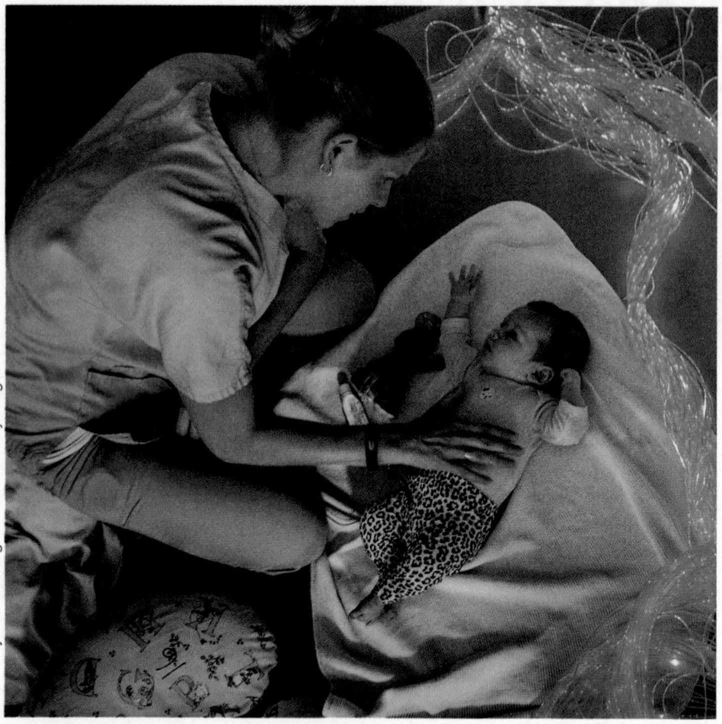
Bill O'Leary/The Washington Post via Getty Images

Addicted at birth Babies of mothers who have opioid or stimulant use disorders during pregnancy may be born with significant physical and psychological problems, including drug addiction. Here, at a pediatric hospital that specializes in weaning newborns off of heroin and methadone, a recreational therapist examines one such infant.

crackling sound as it is inhaled (hence the name). Crack is sold in small quantities at a fairly low cost. Back in the 1980s, its affordability led to an epidemic of use among people who previously could not have afforded cocaine, primarily those in poor, urban areas (Turner, 2017). Although the prevalence of crack use has declined over the past two decades, around 0.3 percent of all people over the age of 11 (almost 1 million individuals) have used it within the past year (SAMHSA, 2018).

What Are the Dangers of Cocaine? Aside from cocaine's harmful effects on behavior, cognition, and emotion, the drug poses serious physical dangers (Chang, 2017; Morgan, 2017). The growth in the use of the powerful forms of cocaine has caused the annual number of cocaine-related emergency room incidents in the United States to multiply more than 125 times since 1982, from around 4,000 cases to 505,000 (Gorelick, 2017). Cocaine use has also been linked to many suicides.

The greatest danger of cocaine use is an overdose (Nelson & Odujebe, 2017). Excessive doses have a strong effect on the respiratory center of the brain, at first stimulating it and then depressing it to the point where breathing may stop. Cocaine can also create major, even fatal, heart irregularities or brain seizures that bring breathing or heart functioning to a sudden stop (Morgan, 2017). In addition, pregnant women who use cocaine run the risk of having a miscarriage and of having children with predispositions to later drug use and with abnormalities in immune functioning, attention and learning, thyroid size, and dopamine and serotonin activity in the brain (Jansson, 2017).

Amphetamines

Amphetamines are stimulant drugs that are manufactured in the laboratory. Some common examples are amphetamine (Benzedrine), dextroamphetamine (Dexedrine), and methamphetamine (Methedrine). First produced in the 1930s to help treat asthma, amphetamines soon became popular among people trying to lose weight; athletes seeking an extra burst of energy; soldiers, truck drivers, and pilots trying to stay awake; and students studying for exams through the night. Physicians now know the drugs are far too dangerous to be used so casually, and they prescribe them much less freely.

Amphetamines are most often taken in pill or capsule form, although some people inject the drugs intravenously or smoke them for a quicker, more powerful effect. Like cocaine, amphetamines increase energy and alertness and reduce appetite when taken in small doses; produce a rush, intoxication, and psychosis in high doses; and cause an emotional letdown as they leave the body. Also like cocaine, amphetamines stimulate the central nervous system by increasing the release of the neurotransmitters dopamine, norepinephrine, and serotonin throughout the brain, although the actions of amphetamines differ somewhat from those of cocaine (Stock, Rädle, & Beste, 2019; Arnold & Ryan, 2017).

One kind of amphetamine, **methamphetamine** (nicknamed *crank*), has surged in popularity over the past decade and so warrants special focus. Almost 6 percent of all people over the age of 11 in the United States have used methamphetamine at least once (SAMHSA, 2018). Around 0.3 currently have methamphetamine use disorder. The drug is available in the form of crystals (also known by the street names *ice* and *crystal meth*), which users smoke.

Most of the nonmedical methamphetamine in the United States is made in small "stovetop laboratories," which typically operate for a few days in a remote area and then move on to a new—safer—location (Boyer et al., 2017). Such laboratories have been

amphetamine A stimulant drug that is manufactured in the laboratory.

methamphetamine A powerful amphetamine drug that has surged in popularity in recent years, posing major health and law enforcement problems.

around since the 1960s, but they have increased eightfold—in number, production, and in being confiscated by authorities—this century. A major health concern is that the secret laboratories expel dangerous fumes and residue.

Since 1989, when the media first began reporting about the dangers of smoking methamphetamine crystals, the rise in usage has been dramatic. Until recently, it had been much more prevalent in western parts of the United States, but its use has now spread east as well. Methamphetamine-linked emergency room visits are rising in hospitals throughout all parts of the country (SAMHSA, 2018).

Methamphetamine is about as likely to be used by women as men. Around 40 percent of current users are women (Paulus, 2017). The drug is popular today among a wide range of people, from biker gangs to rural Americans to urban gay communities, and it has gained wide use as a "club drug," the term for those drugs that regularly find their way to all-night dance parties, or "raves" (NIDA, 2018).

Like other kinds of amphetamines, methamphetamine increases activity of the neurotransmitters dopamine, serotonin, and norepinephrine, producing increased arousal, attention, and related effects (Paulus, 2017). It can have serious negative effects on a user's physical, mental, and social life. Of particular concern is that it damages nerve endings, a problem called *neurotoxicity* (Stock et al., 2019). But users focus more on methamphetamine's immediate positive impact, including perceptions by many that it makes them feel hypersexual and uninhibited (Paulus, 2017).

DON'T LET DRUG DEALERS CHANGE THE FACE OF YOUR NEIGHBOURHOOD.
Call Crimestoppers anonymously on 0800 555 111.
National Pictures/Topham/The Image Works

Methamphetamine dependence: Spreading the word This powerful ad shows the degenerative effects of methamphetamine addiction on a woman over a 4-year period—from age 36 in the top photo to age 40 in the bottom one.

Stimulant Use Disorder

Regular use of either cocaine or amphetamines may lead to *stimulant use disorder.* The stimulant comes to dominate the person's life, and the person may remain under the drug's effects much of each day and function poorly in social relationships and at work. People may develop tolerance and withdrawal reactions to the drug—in order to gain the desired effects, they must take higher doses, and when they stop taking it, they may go through deep depression, fatigue, sleep problems, irritability, and anxiety (Gorelick, 2017). These withdrawal symptoms can last for weeks or even months after drug use has ended. In a given year, 0.1 percent of all people over the age of 11 years display stimulant use disorder that is centered on cocaine, and 0.3 percent display stimulant use disorder centered on amphetamines (SAMHSA, 2018).

...SUMMING UP

STIMULANTS Stimulants, including cocaine, amphetamines, caffeine, and nicotine, are substances that increase the activity of the central nervous system. Abnormal use of cocaine or amphetamines can lead to stimulant use disorder. Stimulants produce their effects by increasing the activity of dopamine, norepinephrine, and serotonin in the brain.

Hallucinogens, Cannabis, and Combinations of Substances

Other kinds of substances may also cause problems for their users and for society. *Hallucinogens* produce delusions, hallucinations, and other sensory changes. *Cannabis* produces sensory changes, but it also has depressant and stimulant effects, and so it is considered apart from hallucinogens in DSM-5. And many people take *combinations of substances.*

#DiagnosticControversy

DSM-5 combines two past disorders, *substance abuse* (excessive and chronic reliance on drugs) and *substance dependence* (excessive reliance accompanied by tolerance and withdrawal symptoms) into a single category—*substance use disorder.* Critics worry that clinicians may now fail to recognize and address the different prognoses and treatment needs of people who abuse substances and those who depend on substances.

Hallucinogens

Hallucinogens are substances that cause powerful changes in sensory perception, from strengthening a person's normal perceptions to inducing illusions and hallucinations. They produce sensations so out of the ordinary that they are sometimes called "trips." The trips may be exciting or frightening, depending on how a person's mind interacts with the drugs. Also called *psychedelic drugs,* the hallucinogens include LSD, mescaline, psilocybin, and MDMA (Ecstasy). Many of these substances come from plants or animals; others are produced in laboratories.

Why do various club drugs (for example, Ecstasy and crystal meth), often used at "raves," fall in and out of favor rather quickly?

LSD (lysergic acid diethylamide), one of the most famous and most powerful hallucinogens, was derived by Swiss chemist Albert Hoffman in 1938 from a group of naturally occurring drugs called *ergot alkaloids.* During the 1960s, a decade of social rebellion and experimentation, millions of people turned to the drug as a way of expanding their experience. Within 2 hours of being swallowed, LSD brings on a state of *hallucinogen intoxication,* sometimes called *hallucinosis,* marked by a general strengthening of perceptions, particularly visual perceptions, along with psychological changes and physical symptoms. People may focus on small details—the pores of the skin, for example, or individual blades of grass. Colors may seem enhanced or take on a shade of purple. People may have illusions in which objects seem distorted and appear to move, breathe, or change shape. A person under the influence of LSD may also hallucinate—seeing people, objects, or forms that are not actually present.

Hallucinosis may also cause one to hear sounds more clearly, feel tingling or numbness in the limbs, or confuse the sensations of hot and cold. Some people have been badly burned after touching flames that felt cool to them under the influence of LSD. The drug may also cause different senses to cross, an effect called *synesthesia.* Colors, for example, may be "heard" or "felt."

LSD can also induce strong emotions, from joy to anxiety or depression. The perception of time may slow dramatically. Long-forgotten thoughts and feelings may resurface. Physical symptoms can include sweating, palpitations, blurred vision, tremors, and poor coordination. All of these effects take place while the user is fully awake and alert, and they wear off in about 6 hours.

Yadid Levy/Anzenberger/Redux

Lingering popularity Although less popular than in the 1960s, LSD continues to be a drug of some favor, especially among younger people at many raves, rock concerts, and similar events. This participant at the annual Burning Man art festival in Nevada's Black Rock Desert has a message written on her back that leaves no doubt about how important the drug is to her.

It seems that LSD produces these symptoms primarily by binding to some of the neurons that normally receive the neurotransmitter *serotonin,* changing the neurotransmitter's activity at those sites (Delgado, 2017). These neurons ordinarily help the brain send visual information and control emotions (as you saw in Chapter 6); thus LSD's activity there produces various visual and emotional symptoms.

More than 15 percent of all people in the United States have used LSD or another hallucinogen at some point in their lives. Around 0.5 percent, or 1.2 million people, are currently using them (SAMHSA, 2018). Although people do not usually develop tolerance to LSD or have withdrawal symptoms when they stop taking it, the drug poses dangers for both one-time and long-term users. It is so powerful that any dose, no matter how small, is likely to produce enormous perceptual, emotional, and behavioral reactions. Sometimes the reactions are extremely unpleasant—a so-called bad trip (when LSD users injure themselves or others, for instance, they are usually in the midst of a bad trip). Witness, for example, this description of a young woman who took LSD during the 1960s when so many people thought of the drug as a problem-free mind expander, only to learn about its dark side through personal use:

> *A 21-year-old woman was admitted to the hospital along with her lover. He had had a number of LSD experiences and had convinced her to take it to make her less constrained sexually. About half an hour after ingestion of approximately 200 micrograms, she noticed that the bricks in the wall began to go in and out and that light affected her strangely. She became frightened when she realized that she was unable to distinguish her body from the chair she was sitting on or from her lover's body. Her fear became more marked after she thought that she would not get back into herself. At the time of admission she was hyperactive and laughed inappropriately. Her stream of talk was illogical and affect labile. Two days later, this reaction had ceased.*
>
> *(Frosch, Robbins, & Stern, 1965)*

Another danger is the long-term effect that LSD may have. Some users eventually develop psychosis or a mood or anxiety disorder. And a number have *flashbacks*—a recurrence of the sensory and emotional changes after the LSD has left the body. Flashbacks may occur days or even months after the last LSD experience (Delgado, 2017).

Cannabis

Cannabis sativa, the hemp plant, grows in warm climates throughout the world. The drugs produced from varieties of hemp are, as a group, called **cannabis.** The most powerful of them is *hashish;* the weaker ones include the best-known form of cannabis, **marijuana,** a mixture derived from the buds, crushed leaves, and flowering tops of hemp plants. More than 22 million people over the age of 11 (8.3 percent of the population) currently smoke marijuana at least monthly (SAMHSA, 2018).

Each of the cannabis drugs is found in various strengths because the potency of a cannabis drug is greatly affected by the climate in which the plant is grown, the way it was prepared, and the manner and duration of its storage. Of the several hundred active chemicals in cannabis, **tetrahydrocannabinol (THC)** appears to be the one

hallucinogen A substance that causes powerful changes primarily in sensory perception, including strengthening perceptions and producing illusions and hallucinations. Also called a *psychedelic drug.*

LSD (lysergic acid diethylamide) A hallucinogenic drug derived from ergot alkaloids.

cannabis Drugs produced from the varieties of the hemp plant *Cannabis sativa.* They cause a mixture of hallucinogenic, depressant, and stimulant effects.

marijuana One of the cannabis drugs, derived from the buds, leaves, and flowering tops of the hemp plant *Cannabis sativa.*

tetrahydrocannabinol (THC) The main active ingredient of cannabis substances.

Adam Glanzman/The New York Times/Redux

The source of marijuana Marijuana is made from the leaves of the hemp plant, *Cannabis sativa,* such as the plants being cultivated in this grow room at a medical marijuana dispensary in Massachusetts. *Cannabis sativa* is grown in a wide range of altitudes, climates, and soils.

#StreetTags

Alcohol	booze, brew
Cocaine	blow, Charlie, rock, snow
Heroin	black tar, horse, smack
Marijuana	grass, Mary Jane, reefer, weed
Amphetamines	bennies, speed, uppers
MDMA	Ecstasy, X, beans, hug
Methamphetamine	meth, crank, crystal, ice
Pain relievers	Oxy, Percs, Vikes

most responsible for its effects. The higher the THC content, the more powerful the cannabis; hashish contains a large portion, while marijuana's is small.

When smoked, cannabis produces a mixture of hallucinogenic, depressant, and stimulant effects. At low doses, the smoker typically has feelings of joy and relaxation and may become either quiet or talkative. Some smokers, however, become anxious, suspicious, or irritated, especially if they have been in a bad mood or are smoking in an upsetting environment. Many smokers report sharpened perceptions and fascination with the intensified sounds and sights around them. Time seems to slow down, and distances and sizes seem greater than they actually are. This overall "high" is technically called *cannabis intoxication*. Physical changes include reddening of the eyes, fast heartbeat, increases in blood pressure and appetite, dryness in the mouth, and dizziness. Some people become drowsy and may fall asleep.

In high doses, cannabis produces odd visual experiences, changes in body image, and hallucinations. Smokers may become confused or impulsive. Some worry that other people are trying to hurt them. Most of the effects of cannabis last 2 to 6 hours. The changes in mood, however, may continue longer.

Cannabis Use Disorder Until the early 1970s, the use of marijuana, the weak form of cannabis, rarely led to a pattern of *cannabis use disorder*. Today, however, many people, including large numbers of high school students, are developing the disorder, getting high on marijuana regularly and finding their social and occupational or academic lives very much affected (Kerridge et al., 2018) (see **Figure 10-3**). Many regular users also develop a tolerance for marijuana and may feel restless and irritable and have flu-like symptoms when they stop smoking (Gorelick, 2018). Around 4 million people, 1.5 percent of all teenagers and adults in the United States, have displayed cannabis use disorder within the past year (SAMHSA, 2018).

Why have more and more marijuana users developed cannabis use disorder over the past three decades? Mainly because marijuana has changed. The marijuana widely available in the United States today is at least four times more powerful than that used in the early 1970s. The average THC content of today's marijuana is 8 percent, compared with 2 percent in the late 1960s. Marijuana is now grown in places with a hot, dry climate, which increases the THC content.

Is Marijuana Dangerous? As the strength and use of marijuana have increased, researchers have discovered that smoking it may pose certain dangers (Wang, 2018; Price, 2011). It occasionally causes panic reactions similar to the ones caused by hallucinogens, and some smokers may fear they are losing their minds. Typically, such reactions end in 2 to 6 hours, along with marijuana's other effects.

Because marijuana can interfere with the performance of complex sensorimotor tasks and with cognitive functioning, it has caused many automobile accidents (Wang,

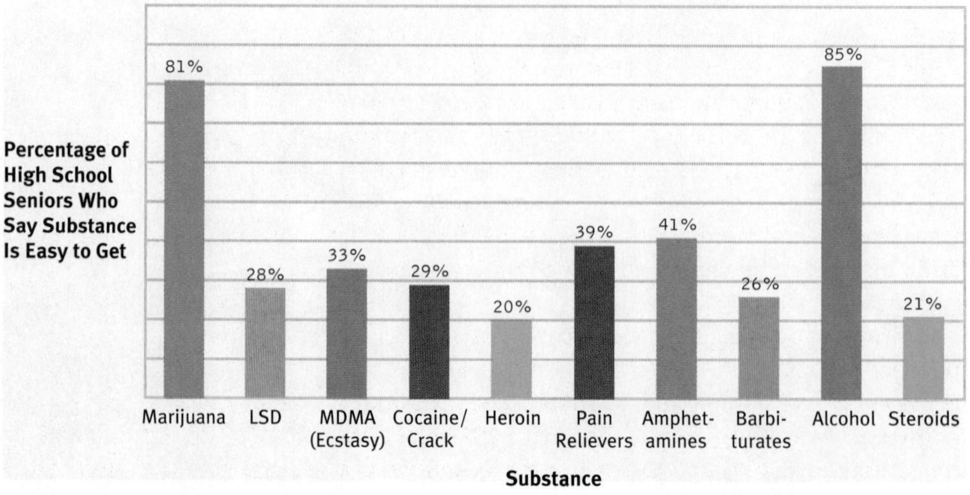

FIGURE 10-3

How Easy Is It for Teenagers to Acquire Substances?

Most surveyed high school seniors say it is easy to get alcohol and marijuana, and more than a third say it is easy to get amphetamines, pain relievers, and Ecstasy. (Information from: Johnston et al., 2017.)

2018; Brady & Li, 2014). And, indeed, 4 percent of adults have driven while under the influence of marijuana at least once during the past year (SAMHSA, 2018). Furthermore, people on a marijuana high often fail to remember information, especially anything that has been recently learned, no matter how hard they try to concentrate; thus, heavy marijuana smokers are at a serious disadvantage at school or work (Gorelick, 2018).

There are research indications that regular marijuana smoking may also lead to long-term health problems (Gorelick, 2018; Hartney, 2014). It may, for example, contribute to lung disease, although there is considerable debate on this issue. Some studies suggest that marijuana smoking reduces the ability to expel air from the lungs, perhaps even more than tobacco smoking does. Another concern is the effect of regular marijuana smoking on human reproduction. Studies since the late 1970s have discovered lower sperm counts in men who are chronic smokers and abnormal ovulation in women who are chronic smokers.

Efforts to educate the public about the dangers of repeated marijuana use appeared to have paid off throughout the 1980s. The percentage of high school seniors who smoked marijuana on a daily basis decreased from 11 percent in 1978 to 2 percent in 1992. Today, however, 6 percent of high school seniors smoke it daily, and 69 percent of seniors do not believe that regular use poses a great risk (Johnston et al., 2017).

#ChangingCourse

In 1907, California was the first state to declare marijuana a poison and to criminalize its sale or possession.

In 1996, California was the first state to legalize medical marijuana.

In 2016, California was the fifth state to legalize recreational marijuana.

Cannabis and Society: A Rocky Relationship For centuries, cannabis played a respected role in medicine. It was recommended as a surgical anesthetic by Chinese physicians 2,000 years ago and was used in other lands to treat cholera, malaria, coughs, insomnia, and rheumatism. When cannabis entered the United States in the early twentieth century, mainly in the form of marijuana, it was likewise used for various medical purposes. Soon, however, more effective medicines replaced it, and the favorable view of cannabis began to change. Marijuana began to be used as a recreational drug, and its illegal distribution became a law enforcement problem. Authorities assumed it was highly dangerous and outlawed the "killer weed."

In the 1980s, researchers developed precise techniques for measuring THC and for extracting pure THC from cannabis; they also developed laboratory forms of THC. These inventions opened the door to new medical applications for cannabis (Wang, 2018), such as its use in treating glaucoma, a severe eye disease. Cannabis was also found to help patients with chronic pain or asthma, to reduce the nausea and vomiting of cancer patients in chemotherapy, and to improve the appetites of people with AIDS and so help them combat weight loss.

In light of these findings, several interest groups campaigned during the late 1980s for the *medical legalization* of marijuana, which operates on the brain and body more quickly than the THC capsules developed in the laboratory. Government agencies resisted this movement, saying prescriptions for pure THC served all needed medical functions. However, medical marijuana advocates pressed on, and in 2009 the U.S. Attorney General directed federal prosecutors to not pursue cases against medical marijuana users or their caregivers who are complying with state laws. Currently, 30 states (plus Washington, D.C., Guam, and Puerto Rico) have laws allowing marijuana to be used for medical purposes, and several more have such laws pending (NCSL, 2018). Medical marijuana is now legal in about a dozen countries (Gorelick, 2018).

Heartened by such developments in the realm of medical marijuana, the U.S. movement to legalize the *recreational* use of marijuana has gained enormous momentum in recent years. In fact, since 2012 residents in eight states have voted to legalize marijuana for use

Sniffing for drugs An increasingly common scene in schools, airports, storage facilities, and similar settings is that of trained dogs sniffing for marijuana, cocaine, opioids, and other substances. Here one such animal sniffs lockers at a school in Texas to see whether students have hidden any illegal substances among their books or other belongings.

Paul S. Howell/Getty Images

Creative protesting People hold a huge cannabis cigarette, or "joint," during a march in Brazil calling for the legalization of marijuana—for both medical and recreational uses.

of any kind—although such state measures still can be blocked by the federal government (Robinson, 2017). Moreover, according to recent polls, 57 percent of respondents believe that marijuana should be made legal, up from 12 percent in 1969 and 41 percent in 2010 (Pew Research Center, 2016). In such polls, more than half of respondents acknowledge they have tried marijuana and most say that the federal government should not enforce federal antimarijuana laws in states where marijuana is legal. Several other countries have moved faster than the United States with regard to the recreational use of marijuana. In 2017, for example, Canada's prime minister introduced legislation to completely legalize marijuana as a consumer product, for any purpose—legislation that now allows legal sales throughout the country (Austen, 2017).

Combinations of Substances

Because people often take more than one drug at a time, a pattern called *polysubstance use*, researchers have studied the ways in which drugs interact with one another (Jarlenski et al., 2017). When different drugs are in the body at the same time, they may *multiply*, or potentiate, each other's effects. The combined impact, called a **synergistic effect,** is often greater than the sum of the effects of each drug taken alone: a small dose of one drug mixed with a small dose of another can produce an enormous change in body chemistry.

One kind of synergistic effect occurs when two or more drugs have *similar actions* (Buckley et al., 2017). For instance, alcohol, benzodiazepines, barbiturates, and opioids—all depressants—may severely depress the central nervous system when mixed. Combining them, even in small doses, can lead to extreme intoxication, coma, and even death. A young man may have just a few alcoholic drinks at a party, for example, and shortly afterward takes a moderate dose of barbiturates to help him fall asleep. He believes he has acted with restraint and good judgment—yet he may never wake up.

A different kind of synergistic effect results when drugs have *opposite*, or *antagonistic, actions*. Stimulant drugs, for example, interfere with the liver's usual disposal of barbiturates and alcohol. Thus, people who combine barbiturates or alcohol with cocaine or amphetamines may build up toxic, even lethal, levels of the depressant drugs in their systems. Students who take amphetamines to help them study late into the night and then take barbiturates to help them fall asleep are unknowingly placing themselves in serious danger.

synergistic effect In pharmacology, an increase of effects that occurs when more than one substance is acting on the body at the same time.

Each year tens of thousands of people are admitted to hospitals with a multiple-drug emergency, and several thousand of them die (SAMHSA, 2018). Sometimes the cause is carelessness or ignorance. Often, however, people use multiple drugs precisely because they enjoy the synergistic effects (Patrick et al., 2018). In fact, as many as 90 percent of those who use one illegal drug are also using another to some extent (Jarlenski et al., 2017; Rosenthal, Levounis, & Herron, 2016).

Fans mourn the deaths of many celebrities who have died from polysubstance use. In the past several years, for example, medical examiners have found multiple drugs in the bodies of actress Carrie Fisher, actor Philip Seymour Hoffman, *Glee* star Cory Monteith, and singers Tom Petty, Whitney Houston, and Michael Jackson—mixtures that may have contributed to their deaths. In the more distant past, Elvis Presley's delicate balancing act of stimulants and depressants, Janis Joplin's mixtures of wine and heroin, and John Belushi's and Chris Farley's liking for the combined effect of cocaine and opioids ("speedballs") each ended in tragedy.

Who has more impact on the drug behaviors of teenagers and young adults: rock performers who speak out against drugs or rock performers who praise drugs?

Yannis Behrakis/Reuters

Easy to make, dangerous to take A drug user in Greece prepares a cocktail known as a speedball, a mixture of cocaine and heroin. The pink capsule in her hand contains heroin and the blue one contains cocaine.

...SUMMING UP

HALLUCINOGENS, CANNABIS, AND COMBINATIONS OF SUBSTANCES

Hallucinogens, such as LSD, are substances that cause powerful changes primarily in sensory perception. People's perceptions are intensified and they may have illusions and hallucinations. LSD apparently causes such effects by disturbing the release of the neurotransmitter serotonin.

The main ingredient of *Cannabis sativa*, a hemp plant, is tetrahydrocannabinol (THC). Marijuana, the most popular form of cannabis, is more powerful today than it was in years past. It can cause intoxication, and regular use can lead to cannabis use disorder.

Many people take more than one drug at a time, and the drugs interact. The use of two or more drugs at the same time—polysubstance use—has become increasingly common.

What Causes Substance Use Disorders?

Clinical theorists have developed sociocultural, psychological, and biological explanations for why people develop substance use disorders. No single explanation, however, has gained broad support. Like so many other disorders, excessive and chronic drug use is increasingly viewed as the result of a combination of these factors.

Sociocultural Views

A number of sociocultural theorists propose that people are most likely to develop substance use disorders when they live under stressful socioeconomic conditions. Studies have found that regions with higher unemployment levels have higher rates of alcohol or opioid use disorder (Khazan, 2017; Marsiglia & Smith, 2010). Similarly, people in lower socioeconomic classes have rates of substance use disorder that are higher than those of the other classes. In a related vein, 18 percent of unemployed adults currently use an illegal drug, compared with 11 percent of full-time employed workers and 13 percent of part-time employees (SAMHSA, 2018).

Sociocultural theorists hold that people confronted regularly by other kinds of stress also have a heightened risk of developing substance use disorders. A range of studies conducted with Hispanic, African American, and LGBTQ individuals, for example, find higher rates of substance use disorders among those participants who live or work in environments of particularly intense discrimination (Rose et al., 2018; Slater et al., 2017).

#

#BadAge

By a strange coincidence, several of rock's most famous stars and substance abusers have died at age 27. They include Jimi Hendrix, Jim Morrison, Janis Joplin, Kurt Cobain, Brian Jones, and Amy Winehouse. The phenomenon has been called "The 27 Club" in some circles.

Still other sociocultural theorists propose that people are more likely to develop substance use disorders if they are part of a family or social environment in which substance use is valued or at least accepted (Mahboubi et al., 2017). Researchers have learned that problem drinking is more common among teenagers whose parents and peers drink, as well as among teenagers whose family environments are stressful and unsupportive (Calhoun et al., 2018; Wilens et al., 2014). Moreover, lower rates of alcoholism are found among Jews and Protestants, groups in which drinking is typically acceptable only as long as it remains within clear limits, whereas alcoholism rates are higher among the Irish and Eastern Europeans, who do not, in general, draw as clear a line (Hart & Ksir, 2017; Ledoux et al., 2002).

What factors might explain the finding that different ethnic, religious, and national groups have different rates of alcohol use disorder?

Psychodynamic Views

Psychodynamic theorists believe that people with substance use disorders have powerful *dependency* needs that can be traced to their early years (Bressert, 2016; Dodes & Khantzian, 2016). They suggest that when parents fail to satisfy a young child's need for nurturance, the child is likely to grow up depending excessively on others for help and comfort, trying to find the nurturance that was lacking during the early years. If this search for outside support includes experimentation with a drug, the person may well develop a dependent relationship with the substance.

Some psychodynamic theorists also believe that certain people respond to their early deprivations by developing a *substance abuse personality* that leaves them particularly prone to drug abuse. Personality inventories, patient interviews, and even animal studies have in fact indicated that individuals who abuse drugs tend to be more dependent, antisocial, impulsive, novelty-seeking, risk-taking, and depressive than other individuals (Martino et al., 2017). However, these findings are correlational (at least, the findings from human studies are), and do not clarify whether such traits lead to chronic drug use or whether repeated drug use causes people to be dependent, impulsive, and the like.

In an effort to establish clearer causation, one pioneering longitudinal study measured the personality traits of a large group of nonalcoholic young men and then kept track of each man's development (Littlefield & Sher, 2010; Jones, 1971, 1968). Years later, the traits of the men who developed alcohol problems in middle age were compared with the traits of those who did not. The men who developed alcohol problems had been more impulsive as teenagers and continued to be so in middle age, a finding suggesting that impulsive men are indeed more prone to develop alcohol problems. Similarly, in various laboratory investigations, "impulsive" rats—those that generally have trouble delaying their rewards—have been found to drink more alcohol when offered it than other rats (Spoelder et al., 2017).

A major weakness of this line of argument is the wide range of personality traits that have been tied to substance use disorders. Different studies point to different "key" traits. Inasmuch as some people with these disorders appear to be dependent, others impulsive, and still others antisocial, researchers cannot presently conclude that any one personality trait or group of traits stands out in the development of the disorders (Garofalo & Wright, 2017).

Feeling the effects Shortly after taking MDMA ("Ecstasy") at a rave, this couple displays a shift in mood, energy, and behavior. Each week, partygoers and other consumers take hundreds of thousands of doses of this drug (Johnston et al., 2017), which is technically a stimulant but also considered a hallucinogenic drug. MDMA produces its effects largely by altering serotonin and dopamine activity in the brain.

Scott Houston/Polaris

Cognitive-Behavioral Views

According to cognitive-behavioral theorists, *operant conditioning* may play a key role in substance use disorders. They argue that the temporary reduction of tension or raising of spirits produced by a drug has a rewarding effect, thus increasing the likelihood that the user will seek this reaction again (Duperrouzel et al., 2018; Nock, Minnes, & Alberts, 2017). Similarly, the rewarding effects may eventually lead users to try higher dosages or more powerful methods of ingestion. Beyond these conditioning explanations, cognitive-behavioral theorists further argue that such rewards eventually produce an *expectancy* that substances will be rewarding, and this expectation helps motivate people to increase drug use at times of tension (Montes et al., 2017).

In support of these views, studies have found that many people do drink more alcohol or seek heroin when they feel tense (Collins et al., 2018; Frone, 2016). In one study, as participants worked on a difficult anagram task, a confederate planted by the researchers unfairly criticized and belittled them. The participants were then asked to participate in an "alcohol taste task," supposedly to compare and rate alcoholic beverages. Those who had been harassed drank more alcohol during the taste task than did the control participants who had not been criticized.

In a manner of speaking, the cognitive-behavioral theorists are arguing that many people take drugs to "medicate" themselves when they feel tense. If so, one would expect higher rates of substance use disorders among people who suffer from anxiety, depression, and other such problems. And, in fact, at least 20 percent of all adults who suffer from psychological disorders also display substance use disorders (Dworkin et al., 2018; SAMHSA, 2018).

A number of cognitive-behavioral theorists have proposed that *classical conditioning* may also play a role in these disorders (Goltseker et al., 2017; O'Brien, 2013). As you'll remember from Chapters 2 and 4, classical conditioning occurs when two stimuli that appear close together in time become connected in a person's mind, so that eventually, the person responds similarly to each stimulus. Cues or objects present in the environment at the time a person takes a drug may act as classically conditioned stimuli and come to produce some of the same pleasure brought on by the drugs themselves. Just the sight of a hypodermic needle, drug buddy, or regular supplier, for example, has been known to comfort people who are addicted to heroin or amphetamines and to relieve their withdrawal symptoms. In a similar manner, cues or objects that are present during withdrawal distress may *produce* withdrawal-like symptoms. One man who had formerly been dependent on heroin became nauseated and had other withdrawal symptoms when he returned to the neighborhood where he had gone through withdrawal in the past—a reaction that led him to start taking heroin again.

#PopularTitles

Substance use is a popular theme in music. Hit songs include Amy Winehouse's "Rehab," the Velvet Underground's "Heroin," the Rolling Stones' "Sister Morphine," Snoop Dogg's "Gin and Juice," Eric Clapton's "Cocaine," Cyprus Hill's "I Wanna Get High," Eminem's "Drug Ballad," Lil' Kim's "Drugs," and Missy Elliott's "Pass That Dutch."

Biological Views

Over the past few decades, researchers have become clear that biological factors play a major role in drug misuse (Volkow et al., 2018). Studies on *genetic predisposition*, *neurotransmitters*, and *brain circuits* have all pointed in this direction.

Genetic Predisposition For years, breeding experiments have been conducted to see whether certain animals are genetically predisposed to become addicted to drugs (Logrip et al., 2018; Weiss, 2011). In several studies, for example, investigators have first identified animals that prefer alcohol to other beverages and then mated them to one another. Generally, the offspring of these animals have been found also to display an unusual preference for alcohol.

Similarly, research with human twins has suggested that people may inherit a predisposition to misuse substances (Stickel et al., 2017; Ystrom et al., 2014). Numerous studies have found an alcoholism *concordance* rate of around 50 percent in identical twins; that is, if one identical twin displays alcoholism, the other twin also does in 50 percent of the cases. In contrast, in these same studies, fraternal twins have a concordance rate of only 30 percent. As you have read, however, such findings do not rule out other

Crack cookies? Researchers at Connecticut College found that the lab-induced addiction of rats to Oreo cookies—particularly the creamy center—was as strong as their lab-induced addiction to cocaine and morphine in many ways. The study was conducted to test the growing theory that many high-fat, high-sugar foods stimulate the brain in the same ways and locations that addictive drugs do.

Photo by Bob MacDonnell, courtesy Connecticut College

interpretations. For one thing, the parenting received by two identical twins may be more similar than that received by two fraternal twins.

A clearer indication that genetics may play a role in substance use disorders comes from studies of alcoholism rates in people adopted shortly after birth (Stickel et al., 2017; Samek et al., 2014). These studies have compared adoptees whose biological parents abuse alcohol with adoptees whose biological parents do not. By adulthood, the individuals whose biological parents abuse alcohol typically show higher rates of alcoholism than those with nonalcoholic biological parents.

Genetic linkage strategies and *molecular biology* techniques provide more direct evidence in support of a genetic explanation (Walker & Nestler, 2018; Way et al., 2017). One line of investigation has found an abnormal form of the so-called *dopamine-2 (D2) receptor gene* in a majority of research participants with substance use disorders but in less than 20 percent of participants who do not have such disorders (Blum et al., 2018, 2015, 1990). Other studies have tied still other genes to substance use disorders (Patriquin et al., 2017; Rezaei et al., 2017).

Neurotransmitters Over the past few decades, some researchers have pieced together a neurotransmitter-focused explanation of drug tolerance and withdrawal symptoms (Lohani et al., 2017; Byrne et al., 2016; Kosten et al., 2011, 2005). These theorists contend that when a particular drug is ingested, it increases the activity of certain neurotransmitters whose normal purpose is to calm, reduce pain, lift mood, or increase alertness. When a person keeps on taking the drug, the brain apparently makes an adjustment and reduces its own production of the neurotransmitters. Because the drug is increasing neurotransmitter activity or efficiency, the brain's release of the neurotransmitter is less necessary. As drug intake increases, the body's production of the neurotransmitters continues to decrease, leaving the person in need of progressively more of the drug to achieve its effects. In this way, drug takers build tolerance for a drug, becoming more and more reliant on it rather than on their own biological processes to feel comfortable, happy, or alert. If they suddenly stop taking the drug, their natural supply of neurotransmitters will be low for a time, producing the symptoms of withdrawal. Withdrawal continues until the brain resumes its normal production of the neurotransmitters.

To some extent, the abused substance dictates which neurotransmitters will be affected. Repeated and excessive use of alcohol or benzodiazepines may lower the brain's production of the neurotransmitter GABA, regular use of opioids may reduce the brain's production of endorphins, and regular use of cocaine or amphetamines may lower the brain's production of dopamine (Vaquero et al., 2017; Kosten et al., 2011, 2005). In addition, researchers have identified a neurotransmitter called *anandamide* that operates much like THC; excessive use of marijuana may reduce the production of anandamide.

Victims of a reward deficiency syndrome? The brain reward circuits of people who develop substance use disorders may be inadequately activated by events in life—a problem called the *reward deficiency syndrome.* With the colors red and orange indicating more brain activity, these PET scans show that before abusers of cocaine, methamphetamine, and alcohol take those substances, their reward circuits (right) are generally less active than the reward circuits of nonabusers (left) (Volkow et al., 2016, 2004, 2002).

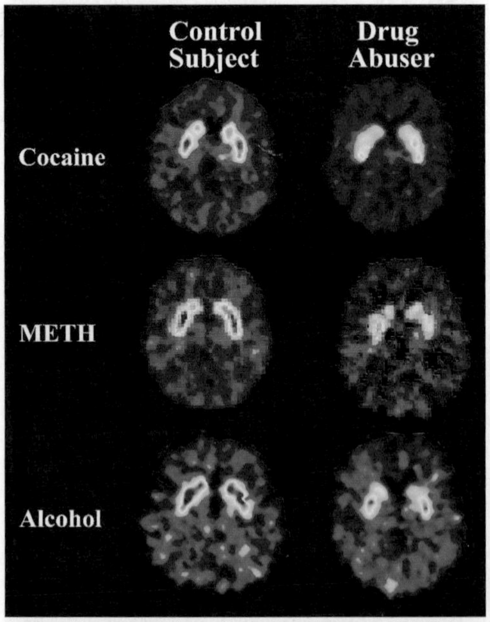

The Brain's Reward Circuit The neurotransmitter-focused explanation of substance abuse helps explain why people who regularly take substances have tolerance and withdrawal reactions. But why are drugs so rewarding, and why do certain people turn to them in the first place? Brain-imaging studies conducted in recent years answer these questions by pointing to the operation of a particular brain circuit—the circuit within which the neurotransmitters under discussion do their work. As you've read earlier, a brain circuit is a network of brain structures that work together, triggering each other into action to produce a distinct behavioral, cognitive, or emotional reaction. The circuit that has been tied to substance misuse is the **reward circuit,** also called the *reward center* and the *pleasure pathway* (Volkow et al., 2018, 2016).

Apparently, whenever a person ingests a substance (from foods to drugs), the substance eventually activates the brain's reward circuit (Hadar et al., 2017). This reward circuit features the brain structure called the *ventral tegmental area* (in the midbrain), a structure known as the *nucleus accumbens,* and the *prefrontal cortex* (see **Figure 10-4**).

In addition, the circuit includes the striatum, hippocampus, and several other important structures (Vaquero et al., 2017). The key neurotransmitter in this circuit is *dopamine* (Volkow et al., 2018, 2016). When dopamine is activated throughout this circuit, a person feels pleasure. Music may activate dopamine in the reward circuit. So may a hug or a word of praise. And so do drugs. Although other neurotransmitters also play roles in the reward circuit, dopamine is the primary one.

Certain drugs directly stimulate the structures in the reward circuit. Remember that cocaine and amphetamines directly increase dopamine activity. Other drugs seem to stimulate it in roundabout ways. The biochemical reactions triggered by alcohol, opioids, and marijuana set in motion a series of chemical events that eventually lead to increased dopamine activity in the reward circuit and, in turn, excessive communications (that is, heightened interconnectivity) between the structures in the reward circuit (Hadar et al., 2017; Vaquero et al., 2017). A number of studies further suggest that as substances repeatedly stimulate this reward circuit, the circuit develops a hypersensitivity to the substances. That is, neurons in the circuit fire more readily when stimulated by the substances, contributing to future desires for them (Moeller & Paulus, 2018).

Still other theorists suspect that people who chronically use drugs may suffer from a *reward deficiency syndrome:* their reward circuit is not readily activated by the usual events in their lives, so they turn to drugs to stimulate this pleasure pathway, particularly in times of stress (Blum et al., 2018, 2016, 2000). Abnormal genes, such as the abnormal D2 receptor gene, have been cited as possible contributors to this syndrome. In short, the chronic intake of certain substances helps to produce a dysfunctional reward circuit in the brain and, along with that, the symptoms of a substance use disorder.

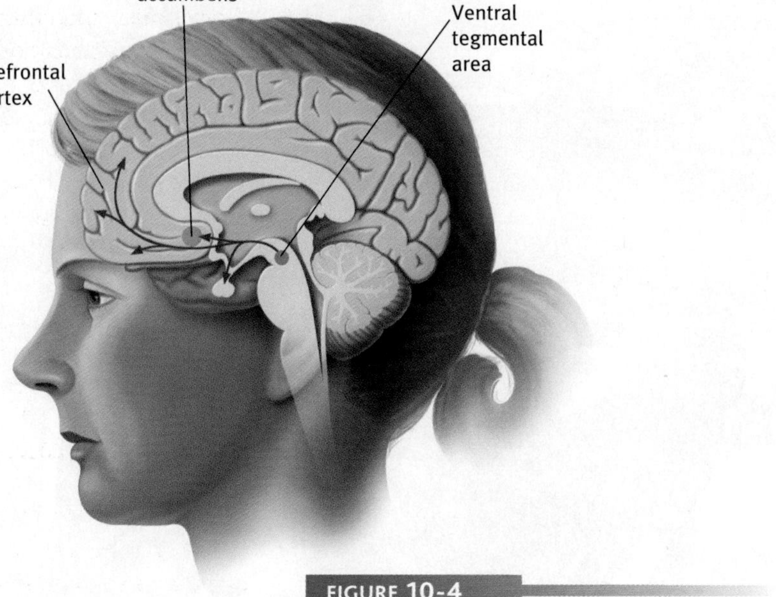

FIGURE 10-4

Pleasure Center in the Brain

One of the reasons substances produce feelings of pleasure is because they increase the activity of the neurotransmitter dopamine in the brain's reward circuit. Chronic dysfunction of this circuit—which includes the ventral tegmental area, nucleus accumbens, and prefrontal cortex—can lead to a substance use disorder.

The Developmental Psychopathology View

Over the years, a list of factors that may contribute to substance use disorders has unfolded, but no single factor fully predicts or explains the disorders. Thus, as with other psychological disorders, a number of substance use theorists have tried to integrate the variables identified by each of the models. Once again, developmental psychopathology theorists have been active in this effort.

According to this perspective, the road to substance use disorders often begins with genetically inherited predispositions—predispositions characterized by a less-than-optimal reward circuit in the brain and by a problematic temperament featuring some of the negative traits discussed earlier in this chapter. Developmental psychopathologists suggest that such predispositions will eventually result in a substance use disorder if the individual further experiences numerous stressors throughout childhood, inadequate parenting (such as substance misuse modeling), satisfying substance use experiences, relationships with peers who use drugs, and/or significant adult stressors (Forster et al., 2018; Zucker et al, 2016). At the same time, individuals who experience *manageable* adversities throughout childhood and adolescence can develop a level of resilience that may help counter such unfavorable predispositions, stressors, and negative family and peer influences.

In short, the developmental psychopathology perspective provides a framework for understanding why the factors discussed in this chapter sometimes lead to substance use disorders and sometimes do not. But the perspective also does more than this: it offers an explanation for seeming contradictions in the substance abuse research literature. Recall, for example, our earlier discussion of substance abuse personalities

reward circuit A dopamine-rich circuit in the brain that produces feelings of pleasure when activated.

Common substance, uncommon danger
A 13-year-old boy sniffs glue as he lies dazed near a garbage heap. In the United States, at least 6 percent of all people have tried to get high by inhaling the hydrocarbons found in common substances such as glue, gasoline, paint thinner, cleaners, and spray-can propellants (APA, 2013). Such behavior may lead to *inhalant use disorder* and poses a number of serious medical dangers.

(see page 314). As you read, a variety of personality traits have been linked to substance use disorders—dependency, antisocial inclinations, impulsivity, novelty seeking, risk taking, and depressive functioning—but different studies have tied different such traits to the disorders. These findings are not conflicting at all, according to developmental psychopathology theorists.

The theorists propose that either of two very different temperaments may set the stage for later substance abuse. On the one hand, some individuals may begin with a *disinhibited* temperament, also called an *externalizing* temperament—featuring impulsivity, aggressiveness, overactivity, limited persistence, low frustration tolerance, and inattention (Trucco et al., 2018; Zucker et al., 2016, 1996). These individuals have great difficulty controlling their behaviors, thus increasing their risk of having early family conflicts, behavioral problems, and school difficulties—variables that may, in turn, lead to social problems, relationships with undesirable peers, rewards from those peers for repeated drug use, and, ultimately, the onset of substance use disorders. Studies have confirmed that this cluster and sequence of variables does indeed unfold in many cases of substance use disorder (Chassin et al., 2016).

On the other hand, according to the developmental psychopathology perspective, other individuals may begin with a temperament of *inhibition* and *negative affectivity*, sometimes called an *internalizing* temperament—characterized by multiple fears, depression, negative thinking, and dependence. This temperament may contribute to worrying and sadness throughout the individuals' development, low self-concept, and interpersonal rejections. These individuals may eventually turn to alcohol and drugs largely because the substances reduce their emotional pain, quiet their troublesome thoughts, and help them through interpersonal difficulties. Studies have indicated that this cluster and sequence of variables may also lead to substance use disorders (Menary, Corbin, & Chassin, 2017; Chassin et al., 2016).

This notion that different temperaments may trigger and interact with different developmental factors to bring about substance use disorders is consistent with one of the key principles of the developmental psychopathology perspective, *equifinality*—the principle that different developmental pathways can lead to the same psychological disorder (see pages 69–70). In short, identifying key factors in substance use disorders is only part of a comprehensive explanation. It is also necessary to identify when and how those factors interact.

...SUMMING UP

WHAT CAUSES SUBSTANCE USE DISORDERS? Several explanations for substance use disorders have been put forward. According to sociocultural theorists, the people most likely to develop these disorders are those living under stressful socioeconomic conditions or those whose families value or tolerate drug use. In the psychodynamic view, people who develop substance use disorders have excessive dependency needs traceable to the early stages of life. Some psychodynamic theorists also believe that certain people have a substance abuse personality that makes them prone to drug use. In the leading cognitive-behavioral views, drug use is seen as being reinforced initially because it reduces tensions, and such reductions lead to an expectancy that drugs will be comforting and helpful.

The biological explanations are supported by twin, adoptee, and genetic studies, suggesting that people may inherit a predisposition to the disorders. Researchers have also learned that drug tolerance and withdrawal symptoms may be caused by cutbacks in the brain's production of particular neurotransmitters during excessive and chronic drug use. Biological studies suggest that many, perhaps all, drugs may ultimately lead to increased dopamine activity in the brain's reward circuit.

Developmental psychopathology theorists suggest that a genetically inherited biological predisposition and temperamental predisposition may interact with life stressors, problematic parenting, and/or other environmental factors to bring about a substance use disorder.

How Are Substance Use Disorders Treated?

Many approaches have been used to treat substance use disorders, including psychodynamic, cognitive-behavioral, and biological approaches, along with several sociocultural therapies. These various approaches are often combined with *motivational interviewing* (see page 283) in which therapists help motivate the clients to make constructive choices and behavioral changes (Kampman, 2018; Ingersoll, 2017). Although treatment sometimes meets with great success, more often it is only moderately helpful (Peavy, 2017; Strain, 2017). Today the various treatments are typically used on either an outpatient or inpatient basis or a combination of the two.

Psychodynamic Therapies

Psychodynamic therapists first guide clients to uncover and work through the underlying needs and conflicts that they believe have led to the substance use disorder. The therapists then try to help the clients change their substance-related styles of living. Although this approach is often used, it has not been found to be particularly effective (Dodes & Khantzian, 2016; McCrady et al., 2014). It may be that substance use disorders, regardless of their causes, eventually become stubborn independent problems that must be the direct target of treatment if people are to become drug-free. Psychodynamic therapy tends to be of more help when it is combined with other approaches in a multidimensional treatment program.

Cognitive-Behavioral Therapies

Cognitive-behavioral treatments for substance use disorders help clients identify and change the behaviors and cognitions that keep contributing to their patterns of substance misuse (Kampman, 2018; Aronson, 2017). The leading cognitive-behavioral interventions for these disorders are *aversion therapy, contingency management, relapse prevention training,* and *acceptance and commitment therapy (ACT).*

Aversion Therapy In **aversion therapy,** a widely used approach based on the behavioral principles of classical conditioning, clients are repeatedly presented with an unpleasant stimulus (for example, an electric shock) at the very moment that they are taking a drug. After repeated pairings, they are expected to react negatively to the substance itself and to lose their craving for it.

Aversion therapy has been used to treat alcoholism more often than it has to treat other substance use disorders. In one version of this therapy, drinking is paired with drug-induced nausea and vomiting (Elkins et al., 2017; Cole, 2016). The pairing of nausea with alcohol is expected to produce negative responses to alcohol itself. Another version of aversion therapy requires people with alcoholism to imagine extremely upsetting, repulsive, or frightening scenes while they are drinking. The pairing of the

#FamousDrugDeaths

- Tom Petty, singer and songwriter (polydrug, 2017)
- Lil Peep, rapper (polydrug, 2017)
- Carrie Fisher, actress (polydrug and sleep apnea, 2017)
- Prince, singer and songwriter (opioid, 2016)
- Philip Seymour Hoffman, actor (polydrug, 2014)
- Cory Monteith, actor (polydrug, 2013)
- Whitney Houston, singer (cocaine and heart disease, 2012)
- Amy Winehouse, singer (alcohol poisoning, 2011)
- Michael Jackson, performer and songwriter (polydrug, 2009)
- Heath Ledger, actor (polydrug, 2008)
- Anna Nicole Smith, model (polydrug, 2007)
- Ol' Dirty Bastard, rapper, Wu-Tang Clan (polydrug, 2004)
- Rick James, singer (cocaine, 2004)

aversion therapy A treatment in which clients are repeatedly presented with unpleasant stimuli while they are performing undesirable behaviors such as taking a drug.

#StayingSober

73% of current AA members have been sober for more than 1 year (AA World Services, 2017).

imagined scenes with alcohol is expected to produce negative responses to alcohol itself. Here is the kind of scene therapists may guide a client to imagine:

> *I'd like you to vividly imagine that you are tasting the (beer, whiskey, etc.). See yourself tasting it, capture the exact taste, color and consistency. Use all of your senses. After you've tasted the drink you notice that there is something small and white floating in the glass—it stands out. You bend closer to examine it more carefully, your nose is right over the glass now and the smell fills your nostrils as you remember exactly what the drink tastes like. Now you can see what's in the glass. There are several maggots floating on the surface. As you watch, revolted, one manages to get a grip on the glass and, undulating, creeps up the glass. There are even more of the repulsive creatures in the glass than you first thought. You realize that you have swallowed some of them and you're very aware of the taste in your mouth. You feel very sick and wish you'd never reached for the glass and had the drink at all.*
>
> *(Clarke & Saunders, 1988, pp. 143–144)*

Aversion therapy for substance use disorders has had only limited success when it is the sole form of treatment (Elkins et al., 2017; Belendiuk & Riggs, 2014). A major problem is that the approach can be effective only if people are motivated to subject themselves to multiple sessions of this unpleasant procedure, and many people are not.

Contingency Management Based on the behavioral principles of operant conditioning, *contingency management* programs offer clients incentives (such as vouchers, prizes, cash, or privileges) that are contingent on the submission of drug-free urine specimens (Rash et al., 2017; Stitzer, Cunningham, & Sweeney, 2017). In essence, this procedure—usually lasting 8 to 16 weeks—is rewarding clients for abstaining from the use of the substances upon which they are dependent.

Studies indicate that clients in contingency management programs maintain a higher attendance record than those in other kinds of programs. However, unless the programs are part of a larger treatment approach, they are at best moderately effective at helping clients abstain from substances for an extended period (Kampman, 2018; Stitzer et al., 2017). As with aversion therapy, a major limitation is that the approach can be effective only when people are motivated to continue despite its unpleasantness or demands.

Better ways to cope Several treatments for substance use disorders, including relapse-prevention training, teach clients alternative—more functional—ways of coping with stress and negative emotions. In that spirit, this patient at a drug rehabilitation center in China developed the practice of kicking a punching dummy to help release his pent-up anger.

©Jason Lee/Reuters/Newscom

Relapse-Prevention Training One of the most prominent cognitive-behavioral approaches to substance misuse is **relapse-prevention training** (Menon & Kandasamy, 2018). The overall goal of this approach is for clients to gain *control* over their substance-related behaviors. To help reach this goal, clients are taught to identify high-risk situations, appreciate the range of decisions that confront them in such situations, change their dysfunctional lifestyles, and learn from mistakes and lapses.

Several strategies typically are included in relapse-prevention training for alcohol use disorder: (1) *Therapists have clients keep track of their drinking.* By writing down the times, locations, emotions, bodily changes, and other circumstances of their drinking, people become more aware of the situations that place them at risk for excessive drinking. (2) *Therapists teach clients coping strategies to use when such situations arise.* Clients learn, for example, to recognize when they are approaching their drinking limits; to control their rate of drinking (perhaps by spacing their drinks or by sipping them rather than gulping); and to practice relaxation techniques, assertiveness skills, and other coping behaviors in situations in which they would otherwise be drinking. (3) *Therapists teach clients to plan ahead of time.* Clients may, for example, determine beforehand how many drinks are appropriate, what to drink, and under which circumstances to drink.

Relapse-prevention training has been found to lower some people's frequency of intoxication and of binge drinking (Menon & Kandasamy, 2018; Hart & Ksir, 2017). People who are young and do not have the tolerance and withdrawal features of chronic alcohol use seem to do best with this approach.

Acceptance and Commitment Therapy Another form of cognitive-behavioral treatment that has been used in cases of substance use disorder is *acceptance and commitment therapy* (*ACT*). As you read in Chapters 2 and 4, ACT therapists use a mindfulness-based approach to help clients become *aware* of their streams of thoughts as they are occurring and to accept such thoughts as mere events of the mind. For people with substance use disorders, that means increasing their awareness and acceptance of their drug cravings, worries, and depressive thoughts. By accepting such thoughts rather than trying to eliminate them, the clients are expected to be less upset by them and less likely to act on them by seeking out drugs. Research indicates that ACT is more effective than placebo treatments and at least as effective as other cognitive-behavioral treatments for substance use disorders, and sometimes more effective (Narayanan & Naaz, 2018; Smallwood et al., 2016).

relapse-prevention training An approach to treating alcohol use disorder in which clients are taught to plan ahead and to apply coping strategies in situations that typically trigger excessive drinking.

detoxification Systematic and medically supervised withdrawal from a drug.

antagonist drugs Drugs that block or change the effects of an addictive drug.

Biological Treatments

Biological treatments may be used to help people withdraw from substances, abstain from them, or simply maintain their level of use without increasing it further. As with the other forms of treatment, biological approaches alone rarely bring long-term improvement, but they can be helpful when combined with other approaches.

Detoxification **Detoxification** is systematic and medically supervised withdrawal from a drug. Some detoxification programs are offered on an outpatient basis. Others are located in hospitals and clinics and may also include individual and group therapy, a "full-service" institutional approach that has become popular. One detoxification approach is to have clients withdraw gradually from the substance, taking smaller and smaller doses until they are off the drug completely. A second—often medically preferred—detoxification strategy is to give clients other drugs that reduce the symptoms of withdrawal (Sevarino, 2018). Antianxiety drugs, for example, are sometimes used to reduce severe alcohol withdrawal reactions such as delirium tremens and seizures. Detoxification programs seem to help motivated people withdraw from drugs. However, relapse rates tend to be high for those who do not receive a follow-up form of treatment—psychological, biological, or sociocultural—after successfully detoxifying (Strain, 2018, 2017).

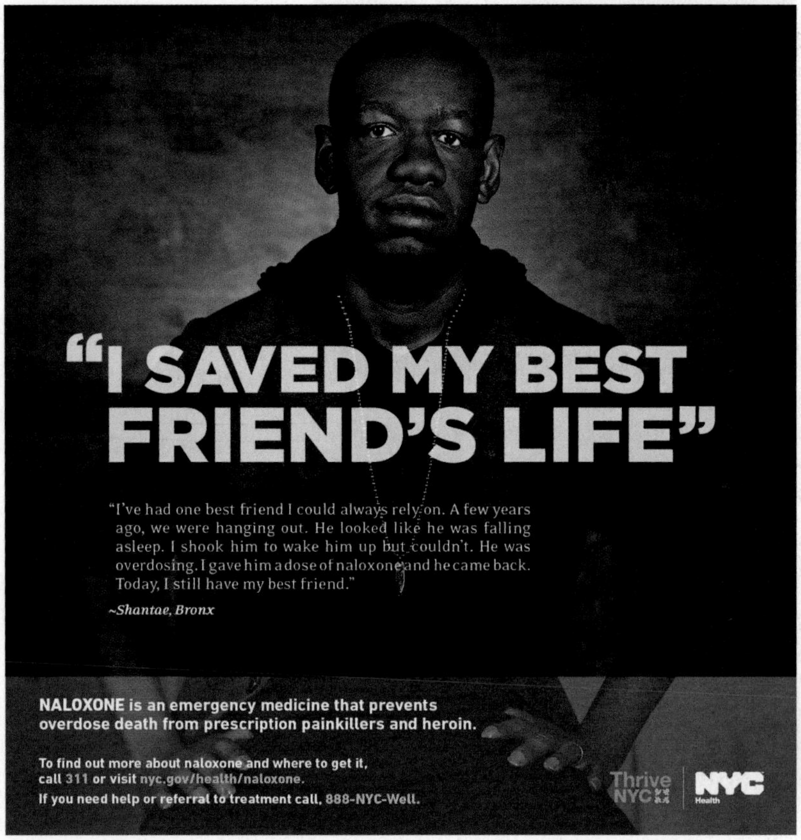
"I SAVED MY BEST FRIEND'S LIFE"
"I've had one best friend I could always rely on. A few years ago, we were hanging out. He looked like he was falling asleep. I shook him to wake him up but couldn't. He was overdosing. I gave him a dose of naloxone and he came back. Today, I still have my best friend."
~Shantae, Bronx
NALOXONE is an emergency medicine that prevents overdose death from prescription painkillers and heroin.
To find out more about naloxone and where to get it, call 311 or visit nyc.gov/health/naloxone.
If you need help or referral to treatment call, 888-NYC-Well.
Thrive NYC
NYC Health

In case of an emergency In 2017 the New York City Health Department launched the "I Saved a Life" public awareness campaign, which urges people to carry the opioid antagonist drug *naloxone* for possible use in opioid-overdose crises. The campaign features powerful posters and stories about real-life people who were able to save the life of a friend or relative by using naloxone. This medication is now available in pharmacies throughout the city.

Antagonist Drugs After successfully stopping a drug, people must avoid falling back into a pattern of chronic use. As an aid to resisting temptation, some people with substance use disorders are given **antagonist drugs,** which block or change the effects of the addictive drug (Strain, 2018; Sofin et al., 2017). *Disulfiram* (Antabuse), for example, is often given to people who are trying to stay away from alcohol. By itself, a low dose of disulfiram seems to have few negative effects, but a person who drinks alcohol while taking it will have intense nausea, vomiting, blushing, a faster heart rate, dizziness, and perhaps fainting. People taking disulfiram are less likely to drink alcohol because they know the terrible reaction that awaits them should they have even one drink. Disulfiram has proved helpful, but again only with people who are motivated to take it as prescribed (Sofin et al., 2017). In addition to disulfiram, several other antagonist drugs are now being tested.

For substance use disorders centered on opioids, several *opioid antagonist drugs*, such as **naloxone,** are used (Strain, 2018). These antagonists attach to *endorphin* receptor sites throughout the brain and make it impossible for the opioids to have their usual effect. Without the rush or high, continued drug use becomes pointless. In addition, by blocking endorphin receptors during an opioid overdose, opioid antagonists can actually reverse the deadly effect of respiratory depression, thus saving the user's life. Research indicates that opioid antagonists may also be useful in the treatment of substance use disorders involving alcohol or cocaine (Busch et al., 2017; Johnson, 2017).

Chau Doan/LightRocket via Getty Images

Drug use . . . under medical supervision Methadone is itself an opioid that can be as dangerous as other opioids when not taken under safe medical supervision. Here a nurse at a methadone treatment facility prepares the drug for administration to clients.

Drug Maintenance Therapy A drug-related lifestyle may be a bigger problem than the drug's direct effects. Much of the damage caused by heroin addiction, for example, comes from overdoses, unsterilized needles, and an accompanying life of crime. Thus, clinicians were very enthusiastic when **methadone maintenance programs** were developed in the 1960s to treat heroin addiction (Dole & Nyswander, 1967, 1965). In these programs, people with an addiction are given the laboratory opioid *methadone* as a substitute, or *agonist,* for heroin. Although they then become dependent on methadone, their new addiction is maintained under safe medical supervision. Unlike heroin, methadone produces a moderate high, can be taken by mouth (thus eliminating the dangers of needles), and needs to be taken only once a day.

Why has the legal, medically supervised use of heroin (in Great Britain) or heroin substitutes (in the United States) sometimes failed to combat drug problems?

At first, methadone programs seemed very effective, and many of them were set up throughout the United States, Canada, and England. These programs became less popular during the 1980s, however, because of the dangers of methadone itself. Many clinicians came to believe that substituting one addiction for another is not an acceptable "solution" for a substance use disorder, and many people with an addiction complained that methadone addiction was creating an additional drug problem that simply complicated their original one (Strain, 2018; Dalsbø et al., 2017).

Despite such concerns, maintenance treatment with methadone has again sparked interest among clinicians in recent years, partly because of new research support (Strain, 2018) and partly because of the rapid spread of the HIV and hepatitis C viruses among intravenous drug abusers and their sex partners and children (Kharasch, 2017). Today thousands of clinics provide methadone treatment across the United States.

Another opioid substitute drug, *buprenorphine*, has also been gaining momentum as a form of maintenance therapy during the past decade (Sevarino, 2018; SAMHSA, 2017). Like methadone, this drug is itself an opioid that is administered to patients as a safer alternative to heroin, painkillers, and the like. However, according to research, buprenorphine is a less potent substitute drug than methadone and produces less tolerance and fewer withdrawal reactions (Strain, 2018; Gowing et al., 2017). For these reasons, buprenorphine is permitted by law to be prescribed by physicians in their offices rather than as part of a highly structured clinic program.

Sociocultural Therapies

As you have read, sociocultural theorists—both *family-social* and *multicultural* theorists—believe that psychological problems emerge in a social setting and are best treated in a social context. Three sociocultural approaches have been used to help people overcome substance use disorders: (1) *self-help programs,* (2) *culture- and gender-sensitive programs,* and (3) *community prevention programs*

Self-Help and Residential Treatment Programs Many people with substance use disorders have organized among themselves to help one another recover without professional assistance (Aronson, 2017). The drug self-help movement dates back to 1935, when two Ohio men suffering from alcoholism met and wound up discussing alternative treatment possibilities. The first discussion led to others and to the eventual formation of a self-help group whose members discussed alcohol-related problems, traded ideas, and provided support. The organization became known as **Alcoholics Anonymous (AA).**

Today AA has approximately 2 million members in 110,000 groups across the world (AA World Services, 2018). It offers peer support along with moral and spiritual guidelines to help people overcome alcoholism. Different members apparently find different aspects of AA helpful. For some it is the peer support; for others it is the spiritual dimension (Kelly, 2017). Meetings take place regularly, and members are available to help each other 24 hours a day.

By offering guidelines for living, the organization helps members abstain "one day at a time," urging them to accept as "fact" the idea that they are powerless over alcohol and that they must stop drinking entirely and permanently if they are to live normal lives. AA views alcoholism as a disease and takes the position that "Once an alcoholic, always an alcoholic." Related self-help organizations, *Al-Anon* and *Alateen,* offer support for people who live with and care about people with alcoholism. Self-help programs such as *Narcotics Anonymous* and *Cocaine Anonymous* have been developed for other substance use disorders (Peavy, 2017; Lembke & Humphreys, 2016).

It is worth noting that the abstinence goal of AA is in direct opposition to the controlled-drinking goal of relapse-prevention training and several other interventions for substance misuse (see pages 320–321). In fact, this issue—abstinence versus controlled drinking—has been debated for years (Zemore, 2017; Rosenthal, 2011). Feelings about it have run so strongly that in the 1980s the people on one side challenged the motives and honesty of those on the other (Sobell & Sobell, 1984, 1973; Pendery et al., 1982).

Research indicates, however, that both controlled drinking and abstinence may be useful treatment goals, depending on the nature of the particular drinking problem (Best, 2017; Zemore, 2017). Studies suggest that abstinence may be a more appropriate goal for people who have a long-standing alcohol use disorder, whereas controlled drinking can be helpful to younger drinkers whose pattern does not include tolerance and withdrawal reactions. Those in the latter group may indeed need to be taught a nonabusive form of drinking.

Many self-help programs have expanded into **residential treatment centers,** or **therapeutic communities**—such as *Daytop Village* and *Phoenix House*—where people formerly addicted to drugs live, work, and socialize in a drug-free environment while undergoing individual, group, and family therapies and making a transition back to community life (Aronson, 2017; Gruenewald et al., 2016).

The evidence that keeps self-help and residential treatment programs going comes largely in the form of individual testimonials. Many tens of thousands of people have revealed that they are members of these programs and credit them with turning their lives around. Studies of the programs have also had favorable findings, but the number of such studies has been limited (Best, 2017; Peavy, 2017).

Culture- and Gender-Sensitive Programs Many people with substance use disorders live in a poor and perhaps violent setting. A growing number of today's treatment programs try to be sensitive to the special sociocultural pressures and problems faced by drug abusers who are poor, homeless, or members of minority groups (Upshur et al., 2018; McKinney & Caetano, 2016). Therapists who are sensitive to their clients' life challenges can do more to address the stresses that often lead to relapse.

Similarly, therapists have become more aware that women often require treatment methods different from those designed for men (Grella, 2018; Gamboa, 2017). Women and men often have different physical and psychological reactions to drugs, for example. In addition, treatment of women with substance use disorders may be complicated

Christian Petersen/Getty Images

End of a dream In 2016, Florida Marlins pitcher Jose Fernandez was killed along with two passengers when he plowed his 32-foot boat into a jetty. A toxicology report showed that the 24-year-old, who defected from Cuba in 2008, was very intoxicated (blood-alcohol level of 0.147) and had cocaine in his system at the time of the pre-dawn accident.

naloxone A widely used opioid antagonist drug.

methadone maintenance program A treatment in which clients are given legally and medically supervised doses of methadone—a heroin substitute—to treat various opioid use disorders.

Alcoholics Anonymous (AA) A self-help organization that provides support and guidance for people with alcohol use disorder.

residential treatment center A place where people who were formerly addicted to drugs live, work, and socialize in a drug-free environment. Also called a *therapeutic community.*

Jonathan Newton/The Washington Post via Getty Images

Fighting drug abuse while in prison
Inmates shake hands during a drug counseling session at a prison in Utah. The session is part of a statewide program—for people living in communities, rehabilitation centers, and prisons—called Addict II Athlete (pronounced "addict-to-athlete"). The program emphasizes exercise and athletic endeavors as an alternative to drug-related behaviors, while also providing support, psychoeducation, and other interventions to help individuals address their substance use disorders.

by the impact of sexual abuse, the possibility that they may be or may become pregnant while taking drugs, the stresses of raising children, and the fear of criminal prosecution for abusing drugs during pregnancy (SAMHSA, 2017). Thus, many women with such disorders feel more comfortable seeking help at gender-sensitive clinics or residential programs; some such programs also allow children to live with their recovering mothers.

Community Prevention Programs Perhaps the most effective approach to substance use disorders is to prevent them (Mewton et al., 2018; Gruenewald et al., 2016). The first drug prevention programs were conducted in schools. Today such programs are also offered in workplaces, activity centers, and other community settings and even through the media (SAMHSA, 2018). Around 12 percent of adolescents report that they have participated in drug prevention programs outside school within the past year. Around 75 percent have seen or heard a substance use prevention message. And almost 60 percent have talked to their parents in the past year about the dangers of alcohol and other drugs.

What impact might admissions by celebrities about past drug use have on people's willingness to seek treatment for a substance use disorder?

Some prevention programs are based on a total abstinence model, while others teach responsible use. Some seek to interrupt drug use; others try to delay the age at which people first experiment with drugs. Programs may also differ in whether they offer drug education, teach alternatives to drug use, try to change the psychological state of the potential user, help people change their peer relationships, or combine these techniques.

Prevention programs may focus on the *individual* (for example, by providing education about unpleasant drug effects), the *family* (by teaching parenting skills), the *peer group* (by teaching resistance to peer pressure), the *school* (by setting up firm enforcement of drug policies), or the *community* at large. The most effective prevention efforts focus on several of these areas in order to provide a consistent message about drug misuse in all areas of people's lives (Mewton et al., 2018). Some prevention programs have even been developed for preschool children.

Two of today's leading community-based prevention programs are TheTruth.com and Above the Influence. The Truth is an antismoking campaign, aimed at young people in particular, that has "edgy" ads on the Web (on YouTube, for instance), on television, and in magazines and newspapers. Above the Influence is a similar advertising campaign that focuses on a range of substances abused by teenagers. Originally created by the U.S. Office of National Drug Control Policy, Above the Influence became a private, not-for-profit program in 2014. A number of studies are being conducted to assess the actual impact of the various community-based prevention programs (SAMHSA, 2017; Allara et al., 2014).

gambling disorder A disorder marked by persistent and recurrent gambling behavior, leading to a range of life problems.

...SUMMING UP

HOW ARE SUBSTANCE USE DISORDERS TREATED? Usually several approaches are combined to treat substance use disorders. Psychodynamic therapists try to help clients become aware of and correct the underlying needs and conflicts that may have led to their use of drugs. Cognitive-behavioral techniques include aversion therapy, contingency management, relapse-prevention training, and acceptance and commitment therapy. Biological treatments include detoxification, antagonist drugs, and drug maintenance therapy. Sociocultural treatments approach substance use disorders in a social context by means of self-help groups (e.g., Alcoholics Anonymous), residential treatment programs, culture- and gender-sensitive treatments, and community prevention programs.

Other Addictive Disorders

As you read at the beginning of this chapter, DSM-5 lists **gambling disorder** as an addictive disorder alongside the substance use disorders. This represents a significant broadening of the concept of addiction, which in previous editions of the DSM referred only to the misuse of substances. In essence, DSM-5 is suggesting that people may become addicted to behaviors and activities beyond substance use.

Gambling Disorder

It is estimated that as many as 4 percent of adults and 3 to 10 percent of teenagers and college students suffer from *gambling disorder* (Floros, 2018; Nowak & Aloe, 2014). Clinicians are careful to distinguish between this disorder and social gambling (APA, 2013). Gambling disorder is defined less by the amount of time or money spent gambling than by the addictive nature of the behavior. People with gambling disorder are preoccupied with gambling and typically cannot walk away from a bet. When they lose money repeatedly, they often gamble more in an effort to win the money back, and continue gambling even in the face of financial, social, occupational, educational, and health problems (see **Table 10-3**). They usually gamble more when feeling distressed, and often lie to cover up the extent of their gambling. Many people with gambling disorder need to gamble with ever-larger amounts of money to reach the desired excitement, and they feel restless or irritable when they try to reduce or stop gambling—symptoms that are similar to the tolerance and withdrawal reactions displayed in substance use disorder (APA, 2013).

The explanations proposed for gambling disorder often parallel those for substance use disorders (Yazdi et al., 2019; Nautiyal et al., 2017). Some studies suggest, for example, that people with gambling disorder may: (1) inherit a genetic predisposition to develop the disorder; (2) experience heightened dopamine activity and dysfunction of the brain's reward circuit when they gamble; (3) have impulsive, novelty-seeking, and other personality styles that leave them prone to gambling disorder; and (4) make repeated and cognitive mistakes such as inaccurate expectations and misinterpretations of their emotions and bodily states. However, the research on these theories has been limited thus far, leaving such explanations tentative for now.

Several of the leading treatments for substance use disorders have been adapted for use with gambling disorder (Choi et al., 2017). These treatments include cognitive-behavioral approaches like relapse-prevention training, and biological approaches such as opioid antagonists. In addition, the self-help group program *Gamblers Anonymous,*

TABLE: 10-3

Dx Checklist

Gambling Disorder
1. Individual displays a maladaptive pattern of gambling, featuring at least 4 of the following symptoms over the course of a full year: • Can achieve excitement only by increasing gambling • Feels restless or irritable during gambling reduction • Repeated failures at controlling gambling • Consumed with gambling thoughts • Gambling often triggered by upset feelings • Frequently returns to gambling to recoup previous losses • Lies to cover up amount of gambling • Gambling puts important relationships, job, or education at risk • Seeks money from others to address gambling debts.
2. Individual experiences significant distress or impairment.

Information from: APA, 2013.

David Sacks/Getty Images

Increase in gambling venues This woman plays a slot machine while vacationing—harmless fun for her, but not for everyone. Some theorists believe that recent increases in the prevalence of gambling disorder are related to the heightened availability of casinos and online gambling sites.

a network modeled after *Alcoholics Anonymous,* is available to the many thousands of people with gambling disorder. People who attend such groups seem to have a better recovery rate.

Internet Gaming Disorder: Awaiting Official Status

As people increasingly turn to the Internet for activities that used to take place in the "real world"—communicating, networking, shopping, playing games, and participating in a community—a new psychological problem has emerged: an uncontrollable need to be online (Lindenberg et al., 2018; Young, 2017). This pattern has been called *Internet use disorder* and *Internet addiction,* among other names.

For people who have this pattern—at least 1 percent of all people—the Internet has become a black hole. They spend all or most of their waking hours texting, tweeting, networking, gaming, Internet browsing, e-mailing, blogging, visiting virtual worlds, shopping online, or viewing online pornography (McNicol & Thorsteinsson, 2017). Specific symptoms of this pattern parallel those found in substance use disorders and gambling disorder, extending from the loss of outside interests to possible withdrawal reactions when Internet use is not possible (APA, 2013).

Although clinicians, the media, and the public have shown enormous interest in this problem, it is not included as a disorder in DSM-5. Rather, the DSM workgroup recommended that one version of the pattern, which it calls *Internet gaming disorder,* receive further study for possible inclusion in future editions (Paulus et al., 2018; APA, 2013). In the meantime, the World Health Organization has indeed decided to include "gaming disorder" as a formal category in its newest edition of the International Classification of Diseases (ICD-11), the classification system used in most countries outside of North America (WHO, 2018).

...SUMMING UP

OTHER ADDICTIVE DISORDERS DSM-5 groups gambling disorder alongside the substance use disorders as an addictive disorder. Treatments for gambling disorder include cognitive-behavioral approaches, opioid antagonists, and self-help groups.

New Wrinkles to a Familiar Story

In some respects, the story of the misuse of drugs is the same today as in the past. Substance use is still rampant, often creating damaging psychological disorders. New drugs keep emerging, and the public goes through periods of believing, naïvely, that the new drugs are "safe." Only gradually do people learn that these, too, pose dangers. And treatments for substance-related disorders continue to have only limited effect.

Yet there are positive new wrinkles in this familiar story. Researchers have begun to develop a clearer understanding of how drugs act on the brain and body. In treatment, self-help groups and rehabilitation programs are flourishing. And preventive education to make people aware of the dangers of drug misuse is also expanding and seems to be having an effect. One reason for these improvements is that investigators and clinicians have stopped working in isolation and are instead looking for intersections between their own work and work from other models. They have come to recognize that social pressures, personality characteristics, rewards, and genetic predispositions all play roles in substance use disorders, and in fact they operate together. Similarly, the various forms of treatment seem to work best when they are combined with approaches from the other models, making integrated treatment the most productive approach.

CLINICAL CHOICES

Now that you've read about substance use and addictive disorders, try the interactive case study for this chapter. See if you are able to identify Jorge's symptoms and suggest a diagnosis based on his symptoms. What kind of treatment would be most effective for Jorge? Go to **LaunchPad** to access *Clinical Choices*.

Yet another new wrinkle to the addiction story is that the clinical field has now formally proclaimed that substances are not the only things to which people may develop an addiction. By grouping gambling disorder with the substance use disorders and targeting Internet gaming disorder for possible inclusion in the future, DSM-5 has opened the door for a broader view and perhaps broader treatments of addictive patterns—whether they are induced by substances or by other kinds of experiences.

...Key Terms

substance intoxication, p. 294
hallucinosis, p. 294
substance use disorder, p. 294
tolerance, p. 294
withdrawal, p. 294
alcohol, p. 295
delirium tremens (DTs), p. 298
cirrhosis, p. 298
Korsakoff's syndrome, p. 299
fetal alcohol syndrome, p. 299
sedative-hypnotic drug, p. 299
barbiturates, p. 299
benzodiazepines, p. 299
opioid, p. 299
opium, p. 299
morphine, p. 300
heroin, p. 300
endorphins, p. 300
cocaine, p. 303
freebasing, p. 304
crack, p. 304
amphetamines, p. 306
methamphetamine, p. 306
hallucinogen, p. 308
LSD (lysergic acid diethylamide), p. 308
cannabis, p. 309
marijuana, p. 309
tetrahydrocannabinol (THC), p. 309
polysubstance use, p. 312
synergistic effect, p. 312
substance abuse personality, p. 314
reward circuit, p. 316
reward-deficiency syndrome, p. 317
aversion therapy, p. 319
contingency management, p. 320
relapse-prevention training, p. 320
detoxification, p. 321
antagonist drug, p. 321
disulfiram (Antabuse), p. 321
opioid antagonist drugs, p. 322
naloxone, p. 322
methadone maintenance program, p. 322
buprenorphine, p. 322
self-help program, p. 322
Alcoholics Anonymous (AA), p. 323
residential treatment center, p. 323
community prevention program, p. 324
gambling disorder, p. 325
Gamblers Anonymous, p. 325
Internet gaming disorder, p. 326

...Quick Quiz

1. What are substance use disorders? *pp. 294–295*
2. How does alcohol act on the brain and body? What are the problems and dangers of alcohol misuse? *pp. 295–299*
3. Describe the features and problems of the misuse of barbiturates and benzodiazepines. *p. 299*
4. Compare the various opioids (opium, heroin, morphine). What problems may result from their use? *pp. 299–303*
5. List and compare two kinds of stimulant drugs. Describe their biological actions and the problems caused by each of them. *pp. 303–307*
6. What are the effects of hallucinogens, particularly LSD? *pp. 307–309*
7. What are the effects of marijuana and other cannabis substances? Why is marijuana a greater danger today than it was decades ago? *pp. 309–311*
8. What special problems does polysubstance use pose? *pp. 312–313*
9. Describe the leading explanations and treatments for substance use disorders. How well supported are these explanations and treatments? *pp. 313–325*
10. Why is gambling disorder categorized as an addictive disorder in DSM-5, alongside substance use disorder? *pp. 325–326*

Visit ***LaunchPad***
to access the e-Book, Clinical Choices, videos, activities, and LearningCurve, as well as study aids including flashcards, FAQs, and research exercises.

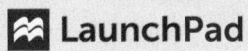

LaunchPad

0,90 m
DOUBLURE
2
1
4
ENVERS TISSU
0,90 m
4
ENVERS TISSU
0,90 m

CHAPTER 11

Sexual Disorders and Gender Variations

TOPIC OVERVIEW

Robert, a 57-year-old man, came to sex therapy with his wife because of his inability to get erections. He had not had a problem with erections until six months earlier, when they attempted to have sex after an evening out, during which he had had several drinks. They attributed his failure to get an erection to his being "a little drunk," but he found himself worrying over the next few days that he was perhaps becoming impotent. When they next attempted intercourse, he found himself unable to get involved in what they were doing because he was so intent on watching himself to see if he would get an erection. Once again he did not, and they were both very upset. His failure to get an erection continued over the next few months. Robert's wife was very upset and frustrated, accusing him of having an affair, or of no longer finding her attractive. Robert wondered if he was getting too old, or if his medication for high blood pressure, which he had been taking for about a year, might be interfering with erections. When they came for sex therapy, they had not attempted any sexual activity for over two months.

Sexual behavior is a major focus of both our private thoughts and public discussions. Sexual feelings are a crucial part of our development and daily functioning, sexual activity is tied to the satisfaction of our basic needs, and sexual performance is linked to our self-esteem. Most people are fascinated by the abnormal sexual behavior of others and worry about the normality of their own sexuality.

Experts recognize two general categories of sexual disorders: sexual dysfunctions and paraphilic disorders. People with *sexual dysfunctions* have problems with their sexual responses. Robert, for example, had a dysfunction known as erectile disorder, a repeated failure to attain or maintain an erection during sexual activity. People with *paraphilic disorders* have repeated and intense sexual urges or fantasies in response to objects or situations that society deems inappropriate, and they may behave inappropriately as well. They may be aroused by the thought of sexual activity with a child, for example, or of exposing their genitals to strangers, and they may act on those urges.

As you will see throughout this chapter, relatively little is known about racial and other cultural differences in sexuality. This is true for normal sexual patterns, sexual dysfunctions, and paraphilic disorders alike. Although different cultural groups have for years been labeled hypersexual, "hot blooded," exotic, passionate, submissive, and the like, such incorrect stereotypes have grown strictly from ignorance or prejudice, not from objective observations or research (McGoldrick et al., 2007). In fact, sex therapists and sex researchers have only recently begun to attend systematically to the importance of culture and race.

After examining the sexual disorders, this chapter will turn to a discussion of *variations in gender*, specifically *transgender* functioning. Transgender people have a sense that their *gender identity* (one's personal experience of one's gender) is different from the gender they were assigned at birth. DSM-5 does not consider such individuals to be abnormal; however, it does include a diagnostic category called *gender dysphoria*, a pattern in which individuals experience significant distress or impairment as a consequence of their transgender feelings. As you will see, the inclusion of this category in the DSM is controversial.

#SexualCensus

The World Health Organization estimates that around 115 million acts of sexual intercourse occur each day.

By convention, sexual disorders and issues of gender are often discussed in the same chapter, and we shall do the same in this chapter. At the same time, it is important to be clear that issues of sex are different from issues of gender. Sexual functioning refers to how one reacts and performs in the sexual realm, whereas gender identity is about whether one considers oneself male or female.

Sexual Dysfunctions

Sexual dysfunctions, disorders in which people cannot respond normally in key areas of sexual functioning, make it difficult or impossible to enjoy sexual intercourse. Studies suggest that as many as 30 percent of men and 45 percent of women around the world suffer from such a dysfunction during their lives (Cunningham & Rosen, 2018). Sexual dysfunctions are typically very distressing, and they often lead to sexual frustration, guilt, loss of self-esteem, and interpersonal problems. Often these dysfunctions are interrelated; many patients with one dysfunction have another as well. Sexual dysfunction is described here for heterosexual couples, the majority of couples seen in therapy. Gay and lesbian couples have the same dysfunctions, however, and therapists use the same basic techniques to treat them.

Rates for sexual behavior are typically based on population surveys. What factors might affect the accuracy of such surveys?

The human sexual response can be described as a *cycle* with four phases: *desire, excitement, orgasm,* and *resolution* (Shifren, 2018) (see **Figure 11-1** and **Figure 11-2**). Sexual dysfunctions affect one or more of the first three phases. Resolution consists simply of the relaxation and reduction in arousal that follow orgasm. Some people struggle with a sexual dysfunction their whole lives; in other cases, normal sexual functioning preceded the dysfunction. In some cases the dysfunction is present during all sexual situations; in others it is tied to particular situations (APA, 2013).

Disorders of Desire

The **desire phase** of the sexual response cycle consists of: an interest in or urge to have sex, sexual attraction to others, and for many people, sexual fantasies. Two dysfunctions affect the desire phase—*male hypoactive sexual desire disorder* and *female sexual interest/arousal disorder.* The latter disorder actually cuts across both the desire and excitement phases of the sexual response cycle. It is considered a single disorder

FIGURE 11-1

The Normal Sexual Response Cycle

Researchers have found a similar sequence of phases in both males and females. Sometimes, however, women do not experience orgasm; in that case, the resolution phase is less sudden. And sometimes women have two or more orgasms in succession before the resolution phase. (Information from: Kaplan, 1974; Masters & Johnson, 1970, 1966.)

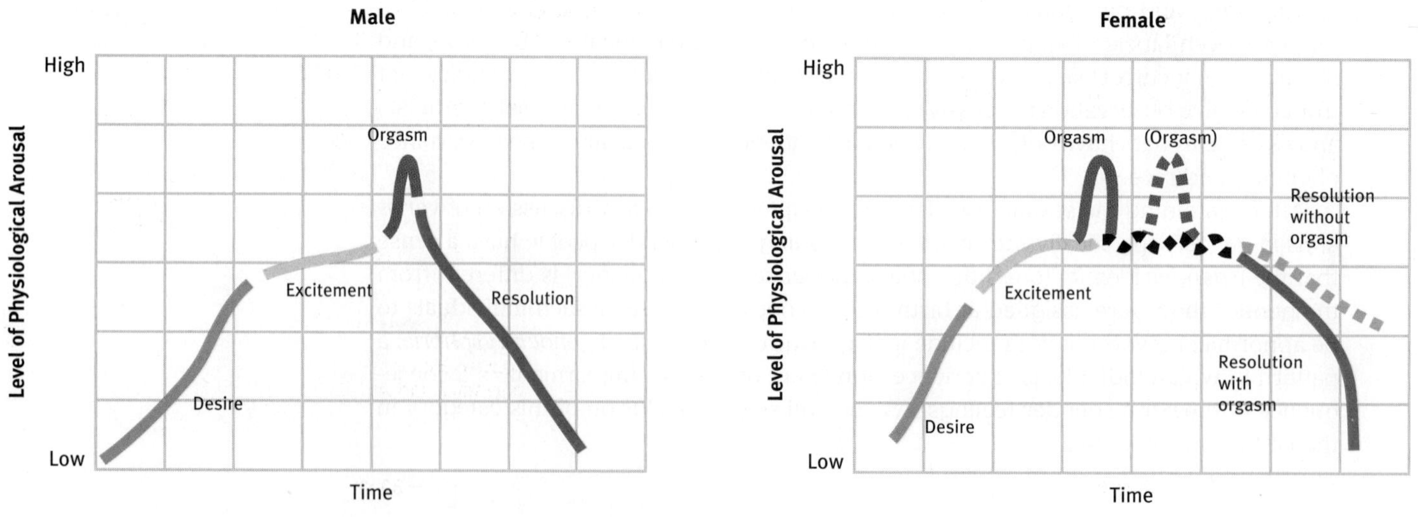

in DSM-5 because, according to research, desire and arousal overlap particularly highly for women, and many women express difficulty distinguishing feelings of desire from those of arousal (APA, 2013).

A number of people have normal sexual interest but choose, as a matter of lifestyle rather than sexual desire, to avoid engaging in sexual relations (see ***InfoCentral*** on page 333). These people are not diagnosed as having one of the sexual desire disorders.

Men with **male hypoactive sexual desire disorder** persistently lack or have reduced interest in sex and engage in little sexual activity (see **Table 11-1**). Nevertheless, when they do have sex, their physical responses may be normal and they may enjoy the experience. While most cultures portray men as wanting all the sex they can get, as many as 18 percent of men worldwide have this disorder, and the number seeking therapy has increased during the past decade (Cunningham & Rosen, 2018; Martin et al., 2014).

Women with **female sexual interest/arousal disorder** also lack normal interest in sex and rarely initiate sexual activity (see Table 11-1 again). In addition, many such women feel little excitement during sexual activity, are unaroused by erotic cues, and have few genital or nongenital sensations during sexual activity (APA, 2013). As many as 39 percent of women worldwide have reduced sexual interest and arousal (Shifren, 2018; Lewis et al., 2010). Around half of those individuals feel significant distress due to their level of arousal, and, as such, they qualify for a diagnosis of female sexual interest/arousal disorder. Note that many sex researchers and therapists believe it is inaccurate to combine desire and excitement symptoms into a single female disorder.

A person's sex drive is determined by a combination of biological, psychological, and sociocultural factors, any of which may reduce sexual desire (Roslan et al., 2017). Most cases of low sexual desire are caused primarily by sociocultural and psychological factors, but biological conditions can also lower sex drive significantly.

Biological Causes of Low Sexual Desire A number of hormones interact to help produce sexual desire and behavior, and abnormalities in their activity can lower a person's sex drive (Cunningham & Rosen, 2018; Shifren, 2018). In both men and women, a high level of the hormone *prolactin*, a low level of the male sex hormone *testosterone*, and either a high or low level of the female sex hormone *estrogen* can lead to low sex drive. Low sex drive has been linked to the high levels of estrogen contained in some birth control pills, for example. Conversely, it has also been tied to the low level of estrogen found in many postmenopausal women or women who have recently given birth.

Clinical practice and research have further indicated that sex drive can be lowered by certain pain medications, psychotropic drugs, and illegal drugs such as cocaine and heroin (Hirsch & Birnbaum, 2018, 2017). Low levels of alcohol may enhance the sex

sexual dysfunction A disorder marked by a persistent inability to function normally in some area of the sexual response cycle.

desire phase The phase of the sexual response cycle consisting of an urge to have sex, sexual fantasies, and sexual attraction to others.

male hypoactive sexual desire disorder A male dysfunction marked by a persistent reduction or lack of interest in sex and hence a low level of sexual activity.

female sexual interest/arousal disorder A female dysfunction marked by a persistent reduction or lack of interest in sex and low sexual activity, as well as, in some cases, limited excitement and few sexual sensations during sexual activity.

FIGURE 11-2

Normal Female Sexual Anatomy

Changes in the female anatomy take place during the different phases of the sexual response cycle. (Information from: Hyde, 1990, p. 200.)

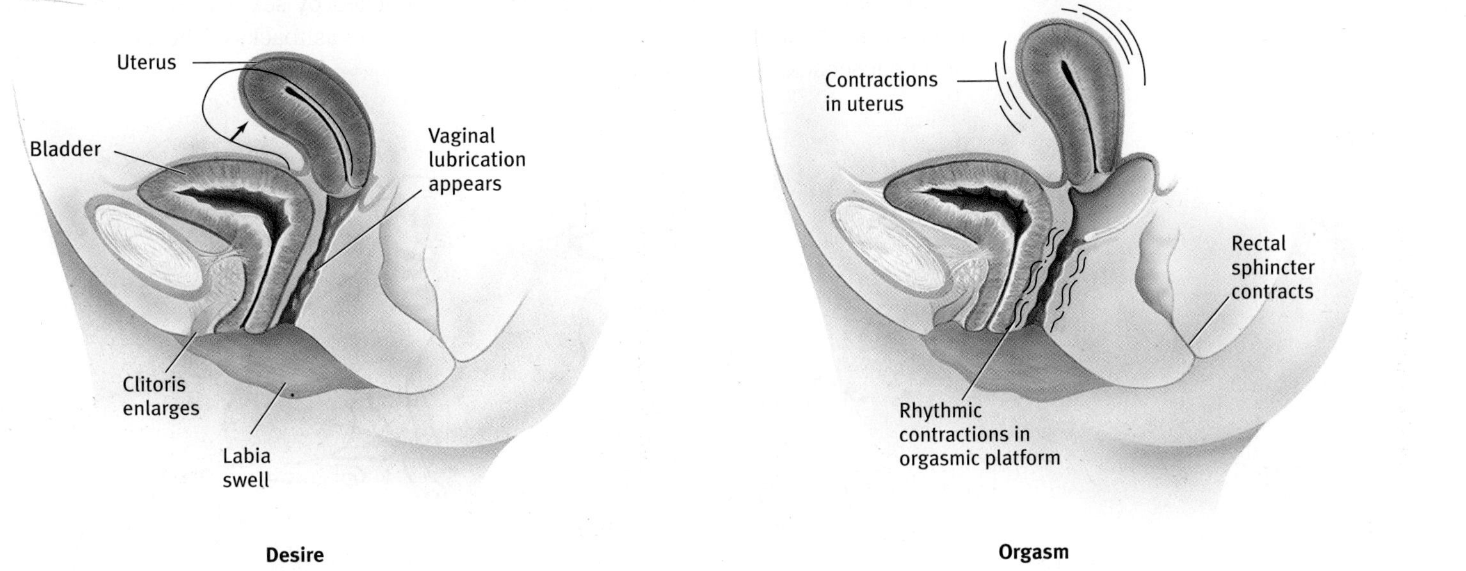

TABLE: 11-1

Dx Checklist

Male Hypoactive Sexual Desire Disorder
1. For at least 6 months, individual repeatedly experiences few or no sexual thoughts, fantasies, or desires.
2. Individual experiences significant distress about this.
Female Sexual Interest/Arousal Disorder
1. For at least 6 months, individual usually displays reduced or no sexual interest and arousal, characterized by the reduction or absence of at least three of the following: • Sexual interest • Sexual thought or fantasies • Sexual initiation or receptiveness • Excitement or pleasure during sex • Responsiveness to sexual cues • Genital or nongenital sensations during sex.
2. Individual experiences significant distress.

Information from: APA, 2013.

drive by lowering a person's inhibitions, but high levels may reduce it (Cunningham & Khera, 2018).

Long-term physical illness can also lower a person's sex drive (Cunningham & Rosen, 2018). The reduced drive may be a direct result of the illness or an indirect result because of stress, pain, or depression brought on by the illness.

Psychological Causes of Low Sexual Desire A general increase in anxiety, depression, or anger may reduce sexual desire in both men and women (Nimbi et al., 2018; Shifren, 2018). Frequently, as cognitive-behavioral theorists have noted, people with low sexual desire have particular attitudes, fears, or memories that contribute to their dysfunction, such as a belief that sex is immoral or dangerous (Nimbi et al., 2018). Other people are so afraid of losing control over their sexual urges that they try to resist them completely. And still others fear pregnancy.

Certain psychological disorders may also contribute to low sexual desire. Even a mild level of depression can interfere with sexual desire, and some people with obsessive-compulsive symptoms find contact with another person's body fluids and odors to be highly unpleasant (Cunningham & Rosen, 2018; Rubio-Aurioles & Bivalacqua, 2013).

Sociocultural Causes of Low Sexual Desire The attitudes, fears, and psychological disorders that contribute to low sexual desire occur within a social context, and thus certain sociocultural factors have also been linked to disorders of sexual desire. Many people who have low sexual desire are feeling situational pressures—divorce, a death in the family, job stress, infertility difficulties, having a baby (Shifren, 2018; Hamilton & Meston, 2013). Other people may be having problems in their relationships. People who are in an unhappy relationship, have lost affection for their partner, or feel powerless and dominated by their partner can lose interest in sex. Even in basically happy relationships, if one partner is a very unskilled, unenthusiastic lover, the other can begin to lose interest in sex (Cunningham & Rosen, 2018; Jiann, Su, & Tsai, 2013). And sometimes partners differ in their needs for closeness. The one who needs more personal space may develop low sexual desire as a way of keeping distance.

Cultural standards can also set the stage for low sexual desire. Some men adopt our culture's double standard and thus cannot feel sexual desire for a woman they love and respect (Nimbi et al., 2018; Antfolk, 2017). More generally, because our society equates sexual attractiveness with youthfulness, many middle-aged and older men and women lose interest in sex as their self-image or their attraction to their partner diminishes with age.

The trauma of sexual molestation or assault is especially likely to produce the fears, attitudes, and memories found in disorders of sexual desire (Shifren, 2018; Giraldi et al., 2013). Some survivors of sexual abuse may feel repelled by sex, sometimes for years, even decades. In some cases, survivors may have vivid flashbacks of the assault during adult consensual sexual activity.

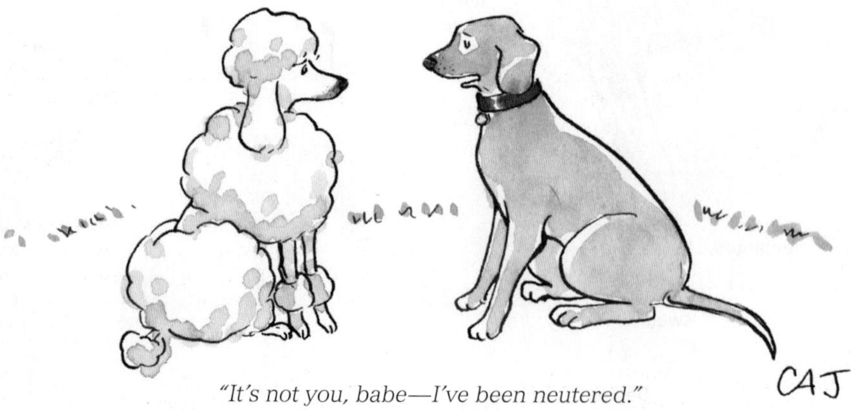

"It's not you, babe—I've been neutered."

SEX THROUGHOUT THE LIFE CYCLE

Sexual dysfunctions are different from the usual patterns of sexual functioning. But in the sexual realm, what is "the usual?" Studies conducted over the past two decades have provided a wealth of enlightening information about sexual behavior in the "normal" populations of North America. As you might expect, sexual behavior often differs by age and by gender.

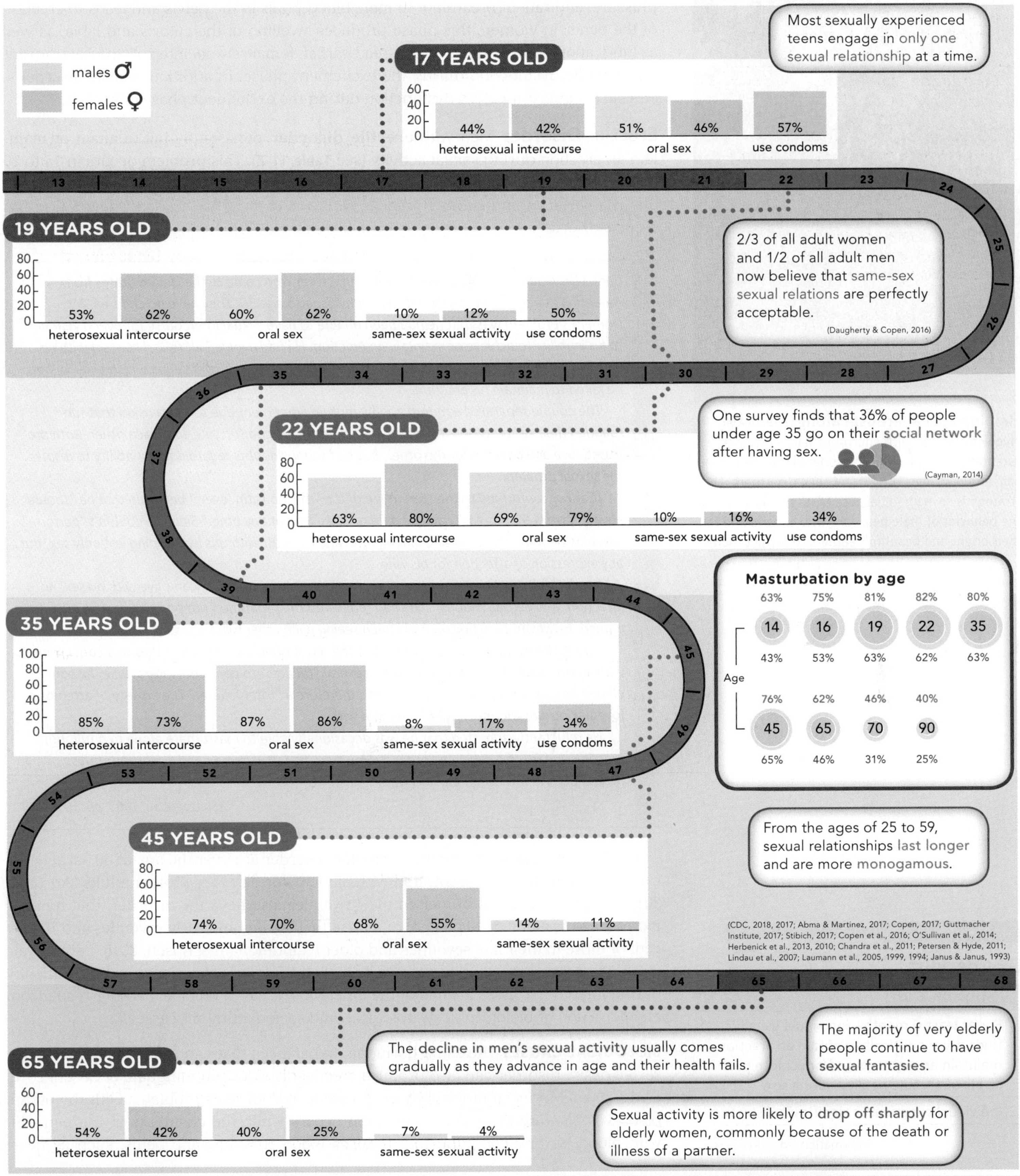

Adrian Lourie/Evening Standard/Redux

Helping sexual arousal along *Peacocking* involves dressing with enormous flair—often in ostentatious ways with accessories like scarves, dyed hair, and piercings—to attract sexual partners. The strategy is so-named because of its similarity to the behavior of male peacocks who expand and fan their bright and beautiful feathers to attract mates.

Disorders of Excitement

The **excitement phase** of the sexual response cycle is marked by changes in the pelvic region, general physical arousal, and increases in heart rate, muscle tension, blood pressure, and rate of breathing. In men, blood pools in the pelvis and leads to erection of the penis; in women, this phase produces swelling of the clitoris and labia, as well as lubrication of the vagina. As you read earlier, female sexual interest/arousal disorder may include dysfunction during the excitement phase. In addition, a male disorder—*erectile disorder*—involves dysfunction during the excitement phase only.

Erectile Disorder Men with **erectile disorder** persistently fail to attain or maintain an erection during sexual activity (see **Table 11-2**). This problem occurs in 15 to 25 percent of the male population, including Robert, the man whose difficulties opened this chapter (Cunningham & Rosen, 2018; Lewis et al., 2010). Carlos Domera also has erectile disorder:

> *Carlos Domera is a 30-year-old dress manufacturer who came to the United States from Argentina at age 22. He is married to . . . Phyllis, also age 30. They have no children. Mr. Domera's problem was that he had been unable to have sexual intercourse for over a year due to his inability to achieve or maintain an erection. He had avoided all sexual contact with his wife for the prior five months, except for two brief attempts at lovemaking which ended when he failed to maintain his erection.*
>
> *The couple separated a month ago by mutual agreement due to the tension that surrounded their sexual problem and their inability to feel comfortable with each other. Both professed love and concern for the other, but had serious doubts regarding their ability to resolve the sexual problem. . . .*
>
> *[Carlos] conformed to the stereotype of the "macho Latin lover," believing that he "should always have erections easily and be able to make love at any time." Since he couldn't "perform" sexually, he felt humiliated and inadequate, and he dealt with this by avoiding not only sex, but any expression of affection for his wife.*
>
> *[Phyllis] felt "he is not trying; perhaps he doesn't love me, and I can't live with no sex, no affection, and his bad moods." She had requested the separation temporarily, and he readily agreed. However, they had recently been seeing each other twice a week. . . .*
>
> *During the evaluation he reported that the onset of his erectile difficulties was concurrent with a tense period in his business. After several "failures" to complete intercourse, he concluded he was "useless as a husband" and therefore a "total failure." The anxiety of attempting lovemaking was too much for him to deal with.*
>
> *He reluctantly admitted that he was occasionally able to masturbate alone to a full, firm erection and reach a satisfying orgasm. However, he felt ashamed and guilty about this . . . feeling that he was "cheating" his wife.*
>
> *(Spitzer et al., 1983, pp. 105–106)*

Unlike Carlos, most men with an erectile disorder are over the age of 50, largely because so many cases are associated with ailments or diseases of older adults (Agronin, 2017). Around 7 percent of men in their twenties also have the disorder; that number increases to as many as 40 percent of men in their sixties and early seventies and 70 percent of those in their late seventies and older (Cunningham & Rosen, 2018; Lewis et al., 2010). Moreover, according to surveys, half of all adult men experience erectile difficulty during intercourse at least some of the time. Most cases of erectile disorder result from an interaction of biological, psychological, and sociocultural processes.

BIOLOGICAL CAUSES The same hormonal imbalances that can cause male hypoactive sexual desire disorder can also produce erectile disorder (Cunningham & Rosen, 2018; Hyde, 2005). More commonly, however, vascular problems—problems with the body's blood vessels—are involved. An erection occurs when the chambers in the penis fill with blood, so any condition that reduces blood flow into the penis, such as heart

TABLE: 11-2

Dx Checklist

Erectile Disorder
1. For at least 6 months, individual usually finds it very difficult to obtain an erection, maintain an erection, and/or achieve past levels of erectile rigidity during sex.
2. Individual experiences significant distress.

Information from: APA, 2013.

disease or clogging of the arteries, may lead to erectile disorder (Hackett et al., 2018). It can also be caused by damage to the nervous system as a result of diabetes, spinal cord injuries, multiple sclerosis, kidney failure, or treatment by dialysis (Gigante et al., 2018; Goldstein et al., 2018). In addition, as is the case with male hypoactive sexual desire disorder, the use of certain medications and various forms of substance abuse, from alcohol abuse to cigarette smoking, may interfere with erections (Hirsch & Birnbaum, 2018, 2017; Mazzilli et al., 2018).

Medical procedures, including ultrasound recordings and blood tests, have been developed for diagnosing biological causes of erectile disorder. Measuring *nocturnal penile tumescence (NPT)*, or erections during sleep, is particularly useful in assessing whether physical factors are responsible. Men typically have erections during *rapid eye movement (REM) sleep*, the phase of sleep in which dreaming takes place. A healthy man is likely to have two to five REM periods each night, and several penile erections as well. Abnormal or absent nightly erections usually (but not always) indicate some physical basis for erectile failure. As a rough screening device, a patient may be instructed to fasten a simple "snap gauge" band around his penis before going to sleep and then check it the next morning. A broken band indicates that he has had an erection during the night. An unbroken band indicates that he did not have nighttime erections and suggests that his general erectile problem may have a physical basis. A newer version of this device further attaches the band to a computer, which provides precise measurements of erections throughout the night (Li et al., 2017).

PSYCHOLOGICAL CAUSES Any of the psychological causes of male hypoactive sexual desire disorder can also interfere with arousal and lead to erectile disorder. As many as 90 percent of all men with severe depression, for example, experience some degree of erectile dysfunction (Cunningham & Rosen, 2018; Montejo et al., 2011).

One well-supported psychological explanation for erectile disorder is the cognitive-behavioral theory developed by William Masters and Virginia Johnson (1970). The explanation emphasizes **performance anxiety** and the **spectator role.** Once a man begins to have erectile problems, for whatever reason, he becomes fearful about failing to have an erection and worries during each sexual encounter (Johnson, 2018). Instead of relaxing and enjoying the sensations of sexual pleasure, he remains distanced from the activity, watching himself and focusing on the goal of reaching erection. Instead of being an aroused participant, he becomes a judge and spectator. Whatever the initial reason for the erectile dysfunction, the resulting spectator role becomes the reason

excitement phase The phase of the sexual response cycle marked by changes in the pelvic region, general physical arousal, and increases in heart rate, muscle tension, blood pressure, and rate of breathing.

erectile disorder A dysfunction in which a man repeatedly fails to attain or maintain an erection during sexual activity.

performance anxiety The fear of performing inadequately and a related tension that are experienced during sex.

spectator role A state of mind that some people experience during sex, focusing on their sexual performance to such an extent that their performance and their enjoyment are reduced.

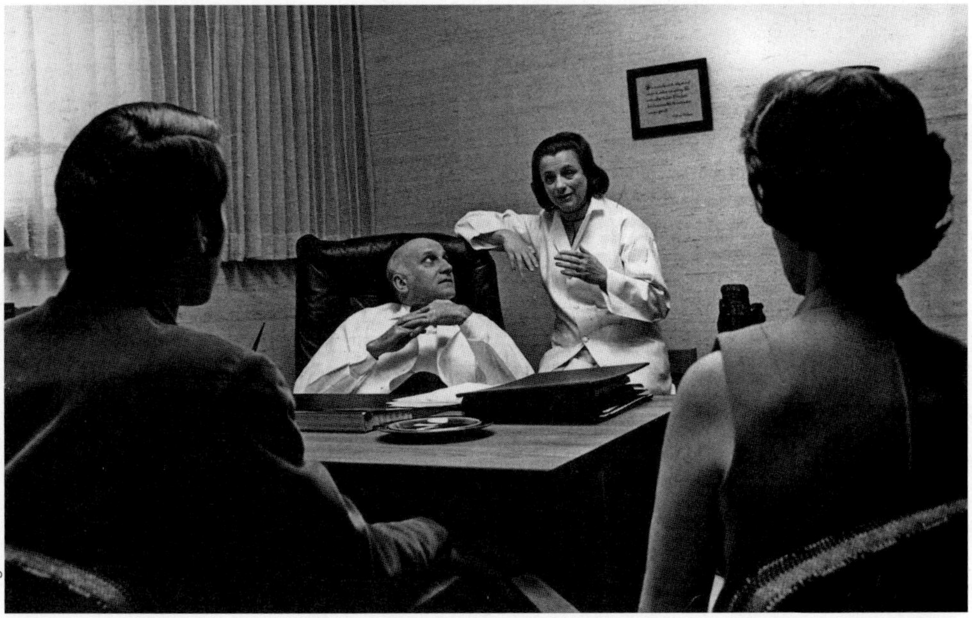

Sexual pioneers William Masters and Virginia Johnson work with a couple in their office. The two researchers, the field's most important figures in the study of the human sexual response and the treatment of sexual dysfunctions, conducted their work from 1967 until the 1990s, writing two classic books, *Human Sexual Response* and *Human Sexual Inadequacy.*

orgasm phase The phase of the sexual response cycle during which a person's sexual pleasure peaks and sexual tension is released as muscles in the pelvic region contract rhythmically.

premature ejaculation A dysfunction in which a man persistently reaches orgasm and ejaculates within 1 minute of beginning sexual activity with a partner and before he wishes to. Also called *early* or *rapid* ejaculation.

delayed ejaculation A male dysfunction characterized by persistent inability to ejaculate or very delayed ejaculations during sexual activity with a partner.

for the ongoing problem. In this vicious cycle, the original cause of the erectile failure becomes less important than fear of failure.

SOCIOCULTURAL CAUSES Each of the sociocultural factors that contribute to male hypoactive sexual desire disorder has also been tied to erectile disorder. Men who have lost their jobs and are under financial stress, for example, are more likely to develop erectile difficulties than other men (Nobre, 2017). Marital stress, too, has been tied to this dysfunction (Cunningham & Rosen, 2018; LoPiccolo, 2004, 1991).

Disorders of Orgasm

During the **orgasm phase** of the sexual response cycle, a person's sexual pleasure peaks and sexual tension is released as the muscles in the pelvic region contract, or draw together, rhythmically (see **Figure 11-3**). The man's semen is ejaculated, and the outer third of the woman's vaginal wall contracts. Dysfunctions of this phase of the sexual response cycle are *early ejaculation* and *delayed ejaculation* in men and *female orgasmic disorder* in women.

Premature Ejaculation Eduardo is typical of many men in his experience of premature ejaculation:

> *Eduardo, a 20-year-old student, sought treatment after his girlfriend ended their relationship because his premature ejaculation left her sexually frustrated. Eduardo had had only one previous sexual relationship, during his senior year in high school. With two friends he would drive to a neighboring town and find a certain prostitute. After picking her up, they would drive to a deserted area and take turns having sex with her, while the others waited outside the car. Both the prostitute and his friends urged him to hurry up because they feared discovery by the police, and besides, in the winter it was cold. When Eduardo began his sexual relationship with his girlfriend, his entire sexual history consisted of this rapid intercourse, with virtually no foreplay. He found caressing his girlfriend's breasts and genitals and her touching of his penis to be so arousing that he sometimes ejaculated before complete entry of the penis, or after at most only a minute or so of intercourse.*

A man suffering from **premature ejaculation** (also called *early,* or *rapid,* ejaculation) persistently reaches orgasm and ejaculates within 1 minute of beginning sexual activity with a partner and before he wishes to (see **Table 11-3**). As many as 30 percent

FIGURE 11-3

Normal Male Sexual Anatomy

Changes in the male anatomy occur during the different phases of the sexual response cycle. (Information from: Hyde, 1990, p. 199.)

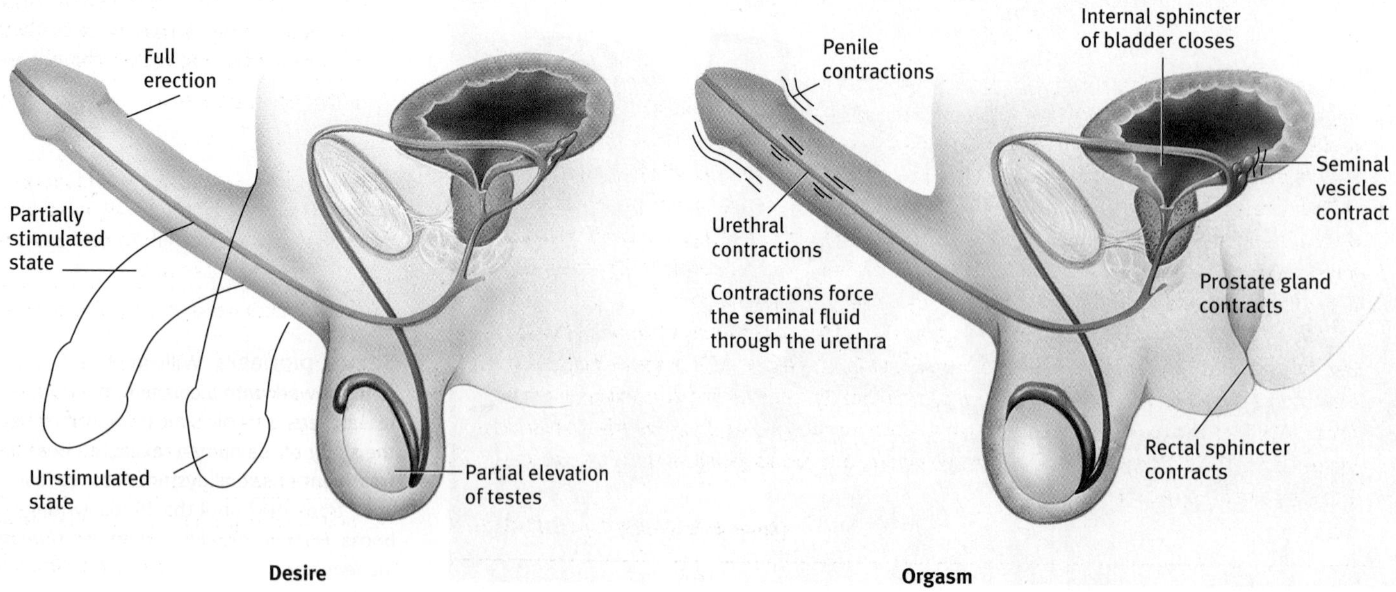

of men worldwide ejaculate early at some time (Cunningham & Rosen, 2018; Lewis et al., 2010). The typical duration of intercourse in our society has increased over the past several decades, which has caused more distress among men who ejaculate prematurely. Although many young men certainly contend with the dysfunction, research suggests that men of any age may suffer from it (Canat et al., 2018).

Psychological, particularly cognitive-behavioral, explanations of premature ejaculation have received more research support than other kinds of explanations. The dysfunction is common, for example, among young, sexually inexperienced men such as Eduardo, who simply have not learned to slow down, control their arousal, and extend the pleasurable process of making love (Cunningham & Rosen, 2018; Althof, 2007). In fact, young men often ejaculate prematurely during their first sexual encounter. With continued sexual experience, most men acquire more control over their sexual responses. Men of any age who have infrequent sex are also prone to ejaculate early.

"Well, how convenient."

Clinicians have also suggested that premature ejaculation may be related to anxiety, hurried masturbation experiences during adolescence (in fear of being "caught" by parents), or poor recognition of one's own sexual arousal. However, these theories have only sometimes received clear research support.

There is a growing belief among many clinical theorists that biological factors may also play a key role in many cases of premature ejaculation. Three biological theories have emerged from the limited investigations done so far. One theory states that some men are born with a genetic predisposition to develop this dysfunction. Indeed, one study found that 91 percent of a small sample of men suffering from early ejaculation had first-degree relatives who also had the dysfunction. A second theory, based on animal studies, argues that the brains of men who ejaculate prematurely contain certain serotonin receptors that are overactive and others that are underactive. A third explanation holds that men with this dysfunction have greater sensitivity or nerve conduction in the area of their penis, a notion that has received inconsistent research support thus far (Roaiah et al., 2018; Guo et al., 2017).

Delayed Ejaculation A man with **delayed ejaculation** (previously called *male orgasmic disorder* or *inhibited male orgasm*) persistently is unable to ejaculate or has very delayed ejaculations during sexual activity with a partner (see Table 11-3 again). As many as 10 percent of men worldwide have this disorder (Morgentaler et al., 2017; Lewis et al., 2010). It is typically a source of great frustration and upset, as in the case of John:

> *John, a 38-year-old sales representative, had been married for 9 years. At the insistence of his 32-year-old wife, the couple sought counseling for their sexual problem—his inability to ejaculate during intercourse. During the early years of the marriage, his wife had experienced difficulty reaching orgasm until he learned to delay his ejaculation for a long period of time. To do this, he used mental distraction techniques and regularly smoked marijuana before making love. Initially, John felt very satisfied that he could make love for longer and longer periods of time without ejaculation and regarded his ability as a sign of masculinity.*
>
> *About 3 years prior to seeking counseling, after the birth of their only child, John found that he was losing his erection before he was able to ejaculate. His wife suggested different intercourse positions, but the harder he tried, the more difficulty he had in reaching orgasm. Because of his frustration, the couple began to avoid sex altogether. John experienced increasing performance anxiety with each successive failure, and an increasing sense of helplessness in the face of his problem.*
>
> *(Rosen & Rosen, 1981, pp. 317–318)*

TABLE: 11-3

Dx Checklist

Premature Ejaculation
1. For at least 6 months, individual usually ejaculates within 1 minute of beginning sex with a partner, and earlier than he wants to.
2. Individual experiences significant distress.
Delayed Ejaculation
1. For at least 6 months, individual usually displays a significant delay, infrequency, or absence of ejaculation during sexual activity with a partner.
2. Individual experiences significant distress.
Female Orgasmic Disorder
1. For at least 6 months, individual usually displays a significant delay, infrequency, or absence of orgasm, and/or is unable to achieve past orgasmic intensity.
2. Individual experiences significant distress.

Information from: APA, 2013.

#GoingNegative

People who are totally unable to find sexual partners sometimes refer to themselves as *incels* ("involuntary celibates"). The number of incel forums on the Internet has grown over the past two decades, as has the mysogynistic and threatening rhetoric of some incels—a subgroup of individuals who contend they are being unfairly deprived of sex and who even endorse violence against sexually active women and men. As a result, this once-supportive online movement has been banned by numerous Web sites.

A low testosterone level, certain neurological diseases, and some head or spinal cord injuries can interfere with ejaculation (Abdel-Hamid & Ali, 2018). Substances that slow down the sympathetic nervous system (such as alcohol, some medications for high blood pressure, and certain psychotropic medications) can also affect ejaculation. For example, certain serotonin-enhancing antidepressant drugs appear to interfere with ejaculation in at least 30 percent of men who take them (Hirsch & Birnbaum, 2018, 2017).

A leading psychological cause of delayed ejaculation appears to be performance anxiety and the spectator role, the cognitive-behavioral factors also involved in erectile disorder (Nimbi et al., 2018). Once a man begins to focus on reaching orgasm, he may stop being an aroused participant in his sexual activity and instead become an unaroused, self-critical, and fearful observer. Another psychological cause of delayed ejaculation may be past masturbation habits. If, for example, a man has masturbated all his life by rubbing his penis against sheets, pillows, or other such objects, he may have difficulty reaching orgasm in the absence of the sensations tied to those objects (Wincze et al., 2008). Finally, delayed ejaculation may develop out of male hypoactive sexual desire disorder. A man who engages in sex without any real desire for it may not get aroused enough to ejaculate.

Are there other problem areas in life that might also be explained by performance anxiety and the spectator role?

Female Orgasmic Disorder Janel and Isaac, married for 3 years, went for sex therapy because of her lack of orgasm.

> *Janel had never had an orgasm in any way, but because of Isaac's concern, she had been faking orgasm during intercourse until recently. Finally she told him the truth, and they sought therapy together. Janel had been raised by a strictly religious family. She could not recall ever seeing her parents kiss or show physical affection for each other. She was severely punished on one occasion when her mother found her looking at her own genitals, at about age 7. Janel received no sex education from her parents, and when she began to menstruate, her mother told her only that this meant that she could become pregnant, so she mustn't ever kiss a boy or let a boy touch her. Her mother restricted her dating severely, with repeated warnings that "boys only want one thing." While her parents were rather critical and demanding of her (asking her why she got one B among otherwise straight A's on her report card, for example), they were loving parents and their approval was very important to her.*

Women with **female orgasmic disorder** persistently fail to reach orgasm, have very low intensity orgasms, or have a very delayed orgasm (see Table 11-3 again). Around 21 percent of women apparently experience this pattern to some degree (Shifren, 2018; Bradford, 2017). Studies indicate that 10 percent or more of women have never had an orgasm, either alone or during intercourse, and at least another 9 percent rarely have orgasms. In one study, when participants with female orgasmic disorder were asked to pick a word that best describes their feelings about it, two-thirds of them chose "frustration" (Kingsberg et al., 2013).

Around 50 to 70 percent of all women experience orgasm in intercourse at least fairly regularly (Frederick et al., 2018; Bancroft et al., 2003). Women who are more sexually assertive tend to have orgasms more regularly. At the same time, most clinicians agree that orgasm during intercourse is not mandatory for normal sexual functioning (Shifren, 2018). Many women instead reach orgasm with their partners by direct stimulation of the clitoris. Although early psychoanalytic theory considered a lack of orgasm during intercourse to be pathological, evidence suggests that women who rely on stimulation of the clitoris for orgasm are entirely normal and healthy (Bradford, 2017; Laan et al., 2013). It is important to note that a number of clinicians further believe that the achievement of orgasm, under any circumstance, is not a defining feature of an acceptable and normal sex life (Shifren, 2018).

female orgasmic disorder A dysfunction in which a woman persistently fails to reach orgasm, has very low intensity orgasms, or has very delayed orgasms.

Biological, psychological, and sociocultural factors may combine to produce female orgasmic disorder. Because arousal plays a key role in orgasms, arousal difficulties often are featured prominently in explanations of female orgasmic disorder.

BIOLOGICAL CAUSES A variety of physiological conditions can affect a woman's orgasm. Diabetes can damage the nervous system in ways that interfere with arousal, lubrication of the vagina, and orgasm. Lack of orgasm has sometimes been linked to multiple sclerosis and other neurological diseases, to the same drugs and medications that may interfere with ejaculation in men, and to changes, often postmenopausal, in skin sensitivity and structure of the clitoris, vaginal walls, or the labia—the folds of skin on each side of the vagina (Hirsch & Birnbaum, 2018, 2017).

PSYCHOLOGICAL CAUSES Research suggests that women with a high level of *sexual inhibition* are particularly likely to experience female orgasmic disorder (Tavares, Laan, & Nobre, 2018). These individuals worry greatly about their sexual performance, have related negative thoughts about it, and are easily distracted during sexual activity.

More generally, the psychological causes of female sexual interest/arousal disorder, including depression, may also lead to female orgasmic disorder (Bradford, 2017). In addition, as both psychodynamic and cognitive theorists might predict, memories of childhood traumas and relationships have sometimes been associated with orgasm problems (Carpenter et al., 2017). In various studies, childhood memories of a dependable father, a positive relationship with one's mother, affection between the parents, the mother's positive personality, and the mother's expression of positive emotions were all predictors of positive orgasm outcomes (Heiman, 2007).

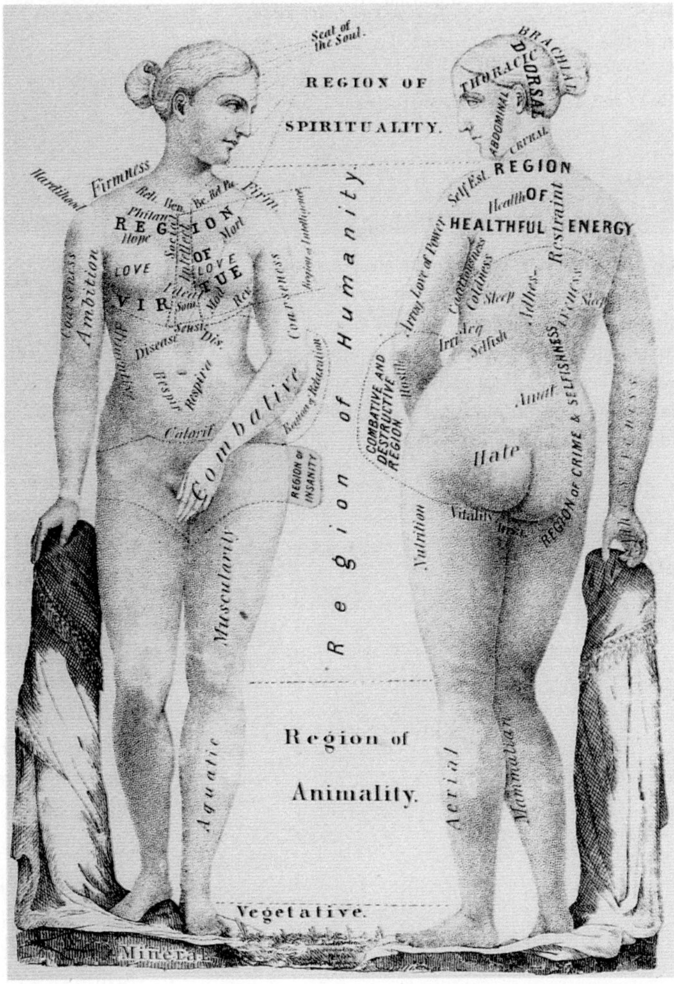

From Joseph R. Buchanan, Outlines of Lectures on the Neurological System of Anthropology, Cincinnati, 1854. The Oskar Diethelm Library, Department of Psychiatry, Cornell University Medical College and The New York Hospital, New York

"The region of insanity" Medical authorities described "excessive passion" in Victorian women as dangerous and as a possible cause of insanity (Gamwell & Tomes, 1995). This illustration from a nineteenth-century medical textbook even labels a woman's reproductive organs as her "region of insanity."

SOCIOCULTURAL CAUSES For years many clinicians have believed that female orgasmic problems may result from society's recurrent message to women that they should repress and deny their sexuality, a message that has often led to "less permissive" sexual attitudes and behavior among women than among men. In fact, many women with both arousal and orgasmic difficulties report that they had an overly strict religious upbringing, were punished for childhood masturbation, received no preparation for the onset of menstruation, were restricted in their dating as teenagers, and were told that "nice girls don't" (Bradford, 2017; Laan et al., 2013).

A sexually restrictive history, however, is just as common among women who function well during sexual activity (LoPiccolo, 2002). In addition, cultural messages about female sexuality have been more positive in recent years, while the rate of arousal and orgasmic problems remains the same for women. Why, then, do some women and not others develop such problems? Researchers suggest that unusually stressful events or traumas may help produce the fears, memories, and attitudes that often characterize these sexual problems (Carpenter et al., 2017; Meana, 2012). For example, many women molested as children or raped as adults have female orgasmic disorder (Hall, 2017, 2007).

Some theorists believe that the women's movement has helped to enlighten clinical views of sexual disorders. How might this be so?

Research has also related orgasmic behavior to certain qualities in a woman's intimate relationships (Bradford, 2017; Kingsberg et al., 2017). Studies have found, for example, that the likelihood of reaching orgasm may be tied to how much emotional involvement and pleasure a woman had during her first experience of intercourse, her current attraction to her partner's body, and her relationship happiness. Interestingly,

AP Photo/Shuji Kajiyama

Grooming is key Humans are not the only animals that follow a sexual response cycle or, for that matter, display sexual dysfunctions. Here a male macaque monkey grooms a female monkey while they sit in a hot spring in the snow in central Japan. Such grooming triples the likelihood that the female will engage in sexual activity with the male.

the same studies have found that orgasmic women more often have erotic fantasies during sex with their current partner than do nonorgasmic women.

Disorders of Sexual Pain

Certain sexual dysfunctions are characterized by enormous physical discomfort during intercourse, a difficulty that does not fit neatly into a specific part of the sexual response cycle. Women have such dysfunctions, collectively called **genito-pelvic pain/penetration disorder,** much more often than men do (Kingsberg & Spadt, 2018; Hellstrom & DeLay, 2017).

For some women with genito-pelvic pain/penetration disorder the muscles around the outer third of the vagina involuntarily contract, preventing entry of the penis (see **Table 11-4**). This problem, known in medical circles as *vaginismus,* can prevent a couple from ever having intercourse. The problem has received relatively little research, but estimates are that fewer than 1 percent of all women have vaginismus (Barbieri, 2017; Christensen et al., 2011). A number of women with vaginismus enjoy sex greatly, have a strong sex drive, and reach orgasm with stimulation of the clitoris (Meana et al., 2017). They just fear the discomfort of penetration of the vagina.

Most clinicians agree with the cognitive-behavioral position that this form of genito-pelvic pain/penetration disorder is usually a learned fear response, set off by a woman's expectation that intercourse will be painful and damaging (Meana et al., 2017; Fugl-Meyer et al., 2013). Alternatively, women may have this form of genito-pelvic pain/penetration disorder because of an infection of the vagina or urinary tract, a gynecological disease such as herpes simplex, or the physical effects of menopause (Kingsberg & Spadt, 2018; Barbieri, 2017). In such cases, the dysfunction can be overcome only if the women receive medical treatment for these conditions.

Other women with genito-pelvic pain/penetration disorder do not have involuntary contractions of their vaginal muscles, but they do experience severe vaginal or pelvic pain during sexual intercourse, a pattern known medically as *dyspareunia* (from Greek words meaning "painful mating"). Surveys suggest that 14 to 16 percent of all women (and 40 percent of all postmenopausal women) suffer from this problem to some degree (Kingsberg & Spadt, 2018; Shifren, 2018). Women with dyspareunia typically enjoy sex and get aroused but find their sex lives very limited by the pain that accompanies what used to be a positive event (Meana et al., 2017).

This form of genito-pelvic pain/penetration disorder usually has a physical cause (Kingsberg & Spadt, 2018). Among the most common is an injury (for example, to the vagina or pelvic ligaments) during childbirth. The scar left by an episiotomy (a cut often made to enlarge the vaginal entrance and ease delivery) also can cause pain. Around 16 percent of women have severe vaginal or pelvic pain during intercourse for up to a year after giving birth (Bertozzi et al., 2010). More generally, such pain has also been tied to the penis colliding with remaining parts of the hymen, vaginal infections, wiry pubic hair rubbing against the labia during intercourse, pelvic diseases, tumors, cysts, allergic reactions to the chemicals in vaginal douches and contraceptive creams, the rubber in condoms and diaphragms, and the protein in semen. Although psychological factors (for instance, heightened anxiety or overattentiveness to one's body) or relationship problems may contribute to dyspareunia, psychosocial factors alone are rarely responsible for it (Kingsberg & Spadt, 2018). It also is the case that 1 to 5 percent of men suffer from pain in the genitals during intercourse, and many of these men also qualify for a diagnosis of genito-pelvic pain/penetration disorder (Hellstrom & DeLay, 2017).

TABLE: 11-4

Dx Checklist

Genito-Pelvic Pain/Penetration Disorder
1. For at least 6 months, individual repeatedly experiences at least one of the following problems: • Difficulty having vaginal penetration during intercourse • Significant vaginal or pelvic pain when trying to have intercourse or penetration • Significant fear that vaginal penetration will cause vaginal or pelvic pain • Significant tensing of the pelvic muscles during vaginal penetration.
2. Individual experiences significant distress from this.

Information from: APA, 2013.

9... SUMMING UP

SEXUAL DYSFUNCTIONS Sexual dysfunctions make it difficult or impossible for a person to have or enjoy sexual activity.

DSM-5 lists two disorders of the desire phase of the sexual response cycle: male hypoactive sexual desire disorder and female sexual interest/arousal disorder. Men with the former disorder persistently lack or have reduced interest in sex and, in turn, engage in little sexual activity. Women with the latter disorder lack normal interest in sex, rarely initiate sexual activity, and may also feel little excitement during sexual activity or in the presence of erotic cues. Biological causes for these disorders include abnormal hormone levels, certain drugs, and some medical illnesses. Psychological and sociocultural causes include specific fears, situational pressures, relationship problems, and the trauma of having been sexually molested or assaulted.

Disorders of the excitement phase include erectile disorder, a repeated inability to attain or maintain an erection during sexual activity. Biological causes of erectile disorder include abnormal hormone levels, vascular problems, medical conditions, and certain medications. Psychological and sociocultural causes include the combination of performance anxiety and the spectator role, situational pressures such as job loss, and relationship problems.

Premature ejaculation, a disorder of the orgasm phase, has been attributed most often to cognitive-behavioral causes, such as inappropriate early learning and inexperience. Delayed ejaculation, a repeated absence of or long delay in reaching orgasm, can have biological causes, such as low testosterone levels, neurological diseases, and certain drugs, and psychological causes, such as performance anxiety and the spectator role. Female orgasmic disorder has been tied to biological causes such as medical diseases and changes that occur after menopause, psychological causes such as memories of childhood traumas, and sociocultural causes such as relationship problems.

Genito-pelvic pain/penetration disorder involves significant pain during intercourse. In one form of this disorder, vaginismus, involuntary contractions of the muscles around the outer third of the vagina prevent entry of the penis. In another form, dyspareunia, the person has severe vaginal or pelvic pain during intercourse. This form of the disorder typically has a physical cause, such as injury resulting from childbirth.

genito-pelvic pain/penetration disorder A sexual dysfunction characterized by significant physical discomfort during intercourse.

Treatments for Sexual Dysfunctions

The last 40 years have brought major changes in the treatment of sexual dysfunctions. A revolution in the treatment of sexual dysfunctions took place with the publication of William Masters and Virginia Johnson's landmark book *Human Sexual Inadequacy* in 1970. The *sex therapy* program they introduced has evolved into a complex approach, which now includes interventions from the various models, particularly cognitive-behavioral, couple, and family systems therapies (Avery-Clark & Weiner, 2017). The goal of sex therapy is to help clients function better sexually and to achieve a higher level of sexual satisfaction and psychological well-being (Peterson, 2017). In recent years, biological interventions, particularly drug therapies, have been added to the treatment arsenal (McCarthy & Wald, 2017).

What Are the General Features of Sex Therapy?

Modern sex therapy is short-term and instructive, typically lasting 15 to 20 sessions. It centers on specific sexual problems rather than on broad personality issues (Peterson, 2017). Carlos Domera, the Argentinian man with erectile disorder whom you met earlier, responded successfully to the multiple techniques of modern sex therapy:

#

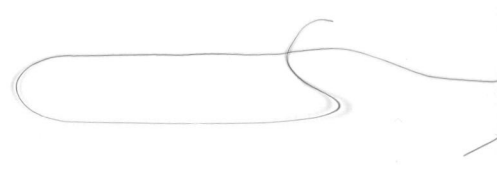

Self-Satisfaction

A large Finnish study found that half of all male and female participants were satisfied with the appearance of their genitals and, in the case of women, of their breasts (Ålgars et al., 2011).

#TheirWords

"Some nights he said that he was tired, and some nights she said that she wanted to read, and other nights no one said anything."

Joan Didion, *Play It as It Lays*

At the end of the evaluation session the psychiatrist reassured the couple that Mr. Domera had a "reversible psychological" sexual problem that was due to several factors, including his depression, but also more currently his anxiety and embarrassment, his high standards, and some cultural and relationship difficulties that made communication awkward and relaxation nearly impossible. The couple was advised that a brief trial of therapy, focused directly on the sexual problem, would very likely produce significant improvement within ten to fourteen sessions. . . .

[T]he couple agreed to commence the therapy on a weekly basis, and they were given a typical first "assignment" to do at home: a caressing massage exercise to try together with specific instructions not to attempt genital stimulation or intercourse at all, even if an erection might occur.

Not surprisingly, during the second session Mr. Domera reported with a cautious smile that they had "cheated" and had had intercourse "against the rules." This was their first successful intercourse in more than a year. Their success and happiness were acknowledged by the therapist, but they were cautioned strongly that rapid initial improvement often occurs, only to be followed by increased performance anxiety in subsequent weeks and a return of the initial problem. They were . . . encouraged to try again to have sexual contact involving caressing and nondemand light genital stimulation, without an expectation of erection or orgasm, and to avoid intercourse.

During the second and fourth weeks [Carlos] did not achieve erections during the love play, and the therapy sessions dealt with helping him to accept himself with or without erections and to learn to enjoy sensual contact without intercourse. His wife helped him to believe genuinely that he could please her with manual or oral stimulation and that, although she enjoyed intercourse, she enjoyed these other stimulations as much, as long as he was relaxed. [Carlos] . . . was encouraged to view his new lovemaking skills as a "success" and to recognize that in many ways he was becoming a better lover than many husbands, because he was listening to his wife and responding to her requests.

By the fifth week the patient was attempting intercourse successfully with relaxed confidence, and by the ninth session he was responding regularly with erections. If they both agreed, they would either have intercourse or choose another sexual technique to achieve orgasm. Treatment was terminated after ten sessions.

(Spitzer et al., 1983, pp. 106–107)

As Carlos Domera's treatment indicates, modern sex therapy includes a variety of principles and techniques. The following ones are used in almost all cases, regardless of the dysfunction:

1. **Assessing and conceptualizing the problem.** Patients are initially given a medical examination and are interviewed concerning their "sex history." The therapist's focus during the interview is on gathering information about past life events and, in particular, current factors that are contributing to the dysfunction (Cunningham & Khera, 2018; Hackett et al., 2018).
2. **Mutual responsibility.** Therapists stress the principle of *mutual responsibility*. Both partners in the relationship share the sexual problem, regardless of who has the actual dysfunction, so treatment is likely to be more successful when both are in therapy (Shifren, 2018; Kingsberg et al., 2017).
3. **Education about sexuality.** Many patients who suffer from sexual dysfunctions know very little about the physiology and techniques of sexual activity (Khera & Cunningham, 2018). Thus sex therapists may discuss these topics and offer educational materials, including instructional books, videos, and Internet sites (van Lankveld, 2017).

Sex is one of the topics most commonly searched on the Internet. Why might it be such a popular search topic?

4. **Emotion identification.** Sex therapists help patients identify and express upsetting emotions tied to past events that may keep interfering with sexual arousal and enjoyment (Johnson, 2017; Kleinplatz, 2010).

#TheirWords

"Whoever called it 'necking' was a poor judge of anatomy."

Groucho Marx, comedian and actor

5. **Attitude change.** Following a cardinal principle of cognitive-behavioral therapy, sex therapists help patients examine and change any beliefs about sexuality that are preventing sexual arousal and pleasure (Bradford, 2017; Kingsberg et al., 2017).
6. **Elimination of performance anxiety and the spectator role.** Therapists often teach couples *sensate focus*, or *nondemand pleasuring*, a series of sensual tasks, sometimes called "petting" exercises, in which the partners focus on the sexual pleasure that can be achieved by exploring and caressing each other's body at home, without demands to have intercourse or reach orgasm—demands that may be interfering with arousal. Couples are told at first to refrain from intercourse at home and to restrict their sexual activity to kissing, hugging, and sensual massage of various parts of the body, but not of the breasts or genitals. Over time, they learn how to give and receive greater sexual pleasure and they build back up to the activity of sexual intercourse (Khera & Cunningham, 2018; Avery-Clark & Weiner, 2017).

"When I touch him he rolls into a ball."

7. **Increasing sexual and communication skills.** Couples are taught to use their sensate-focus skills and apply new sexual techniques and positions at home (Shifren, 2018; Bradford, 2017). They may, for example, try sexual positions in which the person being caressed can guide the other's hands and control the speed, pressure, and location of sexual contact (Heiman, 2007). Couples are also taught to give instructions to each other in a nonthreatening, informative manner ("It feels better over here, with a little less pressure"), rather than a threatening uninformative manner ("The way you're touching me doesn't turn me on").
8. **Changing destructive lifestyles and couple interactions.** A therapist may encourage a couple to change their lifestyle or take other steps to improve a situation that is having a destructive effect on their relationship—to distance themselves from interfering in-laws, for example, or to change a job that is too demanding. Similarly, if the couple's general relationship is marked by conflict, the therapist will try to help them improve it (Kingsberg et al., 2017; Rosen, 2007).
9. **Addressing physical and medical factors.** Systematic increases in physical activity have proved helpful for persons with various kinds of sexual dysfunctions (Khera & Cunningham, 2018). In addition, when sexual dysfunctions are caused by a medical problem, such as disease, injury, medication, or substance abuse, therapists try to address that problem (Shifren, 2018; Korda et al., 2010).

What Techniques Are Used to Treat Particular Dysfunctions?

In addition to the general components of sex therapy, specific techniques can help in each of the sexual dysfunctions.

Disorders of Desire Male hypoactive sexual desire disorder and female sexual interest/arousal disorder are among the most difficult dysfunctions to treat because of the many issues that may feed into them (Both, Schultz, & Laan, 2017). Thus therapists typically use a combination of techniques (Althof & Needle, 2017). In a technique called *affectual awareness*, patients visualize sexual scenes in order to discover any feelings of anxiety, vulnerability, and other negative emotions they may have concerning sex. In another technique, patients receive cognitive *self-instruction training* to help them change their negative reactions to sex. That is, they learn to replace negative statements during sex with "coping statements," such as "I can allow myself to enjoy sex; it doesn't mean I'll lose control."

#

#EarlyPleasure

In some studies, the majority of female participants from sexually positive marriages report that *foreplay* is the most satisfying component of sexual activity with their partner (Herbenick et al., 2018; Basson, 2007; Hurlbert, 1993).

sildenafil One of the drugs used to treat erectile disorder that helps increase blood flow to the penis during sexual activity. Marketed as *Viagra*.

Therapists may also use behavioral approaches to help heighten a patient's sex drive. They may instruct clients to keep a "desire diary" in which they record sexual thoughts and feelings, to read books and view videos with erotic content, and to fantasize about sex. They also may encourage pleasurable shared activities such as dancing and walking together. If the reduced sexual desire has resulted from sexual assault or childhood molestation, additional techniques may be needed (Shifren, 2018; Hall, 2017, 2007). A patient may, for example, be encouraged to remember, talk about, and think about the assault until the memories no longer arouse fear or tension. These and related psychological approaches apparently help many women and men with low sexual desire eventually to have intercourse more than once a week (Khera & Cunningham, 2018; Both et al., 2017).

Finally, biological interventions, such as *hormone* treatments, have been used, particularly for women whose problems arose after removal of their ovaries or later in life. These interventions have received some research support (Shifren, 2018). In addition, several pharmaceutical drugs have been developed specifically for the treatment of these disorders (Khera & Cunningham, 2018).

Erectile Disorder Treatments for erectile disorder focus on reducing a man's performance anxiety, increasing his stimulation, or both, using a range of behavioral, cognitive, and relationship interventions (Nobre, 2017). In one technique, the couple may be instructed to try the *tease technique* during sensate-focus exercises: the partner keeps caressing the man, but if the man gets an erection, the partner stops caressing him until he loses it. This exercise reduces pressure on the man to perform and at the same time teaches the couple that erections occur naturally in response to stimulation, as long as the partners do not keep focusing on performance.

Biological approaches gained great momentum with the development in 1998 of **sildenafil** (trade name Viagra) (Nobre, 2017). This drug increases blood flow to the penis within one hour of ingestion; the increased blood flow enables the user to attain an erection during sexual activity (see ***PsychWatch***). In general, sildenafil appears to be safe; however, it may not be so for men with certain coronary heart diseases and cardiovascular diseases, particularly those who are taking nitroglycerin and other heart medications (Khera & Cunningham, 2018). Soon after Viagra emerged, two other erectile dysfunction drugs were also approved—*tadalafil* (Cialis) and *vardenafil* (Levitra)—and, more recently, yet another such drug, *avanafil* (Stendra), was added to the mix. Collectively, the drugs are the most common form of treatment for erectile disorder. They effectively restore erections and enable sexual intercourse in 60 to 80 percent of men who use them, compared to a rate of 21 percent among men taking placebo drugs (Khera & Cunningham, 2018). Some research, though, suggests that a combination of one of these erectile dysfunction drugs and a psychological intervention such as those mentioned above may be more helpful than either kind of treatment alone (Nobre, 2017; Schmidt et al., 2014).

Viagra around the world Few drugs have had the worldwide impact of Viagra and related erectile dysfunction drugs. Here technicians at a pharmaceutical factory in Cairo sort thousands of Viagra pills for distribution and marketing in Egypt's pharmacies.

AP Photo/Amr Nabil

Prior to the development of Viagra, Cialis, Levitra, and Stendra, a range of other medical procedures were developed for erectile disorder. These procedures are now viewed as "second line"—often costly—treatments that are used primarily when the medications are unsuccessful or too risky for individuals (Lazarou, 2017). Such treatments include gel suppositories, injections of drugs into the penis, a surgical implantation of a penile prosthesis, and a *vacuum erection device (VED)*, a hollow cylinder that is placed over the penis. For the VED, a man uses a hand pump to pump air out of the cylinder, drawing blood into his penis and producing an erection.

Premature Ejaculation Early ejaculation has been treated successfully for years by behavioral procedures (Rowland & Cooper,

PSYCHWATCH

Sexism, Viagra, and the Pill

Most of us would like to believe that we live in an enlightened world, where sexism is declining and where health care and benefits are available to men and women in equal measure. Periodically, however, such illusions are shattered. The responses of government agencies and insurance companies to the discovery and marketing of Viagra in 1998 may be a case in point.

Consider, first, the nation of Japan. In early 1999, just 6 months after it was introduced in the United States, Viagra was approved for use among men in Japan (Goldstein, 2014). In contrast, low-dose contraceptives—"the pill"—were not approved for use among women in Japan until later that same year—a full 40 years after their introduction elsewhere! Some observers believe that birth control pills would still be unavailable to women in Japan had Viagra not received its quick approval.

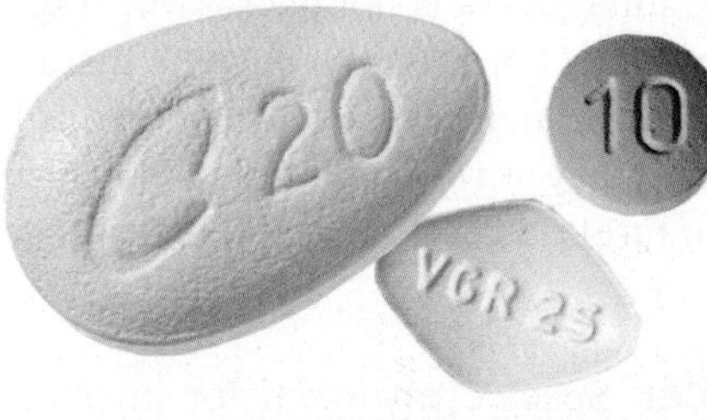

Tony Cenicola/The New York Times/Redux

"The pills": Cialis, Viagra, and Levitra

Has the United States been able to avoid such an apparent double standard in its health care system? Not really. Before Viagra was introduced, insurance companies were not required to reimburse women for the cost of prescription contraceptives. As a result, women had to pay 68 percent more out-of-pocket expenses for health care than did men, largely because of uncovered reproductive health care costs (Hollander, 2006; Hayden, 1998). Some legislators had tried to correct this problem by requiring contraceptive coverage in health insurance plans, but their efforts failed in state after state for more than a decade.

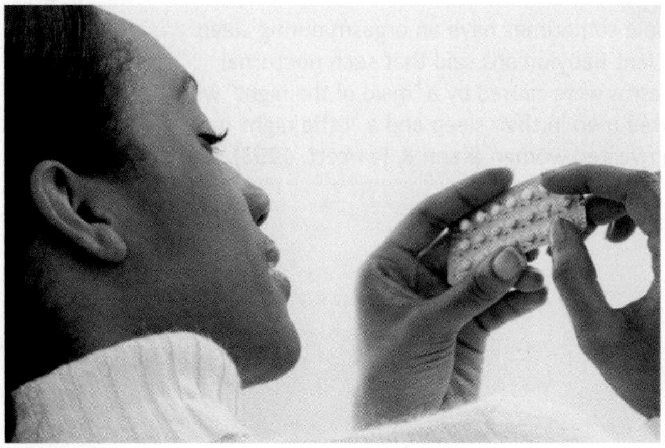
BSIP SA/Alamy

"The pill"

In contrast, when Viagra was introduced in 1998, many insurance companies readily agreed to cover it, and many states included Viagra as part of Medicaid coverage. As the public outcry grew over the contrast between coverage of Viagra for men and lack of coverage of oral contraceptives for women, laws across the country finally began to change.

By the end of 1998, nine states required prescription contraceptive coverage. Today 28 states require such coverage by private insurance companies (Guttmacher Institute, 2018). The Affordable Care Act (ACA)—the federal health care law passed in 2010 and enacted a few years later—includes provisions that require *all* insurance companies to cover contraceptives. However, with Congress repeatedly considering the repeal of the ACA—and possibly, along with it, the elimination of contraceptive coverage requirements—the future of contraceptive insurance coverage is very much at risk.

2017). In one such approach, the *stop-start,* or *pause, procedure,* the penis is manually stimulated until the man is highly aroused. The couple then pauses until his arousal subsides, after which the stimulation is resumed. This sequence is repeated several times before stimulation is carried through to ejaculation, so the man ultimately experiences much more total time of stimulation than he has ever experienced before (LoPiccolo, 2004, 2002). Eventually the couple progresses to putting the penis in the vagina, making sure to withdraw it and to pause whenever the man becomes too highly aroused. According to clinical reports, after 2 or 3 months, many couples can enjoy prolonged intercourse without any need for pauses (Puppo & Sharif, 2017; Althof, 2007).

Many clinicians treat premature ejaculation with SSRIs, the serotonin-enhancing antidepressant drugs (Khera & Cunningham, 2018). Because these drugs often reduce sexual arousal or orgasm, the reasoning goes, they may be helpful to men who ejaculate prematurely. Many studies report positive results with this approach (McMahon et al., 2013).

Delayed Ejaculation Therapies for delayed ejaculation include techniques to reduce performance anxiety and increase stimulation (Rowland & Cooper, 2017; Hartmann & Waldinger, 2007). In one of many such techniques, a man may be instructed to masturbate to orgasm in the presence of his partner or to masturbate just short of orgasm

#

#NightlyVisits

People sometimes have an orgasm during sleep. Ancient Babylonians said that such nocturnal orgasms were caused by a "maid of the night" who visited men in their sleep and a "little night man" who visited women (Kahn & Fawcett, 1993).

before inserting his penis for intercourse (Marshall, 1997). This increases the likelihood that he will ejaculate during intercourse. He then is instructed to insert his penis at ever earlier stages of masturbation.

When delayed ejaculation is caused by physical factors such as neurological damage or injury, treatment may include a drug to increase arousal of the sympathetic nervous system (Khera & Cunningham, 2018). However, few studies have systematically tested the effectiveness of such biological treatments.

Female Orgasmic Disorder Specific treatments for female orgasmic disorder include cognitive-behavioral techniques, self-exploration, enhancement of body awareness, and directed masturbation training (Carpenter et al., 2017; Kingsberg et al., 2017). Biological treatments, including hormone therapy or the use of sildenafil (Viagra), have also been tried, but research has not consistently found these to be helpful (Shifren, 2018; Bradford, 2017).

In **directed masturbation training,** a woman is taught step by step how to masturbate effectively and eventually to reach orgasm during sexual interactions. The training includes the use of diagrams and reading material, private self-stimulation, erotic material and fantasies, "orgasm triggers" such as holding her breath or thrusting her pelvis, sensate focus with her partner, and sexual positioning that produces stimulation of the clitoris during intercourse. This training program appears to be highly effective: over 90 percent of female clients learn to have an orgasm during masturbation, about 80 percent during caressing by their partners, and about 30 percent during intercourse (Bradford, 2017; Laan et al., 2013).

As you read earlier, a lack of orgasm during intercourse is not necessarily a sexual dysfunction, provided the woman enjoys intercourse. For this reason some therapists believe that the wisest course is simply to educate women whose only concern is lack of orgasm during intercourse, informing them that they are quite normal, and to further teach them how to reach orgasm, if they wish, through caressing by their partner or by herself.

Genito-Pelvic Pain/Penetration Disorder Specific treatment for involuntary contractions of the muscles around the vagina typically involves two approaches (Shifren, 2018; Meana et al., 2017). First, a woman may practice tightening and relaxing her vaginal muscles until she gains more voluntary control over them. Second, she may receive gradual behavioral exposure treatment to help her overcome her fear of penetration, beginning, for example, by inserting increasingly large dilators in her vagina at home and at her own pace and eventually ending with the insertion of her partner's penis. Most clients treated with such procedures eventually have pain-free intercourse. Some medical interventions have also been used. For example, several clinical investigators have injected the problematic vaginal muscles with Botox to help reduce spasms in those muscles (Fugl-Meyer et al., 2013). However, studies of this approach have been unsystematic.

Different approaches are used to treat the other form of genito-pelvic pain/penetration disorder—severe vaginal or pelvic pain during intercourse. As you saw earlier, the most common cause of this problem is physical, such as pain-causing scars, lesions, or infection aftereffects. When the cause is known, pain management procedures (see page 340) and sex therapy techniques may be tried, including helping a couple to learn intercourse positions that avoid putting pressure on the injured area (Meana et al., 2017; Fugl-Meyer et al., 2013). Medical interventions—from topical creams to surgery—may also be tried, but typically they must be combined with other sex therapy techniques to overcome the years of sexual anxiety and lack of arousal (Goodman, 2013). Many experts believe that, in most cases, both forms of genito-pelvic pain/penetration disorder are best assessed and treated by a *team* of professionals, including a gynecologist, physical therapist, and sex therapist or other mental health professional (Shifren, 2018; Berry & Berry, 2013).

directed masturbation training A sex therapy approach that teaches women with female arousal or orgasmic problems how to masturbate effectively and eventually to reach orgasm during sexual interactions.

paraphilias Patterns in which a person has recurrent and intense sexual urges, fantasies, or behaviors involving nonhuman objects, children, nonconsenting adults, or experiences suffering or humiliation.

paraphilic disorder A disorder in which a person's paraphilia causes great distress, interferes with social or occupational activities, or places the person or others at risk of harm—either currently or in the past.

What Are the Current Trends in Sex Therapy?

Sex therapists have now moved well beyond the approach first developed by Masters and Johnson. For example, today's sex therapists regularly treat partners who are living together but not married. They also treat sexual dysfunctions that arise from psychological disorders such as depression, mania, schizophrenia, and certain personality disorders (Buehler, 2017). In addition, sex therapists no longer screen out LGBTQ clients, individuals with severe relationship discord, the elderly, the medically ill, the physically handicapped, the intellectually disabled, or individuals who have no long-term sex partner (Cohen & Savin-Williams, 2017; Hough et al., 2017; Zhou & Bober, 2017). Sex therapists are also paying more attention to excessive sexuality, sometimes called *persistent sexuality disorder, hypersexuality,* or *sexual addiction* (Hallberg et al., 2017), although this condition is not listed as a disorder in DSM-5.

Many sex therapists have expressed concern about the sharp increase in the use of drugs and other medical interventions for sexual dysfunctions, particularly for the disorders characterized by low sexual desire and erectile disorder. Their concern is that therapists will increasingly choose the biological interventions rather than integrating biological, psychological, and sociocultural interventions. In fact, a narrow approach of any kind probably cannot fully address the complex factors that cause most sexual problems (McCarthy & Wald, 2017). It took sex therapists years to recognize the considerable advantages of an integrated approach to sexual dysfunctions. The development of new medical interventions should not lead to its abandonment.

#DividedFocus

According to surveys, 1 in 10 respondents admit to having used their cell phones during sex (Archer, 2013).

...SUMMING UP

TREATMENTS FOR SEXUAL DYSFUNCTIONS In the 1970s, the work of William Masters and Virginia Johnson led to the development of sex therapy. Today sex therapy combines a variety of cognitive, behavioral, couple, and family systems therapies. It generally includes features such as careful assessment, education, acceptance of mutual responsibility, attitude changes, sensate-focus exercises, improvements in communication, and couple therapy. In addition, specific techniques have been developed for each of the sexual dysfunctions. The use of biological treatments for sexual dysfunctions is also increasing.

Paraphilic Disorders

Paraphilias are patterns in which people repeatedly have intense sexual urges or fantasies or display sexual behaviors that involve objects or situations outside the usual sexual norms. The sexual focus may, for example, involve nonhuman objects or the experience of suffering or humiliation. Many people with a paraphilia can become aroused only when a paraphilic stimulus is present, fantasized about, or acted out. Others need the stimulus only during times of stress or under other special circumstances. Some people with one kind of paraphilia have others as well. The large consumer market in paraphilic pornography and growing trends such as sexting and cybersex lead clinicians to suspect that paraphilias may be far more common than previously thought (see ***MindTech*** on the next page).

Is the abundance of sexual material on the Internet psychologically healthy or damaging?

According to DSM-5, a diagnosis of **paraphilic disorder** should be applied when paraphilias cause a person significant distress or impairment *or* when the satisfaction of the paraphilias places the person or other people at risk of harm—either currently or in the past (APA, 2013) (see **Table 11-5**). People who initiate sexual contact with children, for example, warrant a diagnosis of *pedophilic disorder,* regardless of how troubled the individuals may or may not be over their behavior. People whose paraphilic disorder

TABLE: 11-5

Dx Checklist

Paraphilic Disorder
1. For at least 6 months, individual experiences recurrent and intense sexually arousing fantasies, urges, or behaviors involving objects or situations outside the usual sexual norms (nonhuman objects; nongenital body parts; the suffering or humiliation of oneself or one's partner; or children or other nonconsenting persons).
2. Individual experiences significant distress or impairment over the fantasies, urges, or behaviors. (In some paraphilic disorders—pedophilic disorder, exhibitionistic disorder, voyeuristic disorder, frotteuristic disorder, and sexual sadism disorder—the performance of the paraphilic behaviors indicates a disorder, even in the absence of distress or impairment.)

Information from: APA, 2013.

MINDTECH

"Sexting": Healthy or Pathological?

"Sexting" is the sending of sexually explicit material—particularly photos or text messages—between cell phones or other digital devices (Moreno, 2018). The term "sexting" did not make its debut until 2005.

One survey of almost 6,000 single adults found that 21 percent of cell phone users have sent a sexually explicit text message and 16 percent have texted a sexually explicit photo of themselves. On the other side of the coin, 28 percent of users have received sext messages and 23 percent have received sexual photos (Madigan et al., 2018; Garcia et al., 2016). In general, half of all people save the sexual images and text messages they receive, and a quarter of recipients—men much more than women—forward the sexual photos that they receive to others (Strassberg et al., 2017, 2013; McAfee, 2014).

Naïve behavior? Not always. The majority of all sexters say they recognize that the act could lead to legal, social, career, or personal problems (Garcia et al., 2016). They are also aware that sexted images sometimes wind up as "revenge porn"—images that are posted on social media by vengeful former friends or relationship partners for all the world to see (LeBlanc, 2017). Young adults (18 to 24 years old) are the largest group of sexters (Englander & McCoy, 2018). And males sext more often than females by a 3 to 2 margin (Frankel et al., 2018).

Is sexting a symptom of abnormal functioning? It depends. Certainly, some sexters—particularly those who sext to nonconsenting recipients—fit the criteria for *exhibitionistic disorder,* the paraphilic pattern in which people act on urges to expose their genitals to others. Sixteen percent of sexters send sexual photos of themselves to complete strangers (McAfee, 2014). And like other forms of exhibitionism, sexting can cause psychological stress for nonconsenting recipients.

There are yet other ways in which sexting may reflect psychological or relationship problems (Weisskirch et al., 2017; Drouin & Landgraff, 2012). According to one study, people who sext to strangers or other nonconsenting recipients are more likely to have general problems with attachment or intimacy than other people. In addition, research indicates that sexting (when done outside of one's marriage or monogamous relationship) is often a step toward infidelity. Some psychologists believe that sexting is itself a form of infidelity even though it does not involve physical contact. It has even been the grounds for divorce in some cases (Cable, 2008).

On the other side of the coin, sexting can be a constructive activity, according to some research (Drouin, Coupe, & Temple, 2017; McDaniel & Drouin, 2015; Wiederhold, 2015). Many couples engage in it as an added dimension to their relationship. According to surveys, more than half of all couples have texted sexual photos or messages to their partners at least once; one-third more than once. Research suggests that this often enhances the in-person romantic relationship, creates more bonding, and heightens sexual satisfaction in the relationship.

What texting activities outside the sexual realm might also have either a negative or positive psychological impact depending on how and when they are performed?

Richard Levine/Alamy

Putting sexting on the map In response to media revelations about his multiple episodes of sexting in 2011 and 2016, former New York congressman Anthony Weiner had to resign his congressional seat and, eventually, give up his political ambitions.

involves children or nonconsenting adults often come to the attention of clinicians as a result of legal issues generated by their inappropriate actions (Brown, 2017).

As you will see, although theorists have proposed various explanations for paraphilic disorders, there is little formal evidence to support such explanations (Martin & Levine, 2018). Moreover, none of the many treatments applied to these disorders has received much research or proved clearly effective (Thibaut et al., 2016). Psychological and sociocultural treatments have been available the longest, but today's professionals are also using biological interventions.

Some practitioners administer drugs called *antiandrogens* that lower the production of testosterone, the male sex hormone, and reduce the sex drive (Turner et al., 2017). Although antiandrogens may indeed reduce paraphilic patterns, several of them disrupt normal sexual feelings and behavior as well (Thibaut et al., 2016, 2010). Thus the drugs tend to be used primarily when the paraphilic disorders are of particular danger either to the individuals themselves or to other people. Clinicians are also increasingly prescribing SSRIs, the serotonin-enhancing antidepressant medications, to treat people with paraphilic disorders, hoping that the SSRIs will reduce these compulsion-like sexual behaviors just as they help reduce other kinds of compulsions (Anupama et al., 2016).

A word of caution is in order before examining the various paraphilic disorders. The definitions of these disorders, like those of sexual dysfunctions, are strongly influenced by the norms of the particular society in which they occur (Fuss, Briken, & Klein, 2018). Some clinicians argue that except when other people are hurt by them, at least some paraphilic behaviors should not be considered disorders at all (Joyal, 2017, 2015; Giami, 2015). Especially in light of the stigma associated with sexual disorders and the self-revulsion that many people feel when they believe they have such a disorder, we need to be very careful about applying these labels to others or to ourselves. Keep in mind that for years clinicians considered homosexuality a paraphilic disorder, and their judgment was used to justify laws and even police actions against gay people. Only in 1987, when the gay rights movement helped change society's understanding of and attitudes toward homosexuality did clinicians officially stop considering it a disorder and remove it entirely from the DSM. Even then, as you read in Chapter 1, many clinicians continued for years to recommend and offer *conversion*, or *reparative, therapy* to "fix" the sexual orientation of gay people. In the meantime, the clinical field had unintentionally contributed to the persecution, anxiety, and humiliation of millions of people because of personal sexual behavior that differed from the conventional norms.

#

#TheirWords

"Erection is chiefly caused by scuraum, eringoes, cresses, crymon, parsnips, artichokes, turnips, asparagus, candied ginger, acorns bruised to powder and drank in muscadel, scallion, sea shell fish, etc."

Aristotle's Masterpiece, 1684

Fetishistic Disorder

One relatively common paraphilic disorder is **fetishistic disorder.** Key features of this disorder are recurrent intense sexual urges, sexually arousing fantasies, or behaviors that involve the use of a nonliving object or nongenital body part, often to the exclusion of all other stimuli (APA, 2013). Usually the disorder, which is far more common in men than in women, begins in adolescence (Martin & Levine, 2018). Almost anything can be a fetish; women's underwear, shoes, and boots are particularly common. Some people with this disorder steal in order to collect as many of the desired objects as possible. The objects may be touched, smelled, worn, or used in some other way while the person masturbates, or the person may ask a partner to wear the object when they have sex (Bressert, 2017). Some of these features are seen in the case of Jaylen, a teenager whose mother, Kiara, discovered his fetishistic disorder over the course of six months:

[Kiara] reported that she first recognized [Jaylen's] sexual interest in women's shoes six months ago. He started to disappear repeatedly from their apartment and [one day, Kiara] found him on the stairs . . . handling the shoes of a female neighbor. Later on, [Kiara] came across [Jaylen] rubbing and smelling the shoes in such a fascinated manner that he did not even recognize his mother's presence. . . . [Kiara] also noticed that [Jaylen] was increasingly staying within their apartment building, taking the neighbor's shoes down to the ground floor rather than going outside. . . . After a week [Jaylen] visited the neighbor's home while helping her carry shopping goods. After an apparently normal visit, the neighbor recognized that her shoes were missing. [Kiara] tried to talk with [her son], but he became agitated and refused to talk. After several weeks, she recognized that her own shoes were missing . . . The mother then started keeping track of [Jaylen] and recognized that he was awaking at night and was . . . rubbing and smelling

(continued on the next page)

fetishistic disorder A paraphilic disorder consisting of recurrent and intense sexual urges, fantasies, or behaviors that involve the use of a nonliving object or nongenital part, often to the exclusion of all other stimuli, accompanied by clinically significant distress or impairment.

her shoes. [Kiara] did not recognize the sexual nature of his behaviors and thought that he had a compulsive interest in shoes. [However, one day] she entered the bathroom and found [Jaylen] there masturbating while he was holding and rubbing her shoe in his hand. At that point, she recognized the sexual nature of his interest in shoes for the first time. Subsequently she came across some videos on his mobile phone. They were recordings of young women's feet with or without shoes, including videos of [Kiara's own] naked feet. There were dozens of these videos, . . . dating back four months.

(Coskun & Ozturk, 2013, p. 199)

Researchers have not been able to pinpoint the causes of fetishistic disorder. Psychodynamic theorists view fetishes as defense mechanisms that help people avoid the anxiety produced by normal sexual contact. Psychodynamic treatment for this problem, however, has met with little success (Martin & Levine, 2016).

Viewing fetishes as learned behaviors, cognitive-behavioral theorists propose that fetishes are acquired through classical conditioning (Martin & Levine, 2018). In a pioneering behavioral study, male participants were shown a series of slides of nude women along with slides of boots (Rachman, 1966). After many trials, the participants became aroused by the boot photos alone. If early sexual experiences similarly occur in the presence of particular objects, perhaps the stage is set for the development of fetishes.

The Everett Collection

Mrs. Robinson's stockings The 1967 film *The Graduate* helped define a generation by focusing on the personal confusion, apathy, and sexual adventures of a young man in search of meaning. Marketers promoted this film by using a fetishistic-like photo of Mrs. Robinson putting on her stockings under Benjamin's watchful eye, a scene forever identified with the movie.

Cognitive-behavioral therapists have sometimes treated fetishistic disorder with *aversion therapy* (Thibaut et al., 2016; Plaud, 2007). In a famous study, an electric shock was administered to the arms or legs of participants with this disorder while they imagined their objects of desire (Marks & Gelder, 1967). After 2 weeks of therapy all men in the study showed at least some improvement. In another aversion technique, *covert sensitization,* people with fetishistic disorder are guided to *imagine* the pleasurable object and repeatedly to pair this image with an *imagined* aversive stimulus until the object of sexual pleasure is no longer desired.

Another cognitive-behavioral treatment for fetishistic disorder is *masturbatory satiation* (Thibaut et al., 2016; Plaud, 2007). In this method, the client masturbates to orgasm while fantasizing about a sexually appropriate object, then switches to fantasizing in detail about fetishistic objects while masturbating again and continues the fetishistic fantasy for an hour. The procedure is meant to produce a feeling of boredom, which in turn becomes linked to the fetishistic object.

Transvestic Disorder

A person with **transvestic disorder,** also known as **transvestism** or **cross-dressing,** feels recurrent and intense sexual arousal from dressing in clothes of the opposite gender—arousal expressed through fantasies, urges, or behaviors (APA, 2013). The individual's transvestic needs and behaviors must cause significant distress or impairment to warrant a diagnosis of transvestic disorder. The typical person with the disorder, almost always a heterosexual male, begins cross-dressing in childhood or adolescence (Brown, 2017; Thibaut et al., 2016). He may be the picture of characteristic masculinity in everyday life and is usually alone when he cross-dresses. A small percentage of such men cross-dress to visit bars or social clubs. Some wear a single item of women's clothing, such as underwear or hosiery, under their masculine clothes. Others wear makeup and dress fully as women. Some married men with transvestic disorder involve their wives in their cross-dressing.

Transvestic disorder is often confused with *transgender* feelings and behaviors, but, as you will see, they are two separate patterns that overlap only in some individuals. Specifically, a transvestic disorder is about the sexual arousal certain persons feel when they dress in opposite-gender clothes, whereas transgender functioning is about the gender a person considers himself or herself to be.

As with fetishes, cognitive-behavioral theorists view transvestic arousal and behavior as learned responses, acquired most often through classical conditioning. That is, if early sexual experiences occur while a person is—out of curiosity, playfulness, or the like—wearing the attire of the other gender, the stage may be set for transvestic arousal and related reactions throughout life. This explanation has, however, received little support in clinical reports or research (Anupama et al., 2016).

Darren McCollester/Getty Images

Playful context Dressing in clothes of the opposite sex does not necessarily convey a paraphilia. Here two members—both male—of Harvard University's Hasty Pudding Theatricals Club, known for staging musicals in which male undergraduates dress like women, plant a kiss on actress Kerry Washington. Washington was receiving the club's 2016 Woman of the Year award.

Exhibitionistic Disorder

A person with **exhibitionistic disorder** experiences recurrent and intense sexual arousal from exposing his genitals to an unsuspecting individual—arousal reflected by fantasies, urges, or behaviors (APA, 2013). Most often, the person wants to provoke shock or surprise rather than initiate sexual activity with the victim. Sometimes an exhibitionist will expose himself in a particular neighborhood at particular hours. In a survey of 2,800 men, 4.3 percent of them reported that they perform exhibitionistic behavior (Långström & Seto, 2006). Yet between one-third and half of all women report having seen or had direct contact with an exhibitionist, or so-called flasher (Marshall et al., 2008). The urge to exhibit typically becomes stronger when the person has free time or is under significant stress.

Generally, exhibitionistic disorder begins before age 18 and usually, but not always, is found among men (Brown, 2017; Thibaut et al., 2016). Some studies suggest that those with the disorder are typically immature in their dealings with the opposite sex and have difficulty in interpersonal relationships (Marshall et al., 2008; Murphy & Page, 2006). Around 30 percent of them are married and another 30 percent divorced or separated; their sexual relations with their wives are not usually satisfactory (Brown, 2017; Doctor & Neff, 2001). Many have doubts or fears about their masculinity, and some seem to have a strong bond to a possessive mother. As with other paraphilic disorders, treatment generally includes aversion therapy, masturbatory satiation, social skills training, and some form of insight therapy (Marshall & Marshall, 2016; Thibaut et al., 2016).

Voyeuristic Disorder

A person with **voyeuristic disorder** experiences recurrent and intense sexual arousal from observing an unsuspecting individual who is naked, disrobing, or engaging in sexual activity. As with other paraphilic disorders, this arousal takes the form of fantasies, urges, or behaviors (APA, 2013). The disorder usually begins before the age of 15 and tends to persist.

A person with voyeuristic disorder may masturbate during the act of observing or when thinking about it afterward but does not generally seek to have sex with the person being spied on (Brown, 2017). The vulnerability of the people being observed and the probability they would feel humiliated if they knew they were under observation are often part of the enjoyment. In addition, the risk of being discovered adds to the excitement, as you can see in 25-year-old Sam's description of his disorder during an interview:

transvestic disorder A paraphilic disorder consisting of repeated and intense sexual urges, fantasies, or behaviors that involve dressing in clothes of the opposite sex, accompanied by clinically significant distress or impairment. Also known as *transvestism* or *cross-dressing*.

exhibitionistic disorder A paraphilic disorder in which persons have repeated sexually arousing urges or fantasies about exposing their genitals to others, and either act on these urges with nonconsenting individuals or experience clinically significant distress or impairment.

voyeuristic disorder A paraphilic disorder in which a person has repeated and intense sexual desires to observe unsuspecting people in secret as they undress or to spy on couples having intercourse, and either acts on these urges with nonconsenting people or experiences clinically significant distress or impairment.

Imagebroker/Alamy

Lady Godiva and "Peeping Tom" According to legend, Lady Godiva (shown in this 1890 illustration) rode naked through the streets of Coventry, England, in order to persuade her husband, the earl of Mercia, to stop taxing the city's poor. Although all townspeople were ordered to stay inside their homes with shutters drawn during her eleventh-century ride, a tailor named Tom "could not contain his sexual curiosity and drilled a hole in his shutter in order to watch Lady Godiva pass by" (Mann et al., 2008). Since then, the term "Peeping Tom" has been used to refer to people with voyeuristic disorder.

I've had girlfriends, but it's not the same. It's fun at first, but I get bored after a while in relationships. I never get that kick, that excitement, that I do when I look at others.

The biggest thrill is when I'm watching my neighbor having sex with one of her boyfriends, or maybe watching Zoe down the block changing her clothes. Neither of them fully shuts their drapes, so there's always a little angle where I can see into their rooms if I get in just the right position on the lawn. Sometimes I'll take a walk and try to find someone I haven't watched before.

Thinking about it afterwards, I also get excited, especially if I came close to getting caught. I realize what a chance I was taking, and it gets my heart going and gets the rest of me going as well. Sometimes I'll make up extra details when remembering what happened, especially details about barely getting away or even being spotted, and that makes it even better. Of course, if I ever did get caught, it would be horrible.

Voyeurism, like exhibitionism, is often a source of sexual excitement in fantasy; it can also play a role in normal sexual interactions if a partner consents to voyeuristic-like behaviors. The clinical disorder of voyeuristic disorder is marked by the repeated invasion of other people's privacy. Some people with the disorder are unable to have normal sexual relations; others have a normal sex life apart from their disorder.

Many psychodynamic clinicians propose that people with voyeuristic disorder are seeking by their actions to gain power over others, possibly because they feel inadequate or are sexually or socially shy (Pfäfflin, 2016). Cognitive-behavioral theorists explain the disorder as a learned behavior that can be traced to a chance and secret observation of a sexually arousing scene (Lavin, 2008). If the onlookers observe such scenes on several occasions while masturbating, they may develop a voyeuristic pattern.

Frotteuristic Disorder

A person with **frotteuristic disorder** experiences repeated and intense sexual arousal from touching or rubbing against a nonconsenting person. The arousal may, like with the other paraphilic disorders, take the form of fantasies, urges, or behaviors. Frottage (from French *frotter,* "to rub") is usually committed in a crowded place, such as a subway or a busy sidewalk (Guterman, Martin, & Rudes, 2011). The person, almost always a male, may rub his genitals against the victim's thighs or buttocks or fondle her genital area or breasts with his hands. Typically he fantasizes during the act that he is having a caring relationship with the victim. This paraphilia usually begins in the teenage years or earlier, often after the person observes others committing an act of frottage. After the age of about 25, people gradually decrease and often cease their acts of frottage (APA, 2000).

Pedophilic Disorder

A person with **pedophilic disorder** experiences equal or greater sexual arousal from children than from physically mature people. This arousal is expressed through fantasies, urges, or behaviors (APA, 2013). Those with the disorder may be attracted to prepubescent children, early pubescent children, or both. Some people with pedophilic disorder are satisfied by child pornography or seemingly innocent material such as children's underwear ads; others are driven to actually watch, touch, fondle, or engage in sexual intercourse with children (Geradt et al., 2018). Some people with the disorder are attracted only to children; others are attracted to adults as well (Brown, 2017; Stephens et al., 2017). Both boys and girls can be pedophilic victims, but there is evidence suggesting that two-thirds are girls (NSOPW, 2018).

People with pedophilic disorder usually develop their pattern of sexual need during adolescence (Thibaut et al., 2016). Some were themselves sexually abused as children, and many were neglected, excessively punished, or deprived of genuinely close relationships during their childhood (Brown, 2017). It is not unusual for them to be married and to have sexual difficulties or other frustrations in life that lead them to seek an area in which they can be masters. Often these individuals are immature: their social and sexual skills may be underdeveloped, they may have limited self-control and poor planning skills, and thoughts of normal sexual relationships fill them with anxiety (Massau et al., 2017; Seto, 2008).

Some people with pedophilic disorder also have distorted thinking, such as, "It's all right to have sex with children as long as they agree" (Geradt et al., 2018; O Ciardha et al., 2016). It is not uncommon for pedophiles to blame the children for adult–child sexual contacts or to assert that the children benefited from the experience.

While many people with this disorder believe that their feelings are indeed wrong and abnormal, others consider adult sexual activity with children to be acceptable and normal. Some even have joined pedophile organizations that advocate abolishing the age-of-consent laws. The Internet has opened the channels of communication among such people, and there is now a wide range of Web sites, newsgroups, chat rooms, forums, and message boards centered on pedophilia and adult–child sex (Pieters, 2018; Durkin & Hundersmarck, 2008).

Studies have found that most men with pedophilic disorder also display at least one additional psychological disorder (Brown, 2017; Farkas, 2013). Some theorists have proposed that pedophilic disorder may be related to biochemical or brain structure abnormalities such as irregular patterns of activity in the amygdala or in the frontal areas of the brain, but such abnormalities have yet to receive consistent research support (Ponseti et al., 2018; Massau et al., 2017).

Most pedophilic offenders are imprisoned or forced into treatment if they are caught (Thibaut et al., 2016). After all, they are committing child sexual abuse when they take any steps toward sexual contact with a child. There are now many residential registration and community notification laws across the United States that help law enforcement agencies and the public account for and control where convicted child sex offenders live and work (NSOPW, 2018).

Treatments for pedophilic disorder include those already mentioned for other paraphilic disorders, such as aversion therapy, masturbatory satiation, cognitive-behavioral therapy, and antiandrogen drugs (Brown, 2017; Marshall & Marshall, 2016, 2015; Thibaut et al., 2016). One widely applied cognitive-behavioral treatment for this disorder, *relapse-prevention training,* is modeled after the relapse-prevention training programs used in the treatment of substance use disorders (see pages 320–321). In this approach, clients identify the kinds of situations that typically trigger their pedophilic fantasies and actions (such as depressed mood or distorted thinking). They then learn strategies for avoiding those situations or coping with them more appropriately and effectively. Relapse-prevention training has sometimes, but not consistently, been of help in this and certain other paraphilic disorders (Laws, 2016; Federoff & Marshall, 2010).

frotteuristic disorder A paraphilic disorder in which a person has repeated and intense sexual urges or fantasies that involve touching and rubbing against a nonconsenting person, and either acts on these urges with the nonconsenting person or experiences clinically significant distress or impairment.

pedophilic disorder A paraphilic disorder in which a person has repeated and intense sexual urges or fantasies about watching, touching, or engaging in sexual acts with children, and either acts on these urges or experiences clinically significant distress or impairment.

Pedophilia, abuse, and justice People enter the courthouse in Angers, France, in 2005, to witness the largest child abuse trial ever held in France. The court found 39 men and 26 women guilty of raping, molesting, and prostituting children. The victims ranged in age from 6 months to 14 years, and the defendants ranged from 27 to 73 years.

Francis Demange/Gamma-Rapho via Getty Images

Sexual Masochism Disorder

A person with **sexual masochism disorder** is repeatedly and intensely sexually aroused by the act of being humiliated, beaten, bound, or otherwise made to suffer (APA, 2013). Again, this arousal may take such forms as fantasies, urges, or behaviors. Many people have fantasies of being forced into sexual acts against their will, but only those who are very distressed or impaired by the fantasies receive this diagnosis. Some people with the disorder act on the masochistic urges by themselves, perhaps tying, sticking pins into, or even cutting themselves. Others have their sexual partners restrain, tie up, blindfold, spank, paddle, whip, beat, electrically shock, "pin and pierce," or humiliate them (APA, 2013).

An industry of products and services has arisen to meet the desires of people with the paraphilia or the paraphilic disorder of sexual masochism. Here a 34-year-old woman describes her work as the operator of a facility that meets those desires:

> *I get people here who have been all over looking for the right kind of pain they feel they deserve. Don't ask me why they want pain, I'm not a psychologist; but when they have found us, they usually don't go elsewhere. . . . Among the things I do, that work really quickly and well, are: I put clothespins on their nipples, or pins in their [testicles]. Some of them need to see their own blood to be able to get off. . . .*
>
> *All the time that a torture scene is going on, there is constant dialogue. . . . I scream at the guy, and tell him what a no-good rotten bastard he is, how this is even too good for him, that he knows he deserves worse, and I begin to list his sins. It works every time . . . I act very tough and hard, but I'm really a very sensitive woman. But you have to watch out for a guy's health . . . you must not kill him, or have him get a heart attack. . . . I know of other places that have had guys die there. I've never lost a customer to death, though they may have wished for it during my "treatment."*
>
> *(Janus & Janus, 1993, p. 115)*

Brant Ward/San Francisco Chronicle/Polaris

A celebration of S/M Sexual sadism and sexual masochism have been viewed by the public with either bemusement or horror, depending on the circumstances surrounding particular acts of these paraphilias. On the light side, the annual Folsom Street Fair in San Francisco celebrates S/M and invites people (like this participant) to go on stage, display their trademark outfits, and in some cases, participate in pseudo whippings or spankings.

In one form of sexual masochism disorder, *hypoxyphilia*, people strangle or smother themselves (or ask their partner to strangle them) in order to enhance their sexual pleasure (Sendler, 2018; Coluccia et al., 2016). There have, in fact, been a disturbing number of clinical reports of autoerotic asphyxia, in which people, usually males and as young as 10 years old, may accidentally induce a fatal lack of oxygen by hanging, suffocating, or strangling themselves while masturbating. There is some debate as to whether the practice should be characterized as sexual masochism disorder, but it is at least sometimes accompanied by other acts of bondage.

Most masochistic sexual fantasies begin in childhood. However, the person does not act out the urges until later, usually by early adulthood. The pattern typically continues for many years. Some people practice more and more dangerous acts over time or during times of particular stress (Frias et al., 2017; Krueger, 2010).

In many cases, sexual masochism disorder seems to have developed through the learning process of classical conditioning (Wylie & Wylie, 2016; Stekel, 2010). A classic case study tells of a teenage boy with a broken arm who was caressed and held close by an attractive nurse as the physician set his fracture, a procedure done in the past without anesthesia (Gebhard, 1965). The powerful combination of pain and sexual arousal the boy felt then may have been the cause of his later masochistic urges and acts.

sexual masochism disorder A paraphilic disorder in which a person has repeated and intense sexual urges, fantasies, or behaviors that involve being humiliated, beaten, bound, or otherwise made to suffer, accompanied by clinically significant distress or impairment.

sexual sadism disorder A paraphilic disorder in which a person has repeated and intense sexual urges or fantasies that involve inflicting suffering on others, and either acts on these urges with nonconsenting individuals or experiences clinically significant distress or impairment.

Sexual Sadism Disorder

A person with **sexual sadism disorder,** usually male, is repeatedly and intensely sexually aroused by the physical or psychological suffering of another individual (APA, 2013). This arousal may be expressed through fantasies, urges, or behaviors, including acts such as dominating, restraining, blindfolding, cutting, strangling, mutilating, or even killing the victim (Longpré et al., 2018, 2017). The label is derived from the name of the famous Marquis de Sade (1740–1814), who tortured others in order to satisfy his sexual desires.

People who fantasize about sexual sadism typically imagine that they have total control over a sexual victim who is terrified by the sadistic act. Many carry out sadistic acts with a consenting partner, often a person with sexual masochism disorder (Joyal, 2017). Some, however, act out their urges on nonconsenting victims. A number of rapists and sexual murderers, for example, exhibit sexual sadism disorder (Longpré et al., 2018, 2017). In all cases, the real or fantasized victim's suffering is the key to arousal.

Fantasies of sexual sadism, like those of sexual masochism, may first appear in childhood or adolescence (Thibaut et al., 2016; Stone, 2010). People who engage in sadistic acts begin to do so by early adulthood (APA, 2013). Some people with the disorder engage in the same level of cruelty in their sadistic acts over time, but often their sadism becomes more and more severe over the years (Robertson & Knight, 2014). Obviously, people with severe forms of the disorder may be highly dangerous to others.

Some cognitive-behavioral theorists believe that classical conditioning is at work in sexual sadism disorder (Akins, 2004). While inflicting pain, perhaps unintentionally, on an animal or person, a teenager may feel intense emotions and sexual arousal. The association between inflicting pain and being aroused sexually sets the stage for a pattern of sexual sadism. Cognitive-behavioral theorists also propose that the disorder may result from modeling, when adolescents observe others achieving sexual satisfaction by inflicting pain. The many Internet sex sites and sexual videos, magazines, and books in our society make such models readily available (Thibaut et al., 2016).

Both psychodynamic and cognitive-behavioral theorists further suggest that people with sexual sadism disorder inflict pain in order to achieve a sense of power or control, necessitated perhaps by underlying feelings of sexual inadequacy. The sense of power in turn increases their sexual arousal (Marshall & Marshall, 2016, 2015). Alternatively, certain biological studies have found signs of possible brain and hormonal abnormalities in people with sexual sadism (Luo et al., 2017; Jacobs, 2011). None of these explanations, however, has been thoroughly investigated.

Cognitive-behavioral therapists have treated the disorder with aversion therapy (Thibaut et al., 2016). The public's view of and distaste for this procedure have been influenced by the novel and 1971 movie *A Clockwork Orange,* which depicts simultaneous presentations of violent images and drug-induced stomach spasms to a sadistic young man until he is conditioned to feel nausea at the sight of such images. It is not clear that aversion therapy is helpful in cases of sexual sadism disorder. However, relapse-prevention training, used in some criminal cases, may be of value (Laws, 2016; Marshall & Marshall, 2016, 2015).

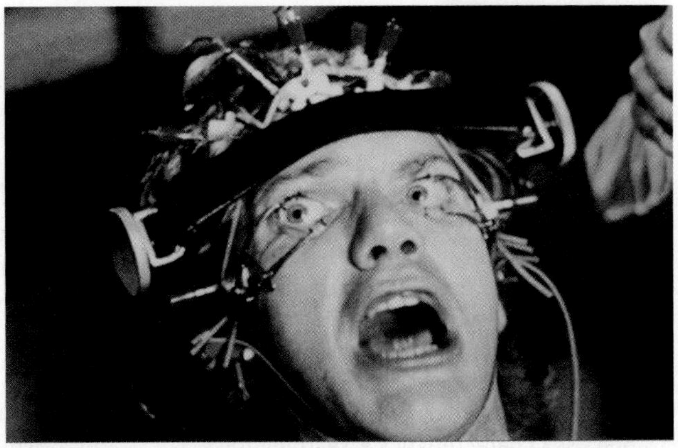

The Everett Collection

Cinematic introduction In one of filmdom's most famous scenes, Alex, the sexually sadistic character in *A Clockwork Orange,* is forced to observe violent images while he experiences painful stomach spasms.

...SUMMING UP

PARAPHILIC DISORDERS Paraphilias are patterns characterized by recurrent and intense sexual urges, fantasies, or behaviors involving objects or situations outside the usual sexual norms—for example, nonhuman objects, children, nonconsenting adults, or experiences of suffering or humiliation. When an individual's paraphilia causes great distress, interferes with social or occupational functioning, or places the individual or others at risk of harm, a diagnosis of paraphilic disorder is applied. Paraphilic disorders are found primarily in men. The paraphilic disorders include fetishistic disorder, transvestic disorder, exhibitionistic disorder, voyeuristic disorder, frotteuristic disorder, pedophilic disorder, sexual masochism disorder, and sexual sadism disorder. Although various explanations have been proposed for paraphilic disorders, research has revealed little about their causes. A range of treatments have been tried, including aversion therapy, masturbatory satiation, and relapse-prevention training.

#

#LegalOption

In 1996 the California state legislature passed the first law in the United States allowing state judges to order *antiandrogen* drug treatments, often referred to as "chemical castration," for repeat sex crime offenders, such as men who repeatedly commit pedophilic acts or rape. At least eight other states now have similar laws.

TABLE: 11-6

Dx Checklist

Gender Dysphoria in Adolescents and Adults
1. For 6 months or more, an individual's gender-related feelings and/or behaviors are at odds with those of his or her assigned gender, as indicated by two or more of the following symptoms: • Gender-related feelings and/or behaviors clearly contradict the individual's primary or secondary sex characteristics • Powerful wish to eliminate one's sex characteristics • Yearning for the sex characteristics of another gender • Powerful wish to be a member of another gender • Yearning to be treated as a member of another gender • Firm belief that one's feelings and reactions are those that characterize another gender.
2. Individual experiences significant distress or impairment.

Information from: APA, 2013.

Gender Variations

As children and adults, most people feel like and identify themselves as males or females—a feeling and identity that is consistent with their *assigned gender* (or *birth anatomy*), the gender to which they are born. But society has come to appreciate that many people do not experience such gender clarity. These people are **transgender,** individuals who have a sense that their *gender identity* (one's personal experience of one's gender) is different from their assigned gender. It is estimated that 25 million people in the world are transgender—0.8 percent of the adult population (Tangpricha & Safer, 2018; Winter et al., 2016). Many transgender people come to terms with their gender inconsistencies. They accept the incongruence or seek out interventions, such as hormone therapy or surgery, to change their birth anatomy into physical characteristics that fit their *gender identity*. Some transgender people, however, may experience extreme distress over the incongruence. DSM-5 categorizes these latter people as having **gender dysphoria** (see **Table 11-6**).

The DSM-5 categorization of gender dysphoria is controversial. Many argue that since a transgender pattern reflects an alternative—not pathological—way of experiencing one's gender identity, it should never be considered a psychological disorder, even if it is accompanied by significant unhappiness. Indeed, this is rapidly becoming the dominant view in the clinical field and society (Russo, 2017). In 2017, for example, Denmark's Parliament actually ruled that transgender individuals should no longer be considered mentally ill in the country's mental health system. And in 2018, the World Health Organization decided to remove transgender functioning from the list of mental disorders in ICD-11, the new edition of its classification system.

In this climate, it is expected that the category of gender dysphoria may be dropped from the next revision of DSM-5. If so, the DSM would be following a route that it travelled in past times with regard to homosexuality. As you read earlier (see page 349), in its first two editions, the developers of the DSM listed homosexuality as a sexual disorder, such as a paraphilic disorder. Protests by gay activist groups and many clinicians eventually led to the DSM's 1973 elimination of this category as a sexual disorder per se, but the DSM did retain a category called *ego dystonic homosexuality*—the experience of extreme distress over one's homosexual orientation. Finally, this latter category too was dropped in a 1987 revision of the DSM. Similarly, in early editions of the DSM, persons with transgender thoughts and needs qualified for a diagnosis of *transgender identity disorder*. This classification was dropped when DSM-5 was published in 2013 and replaced by the current category *gender dysphoria*.

Why might labeling transgender people as mentally ill be harmful to them?

To help distinguish what is known about transgender functioning (an alternative, but not abnormal, pattern) from what is known about gender dysphoria (an abnormal pattern, according to DSM-5), let us look first at transgender functioning, then turn to gender dysphoria.

Transgender Functioning

Given their gender identity, many transgender people would like to get rid of their primary and secondary sex characteristics—some of them find their own genitals repugnant—and to acquire characteristics that correspond to their gender identity (APA, 2013). *Transgender women* (that is, people who identify as female but were assigned male at birth) outnumber *transgender men* (people who identify as male but were assigned female at birth) by around 2 to 1.

Sometimes transgender feelings emerge in children (Olson-Kennedy & Forcier, 2018). Like transgender adults, the children feel uncomfortable with their assigned gender and yearn to be members of another gender. This childhood pattern often

transgender Individuals who have a strong sense that their gender identity is different from their birth anatomy.

gender dysphoria A disorder in which a person persistently feels clinically significant distress or impairment due to his or her assigned gender and strongly wishes to be a member of another gender.

disappears by adolescence or adulthood, but in some cases the individuals do become transgender adults (Forcier & Olson-Kennedy, 2018). Thus transgender adults may have had transgender feelings when they were children, but many children with transgender feelings do not become transgender adults. Surveys of mothers indicate that about 1.5 percent of young boys wish to be a girl, and 3.5 percent of young girls wish to be a boy (Carroll, 2007; Zucker & Bradley, 1995), yet, as we noted earlier, less than 1 percent of adults are transgender (Zucker, 2010). This age shift is, in part, why many experts on transgender functioning strongly recommend against any form of irreversible physical procedures for this pattern until the individual is at least 14 to 16 years of age, except in extraordinary instances (Levine, 2017). Certain kinds of pharmacological interventions are, however, considered acceptable and are being administered increasingly to transgender adolescents (Corathers, 2018; Nahata et al., 2017).

#KeyDistinction

Sexual orientation is about whom one is sexually attracted to. *Gender identity* is about whether one considers oneself male, female, a mixture of the genders, or neither of the genders.

Explanations of Transgender Functioning Increasingly, today's medical and psychological theorists believe that biological factors—perhaps genetic or prenatal—are key to transgender functioning (Burke et al., 2018; Spizzirri et al., 2018). Consistent with a genetic explanation, transgender functioning does sometimes run in families. Research indicates, for example, that people with transgender siblings are more likely to be transgender than are people without such siblings (Gómez-Gil et al., 2010). Indeed, one study of identical twins found that when one of the twins was transgender, the other twin was as well in 9 out of 23 pairs (Heylens et al., 2012).

Biological investigators have uncovered some interesting findings when they examine and compare the brains of transgender and nontransgender individuals. Keeping in mind that male and female brains usually differ slightly, researchers have looked for indications that the brains of transgender people are more similar to brains of the gender with which they identify than the gender to which they were assigned at birth (Mueller, De Cuypere, & T'Sjoen, 2017; Russo, 2017, 2016). For example, using MRI scanning, one team of researchers found that the brains of transgender men (people who identify as male but were assigned female at birth) have relatively thin subcortical areas, much like those of nontransgender men, and the brains of transgender women (people who identify as female but were assigned male at birth) have relatively thin cortical regions in the right hemisphere, much like those of nontransgender women (Guillamon et al., 2016; Luders et al. 2012). Correspondingly, other research has found similarities between transgender individuals and their nontransgender counterparts with regard to the activity and size of brain structures such as the insula, anterior cingulate cortex, and bed nucleus of stria terminalis (BST)—structures known to play roles in gender functioning and consciousness (Spizzirri et al., 2018).

Similar results have been uncovered in studies of brain reactions to strong unpleasant odors. In general, male and female brains react to strong smells differently, particularly in the hypothalamus. Here again, transgender studies have found that, when exposed to strong unpleasant smells, the hypothalamic responses of transgender males are similar to those of nontransgender males, whereas the hypothalamic responses of transgender females are similar to those of nontransgender females (Burke et al., 2018, 2016, 2014; Mueller et al., 2017). Brain response similarities between transgender individuals and their nontransgender counterparts have likewise been found in studies that expose participants to certain sounds, visual stimuli, and memory challenges.

Based on such findings, it might be tempting to conclude that transgender people are individuals whose male brain is simply trapped inside a female body or whose female brain is trapped inside a male body, but, as researcher Antonio Guillamon cautions, "Trans people have brains that are different from males and females, a *unique* kind of brain" (Guillamon, 2016). That is, they do not have a male or female brain, but rather a transgender brain.

A delicate matter A 5-year-old boy (left), who identifies and dresses as a girl and asks to be called "she," plays with a female friend. Sensitive to the gender identity rights movement and to the special needs of children with transgender feelings, a growing number of parents, educators, and clinicians are now supportive of children like this.

Jim Wilson/The New York Times/Redux

gender reassignment surgery A surgical procedure that changes a person's sex organs and gender features. Also known as *gender change surgery*.

Options for Transgender Individuals As you read earlier, transgender people often address the incongruence between their gender identity and birth anatomy through biological procedures. For example, many change their sexual characteristics by means of *hormone administration* (Corathers, 2018; Ferrando & Thomas, 2018). Physicians prescribe the female sex hormone *estrogen* for transgender females, as well as other medications designed to suppress their bodies' production of the male sex hormone testosterone. This leads to breast development, loss of body and facial hair, and changes in body fat distribution. Some of these patients also go to speech therapy, raising their tenor voice to alto through training, and some have facial feminization procedures (Ferrando & Thomas, 2018; Tangpricha & Safer, 2018). In contrast, transgender men are administered the male sex hormone *testosterone*, resulting in a deeper voice, increased muscle mass, and changes in facial and body hair.

Hormone administration enables many transgender persons to lead a fulfilling life in the gender that fits them. For others, however, this is not enough, and they may seek out **gender reassignment surgery,** or **gender change surgery**—also called *gender confirmation surgery* or *gender-affirming surgery* (Crandall, 2018). Such surgery is usually preceded by 1 to 2 years of hormone administration. For transgender women, the surgery can involve one or more of the following procedures: face-changing plastic surgery, breast augmentation, and genital reconstruction (partial removal of the penis and restructuring of its remaining parts into a clitoris and vagina). For transgender men, surgery may include a bilateral mastectomy, chest reconstruction, a hysterectomy, and/or genital reconstruction (the formation of a functioning penis—a procedure not yet perfected—or a silicone prosthesis that can give the appearance of male genitals). Genital reconstruction is performed much less often than the other surgical procedures, especially among transgender men (ASPS, 2017; Mainwaring, 2017). According to a report by the American Society of Plastic Surgeons, more than 3,200 gender reassignment surgeries were performed in the United States in 2016, an increase of 20 percent over the number in 2015. The surgeries were conducted on more transgender women than transgender men. Some insurance companies refuse to cover these (or even nonsurgical) biological treatments for transgender people, but a growing number of states now prohibit such insurance exclusions (Canner et al., 2018; Seelman et al., 2018).

Lea T. Transgender model Lea T. emerged in 2010 as the face of Givenchy, the famous French fashion brand. Born with an assigned gender of male, the Brazilian model has become a leading female figure in runway fashion shows and magazines, including *Vogue Paris*, *Cover* magazine, and *Love* magazine, and she is currently the face of the hair-care brand Redken. In 2012 she underwent gender reassignment surgery.

Splash News/Newscom

Clinicians have debated whether gender change surgery is an appropriate option for transgender persons (à Campo & Nijman, 2016; Gozlan, 2011). Some consider it a humane procedure, perhaps the most satisfying one to many transgender people. Others argue that gender change surgery is a "drastic nonsolution" for a complex issue. Either way, as indicated above, such surgery appears to be on the increase (Crandall, 2018; Ferrando & Thomas, 2018).

Research into the outcomes of gender reassignment surgery has yielded generally positive findings. Across a number of studies, at least 70 percent of patients report satisfaction with the outcome of the surgery, improvement in the quality of their lives, a better psychological state, more positive body satisfaction, better interpersonal interactions, and improvements in sexual functioning (Ferrando & Thomas, 2018; Lindqvist et al., 2017). On the other hand, several studies have yielded less favorable findings. A long-term follow-up study in Sweden, for example, found that gender-reassigned participants had a higher rate of psychological disorders and of suicide attempts than the general population (Dhejne et al., 2011). All of this argues for careful screening prior to surgical interventions, continued research to better understand the long-term impact of the surgical procedures, and, more generally, improved medical and clinical care for transgender people.

Gender Dysphoria

Surveys reveal that 90 percent of transgender persons experience at least a moderate degree of distress or dysfunction at home, school, or work, or in social relationships, especially during adolescence (Billard, 2018; Robles et al., 2016). As you have

read, if that level of distress and impairment becomes significant, DSM-5 categorizes the pattern as gender dysphoria. Some individuals with this disorder—children, adolescents, and adults—feel severe anxiety or depression, display substance abuse, and may have thoughts of suicide (Mueller et al., 2017; Schulman & Erickson-Schroth, 2017).

Although such features of dysphoria have been documented, the cause of gender dysphoria has been hard to sort out. On the one hand, most transgender people do indeed report that the incongruence between their gender identity and birth anatomy directly causes them some distress (Robles et al., 2016). On the other hand, surveys suggest that the primary cause for intense dysphoric reactions is the enormous prejudice that transgender persons typically face. According to surveys across the United States and other countries, for example, 80 to 90 percent of transgender people have been harassed or attacked in their schools, workplaces, or communities (some have even been murdered); 50 percent have been fired from a job, not hired, or not promoted; and 20 percent have been denied a place to live (Wirtz et al., 2018; Steinmetz, 2014). Many have been stigmatized, excluded from social groups, and denied access to appropriate health care (both general health care and care related to their gender needs) (Seelman et al., 2018). This is why so many clinicians favor the elimination of gender dysphoria from the DSM. That is, society's reactions to a transgender person may be much more responsible for the individual's psychological pain than the individual's dismay over transgender issues themselves, difficult though they may be. In fact, more and more studies are finding that when transgender individuals are supported in their identities by their family members and friends, they typically do not experience significant mental health problems (Johns et al., 2018; Seibel et al., 2018).

That said, people in psychological pain still need help, and, indeed, many individuals with gender dysphoria receive psychotherapy (Witcomb et al., 2018; Majumder & Sanyal, 2017, 2016). Here, they typically try to become more aware of their needs and feelings; reduce their feelings of anxiety, depression, and anger; improve their self-image; learn how to cope with the stress caused by their gender issues; and develop a sense of self that also extends beyond gender identity. No single form of psychotherapy has been more widely used than other forms in cases of gender dysphoria. Nor has research indicated that psychotherapy alone consistently brings significant psychological improvement in cases of gender dysphoria.

Actually, the interventions that seem to be of greater help to people with gender dysphoria are the biological gender-change procedures that so many transgender persons undergo. In an analysis of 28 studies—some of them long-term follow-up studies—with a total of 1,833 transgender individuals who received hormone therapy and/or gender reassignment surgery, it was found that 80 percent of participants experienced significant improvements in their symptoms of gender dysphoria as a result of the biological interventions (Tangpricha & Safer, 2018; Murad et al., 2010).

Finally, two positive developments in recent years have been the emergence and growth of transgender education programs and an increase in support programs for transgender people (Valentine & Shipherd, 2018; Vance et al., 2018). Across the world, many hundreds of educational programs, which are offered in locations ranging from schools to workplaces to the Internet, now target transgender persons themselves (both young and old), health care professionals, family members, and the general public. Similarly, numerous support, or mutual help, groups—both in-person and online—are

Walter Iooss Jr./Sports Illustrated/Getty Images

Frazer Harrison/Getty Images

A new audience When he won the gold medal for the decathlon at the 1976 Olympics (left), Bruce Jenner was widely viewed as the personification of masculinity—the world's best male athlete. When in 2015 Jenner appeared in *Vanity Fair* magazine (right) as a transgender woman, Caitlyn, transgender persons hoped that this high-profile revelation would help reduce the public's prejudice against transgender individuals.

#

#GenderTerms

Trans: Short for transgender

Cisgender persons: Individuals whose gender identity matches their assigned gender

A special bond Two men, 64-year-old Juani Santos (left) and 28-year-old Liam Duran (right), catch up on recent events at a cafe in Cuba. Despite a significant age difference, they are close friends, partly because they share an important gender identity experience—they are both transgender men. Santos, one of Cuba's oldest documented transgender individuals, had gender reassignment surgery just a few years ago. He says he first knew he was a boy at the age of 5.

now available for transgender adolescents and adults, providing social support, advice, and relevant information. Research indicates that these various programs help prevent or reduce gender dysphoria or other forms of psychological distress among transgender individuals (Johns et al., 2018; Cipolletta et al., 2017).

...SUMMING UP

GENDER VARIATIONS DSM-5 does not consider transgender functioning to be a psychological disorder, but it does still categorize gender dysphoria—a pattern of significant distress or impairment due to one's transgender feelings and thoughts—as a disorder. Transgender feelings and thoughts in children often disappear by adolescence or adulthood, but in some cases, children with such feelings develop into transgender adults. Hormone treatments have been used to help some people adopt the gender role they believe to be right for them. Gender reassignment surgery has also been performed.

Personal Topics Draw Public Attention

At the beginning of this chapter, we noted that sexual disorders and gender variations are, in fact, very different topics. However, they do share two things. They have both received considerable study over the past few decades, and a key to progress in both areas appears to be public education.

As a result of research in the realm of sexual disorders, people with sexual dysfunctions are no longer doomed to a lifetime of sexual frustration. Studies of sexual dysfunctions have uncovered many psychological, sociocultural, and biological causes. Correspondingly, important progress has been made in the treatment of sexual dysfunctions. At the same time, it has become clear that education about sexual dysfunctions can be as important as therapy. When taken seriously, sexual myths often lead to feelings of shame, self-hatred, isolation, and hopelessness—feelings that themselves contribute to sexual difficulty. Thus public education about sexual functioning—through the Internet, books, television and radio, school programs, group presentations, and the like—has become a major clinical focus.

CLINICAL CHOICES

Now that you've read about sexual disorders and gender variations, try the interactive case study for this chapter. See if you are able to identify Cheryl's issues and suggest a possible diagnosis based on them. What kind of interventions might be most helpful for Cheryl? Go to **LaunchPad** to access ***Clinical Choices***.

Similarly, as a result of research in the realm of gender diversity, transgender persons are no longer doomed to a life of gender confusion and frustration. In addition, the clinical field is now clear that transgender functioning does not represent a mental disorder. And, finally, it has become clear that public education about gender variations is a key to further understanding and progress in this realm. Recent increases in such educational programs have already begun to make some difference in the levels of discrimination, stigmatization, harassment, and hardship faced regularly by transgender people. Clearly, more such education is needed.

...Key Terms

sexual dysfunction, p. 330
desire phase, p. 330
male hypoactive sexual desire disorder, p. 331
female sexual interest/arousal disorder, p. 331
excitement phase, p. 334
erectile disorder, p. 334
nocturnal penile tumescence (NPT), p. 335
performance anxiety, p. 335
spectator role, p. 335
orgasm phase, p. 336
premature ejaculation, p. 336
delayed ejaculation, p. 337
female orgasmic disorder, p. 338
genito-pelvic pain/penetration disorder, p. 340
vaginismus, p. 340
dyspareunia, p. 340
sex therapy, p. 341
sensate focus, p. 343
sildenafil (Viagra), p. 344
directed masturbation training, p. 346
paraphilia, p. 347
paraphilic disorder, p. 347
fetishistic disorder, p. 349
masturbatory satiation, p. 350
transvestic disorder, p. 350
exhibitionistic disorder, p. 351
voyeuristic disorder, p. 351
frotteuristic disorder, p. 352
pedophilic disorder, p. 352
relapse-prevention training, p. 353
sexual masochism disorder, p. 354
sexual sadism disorder, p. 354
transgender, p. 356
gender dysphoria, p. 356
hormone administration, p. 358
gender reassignment surgery, p. 358

...Quick Quiz

1. What sexual dysfunctions are associated with the desire phase of the sexual response cycle? How common are they, and what causes them? *pp. 330–332*
2. What are the symptoms and prevalence of erectile disorder? To which phase of the sexual response cycle is it related? *p. 334*
3. What are the possible causes of erectile disorder? *pp. 334–336*
4. Which sexual dysfunctions seem to involve performance anxiety and the spectator role? *pp. 335, 338*
5. What are the symptoms, rates, and leading causes of premature ejaculation, delayed ejaculation, and female orgasmic disorder? To which phase of the sexual response cycle are they related? *pp. 338–340*
6. Identify, describe, and explain disorders of sexual pain. *p. 340*
7. What are the general features of modern sex therapy? What particular techniques are further used to treat specific sexual dysfunctions? *pp. 341–346*
8. List, describe, and explain the various paraphilic disorders. *pp. 347–355*
9. Describe the treatment techniques of aversion therapy, masturbatory satiation, and relapse-prevention training. Which paraphilic disorders have they been used to treat, and how successful are they? *pp. 350–355*
10. Why is transgender functioning no longer considered a mental disorder, and why is gender dysphoria a controversial diagnostic category? What interventions and options are currently available for transgender individuals? *pp. 356–360*

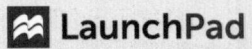

CHAPTER

12

Schizophrenia and Related Disorders

TOPIC OVERVIEW

Laura, 40 years old: Laura's desire was to become independent and leave home . . . as soon as possible. . . . She became a professional dancer at the age of 20 . . . and was booked for . . . theaters in many European countries. . . .

It was during one of her tours in Germany that Laura met her husband. . . . They were married and went to live in a small . . . town in France where the husband's business was. . . . She spent a year in that town and was very unhappy. . . . [Finally] Laura and her husband decided to emigrate to the United States. . . .

They had no children, and Laura . . . showed interest in pets. She had a dog to whom she was very devoted. The dog became sick and partially paralyzed, and veterinarians felt that there was no hope of recovery. . . . Finally [her husband] broached the problem to his wife, asking her "Should the dog be destroyed or not?" From that time on Laura became restless, agitated, and depressed. . . .

Later Laura started to complain about the neighbors. A woman who lived on the floor beneath them was knocking on the wall to irritate her. According to the husband, this woman had really knocked on the wall a few times; he had heard the noises. However, Laura became more and more concerned about it. She would wake up in the middle of the night under the impression that she was hearing noises from the apartment downstairs. She would become upset and angry at the neighbors. . . . Later she became more disturbed. She started to feel that the neighbors were now recording everything she said; maybe they had hidden wires in the apartment. She started to feel "funny" sensations. There were many strange things happening, which she did not know how to explain; people were looking at her in a funny way in the street. . . . She felt that people were planning to harm either her or her husband. . . . In the evening when she looked at television, it became obvious to her that the programs referred to her life. Often the people on the programs were just repeating what she had thought. They were stealing her ideas. She wanted to go to the police and report them.

(Arieti, 1974, pp. 165–168)

Richard, 23 years old: In high school, Richard was an average student. After graduation from high school, he [entered] the army. . . . Richard remembered [the] period . . . after his discharge from the army . . . as one of the worst in his life. . . . Any, even remote, anticipation of disappointment was able to provoke attacks of anxiety in him. . . .

Approximately two years after his return to civilian life, Richard left his job because he became overwhelmed by these feelings of lack of confidence in himself, and he refused to go look for another one. He stayed home most of the day. His mother would nag him that he was too lazy and unwilling to do anything. He became slower and slower in dressing and undressing and taking care of himself. When he went out of the house, he felt compelled "to give interpretations" to everything he looked at. He did not know what to do outside the house, where to go, where to turn. If he saw a red light at a crossing, he would interpret it as a message that he should not go in that direction. If he saw an arrow, he would follow the arrow interpreting it as a sign sent by God that he should go in that direction. Feeling lost and horrified, he would go home and stay there, afraid to go out because going out meant making decisions or choices that he felt unable to make. He reached the point where he stayed home most of the time. But even at home, he was tortured by his symptoms. He could not act; any motion that he felt like making seemed to him an insurmountable obstacle, because he did not know whether he should make it or not. He was increasingly

TABLE: 12-1

Dx Checklist

Schizophrenia
1. For 1 month, individual displays two or more of the following symptoms much of the time: • Delusions • Hallucinations • Disorganized speech • Very abnormal motor activity, including catatonia • Negative symptoms.
2. At least one of the individual's symptoms must be delusions, hallucinations, or disorganized speech.
3. Individual functions much more poorly in various life spheres than was the case prior to the symptoms.
4. Beyond this 1 month of intense symptomology, individual continues to display some degree of impaired functioning for at least 5 additional months.

Information from: APA, 2013.

afraid of doing the wrong thing. Such fears prevented him from dressing, undressing, eating, and so forth. He felt paralyzed and lay motionless in bed. He gradually became worse, was completely motionless, and had to be hospitalized. . . .

Being undecided, he felt blocked, and often would remain mute and motionless, like a statue, even for days.

(Arieti, 1974, pp. 153–155)

Eventually, Laura and Richard each received a diagnosis of **schizophrenia** (APA, 2013). People with schizophrenia, though they previously functioned well or at least acceptably, deteriorate into an isolated wilderness of unusual perceptions, odd thoughts, disturbed emotions, and motor abnormalities. Like Laura and Richard, people with schizophrenia experience **psychosis,** a loss of contact with reality. Their ability to perceive and respond to the environment becomes so disturbed that they may not be able to function at home, with friends, in school, or at work (Marder & Davis, 2017). They may have hallucinations (false sensory perceptions) or delusions (false beliefs), or they may withdraw into a private world. DSM-5 calls for a diagnosis of schizophrenia only after the symptoms continue for six months or more (see **Table 12-1**).

As you saw in Chapter 10, taking LSD or abusing amphetamines or cocaine may also produce psychosis. So may injuries or diseases of the brain. And so may other severe psychological disorders, such as major depressive disorder or bipolar disorder. Most commonly, however, psychosis appears in the form of schizophrenia.

Actually, there are a number of schizophrenia-like disorders listed in DSM-5, each distinguished by particular durations and sets of symptoms (see **Table 12-2**). Because these psychotic disorders all bear a similarity to schizophrenia, they—along with schizophrenia itself—are collectively called *schizophrenia spectrum disorders* (APA, 2013). Schizophrenia is the most prevalent of these disorders. Clinical theorists believe that most of the explanations and treatments offered for schizophrenia are applicable to the other disorders as well (Bole et al., 2017).

Approximately 1 of every 100 people in the world suffers from schizophrenia during his or her lifetime (Fischer & Buchanan, 2018). An estimated 21 million people worldwide are afflicted with it, including 3.6 million in the United States (WHO, 2018; NIMH,

TABLE: 12-2

Schizophrenia Spectrum Disorders: An Array of Psychosis

Disorder	Key Features	Duration	Lifetime Prevalence
Schizophrenia	Various psychotic symptoms, such as delusions, hallucinations, disorganized speech, restricted or inappropriate affect, and catatonia	6 months or more	1.0%
Brief psychotic disorder	Various psychotic symptoms, such as delusions, hallucinations, disorganized speech, restricted or inappropriate affect, and catatonia	Less than 1 month	Unknown
Schizophreniform disorder	Various psychotic symptoms, such as delusions, hallucinations, disorganized speech, restricted or inappropriate affect, and catatonia	1 to 6 months	0.2%
Schizoaffective disorder	Marked symptoms of both schizophrenia and a major depressive episode or a manic episode	6 months or more	Unknown
Delusional disorder	Persistent delusions that are not bizarre and not due to schizophrenia; persecutory, jealous, grandiose, and somatic delusions are common	1 month or more	0.1%
Psychotic disorder due to another medical condition	Hallucinations, delusions, or disorganized speech caused by a medical illness or brain damage	No minimum length	Unknown
Substance/medication-induced psychotic disorder	Hallucinations, delusions, or disorganized speech caused directly by a substance, such as an abused drug	No minimum length	Unknown

Information from: Rosell, 2018; Manschreck, 2017; Marder & Davis, 2017; APA, 2013.

2017). Equal numbers of men and women experience the disorder. The average age of onset for men is 23 years, compared with 28 years for women.

The financial cost of schizophrenia is enormous, and the emotional cost is even greater. As you read in Chapter 7, people with this disorder are much more likely to attempt suicide than the general population. It is estimated that as many as 25 percent of people with schizophrenia attempt suicide and 5 percent die from suicide (SAMHSA, 2018). In addition, people with the disorder have an increased risk of physical—often fatal—illness. On average, they live 10 to 20 fewer years than other people (Fischer & Buchanan, 2018).

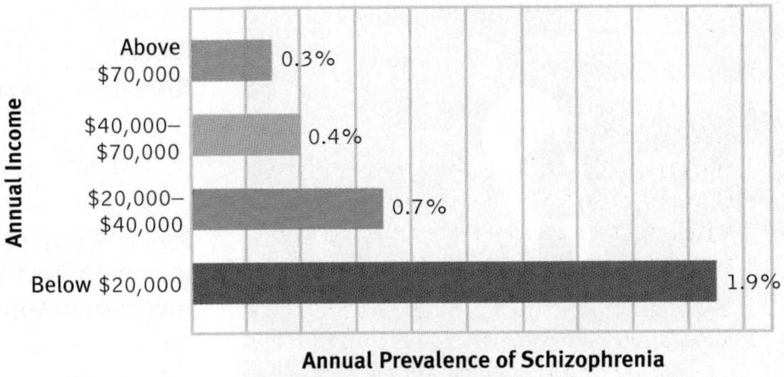

FIGURE 12-1

Socioeconomic Class and Schizophrenia

Poor people in the United States are more likely than wealthy people to experience schizophrenia. (Information from: Gruebner et al., 2017; Uher & Zwicker, 2017; Sareen et al., 2011.)

Although schizophrenia appears in all socioeconomic groups, it is found more frequently in the lower levels (Gruebner et al., 2017; Uher & Zwicker, 2017) (see **Figure 12-1**). This has led some theorists to believe that the stress of poverty is itself a cause of the disorder. However, it could be that schizophrenia causes its sufferers to fall from a higher to a lower socioeconomic level or to remain poor because they are unable to function effectively. This is sometimes called the *downward drift* theory.

People have long shown great interest in schizophrenia, flocking to plays and movies that explore or exploit our fascination with the disorder. Yet, as you will read, all too many people with schizophrenia are neglected in our country, their needs almost entirely ignored. Although effective interventions have been developed, many sufferers live without adequate treatment and never fully achieve their potential as human beings. ■

The Clinical Picture of Schizophrenia

The symptoms of schizophrenia vary greatly from sufferer to sufferer, and so do its triggers, course, and responsiveness to treatment (APA, 2013). In fact, most of today's clinicians believe that schizophrenia is actually a group of distinct disorders that happen to have some features in common (Fischer & Buchanan, 2018). Regardless of whether schizophrenia is a single disorder or several disorders, the lives of people who struggle with its symptoms are filled with pain and turmoil.

What Are the Symptoms of Schizophrenia?

Think back to Laura and Richard, the two people described at the beginning of the chapter. Both of them deteriorated from a normal level of functioning to become ineffective in dealing with the world. Each had some of the symptoms found in schizophrenia. The symptoms can be grouped into three categories: *positive symptoms* (excesses of thought, emotion, and behavior), *negative symptoms* (deficits of thought, emotion, and behavior), and *psychomotor symptoms* (unusual movements or gestures). Some people with schizophrenia are more dominated by positive symptoms and others by negative symptoms, although most tend to have both kinds of symptoms to some degree. In addition, around half of those with schizophrenia have significant difficulties with memory and other kinds of cognitive functioning (Fischer & Buchanan, 2018).

Positive Symptoms

Positive symptoms are "pathological excesses," or bizarre additions, to a person's behavior. *Delusions, disorganized thinking and speech, heightened perceptions and hallucinations,* and *inappropriate affect* are the ones most often found in schizophrenia.

DELUSIONS Many people with schizophrenia develop **delusions,** ideas that they believe wholeheartedly but that have no basis in fact. The deluded person may consider the ideas enlightening or may feel confused by them. Some people hold a single delusion that dominates their lives and behavior; others have many delusions. Delusions

schizophrenia A psychotic disorder in which functioning deteriorates as a result of unusual perceptions, odd thoughts, disturbed emotions, and motor abnormalities.

psychosis A state in which a person loses contact with reality in key ways.

positive symptoms Symptoms of schizophrenia that seem to be excesses of or bizarre additions to thoughts, emotions, or behaviors.

delusion A strange false belief firmly held despite evidence to the contrary.

Paul Brown/REX/Shutterstock

Shared delusions When two or more persons share a delusion or hallucination, it is called *folie à deux* or *shared psychosis*. In an infamous case, two 12-year-old girls recently stabbed a classmate multiple times, saying they were trying to appease and impress *Slender Man*, a mythical "boogie man" whom many internet users report seeing and fearing in their everyday lives. (He is portrayed here at a science fiction convention.) Clinicians later testified that each assailant had a schizophrenia spectrum disorder.

of persecution are the most common in schizophrenia (APA, 2013). People with such delusions believe they are being plotted or discriminated against, spied on, slandered, threatened, attacked, or deliberately victimized. Laura believed that her neighbors were trying to irritate her and that other people were trying to harm her and her husband.

People with schizophrenia may also have *delusions of reference:* they attach special and personal meaning to the actions of others or to various objects or events. Richard, for example, interpreted arrows on street signs as indicators of the direction he should take. People with *delusions of grandeur* believe themselves to be great inventors, religious saviors, or other specially empowered persons. And those with *delusions of control* believe their feelings, thoughts, and actions are being controlled by other people.

Philosopher Friedrich Nietzsche said, "Insanity in individuals is something rare—but in groups, parties, nations and epochs, it is the rule." What did he mean?

DISORGANIZED THINKING AND SPEECH People with schizophrenia may not be able to think logically and may speak in peculiar ways. These difficulties, collectively called **formal thought disorders,** can cause the sufferer great confusion and make communication extremely difficult. Often, such thought disorders take the form of positive symptoms (pathological excesses), as in *loose associations, neologisms, perseveration,* and *clang.*

People who have *loose associations,* or *derailment,* the most common formal thought disorder, rapidly shift from one topic to another, believing that their incoherent statements make sense. A single, perhaps unimportant word in one sentence becomes the focus of the next. One man with schizophrenia, asked about his itchy arms, responded:

> *The problem is insects. My brother used to collect insects. He's now a man 5 foot 10 inches. You know, 10 is my favorite number. I also like to dance, draw, and watch television.*

Some people with schizophrenia use *neologisms,* made-up words that typically have meaning only to the person using them. One person said, for example, "I am here from a foreign university . . . and you have to have a *'plausity'* of all acts of amendment to go through for the children's code . . . it is an *'amorition'* law . . . the children have to have this *'accentuative'* law so they don't go into the *'mortite'* law of the church" (Vetter, 1969, p. 189). Others may have the formal thought disorder of *perseveration,* in which they repeat their words and statements again and again. Finally, some use *clang,* or rhyme, to think or express themselves. When asked how he was feeling, one man replied, "Well, hell, it's well to tell." Another described the weather as "So hot, you know it runs on a cot." Research suggests that some people may have disorganized speech or thinking long before their full pattern of schizophrenia unfolds (Remington et al., 2014).

HEIGHTENED PERCEPTIONS AND HALLUCINATIONS The perceptions and attention of some people with schizophrenia seem to intensify (Spagna et al., 2018). The persons may feel that their senses are being flooded by all the sights and sounds that surround them. This makes it almost impossible for them to attend to anything important. Such problems as these that people with schizophrenia have may develop years before the onset of the actual disorder (Fischer & Buchanan, 2018). It is also possible that such problems further contribute to the memory impairments that are common to many people with schizophrenia (Boudewyn, 2017).

Another kind of perceptual problem in schizophrenia consists of **hallucinations,** perceptions that a person has in the absence of external stimuli (see ***InfoCentral***). People who have *auditory* hallucinations, by far the most common kind in schizophrenia, hear sounds and voices that seem to come from outside their heads. The voices may talk directly to the hallucinator, perhaps giving commands or warning of dangers, or they may be experienced as overheard.

formal thought disorder A disturbance in the production and organization of thought.

hallucination The experiencing of sights, sounds, or other perceptions in the absence of external stimuli.

HALLUCINATIONS

Hallucinations are the experiencing of sights, sounds, smells, and other perceptions that occur in the absence of external stimuli.

TYPES OF HALLUCINATIONS

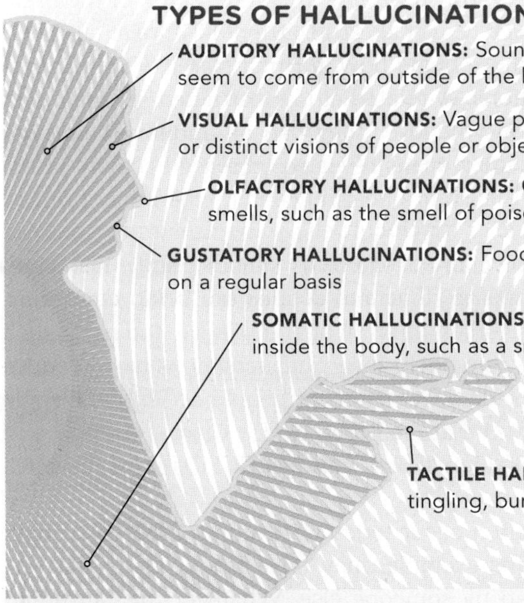

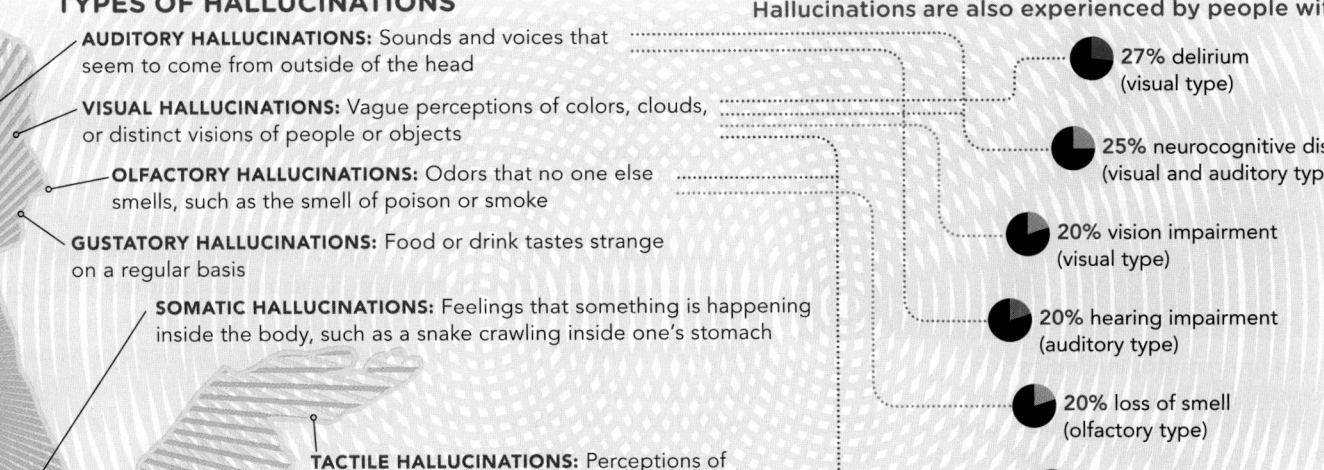

AUDITORY HALLUCINATIONS: Sounds and voices that seem to come from outside of the head

VISUAL HALLUCINATIONS: Vague perceptions of colors, clouds, or distinct visions of people or objects

OLFACTORY HALLUCINATIONS: Odors that no one else smells, such as the smell of poison or smoke

GUSTATORY HALLUCINATIONS: Food or drink tastes strange on a regular basis

SOMATIC HALLUCINATIONS: Feelings that something is happening inside the body, such as a snake crawling inside one's stomach

TACTILE HALLUCINATIONS: Perceptions of tingling, burning, or electric-shock sensations

Hallucinations are also experienced by people with:

- **27% delirium** (visual type)
- **25% neurocognitive disorder** (visual and auditory types)
- **20% vision impairment** (visual type)
- **20% hearing impairment** (auditory type)
- **20% loss of smell** (olfactory type)
- **13% migraines** (visual and olfactory types)

(Linszen et al., 2018; Sacks, 2017, 2012; AFA, 2014; Mandal, 2014; Knott, 2011; Norton, 2011; Frey, 2005)

Hallucinations are different from:

Illusions: Distorted or misinterpreted real perceptions

Imagery: Under voluntary control and does not mimic real perception

Dreaming: Occurs when person is asleep

Pseudohallucinations: Internally triggered, vivid perceptions that are recognized by individual as unreal, and partly under voluntary control

SCHIZOPHRENIC HALLUCINATIONS

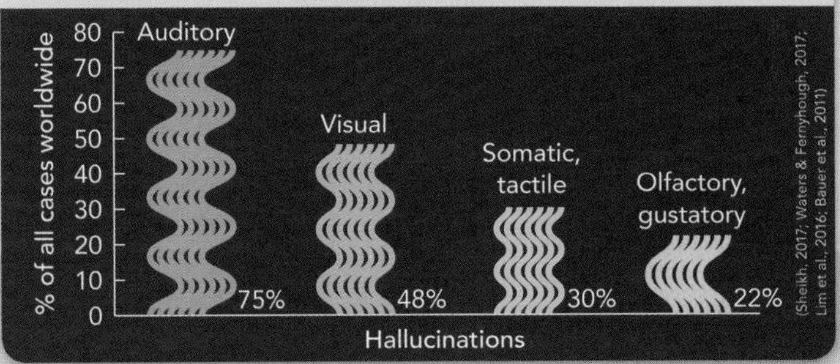

(Sheikh, 2017; Waters & Fernyhough, 2017; Lim et al., 2016; Bauer et al., 2011)

HALLUCINATIONS CAN BE "NORMAL"

Many people experience hallucinations that are unrelated to disorders or substance ingestion. These hallucinations . . .

- affect as many as 10–12% of the population
- occur every 3 days, on average
- last for 2–3 minutes
- can be controlled around 60% of the time
- cause little distress or disruption, unless misinterpreted

(Sheikh, 2017; Read, 2016; de Leede-Smith & Barkus, 2013; Daalman et al., 2011)

37% Hypnagogic hallucinations
Geometric patterns, faces, or landscapes experienced by some people falling asleep

12.5% Hypnopompic hallucinations
Geometric patterns, faces, or landscapes experienced by some people as they are awakening

(Soffer-Dudek, 2017; de Leede-Smith & Barkus, 2013; Daalman et al., 2011)

BRAIN EXPLANATIONS FOR AUDITORY HALLUCINATIONS

ABNORMAL ACTIVATION of the primary **auditory cortex**.

FAILURE to recognize **internally generated speech** as one's own. Cross-activation with the **auditory areas**, so what most people experience as thoughts become "voiced."

ABNORMAL ATTENTION to the **subvocal stream** which accompanies verbal thinking.

MUSICAL HALLUCINATIONS result from activation of the brain network involving **auditory areas, the motor cortex, visual areas, basal ganglia, cerebellum, hippocampus,** and **amygdala.**

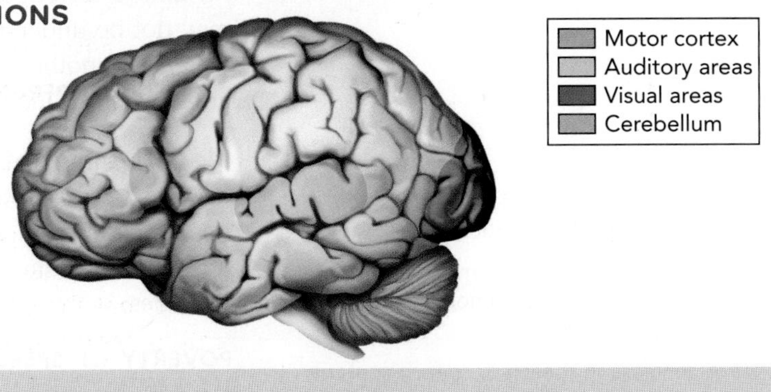

HALLUCINATIONS OVER THE AGES

Ancient times: Attributed to gifts from the gods or the Muses

Prior to 18th century: Caused by supernatural forces, such as gods or demons, angels or djinns

Middle of 18th century: Caused by the overactivity of certain centers in the brain

1990s: Resulting from a circuit of cortical and subcortical structures

(Groopman, 2017; Sacks, 2017, 2012; Shergill et al., 2000)

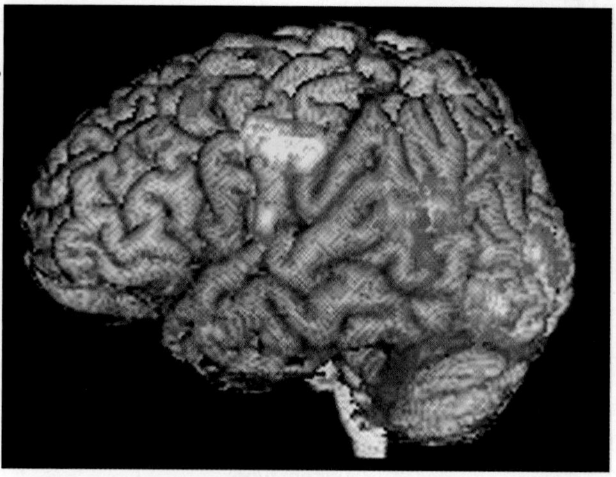

The human brain during hallucinations
This PET scan, taken while a patient was having auditory hallucinations, shows heightened activity (yellow-orange) in Broca's area, a brain region that helps people produce speech, and in the auditory cortex, the brain area that helps people hear sounds. Thus people who are hallucinating seem to hear sounds produced by their own brains (Juckel, 2014; Silbersweig et al., 1995).

Research suggests that people with auditory hallucinations actually produce the nerve signals of sound in their brains, "hear" them, and then believe that external sources are responsible (Hugdahl & Sommer, 2018). One line of research has measured blood flow in *Broca's area,* the region of the brain that helps people produce speech (Cui et al., 2018, 2016; McGuire et al., 1996). The investigators have found more blood flow in Broca's area while patients are having auditory hallucinations. A related study instructed six men with schizophrenia to press a button whenever they had an auditory hallucination (Silbersweig et al., 1995). Brain scans revealed increased activity in the tissues of the auditory cortex, the brain's hearing center, when they pressed the button.

Hallucinations can also involve any of the other senses. *Tactile* hallucinations may take the form of tingling, burning, or electric-shock sensations. *Somatic* hallucinations feel as if something is happening inside the body, such as a snake crawling inside one's stomach. *Visual* hallucinations may produce vague perceptions of colors or clouds or distinct visions of people or objects. People with *gustatory* hallucinations regularly find that their food or drink tastes strange, and people with *olfactory* hallucinations smell odors that no one else does, such as the smell of poison or smoke.

Hallucinations and delusional ideas often occur together (Cutting, 2015). A woman who hears voices issuing commands, for example, may have the delusion that the commands are being placed in her head by someone else. Whatever the cause and whichever comes first, the hallucination and delusion eventually feed into each other.

> *I thought the voices I heard were being transmitted through the walls of my apartment and through the washer and dryer and that these machines were talking and telling me things. I felt that the government agencies had planted transmitters and receivers in my apartment so that I could hear what they were saying and they could hear what I was saying.*
>
> *(Anonymous, 1996, p. 183)*

INAPPROPRIATE AFFECT Many people with schizophrenia display **inappropriate affect,** emotions that are unsuited to the situation (Fischer & Buchanan, 2018). They may smile when making a somber statement or upon being told terrible news, or they may become upset in situations that should make them happy. They may also undergo inappropriate shifts in mood.

In at least some cases, these emotions may be merely a response to other features of the disorder. Consider a woman with schizophrenia who smiles when told of her husband's serious illness. She may not actually be happy about the news; in fact, she may not be understanding or even hearing it. She could, for example, be responding instead to another of the many stimuli flooding her senses, perhaps a joke coming from an auditory hallucination.

Negative Symptoms

Negative symptoms are those that seem to be "pathological deficits," characteristics that are lacking in a person. *Poverty of speech, blunted and flat affect, loss of volition,* and *social withdrawal* are commonly found in schizophrenia (Fischer & Buchanan, 2018; Rocca et al., 2014). Such deficits greatly affect one's life and activities.

POVERTY OF SPEECH People with schizophrenia often have **alogia,** or **poverty of speech,** a reduction in speech or speech content. Some people with this negative kind of formal thought disorder think and say very little. Others say quite a bit but still manage to convey little meaning.

RESTRICTED AFFECT Many people with schizophrenia have a *blunted affect*—they display less anger, sadness, joy, and other feelings than most people. Indeed, a number

inappropriate affect Displays of emotions that are unsuited to the situation.

negative symptoms Symptoms of schizophrenia that seem to be deficits in normal thought, emotions, or behaviors.

alogia A decrease in speech or speech content; a symptom of schizophrenia. Also known as *poverty of speech*.

catatonia A pattern of extreme psychomotor symptoms, found in some forms of schizophrenia, which may include catatonic stupor, rigidity, or posturing.

show almost no emotions at all, a condition known as *flat affect*. Their faces are still, their eye contact is poor, and their voices are monotonous.

Restricted affect of this kind may actually reflect an inability to *express* emotions as others do. One study had participants view very emotional film clips. The participants with schizophrenia showed less facial expression than the others; however, they reported feeling just as much positive and negative emotion and in fact displayed more skin arousal (Kring & Neale, 1996). There is, in fact, a growing recognition in the clinical field that many people with schizophrenia not only experience emotions internally, they grapple with high levels of anxiety and/or depression (Siris & Braga, 2018, 2017).

#TheirWords

"Her face was a solemn mask, and she could neither give nor receive affection."

Mother, 1991, describing her daughter who has schizophrenia

LOSS OF VOLITION Many people with schizophrenia experience *avolition*, or apathy, feeling drained of energy and of interest in normal goals and unable to start or follow through on a course of action. This problem is particularly common in people who have had schizophrenia for many years, as if they have been worn down by it. Similarly, people with schizophrenia may feel *ambivalence*, or conflicting feelings, about most things. The avolition and ambivalence of Richard, the young man you read about earlier, made eating, dressing, and undressing impossible ordeals for him.

SOCIAL WITHDRAWAL People with schizophrenia may withdraw from their social environment and attend only to their own ideas and fantasies (Swain et al., 2017). Because their ideas are illogical and confused, the withdrawal has the effect of distancing them still further from reality. The social withdrawal seems also to lead to a breakdown of social skills, including the ability to recognize other people's needs and emotions accurately (Fischer & Buchanan, 2018).

Psychomotor Symptoms People with schizophrenia sometimes experience *psychomotor symptoms*. Many move relatively slowly, and a number make awkward movements or repeated grimaces and odd gestures that seem to have a private purpose—perhaps ritualistic or magical (Janssens et al., 2018; Grover et al., 2015).

The psychomotor symptoms of schizophrenia may take certain extreme forms, collectively called **catatonia.** Around 10 percent of people with schizophrenia experience some degree of catatonia (Coffey, 2017). People in a *catatonic stupor* stop responding to their environment, remaining motionless and silent for long stretches of time. Recall how Richard would lie motionless and mute in bed for days. People with *catatonic rigidity* maintain a rigid, upright posture for hours and resist efforts to be moved. Still others exhibit *catatonic posturing*, assuming awkward, bizarre positions for long periods of time. Finally, people with *catatonic excitement*, a different form of catatonia, move excitedly, sometimes wildly waving their arms and legs.

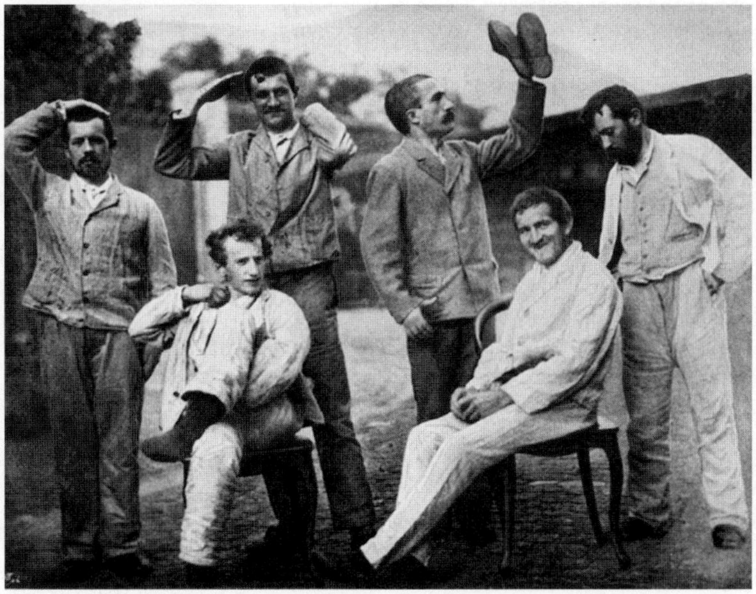

A catatonic pose These patients, photographed in the early 1900s, show features of catatonia, including catatonic posturing, in which they assume bizarre positions for long periods of time.

What Is the Course of Schizophrenia?

Schizophrenia usually first appears between the person's late teens and mid-thirties (Fischer & Buchanan, 2018). Although its course varies widely from case to case, many sufferers seem to go through three phases—prodromal, active, and residual (Lee et al., 2017; Fukumoto et al., 2014). During the *prodromal phase*, symptoms are not yet obvious, but the person is beginning to deteriorate. He or she may withdraw socially, speak in vague or odd ways, develop strange ideas, or express little emotion. During the *active phase*, symptoms become apparent. Sometimes this phase is triggered by stress or trauma in the person's life. For Laura, the middle-aged woman described earlier, the immediate trigger was the loss of her cherished dog. Finally, many people with schizophrenia eventually enter a *residual phase* in which they return to a prodromal-like level

David X Prutting/BFA/REX/Shutterstock

Relationships of the mind Like Taylor Swift, most celebrities grow used to the constant crush of fans and curious onlookers. However, when they are stalked, the matter grows more serious. Some stalkers have *erotomanic delusions*, false beliefs that they are loved by and in a relationship with the object of their attention. In recent years, Swift and other celebrities have had to seek court protection against stalkers who are constantly following them, trying to enter their premises, seeking expressions of love, and threatening them.

of functioning. They may retain some negative symptoms, such as blunted emotion, but have a lessening of the striking symptoms of the active phase. Although 25 percent or more of patients recover completely from schizophrenia, the majority continue to have at least some residual problems for the rest of their lives (Fischer & Buchanan, 2018; an der Heiden & Häfner, 2011).

Each of these phases may last for days or for years. A fuller recovery from schizophrenia is more likely in people who functioned quite well before the disorder; whose initial disorder is triggered by stress, comes on abruptly, or develops during middle age; and who receive early treatment. Relapses are apparently more likely during times of life stress (Lange et al., 2017; Remberk et al., 2015).

Many researchers believe that in order to help predict the course of schizophrenia, there should be a distinction between so-called Type I and Type II schizophrenia. People with *Type I schizophrenia* (80 to 85 percent of cases) seem to be dominated by positive symptoms, such as delusions and hallucinations (Crow, 2008, 1995, 1985, 1980). Those with *Type II schizophrenia* (15 to 20 percent of cases) display mostly negative symptoms, such as restricted affect and poverty of speech.

...SUMMING UP

THE CLINICAL PICTURE OF SCHIZOPHRENIA Schizophrenia is a disorder in which personal, social, and occupational functioning deteriorate as a result of disturbed thought processes, distorted perceptions, unusual emotions, and motor abnormalities. Approximately 1 percent of the world's population suffers from this disorder. The symptoms of schizophrenia fall into three groupings. Positive symptoms include delusions, certain formal thought disorders, hallucinations and other disturbances in perception and attention, and inappropriate affect. Negative symptoms include poverty of speech, restricted affect, loss of volition, and social withdrawal. Schizophrenia may also include psychomotor symptoms, collectively called catatonia in their extreme form. Schizophrenia usually emerges during late adolescence or early adulthood and tends to progress through three phases: prodromal, active, and residual.

How Do Theorists Explain Schizophrenia?

As with many other kinds of disorders, biological, psychological, and sociocultural theorists have each proposed explanations for schizophrenia. So far, the biological explanations have received by far the most research support. This is not to say that psychological and sociocultural factors play no role in the disorder. Rather, a *diathesis–stress relationship* may be at work: people with a biological predisposition (i.e., a diathesis) will develop schizophrenia only if certain kinds of events or stressors are also present (Pruessner et al., 2017). Similarly, a diathesis–stress relationship often seems to be operating in the development of other kinds of psychotic disorders (see ***PsychWatch*** on page 372).

Biological Views

Perhaps the most enlightening research on schizophrenia during the past several decades has come from genetic and biological investigations. These studies have revealed the key roles of inheritance and brain activity in the development of schizophrenia and have opened the door to important treatment changes.

Genetic Factors Following the principles of the diathesis–stress perspective, genetic researchers believe that some people inherit a biological predisposition to schizophrenia and develop the disorder later when they face extreme stress, usually during late

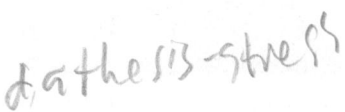

dopamine hypothesis The theory that schizophrenia results from excessive activity of the neurotransmitter dopamine.

antipsychotic drugs Drugs that help correct grossly confused or distorted thinking.

adolescence or early adulthood. The genetic view has been supported by studies of (1) relatives of people with schizophrenia, (2) twins with schizophrenia, (3) people with schizophrenia who are adopted, and (4) schizophrenia-related genes.

What factors, besides genetic ones, might account for the elevated rate of schizophrenia among relatives of people with this disorder?

ARE RELATIVES VULNERABLE? Family pedigree studies have found repeatedly that schizophrenia and schizophrenia-like brain abnormalities are more common among relatives of people with the disorder (Henriksen et al., 2017). And the more closely related the relatives are to the person with schizophrenia, the more likely they are to develop the disorder (see **Figure 12-2**).

IS AN IDENTICAL TWIN MORE VULNERABLE THAN A FRATERNAL TWIN? Twins, who are among the closest of relatives, have in particular been studied by schizophrenia researchers. If both members of a pair of twins have a particular trait, they are said to be *concordant* for that trait. If genetic factors are at work in schizophrenia, identical twins (who share all their genes) should have a higher concordance rate for schizophrenia than fraternal twins (who share only some genes). This expectation has been supported consistently by research (Fischer & Buchanan, 2018; Gottesman, 1991). Studies have found that if one identical twin develops schizophrenia, there is a 48 percent chance that the other twin will do so as well. If the twins are fraternal, on the other hand, the second twin has approximately only a 17 percent chance of developing the disorder.

ARE THE BIOLOGICAL RELATIVES OF AN ADOPTEE VULNERABLE? Adoption studies look at adults with schizophrenia who were adopted as infants and compare them with both their biological and their adoptive relatives. Because they were reared apart from their biological relatives, similar symptoms in those relatives would indicate genetic influences. Conversely, similarities to their adoptive relatives would suggest environmental influences. Researchers have repeatedly found that the biological relatives of adoptees with schizophrenia are more likely than their adoptive relatives to develop schizophrenia or another schizophrenia spectrum disorder (Henriksen et al., 2017).

WHAT DO GENE STUDIES SUGGEST? As with bipolar disorders (see Chapter 6), researchers have run studies of *genetic linkage* and *molecular biology* to pinpoint the possible genetic factors in schizophrenia (Uher & Zwicker, 2017). Using such research procedures, studies have identified possible gene defects on chromosomes 1, 2, 6, 8, 10, 13, 15, 18, 20, and 22 and on the X chromosome, each of which may help predispose a person to develop this disorder (Zhao et al., 2018; Xu et al., 2017). Altogether, the number of specific gene sites linked to schizophrenia is no fewer than 281 to date (Tartakovsky, 2016)! These varied findings may indicate that schizophrenia, like a number of other disorders, is a *polygenic disorder,* caused by a combination of gene defects (Fischer & Buchanan, 2018).

How might genetic factors lead to the development of schizophrenia? Research has pointed to two kinds of biological abnormalities that could conceivably be inherited—*biochemical abnormalities* and *dysfunctional brain circuitry.*

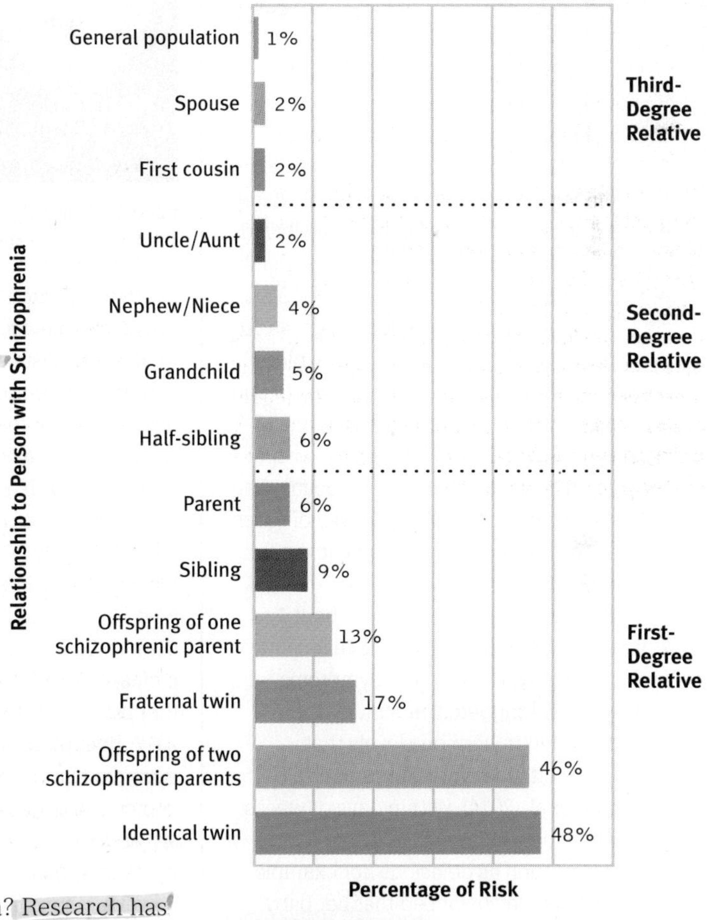

FIGURE 12-2

Family Links

People who are biologically related to someone with schizophrenia have a heightened risk of developing the disorder during their lifetimes. The closer the biological relationship (that is, the more similar the genetic makeup), the greater the risk of developing the disorder. (Information from: Henriksen et al., 2017; Bhatia et al., 2016; Gottesman, 1991, p. 96.)

Biochemical Abnormalities Over the past five decades, researchers have developed a **dopamine hypothesis** to help explain schizophrenia: certain neurons that use the neurotransmitter dopamine fire too often and transmit too many messages to receiving neurons, thus producing the symptoms of schizophrenia (Martino et al., 2018). This hypothesis has undergone challenges and adjustments in recent years, but it is still very influential. As you will see later in this chapter, the chain of events leading to the hypothesis began with the accidental discovery of **antipsychotic drugs,** medications that help remove the symptoms of schizophrenia. The first group of antipsychotic medications,

PSYCHWATCH

Postpartum Psychosis: A Dangerous Syndrome

On the morning of June 20, 2001, the nation's television viewers watched in horror as officials escorted 36-year-old Andrea Yates to a police car. Just minutes before, she had called police and explained that she had drowned her five children in the bathtub because "they weren't developing correctly" and because she "realized [she had not been] a good mother to them."

Homicide sergeant Eric Mehl described how she looked him in the eye, nodded, answered with a polite "Yes, sir" to many of his questions, and twice recounted the order in which the children had died: first 3-year-old Paul, then 2-year-old Luke, followed by 5-year-old John and 6-month-old Mary. She then described how she had had to drag 7-year-old Noah to the bathroom and how he had come up twice as he fought for air. Later she told doctors she wanted her hair shaved so she could see the number 666—the mark of the Antichrist—on her scalp (Roche, 2002).

In Chapter 6 you read that as many as 80 percent of mothers experience "baby blues" soon after giving birth, while between 10 and 30 percent display the clinical syndrome of *postpartum depression*. Yet another postpartum disorder that has become all too familiar to the public in recent times, by way of cases such as that of Andrea Yates, is *postpartum psychosis* (Denno, 2017).

Postpartum psychosis affects about 1 to 2 of every 1,000 mothers who have recently given birth (Payne, 2018). The symptoms apparently are triggered, in part, by the enormous shift in hormone levels that takes place after delivery (Jones et al., 2014; Meinhard et al., 2014). Within days or weeks, the woman develops signs of losing touch with reality, such as delusions (for example, she may become convinced that her baby is the devil); hallucinations (perhaps hearing voices); extreme anxiety, confusion, and disorientation; disturbed sleep; and illogical or chaotic thoughts (for example, thoughts about killing herself or her child). Typically, treatment consists of antipsychotic drugs and psychotherapy, although the effectiveness of this approach has not received much research (Payne, 2017).

Family tragedy In this undated photograph, Andrea Yates poses with her husband and four of the five children she later drowned.

Photo Courtesy of Yates Family/Getty Images

Women with a history of bipolar disorder, schizophrenia, or major depressive disorder are particularly vulnerable to the disorder (Payne, 2018; Di Florio et al., 2014). Women who have previously experienced postpartum depression or postpartum psychosis have an increased likelihood of developing postpartum psychosis after subsequent births (Payne, 2018; Bergink et al., 2012). Andrea Yates, for example, had developed signs of postpartum depression (and perhaps postpartum psychosis) and attempted suicide after the birth of her fourth child (Denno, 2017). At that time, however, she appeared to respond well to a combination of medications, including antipsychotic drugs, and so she and her husband later decided to conceive a fifth child.

After the birth of her fifth child, the depressive symptoms recurred, along with features of psychosis. Yates again attempted suicide. Although she was hospitalized twice and treated with various medications, her condition failed to improve. Six months after giving birth to Mary, her fifth child, she drowned all five of her children. Although relatively few women with the disorder actually try to harm their children (estimates run as high as 4 percent), the Yates case reminds us that such an outcome is possible (Gressier et al., 2015; Posmontier, 2010). The case also reminds us that early detection and treatment are critical (Payne, 2018, 2017; O'Hara & Wisner, 2014).

On July 26, 2006, after an initial conviction for murder was overturned by an appeals court, Yates was found *not guilty by reason of insanity* and sent to a state mental hospital, where she continues to receive treatment today (Denno, 2017).

the **phenothiazines,** were discovered in the 1950s by researchers who were looking for better *antihistamine* drugs to combat allergies. Although phenothiazines failed as antihistamines, it soon became obvious that they were effective in reducing schizophrenic symptoms, and clinicians began to prescribe them widely (Adams et al., 2014).

Researchers later learned that these early antipsychotic drugs often produce troublesome muscular tremors, symptoms that are identical to the central symptom of *Parkinson's disease,* a disabling neurological illness. This undesired reaction to antipsychotic drugs offered the first important clue to the biology of schizophrenia. Scientists already knew that people who suffer from Parkinson's disease have abnormally low levels of the neurotransmitter dopamine in some areas of the brain and that lack of dopamine is the reason for their uncontrollable shaking. If antipsychotic drugs produce Parkinsonian symptoms in people with schizophrenia while removing their psychotic symptoms, perhaps the drugs reduce dopamine activity. And, scientists reasoned further, if lowering dopamine activity helps remove the symptoms of schizophrenia, perhaps schizophrenia is related to excessive dopamine activity in the first place.

Since the 1960s, research has supported and helped clarify the dopamine hypothesis. It has been found, for example, that some people with Parkinson's disease develop schizophrenia-like symptoms if they take too much *L-dopa,* a medication that raises Parkinson's patients' dopamine levels (Hamadjida et al., 2018). The L-dopa apparently raises the dopamine activity so much that it produces psychosis. Support has also come from research on *amphetamines,* drugs that, as you saw in Chapter 10, stimulate the central nervous system by increasing dopamine activity in the brain. Clinical investigators have observed that people who take high doses of amphetamines may develop *amphetamine psychosis*—a syndrome very similar to schizophrenia (McKetin, 2018).

Researchers have located areas of the brain that are rich in dopamine receptors, and they have found that phenothiazines and related antipsychotic drugs bind to many of these receptors, prevent dopamine from binding there, and so prevent the neurons containing those receptors from firing (Wang et al., 2018). As it turns out, there are five kinds of dopamine receptors in the brain—called the D-1, D-2, D-3, D-4, and D-5 receptors—and phenothiazines bind most strongly to the *D-2 receptors.* These and related findings suggest that in schizophrenia, messages traveling from dopamine-sending neurons to dopamine receptors on other neurons, particularly to the D-2 receptors, may be transmitted too easily or too often.

Though enlightening, the dopamine hypothesis has certain problems. The biggest challenge to it has come with the discovery of a new group of drugs called **second-generation antipsychotic drugs,** which are often more effective than the phenothiazines and related early drugs, now collectively called **first-generation antipsychotic drugs.** The newer drugs bind not only to D-2 dopamine receptors, like the first-generation antipsychotic drugs, but also to many D-1 and D-4 receptors and to receptors for other neurotransmitters such as *serotonin* (Fischer & Buchanan, 2018). Thus, it may be that schizophrenia is related to abnormal activity or interactions of both dopamine and other neurotransmitters, rather than to abnormal dopamine activity alone.

Dysfunctional Brain Structures and Circuitry As you have read, reactions of various kinds are tied to *brain circuits*—networks of brain structures that work together, triggering each other into action and producing particular behaviors, cognitions, or emotions. Although research is far from complete, studies have begun to reveal a brain circuit whose dysfunction contributes to schizophrenia (Deng et al., 2019; Lieberman et al., 2018; Chen et al., 2017). The structures that comprise this schizophrenia-related circuit include the prefrontal cortex, hippocampus, amygdala, thalamus, striatum, and substantia nigra, among other brain structures (see **Figure 12-3**). You may notice, once again, that several of the structures in this circuit are also members of brain circuits that contribute to other disorders, but in cases of schizophrenia the structures function and interconnect in problematic ways that are, collectively, unique to this disorder.

phenothiazines A group of antihistamine drugs that became the first group of effective antipsychotic medications.

second-generation antipsychotic drugs A relatively new group of antipsychotic drugs whose biological action is different from that of the first-generation antipsychotic drugs.

first-generation antipsychotic drugs Phenothiazines and other antipsychotic drugs developed throughout the latter half of the twentieth century.

FIGURE 12-3

Biology of Schizophrenia

Studies suggest that a dysfunctional brain circuit may lead to schizophrenia. This circuit includes the prefrontal cortex, hippocampus, amygdala, thalamus, striatum, and substantia nigra, among other structures.

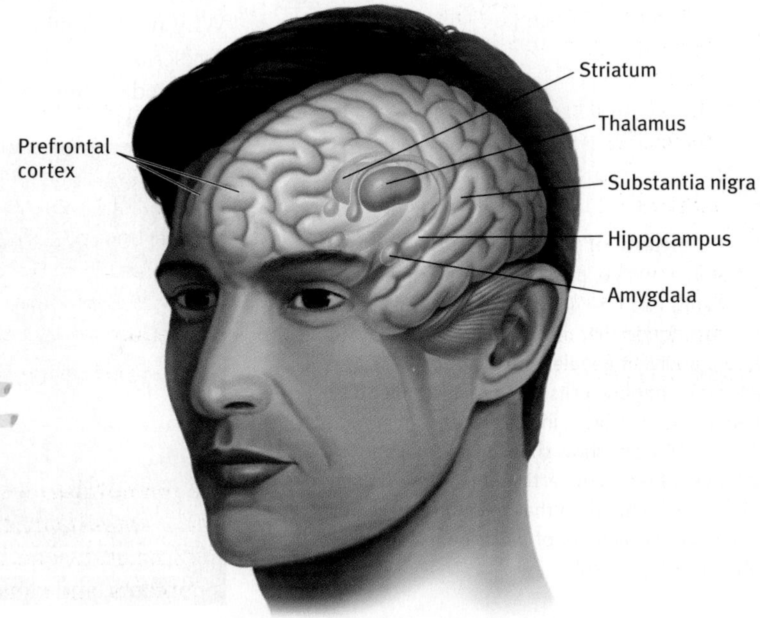

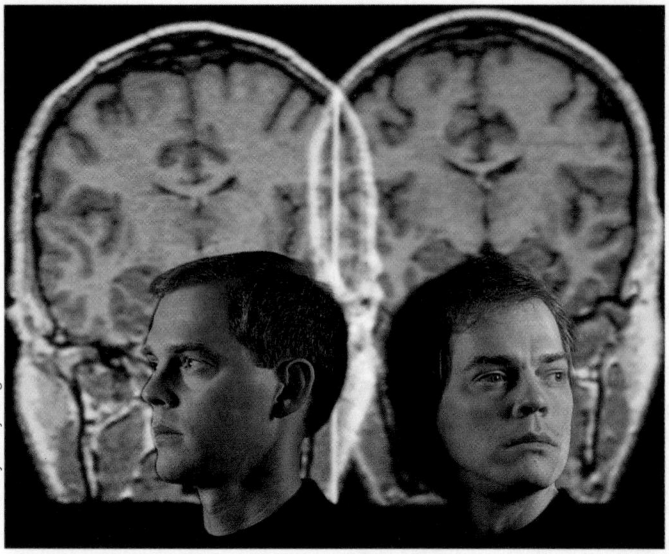

Joe McNally/Getty Images

Not-so-identical twins The man on the left does not have schizophrenia, while his identical twin, on the right, does. MRI scans, shown in the background, clarify that the brain of the twin with schizophrenia is smaller overall and has larger ventricles, brain cavities that contain fluid (indicated by the dark, butterfly-shaped spaces).

The dysfunction of this schizophrenia-related circuit cannot be characterized in broad terms as, for example, a generally "hyperactive" or generally "underactive" circuit. But numerous studies suggest that the circuit does indeed operate abnormally in persons with schizophrenia (Han et al., 2018; Wang, Chen, & Yang, 2017). For example, the *interconnectivity* (flow of communication) is abnormally low between their substantia nigra and prefrontal cortex and between their striatum and thalamus, while it is abnormally high between their substantia nigra and striatum, their thalamus and prefrontal cortex, and their hippocampus and prefrontal cortex (Martino et al., 2018; Wang et al., 2017).

Note that this focus on brain circuitry is compatible with the dopamine hypothesis of schizophrenia that monopolized biological explanations for so many years. After all, dopamine activity is very prominent throughout the schizophrenia-related brain circuit. The key difference between the dopamine hypothesis and the newer brain circuit view is that abnormal activity by this neurotransmitter is now seen as *part of* a broader circuit dysfunction that can propel people toward schizophrenia.

Viral Problems What might cause the biochemical and brain circuit abnormalities found in many cases of schizophrenia? Various studies have pointed to genetic factors, poor nutrition, fetal development, birth complications, immune reactions, and toxins (Fischer & Buchanan, 2018; Uher & Zwicker, 2017). In addition, some investigators contend that the brain abnormalities may result from exposure to *viruses* before birth. Perhaps a viral infection triggers an immune system response in the mother, is passed on to the developing fetus, enters his or her brain, and interrupts proper brain development.

Some of the evidence for the viral theory comes from animal model investigations, while other evidence is circumstantial, such as the finding that an unusually large number of people with schizophrenia are born during the late winter (Fischer & Buchanan, 2018; Patterson, 2012). The late winter birth rate among people with schizophrenia is 5 to 8 percent higher than among other people. This could be because of an increase in fetal or infant exposure to viruses at that time of year. More direct evidence for the viral theory of schizophrenia comes from studies showing that mothers of people with schizophrenia were more likely to have been exposed to the influenza virus during pregnancy than were mothers of people without schizophrenia (Canetta et al., 2014).

Together, the biochemical, brain circuit, and viral findings are shedding much light on the mysteries of schizophrenia. At the same time, it is important to recognize that many people who have these biological abnormalities never develop schizophrenia. Why not? Possibly, as you read earlier, because biological factors merely set the stage for schizophrenia, while key psychological and sociocultural factors must be present for the disorder to appear.

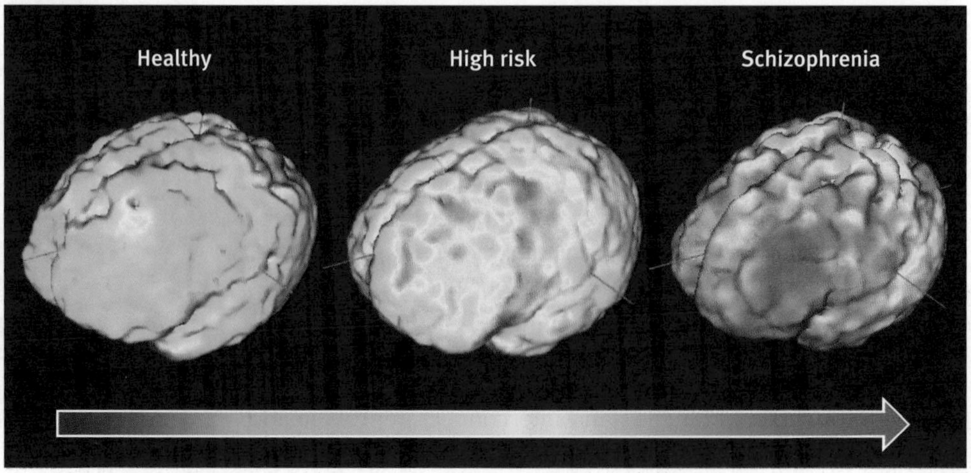

Oliver Howes, Peter Bloomfield and Mattia Veronese

Involvement of the immune system
Consistent with explanations that point to viral infections and immune system reactions, researchers have found that *microglia* are especially active in the brains of people with schizophrenia. Microglia are brain immune cells that provide a first line of defense against brain infections and inflammation. These PET scans show that the microglia activity (orange) of research participants at risk for schizophrenia is higher than that of healthy participants. The microglia activity of participants *with* schizophrenia is higher still.

Psychological Views

When schizophrenia investigators began to identify genetic and biological factors during the 1950s and 1960s, many clinicians abandoned the psychological theories of the disorder. During the past few decades, however, the tables have been turned and psychological factors are once again being considered as important pieces of the schizophrenia puzzle (Uher & Zwicker, 2017). Well-known psychological theories come from the psychodynamic and cognitive-behavioral perspectives.

schizophrenogenic mother A type of mother—supposedly cold, domineering, and uninterested in the needs of her children—who was once thought to cause schizophrenia in her child.

The Psychodynamic Explanation In the middle of the twentieth century, noted psychodynamic clinician Frieda Fromm-Reichmann (1948) elaborated on an earlier notion by Sigmund Freud (1924, 1915, 1914) that cold or unnurturing parents may set schizophrenia in motion. Based on her clinical observations, Fromm-Reichmann described the mothers of people who develop the disorder as cold, domineering, and uninterested in their children's needs. She claimed that these mothers may appear to be self-sacrificing but are actually using their children to meet their own needs. At once overprotective and rejecting, they confuse their children and set the stage for schizophrenic functioning. She called them **schizophrenogenic** (schizophrenia-causing) **mothers.** Although famous, Fromm-Reichmann's theory has received little research support (Seeman, 2016; Harrington, 2012). The majority of people with schizophrenia do not appear to have mothers who fit the schizophrenogenic description.

Why have parents and family life so often been blamed for schizophrenia, and why do such explanations continue to be influential?

Cognitive-Behavioral Explanations Cognitive-behavioral theorists have offered two explanations of how and why people develop schizophrenia. One focuses largely on the behaviors of people with schizophrenia and applies the principles of *operant conditioning.* The other focuses on the unusual thoughts of such individuals and stresses the possible role of *misinterpretations.*

OPERANT CONDITIONING As you have read, operant conditioning is the process by which people learn to perform behaviors for which they have been rewarded frequently. The operant explanation of schizophrenia holds that some people are, for one reason or another, not reinforced during childhood for proper attention to social cues—that is, attention to other people's smiles, frowns, and comments. As a result, they stop attending to such cues and focus instead on irrelevant cues—the brightness of light in a room, a bird flying above, or the sound of a word rather than its meaning. As they attend to irrelevant cues more and more, their responses become increasingly bizarre (Pinkham, 2014). Support for this operant explanation of schizophrenia has been circumstantial, and so the operant view is usually considered at best a partial explanation for schizophrenia.

MISINTERPRETING UNUSUAL SENSATIONS The misinterpretation explanation of schizophrenia begins by accepting the biological position that the brains of people with schizophrenia are actually producing strange and unreal sensations—sensations triggered by biological factors—when they have hallucinations and related experiences. According to the cognitive-behavioral explanation, however, when the individuals attempt to understand their unusual experiences, more features of their disorder emerge (Waters & Fernyhough, 2017). When first confronted by voices or other troubling sensations, these people turn to friends and relatives. Naturally, the friends and relatives deny the reality of the sensations, and eventually the sufferers conclude that the others are trying to hide

Famous, but rare, delusion In MTV's long-running show *Teen Wolf,* a possessed man cries out in terror as his body changes into that of a wolf. *Lycanthropy,* the delusion of being an animal, is a rare psychological syndrome, but it has been the subject of many profitable books, movies, and TV shows over the years.

MGM/The Kobal Collection/Shutterstock

the truth. They begin to reject all feedback, and some develop beliefs (delusions) that they are being persecuted. In short, according to this theory, people with schizophrenia take a "rational path to madness" (Zimbardo, 1976).

Researchers have established that people with schizophrenia do indeed experience sensory and perceptual problems. As you saw earlier, many have hallucinations and most have trouble keeping their attention focused. But researchers have yet to provide clear, direct support for the cognitive-behavioral notion that misinterpretations of such sensory problems actually produce a syndrome of schizophrenia.

Sociocultural Views

Sociocultural theorists, recognizing that people with mental disorders are subject to a wide range of social and cultural forces, believe that *multicultural factors, social labeling,* and *family dysfunction* all contribute to schizophrenia. Research has yet to clarify what the precise causal relationships might be.

How might bias by diagnosticians contribute to race-linked and culture-linked differences in the diagnosis of schizophrenia?

Multicultural Factors Rates of schizophrenia appear to differ between racial and ethnic groups, particularly between African Americans and non-Hispanic white Americans (Coleman et al., 2016). As many as 2.1 percent of African Americans receive a diagnosis of schizophrenia, compared with 1.4 percent of non-Hispanic white Americans. Research also suggests that African Americans with schizophrenia are overrepresented in state hospitals (Durbin el al., 2014; Barnes, 2004). For example, in Tennessee's state hospitals, 48 percent of those with a diagnosis of schizophrenia are African American, although only 16 percent of the state population is African American.

It is not clear why African Americans are more likely than non-Hispanic white Americans to receive this diagnosis. One possibility is that African Americans are more prone to develop schizophrenia. Another is that clinicians from majority groups are unintentionally biased in their diagnoses of African Americans or misread cultural differences as symptoms of schizophrenia.

Yet another explanation for the difference between African Americans and non-Hispanic white Americans may lie in the economic sphere. On average, African Americans are more likely to be poor; when economic differences are controlled for, the prevalence rates of schizophrenia become closer for the two racial groups. Consistent with the economic explanation is the finding that Hispanic Americans, who also tend to be economically disadvantaged, appear to be more likely to be diagnosed with

Silvia Izquierdo/AP Photo

Coming together Different countries and cultures each have their own way of viewing and interacting with people suffering from schizophrenia and other mental disturbances. Here patients and members of the community come together and dance during the annual Carnival parade in front of the Psychiatric Institute in Rio de Janeiro, Brazil. The goal of the carnival is to promote public acceptance by blurring the lines between normal and abnormal functioning.

schizophrenia than non-Hispanic white Americans, although their diagnostic rate is not as high as that of African Americans (Coleman et al., 2016).

It also appears that schizophrenia differs from country to country in key ways (Dein, 2017; McLean et al., 2014). Although the overall prevalence of this disorder is stable—around 1 percent—in countries across the world, the *course* and *outcome* of the disorder may vary considerably. According to a 10-country study conducted by the World Health Organization (WHO), schizophrenic patients who live in *developing* countries have better recovery rates than schizophrenic patients in Western and other *developed* countries (Dein, 2017; Jablensky, 2000). The WHO study followed the progress of 467 patients from developing countries (Colombia, India, and Nigeria) over a two-year period and compared it with that of 603 patients from developed countries (the Czech Republic, Denmark, Ireland, Japan, Russia, the United Kingdom, and the United States). During the course of the study, the schizophrenic patients from the developing countries were more likely than those in the developed countries to recover from their disorder and less likely to have continuing symptoms, to have impaired social functioning, or to require heavy antipsychotic drugs or hospitalization.

Some clinical theorists believe that these differences partly reflect genetic differences from population to population. However, others argue that the psychosocial environments (families and friends) in developing countries tend to be more supportive and therapeutic than those in developed countries, leading to more favorable outcomes for people with schizophrenia (Dein, 2017; Vahia & Vahia, 2008).

#EasyTargets

In the U.S., more than one-third of adults with schizophrenia are victims of violent crime.

In the U.S., adults with schizophrenia are 14 times more likely to be victims of violent crime than to be arrested for committing such a crime.

(MIP, 2017; Kooyman & Walsh, 2011; Cuvelier, 2002; Hiroeh et al., 2001)

Social Labeling Many sociocultural theorists believe that the features of schizophrenia are influenced by the diagnosis itself. In their opinion, society assigns the label "schizophrenic" to people who fail to conform to certain norms of behavior. Once the label is assigned, justified or not, it becomes a self-fulfilling prophecy that promotes the development of many schizophrenic symptoms.

We have already seen the very real dangers of diagnostic labeling. In the famous Rosenhan (1973) study, discussed in Chapter 2, eight normal people presented themselves at various mental hospitals, complaining that they had been hearing voices utter the words "empty," "hollow," and "thud." They were quickly diagnosed as schizophrenic, and all eight were hospitalized. Although the pseudopatients then dropped all symptoms and behaved normally, they had great difficulty getting rid of the label and gaining release from the hospital.

Rosenhan's study is one of the most controversial in the field. What kinds of ethical, legal, and therapeutic concerns does it raise?

The pseudopatients reported that staff members were authoritarian in their behavior toward patients and also treated them as though they were invisible. "A nurse unbuttoned her uniform to adjust her brassiere in the presence of an entire ward of viewing men. One did not have the sense that she was being seductive. Rather, she didn't notice us." In addition, the pseudopatients described feeling powerless, bored, tired, and uninterested. The deceptive design and possible implications of this study have aroused the emotions of clinicians and researchers, pro and con. The investigation does demonstrate, however, that the label "schizophrenic" can itself have a negative effect not just on how people are viewed but also on how they themselves feel and behave.

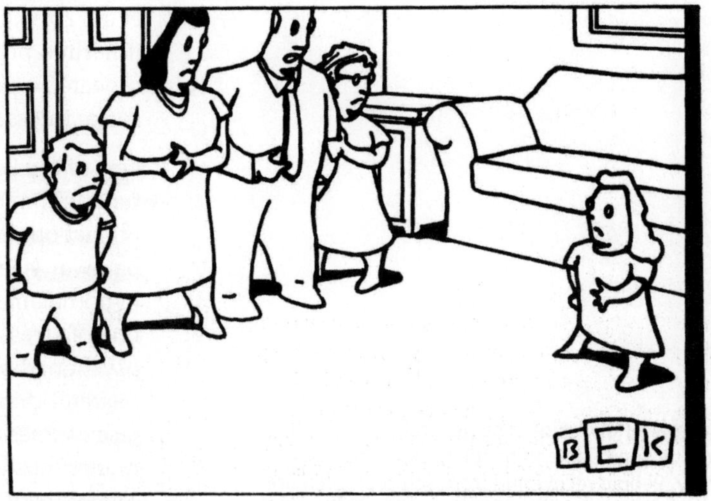

Bruce Eric Kaplan/The New Yorker Collection/The Cartoon Bank

"Bad news—we're all out of our minds. You're going to have to be the lone healthy person in this family."

Family Dysfunction Many studies suggest that schizophrenia, like a number of other mental disorders, is often linked to *family stress* (Gurak & Weisman de Mamani, 2017, 2016). Parents of people with schizophrenia often (1) display more conflict, (2) have more difficulty communicating with one another, and (3) are more critical of and overinvolved with their children than other parents.

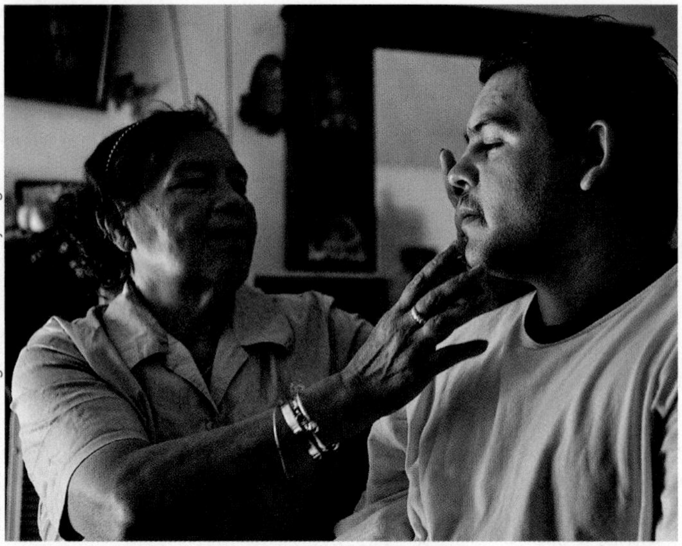

Engaging the family Research indicates that people with schizophrenia make more progress in treatment when they feel positive toward their family. Here a loving mother, Maria Orduna, caresses her son Alfredo during his visit to her apartment. Alfredo has suffered through homelessness, poverty, and jail, largely due to his schizophrenic disorder.

Family theorists have long recognized that some families are high in **expressed emotion**—that is, members frequently express criticism, disapproval, and hostility toward each other and intrude on one another's privacy. People who are trying to recover from schizophrenia are almost four times more likely to relapse if they live with such a family than if they live with one low in expressed emotion (Sadiq et al., 2017; Wang et al., 2017). Do such findings mean that family dysfunction helps cause and maintain schizophrenia? Not necessarily. It is also the case that people with schizophrenia greatly disrupt family life (Yu et al., 2018). In so doing, they themselves may help produce the family problems that clinicians and researchers continue to observe.

Developmental Psychopathology View

As they do with other psychological disorders, developmental psychopathology theorists offer an integrative and developmental framework to explain why and how the factors discussed in this chapter may lead to schizophrenia. The theorists contend that the road to schizophrenia begins with a genetically inherited predisposition to the disorder—a predisposition that is expressed by the dysfunctional brain circuit you read about earlier (Nivard et al., 2018). The theorists further argue that this genetic predisposition may eventually lead to schizophrenia if, over the course of an individual's development, he or she experiences significant life stressors, difficult family interactions, and/or other negative environmental factors (Mayo et al., 2017; Vallejos et al., 2017).

Of course, as you read earlier, theorists of all kinds have, for years, proposed that a *diathesis–stress* relationship is at work in schizophrenia—that is, people with a biological predisposition to this disorder will develop it if they further experience significant life stress or other negative events. What theorists and researchers from the developmental psychopathology perspective have done, however, is provide much more detail about the diathesis–stress processes at work in schizophrenia. In particular, they have clarified two points:

1. Schizophrenia typically begins to unfold long before the actual onset of the disorder in young adulthood. Previously, you read that people with this disorder often display cognitive, perception, and attention problems earlier in their lives. Developmental psychopathology researchers have found that such people also tend to be more socially withdrawn, disagreeable, and disobedient, and to have more motor difficulties, throughout their early development (Walker et al., 2016). Some of those early problems result largely from the individual's inherited predisposition, but, according to research, they may also be due to repeated experiences of childhood stress, family dysfunction, and/or difficult social interactions (Kraan et al., 2018).

2. One of the key ways that a dysfunctional brain circuit may adversely affect the functioning of people who later become schizophrenic is through the circuit's impact on the operation of the hypothalamic-pituitary-adrenal (HPA) stress pathway (see page 142). As you'll recall, whenever we are stressed, the brain's hypothalamus activates this brain–body pathway, leading, in turn, to the secretion of stress hormones and to a broad experience of arousal. Developmental psychopathology researchers have found that dysfunction by the schizophrenia-related brain circuit leads to repeated overreactions by the HPA pathway in the face of stress (Walker et al., 2016). Such chronic overreactions leave individuals highly sensitive to and unsettled by stressors throughout their development. The individuals become all the more inclined to later develop schizophrenia in the face of stress (Pruessner et al., 2017).

expressed emotion The general level of criticism, disapproval, and hostility expressed in a family. People recovering from schizophrenia are considered more likely to relapse if their families rate high in expressed emotion.

Developmental psychopathology researchers and other investigators have further discovered that an overreactive HPA stress pathway and chronic stress reactions lead to the development of a dysfunctional *immune system*, characterized by heightened inflammation throughout the brain (Müller et al., 2015). Thus it is not surprising that numerous studies conducted over the past several years have found significant immune system problems and chronic inflammation throughout the brains of people with schizophrenia (Fries et al., 2018).

In addition to adding depth to the diathesis–stress view of schizophrenia, the developmental psychopathology perspective provides an important service by emphasizing the advantages of *prevention* in dealing with this disorder (Seidman & Nordentoft, 2015). According to this perspective, each of the factors discussed in this chapter (from brain circuit dysfunction to family dynamics to stress reactions) can affect each other. Just as children's overreactive HPA stress pathways can make them particularly vulnerable to stress, so too can their acquisition of resilience and coping skills improve the operation of their HPA pathways. This two-way relationship argues for better identification of children at risk for schizophrenia and for stronger preventive interventions to help reverse the factors predisposing them to schizophrenia (Mayo et al., 2017). Unfortunately, as you will see in the next section, most of today's approaches to schizophrenia involve treatment *after* the onset of the disorder rather than prevention.

Jordi Vidal/Redferns via Getty Images

"The Devil and Daniel Johnston" For decades, singer-songwriter Daniel Johnston has been very influential in the *outsider* and *alternative* music genres. At the same time, he suffers from schizophrenia and bipolar disorder and has been institutionalized several times for these problems. His disorders and their effect on his life and career are chronicled in the film documentary *The Devil and Daniel Johnston*.

...SUMMING UP

HOW DO THEORISTS EXPLAIN SCHIZOPHRENIA Many theorists believe that biological and environmental factors combine in a diathesis–stress relationship to help produce schizophrenia.

The biological explanations of schizophrenia point to genetic, biochemical, brain structure and circuitry, and viral causes. The genetic view is supported by studies of relatives, twins, adoptees, and genes. The leading biochemical explanation holds that dopamine may be overactive in the brains of people with schizophrenia. Studies have also identified a brain circuit whose dysfunction may lead to schizophrenia. Finally, some researchers believe that schizophrenia is related to a virus that settles in the fetus.

The most prominent psychological explanations for schizophrenia come from the psychodynamic and cognitive-behavioral models. One early psychodynamic explanation contended that schizophrenogenic mothers help produce schizophrenia, but this view has received little research support. Contemporary psychodynamic theorists typically ascribe the disorder to a combination of biological and psychodynamic factors. Cognitive-behavioral theorists suggest that people with schizophrenia (1) fail to learn to attend to appropriate social cues and/or (2) misinterpret their strange biological sensations in ways that produce delusional thinking.

One sociocultural explanation holds that multicultural differences may influence the rate and character of schizophrenia, as well as recovery from this disorder, both within the United States and around the world. Another sociocultural explanation says that society expects people who are labeled as having schizophrenia to behave in certain ways and that such expectations actually lead to further symptoms. Other sociocultural theorists point to family dysfunction, including family stress and conflict, as a cause of schizophrenia.

Offering an integrative framework, developmental psychopathology theorists contend that an individual's genetic predisposition—implemented by a dysfunctional brain circuit—may eventually lead to schizophrenia if, over the course of the person's development, he or she also experiences significant life stressors, difficult family interactions, and/or other negative environmental factors.

#PrivateNotions

Surveys suggest that 22 to 37 percent of people in the United States and Britain believe Earth has been visited by aliens from outer space.

Twenty percent of people worldwide believe that aliens walk on Earth disguised as humans.

(Rojas, 2017; MacIsaac, 2014; Reuters, 2010; Spanton, 2008; Andrews, 1998)

How Are Schizophrenia and Other Severe Mental Disorders Treated?

#TreatmentDelay

The average length of time between the first appearance of psychotic symptoms and the initiation of treatment is two years (HN, 2018; Brunet & Birchwood, 2010).

Today's treatment picture for schizophrenia and other severe mental disorders is marked by miraculous triumphs for some, modest success for others, and heartbreaking failure for still others. It is typically characterized by medications, medication-linked health problems, compromised lifestyles, and a mixture of hope and frustration. Let us look at the case of Cathy, whose journey is typical of that of hundreds of thousands of people with schizophrenia and other severe mental disorders. To be sure, there are patients whose efforts to overcome schizophrenia go more smoothly. And at the other end of the spectrum, there are many whose struggles against severe mental dysfunctioning never come close to Cathy's level of success. In between, there are the Cathys.

During [Cathy's] second year in college . . . her emotional troubles worsened. . . . and [she was] put on Haldol and lithium.

For the next sixteen years, Cathy cycled in and out of hospitals. She "hated the meds"—Haldol stiffened her muscles and caused her to drool, while the lithium made her depressed—and often she would abruptly stop taking them. . . . The problem was that off the drugs, she would "start to decompensate and become disorganized."

In early 1994, she was hospitalized for the fifteenth time. She was seen as chronically mentally ill, occasionally heard voices now . . . and was on a cocktail of drugs: Haldol, Ativan, Tegretol, Halcion, and Cogentin, the last drug an antidote to Haldol's nasty side effects. But after she was released that spring, a psychiatrist told her to try Risperdal, a new antipsychotic that had just been approved by the FDA. "Three weeks later, my mind was much clearer," she says. "The voices were going away. I got off the other meds and took only this one drug. I got better. I could start to plan. I wasn't talking to the devil anymore. Jesus and God weren't battling it out in my head." Her father put it this way: "Cathy is back." . . .

She went back to school and earned a degree in radio, film, and television. . . . In 1998, she began dating the man she lives with today. . . . In 2005, she took a part-time job. . . . Still, she remains on SSDI (Social Security Disability Insurance)—"I am a kept woman," she jokes—and although there are many reasons for that, she believes that Risperdal, the very drug that has helped her so much, nevertheless has proven to be a barrier to full-time work. Although she is usually energetic by the early afternoon, Risperdal makes her so sleepy that she has trouble getting up in the morning. . . .

Risperdal has also taken a physical toll. . . . She has . . . developed some of the metabolic problems, such as high cholesterol, that the atypical antipsychotics regularly cause. "I can go toe-to-toe with an old lady with a recital of my physical problems," she says. "My feet, my bladder, my heart, my sinuses, the weight gain—I have it all." . . . But she can't do well without Risperdal. . . .

Such has been her life's course on medications. Sixteen terrible years, followed by fourteen pretty good years on Risperdal. She believes that this drug is essential to her mental health today, and indeed, she could be seen as a local poster child for promoting the wonders of that drug. Still, if you look at the long-term course of her illness . . . you have to ask: Is hers a story of a life made better by our drug-based . . . care for mental disorders, or a story of a life made worse? . . .

Cathy believes that this is a question that psychiatrists never contemplate.

"They don't have any sense about how these drugs affect you over the long term. They just try to stabilize you for the moment, and look to manage you from week to week, month to month. That's all they ever think about."

(Whitaker, 2010)

As Cathy's journey illustrates, schizophrenia is extremely difficult to treat, but clinicians are much more successful at doing so today than they were in the past. Much of the credit goes to *antipsychotic drugs*—imperfect, troubling, and even dangerous

state hospitals Public mental hospitals in the United States, run by the individual states.

though they may be. These medications help many people with schizophrenia and other psychotic disorders to think clearly and profit from psychotherapies that previously would have had little effect for them.

To best convey the plight of people with schizophrenia, this chapter will depart from the usual format and discuss the treatments from a historical perspective. A look at how treatment has changed over the years will help us understand the nature, problems, and promise of today's approaches. As we consider past treatments for schizophrenia, it is important to keep in mind that throughout much of the twentieth century the label "schizophrenia" was assigned to most people with psychosis. Clinical theorists now realize that many people with psychotic symptoms are instead experiencing a severe form of bipolar disorder or major depressive disorder and that such people were in past times inaccurately diagnosed with schizophrenia (Tondo et al., 2015). Thus, our discussions of past treatments for schizophrenia, particularly the failures of institutional care, are as applicable to those other severe mental disorders as they are to schizophrenia (Bustillo & Weil, 2018). Similarly, our discussions about current approaches to schizophrenia, such as the community mental health movement, often apply to other severe mental disorders as well.

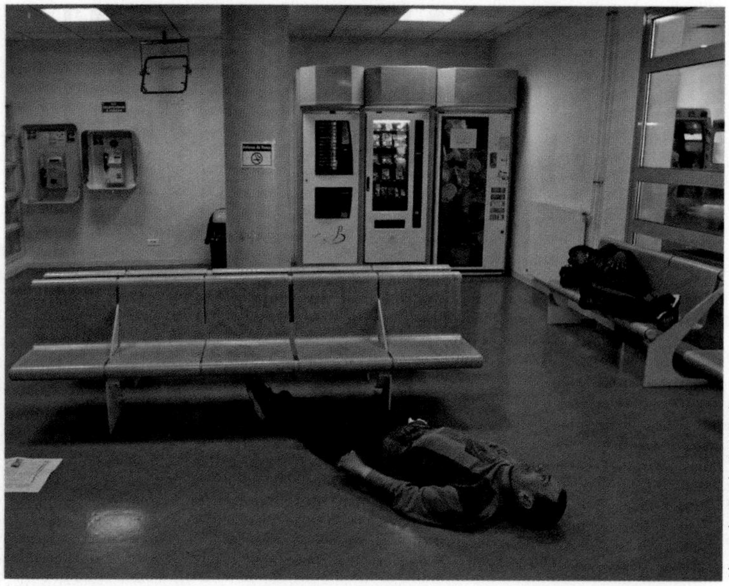

Alexandra Boulat/VII/Redux

A long way to go A man with schizophrenia lies on the floor of the emergency room waiting area at Delafontaine Hospital near Paris, France. The plight of this patient is a reminder that, despite the development of various effective interventions, the overall treatment picture for many people with severe mental disorders leaves much to be desired.

Institutional Care in the Past

For more than half of the twentieth century, most people diagnosed with schizophrenia were *institutionalized* in a public mental hospital. Because patients with schizophrenia did not respond to traditional therapies, the primary goals of these hospitals were to restrain them and give them food, shelter, and clothing. Patients rarely saw therapists and generally were neglected. Many were abused. Oddly enough, this state of affairs unfolded in an atmosphere of good intentions.

As you read in Chapter 1, the move toward institutionalization in hospitals began in 1793 when French physician Philippe Pinel "unchained the insane" at La Bicêtre asylum and began the practice of "moral treatment." For the first time in centuries, patients with severe disturbances were viewed as human beings who should be cared for with sympathy and kindness. As Pinel's ideas spread throughout Europe and the United States, they led to the creation of large mental hospitals rather than asylums to care for those with severe mental disorders (Goshen, 1967).

Why have people with schizophrenia so often been victims of horrific treatments such as overcrowded wards, lobotomy, and, later, deinstitutionalization?

These new mental hospitals, typically located in isolated areas where land and labor were cheap, were meant to protect patients from the stresses of daily life and offer them a healthful psychological environment in which they could work closely with therapists (Grob, 1966). States throughout the United States were even required by law to establish public mental institutions, **state hospitals,** for patients who could not afford private ones.

Eventually, however, the state hospital system encountered serious problems. Between 1845 and 1955, nearly 300 state hospitals opened in the United States, and the number of hospitalized patients on any given day rose from 2,000 in 1845 to nearly 600,000 in 1955. During this expansion, wards became overcrowded, admissions kept rising, and state funding was unable to keep up.

The priorities of the public mental hospitals, and the quality of care they provided, changed over those 110 years. In the face of overcrowding and understaffing, the emphasis shifted from giving humanitarian care to keeping order. In a throwback to the asylum period, difficult patients were restrained, isolated, and punished; individual attention disappeared. Patients were transferred to *back wards,* or chronic wards, if

#TheirWords

"I believe that if you grabbed the nearest normal person off the street and put them in a psychiatric hospital, they'd be diagnosable as mad within weeks."

Clare Allan, novelist, *Poppy Shakespeare*

Institutional life In a scene reminiscent of public mental hospitals in the United States during the first half of the twentieth century, these patients spend their days crowded together on a hospital ward in central Shanghai. Because of a shortage of therapists, only a small fraction of Chinese people with psychological disorders receive proper professional care today.

they failed to improve quickly (Bloom, 1984). Most of the patients on these wards suffered from schizophrenia (Häfner & an der Heiden, 1988). The back wards were human warehouses filled with hopelessness. Staff members relied on straitjackets and handcuffs to deal with difficult patients. More "advanced" forms of treatment included medical approaches such as *lobotomy* (see ***PsychWatch*** on page 384). Many patients not only failed to improve under these conditions but also developed additional symptoms.

Institutional Care Takes a Turn for the Better

In the 1950s, clinicians developed two institutional approaches that finally brought some hope to patients who had lived in institutions for years: *milieu therapy,* based on humanistic principles, and the *token economy program,* based on behavioral principles. These approaches particularly helped improve the personal care and self-image of patients, problem areas that had been worsened by institutionalization. The approaches were soon adopted by many institutions and are now standard features of institutional care.

Milieu Therapy In 1953, Maxwell Jones, a London psychiatrist, converted a ward of patients with various psychological disorders into a therapeutic community—the first application of **milieu therapy** in a hospital setting. The premise of milieu therapy is that institutions can help patients by creating a social climate, or milieu, that promotes productive activity, self-respect, and individual responsibility. In such settings, patients are given the right to run their own lives and make their own decisions. They may participate in community government, working with staff members to establish rules and determine penalties. Patients may also take on special projects, jobs, and recreational activities. In short, their daily schedule is designed to resemble life outside the hospital.

Since Jones's pioneering effort, milieu-style programs have been set up in institutions throughout the Western world. The programs vary from setting to setting, but at a minimum, staff members try to encourage interactions (especially group interactions) between patients and staff, to keep patients active, and to raise their expectations about what they can accomplish.

Research over the years has shown that people with schizophrenia and other severe mental disorders in milieu hospital programs often improve and that they leave the hospital at higher rates than patients in programs offering primarily custodial care (Smith & Spitzmueller, 2016; Paul, 2000). Many remain impaired, however, and must live in sheltered settings after their release. Despite its limitations, milieu therapy continues to be practiced in many institutions, often combined with other hospital approaches. Moreover, you will see later in this chapter that many of today's halfway houses and other community programs for people with severe mental disorders apply the principles of milieu therapy.

The Token Economy In the 1950s, clinicians interested primarily in behaviors and in principles of learning discovered that the systematic use of *operant conditioning* techniques on hospital wards could help change the behaviors of patients with schizophrenia (Ayllon, 1963; Ayllon & Michael, 1959). Programs that apply these techniques are called **token economy programs.**

In token economies, patients are rewarded when they behave acceptably and are not rewarded when they behave unacceptably. The immediate rewards for acceptable behavior are often tokens that can later be exchanged for food, cigarettes, hospital

#TheirWords

"Men will always be mad and those who think they can cure them are the maddest of all."
Voltaire (1694–1778)

privileges, and other desirable items, all of which compose a "token economy." Acceptable behaviors likely to be included are caring for oneself and for one's possessions (making the bed, getting dressed), going to a work program, speaking normally, following ward rules, and showing self-control. Researchers have found that token economies do help reduce psychotic and related behaviors (Ivy et al., 2017; Swartz et al., 2012).

Some clinicians have voiced reservations about the claims made regarding token economy programs. Are operant conditioning procedures changing a patient's psychotic thoughts and perceptions or simply improving the patient's ability to *imitate* normal behavior? This issue is illustrated by the case of a middle-aged man named John, who had the delusion that he was the U.S. government. Whenever he spoke, he spoke as the government. "We are happy to see you. . . . We need people like you in our service. . . . We are carrying out our activities in John's body." When John's hospital ward converted to using a token economy, the staff members targeted his delusional statements and required him to identify himself properly to earn tokens. After a few months, John stopped referring to himself as the government. When asked his name, he would say, "John." Although staff members were understandably pleased with his improvement, John himself had a different view of the situation. In a private discussion he said:

Eitan Abramovich/Getty Images

Milieu philosophy Although less prominent than they once were, milieu principles continue to influence programs in many mental hospitals. At the Borda psychiatric hospital in Buenos Aires, Argentina, patients, therapists, and volunteers take a tango workshop together to help instill in patients a sense of equality, self-respect, and competence.

> *We're tired of it. Every damn time we want a cigarette, we have to go through their bullshit. "What's your name? Who wants the cigarette? Where is the government?" Today, we were desperate for a smoke and went to Simpson, the damn nurse, and she made us do her bidding. "Tell me your name if you want a cigarette. What's your name?" Of course, we said, "John." We needed the cigarettes. If we told her the truth, no cigarettes. But we don't have time for this nonsense. We've got business to do, international business, laws to change, people to recruit. And these people keep playing their games.*
>
> (Comer, 1973)

Token economy programs are no longer as popular as they once were, but they are still used in many mental hospitals, usually along with medication, and in many community residences as well (Ivy et al., 2017). The approach has also been applied to other clinical problems, including intellectual disability, delinquency, and hyperactivity, as well as in other fields, such as education and business (Ivy et al., 2017; Spiegler & Guevremont, 2015).

Antipsychotic Drugs

Milieu therapy and token economy programs helped improve the gloomy outlook for patients diagnosed with schizophrenia, but it was the discovery of *antipsychotic drugs* in the 1950s that truly revolutionized treatment for schizophrenia. These drugs eliminate many of its symptoms and today are almost always a part of treatment (Jibson, 2017).

The discovery of antipsychotic medications dates back to the 1940s, when researchers developed the first *antihistamine drugs* to combat allergies. The French surgeon Henri Laborit soon discovered that one group of antihistamines, *phenothiazines,* could also be used to help calm patients about to undergo surgery. One of the phenothiazines, chlorpromazine, was eventually tested on six patients with psychotic symptoms and was found to reduce their symptoms sharply. In 1954, chlorpromazine was approved for sale in the United States as an antipsychotic drug under the trade name Thorazine.

milieu therapy A humanistic approach based on the premise that institutions can help patients recover by creating a climate that promotes self-respect, responsible behavior, and meaningful activity.

token economy program A program in which a person's desirable behaviors are reinforced systematically by the awarding of tokens that can be exchanged for goods or privileges.

PSYCHWATCH

Lobotomy: How Could It Happen?

In 1935, a Portuguese neurologist named Egas Moniz performed a revolutionary new surgical procedure, which he called a *prefrontal leucotomy*, on a patient with severe mental dysfunction (Wright, 2017; Raz, 2013). The procedure, the first form of *lobotomy*, consisted of drilling two holes in either side of the skull and inserting an instrument resembling an icepick into the brain tissue to cut or destroy nerve fibers. Moniz believed that severe abnormal thinking—such as that on display in schizophrenia, depression, and obsessive-compulsive disorder—was the result of nerve pathways that carried such thoughts from one part of the brain to another. By cutting these pathways, Moniz believed, he could stop the abnormal thinking in its tracks and restore normal mental functioning.

A year after his first leucotomy, Moniz published a monograph in Europe describing his successful use of the procedure on 20 patients (Raz, 2013). An American neurologist, Walter Freeman, read the monograph, called the procedure to the attention of the medical community in the United States, performed the procedure on many patients, and became its foremost supporter. In 1947 he developed a second kind of lobotomy called the *transorbital lobotomy*, in which the surgeon inserted a needle into the brain through the eye socket and rotated it in order to destroy the brain tissue (Collins & Stam, 2015).

From the early 1940s through the mid-1950s, the lobotomy was viewed as a miracle cure by most doctors and became a mainstream part of psychiatry (Wright, 2017; Levinson, 2011). An estimated 50,000 people in the United States alone eventually received lobotomies (Johnson, 2005).

We now know that the lobotomy was hardly a miracle treatment. Far from "curing" people with mental disorders, the procedure left thousands upon thousands extremely withdrawn, subdued, and even stuporous. Why then was the procedure so enthusiastically accepted by the medical community in the 1940s and 1950s? Neuroscientist Elliot Valenstein (1986) points first to the extreme overcrowding in mental hospitals at the time—overcrowding that lobotomies helped to alleviate. Valenstein also points to the personalities of the inventors of the procedure. Although these individuals were gifted and dedicated physicians—in 1949 Moniz was awarded the Nobel Prize for his work—Valenstein believes that their professional ambitions led them to move too quickly and boldly in applying the procedure.

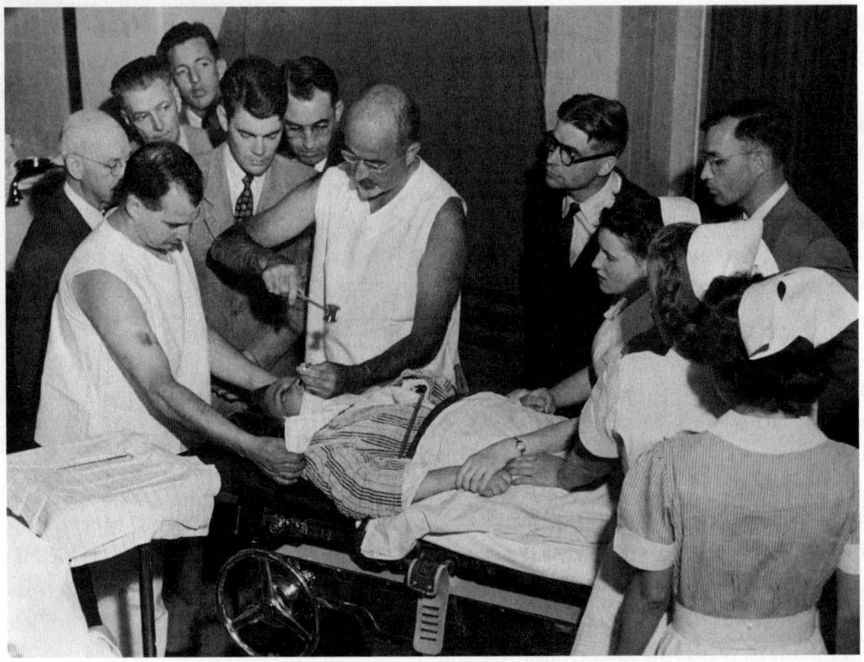

Bettmann/Getty Images

Lessons in psychosurgery Neuropsychiatrist Walter Freeman performs a lobotomy in 1949 before a group of interested onlookers by inserting a needle through a patient's eye socket into the brain.

The prestige of Moniz and Freeman were so great and the field of neurology was so small that their procedures drew little critical review. Physicians may also have been misled by the seemingly positive findings of early studies of the lobotomy, which, as it turned out, were not based on sound methodology (Wright, 2017; Cooper, 2014).

By the 1950s, better studies revealed that in addition to having a fatality rate of 1.5 to 6 percent, lobotomies could cause serious problems such as brain seizures, huge weight gain, loss of motor coordination, partial paralysis, incontinence, endocrine malfunctions, and very poor intellectual and emotional responsiveness (Lapidus et al., 2013). The discovery of effective antipsychotic drugs helped put an end to this inhumane treatment for mental disorders (Krack et al., 2010).

Today's psychosurgical procedures are greatly refined and hardly resemble the lobotomies of 70 years back. Moreover, the procedures are usually reserved for only the most severe cases of disorders such as OCD and depression (Neumaier et al., 2017, 2016; Nair et al., 2014). Even so, many professionals believe that any kind of surgery that destroys brain tissue is inappropriate and perhaps unethical and that it keeps alive one of the clinical field's most shameful and ill-advised efforts at cure.

Since the discovery of the phenothiazines, other kinds of antipsychotic drugs have also been developed. As you read earlier in the chapter, the ones developed throughout the 1960s, 1970s, and 1980s are now referred to as *first-generation antipsychotic drugs* in order to distinguish them from the *second-generation antipsychotics* that have been developed more recently. The first-generation drugs are also known as *neuroleptic drugs* because they often produce undesired movement effects similar to the symptoms of neurological diseases. As you also read earlier, antipsychotic drugs reduce psychotic symptoms at least in part by blocking excessive activity of the neurotransmitter *dopamine* (Jibson, 2018; Wang et al., 2018).

How Effective Are Antipsychotic Drugs? Research has shown that antipsychotic drugs reduce symptoms in around 70 percent of patients diagnosed with schizophrenia (Stroup & Marder, 2017). Moreover, in direct comparisons the drugs appear to be a more effective treatment for schizophrenia than any of the other approaches used alone, such as psychotherapy, milieu therapy, or electroconvulsive therapy.

For patients helped by the drugs, the medications bring about clear improvement within a period of weeks. However, symptoms may return if the patients stop taking the drugs too soon (Tiihonen, Tanskanen, & Taipale, 2018). The antipsychotic drugs, particularly the first-generation ones, reduce the positive symptoms of schizophrenia (such as hallucinations and delusions) more completely, or at least more quickly, than the negative symptoms (such as restricted affect, poverty of speech, and loss of volition) (Jibson, 2018, 2017; Krause et al., 2018).

The Unwanted Effects of First-Generation Antipsychotic Drugs In addition to reducing psychotic symptoms, the first-generation antipsychotic drugs sometimes produce disturbing movement problems (Olten & Bloch, 2018). These effects are called **extrapyramidal effects** because they appear to be caused by the drugs' impact on the extrapyramidal areas of the brain, areas that help control motor activity.

The most common extrapyramidal effects are *Parkinsonian symptoms*, reactions that closely resemble the features of the neurological disorder Parkinson's disease. At least half of patients on first-generation antipsychotic drugs have muscle tremors and muscle rigidity at some point in their treatment; they may shake, move slowly, shuffle their feet, and show little facial expression. Some also have related symptoms such as movements of the face, neck, tongue, and back; and a number experience significant restlessness and discomfort in their limbs.

Whereas most extrapyramidal drug effects appear within days or weeks, a reaction called **tardive dyskinesia** (meaning "late-appearing movement disorder") does not usually unfold until after a person has taken first-generation antipsychotic drugs for more than six months (Tarsy, 2018, 2016). This syndrome may include involuntary

extrapyramidal effects Unwanted movements, such as severe shaking, bizarre-looking grimaces, twisting of the body, and extreme restlessness, sometimes produced by antipsychotic drugs.

tardive dyskinesia Extrapyramidal effects involving involuntary movements that some patients have after they have taken antipsychotic drugs for an extended time.

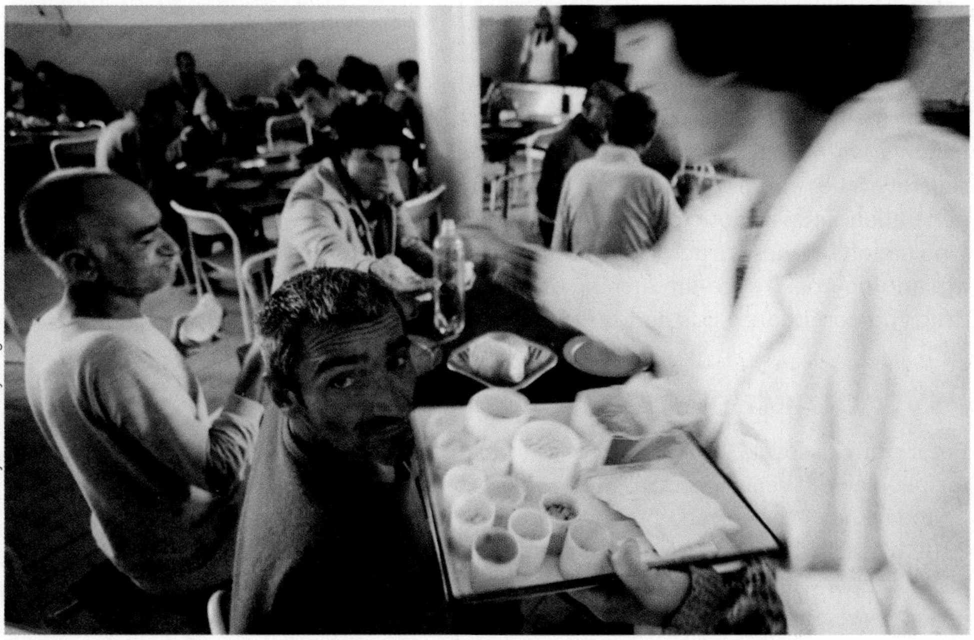

Xavier Rossi/Gamma-Keystone/Getty Images

The drug revolution Since the 1950s, medications have become a central part of treatment for patients with schizophrenia and other severe mental disorders. The medications have resulted in shorter hospitalizations that now last weeks rather than years.

TABLE: 12-3

Some Antipsychotic Drugs

Generic Name	Trade Name
First-generation antipsychotics	
Chlorpromazine	*Thorazine*
Trifluoperazine	*Stelazine*
Fluphenazine	*Prolixin*
Perphenazine	*Trilafon*
Acetophenazine	*Tindal*
Chlorprothixene	*Taractan*
Thiothixene	*Navane*
Haloperidol	*Haldol*
Loxapine	*Loxitane*
Pimozide	*Orap*
Second-generation antipsychotics	
Risperidone	*Risperdal*
Clozapine	*Clozaril*
Olanzapine	*Zyprexa*
Quetiapine	*Seroquel*
Ziprasidone	*Geodon*
Aripiprazole	*Abilify*
Iloperidone	*Fanapt*
Lurasidone	*Latuda*
Paliperidone	*Invega*
Asenapine	*Saphris*

writhing or ticlike movements of the tongue, mouth, face, or whole body; involuntary chewing, sucking, and lip smacking; and jerky movements of the arms, legs, or entire body. It is believed that more than 15 percent of the people who take first-generation antipsychotic drugs, especially the most powerful ones, for an extended time develop tardive dyskinesia to some degree, and the longer the drugs are taken, the higher the risk becomes (Tarsy, 2018, 2016; Achalia et al., 2014). Patients over 50 years of age are at greater risk. Tardive dyskinesia can be difficult, sometimes impossible, to eliminate (Bergman et al., 2018; Soares-Weiser et al., 2018).

Today clinicians are more knowledgeable and more cautious about prescribing first-generation antipsychotic drugs than they were in the past (see **Table 12-3**). Previously, when patients did not improve with such a drug, their clinician would keep increasing the dose; today a clinician will typically add an additional drug to help improve the impact of the antipsychotic drug, stop the drug and try an alternative one, or stop all medications (Tiihonen et al., 2018; Stroup & Marder, 2017). Clinicians try to prescribe the lowest effective doses for each patient and to gradually reduce medications weeks or months after the patient begins functioning normally.

Why did psychiatrists in the past keep administering high dosages of antipsychotic drugs to patients who had adverse effects from the medications?

Second-Generation Antipsychotic Drugs As you read earlier in the chapter, second-generation antipsychotic drugs have been developed in recent decades. The most widely used of these newer drugs are *clozapine* (trade name Clozaril), *risperidone* (Risperdal), *olanzapine* (Zyprexa), *quetiapine* (Seroquel), *ziprasidone* (Geodon), and *aripiprazole* (Abilify). As noted earlier, these drugs are received at fewer dopamine D-2 receptors and at more D-1, D-4, and serotonin receptors than the first-generation drugs (Olten & Bloch, 2018; Tarsy, 2018, 2016).

Second-generation antipsychotic drugs appear to be at least as effective, and often more effective, than the first-generation drugs (Jibson, 2017; Stroup & Marder, 2017). Clozapine is often the most effective such drug, but the other second-generation drugs also bring significant change for many people. Recall, for example, Cathy, the woman whom we met earlier, and how well she responded to risperidone after years of doing poorly on first-generation antipsychotic drugs. Unlike the first-generation drugs, the second-generation ones reduce not only the positive symptoms of schizophrenia, but—to a small degree—the negative ones as well (Krause et al., 2018). Another major benefit is that the second-generation drugs—especially clozapine—cause fewer extrapyramidal symptoms and seem less likely to produce tardive dyskinesia (Tarsy, 2018, 2016).

Given such advantages, more than half of all patients with schizophrenia who are medicated now take the second-generation drugs, which are considered the primary line of treatment for the disorder (Kapitanyan & Su, 2018; Roberts et al., 2018). Many patients with bipolar or other severe mental disorders also seem to be helped by several of these second-generation antipsychotic drugs (Jibson, 2017). Yet the second-generation antipsychotic drugs have serious problems as well. For example, people who use one of these drugs, clozapine, have around a 1 to 1.5 percent risk of developing **agranulocytosis**, a life-threatening drop in white blood cells (other second-generation drugs do not produce this undesired effect) (Coates, 2018; Zhu et al., 2018).

Psychotherapy

Before the discovery of antipsychotic drugs, psychotherapy was not really an option for people with schizophrenia. Most were too far removed from reality to profit from it. Today, however, psychotherapy is helpful to many such patients (Morrison et al., 2018). By helping to relieve thought and perceptual disturbances, antipsychotic drugs allow people with schizophrenia to see themselves more clearly, learn about their disorder, participate actively in therapy (see ***MindTech*** on page 388), make changes in their behavior, and cope with stressors in their lives. The most helpful forms of psychotherapy include cognitive-behavioral therapy and two sociocultural interventions—family therapy and social therapy. Often the various approaches are combined.

Cognitive-Behavioral Therapies Two kinds of cognitive-behavior therapy are now used for people with schizophrenia, (1) *cognitive remediation* and (2) *hallucination reinterpretation and acceptance*. Research indicates that both approaches are helpful, each in a different way (Bustillo & Weil, 2018).

COGNITIVE REMEDIATION **Cognitive remediation** is an approach that focuses on the cognitive impairments that often characterize people with schizophrenia—particularly their difficulties in attention, planning, and memory (Fan, Liao, & Pan, 2017; John et al., 2017). Here clients are required to complete increasingly difficult information-processing tasks on a computer. They may start with a simple task such as responding as quickly as possible to various stimuli that are flashed on the screen—a task designed to improve their attention skills. Once they can perform this task with considerable speed, they move on to more complex computer tasks, such as tasks that challenge their short-term memory. As they master each computer task, they keep moving up the ladder until they eventually reach computer tasks that require planning and social awareness.

Studies indicate that, for many people with schizophrenia, cognitive remediation brings about moderate improvements in attention, planning, memory, and problem-solving—improvements that surpass those produced by other treatment interventions (Bustillo & Weil, 2018; Fan et al., 2017). Moreover, these improvements extend to the client's everyday life and social relationships.

HALLUCINATION REINTERPRETATION AND ACCEPTANCE As you read earlier, the cognitive-behavioral explanation for schizophrenia starts with the premise that people with the disorder do indeed actually hear voices (or experience other kinds of hallucinations) as a result of biologically triggered sensations. According to this theory, the journey into schizophrenia takes shape when people try to make sense of these strange sensations and conclude incorrectly that the voices are coming from external sources, that they are being persecuted, or another such notion. These misinterpretations are essentially delusions.

With this explanation in mind, many clinicians now employ a cognitive-behavioral treatment for schizophrenia that is designed to help change how people view and react to their hallucinations (Lincoln & Peters, 2018; Gottlieb et al., 2017). The therapists believe

Sara Lautman The New Yorker Collection/The Cartoon Bank

"Yes, you've mentioned this 'Facebook' in the past—tell me, is 'Facebook' saying anything right now?"

agranulocytosis A life-threatening drop in white blood cells. This condition is sometimes produced by the second-generation antipsychotic drug *clozapine*.

cognitive remediation A treatment that focuses on the cognitive impairments that often characterize people with schizophrenia—particularly their difficulties in attention, planning, and memory.

#

#TheirWords

"If you talk to God, you are praying. If God talks to you, you have schizophrenia."

Thomas Szasz, psychiatric theorist

MINDTECH

Putting a Face on Auditory Hallucinations

In Chapter 2, you read that a growing number of therapists are using *avatar therapy* to help clients overcome their psychological problems. In this form of virtual reality therapy, clinicians have the clients interact with computer-generated on-screen virtual human figures. Perhaps the boldest application of avatar therapy is its use with people suffering from schizophrenia. Clinical researcher Julian Leff and several colleagues have developed an approach that seems to offer particular promise for such individuals (Craig et al., 2018, 2016; Leff et al., 2014, 2013).

For a pilot study, the researchers selected 16 participants who were being tormented by imaginary voices (auditory hallucinations). In each case, the therapist presented the individual with a mean-sounding and mean-looking avatar. The avatar's voice pitch and appearance were designed based on the patient's description of what he or she was hearing and what the patient believed would be a corresponding face.

The patient was placed alone in a room with the computer simulation while the therapist generated the on-screen avatar from another room. Initially, the avatar spewed all sorts of frightening and upsetting statements at the patient. Then, the therapist encouraged the patient to fight back—to tell the avatar things such as "I will not put up with this, what you are saying is nonsense, I don't believe these things, you must go away and leave me alone, and I do not need this kind of torment" (Rus-Calafell et al., 2015; Kedmey, 2013; Leff et al., 2014, 2013).

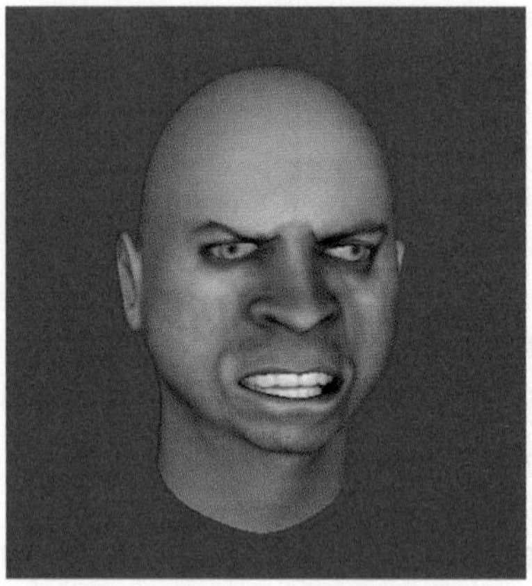

University College London

Voices spring to virtual life This is one of the sinister-looking avatars developed by clinical researcher Julian Leff and his colleagues in their treatment for people with schizophrenia.

Can you think of any negative effects—short-term or long-term—that might result from putting a face on auditory hallucinations?

After seven 30-minute sessions, most of the participants in the pilot study had less frequent and less intense auditory hallucinations and reported being less upset by the voices they did continue to hear. The participants also reported improvements in their feelings of depression and suicidal thinking. Three of the 16 actually reported a total cessation of their auditory hallucinations after the sessions. These promising results have now been followed up by larger studies with more participants—each producing similar findings (Craig et al., 2018, 2016). The collective results of these studies suggest that confronting one's hallucinations in a virtual world can indeed help at least some people with schizophrenia.

that if people can be guided to interpret such experiences in a more accurate way, they will not suffer the fear and confusion produced by their delusional misinterpretations. Thus, the therapists use a combination of behavioral and cognitive techniques:

1. They provide clients with education about the biological causes of hallucinations.
2. They help clients learn more about the "comings and goings" of their own hallucinations and delusions. The clients learn, for example, to identify which kinds of events and situations trigger the voices in their heads.
3. The therapists challenge their clients' inaccurate ideas about the power of their hallucinations, such as the idea that the voices are all-powerful and uncontrollable and must be obeyed. The therapists also have the clients put such notions to the test. What happens, for example, if the clients resist following the orders from their hallucinatory voices?
4. The therapists teach clients to reattribute and more accurately interpret their hallucinations. Clients may, for example, adopt and apply alternative conclusions such as "It's not a real voice, it's my illness."
5. The therapists teach clients techniques for coping with their unpleasant sensations (hallucinations). The clients may, for example, learn ways to reduce the physical arousal that accompanies hallucinations—using special breathing and relaxation techniques, positive self-statements, distraction strategies, and the like.

#TheirWords

"No great genius was ever without some tincture of madness."

Aristotle

These cognitive-behavioral techniques often help people with schizophrenia feel more control over their hallucinations and reduce their delusional ideas (Lincoln & Peters, 2018; Gottlieb et al., 2017). But they do not eliminate the hallucinations. Can anything be done further to lessen the hallucinations' unpleasant impact on the person? Yes, say *new-wave cognitive-behavioral therapists,* including practitioners of *acceptance and commitment therapy.*

As you read in Chapters 2 and 4, new-wave cognitive-behavioral therapists believe that the most useful goal of treatment is often to help clients *accept* their streams of problematic thoughts rather than to judge them, act on them, or try fruitlessly to change them. The therapists, for example, help highly anxious individuals to become simply *mindful* of the worries that engulf their thinking and to *accept* such negative thoughts as harmless events of the mind (see page 110). Similarly, in cases of schizophrenia, new-wave cognitive-behavioral therapists try to help clients become detached and comfortable observers of their hallucinations—merely mindful of the unusual sensations and accepting of them—while otherwise moving forward with the tasks and events of their lives (Gaudiano et al., 2017).

A therapist like myself The AlterEgo project at France's Hospital of Montpellier uses computer-based technology to help people with schizophrenia. Based on the premise that people relate better with and learn more from individuals who resemble them, the program has clients interact with avatars similar to themselves. Here a client helps to program the avatar with whom he will be working by having his body and movements scanned.

Studies indicate that the various cognitive-behavioral treatments are often very helpful to clients with schizophrenia (Lincoln & Peters, 2018; Morrison et al., 2018). Many clients who receive such treatments report that they feel less distressed by their hallucinations and that they have fewer delusions. Indeed, they are often able to shed the diagnosis of schizophrenia. Rehospitalizations decrease by 50 percent among clients treated with cognitive-behavioral therapy.

Family Therapy Many persons who are recovering from schizophrenia and other severe mental disorders live with their families: parents, siblings, spouses, or children. Generally speaking, people with schizophrenia who feel positive toward their relatives do better in treatment (Bustillo & Weil, 2018). As you saw earlier, recovered patients living with relatives who display high levels of *expressed emotion*—that is, relatives who are very critical, emotionally overinvolved, and hostile—often have a much higher relapse rate than those living with more positive and supportive relatives (Joseph, 2018; Wang et al., 2017). Moreover, for their part, family members may be very upset by the social withdrawal and unusual behaviors of a relative with schizophrenia (Lloyd et al., 2017; Yu et al., 2017).

To address such issues, clinicians now commonly include family therapy in their treatment of schizophrenia, providing family members with guidance, training, practical advice, psychoeducation about the disorder, and emotional support and empathy (Brown & Weisman de Mamani, 2018; Bustillo & Weil, 2018). In family therapy, relatives develop more realistic expectations and become more tolerant, less guilt-ridden, and more willing to try new patterns of communication. Family therapy also helps the person with schizophrenia cope with the pressures of family life, make better use of family members, and avoid troublesome interactions. Research has found that family therapy—particularly when it is combined with drug therapy—helps reduce tensions within the family and so helps relapse rates and hospital readmissions go down (Brown & Weisman de Mamani, 2018; Bustillo & Weil, 2018).

The families of people with schizophrenia and other severe mental disorders may also turn to *family support groups* and *family psychoeducational programs* for encouragement and advice (Norman et al., 2017; Bademli & Duman, 2016). In such programs, family members meet with others in the same situation to share their thoughts and emotions, provide mutual support, and learn about schizophrenia.

#

#PaternalImpact

People whose fathers were over 50 years of age when they were born are more likely to develop schizophrenia than people born to fathers under 50 years old. As with bipolar disorder, this may be explained by the tendency of aging men to produce more genetic mutations during the manufacture of sperm cells (Stovall, 2018; Crystal et al., 2012).

Social Therapy Many clinicians believe that the treatment of people with schizophrenia should include techniques that address social and personal difficulties in the clients' lives. These clinicians offer practical advice; work with clients on problem solving, memory enhancement, decision making, and social skills; make sure that the clients are taking their medications properly; and may even help them find work, financial assistance, appropriate health care, and proper housing (Norman et al., 2017; Granholm et al., 2014). Research finds that this practical, active, and broad approach, called *social therapy* or *personal therapy*, does indeed help keep people out of the hospital (Bustillo & Weil, 2018).

Kevin Spear/Orlando Sentinel/TNS via Getty Images

Community outreach Homeless people are more likely to develop schizophrenia, and having schizophrenia increases one's chances of becoming homeless. Thus, extraordinary University of Central Florida graduate student Briana Daniel founded and directs the Street Team Movement, a volunteer program that helps homeless people in Orlando address their clothing, laundry, hygiene, and mental health needs. The 25-year-old woman plans to eventually take the program nationwide.

The Community Approach

The broadest approach for the treatment of schizophrenia and other severe mental disorders is the *community approach*. In 1963, partly in response to the terrible conditions in public mental institutions and partly because of the emergence of antipsychotic drugs, the U.S. government ordered that patients be released and treated in the community. Congress passed the *Community Mental Health Act,* which stipulated that patients with psychological disorders were to receive a range of mental health services—outpatient therapy, inpatient treatment, emergency care, preventive care, and aftercare—in their communities rather than being transported to institutions far from home. Patients diagnosed with schizophrenia and other severe disorders, especially those who had been institutionalized for years, were affected most by this act. Other countries around the world put similar sociocultural treatment programs into action shortly thereafter.

Thus began several decades of **deinstitutionalization,** an exodus of hundreds of thousands of patients with schizophrenia and other long-term mental disorders from state institutions into the community. On a given day in 1955, close to 600,000 patients were living in state institutions; today around 42,000 patients live in such facilities (Statista, 2018; Smith & Milazzo-Sayre, 2014). Clinicians have learned that patients recovering from schizophrenia and other severe disorders can profit greatly from community programs (Joshi et al., 2018; Bustillo & Weil, 2017, 2016). As you will see, however, the actual quality of community care for these people has often been inadequate throughout the United States. The result is a "revolving door" pattern for many patients. They are released to the community, readmitted to an institution within months, released a second time, admitted yet again, and so on, over and over (Allison et al., 2018; Burns & Drake, 2011).

How might the "revolving door" pattern itself worsen the symptoms and outlook of people with schizophrenia?

What Are the Features of Effective Community Care? People recovering from schizophrenia and other severe disorders need medication, psychotherapy, help in handling daily pressures and responsibilities, guidance in making decisions, social skills training, residential supervision, and vocational counseling—a combination of services called *assertive community treatment* (Gaudiano et al., 2017). Those whose communities help them meet these needs make more progress than those living in other communities (Schöttle et al., 2018). Some of the key features of effective community care programs are (1) coordination of patient services, (2) short-term hospitalization, (3) partial hospitalization, (4) supervised residencies, and (5) occupational training.

COORDINATED SERVICES When the Community Mental Health Act was first passed, it was expected that community care would be provided by **community mental health**

centers, treatment facilities that would supply medication, psychotherapy, and inpatient emergency care to people with severe disturbances, as well as coordinate the services offered by other community agencies. When community mental health centers are available and do provide these services, patients with schizophrenia and other severe disorders often make significant progress (Bustillo & Weil, 2018; Joshi et al., 2018). Coordination of services is particularly important for so-called *mentally ill chemical abusers (MICAs)*, patients with psychotic disorders as well as substance use disorders (Campbell, Caroff, & Mann, 2018, 2017).

SHORT-TERM HOSPITALIZATION When people develop severe psychotic symptoms, today's clinicians first try to treat them on an outpatient basis, usually with a combination of antipsychotic medication and psychotherapy. If this approach fails, they may try *short-term hospitalization*—in a mental hospital or a general hospital's psychiatric unit—that lasts a few weeks (rather than months or years) (Gaudiano et al., 2017; Craig & Power, 2010). Soon after the patients improve, they are released for **aftercare,** a general term for follow-up care and treatment in the community.

PARTIAL HOSPITALIZATION People's needs may fall between full hospitalization and outpatient therapy, and so some communities offer **day centers,** or **day hospitals,** all-day programs in which patients return to their homes for the night. Such programs provide patients with daily supervised activities, therapy, and instructions to improve social skills. People recovering from severe disorders in day centers often do better and have fewer relapses than those who spend extended periods in a hospital or in traditional outpatient therapy (Bustillo & Weil, 2018; Bales et al., 2014). Another kind of institution that has become a popular setting for the treatment of people with schizophrenia and other severe disorders is the *semihospital,* or *residential crisis center.* These are houses or other structures in the community that provide 24-hour nursing care for people with severe mental disorders (Zarzar et al., 2018; Soliman et al., 2008).

SUPERVISED RESIDENCES Many people do not require hospitalization but are unable to live alone or with their families. **Halfway houses,** also known as *crisis houses* or *group homes,* often serve individuals well (MHA, 2017; Lindenmayer & Khan, 2012). Such residences may shelter between one and two dozen people. The live-in staff usually are *paraprofessionals*—lay people who receive training and ongoing supervision from outside mental health professionals. The houses are usually run with a *milieu therapy* philosophy that emphasizes mutual support, resident responsibility, and self-government. Research indicates that halfway houses help many people recovering from schizophrenia and other severe disorders adjust to community life and avoid rehospitalization (MHA, 2017; Hansson et al., 2002).

OCCUPATIONAL TRAINING AND SUPPORT Paid employment provides income, independence, self-respect, and the stimulation of working with others. It also brings companionship and order to one's daily life. For these reasons, occupational training and placement are important services for people with schizophrenia and other severe mental disorders (Norman et al., 2017).

Many people recovering from such disorders receive occupational training in a *sheltered workshop*—a supervised workplace for employees who are not ready for competitive or complicated jobs. An alternative work opportunity for people with severe psychological disorders is *supported employment,* in which vocational agencies and counselors help clients find competitive jobs in the community and provide psychological support while the clients are employed (Bustillo & Weil, 2018; Abraham et al., 2017; Solar, 2014). Unfortunately, like sheltered workshops, supported employment

deinstitutionalization The discharge of large numbers of patients from long-term institutional care so that they might be treated in community programs.

community mental health center A treatment facility that provides medication, psychotherapy, and emergency care for psychological problems and coordinates treatment in the community.

aftercare A program of posthospitalization care and treatment in the community.

day center A program that offers hospital-like treatment during the day only. Also known as a *day hospital*.

halfway house A residence for people with schizophrenia or other severe problems, often staffed by paraprofessionals. Also known as a *group home* or *crisis house*.

Craig F. Walker/The Denver Post via Getty Images

They met at a day center Sunday and Sam Duncan pose for a portrait at their home in La Junta, Colorado. The married couple, both of whom have suffered from schizophrenia, met in a day center at Southeast Mental Health Services and, according to them, fell in love at first sight. The day center has received national awards for its innovative approach to schizophrenia.

Craig F. Walker/Getty Images

"Court to Community" Denver, Colorado, has established a program called *Court to Community*, which diverts people with severe mental disorders into court-monitored mental health programs rather than jails. Repeat criminal offenders, like this man with schizophrenia, plead their cases to the program's judges, who determine whether the individuals are taking their medications, avoiding street drugs, and attending therapy. Life in the community is preferable to jail, but it too is difficult. This man told the judge, "I feel like I'm in prison when I'm out there."

opportunities are often in short supply. Fewer than 20 percent of individuals with severe psychological disorders have jobs in the competitive job market.

How Has Community Treatment Failed? There is no doubt that effective community programs can help people with schizophrenia and other severe mental disorders recover. However, fewer than half of all the people who need them receive appropriate community mental health services (Joshi et al., 2018; Addington et al., 2015). In fact, in any given year, 40 to 60 percent of all people with schizophrenia and other severe mental disorders receive no treatment at all (NAMI, 2018; NIMH, 2017). Two factors are primarily responsible: *poor coordination* of services and a *shortage* of services.

POOR COORDINATION OF SERVICES The various mental health agencies in a community often fail to communicate with one another. There may be an opening at a nearby halfway house, for example, and the therapist at the community mental health center may not know about it. Still another problem is poor communication between state hospitals and community mental health centers, particularly at times of discharge (Bonsack et al., 2016; Torrey, 2001).

To help deal with such problems in communication and coordination, a growing number of community therapists have become **case managers** for people with schizophrenia and other severe mental disorders (Schneeberger et al., 2017; Burns, 2010). They try to coordinate available community services and help protect clients' legal rights. Like the social therapists described earlier, they also offer therapy and advice, teach problem-solving and social skills, ensure that clients are taking their medications properly, and keep an eye on possible health care needs. Many professionals now believe that effective case management is the key to success for a community program.

SHORTAGE OF SERVICES The number of community programs—community mental health centers, halfway houses, sheltered workshops—available to people with severe mental disorders falls woefully short (NIMH, 2017; Burns & Drake, 2011). In addition, many of the community mental health centers that do exist generally devote their efforts and money to people with problems such as anxiety disorders or social adjustment difficulties. Only a fraction of the patients treated by such community mental health centers suffer from schizophrenia or other disorders marked by psychosis (NIMH, 2017).

There are various reasons for this shortage of services. Perhaps the primary one is economic. On the one hand, more public funds are available for people with psychological disorders now than in the past. In 1963 a total of \$1 billion was spent in this area, whereas in 2017 approximately \$152 billion in public funding was devoted each year to people with mental disorders (SAMHSA, 2017, 2014). This represents a significant increase even when inflation and so-called real dollars are factored in. On the other hand, rather little of the additional money is going to community treatment programs for people with severe disorders. Much of it goes instead to prescription drugs, monthly income payments such as social security disability income, services for people with mental disorders in nursing homes and general hospitals, and community services for people who are less disturbed (SAMHSA, 2017, 2014). Today, the financial burden of providing community treatment for people with long-term severe disorders often falls on local governments and nonprofit organizations rather than the federal or state government, and such local resources cannot always meet this challenge (SAMHSA, 2017, 2014; Feldman et al., 2014).

case manager A community therapist who offers and coordinates a full range of services for people with schizophrenia or other severe disorders, including therapy, advice, medication, guidance, and protection of patients' rights.

What Are the Consequences of Inadequate Community Treatment? What happens to people with schizophrenia and other severe disorders whose communities do not provide the services they need and whose families cannot afford private treatment? As you have read, a large number receive no treatment at all; many others spend a short time in a state hospital or semihospital and are then discharged prematurely, often without adequate follow-up treatment (NIMH, 2017; Burns & Drake, 2011).

These individuals live in various settings (MIP, 2017; Torrey, 2014, 2001). Many return to their families and receive medication and perhaps emotional and financial support, but little else in the way of treatment. Around 8 percent enter an alternative institution such as a nursing home or rest home, where they receive only custodial care and medication (see **Figure 12-4**). As many as 18 percent are placed in privately run residences where supervision often is provided by untrained staff—foster homes (small or large), boardinghouses, care homes, and similar facilities. These residences vary greatly in quality. Another 34 percent of people with schizophrenia and other severe disorders live in totally unsupervised settings. Some are equal to the challenge of living alone, but others cannot really function independently and wind up in rundown single-room occupancy hotels (SROs) or rooming houses. They may live in conditions that are substandard and unsafe, which may exacerbate their disorder.

Finally, a great number of people with schizophrenia and other severe disorders have become homeless. There are 565,000 homeless people in the United States, and approximately one-fourth of them—a total of 140,000 homeless people—have a severe mental disorder, commonly schizophrenia (NAMI, 2018; MIP, 2017). Many have been released from hospitals. Others are young adults who were never hospitalized in the first place. Another 440,000 or more people with severe mental disorders are in prisons and jails, often because their disorders have led them to break the law (Allison, Bastiampillai, & Fuller, 2017). As many as 26 percent of all persons imprisoned in the United States suffer from schizophrenia or another severe mental disorder (Binswanger & Elmore, 2018; Judd & Parker, 2018). Certainly deinstitutionalization and the community mental health movement have failed these individuals, and many report actually feeling relieved if they are able to return to hospital life.

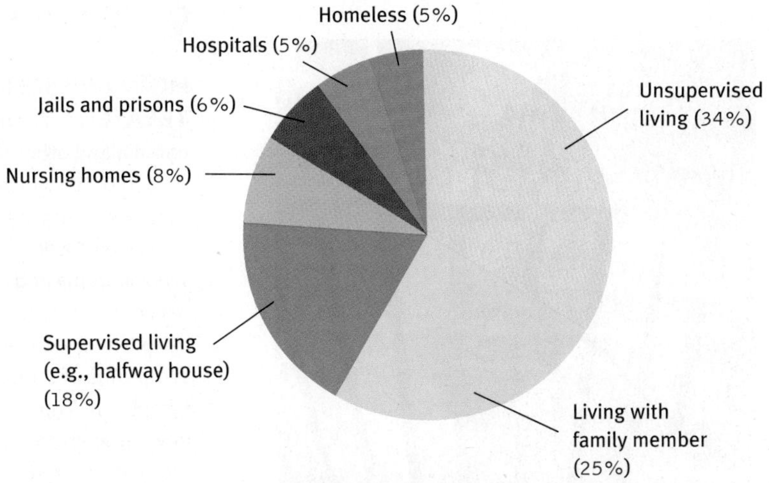

FIGURE 12-4

Where Do People with Schizophrenia Live?

More than one-third live in unsupervised residences, 6 percent are in jails, and 5 percent are homeless. (Information from: Allison et al., 2018, 2017; MIP, 2017; Torrey, 2014, 2001; Kooyman & Walsh, 2011.)

The Promise of Community Treatment Despite these very serious problems, proper community care has shown great potential for assisting people in recovering from schizophrenia and other severe disorders, and clinicians and many government officials continue to press to make it more available. Indeed, in one study of 34 effective community programs across 21 states—programs that properly provide a combination of services (medication, psychotherapy, case management, and assertive community treatment)—clients with schizophrenia were found to make more improvements in their quality of life, symptom reduction, and participation at work and school than did comparable clients in other kinds of treatment or in less-comprehensive community programs (Kane et al., 2016).

In addition, a number of *national interest groups* have formed in countries around the world that push for better community treatment. In the United States, for example, the *National Alliance on Mental Illness* (*NAMI*) began in 1979 with 300 members and has expanded to 200,000 members in more than 1,000 chapters (NAMI, 2018, 2014). Made up largely of families and people affected by severe mental disorders, NAMI has become not only a source of information, support, and guidance for its members but also a powerful lobbying force in state and national legislatures; and it has pressured community mental health centers to treat more people with schizophrenia and other severe disorders.

Today, community care is a major feature of treatment for people recovering from severe mental disorders in countries around the world. Both in the United States and abroad, well-coordinated community treatment is seen as an important part of the solution to the problem of severe mental dysfunction (Bustillo & Weil, 2018; Joshi et al., 2018).

#

#PrisonPopulation

There are more people with schizophrenia and other severe mental disorders in jails and prisons than there are in all hospitals and other treatment facilities.

Chicago's Cook County Jail, where several thousand of the inmates require daily mental health services, is now in effect the largest mental institution in the United States.

(Binswanger & Elmore, 2018; Stürup-Toft et al., 2018; Pruchno, 2014; Balassone, 2011)

AP Photo/Lynsey Addario

Changing the unacceptable A resident of a group home holds a sign during a rally in New York to protest the shortage of appropriate community residences for people with severe mental disorders.

...SUMMING UP

HOW ARE SCHIZOPHRENIA AND OTHER SEVERE MENTAL DISORDERS TREATED? For more than half of the twentieth century, the main treatment for schizophrenia and other severe mental disorders was institutionalization and custodial care. In the 1950s, two in-hospital approaches were developed, milieu therapy and token economy programs. They often brought improvement.

The discovery of antipsychotic drugs in the 1950s revolutionized the treatment of schizophrenia and other disorders marked by psychosis. Today they are almost always a part of treatment. Theorists believe that the first-generation antipsychotic drugs operate by reducing excessive dopamine activity in the brain. These drugs reduce the positive symptoms of schizophrenia more completely, or more quickly, than they do the negative symptoms. The first-generation antipsychotic drugs, however, can also produce dramatic unwanted effects, particularly movement abnormalities called extrapyramidal effects. More recently, second-generation antipsychotic drugs have been developed; these cause fewer extrapyramidal effects.

Psychotherapy is often employed successfully in combination with antipsychotic drugs. Helpful forms include cognitive-behavioral therapy, family therapy, and social therapy. Family support groups and family psychoeducational programs are also growing in number.

A community approach to the treatment of schizophrenia and other severe mental disorders began in the 1960s, when a policy of deinstitutionalization in the United States brought about a mass exodus of hundreds of thousands of patients from state institutions into the community. Among the key elements of effective community care programs are coordination of patient services by a community mental health center, short-term hospitalization (followed by aftercare), day centers, halfway houses, occupational training and support, and case management. However, the quality and funding of community care for people with schizophrenia and other severe disorders have been inadequate, often resulting in a "revolving door" pattern between the community and the hospital. One result is that many people with such disorders are now homeless or in prison.

An Important Lesson

After years of frustration and failure, clinicians now have an arsenal of weapons to use against schizophrenia and other disorders marked by psychosis. It has become clear that antipsychotic medications open the door for recovery from these disorders, but in most cases other kinds of treatment are also needed to help the recovery process along.

Working with schizophrenia and other severe disorders has taught therapists an important lesson: no matter how compelling the evidence for biological causation may be, a strictly biological approach to the treatment of psychological disorders is a mistake more often than not. Largely on the basis of biological discoveries and pharmacological advances, hundreds of thousands of patients with schizophrenia and other severe mental disorders were released to their communities in the 1960s. Little attention was paid to their psychological and sociocultural needs, and many have been trapped in their pathology ever since. Clinicians must remember this lesson, especially in today's climate, when managed care and government priorities often promote medication as the sole treatment for psychological problems.

When the pioneering clinical researcher Emil Kraepelin described schizophrenia at the end of the nineteenth century, he estimated that only 13 percent of its victims ever improved. Today, even with shortages in community care, many more people with schizophrenia—at least three times as many—show improvement. Certainly the clinical field has advanced considerably since Kraepelin's day, but it still has far to go. Studies suggest that the recovery rates—both partial and full—could be considerably higher. It

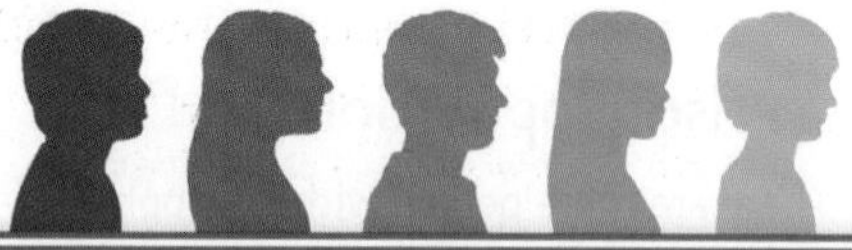

CLINICAL CHOICES

Now that you've read about schizophrenia, try the interactive case study for this chapter. See if you are able to identify Randy's symptoms and suggest a diagnosis based on his symptoms. What kind of treatment would be most effective for Randy? Go to **LaunchPad** to access *Clinical Choices*.

is unacceptable that so many people with this and other severe mental disorders receive few or none of the effective community interventions that have been developed, worse still that hundreds of thousands have become homeless or imprisoned. It is now up to clinicians, along with public officials, to address the needs of all people with schizophrenia and other severe disorders.

Key Terms

schizophrenia, p. 364
psychosis, p. 364
schizophrenia spectrum disorders, p. 364
positive symptoms, p. 365
delusion, p. 365
formal thought disorder, p. 366
loose associations, p. 366
hallucination, p. 366
inappropriate affect, p. 368
negative symptoms, p. 368
alogia, p. 368
restricted affect, p. 368
avolition, p. 369
catatonia, p. 369
dopamine hypothesis, p. 371
antipsychotic drug, p. 371
phenothiazines, p. 372
second-generation antipsychotic drugs, p. 373
first-generation antipsychotic drugs, p. 373
schizophrenia-related brain circuit, p. 374
schizophrenogenic mother, p. 375
expressed emotion, p. 378
state hospital, p. 381
milieu therapy, p. 382
token economy program, p. 382
neuroleptic drugs, p. 385
extrapyramidal effects, p. 385
tardive dyskinesia, p. 385
agranulocytosis, p. 386
cognitive remediation, p. 387
social therapy, p. 390
deinstitutionalization, p. 390
assertive community treatment, p. 390
community mental health center, p. 390
mentally ill chemical abuser (MICA), p. 391
aftercare, p. 391
day center, p. 391
halfway house, p. 391
sheltered workshop, p. 391
case manager, p. 392
national interest groups, p. 393

Quick Quiz

1. What is schizophrenia, and how prevalent is it? What is its relation to socioeconomic class and gender? *pp. 364–365*
2. What are the positive, negative, and psychomotor symptoms of schizophrenia? *pp. 365–369*
3. Describe the genetic, biochemical, brain circuitry, and viral explanations of schizophrenia, and discuss how they have been supported in research. *pp. 370–374*
4. What are the key features of the psychodynamic, cognitive-behavioral, multicultural, social labeling, family, and developmental psychopathology explanations of schizophrenia? *pp. 375–379*
5. Describe institutional care for people with schizophrenia and other severe mental disorders over the course of the twentieth century. How effective are the milieu and token economy treatment programs? *pp. 381–383*
6. How do antipsychotic drugs operate on the brain? How do first-generation antipsychotic and second-generation antipsychotic drugs differ? *pp. 383–385*
7. How effective are antipsychotic drugs in the treatment of schizophrenia? What are the unwanted effects of first-generation antipsychotic drugs? *pp. 385–386*
8. What kinds of psychotherapy seem to help people with schizophrenia and other disorders marked by psychosis? *pp. 386–390*
9. What is deinstitutionalization? What features of community care seem critical for helping people with schizophrenia and other severe mental disorders? *pp. 390–392*
10. How and why has the community mental health approach been inadequate for many people with severe mental disorders? *pp. 392–393*

Richtigkeit bescheinigt
Kunde
Datum
Best.-Nr. 8934 (V 6-54) VLV
5
4
6
1
3
TABLE No 2
3
GE4Y
1,40 m
DATE
INITIALS

CHAPTER

13

Personality Disorders

TOPIC OVERVIEW

While interviewing for the job of editor of a start-up news Web site, Frederick said, "This may sound self-serving, but I am extraordinarily gifted. I am certain that I will do great things in this position. I and the Osterman Post will soon set the standard for journalism and blogging in the country. Within a year, we'll be looking at the Huffington Post in the rearview mirror." The committee was impressed. Certainly, Frederick's credentials were strong, but even more important, his self-confidence and boldness had wowed them.

A year later, many of the same individuals were describing Frederick differently—arrogant, self-serving, cold, egomaniacal, draining. He had performed well as editor (though not as spectacularly as he seemed to think), but that performance could not outweigh his impossible personality. Colleagues below and above him had grown weary of his manipulations, his emotional outbursts, his refusal ever to take the blame, his nonstop boasting, and his grandiose plans. Once again Frederick had outworn his welcome.

To be sure, Frederick had great charm, and he knew how to make others feel important, when it served his purpose. Thus he always had his share of friends and admirers. But in reality they were just passing through, until Frederick would tire of them or feel betrayed by their lack of enthusiasm for one of his self-serving interpretations or grand plans. Or until they simply could take Frederick no longer.

Bright and successful though he was, Frederick always felt entitled to more than he was receiving—to higher grades at school, greater compensation at work, more attention from girlfriends. If criticized even slightly, he reacted with fury, and was certain that the critic was jealous of his superior intelligence, skill, or looks. At first glance, Frederick seemed to have a lot going for him socially. Typically, he could be found in the midst of a deep, meaningful romantic relationship—in which he might be tender, attentive, and seemingly devoted to his partner. But Frederick would always tire of his partner within a few weeks or months and would turn cold or even mean. Often he started affairs with other women while still involved with the current partner. The breakups—usually unpleasant and sometimes ugly—rarely brought sadness or remorse to him, and he would almost never think about his former partner again. He always had himself.

Each of us has a *personality*—a set of uniquely expressed characteristics that influence our behaviors, emotions, thoughts, and interactions. Our particular characteristics, often called *personality traits,* lead us to react in fairly predictable ways as we move through life. Yet our personalities are also flexible. We learn from experience. As we interact with our surroundings, we try out various responses to see which feel better and which are more effective. This is a flexibility that people who suffer from a personality disorder usually do not have.

People with a **personality disorder** display an enduring, rigid pattern of inner experience and outward behavior that impairs their sense of self, emotional experiences, goals, capacity for empathy, and/or capacity for intimacy (APA, 2013) (see **Table 13-1**). Put another way, they have personality traits that are much more extreme and dysfunctional than those of most other people in their culture, leading to significant problems and psychological pain for themselves or others.

Frederick appears to display a personality disorder. For most of his life, his extreme narcissism, grandiosity, and insensitivity have led to poor functioning in both the personal and social realms. They have caused him to repeatedly feel angry and unappreciated,

TABLE: 13-1

Dx Checklist

Personality Disorder
1. Individual displays a long-term, rigid, and wide-ranging pattern of inner experience and behavior that leads to dysfunction in at least two of the following realms: • Cognition • Emotion • Social interactions • Impulsivity.
2. The individual's pattern is significantly different from ones usually found in his or her culture.
3. Individual experiences significant distress or impairment.

Information from: APA, 2013.

deprived him of close personal relationships, and brought considerable pain to others. Witness the upset and turmoil felt by Frederick's coworkers and girlfriends.

The symptoms of personality disorders last for years and typically become recognizable in adolescence or early adulthood, although some start during childhood (Skodol, 2017). These disorders are among the most difficult psychological disorders to treat. Surveys indicate that around 15 percent of all adults in the United States display a personality disorder at some point in their lives (Skodol, 2017; APA, 2013).

It is common for a person with a personality disorder to also suffer from another disorder, a relationship called *comorbidity.* As you will see later in this chapter, for example, many people with avoidant personality disorder, who fearfully shy away from all relationships, also display social anxiety disorder. Research indicates that the presence of a personality disorder complicates a person's chances for a successful recovery from other psychological problems (Caligor & Petrini, 2018; Silverman & Krueger, 2018).

DSM-5 identifies 10 personality disorders (APA, 2013). Often these disorders are separated into three groups, or *clusters.* One cluster, marked by odd or eccentric behavior, consists of the *paranoid, schizoid,* and *schizotypal* personality disorders. A second cluster features dramatic behavior and consists of the *antisocial, borderline, histrionic,* and *narcissistic* personality disorders. The final cluster features a high degree of anxiety and includes the *avoidant, dependent,* and *obsessive-compulsive* personality disorders.

These 10 personality disorders are each characterized by a group of problematic personality symptoms. For example, as you will soon see, *paranoid personality disorder* is diagnosed when a person has unjustified suspicions that others are harming him or her, has persistent unfounded doubts about the loyalty of friends, reads threatening meanings into benign events, persistently bears grudges, and has recurrent unjustified suspicions about the faithfulness of life partners.

The DSM's listing of 10 distinct personality disorders is called a *categorical* approach. Like a light switch that is either on or off, this kind of approach assumes that (1) problematic personality traits are either present or absent in people, (2) a personality disorder is either displayed or not displayed by a person, and (3) a person who suffers from a personality disorder is not markedly troubled by personality traits outside of that disorder.

It turns out, however, that these assumptions are frequently contradicted in clinical practice. In fact, the symptoms of the personality disorders listed in DSM-5 overlap so much that clinicians often find it difficult to distinguish one disorder from another, resulting in frequent disagreements about which diagnosis is correct for a person with a personality disorder. Diagnosticians sometimes even determine that particular people have more than one personality disorder (Lilienfeld & Latzman, 2018). This lack of agreement has raised serious questions about the *validity* (accuracy) and *reliability* (consistency) of the 10 DSM-5 personality disorder categories.

Given this state of affairs, many theorists have challenged the use of a categorical approach to personality disorders. They believe that personality disorders differ more in *degree* than in type of dysfunction and should instead be classified by the severity of personality traits rather than by the presence or absence of specific traits—a procedure called a *dimensional* approach (Anderson et al., 2018, 2014; Skodol, 2018). In a dimensional approach, each trait is seen as varying along a continuum extending from nonproblematic to extremely problematic. People with a personality disorder are those who display extreme degrees of problematic traits—degrees not commonly found in the general population.

Given the inadequacies of a categorical approach and the growing enthusiasm for a dimensional one, the framers of DSM-5 initially proposed significant changes in how personality disorders should be classified. After much debate, they decided to retain a classic 10-disorder categorical approach in the current DSM. At the same time, however, the framers acknowledged the likely future direction of personality disorder classifications by also describing an *alternative* dimensional approach. Most of the discussions in this chapter are organized around the 10-disorder categorical approach used in DSM-5.

personality disorder An enduring, rigid pattern of inner experience and outward behavior that repeatedly impairs a person's sense of self, emotional experiences, goals, capacity for empathy, and/or capacity for intimacy.

paranoid personality disorder A personality disorder marked by a pattern of distrust and suspiciousness of others.

Later in the chapter, we will examine possible alternative—dimensional—approaches of the future, including the one presented in DSM-5.

As you read about the various personality disorders, you should be clear that diagnoses of such disorders can be assigned too often. We may catch glimpses of ourselves or of people we know in the descriptions of these disorders and be tempted to conclude that we or they have a personality disorder. In the vast majority of instances, such interpretations are incorrect. We all display personality traits. Only occasionally are they so maladaptive, distressing, and inflexible that they can be considered disorders. ■

Why do you think personality disorders attract so many efforts at amateur psychology?

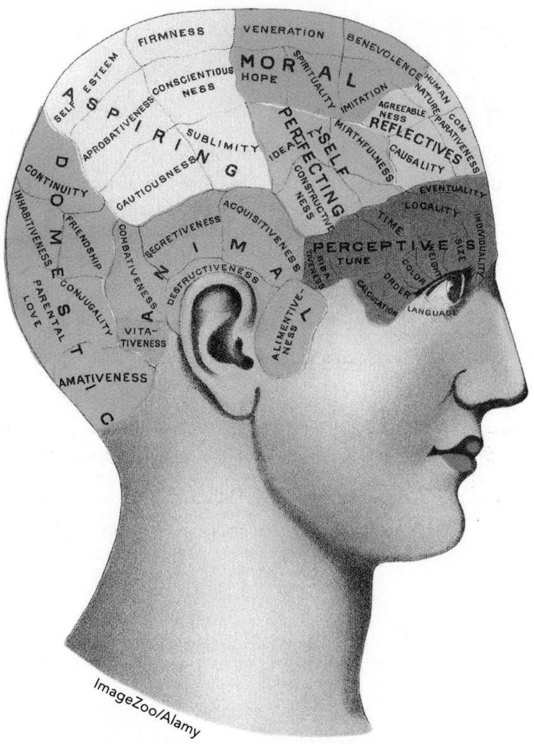

ImageZoo/Alamy

Early notions of personality In the popular nineteenth-century theory of phrenology, Franz Joseph Gall (1758–1828) suggested that the brain consists of distinct portions, each responsible for some aspect of personality. Phrenologists tried to assess personality by feeling bumps and indentations on a person's head.

9... SUMMING UP

PERSONALITY DISORDERS AND DSM-5 People with a personality disorder display an enduring, rigid pattern of inner experience and outward behavior. Their personality traits are much more extreme and dysfunctional than those of most other people in their culture, resulting in significant problems for them or those around them. It has been estimated that as many as 15 percent of adults develop such a disorder at some point in their lives. DSM-5 uses a categorical approach that lists 10 distinct personality disorders. In addition, the framers of DSM-5 have proposed a dimensional approach to the classification of personality disorders.

"Odd" Personality Disorders

The cluster of "odd" personality disorders consists of the *paranoid, schizoid,* and *schizotypal* personality disorders. People with these disorders typically have odd or eccentric behaviors that are similar to but not as extensive as those seen in schizophrenia, including extreme suspiciousness, social withdrawal, and peculiar ways of thinking and perceiving things. Such behaviors often leave the person isolated. Some clinicians believe that these personality disorders are related to schizophrenia. In fact, schizotypal personality disorder is listed twice in DSM-5—as one of the schizophrenia spectrum disorders and as one of the personality disorders. Directly related or not, people with an odd-cluster personality disorder often qualify for an additional diagnosis of schizophrenia or have close relatives with schizophrenia (Lenzenweger, 2018).

Clinicians have learned much about the symptoms of the odd-cluster personality disorders but have not been so successful in determining their causes or how to treat them. In fact, as you'll soon see, people with these disorders rarely seek treatment.

Paranoid Personality Disorder

As you read earlier, people with **paranoid personality disorder** deeply distrust other people and are suspicious of others' motives (APA, 2013). Because they believe that everyone intends them harm, they shun close relationships. Their trust in their own ideas and abilities can be excessive, though, as you can see in the case of Eduardo:

For Eduardo, a researcher at a genetic engineering company, this was the last straw. He had been severely chastised by his supervisor for deviating from the research procedure on a major study. He knew where this was coming from. He had been "ratted out" by his jealous, conniving lab colleagues. This time, Eduardo would not sit back quietly. He demanded a meeting with his supervisor and the three other researchers in the lab.

At the outset of the meeting, Eduardo insisted that he would not leave the room until he was told the name of the person who had ratted him out. He acknowledged that he had, in

(continued on the next page)

#

#BigOverlap

Suspiciousness, self-absorption, anxiety, and depression are prominent features in almost all 10 personality disorders in DSM-5.

fact, changed the study's design in key ways, maintaining that these changes would open the door to enormous medical gains. Eduardo quickly shifted the focus onto his lab colleagues. He stated that the other scientists were intimidated by his visionary ideas, and he accused them of trying to get him out of the way so they could continue to work in an unproductive, low-pressure atmosphere. He said that their desire to get rid of him was always apparent to him, revealed by their coldness toward him each and every day and their outright nastiness whenever he tried to correct them or offer constructive criticism. Nor did it escape his attention that they were always laughing at him, talking about him behind his back, and, on more than one occasion, trying to copy or destroy his notes.

The other researchers were aghast as Eduardo laid out his suspicions. They pointed out that it was Eduardo, not they, who was always behaving in an unfriendly manner. He had stopped speaking to all of them two months ago and he regularly tried to antagonize them—giving them dirty looks and slamming doors.

Next, Eduardo's supervisor, Lisa, spoke up. She said that in her objective opinion, none of Eduardo's accusations were true. First, none of his colleagues had informed on him. She herself had reviewed videos from the lab cameras as a matter of routine and had noticed him feeding rats that were supposed to be left hungry. Second, she said that it was his coworkers' account, not Eduardo's, that rang true. In fact, she had received many complaints from people outside the lab about Eduardo's cold and aloof manner.

Later, in the privacy of her office, Lisa told Eduardo that she had no choice but to let him go. Eduardo was furious, but not completely surprised. His past two jobs had ended badly as well.

Ever on guard and cautious and seeing threats everywhere, people like Eduardo continually expect to be the targets of some trickery (see **Figure 13-1**). They find "hidden" meanings, which are usually belittling or threatening, in everything. In an early study that required people to role-play, participants with paranoia were more likely than control participants to read hostile intentions into the actions of others (Turkat et al., 1990). In addition, they more often chose anger as the appropriate role-play response.

Quick to challenge the loyalty or trustworthiness of acquaintances, people with paranoid personality disorder remain cold and distant. A woman might avoid confiding in anyone, for example, for fear of being hurt; or a husband might, without any justification, persist in questioning his wife's faithfulness. Although inaccurate and inappropriate, their suspicions are not usually *delusional;* the ideas are not so bizarre or so firmly held as to clearly remove the individuals from reality (Lee, 2017).

People with this disorder are critical of weakness and fault in others, particularly at work (McGurk et al., 2013). They are unable to recognize their own mistakes, though, and are extremely sensitive to criticism. They often blame others for the things that go wrong in their lives, and they repeatedly bear grudges. As many as 4.4 percent of adults experience this disorder, which is apparently more common in men than in women (Quirk et al., 2017, 2016; APA, 2013).

Jason Adam Katzenstein/The New Yorker Collection/The Cartoon Bank

How Do Theorists Explain Paranoid Personality Disorder? The theories that have been proposed to explain paranoid personality disorder, like those about most other personality disorders, have received little systematic research. Psychodynamic theories, the oldest of these explanations, trace the pattern to early interactions with demanding parents, particularly distant, rigid fathers and overcontrolling, rejecting mothers (Paris, 2018; Williams, 2010). (You will see that psychodynamic explanations for almost all the personality disorders begin the same way—with repeated mistreatment during childhood and lack of love.) According to one psychodynamic view, some people come to view their environment as hostile as a result of their parents' persistently unreasonable demands. They must always be on the alert because they cannot trust others, and they are likely to develop feelings of extreme anger. They also project these feelings onto others and, as a result, feel increasingly persecuted (Geoffreys, 2015; Koenigsberg et al., 2001). Similarly, some cognitive-behavioral theorists suggest that people with paranoid personality disorder generally hold broad maladaptive assumptions, such as "People are evil" and "People will attack you if given the chance" (Beck, Davis, & Freeman, 2015).

Biological theorists propose that paranoid personality disorder has genetic causes (Haghighatfard et al., 2018). A widely reported study that looked at self-reports of suspiciousness in 3,810 Australian twin pairs found that if one twin was excessively suspicious, the other had an increased likelihood of also being suspicious (Kendler et al., 1987). Once again, however, it is important to note that such similarities between twins might also be the result of common environmental experiences.

Treatments for Paranoid Personality Disorder People with paranoid personality disorder do not typically see themselves as needing help, and few come to treatment willingly (Skodol, 2017; Kellett & Hardy, 2014). Furthermore, many who are in treatment view the role of patient as inferior and distrust and rebel against their therapists. Thus it is not surprising that therapy for this disorder has limited effect and moves slowly.

Object relations therapists—the psychodynamic therapists who give center stage to relationships—try to see past the patient's anger and work on what they view as his or her deep wish for a satisfying relationship (Caligor et al., 2018; Kernberg, 2018). Cognitive-behavioral therapy has also been used to treat people with paranoid personality disorder. On the behavioral side, therapists help clients to master anxiety-reduction techniques and to improve their skills at solving interpersonal problems. On the cognitive side, therapists guide the clients to develop more realistic interpretations of other people's words and actions and to become more aware of other people's points of view (Davidson, 2018). Antipsychotic drug therapy seems to be of limited help (Markovitz, 2018; Skodol, 2017).

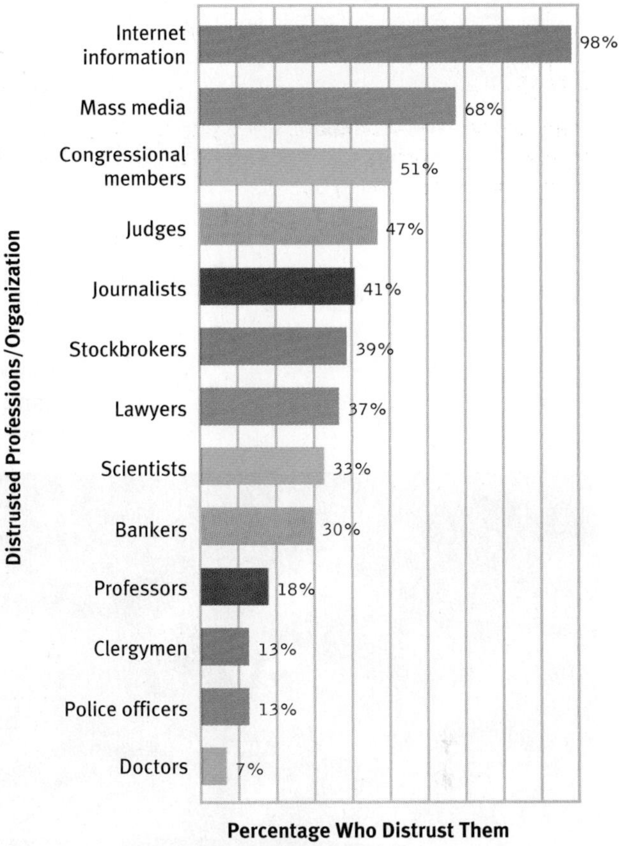

FIGURE 13-1

Whom Do You Distrust?

Although distrust and suspiciousness are the hallmarks of paranoid personality disorder, even people without this disorder are often untrusting. In various surveys, the majority of respondents have said they distrust Internet information, the mass media (newspapers, TV, and radio), and members of Congress. (Information from: Gallup Poll, 2018, 2016, 2015; Bernstein, 2017; Pew Research, 2017, 2016; Swift, 2016; Ho, 2012.)

Schizoid Personality Disorder

People with **schizoid personality disorder** persistently avoid and are removed from social relationships and demonstrate little in the way of emotion (APA, 2013). Like people with paranoid personality disorder, they do not have close ties with other people. The reason they avoid social contact, however, has nothing to do with paranoid feelings of distrust or suspicion; it is because they genuinely prefer to be alone. Take Eli:

Eli, a student at the local technical institute, had been engaged in several different Internet certificate programs over the past few years, and was about to engage in yet another, when his mother, confused as to why he would not apply for a traditional degree at a "real" college, insisted he seek therapy. A loner by nature, Eli preferred not to socialize in any traditional sense, having little to no desire to get to know much about the people in his immediate social context. The way Eli saw it, . . . "at least at my school you just go to class and go home."

Routinely, he slept through much of his day and then spent his evenings, nights, and weekends at the school's computer lab, "chatting" with others over the Internet while not in class. Notably, people that he chatted with often sought to meet Eli, but he always declined these invitations, stating that he didn't really have any desire to learn more about them than what they shared over the computer in the chat rooms. He described a family life that was similar to that of his social surroundings; he was mostly oblivious of his younger brother and sister, two outgoing teens, despite the fact that they seemed to hold him in the highest regard, and he had recently alienated himself entirely from his father, who had left the family several years earlier. . . .

(continued on the next page)

schizoid personality disorder A personality disorder featuring persistent avoidance of social relationships and little expression of emotion.

> *A marked deficit in social interest was notable in Eli, as were frequent behavioral eccentricities. . . . At best, he had acquired a peripheral . . . role in social and family relationships. . . . Rather than venturing outward, he had increasingly removed himself from others and from sources of potential growth and gratification. Life was uneventful, with extended periods of solitude interspersed.*
>
> (Millon, 2011)

People like Eli, often described as "loners," make no effort to start or keep friendships, take little interest in having sexual relationships, and even seem indifferent to their families. They seek out jobs that require little or no contact with others. When necessary, they can form work relations to a degree, but they prefer to keep to themselves. Many live by themselves as well. Not surprisingly, their social skills tend to be weak. If they marry, their lack of interest in intimacy may create marital or family problems.

People with schizoid personality disorder focus mainly on themselves and are generally unaffected by praise or criticism. They rarely show any feelings, expressing neither joy nor anger. They seem to have no need for attention or acceptance; are typically viewed as cold, humorless, or dull; and generally succeed in being ignored. This disorder is present in 3.1 percent of the adult population (Morgan & Zimmerman, 2018; APA, 2013). Men are slightly more likely to experience it than are women.

A darker knight In recent years, Batman movies have presented the crime fighter as a singularly driven loner incapable of forming or sustaining relationships, a portrayal true to the original comic book presentation. In the 2016 film *Batman v Superman: Dawn of Justice*, for example, Batman's asocial personality, including his hatred and distrust of Superman, is evident. A number of clinical observers have argued that in these recent presentations, Batman displays some of the symptoms of schizoid personality disorder.

How Do Theorists Explain Schizoid Personality Disorder?

Many psychodynamic theorists, particularly object relations theorists, propose that schizoid personality disorder has its roots in an unsatisfied need for human contact (Kernberg, 2018). The parents of people with this disorder, like those of people with paranoid personality disorder, are believed to have been unaccepting or even abusive of their children. Whereas people with paranoid symptoms react to such parenting chiefly with distrust, those with schizoid personality disorder are left unable to give or receive love. They cope by avoiding all relationships.

Cognitive-behavioral theorists propose, not surprisingly, that people with schizoid personality disorder suffer from deficiencies in their thinking. Their thoughts tend to be vague, empty, and without much meaning, and they have trouble scanning the environment to arrive at accurate perceptions (Chadwick, 2014). Unable to pick up emotional cues from others, they simply cannot respond to emotions. As this theory might predict, children with schizoid personality disorder develop language and motor skills very slowly, whatever their level of intelligence (APA, 2013).

Treatments for Schizoid Personality Disorder Their social withdrawal prevents most people with schizoid personality disorder from entering therapy unless some other disorder, such as alcoholism, makes treatment necessary (Skodol & Bender, 2018, 2016). These clients are likely to remain emotionally distant from the therapist, seem not to care about their treatment, and make limited progress at best (Sperry, 2016; Colli et al., 2014).

Cognitive-behavioral therapists have sometimes been able to help people with this disorder experience more positive emotions and more satisfying social interactions (Davidson, 2018; Beck et al., 2015). On the cognitive end, their techniques include presenting clients with lists of emotions to think about or having them write down and remember pleasurable experiences. On the behavioral end, therapists have sometimes had success teaching social skills to such clients, using role-playing, exposure techniques, and homework assignments as tools. Group therapy is apparently useful when it offers a safe setting for social contact, although people with schizoid personality disorder may resist pressure to take part (Bressert, 2016). As with paranoid personality disorder, drug therapy seems to offer limited help (Markovitz, 2018; Skodol, 2017).

schizotypal personality disorder A personality disorder characterized by extreme discomfort in close relationships, very odd patterns of thinking and perceiving, and behavioral eccentricities.

Schizotypal Personality Disorder

People with **schizotypal personality disorder** display a range of interpersonal problems marked by extreme discomfort in close relationships, very odd patterns of thinking and perceiving, and behavioral eccentricities (APA, 2013). Anxious around others, they seek isolation and have few close friends. Some feel intensely lonely. The disorder is more severe than the paranoid and schizoid personality disorders, as we see in the case of 41-year-old Kevin:

Kevin was a night security guard at a warehouse, where he had worked since his high school graduation more than 20 years ago. His parents, both successful professionals, had been worried for many years, as Kevin seemed entirely disconnected from himself and his surroundings and had never taken initiative to make any changes, even toward a shift supervisory position. They therefore made the referral for therapy, and Kevin simply acquiesced. He explained that he liked his work, as it was a place where he could be by himself in a quiet atmosphere, away from anyone else. He described where he worked as "an empty warehouse; they don't use it no more but they don't want no one in there. It's nice; 'homey.'"

Throughout the . . . interview, Kevin remained aloof, never once looking at the counselor, usually answering questions with either one-word responses or short phrases, and usually waiting to respond until a second question was asked or the first question was repeated. He described, in . . . short, bizarre answers, a life devoid of almost any human interconnectedness, almost his only tangible contact being his brother, whom he saw only during major holidays. Living alone, he could only remember one significant relationship, and that was with a girl in high school. Very simply, he stated, "We graduated, and then I didn't see her anymore." He expressed no apparent loneliness, however, and appeared entirely emotionless regarding any aspect of his life. . . .

Kevin . . . often seemed to experience a separation between his mind and his physical body. There was a strange sense of nonbeing or nonexistence, as if his floating conscious awareness carried with it a depersonalized or identityless human form. Behaviorally, his tendency was to be drab, sluggish, and inexpressive. He . . . appeared bland, indifferent, unmotivated, and insensitive to the external world. . . . Most people considered him to be [a] strange person . . . who faded into the background, self-absorbed . . . and lost to the outside world. . . . Bizarre "telepathic" powers enabled him to communicate with mythical or distant others. . . . Kevin also occasionally decompensated when faced with too much, rather than too little, stimulation. . . . He would simply fade out, becoming blank, losing conscious awareness, and turning off the pressures of the outer world.

(Millon, 2011)

As with Kevin, the thoughts and behaviors of people with schizotypal personality disorder can be noticeably disturbed. These symptoms may include *ideas of reference*—beliefs that unrelated events pertain to them in some important way—and *bodily illusions*, such as sensing an external "force" or presence. A number of people with this disorder see themselves as having special extrasensory abilities, and some believe that they have magical control over others. Examples of schizotypal eccentricities include repeatedly arranging cans to align their labels, organizing closets extensively, or wearing an odd assortment of clothing. The emotions of these individuals may be inappropriate, flat, or humorless.

People with schizotypal personality disorder often have great difficulty keeping their attention focused. Correspondingly, their conversation is typically digressive and vague, even sprinkled with loose associations (Lenzenweger, 2018; Rabella et al., 2016). Like Kevin, they tend to drift aimlessly and lead an idle, unproductive life. They are

#CommonBelief

People who think that they have extrasensory abilities are not necessarily suffering from schizotypal personality disorder. In fact, according to surveys, more than 73 percent of adults believe in some form of the paranormal or occult—ESP, astrology, ghosts, communicating with the dead, or psychics (Gray & Gallo, 2016; Austin, 2015; Gallup Poll, 2005).

likely to choose undemanding jobs in which they can work below their capacity and are not required to interact with other people. Surveys suggest that 3.9 percent of adults—slightly more males than females—display schizotypal personality disorder (Rosell, 2017; APA, 2013).

How Do Theorists Explain Schizotypal Personality Disorder? Because the symptoms of schizotypal personality disorder so often resemble those of schizophrenia, researchers have hypothesized that similar factors may be at work in both disorders. A range of studies have supported such expectations (Lenzenweger, 2018; Rosell, 2017). Investigators have found that schizotypal symptoms, like schizophrenic patterns, are often linked to family conflicts and to psychological disorders in parents. They have also learned that defects in attention and short-term memory may contribute to schizotypal personality disorder, just as they apparently do to schizophrenia. For example, research participants with either disorder perform poorly on *backward masking*, a laboratory test of attention that requires a person to identify a visual stimulus immediately after a previous stimulus has flashed on and off the screen. People with these disorders have a hard time shutting out the first stimulus in order to focus on the second. Finally, researchers have linked schizotypal personality disorder to some of the same biological factors found in schizophrenia, such as high activity of the neurotransmitter dopamine, enlarged brain ventricles, smaller temporal lobes, and loss of gray matter (Chan et al., 2018; Lenzenweger, 2018). As you read in Chapter 12, there are indications that these biological factors may have a genetic basis.

Although these findings do suggest a close relationship between schizotypal personality disorder and schizophrenia, the personality disorder also has been linked to disorders of mood. Around two-thirds of people with schizotypal personality disorder also suffer from major depressive disorder or bipolar disorder at some point in their lives (Rosell, 2017). Thus, at the very least, this personality disorder is not tied exclusively to schizophrenia.

Sipa Press

When personality disorders explode
In this 2007 video, Seung-Hui Cho, a student at Virginia Tech, described the slights he experienced throughout his life. After mailing the video to NBC News, he proceeded to kill 32 people, including himself, and to wound 25 others in a massive campus shooting. Most clinicians agree that he displayed a combination of features from the schizotypal, paranoid, schizoid, antisocial, borderline, and narcissistic personality disorders, including strange thinking, extreme social withdrawal, persistent distrust, boundless fury and hatred, intimidating behavior, arrogance, and disregard for others.

Treatments for Schizotypal Personality Disorder Therapy is as difficult in cases of schizotypal personality disorder as it is in cases of paranoid and schizoid personality disorders. Most therapists agree on the need to help these clients "reconnect" with the world and recognize the limits of their thinking and their powers. The therapists may thus try to set clear limits—for example, by requiring punctuality—and work on helping the clients recognize where their views end and those of the therapist begin. Other therapy goals are to increase positive social contacts, ease loneliness, reduce overstimulation, and help the individuals become more aware of their personal feelings (Sperry, 2016; Colli et al., 2014).

Cognitive-behavioral therapists further try to teach clients to evaluate their unusual thoughts or perceptions objectively and to ignore the inappropriate ones (Davidson, 2018; Beck et al., 2015). The therapists may keep track of clients' odd or magical predictions, for example, and later point out their inaccuracy. When clients are speaking and begin to digress, the therapists might ask them to sum up what it is they are trying to say. In addition, specific behavioral methods, such as speech lessons, social skills training, and tips on appropriate dress and manners, have sometimes helped clients learn to blend in better with and be more comfortable around other people (Skodol, 2017; Bressert, 2016).

Antipsychotic drugs have been given to people with schizotypal personality disorder, again because of the disorder's similarity to schizophrenia. In low doses the drugs appear to have helped some people, usually by reducing certain of their thought problems (Jakobsen et al., 2017; Skodol, 2017).

9... SUMMING UP

"ODD" PERSONALITY DISORDERS Three of the personality disorders in DSM-5 are marked by the kinds of odd or eccentric behavior often seen in schizophrenia. People with paranoid personality disorder display a broad pattern of distrust and suspiciousness. Those with schizoid personality disorder persistently avoid social relationships, have little or no social interest, and show little emotional expression. People with schizotypal personality disorder display a range of interpersonal problems marked by extreme discomfort in close relationships, very odd forms of thinking and behavior, and behavioral eccentricities. Treatment gains for people with these disorders tend to be modest at best.

"Dramatic" Personality Disorders

The cluster of "dramatic" personality disorders includes the *antisocial, borderline, histrionic,* and *narcissistic* personality disorders. The behaviors of people with these problems are so dramatic, emotional, or erratic that it is almost impossible for them to have relationships that are truly giving and satisfying.

These personality disorders are more commonly diagnosed than the others. However, only the antisocial and borderline personality disorders have received much study, partly because they create so many problems for other people. The causes of the disorders, like those of the odd personality disorders, are not well understood. Treatments range from ineffective to moderately effective.

Don Emmert/AFP/Getty Images

Notorious disregard In 2009, financier Bernard Madoff was sentenced to 150 years in prison after defrauding thousands of investors, including many charities, of billions of dollars. Given his overwhelming disregard for people and related qualities, some clinicians suggest that Madoff displays antisocial personality disorder.

Antisocial Personality Disorder

Sometimes described as "psychopaths" or "sociopaths," people with **antisocial personality disorder** persistently disregard and violate others' rights (APA, 2013). Aside from substance use disorders, this is the disorder most closely linked to adult criminal behavior. DSM-5 stipulates that a person must be at least 18 years of age to receive this diagnosis; however, most people with antisocial personality disorder displayed some patterns of misbehavior before they were 15, including truancy, running away, cruelty to animals or people, and destroying property.

Robert Hare, a leading clinician and researcher in this realm, recalls an early professional encounter with a prison inmate named Ray:

In the early 1960s, I found myself employed as the sole psychologist at the British Columbia Penitentiary. . . . I wasn't in my office for more than an hour when my first "client" arrived. He was a tall, slim, dark-haired man in his thirties. The air around him seemed to buzz, and the eye contact he made with me was so direct and intense that I wondered if I had ever really looked anybody in the eye before. That stare was unrelenting—he didn't indulge in the brief glances away that most people use to soften the force of their gaze.

Without waiting for an introduction, the inmate—I'll call him Ray—opened the conversation: "Hey, Doc, how's it going? Look, I've got a problem. I need your help. I'd really like to talk to you about this."

Eager to begin work as a genuine psychotherapist, I asked him to tell me about it. In response, he pulled out a knife and waved it in front of my nose, all the while smiling and maintaining that intense eye contact.

Once he determined that I wasn't going to push the button, he explained that he intended to use the knife not on me but on another inmate who had been making overtures to his "protégé," a prison term for the more passive member of a homosexual pairing. . . . From that first meeting on, Ray managed to make my eight-month stint at the prison miserable. His constant demands on my time and his attempts to manipulate me into doing things for him were unending. On one

(continued on the next page)

antisocial personality disorder A personality disorder marked by a general pattern of disregard for and violation of other people's rights.

#PreviousIdentity

Antisocial personality disorder was referred to as "moral insanity" during the nineteenth century (Jones, 2017).

occasion, he convinced me that he would make a good cook . . . and I supported his request for a transfer from the machine shop (where he had apparently made the knife). . . . Several months after I had recommended the transfer, there was a mighty eruption below the floorboards directly under the warden's [dining] table. When the commotion died down, we found an elaborate system for distilling alcohol below the floor. Something had gone wrong and one of the pots had exploded. There was nothing unusual about the presence of a still in a maximum-security prison, but the audacity of placing one under the warden's seat shook up a lot of people. When it was discovered that Ray was the brains behind the bootleg operation, he spent some time in solitary confinement.

Once out of "the hole," Ray appeared in my office as if nothing had happened and asked for a transfer from the kitchen to the auto shop—he really felt he had a knack, he saw the need to prepare himself for the outside world . . . eventually he wore me down.

Soon afterward I decided to leave the prison to pursue a Ph.D. in psychology, and about a month before I left Ray almost persuaded me to ask my father, a roofing contractor, to offer him a job as part of an application for parole.

Ray had an incredible ability to con not just me but everybody. He could talk, and lie, with a smoothness and a directness that sometimes momentarily disarmed even the most experienced and cynical of the prison staff. When I met him he had a long criminal record behind him (and, as it turned out, ahead of him); about half his adult life had been spent in prison, and many of his crimes had been violent. . . . He lied endlessly, lazily, about everything, and it disturbed him not a whit whenever I pointed out something in his file that contradicted one of his lies. He would simply change the subject and spin off in a different direction. Finally convinced that he might not make the perfect job candidate in my father's firm, I turned down Ray's request—and was shaken by his nastiness at my refusal.

Before I left the prison for the university, I took advantage of the prison policy of letting staff have their cars repaired in the institution's auto shop—where Ray still worked, thanks (he would have said no thanks) to me. The car received a beautiful paint job and the motor and drivetrain were reconditioned.

With all our possessions on top of the car and our baby . . . in the backseat, my wife and I headed for Ontario. The first problems appeared soon after we left Vancouver, when the motor seemed a bit rough. Later, when we encountered some moderate inclines, the radiator boiled over. A garage mechanic discovered ball bearings in the carburetor's float chamber; he also pointed out where one of the hoses to the radiator had clearly been tampered with. These problems were repaired easily enough, but the next one, which arose while we were going down a long hill, was more serious. The brake pedal became very spongy and then simply dropped to the floor—no brakes, and it was a long hill. Fortunately, we made it to a service station, where we found that the brake line had been cut so that a slow leak would occur. Perhaps it was a coincidence that Ray was working in the auto shop when the car was being tuned up, but I had no doubt that the prison [pipeline] had informed him of the owner of the car.

(Hare, 1993)

Like Ray, people with antisocial personality disorder lie repeatedly (APA, 2013). Many cannot work consistently at a job; they are absent frequently and are likely to quit their jobs altogether (Black, 2017). Usually they are also careless with money and frequently fail to pay their debts. They are often impulsive, taking action without thinking of the consequences (Olson & Patrick, 2018). Correspondingly, they may be irritable, aggressive, and quick to start fights.

How do various institutions in our society—business, government, science, religion—view lying? How might such views affect lying by individuals?

Recklessness is another common trait: people with antisocial personality disorder have little regard for their own safety or for that of others, even their children. They are self-centered as well, and are likely to have trouble maintaining close relationships. Usually they develop a knack for gaining personal profit at the expense of others. Because the pain or damage they cause seldom concerns them, clinicians often say that they lack a moral conscience (see **Table 13-2**).

#CharacterIngestion

As late as the Victorian era, many English parents believed babies absorbed personality and moral uprightness as they took in milk. Thus, if a mother could not nurse, it was important to find a wet nurse of good character (Asimov, 1997).

They think of their victims as weak and deserving of being conned, robbed, or even physically harmed (see ***Trending*** on the next page).

Surveys indicate that 3.6 percent of adults in the United States meet the criteria for antisocial personality disorder (Black, 2017; APA, 2013). The disorder is as much as four times more common among men than women.

Because people with this disorder are often arrested, researchers frequently look for people with antisocial patterns in prison populations (Azevedo et al., 2018). It is estimated that at least 35 percent of people in prison meet the diagnostic criteria for this disorder. The criminal behavior of many people with this disorder declines after the age of 40; some, however, continue their criminal activities throughout their lives (Holzer & Vaughn, 2017; APA, 2013).

Studies and clinical observations also indicate that people with antisocial personality disorder have higher rates of alcoholism and other substance use disorders than do the rest of the population (Black, 2017; Robitaille et al., 2017). Thus some theorists speculate that antisocial personality disorder and substance use disorders both have the same cause, such as a deep-seated need to take risks. Consistent with this notion, a number of people with antisocial personality disorder also display gambling disorder (Chamberlain et al., 2017).

How Do Theorists Explain Antisocial Personality Disorder? Most explanations of antisocial personality disorder come from the psychodynamic, cognitive-behavioral, and biological models. As with many other personality disorders, *psychodynamic* theorists propose that this one begins with an absence of parental love during infancy, leading to a lack of basic trust (Paris, 2018; Meloy & Yakeley, 2010). In this view, some children—the ones who develop antisocial personality disorder—respond to the early inadequacies by becoming emotionally distant, and they bond with others through the use of power and destructiveness. In support of the psychodynamic explanation, researchers have found that people with this disorder are more likely than others to have had significant stress in their childhoods, particularly in such forms as family poverty, family violence, child abuse, and parental conflict or divorce (Black, 2017; Gard et al., 2017).

Cognitive-behavioral theorists have argued that a combination of behavioral and cognitive factors contribute to antisocial personality disorder. On the behavioral side, they suggest that antisocial symptoms may be learned through principles of conditioning, particularly *modeling*, or imitation (Cabrera et al., 2017). As evidence, they point to the higher rate of antisocial personality disorder found among the parents and close relatives of people with this disorder (Black, 2017). The modeling explanation is also supported by studies of friends and associates of people with antisocial personality disorder (McKeown & Taylor, 2018). For example, one investigation found that middle school students who were attracted to antisocial peers went on to engage in antisocial behavior themselves in order to gain acceptance (Juvonen & Ho, 2008).

Cognitive-behavioral theorists also point to *operant conditioning* to help explain this disorder. They suggest that some parents unintentionally teach antisocial behavior by regularly rewarding a child's aggressive behavior (Black, 2017; Kazdin, 2005). When the child misbehaves

TABLE: 13-2

Annual Hate Crimes in the United States

Group Attacked	Number of Reported Incidents
Racial/ethnic groups	4,216
LGBT groups	1,410
Religious groups	1,402
Groups with disability	85

Information from: FBI, 2017, 2016.

Popular sociopaths Television audiences seem to love characters with the symptoms of antisocial personality disorder. Legendary character Walter White (left), the ruthless meth manufacturer and dealer in *Breaking Bad*, and the equally legendary Joffrey Baratheon (right), the amoral and cruel king in *Game of Thrones*, are two of this decade's most popular villains.

Ursula Coyote/© AMC/Courtesy Everett Collection

HBO/Photofest

...TRENDING

Mass Murders: Where Does Such Violence Come From?

At 2:00 A.M. on June 12, 2016, a 29-year-old man entered Pulse, a gay nightclub in Orlando, Florida, and, using two semi-automatic weapons, proceeded to shoot 100 patrons, killing 49 of them. The mass killing, considered a terrorist-hate attack, was one of the deadliest by a single shooter in U.S. history. But it was certainly not the only mass killing. The Orlando horror has been followed by numerous other mass shootings, including ones at a country music concert in Las Vegas, Nevada, in 2017, and at the Marjory Stoneman Douglas High School in Parkland, Florida, in 2018. Similarly, it was preceded by numerous mass killings across the country and the world, including the 2015 killings of 9 Bible study members at a church in Charleston, South Carolina; the 2012 killings of 26 students and teachers at the Sandy Hook Elementary School in Newtown, Connecticut; and the 2012 murders of 12 moviegoers at a *Batman* movie in Aurora, Colorado.

These numbers are numbing, and the public has looked to the clinical field to help it understand why mass killings occur and why they are on the increase. Clinical theorists and researchers have offered various theories about why individuals commit such murders, but enlightening research and effective interventions have been elusive (Fox, Levin, & Fridel, 2018; Abe, 2017).

What do we know about mass killings? We know they involve, by definition, the murder of four or more people in the same location and at around the same time. FBI records also indicate that, on average, mass killings occur in the United States every two weeks, 75 percent of them feature a lone killer, 67 percent involve the use of guns, and most are committed by males (FBI, 2017; Hoyer & Heath, 2012).

We also know that despite public perceptions, mass killings are not a new phenomenon. They have occurred—with regularity—for centuries (Bonn, 2017, 2015). What is new, however, is the increasing frequency of mass *public* shootings (for example, schools, shopping malls, and workplaces) and the emergence of certain patterns of mass murder (Fox et al., 2018; Wilson, 2016). Although specific issues vary from mass murder to mass murder—racial or religious hatred, for example—two general patterns are on the rise (Abe, 2017). In one pattern, so-called "pseudocommando" mass murders, the murderer "kills in public, often during the daytime, plans his offense well in advance, and comes prepared with a powerful arsenal of weapons. He has no escape planned and expects to be killed during the incident" (Knoll, 2010). In another pattern, "autogenic" (self-generated) massacres, individuals kill people indiscriminately to fulfill a personal agenda.

Melissa Lyttle for The Washington Post via Getty Images

Unthinkable Friends of the victims of the 2016 mass shooting at Pulse nightclub gather in Orlando to embrace, cry, and show support for those who died or were injured in the mass murder.

Theorists have suggested a number of factors to help explain pseudocommando, autogenic, and other mass killings, including the availability of guns, bullying behavior, substance abuse, the proliferation of violent media and video games, dysfunctional homes, and contagion effects (Lankford & Tomek, 2018; Singal, 2017). Moreover, regardless of one's position on gun control, media violence, or the like, almost everyone, including most clinicians, believe that mass killers typically suffer from a mental disorder (Fox et al., 2018; Winegard & Ferguson, 2016). Which mental disorder? On this, there is little agreement (Carey, 2016). Each of the following has been suggested:

- Antisocial, borderline, paranoid, or schizotypal personality disorder
- Schizophrenia or severe bipolar disorder
- Intermittent explosive disorder—an impulse-control disorder featuring repeated, unprovoked verbal and/or behavioral outbursts
- Severe depression, stress, or anxiety

Although these and yet other disorders have been proposed, none has received clear support in the limited research conducted on mass killings. On the other hand, several psychological variables have emerged as a common denominator across the various studies: severe feelings of anger and resentment, feelings of being persecuted or grossly mistreated, and desires for revenge (Fox et al., 2018). That is, regardless of which mental disorder a mass killer may display, he usually is driven by this set of feelings. For a growing number of clinical researchers, this repeated finding suggests that research should focus less on diagnosis and much more on identifying and understanding these particular feelings.

Clearly, clinical research must expand its focus on this area of enormous social concern. It is a difficult problem to investigate, partly because so few mass killers survive their crimes, but the clinical field has managed to gather useful insights about other elusive areas. And, indeed, in the aftermath of the horrific murders mentioned at the beginning of this box, a wave of heightened determination and commitment seems to have seized the clinical community.

or becomes violent in reaction to the parents' requests or orders, for example, the parents may give in to restore peace. Without meaning to, they may be teaching the child to be stubborn and perhaps even violent.

On the cognitive side, cognitive-behavioral theorists say that people with antisocial personality disorder often hold attitudes that trivialize the importance of other people's needs (Elwood et al., 2004). They believe that such a philosophy of life may be far more common in our society than people recognize. In a related explanation, a number of cognitive-behavioral theorists propose that people with this disorder have genuine difficulty recognizing points of view or feelings other than their own (Igoumenou et al., 2017).

Finally, studies suggest that *biological* factors play an important role in antisocial personality disorder. Genetic research suggests that the disorder may be linked to particular genes (Raine, 2018; Rosenström et al., 2017). In addition, researchers have found that antisocial people, particularly those who are highly impulsive and aggressive, have lower activity of the neurotransmitter serotonin than other people (Eisner et al., 2017). As you'll recall (see page 224), in other kinds of studies both impulsivity and aggression have been linked to low serotonin activity, so the presence of this biological factor in people with antisocial personality disorder is not surprising.

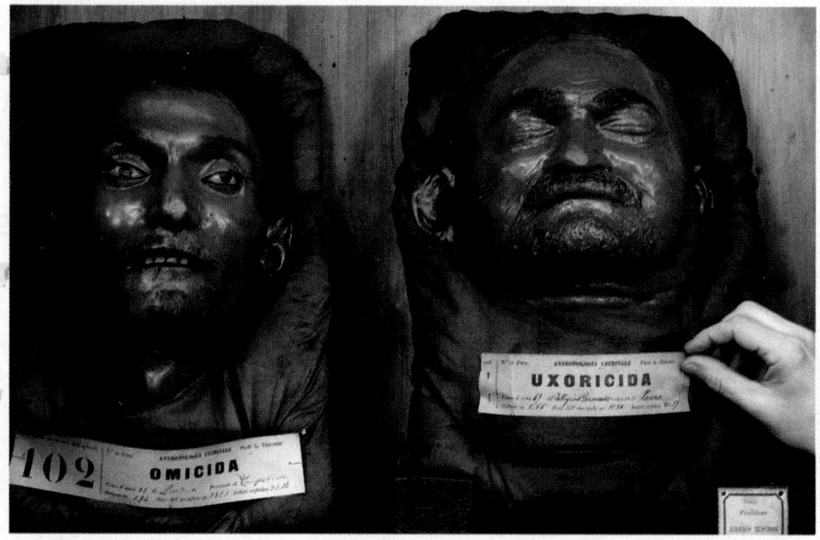

Reuters/Stefano Rellandini

Hardly a new disorder A worker attaches a tag that translates as "Killer of a Wife" to a wax-covered head at the Lombroso Museum in Turin, Italy. Hundreds of such heads, taken from prisons throughout Europe, line the museum's shelves, each with tags like "Ladro" ("Thief") or "Omicida" ("Murderer"). The display comes from nineteenth-century psychiatrist Cesare Lombroso's crude but pioneering research into the nature of criminal and related antisocial behavior.

In related work, studies indicate that individuals with this disorder display deficient functioning in their *prefrontal cortex, anterior cingulate cortex, amygdala, hippocampus,* and *temporal cortex*—brain structures that, collectively, help people follow rules; plan and execute realistic strategies; and display sympathy, judgment, and empathy (Gard et al., 2017; Schiffer et al., 2017). These are, of course, all abilities found wanting in people with antisocial personality disorder.

A different line of biological research has found that research participants with this disorder often respond to warnings or expectations of stress with low brain and bodily arousal (Thompson et al., 2014; Perdeci et al., 2010). It is believed that such underarousal may enable people with the disorder to readily tune out threatening or emotional situations and so be unaffected by them. This could help explain a phenomenon often observed by clinicians—that people with antisocial personality disorder seem to feel less anxiety than other people, and so lack a key ingredient for learning from negative life experiences or tuning in to the emotional cues of others (Black, 2017; Blair et al., 2005). Such physical underarousal may also help explain why people with antisocial personality disorder take more risks and seek more thrills than other people do.

These numerous biological factors may be connected more closely than first meets the eye. Consistent with the field's increasing emphasis on dysfunctional brain circuits, many theorists now suspect that antisocial personality disorder is ultimately related to poor functioning by a brain circuit consisting of the structures mentioned above. Poor communication (that is, poor *interconnectivity*) between those structures in the circuit may produce chronic low reactions to stress by the two brain–body stress pathways—the *sympathetic nervous system pathway* and the *hypothalamic-pituitary-adrenal pathway*—leading, in turn, to a state of low arousal, weak stress reactions, poor empathy for the pain of others, and other features of antisocial personality disorder (Aghajani et al., 2017; Glenn et al., 2017, 2015). Although enthusiasm for this circuit-centered explanation is growing, research regarding its specifics and merits has been limited to date.

Treatments for Antisocial Personality Disorder Treatments for people with antisocial personality disorder are typically ineffective (Skodol & Bender, 2018, 2016). Major obstacles to treatment include the individual's lacking a conscience, a desire to

borderline personality disorder A personality disorder characterized by repeated instability in interpersonal relationships, self-image, and mood and by impulsive behavior.

change, or respect for therapy (Sperry, 2016). Most of those in therapy have been forced to participate by an employer, their school, or the law, or they come to the attention of therapists when they also develop another psychological disorder (Bressert, 2016).

Cognitive-behavioral therapists may try to guide clients with antisocial personality disorder to think about moral issues and about the needs of other people. However, research has not found this approach to be particularly helpful (Black, 2017). In a similar vein, a number of hospitals and prisons have tried to create a therapeutic community for people with this disorder, a structured environment that teaches responsibility toward others (Bressert, 2016). Some such individuals seem to profit from approaches of this kind, but it appears that most do not. In recent years, clinicians have also used psychotropic medications, particularly antipsychotic drugs, to treat people with antisocial personality disorder. However, research has not found medication to be consistently useful in addressing the overall antisocial pattern (Black, 2017).

Borderline Personality Disorder

People with **borderline personality disorder** display great instability, including major shifts in mood, an unstable self-image, and impulsivity (APA, 2013). These characteristics combine to make their relationships very unstable as well (Paris, 2018). In her first treatment session, Dal displays or reveals all of these difficulties, as described by her therapist:

Dal . . . seems to be unable to maintain a stable sense of self-worth and self-esteem. Her confidence in her ability to "hold on to men" is at a low ebb, having just parted ways with "the love of her life." In the last year alone she confesses to having had six "serious relationships."

. . . The commencement of each affair was "a dream come true" and the men were all and one "Prince Charming." But then she invariably found herself in the stormy throes of violent fights over seeming trifles. She tried to "hang in there," but the more she invested in the relationships, the more distant and "vicious" her partners became. Finally, they abandoned her. . . .

*She shrugs and . . . her posture [becomes] almost violent: "No one f***s with me. I stand my ground, you get my meaning?" She admits that she physically assaulted three of her last six paramours, hurled things at them, and, amidst uncontrollable rage attacks and temper tantrums, even threatened to kill them. What made her so angry? She can't remember now . . .*

As she recounts these sad exploits, she alternates between boastful swagger and self-chastising, biting criticism of her own traits and conduct. Her affect swings wildly, in the confines of a single therapy session, between exuberant and fantastic optimism and unbridled gloom.

One minute she can conquer the world, careless and "free at last" ("It's their loss. . . .")— the next instant, she hyperventilates with unsuppressed anxiety, bordering on a panic attack . . .

Dal likes to "live dangerously, on the edge." She does drugs occasionally—"not a habit, just for recreation," she assures me. She is a shopaholic and often finds herself mired in debts. She went through three personal bankruptcies . . . She also binges on food, especially when she is stressed or depressed which seems to occur quite often.

She sought therapy because she is having intrusive thoughts about killing herself. [She often performs] self-injury and self-mutilation (she shows me a pair of pale, patched wrists, more scratched than slashed).

(Vaknin, 2016, 2015)

Like Dal, people with borderline personality disorder swing in and out of very depressive, anxious, and irritable states that last anywhere from a few hours to a few days or more (see **Table 13-3**). Their emotions seem to be always in conflict with the world around them. They are prone to bouts of anger, which sometimes result in physical aggression and violence (Zanarini et al., 2017). Just as often, however, they direct their impulsive anger inward and inflict bodily harm on themselves. Many seem troubled by deep feelings of emptiness (Zandersen & Parnas, 2018).

#

#TheirWords

"Anger is a brief lunacy."

Horace, Roman poet

Borderline personality disorder is a complex disorder, and it is fast becoming one of the more common conditions seen in clinical practice. As many as 85 percent of individuals with this syndrome also experience another psychological disorder, such as major depressive disorder or an eating disorder, at some point in their lives (Silverman & Krueger, 2018). Their impulsive, self-destructive activities may range from substance abuse to delinquency, unsafe sex, and reckless driving (Friedel, 2018; Kienast et al., 2014). Many engage in behaviors that involve self-injury or self-mutilation, such as cutting or burning themselves or banging their heads. As you saw in Chapter 7, such behaviors typically cause immense physical suffering, but those with borderline personality disorder often feel as if the physical discomfort offers relief from an "emotional overload" (Skodol, 2018, 2017; Sadeh et al., 2014). Many try to hurt themselves as a way of dealing with their chronic feelings of emptiness, boredom, and identity confusion.

Suicidal threats and actions are also common (Soloff & Chiappetta, 2018; Amore et al., 2014). Studies suggest that around 75 percent of people with borderline personality disorder attempt suicide at least once in their lives; as many as 10 percent actually die of suicide. It is common for people with this disorder to enter clinical treatment by way of the emergency room after a suicide attempt (Hong, 2016).

TABLE: 13-3

Comparison of Personality Disorders

	Cluster	Similar Disorders	Responsiveness to Treatment
Paranoid	Odd	Schizophrenia; delusional disorder	Modest
Schizoid	Odd	Schizophrenia; delusional disorder	Modest
Schizotypal	Odd	Schizophrenia; delusional disorder	Modest
Antisocial	Dramatic	Conduct disorder	Poor
Borderline	Dramatic	Depressive disorder; bipolar disorder	Moderate
Histrionic	Dramatic	Somatic symptom disorder; depressive disorder	Modest
Narcissistic	Dramatic	Cyclothymic disorder (mild bipolar disorder)	Poor
Avoidant	Anxious	Social anxiety disorder	Moderate
Dependent	Anxious	Separation anxiety disorder; depressive disorder	Moderate
Obsessive-Compulsive	Anxious	Obsessive-compulsive disorder	Moderate

People with borderline personality disorder frequently form intense, conflict-ridden relationships in which their feelings are not necessarily shared by the other person (Skodol, 2018, 2017). They may come to idealize another person's qualities and abilities after just a brief first encounter. They also may violate the boundaries of relationships. Thinking in dichotomous (black-and-white) terms, they quickly feel rejected and become furious when their expectations are not met; yet they remain very attached to the relationships (Miano et al., 2017). In fact, they have recurrent fears of impending abandonment and frequently engage in frantic efforts to avoid real or imagined separations from important people in their lives (Skodol, 2018, 2017). Sometimes they cut themselves or carry out other self-destructive acts to prevent partners from leaving.

People with borderline personality disorder typically have dramatic identity shifts. Because of this unstable sense of self, their goals, aspirations, friends, and even sexual orientation may shift rapidly. They may also occasionally have a sense of dissociation, or detachment, from their own thoughts or bodies (Krause-Utz et al., 2017). At times they may have no sense of themselves at all, leading to the feelings of emptiness described earlier.

According to surveys, 5.9 percent of the adult population display borderline personality disorder (Skodol, 2018, 2017; APA, 2013). Close to 75 percent of the patients who receive the diagnosis are women. The course of the disorder varies from person to person. In the most common pattern, the person's instability and risk of suicide peak during young adulthood and then gradually wane with advancing age.

How Do Theorists Explain Borderline Personality Disorder? Theorists have pointed to a range of possible psychological, biological, and sociocultural factors in their explanations of borderline personality disorder. In addition, over the past several years, there have been productive efforts to determine how such factors may interact to produce the disorder.

PSYCHOLOGICAL, BIOLOGICAL, AND SOCIOCULTUAL FACTORS Because a fear of abandonment tortures so many people with borderline personality disorder, *psychodynamic* theorists have looked once again to early parental relationships to explain the disorder.

#

#ExpressingAnger

23% Percentage of adults who report openly expressing their anger

39% Percentage who say they hide or contain their anger

(Information from: BAAM, 2017, 2016; Kanner, 2005, 1995)

Troubled princess Princess Diana, shown here embracing schoolchildren at a Hindu temple in northern London, was admired by millions during her short life, particularly for her numerous charitable efforts and humane acts. However, she also had a range of psychological problems that she herself disclosed in books and interviews. Diagnosing and explaining the princess's problems has become a common practice—both inside and outside the clinical field—since her death in 1997. Her self-cutting, possible borderline personality functioning, and disordered eating behaviors have received the most attention.

Object relations theorists, for example, propose that an early lack of acceptance by parents may lead to a loss of self-esteem, increased dependence, and an inability to cope with separation (Kernberg, 2018; Huprich et al., 2017). In support of this theory, research has found that the parents of many people with borderline personality disorder did indeed neglect or reject them during their childhood, verbally abuse them, or otherwise behave inappropriately (Parker, McCraw, & Bayes, 2018; Skodol, 2018, 2017). The childhoods were often marked by multiple parent substitutes, divorce, death, or traumas such as physical or sexual abuse.

Borderline personality disorder also has been linked to *biological* factors. There are indications that people may inherit a biological predisposition to this disorder. Research has revealed, for example, that close relatives of those with the disorder are five times more likely than the general population to have the same disorder (Bassir Nia et al., 2018; Amad et al., 2014). In a similar vein, research suggests that the disorder may be linked to particular genes (Agha et al., 2017).

Beyond genetic studies, researchers have found that people with borderline personality disorder, particularly those who are most impulsive—individuals who attempt suicide or are very aggressive toward others—have lower brain serotonin activity (Skodol, 2018, 2017; Soloff et al., 2014). Recall, once again, from Chapters 6 and 7, that low serotonin activity has been linked repeatedly to depression, suicide, aggression, and impulsivity (see pages 178–180 and 224).

Borderline personality disorder also has been tied to abnormal activity in certain brain structures, including the amygdala (hyperactive), hippocampus (underactive), prefrontal cortex (underactive), and other structures in the frontal lobes (Skodol, 2018, 2017; Soloff et al., 2017). A number of theorists further believe that these structures are members of a particular brain circuit and that the problems displayed by each structure actually reflect dysfunction (that is, poor interconnectivity) throughout that entire brain circuit, dysfunction that results in frequent emotional outbursts, impulsive acts, wrong judgments, and bad decisions (Agha et al., 2017; Krause-Utz et al., 2017).

Finally, some *sociocultural* theorists suggest that cases of borderline personality disorder are particularly likely to emerge in cultures that change rapidly. As a culture loses its stability, they argue, it inevitably leaves many of its members with problems of identity, a sense of emptiness, high anxiety, and fears of abandonment. Family units may come apart, leaving people with little sense of belonging. Changes of this kind in society today may explain growing reports of the disorder (Paris, 2018, 2010; Lazzari et al., 2017).

#

#VentingMyth

Contrary to the notion that "letting off steam" reduces anger, angry participants in one study acted much more aggressively after hitting a punching bag than did angry participants who sat quietly for a while (Bushman et al., 1999).

INTEGRATIVE EXPLANATIONS In recent years, two explanations—the *biosocial* and the *developmental psychopathology* explanations—have examined how these various factors might intersect to more fully account for borderline personality disorder.

According to the *biosocial* explanation, the disorder results from a combination of internal forces (for example, difficulty identifying and controlling one's emotions, social skill deficits, abnormal neurotransmitter activity) and external forces (for example, an environment in which a child's emotions are punished, ignored, trivialized, or disregarded) (Elzy & Karver, 2018; Neacsiu & Linehan, 2014). Most of the internal and external factors cited by biosocial theorists are the very factors focused upon in the preceding section. According to biosocial theorists, the more such factors people experience over the course of life, the more inclined they are to develop borderline personality disorder. This theory has received some, but not consistent, research support (Elzy & Karver, 2018; Gill & Warburton, 2014).

Proponents of the other integrative explanation of borderline personality disorder, the *developmental psychopathology* explanation, build on and add details to the biosocial view. Like the biosocial theorists, developmental psychopathologists believe that internal and external factors may intersect over the course of a person's life to help produce this disorder (Lenzenweger & Depue, 2016; Tackett et al., 2016). While these theorists are interested in all such factors—from genetic to environmental—they believe that early parent–child relationships are particularly influential in the development of borderline personality disorder. Consistent with the psychodynamic model's *object relations* theorists, developmental psychopathologists contend that children who experience early trauma and abuse and whose parents are markedly inattentive, uncaring, confusing, threatening, and dismissive are likely to enter adulthood with a *disorganized attachment style*—a severely flawed capacity for healthy relationships (Fonagy & Luyten, 2018, 2016). Unless such individuals are fortunate enough to further experience significant positive factors throughout their development (positive genetic predispositions, positive life events, sensitive role models, opportunities to build resilience, and the like), they will become, say developmental psychopathologists, high-risk candidates for borderline personality disorder (Fonagy et al., 2017). In support of this theory, studies have found clear ties between poor parent–child attachments and the development of disorganized attachment styles and between disorganized attachment styles and borderline personality disorders (Shiner & Allen, 2018; Beeney et al., 2017).

In recent years, developmental psychopathologists have also come to believe that a central psychological deficit in borderline personality disorder is the person's inability to *mentalize* (Bateman, Fonagy, & Campbell, 2018). **Mentalization** refers to people's capacity to understand their own mental states and those of other people—that is, to recognize needs, desires, feelings, beliefs, and goals. When people mentalize effectively, they can predict the behaviors of other people, and they can react to others in appropriate and trusting ways. These theorists suspect that persons who emerge from childhood with a disorganized attachment style have a weakened ability to mentalize and, correspondingly, a poor ability to control their own emotions, attention, thinking, and behavior, and their relationships (Fonagy & Luyten, 2018, 2016; Quek et al., 2017). Consistent with this notion, studies have consistently found poor mentalization skills in people with borderline personality disorder (Badoud et al., 2018; Fonagy et al., 2017).

The developmental psychopathology explanation of borderline personality disorder has excited many in the clinical field. However, it is important to recognize that the explanation's supportive research has not actually shown early parent–child attachments to be the *primary* factor in the development of this disorder. Nor is it clear that mentalization

mentalization The capacity to understand one's own mental states and those of other people.

"Zero Degrees of Empathy" Psychologist Simon Baron-Cohen has argued in his book *Zero Degrees of Empathy* that a common element in many personality disorders is a total lack of empathy. Of course, people without such disorders may also have empathy difficulties. Thus, in 2017, as part of a film project, 20 actors walked around New York City wearing mirrored cubes over their heads. Passersby saw only their own reflected faces while they were interacting with the actors—an exercise designed to increase the pedestrians' empathy for others by forcing them to "see themselves in others."

Damon Winter/The New York Times/Redux

#

#WhitherBorderline?

In 1938 the term "borderline" was introduced by psychoanalyst Adolph Stern. He used it to describe patients who were more disturbed than "neurotic" patients, yet not psychotic (Bateman, 2011; Stern, 1938). The term has since evolved to its present usage.

deficits are at the center of the disorder. Those important issues are currently being investigated in a range of studies.

Treatments for Borderline Personality Disorder It appears that psychotherapy can eventually lead to some degree of improvement for people with borderline personality disorder (Livesley, 2017). It is, however, extraordinarily difficult for a therapist to strike a balance between empathizing with the borderline client's dependency and anger and challenging his or her way of thinking (Skodol, 2018; Sperry, 2016). Moreover, clients with borderline personality disorder may violate the boundaries of the client–therapist relationship (for example, repeatedly calling the therapist's emergency contact number to discuss matters of a less urgent nature) (Skodol, 2018; Colli et al., 2014).

Traditional psychoanalytic therapy has not been effective for people with borderline personality disorder (Doering et al., 2010). However, contemporary psychodynamic approaches, particularly *relational psychoanalytic therapy* (see pages 47–48), in which therapists take a more supportive posture and focus primarily on the therapist–patient relationship, have had some success (Clarkin et al., 2018; Cristea et al., 2017). In approaches of this kind, therapists work to provide an empathic setting within which borderline clients can explore their unconscious conflicts and pay attention to their central relationship disturbance, poor sense of self, and pervasive loneliness and emptiness.

Over the past two decades, a new-wave cognitive-behavioral therapy for borderline personality disorder, called **dialectical behavior therapy (DBT),** has received considerable research support and is now considered the treatment of choice for people with borderline personality disorder (Robins et al., 2018; Linehan et al., 2015, 2002, 2001). DBT, developed by psychologist Marsha Linehan, consists of weekly individual therapy and group skill-building sessions that last for approximately one year. While targeting all of the features of borderline personality disorder, DBT places special emphasis on clients' efforts at self-harm and/or suicide.

The individual therapy sessions of DBT include many of the same behavioral and cognitive techniques that are applied to other disorders: homework assignments, psychoeducation, the teaching of coping and related skills, modeling by the therapist, clear goal setting, reinforcements for appropriate behaviors, mindfulness skill training, ongoing assessment of the client's behaviors and treatment progress, and collaborative examinations by the client and therapist of the client's ways of thinking.

Although primarily cognitive-behavioral, the individual DBT sessions also borrow heavily from the contemporary psychodynamic and humanistic approaches, placing the client–therapist relationship itself at the center of treatment interactions, making sure that appropriate treatment boundaries are adhered to, and providing an environment of acceptance and validation of the client. Indeed, DBT therapists regularly empathize with their borderline clients and with the emotional turmoil they are experiencing, locate kernels of truth in the clients' complaints or demands, and examine alternative ways for them to address valid needs (Skodol, 2018).

DBT clients also participate in social skill–building groups. In these groups, clients practice new ways of relating to other people in a safe environment and receive validation and support from other group members.

DBT has received more research support than any other treatment for borderline personality disorder (Robins et al., 2018; Rudge et al., 2018). Many clients who undergo DBT become more able to tolerate stress, develop more social skills, respond more effectively to life situations, and develop a more stable identity. They also display significantly fewer self-harm and suicidal behaviors and require fewer hospitalizations than those who receive other forms of treatment. In addition, they are more likely to remain in treatment and to report less anger, more

Bruce Eric Kaplan/The New Yorker Collection/The Cartoon Bank

"I wish my identity weren't so wrapped up with who I am."

social gratification, improved work performance, and reductions in substance abuse (Skodol, 2018; Linehan et al., 2015).

Antidepressant, antibipolar, antianxiety, and antipsychotic drugs have helped calm the emotional and aggressive storms of some people with borderline personality disorder (Markovitz, 2018; Bridler et al., 2015). Most professionals believe that psychotropic drug treatment for this disorder should be used largely as an adjunct to psychotherapy approaches, and indeed many clients seem to benefit from a combination of psychotherapy and drug therapy (Skodol, 2018).

Histrionic Personality Disorder

People with **histrionic personality disorder,** once called *hysterical personality disorder,* are extremely emotional—they are typically described as "emotionally charged"—and continually seek to be the center of attention (APA, 2013). Their exaggerated moods and neediness can complicate life considerably, as we see in the case of Lucinda:

Unhappy over her impending divorce, Lucinda decided to seek counseling. She arrived at her first session wearing a very provocative outfit, including a revealing blouse and extremely short skirt. Her hair had been labored over, and she had on an excessive amount of makeup—very carefully applied.

When asked to discuss her separation, Lucinda first insisted that the therapist call her Cindy, saying, "All my close friends call me that, and I like to think that you and I will become very good friends here." She said that her husband, Morgan, had suddenly abandoned her—"probably brainwashed by some young trollop." She proceeded to describe their break-up in a theatrical manner. Over a span of five minutes, her voice ranged from whispers to cries of agony and back again to whispers; she waved her arms dramatically while making some points and sat totally still while making others.

Lucinda said that when Morgan first told her that he wanted a divorce, she did not know whether she could go on. The pain was palpable. After all, they had been so "incredibly and irrevocably" close, and he had been so very devoted to her. She said that initially she even had thoughts of doing away with herself. But, of course, she knew that she had to pull herself together. So many people needed her to be strong. So many people relied on her, particularly her "dear friends" and her sister. She had deep and special relationships with them all.

She told the therapist that without Morgan she would now need a man to take care of her—emotionally and every other way. She asked the therapist if she looked like a 30-year-old woman. When he declined to answer, she said, "I know you're not supposed to say."

When the therapist attempted to steer the conversation back to Morgan, Lucinda became petulant and asked, "Do we really need to talk about that abusive lout?" Pressed on the word "abusive," Lucinda replied that she was referring to "mental cruelty." Morgan had, after all, called her inadequate and worthless throughout their marriage and told her that everything good in her life had been due to him. When her therapist pointed out that this seemed to contradict the rosy picture she had just painted of Morgan and their married life, she quickly changed the subject.

As the session came to a close, Lucinda's therapist suggested that it might be useful for him to meet with Morgan. She loved the idea, saying, "Then he'll know the competition he has!"

When he met with Morgan a few days later, the therapist heard a very different story than the one presented by Lucinda. Morgan said, "I really loved Cindy—still do—but she was always flying off the handle, telling me I'm no good or that I didn't care about her. She would often complain that I spent too much time at work—keep in mind that I never work more than 30 hours a week—and too little time attending to her and her needs. I just can't take life with her anymore. It's too draining."

Morgan also indicated that Lucinda had virtually no close friends. She and her sister might talk on the phone once a month and get together in person twice a year. He acknowledged that she drew a lot of attention from people. But, he noted. "Look at the way she dresses and her constant flirting. That'll certainly get people's attention, keep them around for a while."

#TheirWords

"I honestly didn't realize at the time that I was dealing with myself. . . . But I suppose it's true that I developed a therapy [DBT] that provides the things I needed for so many years and never got."

Marsha Linehan, psychologist, 2011

dialectical behavior therapy (DBT) A comprehensive treatment approach, applied particularly in cases of borderline personality disorder and/or suicidal intent; includes both individual therapy sessions and group sessions.

histrionic personality disorder A personality disorder characterized by a pattern of excessive emotionality and attention seeking. Once called *hysterical personality disorder.*

Jim Sugar/Getty Images

Transient hysterical symptoms These avid Harry Potter fans expressed themselves with exaggerated emotionality and lack of restraint at the midnight launch of one of the books in the series. Similar reactions, along with fainting, tremors, and even convulsions, have been common at concerts by musical idols dating back to the 1940s. Small wonder that expressive fans of this kind are regularly described as "hysterical" or "histrionic" by the press—the same labels applied to the personality disorder that is marked by such behaviors and symptoms.

People with histrionic personality disorder are always "on stage," using theatrical gestures and mannerisms and grandiose language to describe ordinary everyday events. Like chameleons, they keep changing themselves to attract and impress an audience, and in their pursuit they change not only their surface characteristics—according to the latest fads—but also their opinions and beliefs. In fact, their speech is actually scanty in detail and substance, and they seem to lack a sense of who they really are.

Approval and praise are their lifeblood; they must have others present to witness their exaggerated emotional states. Vain, self-centered, demanding, and unable to delay gratification for long, they overreact to minor events that get in the way of their quest for attention. Some make suicide attempts, often to manipulate others (Bressert, 2016; APA, 2013).

People with histrionic personality disorder may draw attention to themselves by exaggerating their physical illnesses or fatigue (Kayhan et al., 2016). They may also behave very provocatively and try to achieve their goals through sexual seduction. Most obsess over how they look and how others will perceive them, often wearing bright, eye-catching clothes. They exaggerate the depth of their relationships, considering themselves to be the intimate friends of people who see them as no more than casual acquaintances.

This disorder was once believed to be more common in women than in men, and clinicians long described the "hysterical wife" (Novais et al., 2015). Research, however, has revealed gender bias in past diagnoses (APA, 2013). When evaluating case studies of people with a mixture of histrionic and antisocial traits, clinicians in several studies gave a diagnosis of histrionic personality disorder to women more than men. Surveys suggest that 1.8 percent of adults have this personality disorder, with males and females equally affected (Morgan & Zimmerman, 2018; APA, 2013).

How Do Theorists Explain Histrionic Personality Disorder? The psychodynamic perspective was originally developed to help explain cases of hysteria (see Chapter 8), so it is no surprise that psychodynamic theorists continue to have a strong interest in histrionic personality disorder. Most psychodynamic theorists believe that as children, people with this disorder had cold and controlling parents who left them feeling unloved and afraid of abandonment (Paris, 2018; Horowitz & Lerner, 2010). To defend against deep-seated fears of loss, the children learned to behave dramatically, inventing crises that would require other people to act protectively.

#

#TheirWords

"The hysterical find too much significance in things. The depressed find too little."

Mason Cooley, American aphorist

Cognitive-behavioral explanations look instead at the lack of substance and extreme suggestibility that people with histrionic personality disorder have (Novais et al., 2015; Blagov et al., 2007). Cognitive-behavioral theorists see these individuals as becoming less and less interested in knowing about the world at large because they are so self-focused and emotional. With no detailed memories of what they never learned, they must rely on hunches or on other people to provide them with direction in life. Some such theorists also believe that people with this disorder hold a general assumption that they are helpless to care for themselves, and so they constantly seek out others who will meet their needs (Beck et al., 2015; Weishaar & Beck, 2006).

Sociocultural, particularly multicultural, theorists believe that histrionic personality disorder is produced in part by cultural norms and expectations (Mulder, 2018; Novais et al., 2015). Until recent decades, our society encouraged women to hold on to childlike dependency throughout their development. The vain, dramatic, and selfish behavior of the histrionic personality may actually be an exaggeration of femininity as our culture once defined it. Similarly, some clinical observers claim that histrionic personality disorder is diagnosed less often in Asian and other cultures that discourage overt sexualization and more often in Hispanic American and Latin American cultures that are more tolerant of overt sexualization (Patrick, 2007; Trull & Widiger, 2003). Researchers have not, however, investigated this claim systematically.

#VainPortrait

King Frederick V, ruler of Denmark from 1746 to 1766, had his portrait painted at least 70 times by the same artist, Carl Pilo (Shaw, 2004).

Treatments for Histrionic Personality Disorder Working with clients with histrionic personality disorder can be very difficult because of the demands, tantrums, and seductiveness they may deploy. Another problem is that these individuals may pretend to have important insights or to change during treatment merely to please the therapist. To head off such problems, therapists must remain objective and maintain strict professional boundaries (Sperry, 2016).

Cognitive-behavioral therapists have tried to help people with this disorder change their belief that they are helpless and also to develop better, more deliberate ways of thinking and solving problems (Davidson, 2018; Beck et al., 2015). Psychodynamic therapy and various group therapy formats have also been used (Caligor et al., 2018; Novais et al., 2015). In all of these approaches, therapists ultimately aim to help the clients recognize their excessive dependency, find inner satisfaction, and become more self-reliant. Clinical case reports suggest that each of the approaches can be useful. Drug therapy tends to be of limited help except as a means of relieving the depressive symptoms some patients have (Markovitz, 2018; Bock et al., 2010).

Narcissistic Personality Disorder

People with **narcissistic personality disorder** are generally grandiose, need much admiration, and feel no empathy with others (APA, 2013). Convinced of their own great success, power, or beauty, they expect constant attention and admiration from those around them. Frederick, the man we met at the beginning of this chapter, was one such person. So is Steven, a 30-year-old artist, married, with one child:

Steven came to the attention of a therapist when his wife insisted that they seek marital counseling. According to her, Steven was "selfish, ungiving and preoccupied with his work." Everything at home had to "revolve about him, his comfort, moods and desires, no one else's." She claimed that he contributed nothing to the marriage, except a rather meager income. He shirked all "normal" responsibilities and kept "throwing chores in her lap," and she was "getting fed up with being the chief cook and bottlewasher, tired of being his mother and sleep-in maid."

On the positive side, Steven's wife felt that he was basically a "gentle and good-natured guy with talent and intelligence." But this wasn't enough. She wanted a husband, someone with whom she could share things. In contrast, he wanted, according to her, "a mother, not a

(continued on the next page)

narcissistic personality disorder A personality disorder marked by a broad pattern of grandiosity, need for admiration, and lack of empathy.

wife"; he didn't want "to grow up, he didn't know how to give affection, only to take it when he felt like it, nothing more, nothing less."

Steven presented a picture of an affable, self-satisfied and somewhat disdainful young man. He was employed as a commercial artist, but looked forward to his evenings and weekends when he could turn his attention to serious painting. He claimed that he had to devote all of his spare time and energies to "fulfill himself," to achieve expression in his creative work. . . .

His relationships with his present co-workers and social acquaintances were pleasant and satisfying, but he did admit that most people viewed him as a "bit self-centered, cold and snobbish." He recognized that he did not know how to share his thoughts and feelings with others, that he was much more interested in himself than in them and that perhaps he always had "preferred the pleasure" of his own company to that of others.

(Millon, 1969, pp. 261–262)

People with narcissistic personality disorder have a grandiose sense of self-importance. They exaggerate their achievements and talents, expecting others to recognize them as superior, and often appear arrogant. They are very choosy about their friends and associates, believing that their problems are unique and can be appreciated only by other "special," high-status people. Because of their charm, they often make favorable first impressions, yet they can rarely maintain long-term relationships (Caligor & Petrini, 2018).

Why do people often admire arrogant deceivers—art forgers, jewel thieves, or certain kinds of "con" artists, for example?

Like Steven, people with narcissistic personality disorder are seldom interested in the feelings of others. They may not even be able to empathize with such feelings (Marcoux et al., 2014). Many take advantage of other people to achieve their own ends, perhaps partly out of envy; at the same time they believe others envy them. Though grandiose, some react to criticism or frustration with rage, a sense of inadequacy, humiliation, or embitterment (Caligor & Petrini, 2018; Miller et al., 2017). Others may react with cold indifference. And still others experience a sense of inadequacy, pessimism, or depression (Stanton & Zimmerman, 2018; Gore & Widiger, 2016). They may have periods of zest that alternate with periods of disappointment (Ronningstam, 2017, 2011).

As many as 6.2 percent of adults display narcissistic personality disorder, up to 75 percent of them men (Caligor & Petrini, 2018; APA, 2013). Narcissistic-type behaviors and thoughts are common and normal among teenagers and do not usually lead to adult narcissism (see ***MindTech***).

Richard Cline/The New Yorker Collection/The Cartoon Bank

"I'm attracted to you, but then I'm attracted to me, too."

How Do Theorists Explain Narcissistic Personality Disorder? Psychodynamic theorists more than others have theorized about narcissistic personality disorder, and they again propose that the problem begins with cold, rejecting parents (Miller et al., 2017; Roepke & Vater, 2014). They argue that some people with this background spend their lives defending against feeling unsatisfied, rejected, unworthy, ashamed, and wary of the world. They do so by repeatedly telling themselves that they are actually perfect and desirable, and also by seeking admiration from others. Object relations theorists—the psychodynamic theorists who emphasize relationships—interpret the grandiose self-image as a way for these people to convince themselves that they are totally self-sufficient and without need of warm relationships with their parents or anyone else (Kernberg, 2018). In support of the psychodynamic theories, research has found that children who are neglected and/or abused or who lose parents through adoption, divorce, or death are at particular risk for the later development of narcissistic personality disorder (Caligor & Petrini, 2018). Studies also show that people with this disorder do indeed earn relatively high shame and rejection scores on various scales and believe that other people are basically unavailable to them (Stanton & Zimmerman, 2018; Miller et al., 2017).

A number of cognitive-behavioral theorists propose that narcissistic personality disorder may develop when people are treated *too positively* rather

MINDTECH

Selfies: Narcissistic or Not?

Peter Bernik/Shutterstock

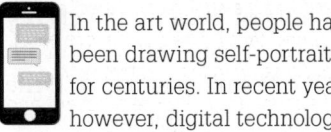

In the art world, people have been drawing self-portraits for centuries. In recent years, however, digital technology has ushered in the era of the *selfie*, a cousin to the self-portrait. Safe to say, just about every cell phone user has taken a selfie. In fact, more than 90 percent of all teens have now posted a photo of themselves online (SMA, 2017; Pew Research Center, 2014), and, according to some estimates, 93 million selfies are posted online every day (Weigold, 2018; Whitbourne, 2016). These self-photos have created such a stir that the word "selfie" was elected "Word of the Year" by the Oxford English Dictionary a few years back.

As the selfie phenomenon has grown, opinions about selfies have intensified (Diefenbach & Christoforakos, 2017). It seems like people either love them or hate them. This is true in the field of psychology as well. Some psychologists view taking selfies as a form of narcissistic behavior, while others view them more positively.

First, the negative perspective. Many sociocultural theorists see a link between narcissistic personality disorder and "eras of narcissism" in society (Paris, 2014). They suggest that social values in society break down periodically, producing generations of self-centered, materialistic youth. Some of these theorists consider today's selfie generation a perfect example of a current era of narcissism. This theory has gained a large following, but it is not supported by research. Several teams of investigators have found no relationship at all between how many selfies people post and how high they score on narcissism personality scales (Etgar & Amichai-Hamburger, 2017; Alloway, 2014). Other researchers have found that people who score high on narcissism scales do, on average, like to take selfies, but many such individuals do not (Kim et al., 2016; Whitbourne, 2016). Moreover, the vast majority of people who post selfies do not score especially high on narcissism scales.

This lack of support for the narcissism viewpoint does not mean that selfies, especially repeated selfie behaviors, are completely harmless. Sherry Turkle, an influential technology psychologist, believes that the near-reflexive instinct to photograph oneself may limit deeper engagements with the environment or prevent a full experience of events (Turkle, 2017, 2015, 2013; Eisold, 2013). Turkle also suggests that people who post an endless stream of selfies are often seeking external validation of their self-worth, even if that pursuit may not rise to a level of clinical narcissism.

Psychologists also observe that posting too many "selfies" may alienate those who view the poster's social media profile (Miller, 2013). Studies have found, for example, that people often take a negative view of friends and family members who excessively post photos to their Facebook sites (Houghton, 2013).

On the positive side, a number of psychologists believe that the criticisms and concerns about the selfie movement have been overstated. They agree with media psychologist Pamela Rutledge (2013) that, for the most part, selfies are an inevitable by-product of "technology-enabled self-expression." Rutledge contends that selfie behaviors are simply confusing to individuals of a predigital generation. Moreover, she concludes that the selfie trend can enhance explorations of identity, help identify one's interests, develop artistic expression, help people craft a meaningful narrative of their life experiences, and even reflect more realistic body images (for example, posting "selfies" without makeup). Indeed, several studies have supported these points and have also uncovered additional positive motives and effects of selfie taking (Christensen, 2017).

In short, like other technological trends you've read about, the selfie phenomenon has received mixed grades from psychology researchers and practitioners so far.

than too negatively in early life. They hold that certain children acquire a superior and grandiose attitude when their "admiring or doting parents" teach them to "overvalue their self-worth," repeatedly rewarding them for minor accomplishments or for no accomplishment at all (Caligor & Petrini, 2018; Miller et al., 2017).

Many sociocultural theorists see a link between narcissistic personality disorder and "eras of narcissism" in society (Paris, 2014). They suggest that family values and social ideals in certain societies periodically break down, producing generations of young people who are self-centered and materialistic and have short attention spans. Western cultures in particular, which encourage self-expression, individualism, and competitiveness, are considered likely to produce such generations of narcissism. In fact, one worldwide study found that respondents from the United States had the highest

#

#StolenGlances

22%	Percentage of people who regularly check their reflections in store windows and the like
69%	Those who steal glances at least occasionally
9%	Those who never look at themselves in public mirrors or windows

(Information from: Kanner, 2005, 1995)

narcissism scores, followed, in descending order, by those from Europe, Canada, Asia, and the Middle East (Foster, Campbell, & Twenge, 2003).

Treatments for Narcissistic Personality Disorder Narcissistic personality disorder is one of the most difficult personality patterns to treat because the clients are unable to acknowledge weaknesses, to appreciate the effect of their behavior on others, or to incorporate feedback from others (Tanzilli et al., 2017; Ronningstam, 2017). The clients who consult therapists usually do so because of a related disorder such as depression (Caligor & Petrini, 2018). Once in treatment, the clients may try to manipulate the therapist into supporting their sense of superiority (Skodol & Bender, 2018, 2016). Some also seem to project their grandiose attitudes onto their therapists and develop a love-hate stance toward them (Sperry, 2016; Colli et al., 2014).

Psychodynamic therapists seek to help people with this disorder recognize and work through their underlying insecurities and defenses (Caligor et al., 2018; Diamond & Meehan, 2013). Cognitive-behavioral therapists, focusing on the self-centered thinking of such individuals, try to redirect the clients' focus onto the opinions of others, teach them to interpret criticism more rationally, increase their ability to empathize, and change their all-or-nothing notions (Caligor & Petrini, 2018; Beck et al., 2015). None of the approaches have had clear success, however (Paris, 2018, 2014).

...SUMMING UP

"DRAMATIC" PERSONALITY DISORDERS Four of the personality disorders in DSM-5 are marked by highly dramatic, emotional, or erratic symptoms. People with antisocial personality disorder display a pattern of disregard for and violation of the rights of others. Explanations for this disorder point to psychodynamic, cognitive-behavioral, and biological factors, including a growing emphasis on a dysfunctional brain circuit. No known treatment is notably effective. People with borderline personality disorder display a pattern of instability in interpersonal relationships, self-image, and mood, along with extreme impulsivity. Explanations for this disorder have focused on psychological, biological, and sociocultural factors, and, prominently, on integrative perspectives such as a biosocial explanation and a developmental psychopathology perspective. Treatment, particularly dialectical behavior therapy, apparently can be helpful and lead to some improvement. People with histrionic personality disorder display a pattern of extreme emotionality and attention seeking. Clinical case reports suggest that treatment is helpful on occasion. Finally, people with narcissistic personality disorder display a pattern of grandiosity, need for admiration, and lack of empathy. It is one of the most difficult disorders to treat.

"Anxious" Personality Disorders

The cluster of "anxious" personality disorders includes the *avoidant, dependent,* and *obsessive-compulsive personality disorders*. People with these patterns typically display anxious and fearful behavior. As with most of the other personality disorders, research support for the various explanations is very limited. At the same time, treatments for these disorders appear to be modestly to moderately helpful—considerably better than for other personality disorders.

Avoidant Personality Disorder

avoidant personality disorder A personality disorder characterized by consistent discomfort and restraint in social situations, overwhelming feelings of inadequacy, and extreme sensitivity to negative evaluation.

People with **avoidant personality disorder** are very uncomfortable and inhibited in social situations, overwhelmed by feelings of inadequacy, and extremely sensitive to negative evaluation (APA, 2013). They are so fearful of being rejected that they give no one an opportunity to reject them—or to accept them either:

Perhaps what made Malcolm pursue counseling was the painful awareness of his inability to socialize at a party hosted by a professor. A first-semester computer science graduate student, Malcolm watched other new students in his program fraternize at this gathering while he suffered in silence. He wanted desperately to join [in], but, as he described it, "I was totally at a loss as to how to go about talking to anyone." The best feeling in the world, he stated, was getting out of there. The following Monday, he came to the university counseling center, realizing he would have to be able to function in this group, but not before his first teaching experience that morning, which he described as "the most terrifying feeling I have ever encountered." As an undergrad, he spent most of his time alone in the computer lab working on new programs, which was what he most enjoyed as "no one was looking over my shoulder or judging me." In contrast to this, with his teaching assistantship duties . . . he felt he constantly ran the risk of being made to look like a fool in front of a large audience.

When asked about personal relationships he had previously enjoyed, Malcolm admitted that any interaction was a source of frustration and worry. From the moment he left home for undergraduate school, he lived alone, attended functions alone, and found it nearly impossible to make conversation with anyone. . . . The expectancy that people would be rejecting . . . precipitated profound gloom. . . . Despite a longing to relate and be accepted, Malcolm . . . maintained a safe distance from all emotional involvement. [He] became remote from others and from needed sources of support. He . . . had learned to be watchful, on guard against ridicule, and ever alert . . . to the most minute traces of annoyance expressed by others.

(Millon, 2011)

#ShynessAlert

Between 40 and 60 percent of people in the United States consider themselves to be shy (Bressert, 2016).

People like Malcolm actively avoid occasions for social contact. At the center of this withdrawal lies not so much poor social skills as a dread of criticism, disapproval, or rejection. They are timid and hesitant in social situations, afraid to say something foolish or to embarrass themselves by blushing or acting nervous. Even in intimate relationships they express themselves very carefully, afraid of being shamed or ridiculed.

People with this disorder believe themselves to be unappealing or inferior to others. They exaggerate the potential difficulties of new situations, so they seldom take risks or try out new activities. They usually have few or no close friends, though they actually yearn for intimate relationships, and frequently feel depressed and lonely. As

Michael Prince

Just a stage This child sits alone on the steps of his school as other children pass by. That behavior could be a sign of being painfully shy, withdrawn, easily embarrassed, and uncomfortable with people. Early temperament is often linked to adult personality traits, but research has not shown that extreme shyness, a common and normal part of childhood, necessarily predicts the development of avoidant or dependent personality disorder in adulthood.

a substitute, some develop an inner world of fantasy and imagination (Bressert, 2017; Millon, 2011).

Avoidant personality disorder is similar to *social anxiety disorder* (see Chapter 4), and many people with one of these disorders also experience the other (Pellecchia et al., 2018). The similarities include a fear of humiliation and low confidence. Some theorists believe that there is a key difference between the two disorders—namely, that people with social anxiety disorder primarily fear social *circumstances,* while people with the personality disorder tend to fear close social *relationships.* Other theorists, however, believe that the two disorders reflect the same core psychopathology and should be combined.

At least 2.4 percent of adults have avoidant personality disorder, men as frequently as women (Lampe & Malhi, 2018; APA, 2013). Many children and teenagers are also painfully shy and avoid other people, but this is usually just a normal part of their development.

How Do Theorists Explain Avoidant Personality Disorder? Theorists often assume that avoidant personality disorder has the same causes as anxiety disorders—such as early traumas, conditioned fears, upsetting beliefs, or biochemical abnormalities. However, with the exception of social anxiety disorder, research has not clearly tied the personality disorder directly to the anxiety disorders (Herbert, 2007). Psychodynamic and cognitive-behavioral explanations of avoidant personality disorder are the most popular among clinicians.

Psychodynamic theorists focus mainly on the general feelings of shame and insecurity that people with avoidant personality disorder have (Lampe & Malhi, 2018; Svartberg & McCullough, 2010). Some trace the shame to childhood experiences such as early bowel and bladder accidents. If parents repeatedly punish or ridicule a child for having such accidents, the child may develop a negative self-image. This may lead to the child's feeling unlovable throughout life and distrusting the love of others.

Similarly, cognitive-behavioral theorists believe that harsh criticism and rejection in early childhood may lead certain people to assume that others in their environment will always judge them negatively. These people come to expect rejection, misinterpret the reactions of others to fit that expectation, discount positive feedback, and generally fear social involvements—setting the stage for avoidant personality disorder (Lampe & Malhi, 2018; Weishaar & Beck, 2006). In several studies, when participants with this disorder were asked to recall their childhood, their descriptions supported both the psychodynamic and cognitive-behavioral predictions (Carr & Francis, 2010; Herbert, 2007). They remembered, for example, feeling criticized, rejected, and isolated; receiving little encouragement from their parents; and experiencing few displays of parental love or pride.

Cognitive-behavioral theorists also suggest that most people with avoidant personality disorder fail to develop effective social skills, a failure that helps maintain the disorder. In support of this position, several studies have found social skills deficits among people with avoidant personality disorder (Moroni et al., 2016; Kantor, 2010). Most of the theorists agree, however, that these deficits first develop as a result of the individuals avoiding so many social situations.

Treatments for Avoidant Personality Disorder People with avoidant personality disorder come to therapy in the hope of finding acceptance and affection. At the same time, they may distrust the therapist's sincerity and start to fear his or her rejection (Skodol & Bender, 2018, 2016). Thus, as with several of the other personality disorders, a key task of the therapist is to gain the person's trust (Skodol, 2017; Sperry, 2016).

Beyond building trust, therapists tend to treat people with avoidant personality disorder much as they treat people with social anxiety disorder and other anxiety disorders. Such approaches have had at least modest success (Bernecker et al., 2017; Lampe, 2016). Psychodynamic therapists try to help clients recognize and resolve the unconscious conflicts that may be operating (Caligor et al., 2018; Leichsenring & Salzer, 2014). Cognitive-behavioral therapists help the individuals change their distressing beliefs and thoughts,

#

#ShynessRocks

Rock music has been strongly influenced by stars with extremely shy, reticent demeanors.

Meg White, drummer for the popular rock band The White Stripes, described herself as "very shy" and frequently appeared uncomfortable both onstage and during her rare interviews. The group disbanded after "acute anxiety" caused her to cancel a 2007 tour.

The alternative rock band My Bloody Valentine often plays with their backs to the audience and spearheaded an influential pop movement called "shoegaze" based on their tendency to look away or at the floor during shows.

For many of her initial concerts, folk singer Cat Power (Chan Marshall) would not look at the audience and would weep or run offstage during shows.

carry on in the face of painful emotions, and improve their self-image (Davidson, 2018; Lampe, 2016). They also provide social skills training and exposure treatments that require people to gradually increase their social contacts (Kampmann et al., 2016). Group therapy formats, especially groups that follow cognitive and behavioral principles, have the added advantage of providing clients with practice in social interactions (Bressert, 2017). Antianxiety and antidepressant drugs are sometimes useful in reducing the social anxiety of people with the disorder (Markovitz, 2018; Skodol, 2017).

#TheirWords

"We continue to shape our personality all our life."

Albert Camus

Dependent Personality Disorder

People with **dependent personality disorder** have a pervasive, excessive need to be taken care of (APA, 2013). As a result, they are clinging and obedient, fearing separation from their parent, spouse, or other person with whom they are in a close relationship. They rely on others so much that they cannot make the smallest decision for themselves. Lucas is a case in point.

Lucas, an assistant graphics programmer, is a 42-year-old single man who lives with his father. He is currently grappling with significant feelings of depression and anxiety. These feelings began when he ended his relationship of two years with Orena, whom he had viewed as the woman of his dreams and his future wife. But Lucas's father just didn't like Orena, and he certainly didn't like the idea of Lucas marrying her. In fact, he forbid it—forbid his middle-aged son from marrying the woman of his dreams.

Inside, Lucas was furious at his father, although he knew he could never express his anger. Not that he was afraid of his father physically. His fear was in the psychological sphere. He simply could not—now or ever—risk his father getting angry at him, being disappointed in him, not talking to him, or being unsupportive. Then he might have to fend for himself, and that was unthinkable. At some level, he also thought that maybe his father was right, maybe he should not marry Orena. He always went along with his father's advice and decisions. He thought of himself as a person of poor judgment—too poor to make a decision, big or small, on his own.

So eventually Lucas did what he always knew he would have to do—he broke up with Orena. He was more than ashamed and critical of himself, for hurting Orena, for being such a weakling, for giving up his dream so readily. But what could he do? He felt helpless and incapable of taking any other course of action.

Lucas is not particularly accomplished in the various areas of his life. His job of 15 years is at least two levels below what he is capable of. Over the years, he has rejected promotion offers and has not responded to overtures from other graphic design companies. The reason was always the same: he didn't want—no, he was afraid to take on—additional responsibilities, especially responsibilities for making decisions and leading a team of workers. So he continues to work at the same job, for the same boss, in the same routine. He is considered dependable and hard-working—a never-changing fixture in the work setting.

His social life is similarly modest and uneventful. Outside of Orena, his social life is limited to a single lifelong friend. They get together for dinner and an activity three nights a week. If his friend ever cancels, Lucas feels lost.

Growing up, Lucas's older sisters, mother, and father always pampered and protected him, catering to his every need. Still he remembers being fearful and tentative throughout his childhood, always wanting to hold a family member's hand, afraid to do anything on his own. When his sisters grew older and moved away and after his mother died, it became just him and his father. Going away to college in another city was unthinkable. Without question, his father is now the most important person in his life. Although more than a little domineering, he loves Lucas and continues the family tradition of protecting and guiding him.

It is normal and healthy to depend on others, but those with dependent personality disorder constantly need assistance with even the simplest matters and have extreme feelings of inadequacy and helplessness. Afraid that they cannot care for themselves, they cling desperately to friends or relatives.

dependent personality disorder A personality disorder characterized by a pattern of clinging and obedience, fear of separation, and an ongoing need to be taken care of.

#TheirWords

"The deepest principle of human nature is the craving to be appreciated."

William James, psychologist, 1896

As you observed previously, people with avoidant personality disorder have difficulty *initiating* relationships. In contrast, people with dependent personality disorder have difficulty with *separation*. They feel completely helpless and devastated when a close relationship ends, and they quickly seek out another relationship to fill the void. Many cling persistently to relationships with partners who physically or psychologically abuse them (Leemans & Loas, 2016).

Lacking confidence in their own ability and judgment, people with this disorder seldom disagree with others and allow even important decisions to be made for them (Bressert, 2017; Gore & Widiger, 2015). They may depend on a parent or spouse to decide where to live, what job to have, and which neighbors to befriend. Because they so fear rejection, they are overly sensitive to disapproval and keep trying to meet other people's wishes and expectations, even if it means volunteering for unpleasant or demeaning tasks.

Many people with dependent personality disorder feel distressed, lonely, and sad; often they dislike themselves. Thus they are at risk for depressive, anxiety, and eating disorders (Bornstein, 2016, 2012, 2007). Their fear of separation and their feelings of helplessness may leave them particularly prone to suicidal thoughts, especially when they believe that a relationship is about to end.

Surveys suggest that fewer than 1 percent of the population experience dependent personality disorder (Morgan & Zimmerman, 2018; APA, 2013). For years, clinicians have believed that more women than men display this pattern, but some research suggests that the disorder is just as common in men (APA, 2013).

How Do Theorists Explain Dependent Personality Disorder? Psychodynamic explanations for dependent personality disorder are similar to those for depression (Sperry, 2016; Svartberg & McCullough, 2010). Freudian theorists argue, for example, that unresolved conflicts during the oral stage of development can give rise to a lifelong need for nurturance, thus heightening the likelihood of a dependent personality disorder (Bornstein, 2012, 2007, 2005). Similarly, object relations theorists say that early parental loss or rejection may prevent normal experiences of *attachment* and *separation*, leaving some children with fears of abandonment that persist throughout their lives (Kernberg, 2018; Caligor & Clarkin, 2010). Still other psychodynamic theorists suggest that, to the contrary, many parents of people with this disorder were overinvolved and overprotective, thus increasing their children's dependency, insecurity, and separation anxiety (Sperry, 2016).

Bruce Eric Kaplan/The New Yorker Collection/The Cartoon Bank

"My self-esteem was so low I just followed her around everywhere she would go."

Cognitive-behavioral theorists point to both behavioral and cognitive factors in their explanation of dependent personality disorder. In the behavioral realm, they propose that parents of people with dependent personality disorder unintentionally rewarded their children's clinging and "loyal" behavior, while at the same time punishing acts of independence, perhaps through the withdrawal of love. Alternatively, some parents' own dependent behaviors may have served as models for their children (Bornstein, 2012, 2007). In the cognitive realm, the theorists identify two maladaptive attitudes as further helping to produce and maintain this disorder: (1) "I am inadequate and helpless to deal with the world," and (2) "I must find a person to provide protection so I can cope." Dichotomous (black-and-white) thinking may also play a key role: "If I am to be dependent, I must be completely helpless," or "If I am to be independent, I must be alone." Such thinking prevents sufferers from making efforts to be autonomous (Beck et al., 2015; Borge et al., 2010).

Treatments for Dependent Personality Disorder In therapy, people with dependent personality disorder usually place all responsibility for their treatment and well-being on the clinician. Thus a key task of therapy is to help patients accept responsibility for themselves (Bressert, 2017; Sperry, 2016). Because the domineering behaviors of a spouse or parent may help foster a patient's symptoms, some clinicians suggest couple or family therapy as well, or even separate therapy for the partner or parent (Lebow & Uliaszek, 2010).

Treatment for dependent personality disorder can be at least modestly helpful. Psychodynamic therapy for this pattern focuses on many of the same issues as therapy for depressed people, including the *transference* of dependency needs onto the therapist (Caligor et al., 2018). Cognitive-behavioral therapists combine behavioral and cognitive interventions to help the clients take control of their lives. On the behavioral end, the therapists often provide assertiveness training to help the individuals better express their own wishes in relationships (Bressert, 2017; Farmer & Nelson-Gray, 2005). On the cognitive end, the therapists also try to help the clients challenge and change their assumptions of incompetence and helplessness (Beck et al., 2015). As with avoidant personality disorder, a group therapy format can be useful because it provides opportunities for clients to receive support from a number of peers rather than from a single dominant person (Bressert, 2017). Antidepressant drug therapy has been helpful for people whose personality disorder is accompanied by depression (Markovitz, 2018; Skodol, 2017).

#AnimalTraits

Researchers have found that animals of every kind—from spiders to lions—display distinct differences in their personalities, behaviors, and preferences. Among sheep, for example, some are leaders and others followers. Similarly, sheep differ in their individual levels of fearfulness, vocalization, friendliness, and distraction. These differences often hold steady throughout their lives (Cherry, 2017; Angier, 2010).

Obsessive-Compulsive Personality Disorder

People with **obsessive-compulsive personality disorder** are so preoccupied with order, perfection, and control that they lose all flexibility, openness, and efficiency (APA, 2013). Their concern for doing everything "right" impairs their productivity, as in the case of Joseph:

Joseph was advised to seek assistance from a therapist following several months of relatively sleepless nights and a growing immobility and indecisiveness at his job. When first seen, he reported feelings of extreme self-doubt and guilt and prolonged periods of tension and diffuse anxiety. It was established early in therapy that he always had experienced these symptoms; they were now merely more pronounced than before.

The precipitant for this sudden increase in discomfort was a forthcoming change in his academic post. New administrative officers had assumed authority at the college, and he was asked to resign his deanship to return to regular departmental instruction. In the early sessions, Joseph spoke largely of his fear of facing classroom students again, wondered if he could organize his material well, and doubted that he could keep classes disciplined and interested in his lectures. It was his preoccupation with these matters that he believed was preventing him from concentrating and completing his present responsibilities.

At no time did Joseph express anger toward the new college officials for the demotion he was asked to accept; he repeatedly voiced his "complete confidence" in the "rationality of their decision." Yet, when face-to-face with them, he observed that he stuttered and was extremely tremulous.

Joseph was the second of two sons, younger than his brother by three years. His father was a successful engineer, and his mother a high school teacher. Both were "efficient, orderly, and strict" parents. Life at home was "extremely well planned," with "daily and weekly schedules of responsibility posted" and "vacations arranged a year or two in advance." Nothing apparently was left to chance. . . . Joseph adopted the "good boy" image. Unable to challenge his brother either physically, intellectually, or socially, he became a "paragon of virtue." By being punctilious, scrupulous, methodical, and orderly, he could avoid antagonizing his perfectionistic parents, and would, at times, obtain preferred treatment from them. He obeyed their advice, took their guidance as gospel, and hesitated making any decision before gaining their approval. Although he recalled "fighting" with his brother before he was 6 or 7, he "restrained my anger from that time on and never upset my parents again."

(Millon, 2011, 1969, pp. 278–279)

obsessive-compulsive personality disorder A personality disorder marked by such an intense focus on orderliness, perfectionism, and control that the person loses flexibility, openness, and efficiency.

#CriticalDifference

People with obsessive-compulsive disorder typically do not want or like their symptoms; those with obsessive-compulsive personality disorder often embrace their symptoms and rarely wish to resist them.

In Joseph's concern with rules and order and doing things right, he has trouble seeing the larger picture. When faced with a task, he and others who have obsessive-compulsive personality disorder may become so focused on organization and details that they fail to grasp the point of the activity. As a result, their work is often behind schedule (some seem unable to finish any job), and they may neglect leisure activities and friendships (Mike et al., 2017).

People with this personality disorder set unreasonably high standards for themselves and others. Their behaviors extend well beyond the realm of conscientiousness. They can never be satisfied with their performance, but they typically refuse to seek help or to work with a team, convinced that others are too careless or incompetent to do the job right. Because they are so afraid of making mistakes, they may be reluctant to make decisions (Wheaton & Pinto, 2017).

They also tend to be rigid and stubborn, particularly in their morals, ethics, and values. They live by a strict personal code and use it as a yardstick for measuring others. They may have trouble expressing much affection, and their relationships are sometimes stiff and superficial. In addition, they are often stingy with their time or money. Some cannot even throw away objects that are worn out or useless (Pinto et al., 2018; Riddle et al., 2016).

According to surveys, as many as 7.9 percent of the adult population display obsessive-compulsive personality disorder, with white, educated, married, and employed people receiving the diagnosis most often (Skodol, 2017; APA, 2013). Men are twice as likely as women to display the disorder.

Many clinicians believe that obsessive-compulsive personality disorder and *obsessive-compulsive disorder* are closely related. Certainly, the two disorders share a number of features, and many people who suffer from one of the disorders meet the diagnostic criteria for the other disorder (Starcevic & Brakoulias, 2017). However, it is worth noting that people with the personality disorder are more likely to suffer from either major depressive disorder, an anxiety disorder, or a substance use disorder than from obsessive-compulsive disorder (Brakoulias et al., 2017). In fact, researchers have not consistently found a specific link between obsessive-compulsive personality disorder and obsessive-compulsive disorder (Starcevic & Brakoulias, 2017, 2014).

How Do Theorists Explain Obsessive-Compulsive Personality Disorder?

Most explanations of obsessive-compulsive personality disorder borrow heavily from those of obsessive-compulsive disorder, despite the doubts concerning a link between the two disorders. Research evidence for these explanations is limited.

Freudian theorists suggest that people with obsessive-compulsive personality disorder are *anal retentive*. That is, because of overly harsh toilet training during the anal stage, they become filled with anger, and they remain *fixated* at this stage. To keep their anger under control, they persistently resist both their anger and their instincts to have bowel movements. In turn, they become extremely orderly and restrained; many become passionate collectors. Other psychodynamic theorists suggest that any early struggles with parents over control and independence may ignite the aggressive impulses at the root of this personality disorder (Kanehisa et al., 2017; Bartz et al., 2007).

Toilet trouble According to Freud, toilet training often produces rage in a child. If parents are too harsh in their approach, the child may become fixated at the anal stage and prone to obsessive-compulsive functioning later in life.

Design Pics/Misty Bedwell/Getty Images

Cognitive-behavioral theorists have little to say about the origins of obsessive-compulsive personality disorder, but they do propose that illogical thinking processes help keep it going (Paast et al., 2016; Weishaar & Beck, 2006). They point, for example, to dichotomous thinking, which may produce rigidity and perfectionism. Similarly, they note that people with this disorder tend to misread or exaggerate the potential outcomes of mistakes or errors.

Treatments for Obsessive-Compulsive Personality Disorder

People with obsessive-compulsive personality disorder do not usually believe there is anything wrong with them. They therefore are not likely to seek treatment unless they are also suffering from another disorder, most frequently an anxiety disorder or depression, or unless someone close to them insists that they get treatment (Smith et al., 2017; Bartz et al., 2007).

People with obsessive-compulsive personality disorder sometimes respond well to psychodynamic or cognitive-behavioral therapy (Smith et al., 2017; Kikkert et al., 2016). Psychodynamic therapists typically try to help these clients recognize, experience, and accept their underlying feelings and insecurities, and perhaps take risks and accept their personal limitations (Caligor et al., 2018; Bressert, 2016). Cognitive-behavioral therapists focus on helping the clients to change their dichotomous—"all or nothing"—thinking, perfectionism, indecisiveness, procrastination, and chronic worrying (Davidson, 2018; Beck et al., 2015). A number of clinicians report that people with obsessive-compulsive personality disorder, like those with obsessive-compulsive disorder, respond well to SSRIs, the serotonin-enhancing antidepressant drugs; however, researchers have yet to study this issue fully (Markovitz, 2018; Pinto et al., 2018, 2008).

9... SUMMING UP

"ANXIOUS" PERSONALITY DISORDER Three of the personality disorders in DSM-5 are marked by anxious and fearful behavior. People with avoidant personality disorder are consistently uncomfortable and inhibited in social situations, overwhelmed by feelings of inadequacy, and extremely sensitive to negative evaluation. People with dependent personality disorder have a persistent need to be taken care of, are submissive and clinging, and fear separation. People with obsessive-compulsive personality disorder are so preoccupied with order, perfection, and control that they lose their flexibility, openness, and efficiency. A variety of treatment strategies have been used for people with these disorders and have been modestly to moderately helpful.

#TheirWords

"In most of us, by the age of thirty, the character has set like plaster and will never soften again."
William James, psychologist, 1887

Multicultural Factors: Research Neglect

According to the current criteria of DSM-5, a pattern diagnosed as a personality disorder must "deviate markedly from the expectations of the individual's culture" (APA, 2013). Given the importance of culture in this diagnosis, and given the enormous clinical interest in personality disorders, it is striking how little multicultural research has been conducted on these problems. Clinical theorists have suspicions but little compelling evidence that there are cultural differences in this realm (Mulder, 2018; Ascoli et al., 2017).

The lack of multicultural research is of special concern with regard to borderline personality disorder, the pattern characterized by extreme mood fluctuations, outbursts of intense anger, self-injurious behavior, fear of abandonment, feelings of emptiness, problematic relationships, and identity confusion, because many theorists are convinced that gender and other cultural differences may be particularly important in both the development and diagnosis of this disorder.

As you read earlier, around 75 percent of all people who receive a diagnosis of borderline personality disorder are female (Skodol, 2018, 2017). Although it may be that women are biologically more prone to the disorder or that diagnostic bias is at work, this gender difference may instead be a reflection of the extraordinary traumas to

Understudied As illustrated by this diverse group of people, we live in a multicultural nation and world. Nevertheless, psychologists have devoted relatively little study to cultural and racial differences in the development, features, and treatment of personality disorders.

digitalskillet/Shutterstock

which many women are subjected as children (Daigre et al., 2015). Recall, for example, that the childhoods of some people with borderline personality disorder are filled with emotional trauma, victimization, violence, and abuse, at times sexual abuse. It may be, a number of theorists argue, that experiences of this kind are *prerequisites* to the development of borderline personality disorder, that women in our society are particularly subjected to such experiences, and that, in fact, the disorder should more properly be viewed and treated as a special form of posttraumatic stress disorder (Kulkarni, 2017; Sherry & Whilde, 2008). In the absence of systematic research, however, alternative explanations like this remain untested and corresponding treatments undeveloped.

#TheirWords

"She is still a prisoner of her childhood; attempting to create a new life, she reencounters the trauma."

Judith L. Herman, psychiatrist and author, 2015, 1992

Why have researchers given relatively little attention to the study of cultural, racial, and gender differences in personality disorders?

In a related vein, given the childhood experiences that typically precede borderline personality disorder, some multicultural theorists believe that the disorder may actually be a reaction to persistent feelings of marginality, powerlessness, and social failure (Sherry & Whilde, 2008). That is, the disorder may be attributable more to social inequalities (including sexism, racism, or homophobia) than to psychological factors.

Given such possibilities, it is most welcome that a few multicultural studies of borderline personality disorder have been conducted over the past decade (Skodol, 2017; De Genna & Feske, 2013). In these undertakings, researchers assessed the prevalence of the personality disorder in diverse clinical populations (Meaney et al., 2016; Trull et al., 2010; Chavira et al., 2003). They found that Hispanic American individuals qualified for a diagnosis of borderline personality disorder more often than non-Hispanic white American or African American individuals did. Could it be that Hispanic Americans generally are more likely than other cultural groups to display this disorder, and—if so—why? Questions of this kind underline once again the need for more multicultural research into personality disorders.

Are There Better Ways to Classify Personality Disorders?

As you read earlier, DSM-5's personality disorders are often hard to diagnose and easy to misdiagnose, difficulties that indicate serious problems with the validity and reliability of these categories. In light of such problems, the leading criticism of DSM-5's approach to personality disorders is, as noted previously, that the classification system defines such disorders by using *categories*—rather than *dimensions*—of personality. Many of today's theorists believe that personality disorders differ more in *degree* than in type of dysfunction. Therefore, they propose that the disorders should be classified by the severity of key personality traits (or dimensions) rather than by the presence or absence of specific traits (Anderson et al., 2018, 2016; Skodol, 2018). In such an approach, each key trait (for example, disagreeableness, dishonesty, or self-absorption) would be seen as varying along a continuum in which there is no clear boundary between normal and abnormal. People with a personality disorder would be those who display extreme degrees of several of these key traits—degrees not commonly found in the general population (see ***InfoCentral***).

Bruce Eric Kaplan/The New Yorker Collection/The Cartoon Bank

"You'll have to excuse me—I'm myself today."

Which key personality dimensions should clinicians use to help identify people with personality problems? Some theorists believe that they should rely on the dimensions identified in the "Big Five" theory of personality, dimensions that have received enormous attention by personality psychologists over the years.

THE DARK TRIAD

Over the past 15 years, researchers have studied the **Dark Triad**, a trio of "malicious" traits that work together to produce socially offensive behaviors (Garcia et al., 2018; Muris et al., 2017). People with these traits—*narcissism*, *psychopathy*, and *Machiavellianism*—tend to undermine others, perhaps secretly, in order to achieve their own ends (Whitbourne, 2013).

Individuals with just one of these traits often offend, manipulate, or disregard the needs of others. But those with **all three** traits are particularly self-absorbed and create serious problems for others. People who score high on Dark Triad rating scales may display a personality disorder, but more often, they experience little distress or impairment and function adequately, sometimes quite effectively, in the personal, social, and occupational realms.

WHAT IS THE DARK TRIAD?

Narcissism
Self-admiring
Self-absorbed
Admiration-seeking
Special treatment–seeking
Overly entitled
Gratification-seeking

Psychopathy
Callous
Insensitive
Antisocial
Unempathetic
Remorseless
Disinhibited

Machiavellianism
Manipulative
Self-interested
Duplicitous
Cynical
Amoral
Focused on personal gain

(Jones & Paulhus, 2017; Muris et al., 2017; Whitbourne, 2013)

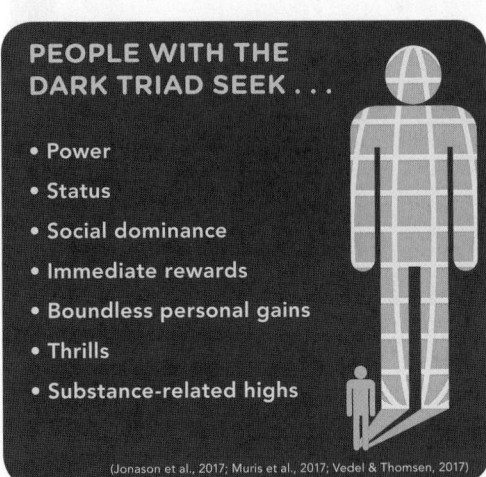

PEOPLE WITH THE DARK TRIAD SEEK . . .

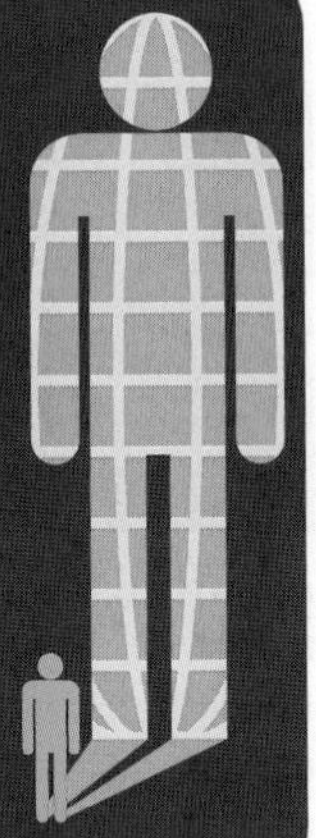

- Power
- Status
- Social dominance
- Immediate rewards
- Boundless personal gains
- Thrills
- Substance-related highs

(Jonason et al., 2017; Muris et al., 2017; Vedel & Thomsen, 2017)

THE DARK TRIAD AFFECTS ALL SPHERES OF LIFE

The PERSONAL realm

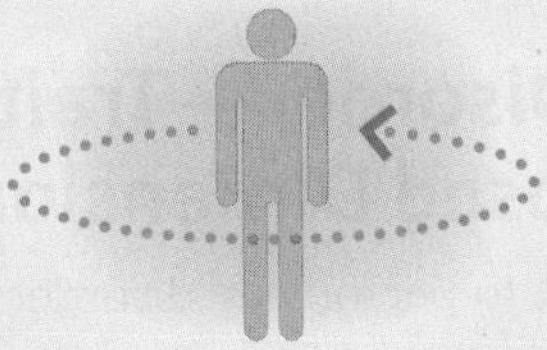

People are more likely to be...

Immodest
Disagreeable
Greedy
Suspicious
Dishonest
Substance abusers
Aggressive drivers

(Jones & Paulhus, 2017; Muris et al., 2017; Burtăverde et al., 2016; Sabouri et al., 2016; Furnham et al., 2013)

The SOCIAL sphere

People are more likely to be...

Dominant
Prejudiced
Unethical
Bullies
Extroverted
Aggressive
Insensitive

(Muris et al., 2017; Furnham et al., 2013)

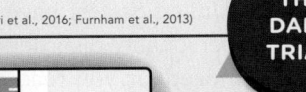

The SEXUAL realm

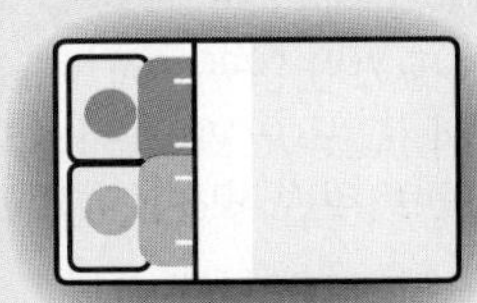

People are more likely to...

Pursue quick gratification
Seek casual sex
Display aggressive strategies
Exhibit sexual opportunism
Seek more sexual partners
Commit sexual infidelities
Poach mates from others

(Tsoukas & March, 2018; Jonason et al., 2017, 2011, 2010, 2009; Furnham et al., 2013; Whitbourne, 2013)

At WORK

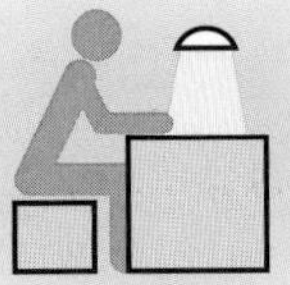

People are more likely to...

Have troubled work relationships
Exhibit toxic leadership
Ruthlessly seek self-advancement
Cheat
Commit sexual harassment
Hinder career success of subordinates
Adversely affect personal well-being of subordinates

(de Vries, 2018; Jones & Paulhus, 2017; Muris et al., 2017; Volmer et al., 2016; Zeigler-Hill et al., 2016)

WHO IS MORE LIKELY TO DISPLAY THE DARK TRIAD?

Men > Women
Non-Hispanic white Americans > Ethnic/racial minorities
CEOs/upper managers > Nonmanagement workers
Internet trolls > Nonmalevolent users

(Lopes & Yu, 2017; Muris et al., 2017; Vedel & Thomsen, 2017; Dahling et al., 2008; Twenge & Foster, 2008)

THE DARK TRIAD AND SUCCESS

People tend to...

- Attain leadership positions
- Earn higher salaries
- Experience career satisfaction
- Negotiate effectively

(Volmer et al., 2016; Lilienfeld et al., 2015; Spurk et al., 2015; Furnham et al., 2013)

The "Big Five" Theory of Personality and Personality Disorders

Reuters/Matthias Hiekel/Pool

Is hatred a disorder? With the term "Skinhead" tattooed on the back of his head, this man awaits trial in Germany for committing neo-Nazi crimes against foreigners and liberals. Clinicians sometimes confront extreme racism and intolerance, particularly among clients with paranoid, antisocial, and certain other personality disorders. There is a small but growing movement to classify extreme hatred and prejudice as a psychological disorder.

A large body of research conducted with diverse populations consistently suggests that the basic structure of personality may consist of five "supertraits," or factors—*neuroticism, extroversion, openness to experiences, agreeableness,* and *conscientiousness* (Wilt & Revelle, 2019; Chapman et al., 2017). Each of these factors, which are frequently referred to as the "Big Five," consists of a number of subfactors. Anxiety and hostility, for example, are subfactors of the neuroticism factor, while optimism and friendliness are subfactors of the extroversion factor. Theoretically, everyone's personality can be summarized by a combination of these supertraits. One person may display high levels of neuroticism and agreeableness, medium extroversion, and low conscientiousness and openness to experiences. In contrast, another person may display high levels of agreeableness and conscientiousness, medium neuroticism and extroversion, and low openness to experiences. And so on.

Many proponents of the Big Five model have argued further that it would be best to describe all people with personality disorders as being high, low, or in between on the five supertraits and to drop the use of personality disorder categories altogether (Song & Shi, 2017; Glover et al., 2011). Thus a particular person who currently qualifies for a diagnosis of avoidant personality disorder might instead be described as displaying a high degree of neuroticism, medium degrees of agreeableness and conscientiousness, and very low degrees of extroversion and openness to new experiences. Similarly, a person currently diagnosed with narcissistic personality disorder might be described in the Big Five approach as displaying very high degrees of neuroticism and extroversion, medium degrees of conscientiousness and openness to new experiences, and a very low degree of agreeableness.

"Personality Disorder—Trait Specified": DSM-5's Proposed Dimensional Approach

The "Big Five" approach to personality disorders has received considerable study, and some theorists would like it to be used as the official classification approach in the United States and around the world. Instead, the framers of the ICD (the classification system used in most countries outside the United States) and the DSM (the classification system used in the United States) have each developed their own dimensional approach for classifying personality disorders, and they plan to use those approaches in their future editions. Indeed, as you read earlier, the DSM-5 framers have already included a detailed description of their proposed dimensional approach in DSM-5 so that it can be examined by clinicians and studied and tested by researchers (Hopwood & Waugh, 2018).

DSM-5's proposed dimensional approach to personality disorders begins with the notion that people whose traits significantly impair their functioning should receive a diagnosis called **personality disorder—trait specified (PDTS)** (APA, 2013). When assigning this diagnosis, clinicians would also identify and list the problematic traits and rate the severity of impairment caused by them. According to the proposal, five groups of problematic traits would be eligible for a diagnosis of PDTS: *negative affectivity, detachment, antagonism, disinhibition,* and *psychoticism.*

- **Negative Affectivity** People who display negative affectivity experience negative emotions frequently and intensely. In particular, they exhibit one or more of the following traits: *emotional lability* (unstable emotions), *anxiousness, separation insecurity, perseveration* (repetition of certain behaviors despite repeated failures), *submissiveness, hostility, depressivity, suspiciousness,* and *strong emotional reactions* (overreactions to emotionally arousing situations).

© Joshua Sudock/ZUMA Press/Newscom

Photo courtesy of Everett Collection

Dysfunctional toons Today's animated film characters often display significant personality flaws or disorders. Some have a single dysfunctional trait, as is the case for Angry Birds, while others may have "clusters" of problematic traits, as shown by the *South Park* kids. Some observers suggest that the latter (especially Cartman, second from left) show enduring grumpiness, disrespect for authority, irreverence, self-absorption, disregard for the feelings of others, general lack of conscience, and a tendency to get into trouble.

- **Detachment** People who manifest detachment tend to withdraw from other people and social interactions. They may exhibit any of the following traits: *restricted emotional reactivity* (little reaction to emotionally arousing situations), *depressivity, suspiciousness, withdrawal, anhedonia* (inability to feel pleasure or take interest in things), and *intimacy avoidance*. You'll note that two of the traits in this group—depressivity and suspiciousness—are also found in the negative affectivity group.
- **Antagonism** People who display antagonism behave in ways that put them at odds with other people. They may exhibit any of the following traits: *manipulativeness, deceitfulness, grandiosity, attention seeking, callousness,* and *hostility*. Hostility is also found in the negative affectivity group.
- **Disinhibition** People who manifest disinhibition behave impulsively, without reflecting on potential future consequences. They may exhibit any of the following traits: *irresponsibility, impulsivity, distractibility, risk taking,* and *imperfection/disorganization*.
- **Psychoticism** People who display psychoticism have unusual and bizarre experiences. They may exhibit any of the following traits: *unusual beliefs and experiences, eccentricity,* and *cognitive and perceptual dysregulation* (odd thought processes and sensory experiences).

If a person is impaired significantly by any of the five trait groups, or even by just 1 of the 25 traits that make up those groups, he or she would qualify for a diagnosis of *personality disorder—trait specified*. In such cases, the diagnostician would indicate which traits are impaired.

Consider, for example, Lucas, the unhappy 42-year-old assistant graphics programmer described on page 423. As you'll recall, Lucas meets the criteria for a diagnosis of dependent personality disorder under DSM-5's current categorical approach, based largely on his lifetime of extreme dependence on his father, mother, sisters, friends, and coworkers. Using the alternative dimensional approach presented in DSM-5, a diagnostician would instead observe that Lucas is significantly impaired by several of the traits that characterize the negative affectivity trait group. He is, for example, greatly impaired by "separation insecurity." This trait has prevented him from ever living on his own, marrying his girlfriend, disagreeing with his father, advancing at work, and broadening his social life. In addition, Lucas seems to be impaired significantly by the traits of "submissiveness," "anxiousness," and "depressivity." Given this picture, his therapist might assign him a diagnosis of *personality disorder—trait specified, with problematic traits of separation insecurity, submissiveness, anxiousness, and depressivity.*

personality disorder—trait specified (PDTS) A personality disorder undergoing study for possible inclusion in the DSM. People would receive this diagnosis if they had significant impairment in functioning as a result of one or more very problematic traits.

#AsSuspected

For years, people have suspected that individuals who like dogs may be psychologically different from those who like cats. Research supports such speculation (Cherry, 2017; Gosling et al., 2015). Almost 5,000 participants filled out a Big Five personality inventory. On average, the "dog people" scored higher than the "cat people" on extroversion, agreeableness, and conscientiousness. In contrast, the cat people scored higher on introversion and curiosity (i.e., openness to experiences).

According to this dimensional approach, when clinicians assign a diagnosis of personality disorder—trait specified, they also must rate the degree of dysfunction caused by each of the person's traits, using a five-point scale ranging from "little or no impairment" (Rating = 0) to "extreme impairment" (Rating = 4).

Consider Lucas once again. He would probably warrant a rating of "0" on most of the 25 traits listed in the DSM-5 proposal, a rating of "3" on the traits of anxiousness and depressivity, and a rating of "4" on the traits of separation insecurity and submissiveness. Altogether, he would receive the following cumbersome, but informative, diagnosis:

Diagnosis: *Personality Disorder—Trait Specified*
Separation insecurity: Rating 4
Submissiveness: Rating 4
Anxiousness: Rating 3
Depressivity: Rating 3
Other traits: Rating 0

This dimensional approach to personality disorders may indeed prove superior to DSM-5's current categorical approach. Thus far, however, it has caused its own stir in the clinical community. Many clinicians believe that the proposed changes would give too much latitude to diagnosticians—allowing them to apply diagnoses of personality disorder to an enormous range of personality patterns. Still others worry that the requirements of the newly proposed system are too cumbersome or complicated. Thus a number of researchers are currently conducting studies to clarify the merits and drawbacks of the proposed system (Anderson et al., 2018, 2016; Skodol, 2018). Only time and continued research will determine whether the alternative system is indeed a useful approach to the classification and diagnosis of personality disorders.

... SUMMING UP

MULTICULTURAL FACTORS AND DIMENSIONAL CLASSIFICATIONS Despite the field's growing focus on personality disorders, relatively little research has been done on gender and other multicultural influences.

Given the significant problems posed by DSM-5's current categorical approach, a number of today's theorists believe that personality disorders should instead be described and classified by a dimensional approach. Thus, the framers of DSM-5 have developed a dimensional approach called the "personality disorder—trait specified" model. A description of this approach is under study for possible inclusion in a future revision of DSM-5.

Rediscovered, Then Reconsidered

During the first half of the twentieth century, clinicians believed deeply in the unique, enduring patterns we call personality, and they tried to define important personality traits. They then discovered how readily people can be shaped by the situations in which they find themselves, and a backlash developed. The concept of personality seemed to lose legitimacy, and for a while it became almost an obscene word in some circles. The clinical category of personality disorders went through a similar rejection. When psychodynamic and humanistic theorists dominated the clinical field, *neurotic character disorders*—a set of diagnoses similar to today's personality disorders—were considered useful clinical categories, but their popularity declined as other models grew in influence.

During the past 25 years, serious interest in personality and personality disorders has rebounded. In case after case, clinicians have concluded that

CLINICAL CHOICES

Now that you've read about personality disorders, try the interactive case study for this chapter. See if you are able to identify Alicia's symptoms and suggest a diagnosis based on her symptoms. What kind of treatment would be most effective for Alicia? Go to **LaunchPad** to access ***Clinical Choices***.

rigid personality traits do seem to pose special problems, and they have developed new objective tests and interview guides to assess these disorders, setting in motion a wave of systematic research (Clarkin, Livesley, & Meehan, 2018). So far, the antisocial and borderline personality disorders have received the most study. However, with DSM-5 now considering a new—dimensional—classification approach for possible use in the future, additional research is likely to follow. This may allow clinicians to better answer some pressing questions: How common are the various personality disorders? How useful are personality disorder categories? How effective is a dimensional approach to diagnosing these disorders? And which treatments are most effective?

...Key Terms

personality, p. 397
personality traits, p. 397
personality disorder, p. 397
comorbidity, p. 398
categorical, p. 398
dimensional, p. 398
paranoid personality disorder, p. 399
schizoid personality disorder, p. 401
schizotypal personality disorder, p. 403
antisocial personality disorder, p. 405
borderline personality disorder, p. 410
biosocial explanation, p. 413
developmental psychopathology, p. 413
disorganized attachment style, p. 413
mentalization, p. 413
relational psychoanalytic therapy, p. 414
dialectical behavior therapy (DBT), p. 414
histrionic personality disorder, p. 415
narcissistic personality disorder, p. 417
avoidant personality disorder, p. 420
dependent personality disorder, p. 423
obsessive-compulsive personality disorder, p. 425
anal retentive, p. 426
Big Five theory, p. 430
personality disorder—trait specified (PDTS), p. 430

...Quick Quiz

1. What is a personality disorder? *pp. 397–398*
2. Describe the social relationship problems caused by each of the personality disorders. *pp. 397–427*
3. What are the three "odd" personality disorders, and what are the symptoms of each? *pp. 399–404*
4. What explanations and treatments have been applied to the paranoid, schizoid, and schizotypal personality disorders? *pp. 400–404*
5. What are the "dramatic" personality disorders, and what are the symptoms of each disorder? *pp. 405–418*
6. How have theorists explained antisocial personality disorder and borderline personality disorder? What are the leading treatments for these disorders, and how effective are they? *pp. 407–415*
7. What are the leading explanations and treatments for the histrionic and narcissistic personality disorders? How strongly does research support these explanations and treatments? *pp. 416–420*
8. What is the name of the cluster that includes the avoidant, dependent, and obsessive-compulsive personality disorders? What are the leading explanations and treatments for these disorders, and to what extent are they supported by research? *pp. 420–427*
9. How comprehensively have researchers studied cultural and racial differences in the various kinds of personality disorders? *pp. 427–428*
10. Describe two of the dimensional approaches that have been proposed to identify and describe personality disorders. *pp. 430–432*

bas poignet
4
4
5
3
4
4
3
AF6Z ZE4Y

CHAPTER

14

Disorders Common Among Children and Adolescents

TOPIC OVERVIEW

When Cameron was eight years old, his mother started to worry about him. Not so coincidentally, his teacher was becoming concerned at the same time. What they both saw was a sad, and seemingly lost, little boy. At home Cameron just wanted to lie around and watch TV. He would do his chores, and answer his parents' questions—in as few words as possible—but he initiated almost nothing. He ate only when told to eat. He showed little interest in his beloved iPad, and stopped playing computer games. Nor did Cameron seek out playmates anymore. His mother had to virtually drag him to their houses. Nothing gave him pleasure. Cameron also seemed to have more than a few physical problems—from headaches to stomach pains, it was always something, yet the doctor said he checked out fine.

The story was similar at school. Cameron was obedient and compliant, always did what his teacher asked, but he seemed sad and joyless. He rarely joined in class discussions. He stayed in a group with the other kids as they travelled from the classroom to the cafeteria or the schoolyard, but he interacted very little with anyone in particular. When the school psychologist interviewed him, she noticed that he made no eye contact, offered little, and rarely smiled.

When the counselor asked Cameron's mother and teacher if anything special had triggered his unhappiness, they both pointed to the departure of his two best friends—twins who had moved to another state two months ago. But, at the same time, the more they thought about it, that was not really the beginning of Cameron's slide. It certainly worsened things, but his sad mood, inactivity, and isolation had been increasing for quite a while before that.

Ricky Smith was a 7-year-old. . . . During her initial call to the clinic, Mrs. Smith said her son was "out of control." She said Ricky "was all over the place" and "constantly getting into trouble." . . .

Ricky . . . said his teacher, Mrs. Candler, was always yelling at him and sending notes home to his mother. Ricky initially said he did not know why the teacher yelled at him but then said it was mostly about not paying attention or following class rules. . . .

Ricky . . . said he had a few friends but often had to keep to himself. This was because Mrs. Candler made him spend much of the school day in a corner of the classroom to complete his work. Unfortunately, little of the work was successfully finished. Ricky said he felt bored, sad, tired, and angry in the classroom. . . .

Ricky said his mother yelled at him a lot. . . . He said he felt happiest when riding his bike because nobody yelled at him and he could "go wherever I want." . . .

Mrs. Smith said Ricky was almost intolerable in the classroom, . . . crying when asked to do something, stomping his feet, and being disrespectful to the teacher. . . . [She also said] her son was generally "out of control" at home. He would not listen to her commands and often ran around the house until he got what he wanted. She and her son often argued about his homework, chores, [and] misbehavior. . . [In addition,] Ricky often fidgeted and lost many of his school materials. He was disorganized and paid little attention to long-term consequences. The child was also difficult to control in public places, such as a supermarket or church. . . .

Ricky's teacher . . . added that Ricky's academic performance was below average . . . He understood and completed his reading and math assignments when motivated to do so but his attention was sporadic and insufficient. . . . Ricky was [also] getting out of his seat more and more, requiring a constant response. . . .

(Kearney, 2013, pp. 62–64)

#TheirWords

"It is an illusion that youth is happy, an illusion of those who have lost it."
W. Somerset Maugham, playwright and novelist

Cameron and Ricky are both displaying psychological disorders. Their disorders are disrupting the boys' family ties, school performances, and social relationships, but each disorder does so in a particular way and for particular reasons. Cameron, who may qualify for a diagnosis of *major depressive disorder*, struggles constantly with sadness, disinterest in other people and activities, and lack of pleasure, along with stomachaches and other physical ailments. Ricky's main problems, on the other hand, are that he cannot concentrate and is overly active and impulsive—difficulties that characterize attention-deficit/hyperactivity disorder (ADHD).

Abnormal functioning can occur at any time in life. Some patterns of abnormality, however, are more likely to emerge during particular periods—during childhood for example, or, at the other end of the spectrum, during old age. In this chapter you will read about disorders that commonly have their onset during childhood or early adolescence. In the next chapter you'll learn about problems that are more prevalent among the elderly.

Childhood and Adolescence

People often think of childhood as a carefree and happy time—yet it can also be frightening and upsetting (see **Figure 14-1**). In fact, children of all cultures typically have at least some emotional and behavioral problems as they encounter new people and situations. Surveys reveal that *worry* is a common experience: close to half of all children in the United States have multiple fears, particularly concerning school, health, and personal safety (Fernandez, 2017; Jovanovic et al., 2014). Bed-wetting, nightmares, temper tantrums, and restlessness are other problems that many children contend with.

Adolescence can also be a difficult period. Physical and sexual changes, social and academic pressures, school violence, personal doubts, and temptations cause many teenagers to feel nervous, confused, and depressed.

Most people who are bullied are upset by it, but some seem to be more traumatized by the experience than others. Why might that be?

A particular concern among children and adolescents is that of being bullied (see ***InfoCentral***). Surveys throughout the world have revealed repeatedly that bullying ranks as a major problem in the minds of most young respondents, often a bigger problem than racism, AIDS, and peer pressure to try sex or alcohol (Hymel & Swearer, 2015). More generally, over 20 percent of students report being bullied frequently, and more than 50 percent report having been bullied at least once (DTL, 2017). Typically, kids who have been bullied react with feelings of humiliation, anxiety, or dislike for school (Eastman et al., 2018). In extreme cases, they

Jason Szenes/EPA/Redux

It gets better Gay activist and journalist Dan Savage accepts a Webby Special Achievement award for co-founding "It Gets Better"—an Internet outreach program that tells LGBTQ teenagers their lives will get better as they move toward adulthood and find support from their communities. The project was started in 2010 by Savage and his husband Terry Miller after a number of gay teens had killed themselves in response to bullying. It now has a Web site featuring more than 50,000 messages of support and inspiration to beleaguered LGBTQ teens.

CHILD AND ADOLESCENT BULLYING

Bullying is the repeated infliction of force, threats, or coercion in order to intimidate, hurt, or dominate another, less powerful person. It is particularly common among children and adolescents. Members of certain minority groups, such as LGBTQ individuals, are much more likely to be bullied. Over the past decade, clinicians and educators have learned that bullying is much more common and more harmful than previously thought. (Kaess, 2018; Pontes et al., 2018; USDHHS, 2017)

TYPES OF BULLYING

Physical — hitting, pushing, tripping

Verbal — name-calling, mean taunting, sexual comments, threatening

Relational/Social — spreading rumors, posting embarrassing images, rejecting from group

BULLYING IS ON THE RISE...

39%	54%
over age 50	under age 50

people bullied as teenagers

(DTL, 2017; Harris Interactive, 2014; Ratcliffe, 2014; NFER, 2010)

BULLIES TEND TO:

- Display antisocial behaviors
- Perform poorly in school
- Drop out of school
- Bring weapons to school
- Drink alcohol
- Smoke cigarettes
- Use drugs

(BSA, 2017; CDC, 2017; Hertz & Donato, 2013)

EFFECTS OF BULLYING

- Depression
- Suicidal thinking and attempts
- Anxiety
- Low self-esteem
- Sleep problems
- Somatic symptoms
- Substance use and abuse
- School problems and/or phobias
- Antisocial behavior

(Gordon, 2018; APA, 2017; Barzilay et al., 2017; BSA, 2017; CDC, 2017, 2016; CRC, 2017; UNESCO, 2017)

SCHOOL BULLYING

Much bullying takes place at school. Around **2/3** of all school bullying occurs in hallways, schoolyards, bathrooms, cafeterias, or buses. A full **1/3** occurs in classrooms, while teachers are present (BSA, 2014). It is estimated that **30% to 40%** of school bullying goes unreported. (BSA, 2017; NB, 2017; UNESCO, 2017; USDHHS, 2017)

The Nature of School Bullying

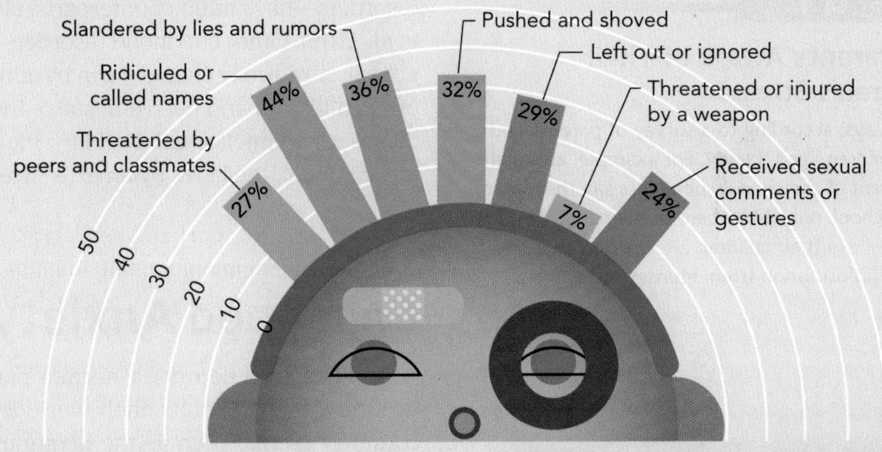

(BSA, 2017, 2014; NB, 2017; USDHHS, 2017; UNESCO, 2017; CDC, 2013)

Features of School Anti-Bullying Programs

- Increased supervision of students
- Delivery of consequences for bullying
- School-wide implementation of anti-bullying policies
- Cooperation among school staff, parents, and professionals across disciplines
- Identification of risk factors for bullying

(CDC, 2017, 2013)

Bullying prevention programs in schools reduce bullying between **25% and 50%.** (NB, 2017, 2016; UNESCO, 2017; NBPC, 2016)

CYBERBULLYING

Like

Cyberbullying takes place through e-mail, text messaging, Web sites and apps, instant messaging, chat rooms, or posted videos or photos. Between **40% and 50%** of all children and teens have been bullied online at least once. About **21%** are bullied online frequently. Girls are at least **50%** more likely than boys to be cyberbullied on a regular basis. (Kim et al., 2018; DTL, 2017; EIE, 2017; NB, 2017; Pew Research Center, 2017; CRC, 2016; BSA, 2014; NSPCC, 2013; Sedghi, 2013)

Why Do Teens Cyberbully?

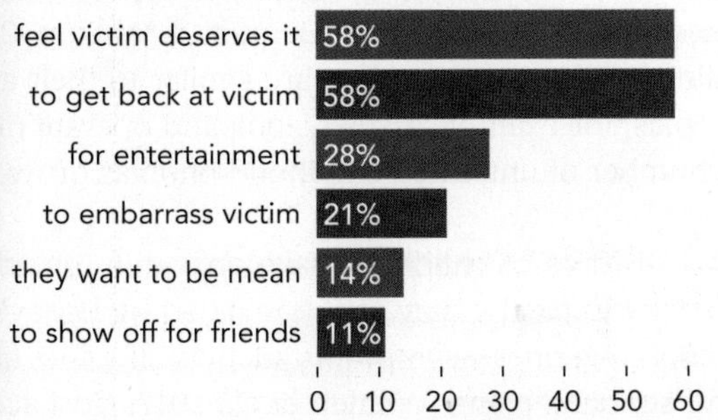

(NB, 2017; BSA, 2014; Knowthenet, 2013)

Social Media and Cyberbullying

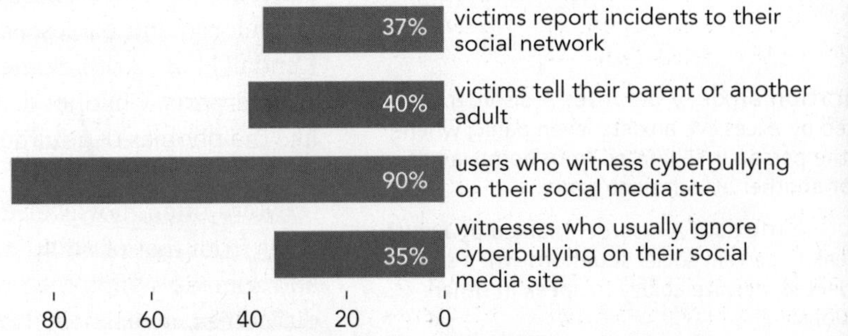

(EIE, 2017; NB, 2017; Pew Research Center, 2017; BSA, 2014; Knowthenet, 2013)

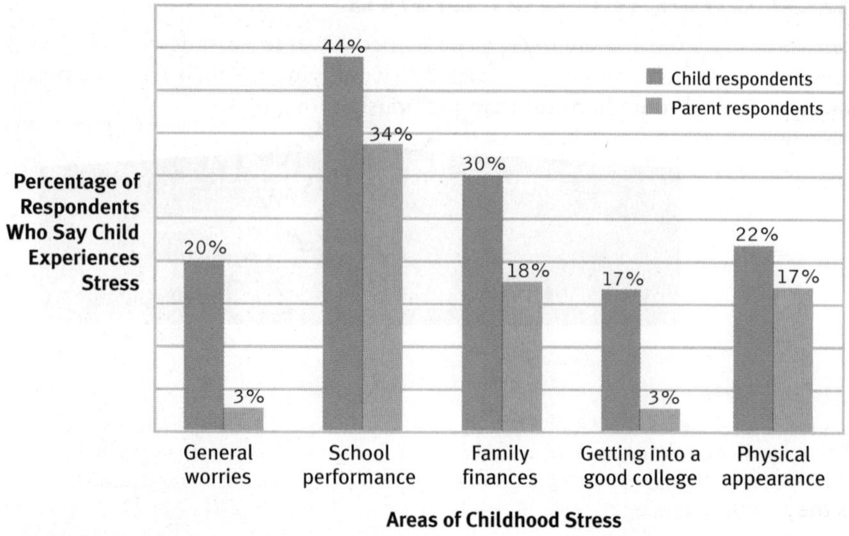

FIGURE 14-1

Are Parents Aware of Their Children's Stress?

Not always, according to a survey of parents and their children aged 8 to 17. For example, although 44 percent of the child respondents say they worry about school, only 34 percent of the parent respondents believe their children are worried about school. (Information from: Munsey, 2010.)

may attempt suicide (Ford et al., 2017). Moreover, the psychological effects of being bullied can reach far into adulthood (Arseneault, 2017). Also troubling, the technological advances of today's world have broadened the ways in which children and adolescents can be bullied, and *cyberbullying*—bullying and humiliating by e-mail, text messages, and social media—is now on the rise (Ferrara et al., 2018; Kim et al., 2018).

Beyond these common concerns and psychological difficulties, at least one-fifth of all children and adolescents in North America also experience a diagnosable psychological disorder (CDC, 2017; Costello & Angold, 2016). Boys with disorders outnumber girls, even though most of the adult psychological disorders are more common among women.

Some disorders displayed by children—childhood anxiety disorders, childhood depression, and disruptive disorders—have adult counterparts, although they are also distinct in certain ways (Rice et al., 2019). Other childhood disorders—elimination disorders, for example—usually disappear or radically change form by adulthood. There are also disorders that begin at birth or in childhood and persist in stable forms into adult life. These include autism spectrum disorder and intellectual disability, the former marked by a lack of responsiveness to the environment, the latter by an extensive disturbance in intellect and adaptive functioning.

Childhood Anxiety Disorders

Anxiety is, to a degree, a normal part of childhood. Since children have had fewer experiences than adults, their world is often new and scary. They may be frightened by common events, such as the beginning of school, or by special upsets, such as moving to a new house or becoming seriously ill. In addition, each generation of children is confronted by new sources of anxiety. Today's children, for example, are repeatedly warned, both at home and at school, about the dangers of Internet browsing and online predators, child abduction, drugs, school shootings, and terrorism.

Children may also be strongly affected by parental problems or inadequacies. If, for example, parents typically react to events with high levels of anxiety or uncertainty, or if they overprotect their children, the children may be more likely to respond to the world with anxiety (Kendall et al., 2018; Kerns et al., 2017, 2014). And if parents are divorced, become seriously ill, or must be separated from their children for a long period, childhood anxiety may result. Beyond such environmental problems, genetic studies suggest that some children are prone to an anxious temperament (Buzzell et al., 2017; Tone, Garn, & Pine, 2016).

For some children, these anxieties become long-lasting and debilitating, interfering with their daily lives and their ability to function appropriately. These children may be suffering from an *anxiety disorder*. Surveys indicate that between 14 and 25 percent of all children and adolescents experience an anxiety disorder (Bennett & Walkup, 2018; Kendall et al., 2018). Some of the childhood anxiety disorders are similar to their adult counterparts. Childhood specific phobias, for example, usually look and operate much like the phobias of adulthood, and a number of untreated childhood phobias grow into adult ones.

More often, however, the anxiety disorders of childhood take on a different character from that of adult anxiety disorders. Typically they are dominated by behavioral and somatic symptoms rather than cognitive ones—symptoms such as clinging, sleep difficulties, avoidance, irritability, and stomach pains (Whalen et al., 2017; Cornacchio

separation anxiety disorder A disorder marked by excessive anxiety, even panic, whenever the person is separated from home, a parent, or another attachment figure.

selective mutism A disorder marked by failure to speak in certain social situations when speech is expected, despite ability to speak in other situations.

et al., 2016). They tend to center on specific, sometimes imaginary, objects and events, such as monsters, ghosts, or thunderstorms, rather than broad concerns about the future or one's place in the world (Kendall et al., 2018). Similarly, the anxiety symptoms are more often than not triggered by immediate situations and surroundings, rather than by thoughts about events that could happen in the future.

© Melissa Lyttle

Reluctant to speak Children with selective mutism fail to speak in their classrooms and/or other social situations. Often the children use whispering, either directly to a teacher or through a go-between, to communicate important messages. Here, a child with the disorder whispers to her counselor at Florida International University's Center for Children and Families.

Separation Anxiety Disorder and Selective Mutism

Two patterns of childhood anxiety, *separation anxiety disorder* and *selective mutism*, have received considerable attention in recent years, partly because they cause children emotional pain and partly because they leave the parents feeling helpless as they try to help their children.

Separation anxiety disorder, which you read about in Chapter 4, is one of the most common anxiety disorders among children (see page 104). The disorder often begins as early as the preschool years, and at least 4 percent of all children experience it (Hannesdottir et al., 2018). As you'll recall, children suffering from this disorder have enormous difficulty being away from their parents or other major attachment figures, and they are often reluctant—or outright refuse—to go anywhere where they might be separated from their parents—friends' houses, birthday parties, or even their own bedrooms. Separation anxiety disorder in childhood may further take the form of *school refusal*, in which children fear going to school and often stay home for a long period (Nayak, Sangoi, & Nachane, 2018). However, many cases of school refusal, particularly those in later childhood, have causes other than separation fears, such as social or academic concerns, depression, fears of specific objects or persons at school, or a desire to be defiant.

In **selective mutism**, children consistently fail to speak in certain social situations but show no difficulty at all speaking in others (Furr et al., 2019; Rogoll, Petzold, & Strohle, 2018). A child with this disorder may have no problem talking, laughing, or singing at home with family members but will offer absolutely no words in other key situations, such as the classroom (see **Table 14-1**). Some go an entire school year without speaking a word to their teacher or classmates. Many have a special friend in the classroom to whom they will discreetly whisper important things to be communicated to the class, such as answers to a teacher's questions or the need to use the restroom. People who only see a selectively mute child at school often find it hard to believe that the child is an absolute chatterbox at home. Almost 1 percent of all children display this disorder (SMA, 2018; Hua & Major, 2016).

Many researchers believe that selective mutism is an early version of *social anxiety disorder*, appearing in children before they have fully developed the cognitive capacities to worry about future embarrassment or anticipate potential judgment from others (see pages 120–123). Indeed, some, but far from all, older children with selective mutism do develop social anxiety disorder (Rogoll et al., 2018). At the same time, there are many features unique to selective mutism. For example, some children with this disorder have significant delays in their development of communication and language skills (Hua & Major, 2016).

Educators and clinicians can underestimate a child's capabilities when he or she refuses to speak during an evaluation. Thus some children with selective mutism are misclassified as having an *intellectual disability* (which you will read about later in this chapter).

TABLE: 14-1

DX Checklist

Selective Mutism
1. Individual persistently does not speak in certain social situations in which speech is expected, although speaking in other situations presents no problem.
2. Academic or social interference.
3. Individual's symptoms last 1 month or more, and are not limited to the first 4 weeks of a new school year.
4. Symptoms not due to autism spectrum disorder, thought disorder, or language or communication disorder.

Information from: APA, 2013.

This can, in turn, lead to incorrect interventions that focus on intellectual functioning and language development rather than on anxiety difficulties.

cognitive behavioral therapy works best

Treatments for Childhood Anxiety Disorders

Despite the high prevalence of childhood and adolescent anxiety disorders, around two-thirds of anxious children go untreated (NIMH, 2017). Among the children who do receive treatment, psychodynamic, cognitive-behavioral, family, and group therapies, separately or in combination, have been used most often. Each approach has had some degree of success; however, studies have found that cognitive-behavioral therapy fares best (Comer et al., 2019; Oerbeck et al., 2018). These various therapies parallel the adult anxiety approaches you read about in Chapter 4, but they are tailored to the child's cognitive abilities, unique life situation, and limited control over his or her life. In addition, clinicians may offer psychoeducation, provide parent training, and arrange school interventions to treat anxious children (Sanchez et al., 2018; Cornacchio et al., 2017).

Clinicians have also used drug therapy in a number of cases of childhood anxiety disorders, often in combination with psychotherapy. Not only do they prescribe antianxiety drugs, but antidepressant and antipsychotic drugs as well (Comer et al., 2019, 2011, 2010; Wang et al., 2017). Studies suggest that antidepressant drugs, in particular, are helpful for severely anxious children, often as helpful as cognitive-behavioral therapy (Albano et al., 2018). In a landmark study called the *Child/Adolescent Anxiety Multimodal Study* (*CAMS*), clinicians treated almost 500 children and adolescents with anxiety disorders across the United States, and compared the effectiveness of cognitive-behavioral therapy alone, antidepressant therapy alone, cognitive-behavioral and antidepressant therapy combined, and placebo therapy. They found that combining cognitive-behavioral and antidepressant therapy led to the most favorable outcomes. Around 80 percent of the anxious children and adolescents receiving the combination treatment showed substantial clinical improvement (Piacentini et al., 2014; Walkup et al., 2008).

Al Diaz/Miami Herald/TNS via Getty Images

Never too young? Young campers at the Camp Honey Shine in Miami, Florida, learn mindfulness meditation and other techniques for dealing with stress.

Because children typically have difficulty recognizing and understanding their feelings and motives, many therapists, particularly psychodynamic therapists, use **play therapy** as part of treatment. In this approach, the children play with toys, draw, and make up stories; in doing so, they are thought to reveal the conflicts in their lives and their related feelings. Over the course of therapy, the therapists introduce more play and fantasy to help the children work through their conflicts and change their emotions and behavior. In addition, humanistic therapists conduct *child-centered therapy* with anxious children, in which, as you read in Chapter 2, the clinician listens carefully to the child, reflects on what the child is saying, shows empathy, and gives unconditional positive regard (Silk et al., 2018).

Depressive and Bipolar Disorders During Childhood

Like Cameron, the boy you read about at the beginning of this chapter, around 2 percent of children and 8 percent of adolescents currently experience a major depressive disorder (NIMH, 2017, 2016; Avenevoli et al., 2015). As many as 20 percent of adolescents experience at least one depressive episode during their teen years. In addition, a number of clinicians believe that children can experience a bipolar disorder.

play therapy An approach to treating childhood disorders that helps children express their conflicts and feelings indirectly by drawing, playing with toys, and making up stories.

Major Depressive Disorder

Very young children lack some of the cognitive skills that help produce clinical depression, thus accounting for the relatively low rate of depression among the very young (Wesselhoeft et al., 2016). For example, in order to experience the sense of hopelessness typically found in depressed adults, children must be able to hold expectations about the future, a skill rarely in full bloom before the age of 7.

Nevertheless, if life situations or biological predispositions are significant enough, even very young children sometimes have severe downward turns of mood (Whalen et al., 2017). Depression in the young may be triggered by negative life events (particularly losses), major changes, rejection, or ongoing abuse (see ***PsychWatch*** on the next page). Childhood depression commonly features symptoms such as irritability, headaches, stomach pain, and a disinterest in toys and games (Fristad & Black, 2018; Whalen et al., 2017).

AP Photo/The Free Lance-Star, Mike Morones

Separation and depression This 3-year-old boy hugs his father as the soldier departs for overseas military duty. Given evidence that extended family separations often produce depression in children, clinical theorists have been particularly worried about the thousands of children affected by military deployments, refugee and immigrant detentions, and parent incarcerations (Kritikos et al., 2019).

Clinical depression is much more common among teenagers than among young children. Adolescence is, under the best of circumstances, a difficult and confusing time, marked by angst, hormonal and bodily changes, mood changes, complex relationships, and new explorations. For some teens, these "normal" upsets of adolescence cross the line into clinical depression. As you read in Chapter 7, suicidal thoughts and attempts are particularly common among adolescents—one in eight teens persistently thinks about suicide each year—and depression is the leading cause of such thoughts and attempts (Kennebeck & Bonin, 2017; Nock et al., 2013).

Interestingly, while there is no difference between the rates of depression in boys and girls before the age of 13, girls are twice as likely as boys to be depressed by the age of 16 (Breslau et al., 2017). Why this gender shift? Several factors have been suggested, including hormonal changes, the fact that females increasingly experience more stressors than males, and the tendency of girls to become more emotionally invested than boys in social and intimate relationships as they mature. One explanation also focuses on teenage girls' growing dissatisfaction with their bodies. Whereas boys tend to like the increase in muscle mass and other body changes that accompany puberty, girls often detest the increases in body fat and weight gain that they experience during puberty and beyond. Raised in a society that values and demands extreme thinness as the aesthetic female ideal, many adolescent girls feel imprisoned by their own bodies, have low self-esteem, and become depressed (Klein & Attia, 2017). Many also develop eating disorders, as you saw in Chapter 9.

For years, it was generally believed that childhood and teenage depression would respond well to the same treatments that have been of help to depressed adults—particularly, cognitive-behavioral therapy, interpersonal psychotherapy, and antidepressant drugs—and, in fact, many studies have indicated the effectiveness of such approaches (Weersing et al., 2017). Moreover, clinicians have often found success treating children and adolescents with family-focused approaches that aim to improve parent–child relationships, increase shared family activities, and build child coping skills (Tompson et al., 2017). At the same time, one development over the past 15 years has raised significant questions about the treatment of depressed teenagers. This is the discovery that antidepressant drugs may be dangerous for some depressed children and teenagers.

Throughout the 1990s, most psychiatrists believed that second-generation antidepressants were safe and effective for children and adolescents, and they prescribed them readily. However, the U.S. Food and Drug Administration (FDA) concluded in 2004, based on a number of clinical reports, that the drugs may produce a real, though small, increase in the risk of suicidal behavior for certain children and adolescents, especially during the first few months of treatment. Thus, the FDA ordered that all

#

#CounselingDeficit

Currently there is 1 school counselor for every 491 students in the United States. The recommended ratio is 1 per 250 students (ASCA, 2017, 2016).

PSYCHWATCH

Child Abuse

A problem that affects all too many children and has an enormous impact on their psychological development is *child abuse,* the nonaccidental use of excessive physical or psychological force by an adult on a child, often with the intention of hurting or destroying the child. Between 5 and 16 percent of children in the United States are physically abused each year (Wherry, 2018; Boos, 2017). Surveys suggest that 1 of every 10 children is the victim of severe violence, such as being kicked, bitten, hit, beaten, or threatened with a knife or a gun. Although child abuse is perpetrated in all socioeconomic groups, it is apparently more common among the poor (Boos, 2017; Romero-Martínez et al., 2014).

Abusers are usually the child's parents (Christian, 2017; Ben-Natan et al., 2014). Clinical investigators have learned that abusive parents often have poor impulse control, low self-esteem, higher levels of depression, and weak parenting skills (Boos, 2017). Many were abused themselves as children and have had poor role models. In some cases, they are dealing with stressors such as marital discord or unemployment (Christian, 2017).

Studies suggest that the victims of child abuse may suffer both immediate and long-term psychological effects (Kolko & Berkout, 2017). Research has shown, for example, that they may experience psychological symptoms such as anxiety, depression, or bed-wetting, and display performance and behavior problems in school (Martin, Kidd, & Seedat, 2019; Keeshin et al., 2014). Long-term negative effects include lack of social acceptance, a higher number of medical and psychological disorders during adulthood, more abuse of alcohol and other substances, more impulsive and risk-taking behaviors, more arrests during adolescence and adulthood, a greater risk of becoming criminally violent, a higher unemployment rate, and a higher suicide rate (Kolko & Berkout, 2017; Afifi et al., 2014). Finally, as many as one-third of those who are abused grow up to be abusive, neglectful, or inadequate parents themselves (Romero-Martínez et al., 2014).

Jill Toyoshiba/Kansas City Star/TNS via Getty Images

Lingering impact A mother prepares her adopted 5-year-old son for pajama day at a trauma treatment program in which the child participates. The program addresses issues that the boy is still dealing with as a result of abuse or neglect in an earlier family.

Two forms of child abuse have received special attention: psychological and sexual abuse. *Psychological abuse* may include severe rejection, excessive discipline, scapegoating and ridicule, isolation, and refusal to provide help for a child with psychological problems (Endom, 2017). It probably accompanies all forms of physical abuse and neglect and often occurs by itself. *Child sexual abuse,* the use of a child for gratification of adult sexual desires, may occur outside or within the home (Bechtel & Bennett, 2017; Murray, Nguyen, & Cohen, 2014). Surveys suggest that, worldwide, as many as 25 percent of women were forced into sexual contact with an adult male during childhood, many of them with a parent or stepparent. As many as 9 percent of men were also sexually abused during childhood. Child sexual abuse appears to be equally common across all socioeconomic classes, races, and ethnic groups.

A variety of therapies have been used in cases of child abuse, including groups sponsored by *Parents Anonymous,* which help parents develop insight into their behavior, provide training on alternatives to abuse, and teach coping and parenting skills (PA, 2017; Miller et al., 2007). In addition, prevention programs, often in the form of home visitations and parent training, have proved promising (Beasley et al., 2014; Rubin et al., 2014).

Research suggests that the psychological needs of children who have been abused should be addressed as early as possible (PA, 2017; Murray et al., 2014). Clinicians and educators have launched valuable *early detection programs* that (1) educate all children about child abuse, (2) teach them skills for avoiding or escaping from abusive situations, (3) encourage children to tell another adult if they are abused, and (4) assure them that abuse is never their fault (PA, 2017; Miller et al., 2007).

antidepressant containers carry "black box" warnings stating that the drugs "increase the risk of suicidal thinking and behavior in children" (Morkem et al., 2017). Arguments about the wisdom of this FDA order have since ensued. Although most clinicians agree that the drugs may increase the risk of suicidal thoughts and attempts in as many as 2 percent of young patients, some have noted that the overall risk of suicide may actually be reduced for the vast majority of children who take the drugs (Pozzi et al., 2016; Isacson & Rich, 2014). They point out, for example, that suicides among children and teenagers decreased by 30 percent in the decade leading up to 2004, as the number of antidepressant prescriptions provided to children and teenagers was soaring. Today's medicators seem to agree that, on balance, antidepressants are indeed a useful and

disruptive mood dysregulation disorder A childhood disorder marked by severe recurrent temper outbursts along with a persistent irritable or angry mood.

relatively safe treatment for most depressed children and adolescents. In the five years following the initial black box warnings, prescriptions of these drugs for young persons declined significantly, but, over the past decade, such prescriptions have steadily increased once again (Morkem et al., 2017).

AP Photo/Al Grillo

Grief camp "Grief camps" have been developed for children and teenagers who have lost a loved one. At one such program, this young girl, whose uncle was killed while fighting in Iraq, puts a clipping representing what she feels about his death into a bag.

Bipolar Disorder and Disruptive Mood Dysregulation Disorder

For decades, bipolar disorder was thought to be almost exclusively an *adult* disorder, and that its earliest age of onset is the late teens (APA, 2013). However, beginning in the mid-1990s, clinical theorists did an about-face, and a large number of them came to believe that many children display bipolar disorder (Van Meter et al., 2016). Indeed, one review of national diagnostic trends found that the number of children and adolescents diagnosed and treated for bipolar disorder in the United States increased 40-fold from 1994 to 2003 (Moreno et al., 2007). Moreover, this trend continued during the decade following that review (Mash & Wolfe, 2018; Ryles et al., 2017).

During that period, some theorists came to suspect that such increases reflected not a rise in the prevalence of bipolar disorders among children but rather a new—often inaccurate—diagnostic trend (Van Meter et al., 2016). They believed that the diagnosis of bipolar disorder was being overapplied to children and adolescents and being assigned to the majority of extremely explosive, aggressive children. In support of these claims, studies revealed that symptoms of rage and aggression, along with depression, were in fact dominating the clinical picture of most children who were receiving a bipolar diagnosis (Hernandez et al., 2017; Ryles et al., 2017). Many such children were not even displaying the symptoms of mania or the mood swings that characterize adult bipolar disorder.

The task force of DSM-5 came to the same conclusion—that the childhood bipolar label had been overapplied. In an attempt to rectify this, DSM-5 now includes a new category, **disruptive mood dysregulation disorder,** which is used to describe children with patterns of severe rage (see **Table 14-2**). It is expected that, henceforth, most children with severe anger and temper outbursts will receive this diagnosis and that the number of childhood bipolar disorder diagnoses will decrease correspondingly.

This diagnostic issue is particularly important because the rise in diagnoses of bipolar disorder has been accompanied by an increase in the number of children prescribed medications (Duffy & Grof, 2018; Cervesi et al., 2017). Although several psychological approaches seem to be helpful for children with a diagnosis of bipolar disorder, fully half of those in treatment receive an antipsychotic drug, a third receive an antibipolar drug, and many others receive antidepressant or stimulant drugs (Vallarino et al., 2015). Yet relatively few of these drugs or drug combinations have been tested for such use with children.

... SUMMING UP

CHILDHOOD ANXIETY, DEPRESSIVE, AND BIPOLAR DISORDERS Emotional and behavioral problems are common in childhood and adolescence, but in addition, at least 20 percent of all children and adolescents in the United States have a diagnosable psychological disorder. A particular concern among children is that of being bullied.

Anxiety disorders are particularly common among children and adolescents. This group of problems includes adultlike disorders (such as generalized anxiety disorder and social anxiety disorder), the childhood form of separation anxiety disorder, and selective mutism.

Two percent of children and 8 percent of adolescents experience depression. Childhood depression is often characterized by such symptoms as irritability, headaches, stomach pain, and a disinterest in toys and games. In addition, over the past two decades, there has also been an enormous increase in the number of children and adolescents who receive diagnoses of bipolar disorder. Such diagnoses are expected to decrease now that DSM-5 has added a new childhood category, disruptive mood dysregulation disorder.

TABLE: 14-2

Dx Checklist

Disruptive Mood Dysregulation Disorder
1. For at least a year, child frequently has severe outbursts of temper that are extremely out of proportion to triggering situations.
2. The outbursts occur in at least two settings (home, school, with peers).
3. Individual repeatedly is irritable or angry between the outbursts.
4. Individual receives initial diagnosis between 6 and 18 years of age.

Information from: APA, 2013.

oppositional defiant disorder A disorder in which children are repeatedly argumentative, defiant, angry, irritable, and perhaps vindictive.

conduct disorder A disorder in which children repeatedly violate the basic rights of others and display significant aggression.

Oppositional Defiant Disorder and Conduct Disorder

Most children break rules or misbehave on occasion. If they consistently display extreme hostility and defiance, however, they may qualify for a diagnosis of oppositional defiant disorder or conduct disorder. Those with **oppositional defiant disorder** are argumentative and defiant, angry, and irritable, and in some cases, vindictive (Matthys & Lochman, 2017). They may argue repeatedly with adults, ignore adult rules and requests, deliberately annoy other people, and feel much anger and resentment. As many as 10 percent of children qualify for a diagnosis of oppositional defiant disorder (Mash & Wolfe, 2018, 2015). The disorder is more common in boys than in girls before puberty but equal in both genders after puberty.

Children with **conduct disorder,** a more severe problem, repeatedly violate the basic rights of others (APA, 2013). They are often aggressive and may be physically cruel to people or animals, deliberately destroy other people's property, steal or lie, skip school, or run away from home (see **Table 14-3**). Many threaten or harm their victims, committing such crimes as firesetting, shoplifting, forgery, breaking into buildings or cars, mugging, and armed robbery. As they get older, their acts of physical violence may include rape or, in rare cases, homicide. The symptoms of conduct disorder are apparent in this summary of a clinical interview with a 15-year-old boy named Derek:

Questioning revealed that Derek was getting into . . . serious trouble of late, having been arrested for shoplifting 4 weeks before. Derek was caught with one other youth when he and a dozen friends swarmed a convenience store and took everything they could before leaving in cars. This event followed similar others at [an electronics] store and a . . . clothing store. Derek blamed his friends for his arrest because they apparently left him behind as he straggled out of the store. He was charged only with shoplifting, however, after police found him holding just three candy bars and a bag of potato chips. Derek expressed no remorse for the theft or any care for the store clerk who was injured when one of the teens pushed her into a glass case. When informed of the clerk's injury, for example, Derek replied, "I didn't do it, so what do I care?"

The psychologist questioned Derek further about other legal violations and discovered a rather extended history of trouble. Derek was arrested for vandalism 10 months earlier for breaking windows and damaging cars on school property. He received probation for 6 months because this was his first offense. Derek also boasted of other exploits for which he was not caught, including several shoplifting episodes, . . . joyriding, and missing school. Derek missed 23 days (50 percent) of school since the beginning of the academic year. In addition, he described break-in attempts of his neighbors' apartments. . . . Only rarely during the interview did Derek stray from his bravado.

(Kearney, 2013, pp. 87–88)

Conduct disorder usually begins between 7 and 15 years of age (APA, 2013). Between 5 and 10 percent of children, three-quarters of them boys, qualify for this diagnosis (Matthys & Lochman, 2017). Children with a relatively mild conduct disorder often improve over time, but a severe case may continue into adulthood and develop into antisocial personality disorder, another psychological problem, and/or a criminal lifestyle (Rivenbark et al., 2018; Dishion & Patterson, 2016). Research indicates that more than 80 percent of those who develop conduct disorder first display a pattern of oppositional defiant disorder (APA, 2013). More than one-third of children with conduct disorder also display attention-deficit/hyperactivity disorder (ADHD), a disorder that you will read about shortly, and a number experience depression and anxiety (Wichstrom, Belsky, & Steinsbekk, 2017).

Some clinical theorists believe that there are actually several kinds of conduct disorder, including (1) the *overt-destructive* pattern, in which individuals display openly

TABLE: 14-3

Dx Checklist

Conduct Disorder
1. Individual repeatedly violates the rights of others or ignores the norms or rules of society, beyond the violations displayed by most people of his or her age.
2. At least three of the following features are present over the past year (and at least one in the past 6 months): • Frequent bullying or threatening • Frequent provoking of physical fights • Using dangerous weapons • Physical cruelty to people • Physical cruelty to animals • Stealing during confrontations • Forcing someone into sexual activity • Firesetting • Deliberately destroying others' property • Breaking into a house, building, or car • Frequent lying • Stealing under nonconfrontational circumstances • Frequent staying out beyond curfews, starting before the age of 13 • Running away from home overnight at least twice • Frequent truancy, starting before adolescence.
3. Significant impairment.

Information from: APA, 2013.

aggressive and confrontational behaviors; (2) the *overt-nondestructive* pattern, dominated by openly offensive but nonconfrontational behaviors such as lying; (3) the *covert-destructive* pattern, characterized by secretive destructive behaviors such as violating other people's property, breaking and entering, and setting fires; and (4) the *covert-nondestructive* pattern, in which individuals secretly commit nonaggressive behaviors, such as being truant from school (Renk et al., 2017; McMahon & Frick, 2007, 2005).

A number of researchers distinguish yet another pattern of aggression found in certain cases of conduct disorder, *relational aggression,* in which the individual is socially isolated and primarily performs social misdeeds such as slandering others, spreading rumors, and manipulating friendships (Perry & Ostrov, 2018; Murray-Close et al., 2016). Relational aggression is more common among girls than boys.

Many children with conduct disorder are suspended from school, placed in foster homes, or incarcerated (Matthys & Lochman, 2017). When children between the ages of 8 and 18 break the law, the legal system often labels them *juvenile delinquents* (Krisberg, 2018). Boys are much more involved in juvenile crime than girls, although the gap between them is narrowing. It is encouraging that the number of arrests of teenagers for serious crimes has fallen by one-third since the turn of the century (DOJ, 2017, 2014, 2010).

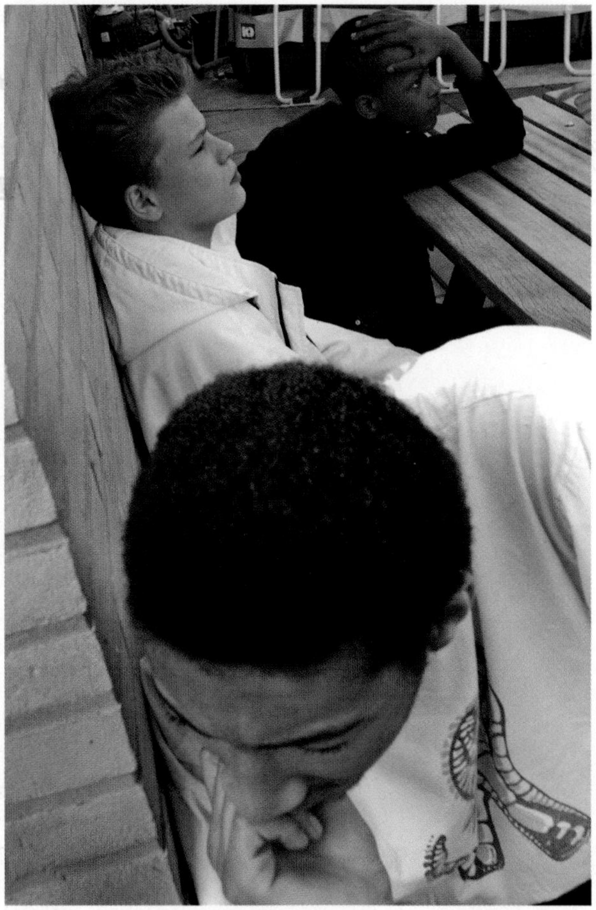

Thierry Dudoit/EXPRESS-REA/Redux

Antisocial behavior and the law Many children and adolescents with conduct disorder wind up incarcerated in *juvenile detention,* or *juvenile training, centers* when their antisocial behaviors place them in conflict with the law. Here inmates at one such center in Holland spend many hours sitting around, staring, and thinking—hardly a prescription for improvements in their behaviors or mental health.

What Are the Causes of Conduct Disorder?

Many cases of conduct disorder, particularly those marked by destructive behaviors, have been linked to genetic and biological factors (Matthys & Lochman, 2017). A number of cases have also been tied to drug abuse, poverty, traumatic events, and exposure to violent peers or community violence (McCloskey & Drabick, 2018; Wymbs et al., 2014). In addition, conduct disorder is often related to troubled parent–child relationships, inadequate parenting, family conflict, marital conflict, and family hostility (Mash & Wolfe, 2018; Dishion & Patterson, 2016). Children whose parents reject, leave, coerce, or abuse them or fail to provide appropriate and consistent supervision are apparently more likely to develop conduct problems. Children also seem more prone to this disorder when their parents themselves are antisocial, display excessive anger, or have substance use, mood, or schizophrenic disorders (Wilson, 2017).

As they do with regard to other psychological disorders, developmental psychopathologists explain conduct disorder by pointing to *interactions* between these various factors (Fonagy & Luyten, 2018; Holz et al., 2018). Research shows, for example, that some, but not all, children who are maltreated go on to develop conduct disorder. Why only some? According to several studies, maltreated individuals are especially likely to develop conduct problems if they were also born with a particular variation of a gene called the *MAOA gene* (nicknamed the "human warrior gene") (Byrd et al., 2018; Taylor & Kim-Cohen, 2007). On the other hand, children who are similarly maltreated but who do *not* carry this particular genetic vulnerability are not nearly as likely to develop conduct disorder. And, finally, *unless* they are maltreated, people with this genetic variability do not have a particularly high risk for developing conduct disorder. In short, children with a problematic variation of the MAOA gene *and* a childhood filled with maltreatment are at high risk for conduct disorder, but children with only one of these factors are significantly less likely to develop the disorder.

#GenderGap

Today, one of every five teens arrested for violent crimes is female (DOJ, 2017).

How Do Clinicians Treat Conduct Disorder?

Because aggressive behaviors become more locked in with age, treatments for conduct disorder are generally most effective with children younger than age 13 (Cornacchio et al., 2017; Comer et al., 2013). Several different treatments have had moderate success,

parent management training A treatment approach for conduct disorder in which therapists combine family and cognitive-behavioral interventions to help improve family functioning and help parents deal with their children more effectively.

but no one of them alone appears to be the answer for this difficult problem (Bakker et al., 2017). Today's clinicians are increasingly combining several such approaches into a wide-ranging treatment program.

Parent Management Training Given the importance of family factors in conduct disorder, many therapists use a combination of family and cognitive-behavioral interventions, collectively known as **parent management training,** to help improve family functioning and help parents deal with their children more effectively (He et al., 2018; Kaminski & Claussen, 2017). Parent management training takes various forms, depending on the age of the child with conduct problems.

One form of parent management training, used with preschoolers, is called *parent–child interaction therapy* (Elkins et al., 2017; Hembree-Kigin & McNeil, 2013). Here therapists teach parents to work with their child positively, set appropriate limits, act consistently, be fair and structured in their discipline, and establish appropriate expectations regarding the child. Ideally, these efforts strengthen the parent–child relationship, improve the parents' attitudes, increase parental control, promote a consistent home environment, and produce improvements in the child's behavior. A related family intervention for preschoolers, *video modeling,* uses video tools to help achieve the same goals (Webster-Stratton, 2016).

In recent years, researchers have successfully used *videoconferencing* technology to offer parent–child interaction therapy in the actual homes of children with severe conduct problems. Using webcams, parents stream their home family interactions in real-time to a therapist located elsewhere, and the therapist, in turn, coaches the parents through a Bluetooth earpiece. Research suggests that this videoconferencing technique may lead to even more positive child improvements than those seen in parent–child interaction therapy delivered in a clinic (Comer et al., 2017, 2015).

Why might some children show more positive improvements when their therapist uses technology to treat them in their own homes?

If children with conduct problems are of school age, therapists may further engage the parents and child in *family therapy* (Vuori et al., 2017, 2015; Kazdin, 2012, 2010, 2002). They may guide the family to identify behaviors that are in need of change and then—with the aid of written manuals, rehearsals, practice, and homework—teach the parents how to stop rewarding unwanted behaviors and consistently reward proper behaviors. Like parent management training for preschoolers with conduct disorder, this enhanced approach for school-age children has often achieved a measure of success (Kaminski & Claussen, 2017; Forgatch & Patterson, 2010).

Many therapists further supplement parent management training with interventions in the children's schools, social lives, and the broader community—a combination of interventions called *multisystemic therapy.* Multisystemic therapists not only treat family dynamics; they also work to increase the amount of time children spend with positive children and role models instead of delinquent peers. Treatment goals may include improving grades or helping the child develop vocational skills, as well as promoting the child's participation in positive and structured activities, such as sports, school clubs, or neighborhood organizations. Although multisystemic therapy is typically applied to severe and complex cases of conduct disorder, research finds that this integrative approach often results in small but long-lasting positive effects (Bakker et al., 2017; Tan & Fajardo, 2017).

Lee Lorenz/The New Yorker Collection/The Cartoon Bank

"Is this the story you want to tell on your college application?"

AP Photo/Charles Krupa

Multiple traumas A number of children in the Boston area developed posttraumatic stress disorder and/or other psychological disorders in the aftermath of the Boston Marathon bombing in 2013. It turns out that their disorders were triggered not only by witnessing (in person or on television) the devastation produced by the bombing but also by the door-to-door searches for the suspects conducted by police in the days following the bombing (Comer et al., 2019, 2014). Here a woman carries her child from their home as a SWAT team enters to conduct one such search.

Child-Focused Treatments Treatments that focus primarily on the child with conduct disorder, particularly cognitive-behavioral interventions, have sometimes been helpful (Bakker et al., 2017; Kaminski & Claussen, 2017). In an approach called *problem-solving skills training,* therapists combine modeling, practice, role-playing, and systematic rewards to teach children constructive thinking and positive social behaviors. The therapists may play games and solve tasks with the children, and later help them apply the lessons and skills derived from the games and tasks to real-life situations.

In another child-focused approach, the *Coping Power Program,* children with conduct problems participate in group sessions that teach them to manage their anger more effectively, view situations in perspective, solve problems, become aware of their emotions, build social skills, set goals, and handle peer pressure. Studies indicate that this kind of approach does indeed help reduce aggressive behaviors and prevent substance use in adolescence (Helander et al., 2018; Powell et al., 2017).

Drug therapy has also been used for some children with conduct disorder. *Stimulant drugs* may help reduce their aggressive behaviors at home and at school, particularly if the children's symptoms further include impulsivity and overactivity (Balia et al., 2018; Haggerty, 2017).

Residential Treatment Residential treatment in the community has also helped some children. In one such approach, *treatment foster care,* delinquent boys and girls with conduct disorder are assigned to a foster home in the community by the juvenile justice system (Sinclair et al., 2016; Henggeler & Sheidow, 2012). While there, the children, foster parents, and birth parents all receive training and treatment interventions, including family therapy with both sets of parents, individual treatment for the child, and meetings with the school and with parole and probation officers. In addition, the children and their parents continue to receive treatment and support after the children leave foster care. In contrast to this form of residential treatment, institutionalization in so-called *juvenile training centers* has not met with much success (Stahlberg et al., 2010; Heilbrun et al., 2005). In fact, such institutions frequently serve to strengthen delinquent behavior rather than resocialize young offenders.

How might juvenile training centers themselves contribute to the high recidivism rate among teenage criminal offenders?

#HelpNeeded

Around 70 percent of children and teens in the juvenile justice system have at least one mental health condition (NAMI, 2018).

Prevention It may be that the best hope for dealing with the problem of conduct disorder lies in *prevention* programs that begin in the earliest stages of childhood (CDC, 2018; Toth et al., 2016). These programs try to change unfavorable social conditions before a conduct disorder is able to develop. Typically, the programs offer training opportunities for young people, recreational facilities, and health care. They may also seek to ease the stresses of poverty, promote more positive school environments, and improve parents' child-rearing skills. All such approaches work best when they educate and involve the family.

Elimination Disorders

Children with elimination disorders repeatedly urinate or pass feces in their clothes, in bed, or on the floor. They already have reached an age at which they are expected to control these bodily functions, and their symptoms are not caused by physical illness.

Enuresis

Enuresis is repeated involuntary (or in some cases intentional) bed-wetting or wetting of one's clothes. It typically occurs at night during sleep but may also occur during the day. Children must be at least 5 years of age to receive this diagnosis (Tu, Baskin, & Arnhym, 2017; APA, 2013). The problem may be triggered by stressful events, such as a hospitalization, entrance into school, or family problems.

The prevalence of enuresis decreases with age. As many as 33 percent of 5-year-old children have some bed-wetting and 16 percent meet the criteria for enuresis; in contrast, 5 percent of 10-year-olds and less than 2 percent of 15-year-olds have enuresis (Kosilov et al., 2018; Tu et al., 2017). Boys with the disorder outnumber girls by 2 to 1. Those with enuresis typically have a close relative (parent, sibling) who has had or will have the same disorder.

AP Photo/Katy Winn

The Bedwetter Outrageous comedian Sarah Silverman holds up a copy of her best-selling book *The Bedwetter.* In this memoir, she writes extensively about her childhood experiences with enuresis and other emotional difficulties—always with a blend of self-revelation, pain, and humor.

Theorists have proposed a range of possible causes for enuresis, but none of them has received strong research support (Tu et al., 2017; Kim et al., 2014). Most cases of the disorder correct themselves even without treatment. However, treatments, particularly cognitive-behavioral therapy, can speed up the process (Tu & Baskin, 2018). In a widely used classical conditioning approach, the *bell-and-battery technique,* a bell and a battery are wired to a pad consisting of two metallic foil sheets, and the entire apparatus is placed under the child at bedtime (Kosilov et al., 2018; Mowrer & Mowrer, 1938). A single drop of urine sets off the bell, awakening the child as soon as he or she starts to wet. Thus the bell (unconditioned stimulus) paired with the sensation of a full bladder (conditioned stimulus) produces the response of waking. Eventually, a full bladder alone awakens the child.

Another effective cognitive-behavioral treatment method is *dry-bed training.* In this approach children receive training in retention control, are awakened periodically during the night, practice getting out of bed and going to the bathroom, and are appropriately rewarded. Like the bell-and-battery technique, this behavioral approach is often effective.

Encopresis

Children with **encopresis,** also called soiling, repeatedly defecate into their clothing. The disorder is less common than enuresis, and it is also less well researched (Mash & Wolfe, 2018; Sood, 2018). This problem seldom occurs at night during sleep. It is usually involuntary, starts at the age of 4 or older, and affects about 1.5 to 4 percent of all children (see **Table 14-4**). The disorder is much more common in boys than in girls.

TABLE: 14-4

Comparison of Childhood Disorders

Disorder	Usual Age of Identification	Prevalence Among All Children	Gender with Greater Prevalence	Elevated Family History	Recovery by Adulthood
Separation anxiety disorder	Before 12 years	4%–10%	Females	Yes	Usually
Selective mutism	2–4 years	1%	Females	Yes	Often
Conduct disorder	7–15 years	5%–10%	Males	Yes	Often
Enuresis	5–8 years	7%	Males	Yes	Usually
Encopresis	After 4 years	1.5%–4%	Males	Unclear	Usually
ADHD	Before 12 years	7%	Males	Yes	Often
Autism spectrum disorder	0–3 years	2%	Males	Yes	Sometimes
Specific learning disorder	6–9 years	5%–10%	Males	Yes	Often
Intellectual disability	Before 10 years	1%–3%	Males	Unclear	Sometimes

Information from: AAIDD, 2018; Augustyn, 2018; CDC, 2018, 2017; Hamilton, 2018, 2017; Hannesdottir, 2018; Krull, 2018; Lerner et al., 2018; Pivalizza & Lalani, 2018; SMA, 2018; Sood, 2018; von Hahn, 2018, 2017; Matthys & Lochman, 2017; Tu et al., 2017; APA, 2013.

Encopresis causes intense social problems, shame, and embarrassment (Sood, 2018; NLM, 2015). Children who suffer from it usually try to hide their condition and to avoid situations, such as camp or school, in which they might embarrass themselves. It may stem from biological factors such as constipation, stress, improper toilet training, or a combination of these factors (Sood, 2018). Constipation, by far the most common cause, is a factor in 80 percent of cases. Because physical problems are so often linked to this disorder, a medical examination is typically conducted first.

The most common and successful treatments for encopresis are cognitive-behavioral and medical approaches or a combination of the two (Sood, 2018; Call et al., 2017). Treatment may include interventions to eliminate the children's constipation; biofeedback (see pages 259–260) to help the children better detect when their bowels are full; and the stimulation of regular bowel functioning with high-fiber diets, mineral oil, laxatives, and lubricants. Family therapy has also proved helpful.

... SUMMING UP

OPPOSITIONAL DEFIANT, CONDUCT, AND ELIMINATION DISORDERS

Children with oppositional defiant disorder argue repeatedly with adults, ignore adult rules and requests, and feel intense anger and resentment. Those with conduct disorder, a more severe pattern of rule breaking and aggressiveness, repeatedly violate the basic rights of others. These latter children often are violent and cruel and may deliberately destroy property, steal, and run away from home. Several kinds of conduct disorders have been identified, including an overt-destructive pattern, overt-nondestructive pattern, covert-destructive pattern, covert-nondestructive pattern, and relational aggression pattern. Clinicians have treated children with conduct disorder by using approaches such as parent management training (including parent–child interaction therapy), multisystemic therapy, problem-solving skills training, the Coping Power Program, and treatment foster care. A number of prevention programs have also been developed.

Children with an elimination disorder—enuresis or encopresis—repeatedly urinate or pass feces in inappropriate places. Cognitive-behavioral approaches, such as the bell-and-battery technique, are effective treatments for enuresis.

enuresis A childhood disorder marked by repeated bed-wetting or wetting of one's clothes.

encopresis A childhood disorder characterized by repeated defecating in inappropriate places, such as one's clothing.

neurodevelopmental disorders A group of disabilities—including ADHD, autism spectrum disorder, and intellectual disability—in the functioning of the brain that emerge at birth or during very early childhood and affect one's behavior, memory, concentration, or ability to learn.

attention-deficit/hyperactivity disorder (ADHD) A disorder marked by the inability to focus attention, or by overactive and impulsive behavior, or both.

Neurodevelopmental Disorders

Neurodevelopmental disorders are a group of disabilities in the functioning of the brain that emerge at birth or during very early childhood and affect the individual's behavior, memory, concentration, and/or ability to learn. As you read at the beginning of this chapter, some disorders first displayed during childhood subside as the person ages. However, the neurodevelopmental disorders often have a significant impact throughout the person's life.

Three of the most prominent neurodevelopmental disorders are *attention-deficit/hyperactivity disorder, autism spectrum disorder,* and *intellectual disability*. Each of these problems has been studied extensively. In addition, although this was not always so, clinicians now have a range of treatment approaches that can make a major difference in the lives of people with the disorders.

Attention-Deficit/Hyperactivity Disorder

Children with **attention-deficit/hyperactivity disorder (ADHD)** have great difficulty attending to tasks, or behave overactively and impulsively, or both (APA, 2013) (see **Table 14-5**). ADHD often appears before the child starts school, as with Ricky, one of the boys we met at the beginning of this chapter. Steven is another child whose symptoms began very early in life:

Steven's mother cannot remember a time when her son was not into something or in trouble. As a baby he was incredibly active, so active in fact that he nearly rocked his crib apart. All the bolts and screws became loose and had to be tightened periodically. Steven was also always into forbidden places, going through the medicine cabinet or under the kitchen sink. He once swallowed some washing detergent and had to be taken to the emergency room. As a matter of fact, Steven had many more accidents and was more clumsy than his older brother and younger sister. . . . He always seemed to be moving fast. His mother recalls that Steven progressed from the crawling stage to a running stage with very little walking in between.

Trouble really started to develop for Steven when he entered kindergarten. Since his entry into school, his life has been miserable and so has the teacher's. Steven does not seem capable of attending to assigned tasks and following instructions. He would rather be talking to a neighbor or wandering around the room without the teacher's permission. When he is seated and the teacher is keeping an eye on him to make sure that he works, Steven's body still seems to be in motion. He is either tapping his pencil, fidgeting, or staring out the window and daydreaming. Steven hates kindergarten and has few long-term friends; indeed, school rules and demands appear to be impossible challenges for him. The effects of this mismatch are now showing in Steven's schoolwork and attitude. He has fallen behind academically and has real difficulty mastering new concepts; he no longer follows directions from the teacher and has started to talk back.

(Gelfand, Jenson, & Drew, 1982, p. 256)

The symptoms of ADHD often feed into one another. Children who have trouble focusing attention may keep turning from task to task until they end up trying to run in several directions at once. Similarly, children who move constantly may find it hard to attend to tasks or show good judgment. In many cases, one of these symptoms stands out much more than the other. About half of the children with ADHD also have learning or communication problems; many perform poorly in school; a number have difficulty interacting with other children, and about 80 percent misbehave, often quite seriously (Mash & Wolfe, 2018). The children may also have great difficulty controlling their emotions, and some have anxiety or mood problems (Musser & Nigg, 2018).

Around 7 percent of all children display ADHD at any given time, as many as 70 percent of them boys (Krull, 2018; APA, 2013). Those whose parents have had ADHD

#SchoolPerformance

More than 90 percent of children with ADHD underachieve scholastically.

Between 23 and 32 percent of children with ADHD do not complete high school.

(ADDitude, 2017; Dendy, 2016; Rapport et al., 2008)

TABLE: 14-5

Dx Checklist

Attention-Deficit/Hyperactivity Disorder

1. Individual presents one or both of the following patterns:
   (a) For 6 months or more, individual frequently displays at least six of the following symptoms of inattention, to a degree that is maladaptive and beyond that shown by most similarly aged persons: • Unable to properly attend to details, or frequently makes careless errors • Finds it hard to maintain attention • Fails to listen when spoken to by others • Fails to carry out instructions and finish work • Disorganized • Dislikes or avoids mentally effortful work • Loses items that are needed for successful work • Easily distracted by irrelevant stimuli • Forgets to do many everyday activities.
   (b) For 6 months or more, individual frequently displays at least six of the following symptoms of hyperactivity and impulsivity, to a degree that is maladaptive and beyond that shown by most similarly aged persons: • Fidgets, taps hands or feet, or squirms • Inappropriately wanders from seat • Inappropriately runs or climbs • Unable to play quietly • In constant motion • Talks excessively • Interrupts questioners during discussions • Unable to wait for turn • Barges in on others' activities or conversations.
2. Individual displayed some of the symptoms before 12 years of age.
3. Individual shows symptoms in more than one setting.
4. Individual experiences impaired functioning.

Information from: APA, 2013.

are more likely than others to develop it. The disorder usually persists throughout childhood. Many children show a lessening of symptoms as they move into mid-adolescence, but as many as 60 percent of them, particularly those with more severe symptoms, continue to have ADHD as adults (Bukstein, 2018; APA, 2013). The symptoms of restlessness and overactivity are not usually as pronounced in adult cases.

ADHD is difficult to assess properly (Sibley, Campez, & Raiker, 2018). Ideally, the child's behavior should be observed in several environments (school, home, with friends) because the symptoms of hyperactivity and inattentiveness must be present across multiple settings in order for ADHD to be diagnosed (APA, 2013). A range of diagnostic interviews, ratings scales, and psychological tests should be used, but many children receive their diagnosis from pediatricians or family physicians rather than from a systematic mental health assessment. At most one-third of ADHD diagnoses are based on psychological or educational testing (Mattingly, Wilson, & Rostain, 2017; Millichap, 2010). Extensive studies indicate that ADHD is, in fact, overdiagnosed in the United States (Krull, 2018; Rydell et al., 2018).

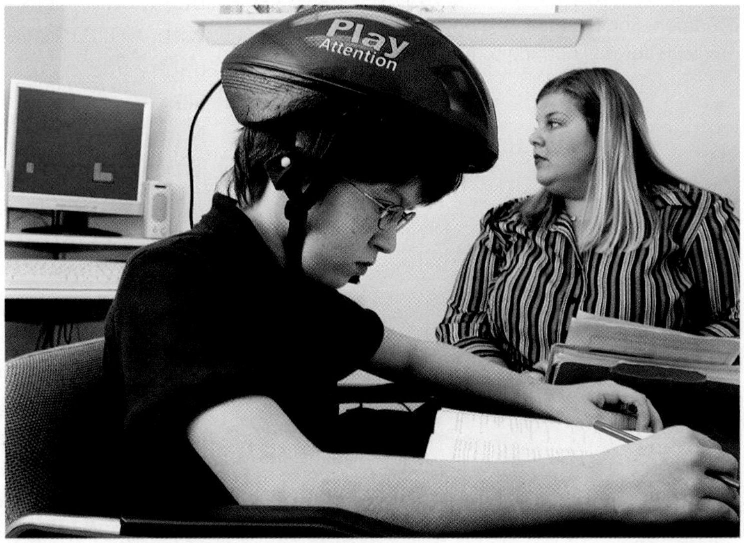

AP Photo/The Patriot-News, Dan Gleiter

"Playing" attention A range of techniques have been used to help understand and treat children with ADHD, including a computer program called *Play Attention*. Here, under the watchful eye of a behavior specialist, a child wears a bike helmet that measures brain waves while she performs tasks that require attention.

What Are the Causes of ADHD? Most of today's clinicians consider ADHD to result from several interacting causes. Biological factors have, for example, been identified in many cases (Baykal et al., 2019; Krull, 2018). To appreciate the brain factors that may contribute to ADHD, it is necessary to first understand normal human attention. There are two complementary processes that make up our moment-to-moment attention (Nigg, 2017, 2016). *Type 1 attention processes* are beyond our voluntary control and focus our attention on unexpected things that occur in our surroundings, such as sudden sounds or startling information. In contrast, *Type 2 attention processes* are mental activities that we control, and they involve our effortful focus of attention. In order to attend to our environment properly, we must have an appropriate interplay between our Type 1 and Type 2 attention processes. In many situations, for example,

Laurence Griffiths/Getty Images

Competition of another kind Simone Biles, the most decorated American gymnast in history, performs in the balance beam competition at the 2016 Olympic Games at the age of 19. After hackers revealed her medical records, Biles proudly announced that she suffers from ADHD and has received an exemption from the World Anti-Doping Association (WADA) to take methylphenidate for her condition. She tweeted: "Having ADHD and taking medicine for it is nothing to be ashamed of."

it is important that our Type 2 attention processes suppress our Type 1 attention alerts so that we can achieve our goals. If you were reading a book and suddenly there was lightning and thunder outside, your Type 1 attention processes might automatically reorient your focus momentarily to the unanticipated sight and sound. In order to resume reading, however, you would need to engage your Type 2 attention processes to consciously divert your attention from the distracting weather outside back to your book.

The symptoms of poor attention found in ADHD are commonly understood as a breakdown in the balance between Type 1 and Type 2 attention processes (Nigg, 2017, 2016). Children with ADHD have particular difficulty engaging Type 2 attention processes to override Type 1 "emergency alarms," and as a result they have trouble deliberately refocusing their attention to successfully function at home, at school, and in social situations.

Brain scan studies have identified an *attention circuit*—a number of structures that work together throughout the brain to bring about attention and to maintain a proper balance between Type I and Type 2 attention processes. You have read about some of the brain structures in this circuit (the *prefrontal cortex*, *anterior cingulate*, and *striatum*, for example) in our earlier discussions of other brain circuits. Other structures in the attention circuit, such as the *corona radiata* and the *longitudinal fasciculus*, are new to your reading. Research on the possible ties between the attention circuit and ADHD is still unfolding, but indications are that individuals with ADHD have a dysfunctional attention circuit, marked by poor communication (faulty *interconnectivity*) between the structures in this circuit, as well as by abnormal activity of the neurotransmitter *dopamine* throughout the circuit (Gehricke et al., 2017; Nigg, 2017, 2016). Given the dysfunctional attention circuit of these individuals, their Type 2 attention processes are, more often than not, simply unable to override their Type 1 attention processes.

In addition to biological factors, ADHD has been linked to high levels of stress and to family dysfunction (Krull, 2018). In fact, some studies suggest that these negative factors interfere with the development of effective Type 2 attention processes (Nigg, 2017, 2016). In addition, sociocultural theorists have noted that ADHD symptoms and a diagnosis of ADHD may themselves create interpersonal problems and produce further symptoms in the child. That is, children who are hyperactive tend to be viewed negatively by their peers and parents, have impaired peer relationships, and, in turn, come to view themselves negatively (Ros & Graziano, 2018).

How Is ADHD Treated? Almost 80 percent of all children and adolescents with ADHD receive treatment (CDC, 2018). The most commonly used approaches are drug therapy, cognitive-behavioral therapy, or a combination of the two (Krull, 2018).

Millions of children and adults with ADHD are currently treated with **methylphenidate,** a stimulant drug that actually has been available for decades, or with certain other stimulants. Although a variety of manufacturers now produce methylphenidate, the drug is often known to the public by its famous trade names, *Ritalin* or *Concerta*. As researchers have confirmed methylphenidate's quieting effects on children with ADHD and its ability to help them focus, solve complex tasks, perform better at school, and control aggression, use of the drug has increased enormously—according to some estimates, at least a threefold increase since 1990 alone (Hawk et al., 2018; Krull, 2018). Around 2.2 million children in the United States, 3 percent of all schoolchildren, regularly take methylphenidate for ADHD, a number that keeps rising

Why has there been a sizable increase in the diagnosis and treatment of ADHD over the past few decades?

#TheirWords

"I want to thank my mom and my dad up in heaven for disobeying the doctor's orders and not medicating their hyperactive girl and finding out what she was into instead."

Audra McDonald,
Tony Award–winning actress and singer

(Bachmann et al., 2017; Olfson et al., 2016). It is now the most common treatment for the disorder, although amphetamines such as *Adderall* are being increasingly prescribed for children with ADHD (Safer, 2016).

methylphenidate A stimulant drug, better known by the trade names *Ritalin* or *Concerta*, commonly used to treat ADHD.

Although widely used, methylphenidate has raised certain concerns. First, many clinicians worry about the possible long-term effects of these various stimulants, and others question whether the favorable findings of the drug studies (most of which have been done on non-Hispanic white American children) are applicable to children from minority groups (Ji et al., 2018; Cummings et al., 2017). Second, because ADHD is overdiagnosed in the United States, many children who are receiving stimulants may in fact have been inaccurately diagnosed (Rydell et al., 2018; Merten et al., 2017). Third, although stimulant medication can improve children's attention and behavioral control in the short term, studies do not always find that such treatment leads to meaningful long-term improvements or to positive changes in peer relationships or family dynamics (Rajeh et al., 2017).

Cognitive-behavioral therapy is often used for individuals with ADHD. In many cases, parents and teachers are taught how to apply the principles of operant conditioning—systematically rewarding the children for attentiveness or self-control. They may, for example, set up a *token economy program* in which the children receive tokens whenever they attend and respond appropriately—tokens that can later be exchanged for rewards of various kinds (Krull, 2018). Many children with ADHD also participate in eight-week therapeutic summer camps that provide systematic cognitive-behavioral interventions in classroom-like formats (Sibley et al., 2018; Evans, Owens, & Bunford, 2014).

Parents of children with ADHD may also receive *parent management training*, in which cognitive-behavioral techniques are combined with family interventions to help them deal with their children more effectively, similar to the training received by parents of children with conduct disorder. Moreover, parent management training and operant techniques may be combined with *school interventions* (Sanchez et al., 2018). In one such combination program, the *Daily Report Card* (*DRC*), a child's target behaviors—staying in his or her classroom seat, raising a hand to speak, and using an "inside voice"—are carefully evaluated, recorded on a DRC, and reinforced by teachers throughout the school day. At the end of the day, the teacher further provides the report card for the parents to see, and, if a sufficient number of target behaviors had been performed satisfactorily that day, the child is also given rewards at home (Cornacchio et al., 2017).

Jose Azel/Aurora

Cognitive-behavioral interventions Educational programs often use operant conditioning principles that clearly spell out targeted behaviors and rewards and systematically reinforce appropriate behaviors. Such programs can be particularly helpful for children with ADHD.

Research suggests that children with ADHD may improve most when they receive a combination of stimulant drug therapy and the cognitive-behavioral treatments we have been discussing (Kemper et al., 2018; Pelham et al., 2016). Combining drug therapies and cognitive-behavioral therapy is also desirable because, according to research, children who receive both treatments require lower levels of medication, meaning, of course, that they are less subject to the medication's undesired effects (Page et al., 2016).

Multicultural Factors and ADHD Throughout this book, you have seen that race and ethnicity often affect how people are diagnosed and treated for various psychological disorders. Thus, you should not be totally surprised that race and ethnicity also seem important with regard to ADHD.

A number of studies indicate that African American and Hispanic American children with significant attention and activity problems are less likely than non-Hispanic white American children with similar symptoms to be assessed for ADHD or receive a diagnosis of ADHD (Coker et al., 2016; Morgan & Farkas, 2016). Moreover, among those who do receive an ADHD diagnosis, children from racial/ethnic minorities are less

autism spectrum disorder A developmental disorder marked by extreme unresponsiveness to others, severe communication deficits, and highly repetitive and rigid behaviors, interests, and activities.

likely than non-Hispanic white American children to be treated with stimulant drugs or a combination of stimulants and cognitive-behavioral therapy—the interventions that seem to be of most help to individuals with ADHD (Ji et al., 2018; Pham et al., 2010). They are also less likely to receive adequate follow-up care to monitor their medication responses (Cummings et al., 2017).

In part, these racial and ethnic differences are tied to economic factors. Studies consistently show that poorer children are less likely than wealthier ones to be identified as having ADHD and are less likely to receive effective treatment; and racial/ethnic minority families have, on average, lower incomes and weaker insurance coverage. Some clinical theorists further believe that social bias and stereotyping may contribute to the racial and ethnic differences in diagnosis and treatment. They argue that our society often views the symptoms of ADHD as medical problems when exhibited by non-Hispanic white American children, but as indicators of poor parenting, lower IQ, substance use, or violence when displayed by African American and Hispanic American children (Duval-Harvey & Rogers, 2010; Kendall & Hatton, 2002). This notion has been supported by the finding that, all symptoms being equal, teachers and parents are more likely to conclude that overactive non-Hispanic white American children have ADHD, but that overactive African American or Hispanic American children have other kinds of difficulties (Alvarado & Modesto-Lowe, 2017; Hillemeier et al., 2007).

Whatever the precise reasons may be, it appears that children from racial and ethnic minority groups are less likely to receive a proper ADHD diagnosis and treatment. While many of today's clinical theorists correctly alert us to the possibility that ADHD may be generally overdiagnosed and overtreated, it is important to also recognize that children from minority backgrounds may, in fact, be underdiagnosed and undertreated.

Autism Spectrum Disorder

Autism spectrum disorder, a pattern first identified by psychiatrist Leo Kanner in 1943, is marked by extreme unresponsiveness to other people, severe communication deficits, and highly rigid and repetitive behaviors, interests, and activities (APA, 2013) (see **Table 14-6**). These symptoms appear early in life, typically before 3 years of age. Just two decades ago, the disorder seemed to affect around 1 out of every 2,000 children. However, in recent years there has been a steady increase in the number of children diagnosed with autism spectrum disorder, and it now appears that as many as 1 in 50 children display this pattern (Augustyn, 2018). Jennie is one such child:

Ms. D'Angelo [a special education teacher] first observed Jennie in a small classroom over a 5-day period. Jennie was often nonresponsive to others, especially her classmates, and rarely made eye contact with anyone. When left alone, Jennie would usually stand, put her hands over her throat, stick out her tongue, and make strange but soft noises. This would last for hours if she were left alone. When seated, Jennie rocked back and forth in her chair but never fell. Her motor skills seemed excellent and she could use crayons and manipulate paper when asked to do so. Her dexterity was also evident in her aggression, however. Jennie often grabbed people's jewelry and eyeglasses and flung them across the room. She moved quickly enough to accomplish this in less than two seconds. . . . Ms. D'Angelo noticed that Jennie was most aggressive when introduced to something or someone new. . . .

Ms. D'Angelo noticed that Jennie did not speak and vocalized only when making her soft sounds. . . [She] made no effort to communicate with others and was often oblivious to others. . . . Despite her lack of expressiveness, Jennie did understand and adhere to simple requests from others. She complied readily when told to get her lunch, use the bathroom, or retrieve an item in the classroom. . . .

Jennie had a "picture book" with photographs of items she might want or need. . . . When shown the book and asked to point, Jennie either pushed the book onto the desk if she did not want anything or pointed to one of five photographs (i.e., a lunch box, cookie, glass of water, favorite toy, or toilet) if she did want something. . . .

#StunningNumbers

Approximately 100 individuals are diagnosed with autism every day in the United States.

Each year, more children are diagnosed with autism than with cancer, diabetes, and AIDS combined.

(Information from: TACA, 2017)

> *[Her parents] said Jennie "had always been like this" and gave examples of her early impairment. Both said Jennie was "different" as a baby when she resisted being held and when she failed to talk by age 3 years. . . .*
>
> (Kearney, 2013, pp. 125–126)

Around 80 percent of all cases of autism spectrum disorder occur in boys. As many as 90 percent of children with the disorder remain significantly disabled into adulthood. They have enormous difficulty maintaining employment, performing household tasks, and leading independent lives (Lerner et al., 2018). Even the highest-functioning adults with autism typically have problems with closeness and empathy and have restricted interests and activities.

The individual's *lack of responsiveness and social reciprocity*—extreme aloofness, lack of interest in other people, low empathy, and inability to share attention with others—has long been considered a central feature of autism. Like Jennie, children with this disorder typically do not reach for their parents during infancy. Instead they may arch their backs when they are held and appear not to recognize or care about those around them. In a similar vein, unlike other children of the same age, children with autism typically do not include others in their play and do not represent social experiences when they are playing; they often fail to see themselves as others see them and have no desire to imitate or be like others (Augustyn, 2017).

Communication problems take various forms in autism spectrum disorder (Shire et al., 2018). Many people with the disorder have great difficulty understanding speech or using language for conversational purposes. In fact, like Jennie, at least a third fail to speak or develop language skills (Autism Speaks, 2018). Those who do talk may have rigid and repetitious speech patterns. One of the most common speech peculiarities is *echolalia,* the exact echoing of phrases spoken by others. The individuals repeat the words with the same accent or inflection, but with no sign of understanding or intent of communicating. Another speech oddity is *pronominal reversal,* or confusion of pronouns—for example, the use of "you" instead of "I." When hungry, a child with autism spectrum disorder might say, "Do you want dinner?"

The nonverbal behaviors of these individuals are often at odds with their efforts at verbal communication. They may not, for example, use a proper tone when talking. They may display few or no facial expressions or body gestures. And they may be incapable of maintaining proper eye contact during interactions. Recall, for example, that Jennie "rarely made eye contact with anyone."

People with autism also display a wide range of *highly rigid and repetitive behaviors, interests, and activities* that extend beyond speech patterns (Lerner et al., 2018). Typically they become very upset at minor changes in objects, persons, or routines and resist any efforts to change their own repetitive behaviors. Jennie's special education teacher noticed that she was most aggressive when introduced to something or someone new.

Similarly, some children with the disorder react with tantrums if a parent wears an unfamiliar pair of glasses, a chair is moved to a different part of the room, or a word in a song is changed. Many also become strongly attached to particular objects—plastic lids, rubber bands, buttons, water. They may collect these objects, carry them, or play with them constantly. Some are fascinated by movement and may watch spinning objects, such as fans, for hours.

People with autism may display *motor movements* that are unusual, rigid, and repetitive. They may jump, flap their arms, twist their hands and fingers, rock, walk on their toes, spin, and make faces. These acts are called *self-stimulatory*

TABLE: 14-6

Dx Checklist

Autism Spectrum Disorder
1. Individual displays continual deficiencies in various areas of communication and social interaction, including the following: • Social-emotional reciprocity • Nonverbal communication • Development and maintenance of relationships.
2. Individual displays significant restriction and repetition in behaviors, interests, or activities, including two or more of the following: • Exaggerated and repeated speech patterns, movements, or object use • Inflexible demand for same routines, statements, and behaviors • Highly restricted, fixated, and overly intense interests • Over- or underreactions to sensory input from the environment.
3. Individual develops symptoms by early childhood.
4. Individual experiences impaired functioning.

Information from: APA, 2013.

Blocking out the world An 8-year-old child with autism spectrum disorder peers vacantly through a hole in the netting of a baseball batting cage, seemingly unaware of other children and activities at the playground.

theory of mind An awareness that other people base their behaviors on their own beliefs, intentions, and other mental states, not on information that they have no way of knowing.

joint attention Sharing focus with other people on items or events in one's immediate surroundings, whether through shared eye-gazing, pointing, referencing, or other verbal or nonverbal indications that one is paying attention to the same object.

behaviors. Some individuals with the disorder also perform *self-injurious behaviors,* such as repeatedly lunging into or banging their head against a wall, pulling their hair, or biting themselves (Oliver et al., 2017).

The symptoms of autism spectrum disorder suggest a very disturbed and contradictory pattern of reactions to stimuli. Sometimes the individuals seem overstimulated by sights and sounds and appear to be trying to block them out (called *hyperreactivity*), while at other times they seem understimulated and appear to be performing self-stimulatory actions (called *hyporeactivity*). They may, for example, fail to react to loud noises yet turn around when they hear soda being poured.

What Are the Causes of Autism Spectrum Disorder? A variety of explanations have been offered for autism spectrum disorder. This is one disorder for which sociocultural explanations have probably been overemphasized. In fact, such explanations initially led investigators in the wrong direction. More recent work in the psychological and biological spheres has persuaded clinical theorists that cognitive limitations and brain abnormalities are the primary causes of the disorder.

SOCIOCULTURAL CAUSES At first, theorists thought that family dysfunction was the primary cause of autism spectrum disorder. When he first identified this disorder, for example, Kanner argued that particular personality characteristics of the parents created an unfavorable climate for development and contributed to the disorder (Kanner, 1954, 1943). He saw these parents as very intelligent yet cold—"refrigerator parents." These claims had enormous influence on the public and on the self-image of the parents themselves, but research has totally failed to support a picture of rigid, cold, rejecting, or disturbed parents (Lerner et al., 2018; Sicile-Kira, 2014).

PSYCHOLOGICAL CAUSES According to certain theorists, people with autism spectrum disorder have a central cognitive disturbance that makes normal communication and interactions impossible. One influential explanation holds that those with the disorder fail to develop a **theory of mind**—an awareness that other people base their behaviors on their own beliefs, intentions, and other mental states, not on information that they have no way of knowing (Jones et al., 2018; Mazza et al., 2017). (You may notice that theory of mind is similar to *mentalization,* which was discussed on page 413 in Chapter 13).

By 3 to 5 years of age, most normal children can take the perspective of another person into account and use it to anticipate what the person will do. In a way, they learn to read others' minds. Let us say, for example, that we watch Jessica place a marble in a container and then we observe Frank move the marble to a nearby room while Jessica is taking a nap. We know that later Jessica will search first in the container for the marble because she is not aware that Frank moved it. We know that because we take Jessica's perspective into account. A normal child would also anticipate Jessica's search correctly. A child with autism would not. He or she would expect Jessica to look in the nearby room because that is where the marble actually is. Jessica's own mental processes would be unimportant to the child.

Studies show that people with autism spectrum disorder do indeed have this kind of "mind-blindness," although they are not the only kinds of individuals with this limitation (Jones et al., 2018). They thus have great difficulty taking part in make-believe play, using language in ways that include the perspectives of others, developing relationships, or participating in human interactions.

People with autism also display deficiencies in **joint attention,** a cognitive limitation that is probably related to their theory of mind deficiency. They have great difficulty sharing focus with other people on items and events in their immediate surroundings, through mutual eye-gazing, making reference to observed objects, pointing, or other such acts (Mundy, 2018; Van Hecke, Oswald, & Mundy, 2016). When individuals with severe autism are around other people, they simply are not having a "shared" experience. Deficiencies in joint attention can greatly impair proper language development, since a core function of language is to direct someone else's attention.

The iPad breakthrough A child with autism works on an iPad as his teacher looks on. Electronic tablets provide enormous cognitive stimulation and pleasure for people with this disorder and often serve as helpful communication devices.

AP Photo/Daily Herald, Bev Horne

Linda Davidson/The Washington Post via Getty Images

Autistic and artistic High school student Austin Morrison (standing) rehearses for the play *Nerdicus (My Brother with Autism)*. Morrison, who himself has autism, stars in the play, which is about a child whose intellectual, adaptive, and language skills remain relatively strong despite his severe social interaction deficits and his highly rigid and repetitive behaviors. This higher-functioning pattern of autism was previously called *Asperger's disorder*, but it is now classified as autism spectrum disorder along with lower-functioning patterns.

Why do people with autism have these cognitive limitations? Most theorists point to biological factors that prevent proper cognitive development and functioning.

BIOLOGICAL CAUSES For years researchers have tried to determine what biological abnormalities might cause theory-of-mind deficits and the other features of autism spectrum disorder. They have not yet developed a complete biological explanation, but they have uncovered promising leads. First, examinations of the relatives of people with autism keep suggesting a *genetic factor* in this disorder. The prevalence of autism among their siblings, for example, is 10 to 20 percent, a rate much higher than the general population's (Autism Speaks, 2018). Moreover, the prevalence of autism among the identical twins of people with the disorder is 60 percent. Genetic studies are increasingly identifying specific genes that, in combination, increase the likelihood of developing autism spectrum disorder (Fakhoury, 2018).

Some studies have also linked autism spectrum disorder to *prenatal difficulties* or *birth complications* (Hisle-Gorman et al., 2018; Bernier & Dawson, 2016). For example, the chances of developing the disorder are higher when the mother had rubella (German measles) during pregnancy, was exposed to toxic chemicals before or during pregnancy, or had complications during labor or delivery.

In addition, researchers have identified specific *biological factors* that may contribute to autism spectrum disorder. Initially, investigators believed that the abnormal activity or anatomy of a single brain structure, the *cerebellum*, might be responsible for the disorder, partly because this structure helps control a person's ability to rapidly shift attention (Bernier & Dawson, 2016). Cerebellum abnormalities are still considered a possible factor in the development of autism spectrum disorder, but research over the past two decades has also tied the disorder to other brain structures, including the *corpus callosum, prefrontal cortex, amygdala, orbitofrontal cortex, cingulate cortex, striatum*, and *thalamus* (Mundy, 2018; Kim et al., 2016). Dysfunction by any of these brain structures may contribute to the disorder. However, in line with scientists' growing appreciation of the importance of brain circuits, a growing number of theorists believe that flawed communication (flawed *interconnectivity*) among these and perhaps other brain structures may be the key to autism spectrum disorder. In support of this belief, many studies of people with autism and of animals that display autistic-like behavior indicate poor interconnectivity—sometimes hyperconnectivity and sometimes hypoconnectivity—between these various structures (Xu et al., 2018; Fingher et al., 2017). It is tempting to

#

#FamilyCost

On average, the lifetime cost of rearing an individual with autism ranges from $3.5 million to $5 million—at least 3 times the cost of rearing a nonautistic individual (Autism Speaks, 2018; NAN, 2017).

#

#TheirWords

"The one common denominator for all of the young children [with autism] is that early intervention does work, and it seems to improve the prognosis."

Temple Grandin, professor and individual with autism

conclude from such findings that there is an autism-related brain circuit whose dysfunction is the key to autism spectrum disorder, but research has yet to establish the existence or nature of such a circuit (Muhle et al., 2018; Twining et al., 2017).

Finally, because it has received so much attention over the past 20 years, it is worth mentioning a biological explanation for autism spectrum disorder that has *not* been borne out—the *MMR vaccine* theory. In 1998 a team of investigators published a study suggesting that a *postnatal event*—the vaccine for measles, mumps, and rubella (*MMR vaccine*)—might produce autistic symptoms in some children (Wakefield et al., 1998). Specifically, the researchers thought that for certain children, this vaccine, which is usually given to children between the ages of 12 and 15 months, produces an increase in the measles virus throughout the body, which in turn causes the onset of a powerful stomach disease and, ultimately, autism spectrum disorder.

However, virtually all research conducted since 1998 has argued against this theory (Drutz, 2017; Taylor, Swerdfeger, & Eslick, 2014). For example, epidemiological studies repeatedly have found that children throughout the world who receive the MMR vaccine have the same prevalence of autism as those who do not receive the vaccine. Moreover, careful reexaminations of the original study have indicated that it was methodologically flawed, perhaps even manipulated, and that it failed to demonstrate any relationship between the MMR vaccine and the development of autism spectrum disorder (*Lancet*, 2010). Unfortunately, despite this clear refutation, many concerned parents now choose to withhold the MMR vaccine from their young children, leaving them highly vulnerable to diseases that can be very dangerous.

Why do many people still believe that the MMR vaccine causes autism spectrum disorder, despite so much evidence to the contrary?

How Do Clinicians and Educators Treat Autism Spectrum Disorder?

Treatment can help people with autism spectrum disorder adapt better to their environment, although no treatment yet known totally reverses the autistic pattern. Treatments of particular help are *cognitive-behavioral therapy, communication training, parent training,* and *community integration.* In addition, psychotropic drugs and certain vitamins have sometimes helped when combined with other approaches (Weissman & Bridgemohan, 2018).

COGNITIVE-BEHAVIORAL THERAPY For more than 50 years, cognitive-behavioral approaches have been used in cases of autism, particularly behavior-focused interventions that teach the individuals new, appropriate behaviors—including speech, social skills, classroom skills, and self-help skills—while seeking to reduce their negative, dysfunctional behaviors. Using the principles of *modeling,* therapists often demonstrate desired behaviors and guide the persons with autism to imitate them. Using the principles of *operant conditioning,* the clinicians reinforce desired behaviors, first by "shaping" them—breaking them down so they can be learned step by step—and then rewarding each step clearly and consistently. With careful planning and execution, these procedures often produce new, more functional behaviors.

Learning to communicate Cognitive-behavioral clinicians and educators have had success teaching many children with autism spectrum disorder to communicate. Here a speech language specialist combines cognitive-behavioral techniques with the use of a communication board to teach a 3-year-old child how to express herself better and understand others.

AP Photo/Albuquerque Journal, Pat Vasquez-Cunningham

A pioneering, long-term study compared the progress of two groups of children with autism spectrum disorder (Lovaas, 2003, 1987; McEachin et al., 1993). Nineteen received the treatments described above, and 19 served as a control group. Treatment began when the children were 3 years old and continued until they were 7. By the age of 7, the group that received behavior-focused interventions was doing better in school and scoring higher on intelligence tests than the control group. Many were able to go to school in regular classrooms. The gains continued into the research participants' teenage years. Given the favorable findings of this and similar studies, many clinicians now consider early intensive behavior-focused programs to be the preferred treatment for autism spectrum disorder (Rivard et al., 2018; Weissman & Bridgemohan, 2018, 2017).

Therapies for individuals with this disorder tend to provide the most benefit when they are started early in life (Green & Garg, 2018; Landa, 2018). Very young children with autism often begin with services at home, but ideally, by the age of 3 they attend special programs outside the home. Typically, services are provided by education, health, or social service agencies until the children reach 3; then the department of education for each state determines which specific services the children will receive.

Given the recent increases in the prevalence of this disorder, many school districts are now trying to provide education and training for the children in special classes that operate at the district's own facilities (Smith et al., 2017; Iadarola et al., 2015). However, most school districts remain ill-equipped to meet the profound needs of students with autism. The most fortunate of these students are sent by their school districts to attend special schools, where education and therapy are combined. At such schools, specially trained teachers help the children improve their skills, behaviors, and interactions with the world. Higher-functioning students with autism may eventually spend at least part of their school day returning to standard classrooms in their own school district (Weissman & Bridgemohan, 2018, 2017).

augmentative communication system A method for enhancing the communication skills of people with autism spectrum disorder, intellectual disability, or cerebral palsy by teaching them to point to pictures, symbols, letters, or words on a communication board or computer.

COMMUNICATION TRAINING As you read earlier, even when given intensive treatment, at least a third of people with autism spectrum disorder remain speechless. To help address this, they are often taught other forms of communication, including *sign language* and *simultaneous communication,* a method combining sign language and speech. They may also learn to use **augmentative communication systems,** such as "communication boards" or computers that use pictures, symbols, or written words to represent objects or needs (Weissman & Bridgemohan, 2018). A child may point to a picture of a fork to give the message "I am hungry," for instance, or point to a radio for "I want music." Recall, for example, the use of a "picture book" by Jennie, the child whose case introduced this section.

Some autism programs further try to improve language and communication skills by working on the individual's capacity for *joint attention,* the cognitive ability that you read about above. The clinician teaches the individual to gaze into the eyes of others, make reference to observed objects, point at objects, and perform other "sharing" behaviors when he or she is involved in joint activities with other people. Studies have

AP Photo/Javier Galeano

Animal connection At the National Aquarium in Havana, Cuba, therapists host regular sessions of stroking and touching dolphins, sea tortoises, and sea lions for children. These sessions have helped many children with autism spectrum disorder and others with intellectual disability to become more spontaneous, independent, and sociable.

found that treating joint attention deficiencies during the preschool years can have a positive impact on communication and language development as well as other features of autism (Shire et al., 2017).

PARENT TRAINING Today's treatment programs for autism spectrum disorder involve parents in a variety of ways. Cognitive-behavioral programs, for example, often train parents so that they can apply conditioning and skill-building techniques at home (Smith et al., 2018; Ginn et al., 2017). Instruction manuals for parents and home visits by teachers and other professionals are typically included in such programs. Research consistently has demonstrated that the improvements in behavior produced by trained parents are often equal to or greater than those generated by teachers.

In addition to parent-training programs, individual therapy and support groups are becoming more available to help the parents of children with autism deal with their own emotions and needs (Da Paz & Wallander, 2017). A number of parent associations and lobbies also offer emotional support and practical help.

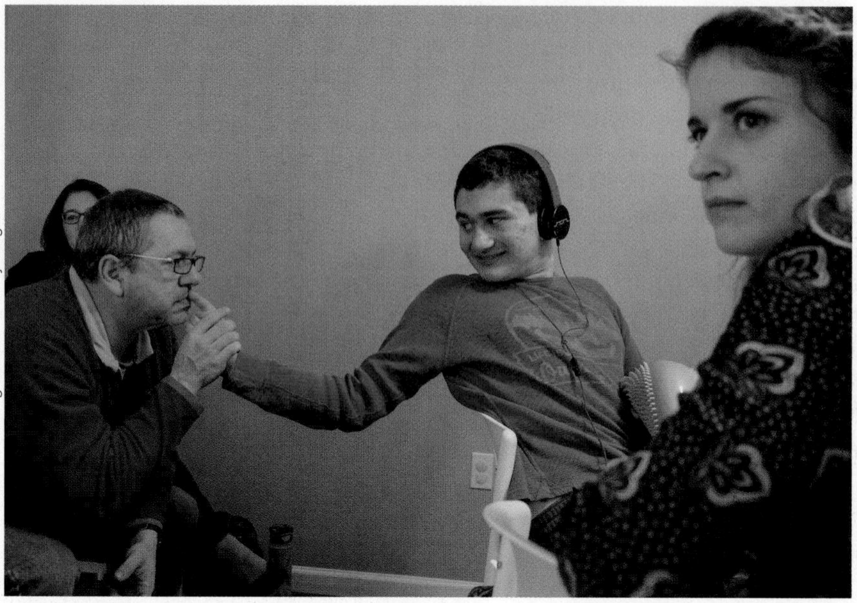
Jahi Chikwendiu/The Washington Post via Getty Images

A special bond Given the hard road they must travel together, the bond between children with autism and their parents is often especially close and intense. Here Gordy Baylinson, who has autism and is nonverbal, reaches back to caress the face of his father during a therapy session at Growing Kids Therapy Center in Herndon, Virginia.

COMMUNITY INTEGRATION Many of today's school-based and home-based programs for autism spectrum disorder teach self-help, self-management, and living, social, and work skills as early as possible to help the individuals function better in their communities. In addition, greater numbers of carefully run *group homes* and *sheltered workshops* are now available for teenagers and adults with autism. These and related programs help the individuals become a part of their community; they also reduce the concerns of aging parents whose children will always need supervision.

Intellectual Disability

Ed Murphy, aged 26, can tell us what it's like to be considered intellectually disabled or, as it was called in his day, "mentally retarded":

> *What is retardation? It's hard to say. I guess it's having problems thinking. Some people think that you can tell if a person is retarded by looking at them. If you think that way you don't give people the benefit of the doubt. You judge a person by how they look or how they talk or what the tests show, but you can never really tell what is inside the person.*
>
> *(Bogdan & Taylor, 1976, p. 51)*

For much of his life Ed was considered intellectually disabled and was educated and cared for in special institutions. During his adult years, clinicians discovered that Ed's intellectual ability was in fact higher than had been assumed. In the meantime, however, he had lived the childhood and adolescence of an intellectually disabled person, and his statement reveals the kinds of difficulties often faced by people with this disability.

In DSM-5, the term "mental retardation" has been replaced by *intellectual disability*. This term is applied to a varied population, including children in institutional wards who rock back and forth, young people who work in special job programs, and men and women who raise and support their families by working at jobs that are modestly demanding. As many as 3 of every 100 people meet the criteria for this diagnosis (Baldor, 2018). Around three-fifths of them are male, and the vast majority display a *mild* level of the disability.

People receive a diagnosis of **intellectual disability (ID)** when they display general *intellectual functioning* that is well below average, in combination with poor *adaptive*

intellectual disability (ID) A disorder marked by intellectual functioning and adaptive behavior that are well below average. Previously called *mental retardation.*

intelligence quotient (IQ) A score derived from intelligence tests that theoretically represents a person's overall intellectual capacity.

behavior (APA, 2013). That is, in addition to having a low IQ (a score of 70 or below), a person with intellectual disability has great difficulty in areas such as communication, home living, self-direction, work, or safety. The symptoms also must appear before the age of 18 (see **Table 14-7**).

Ben McCanna/Portland Press Herald via Getty Images

Normal needs People with intellectual disability have normal interpersonal and sexual needs—needs for which they may receive training and supervision in various clinical programs. Here a couple with Down syndrome twirl each other on the dance floor during the Night to Shine—a dance party in Portland, Maine, for people with special needs.

Assessing Intelligence Educators and clinicians administer intelligence tests to measure intellectual functioning (see Chapter 3). These tests consist of a variety of questions and tasks that rely on different aspects of intelligence, such as knowledge, reasoning, and judgment. Having difficulty in just one or two of these subtests or areas of functioning does not necessarily reflect low intelligence (see ***PsychWatch*** on page 463). It is an individual's overall test score, or **intelligence quotient (IQ),** that is thought to indicate general intellectual ability.

Many theorists have questioned whether IQ tests are indeed valid. Do they actually measure what they are supposed to measure? The correlation between IQ and school performance is rather high—around .50—indicating that many children with lower IQs do, as one might expect, perform poorly in school, while many of those with higher IQs perform better (Sternberg et al., 2001). At the same time, the correlation also suggests that the relationship is far from perfect. That is, a particular child's school performance is often higher or lower than his or her IQ might predict. Moreover, the accuracy of IQ tests at measuring extremely low intelligence has not been evaluated adequately, so it is difficult to properly assess people with severe intellectual disability (AAIDD, 2018).

Are there other kinds of intelligence that IQ tests might fail to assess? What might that suggest about the validity and usefulness of these tests?

Intelligence tests also appear to be socioculturally biased, as you read in Chapter 3. Children reared in households at the middle and upper socioeconomic levels tend to have an advantage on the tests because they are regularly exposed to the kinds of language and thinking that the tests evaluate. The tests rarely measure the "street sense" needed for survival by people who live in poor, crime-ridden areas—a kind of knowhow that certainly requires intellectual skills. Members of cultural minorities and people for whom English is a second language also often appear to be at a disadvantage in taking these tests.

If IQ tests do not always measure intelligence accurately and objectively, then the diagnosis of intellectual disability also may be biased. That is, some people may receive the diagnosis partly because of test inadequacies, cultural differences, discomfort with the testing situation, or the bias of a tester.

Assessing Adaptive Functioning Diagnosticians cannot rely solely on a cutoff IQ score of 70 to determine whether a person suffers from intellectual disability. Some people with a low IQ are quite capable of managing their lives and functioning independently, while others are not. The cases of Brian and Jeffrey show the range of adaptive abilities.

Brian comes from a lower-income family. He always has functioned adequately at home and in his community. He dresses and feeds himself and even takes care of himself each day until his mother returns home from work. He also plays well with his friends. At school, however, Brian refuses to participate or do his homework. He seems ineffective, at times lost, in the classroom. Referred to a school psychologist by his teacher, he received an IQ score of 60.

Jeffrey comes from an upper-middle-class home. He was always slow to develop, and sat up, stood, and talked late. During his infancy and toddler years, he was put in a special stimulation

(continued on the next page)

TABLE: 14-7

Dx Checklist

Intellectual Disability

1. Individual displays deficient intellectual functioning, as reflected by clinical assessment and intelligence tests.
2. Individual displays deficient adaptive functioning in at least one area of daily life, such as communication, social involvement, or personal independence, across home, school, work, or community settings. The limitations extend beyond those of most similarly aged persons and necessitate ongoing support at school or work, or with independent living.
3. The deficits begin during the developmental period (before the age of 18).

Information from: APA, 2013.

program and given special help and attention at home. Still Jeffrey has trouble dressing himself today and cannot be left alone in the backyard lest he hurt himself or wander off into the street. Schoolwork is very difficult for him. The teacher must work slowly and provide individual instruction for him. Tested at age 6, Jeffrey received an IQ score of 60.

Brian seems well adapted to his environment outside school. Jeffrey's limitations, however, are pervasive. In addition to his low IQ score, Jeffrey has difficulty meeting challenges at home and elsewhere. Thus a diagnosis of intellectual disability may be more appropriate for Jeffrey than for Brian.

Several scales have been developed to assess adaptive behavior. Here again, however, some people function better in their lives than the scales predict, while others fall short. Thus to properly diagnose intellectual disability, clinicians should probably observe the adaptive functioning of each individual in his or her everyday environment, taking both the person's background and the community's standards into account. Even then, such judgments may be subjective, as clinicians may not be familiar with the standards of a particular culture or community.

#TheirWords

"The IQ test was invented to predict academic performance, nothing else. If we wanted something that would predict life success, we'd have to invent another test completely."

Robert Zajonc, psychologist, 1984

What Are the Features of Intellectual Disability? The most consistent feature of intellectual disability is that the person learns very slowly (AAIDD, 2018; Sturmey & Didden, 2014). Other areas of difficulty are attention, short-term memory, planning, and language (Burack et al., 2016). Those who are institutionalized with this disability are particularly likely to have these limitations. It may be that the unstimulating environment and minimal interactions with staff in many institutions contribute to such difficulties. Traditionally, four levels of intellectual disability have been distinguished: *mild* (IQ 50–70), *moderate* (IQ 35–49), *severe* (IQ 20–34), and *profound* (IQ below 20).

Mild ID Some 80 to 85 percent of all people with intellectual disability fall into the category of *mild ID* (IQ 50–70). This is sometimes called the "educable" level because the individuals can benefit from schooling and can support themselves as adults. Mild ID is not usually recognized until children enter school and are assessed there. These children demonstrate rather typical language, social, and play skills, but they need assistance when under stress (Pivalizza & Lalani, 2018). The intellectual performance of individuals with mild ID often seems to improve with age; some even seem to leave the label behind when they leave school, and they go on to function well in the community (Sturmey & Didden, 2014). Their jobs tend to be unskilled or semiskilled.

Breaking the barrier Thirty-one-year-old Noelia Garella (center) reads a book to her preschool students in Cordoba, Argentina. She is one of but a few persons in the world with intellectual disability who work as public school teachers. When she was a child, a nursery school rejected her as "a monster."

Diego Lima/AFP/Getty Images

Research has often linked mild ID to sociocultural and psychological causes, particularly poor and unstimulating environments during a child's early years, inadequate parent–child interactions, and insufficient learning experiences (Pivalizza & Lalani, 2018). These relationships have been observed in studies comparing deprived and enriched environments. In fact, some community programs have sent workers into the homes of young children with low IQ scores to help enrich the environment there, and their interventions have often improved the children's functioning. When continued, programs of this kind also help improve the person's later performance in school and adulthood (Ramey, 2018; Ramey & Ramey, 2007, 2004).

Although sociocultural and psychological factors seem to be key causes of mild ID, at least some biological factors also may be operating. Studies

PSYCHWATCH

Reading and 'Riting and 'Rithmetic

Around 15 to 20 percent of all children, boys more often than girls, develop particularly slowly and function poorly in a single area such as learning, communication, or motor coordination (Poletti et al., 2018; CDC, 2017). The children do not suffer from intellectual disability, and in fact they are often very bright, yet their problems may interfere with school performance, daily living, and in some cases social interactions. Similar difficulties may be seen in the children's close biological relatives (von Hahn, 2017, 2016). According to DSM-5, many of these children are suffering from a specific learning disorder, communication disorder, or developmental coordination disorder—each a kind of neurodevelopmental disorder.

Children with a *specific learning disorder* have significant difficulties acquiring reading, writing, arithmetic, or mathematical reasoning skills (Poletti et al., 2018). Across the United States, children with such problems comprise the largest subgroup of those placed in special education classes (von Hahn, 2017). Some of these children read slowly or inaccurately or have difficulty understanding the meaning of what they are reading, difficulties also known as *dyslexia* (Hamilton, 2018). Others spell or write very poorly. And still others have great trouble remembering number facts, performing calculations, or reasoning mathematically.

Libor Sojka/CTK via AP Images

A special pair of glasses One of several explanations for dyslexia is that some people with this disorder have a significant visual processing problem. Thus various kinds of special 3D glasses, modeled here by this child, have been developed to help diagnose and treat the disorder.

The *communication disorders* include language disorder, speech sound disorder, and childhood-onset fluency disorder (stuttering) (Lieberman, 2018; APA, 2013; Gillam & Petersen, 2011). Children with *language disorder* may have persistent trouble using language to express themselves, struggle at learning new words, or confine their speech to short simple sentences. Children with *speech sound disorder* may have persistent difficulties in speech production or speech fluency. Some, for example, cannot make correct speech sounds at an appropriate age, resulting in speech that sounds like baby talk. People who display *stuttering* may frequently repeat, prolong, or interject sounds when they speak, pause before finishing a word, or experience excessive tension in the muscles they use for speech.

Finally, children with *developmental coordination disorder* perform coordinated motor activities at a level well below that of others their age (Hamilton, 2017; APA, 2013). Younger children with this disorder are clumsy and slow to master skills such as tying shoelaces, buttoning shirts, and zipping pants. Older children with the disorder may have great difficulty assembling puzzles, building models, playing ball, and printing or writing.

Studies have linked these various disorders to genetic factors, brain abnormalities, birth injuries, lead poisoning, inappropriate diet, sensory or perceptual dysfunction, and poor teaching (Hamilton, 2018, 2017; von Hahn, 2018, 2017, 2016). Some of the disorders respond to special treatment approaches. Reading therapy, for example, is very helpful in mild cases of dyslexia, and speech therapy brings about complete recovery in many cases of speech sound disorder. Furthermore, the various disorders often disappear before adulthood, even without any treatment.

suggest, for example, that a mother's moderate drinking, drug use, or malnutrition during pregnancy may lower her child's intellectual potential (CDC, 2017; Popova et al., 2017). Malnourishment during a child's early years also may hurt his or her intellectual development, although this effect can usually be reversed at least partly if a child's diet is improved before too much time goes by.

Moderate, Severe, and Profound ID Approximately 10 percent of those with intellectual disability function at a level of *moderate ID* (IQ 35–49). They typically receive their diagnosis earlier in life than do individuals with mild ID, as they demonstrate clear deficits in language development and play during their preschool years. By middle school they further show significant delays in their acquisition of reading and number skills and adaptive skills. By adulthood, however, many individuals with moderate ID manage to develop a fair degree of communication skill, learn to care for themselves, benefit from vocational training, and can work in unskilled or semiskilled jobs, usually under supervision. Most also function well in the community if they have supervision (AAIDD, 2018).

#

#TheirWords

"Intelligence is the ability to adapt to change."
Stephen Hawking, physicist

Approximately 3 to 4 percent of people with intellectual disability display *severe ID* (IQ 20–34). They typically demonstrate basic motor and communication deficits during infancy. Many also show signs of neurological dysfunction and have an increased risk for brain seizure disorder. In school, they may be able to string together only two or three words when speaking. They usually require careful supervision, profit somewhat from vocational training, and can perform only basic work tasks in structured and sheltered settings. Their understanding of communication is usually better than their speech. Most are able to function well in the community if they live in group homes, in community nursing homes, or with their families (AAIDD, 2018).

Around 1 to 2 percent of all people with intellectual disability function at a level of *profound ID* (IQ below 20). This level is very noticeable at birth or early infancy. With training, people with profound ID may learn or improve basic skills such as walking, some talking, and feeding themselves. They need a very structured environment, with close supervision and considerable help, including a one-to-one relationship with a caregiver, in order to develop to the fullest (AAIDD, 2018). Profound (and severe) levels of intellectual disability often appear as part of larger syndromes that include severe physical handicaps.

What Are the Biological Causes of Intellectual Disability? As you read earlier, the primary causes of mild ID are environmental, although biological factors may also be operating in many cases. In contrast, the main causes of moderate, severe, and profound ID are biological, although people who function at these levels also are strongly affected by their family and social environment (Mary et al., 2018; Reichenberg et al., 2016). The biological causes include chromosomal abnormalities, metabolic disorders, prenatal problems, birth complications, and childhood diseases and injuries.

CHROMOSOMAL CAUSES The most common of the chromosomal disorders that lead to intellectual disability is **Down syndrome,** named after Langdon Down, the British physician who first identified it. Down syndrome occurs in fewer than 1 of every 1,000 live births, but the rate increases significantly when the mother's age is over 35. Many older expectant mothers are now encouraged to undergo prenatal testing during the early months of pregnancy to identify Down syndrome and other chromosomal abnormalities.

People with Down syndrome may have a small head, flat face, slanted eyes, high cheekbones, and, in some cases, protruding tongue. The latter may affect their ability to pronounce words clearly. They are often very affectionate with family members but in general display the same range of personality characteristics as people in the general population.

Several types of chromosomal abnormalities may cause Down syndrome. The most common type (94 percent of cases) is *trisomy 21,* in which the person has three free-floating 21st chromosomes instead of two (Weremowicz, 2018). Most people with Down syndrome range in IQ from 35 to 55. The individuals appear to age early, and many even show signs of neurocognitive decline as they approach 40 (Ostermaier, 2018). It appears that Down syndrome and early neurocognitive decline often occur together because the genes that produce them are located close to each other on chromosome 21 (Hithersay et al., 2017).

Fragile X syndrome is the second most common chromosomal cause of intellectual disability. Children born with a fragile X chromosome (that is, an X chromosome with a genetic abnormality that leaves it prone to breakage and loss) generally display mild to moderate degrees of intellectual dysfunction, language impairments, and in some cases, behavioral problems (Dahlhaus, 2018). Typically, they are shy and anxious.

#

#SexChromosomes

The 23rd chromosome, whose abnormality causes fragile X syndrome, is the smallest chromosome.

The 23rd chromosome determines a person's sex and so is also referred to as the sex chromosome.

In males, the 23rd chromosome pair consists of an X chromosome and a Y chromosome.

In females, the 23rd chromosome pair consists of two X chromosomes.

METABOLIC CAUSES In metabolic disorders, the body's breakdown or production of chemicals is disturbed. The metabolic disorders that affect intelligence and development are typically caused by the pairing of two defective *recessive* genes, one from each

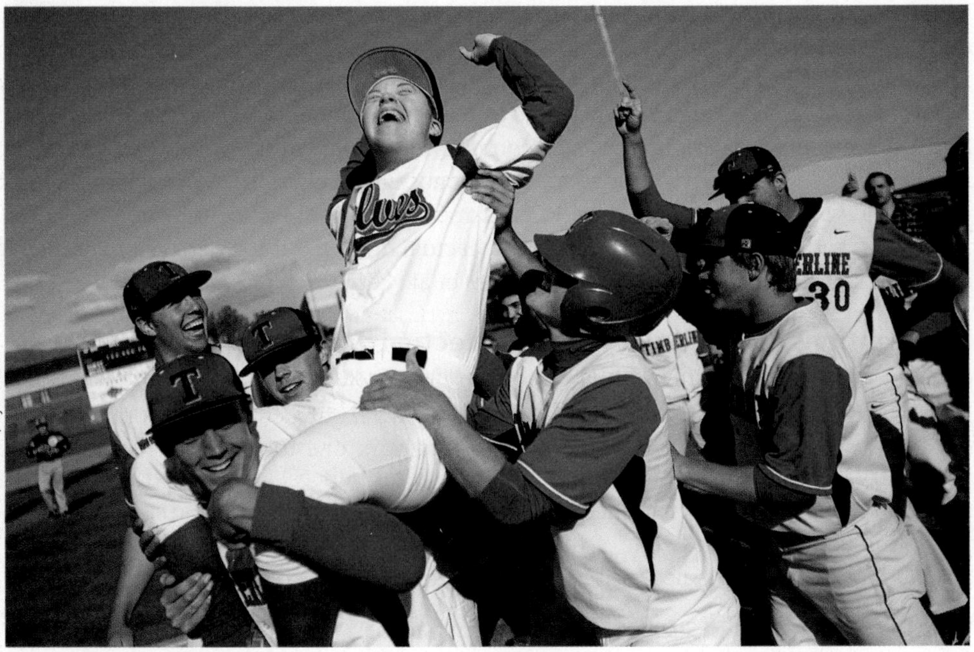

AP Photo/The Idaho Statesman, Kyle Green

Reaching higher Today people with Down syndrome are viewed as individuals who can learn and accomplish many things in their lives. Eddie Gordon, a teenager with Down syndrome, is lifted into the air in celebration by his Timberline High School baseball teammates. He has just rounded the bases during his turn as an honorary lead-off batter.

parent. Although one such gene would have no influence if it were paired with a normal gene, its pairing with another defective gene leads to major problems for the child.

The most common metabolic disorder to cause intellectual disability is *phenylketonuria (PKU)*, which strikes 1 of every 14,000 children. Babies with PKU appear normal at birth but cannot break down the amino acid *phenylalanine*. The chemical builds up and is converted into substances that poison the system, causing severe intellectual dysfunction and several other symptoms. Today infants can be screened for PKU, and if started on a special diet before 3 months of age, they may develop normal intelligence (van Spronsen et al., 2017).

PRENATAL AND BIRTH-RELATED CAUSES As a fetus develops, major physical problems in the pregnant mother can threaten the child's prospects for a normal life (AAIDD, 2018). When a pregnant woman has too little iodine in her diet, for example, her child may be born with *cretinism*, also called *severe congenital hypothyroidism*, marked by an abnormal thyroid gland, slow development, intellectual disability, and a dwarflike appearance. This condition is rare today because the salt in most diets now contains extra iodine. Also, any infant born with this problem may quickly be given thyroid extract to bring about normal development.

Other prenatal problems may also cause intellectual disability. As you read in Chapter 10, children whose mothers drink too much alcohol during pregnancy may be born with **fetal alcohol syndrome,** a group of very serious problems that includes mild to severe ID (CDC, 2018; Popova et al., 2017). It is estimated that 120,000 children are born with fetal alcohol syndrome each year (Popova et al., 2017). In fact, a generally safe level of alcohol consumption during pregnancy has not been established by research. In addition, certain maternal infections during pregnancy—*rubella* (German measles) and *syphilis*, for example—may cause childhood problems that include intellectual disability.

Birth complications also can lead to problems in intellectual functioning. A prolonged period without oxygen (*anoxia*) during or after delivery can cause brain damage and intellectual disability in a baby. In addition, although premature birth does not necessarily lead to long-term problems for children, researchers have found that some babies with a premature birth weight of less than 3.5 pounds display low intelligence (Oudgenoeg-Paz et al., 2017).

Down syndrome A form of intellectual disability caused by an abnormality in the 21st chromosome.

fetal alcohol syndrome A group of problems in a child, including lower intellectual functioning, low birth weight, and irregularities in the hands and face, that result from excessive alcohol intake by the mother during pregnancy.

CHILDHOOD PROBLEMS After birth, particularly up to age 6, certain injuries and accidents can affect intellectual function and in some cases lead to intellectual disability. Poisonings, serious head injuries caused by accident or abuse, excessive exposure to X-rays, and excessive use of certain drugs pose special dangers (AAIDD, 2018; Kirkham, 2017). For example, a serious case of *lead poisoning,* from eating lead-based paints or inhaling high levels of automobile fumes, can cause ID in children. Mercury, radiation, nitrite, and pesticide poisoning may do the same. In addition, certain infections, such as *meningitis* and *encephalitis,* can lead to intellectual disability if they are not diagnosed and treated in time (AAIDD, 2018; Khandaker et al., 2016).

Attila Balazs/EPA/Redux

The power of mainstreaming The goal of mainstreaming, or inclusion, programs—in which children with intellectual disability are placed in regular classes with the general school population—is apparent in this photo. Here, Nandor Szecsi (front), who has Down syndrome and is mainstreamed, is hugged lovingly by his primary school classmate in Budapest, Hungary.

Interventions for People with Intellectual Disability

The quality of life attained by people with intellectual disability depends largely on sociocultural factors: where they live and with whom, how they are educated, and the growth opportunities available at home and in the community. Thus intervention programs for these individuals try to provide comfortable and stimulating residences, a proper education, and social and economic opportunities. At the same time, the programs seek to improve the self-image and self-esteem of those with intellectual disability. Once these needs are met, formal psychological or biological treatments are also of help in some cases.

WHAT IS THE PROPER RESIDENCE? Until recent decades, parents of children with intellectual disability would send them to live in public institutions—**state schools**—as early as possible (Harris, 2010). These overcrowded institutions provided basic care, but residents were neglected, often abused, and isolated from society.

During the 1960s and 1970s, the public became more aware of these sorry conditions and, as part of the broader *deinstitutionalization* movement (see Chapter 12), demanded that many people with intellectual disability be released from the state schools (Harris, 2010). In many cases, the releases were done without adequate preparation or supervision. Like people with schizophrenia who were suddenly deinstitutionalized, those with intellectual disability were virtually dumped into the community. Often they failed to adjust and had to be institutionalized once again.

Since that time, reforms have led to the creation of *small institutions* and other *community residences* that teach self-sufficiency, devote more staff time to patient care, and offer educational and medical services. The community residences range from fully supervised group homes to semi-independent residences to local branches of larger institutions. Many of these settings follow the principles of **normalization** first started in Denmark and Sweden—they attempt to provide living conditions similar to those enjoyed by the rest of society; flexible routines; and normal developmental experiences, including opportunities for self-determination, sexual fulfillment, and economic freedom (Pivalizza, 2017).

Today the vast majority of children with intellectual disability live at home rather than in an institution. During adulthood and as their parents age, however, some people with intellectual disability require levels of assistance and opportunities that their families are unable to provide. A community residence becomes an appropriate alternative for them. Most people with intellectual disability, including almost all with mild ID, now spend their adult lives either in the family home or in a community residence (NCD, 2018; Sturmey & Didden, 2014).

WHICH EDUCATIONAL PROGRAMS WORK BEST? Because early intervention seems to offer such great promise, educational programs for people with intellectual disability may begin during the earliest years. The appropriate education depends on the person's level of functioning. Educators hotly debate whether special classes or mainstreaming is most effective once the children enter school (Malki & Einat, 2017; Bouck & Park, 2016). In **special education,** children with intellectual disability are grouped together in a separate, specially designed educational program. In contrast, in **mainstreaming,** or **inclusion,** they are placed in regular classes with students from the general school population. Neither approach seems consistently superior. It may well be that mainstreaming is better for some areas of learning and for some children, and special classes are better for others.

Teachers who work with students with intellectual disability often use operant conditioning principles to improve their students' self-help, communication, social, and academic skills (Mader, 2017; Pivalizza, 2017). They break learning tasks down into small steps, giving positive reinforcement for each increment of progress. Additionally, many institutions, schools, and private homes have set up *token economy programs*—the operant conditioning programs that have also been used to treat children with ADHD and institutionalized patients who have schizophrenia.

What might be the benefits of mainstreaming compared with special education classes, and vice versa?

WHEN IS THERAPY NEEDED? Like anyone else, people with intellectual disability sometimes have emotional and behavioral problems (Sutton & Gates, 2019). Around 30 percent or more have a psychological disorder other than intellectual disability (Bratek, Krysta, & Kucia, 2017; Bouras & Holt, 2010). Furthermore, some suffer from low self-esteem, interpersonal problems, and difficulties adjusting to community life. These problems are helped to some degree by either individual or group therapy (Cooney et al., 2018). Large numbers of people with intellectual disability also take psychotropic medications (Bowring et al., 2017). Many clinicians argue, however, that too often the medications are used simply for the purpose of making the individuals easier to manage.

PROMOTING PERSONAL, SOCIAL, AND OCCUPATIONAL GROWTH People need to feel effective and competent in order to move forward in life. Those with intellectual disability are most likely to feel effective and competent if their communities allow them to grow and to make many of their own choices. Denmark and Sweden, where the normalization movement began, have again been leaders in this area, developing youth clubs that encourage those with intellectual disability to take risks and function independently. The Special Olympics program has also encouraged those with intellectual disability to be active in setting goals, to participate in their environment, and to interact socially with others (Tint et al., 2017; Crawford et al., 2015).

Socializing, sex, and marriage are difficult issues for people with intellectual disability and their families, but with proper training and practice, they usually can learn to use contraceptives and carry out responsible family planning (Gil-Llario et al., 2018). National advocacy organizations and a number of clinicians currently offer guidance in these matters, and some have developed *dating skills programs* (AAIDD, 2018).

Some states restrict marriage for people with intellectual disability. These laws are rarely enforced, though, and in fact many people with mild ID marry. Contrary to popular myths, the marriages can be very successful. And although some may be incapable of raising children, many are quite able to do so, either on their own or with special help and community services (McConnell et al., 2017).

Finally, adults with intellectual disability—whatever the severity—need the personal and financial rewards that come with holding a job (AAIDD, 2018; Park & Bouck, 2018). Many work in *sheltered workshops,* protected and supervised workplaces that train them at a pace and level tailored to their abilities. After training in the workshops, a number of people with mild or moderate ID move on to hold regular jobs. Although training programs for people with intellectual disability have improved greatly in quality over the past 40 years, there are too few of them. Additional programs are required so that more people with intellectual disability may achieve their full potential, as workers and as human beings.

state school A state-supported institution for people with intellectual disability.

normalization The principle that institutions and community residences for people with intellectual disability should provide living conditions and opportunities similar to those enjoyed by the rest of society.

special education An approach to educating children with intellectual disability in which they are grouped together and given a separate, specially designed education.

mainstreaming The placement of children with intellectual disability in regular school classes. Also known as *inclusion*.

Working for money, independence, and self-respect Simone Ippoliti pours a beer for a patron at Locanda dei Sunflowers, a restaurant in Rome. The restaurant promotes the employment of individuals with intellectual disability, like Simone—providing them with job opportunities and dignity through training and placement.

Gabriel Bouys/AFP/Getty Images

#WorstWord

Surveys of the general population earlier this century found "retarded" to be the single most offensive disability-related word. Thus in 2010, Congress passed Rosa's Law, which ruled that the term "intellectual disability" must replace "mental retardation" in many areas of government. DSM-5 followed suit with this label change in 2013.

9... SUMMING UP

NEURODEVELOPMENTAL DISORDERS Neurodevelopmental disorders are a group of disabilities in the functioning of the brain that emerge at birth or during very early childhood and affect the person's behavior, memory, concentration, and/or ability to learn.

Children with attention-deficit/hyperactivity disorder (ADHD) attend poorly to tasks, behave overactively and impulsively, or both. Many of the attention difficulties seen in ADHD may be associated with a dysfunctional attention brain circuit whose structures display problematic interconnectivity. Drug therapy—methylphenidate, amphetamine, or other stimulant drugs—and cognitive-behavioral programs can be effective treatments.

People with autism spectrum disorder are extremely unresponsive to others, have severe communication deficits, and display very rigid and repetitive behaviors, interests, and activities. The leading explanations of this disorder point to cognitive deficits, such as failure to develop a theory of mind and joint attention skills, and biological abnormalities, including, perhaps, a dysfunctional brain circuit. Although no treatment totally reverses the autistic pattern, significant help is available in the form of cognitive-behavioral treatments, communication training, training and treatment for parents, and community integration.

People with intellectual disability are significantly below average in intelligence and adaptive ability. Mild ID, by far the most common level of intellectual disability, has often been linked to environmental factors such as unstimulating environments during a child's early years, inadequate parent–child interactions, and insufficient learning experiences. Moderate, severe, and profound ID are caused primarily by biological factors. The leading biological causes of intellectual disability are chromosomal abnormalities, metabolic disorders, prenatal problems, birth complications, and childhood diseases and injuries.

Today's intervention programs for people with intellectual disability typically emphasize the importance of a comfortable and stimulating residence—either the family home, a small institution or group home, or a semi-independent residence—that follows the principles of normalization. Other important interventions include proper education, therapy for psychological problems, and programs offering training in socializing, sex, marriage, parenting, and occupational skills. A key debate centers on whether people with intellectual disability profit more from special classes or from mainstreaming.

Clinicians Discover Childhood and Adolescence

Early in the twentieth century, mental health professionals virtually ignored children. At best, they viewed them as small adults and treated their psychological disorders as they would adult problems. Today the problems and needs of young people have caught the attention of researchers and clinicians.

This increased attention has zeroed in on the importance of the family. Because children and adolescents have limited control over their lives, they are particularly affected by the attitudes and reactions of family members. Clinicians must therefore deal with those attitudes and reactions as they try to address the problems of the young. Treatments for conduct disorder, ADHD, intellectual disability, and other problems of childhood and adolescence typically fall short unless clinicians educate and work with the family as well. At the same time, clinicians who work with children and adolescents have learned that a narrow focus on any one model can lead to problems. For years, autism spectrum disorder was explained exclusively by family factors, misleading theorists and therapists alike and adding to the pain of parents already devastated by their child's disorder.

The increased clinical focus on the young has also been accompanied by more attention to young people's human and legal rights. More and more

CLINICAL CHOICES

Now that you've read about disorders common among children and adolescents, try the interactive case study for this chapter. See if you are able to identify Gabriel's symptoms and suggest a diagnosis based on his symptoms. What kind of treatment would be most effective for Gabriel? Go to **LaunchPad** to access ***Clinical Choices***.

clinicians have called on government agencies to protect the rights and safety of this often-powerless group. In doing so, they hope to fuel the fights for better educational resources and against child abuse and neglect, sexual abuse, malnourishment, and fetal alcohol syndrome.

As the problems and, at times, mistreatment of young people receive more attention, the special needs of these individuals are becoming more visible. Thus the study and treatment of psychological disorders among children and adolescents are likely to continue at a rapid pace. Now that clinicians and public officials have "discovered" this population, they are not likely to underestimate their needs and importance again.

...Key Terms

bullying, p. 437
separation anxiety disorder, p. 439
selective mutism, p. 439
play therapy, p. 440
disruptive mood dysregulation disorder, p. 443
oppositional defiant disorder, p. 444
conduct disorder, p. 444
parent management training, p. 446
parent–child interaction therapy, p. 446
multisystemic therapy, p. 446
enuresis, p. 448
encopresis, p. 448
neurodevelopmental disorders, p. 450
ADHD, p. 450
Type 1 attention processes, p. 451
Type 2 attention processes, p. 451
attention circuit, p. 452
methylphenidate, p. 452
autism spectrum disorder, p. 454
echolalia, p. 455
theory of mind, p. 456
joint attention, p. 456
augmentative communication system, p. 459
intellectual disability (ID), p. 460
intelligence quotient (IQ), p. 461
mild ID, p. 462
moderate ID, p. 463
severe ID, p. 464
profound ID, p. 464
Down syndrome, p. 464
fragile X syndrome, p. 464
recessive genes, p. 464
phenylketonuria (PKU), p. 465
fetal alcohol syndrome, p. 465
state school, p. 466
normalization, p. 466
special education, p. 466
mainstreaming, p. 466
sheltered workshop, p. 467

...Quick Quiz

1. What are the prevalence rates and gender ratios for the various disorders common among children and adolescents? *pp. 436–468*
2. What are the different kinds of childhood anxiety and depressive disorders? What are today's leading explanations and treatments for these disorders? *pp. 438–443*
3. What is disruptive mood dysregulation disorder, and why might DSM-5's addition of this new category affect diagnoses of childhood bipolar disorder? *p. 443*
4. Describe oppositional defiant disorder and conduct disorder. What factors help cause conduct disorder, and how is this disorder treated? *pp. 444–448*
5. What are enuresis and encopresis? How are these disorders treated? *pp. 448–449*
6. What are the symptoms of attention-deficit/hyperactivity disorder? What are today's leading explanations for it? What are the current treatments for ADHD, and how effective are they? *pp. 450–454*
7. What is autism spectrum disorder, and what are its possible causes? What are the overall goals of treatment for this disorder, and which interventions have been most helpful? *pp. 454–460*
8. Describe the different levels of intellectual disability. *pp. 460–464*
9. What are the leading environmental and biological causes of intellectual disability? *pp. 462–466*
10. What kinds of residences, educational programs, treatments, and community programs are helpful to persons with intellectual disability? *pp. 466–468*

Visit ***LaunchPad***
to access the e-Book, Clinical Choices, videos, activities, and LearningCurve, as well as study aids including flashcards, FAQs, and research exercises.

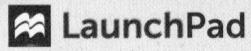

LaunchPad

CHAPTER

15

Disorders of Aging and Cognition

TOPIC OVERVIEW

Harry appeared to be in perfect health at age 58. . . . He worked in the municipal water treatment plant of a small city, and it was at work that the first overt signs of Harry's mental illness appeared. While responding to a minor emergency, he became confused about the correct order in which to pull the levers that controlled the flow of fluids. As a result, several thousand gallons of raw sewage were discharged into a river. Harry had been an efficient and diligent worker, so after puzzled questioning, his error was attributed to the flu and overlooked.

Several weeks later, Harry came home with a baking dish his wife had asked him to buy, having forgotten that he had brought home the identical dish two nights before. Later that week, on two successive nights, he went to pick up his daughter at her job in a restaurant, apparently forgetting that she had changed shifts and was now working days. A month after that, he quite uncharacteristically argued with . . . the phone company; he was trying to pay a bill that he had already paid three days before. . . .

Months passed and Harry's wife was beside herself. She could see that his problem was worsening. Not only had she been unable to get effective help, but Harry himself was becoming resentful and sometimes suspicious of her attempts. He now insisted there was nothing wrong with him, and she would catch him narrowly watching her every movement. . . . Sometimes he became angry—sudden little storms without apparent cause. . . . More difficult for his wife was Harry's repetitiveness in conversation: He often repeated stories from the past and sometimes repeated isolated phrases and sentences from more recent exchanges. There was no context and little continuity to his choice of subjects. . . .

Two years after Harry had first allowed the sewage to escape, he was clearly a changed man. Most of the time he seemed preoccupied; he usually had a vacant smile on his face, and what little he said was so vague that it lacked meaning. . . . Gradually his wife took over getting him up, toileted, and dressed each morning. . . .

Harry's condition continued to worsen slowly. When his wife's school was in session, his daughter would stay with him some days, and neighbors were able to offer some help. But occasionally he would still manage to wander away. On those occasions he greeted everyone he met—old friends and strangers alike—with "Hi, it's so nice." That was the extent of his conversation, although he might repeat "nice, nice, nice" over and over again. . . . When Harry left a coffee pot on a unit of the electric stove until it melted, his wife, desperate for help, took him to see another doctor. Again Harry was found to be in good health. [However] the doctor ordered a [brain scan and eventually concluded] that Harry had "Pick-Alzheimer disease." . . . Because Harry was a veteran . . . [he qualified for] hospitalization in a . . . veterans' hospital about 400 miles away from his home. . . .

At the hospital the nursing staff sat Harry up in a chair each day and, aided by volunteers, made sure he ate enough. Still, he lost weight and became weaker. He would weep when his wife came to see him, but he did not talk, and he gave no other sign that he recognized her. After a year, even the weeping stopped. Harry's wife could no longer bear to visit. Harry lived on until just after his sixty-fifth birthday, when he choked on a piece of bread, developed pneumonia as a consequence, and soon died.

(Heston, 1992, pp. 87–90)

Harry suffered from a form of *Alzheimer's disease*. This term is familiar to almost everyone in our society. It seems as if each decade is marked by a disease that everyone dreads—a diagnosis no one wants to hear because it feels like a death sentence. Cancer used to be such a diagnosis, then AIDS. But medical science

geropsychology The field of psychology concerned with the mental health of elderly people.

has made remarkable strides with those diseases, and patients who now develop them have reason for great hope. Alzheimer's disease, on the other hand, remains incurable and almost untreatable, although, as you will see later, researchers are currently making enormous progress toward understanding it and reversing, or at least slowing, its march.

What makes Alzheimer's disease particularly frightening is that it means not only eventual physical death but also, as in Harry's case, a slow psychological death—a progressive deterioration of one's memory and related cognitive faculties. Significant cognitive deterioration, previously called *dementia,* is now categorized as *neurocognitive disorder.* There are many types of neurocognitive disorders listed in DSM-5 (APA, 2013). Alzheimer's disease is the most common one (Wolk & Dickerson, 2017).

Although neurocognitive disorders are currently the most publicized and feared psychological problems among the elderly, they are hardly the only ones. A variety of psychological disorders are tied closely to later life. As with childhood disorders, some of the disorders of old age are caused primarily by pressures that are particularly likely to appear at that time of life, others by unique traumatic experiences, and still others—like neurocognitive disorders—by biological abnormalities.

Old Age and Stress

Old age is usually defined in our society as the years past age 65. By this account, around 46 million people in the United States are "old," representing 14.5 percent of the total population; this is a 15-fold increase since 1900 (U.S. Census Bureau, 2018, 2016; Mather, 2016). It has also been estimated that there will be 70 million elderly people in the United States by the year 2030—21 percent of the population. Not only is the overall population of the elderly on the rise, but also the number of people over 85 will double in the next 10 years. Indeed, people over 85 represent the fastest-growing segment of the population in the United States and in most countries around the world. Older women outnumber older men by almost 3 to 2.

Like childhood, old age brings special pressures, unique upsets, and major biological changes (Heflin, 2018). People become more prone to illness and injury as they age. About half of adults over 65 have two or three chronic illnesses, and 15 percent have

Owen Franken/Getty Images

Making a difference To help prevent feelings of unimportance and low self-esteem, some older people now offer their expertise to young people who are trying to master new skills, undertake business projects, and the like. This elderly man, who volunteers regularly at an elementary school, is teaching math to a first-grader.

four or more. And at least half of elderly people have some measure of insomnia or other sleep problems (APA, 2018, 2017; Winkelman, 2018). In addition, elderly people are likely to be contending with the stress of loss—the loss of spouses, friends, and adult children; of former activities and roles; of hearing and vision. Many lose their sense of purpose after they retire. Some also have to adjust to the loss of favored pets and possessions.

The stresses of aging need not necessarily cause psychological problems (see ***PsychWatch***). In fact, some older people, particularly those who seek social contacts and those who maintain a sense of control over their lives, use the changes that come with aging as opportunities for learning and growth (Espinoza & Unützer, 2017). For example, two-thirds of elderly people now use the Internet to connect with people of similar ages and interests, a 16-fold increase since the year 2000 (Pew Research Center, 2017; Oinas-Kukkonen & Mantila, 2009). Indeed, 34 percent of persons over age 65 use social media. For other elderly people, however, the stresses of old age do lead to psychological difficulties. Studies indicate that more than 20 percent of elderly people meet the criteria for a mental disorder and as many as half of all elderly people would benefit from some degree of mental health services, yet fewer than 20 percent actually receive them (APA, 2018, 2017). **Geropsychology,** the field of psychology dedicated to the mental health of elderly people, has developed almost entirely within the last

What kinds of attitudes and activities might help people enter old age with peace of mind and positive anticipation?

PSYCHWATCH

The Oldest Old

Clinicians suggest that aging need not inevitably lead to psychological problems. Nor apparently does it always lead to physical problems.

There are currently 72,000 *centenarians* in the United States—people who are 100 years old or older. When researchers have studied these people—often called the "oldest old"—they have been surprised to learn that centenarians are on average more healthy, positive, clearheaded, and agile than those in their 80s and early 90s (Etxeberria et al., 2017; Rea, 2017). Although some certainly experience cognitive decline, more than half remain perfectly alert. Many of the oldest old are, in fact, still employed, sexually active, and able to enjoy the outdoors and the arts. What is their greatest fear? The fear of significant cognitive decline. According to some studies, many people in their 90s and older fear the prospect of mental deterioration more than they fear death (Arosio et al., 2017; Boeve et al., 2003).

Some scientists believe that people who live this long carry "longevity" genes that make them resistant to disabling or terminal infections (Grossi et al., 2018; Hao et al., 2018). Research also points to engaged lifestyles and "robust" personalities that help the oldest old meet life's challenges with optimism and a sense of challenge (Etxeberria et al., 2017; da Rosa et al., 2014). The centenarians themselves often credit a good frame of mind or regular behaviors that they have maintained for many years—for example, eating healthful food, getting regular exercise, and not smoking (da Silva et al., 2018; Rea, 2017). Said one very elderly retired math and science teacher, "You can't sit. . . . You have to keep moving" (Duenwald, 2003).

Dream of a (long) lifetime Since 2008, it had been 107-year-old Virginia McLaurin's dream to meet President Barack Obama. That wish came true in 2016 when the centenarian was invited to a reception at the White House celebrating African American History Month. McLaurin not only met with then-President Obama but got to dance with then-First Lady Michelle Obama.

#

#PovertyPressure

10%	Percentage of elderly non-Hispanic white Americans who live below the poverty line
21%	Percentage of elderly Hispanic Americans who live below the poverty line
24%	Percentage of elderly African Americans who live below the poverty line

(Information from: Heflin, 2018)

four decades, and at present only 4.2 percent of clinicians work primarily with elderly persons (APA, 2018, 2017).

The psychological problems of elderly people may be divided into two groups. One group consists of disorders that may be common among people in all age groups but are often connected to the process of aging when they occur in an elderly person. These include *depressive, anxiety,* and *substance use disorders*. The other group consists of disorders of cognition, such as *delirium, mild neurocognitive disorders,* and *major neurocognitive disorders* that result from brain abnormalities. As in Harry's case, these brain abnormalities are most often tied to aging, but they also can sometimes occur when people are younger. Elderly people with one of these psychological problems often display other such problems. For example, many who suffer from neurocognitive disorders also deal with depression and anxiety (APA, 2018).

Depression in Later Life

Depression is one of the most common mental health problems of older adults. The features of depression are the same for elderly people as for younger people, including feelings of profound sadness and emptiness; low self-esteem, guilt, and pessimism; and loss of appetite and sleep disturbances. Depression is particularly common among those who have recently undergone a trauma, such as the loss of a spouse or close friend or the development of a serious physical illness (APA, 2018; Espinoza & Unützer, 2017).

[Oscar] was an 83-year-old married man with an episode of major depressive disorder. . . . He said that about one and one-half years prior to beginning treatment, his brother had died. In the following months, two friends whom he had known since childhood died. Following these losses, he became increasingly anxious [and] grew more and more pessimistic. Reluctantly, he acknowledged, "I even thought about ending my life." . . .

During . . . treatment, [Oscar] discussed his relationship with his brother. He discussed how distraught he was to watch his brother's physical deterioration from an extended illness. He described the scene at his brother's deathbed and the moment "when he took his final breath." He experienced guilt over the failure to carry out his brother's funeral services in a manner he felt his brother would have wanted. While initially characterizing his relationship with his brother as loving and amiable, he later acknowledged that he disapproved of many ways in which his brother acted. Later in therapy, he also reviewed different facets of his past relationships with his two deceased friends. He expressed sadness that the long years had ended. . . . [Oscar's] life had been organized around visits to his brother's home and outings with his friends. . . . [While] his wife had encouraged him to visit with other friends and family, it became harder and harder to do so as he became more depressed.

(Hinrichsen, 1999, p. 433)

Overall, as many as 20 percent of people become depressed at some point during old age (APA, 2018). The rate is highest in older women. This rate among the elderly is about the same as that among younger adults—even lower, according to some studies. However, it climbs much higher (32 percent or more) among aged people who live in nursing homes, as opposed to those in the community (Espinoza & Unützer, 2017; Seitz et al., 2010).

Is it more likely that positive thinking leads to good health or that good health produces positive thinking?

Several studies suggest that depression raises an elderly person's chances of developing significant medical problems (Heflin, 2018; Taylor, 2014). For example, older depressed people with high blood pressure are almost three times as likely to suffer a stroke as older nondepressed people with the same condition. Similarly, elderly people who are depressed recover more slowly and less completely from heart attacks, hip fractures, pneumonia, and

#

#SpousalLoss

9.0 million	Number of widows in the U.S.
2.1 million	Number of widowers in the U.S.

(Information from: U.S. Census Bureau, 2018, 2017)

© Matthew A. Turner 2013

© Mitch Wojnarowicz/The Image Works

Racing to mental health Gerontologists propose that elderly people need to pursue pleasurable and personally meaningful activities. The elderly women on the left compete in a race at the National Senior Games. In contrast, the elderly gentleman on the right, also interested in racing, watches a competition at the Saratoga Springs horse racing track with the daily racing form on his head. Which of these two activities might be more likely to contribute to successful psychological functioning during old age?

other infections and illnesses. Small wonder that among the elderly, increases in clinical depression are tied to increases in the death rate.

As you read in Chapter 7, elderly people are also more likely to die from suicide than young people, and often their suicides are related to depression (APA, 2018). The overall rate of suicide in the United States is 12.6 per 100,000 people; among those over 65 years of age, it is more than 16 per 100,000, and among those over 75, it is more than 24 per 100,000 (CDC, 2017, 2016; WHO, 2017).

Like younger adults, older people who are depressed may be helped by cognitive-behavioral therapy, interpersonal psychotherapy, antidepressant medications, or a combination of these approaches (Espinoza & Unützer, 2017). Both individual and group therapy formats have been used. More than half of elderly patients with depression improve with these various treatments. It is, however, sometimes difficult for older people to use antidepressant drugs effectively and safely because the body breaks the drugs down differently in later life (Rochon, 2018). Moreover, among elderly people, antidepressant drugs have a higher risk of causing some cognitive impairment. Electroconvulsive therapy, applied with certain modifications, has been used for elderly people who are severely depressed and have not been helped by other approaches (Kellner, 2018).

Some elderly people experience depression as part of a bipolar disorder rather than a unipolar type of depressive disorder (Sajatovic & Chen, 2017). Around 1 percent of all persons over 65 years of age display a bipolar disorder in any given year. Usually, the disorder began well before they reached old age. In most cases, the individuals receive the kinds of treatment that younger individuals with bipolar disorder receive—mood-stabilizing medications and adjunctive psychotherapy.

Anxiety Disorders in Later Life

Anxiety is also common among elderly people (APA, 2018, 2017). At any given time, as many as 11 percent of elderly individuals in the United States experience at least one of the anxiety disorders (ADAA, 2017; Zhang et al., 2015). Surveys indicate that generalized anxiety disorder is particularly common (Baldwin, 2018). The prevalence of anxiety also increases throughout old age. For example, people over 85 years of age report higher rates of anxiety than those between 65 and 84 years. In fact, all of these numbers may be

"All of a sudden, everyone seems younger than I am."

Mike Twohy/The New Yorker Collection/ www.cartoonbank.com

low, as anxiety in the elderly tends to be underreported (APA, 2018). Both the elderly patient and the clinician may interpret physical symptoms of anxiety, such as heart palpitations and perspiring, as symptoms of a medical condition.

There are many things about aging that may heighten the anxiety levels of certain people (APA, 2018; Bower et al., 2015). Declining health, for example, has often been pointed to, and in fact, older persons who have significant medical illnesses or injuries report more anxiety than those who are healthy or injury-free. Researchers have not, however, been able to determine why some people who face such problems in old age become anxious while others in similar circumstances remain relatively calm (see ***InfoCentral***).

Older adults with anxiety disorders have been treated with psychotherapy of various kinds, particularly cognitive-behavioral therapy (APA, 2017; Hui & Zhihui, 2017). Many also receive benzodiazepines or other antianxiety medications, just as younger sufferers do. And a number are treated with serotonin-enhancing antidepressant drugs. Again, however, all such drugs must be used cautiously with older people (Rochon, 2018).

Substance Misuse in Later Life

Although alcohol use disorder and other substance use disorders are significant problems for many older persons, the prevalence of such patterns actually appears to decline after age 65, perhaps because of declining health or reduced income (APA, 2018, 2017; Li & Caltabiano, 2017). The majority of older adults do not misuse alcohol or other substances, despite the fact that aging can sometimes be a time of considerable stress and in our society people often turn to alcohol and drugs during times of stress. Accurate data about the rate of substance abuse among older adults are difficult to gather because many elderly people do not suspect or admit that they have such a problem.

Surveys find that 3 to 7 percent of older people, particularly men, have alcohol use disorder in a given year (APA, 2018; Li & Caltabiano, 2017). Men under 30 are four times as likely as men over 60 to display a behavioral problem associated with excessive alcohol use, such as repeated falling, spells of dizziness or blacking out, secretive drinking, or social withdrawal. Older patients who are institutionalized, however, do display high rates of problem drinking. For example, alcohol problems among older people admitted to general and mental hospitals are at least 15 percent, and estimates of alcohol-related problems among patients in nursing homes are as high as 50 percent (Li & Caltabiano, 2017; McConnaughey, 2014).

Researchers often distinguish between older problem drinkers who have had alcohol use disorder for many years, perhaps since their 20s, and those who do not start abusing alcohol until their 50s or 60s (in what is sometimes called "late-onset alcoholism"). The latter group typically begins abusive drinking as a reaction to the negative events and pressures of growing older, such as the death of a spouse, living alone, or unwanted retirement. Alcohol use disorder in elderly people is treated much as it is in younger adults (see Chapter 10): through such interventions as detoxification, Antabuse, Alcoholics Anonymous, and cognitive-behavioral therapy (APA, 2017).

A leading substance problem in the elderly is the *misuse of prescription drugs* (APA, 2018; Rochon, 2018). Most often the misuse is unintentional. In the United States, people over the age of 65 buy more than one-third of all prescription drugs (NIDA, 2016). At any given time, elderly people are taking, on average, three to five prescription drugs and two over-the-counter drugs (Heflin, 2018; NCHS, 2014). Thus their risk of confusing

#LateLifeMeds

66%	Percentage of elderly persons who take blood pressure drugs
47%	Percentage of elderly persons who take cholesterol drugs
19%	Percentage of elderly persons who take diabetes drugs
17%	Percentage of elderly persons who take antidepressant drugs
9%	Percentage of elderly persons who take antianxiety drugs

(Information from: Kantor et al., 2015)

THE AGING POPULATION

The number and proportion of elderly people in the United States and around the world are ever-growing. This acceleration has important consequences, requiring each society to pay particular attention to aging-related issues in healthcare, housing, the economy, and other such realms. In particular, as the number and proportion of elderly people increases, so too do the number and proportion of the population who experience aging-related psychological difficulties.

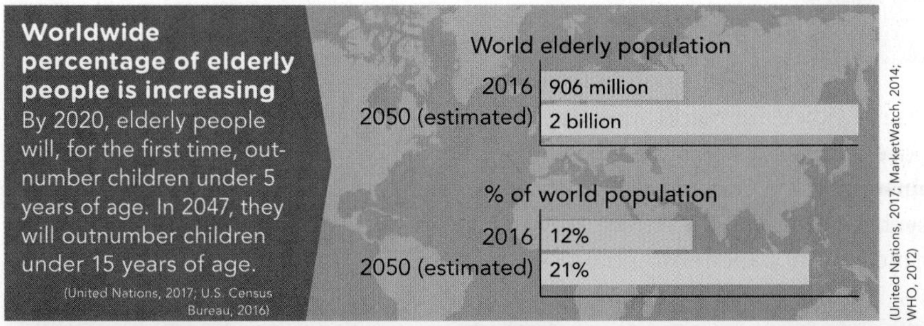

Worldwide percentage of elderly people is increasing
By 2020, elderly people will, for the first time, outnumber children under 5 years of age. In 2047, they will outnumber children under 15 years of age.
(United Nations, 2017; U.S. Census Bureau, 2016)
World elderly population
2016 906 million
2050 (estimated) 2 billion
% of world population
2016 12%
2050 (estimated) 21%
(United Nations, 2017; MarketWatch, 2014; WHO, 2012)

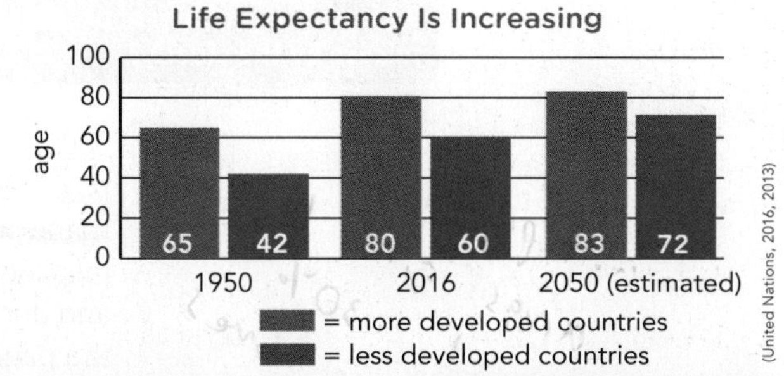

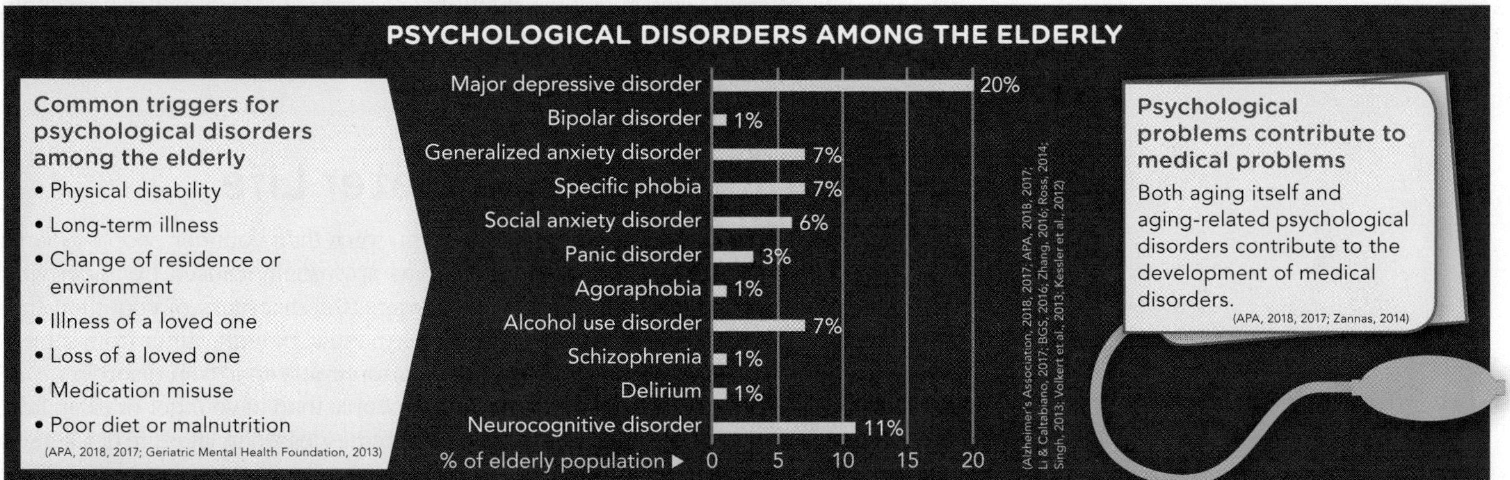

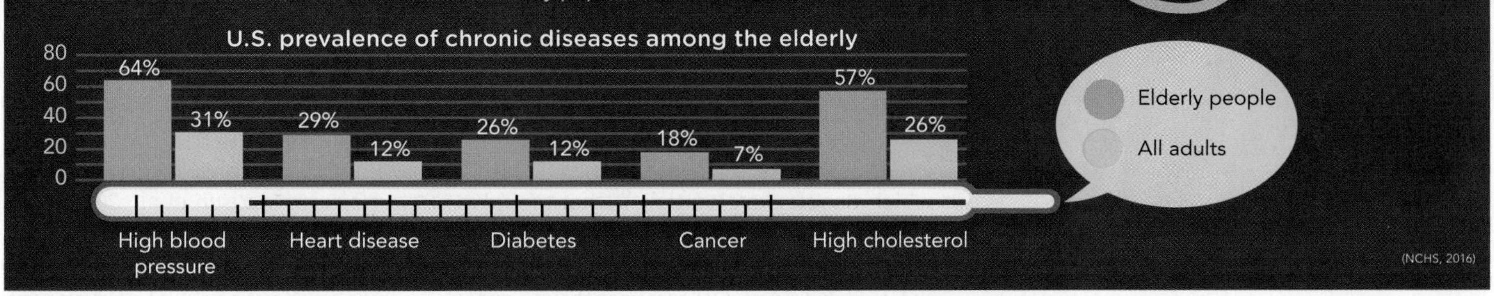

THE ELDERLY POPULATION IS ITSELF AGING

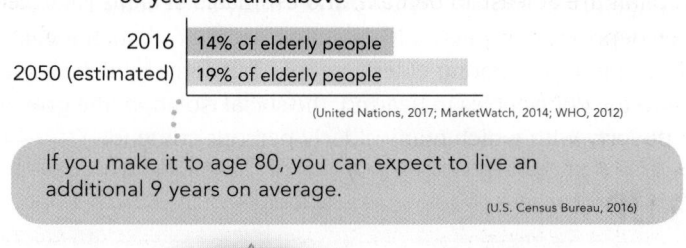

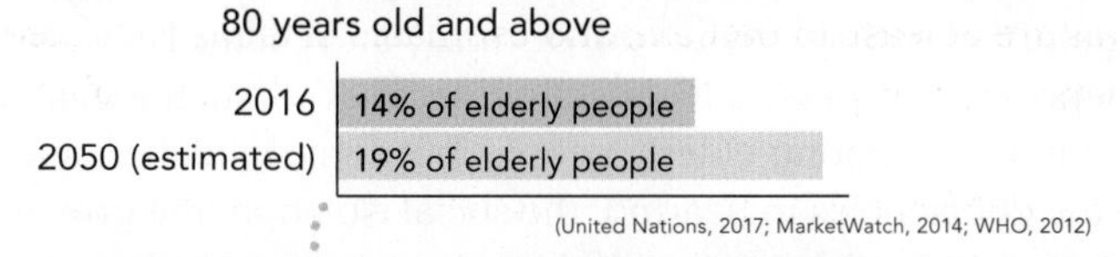

If you make it to age 80, you can expect to live an additional 9 years on average. (U.S. Census Bureau, 2016)

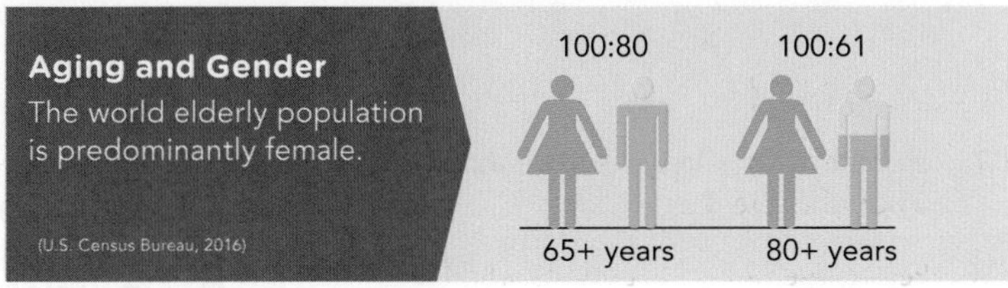

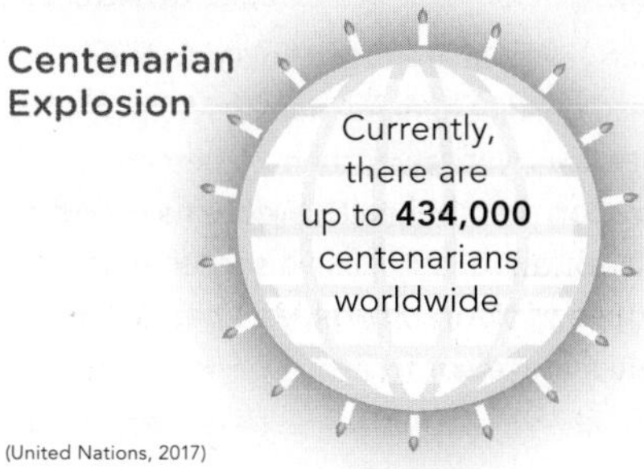

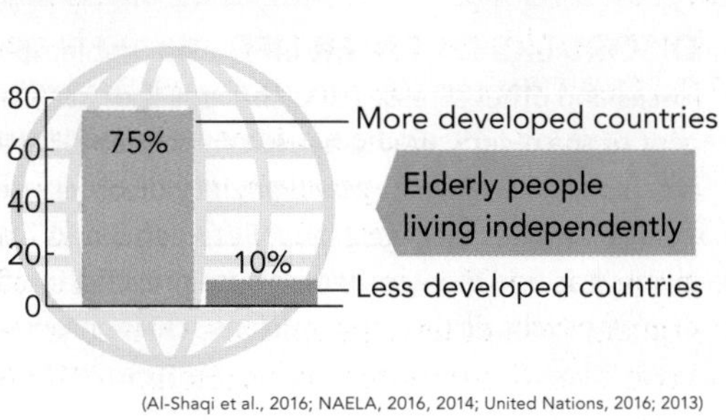

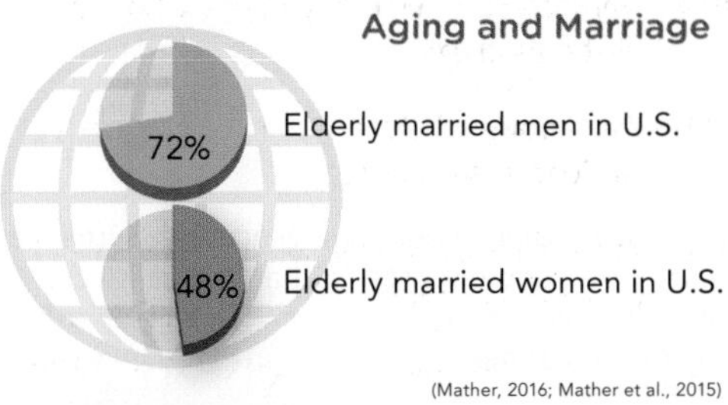

medications or skipping doses is high. To help address this problem, physicians and pharmacists often try to simplify medications, educate older patients about their prescriptions, clarify directions, and teach patients to watch for undesired effects. However, physicians themselves are sometimes to blame in cases of prescription drug misuse, perhaps overprescribing medications for elderly patients or unwisely mixing certain medicines (Rochon, 2018).

What changes in medical practice, patient education, or family interactions might address the problem of prescription drug misuse by the elderly?

Yet another drug-related problem, apparently on the increase, is the misuse of powerful medications at nursing homes. Research indicates that antipsychotic drugs are currently being given to almost 30 percent of the total nursing home population in the United States, despite the fact that many of the residents do not display psychotic functioning (HRW, 2018; Rochon, 2018). Apparently, these powerful and (for some elderly patients) dangerous drugs are often given to sedate and manage the patients. Indeed, research suggests that 17 percent of new nursing home patients who have never before taken an antipsychotic drug are administered such drugs within 100 days of admission (Rochon, 2018; Bronskill et al., 2004).

Psychotic Disorders in Later Life

Elderly people have a higher rate of psychotic symptoms than younger people (Soares et al., 2017). Among aged people, these symptoms are usually caused by underlying medical conditions such as neurocognitive disorders, the disorders of cognition that you will read about in the next section. Some elderly people, though, suffer from *schizophrenia* or *delusional disorder,* one of the other schizophrenia spectrum disorders.

Actually, schizophrenia is less common in older people than in younger ones. In fact, many people with schizophrenia find that their symptoms lessen in later life (Dickerson et al., 2014). Improvement can occur in people who have had schizophrenia for 30 or more years, particularly in such areas as social skills and work capacity, as we are reminded by the remarkable late-life improvement of the Nobel Prize recipient John Nash, the subject of the book and movie *A Beautiful Mind*. It is uncommon for *new* cases of schizophrenia to emerge in late life (Feki et al., 2017).

Another kind of psychotic disorder found among the elderly is *delusional disorder,* in which people develop beliefs that are false but not bizarre (Jagsch et al., 2018; APA, 2013). This disorder, which you read about in Chapter 12, is rare in most age groups—around 2 of every 1,000 persons—but its prevalence appears to increase in the elderly population. Older people with a delusional disorder may develop deeply held suspicions of persecution; they believe that other people—often family members, doctors, or friends—are conspiring against, cheating, spying on, or maligning them. They may become irritable, angry, or depressed or pursue legal action because of such ideas. It is not clear why this disorder increases among elderly people, but some clinicians suggest that the rise is related to the deficiencies in hearing, the social isolation, the greater stress, or the heightened poverty with which many elderly persons contend.

...SUMMING UP

DISORDERS OF LATER LIFE The problems of elderly people are often linked to the losses and other stresses and changes that accompany advancing age. As many as 50 percent of the elderly would benefit from mental health services, yet fewer than 20 percent receive them. Depressive and anxiety disorders are common mental health problems among those in this age group. Between 3 and 7 percent exhibit alcohol use disorder in any given year, and many others misuse prescription drugs. In addition, some elderly people display psychotic disorders such as schizophrenia or delusional disorder.

delirium A rapidly developing, acute disturbance in attention and orientation that makes it very difficult to concentrate and think in a clear and organized manner

Disorders of Cognition

Most of us worry from time to time that we are losing our memory and other mental abilities. You rush out the door without your keys, you meet a familiar person and cannot remember her name, or you forget that you have seen a particular film. Actually such mishaps are a common and quite normal feature of stress or of aging. As people move through middle age, these memory difficulties and lapses of attention increase, and they may occur regularly by the age of 60 or 70 (see ***MindTech*** on the next page). Sometimes, however, people have memory and other cognitive changes that are far more extensive and problematic.

In Chapter 5 you saw that problems in memory and related cognitive processes can occur without biological causes, in the form of *dissociative disorders*. More often, though, cognitive problems do have organic roots, particularly when they appear late in life. The leading such disorders among the elderly are *delirium, major neurocognitive disorder,* and *mild neurocognitive disorder.*

Sean Gallup/Getty Images

Affection is not forgotten Clinicians have found that elderly people in senior care facilities are uplifted and stimulated by interactions with cats, dogs, parakeets, and other pets. In apparent agreement with Sigmund Freud's declaration that "time spent with cats is never wasted," Edith Ehninger, age 95, talks to her regular visitor Mogli. Ehninger has a neurocognitive disorder.

Delirium

occurs over hours or days (short)

Delirium is a major disturbance in attention and orientation to the environment (see **Table 15-1**). As the person's focus becomes less clear, he or she has great difficulty concentrating and thinking in an organized way, leading to misinterpretations, illusions, and on occasion, hallucinations. Sufferers may believe that it is morning in the middle of the night or that they are home when actually they are in a hospital room.

This state of massive confusion typically develops over a short period of time, usually hours or days. Delirium may occur in any age group, including children, but is most common in elderly people (Grover & Avasthi, 2018). Fewer than 0.5 percent of the nonelderly population experience delirium, compared with 1 percent of people over 55 years of age and 14 percent of those over 85 years of age (Hshieh, Inouye, & Oh, 2018; Tune & DeWitt, 2011). When elderly people enter a hospital—which represents a major change in their environment and routine—to be treated for a general medical condition, 10 percent of them show the symptoms of delirium (Blazer, 2018; Grover & Avasthi, 2018). At least another 10 to 20 percent develop delirium during their stay in the hospital (Blazer, 2018; Francis & Young, 2014). Around 17 percent of elderly patients admitted for surgery develop delirium (Wang et al., 2017; de Castro et al., 2014). That number rises to 23 percent among those admitted suddenly for acute surgery. Between 18 and 50 percent of elderly nursing home residents have some delirium (Blazer, 2018; Forsberg, 2017).

Newly, living in hospital

causes of delirium

Fever, certain diseases and infections, poor nutrition, head injuries, strokes, and stress (including the trauma of surgery) may all cause delirium (Magny et al., 2018; Paulo et al., 2017). So may intoxication by certain substances, such as prescription drugs. Partly because older people face so many of these problems, they are more likely than younger ones to experience delirium. If a clinician accurately identifies delirium, it can often be relatively easy to correct—by treating the underlying infection, for example, or changing the patient's drug prescription (Hshieh et al., 2018). However, the syndrome typically fails to be recognized for what it is (Baten et al., 2018). One pioneering study on a medical ward, for example, found that admission doctors detected only 1 of 15 consecutive cases of delirium (Cameron et al., 1987). Incorrect diagnoses of this kind may contribute to a high death rate for older people with delirium (Grover & Avasthi, 2018).

TABLE: 15-1

Dx Checklist

Delirium
1. Over the course of hours or a few days, individual experiences fast-moving and fluctuating disturbances in attention and orientation to the environment.
2. Individual also displays a significant cognitive disturbance.

Information from: APA, 2013.

MINDTECH

Remember to Tweet; Tweet to Remember

Social media sites, and the Internet in general, are often thought of as the province of the young. However, elderly people are also going online and joining social networking sites at increasing rates. Two-thirds of people over age 65 now use the Internet, and 62 percent of those users are Facebook members (Pew Research Center, 2017; Wayne, 2017).

Social networking among the elderly is much more than just an interesting statistic; it may be downright therapeutic. Several studies have found that online activity actually helps elderly people maintain and possibly improve their cognitive skills, coping skills, social pleasures, and emotions (GCBH, 2017; Wayne, 2017). In one study, for example, researchers recruited 42 adults, aged 68 to 91, and trained 14 of them on Facebook. The study found a 25 percent improvement in the cognitive performances of the 14 participants, including improvements in their mental "updating" skills—the ability to quickly add or delete material from their working memory (Piatt, 2013; Wohltmann, 2013).

What other factors might help explain the link between social networking and better coping, social functioning, and emotions among the elderly?

Clinical theorists have offered several explanations for the positive effects of social media on elderly people. It may be, for example, that the cognitive stimulation derived from Internet use activates memory and other cognitive faculties or that the engagement with the world and family provided by the Internet directly satisfies social and emotional needs. Whatever the reason, more and more studies indicate that elderly people who are online often function and feel better than those who do not pursue online activities.

Because older persons often find it intimidating to go online, many elderly people resist the Internet and social networking, saying things like "It's not for me," "It overwhelms me," or "You can't teach an old dog new tricks" (Tsai et al., 2017). However, the growing body of research suggests that they may want to embrace social networking and the Internet for better functioning and for better mental health.

Dieter Nagl/AFP/Getty Images

A new world A young volunteer teaches this elderly man how to use modern communication devices such as computers and smartphones.

Alzheimer's Disease and Other Neurocognitive Disorders

People with a **neurocognitive disorder** experience a significant decline in at least one (often more than one) area of cognitive functioning, such as memory, attention, visual perception, planning and decision making, language ability, or social awareness (APA, 2013). Those who have certain types of neurocognitive disorders may also undergo personality changes—they may behave inappropriately, for example—and their symptoms may worsen steadily.

If the person's cognitive decline is substantial and interferes significantly with his or her ability to be independent, a diagnosis of **major neurocognitive disorder** is in order. If the decline is modest and does not interfere with independent functioning, the appropriate diagnosis is **mild neurocognitive disorder** (see **Table 15-2**).

There are currently 47 million people with neurocognitive disorders around the world, with 4.6 million new cases emerging each year (Keene, Montine, & Kuller, 2018). The number of cases is expected to reach 135 million by 2050 unless a cure is found.

TABLE: 15-2

Dx Checklist

Major Neurocognitive Disorder
1. Individual displays substantial decline in at least one of the following areas of cognitive function: • Memory and learning • Attention • Perceptual-motor skills • Planning and decision-making • Language ability • Social awareness.
2. Cognitive deficits interfere with the individual's everyday independence.
Mild Neurocognitive Disorder
1. Individual displays modest decline in at least one of the following areas of cognitive function: • Memory and learning • Attention • Perceptual-motor skills • Planning and decision-making • Language ability • Social awareness.
2. Cognitive deficits do not interfere with the individual's everyday independence.
Neurocognitive Disorder Due to Alzheimer's Disease
1. Individual displays the features of major or mild neurocognitive disorder.
2. Memory impairment is a prominent feature, and genetic indications often underscore diagnosis.
3. Symptoms are not due to other types of disorders or medical problems.

Information from: APA, 2013.

The occurrence of neurocognitive disorders is closely related to age (see **Figure 15-1** on the next page). Among people 65 years of age, the prevalence is around 1 to 2 percent, increasing to as much as 50 percent for those over the age of 85 (Heflin, 2018).

As you read earlier, **Alzheimer's disease** is the most common type of neurocognitive disorder, accounting for at least two-thirds of all cases. Around 5.4 million people in the United States currently have this disease, a number that is expected to triple by the year 2050 (Alzheimer's Association, 2018, 2017; Wolk & Dickerson, 2017). Alzheimer's disease sometimes appears in middle age, but in the vast majority of cases it occurs after the age of 65, and its prevalence increases markedly among people in their late 70s. Altogether, 11 percent of all people over 65 have Alzheimer's disease.

African Americans and Hispanic Americans are twice as likely as non-Hispanic white Americans to develop this disease (Alzheimer's Association, 2018, 2017). The reasons for this significant difference are not known (Keene et al., 2018).

Alzheimer's disease is a gradually progressive disease in which memory impairment is, by far, the most prominent cognitive dysfunction. Technically, sufferers receive a DSM-5 diagnosis of *mild neurocognitive disorder due to Alzheimer's disease* during the early and mild stages of the syndrome and *major neurocognitive disorder due to Alzheimer's disease* during the later, more severe stages (see Table 15-2 again).

Alzheimer's disease is named after Alois Alzheimer, the German physician who formally identified it in 1907. Alzheimer first became aware of the syndrome in 1901 when a new patient, Auguste D., was placed under his care:

> *On November 25, 1901, a . . . woman with no personal or family history of mental illness was admitted to a psychiatric hospital in Frankfurt, Germany, by her husband, who could no longer ignore or hide quirks and lapses that had overtaken her in recent months. First, there were unexplainable bursts of anger, and then a strange series of memory problems. She became increasingly unable to locate things in her own home and began to make surprising mistakes in the kitchen. By the time she arrived at Städtische Irrenanstalt, the Frankfurt Hospital for the Mentally Ill and Epileptics, her condition was as severe as it was curious. The attending doctor, senior physician Alois Alzheimer, began the new file with these notes. . . .*
>
> *She sits on the bed with a helpless expression.*
> *"What is your name?"*

(continued on the next page)

#

#CostlyDisease

In the U.S., the total annual cost for Alzheimer's disease and other neurocognitive disorders is $236 billion (Alzheimer's Association, 2018, 2017).

Blacks + Hispanics twice as likely to get alzheimers than whites

neurocognitive disorder A disorder marked by a significant decline in cognitive functioning.

major neurocognitive disorder A neurocognitive disorder in which the cognitive decline is substantial and interferes with one's independence.

mild neurocognitive disorder A neurocognitive disorder in which the cognitive decline is modest and does not interfere with one's independence.

Alzheimer's disease The most common type of neurocognitive disorder, marked most prominently by memory impairment.

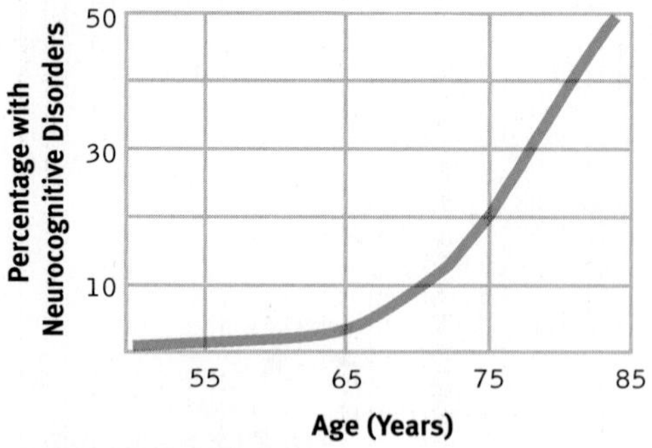

FIGURE 15-1

Neurocognitive Disorders and Age

Fewer than 1 percent of 60-year-olds have neurocognitive disorders, compared with as many as 50 percent of those who are 85. (Information from: Heflin, 2018; Keene et al., 2018.)

3-8 years for death

Auguste.
"Last name?"
Auguste.
"What is your husband's name?"
Auguste, I think.
"How long have you been here?"
(She seems to be trying to remember.)
Three weeks.

It was her second day in the hospital. Dr. Alzheimer, a thirty-seven-year-old neuropathologist and clinician, . . . observed in his new patient a remarkable cluster of symptoms: severe disorientation, reduced comprehension, aphasia (language impairment), paranoia, hallucinations, and a short-term memory so incapacitated that when he spoke her full-name, Frau Auguste D____, and asked her to write it down, the patient got only as far as "Frau" before needing the doctor to repeat the rest.

He spoke her name again. She wrote "Augu" and again stopped.

When Alzheimer prompted her a third time, she was able to write her entire first name and the initial "D" before finally giving up, telling the doctor, "I have lost myself."

Her condition did not improve. It became apparent that there was nothing that anyone at this or any other hospital could do for Frau D. except to ensure her safety and try to keep her as clean and comfortable as possible for the rest of her days. Over the next four and a half years, she became increasingly disoriented, delusional, and incoherent. She was often hostile.

"Her gestures showed a complete helplessness," Alzheimer later noted in a published report. "She was disoriented as to time and place. From time to time she would state that she did not understand anything, that she felt confused and totally lost. . . . Often she would scream for hours and hours in a horrible voice."

By November 1904, three and a half years into her illness, Auguste D. was bedridden, incontinent, and largely immobile. . . . Notes from October 1905 indicate that she had become permanently curled up in a fetal position with her knees drawn up to her chest, muttering but unable to speak, and requiring assistance to be fed.

(Shenk, 2001, pp. 12–14)

Although some people with Alzheimer's disease may survive for as many as 20 years, the time between onset and death is typically 3 to 8 years (Wolk & Dickerson, 2017). It usually begins with mild memory problems, lapses of attention, and difficulties in language and communication. As symptoms worsen, the person has trouble completing complicated tasks or remembering important appointments. Eventually sufferers also have difficulty with simple tasks, forget distant memories, and have changes in personality that often become very noticeable. For example, a gentle man may become uncharacteristically aggressive.

People with Alzheimer's disease may at first deny that they have a problem, but they soon become anxious or depressed about their state of mind; many also become agitated. At least 17 percent of them develop major depressive disorder (APA, 2018; Chi et al., 2014). A woman from Virginia describes her memory loss as the disease progresses:

Very often I wander around looking for something which I know is very pertinent, but then after a while I forget about what it is I was looking for. . . . Once the idea is lost, everything is lost and I have nothing to do but wander around trying to figure out what it was that was so important earlier.

(Shenk, 2001, p. 43)

Jim Davis/The Boston Globe via Getty Images

Slipping away Because of their short-term memory problems, people with advanced cases of Alzheimer's disease are often unable to easily draw or paint or do simple tasks. In addition, their long-term memory deficits may prevent them from recognizing even close relatives or friends.

As the neurocognitive symptoms intensify, people with Alzheimer's disease show less and less awareness of their limitations. They may withdraw from others during the late stages of the disorder, become more confused about time and place, wander, speak little, and show very poor judgment (Wolk & Dickerson, 2017). Eventually they become fully dependent on other people. They may lose almost all knowledge of the past and fail to recognize the faces of even close relatives. They also become increasingly uncomfortable at night and take frequent naps during the day (Neikrug & Ancoli-Israel, 2017). During the late phases of the disorder, they require constant care.

People with Alzheimer's usually remain in fairly good health until the later stages of the disease. As their mental functioning declines, however, they become less active and spend much of their time just sitting or lying in bed. This makes them prone to develop serious infections such as pneumonia, which can result in death (Mitchell, 2018). Alzheimer's disease is currently responsible for almost 94,000 deaths each year in the United States, a number more than 40 percent higher than it was a decade ago (CDC, 2017, 2015). It is the sixth leading cause of death in the country, the third leading cause among the elderly.

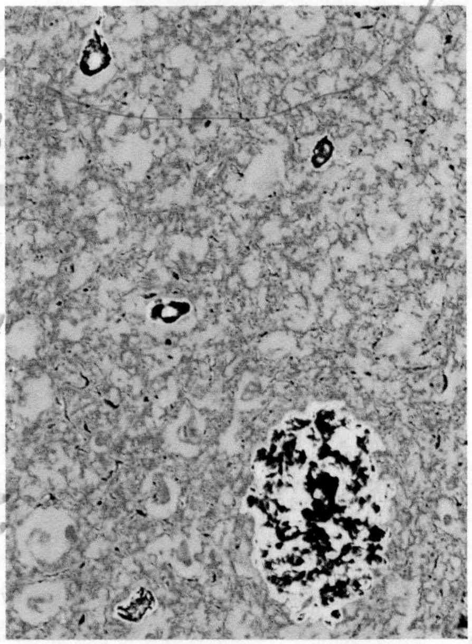

Simon Fraser/Science Source

Biological culprits Tissue from the brain of a person with Alzheimer's disease shows excessive amounts of plaque (large yellow-black sphere at lower right of photo) and neurofibrillary tangles (several smaller yellow blobs throughout photo).

In most cases, Alzheimer's disease can be diagnosed with certainty only after death, when structural changes in the person's brain, such as excessive *senile plaques* and *neurofibrillary tangles*, can be fully examined. **Senile plaques** are sphere-shaped deposits of a small molecule known as the *beta-amyloid protein* that form in the spaces *between* neurons in the hippocampus, cerebral cortex, and certain other brain structures, as well as in some nearby blood vessels. The formation of plaques is a normal part of aging, but it is exceptionally high in people with Alzheimer's disease (Keene et al., 2018). **Neurofibrillary tangles,** twisted protein fibers found *within* the neurons of the hippocampus and certain other brain structures, also occur in all people as they age, but, again, people with Alzheimer's disease form an extraordinary number of them.

Scientists do not fully understand what role excessive numbers of plaques and tangles play in Alzheimer's disease, but most agree that they both do their ultimate damage by contributing to the death of neurons. The plaques (which occur between neurons) accomplish this by interfering with neuron-to-neuron communications, while the tangles (which occur inside neurons) accomplish it by blocking the transportation of essential molecules within neurons (Alzheimer's Association, 2018, 2017). Today's leading explanations for Alzheimer's disease center on plaques and tangles and on the various factors that may contribute to their formation and excessive buildup.

What Are the Genetic Causes of Alzheimer's Disease? To understand the genetic theories of Alzheimer's disease, we must first appreciate the nature and role of *proteins*. Proteins are fundamental components of all living cells, including, of course, brain cells. They are large molecules made up of chains of carbon, hydrogen, oxygen, nitrogen, and sulfur. There are many different kinds of proteins, each with a different function. Collectively, they are essential for the proper functioning of an organism.

The plaques and tangles that are so plentiful in the brains of Alzheimer's patients seem to occur when two important proteins start acting in a frenzied manner. Abnormal activity by the beta-amyloid protein is, as you just read, key to the repeated formation of plaques. Abnormal activity by another protein, *tau*, is key to the excessive formation of tangles. One of the leading theories holds that the many plaques formed by beta-amyloid proteins also cause tau proteins within neurons to start breaking down, resulting in tangles and the death of many neurons (Keene et al., 2018; Hughes, 2011).

What causes this chain of events? Genetic factors are a major culprit (Sweeney et al., 2019). However, the genetic factors that are responsible differ for the early-onset and late-onset types of Alzheimer's disease.

senile plaques Sphere-shaped deposits of beta-amyloid protein that form in the spaces between certain neurons and in certain blood vessels of the brain as people age. People with Alzheimer's disease have an excessive number of such plaques.

neurofibrillary tangles Twisted protein fibers that form within certain neurons as people age. People with Alzheimer's disease have an excessive number of such tangles.

Lucas Oleniuk/Toronto Star via Getty Images

An early good-bye Lyndon Blackbird (left) takes a leave of absence from work to spend what he suspects will be the last summer with his 54-year-old wife, Evelyn Davis. Davis suffers from early-onset Alzheimer's disease, a relatively uncommon form of this neurocognitive disorder.

EARLY-ONSET ALZHEIMER'S DISEASE Alzheimer's disease occurs before the age of 65 in fewer than 1 percent of cases. This relatively rare form of the disorder typically runs in families. Researchers have learned that it is caused by abnormalities in genes responsible for the production of two proteins—the *beta-amyloid precursor protein* (*beta-APP*) and the *presenilin protein*. Apparently, some families transmit mutations, or abnormal forms, of one or both of these genes—mutations that lead ultimately to abnormal beta-amyloid protein buildups and, in turn, to plaque formations (Sherva & Kowall, 2018).

LATE-ONSET ALZHEIMER'S DISEASE The vast majority of Alzheimer cases develop after the age of 65 and do not typically run in families (Wolk & Dickerson, 2017). This late-onset form of the disease appears to result from a combination of genetic, environmental, and lifestyle factors. However, the genetic factors at play in late-onset Alzheimer's disease are different from those involved in early-onset Alzheimer's disease. The genetic factor that has received the most attention from clinical theorists and researchers is a gene called the *apolipoprotein E* (*ApoE*) *gene*.

The ApoE gene, located on chromosome 19, is normally responsible for the production of a protein that helps carry various fats into the bloodstream. This gene comes in various forms. About 30 percent of the population inherit the form called *ApoE-4*, and those people may be particularly vulnerable to the development of Alzheimer's disease (Keene et al., 2018; Sherva & Kowall, 2018). Apparently, this ApoE-4 gene form promotes the excessive formation of beta-amyloid proteins, helping to spur the formation of plaques and, in turn, the breakdown of the tau protein, the formation of numerous tangles, the death of many neurons, and, ultimately, the onset of Alzheimer's disease.

Although the ApoE-4 gene form appears to be a major contributor to the development of Alzheimer's disease, it is important to recognize that not everyone with this form of the gene develops the disease. Other factors—perhaps environmental, lifestyle, or stress-related—may also have a significant impact in the development of late-onset Alzheimer's disease (Alzheimer's Association, 2018, 2017).

AN ALTERNATIVE GENETIC THEORY OF ALZHEIMER'S DISEASE As you have just read, a number of genetic theories of Alzheimer's disease point to gene forms—most often ApoE-4—that produce abnormal beta-amyloid protein buildups and plaque formations. These gene forms, in turn, lead to abnormal activity of tau proteins and the formation of numerous tangles. In recent years, however, some researchers have come to believe that abnormal tau protein activity is not always the result of these abnormal beta-amyloid protein buildups (DeVos et al., 2018; Smolek et al., 2018). These researchers have identified other gene forms in Alzheimer's patients that seem to be directly associated with tau protein abnormalities and tangle formations within neurons. Thus it may be that there are multiple genetic causes for the formation of numerous tangle formations and the onset of Alzheimer's disease: (1) gene forms that start the ball rolling by first promoting beta-amyloid protein formations and plaques, and (2) gene forms that more directly promote tau protein abnormalities and tangle formations.

#

#EarlyDebut

People with early-onset Alzheimer's disease may develop symptoms as early as 30 years of age (Alzheimer's Association, 2018).

How Does Brain Structure Relate to Alzheimer's Disease? Granting that genetic factors may predispose people to Alzheimer's disease, we still need to know what abnormalities in brain structure eventually result from such factors and help promote Alzheimer's disease. Researchers have identified a number of possibilities.

Certain brain structures seem to be especially important in memory. Among the most important structures in short-term memory is the *prefrontal cortex*. Among the most

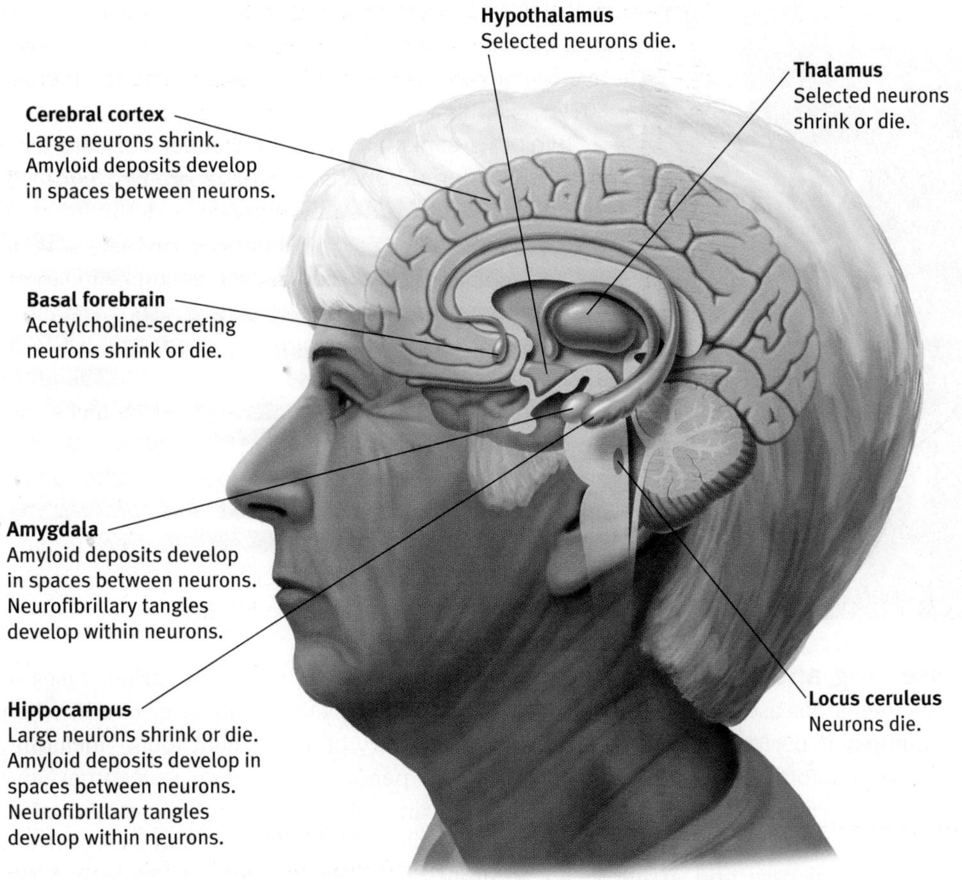
Hypothalamus
Selected neurons die.
Thalamus
Selected neurons shrink or die.
Cerebral cortex
Large neurons shrink. Amyloid deposits develop in spaces between neurons.
Basal forebrain
Acetylcholine-secreting neurons shrink or die.
Amygdala
Amyloid deposits develop in spaces between neurons. Neurofibrillary tangles develop within neurons.
Hippocampus
Large neurons shrink or die. Amyloid deposits develop in spaces between neurons. Neurofibrillary tangles develop within neurons.
Locus ceruleus
Neurons die.

FIGURE 15-2

The Aging Brain

In old age, the brain undergoes changes that affect cognitive functions such as memory, learning, and reasoning to some degree. The same changes occur to an excessive degree in people with Alzheimer's disease. (Information from: Bauer, Cabral, & Killiany, 2018; Zheng et al. 2018; Mu et al., 2017; Nomi et al., 2017; Selkoe, 2011, 1992.)

important structures in transforming short-term memory into long-term memory are the *temporal lobes* (which include the *hippocampus* and *amygdala*) and the *diencephalon* (which includes the *mammillary bodies, thalamus,* and *hypothalamus*). Research indicates that Alzheimer's disease involves improper functioning of one or more of these brain structures (Giraldo et al., 2018; Wolk & Dickerson, 2017) (see **Figure 15-2**).

What Biochemical Changes in the Brain Relate to Alzheimer's Disease?

In order for new information to be acquired and remembered, certain proteins must be produced in key brain cells. Several brain chemicals—for example, *acetylcholine, glutamate, RNA* (*ribonucleic acid*), and *calcium*—are responsible for the production of the memory-linked proteins. If the activity of any of these chemicals is disturbed, the proper production of proteins may be prevented and the formation of memories interrupted (Gallegos et al., 2018; More et al., 2018). Correspondingly, researchers have found that abnormal activity by these may contribute to the symptoms of Alzheimer's disease (Hoshi et al., 2018; Sabri et al., 2018).

Other Explanations of Alzheimer's Disease Several lines of investigation suggest that certain substances found in nature may act as toxins, damage the brain, and contribute to the development of Alzheimer's disease. For example, researchers have detected high levels of *zinc* in the brains of some Alzheimer's patients (Lee et al., 2018; Khan, 2016). This finding has gained particular attention because in some animal studies zinc has been observed to trigger a clumping of the beta-amyloid protein, similar to the plaques found in the brains of Alzheimer's patients.

Still other studies suggest that the environmental toxin *lead* may contribute to the development of Alzheimer's disease (Lee, Peterson, & Freeman, 2017; Lee & Freeman, 2016, 2014). Many of today's elderly were exposed to high levels of lead in the 1960s and 1970s, regularly inhaling air pollution from vehicle exhausts. Several studies suggest

#BusyBrains

Researchers have found fewer plaques and tangles in the brains of lab mice that live in intellectually and physically stimulating environments—with chew toys, running wheels, and tunnels—than in those of mice that live in less stimulating settings (Li et al., 2017; Lazarov et al., 2005).

Jens Büttner/picture-alliance/dpa/AP Images

More than a dance Carmen Dunkelmann, who suffers from an advanced neurocognitive disorder, dances with her husband, Peter, at the "dance cafe" of her treatment center. The couple always loved dancing and, as Carmen's memories and abilities slip away all too fast, this is an activity and form of intimacy they can still share. In addition, the exercise, stimulation, and joy that accompany dancing are thought to be helpful in Carmen's struggle against her progressive disorder.

that this earlier absorption of lead and other pollutants may be having a negative effect on the current cognitive functioning of these individuals (Richardson et al., 2014).

Two other explanations for Alzheimer's disease have also been offered. One is the *autoimmune theory.* On the basis of certain irregularities found in the immune systems of people with Alzheimer's disease, several researchers have speculated that changes in aging brain cells may trigger an *autoimmune response* (that is, a mistaken attack by the immune system against itself) that helps lead to the disease (Walton, 2018). The other explanation is a *viral theory.* Because Alzheimer's disease resembles *Creutzfeldt-Jakob disease,* another type of neurocognitive disorder that is known to be caused by a slow-acting virus, some researchers propose that a similar virus may cause Alzheimer's disease. To date, however, no such virus has been detected in the brains of Alzheimer's victims (Zafar et al., 2017).

Assessing and Predicting Alzheimer's Disease As you read earlier, cases of Alzheimer's disease can be diagnosed with absolute certainty only after death, when an autopsy is performed. However, by using a battery of assessment tools—including neuropsychological tests (tests that measure a person's cognitive, perceptual, and motor performances on certain tasks), brain scans, blood tests and other laboratory work, and careful history taking—diagnosticians are usually able to build a very strong circumstantial case and arrive at an accurate diagnosis (Knezevic & Mizrahi, 2018; Larson, 2018).

When diagnosticians administer brain scans, laboratory tests, and other biological tests, they are looking for **biomarkers**—biochemical, molecular, genetic, or structural characteristics that usually accompany Alzheimer's disease (Blennow & Zetterberg, 2018). It turns out that many of these biomarkers appear in the brain long before the obvious onset of Alzheimer's disease. Thus many researchers have tried to determine whether certain combinations of biomarkers might be able to *predict* cases of Alzheimer's disease and other neurocognitive disorders—perhaps even years before the onset of symptoms (Perpetuini et al., 2018; Sheng et al., 2018). One promising line of work comes from the laboratory of neuroscientist Lisa Mosconi and her colleagues (Mosconi et al., 2018, 2014, 2010, 2008). Using brain scans and other biological tests, this research team measured a combination of biomarkers in dozens of elderly research participants—all of them seemingly healthy—and then conducted follow-up studies of them for up to 24 years. Eventually, 43 percent of the study's participants developed either a mild or major neurocognitive disorder due to Alzheimer's disease. The researchers found that those who developed such disorders had displayed more biomarker abnormalities on their initial brain tests than the participants who remained healthy. Overall, the biomarker tests, administered years before the onset of symptoms, predicted mild neurocognitive impairment with an accuracy rate of 71 percent and major neurocognitive impairment with an accuracy rate of 83 percent.

Would people be better off knowing that they will eventually develop a disease that has no known cure?

Other Types of Neurocognitive Disorders There are a number of neurocognitive disorders in addition to Alzheimer's disease (APA, 2013). *Vascular neurocognitive disorder* follows a cerebrovascular accident, or *stroke,* during which blood flow to specific areas of the brain was cut off, thus damaging the areas (Wright, 2017). *Frontotemporal neurocognitive disorder,* also known as *Pick's disease,* affects the frontal and temporal

biomarkers Biochemical, molecular, genetic, or structural characteristics that usually accompany a disease.

Neuro cog - disorde ... spasms of body

lobes (Che et al., 2018). *Neurocognitive disorder due to prion disease,* also called *Creutzfeldt-Jakob disease,* has symptoms that include spasms of the body. As we observed earlier, this disorder is caused by a virus that may live in the body for years before the disease develops. *Neurocognitive disorder due to Huntington's disease* is an inherited progressive syndrome in which memory problems, along with personality changes, mood difficulties, and severe twitching and spasms, worsen over time (Suchowersky, 2018). *Parkinson's disease,* the slowly progressive neurological disorder marked by tremors, rigidity, and unsteadiness, can result in *neurocognitive disorder due to Parkinson's disease,* particularly in older people or those whose cases are advanced (Rodnitzky, 2018). *Neurocognitive disorder due to Lewy body disease* involves the buildup of clumps of protein deposits, called Lewy bodies, within many neurons (Farlow, 2018). Finally, yet other neurocognitive disorders may be caused by *HIV infections, traumatic brain injury, substance abuse,* or various *medical conditions* such as meningitis or advanced syphilis (Price, 2018, 2017) (see ***Trending*** on the next page).

BSIP/UIG via Getty Images

A therapeutic environment In this long-term care facility, a woman with Alzheimer's disease is drawn to and touches some of her room's stimulating objects and is, at the same time, comforted by the room's soothing colors and decorations.

What Treatments Are Currently Available for Alzheimer's Disease and Other Neurocognitive Disorders?

Treatments for the cognitive features of Alzheimer's disease and most other types of neurocognitive disorders have been at best modestly helpful. A number of approaches have been applied, including drug therapy, cognitive-behavioral interventions, support for caregivers, and sociocultural approaches. None of these interventions stops the progression of the disorder (Wolk & Dickerson, 2017).

DRUG TREATMENT The drugs currently prescribed for Alzheimer's patients are designed to affect acetylcholine and glutamate, the neurotransmitters that play important roles in memory. Such drugs include donepezil (Aricept), rivastigmine (Exelon), galantamine (Reminyl), and memantine (Namenda). The short-term memory and reasoning ability of some Alzheimer's patients who take these drugs improve slightly, as do their use of language and their ability to cope under pressure (Press & Alexander, 2018). Although the benefits of the drugs are limited and their side effects can be problematic, they have been approved by the FDA. Clinicians believe that they may be of greatest use to people in the early, mild stage of Alzheimer's disease. There is a popular belief that another approach, taking vitamin E, either alone or in combination with one of these drugs, will help slow down some of the cognitive difficulties experienced by people in the mild stage of Alzheimer's disease; however, as it turns out, this notion is, at best, modestly supported by various studies (Press & Alexander, 2018).

increase short term memory

Rejoining the world Virtual reality technology can help improve the cognitive and physical functioning of elderly people and Alzheimer's sufferers. Here a retirement home resident takes a virtual bike ride through various environments and performs valuable exercise (she's also on a stationary bike).

BSIP/UIG via Getty Images

...TRENDING

Damaging the Brain: Football and CTE

AP Photo/Steve Ruark

Part of the game? National Football League great John Mackey shows off his Super Bowl V and Hall of Fame rings. Mackey died at age 69 in 2011 of a major neurocognitive disorder, apparently caused by repeated sports injuries to his head. The link between football and such disorders was implicitly acknowledged by the NFL with their implementation of the "88 Plan" (named after Mackey's jersey number), which helps pay the cost of care for football veterans with such problems.

Tens of millions of people in the United States build their Sunday schedules around professional football. They watch their favorite National Football League (NFL) teams go "head-to-head" in what has arguably become America's favorite viewer pastime. For years it was generally believed that the obvious dangers of this sport were outweighed by the enjoyment it brought to so many and the riches it offered the players. But that thinking has changed dramatically over the past decade. The reason? The discovery that *chronic traumatic encephalopathy (CTE)*, a degenerative brain disease, is suffered by many NFL players, largely as a result of the repeated head blows they receive over the course of their years in the game (Solomon, 2018; Rabinovici, 2017).

Research has clarified that, like various other neurocognitive disorders, CTE features excessive formations of *tangles*—produced by the *tau protein*—in neurons throughout the brain (Lepage et al., 2018; Ling, 2018). These tangles, along with related abnormalities in brain structures such as the hippocampus, thalamus, substantia nigra, and amygdala, produce a range of neurocognitive symptoms that unfold over a period of years—disorientation, memory loss, erratic behavior, personality changes, progressive cognitive decline, suicidal thinking, and death (Larson, 2018, 2017; Brosch & Farlow, 2017).

CTE and its lethal impact were not identified until 2005 when neuropathologist Bennet Omalu was conducting an autopsy on former NFL player Mike Webster and discovered indications of this "new" disease in Webster's brain. Webster had displayed severe cognitive, behavioral, and emotional deterioration prior to his death, but his symptoms had been a mystery to medical professionals. Since Omalu's breakthrough discovery, CTE has been identified in the autopsied brains of many dozens of former football, hockey, soccer, and rugby players, as well as boxers, wrestlers, martial artists, and military personnel (Solomon, 2018; Lindsley, 2017).

The recognition of CTE and its impact unfolded slowly for several reasons (Lee et al., 2018; Mez et al., 2017). One, it is caused by multiple relatively mild concussions and mild blows to the head, rather than by one obvious episode of major brain trauma. Two, brain scans of living persons cannot detect the disease in progress because mild concussions do not result in bleeding or obvious brain structure damage. Like Alzheimer's disease, a definitive diagnosis of CTE can be made only when the brain is examined after death. However, what *is* clear while the sufferers are still alive is that something profoundly wrong is happening to them.

Now that CTE is "on the map," a growing number of precautions and actions are being taken—by individuals and officials alike (Oliver et al., 2018; Lindsley, 2017). For example, the NFL has changed its "return-to-play" procedures, making sure that players fully recover from all symptoms of even mild concussions before they resume playing. The league has also reduced the number of "contact" practice sessions a team may conduct. Moreover, the NFL has created a multimillion-dollar CTE compensation fund from which former players and their families can collect as their symptoms unfold and/or after their deaths. Changes of this kind did not necessarily come about easily or cooperatively—multiple lawsuits and collective bargaining pressures preceded them. Nevertheless, they and other such improvements are now unfolding.

In the meantime, we are reminded all too often that neurocognitive disorders are not only the result of genetic and/or lifestyle factors. They can also be brought about by head injuries—even seemingly mild ones—or, for that matter, by drugs, brain surgery, or factors yet to be determined.

The drugs just discussed are each prescribed *after* a person has developed Alzheimer's disease. In contrast, studies suggest that certain substances now available on the marketplace for other kinds of problems may help prevent or delay the onset of Alzheimer's disease. For example, some studies have found that women who took *estrogen,* the female sex hormone, for years after menopause cut their risk of developing

© Christina Koci Hernandez/SFC/San Francisco Chronicle/Polaris

Al Schaben/Los Angeles Times via Getty Images

Fitness of all kinds Clinicians have stressed the value of *cognitive fitness* to help prevent or slow down the cognitive decline seen in old age and/or neurocognitive disorders. Thus, many senior community programs now include facilities (left) where elderly people can work on cognitive computer programs. Research further suggests that *physical exercise* may be even more effective at slowing cognitive decline. Thus, the elderly identical twins on the right, both of whom have Alzheimer's disease, participate regularly in a physical exercise program.

Alzheimer's disease in half (Grodstein, 2018; Li et al., 2017, 2014). Other studies have suggested that the long-term use of *nonsteroidal anti-inflammatory drugs* such as *ibuprofen* and *naprosyn* (drugs found in Advil, Motrin, Nuprin, and other pain relievers) may help reduce the risk of Alzheimer's disease, although recent findings on this possibility have been mixed (Press & Alexander, 2018).

COGNITIVE-BEHAVIORAL TECHNIQUES Cognitive-behavioral treatments have been used in cases of Alzheimer's disease, with some degree of success. In Japan, for example, a number of people with the disease meet regularly in classes, performing simple calculations and reading essays and novels aloud. Similarly, research suggests that cognitive activities, including computer-based cognitive stimulation programs, sometimes help prevent or delay the onset of Alzheimer's disease (Ko et al., 2018; Press & Alexander, 2018). For example, one study of 700 people in their 80s found that those research participants who had pursued cognitive activities over a five-year period (for example, writing letters, following the news, reading books, or attending concerts or plays) were less likely to develop Alzheimer's disease than were mentally inactive participants (Arfanakis et al., 2016; Wilson et al., 2012, 2007).

cog-nitive behav. techniques

Interestingly, cognitive-behavioral strategies that focus primarily on behaviors rather than on cognitions seem to be even more useful in preventing and managing this disease. It has become clear across many studies that physical exercise helps improve cognitive functioning—for people of all ages and states of health (Mandolesi et al., 2018; McDade & Petersen, 2018). There is evidence that regular physical exercise may also help reduce the risk of developing Alzheimer's disease and other neurocognitive disorders (Keene et al., 2018; Press & Alexander, 2018). Thus physical exercise is often a part of treatment programs for people with the disorders.

Behavior-focused interventions of a different kind have been used to help improve specific symptoms displayed by Alzheimer's patients. The approaches typically focus on changing everyday patient behaviors that are stressful for the family, such as wandering at night, loss of bladder control, demands for attention, and inadequate personal care (Press & Alexander, 2018, 2017; Lancioni et al., 2011). The therapists use a combination of role-playing exercises, modeling, and practice to teach family members how and when to use reinforcement in order to shape more positive behaviors.

SUPPORT FOR CAREGIVERS Caregiving can take a heavy toll on the close relatives of people with Alzheimer's disease and other neurocognitive disorders (Alzheimer's Association, 2018, 2017). Almost 90 percent of all people with Alzheimer's disease are cared for by their relatives, usually their adult children or spouses. It is hard to take care of

#GenderPressure

Two-thirds of caregivers for Alzheimer sufferers are women. One-third of the caregivers are daughters.

Daughters provide an average of 102 caregiving hours per month for their parents with Alzheimer's disease. Sons provide 80 hours per month.

(Information from: Alzheimer's Association, 2018, 2017)

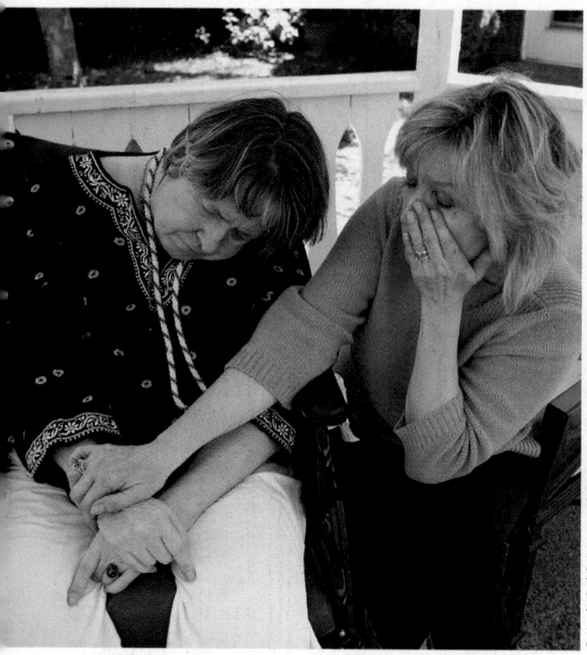

© Jodi Cobb/National Geographic Creative

Toll on caregivers A woman comforts her twin sister, who suffers from Alzheimer's disease. The psychological and physical burdens of caring for close relatives with neurocognitive disorders typically take a heavy toll on caregivers.

someone who is becoming increasingly lost, helpless, and medically ill. And it is very painful to witness mental and physical decline in someone you love.

One of the most frequent reasons for the institutionalization of people with Alzheimer's disease is that overwhelmed caregivers can no longer cope with the difficulties of keeping them at home (Alzheimer's Association, 2018, 2017; Di Rosa et al., 2011). Many caregivers experience anger and depression, and their own physical and mental health often declines (Kang et al., 2014). A number of them are, in fact, "sandwich generation" caregivers, meaning they must care not only for their parents with Alzheimer's disease but also for their teenage children. Clinicians now recognize that one of the most important aspects of treating Alzheimer's disease and other types of neurocognitive disorders is to focus on the emotional needs of the caregivers, including their needs for regular time out, education about the disease, and psychotherapy (Merlo et al., 2018; Piersol et al., 2017). Some clinicians also provide caregiver support groups.

SOCIOCULTURAL APPROACHES Sociocultural approaches play an important role in treatment (Alzheimer's Association, 2018, 2017). A number of day-care facilities for patients with neurocognitive disorders have been developed, providing treatment programs and activities for outpatients during the day and returning them to their homes and families at night. There are also many assisted-living facilities in which those suffering from neurocognitive impairment live in cheerful apartments, receive needed supervision, and take part in stimulating activities. These apartments are typically designed to meet the special needs of the residents—providing more light, for example, or enclosing gardens with circular paths so the residents can go for strolls alone without getting lost. Studies suggest that such facilities bring some degree of improvement to the cognitive deficits of residents and enhance their enjoyment of life. In addition, a growing number of practical devices, such as tracking beacons worn on the wrists of Alzheimer's patients and shoes that contain a GPS tracker, have been developed to help locate patients who may wander off (Jensen & Padilla, 2017; Press & Alexander, 2017).

If Alzheimer's disease is a cognitive disorder, and biologically caused, why would increasing patients' comfort levels make a difference?

Given the progress now unfolding in the understanding and treatment of Alzheimer's disease and other neurocognitive disorders, researchers are looking forward to life-changing advances in the coming years. The brain changes responsible for these disorders are tremendously complex, but most investigators believe that exciting breakthroughs are just over the horizon.

#NormalDecline?

DSM-5 has added the category *mild neurocognitive disorder* in order to help clinicians detect individuals in the early stages of *major neurocognitive disorder* (e.g., *Alzheimer's disease*). Critics worry, however, that many people who display normal forgetfulness and other normal features of aging will incorrectly receive a diagnosis of mild neurocognitive disorder.

...SUMMING UP

DISORDERS OF COGNITION Older people have an increased risk for experiencing delirium, a disturbance marked by major disturbances in attention and orientation.

Neurocognitive disorders, characterized by a significant decline in cognitive function, become increasingly common in older age groups. There are many types of neurocognitive disorders, the most common being Alzheimer's disease. This disease has been linked to an unusually high number of senile plaques and neurofibrillary tangles in the brain. According to a leading explanation of late-onset Alzheimer's disease, people who inherit ApoE-4, a particular form of the apolipoprotein E (ApoE) gene, are particularly vulnerable to Alzheimer's disease.

A number of other causes have also been proposed for this disease, including high levels of zinc, lead, or other toxins; immune system problems; and a virus of some kind.

Researchers are making significant strides at better assessing Alzheimer's disease and other neurocognitive disorders and even at identifying those who will develop these disorders. Drug therapy and cognitive-behavioral therapies have been used to treat Alzheimer's disease, with limited success. Addressing the needs of caregivers is a key part of treatment. In addition, sociocultural approaches such as day-care facilities are on the rise.

Issues Affecting the Mental Health of the Elderly

As the study and treatment of elderly people have progressed, three issues have raised concern among clinicians: the special problems faced by elderly members of racial and ethnic minority groups, the inadequacies of long-term care, and the need for a health-maintenance approach to medical care in an aging world.

First, *discrimination based on race and ethnicity* has long been a problem in the United States (see Chapter 2), and many people suffer as a result, particularly those who are old. To be both old and a member of a minority group is considered a kind of "double jeopardy" by many observers. For older women in minority groups, the difficulties are sometimes termed "triple jeopardy," as many more older women than older men live alone, are widowed, and are poor. Clinicians must take into account their older patients' race, ethnicity, and gender as they try to diagnose and treat their mental health problems (Heflin, 2018; Ng et al., 2014) (see **Figure 15-3**).

Kyodo News/Getty Images

First things first Self-care and self-concern may decline over the course of a major neurocognitive disorder. Thus these elderly women at a treatment facility in Japan are receiving hygiene and make-up lessons, part of their "cosmetic therapy program."

Some elderly people in minority groups face language barriers that interfere with their medical and mental health care. Others may hold cultural beliefs that prevent them from seeking services. Additionally, many members of minority groups do not trust the majority establishment or do not know about medical and mental health services that are sensitive to their culture and their particular needs (Lines & Wiener, 2014). As a result, it is common for elderly members of racial and ethnic minority groups to rely largely on family members or friends for remedies and health care. Today, around 20 percent of all elderly people live with their children or other relatives, usually because of increasing health problems (Pew Research Center, 2017; Keefer, 2015). In the United States, this living arrangement is more common for families from racial and ethnic minority groups.

Second, many older people require *long-term care*, a general term that may refer variously to the services offered outside the family in a partially supervised apartment, a senior housing complex for mildly impaired elderly persons, or a nursing home where skilled medical and nursing care is available around the clock. The quality of care in such residences varies widely.

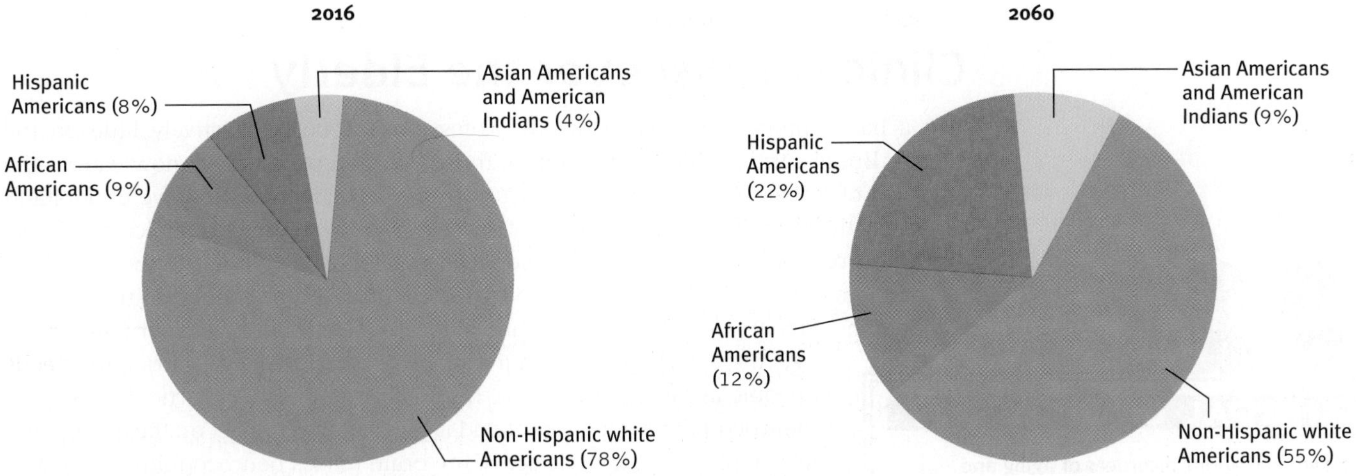

FIGURE 15-3

Ethnicity and Old Age

The elderly population is becoming racially and ethnically more diverse. In the United States today, almost 80 percent of all people over the age of 65 are non-Hispanic white Americans. By 2060, non-Hispanic white Americans will comprise only 55 percent of the elderly. (Information from: Frey, 2018; Mather, 2016; PRB, 2015.)

Paula Solloway/Alamy

Every little bit helps In line with findings that all kinds of physical exercise may help improve cognitive functioning and/or slow down cognitive decline, these elderly persons participate in an "armchair" exercise program at a community center in England.

At any given time in the United States, only about 4 percent of the entire elderly population actually live in nursing homes (1.5 million people), but as many as 20 percent of people 85 years and older do eventually wind up being placed in such facilities (CDC, 2017). Thus many older adults live in fear of being "put away." They fear having to move, losing independence, and living in a medical environment. Many also worry about the cost of long-term care facilities. Around-the-clock nursing care is expensive, and nursing home costs continue to rise. The average cost for a private room in a nursing home in the United States is over $90,000 per year; for a semi-private room it is over $80,000 (Alzheimer's Association, 2018, 2017). Most health insurance plans available today do not adequately cover the costs of long-term or permanent placement. Worry over these issues can greatly harm the mental health and/or family harmony of older adults.

Finally, clinical scientists suggest that the current generation of young adults should take a *health-maintenance, or wellness promotion, approach* to their own aging process (Heflin, 2018; Libman et al., 2017). In other words, they should do things that promote physical and mental health—avoid smoking, eat well-balanced and healthful meals, exercise regularly, engage in positive social relationships, and take advantage of psychoeducational, stress management, and other mental health programs. There is a growing belief that older adults will adapt more readily to changes and negative events if their physical and psychological health is good.

...SUMMING UP

ISSUES AFFECTING THE MENTAL HEALTH OF THE ELDERLY In studying and treating the problems of old age, clinicians have become concerned about three issues: the problems of elderly members of racial and ethnic minority groups, inadequacies of long-term care, and the need for health maintenance by young adults.

Clinicians Discover the Elderly

Just a half century ago, mental health professionals focused relatively little on the elderly. But like the problems of children, those of aging people have now caught the attention of researchers and clinicians. Current work is changing how we understand and treat the psychological problems of the elderly. No longer do clinicians simply accept depression or anxiety in older people as inevitable. No longer do they overlook the dangers of prescription drug misuse by the elderly. And no longer do they underestimate the dangers of delirium or the prevalence of neurocognitive disorders.

As the elderly population lives longer and grows ever larger, the needs of people in this age group are becoming more visible. Particularly urgent is neurocognitive impairment and its devastating impact on the elderly and their families. The complexity of the brain makes neurocognitive disorders difficult to understand, diagnose, and treat. However, researchers are now making important discoveries on a regular basis. To date, this research has largely focused on the biological aspects of the disorders, but the disorders have such a powerful impact on patients and their families that psychological and sociocultural investigations are also now growing by leaps and bounds.

CLINICAL CHOICES

Now that you've read about disorders of aging and cognition, try the interactive case study for this chapter. See if you are able to identify Fred's symptoms and suggest a diagnosis based on his symptoms. What kind of treatment would be most effective for Fred? Go to **LaunchPad** to access ***Clinical Choices***.

... Key Terms

geropsychology, p. 473
delirium, p. 479
neurocognitive disorder, p. 480
major neurocognitive disorder, p. 480
mild neurocognitive disorder, p. 480
Alzheimer's disease, p. 481
senile plaques, p. 483
beta-amyloid protein, p. 483
neurofibrillary tangles, p. 483
tau protein, p. 483
early-onset Alzheimer's disease, p. 484
beta-amyloid precursor protein, p. 484
presenilin protein, p. 484
late-onset Alzheimer's disease, p. 484
apolipoprotein E (ApoE) gene, p. 484
ApoE-4, p. 484
prefrontal cortex, p. 484
temporal lobes, p. 485
diencephalon, p. 485
acetylcholine, p. 485
glutamate, p. 485
ribonucleic acid (RNA), p. 485
calcium, p. 485
zinc, p. 485
lead, p. 485
autoimmune theory, p. 486
viral theory, p. 486
Creutzfeldt-Jakob disease, p. 486
biomarkers, p. 486
vascular neurocognitive disorder, p. 486
Huntington's disease, p. 487
Lewy body disease, p. 487
donepezil, p. 487
rivastigmine, p. 487
galantamine, p. 487
memantine, p. 487
vitamin E, p. 487
day-care facilities, p. 490
assisted-living facilities, p. 490
discrimination, p. 491
long-term care, p. 491
health-maintenance approach, p. 492

... Quick Quiz

1. What is geropsychology? What kinds of special pressures and upsets are faced by elderly persons? *pp. 472–474*
2. How common is depression among the elderly? What are the possible causes of this disorder in aged persons, and how is it treated? *pp. 474–475*
3. How prevalent are anxiety disorders among the elderly? How do theorists explain the onset of these disorders in aged persons, and how do clinicians treat them? *pp. 475–476*
4. Describe and explain the kinds of substance misuse patterns that sometimes emerge among the elderly. *pp. 476–478*
5. What kinds of psychotic disorders may be experienced by elderly persons? *p. 478*
6. What is delirium? *p. 479*
7. How common are neurocognitive disorders among the elderly? Describe the clinical features and course of Alzheimer's disease. *pp. 480–483*
8. What are the possible causes of Alzheimer's disease? *pp. 483–486*
9. Can Alzheimer's disease be predicted? What kinds of interventions are applied in cases of this and other neurocognitive disorders? *pp. 486–490*
10. What issues regarding aging have raised particular concern among clinicians? *pp. 491–492*

CHAPTER

16

...Law, Society, and the Mental Health Profession

TOPIC OVERVIEW

Dear Jodie:

There is a definite possibility that I will be killed in my attempt to get Reagan. It is for this very reason that I am writing you this letter now. As you well know by now, I love you very much. The past seven months I have left you dozens of poems, letters and messages in the faint hope you would develop an interest in me. . . . Jodie, I would abandon this idea of getting Reagan in a second if I could only win your heart and live out the rest of my life with you, whether it be in total obscurity or whatever. I will admit to you that the reason I'm going ahead with this attempt now is because I just cannot wait any longer to impress you. I've got to do something now to make you understand in no uncertain terms that I am doing all of this for your sake. By sacrificing my freedom and possibly my life I hope to change your mind about me. This letter is being written an hour before I leave for the Hilton Hotel. Jodie, I'm asking you please to look into your heart and at least give me the chance with this historical deed to gain your respect and love. I love you forever.

John Hinckley

John W. Hinckley Jr. wrote this letter to actress Jodie Foster in March 1981. Soon after writing it, he stood waiting, pistol ready, outside the Washington Hilton Hotel. Moments later, President Ronald Reagan came out of the hotel, and the popping of pistol fire was heard. As his Secret Service detail pushed Reagan into the limousine, a police officer, the president's press secretary, and a Secret Service agent fell to the pavement. The president had been shot, and by nightfall most of America had seen the face and heard the name of the disturbed young man from Colorado.

As you have seen throughout this book, the psychological dysfunction of an individual does not occur in isolation. It is influenced—sometimes caused—by societal and social factors, and it affects the lives of relatives, friends, and acquaintances. The case of John Hinckley demonstrates in powerful terms that individual dysfunction may, in some cases, also affect the well-being and rights of people the person does not know.

By the same token, clinical scientists and practitioners do not conduct their work in isolation. As they study and treat people with psychological problems, they affect and are affected by other institutions of society. We have seen, for example, how the government regulates the use of psychotropic medications, how clinicians helped carry out the government's policy of deinstitutionalization, and how clinicians have called the psychological ordeals of Vietnam, Iraq, and Afghanistan combat veterans to the attention of society.

In short, like their clients, clinical professionals operate within a complex social system—for clinicians, it is the system that defines and often regulates their professional responsibilities. Just as we must understand the social context in which abnormal behavior occurs in order to understand the behavior, so must we understand the context in which this behavior is studied and treated. This chapter focuses on the relationship between the mental health field and three major forces in society—the *legislative/judicial system*, the *business/economic* arena, and the world of *technology*.

#

#TheirWords

"I think John Hinckley will be a threat the rest of his life. He is a time bomb."

U.S. Attorney, 1982

"Without doubt, [John Hinckley] is the least dangerous person on the planet."

Attorney for John Hinckley, 2003

Law and Mental Health

Two social institutions have a particularly strong impact on the mental health profession: the legislative and judicial systems. These institutions—collectively, the *legal field*—have long been responsible for protecting both the public good and the rights of individuals. Sometimes the relationship between the legal field and the mental health field has been friendly, and those in the two fields have worked together to protect the rights and meet the needs of troubled people and of society at large. At other times they have clashed, and one field has imposed its will on the other.

This relationship has two distinct aspects. On the one hand, mental health professionals often play a role in the criminal justice system, as when they are called upon to help the courts assess the mental stability of people accused of crimes. They responded to this call in the Hinckley case, as you will see, and in thousands of other cases. This aspect of the relationship is sometimes termed *psychology in law;* that is, clinical practitioners and researchers operate within the legal system. On the other hand, there is another aspect to the relationship, called *law in psychology*. The legislative and judicial systems act upon the clinical field, regulating certain aspects of mental health care. The courts may, for example, force some people to enter treatment, even against their will. In addition, the law protects the rights of patients.

The intersections between the mental health field and the legal and judicial systems are collectively referred to as **forensic psychology** (Neal, 2018). Forensic psychologists or psychiatrists (or related mental health professionals) may perform such varied activities as testifying in trials, researching the reliability of eyewitness testimony, or helping police profile the personality of a serial killer on the loose.

How Do Clinicians Influence the Criminal Justice System?

To arrive at just and appropriate punishments, the courts need to know whether defendants are *responsible* for the crimes they commit and *capable* of defending themselves in court. If not, it would be inappropriate to find defendants guilty or punish them in the usual manner. The courts have decided that in some instances people who suffer from severe *mental instability* may not be responsible for their actions or may not be able to defend themselves in court, and so should not be punished in the usual way. Although the courts make the final judgment as to mental instability, their decisions are guided to a large degree by the opinions of mental health professionals.

When people accused of crimes are judged to be mentally unstable, they are usually sent to a mental institution for treatment, a process called **criminal commitment.** Actually there are several forms of criminal commitment. In one, people are judged mentally unstable *at the time of their crimes* and so innocent of wrongdoing. They may plead **not guilty by reason of insanity (NGRI)** and bring mental health professionals into court to support their claim. When people are found not guilty on this basis, they are committed for treatment until they improve enough to be released.

In a second form of criminal commitment, people are judged mentally unstable *at the time of their trial* and so are considered unable to understand the trial procedures and to defend themselves in court. They are committed for treatment until they are competent to stand trial. Once again, the testimony of mental health professionals helps determine the defendant's psychological functioning.

These judgments of mental instability have stirred many arguments. Some people consider the judgments to be loopholes in the legal system that allow criminals to escape proper punishment for wrongdoing. Others argue that a legal system simply cannot be just unless it allows for extenuating circumstances, such as mental instability. The practice of criminal commitment differs from country to country. In this chapter you

forensic psychology The branch of psychology concerned with intersections between psychological practice and research and the judicial system. Also related to the field of *forensic psychiatry.*

criminal commitment A legal process by which people accused of a crime are instead judged mentally unstable and sent to a treatment facility.

not guilty by reason of insanity (NGRI) A verdict stating that defendants are not guilty of a crime because they were insane at the time of the crime.

will see primarily how it operates in the United States. Although the specific principles and procedures of each country may differ, most countries grapple with the same issues, concerns, and decisions that you will read about here.

Would-be assassin Few courtroom decisions have spurred as much debate or legislative action as the jury's verdict that John Hinckley, having been captured in the act of shooting President Ronald Reagan, was not guilty by reason of insanity.

Criminal Commitment and Insanity During Commission of a Crime Consider once again the case of John Hinckley. Was he insane at the time he shot the president? If insane, should he be held responsible for his actions? On June 21, 1982, fifteen months after he shot four men in the nation's capital, a jury pronounced Hinckley not guilty by reason of insanity. Hinckley thus joined Richard Lawrence, a house painter who shot at Andrew Jackson in 1835, and John Schrank, a saloonkeeper who shot former president Teddy Roosevelt in 1912, as a would-be assassin who was found not guilty by reason of insanity.

It is important to recognize that "insanity" is a *legal* term (Brown, 2018; Hallevy, 2017). That is, the definition of "insanity" used in criminal cases was written by legislators, not by clinicians. Defendants may have mental disorders but not necessarily qualify for a legal definition of insanity. Modern Western definitions of insanity can be traced to the murder case of Daniel M'Naghten in England in 1843. M'Naghten shot and killed Edward Drummond, the secretary to British prime minister Robert Peel, while trying to shoot Peel. Because of M'Naghten's apparent delusions of persecution, the jury found him to be not guilty by reason of insanity. The public was outraged by this decision, and their angry outcry forced the British law lords to define the insanity defense more clearly. This legal definition, known as the **M'Naghten test,** or **M'Naghten rule,** stated that having a mental disorder at the time of a crime does not by itself mean that the person was insane; the defendant also had to be *unable to know right from wrong*. The state and federal courts in the United States adopted this test as well.

In the late nineteenth century some state and federal courts in the United States, dissatisfied with the M'Naghten rule, adopted a different test—the **irresistible impulse test.** This test, which had first been used in Ohio in 1834, emphasized the inability to control one's actions. A person who committed a crime during an uncontrollable "fit of passion" was considered insane and not guilty under this test.

For years state and federal courts chose between the M'Naghten test and the irresistible impulse test to determine the sanity of criminal defendants. For a while a third test, called the **Durham test,** also became popular, but it was soon replaced in most courts. This test, based on a decision handed down by the Supreme Court in 1954 in the case of *Durham v. United States,* stated simply that people are not criminally responsible if their "unlawful act was the product of mental disease or mental defect." This test was meant to offer more flexibility in court decisions, but it proved too flexible. Insanity defenses could point to such problems as alcoholism or other forms of substance abuse and conceivably even headaches or ulcers, which were listed as psychophysiological disorders in DSM-I (Covey, 2017).

In 1955 the American Law Institute (ALI) formulated a test that combined aspects of the M'Naghten, irresistible impulse, and Durham tests. The **American Law Institute test** held that people are not criminally responsible if at the time of a crime they had a mental disorder or defect that prevented them from knowing right from wrong *or* from being able to control themselves and to follow the law. For a time the new test became the most widely accepted legal test of insanity. After the Hinckley verdict, however, there was a public uproar over the "liberal" ALI guidelines, and people called for tougher standards.

Partly in response to this uproar, the American Psychiatric Association recommended in 1983 that people should be found not guilty by reason of insanity *only* if they did not know right from wrong at the time of the crime; an inability to control themselves and to follow the law should no longer be sufficient grounds for a judgment of insanity. In short, the association was calling for a return to the M'Naghten test. This test is now

M'Naghten test A legal test that holds people to be insane at the time they committed a crime if, because of a mental disorder, they did not know the nature of the act or did not know right from wrong.

irresistible impulse test A legal test that holds people to be insane at the time they committed a crime if they were driven to do so by an uncontrollable "fit of passion."

Durham test A legal test that holds people to be insane at the time they committed a crime if their act was the result of a mental disorder.

American Law Institute test A legal test for insanity that holds people to be insane at the time they committed a crime if, because of a mental disorder, they did not know right from wrong or could not resist an uncontrollable impulse to act.

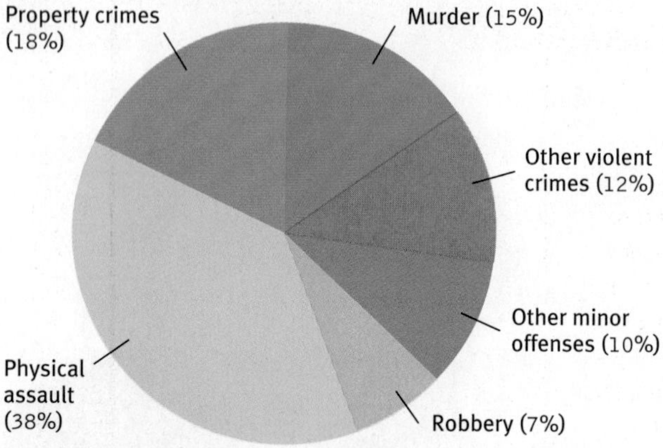

FIGURE 16-1

Crimes for Which People Are Found Not Guilty by Reason of Insanity (NGRI)

Reviews of NGRI verdicts in a number of states show that most people who are acquitted on this basis had been charged with a violent crime. (Information from: Melton et al., 2017, 2007; Perlin, 2017; Steadman et al., 1993; Callahan et al., 1991.)

used in all cases tried in federal courts and in about half of the state courts. The more liberal ALI standard is still used in the remaining state courts, except in Idaho, Kansas, Montana, and Utah, which have more or less done away with the insanity plea altogether.

People suffering from severe mental disorders in which confusion is a major feature may not be able to tell right from wrong or to control their behavior. It is therefore not surprising that more than 80 percent of defendants who are acquitted of a crime by reason of insanity qualify for a diagnosis of schizophrenia or another form of psychosis (Melton et al., 2017, 2007). The majority of these acquitted defendants have a history of past hospitalization, arrest, or both. About half who successfully plead insanity are white, and 86 percent are male. Their mean age is 32 years. The crimes for which defendants are found not guilty by reason of insanity vary greatly, although approximately 70 percent are violent crimes of some sort. At least 15 percent of those acquitted are accused specifically of murder (see **Figure 16-1**).

WHAT CONCERNS ARE RAISED BY THE INSANITY DEFENSE? Despite the changes in the insanity criteria, criticism of the insanity defense continues (Krauss et al., 2018; Perlin, 2017). One concern is the fundamental difference between the law and the science of human behavior. The law assumes that individuals have free will and are generally responsible for their actions. Several models of human behavior, in contrast, assume that physical or psychological forces act to determine the individual's behavior. Inevitably, then, legal definitions of insanity and responsibility will differ from those suggested by clinical research.

A second criticism points to the uncertainty of scientific knowledge about abnormal behavior. During a typical insanity defense trial, the testimony of defense clinicians conflicts with that of clinicians hired by the prosecution, and so the jury must weigh the claims of "experts" who disagree in their assessments (Krauss et al., 2018). Some people see this lack of professional agreement as evidence that clinical knowledge in some areas may be too incomplete to be allowed to influence important legal decisions. Others counter that the field has made great strides—for example, developing several psychological scales to help clinicians discriminate more consistently between the sane and insane as defined by the M'Naghten standard (Brown, 2018; Melton et al., 2017, 2007).

Even with helpful scales in hand, however, clinicians making judgments of legal insanity face a problem that is difficult to overcome: They must evaluate a defendant's state of mind during an event that took place weeks, months, or years earlier. Because mental states can and do change over time and across situations, clinicians can never be entirely certain that their assessments of mental instability at the time of the crime are accurate.

Perhaps the most common criticism of the insanity defense is that it allows criminals to escape punishment. Granted, some people who successfully plead insanity are released from treatment facilities just months after their acquittal. Yet the number of such cases is quite small (MHA, 2018; Melton et al., 2017, 2007; Steadman et al., 1993; Callahan et al., 1991). According to surveys, the public dramatically overestimates the percentage of defendants who plead insanity, guessing it to be 30 to 40 percent, when in fact it is less than 1 percent. Moreover, only a minority of these defendants fake or exaggerate their psychological symptoms, and only 26 percent of those who plead insanity are actually found not guilty on this basis. In all, less than 1 of every 400 defendants in the United States is found not guilty by reason of insanity (see ***PsychWatch***). It is also worth noting that in 80 percent of those cases in which defendants are acquitted by reason of insanity, the prosecution has agreed to the appropriateness of the plea (Gardner, Murrie, & Torres, 2018; MHA, 2018).

During most of U.S. history, a successful insanity plea amounted to the equivalent of a long-term prison sentence. In fact, on average, treatment in a mental hospital resulted in confinement that was twice as long as imprisonment for the same crime would have

#TheAftermath

Daniel M'Naghten Judged not guilty by reason of insanity in 1843, M'Naghten lived in a mental hospital until his death 22 years later.

John Hinckley Judged not guilty by reason of insanity in 1982, Hinckley lived in a mental hospital until his release by a federal judge in 2016.

PSYCHWATCH

Famous Insanity Defense Cases

Although the plea of not guilty by reason of insanity is used infrequently, some of the most famous cases in history have featured this defense strategy. You have already read about the cases of John Hinckley (see page 497) and Andrea Yates (see page 372). Here are some other famous insanity defense cases:

1977 In Michigan, Francine Hughes poured gasoline around the bed where her husband lay in a drunken stupor. Then she lit a match and set him on fire. At her trial she explained that he had beaten her repeatedly for 14 years and had threatened to kill her if she tried to leave him. The jury found her not guilty by reason of insanity, making her into a symbol for many abused women across the nation.

1978 David "Son of Sam" Berkowitz, a serial killer in New York City, explained that a barking dog had sent him demonic messages to kill. Although two psychiatrists assessed him as psychotic, he was found guilty of his crimes. Long after his trial, he said that he had actually made up the delusions.

1979 Kenneth Bianchi, one of the pair known as the Hillside Strangler, entered a plea of not guilty by reason of insanity but was found guilty, along with his cousin, of sexually assaulting and murdering women in the Los Angeles area in late 1977 and early 1978. He claimed that he had multiple personalities.

1980 In December, Mark David Chapman murdered John Lennon. Chapman later explained that he had killed the rock music legend because he believed Lennon to be a "sell-out." Pleading not guilty by reason of insanity, he also described hearing the voice of God and compared himself with Moses. Chapman was convicted of murder.

1992 Jeffrey Dahmer, a 31-year-old mass murderer in Milwaukee, was tried for the killings of 15 young men. Dahmer drugged some of his victims, performed crude lobotomies on them, and dismembered their bodies and stored their parts to be eaten. Despite a plea of not guilty by reason of insanity, the jury found him guilty as charged. He was beaten to death by another inmate in 1995.

1994 On June 23, 1993, twenty-four-year-old Lorena Bobbitt cut off her husband's penis with a 12-inch kitchen knife while he slept. During her trial, defense attorneys argued that after years of abuse by John Bobbitt, his wife suffered a brief psychotic episode and was seized by an "irresistible impulse" to cut off his penis after he raped her. In 1994, the jury found her not guilty by reason of insanity. She was committed to a state mental hospital and released a few months later.

2011 In 2002, Brian David Mitchell abducted a 14-year-old teenager named Elizabeth Smart from her home and held her until she was rescued nine months later. After years of trial delays, Mitchell pleaded not guilty by reason of insanity in 2010, saying that he was acting out delusions ("revelations from God") when he committed this crime. The jury found him guilty of kidnapping in 2011 and sentenced him to life in prison without parole.

2015 In 2012, James Holmes, a 25-year-old neuroscience doctoral student, entered a cinema in Aurora, Colorado, and opened fire on the moviegoers, killing 12 and wounding 20. In the months after his arrest, Holmes, who had no prior criminal record, tried to kill himself three times. Holmes pleaded not guilty by reason of insanity, but a jury found him guilty of murder in 2015 and sentenced him to life in prison without parole.

AP Photo/Denver Post, RJ Sangosti

Plea rejected James Holmes sits in a courtroom in Colorado in 2012, a few days after killing 12 moviegoers and wounding 20 in the town of Aurora. In 2015, a jury rejected his plea of not guilty by reason of insanity and instead found him guilty of murder and attempted murder.

2017 In 2014 two 12-year-old girls stabbed a classmate multiple times, saying they were trying to appease and impress Slender Man, a mythical "boogie man" whom a number of Internet users report seeing and fearing in their everyday lives. In separate 2017 trials, each of the assailants pleaded guilty to attempted intentional homicide, but in each case they were further deemed to have been mentally ill at the time of the attack and were assigned to extended treatment in a mental hospital rather than imprisonment.

brought (Perlin, 2017). Because hospitalization resulted in little if any improvement, clinicians were reluctant to predict that the offenders would not repeat their crimes.

Today, however, offenders are being released from mental hospitals earlier and earlier. This trend is the result of the increasing effectiveness of drug therapy and other treatments in institutions, the growing reaction against extended institutionalization, and more emphasis on patients' rights (Gowensmith et al., 2017). In 1992, in the case of *Foucha v. Louisiana,* the U.S. Supreme Court clarified that the *only* acceptable

AP Photo/Douglas D. Pizac

"Effectively misleading psychopath" In 2002 Brian David Mitchell abducted a 14-year-old teenager named Elizabeth Smart at knifepoint from her home and held her until she was rescued nine months later. For seven years following his capture, Mitchell was declared incompetent to stand trial. Finally, in 2010, a federal court judge called him an "effectively misleading psychopath" and scheduled him for trial. Mitchell was found guilty of kidnapping and sentenced to life in prison, despite his not guilty by reason of insanity plea.

basis for determining the release of hospitalized offenders is whether or not they are still "insane"; they cannot be kept indefinitely in mental hospitals solely because they are dangerous. Some states are able to maintain control over offenders even after their release from hospitals. Adopting a procedure called "outpatient commitment," the states may insist on community treatment, monitor the patients closely, and rehospitalize them if necessary (Corring et al., 2018; Gowensmith et al., 2017).

After patients have been criminally committed to institutions, why might clinicians be hesitant to later declare them unlikely to commit the same crime again?

WHAT OTHER VERDICTS ARE AVAILABLE? Over the past four decades, at least 20 states have added another verdict option—**guilty but mentally ill.** Defendants who receive this verdict are found to have had a mental illness at the time of their crime, but the illness was not fully related to or responsible for the crime. The option of guilty but mentally ill enables jurors to convict a person they view as dangerous while also suggesting that the individual receive needed treatment. Defendants found to be guilty but mentally ill are given a prison term with the added recommendation that they also undergo treatment if necessary.

After initial enthusiasm for this verdict option, legal and clinical theorists have increasingly found it unsatisfactory. According to research, it has not reduced the number of not guilty by reason of insanity verdicts, and it often confuses jurors (MHA, 2018; Bartol & Bartol, 2015). In addition, as critics point out, appropriate mental health care is supposed to be available to all prisoners anyway, regardless of the verdict. That is, the verdict of guilty but mentally ill may differ from a guilty verdict in name only.

Some states allow still another kind of defense, *guilty with diminished capacity,* in which a defendant's mental dysfunction is viewed as an extenuating circumstance that the court should take into consideration in determining the precise crime of which he or she is guilty (ABA, 2018, 2017; Slovenko, 2011). The defense lawyer argues that because of mental dysfunction, the defendant could not have *intended* to commit a particular crime. The person can then be found guilty of a lesser crime—of manslaughter (unlawful killing without intent), say, instead of murder in the first degree (planned murder). The famous case of Dan White, who shot and killed Mayor George Moscone and City Supervisor Harvey Milk of San Francisco in 1978, illustrates the use of this verdict.

Defense attorney Douglas Schmidt argued that a patriotic, civic-minded man like Dan White—high school athlete, decorated war veteran, former fireman, policeman, and city supervisor—could not possibly have committed such an act unless something had snapped inside him. The brutal nature of the two final shots to each man's head only proved that White had lost his wits. White was not fully responsible for his actions because he suffered from "diminished capacity." Although White killed Mayor George Moscone and Supervisor Harvey Milk, he had not planned his actions. On the day of the shootings, White was mentally incapable of planning to kill, or even of wanting to do such a thing.

Well known in forensic psychiatry circles, Martin Blinder, professor of law and psychiatry at the University of California's Hastings Law School in San Francisco, brought a good measure of academic prestige to White's defense. White had been, Blinder explained to the jury, "gorging himself on junk food: Twinkies, Coca-Cola. . . . The more he consumed, the worse he'd feel and he'd respond to his ever-growing depression by consuming ever more junk food." Schmidt later asked Blinder if he could elaborate on this. "Perhaps if it were not for the ingestion of this junk food," Blinder responded, "I would suspect that these homicides would not have taken place." From that moment on, Blinder became known as the author of the Twinkie defense. . . .

Dan White was convicted only of voluntary manslaughter, and was sentenced to seven years, eight months. (He was released on parole January 6, 1984.) Psychiatric testimony convinced the jury that White did not wish to kill George Moscone or Harvey Milk.

The angry crowd that responded to the verdict by marching, shouting, trashing City Hall, and burning police cars was in good part homosexual. Gay supervisor Harvey Milk had worked

#FollowUp

Released from prison in 1984, Dan White died by suicide in 1985.

Bill Nation

Justice served? People held mass protests in San Francisco after Dan White was convicted of voluntary manslaughter rather than premeditated murder in the 1978 killings of Mayor George Moscone and Supervisor Harvey Milk, who was one of the nation's leading gay activists. The verdict highlighted the serious pitfalls of the "diminished capacity" defense and has led to a significant decrease in its use.

well for their cause, and his loss was a serious setback for human rights in San Francisco. Yet it was not only members of the gay community who were appalled at the outcome. Most San Franciscans shared their feelings of outrage.

(Coleman, 1984, pp. 65–70)

Because of possible miscarriages of justice, many legal experts have argued against the "diminished capacity" defense. A number of states have even eliminated it, including California shortly after the Dan White verdict (MHA, 2018).

WHAT ARE SEX-OFFENDER STATUTES? Since 1937, when Michigan passed the first "sexual psychopath" law, a number of states have placed sex offenders in a special legal category (Lewis & Dwyer, 2018; Sanders, 2016). These states believe that some of those who are repeatedly found guilty of sex crimes have a mental disorder, so the states categorize them as *mentally disordered sex offenders*.

People classified in this way are convicted of a criminal offense and are thus judged to be responsible for their actions. Nevertheless, mentally disordered sex offenders are sent to a mental health facility instead of a prison. In part, such laws reflect a belief held by many legislators that such sex offenders are psychologically disturbed. On a practical level, the laws help protect sex offenders from the physical abuse that they often receive in prison society.

Over the past two decades, however, most states have been changing or abolishing their mentally disordered sex offender laws, and at this point only a handful still have them. There are several reasons for this trend. First, the state laws often declare that in order to be classified as a mentally disordered sex offender, the person must be a good candidate for treatment, another judgment that is difficult for clinicians to make, especially for this population (Marshall & Marshall, 2016; Marshall et al., 2011). Second, there is evidence that racial bias often affects the use of the mentally disordered sex offender classification. From a defendant's perspective, this classification is considered an attractive alternative to imprisonment—an alternative available to non-Hispanic white Americans much more often than to members of racial and ethnic minority groups. Non-Hispanic white Americans are twice as likely as African Americans or Hispanic Americans who have been convicted of similar crimes to be granted mentally disordered sex offender status.

guilty but mentally ill A verdict stating that defendants are guilty of committing a crime but are also suffering from a mental illness that should be treated during their imprisonment.

But perhaps the primary reason that mentally disordered sex offender laws have lost favor is that state legislatures and courts are now less concerned than they used to be about the rights and needs of sex offenders, given the growing number of sex crimes taking place across the country (Feldman, 2017), particularly ones in which children are victims. In fact, in response to public outrage over the high number of sex crimes, 21 states and the federal government have instead passed *sexually violent predator* laws (or *sexually dangerous persons* laws) (MHA, 2018). These relatively new laws call for certain sex offenders who have been convicted of sex crimes and have served their sentence in prison to be removed from prison before their release and committed involuntarily to a mental hospital for treatment if a court judges them likely to engage in further "predatory acts of sexual violence" as a result of "mental abnormality" or "personality disorder" (MHA, 2018). That is, in contrast to the mentally disordered sex offender laws, which call for sex offenders to receive treatment *instead* of imprisonment, the sexually violent predator laws require certain sex offenders to receive imprisonment and then, *in addition*, be committed for a period of involuntary treatment. The constitutionality of the sexually violent predator laws was upheld by the Supreme Court in the 1997 case of *Kansas v. Hendricks* by a 5-to-4 margin.

AP Photo/Sue Ogrocki

Incompetent to stand trial In 2014, Alton Nolen beheaded a co-worker and tried to behead another at a food plant in Oklahoma. The defendant was ruled incompetent to stand trial until 2017, at which time he pled guilty and requested to receive the death penalty.

Criminal Commitment and Incompetence to Stand Trial Regardless of their state of mind at the time of a crime, defendants may be judged to be **mentally incompetent** to stand trial. The competence requirement is meant to ensure that defendants understand the charges they are facing and can work with their lawyers to prepare and conduct an adequate defense (Reisner & Piel, 2018). This minimum standard of competence was specified by the Supreme Court in the case of *Dusky v. United States* (1960).

The issue of competence is most often raised by the defendant's attorney, although prosecutors, arresting police officers, and even the judge may raise it as well (Judd & Parker, 2018; Reisner & Piel, 2018). When the issue of competence is raised, the judge orders a psychological evaluation, usually on an inpatient basis (see **Table 16-1**). As many as 60,000 competency evaluations are conducted in the United States each year (Faubion, 2016; Bartol & Bartol, 2015). Approximately 20 to 25 percent of defendants who receive such an evaluation are found to be incompetent to stand trial. If the court decides that the defendant is incompetent, he or she is typically assigned to a mental health facility until competent to stand trial.

A famous case of incompetence to stand trial is that of Jared Lee Loughner. On January 8, 2011, Loughner went to a political gathering at a shopping center in Tucson, Arizona, and opened fire on 20 persons. Six people were killed and 14 injured, including U.S. representative Gabrielle Giffords. Giffords, the apparent target of the attack,

TABLE: 16-1

Race and Forensic Psychology

Racial/Ethnic Minority Individuals	Non-Hispanic White Individuals
• Psychologically disturbed law breakers *more* likely to be sent to prison.	• Psychologically disturbed law breakers *more* likely to be sent to mental health facilities.
• Defendants *more* likely to be judged incompetent to stand trial.	• Defendants *less* likely to be judged incompetent to stand trial.
• Individuals *more* likely to be ordered into involuntary mental hospital commitment.	• Individuals *less* likely to be ordered into involuntary mental hospital commitment.
• Individuals *more* likely to be ordered into involuntary outpatient commitment.	• Individuals *less* likely to be ordered into involuntary outpatient commitment.

Information from: Judd & Parker, 2018; APA, 2017; Kisely & Xiao, 2017; Fraser, 2016; NCBH, 2015; Zaejian, 2014; Swanson et al., 2009; Haroules, 2007; Pinals et al., 2004.

survived, although she was shot in the head. After Loughner underwent five weeks of psychiatric assessment, a judge ruled that he was incompetent to stand trial. It was not until 18 months later, after extended treatment with antipsychotic drugs, that Loughner was ruled competent to stand trial. In November 2012, he pleaded guilty to murder and was sentenced to life imprisonment.

Many more cases of criminal commitment result from decisions of mental incompetence than from verdicts of not guilty by reason of insanity (Kaneya, 2017; Roesch, 2016). However, the majority of criminals currently institutionalized for psychological treatment in the United States are not from either of these two groups. Rather, they are convicted inmates whose psychological problems have led prison officials to decide they need treatment, either in mental health units within the prison or in mental hospitals (Ollove, 2017; Fazel et al., 2016) (see **Figure 16-2**).

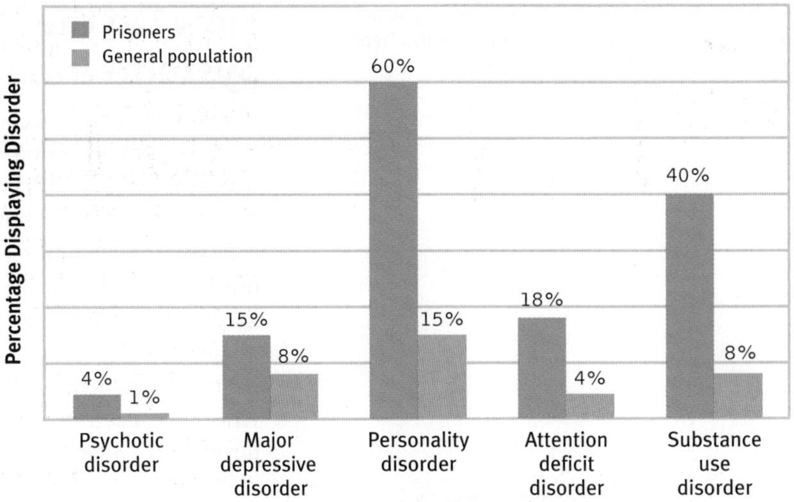

FIGURE 16-2

Prison and Mental Health

According to studies in several Western countries, psychological disorders are much more prevalent in prison populations than in the general population. For example, schizophrenia and personality disorders (particularly antisocial personality disorder) are each four times more common among prisoners than among nonprisoners. (Information from: Stürup-Toft, O'Moore, & Plugge, 2018; NIMH, 2017; Bukstein, 2016; Fazel et al., 2016.)

It is possible that an innocent defendant, ruled incompetent to stand trial, could spend years in a mental health facility with no opportunity to disprove the criminal accusations against him or her. Some defendants have, in fact, served longer "sentences" in mental health facilities awaiting a ruling of competence than they would have served in prison had they been convicted. Such a possibility was reduced when the Supreme Court ruled, in the case of *Jackson v. Indiana* (1972), that an incompetent defendant cannot be indefinitely committed. After a reasonable amount of time, he or she should either be found competent and tried, set free, or transferred to a mental health facility under *civil* commitment procedures.

Until the early 1970s, most states required that mentally incompetent defendants be committed to maximum security institutions for the "criminally insane." Under current law, however, the courts have more flexibility. In fact, when the charges are relatively minor, such defendants are often treated on an outpatient basis, an arrangement often called *jail diversion* because the disturbed person is "diverted" from jail to the community for mental health care (Boutros, Kang, & Boutros, 2018).

9... SUMMING UP

HOW DO CLINICIANS INFLUENCE THE CRIMINAL JUSTICE SYSTEM?

Mental health professionals may help assess the mental stability of people accused of crimes. If defendants are judged to have been mentally unstable at the time they committed a crime, they may be found not guilty by reason of insanity and placed in a treatment facility rather than a prison. In federal courts and about half the state courts, insanity is judged in accordance with the M'Naghten test, which holds that defendants were insane at the time of a criminal act if they did not know the nature or quality of the act or did not know right from wrong at the time they committed it. Other states use the broader American Law Institute test.

The insanity defense has been criticized on several grounds, and some states have added an additional option, guilty but mentally ill. Another verdict option is guilty with diminished capacity. Depending on state laws, it is also the case that sex offenders may receive treatment as mentally disordered sex offenders, or, more commonly, under the state's sexually violent predator law.

Regardless of their state of mind at the time of the crime, defendants may be found mentally incompetent to stand trial, that is, incapable of fully understanding the charges or legal proceedings that confront them. These defendants are commonly sent to a mental hospital until they are competent to stand trial.

mental incompetence A state of mental instability that leaves defendants unable to understand the legal charges and proceedings they are facing and unable to prepare an adequate defense with their attorney.

civil commitment A legal process by which a person can be forced to undergo mental health treatment.

How Do the Legislative and Judicial Systems Influence Mental Health Care?

Just as clinical science and practice have influenced the legal system, so the legal system has had a major impact on clinical practice. First, courts and legislatures have developed the process of **civil commitment,** which allows certain people to be forced into mental health treatment. Although many people who show signs of mental disturbance seek treatment voluntarily, a large number are not aware of their problems or are simply not interested in undergoing therapy. For such people, civil commitment procedures may be put into action.

Second, the legal system, on behalf of the state, has taken on the responsibility of protecting patients' rights during treatment. This protection extends not only to patients who have been involuntarily committed but also to those who seek treatment voluntarily, even on an outpatient basis.

Civil Commitment Every year in the United States, large numbers of people with mental disorders are involuntarily committed to treatment. Typically they are committed to *mental institutions,* but 46 states also have some form of *outpatient* civil commitment laws that allow patients to be forced into community treatment programs (Tabas et al., 2017; TAC, 2017). Canada and Great Britain have similar laws. Civil commitments have long caused controversy and debate. In some ways the law provides more protection for people suspected of being criminals than for people suspected of being psychotic.

WHY COMMIT? Generally our legal system permits involuntary commitment of individuals when they are considered to be *in need of treatment* and *dangerous to themselves or others.* People may be dangerous to themselves if they are suicidal or if they act recklessly (for example, drinking a drain cleaner to prove that they are immune to its chemicals). They may be dangerous to others if they seek to harm them or if they unintentionally place others at risk. The state's authority to commit disturbed people rests on its duties to protect the interests of the individual and of society.

"The Taser solution" Police often use Tasers—stun guns that affect neuromuscular control and temporarily incapacitate individuals—to subdue people with mental disorders. To help officers appreciate the impact of this weapon, the Los Angeles Police Department has new recruits—such as Officer Vanessa Lopez—receive a Taser charge during training. Mental health advocates view Tasers as an inhumane intervention when dealing with extremely confused or frightened people.

Brian van der Brug/Los Angeles Times via Getty Images

WHAT ARE THE PROCEDURES FOR CIVIL COMMITMENT? Civil commitment laws vary from state to state. Some basic procedures, however, are common to most of these laws. Often family members begin commitment proceedings. In response to a son's psychotic behavior and repeated assaults on other people, for example, his parents may try to persuade him to seek admission to a mental institution. If the son refuses, the parents may go to court and seek an involuntary commitment order. If the son is a minor, the process is straightforward. The Supreme Court has ruled that a hearing is not necessary in such cases, as long as a qualified mental health professional considers commitment necessary. If the son is an adult, however, the process is more involved. The court usually will order a mental examination and allow the person to contest the commitment in court, often represented by a lawyer.

The Supreme Court has ruled that before an individual can be committed, there must be "clear and convincing" proof that he or she is mentally ill and has met the state's criteria for involuntary commitment. That is, whatever the state's criteria, clinicians must offer clear and convincing proof that the person meets those criteria (Hille, 2017). When is proof clear and convincing, according to the court? When it provides 75 percent certainty that the criteria of commitment have been met. This is far less than the near-total certainty ("beyond a reasonable doubt") required to convict people of committing a crime.

EMERGENCY COMMITMENT Many situations require immediate action; no one can wait for commitment proceedings when a life is at stake. Consider, for example, an emergency patient who is suicidal or hearing voices demanding hostile actions against others. He or she may need immediate treatment and round-the-clock supervision. If treatment could not be given in such situations without the patient's full consent, the consequences could be tragic.

Therefore, many states give clinicians the right to certify that certain patients need temporary commitment and medication. In past years, these states required certification by two *physicians* (not necessarily psychiatrists in some of the states). Today states may allow certification by other mental health professionals as well. The clinicians must declare that the state of mind of the patients makes them dangerous to themselves or others. By tradition, the certifications are often referred to as *two-physician certificates,* or *2 PCs.* The length of such emergency commitments varies from state to state, but three days is often the limit (Frances & Ruffalo, 2018; Hedman et al., 2016). Should clinicians come to believe that a longer stay is necessary, formal commitment proceedings may be initiated during the period of emergency commitment.

AFP/Getty Images

Dangerous to oneself There are various ways that people may be dangerous to themselves, in need of treatment, and subject to civil commitment. This sequence of photos shows a man being attacked by a lion at the zoo after he crossed a barbed wire fence to "preach" to two of the animals.

WHO IS DANGEROUS? In the past, people with mental disorders were actually less likely than others to commit violent or dangerous acts. This low rate of violence was apparently related to the fact that so many such people lived in institutions. As a result of deinstitutionalization, however, hundreds of thousands of people with severe disturbances now live in the community, and many of them receive little, if any, treatment. Some are indeed dangerous to themselves or others.

It is important to be clear that, according to research, the vast majority of people with mental disorders (90 percent) are in no way violent or dangerous, and only a small percentage of all violent acts (3 percent) are committed by people with mental disorders (HHS, 2017; Frances, 2016). That said, recent studies do suggest that people with severe mental disorders are somewhat more likely than the general population to perform violent behaviors (Dai et al., 2017). The disorders with the strongest relationships to violence are severe substance use disorder, impulse control disorder, antisocial personality disorder, and psychotic disorders (Bonnet et al., 2017; Moore & Pfaff, 2017). Of these, substance use disorder appears to be the single most influential factor. For example, schizophrenia compounded by substance use disorder has a stronger relationship to violence than schizophrenia alone does.

A determination of *dangerousness* is often required for involuntary civil commitment. But can mental health professionals accurately predict who will commit violent acts? Research suggests that psychiatrists and psychologists are wrong more often than right when they make *long-term* predictions of violence (Galán et al., 2018; Miller & Hanson, 2016). Most often they overestimate the likelihood that a patient will eventually be violent. Their *short-term* predictions—that is, predictions of imminent violence—tend to be more accurate (Fazel et al., 2017). Researchers are now working, with some success, to develop new assessment techniques that use statistical approaches and are more objective in their predictions of dangerousness than are the subjective judgments of clinicians (Ramesh et al., 2018).

WHAT ARE THE PROBLEMS WITH CIVIL COMMITMENT? Civil commitment has been criticized on several grounds (Jain, Christopher, & Appelbaum, 2018; Miller & Hanson, 2016). First is the difficulty of assessing a person's dangerousness. If judgments of

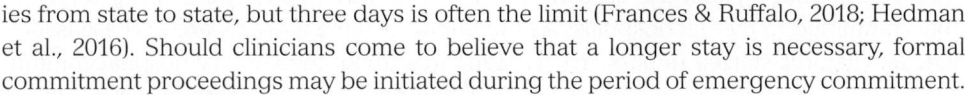

#BetterInterventions

Many police now receive *Crisis Intervention Team (CIT)* training to help them respond more knowledgeably and effectively when dealing with people who have mental disorders. The police undergo 40 hours of intensive training regarding mental conditions, medications, and community resources, and they develop skills at *verbal de-escalation.* There are now 2,800 CIT programs across the United States—offered in 15 percent of all police jurisdictions (NAMI, 2018; Lucas, 2016).

right to treatment The legal right of patients, particularly those who are involuntarily committed, to receive adequate treatment.

right to refuse treatment The legal right of patients to refuse certain forms of treatment.

dangerousness are often inaccurate, how can one justify using them to deprive people of liberty? Second, the legal definitions of "mental illness" and "dangerousness" are vague. The terms may be defined so broadly that they could be applied to almost anyone an evaluator views as undesirable. Indeed, many civil libertarians worry about involuntary commitment being used to control people, as is often done in countries ruled by authoritarian governments, where mental hospitals house people with unpopular political views. A third problem is the sometimes questionable therapeutic value of civil commitment. Research suggests that many people committed involuntarily do not respond well to therapy.

How are people who have been institutionalized viewed and treated by other people in society today?

TRENDS IN CIVIL COMMITMENT The flexibility of the involuntary commitment laws probably reached a peak in 1962. That year, in the case of *Robinson v. California,* the Supreme Court ruled that imprisoning people who suffered from substance use disorders might violate the Constitution's ban on cruel and unusual punishment, and it recommended involuntary civil commitment to a mental hospital as a more reasonable action. This ruling encouraged the civil commitment of many kinds of "social deviants," and many such individuals found it difficult to obtain release from the hospitals to which they were committed.

During the late 1960s and early 1970s, reporters, novelists, civil libertarians, and others spoke out against the ease with which so many people were being unjustifiably committed to mental hospitals. As the public became more aware of these issues, state legislatures started to pass stricter standards about involuntary hospital commitment, and, as mentioned earlier, many launched *outpatient commitment* programs in which courts may order people with severe mental disorders into community treatment (Corring et al., 2018). In turn, rates of involuntary hospital commitment declined, and release rates rose. Fewer people are institutionalized through civil commitment procedures today than in the past.

Protecting Patients' Rights

Over the past two decades, court decisions and state and federal laws have significantly expanded the rights of patients with mental disorders, in particular the *right to treatment* and the *right to refuse treatment* (Tingle, 2018; Miller & Hanson, 2016).

HOW IS THE RIGHT TO TREATMENT PROTECTED? When people are committed to mental institutions and do not receive treatment, the institutions become, in effect, prisons for the unconvicted. To many patients in the late 1960s and the 1970s, large state mental institutions were just that, and some patients and their attorneys began to demand that the state honor the patients' **right to treatment.** In the landmark case of *Wyatt v. Stickney,* a suit on behalf of institutionalized patients in Alabama in 1972, a federal court ruled that the state was constitutionally obligated to provide "adequate treatment" to all people who had been committed involuntarily. Because conditions in the state's hospitals were so terrible, the judge laid out goals that state officials had to meet, including more therapists, better living conditions, more privacy, more social interactions and physical exercise, and a more proper use of physical restraint and medication. Other states have since adopted many of these standards.

Another important decision was handed down in 1975 by the Supreme Court in the case of *O'Connor v. Donaldson.* After being held in a Florida mental institution for more than 14 years, Kenneth Donaldson sued for release. Donaldson repeatedly had sought release and had been overruled

John Stanmeyer/VII/Redux

Hospital neglect While some countries increasingly have attended to the rights of patients, including their rights to treatment and to humane treatment conditions, other countries, especially poor ones, have lagged behind. For example, although the government of Indonesia banned *pasung*—the chaining or close-quarter confinement of mentally ill persons—back in 1977, the practice apparently continues today. This scene inside a center for mental patients in Jakarta underscores the point.

by the institution's psychiatrists. He argued that he and his fellow patients were receiving poor treatment, were being largely ignored by the staff, and were allowed little personal freedom. The Supreme Court ruled in his favor, fined the hospital's superintendent, and said that such institutions must review patients' cases periodically. The justices also ruled that the state cannot continue to institutionalize people against their will if they are not dangerous and are capable of surviving on their own or with the willing help of responsible family members or friends.

To help protect the rights of patients, Congress passed the Protection and Advocacy for Mentally Ill Individuals Act in 1986. This law set up *protection and advocacy systems* in all states and U.S. territories and gave public advocates who worked for patients the power to investigate possible abuse and neglect and to correct those problems legally.

In more recent years, public advocates have argued that the right to treatment also should be extended to the tens of thousands of people with severe mental disorders who are repeatedly released from hospitals into communities ill-equipped to care for them. Many such people have no place to go and are unable to care for themselves, often winding up homeless or in prisons (Allison et al., 2017; MIP, 2017). A number of advocates are now suing federal and state agencies throughout the country, demanding that they fulfill the promises of the community mental health movement (see Chapter 12).

Don Bartletti/Los Angeles Times via Getty Images

Prisoners also have a right to treatment These prisoners, all military veterans, at the San Diego County jail are receiving day-long classes on subjects like anger management and PTSD. Many prisoners in the United States have psychological disorders, and the Supreme Court has upheld their right to receive treatment during their incarceration. However, prison systems are often ill-equipped to provide proper care.

HOW IS THE RIGHT TO REFUSE TREATMENT PROTECTED? During the past two decades, the courts have also decided that patients, particularly those in institutions, have the **right to refuse treatment.** Most of the right-to-refuse-treatment rulings center on *biological treatments*. These treatments are easier to impose on patients without their cooperation than psychotherapy, and they often are more hazardous. For example, state rulings have consistently granted patients the right to refuse *psychosurgery*, the most irreversible form of physical treatment—and often the most dangerous.

Some states have also acknowledged a patient's right to refuse *electroconvulsive therapy (ECT)*, the treatment used in many cases of severe depression (see Chapter 6). However, the right-to-refuse issue is more complex with regard to ECT than to psychosurgery. ECT is very effective for many people with severe depression, but it can cause great upset and can also be misused. Today many states grant patients—particularly voluntary patients—the right to refuse ECT (NARPA, 2018; OPA, 2016). Usually a patient must be informed fully about the nature of the treatment and must give written consent to it. A number of states continue to permit ECT to be forced on committed patients, whereas others require the consent of a close relative or other third party in such cases.

In the past, patients did not have the right to refuse *psychotropic medications*. As you have read, however, many psychotropic drugs are very powerful, and some produce effects that are unwanted and dangerous. As these harmful effects have become more apparent, some states have granted patients the right to refuse medication (Virdi & Weiss, 2017; OPA, 2016). Typically, these states require physicians to explain the purpose of the medication to patients and obtain their written consent. If a patient's refusal is considered incompetent, dangerous, or irrational, the state may allow it to be overturned by an independent psychiatrist, medical committee, or local court. However, the refusing patient is supported in this process by a lawyer or other patient advocate.

WHAT OTHER RIGHTS DO PATIENTS HAVE? Court decisions have protected still other patient rights over the past several decades. Patients who perform work in mental

Neemah Aaron/AP Photo

Executing the mentally ill Charles Singleton, a man who killed a store clerk in Arkansas, was sentenced to death in 1979, and then he developed schizophrenia at some point after the trial. Since the United States does not allow executions if persons cannot understand why they are being executed, state officials wanted Singleton to take medications to clear up his psychosis. Eventually, Singleton chose to take medications voluntarily, showed psychological improvement, and was executed by lethal injection in 2004.

institutions, particularly private institutions, are now guaranteed at least a *minimum wage*. In addition, according to a court decision, patients released from state mental hospitals have a right to *aftercare* and to an *appropriate community residence*, such as a group home. And, more generally, people with psychological disorders should receive treatment in the *least restrictive facility* available. If an inpatient program at a community mental health center is available and appropriate, for example, then that is the facility to which they should be assigned, not a mental hospital.

THE "RIGHTS" DEBATE Certainly, people with psychological disorders have civil rights that must be protected at all times. However, many clinicians express concern that the patients' rights rulings and laws may unintentionally deprive these patients of opportunities for recovery. Consider the right to refuse medication. If medications can help a patient with a severe mental disorder to recover, doesn't the patient have the right to that recovery? If confusion causes the patient to refuse medication, can clinicians in good conscience delay medication while legal channels are being cleared?

Despite such legitimate concerns, keep in mind that the clinical field has not always done an effective job of protecting patients' rights. Over the years, many patients have been overmedicated and received improper treatments. Furthermore, one must ask whether the field's present state of knowledge justifies clinicians' overriding of patients' rights. Can clinicians confidently say that a given treatment will help a patient? Can they predict when a treatment will have harmful effects? Since clinicians themselves often disagree, it seems appropriate for patients, their advocates, and outside evaluators to also play key roles in decision-making.

9... SUMMING UP

HOW DOES THE LEGAL SYSTEM INFLUENCE MENTAL HEALTH CARE?

Courts may be called upon to commit noncriminals to mental hospitals for treatment, a process called civil commitment. Society allows involuntary commitment of people considered to be in need of treatment and dangerous to themselves or others. Laws governing civil commitment procedures vary from state to state, but the Supreme Court has ruled that in order for individuals to be committed there must be clear and convincing proof that they are mentally ill and meet their state's criteria for involuntary commitment. In addition to mental hospital commitment, many states have established outpatient civil commitment programs.

The courts and legislatures significantly affect the mental health profession by specifying legal rights to which patients are entitled, including the right to treatment and the right to refuse treatment.

In What Other Ways Do the Clinical and Legal Fields Interact?

Mental health and legal professionals may influence each other's work in other ways as well. During the past 25 years, their paths have crossed in four key areas: *malpractice suits, professional boundaries, jury consultation,* and *psychological research of legal topics*.

malpractice suit A lawsuit charging a therapist with improper conduct in the course of treatment.

Malpractice Suits The number of **malpractice suits** against therapists has risen sharply in recent years. Claims have been made against clinicians in response to a patient's attempted suicide, sexual activity with a patient, failure to obtain informed consent for a treatment, negligent drug therapy, omission of drug therapy that would speed improvement, improper termination of treatment, and wrongful commitment

(Reuveni et al., 2017; Pope & Vasquez, 2016). Studies suggest that malpractice suits, or the fear of them, can have significant effects on clinical decisions and practice, for better or for worse.

Professional Boundaries Over the past 25 years, the legislative and judicial systems have helped change the *boundaries* that distinguish one clinical profession from another. In particular, they have given more authority to psychologists and blurred the lines that once separated psychiatry from psychology. A growing number of states, for example, are ruling that psychologists can admit patients to hospitals, a power previously held only by psychiatrists.

In 1991, with the blessing of Congress, the Department of Defense (DOD) started to reconsider the biggest difference of all between the practices of psychiatrists and psychologists—the authority to prescribe drugs, a role previously denied to psychologists. The DOD set up a trial training program for Army psychologists. Given the apparent success of this trial program, the American Psychological Association later recommended that all psychologists be allowed to pursue extensive educational and training programs in prescription services and receive certification to prescribe medications if they pass. New Mexico, Louisiana, Illinois, Iowa, Idaho, and the U.S. territory of Guam now do grant prescription privileges to psychologists who receive special pharmacology training (APA, 2018, 2017).

Most psychiatrists oppose the idea of prescription rights for psychologists. Why do some psychologists also oppose the idea?

#FamousCase

After shooting and killing two men on a busy street in 1995, delusional law student Wendell Williamson was found not guilty by reason of insanity and institutionalized for treatment. He later sued the psychiatrist who had been treating him before the killings, contending that the therapist had made an incorrect diagnosis and failed to arrange follow-up services when therapy ended. In 1998 a jury awarded Williamson a judgment of $500,000.

Jury Consultation During the past 30 years, more and more lawyers have turned to clinicians for psychological advice in conducting trials (Kovera, 2017; Gomez, 2016). A new breed of clinical specialists, known as "jury specialists," has evolved. They advise lawyers about which potential jurors are likely to favor their side and which strategies are likely to win jurors' support during trials. The jury specialists make their suggestions on the basis of surveys, interviews, analyses of jurors' backgrounds and attitudes, and laboratory simulations of upcoming trials. However, it is not clear that a clinician's advice is more valid than a lawyer's instincts or that the judgments of either are particularly accurate.

Psychological Research of Legal Topics Psychologists have sometimes conducted studies and developed expertise on topics of great importance to the criminal justice system. In turn, these studies influence how the system carries out its work. Psychological investigations of two topics, *eyewitness testimony* and *patterns of criminality*, have gained particular attention.

EYEWITNESS TESTIMONY In criminal cases, testimony by eyewitnesses is extremely influential. It often determines whether a defendant will be found guilty or not guilty. But how accurate is eyewitness testimony? This question has become urgent, as a troubling number of prisoners (many on death row) have had their convictions overturned after DNA evidence revealed that they could not have committed the crimes of which they had been convicted. It turns out that more than 70 percent of such wrongful convictions were based in large part on mistaken eyewitness testimony (Innocence Project, 2017).

Most eyewitnesses undoubtedly try to tell the truth about what or whom they saw. Yet research indicates that eyewitness testimony can be highly unreliable, partly because eyewitnesses sometimes hold subtle biases and partly because most crimes are unexpected and fleeting and therefore not the sort of events remembered well (Carpenter & Krendl, 2018; Wade, Nash, & Lindsay, 2018). During the crime, for example, lighting may be poor or other distractions may be present. Witnesses may have had other things on their

Eyewitness error Psychological research indicates that eyewitness testimony is often invalid. Here a woman talks to the man whom she had identified as her rapist back in 1984. DNA testing eventually proved that a different person had raped her, and the incorrectly identified man was released. In the meantime, however, he had served 11 years of a life sentence in prison.

Chuck Burton/AP Photo

#TVProfilers

Criminal Minds (current)

Mindhunter (current)

Killing Eve (current)

Luther (current)

Law and Order: SVU (current)

The Mentalist (recent)

Psych (recent)

minds, such as concern for their own safety or that of bystanders. Such concerns may greatly impair later memory.

In laboratory studies, researchers have found it easy to fool participants who are trying to recall the details of an observed event simply by introducing misinformation (Loftus, 2017; Rindal et al., 2017). After a suggestive description by the researcher, stop signs can be transformed into yield signs, white cars into blue ones, and Mickey Mouse into Minnie Mouse. In addition, laboratory studies indicate that persons who are highly suggestible have the poorest recall of observed events (Liebman et al., 2002).

As for identifying actual perpetrators, research has found that accuracy is heavily influenced by the method used in identification (Smith et al., 2018; Wixted & Wells, 2017). For example, police lineups, particularly ones conducted poorly, are not always reliable, and the errors that witnesses make when looking at lineups tend to stick (Taubert, van Golde, & Verstraten, 2017; Wells et al., 2015, 2011). Researchers have also learned that the confidence of witnesses is not consistently related to accuracy (Wixted & Wells, 2017). Witnesses who are "absolutely certain" may be no more correct in their recollections than those who are only "fairly sure." Yet the degree of a witness's confidence often influences whether jurors believe his or her testimony (Loftus & Greenspan, 2017).

Psychological investigations into the memories of eyewitnesses have not yet undone the judicial system's reliance on or respect for those witnesses' testimony. Nor should it. The distance between laboratory studies and real-life events is often great, and the findings from such studies must be applied with care. Still, eyewitness research has begun to make an impact. Instructions to jurors about the accuracy of eyewitness confidence may now be included in eyewitness cases (Cash & Lane, 2017). In addition, studies of hypnosis and of its ability to create false memories have led most states to prohibit eyewitnesses from testifying about events or details if their recall of the events was initially helped by hypnosis.

PATTERNS OF CRIMINALITY A growing number of television shows, movies, and books suggest that clinicians often play a major role in criminal investigations by providing police with *psychological profiles* of perpetrators—"He's probably white, in his thirties, has a history of animal torture, has few friends, and is subject to emotional outbursts." The study of criminal behavior patterns and of profiling has increased in recent decades; however, it is not nearly as revealing or influential as the media and the arts would have us believe (Keatley et al., 2018; Kapardis, 2017).

On the positive side, researchers have gathered information about the psychological features of various criminals, and they have indeed found that perpetrators of particular kinds of crimes—serial murder or serial sexual assault, for example—frequently share a number of traits and background features (see ***PsychWatch***). But while such traits are *often* present, they are not *always* present, and so applying profile information to a particular crime can be wrong and misleading (Fox, Levin, & Fridel, 2018). Increasingly, police are consulting psychological profilers, and this practice appears to be helpful as long as the limitations of profiling are recognized.

A reminder of the limitations of profiling comes from the case of the snipers who terrorized the Washington, DC, area for three weeks in October 2002, shooting 10 people dead and seriously wounding 3 others. Most of the profiling done by FBI psychologists had suggested that the sniper was acting alone; it turned out that the attacks were conducted by a pair: a middle-aged man, John Allen Muhammad, and a teenage boy, Lee Boyd Malvo. Although profiles had suggested a young thrill-seeker, Muhammad was 41. Profilers had believed the attacker to be non-Hispanic white, but neither Muhammad nor Malvo was white. The prediction of a *male* attacker was correct, but then again female serial killers are relatively rare.

Misleading profile Police search for clues outside a Home Depot in Virginia in 2002, hoping to identify and capture the serial sniper who killed 10 people and terrorized residents throughout Washington, DC, Maryland, and Virginia. As it turned out, psychological profiling in this famous case offered little help and even misled the police.

AP Photo/Doug Mills

PSYCHWATCH

Serial Murderers: Madness or Badness?

On April 24, 2018, police arrested former police officer Joseph James DeAngelo outside his home near Sacramento, California. Based on DNA evidence, they accused DeAngelo of being the so-called Golden State Killer, a murderer of at least 12 people in separate incidents during a crime spree that terrorized Californians from 1974 to 1986. If convicted, DeAngelo would join a growing list of serial killers who have fascinated and horrified the public over the years: Bruce Ivins ("anthrax killer"), Theodore Kaczynski ("Unabomber"), Ted Bundy, David Berkowitz ("Son of Sam"), Albert DeSalvo ("Boston Strangler"), John Wayne Gacy ("Killer Clown"), Jeffrey Dahmer ("Milwaukee Cannibal"), Dennis Rader ("BTK killer"), and more.

By definition, serial killers commit a series of murders (3 or more) in separate incidents over an extended period of time. They are different from mass killers, whom you read about in Chapter 13—individuals who murder four or more people at a single time, usually in a single location (see page 408).

The FBI estimates that there are between 25 and 50 serial killers at large in the United States at any given time (FBI, 2017, 2014). Worldwide, 4,500 such killers have been identified since the year 1900 (Aamodt, 2016, 2014).

Each serial killer follows his or her own pattern, but many of them appear to have certain characteristics in common (Fox et al., 2018; Johnston, 2017). The majority—but certainly not all—are non-Hispanic white males between 30 and 45 years old, of average to high intelligence, seemingly clean-cut, smooth-talking, attractive, and skillful manipulators.

Close to half of serial killers seem to have severe personality disorders (Fox et al., 2018; FBI, 2017, 2014). Lack of conscience and an utter disregard for people and the rules of society—key features of antisocial personality disorder—are typical. Narcissistic thinking is quite common as well. Feelings of being special may even give the killers an unrealistic belief that they will not get caught (Fox et al., 2018; Kocsis, 2008). Often it is this sense of invincibility that leads to their capture.

Sexual dysfunctions, paraphilic disorders, and fantasies also seem to play a part (Fox et al., 2018; FBI, 2017, 2014). Studies have found that vivid fantasies, often sexual and sadistic, may help drive the killer's behavior. Some clinicians also believe that the killers may be trying to overcome general feelings of powerlessness by controlling, hurting, or eliminating those who are momentarily weaker. A number of the killers were abused as children—physically, sexually, and/or emotionally (Keatley et al., 2018).

Law enforcement agencies and behavioral researchers have gathered an impressive body of statistical information about serial killings and killers in recent years. This data is often of help to criminal investigators as they seek to capture these repeat perpetrators of particularly heinous acts. At the same time, it would be inaccurate to say that clinical theorists understand why serial killers behave as they do.

Bill O'Leary/The Washington Post via Getty Images

Serial sentences for serial murders During a trial in 2016, court deputies watch over Charles Severance, an eccentric history buff accused of killing three people in Alexandria, Virginia, between 2003 and 2014 simply because they were relatively affluent. Severance was found guilty for his serial killings and given three consecutive life sentences.

9... SUMMING UP

OTHER CLINICAL–LEGAL INTERACTIONS Mental health and legal professionals also cross paths in four other areas. First, malpractice suits against therapists have increased in recent years. Second, the legislative and judicial systems help define professional boundaries. Third, lawyers may solicit the advice of mental health professionals regarding the selection of jurors and case strategies. Fourth, psychologists may investigate legal phenomena such as eyewitness testimony and patterns of criminality.

What Ethical Principles Guide Mental Health Professionals?

Discussions of the legal and mental health systems may sometimes give the impression that clinicians as a group are uncaring and are considerate of patients' rights and needs only when they are forced to be. This, of course, is not true. Most clinicians care greatly about their clients and strive to help them while at the same time respecting their rights and dignity (Mazulla & LiVecchi, 2018; Pope & Vasquez, 2016, 2011). In fact, clinicians do not rely exclusively on the legislative and court systems to ensure proper and effective clinical practice. They also regulate themselves by continually developing and revising ethical guidelines for their work and behavior. Many legal decisions do nothing more than place the power of the law behind these already existing professional guidelines.

Each profession within the mental health field has its own **code of ethics.** The code of the American Psychological Association (2017, 2010, 2002) is typical. This code, highly respected by other mental health professionals and public officials, includes specific guidelines:

1. **Psychologists are permitted to offer advice** online, in self-help books, on DVDs, on television and radio programs, in newspapers and magazines, through mailed material, and in other places, provided they do so responsibly and professionally and base their advice on appropriate psychological literature and practices. Of these, Internet-based professional advice has proved particularly difficult to regulate, because the number of online clinical offerings keeps getting larger and larger and so many advice-givers do not appear to have any professional training or credentials.

2. **Psychologists may not conduct fraudulent research, plagiarize the work of others, or publish false data.** During the past 30 years, cases of scientific fraud or misconduct have been discovered in all of the sciences, including psychology. These acts have led to misunderstandings of important issues, taken scientific research in the wrong direction, and damaged public trust. Unfortunately, the impressions created by false findings may continue to influence the thinking of both the public and other scientists for years.

3. **Psychologists must acknowledge their limitations** with regard to patients who are disabled or whose gender, ethnicity, language, socioeconomic status, or sexual orientation differs from that of the therapist. This guideline often requires psychotherapists to obtain additional training or supervision, consult with more knowledgeable colleagues, or refer clients to more appropriate professionals.

4. **Psychologists who make evaluations and testify in legal cases must base their assessments on sufficient information and substantiate their findings appropriately.** If an adequate examination of the individual in question is not possible, psychologists must make clear the limited nature of their testimony.

5. **Psychologists may not participate or assist in torture—acts in which severe pain, suffering, or degradation is intentionally inflicted on people.** This guideline was added to the code of ethics in 2017, a year after an APA-sponsored evaluation revealed that, over a period of several years, the APA had aided and advised the Department of Defense and the Central Intelligence Agency in the development of "enhanced interrogation" techniques (that is, torture-based questioning) and had adjusted professional guidelines to allow psychologist involvement in such interrogations (see ***Trending*** on page 514).

Barry Brecheisen/Getty Images

The ethics of giving professional advice
Today's psychologists are bound by the field's ethics code to base their advice on psychological theories and findings. In 2006, the enormously popular Phil McGraw ("Dr. Phil") surrendered his Texas psychologist license so that he could be free to use his own best judgment when giving advice on television and in books.

6. **Psychologists may not take advantage of clients and students, sexually or otherwise.** This guideline relates to the widespread social problem of sexual harassment, as well as the problem of therapists who take sexual advantage of clients in therapy. The code specifically forbids a sexual relationship with a present or former therapy client for at least two years after the end of treatment—and even then such a relationship is permitted only in "the most unusual circumstances." Furthermore, psychologists may not accept as clients people with whom they have previously had a sexual relationship.

   Research has clarified that clients may suffer great emotional damage from sexual involvement with their therapists (Pope & Wedding, 2019; Pope & Vasquez, 2016, 2011). How many therapists actually have a sexual relationship with a client? On the basis of various surveys, reviewers have estimated that 4 to 5 percent of today's therapists engage in some form of sexual misconduct with patients, down from 10 percent more than a decade ago.

   Although the vast majority of therapists do not engage in sexual behavior of any kind with clients, their ability to control private feelings is apparently another matter. In surveys, more than 80 percent of therapists reported having been sexually attracted to a client, at least on occasion (Pope & Wedding, 2019; Pope & Vasquez, 2016, 2011). Although few of these therapists acted on their feelings, most of them felt guilty, anxious, or concerned about the attraction. Given such issues, it is not surprising that sexual ethics training is given high priority in many of today's clinical training programs.

7. **Psychologists must follow the principle of confidentiality.** All of the state and federal courts have upheld laws protecting therapy **confidentiality** (Ashton & Sullivan, 2018; Skodol & Bender, 2018). For peace of mind and to ensure effective therapy, clients must be able to trust that their private exchanges with a therapist will not be repeated to others. There are times, however, when the principle of confidentiality must be compromised (Pope & Wedding, 2019; Middleman & Olson, 2017). A therapist in training, for example, must discuss cases on a regular basis with a supervisor, and clients must be informed that such discussions are taking place.

   A second exception arises in cases of outpatients who are clearly dangerous. The 1976 case of *Tarasoff v. Regents of the University of California,* one of the most important cases to affect client–therapist relationships, concerned an outpatient at a University of California hospital. He had confided to his therapist that he wanted to harm his former girlfriend, Tanya Tarasoff. Several days after ending therapy, the former patient fulfilled his promise. He stabbed Tanya Tarasoff to death.

   Can you think of other instances in which the principle of therapy confidentiality should be broken?

   Should confidentiality have been broken in this case? The therapist, in fact, felt that it should. Campus police were notified, but the patient was released after some questioning. In their suit against the hospital and therapist, the victim's parents argued that the therapist should have also warned them and their daughter that the patient intended to harm Ms. Tarasoff. The California Supreme Court agreed: "The protective privilege ends where the public peril begins."

   The current code of ethics for psychologists thus declares that therapists have a **duty to protect**—a responsibility to break confidentiality, even without the client's consent, when it is necessary "to protect the client or others from harm." Since the *Tarasoff* ruling, most states have passed "duty to protect" bills that clarify the rules of confidentiality for therapists and protect them from certain civil suits (Adi & Mathbout, 2018; Middleman & Olson, 2017).

code of ethics A body of principles and rules for ethical behavior, designed to guide decisions and actions by members of a profession.

confidentiality The principle that certain professionals will not divulge the information they obtain from a client.

duty to protect The principle that therapists must break confidentiality in order to protect a person who may be the intended victim of a client.

#

#LegalKnowledge

75%	Percentage of psychologists who are misinformed about their legal responsibilities regarding potentially dangerous clients.
90%	Percentage of same psychologists who feel confident that their legal knowledge in this realm is accurate.

(Information from: Thomas, 2014)

...TRENDING

Doctor, Do No Harm

The Hippocratic Oath requires that doctors, first and foremost, "do no harm"—a principle also embraced by the code of ethics for each mental health profession. However, recent developments suggest that in the realm of torture, some psychologists have indeed done harm to individuals.

A 2014 book entitled *Pay Any Price,* a 2015 Senate Select Committee investigation, a 2015 report called the Hoffman Report, and a 2017 lawsuit have collectively indicated that certain psychologists and, indeed, the American Psychological Association (APA) participated for several years in the Central Intelligence Agency's program of *enhanced interrogation,* or *torture-based questioning,* to obtain information from suspected terrorists (Wise, 2018; APA, 2017; Bailey, 2017; Fink & Risen, 2017; Melechi, 2016; Patel & Elkin, 2015). Here are key events revealed by these sources:

In 2002, shortly after the September 11, 2001 terrorist attacks in New York City and Washington, DC, the White House gave approval to a CIA program of "enhanced interrogation" of national security prisoners, or "detainees." In a series of so-called torture memos, it stated that enhanced interrogations could indeed proceed if consulting mental health experts indicated the procedures were not causing or likely to cause significant physical injury or severe mental distress.

Later in 2002, two psychologists, commissioned by the CIA, developed a package of enhanced interrogation procedures (including sleep deprivation, repeated waterboarding, physical assault, binding in stressful positions, deafening noise, and imprisonment in a box), and the CIA tested those procedures on a prisoner with possible ties to the terrorist organization Al Qaeda. Officials declared the test a success and, from that point forward, enhanced interrogations became an accepted national security policy. The two psychologists continued to serve as major advisers for the CIA program.

In order for the enhanced interrogation program to proceed, the CIA needed a number of psychologists to observe the interrogations and declare them acceptable, as well as ongoing advice and input from various psychologists to further develop the program. As a result, the CIA and key administrators at the APA developed a cooperative relationship that continued for several years. Although the APA did not participate in the actual administration of torture procedures, some of its administrators did have a series of communications, discussions, and brainstorming sessions with the CIA about the enhanced interrogation program and the possible role of psychologists.

Perhaps most damning, certain APA administrators manipulated the language of the organization's code of ethics, apparently to allow individual psychologists to participate in the enhanced interrogation program without fear of being accused of professional wrongdoing. After all, psychologists could not work with the program if that meant they were violating their profession's ethical standards. This concern disappeared in 2005 when the APA's "Presidential Task Force on Ethics and National Security" (PENS) ruled, in subtle language, that psychologists are not violating their "do no harm" obligation if they do not break any laws in their work, including possible work in the realm of enhanced interrogations. That is, even if their enhanced interrogation involvement contributed to the development of PTSD, anxiety disorders, depression, or the like, the psychologists would not be violating their profession's ethical principles.

Some members of the APA recognized that the subtly worded PENS ruling allowed psychologists to participate in the CIA torture-based program, and, in the ensuing years, as the relationship between certain APA officials and the CIA continued and while the APA continued to deny the organization's involvement in or endorsement of the torture-based program, these astute APA members protested the APA's likely involvement with the CIA.

All this came to a head in 2014, when the stunning developments mentioned earlier began to unfold in quick succession. Since those revelations, several of the APA administrators linked to the enhanced interrogation discussions have resigned. (In 2017, those former administrators sued the authors of the Hoffman Report for incorrectly characterizing their actions and for defaming them.) Also in 2017, the two psychologists who initiated and implemented the CIA's enhanced interrogation program beginning back in 2002 reached a court settlement with three tortured national security prisoners who had sued them.

Finally, the APA, with its members now fully informed about what had unfolded, sought to end this ugly episode and to ensure that it would not occur again. Most importantly, the entire APA membership voted to bar psychologists from direct and indirect involvement in any national security interrogations—both enhanced and noncoercive. In so doing, it was reaffirming that, even in a complex and dangerous world, a primary obligation of psychologists is to "do no harm" of any kind to individuals.

AP Photo/Jeff Chiu

No place for psychologists Protestors at an APA conference rally against psychologist involvement in CIA enhanced interrogation programs.

Mental Health, Business, and Economics

The legislative and judicial systems are not the only social institutions with which mental health professionals interact. *Business* and *economic* fields are two other sectors that influence and are influenced by clinical practice and study.

Bringing Mental Health Services to the Workplace

According to numerous surveys, work is by far the leading source of stress for people (APA, 2018; AIS, 2017). Over 40 percent of workers find their jobs very stressful and believe them to be bad for their mental health and general health (AIS, 2017; HSPH, 2016). Stressed-out workers report that the primary causes of their upsets are excessive workload (46 percent of workers), people and personnel issues (28 percent), difficulties balancing work with home life (20 percent), and lack of job security (6 percent) (APA, 2018; AIS, 2017).

All this stress not only affects the home life and personal functioning of employees. It also impairs performance in the workplace. Indeed, 60 percent of absences from work can be traced, directly or indirectly, to stress and related mental health issues (APA, 2018; HSPH, 2016). Furthermore, studies find that stress at work contributes to poorer productivity and more accidents, employee mistakes, employee departures, insurance costs, and worker compensation expenses (AIS, 2017; White, 2015).

William Haefeli/The New Yorker Collection/The Cartoon Bank

"My life has become a tangled web of fictitious user names and fiendishly clever passwords."

For both humane and financial reasons, many employers try to address the work-related stress and other mental health needs of their employees. Two common approaches, provided by about half of employers, are *employee assistance programs* and *stress reduction programs* (McRee, 2017; HSPH, 2016). **Employee assistance programs** are mental health services made available by a place of business. They are run either by mental health professionals who work directly for a company or by outside mental health agencies. **Stress-reduction and problem-solving programs** are workshops or group sessions in which mental health professionals teach employees techniques for coping, solving problems, and handling and reducing stress. As you read in Chapter 2, one of today's most common such techniques is *mindfulness training*, offered by around one-third of employers (see pages 53–54). Businesses believe that employee assistance and stress reduction programs save them money in the long run by preventing psychological problems from interfering with work performance and by reducing employee insurance claims, a notion that has been supported in various studies (Richmond et al., 2017). And, for their part, at least half of workers agree that they need help learning how to manage stress (AIS, 2017).

The Economics of Mental Health

You have already seen how economic decisions by the government may influence the clinical field's treatment of people with severe mental disorders. For example, the desire of the state and federal governments to reduce costs was an important consideration in the country's deinstitutionalization movement, which contributed to the premature release of hospital patients into the community. Economic decisions by government agencies may affect other kinds of clients and treatment programs as well.

As you read in Chapter 12, government funding for services to people with psychological disorders has risen sharply over the past five decades, from $1 billion in 1963 to around $152 billion today (SAMHSA, 2017, 2014). Around 28 percent of that money is spent on prescription drugs, but much of the rest is targeted for income support, housing subsidies, and other such expenses rather than direct mental health services.

employee assistance program A mental health program offered by a business to its employees.

stress-reduction and problem-solving program A workshop or series of group sessions offered by a business, in which mental health professionals teach employees how to cope with and solve problems and reduce stress.

AP Photo/Gerry Broome

Caught in an economic spiral Group home residents and mental health advocates rally at the legislative office building in Raleigh, North Carolina, to protest a Medicaid payment law change. This change could result in residents with severe mental disorders losing their group homes and having nowhere to live.

The result is that government funding for mental health services is, in fact, insufficient. People with severe mental disorders are hit hardest by the funding shortage. The number of people on waiting lists for community-based services grew from 200,000 in 2002 to 393,000 in 2008, and that number has increased still more over the past decade, according to individual state reports (Morris, 2017; NCBH, 2017).

Government funding currently covers 63 percent of all mental health services, leaving a mental health expense of tens of billions of dollars for individual patients and their private insurance companies (SAMHSA, 2017, 2014). This large economic role of private insurance companies has had a significant effect on the way clinicians go about their work. As you'll remember from Chapter 1, to reduce their expenses, most of these companies have developed **managed care programs,** in which the insurance company determines which therapists clients may choose from, the cost of sessions, and the number of sessions for which a client may be reimbursed (Bowers et al., 2017, 2016). These and other insurance plans may also control expenses through the use of **peer review systems,** in which clinicians who work for the insurance company periodically review a client's treatment program and recommend that insurance benefits be either continued or stopped. Typically, insurers require reports or session notes from the therapist, often including intimate personal information about the patient.

As you also read in Chapter 1, many therapists and clients dislike managed care programs and peer reviews (Kornack, Herscovich, & Williams, 2017; Decker, 2016). They believe that the reports required of therapists breach confidentiality, even when efforts are made to protect anonymity, and that the importance of therapy in a given case is sometimes difficult to convey in a brief report. They also argue that the priorities of managed care programs inevitably shorten therapy, even if longer-term treatment would be advisable in particular cases. The priorities may also favor treatments that offer short-term results (for example, drug therapy) over more costly approaches that might yield more promising long-term improvement (Bowers et al., 2017, 2016). As in the medical field, there are disturbing stories about patients who are prematurely cut off from mental health services by their managed care programs.

What are the costs to clients and practitioners when insurance companies make decisions about the methods, frequency, and duration of treatment?

Yet another major problem with insurance coverage in the United States—whether managed care or other kinds of insurance programs—is that reimbursements for mental disorders are, on average, lower than those for physical disorders, placing people with psychological difficulties at a significant disadvantage (Thalmayer et al., 2018). As you have read, the federal government tried to address this problem from 2008 through 2016 (see page 18). In 2008 Congress passed a *parity* law that mandated equal insurance coverage for mental and physical problems, and in 2014 the mental health provisions of the Affordable Care Act ("Obamacare") expanded the reach of the earlier bill. If, however, efforts in Congress to change or repeal the Affordable Care Act eventually succeed, it is possible that the federal mandates for parity in mental health insurance coverage will, likewise, be discontinued.

#

#InsuranceRejection

55%	Percentage of psychiatrists willing to accept insurance payments.
93%	Percentage of all other kinds of physicians who accept insurance payments.

(Information from: Pettypiece, 2015; Pear, 2013)

Technology and Mental Health

As you have seen throughout this book, today's ever-changing technology has had significant effects—both positive and negative—on the mental health field, and it will undoubtedly affect the field even more in the coming years.

Our digital world provides new *triggers* for the expression of abnormal behavior. The maladaptive functioning of many persons with gambling disorder, for example, has been exacerbated by the ready availability of Internet gambling (see page 325). Similarly, the Internet, texting, and social networking are now used frequently by those who wish to stalk or bully others, express sexual exhibitionism, pursue pedophilic desires, or satisfy other paraphilic disorders (see pages 348, 437). And, in the opinion of many clinicians, constant texting, tweeting, and Internet browsing may help shorten people's attention spans and establish a foundation for attention problems.

Beyond providing new triggers for abnormal behavior, research indicates that today's technology also is helping to produce *new* psychological disorders. As you read in Chapter 10, one such pattern is *Internet use disorder*, a problem marked by excessive and dysfunctional levels of texting, tweeting, networking, Internet browsing, e-mailing, blogging, online shopping, or online pornographic use (Lindenberg et al., 2018) (see page 326). The framers of DSM-5 have suggested that this disorder be considered for possible inclusion in future revisions of the DSM. Similarly, the Internet has brought a new exhibitionistic feature to certain kinds of abnormal behavior. For example, as you read in Chapter 7, a growing number of people now use social networking to post videos of themselves engaging in self-cutting or suicidal acts, acts that traditionally had been conducted in private (see pages 214–216).

There is also a growing recognition among clinical practitioners and researchers that even everyday social networking can contribute to psychological dysfunction. In addition to its many virtues, social networking may, according to research, provide a new venue for peer pressure and social anxiety in some adolescents (Gao et al., 2018; Levula et al., 2018). It may, for example, cause some people to develop fears that others in their network will exclude them socially. Similarly, clinicians worry that social networking may lead shy or socially anxious people to withdraw from valuable face-to-face relationships.

As you have read throughout this textbook, the face of clinical treatment has also expanded in our fast-moving digital world. *Telemental health*, the use of various technologies to deliver mental health services without the therapist being physically present, is now common (Comer et al., 2019, 2017; Adams et al., 2018). It takes such forms as long-distance therapy between clients and therapists using videoconferencing (see page 446), therapy offered by computer programs, treatment enhanced by the use of video game–like avatars and other virtual reality experiences (see pages 63, 118, 155), and Internet-based support groups (see pages 20, 63). In addition, of the hundreds of thousands of new apps created over the past five years, a number are devoted to helping people relax, cheer up, or track their shifting moods and thoughts (see pages 193–194). And many computer exercise programs—cognitive and physical—have been developed with the goal of improving both mental health (particularly, cognitive functioning and mood) and physical health (see page 489).

Similarly, numerous Web sites now offer useful mental health information, enabling people to better inform themselves, their friends, and their family members about psychological problems and treatment options (see page 20). Unfortunately, along with this wealth of online information comes considerable misinformation about psychological problems and their treatments, offered by persons and sites that are far from knowledgeable or noble. The issue of quality control is also a major problem for Internet-based therapy, support groups, and the like, and there are now numerous antitreatment networks, such as the pro-suicide and pro-Ana networks you read about in Chapters 7 and 9, that try to guide people away from seeking help for their psychological problems (see pages 216, 277).

managed care program An insurance program in which the insurance company decides the cost, method, provider, and length of treatment.

peer review system A system by which clinicians paid by an insurance company may periodically review a patient's progress and recommend the continuation or termination of insurance benefits.

Extending psychology's reach A child meets with a psychologist (left on screen) and physician (right) located several towns away. Long-distance therapy by videoconferencing is an increasingly used form of telemental health.

AP Photo/Nati Harnik

What ethical concerns or problems might emerge as a result of the mental health field's increasing use of new technologies?

Clearly, the growing impact of technological change on the mental health field presents formidable challenges for clinicians and researchers alike. Few of the technological applications discussed throughout this book are well understood, and few have been subjected to comprehensive research. Yet, as we mentioned earlier, the relationship between technology and mental health is growing precipitously. It behooves everyone in the field to understand this growth and its implications.

The Person Within the Profession

The actions of clinical researchers and practitioners not only influence and are influenced by other forces in society but also are closely tied to their personal needs and goals (see ***InfoCentral***). You have seen that the human strengths, imperfections, wisdom, and clumsiness of clinical professionals may affect their theoretical orientations, their interactions with clients, and the kinds of clients with whom they choose to work. You have also seen how personal leanings may sometimes override professional standards and scruples and, in extreme cases, lead clinical scientists to commit research fraud and clinical practitioners to engage in sexual misconduct with clients.

Surveys of the mental health of therapists have found that as many as 84 percent report having been in therapy at least once (Pope & Wedding, 2019; Pope & Vasquez, 2016). Their reasons are largely the same as those of other clients, with relationship problems, depression, and anxiety topping the list. And, like other people, therapists often are reluctant to acknowledge their psychological problems.

#TheirWords

"After doing psychology for half a century, my passion for all of it is greater than ever."
Phillip Zimbardo, influential psychologist, Stanford Prison Experiment

It is not clear why so many therapists have psychological problems. Perhaps it is because their jobs are highly stressful; research suggests that therapists often experience some degree of job burnout (Hammond, Crowther, & Drummond, 2018). Or perhaps therapists are simply more aware of their own negative feelings or are more likely to pursue treatment for their problems. Alternatively, people with personal concerns may be more inclined to choose clinical work as a profession. Whatever the reason, clinicians bring to their work a set of psychological issues that may, along with other important factors, affect how they listen and respond to clients.

The science and profession of abnormal psychology seek to understand, predict, and change abnormal functioning. But we must not lose sight of the fact that mental health

"Oops! I just deleted all your files. Can you repeat everything you've ever told me?"

PERSONAL AND PROFESSIONAL ISSUES

Like everyone else, clinicians have personal needs, perspectives, goals, and problems, each of which may affect their work. Therapists typically try to minimize the impact of such variables on their interactions with clients—called **countertransference** by Freud. However, research suggests that, to at least some degree, personal therapist issues influence how clinicians deal with clients.

THE EARLY YEARS

Common events in the early lives of therapists

- Experiencing personal distress
- Witnessing the distress of others
- Observing the behaviors and emotions of others; becoming psychologically minded
- Reading
- Being in therapy
- Being a confidant to others
- Modeling the behavior of others
- Learning from a mentor

(Miller, 2017; Pope & Vasquez, 2016; Farber et al., 2005)

Top 5 reasons people become therapists

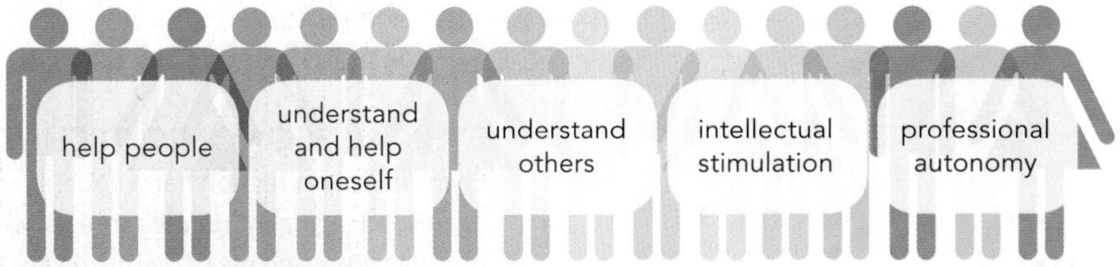

(Miller, 2017; Waters, 2015; Farber et al., 2005; Norcross & Farber, 2005)

CLINICAL CAREERS

How satisfied are clinical psychologists with their careers?

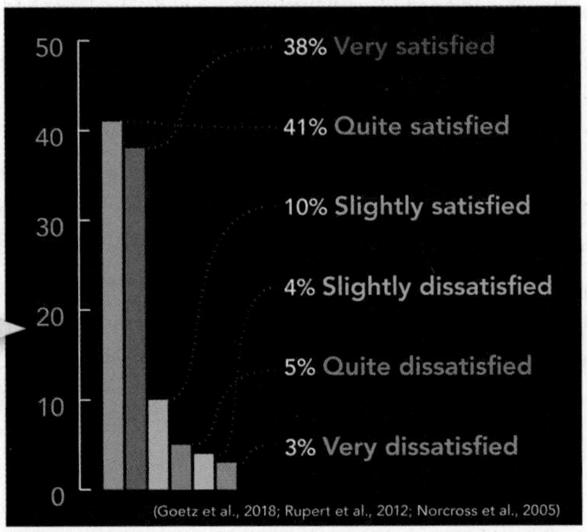

(Goetz et al., 2018; Rupert et al., 2012; Norcross et al., 2005)

How do clinical psychologists spend their professional time?

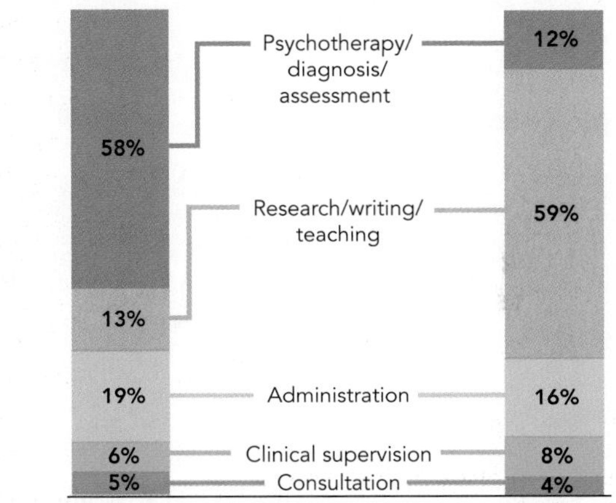

(APA, 2016; Norcross et al., 2009, 2005)

ETHICS IN CLINICAL PRACTICE

Although the field's code of ethics explicitly forbids it, some therapists engage in sexual relationships with their clients. This is the profession's most egregious violation of trust and boundaries and typically causes significant psychological harm to clients.

Who has had a sexual relationship with a client?

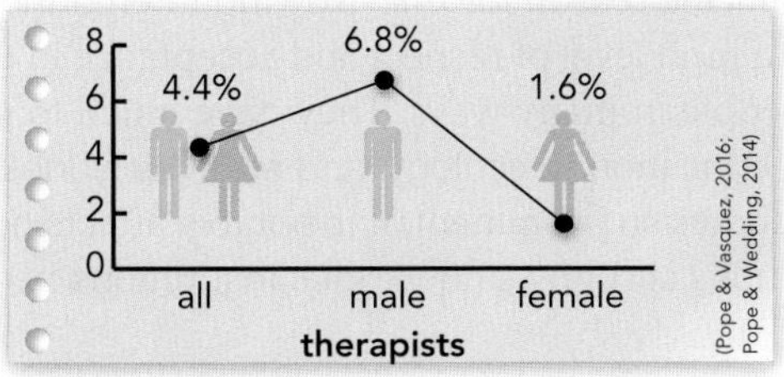

(Pope & Vasquez, 2016; Pope & Wedding, 2014)

Effects on clients

- Ambivalence
- Guilt
- Emptiness and isolation
- Sexual confusion
- Inability to trust
- Confusion of roles and boundaries
- Emotional damage
- Suppressed rage
- Heightened risk of suicide
- Cognitive dysfunction

(Pope & Wedding, 2019; Pope & Vasquez, 2016; Pope, 1994, 1988)

CLINICIANS IN THERAPY

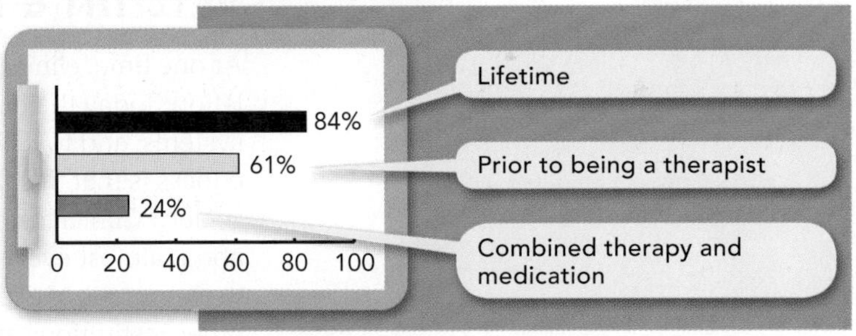

(Pope & Vasquez, 2016; Bearse et al., 2014)

Top qualities clinicians look for in choosing a therapist

- Competence
- Warmth and caring
- Clinical experience and professional reputation
- Openness
- Active therapeutic style
- Flexibility

(Hill et al., 2017; Norcross et al., 2009, 2005)

THE EMOTIONAL SIDE

Therapists' fears regarding clients

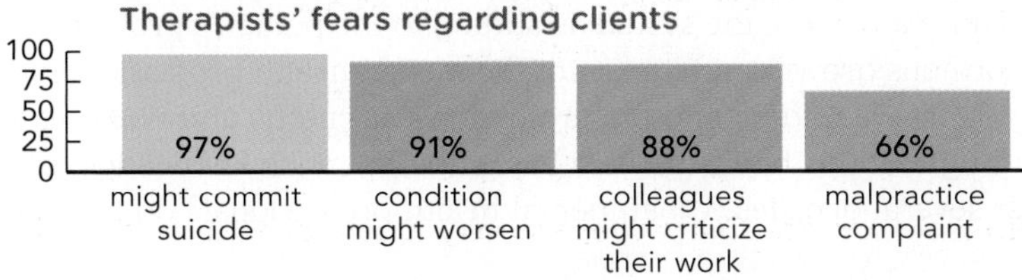

Therapists' anger toward clients

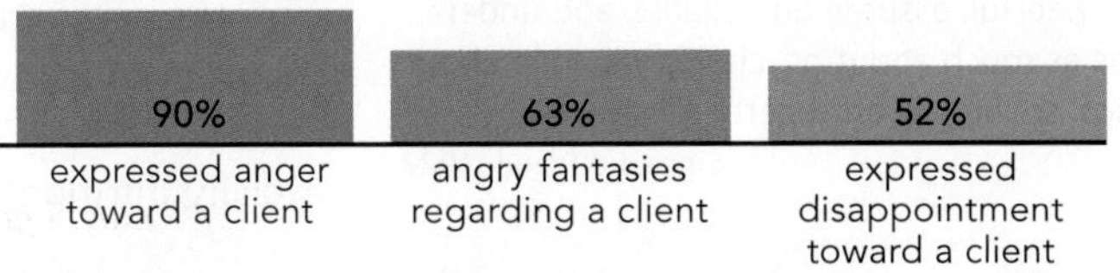

(Pope & Vasquez, 2016; Pope & Tabachnick, 1993; Pope et al., 1987)

researchers and clinicians are human beings, living within a society of human beings, working to serve human beings. The mixture of discovery, misdirection, promise, and frustration that you have encountered throughout this book is thus to be expected. When you think about it, could the study and treatment of human behavior really proceed in any other way?

... SUMMING UP

ETHICAL, ECONOMIC, TECHNOLOGICAL, AND PERSONAL FACTORS Each clinical profession has a code of ethics. The psychologists' code includes prohibitions against engaging in fraudulent research, taking advantage of clients and students (sexually or otherwise), and participating or assisting in enhanced interrogation programs. It also establishes guidelines for respecting patient confidentiality. The case of *Tarasoff v. Regents of the University of California* helped determine the circumstances in which therapists have a duty to protect the client or others from harm and must break confidentiality.

Clinical practice and study also intersect with the business and economic worlds. Clinicians may be called upon to address psychological problems in the workplace. In addition, private insurance companies often set up managed care programs whose procedures influence—sometimes adversely—the length, focus, confidentiality, and quality of therapy.

The technological advances of recent times have affected the mental health field by contributing to new triggers for psychopathology, new forms of psychopathology, and various kinds of telemental health.

Mental health activities are affected by the personal needs, values, and goals of the human beings who provide the clinical services. These factors inevitably affect the direction and even quality of their work.

#TheirWords

"Relativity applies to physics, not ethics."

Albert Einstein, physicist, Theory of Relativity

Within a Larger System

At one time, clinical researchers and professionals conducted their work largely in isolation. Today their activities have numerous ties to the legislative, judicial, and economic systems, and to technological forces as well. One reason for this growing interconnectedness is that the clinical field has reached a high level of respect and acceptance in our society. Clinicians now serve millions of people in many ways. They have much to say about almost every aspect of society, from education to ecology, and are widely looked to as sources of expertise. When a field becomes so prominent, it inevitably affects how other institutions are run. It also attracts public scrutiny, and various institutions begin to keep an eye on its activities.

When people with psychological problems seek help from a therapist, they are entering a complex system consisting of many interconnected parts. Just as their personal problems have grown within a social structure, so will their treatment be affected by the various parts of a larger system—the therapist's values and needs, legal and economic factors, societal attitudes, technological changes, and yet other forces. These many forces influence clinical research as well.

The effects of this larger system on an individual's psychological needs can be positive or negative, like a family's impact on each of its members. When the system protects a client's rights and confidentiality, for example, it is serving the client well. When economic, legal, or other societal forces limit treatment options, cut off treatment prematurely, or stigmatize a person, the system is adding to the person's problems.

Because of the enormous growth and impact of the mental health profession in our society, it is important that we understand the profession's strengths and weaknesses. As you have seen throughout this book, the field has gathered much knowledge, especially during the past several decades. What mental health professionals do not know

#TheirWords

"I spent . . . two hours chatting with Einstein. . . . He is cheerful, assured and likable, and understands as much about psychology as I do about physics, so we got on together very well."

Sigmund Freud, 1927

and cannot do, however, still outweighs what they do know and can do. Everyone who turns to the clinical field—directly or indirectly—must recognize that it is young and imperfect. Society is vastly curious about behavior and often in need of information and help. What we as a society must remember, however, is that the field is still unfolding.

Key Terms

forensic psychology, p. 496
criminal commitment, p. 496
not guilty by reason of insanity (NGRI), p. 496
M'Naghten test, p. 497
irresistible impulse test, p. 497
Durham test, p. 497
American Law Institute (ALI) test, p. 497
guilty but mentally ill, p. 500
guilty with diminished capacity, p. 500
mentally disordered sex offenders, p. 501
sexually violent predator laws, p. 502
mental incompetence, p. 502
civil commitment, p. 504
outpatient civil commitment, p. 504
two-physician certificate (2 PC), p. 505
dangerousness, p. 505
right to treatment, p. 506
right to refuse treatment, p. 507
malpractice suit, p. 508
professional boundaries, p. 509
jury consultation, p. 509
eyewitness testimony, p. 509
psychological profiles, p. 510
code of ethics, p. 512
enhanced interrogation, p. 512
confidentiality, p. 513
duty to protect, p. 513
employee assistance programs, p. 515
stress-reduction and problem-solving programs, p. 515
managed care program, p. 516
peer review system, p. 516
telemental health, p. 517

Quick Quiz

1. Briefly explain the M'Naghten, irresistible impulse, Durham, and ALI tests of insanity. Which tests are used today to determine whether defendants are not guilty by reason of insanity? *pp. 496–498*
2. Explain the guilty but mentally ill, diminished capacity, mentally disordered sex offender, and sexually violent predator verdicts and laws. *pp. 501–502*
3. What are the reasons behind and the procedures for determining whether defendants are mentally incompetent to stand trial? *pp. 502–503*
4. What are the reasons for civil commitment, and how is it carried out? What criticisms have been made of civil commitment? *pp. 504–506*
5. What rights have court rulings and legislation guaranteed to patients with psychological disorders? *pp. 506–508*
6. How do the legislative and judicial systems affect the issue of professional boundaries of clinical practice? *p. 509*
7. What have clinical researchers learned about eyewitness memories and about patterns of criminality? How accurate and influential is the practice of psychological profiling in criminal cases? *pp. 509–511*
8. What key issues are covered by the psychologist's code of ethics? Under what conditions must therapists break the principle of confidentiality? *pp. 512–513*
9. What kinds of programs for the prevention and treatment of psychological problems have been established in business settings? What trends have emerged in recent years in the funding and insurance of mental health care? *pp. 515–516*
10. Describe how the mental health field has been affected by and dealt with the technological advances of recent years. *pp. 516–518*

Visit ***LaunchPad***
to access the e-Book, Clinical Choices, videos, activities, and LearningCurve, as well as study aids including flashcards, FAQs, and research exercises.

LaunchPad

Glossary

ABAB design A single-subject experimental design in which behavior is measured during a baseline period, after a treatment has been applied, after baseline conditions have been reintroduced, and after the treatment has been reintroduced. Also called a *reversal design*.

Abnormal psychology The scientific study of abnormal behavior undertaken to describe, predict, explain, and change abnormal patterns of functioning.

Acceptance and commitment therapy (ACT) A cognitive-behavioral therapy that teaches clients to accept and be mindful of (i.e., just notice) their dysfunctional thoughts or worries.

Acetylcholine A neurotransmitter that has been linked to depression and dementia.

Acute stress disorder A disorder in which fear and related symptoms are experienced soon after a traumatic event and last less than a month.

Addiction Persistent, compulsive dependence on a substance or behavior.

Adjustment disorders Disorders characterized by clinical symptoms such as depressed mood or anxiety in response to significant stressors.

Affect An experience of emotion or mood.

Aftercare A program of posthospitalization care and treatment in the community.

Agoraphobia An anxiety disorder in which a person is afraid to be in public places or situations from which escape might be difficult (or embarrassing) or help unavailable if panic-like symptoms were to occur.

Agranulocytosis A life-threatening drop in white blood cells. This condition is sometimes produced by the second-generation antipsychotic drug *clozapine*.

Alcohol Any beverage containing ethyl alcohol, including beer, wine, and liquor.

Alcohol dehydrogenase An enzyme that breaks down alcohol in the stomach before it enters the blood.

Alcohol use disorder A pattern of behavior in which a person repeatedly abuses or depends on alcohol. Also known as *alcoholism*.

Alcoholics Anonymous (AA) A self-help organization that provides support and guidance for people with alcoholism.

Alcoholism A pattern of behavior in which a person repeatedly abuses or depends on alcohol. Also known as *alcohol use disorder*.

Alogia A decrease in speech or speech content; a symptom of schizophrenia. Also known as *poverty of speech*.

Alprazolam A benzodiazepine drug shown to be effective in the treatment of anxiety disorders. Marketed as *Xanax*.

Altruistic suicide Suicide committed by people who intentionally sacrifice their lives for the well-being of society.

Alzheimer's disease The most common type of neurocognitive disorder, usually occurring after the age of 65, marked most prominently by memory impairment.

Amenorrhea The absence of menstrual cycles.

American Law Institute test A legal test for insanity that holds people to be insane at the time of committing a crime if, because of a mental disorder, they did not know right from wrong or could not resist an uncontrollable impulse to act.

Amnesia Loss of memory.

Amphetamines Stimulant drugs that are manufactured in the laboratory.

Amphetamine psychosis A syndrome characterized by psychotic symptoms brought on by high doses of amphetamines. Similar to *cocaine psychosis*.

Amygdala A structure in the brain that plays a key role in emotion and memory.

Analog observation A method for observing behavior in which people are observed in artificial settings such as clinicians' offices or laboratories.

Analogue experiment A research method in which the experimenter produces abnormal-like behavior in laboratory participants and then conducts experiments on the participants.

Anal stage In psychoanalytic theory, the second 18 months of life, during which the child's focus of pleasure shifts to the anus.

Anesthesia A lessening or loss of sensation of touch or of pain.

Anomic suicide Suicide committed by individuals whose social environment fails to provide stability, thus leaving them without a sense of belonging.

Anorexia nervosa A disorder marked by the pursuit of extreme thinness and by an extreme loss of weight.

Anoxia A complication of birth in which the baby is deprived of oxygen.

Antabuse (disulfiram) A drug that causes intense nausea, vomiting, increased heart rate, and dizziness when taken with alcohol. It is often taken by people who are trying to refrain from drinking alcohol.

Antagonist drugs Drugs that block or change the effects of an addictive drug.

Antianxiety drugs Psychotropic drugs that help reduce tension and anxiety. Also called *minor tranquilizers* or *anxiolytics*.

Antibipolar drugs Psychotropic drugs that help stabilize the moods of people suffering from a bipolar disorder. Also known as *mood stabilizers*.

Antibodies Bodily chemicals that seek out and destroy foreign invaders such as bacteria or viruses.

Antidepressant drugs Psychotropic drugs that improve the mood of people with depression.

Antigen A foreign invader of the body, such as a bacterium or virus.

Antipsychotic drugs Drugs that help correct grossly confused or distorted thinking.

Antisocial personality disorder A personality disorder marked by a general pattern of disregard for and violation of other people's rights.

Anxiety The central nervous system's physiological and emotional response to a vague sense of threat or danger.

Anxiety disorder A disorder in which anxiety is a central symptom.

Anxiety sensitivity A tendency to focus on one's bodily sensations, assess them illogically, and interpret them as harmful.

Anxiolytics Drugs that reduce anxiety.

ApoE-4 gene One form of the ApoE gene that is inherited by about 30 percent of the population. Those people may be particularly vulnerable to the development of Alzheimer's disease.

Arbitrary inference An error in logic in which a person draws negative conclusions on the basis of little or even contrary evidence.

Aripiprazole A second-generation antipsychotic drug whose brand name is Abilify.

Asperger's disorder The term previously applied to persons with autism spectrum disorder who display profound social impairment yet maintain a relatively high level of cognitive functioning and language skills.

Assertiveness training A cognitive-behavioral approach to increasing assertive behavior that is socially desirable.

Assessment The process of collecting and interpreting relevant information about a client or research participant.

Asthma A medical problem marked by narrowing of the trachea and bronchi, which results in shortness of breath, wheezing, coughing, and a choking sensation.

Asylum A type of institution that first became popular in the sixteenth century to provide care for persons with mental disorders. Most became virtual prisons.

Attention circuit A number of brain structures that work together to bring about attention and to maintain a proper balance between Type 1 and Type 2 attention processes.

Attention-deficit/hyperactivity disorder (ADHD) A disorder marked by the inability to focus attention, or overactive and impulsive behavior, or both.

Attribution An explanation of things we see going on around us that points to particular causes.

Auditory hallucination A hallucination in which a person hears sounds or voices that are not actually present.

Augmentative communication system A method for enhancing the communication skills of people with autism spectrum disorder, intellectual developmental disorder, or cerebral palsy by teaching them to point to pictures, symbols, letters, or words on a communication board or computer.

Aura A warning sensation that may precede a migraine headache.

Autism spectrum disorder A developmental disorder marked by extreme unresponsiveness to others, severe communication deficits, and highly repetitive and rigid behaviors, interests, and activities.

Autoerotic asphyxia A fatal lack of oxygen that people may unintentionally produce while hanging, suffocating, or strangling themselves during masturbation.

Autogenic mass killing Mass murder in which an individual kills people indiscriminately to fulfill a personal agenda.

Automatic thoughts Numerous unpleasant thoughts that help to cause or maintain depression, anxiety, or other forms of psychological dysfunction.

Autonomic nervous system (ANS) The network of nerve fibers that connect the central nervous system to all the other organs of the body.

Aversion therapy A treatment in which clients are repeatedly presented with unpleasant stimuli while performing undesirable behaviors such as taking a drug.

Avoidant personality disorder A personality disorder characterized by consistent discomfort and restraint in social situations, overwhelming feelings of inadequacy, and extreme sensitivity to negative evaluation.

Avolition A symptom of schizophrenia marked by apathy and an inability to start or complete a course of action.

Axon A long fiber extending from the body of a neuron.

Barbiturates One group of sedative-hypnotic drugs that reduces anxiety and helps produce sleep.

Baseline data A person's initial response level on a test or scale.

Basic irrational assumptions The inaccurate and inappropriate beliefs held by people with various psychological problems, according to Albert Ellis.

Battery A series of tests, each of which measures a specific skill area.

B-cell A lymphocyte that produces antibodies.

Behavioral activation A therapy for depression in which the client is guided to systematically increase the number of constructive and pleasurable activities and events in his or her life.

Behavioral medicine A field that combines psychological and physical interventions to treat or prevent medical problems.

Behavior-focused therapy A therapeutic approach that seeks to identify problem-causing behaviors and change them. Also known as *behavior modification*.

Behaviors The responses an organism makes to its environment.

Bender Visual-Motor Gestalt Test A neuropsychological test in which a subject is asked to copy a set of nine simple designs and later reproduce the designs from memory.

Benzodiazepines The most common group of antianxiety drugs, which includes Valium and Xanax.

Bereavement The process of working through the grief that one feels when a loved one dies.

Beta-amyloid protein A small molecule that forms sphere-shaped deposits called senile plaques, linked to aging and to Alzheimer's disease.

"Big Five" theory of personality A leading theory that holds that personality can be effectively organized and described by five broad dimensions of personality—openness, conscientiousness, extroversion, agreeableness, and neuroticism.

Binge An episode of uncontrollable eating during which a person ingests a very large quantity of food.

Binge drinking A pattern of alcohol consumption in which a person consumes five or more drinks on a single occasion.

Binge-eating disorder A disorder marked by frequent binges but not extreme compensatory behaviors.

Binge-eating/purging-type anorexia nervosa A type of anorexia nervosa in which people have eating binges but still lose excessive weight by forcing themselves to vomit after meals or by abusing laxatives or diuretics.

Biofeedback A technique in which a client is given information about physiological reactions as they occur and learns to control the reactions voluntarily.

Biological challenge test A procedure used to produce panic in participants or clients by having them exercise vigorously or perform some other potentially panic-inducing task in the presence of a researcher or therapist.

Biological model The theoretical perspective that points to biological processes as the key to human behavior.

Biological therapy The use of physical and chemical procedures to help people overcome psychological problems.

Biomarkers Biochemical, molecular, genetic, or structural characteristics that usually accompany a disease.

Biopsychosocial theories Explanations that attribute the cause of abnormality to an interaction of genetic, biological, developmental, emotional, behavioral, cognitive, social, and societal influences.

Bipolar disorder A disorder marked by alternating or intermixed periods of mania and depression.

Bipolar I disorder A type of bipolar disorder marked by full manic and major depressive episodes.

Bipolar II disorder A type of bipolar disorder marked by mild manic (hypomanic) and major depressive episodes.

Birth complications Problematic biological conditions during birth that can affect the physical and psychological well-being of the child.

Blind design An experiment in which participants do not know whether they are in the experimental or the control condition. Also known as *masked design*, now the preferred term.

Blunted affect A symptom of schizophrenia in which a person shows less emotion than most people.

Body dysmorphic disorder A disorder in which individuals become preoccupied with the belief that they have certain defects or flaws in their physical appearance. The perceived defects or flaws are imagined or greatly exaggerated.

Body shaming The practice of criticizing people publicly for being overweight, or, less frequently, underweight.

Borderline personality disorder A personality disorder characterized by repeated instability in interpersonal relationships, self-image, and mood, and by impulsive behavior.

Brain circuit A network of particular brain structures that work together, triggering each other into action to produce a distinct kind of behavioral, cognitive, or emotional reaction.

Brain stimulation Interventions that directly or indirectly stimulate the brain in order to bring about psychological improvement.

Brain structure A distinct area or region of the brain formed by a large group of neurons.

Brain wave The fluctuations of electrical potential that are produced by neurons in the brain.

Breathing-related sleep disorder A sleep disorder in which sleep is frequently disrupted by a breathing problem, causing excessive sleepiness or insomnia.

Brief psychotic disorder Psychotic symptoms that appear suddenly after a very stressful event or a period of emotional turmoil and last anywhere from a few hours to a month.

Brodmann Area 25 A brain structure whose abnormal activity has been linked to depression. Also called the *subgenual cingulate*.

Bulimia nervosa A disorder marked by frequent eating binges that are followed by forced vomiting or other extreme compensatory behaviors to avoid gaining weight. Also known as *binge-purge syndrome*.

Buprenorpine An opioid substitute drug that is administered as a form of maintenance therapy for substance use disorder.

Caffeine The world's most widely used stimulant, most often consumed in coffee.

Cannabis Substance produced from the varieties of the hemp plant, *Cannabis sativa*. It causes a mixture of hallucinogenic, depressant, and stimulant effects.

Case manager A community therapist who offers a full range of services for people with schizophrenia or other severe disorders, including therapy, advice, medication, guidance, and protection of patients' rights.

Case study A detailed account of a person's life and psychological problems.

Catatonia A pattern of extreme psychomotor symptoms, found in some forms of schizophrenia, that may include catatonic stupor, rigidity, or posturing.

Catatonic excitement A form of catatonia in which a person moves excitedly, sometimes with wild waving of the arms and legs.

Catatonic stupor A symptom associated with schizophrenia in which a person becomes almost totally unresponsive to the environment, remaining motionless and silent for long stretches of time.

Catharsis The reliving of past repressed feelings in order to settle internal conflicts and overcome problems.

Caudate nuclei Structures in the brain, within the region known as the basal ganglia, that help convert sensory information into thoughts and actions.

Central nervous system The brain and spinal cord.

Cerebellum An area of the brain that coordinates movement in the body and perhaps helps control a person's ability to shift attention rapidly.

Checking compulsion A compulsion in which people feel compelled to check the same things over and over.

Child abuse The nonaccidental use of excessive physical or psychological force by an adult on a child, often aimed at hurting or destroying the child.

Chlorpromazine A phenothiazine drug commonly used for treating schizophrenia. Marketed as *Thorazine*.

Chromosomes The structures, located within a cell, that contain genes.

Chronic headaches A medical problem marked by frequent intense aches in the head or neck that are not caused by another medical disorder.

Chronic traumatic encephalopathy (CTE) A degenerative brain disease that is suffered by many NFL players, among others, that is caused by repeated head blows over the course of time.

Circadian rhythm disorder A sleep-wake disorder characterized by a mismatch between a person's sleep-wake pattern and the sleep-wake schedule of most other people.

Circadian rhythms Internal "clocks" consisting of repeated biological fluctuations.

Cirrhosis An irreversible condition, often caused by excessive drinking, in which the liver becomes scarred and begins to change in anatomy and functioning.

Civil commitment A legal process by which an individual can be forced to undergo mental health treatment.

Clang A rhyme used by some people with schizophrenia as a guide to forming thoughts and statements.

Classical conditioning A process of learning in which two events that repeatedly occur close together in time become tied together in a person's mind and so produce the same response.

Classification system A list of disorders, along with descriptions of symptoms and guidelines for making appropriate diagnoses.

Cleaning compulsion A common compulsion in which people feel compelled to keep cleaning themselves, their clothing, and their homes.

Client-centered therapy The humanistic therapy developed by Carl Rogers in which clinicians try to help clients by being accepting, empathizing accurately, and conveying genuineness.

Clinical interview A face-to-face encounter in which clinicians ask questions of clients, weigh their responses and reactions, and learn about them and their psychological problems.

Clinical psychologist A mental health professional who has earned a doctorate in clinical psychology.

Clinical psychology The study, assessment, treatment, and prevention of abnormal behavior.

Clinical social worker A mental health specialist who is qualified to conduct psychotherapy upon earning a master's degree or doctorate in social work.

Clitoris The female sex organ located in front of the urinary and vaginal openings. It becomes enlarged during sexual arousal.

Clozapine A commonly prescribed second-generation antipsychotic drug.

Cocaine An addictive stimulant obtained from the coca plant. It is the most powerful natural stimulant known.

Code of ethics A body of principles and rules for ethical behavior, designed to guide decisions and actions by members of a profession.

Cognition The capacity to think, remember, and anticipate.

Cognitive-behavioral model A theoretical perspective that emphasizes both behavior and the process and content of thinking as causes of psychological problems.

Cognitive-behavioral therapies Therapy approaches that seek to help clients change both counterproductive behaviors and dysfunctional ways of thinking.

Cognitive processing therapy A cognitive-focused intervention for people with PTSD in which therapists guide individuals to examine and change the dysfunctional attitudes and styles of interpretation they have developed as a result of their traumatic experiences, thus enabling them to deal with difficult memories and feelings.

Cognitive remediation A treatment that focuses on the cognitive impairments that often characterize people with schizophrenia, particularly their difficulties in attention, planning, and memory.

Cognitive therapy A therapy developed by Aaron Beck that helps people identify and change the maladaptive assumptions and ways of thinking that help cause their psychological disorders.

Cognitive triad The three forms of negative thinking that theorist Aaron Beck theorizes lead people to feel depressed. The triad consists of a negative view of one's experiences, oneself, and the future.

Coitus Sexual intercourse.

Communication disorders Neurodevelopmental disorders characterized by marked impairment in language and/or speech.

Community mental health center A treatment facility that provides medication, psychotherapy, and emergency care to patients, and coordinates treatment in the community.

Community mental health treatment A treatment approach that emphasizes community care.

Comorbidity The occurrence of two or more disorders in the same person.

Compulsion A repetitive and rigid behavior or mental act that persons feel driven to perform in order to prevent or reduce anxiety.

Compulsive ritual A detailed, often elaborate, set of actions that a person often feels compelled to perform, always in an identical manner.

Computerized axial tomography (CT scan) A composite image of the brain created by compiling X-ray images taken from many angles.

Concerta A trade name of methylphenidate, a stimulant drug that is helpful in many cases of attention-deficit/hyperactivity disorder (ADHD).

Concordance A statistical measure of the frequency with which family members (often both members of a pair of twins) have the same particular characteristic.

Concurrent validity The degree to which the measures gathered from one assessment tool agree with the measures gathered from other assessment techniques.

Conditioned response (CR) A response previously associated with an unconditioned stimulus that comes to be produced by a conditioned stimulus.

Conditioned stimulus (CS) A previously neutral stimulus that comes to be associated with a nonneutral stimulus, and it can then produce responses similar to those produced by the nonneutral stimulus.

Conditioning A simple form of learning.

Conditions of worth According to client-centered theorists, the internal standards by which a person judges his or her own lovability and acceptability, determined by the standards to which the person was held as a child.

Conduct disorder A disorder in which a child repeatedly violates the basic rights of others and displays aggression, characterized by symptoms such as physical cruelty to people or animals, the deliberate destruction of other people's property, and the commission of various crimes.

Confabulation A made-up description of one's experience to fill in a gap in one's memory.

Confederate An experimenter's accomplice, who helps create a particular impression in a study while pretending to be just another research participant.

Confidentiality The principle that certain professionals will not divulge the information they obtain from a client.

Confound In an experiment, a variable other than the independent variable that is also acting on the dependent variable.

Contingency management An operant conditioning treatment program that offers clients incentives (such as vouchers, prizes, cash, or privileges) that are contingent on the submission of drug-free urine specimens.

Continuous amnesia An inability to recall newly occurring events as well as certain past events.

Control group In an experiment, a group of participants who are not exposed to the independent variable.

Conversion disorder A disorder in which bodily symptoms affect voluntary motor and sensory functions, but the symptoms are inconsistent with known medical diseases.

Conversion therapy A treatment approach, widely discredited, that attempts to change the sexual orientation of a person from homosexual or bisexual to heterosexual. Also called *reparative therapy*.

Convulsion A brain seizure.

Coronary arteries Blood vessels that surround the heart and are responsible for carrying oxygen to the heart muscle.

Coronary heart disease Illness of the heart caused by a blockage in the coronary arteries.

Correlation The degree to which events or characteristics vary along with each other.

Correlation coefficient (*r*) A statistical term that indicates the direction and the magnitude of a correlation, ranging from –1.00 to +1.00.

Correlational method A research procedure used to determine how much events or characteristics vary along with each other.

Corticosteroids A group of hormones, including cortisol, released by the adrenal glands at times of stress.

Cortico-striato-thalamo-cortical brain circuit A brain circuit that includes such brain structures as the orbitofrontal cortex (just above each eye), cingulate cortex, striatum (including the caudate nucleus and putamen, two other structures at the back of the striatum), and thalamus. The circuit is hyperactive in people with obsessive-compulsive disorder, making it difficult for them to turn off or dismiss their various impulses, needs, and related thoughts.

Cortisol A hormone released by the adrenal glands when a person is under stress.

Counseling psychology A mental health specialty similar to clinical psychology that offers its own graduate training program.

Countertransference A phenomenon of psychotherapy in which a therapist's own feelings, history, and values subtly influence the way he or she interprets a patient's problems.

Couple therapy A therapy format in which the therapist works with two people who share a long-term relationship.

Covert desensitization Desensitization that focuses on imagining confrontations with frightening objects or situations while in a state of relaxation.

Covert sensitization A treatment for eliminating unwanted behavior by pairing the behavior with unpleasant mental images.

Crack A powerful, ready-to-smoke freebase cocaine.

C-reactive protein (CRP) A protein that spreads throughout the body and causes inflammation and various illnesses and disorders.

Cretinism A disorder marked by intellectual deficiencies and physical abnormalities; caused by low levels of iodine in the mother's diet during pregnancy. Also known as *severe congenital hypothyroidism*.

Creutzfeldt–Jakob disease A form of neurocognitive disorder caused by a slow-acting virus that may live in the body for years before the disease unfolds.

Criminal commitment A legal process by which people accused of a crime are instead judged mentally unstable and sent to a mental health facility for treatment.

Crisis intervention A treatment approach that tries to help people in a psychological crisis view their situation more accurately, make better decisions, act more constructively, and overcome the crisis.

Critical incident stress debriefing Training in how to help victims of disasters or other horrifying events talk about their feelings and reactions to the traumatic incidents.

Cross-tolerance Tolerance that a person develops for a substance as a result of regularly using another substance similar to it.

Culture A people's common history, values, institutions, habits, skills, technology, and arts.

Culture-sensitive therapies Approaches that are designed to address the unique issues faced by members of minority groups.

Cyberbullying The use of e-mail, texting, chat rooms, cell phones, or other digital devices to harass, threaten, or intimidate people.

Cyclothymic disorder A disorder marked by numerous periods of hypomanic symptoms and mild depressive symptoms.

Daily Report Card (DRC) A treatment for ADHD in which a child's target classroom behaviors—staying in his or her classroom seat, raising a hand to speak, and using an "inside voice"—are carefully evaluated, recorded on a DRC, and reinforced by teachers throughout the school day. At the end of the day, the teacher further provides the report card for the parents to see, and, if a sufficient number of target behaviors had been performed satisfactorily that day, the child is also given rewards at home.

Day center A program that offers hospital-like treatment during the day only. Also known as a *day hospital*.

Death darer A person who is ambivalent about the wish to die even as he or she attempts suicide.

Death ignorer A person who attempts suicide without recognizing the finality of death.

Death initiator A person who attempts suicide believing that the process of death is already under way and that he or she is simply quickening the process.

Death seeker A person who clearly intends to end his or her life at the time of a suicide attempt.

Deep brain stimulation (DBS) A treatment procedure for depression in which a pacemaker powers electrodes that have been implanted in the subgenual cingulate, thus stimulating that brain structure.

Deinstitutionalization The discharge, begun during the 1960s, of large numbers of patients from long-term institutional care so that they might be treated in community programs.

Déjà vu The haunting sense of having previously seen or experienced a new scene or situation.

Delayed ejaculation A male sexual dysfunction characterized by persistent inability to ejaculate or very delayed ejaculations during sexual activity with a partner.

Delirium A rapidly developing, acute disturbance in attention and orientation that makes it very difficult to concentrate and think in a clear and organized manner.

Delirium tremens (DTs) A dramatic withdrawal reaction experienced by some people with alcohol use disorder. It consists of confusion, clouded consciousness, and terrifying visual hallucinations.

Delusion A strange false belief firmly held despite evidence to the contrary.

Delusion of control The belief that one's impulses, feelings, thoughts, or actions are being controlled by other people.

Delusion of grandeur The belief that one is a great inventor, historical figure, or other specially empowered person.

Delusion of persecution The belief that one is being plotted or discriminated against, spied on, slandered, threatened, attacked, or deliberately victimized.

Delusion of reference A belief that attaches special and personal meaning to the actions of others or to various objects or events.

Delusional disorder A disorder consisting of persistent, nonbizarre delusions that are not part of a schizophrenic disorder.
Demonology The belief that abnormal behavior results from supernatural causes such as evil spirits.
Dendrite An extension located at one end of a neuron that receives impulses from other neurons.
Denial An ego defense mechanism in which a person fails to acknowledge unacceptable thoughts, feelings, or actions.
Dependent personality disorder A personality disorder characterized by a pattern of clinging and obedience, fear of separation, and an ongoing need to be taken care of.
Dependent variable The variable in an experiment that is expected to change as the independent variable is manipulated.
Depersonalization–derealization disorder A dissociative disorder marked by the presence of persistent and recurrent episodes of depersonalization, derealization, or both.
Depressant A substance that slows the activity of the central nervous system and in sufficient dosages causes a reduction of tension and inhibitions.
Depression A low, sad state marked by significant levels of sadness, lack of energy, low self-worth, guilt, or related symptoms.
Depression-related brain circuit A brain circuit whose dysfunction contributes to unipolar depression. It includes the prefrontal cortex, hippocampus, amygdala, and subgenual cingulate (also called Brodmann Area 25), among other structures.
Depressive disorders The group of disorders marked by unipolar depression.
Derailment A common thinking disturbance in schizophrenia, involving rapid shifts from one topic of conversation to another. Also called *loose associations*.
Desensitization *See* Systematic desensitization.
Desire phase The phase of the sexual response cycle consisting of an urge to have sex, sexual fantasies, and sexual attraction.
Detoxification Systematic and medically supervised withdrawal from a drug.
Developmental coordination disorder Neurodevelopmental disorder characterized by marked impairment in the development and performance of coordinated motor activities.
Developmental psychopathology A perspective that uses a developmental framework to understand how factors and principles from the various models may intersect at points throughout the life span to help produce both normal and abnormal functioning.
Deviance Variance from common patterns of behavior.
Diagnosis A determination that a person's problems reflect a particular disorder.
Diagnostic and Statistical Manual of Mental Disorders (DSM) The classification system for mental disorders developed by the American Psychiatric Association.
Dialectical behavior therapy (DBT) A comprehensive treatment approach developed by psychologist Marsha Linehan, applied particularly in cases of borderline personality disorder and/or suicidal intent. The approach includes both individual therapy sessions and group sessions and features cognitive-behavioral techniques, social skill building, and various emotion regulation, mindfulness, humanistic, and other techniques.
Diathesis–stress view The view that a person must first have a predisposition to a disorder and then be subjected to immediate psychosocial stress in order to develop the disorder.
Diazepam A benzodiazepine drug, marketed as *Valium*.
Dichotomous thinking Viewing problems and solutions in rigid "either/or" terms.
Diencephalon A brain area (consisting of the mammillary bodies, thalamus, and hypothalamus) that plays a key role in transforming short-term to long-term memory, among other functions.
Directed masturbation training A sex therapy approach that teaches women with female arousal or orgasmic disorders how to masturbate effectively and eventually reach orgasm during sexual interactions.
Disaster Response Network (DRN) A network of thousands of volunteer mental health professionals who mobilize to provide free emergency psychological services at disaster sites throughout North America.
Displacement An ego defense mechanism that channels unacceptable id impulses toward a safer substitute.
Disruptive mood dysregulation disorder A childhood disorder marked by severe recurrent temper outbursts along with a persistent irritable or angry mood.
Dissociative amnesia A dissociative disorder marked by an inability to recall important personal events and information.
Dissociative disorders A group of disorders in which some parts of one's memory or identity seem to be dissociated, or separated, from other parts of one's memory or identity.
Dissociative fugue A form of dissociative amnesia in which a person travels to a new location and may assume a new identity, simultaneously forgetting his or her past.
Dissociative identity disorder A disorder in which a person develops two or more distinct personalities. Previously known as *multiple personality disorder*.
Disulfiram (Antabuse) An antagonist drug used in treating alcohol abuse or dependence.
Dopamine The neurotransmitter whose high activity has been shown to be related to schizophrenia.
Dopamine hypothesis The theory that schizophrenia results from excessive activity of the neurotransmitter dopamine.
Double-bind hypothesis A theory that some parents repeatedly communicate pairs of messages that are mutually contradictory, helping to produce schizophrenia in their children.
Double-masked design Experimental procedure in which neither the participant nor the experimenter knows whether the participant has received the experimental treatment or a placebo.
Down syndrome A form of intellectual disability caused by an abnormality in the 21st chromosome.
Dream A series of ideas and images that form during sleep.
Drug Any substance other than food that affects the body or mind.
Drug maintenance therapy An approach to treating substance dependence in which clients are given legally and medically supervised doses of the drug on which they are dependent, or a substitute drug.
Drug therapy The use of psychotropic drugs to reduce the symptoms of psychological disorders.
DSM-5 (*Diagnostic and Statistical Manual of Mental Disorders,* Fifth Edition) The newest edition of the DSM, published in 2013.
Durham test A legal test for insanity that holds people to be insane at the time they committed a crime if their act was the result of a mental disorder or defect.
Duty to protect The principle that therapists must break confidentiality in order to protect a person who may be the intended victim of a client.
Dyslexia A type of specific learning disorder in which people show a marked impairment in the ability to recognize words and to comprehend what they read.
Dyssomnias Sleep-wake disorders, such as insomnia disorder and hypersomnolence disorder, in which the amount, quality, or timing of sleep is disturbed.
Dysthymia A pattern of persistent depressive disorder that is chronic but less severe and less disabling than repeated episodes of major depression.

Early-onset Alzheimer's disease A relatively rare form of Alzheimer's disease that occurs before the age of 65. It typically runs in families.
Eccentric A person who deviates from conventional norms in odd, irregular, or even bizarre ways, but who is not displaying a psychological disorder.
Echolalia A symptom of autism or schizophrenia in which a person responds to statements by repeating the other person's words.
Ecstasy (MDMA) A drug chemically related to amphetamines and hallucinogens, used illicitly for its euphoric and hallucinogenic effects.
Ego According to Freud, the psychological force that employs reason and operates in accordance with the reality principle.

Ego defense mechanisms According to psychoanalytic theory, strategies developed by the ego to control unacceptable id impulses and to avoid or reduce the anxiety they arouse.

Egoistic suicide Suicide committed by people over whom society has little or no control, people who are not concerned with the norms or rules of society.

Eidetic imagery A strong visual image of an object or scene that persists in some persons long after the object or scene is removed.

Ejaculation Contractions of the muscles at the base of the penis that cause sperm to be ejected.

Electra complex According to Freud, the pattern of desires all girls experience during the phallic stage, in which they develop a sexual attraction to their father.

Electroconvulsive therapy (ECT) A treatment for depression in which electrodes attached to a patient's head send an electrical current through the brain, causing a seizure.

Electroencephalograph (EEG) A device that records electrical impulses in the brain.

Electromyograph (EMG) A device that provides feedback about the level of muscular tension in the body.

Emergency commitment The temporary commitment to a mental hospital of a patient who is behaving in a bizarre or violent way.

Empirically supported treatment A movement in the clinical field that seeks to identify which therapies have received clear research support for each disorder, to develop corresponding treatment guidelines, and to spread such information to clinicians. Also known as *evidence-based treatment*.

Employee assistance program A mental health program offered by a business to its employees.

Encopresis A disorder characterized by repeated defecating in inappropriate places, such as one's clothing.

Endocrine system The system of glands located throughout the body that help control important activities such as growth and sexual activity.

Endogenous depression A depression that appears to develop without external reasons and is assumed to be caused by internal factors.

Endorphins Neurotransmitters that help relieve pain and reduce emotional tension. They are sometimes referred to as the body's own opioids.

Enhanced interrogation program A torture-based form of questioning that has been used to try to obtain information from suspected terrorists.

Enmeshed family pattern A family system in which members are overinvolved with each other's affairs and overconcerned about each other's welfare.

Enuresis A disorder marked by repeated bed-wetting or wetting of one's clothes.

Epidemiological study A study that measures the incidence and prevalence of a disorder in a given population.

Equifinality The principle that a number of different developmental pathways can lead to the same psychological disorder.

Erectile disorder A sexual dysfunction in which a man persistently fails to attain or maintain an erection during sexual activity.

Ergot alkaloid A naturally occurring compound from which LSD is derived.

Erotomanic delusions Delusional beliefs held by some individuals that they are loved by and in a relationship with a person on whom they focus their attention (for example, a celebrity), a person with whom they have no relationship.

Essential hypertension High blood pressure caused by a combination of psychosocial and physiological factors.

Estrogen The primary female sex hormone.

Ethyl alcohol The chemical compound in all alcoholic beverages that is rapidly absorbed into the blood and immediately begins to affect the person's functioning.

Evoked potentials The brain response patterns recorded on an electroencephalograph while a person performs a task such as observing a flashing light.

Excitement phase The phase of the sexual response cycle marked by changes in the pelvic region, general physical arousal, and increases in heart rate, muscle tension, blood pressure, and rate of breathing.

Excoriation disorder A disorder in which persons repeatedly pick at their skin, resulting in significant sores or wounds. Also called *skin-picking disorder*.

Exhibitionistic disorder A paraphilic disorder in which persons have repeated sexually arousing urges or fantasies about exposing their genitals to others, and either act on these urges with nonconsenting individuals or experience clinically significant distress or impairment.

Existential anxiety According to existential theorists, a universal fear of the limits and responsibilities of one's existence.

Existential model The theoretical perspective that human beings are born with the total freedom either to face up to one's existence and give meaning to one's life or to shrink from that responsibility.

Existential therapy A therapy that encourages clients to accept responsibility for their lives and to live with greater meaning and value.

Exorcism The practice, common in early societies, of treating abnormality by coaxing evil spirits to leave the person's body.

Experiment A research procedure in which a variable is manipulated and the effect of the manipulation is observed.

Experimental group In an experiment, the participants who are exposed to the independent variable under investigation.

Exposure and response prevention A treatment for obsessive-compulsive disorder that exposes a client to anxiety-arousing thoughts or situations and then prevents the client from performing his or her compulsive acts. Also called *exposure and ritual prevention*.

Exposure therapy A behavior-focused intervention in which fearful persons are repeatedly exposed to the objects or situations they dread.

Expressed emotion The general level of criticism, disapproval, hostility, and intrusiveness expressed in a family. People recovering from schizophrenia are considered more likely to relapse if their families rate high in expressed emotion.

External validity The degree to which the results of a study may be generalized beyond that study.

Extrapyramidal effects Unwanted movements—such as severe shaking, bizarre-looking grimaces, twisting of the body, and extreme restlessness—sometimes produced by antipsychotic drugs.

Eye movement desensitization and reprocessing (EMDR) An exposure treatment in which clients move their eyes in a rhythmic manner from side to side while flooding their minds with images of objects and situations they ordinarily avoid.

Factitious disorder A disorder in which a person feigns or induces symptoms, typically for the purpose of assuming the role of a sick person.

Family pedigree study A research design in which investigators determine how many and which relatives of a person with a disorder have the same disorder.

Family systems theory A theory that views the family as a system of interacting parts whose interactions exhibit consistent patterns and unstated rules.

Family therapy A therapy format in which the therapist meets with all members of a family and helps them to change in therapeutic ways.

Fantasy An ego defense mechanism in which a person uses imaginary events to satisfy unacceptable impulses.

Fear The central nervous system's physiological and emotional response to a serious threat to one's well-being.

Fear brain circuit The brain circuit that produces and manages fear reactions. Generalized anxiety disorder is related to dysfunction in this circuit, which includes such brain structures as the prefrontal cortex, anterior cingulate cortex, insula, and amygdala.

Fear hierarchy A list of objects or situations that frighten a person, starting with those that are slightly feared and ending with those that are feared greatly; used in systematic desensitization.

Female orgasmic disorder A dysfunction in which a woman persistently fails to reach orgasm, has very low intensity orgasms, or has very delayed orgasms.

Female sexual interest/arousal disorder A female dysfunction marked by a persistent reduction or lack of interest in sex and low sexual activity, as well as, in some cases, limited excitement and few sexual sensations during sexual activity.

Fentanyl A powerful opioid pain relief drug that is 50 to 100 times more powerful than morphine and 20 to 35 times more powerful than heroin. It is by far the painkiller most commonly linked to overdose deaths.

Fetal alcohol syndrome A cluster of problems in a child, including low birth weight, irregularities in the hands and face, and intellectual deficits, caused by excessive alcohol intake by the mother during pregnancy.

Fetishistic disorder A paraphilic disorder consisting of recurrent and intense sexual urges, fantasies, or behaviors that involve the use of a nonliving object or nongenital part, often to the exclusion of all other stimuli, accompanied by significant distress or impairment.

First-generation antipsychotic drugs A group of drugs, including phenothiazines, that comprised the first wave of antipsychotic drugs and are still in use today.

Fixation According to Freud, a condition in which the id, ego, and superego do not mature properly and are frozen at an early stage of development.

Flashback The recurrence of LSD-induced sensory and emotional changes long after the drug has left the body, or, in posttraumatic stress disorder, the reexperiencing of past traumatic events.

Flat affect A symptom of schizophrenia in which the person shows almost no emotion at all.

Flooding An exposure therapy in which clients are exposed repeatedly and intensively to a feared object and made to see that it is actually harmless.

Forensic psychology The branch of psychology concerned with intersections between psychological practice and research and the judicial system. Also related to the field of *forensic psychiatry*.

Formal thought disorder A disturbance in the production and organization of thought.

Free association A psychodynamic technique in which the patient describes any thought, feeling, or image that comes to mind, even if it seems unimportant.

Freebase A technique for ingesting cocaine in which the pure cocaine basic alkaloid is chemically separated from processed cocaine, vaporized by heat from a flame, and inhaled through a pipe.

Free-floating anxiety Chronic and persistent feelings of anxiety that are not clearly attached to a specific, identifiable threat.

Frotteuristic disorder A paraphilic disorder in which a person has repeated and intense sexual urges or fantasies that involve touching and rubbing against a nonconsenting person, and either acts on these urges with nonconsenting individuals or experiences clinically significant distress or impairment.

Functional magnetic resonance imaging (fMRI) A neuroimaging technique used to visualize internal functioning of the brain or body.

Fusion The final merging of two or more subpersonalities in multiple personality disorder.

GABA *See* Gamma-aminobutyric acid.

Gambling disorder A disorder marked by persistent and recurrent gambling behavior, leading to a range of life problems.

Gamma-aminobutyric acid (GABA) A neurotransmitter whose low activity has been linked to generalized anxiety disorder.

Gender-change surgery A surgical procedure that changes a person's sex organs and gender features. Also known as *gender reassignment surgery*, *gender confirmation surgery*, and *gender-affirming surgery*.

Gender dysphoria A disorder in which a transgender individual persistently experiences clinically significant distress or impairment due to his or her assigned gender.

Gender reassignment surgery A surgical procedure that changes a person's sex organs and gender features. Also known as *gender change surgery*, *gender confirmation surgery*, and *gender-affirming surgery*.

Gender-sensitive therapies Approaches geared to the pressures of being a woman in Western society. Also called *feminist therapies*.

Gene Chromosome segments that control the characteristics and traits we inherit.

General paresis An irreversible medical disorder whose symptoms include psychological abnormalities, such as delusions of grandeur; caused by syphilis.

Generalized amnesia A loss of memory for events that occurred over a limited period of time as well as for certain events that occurred prior to that period.

Generalized anxiety disorder A disorder marked by persistent and excessive feelings of anxiety and worry about numerous events and activities.

Generic drug A marketed drug that is comparable to a trade-named drug in dosage form, strength, and performance.

Genetic linkage study A research approach in which extended families with high rates of a disorder over several generations are observed in order to determine whether the disorder closely follows the distribution pattern of other family traits.

Genital stage In Freud's theory, the stage beginning at approximately 12 years old, when the child begins to find sexual pleasure in heterosexual relationships.

Genito-pelvic pain/penetration disorder A sexual dysfunction characterized by significant physical discomfort during intercourse.

Geropsychology The field of psychology concerned with the mental health of elderly people.

Gestalt therapy The humanistic therapy developed by Fritz Perls in which clinicians actively move clients toward self-recognition and self-acceptance by using techniques such as role-playing and self-discovery exercises.

Glia Brain cells that support the neurons.

Glutamate A common neurotransmitter that has been linked to memory and to dementia.

Grief The reaction a person experiences when a loved one is lost.

Group home A special home where people with disorders or disabilities live and are taught self-help, living, and working skills.

Group therapy A therapy format in which a group of people with similar problems meet together with a therapist to work on those problems.

Guided participation A modeling technique in which a client systematically observes and imitates the therapist while the therapist confronts feared items.

Guilty but mentally ill A verdict stating that defendants are guilty of committing a crime but are also suffering from a mental illness that should be treated during their imprisonment.

Guilty with diminished capacity A legal defense argument that states that because of limitations posed by mental dysfunction, a defendant could not have intended to commit a particular crime and thus should be convicted of a lesser crime.

Halfway house A residence for people with schizophrenia or other severe problems, often staffed by paraprofessionals. Also known as a *group home* or *crisis house*.

Hallucination The experiencing of imagined sights, sounds, or other perceptions in the absence of external stimuli.

Hallucinogen A substance that causes powerful changes, primarily in sensory perception, including strengthening perceptions and producing illusions and hallucinations. Also called a *psychedelic drug*.

Hallucinosis A form of intoxication caused by hallucinogens, consisting of perceptual distortions and hallucinations.

Hardiness A set of positive attitudes and reactions in response to stress.

Health maintenance The principle that young adults should act to promote their physical and mental health to best prepare for the aging process. Also called *wellness*.

Helper T-cell A lymphocyte that identifies foreign invaders and then both multiplies and triggers the production of other kinds of immune cells.

Heroin One of the most addictive substances derived from opium.

High The pleasant feeling of relaxation and euphoria that follows the rush from certain recreational drugs.

Hippocampus A brain structure located below the cerebral cortex that is involved in memory.

Histrionic personality disorder A personality disorder in which an individual displays a pattern of excessive emotionality and attention seeking. Once called *hysterical personality disorder*.

Hoarding disorder A disorder in which people feel compelled to save items and experience significant distress if they try to discard them, resulting in an excessive accumulation of items and possessions.

Hopelessness A pessimistic belief that one's present circumstances, problems, or mood will never change.

Hormones The chemicals released by endocrine glands into the bloodstream.

Humanistic model The theoretical perspective that human beings are born with a natural inclination to be friendly, cooperative, and constructive, and are driven to self-actualize.

Humanistic therapy A system of therapy in which clinicians try to help clients look at themselves accurately and acceptingly so that they can fulfill their positive inborn potential.

Humors According to the Greeks and Romans, bodily chemicals that influence mental and physical functioning.

Huntington's disease An inherited disease, characterized by progressive problems in cognition, emotion, and movement, that results in a neurocognitive disorder.

Hypersomnolence disorder A sleep-wake disorder characterized by an extreme need for extra sleep and feelings of excessive sleepiness.

Hypertension Chronic high blood pressure.

Hypnosis A sleeplike suggestible state during which a person can be directed to act in unusual ways, to experience unusual sensations, to remember seemingly forgotten events, or to forget remembered events.

Hypnotic amnesia Loss of memory produced by hypnotic suggestion.

Hypnotic therapy A treatment in which the patient undergoes hypnosis and is then guided to recall forgotten events or perform other therapeutic activities. Also known as *hypnotherapy*.

Hypnotism A procedure that places people in a trancelike mental state during which they become extremely suggestible.

Hypochondriasis A disorder in which people mistakenly fear that minor changes in their physical functioning indicate a serious disease. Now known as *illness anxiety disorder*.

Hypomanic episode An episode of mania in which the symptoms cause relatively little impairment.

Hypomanic pattern A pattern in which a person displays symptoms of mania, but the symptoms are less severe and cause less impairment than those of a manic episode.

Hypothalamic-pituitary-adrenal (HPA) pathway One of the two major routes by which the brain and body produce arousal and fear.

Hypothalamus A brain structure that helps maintain various bodily functions, including eating and hunger.

Hypothesis A hunch or prediction that certain variables are related in certain ways.

Hypoxyphilia A pattern in which people strangle or smother themselves, or ask their partners to strangle or smother them, to increase their sexual pleasure.

Hysteria A term once used to describe what are now known as conversion disorder, somatic symptom disorder, and illness anxiety disorder.

Hysterical disorder A disorder in which physical functioning is changed or lost, without an apparent physical cause.

Iatrogenic Produced or caused inadvertently by a clinician.

Id According to Freud, the psychological force that produces instinctual needs, drives, and impulses.

Ideas of reference Beliefs that unrelated events pertain to oneself in some important way.

Identification Unconsciously incorporating the values and feelings of one's parents and fusing them with one's identity. Also, an ego defense mechanism in which a person takes on the values and feelings of a person who is causing them anxiety.

Idiographic understanding An understanding of the behavior of a particular individual.

Illness anxiety disorder A disorder in which people are chronically anxious about and preoccupied with the notion that they have or are developing a serious medical illness, despite the absence of somatic symptoms. Previously known as *hypochondriasis*.

Illogical thinking According to cognitive theories, illogical ways of thinking that may lead to self-defeating conclusions and psychological problems.

Immune system The body's network of activities and cells that identify and destroy antigens and cancer cells.

Inappropriate affect Display of emotions that are unsuited to the situation; a symptom of schizophrenia.

Incidence The number of new cases of a disorder occurring in a population over a specific period of time.

Independent variable The variable in an experiment that is manipulated to determine whether it has an effect on another variable.

Individual therapy A therapeutic approach in which a therapist sees a client alone for sessions that may last from 15 minutes to 2 hours.

Informed consent The requirement that researchers provide sufficient information to participants about the purpose, procedure, risks, and benefits of a study.

Insanity defense A legal defense in which a person charged with a criminal offense claims to be not guilty by reason of insanity at the time of the crime.

Insomnia Difficulty falling or staying asleep.

Insomnia disorder A sleep-wake disorder characterized by severe difficulty falling asleep or maintaining sleep at least three nights per week.

Institutional Review Board (IRB) An ethics committee formed in a research facility that is empowered to protect the rights and safety of human research participants. It reviews and may require changes in each proposed study at the facility before approving or disapproving the study.

Integrity test A test that is designed to measure whether the test taker is generally honest or dishonest.

Intellectual disability (ID) A disorder marked by intellectual functioning and adaptive behavior that are well below average. Previously called *mental retardation*.

Intelligence quotient (IQ) A score derived from intelligence tests that theoretically represents a person's overall intellectual capacity.

Intelligence test A test designed to measure a person's intellectual ability.

Intermittent explosive disorder An impulse-control disorder in which people periodically fail to resist aggressive impulses and commit serious assaults on others or destroy property.

Internal validity The accuracy with which a study can pinpoint one of various possible factors as the cause of a phenomenon.

International Classification of Diseases (ICD) The classification system for medical and mental disorders that is used by the World Health Organization.

Internet gaming disorder A disorder marked by persistent, recurrent, and excessive Internet gaming activity. Recommended for further study by the DSM-5 study group.

Interpersonal psychotherapy (IPT) A treatment for unipolar depression that is based on the belief that clarifying and changing one's interpersonal problems will help lead to recovery.

Interpersonal theory of suicide A theory asserting that people with perceived burdensomeness, thwarted belongingness, and a psychological capability to carry out suicide are the most likely to attempt suicide. Also called *interpersonal-psychological theory*.

Interrater reliability A measure of the reliability of a test or of research results in which the consistency of evaluations across different judges is assessed. Also called *interjudge reliability*.

Intolerance of uncertainty theory An explanation for generalized anxiety disorder that states that certain individuals cannot tolerate the knowledge that negative events may occur, even if the possibility of occurrence is very small.

Intoxication A cluster of undesirable behavioral or psychological changes, such as slurred speech or mood changes, that may develop during or shortly after the ingestion of a substance.

In vivo desensitization Desensitization that makes use of actual objects or situations, as opposed to imagined ones.

Ion An atom or group of atoms that has a positive or negative electrical charge.

Irresistible impulse test A legal test for insanity that holds people to be insane at the time they committed a crime if they were driven to do so by an uncontrollable "fit of passion."

Isolation An ego defense mechanism in which people unconsciously isolate and disown undesirable and unwanted thoughts, experiencing them as foreign intrusions.

Jail diversion An arrangement in which mentally disturbed criminal defendants are treated for their disorders on an outpatient basis. That is, they are diverted from jail to the community for mental health care.

Joint attention Sharing focus with other people on items or events in one's immediate surroundings, through shared eye-gazing, pointing, referencing, or other verbal or nonverbal indications that one is paying attention to the same object.

Korsakoff's syndrome An alcohol-related disorder marked by extreme confusion, memory impairment, and other neurological symptoms.

Late-onset Alzheimer's disease By far, the most common form of Alzheimer's disease, developing after the age of 65 and not typically running in families.

Latent content The symbolic meaning behind a dream's content.

Lateral hypothalamus (LH) A brain region that produces hunger when activated.

L-dopa A drug used in the treatment of Parkinson's disease, a disease in which dopamine is low.

Learned helplessness The perception, based on past experiences, that one has no control over one's reinforcements.

Lewy body disease A type of neurocognitive disorder that involves a buildup of clumps of protein deposits, called Lewy bodies, within many neurons. In addition to progressive cognitive problems, this disease features significant movement difficulties.

Libido The sexual energy that fuels the id.

Life change units (LCUs) A system for measuring the stress associated with various life events.

Light therapy A treatment for seasonal affective disorder in which patients are exposed to extra light for several hours. Also called *phototherapy*.

Lithium A metallic element that occurs in nature as a mineral salt and is an effective treatment for bipolar disorders.

Lobotomy Psychosurgery in which a surgeon cuts the connections between the brain's frontal lobes and the lower centers of the brain.

Localized amnesia An inability to recall any of the events that occurred over a limited period of time.

Locus ceruleus A small brain structure that seems to be active in the regulation of emotions. Many of its neurons use norepinephrine.

Longitudinal study A study that observes the same participants on many occasions over a long period of time.

Long-term care Extended personal and medical support provided to elderly and other persons who may be impaired. It may range from partial support in a supervised apartment to intensive care at a nursing home.

Long-term memory The memory system that contains all the information that a person has stored over the years.

Loose associations A common thinking disturbance in schizophrenia, characterized by rapid shifts from one topic of conversation to another. Also known as *derailment*.

LSD (lysergic acid diethylamide) A hallucinogenic drug derived from ergot alkaloids.

Lycanthropy A condition in which persons believe themselves to be possessed by wolves or other animals.

Lymphocytes White blood cells that circulate through the lymph system and bloodstream, helping the body identify and destroy antigens and cancer cells.

Magnetic resonance imaging (MRI) A neuroimaging technique used to visualize internal structures of the brain or body.

Mainstreaming The placement of children with intellectual disability in regular school classes. Also known as *inclusion*.

Major depressive disorder A severe pattern of unipolar depression that is disabling and is not caused by such factors as drugs or a general medical condition.

Major neurocognitive disorder A neurocognitive disorder in which the decline in cognitive functioning is substantial and interferes with the ability to be independent.

Male hypoactive sexual desire disorder A male dysfunction marked by a persistent reduction or lack of interest in sex and hence a low level of sexual activity.

Malingering Intentionally faking illness to achieve some external gains, such as financial compensation or military deferment.

Malpractice suit A lawsuit charging a therapist with improper conduct or decision making in the course of treatment.

Managed care program A system of health care coverage in which the insurance company largely controls the nature, scope, and cost of medical or psychological services.

Mania A state or episode of euphoria or frenzied activity in which people may have an exaggerated belief that the world is theirs for the taking.

Manifest content The consciously remembered content of a dream.

Mantra A sound, uttered or thought, used to focus one's attention and to turn away from ordinary thoughts and concerns during meditation.

MAO inhibitor An antidepressant drug that prevents the action of the enzyme monoamine oxidase.

Marijuana One of the cannabis drugs, derived from the buds, leaves, and flowering tops of the hemp plant *Cannabis sativa*.

Marital therapy A therapy approach in which the therapist works with two people who share a long-term relationship. Also known as *couple therapy*.

Masked design An experiment in which participants do not know whether they are in the experimental or the control condition. Previously called a *blind design*.

Masturbation Self-stimulation of the genitals to achieve sexual arousal.

Masturbatory satiation A behavioral treatment in which a client masturbates for a very long period of time while fantasizing in detail about a paraphilic object. The procedure is expected to produce a feeling of boredom that becomes linked to the object.

Matched design A research design that matches the experimental participants with control participants who are similar on key characteristics.

Mean The average of a group of scores.

Meditation A technique of turning one's concentration inward and achieving a slightly changed state of consciousness.

Melancholia A condition described by early Greek and Roman philosophers and physicians as consisting of unshakable sadness. Today it is known as *depression*.

Melatonin A hormone released by the pineal gland when a person's surroundings are dark.

Memory The faculty for recalling past events and past learning.

Mental incompetence A state of mental instability that leaves defendants unable to understand the legal charges and proceedings they are facing and unable to prepare an adequate defense with their attorney.

Mentalization The capacity to understand one's own mental states and those of other people.

Mental status exam A set of interview questions and observations designed to reveal the degree and nature of a client's psychological functioning.

Mentally disordered sex offender A legal category that some states apply to certain people who are repeatedly found guilty of sex crimes.

Mentally ill chemical abusers (MICAs) People suffering from both schizophrenia (or another severe psychological disorder) and a substance use disorder. Also called *dual-diagnosis patients*.

Mesmerism The method employed by Austrian physician F. A. Mesmer to treat hysterical disorders; a precursor of *hypnotism*.

Meta-analysis A statistical method that combines results from multiple independent studies.

Metabolism An organism's chemical and physical breakdown of food and the process of converting it into energy. Also, an organism's biochemical transformation of various substances, as when the liver breaks down alcohol into acetylaldehyde.

Metacognitive theory A theory suggesting that people with generalized anxiety disorder implicitly hold both positive and negative beliefs about worrying.

Metaworry Worrying about the fact that one is worrying so much.

Methadone A laboratory-made opioid-like drug.

Methadone maintenance program An approach to treating opioid-centered substance use in which clients are given legally and medically supervised doses of a substitute drug, methadone.

Methamphetamine A powerful amphetamine drug that has experienced a surge in popularity in recent years, posing major health and law enforcement problems.

Methylphenidate A stimulant drug, known better by the trade names *Ritalin* and *Concerta,* commonly used to treat ADHD.

Migraine headache A very severe headache that occurs on one side of the head, often preceded by a warning sensation and sometimes accompanied by dizziness, nausea, or vomiting.

Mild intellectual disability A level of intellectual disability (IQ between 50 and 70) at which people can benefit from education and can support themselves as adults.

Mild neurocognitive disorder Neurocognitive disorder in which the decline in cognitive functioning is modest and does not interfere with the ability to be independent.

Milieu therapy A humanistic approach to institutional treatment based on the premise that institutions can help patients recover by creating a climate that promotes self-respect, individual responsible behavior, and meaningful activity.

Mind-body dualism The position advocated by the seventeenth-century French philosopher René Descartes that the mind is separate from the body.

Mindfulness-based cognitive-behavioral therapy A type of therapy that teaches clients to be mindful of (just notice and accept) their dysfunctional thoughts or worries.

Mindfulness meditation A type of meditation in which people are mindful of (just notice) the various thoughts, emotions, sensations, and other private experiences that pass through their minds and bodies.

Minnesota Multiphasic Personality Inventory (MMPI) A widely used personality inventory consisting of a large number of statements that subjects mark as being true or false for them.

Mixed design A research design that intermixes elements of both experimental and correlational studies. Also known as *quasi-experimental design*.

M'Naghten test A widely used legal test for insanity that holds people to be insane at the time they committed a crime if, because of a mental disorder, they did not know the nature of the act or did not know right from wrong. Also known as the *M'Naghten rule*.

Model A set of assumptions and concepts that help scientists explain and interpret observations. Also called a *paradigm*.

Modeling A process of learning in which a person acquires responses by observing and imitating others. Also, a therapy approach based on the same principle.

Moderate intellectual disability A level of intellectual disability (IQ between 35 and 49) at which people can learn to care for themselves and can benefit from vocational training.

Monoamine oxidase (MAO) A body chemical that destroys the neurotransmitter norepinephrine.

Monoamine oxidase (MAO) inhibitors Antidepressant drugs that lower MAO activity and thus increase the level of norepinephrine activity in the brain.

Mood disorder A disorder affecting one's emotional state, including major depressive disorder and bipolar disorders.

Mood stabilizing drugs Psychotropic drugs that help stabilize the moods of people suffering from a bipolar disorder. Also known as *antibipolar drugs*.

Moral treatment A nineteenth-century approach to treating people with mental dysfunction that emphasized moral guidance and humane and respectful treatment.

Morphine A highly addictive substance derived from opium that is particularly effective in relieving pain.

Motivational interviewing A treatment intervention that uses a mixture of empathy and inquiring review to help motivate clients to recognize they have a serious psychological problem and to commit to making constructive choices and behavior changes.

Multicultural perspective The view that each culture within a larger society has a particular set of values and beliefs, as well as special external pressures, that help account for the behavior and functioning of its members. Also called *culturally diverse perspective*.

Multicultural psychology The field of psychology that examines the impact of culture, race, ethnicity, gender, and similar factors on our behaviors and thoughts and focuses on how such factors may influence the origin, nature, and treatment of abnormal behavior.

Multidimensional risk perspective A theory that identifies several kinds of risk factors that are thought to combine to help cause a disorder. The more factors present, the greater the risk of developing the disorder.

Multifinality The principle that persons with a similar developmental history may nevertheless react to similar current situations in very different ways.

Munchausen syndrome An extreme and long-term form of factitious disorder in which a person produces symptoms, gains admission to a hospital, and receives treatment.

Munchausen syndrome by proxy A factitious disorder in which parents make up or produce physical illnesses in their children.

Muscle contraction headache A headache caused by the narrowing of muscles surrounding the skull. Also known as *tension headache*.

Muscle dysmorphia Disorder in which people become obsessed with the incorrect belief that they are not muscular enough.

Naloxone One of the most widely used opioid antagonist drugs.

Narcissistic personality disorder A personality disorder marked by a broad pattern of grandiosity, need for admiration, and lack of empathy.

Narcolepsy A sleep-wake disorder characterized by a repeated sudden and irrepressible need to sleep during waking hours.

Narcotic Any natural or synthetic opioid-like drug.

National Alliance on Mental Illness (NAMI) A nationwide grassroots organization that provides support, education, advocacy, and research for people with severe mental disorders and their families.

National interest groups Groups and organizations such as NAMI that have formed in countries around the world to push for better community treatment.

Natural experiment An experiment in which nature, rather than an experimenter, manipulates an independent variable.

Naturalistic observation A method of observing behavior, in which clinicians or researchers observe people in their everyday environments.

Negative correlation A statistical relationship in which the value of one variable increases while the other variable decreases.

Negative symptoms Symptoms of schizophrenia that seem to be deficits in normal thought, emotions, or behaviors.

Neologism A made-up word that has meaning only to the person using it.

Nerve ending The region at the end of a neuron from which an impulse is sent to a neighboring neuron.

Neurocognitive disorder A disorder marked by a significant decline in at least one area of cognitive functioning.

Neurodevelopmental disorders A group of disorders—including ADHD, autism spectrum disorder, and intellectual disability—in the functioning of the brain that emerge at birth or during very early childhood and that affect an individual's behavior, memory, concentration, and/or ability to learn.

Neurofibrillary tangles Twisted protein fibers that form within certain brain cells as people age. People with Alzheimer's disease have an excessive number of such tangles.

Neuroimaging techniques Neurological tests that provide images of brain structure or activity, such as CT scans, PET scans, and MRIs. Also called *brain scans*.

Neuroleptic drugs An alternative term for first-generation antipsychotic drugs, so called because they often produce undesired effects similar to the symptoms of neurological disorders.

Neuroleptic malignant syndrome A severe, potentially fatal reaction to antipsychotic drugs, marked by muscle rigidity, fever, altered consciousness, and autonomic dysfunction.

Neurological Relating to the structure or activity of the brain.

Neurological test A test that directly measures brain structure or activity.

Neuromodulator A neurotransmitter that helps modify or regulate the effect of other neurotransmitters.

Neuron A nerve cell.

Neuropsychological test A test that detects brain impairment by measuring a person's cognitive, perceptual, and motor performances.

Neurosis Freud's term for disorders characterized by intense anxiety, attributed to failure of a person's ego defense mechanisms to cope with unconscious conflicts.

Neurotransmitter A chemical that, released by one neuron, crosses the synaptic space to be received at receptors on the dendrites of neighboring neurons.

Neutralizing Attempting to eliminate thoughts that one finds unacceptable by thinking or behaving in ways that make up for those thoughts and so put matters right internally.

New wave cognitive-behavioral therapies A group of relatively new approaches, including acceptance and commitment therapy (ACT), that help clients to accept many of their problematic thoughts rather than judge them, act on them, or try fruitlessly to change them.

Nicotine An alkaloid (nitrogen-containing chemical) derived from tobacco or produced in the laboratory.

Nicotine patch A patch attached to the skin like a Band-Aid, with nicotine content that is absorbed through the skin; it may ease the withdrawal reaction of an individual who has quit cigarette smoking.

Nightmare disorder A parasomnia characterized by chronic distressful, frightening dreams.

Nocturnal penile tumescence (NPT) Erection during sleep.

Nomothetic understanding A general understanding of the nature, causes, and treatments of abnormal psychological functioning, in the form of laws or principles.

Nonsuicidal self-injury (NSSI) A disorder that is being studied for possible inclusion in a future edition of DSM-5, characterized by persons intentionally injuring themselves on five or more occasions over a 1-year period, without the conscious intent of killing themselves.

Norepinephrine A neurotransmitter whose abnormal activity is linked to panic disorder and depression.

Normalization The principle that institutions and community residences should provide people with intellectual disability with types of living conditions and opportunities that are similar to those enjoyed by the rest of society.

Norms A society's stated and unstated rules for proper conduct.

Not guilty by reason of insanity (NGRI) A verdict stating that defendants are not guilty of committing a crime because they were insane at the time of the crime.

Nutritional rehabilitation An initial phase of treatment in a number of cases of anorexia nervosa that includes supportive nursing care, day-to-day increased caloric intake, nutrition counseling, support, and, in some programs, motivational interviewing.

Object relations theory The psychodynamic theory that views the desire for relationships as the key motivating force in human behavior.

Observer drift The tendency of an observer who is rating subjects in an experiment to change criteria gradually and involuntarily, thus making the data unreliable.

Obsession A persistent thought, idea, impulse, or image that is experienced repeatedly, feels intrusive, and causes anxiety.

Obsessive-compulsive disorder (OCD) A disorder in which a person has recurrent and unwanted thoughts and/or a need to perform repetitive and rigid actions.

Obsessive-compulsive personality disorder A personality disorder marked by such an intense focus on orderliness, perfectionism, and control that the person loses flexibility, openness, and efficiency.

Obsessive-compulsive-related disorders A group of disorders in which obsessive-like concerns drive people to repeatedly and excessively perform specific patterns of behavior that greatly disrupt their lives.

Oedipus complex In Freudian theory, the pattern of desires emerging during the phallic stage in which boys become attracted to their mother as a sexual object and see their father as a rival they would like to push aside.

Olanzapine A second-generation antipsychotic drug whose brand name is Zyprexa.

Operant conditioning A process of learning in which behavior that leads to satisfying consequences is likely to be repeated.

Opioid Opium, drugs derived from opium, and similar synthetic drugs. Also known collectively as *narcotics*.

Opioid antagonist A substance that attaches to opioid receptors in the brain and, in turn, blocks the effects of opioids.

Opium A highly addictive substance made from the sap of the opium poppy seed.

Oppositional defiant disorder A disorder in which children are repeatedly argumentative and defiant, angry and irritable, and, in some cases, vindictive.

Oral stage The earliest developmental stage in Freud's conceptualization of psychosexual development, during which the infant's main gratification comes from feeding and from the body parts involved in feeding.

Orbitofrontal cortex A brain structure in which impulses involving excretion, sexuality, violence, and other primitive activities normally arise.

Orgasm A peaking of sexual pleasure, consisting of rhythmic muscular contractions in the pelvic region, during which a man's semen is ejaculated and the outer third of a woman's vaginal wall contracts.

Orgasm phase The phase of the sexual response cycle during which a person's sexual pleasure peaks and sexual tension is released as muscles in the pelvic region contract rhythmically.

Outpatient A person who receives a diagnosis or treatment in a clinic, hospital, or therapist's office but is not hospitalized overnight.

Outpatient civil commitment program A legal process in which courts order people with severe mental disorders into community treatment.

Oxycodone The key ingredient in OxyContin and Percocet, medical opioids prescribed to relieve pain.

Panic attacks Periodic, short bouts of panic that occur suddenly, reach a peak within minutes, and gradually pass.

Panic brain circuit The brain circuit that helps produce panic reactions, consisting of structures such as the amygdala, hippocampus, ventromedial nucleus of the hypothalamus, central gray matter, and locus coeruleus.

Panic disorder An anxiety disorder marked by recurrent and unpredictable panic attacks.

Paranoid personality disorder A personality disorder marked by a pattern of extreme distrust and suspiciousness of others.

Paraphilias Patterns in which a person has recurrent and intense sexual urges, fantasies, or behaviors involving nonhuman objects, children, nonconsenting adults, or experiences of suffering or humiliation.

Paraphilic disorder A disorder in which a person's paraphilia causes great distress, interferes with social or occupational activities, or places the person or others at risk of harm—either currently or in the past.

Paraprofessional A person without previous professional training who provides services under the supervision of a mental health professional.

Parasomnias Sleep-wake disorders, such as sleepwalking, sleep terrors, and nightmare disorder, characterized by the occurrence of abnormal events during sleep.

Parasuicide A suicide attempt that does not result in death.

Parasympathetic nervous system The nerve fibers of the autonomic nervous system that help return bodily processes to normal.

Parent management training A treatment approach for conduct disorder in which therapists combine family and cognitive-behavioral interventions to improve family functioning and help parents deal with their children more effectively.

Parity laws Laws that direct insurance companies to provide equal coverage for mental and physical problems.

Parkinsonian symptoms Symptoms similar to those found in Parkinson's disease. Patients with schizophrenia who take antipsychotic medications may display one or more of these symptoms.

Parkinson's disease A slowly progressive neurological disease, marked by tremors and rigidity, that may also cause a neurocognitive disorder.

Participant An individual chosen to participate in a study. Also called a *subject*.

Participant modeling A behavioral treatment in which people with fears observe a therapist (model) interacting with a feared object and then interact with the object themselves.

Pedophilic disorder A paraphilic disorder in which a person has repeated and intense sexual urges or fantasies about watching, touching, or engaging in sexual acts with children, and either acts on these urges or experiences clinically significant distress or impairment.

Peer review system A system by which clinicians paid by an insurance company may periodically review a patient's progress and recommend the continuation or termination of insurance benefits.

Penile prosthesis A surgical implant consisting of a semirigid rod that produces an artificial erection.

Performance anxiety The fear of performing inadequately and a related tension experienced during sex.

Perseveration The persistent repetition of words and statements.

Persistent depressive disorder A chronic form of unipolar depression marked by ongoing and repeated symptoms of either major or mild depression.

Personality A unique and long-term pattern of inner experience and outward behavior that leads to consistent reactions across various situations.

Personality disorder An enduring, rigid pattern of inner experience and outward behavior that repeatedly impairs a person's sense of self, emotional experiences, goals, capacity for empathy, and/or capacity for intimacy.

Personality disorder—trait specified (PDTS) A personality disorder currently undergoing study for possible inclusion in a future revision of DSM-5. Individuals would receive this diagnosis if they display significant impairment in functioning as a result of one or more very problematic traits.

Personality inventory A test designed to measure broad personality characteristics, consisting of statements about behaviors, beliefs, and feelings that people evaluate as either characteristic or uncharacteristic of them.

Phallic stage In psychoanalytic theory, the period between the third and fourth years when the focus of sexual pleasure shifts to the genitals.

Phalloplasty A surgical procedure designed to create a functional penis.

Phenothiazines A group of antihistamine drugs that became the first group of effective antipsychotic medications.

Phenylketonuria (PKU) A metabolic disorder caused by the body's inability to break down the amino acid phenylalanine, resulting in intellectual disability and other symptoms.

Phobia A persistent and unreasonable fear of a particular object, activity, or situation.

Pick's disease A neurological disease that affects the frontal and temporal lobes, causing a neurocognitive disorder.

Placebo therapy A simulated treatment that the participant in an experiment believes to be genuine.

Play therapy An approach to treating childhood disorders that helps children express their conflicts and feelings indirectly by drawing, playing with toys, and making up stories.

Pleasure principle The pursuit of gratification that characterizes id functioning.

Plethysmograph A device used to measure sexual arousal.

Polygraph test A test that seeks to determine whether the test taker is telling the truth by measuring physiological responses such as respiration level, perspiration level, and heart rate. Also known as a *lie detector test*.

Polysubstance use The use of two or more substances at the same time.

Positive correlation A statistical relationship in which the values of two variables increase together or decrease together.

Positive psychology The study and enhancement of positive feelings, traits, and abilities.

Positive symptoms Symptoms of schizophrenia that seem to be excesses of or bizarre additions to normal thoughts, emotions, or behaviors.

Positron emission tomography (PET scan) A computer-produced motion picture showing rates of metabolism throughout the brain.

Postpartum depression An episode of depression experienced by some new mothers that begins within four weeks after giving birth.

Postpartum psychosis An episode of psychosis experienced by a small percentage of new mothers that begins within days or weeks after giving birth.

Posttraumatic stress disorder (PTSD) A disorder in which fear and related symptoms continue to be experienced long after a traumatic event.

Poverty of speech A decrease in speech or speech content found in some people with schizophrenia. Also known as *alogia*.

Predictive validity The ability of a test or other assessment tools to predict future characteristics or behaviors.

Predisposition An inborn or acquired vulnerability for developing certain symptoms or disorders.

Prefrontal lobes Structures of the brain that play a key role in short-term memory, among other functions.

Premature ejaculation A dysfunction in which a man persistently reaches orgasm and ejaculates within one minute of beginning sexual activity with a partner and before he wishes to. Also called *early* or *rapid ejaculation*.

Premenstrual dysphoric disorder A disorder marked by repeated experiences of significant depression and related symptoms during the week before menstruation.

Premenstrual syndrome (PMS) A common and normal cluster of psychological and physical discomforts that precede menses.

Premorbid The period prior to the onset of a disorder.

Preparedness A predisposition to develop certain fears.

Prevalence The total number of cases of a disorder occurring in a population over a specific period of time.

Prevention A key feature of community mental health programs that seek to prevent or minimize psychological disorders.

Primary gain In psychodynamic theory, the gain people achieve when their somatic symptoms keep their internal conflicts out of awareness.

Primary personality The subpersonality that appears more often than the others in individuals with dissociative identity disorder.

Primary prevention Prevention interventions that are designed to prevent disorders altogether.

Private psychotherapy An arrangement in which a person directly pays a therapist for counseling services.

Proband The person who is the focus of a genetic study.

Procedural memory Memory of learned skills that a person performs without needing to think about them.

Prodromal phase The period during which the symptoms of schizophrenia are not yet prominent, but the person has begun to deteriorate from previous levels of functioning.
Profound intellectual disability A level of intellectual disability (IQ below 20) at which people need a very structured environment with close supervision.
Projection An ego defense mechanism whereby individuals attribute to other people characteristics or impulses they do not wish to acknowledge in themselves.
Projective test A test consisting of ambiguous material that people interpret or respond to.
Prolonged exposure An exposure treatment in which clients confront not only trauma-related objects and situations but also their painful memories of traumatic experiences.
Protection and advocacy system The system by which lawyers and advocates who work for patients may investigate the patients' treatments and protect their rights.
Prozac The trade name for fluoxetine, a second-generation antidepressant.
Pseudocommando mass killing Mass murder in which an individual kills in public, often during the daytime, plans his offense well in advance, and comes prepared with a powerful arsenal of weapons. The killer has no escape planned and expects to be killed during the incident.
Psychedelic drugs Substances such as LSD that cause profound perceptual changes. Also called *hallucinogenic drugs*.
Psychiatrist A physician who in addition to medical school has completed three to four years of residency training in the treatment of abnormal mental functioning.
Psychoanalysis Either the theory or the treatment of abnormal mental functioning that emphasizes unconscious psychological forces as the cause of psychopathology.
Psychodynamic model The theoretical perspective that sees all human functioning as being shaped by dynamic (interacting) psychological forces and explains people's behavior by reference to unconscious internal conflicts.
Psychodynamic therapy A system of therapy whose goals are to help clients uncover past traumatic events and the inner conflicts that have resulted from them, settle those conflicts, and resume personal development.
Psychogenic perspective The view that the chief causes of abnormal functioning are psychological.
Psychological autopsy A procedure used to analyze information about a deceased person, for example, in order to determine whether the person's death was a suicide.
Psychological debriefing A form of crisis intervention in which victims are helped to talk about their feelings and reactions to traumatic incidents. Also called *critical incident stress debriefing*.
Psychological profile A method of suspect identification that seeks to predict an unknown criminal's psychological, emotional, and personality characteristics based on the individual's pattern of criminal behavior and on research into the psychological characteristics of people who have committed similar crimes.
Psychology The study of mental processes and behaviors.
Psychomotor symptoms Disturbances in movement sometimes found in certain disorders such as schizophrenia.
Psychoneuroimmunology The study of the connections among stress, the body's immune system, and illness.
Psychopathology An abnormal pattern of functioning that may be described as deviant, distressful, dysfunctional, and/or dangerous.
Psychopathy *See* antisocial personality disorder.
Psychopharmacologist A psychiatrist who primarily prescribes medications. Also called *pharmacotherapist*.
Psychophysiological disorders Disorders in which biological, psychological, and sociocultural factors interact to cause or worsen a physical illness. Also known as *psychological factors affecting other medical conditions*.
Psychophysiological test A test that measures physical responses (such as heart rate and muscle tension) as possible indicators of psychological problems.
Psychosexual stages The developmental stages defined by Freud in which the id, ego, and superego interact.
Psychosis A state in which a person loses contact with reality in key ways.
Psychosurgery Brain surgery for mental disorders.
Psychotherapy A treatment system in which words and acts are used by a client (patient) and therapist in order to help the client overcome psychological difficulties.
Psychotropic medications Drugs that mainly affect the brain and reduce many symptoms of mental dysfunction.

Quasi-experimental design A research design that fails to include key elements of a "pure" experiment and/or intermixes elements of both experimental and correlational studies. Also called a *mixed design*.

Random assignment A selection procedure that ensures that participants are randomly placed either in the control group or in the experimental group.
Rap group The initial term for group therapy sessions among veterans, in which members meet to talk about and explore problems in an atmosphere of mutual support.
Rape Forced sexual intercourse or another sexual act committed against a nonconsenting person or intercourse with an underage person.
Rapid eye movement (REM) sleep The period of the sleep cycle during which the eyes move quickly back and forth, indicating that the person is dreaming.
Rapprochement movement An effort to identify a set of common strategies that run through the work of all effective therapists.
Rational-emotive therapy A cognitive-behavioral therapy developed by Albert Ellis that helps clients identify and change the irrational assumptions and thinking that help cause their psychological disorder.
Rationalization An ego defense mechanism in which one creates acceptable reasons for unwanted or undesirable behavior.
Reaction formation An ego defense mechanism whereby a person counters an unacceptable desire by taking on a lifestyle that directly opposes the unwanted impulse.
Reactive depression A depression that appears to be triggered by clear events. Also known as *exogenous depression*.
Reactivity The extent to which the very presence of an observer affects a person's behavior.
Reality principle The recognition, characterizing ego functioning, that we cannot always express or satisfy our id impulses.
Receptor A site on a neuron that receives a neurotransmitter.
Regression An ego defense mechanism in which a person returns to a more primitive mode of interacting with the world.
Reinforcement The desirable or undesirable stimuli that result from an organism's behavior.
Relapse-prevention training A cognitive-behavioral approach to treating alcohol use disorder (and applied to certain other disorders) in which clients are taught to keep track of their drinking behavior, apply coping strategies in situations that typically trigger excessive drinking, and plan ahead for risky situations and reactions.
Relational psychoanalytic therapy A form of psychodynamic therapy that considers therapists to be active participants in the formation of patients' feelings and reactions and therefore calls for therapists to disclose their own experiences and feelings in discussions with patients.
Relaxation training A treatment procedure that teaches clients to relax at will so they can calm themselves in stressful situations.
Reliability A measure of the consistency of test or research results.
Repression A defense mechanism whereby the ego prevents unacceptable impulses from reaching consciousness.
Residential treatment center A place where people formerly addicted to drugs live, work, and socialize in a drug-free environment. Also called a *therapeutic community*.
Resilience The ability to avoid or recover from the effects of negative circumstances.

Resistance An unconscious refusal to participate fully in therapy.
Resolution phase The fourth phase in the sexual response cycle, characterized by relaxation and a decline in arousal following orgasm.
Response inventories Tests designed to measure a person's responses in one specific area of functioning, such as affect, social skills, or cognitive processes.
Restricting-type anorexia nervosa A type of anorexia nervosa in which people reduce their weight by severely restricting their food intake.
Reticular formation The brain's arousal center, which helps people to be awake, alert, and attentive.
Retrograde amnesia A lack of memory about events that occurred before the event that triggered amnesia.
Retrospective analysis A psychological autopsy in which clinicians and researchers piece together information about a person's suicide from the person's past.
Reversal design A single-subject experimental design in which behavior is measured to provide a baseline (A), then again after the treatment has been applied (B), then again after the conditions during baseline have been reintroduced (A), and then once again after the treatment is reintroduced (B). Also known as *ABAB design*.
Reward A pleasurable stimulus given to an organism that encourages a specific behavior.
Reward circuit A dopamine-rich circuit in the brain that produces feelings of pleasure when activated.
Reward-deficiency syndrome A condition, suspected to be present in some people, in which the brain's reward circuit is not readily activated by the usual events in their lives.
Right to refuse treatment The legal right of patients to refuse certain forms of treatment.
Right to treatment The legal right of patients, particularly those who are involuntarily committed, to receive adequate treatment.
Risperidone A commonly prescribed second-generation antipsychotic drug.
Ritalin A trade name of methylphenidate, a stimulant drug that is helpful in many cases of attention-deficit/hyperactivity disorder (ADHD).
Role-playing A therapy technique in which clients are instructed to act out roles assigned to them by the therapist.
Rorschach test A projective test, in which a person reacts to inkblots designed to help reveal psychological features of the person.
Rosenthal effect The general finding that the results of any experiment often conform to the expectations of the experimenter.
Rush A spasm of warmth and ecstasy that occurs when certain drugs, such as heroin, are ingested.
Savant A person with a mental disorder or with significant intellectual deficits who has some extraordinary ability despite the disorder or deficits.
Schizoaffective disorder A disorder in which symptoms of both schizophrenia and a mood disorder are prominent.
Schizoid personality disorder A personality disorder in which a person persistently avoids social relationships and shows little emotional expression.
Schizophrenia A psychotic disorder in which personal, social, and occupational functioning deteriorate as a result of strange perceptions, disturbed thought processes, unusual emotions, and motor abnormalities.
Schizophrenia-related brain circuit A brain circuit whose dysfunction contributes to schizophrenia. It includes the prefrontal cortex, hippocampus, amygdala, thalamus, striatum, and substantia nigra, among other brain structures.
Schizophreniform disorder A disorder in which all of the key features of schizophrenia are present but last only between one and six months.
Schizophrenogenic mother A type of mother—supposedly cold, domineering, and uninterested in the needs of her children—who was once thought to cause schizophrenia in her child.
Schizotypal personality disorder A personality disorder characterized by extreme discomfort in close relationships, odd forms of thinking and perceiving, and behavioral eccentricities.
School refusal A pattern in which children fear going to school and often stay home for a long period of time. Also called *school phobia*.
Scientific method The process of systematically gathering and evaluating information through careful observations to gain an understanding of a phenomenon.
Seasonal affective disorder (SAD) A mood disorder in which mood episodes are related to changes in season.
Second-generation antidepressant drugs A relatively new group of antidepressant drugs that differ structurally from tricyclics and MAO inhibitors.
Second-generation antipsychotic drugs A relatively new group of antipsychotic drugs whose biological action is different from that of the first-generation antipsychotic drugs.
Second messengers Chemical changes within a neuron just after the neuron receives a neurotransmitter message and just before it responds.
Secondary gain In psychodynamic theory, the gain people achieve when their somatic symptoms elicit kindness from others or provide an excuse for avoiding unpleasant activities.
Secondary prevention Prevention interventions that are designed to address disorders quickly, before they become more serious problems.
Sedative-hypnotic drugs Drugs used in low doses to calm people and in higher doses to help people sleep.
Selective amnesia An inability to recall some of the events that occurred over a limited period of time.
Selective mutism A disorder marked by failure to speak in certain social situations when speech is expected, despite an ability to speak in other situations.
Selective serotonin reuptake inhibitors (SSRIs) A group of second-generation antidepressant drugs that increase serotonin activity specifically, without affecting other neurotransmitters.
Self-actualization The humanistic process by which people fulfill their potential for goodness and growth.
Self-efficacy The belief that one can master and perform needed behaviors whenever necessary.
Self-help group A group made up of people with similar problems who help and support one another without the direct leadership of a clinician. Also called a *mutual help group*.
Self-hypnosis The process of hypnotizing oneself, sometimes for the purpose of forgetting unpleasant events.
Self-Injury Implicit Association Test A cognitive test used to help assess suicidal risk. Rather than asking people if they plan to attempt suicide, this test instructs them to pair various suicide-related words (for example, "dead," "lifeless," "suicide") with words that are personally relevant ("I," "myself," "mine") and with words that are not personally relevant ("they," "them," "other").
Self-instruction training A treatment developed by Donald Meichenbaum that teaches people to use coping self-statements at times of stress, discomfort, or significant pain. Also called *stress inoculation training*.
Self-monitoring Clients' observation of their own behavior.
Self-statements According to some theorists, statements about oneself, sometimes counterproductive, that come to mind during stressful situations.
Self-theory The psychodynamic theory that emphasizes the role of the self—a person's unified personality.
Senile plaques Sphere-shaped deposits of beta-amyloid protein that form in the spaces between certain brain cells and in certain blood vessels as people age. People with Alzheimer's disease have an excessive number of such plaques.
Sensate focus A treatment for sexual disorders that instructs couples to take the focus away from orgasm or intercourse and instead spend time concentrating on the pleasure achieved by such acts as kissing, hugging, and mutual massage. Also known as *nondemand pleasuring*.
Separation anxiety disorder A disorder marked by excessive anxiety, even panic,

whenever the individual is separated from home, a parent, or another attachment figure.

Serial murders A series of three or more killings carried out separately by the same individual(s) over a period of time—usually a month or more.

Serotonin A neurotransmitter whose abnormal activity is linked to depression, obsessive-compulsive disorder, and eating disorders.

Severe intellectual disability A level of intellectual disability (IQ between 20 and 34) at which individuals require careful supervision and can learn to perform basic work in structured and sheltered settings.

Sex offender statute The presumption by some state legislatures that people who are repeatedly found guilty of certain sex crimes have a mental disorder and should be categorized as "mentally disordered sex offenders." Such laws have been changed or abolished by many states over the past two decades.

Sexting The sending of sexually explicit material—particularly photos or text messages—between cell phones or other digital devices.

Sexual dysfunction A disorder marked by a persistent inability to function normally in some area of the human sexual response cycle.

Sexual masochism disorder A paraphilic disorder in which a person has repeated and intense sexual urges, fantasies, or behaviors that involve being humiliated, beaten, bound, or otherwise made to suffer, accompanied by clinically significant distress or impairment.

Sexual response cycle The general sequence of behavior and feelings that occurs during sexual activity, consisting of desire, excitement, orgasm, and resolution.

Sexual sadism disorder A paraphilic disorder in which a person has repeated and intense sexual urges or fantasies that involve inflicting suffering on others, and either acts on these urges with nonconsenting individuals or experiences clinically significant distress or impairment.

Sexually violent predator laws Laws passed by the federal government and many states that call for certain sex offenders who have been convicted of sex crimes and have served their sentence in prison to be removed from prison before their release and committed involuntarily to a mental hospital for treatment if a court judges them likely to engage in further acts of sexual violence due to a mental or personality abnormality. Also called *sexually dangerous persons laws*.

Shaping A learning procedure in which successive approximations of the desired behavior are rewarded until finally the exact and complete behavior is learned.

Sheltered workshop A supervised workplace for people who are not yet ready for competitive jobs.

Short-term memory The memory system that collects new information. Also known as *working memory*.

Shuttle box A box separated in the middle by a barrier that an animal can jump over in order to escape or avoid a shock.

Sildenafil A drug used to treat erectile disorder that helps increase blood flow to the penis during sexual activity. Marketed as *Viagra*.

Single-subject experimental design A research method in which a single participant is observed and measured both before and after the manipulation of an independent variable.

Sleep apnea disorder A sleep-wake disorder characterized by frequent awakenings each night due to periodic deprivation of oxygen to the brain during sleep.

Sleep terror disorder A parasomnia in which a person awakens suddenly during the first third of sleep, screaming out in extreme fear and agitation.

Sleepwalking disorder A parasomnia in which people repeatedly leave their beds and walk around without being conscious of the episode or remembering it later.

Social anxiety disorder A severe and persistent fear of social or performance situations in which embarrassment may occur.

Social communication disorder A disorder marked by persistent problems in communication and social relationships, but without significant language difficulties or cognitive impairment. The communication and social problems are different in nature and less severe than those in autism spectrum disorder.

Social skills training A therapy approach that helps people learn or improve social skills and assertiveness through role-playing and rehearsing of desirable behaviors.

Social therapy An approach to therapy in which the therapist makes practical advice and life adjustment a central focus of treatment for schizophrenia. Therapy also focuses on problem solving, decision making, memory enhancement, development of social skills, and management of medications. Also known as *personal therapy*.

Sociocultural model The theoretical perspective that emphasizes the effects of society, culture, and social and family groups on individual behavior.

Sociopathy *See* antisocial personality disorder.

Sodium amobarbital (Amytal) A drug used to put people into a near-sleep state during which some can better recall forgotten events.

Sodium pentobarbital (Pentothal) A drug used to put people into a near-sleep state during which some can better recall forgotten events.

Somatic symptom disorder A disorder in which people become excessively distressed, concerned, and anxious about bodily symptoms that they are experiencing, with their lives greatly and disproportionately disrupted by the symptoms.

Somatogenic perspective The view that abnormal psychological functioning has physical causes.

Special education An approach to educating children with intellectual disability in which they are grouped together and given a separate, specially designed education.

Specific learning disorder A neurodevelopmental disorder marked by impairments in cognitive skills such as reading, writing, arithmetic, or mathematical skills.

Specific phobia A severe and persistent fear of a specific object or situation (does not include agoraphobia and social anxiety disorder).

Spectator role A state of mind that some people experience during sex, in which they focus on their sexual performance to such an extent that their performance and their enjoyment are reduced.

Standardization The process in which a test is administered to a large group of people whose performance then serves as a standard or norm against which any individual's score can be measured.

State-dependent learning Learning that becomes associated with the conditions under which it occurred, so that it is best remembered under the same conditions.

State hospitals Public mental institutions in the United States, run by the individual states.

State school A state-supported institution for people with intellectual disability.

Statistical analysis The application of principles of probability to the findings of a study in order to learn how likely it is that the findings have occurred by chance.

Statistical significance A measure of the probability that a study's findings occurred by chance rather than because of the experimental manipulation.

Stimulant drug A substance that increases the activity of the central nervous system.

Stimulus generalization A phenomenon in which responses to one stimulus are also produced by similar stimuli.

Stress brain circuit The brain circuit whose dysfunction contributes to PTSD. It includes such brain structures as the amygdala, prefrontal cortex, anterior cingulate cortex, insula, and hippocampus, among others.

Stress-management program An approach to treating generalized and other anxiety disorders that teaches clients techniques for reducing and controlling stress.

Stressor An event that creates a sense of threat by confronting a person with a demand or opportunity for change of some kind.

Stress-reduction and problem-solving programs Workshops or group sessions offered by a business, in which mental health professionals teach employees techniques for coping, solving problems, and handling and reducing stress.

Stress response A person's particular reactions to stress.

Structured interview An interview format in which the clinician asks prepared questions.

Subgenual cingulate A brain structure whose abnormal activity has been linked to depression. Also called *Brodmann Area 25.*

Subintentional death A death in which the victim plays an indirect, hidden, partial, or unconscious role.

Subject An individual chosen to participate in a study. Also called a *participant.*

Sublimation In psychoanalytic theory, the rechanneling of id impulses into endeavors that are both socially acceptable and personally gratifying. Sublimation can also be used as an ego defense mechanism.

Subpersonalities The two or more distinct personalities found in individuals suffering with dissociative identity disorder. Also known as *alternate personalities.*

Substance use disorder A pattern of maladaptive behaviors and reactions brought about by repeated use of a substance, sometimes also including tolerance for the substance and withdrawal reactions.

Suicidal behavior disorder A classification being studied for possible inclusion in a future revision of DSM-5, in which individuals have tried to die by suicide within the last two years.

Suicide A self-inflicted death in which the person acted intentionally, directly, and consciously.

Suicide education programs Suicide prevention programs that usually take place in schools and concentrate on students and their teachers. There are also a growing number of online sites that provide education about suicide—targeting troubled persons, their family members, and friends.

Suicide prevention program A program that tries to identify people who are at risk of killing themselves and to offer them crisis intervention.

Superego According to Freud, the psychological force that represents a person's values and ideals.

Symbolic loss According to Freudian theory, the loss of a valued object (for example, a loss of employment) that is unconsciously interpreted as the loss of a loved one. Also called *imagined loss.*

Sympathetic nervous system The nerve fibers of the autonomic nervous system that quicken the heartbeat and produce other changes experienced as arousal and fear. One of the two major routes by which the brain and body produce arousal and fear.

Symptom A physical or psychological sign of a disorder.

Synapse The tiny space between the nerve ending of one neuron and the dendrite of another.

Syndrome A cluster of symptoms that usually occur together.

Synergistic effect In pharmacology, an increase of effects that occurs when more than one substance is acting on the body at the same time.

Synesthesia A crossing over of sensory perceptions. For example, a loud sound may be seen or a color may be felt.

Systematic desensitization An exposure therapy that uses relaxation training and a fear hierarchy to help clients with phobias react calmly to the objects or situations they dread.

Tarantism A disorder occurring throughout Europe between 900 and 1800 A.D. in which people would suddenly start to jump around, dance, and go into convulsions. Also known as *St. Vitus's dance.*

Tardive dyskinesia Extrapyramidal effects that appear in some patients after they have taken antipsychotic drugs for an extended time.

Telemental health The use of digital technologies to deliver mental health services without the therapist being physically present.

Temporal lobes Regions of the brain that play a key role in transforming short-term memory to long-term memory, among other functions.

Tension headache *See* Muscle contraction headache.

Tertiary prevention Prevention interventions that are designed to provide effective treatment for moderate or severe disorders as soon as it is needed so that the disorders do not become long-term problems.

Test A device for gathering information about a few aspects of a person's psychological functioning from which broader information about the person can be inferred.

Testosterone The principal male sex hormone.

Tetrahydrocannabinol (THC) The main active ingredient of cannabis.

Thanatos According to the Freudian view, the basic death instinct that functions in opposition to the life instinct.

Thematic Apperception Test (TAT) A projective test consisting of pictures that show people in ambiguous situations that the client is asked to interpret.

Theory of mind One's awareness that other people base their behaviors on their own beliefs, intentions, and mental states, not on information they have no way of knowing.

Therapist A professional clinician who applies a system of therapy to help a person overcome psychological difficulties.

Therapy A systematic process for helping people overcome their psychological problems. Therapy consists of a client (patient), a trained therapist, and a series of contacts between them.

Token economy program A behavior-focused program in which a person's desirable behaviors are reinforced systematically throughout the day by the awarding of tokens that can be exchanged for goods or privileges.

Tolerance The adjustment that the brain and the body make to the regular use of certain drugs so that ever larger doses are needed to achieve the earlier effects.

Torture The use of brutal, degrading, and disorienting strategies to reduce victims to a state of utter helplessness.

Tranquilizer A drug that reduces anxiety.

Transcranial magnetic stimulation (TMS) A treatment procedure for depression and certain other disorders in which an electromagnetic coil, which is placed on or above a person's head, sends a current into the person's brain.

Transference According to psychodynamic theorists, the redirection toward the psychotherapist of feelings associated with important figures in a patient's life, now or in the past.

Transgender Individuals who have a strong sense that their gender identity is different from their birth anatomy.

Transvestic disorder A paraphilic disorder consisting of repeated and intense sexual urges, fantasies, or behaviors that involve dressing in clothes of the opposite sex, accompanied by clinically significant distress or impairment. Also known as *transvestism* or *cross-dressing.*

Treatment A systematic procedure designed to help change abnormal behavior into more normal behavior. Also called *therapy.*

Trephination An ancient operation in which a stone instrument was used to cut away a circular section of the skull, perhaps to treat abnormal behavior.

Trichotillomania A disorder in which people repeatedly pull out hair from their scalp, eyebrows, eyelashes, or other parts of their body. Also called *hair-pulling disorder.*

Tricyclic An antidepressant drug such as imipramine that has three rings in its molecular structure.

Trisomy A chromosomal abnormality in which a person has three chromosomes of one kind rather than the usual two.

Tube and intravenous feeding Forced nourishment sometimes provided to people with anorexia nervosa when their condition becomes life-threatening.

Type A personality style A personality pattern characterized by hostility, cynicism, drivenness, impatience, competitiveness, and ambition.

Type B personality style A personality pattern in which a person is more relaxed, less aggressive, and less concerned about time.

Type I schizophrenia According to some theorists, a type of schizophrenia dominated by positive symptoms, such as delusions, hallucinations, and certain formal thought disorders.

Type II schizophrenia According to some theorists, a type of schizophrenia dominated by negative symptoms, such as flat affect, poverty of speech, and loss of volition.

Tyramine A chemical that, if allowed to accumulate, can raise blood pressure dangerously. It is found in many common foods and is broken down by MAO.

Ulcer A lesion that forms in the wall of the stomach or of the duodenum.

Unconditional positive regard Full, warm acceptance of a person regardless of what he or she says, thinks, or feels; a critical component of client-centered therapy.

Unconditioned response (UCR) The natural, automatic response produced by an unconditioned stimulus.

Unconditioned stimulus (UCS) A stimulus that produces an automatic, natural response.

Unconscious The deeply hidden mass of memories, experiences, and impulses that is viewed in Freudian theory as the source of much behavior.

Undoing An ego defense mechanism in which a person unconsciously cancels out an unacceptable desire or act by performing another act.

Unipolar depression Depression without a history of mania.

Unstructured interview An interview format in which the clinician asks spontaneous questions that are based on issues that arise during the interview.

Vagus nerve stimulation A treatment procedure for depression in which an implanted pulse generator sends regular electrical signals to a person's vagus nerve; the nerve, in turn, stimulates the brain.

Validity The accuracy of a test's or study's results; that is, the extent to which the test or study actually measures or shows what it claims.

Valium The trade name of diazepam, an antianxiety drug.

Variable Any characteristic or event that can vary across time, locations, or persons.

Ventromedial hypothalamus (VMH) A brain region that depresses hunger when activated.

Virtual reality treatment Cognitive-behavioral intervention that uses virtual reality—3D computer graphics that simulate real-world objects and situations—as an exposure tool.

Visual hallucinations Hallucinations in which a person may either experience vague visual perceptions, perhaps of colors or clouds, or have distinct visions of people, objects, or scenes that are not there.

Voyeuristic disorder A paraphilic disorder in which a person has repeated and intense sexual desires to observe unsuspecting people in secret as they undress or to spy on couples having intercourse, and either acts on these urges with nonconsenting individuals or experiences clinically significant distress or impairment.

Weight set point The weight level that a person is predisposed to maintain, controlled in part by the hypothalamus.

Withdrawal Unpleasant, sometimes dangerous reactions that may occur when people who use a drug regularly stop taking or reduce their dosage of the drug.

Working through The psychoanalytic process of facing conflicts, reinterpreting feelings, and overcoming one's problems.

References

AA World Services. (2017, April). Estimated worldwide A.A. individual and group membership (SM F-132). A.A. Retrieved from http://www.aa.org/assets.

AA World Services. (2018, April). Estimated worldwide A.A. individual and group membership (SMF-132). A.A. Retrieved from http://www.aa.org/assets.

AAC (American Addiction Centers). (2018). *Dangers of snorting, smoking, or injecting cocaine*. Brentwood, TN: AAC.

AAFPRS (American Academy of Facial Plastic and Reconstructive Surgery). (2017, January 26). AAFPRS Annual Survey unveils rising trends in facial plastic surgery. Retrieved from http://www.aafprs.org/media/stats_polls/m_stats.html.

AAIDD (American Association of Intellectual and Developmental Disabilities). (2018). Definition of intellectual disability. *AAIDD*. Retrieved from http://www.aaidd.org.

Aalami, M., Jafarnejad, F., & Modarres Gharavi, M. (2016). The effects of progressive muscular relaxation and breathing control technique on blood pressure during pregnancy. *Iranian Journal of Nursing and Midwifery Research, 21*(3), 331–336.

AAMFT (American Association of Marriage and Family Therapy). (2018). *Rape trauma*. Alexandria, VA: AAMFT

Aamodt, M. G. (2014, September 6). *Serial killer statistics*. Retrieved from Aamodt website: http://maamodt.asp.radford.edu/serial_killer_information_center/project_description.htm.

Aamodt, M. G. (2016, September 4). *Serial killer statistics*. Retrieved from http://maamodt.asp.radford.edu/serial_killer_information_center/project description.htm.

Aaronson, S. T., Sears, P., Ruvunaq, F., Bunker, M., Conway, C. R., Dougherty, D. D., . . . Zajecka, J. M. (2017). A 5-year observational study of patients with treatment-resistant depression treated with vagus nerve stimulation or treatment as usual: Comparison of response, remission, and suicidality. *American Journal of Psychiatry, 174*, 640–648.

ABA (American Bar Association). (2017). *Court cases by diminished capacity/guilt*. Washington, DC: ABA (Center on Children and the Law).

ABA (American Bar Association). (2018). *Rule 1.14: Client with diminished capacity*. Chicago, IL: ABA.

Abbey, A. (2002). Alcohol-related sexual assault: A common problem among college students. *Journal of Studies on Alcohol, 14*, 118–128.

Abbey, S. E. (2005). Somatization and somatoform disorders. In J. L. Levenson (Ed.), *The American Psychiatric Publishing textbook of psychosomatic medicine* (pp. 271–296). Washington, DC: American Psychiatric Publishing.

Abdel-Hamid, I. A., & Ali, O. I. (2018). Delayed ejaculation: Pathophysiology, diagnosis, and treatment. *World Journal of Men's Health, 36*(1), 22–40.

Abe, K. (2017). What is a serial killer? What is a mass murderer? How do they differ? *European Journal of Academic Essays, 4*(4), 187–198.

Abel, G. G., Jordan, A., Hand, C. G., Holland, L. A., & Phipps, A. (2001). Classification models of child molesters utilizing the Abel Assessment for child sexual abuse interest. *Child Abuse and Neglect, 25*(5), 703–718.

Abma, J. C., & Martinez, G. M. (2017, June 22). Sexual activity and contraceptive use among teenagers in the United States, 2011–2015. Atlanta, GA: CDC, National Health Statistics Report, No. 104.

Abraham, K. (1911). Notes on the psychoanalytic investigation and treatment of manic-depressive insanity and allied conditions. In *Selected papers on psychoanalysis* (pp. 137–156). New York: Basic Books. [Work republished 1960.]

Abraham, K. (1916). The first pregenital stage of the libido. In *Selected papers on psychoanalysis* (pp. 248–279). New York: Basic Books. [Work republished 1960.]

Abraham, K. M., Yosef, M., Resnick, S. G., & Zivin, K. (2017). Competitive employment outcomes among veterans in VHA therapeutic and supported employment services programs. *Psychiatry Services, 68*(9), 938–946.

Abramowitz, J. (2017, October 23). Psychotherapy for obsessive-compulsive disorders in adults. *UpToDate*. Retrieved from http://www.uptodate.com.

Abramowitz, J. S., & Braddock, A. E. (2011). *Hypochondriasis and health anxiety. Advances in psychotherapy—Evidence-based practice*. Cambridge, MA: Hogrefe Publishing.

Abramson, L. Y., Alloy, L. B., Hankin, B. L., Haeffel, G. J., MacCoon, D. G., & Gibb, B. E. (2002). Cognitive vulnerability—Stress models of depression in a self-regulatory and psychobiological context. In I. H. Gotlib & C. L. Hammen (Eds.), *Handbook of depression* (pp. 268–294). New York: Guilford Press.

Abramson, L. Y., Metalsky, G. I., & Alloy, L. B. (1989). Hopelessness depression: A theory-based subtype of depression. *Psychological Review, 96*(2), 358–372.

Abramson, L. Y., Seligman, M. E., & Teasdale, J. D. (1978). Learned helplessness in humans: Critique and reformulation. *Journal of Abnormal Psychology, 87*(1), 49–74.

Abulizi, X., Pryor, L., Michel, G., Melchior, M., van der Waerden, J., & EDEN Mother–Child Cohort Study Group. (2017). Temperament in infancy and behavioral and emotional problems at age 5.5: The EDEN mother-child cohort. *PLoS ONE, 12*(2), e0171971.

à Campo, J. M. L. G., & Nijman, H. (2016). Gender dysphoria and psychiatric symptoms. *Journal of Nervous & Mental Disease, 204*(7), 558.

Achalia, R. M., Chaturvedi, S. K., Desai, G., Rao, G. N., & Prakash, O. (2014). Prevalence and risk factors associated with tardive dyskinesia among Indian patients with schizophrenia. *Asian Journal of Psychiatry, 9*, 31–35.

Acierno, R., Knapp, R., Tuerk, P., Gilmore, A. K., Lejuez, C., Ruggiero, K., . . . Foa, E. B. (2017). A non-inferiority trial of prolonged exposure for posttraumatic stress disorder: In person versus home-based telehealth. *Behaviour Research and Therapy, 89*, 57–65.

Ackerman, C. (2017, January 18). 22 mindfulness exercises, techniques & activities for adults (+PDF's). *Positive Psychology Program*. Retrieved from https://positivepsychologyprogram.com.

Ackland, G. L., Whittle, J., Toner, A., Machhada, A., Del Arroyo, A. G., Sciuso, A., . . . Gourine, A. V. (2016). Molecular mechanisms linking autonomic dysfunction and impaired cardiac contractility in critical illness. *Critical Care Medicine, 44*(8), e614–e624.

ACOG (American Congress of Obstetricians and Gynecologists). (2016). *Committee opinion: Concerns regarding social media and health issues in adolescents and young adults* (No. 653). Washington, DC: ACOG.

ADAA (Anxiety and Depression Association of America). (2017). *About ADA: Facts & statistics*. Silver Springs, MD: ADAA.

Adam, K. S., Bouckoms, A., & Streiner, D. (1982). Parental loss and family stability in attempted suicide. *Archives of General Psychiatry, 39*(9), 1081–1085.

Adamowicz, M. W. (2016). Psychological Testing. *Mentalhelp.net*

Adams, C. E., Awad, G. A., Rathbone, J., Thornley, B., & Soares-Weiser, K. (2014). Chlorpromazine versus placebo for schizophrenia. *Cochrane Database of Systematic Reviews, 1*, CD000284.

Adams, J. G. (2013). Sexual assault (Chap. 128). In J. G. Adams (Ed.), *Emergency medicine: Clinical essentials* (2nd ed.). Elsevier Health Services. [Kindle edition]

Adams, R. E., & Boscarino, J. A. (2005). Stress and well-being in the aftermath of the World Trade Center attack: The continuing effects of a communitywide disaster. *Journal of Community Psychology, 33*(2), 175–190.

Adams, S. M., Rice, M. J., Jones, S. L., Herzog, E., Mackenzie, L. J., & Oleck, L. G. (2018, March 1). Telemental health standards: Standards, reimbursement, and interstate practice. *Journal of the American Psychiatric Nurses Association*. [Epub ahead of print]

Addington, J., Heinssen, R. K., Robinson, D. G., Schooler, N. R., Marcy, P., Brunette, M. F., . . . Kane, J. M. (2015). Duration of untreated psychosis in community treatment settings in the United States. *Psychiatric Services* (Washington, D.C.), *66*(7), 753–756.

ADDitude. (2017). ADHD, by the numbers. *ADDitude Magazine*.

Adebäck, P., Schulman, A., & Nilsson, D. (2018). Children exposed to a natural disaster: Psychological consequences eight years after 2004 tsunami. *Nordic Journal of Psychiatry, 72*(1), 75–81.

Adi, A., & Mathbout, M. (2018, April). The duty to protect: Four decades after Tarasoff. *Psychiatry Online* (American Psychiatric Association). Retrieved from https://ajp.psychiatryonline.org.

AFA (Alzheimer's Foundation of America). (2014). *About dementia*. New York: AFA.

Afifi, T. O., MacMillan, H. L., Boyle, M., Taillieu, T., Cheung, K., & Sareen, J. (2014). Child abuse and mental disorders in Canada. *Canadian Medical Association Journal, 186*(9), E324–E332.

AFSP (American Foundation for Suicide Prevention). (2014). Facts and figures for 2010: Suicide deaths. Retrieved from https://www.afsp.org/understanding-suicide/facts-and-figures.

AFSP (American Foundation for Suicide Prevention). (2014). Facts and figures for 2011: Suicide deaths. Retrieved from https://www.afsp.org/understanding-suicide/facts-and-figures.

AFSP (American Foundation for Suicide Prevention). (2017). *Suicide statistics.* Retrieved from https://www.afsp.org/about-suicide/suicide-statistics/.

AFSP (American Foundation for Suicide Prevention). (2018). *Suicide prevention in schools.* New York: AFSP.

AFSP (American Foundation for Suicide Prevention). (2018). *Suicide statistics.* Retrieved from https://www.afsp.org/about-suicide/suicide-statistics/.

AFSP (American Foundation for Suicide Prevention). (2018). *Suicide statistics.* New York: AFSP.

Aggarwal, N. K. (2017). Culture, communication, and DSM-5 diagnostic reliability. *Journal of the National Medical Association, 109*(3), 150–152.

Agha, M., Nisar, A., Liaqat, H., Choudry, U. K., Choudry, A. K., & Shoaib, M. (2017). Neurophysiological perspectives of borderline personality disorders. *Acta Psychopathologica, 3*(3), 21.

Aghajani, M., Klapwijk, E. T., van der Wee, N. J., Veer, I. M., Rombouts, S. A. R. B., Boon, A. E., . . . Colins, O. F. (2017). Disorganized amygdala networks in conduct-disordered juvenile offenders with callous-unemotional traits. *Biological Psychiatry, 82*(4), 283–293.

Agras, S. (1985). *Panic: Facing fears, phobias, and anxiety.* New York: W. H. Freeman.

Agras, W. S., Fitzsimmons-Craft, E. E., & Wilfley, D. E. (2017). Evolution of cognitive-behavioral therapy for eating disorders. *Behaviour Research and Therapy, 88,* 26–36.

Agrawal, A., Tillman, R., Grucza, R. A., Nelson, E. C., McCutcheon, V. V., Few, L., . . . Bucholz, K. K. (2017). Reciprocal relationships between substance use and disorders and suicidal ideation and suicide attempts in the Collaborative Study of the Genetics of Alcoholism. *Journal of Affective Disorders, 213,* 96–104.

Agronin, M. (2017, October 24). Sexual dysfunction in older adults. *UpToDate.* Retrieved from http://www.uptodate.com.

Aguilera, A., Bruehlman-Senecal, E., Demasi, O., & Avila, P. (2017). Automated text messaging as an adjunct to cognitive behavioral therapy for depression: A clinical trial. *Journal of Medical Internet Research, 19*(5), e148.

Aguilera, A., Garza, M. J., & Muñoz, R. F. (2010). Group cognitive-behavioral therapy for depression in Spanish: Culture-sensitive manualized treatment in practice. *Journal of Clinical Psychology, 66*(8), 857–867.

Ahmadi, K. (2016). What is a self-help group? *Psych Central.* Retrieved from https://psychcentral.com/lib.

Aiken, L. R. (1985). *Psychological testing and assessment* (5th ed.). Boston: Allyn & Bacon.

Aikin, K. J., Sullivan, H. W., Dolina, S., Lynch, M., & Squiers, L. B. (2017). Direct-to-consumer promotion of prescription drugs on mobile devices: Content analysis. *Journal of Medical Internet Research, 19*(7), e225.

AIS (American Institute of Stress). (2017). *Transforming stress through awareness, education and collaboration.* Fort Worth, TX: AIS.

Akhtar, S., Wig, N. H., Verma, V. K., Pershod, D., & Verma, S. K. (1975). A phenomenological analysis of symptoms in obsessive-compulsive neuroses. *British Journal of Psychiatry, 127,* 342–348.

Akin, O., Yesilkaya, E., Sari, E., Akar, C., Basbozkurt, G., Macit, E., . . . Gül, H. (2016). A rare reason of hyperinsulinism: Munchausen syndrome by proxy. *Hormone Research in Paediatrics, 86*(6), 416–419.

Akins, C. K. (2004). The role of Pavlovian conditioning in sexual behavior: A comparative analysis of human and nonhuman animals. *International Journal of Comparative Psychology, 17*(2–3), 241–262.

Albano, A. M., Comer, J. S., Compton, S. N., Piacentini, J., Kendall, P. C., Birmaher, B., . . . Sherrill, J. T. (2018). Secondary outcomes from the Child/Adolescent Anxiety Multimodal Study (CAMS): Implications for clinical practice. *Evidence-Based Practice in Child and Adolescent Mental Health, 3*(1), 30–41.

Alderson-Day, B., & Jones, N. (2018). Understanding AVATAR therapy: Who, or what, is changing? *Lancet Psychiatry, 5*(1), 2–3.

Alegría, M., Alvarez, K. Ishikawa, R. Z., DiMarzio, K., & McPeck, S. (2016). Removing obstacles to eliminating racial and ethnic disparities in behavioral health care. *Health Affairs, 35*(6), 991–999.

Alegría, M., Nakash, O., & NeMoyer, A. (2018). Increasing equity in access to mental health care: A critical first step in improving service quality. *World Psychiatry, 17*(1), 43–44.

Alegría, M., Atkins, M., Farmer, E., Slaton, E., & Stelk, W. (2010). One size does not fit all: Taking diversity, culture and context seriously. *Administration and Policy in Mental Health and Mental Health Service Research, 37*(1-2), 48–60.

Alegría, M., Fortuna, L. R., Lin, J. Y., Norris, F. H., Gao, S., Takeuchi, D. T., . . . Valentine, A. (2013). Prevalence, risk, and correlates of posttraumatic stress disorder across ethnic and racial minority groups in the United States. *Medical Care, 51*(12), 1114–1123.

Alegría, M., Molina, K. M., & Chen, C. (2014). Neighborhood characteristics and differential risk for depressive and anxiety disorders across racial/ethnic groups in the United States. *Depression and Anxiety, 31*(1), 27–37.

Alexander, J. R., Houghton, D. C., Twohig, M. P., Franklin, M. E., Saunders, S. M., Neal-Barnett, A. M., . . . Woods, D. W. (2017). Clarifying the relationship between trichotillomania and anxiety. *Journal of Obsessive-Compulsive and Related Disorders, 13,* 30–34.

Ålgars, M., Santtila, P., Jern, P., Johansson, A., Westerlund, M., & Sandnabba, N. K. (2011). Sexual body image and its correlates: A population-based study of Finnish women and men. *International Journal of Sexual Health, 23*(1), 26–34.

Ali, M. M., Dwyer, D. S., & Rizzo, J. A. (2011). The social contagion effect of suicidal behavior in adolescents: Does it really exist? *Journal of Mental Health Policy and Economics, 14*(1), 3–12.

Allara, E., Ferri, M., Bo, A., Gasparrini, A., Faggiano, F. (2014). Are mass-media campaigns effective in preventing drug use: A Cochrane systematic review and meta-analysis. *BMJ.* Retrieved from http://bmjopen.bmj.com.

Allderidge, P. (1979). Hospitals, madhouses and asylums: Cycles in the care of the insane. *British Journal of Psychiatry, 134,* 321–334.

Allen, A. P., Curran, E. A., Duggan, A., Cryan, J. F., Chorcoráin, A. N., Dinan, T. G., . . . Clarke, G. (2017). A systematic review of the psychobiological burden of informal caregiving for patients with dementia: Focus on cognitive and biological markers of chronic stress. *Neuroscience & Biobehavioral Reviews, 73,* 123–164.

Allen, D. F. (Ed.). (1985). *The cocaine crisis.* Plenum Press: New York.

Allen, M. T., Jameson, M. M., & Myers, C. E. (2017). Beyond behavioral inhibition: A computer avatar task designed to assess behavioral inhibition extends to harm avoidance. *Frontiers in Pharmacology, 8,* 1560.

Allison, S., Bastiampillai, T., & Fuller, D. A. (2017). Mass incarceration and severe mental illness in the USA. *The Lancet, 390*(1009), 25.

Allison, S., Bastiampillai, T., Licinio, J., Fuller, D. A., Bidargaddi, N., & Sharfstein, S. S. (2018). When should governments increase the supply of psychiatric beds? *Molecular Psychiatry, 23*(4), 796–800.

Alloway, T. P. (2014, May 11). Selfies, Facebook, and narcissism: What's the link? *Psychology Today.*

Alloway, T. P., Runac, R., Qureshi, M., & Kemp, G. (2014). Is Facebook linked to selfishness? Investigating the relationships among social media use, empathy, and narcissism. *Social Networking, 3*(3), 150–158.

Alridge, J. (2012, May 17). How many people commit suicide due to depression? *Examiner.com.*

Al-Shaqi, R., Mourshed, M., & Rezgui, Y. (2016). Progress in ambient assisted systems for independent living by the elderly. *Springerplus, 5,* 624.

Althof, S. E., & Needle, R. B. (2017). Treating low sexual desire in men. In Z. D. Peterson, *The Wiley-Blackwell handbook of sex therapy* (Chap. 3, pp. 32–39). Hoboken, NJ: Wiley-Blackwell.

Althof, S. E. (2007). Treatment of rapid ejaculation: Psychotherapy, pharmacotherapy, and combined therapy. In S. R. Leiblum, *Principles and practice of sex therapy* (4th ed., pp. 212–240). New York: Guilford Press.

Altinay, M., Karne, H., & Anand, A. (2018). Lithium monotherapy associated clinical improvement effects on amygdala-ventromedial prefrontal cortex resting state connectivity in bipolar disorder. *Journal of Affective Disorders, 225,* 4–12.

Altszyler, E., Ribeiro, S., Sigman, M., & Fernández Slezak, D. (2017). The interpretation of dream meaning: Resolving ambiguity using Latent Semantic Analysis in a small corpus of text. *Consciousness and Cognition, 56,* 178–187.

Alvarado, C., & Modesto-Lowe, V. (2017). Improving treatment in minority children with attention deficit/hyperactivity disorder. *Clinical Pediatrics, 56*, 171–176.

Alzheimer's Association. (2017). *2017 Alzheimer's disease facts and figures*. Chicago, IL: Alzheimer's Association.

Alzheimer's Association. (2018). *2018 Alzheimer's disease facts and figures*. Chicago, IL: Alzheimer's Association.

AMA (American Medical Association). (2015). *AMA calls for ban on DTC ads of prescription drugs and medical devices*. Washington, DC: Author

Amad, A., Ramoz, N., Thomas, P., Jardri, R., & Gorwood, P. (2014). Genetics of borderline personality disorder: Systematic review and proposal of an integrative model. *Neuroscience and Biobehavioral Reviews, 40*, 6–19.

Amadeo, K. (2017, July 11). *Deinstitutionalization: How does it affect you today?* Retrieved from https://www.thebalance.com/deinstitutionalization-3306067.

Amirkhan, J. H., Urizar, G. G., & Clark, S. (2015). Criterion validation of a stress measure: The Stress Overload Scale. *Psychological Assessment, 27*(3), 985–996.

Amore, M., Innamorati, M., Vittorio, C. D., Weinberg, I., Turecki, G., Sher, L., . . . Pompili, M. (2014). Suicide attempts in major depressed patients with personality disorder. *Suicide and Life-Threatening Behavior, 44*(2), 155–166.

Amsel, T. T. (2017). *Practicing polygraph: Best practice guide*. CreateSpace.

an der Heiden, W., & Häfner, H. (2011). Course and outcomes. In D. R. Weinberg & P. Harrison (Eds.), *Schizophrenia* (pp. 104–141). Hoboken, NJ: Wiley-Blackwell.

ANAD (National Association of Anorexia Nervosa and Associated Disorders). (2018). *Eating disorder types and symptoms*. Chicago, IL: ANAD. Retrieved from http://www.anad.org/education-and-awareness.

ANAD (National Association of Anorexia Nervosa and Associated Disorders). (2014). Binge eating disorder: The "new" eating disorder: Binge eating disorder (BED). Retrieved from http://www.anad.org/get-information/get-informationbinge-eating.

Anderson, A. P. A., Feldman, M. D., & Bryce, J. (2018). Munchausen by proxy: A qualitative investigation into online perceptions of medical child abuse. *Journal of Forensic Science, 63*(3), 771–775.

Anderson, G. (2018). Linking the biological underpinnings of depression: Role of mitochondria interactions with melatonin, inflammation, sirtuins, tryptophan catabolites, DNA repair and oxidative and nitrosative stress, with consequences for classification and cognition. *Progress in Neuro-Psychopharmacology and Biological Psychiatry, 80*(Pt C), 255–266.

Anderson, J. L., Sellbom, M., & Shealy, R. C. (2017). Clinician perspectives of antisocial and borderline personality disorders using DSM-5 Section III dimensional personality traits. *Journal of Personality Disorders, 31*, 1–15.

Anderson, J. L., Wood, M. E., Tarescavage, A. M., Burchett, D., & Glassmire, D. M. (2018). The role of dimensional personality psychopathology in a forensic inpatient psychiatric setting. *Journal of Personality Disorders*. [Manuscript in press]

Anderson, J., Snider, S., Sellbom, M., Krueger, R., & Hopwood, C. (2014). A comparison of the DSM-5 Section II and Section III personality disorder structures. *Psychiatry Research, 216*(3), 363–372.

Andrade, C. (2016). Antipsychotic drugs in schizophrenia: Relative effects in patients with and without treatment resistance. *Journal of Clinical Psychiatry, 77*(12), e1656–e1660.

Andrews, B., & Brewin, C.R. (2017). False memories and free speech: Is scientific debate being suppressed? *Applied Cognitive Psychology, 31*(1), 45–49.

Andrews, V. (1998, December 14). Abducted by aliens? Or just a little schizoid? *HealthScout*.

Anestis, M. D., & Houtsma, C. (2018). The association between gun ownership and statewide overall suicide rates. *Suicide and Life-Threatening Behavior*. [Manuscript in press]

Angier, N. (2010, April 5). Even among animals: Leaders, followers and schmoozers. *New York Times*.

Anheyer, D., Haller, H., Barth, J., Lauche, R., Dobos, G., & Cramer, H. (2017, April 25). Mindfulness-based stress reduction for treating low back pain: A systematic review and meta-analysis. *Annals of Internal Medicine*, 1–9. [Epub ahead of print]

Anonymous. (1996). First person account: Social, economic, and medical effects of schizophrenia. *Schizophrenia Bulletin, 22*(1), 183.

Anonymous. (2006). On madness: A personal account of rapid cycling bipolar disorder. *British Journal of General Practice, 56*(530), 726–728.

Anson, P. (2017, February 9). Sex, poverty and education linked to chronic pain. *Pain News Network*. Retrieved from https://www.painnewsnetwork.org.

Antal, H., Hossain, M. J., Hassink, S., Henry, S., Fuzzell, L., Taylor, A., & Wysocki, T. (2015). Audio-video recording of health care encounters for pediatric chronic conditions: Observational reactivity and its correlates. *Journal of Pediatric Psychology, 40*(1), 144–153.

Antfolk, J. (2017, January 25). Age limits. *Evolutionary Psychology, 15*(1).

Antony, M. M. (2019). Behavior therapy. In D. Wedding & R. J. Corsini (Eds.), *Current psychotherapies* (11th ed., Ch. 6). Independence, KY: Cengage Publications.

Anupama, M., Gangadhar, K. H., Shetty, V. B., & Dip, P. B. (2016). Transvestism as a symptom: A case series. *Indian Journal of Psychological Medicine, 38*(1), 78–80.

APA (American Psychiatric Association). (2000). *DSM-IV text revision*. Washington, DC: Author.

APA (American Psychiatric Association). (2013). *Diagnostic and statistical manual of mental disorders* (5th ed.). Washington, DC: Author.

APA (American Psychiatric Association). (2013). *The people behind DSM-5*. Washington, DC: Author.

APA (American Psychiatric Association). (2013, May 13). *DSM-5 field trials*. Washington, DC: Author.

APA (American Psychiatric Association). (2017). *DSM history*. Arlington, VA: APA.

APA (American Psychological Association). (2002). *Ethical principles of psychologists and code of conduct*. Washington, DC: Author.

APA (American Psychological Association). (2010). *Ethical principles of psychologists and code of conduct*. Washington, DC: Author.

APA (American Psychological Association). (2014). *Ethical principles of psychologists and code of conduct*. Washington, DC: Author.

APA (American Psychological Association). (2014). *Mental and behavioral health and older Americans*. Washington, DC: American Psychiatric Publishing, Inc. Retrieved from http://www.apa.org/about/gr/issues/aging/mental-health.aspx.

APA (American Psychological Association). (2014, July/August). How many psychology doctorates are awarded by U.S. institutions? *Monitor, 45*(7), 13.

APA (American Psychological Association). (2015). *2005–13: Demographics of the U.S. psychology workforce*. Washington, DC: American Psychological Association.

APA (American Psychological Association). (2016). *Data on behavioral health in the United States*. Washington, DC: American Psychological Association.

APA (American Psychological Association). (2016, September). *2015 APA survey of psychology health service providers. Times Higher Education*. Retrieved from https://www.timeshighereducation.com.

APA (American Psychological Association). (2017). *Depression*. Washington, DC: Author.

APA (American Psychological Association). (2017). *Ethical principles of psychologists and code of conduct*. Washington, DC: Author.

APA (American Psychological Association). (2017). *Ethnic and racial minorities & socioeconomic status*. Washington, DC: Author.

APA (American Psychological Association). (2017). *Mental and behavioral health and older Americans*. Washington, DC: APA.

APA (American Psychological Association). (2017, April 5). *Idaho becomes fifth state to allow psychologists to prescribe medications*. Washington, DC: Author.

APA (American Psychological Association). (2017, August 17). *APA reaction to settlement of torture case against psychologists Mitchell, Jessen*. Washington, DC: APA.

APA (American Psychological Association). (2017, January 1). *Introduction and applicability* (Amendment). Washington, DC: Author.

APA (American Psychological Association). (2017, January 30). *School bullying linked to lower academic achievement, research finds*. Retrieved from http://www.apa.org/news/press/releases.

APA (American Psychological Association). (2017, November 1). *Stress in America: State of our nation*. Washington, DC: Author.

APA (American Psychological Association). (2018). *Coping with stress at work*. Washington, DC: APA.

APA (American Psychological Association). (2018). *Growing mental and behavioral health concerns facing older Americans*. Washington, DC: APA.

APA (American Psychological Association). (2018). *Higher stress among minority and low-income populations can lead to health disparities, says report*. Washington, DC: Author.

APA (American Psychological Association). (2018, June 4). *Prescriptive authority*.

Washington, DC: APA. Retrieved from http://www.apapracticecentral.org/advocacy.

APA (American Psychological Association). (2015, February 4). Stress in America: Paying with our health. Washington, DC: Author.

Apter, A., & Wasserman, D. (2007). Suicide in psychiatric disorders during adolescence. In R. Tatarelli, M. Pompili, & P. Girardi (Eds.), *Suicide in psychiatric disorders*. New York: Nova Science Publishers.

Archer, D. (2013). Reading between the (head)lines: Smartphone addiction. *Psychology Today*. Retrieved from https://www.psychologytoday.com/us/blog/reading-between-the-headlines/201307/smartphone-addiction.

Arfanakis, K., Wilson, R. S., Barth, C. M., Capuano, A. W., Vasireddi, A., Zhang, S., . . . Bennett, D. A. (2016). Cognitive activity, cognitive function, and brain diffusion characteristics in old age. *Brain Imaging and Behavior, 10*(2), 455–463.

Arie, S. (2016, September 21). Beyond Bedlam. *BMJ*, 354:i5115.

Arieti, S. (1974). *Interpretation of schizophrenia*. New York: Basic Books.

Arieti, S., & Bemporad, J. R. (1978). *Severe and mild depression: The psychotherapeutic approach*. New York: Basic Books.

Aring, C. D. (1974). The Gheel experience: Eternal spirit of the chainless mind! *Journal of the American Medical Association, 230*(7), 998–1001.

Aring, C. D. (1975). Gheel: The town that cares. *Family Health, 7*(4), 54–55, 58, 60.

Arnold, T. C., & Ryan, M. L. (2017, November 6). Acute amphetamine and synthetic cathinone ("bath salt") intoxication. *UpToDate*. Retrieved from http://www.uptodate.com.

Aronson, M. D. (2017, June 22). Psychosocial treatment of alcohol use disorder. *UpToDate*. Retrieved from http://www.uptodate.com.

Arosio, B., Ostan, R., Mari, D., Damanti, S., Ronchetti, F., Arcudi, S., . . . Monti, D. (2017). Cognitive status in the oldest old and centenarians: A condition crucial for quality of life methodologically difficult to assess. *Mechanisms of Ageing and Development, 165*(Part B), 185–194.

Arseneault, L. (2017). The long-term impact of bullying victimization on mental health. *World Psychiatry, 16*, 27–28.

ASA (American Sleep Association). (2017). Sleep and sleep disorder statistics. *Sleep Association*. Retrieved from https://www.sleepassociation.org/sleep/sleep-statistics.

Asarnow, J. R., Hughes, J. L., Babeva, K., & Sugar, C. A. (2017). Cognitive-behavioral family treatment for suicide attempt prevention: A randomized controlled trial. *Journal of the American Academy of Child and Adolescent Psychiatry, 56*(6), 506–514.

ASCA (American School Counselor Association). (2016). *Student-to-school-counselor ratio 2013–2014*. Alexandria, VA: ASCA.

ASCA (American School Counselor Association). (2017). *Student-to-school-counselor ratio*. Alexandria, VA: ASCA.

Ascoli, M., Lee, T., Warfa, N., Mairura, J., Persaud, A., & Bhui, K. (2017, March 31). Race, culture, ethnicity and personality disorder: Group Careif position paper. *Psycheblog*. Retrieved from http://psycheblog.uk.

Ash, R. (2001). *The top 10 of everything 2002* (American ed.). New York: DK Publishing.

Ashford, M. T., Olander, E. K., Rowe, H., Fisher, J. R. W., & Ayers, S. (2017). Internet-based interventions for postpartum anxiety: Exploring health visitors' views. *Journal of Reproductive and Infant Psychology, 35*(3), 298–308.

Ashraf, N., & Thevasagayam, M. S. (2014). Munchausen syndrome by proxy presenting as hearing loss., *Journal of Laryngology and Otology, 128*(6), 540–542.

Ashton, K., & Sullivan, A. (2018, February 15). Ethics and confidentiality for psychologists in academic health centers. *Journal of Clinical Psychology in Medical Settings*. [Epub ahead of print]

Asimov, I. (1997). *Isaac Asimov's book of facts*. New York: Random House (Wings Books).

ASPS (American Society of Plastic Surgeons). (2017). *2016 plastic surgery statistics*. Retrieved from https://www.plasticsurgery.org/news.

ASPS (American Society of Plastic Surgeons). (2017, May 22). *Gender confirmation surgeries rise 20% in first ever report*. Retrieved from https://www.plasticsurgery.org/news/press-releases.

Assari, S. (2017). Social determinants of depression: The intersections of race, gender, and socioeconomic status. *Brain Sciences, 7*(12), 156.

Asselmann, E., Stender, J., Grabe, H. J., König, J., Schmidt, C. O., Hamm, A. O., & Pané-Farré, C. A. (2018). Assessing the interplay of childhood adversities with more recent stressful life events and conditions in predicting panic pathology among adults from the general population. *Journal of Affective Disorders, 225*, 715–722.

Augustyn, M. (2017, March 7). Autism spectrum disorder: Terminology, epidemiology, and pathogenesis. *UpToDate*. Retrieved from http://www.uptodate.com.

Augustyn, M. (2017, March 8). Autism spectrum disorder: Clinical features. *UpToDate*. Retrieved from http://www.uptodate.com.

Augustyn, M. (2018, January 4). Autism spectrum disorder: Clinical features. *UpToDate*. Retrieved from http://www.uptodate.com.

Augustyn, M. (2018, May 8). Autism spectrum disorder: Terminology, epidemiology, and pathogenesis. *UpToDate*. Retrieved from http://www.uptodate.com.

Austen, I. (2017, April 13). Trudeau unveils bill legalizing recreational marijuana in Canada. *New York Times*.

Austin, J. (2015). More than half of Britons claim to have had contact with ghosts. *The Independent*. Retrieved from http://www.theindependentbd.com.

Autism Speaks. (2018). *Facts about autism*. New York: Autism Speaks.

Autism Speaks. (2018). *Increased risk of autism in siblings news coverage*. New York: Autism Speaks.

Autism Speaks. (2018). *What is autism?* New York: Autism Speaks.

Avenevoli, S., Swendsen, J., He, J. P., Burstein, M., & Merikangas, K. R. (2015). Major depression in the National Comorbidity Survey-Adolescent Supplement: Prevalence, correlates, and treatment. *Journal of the American Academy of Child and Adolescent Psychiatry, 54*, 37–44.

Avery-Clark, C., & Weiner, L. (2017). A traditional Masters and Johnson behavioral approach to sex therapy. In Z. D. Peterson, *The Wiley-Blackwell handbook of sex therapy* (Chap. 11, pp. 165–189). Hoboken, NJ: Wiley-Blackwell.

Avraham, Y., Hants, Y., Vorobeiv, L., Staum, M., Abu Ahmad, W., Mankuta, D., . . . Arbel-Alon, S. (2017). Brain neurotransmitters in an animal model with postpartum depressive-like behavior. *Behavioural Brain Research, 326*, 307–321.

Ayd, F. J., Jr. (1956). A clinical evaluation of Frenquel. *Journal of Nervous and Mental Disease, 124*, 507–509.

Ayhan, G., Arnal, R., Basurko, C., About, V., Pastre, A., Pinganaud, E., . . . Nacher, M. (2017). Suicide risk among prisoners in French Guiana: Prevalence and predictive factors. *BMC Psychiatry, 17*(1), 156.

Ayllon, T. (1963). Intensive treatment of psychotic behavior by stimulus satiation and food reinforcement. *Behavioral Research and Therapy, 1*, 53–62.

Ayllon, T., & Michael, J. (1959). The psychiatric nurse as a behavioural engineer. *Journal of Experimental Analytical Behavior, 2*, 323–334.

Ayoub, C. C. (2006). Munchausen by proxy. In T. G. Plante (Ed.), *Mental disorders of the new millenium: Biology and function* (Vol. 3, pp. 173–193). Westport, CT: Praeger Publishers/Greenwood Publishing.

Ayoub, C. C. (2010). Munchausen by proxy. In J. M. Brown & E. A. Campbell (Eds.), *The Cambridge handbook of forensic psychology* (pp. 690–699). New York: Cambridge University Press.

Azevedo, J. C., Pais-Ribeiro, J. L., Coelho, R., & Figueiredo-Braga, M. (2018). Validation of the Portuguese version of impulsive-premeditated aggression scale in an inmate population. *Frontiers in Psychiatry, 9*, 10.

BAAM (British Association of Anger Management). (2016). Mental health organization: Boiling point report 2008. *BAAM*. Retrieved from https://www.angermanage.co.uk/anger-statistics.

BAAM (British Association of Anger Management). (2017). Mental health organization: Boiling point report 2008. *BAAM*. Retrieved from https://www.angermanage.co.uk/anger-statistics.

Bachhuber, M. A., Hennessy, S., Cunningham, C. O., & Starrels, J. L. (2016). Increasing benzodiazepine prescriptions and overdose mortality in the United States, 1996–2013. *American Journal of Public Health, 106*, 686–688.

Bachmann, C. J., Wijilaars, L. P., Kalverdijk, L. J., Burcu, M., Glaeske, G., Schuiling-Beninga, C. C. M., Hoffmann, F., Aagaard, L., & Zito, J. M. (2017). Trends in ADHD medication use in children and adolescents in five western countries, 2005–2012. *European Neuropsychopharmacology, 27*, 484–493.

Bademli, K., & Duman, Z. C. (2016). Emotions, ideas and experiences of caregivers of patients with schizophrenia about "family to family support program." *Archives of Psychiatric Nursing, 30*(3), 329–333.

Badr, L. K. (2018). Is the effect of postpartum depression on mother-infant bonding universal? *Infant Behavior and Development, 51,* 15–23.

Bagayogo, I. P., Interian, A., & Escobar, J. I. (2013). Transcultural aspects of somatic symptoms in the context of depressive disorders. *Advances in Psychosomatic Medicine, 33,* 64–74.

Bagby, E. (1922). The etiology of phobias. *Journal of Abnormal Psychology, 17,* 16–18.

Bagot, R. C., Cates, H. M., Purushothaman, I., Lorsch, Z. S., Walker, D. M., Wang, J., . . . Nestler, E. J. (2016). Circuit-wide transcriptional profiling reveals brain region-specific gene networks regulating depression susceptibility. *Neuron, 90*(5), 969–983.

Bailey, L. (2017, February 21). Psychologists refute report on collusion with Feds. *Courthouse News.* Retrieved from https://www.courthousenews.com.

Bakalar, N. (2013, July 31). Moon phases tied to sleep cycles. *New York Times.*

Bakker, M. J., Greven, C. U., Buitelaar, J. K., & Glennon, J. C. (2017). Practitioner review: Psychological treatments for children and adolescents with conduct disorder problems: A systematic review and meta-analysis. *Journal of Child Psychology and Psychiatry, 58*(1), 4–18.

Balassone, M., (2011). Jails, prisons increasingly taking care of mentally ill. *Washington Post, 134*(49).

Baldor, R. (2018, January 16). Primary care of the adult with intellectual and developmental disabilities. *UpToDate.* Retrieved from http://www.uptodate.com.

Baldwin, D. (2018, April 3). Generalized anxiety disorder in adults: Epidemiology, pathogenesis, clinical manifestations, course, assessment, and diagnosis. *UpToDate.* Retrieved from http://www.uptodate.com.

Baldwin, D. S., Gordon, R., Abelli, M., & Pini, S. (2016). The separation of adult separation anxiety disorder. *CNS Spectrums, 21*(4), 289–294.

Bales, D. L., Timman, R., Andrea, H., Busschbach, J. V., Verheul, R., & Kamphuis, J. H. (2014). Effectiveness of day hospital mentalization-based treatment for patients with severe borderline personality disorder: A matched control study. *Clinical Psychology and Psychotherapy.* [Advance online publication]

Balia, C., Carucci, S., Coghill, D., & Zuddas, A. (2018). The pharmacological treatment of aggression in children and adolescents with conduct disorder. Do callous-unemotional traits modulate the efficacy of medication? *Neuroscience & Biobehavioral Reviews, 91,* 218–238.

Balmer, A. (2018). *Lie detection and the law: Torture, technology and truth (law, science and society).* New York: Routledge.

Bancroft, J., Loftus, J., & Long, J. S. (2003). Distress about sex: A national survey of women in heterosexual relationships. *Archives of Sexual Behavior, 32*(3), 193–208.

Bandelow, B., & Michaelis, S. (2015). Epidemiology of anxiety disorders in the 21st century. *Dialogues in Clinical Neuroscience, 17,* 327–335.

Bandura, A. (1971). Psychotherapy based upon modeling principles. In A. E. Bergin & S. L. Garfield (Eds.), *Handbook of psychotherapy and behavior change.* New York: Wiley.

Bandura, A. (1977). Self-efficacy: Toward a unifying theory of behavioral change. *Psychological Review, 84*(2), 191–215.

Bandura, A. (2011). But what about that gigantic elephant in the room? In R. M. Arkin (Ed.), *Most underappreciated: 50 prominent social psychologists describe their most unloved work* (pp. 51–59). New York: Oxford University Press.

Bandura, A., & Rosenthal, T. (1966). Vicarious classical conditioning as a function of arousal level. *Journal of Personality and Social Psychology, 3,* 54–62.

Bandura, A., Adams, N. E., & Beyer, J. (1977). Cognitive processes mediating behavioral change. *Journal of Personality and Social Psychology, 35*(3), 125–139.

Barbieri, R. I. (2017, October 3). Differential diagnosis of sexual pain in women. *UpToDate.* Retrieved from http://www.uptodate.com.

Bareggi, S. R., Bianchi, L., Cavallaro, R., Gervasoni, M., Siliprandi, F., & Bellodi, L. (2004). Citalopram concentrations and response in obsessive-compulsive disorder: Preliminary results. *CNS Drugs, 18*(5), 329–335.

Bari, A. A., Mikell, C. B., Abosch, A., Ben-Haim, S., Buchanan, R. J., Burton, A. W., . . . Sheth, S. A. (2018, January 25). Charting the road forward in psychiatric neurosurgery: Proceedings of the 2016 American Society for Stereotactic and Functional Neurosurgery workshop on neuromodulation for psychiatric disorders. *Journal of Neurology, Neurosurgery & Psychiatry.* [Epub ahead of print]

Barker, E. D. (2018). Epigenetics, early adversity and child and adolescent mental health. *Psychopathology, 51*(2), 71–75.

Barlow, M. R. (2011). Memory for complex emotional material in dissociative identity disorder. *Journal of Trauma & Dissociation, 12*(1), 53–66.

Barnes, A. (2004). Race, schizophrenia, and admission to state psychiatric hospitals. *Administration and Policy in Mental Health, 31*(3), 241–252.

Barnes, M. (2017, March 14). Mom thought daughter's Facebook suicide was fake, posts cruel comment. *Rolling Out.* Retrieved from http://rollingout.com.

Barnes, N., Hattan, P., Black, D. S., & Schuman-Olivier, Z. (2016). An examination of mindfulness-based programs in US medical schools. *Biomind.* Retrieved from http://www.biomind.usc.edu.

Barnes, S. M., Bahraini, N. H., Forster, J. E., Stearns-Yoder, K. A., Hostetter, T. A. Smith, G., . . . Nock, M. K. (2017). Moving beyond self-report: Implicit associations about death/life prospectively predict suicidal behavior among veterans. *Suicide and Life-Threatening Behavior, 47*(1), 67–77.

Barnett, J. E. (2018). Integrating spirituality and religion into psychotherapy practice. *Society for the Advancement of Psychotherapy, Division 29 of the American Psychological Association.* (Web article.)

Barrera, T. L., Wilson, K. P., & Norton, P. J. (2010). The experience of panic symptoms across racial groups in a student sample. *Journal of Anxiety Disorders, 24*(8), 873–878.

Barsky, A. J. (2016). Assessing the new DSM-5 diagnosis of somatic symptom disorder. *Psychosomatic Medicine, 78*(1), 2–4.

Bartholomew, R. (2014). *Mass hysteria in schools: Worldwide since 1566.* Jefferson, NC: McFarland.

Bartlett, S. C. (2017). A path towards abuse—the decline of moral treatment in the Utica Lunatic Asylum. *Global Tides, 11*(1).

Bartol, C. R., & Bartol, A. M. (2015). *Psychology and law: Research and practice.* Los Angeles: Sage Publications.

Bartoli, F., Pompili, M., Lillia, N., Crocamo, C., Salemi, G., Clerici, M., Carrà, G. (2017). Rates and correlates of suicidal ideation among stroke survivors: A meta-analysis. *Journal of Neurology, Neurosurgery & Psychiatry, 88,* 498–504.

Bartz, J., Kaplan, A., & Hollander, E. (2007). Obsessive-compulsive personality disorder. In W. O'Donohue, K. A. Fowler, S. O. Lilienfeld (Eds.). *Personality disorders: Toward the DSM-V.* Los Angeles: Sage Publications.

Basile, J., & Bloch, M. J. (2018, January 18). Overview of hypertension in adults. *UpToDate.* Retrieved from http://www.uptodate.com.

Basoglu, M., Jaranson, J. M., Mollica, R., & Kastrup, M. (2001). Torture and mental health: A research overview. In E. Gerrity, T. M. Keane, & F. Tuma (Eds.), *The mental health consequences of torture* (pp. 35–62). New York: Kluwer Academic/Plenum Publishers.

Bass, C., & Glaser, D. (2014). Early recognition and management of fabricated or induced illness in children. *Lancet, 383*(9926), 1412–1421.

Bassir Nia, A., Eveleth, M. C., Gabbay, J. M., Hassan, Y. J., Zhang, B., & Perez-Rodriguez, M. M. (2018). Past, present, and future of genetic research in borderline personality disorder. *Current Opinion in Psychology, 21,* 60–68.

Basso, J. C., McHale, A., Ende, V., Oberlin, D. J., & Suzuki, W. A. (2019). Brief, daily meditation enhances attention, memory, mood, and emotional regulation in non-experienced meditators. *Behavioural Brain Research, 356,* 208–220.

Basson, R. (2007). Sexual desire/arousal disorders in women. In S. R. Leiblum (Ed.), *Principles and practice of sex therapy* (4th ed., pp. 25–53). New York: Guilford Press.

Bateman, A. W., Fonagy, P., & Campbell, C. (2018). Mentalization-based treatment. In W. J. Livesley & R. Larstone (Eds.), *Handbook of personality disorders: Theory, research, and treatment* (2nd ed., Ch. 30). New York: Guilford Press.

Bateman, A. W. (2011). Borderline personality disorder. In J. C. Norcross, G. R. VandenBos, & D. K. Freedheim (Eds.), *History of psychotherapy: Continuity and change* (2nd ed., pp. 588–600). Washington, DC: American Psychological Association.

Baten, V., Busch, H. J., Busche, C., Schmid, B., Heupel-Reuter, M., Perlov, E., . . . Klöppel, S. (2018, May 8). Validation of the brief confusion assessment method for screening delirium in elderly medical patients in a German emergency department. *Academic Emergency Medicine.* [Epub ahead of print]

Bates, C. K. (2017, April 6). Evaluation and management of adult and adolescent sexual assault victims. *UpToDate.* Retrieved from http://www.uptodate.com.

Bates, G. W., Thompson, J. C., & Flanagan, C. (1999). The effectiveness of individual versus group induction of depressed mood. *Journal of Psychology, 133*(3), 245–252.

Baucom, B. R., Atkins, D. C., Rowe, L. S., Doss, B. D., & Christensen, A. (2015). Prediction of treatment response at 5-year follow-up in a randomized clinical trial of behaviorally based couple therapies. *Journal of Consulting and Clinical Psychology, 83*(1), 103–114.

Baucom, D. H., Fischer, M. S., Worrell, M., Corrie, S., Belus, J. M., Molyva, E., & Boeding, S. E. (2018). Couple-based intervention for depression: An effectiveness study in the National Health Service in England. *Family Process, 57*(2), 275–292.

Baucom, D. H., Epstein, N. B., Kirby, J. S., & LaTaillade, J. J. (2010). Cognitive-behavioral couple therapy. In K. S. Dobson (Ed.), *Handbook of cognitive-behavioral therapies* (3rd ed., pp. 411–444). New York: Guilford Press.

Bauer, C. M., Cabral, H. J., & Killiany, R. J. (2018). Multimodal discrimination between normal aging, mild cognitive impairment and Alzheimer's disease and prediction of cognitive decline. *Diagnostics* (Basel), *8*(1).

Bauer, S. M., Schanda, H., Karakula, H., Olajossy-Hilkesberger, L., Rudaleviciene, P., Okribelashvili, N., . . . Stompe, T. (2011). Culture and the prevalence of hallucinations in schizophrenia. *Comprehensive Psychiatry,* 52(3), 319–325.

Baum, A., Trevino, L. A., & Dougall, A. L. (2011). Stress and the cancers. In R. J. Contrada & A. Baum (Eds.), *The handbook of stress science: Biology, psychology, and health* (pp. 411–423). New York: Springer Publishing.

Baune, B. T., Malhi, G. S., Morris, G., Outhred, T., Hamilton, A., Das, P., . . . Singh, A. B. (2018). Cognition in depression: Can we THINC-it better? *Journal of Affective Disorders, 225,* 559–562.

Baykal, S., Batar, B., Nalbantoglu, A., Albayrak, Y., Hanci, H., Potas, N., . . . Beyanzyüz, M. (2019). Altered methyltetrahydrofolate reductase gene polymorphism in mothers of children with attention deficit and hyperactivity disorder. *Progress in Neuro-Psychopharmacology & Biological Psychiatry, 88,* 215–221.

Bearse, J. L., McMinn, M. R., Seegobin, W., & Free, K. (2014). Healing thyself: What barriers do psychologists face when considering personal psychotherapy and how can they be overcome? *APA, 45*(49), 62.

Beasley, L. O., Silovsky, J. F., Owora, A., Burris, L., Hecht, D., DeMoraes-Huffine, P., . . . Tolma, E. (2014). Mixed-methods feasibility study on the cultural adaptation of a child abuse prevention model. *Child Abuse and Neglect.* [Electronic publication]

Beatty Moody, D. L., Waldstein, S. R., Tobin, J. N., Cassells, A., Schwartz, J. C., & Brondolo, E. (2016). Lifetime racial/ethnic discrimination and ambulatory blood pressure: The moderating effect of age. *Health Psychology, 35*(4), 333–342.

Beblo, T., Kater, L., Baetge, S., Driessen, M., & Piefke, M. (2017). Memory performance of patients with major depression in an everyday life situation. *Psychiatry Research, 248,* 28–34.

Bechtel, K., & Bennett, B. L. (2017, March 15). Evaluation of sexual abuse in children and adolescents. *UpToDate.* Retrieved from http://www.uptodate.com.

Beck, A. T. (2016). Cognitive therapy: Nature and relation to behavior therapy (Republished article). *Behavior Therapy, 47*(6), 776–784.

Beck, A. T., & Weishaar, M. E. (2019). Cognitive therapy. In D. Wedding & R. J. Corsini (Eds.), *Current psychotherapies* (11th ed., Ch. 7). Independence, KY: Cengage Publications.

Beck, A. T., Davis, D. D., & Freeman, A. (Eds.). (2015). *Cognitive therapy of personality disorders* (3rd ed.). New York: Guilford Press.

Beck, A. T. (1967). *Depression: Clinical, experimental and theoretical aspects.* New York: Harper & Row.

Beck, A. T. (2002). Cognitive models of depression. In R. L. Leahy & E. T. Dowd (Eds.), *Clinical advances in cognitive psychotherapy: Theory and application* (pp. 29–61). New York: Springer.

Beck, A. T., Rush, A. J., Shaw, B. F., & Emery, G. (1979). *Cognitive therapy of depression.* New York: Guilford Press.

Beck, A. T., Ward, C. H., Mendelson, M., Mock, J. E., & Erbaugh, J. (1962). Reliability of psychiatric diagnosis: 2. A study of consistency of clinical judgments and ratings. *American Journal of Psychiatry, 119,* 351–357.

Becker, C. B., Perez, M., Kilpela, L. S., Diedrichs, P. C., Trujillo, E., & Stice, E. (2017). Engaging stakeholder communities as body image intervention partners: The Body Project as a case example. *Eating Behaviors, 25,* 62–67.

Becker, P. M. (2015). Hypnosis in the management of sleep disorders. *Sleep Medicine Clinics, 10*(1), 85–92.

Becker, W. C., & Starrels, J. L. (2018, January 4). Prescription drug misuse: Epidemiology, prevention, identification, and management. *UpToDate.* Retrieved from http://www.uptodate.com.

Beckman, K., Lindh, A. U., Waern, M., Stromsten, L., Renberg, E. S., Runeson, B., & Dahlin, M. (2019). Impulsive suicide attempts among young people: A prospective multicentre cohort study in Sweden. *Journal of Affective Disorders, 243,* 421–426.

Beelmann, A., Malti, T., Noam, G. G., & Sommer, S. (2018, January 25). Innovation and integrity: Desiderata and future directions for prevention and intervention science. *Prevention Science.* [Epub ahead of print]

Beeney, J. E., Wright, A. G. C., Stepp, S. D., Hallquist, M. N., Lazarus, S. A., Beeney, J. R. S., . . . Pilkonis, P. A. (2017). Disorganized attachment and personality functioning in adults: A latent class analysis. *Personality Disorders, 8*(3), 206–216.

Beidel, D. C., Alfano, C. A., Kofler, M. J., Rao, P. A., Scharfstein, L., & Wong Sarver, N. (2014). The impact of social skills training for social anxiety disorder: A randomized controlled trial. *Journal of Anxiety Disorders, 28*(8), 908–918.

Beier, E. G., & Young, D. M. (1984). *The silent language of psychotherapy: Social reinforcement of the unconscious processes* (2nd ed.). Hawthorne, New York: Aldine.

Bekker, J. (2017, October 6). 28 percent of mass shooting survivors experience PTSD. *Las Vegas Review-Journal.*

Belendiuk, K. A., & Riggs, P. (2014). Treatment of adolescent substance use disorders. *Current Treatment Options in Psychiatry, 1*(2), 175–188.

Beletsky, L., & Davis, C. S. (2017). Today's fentanyl crisis: Prohibition's iron law, revisited. *International Journal of Drug Policy, 46,* 156–159.

Bemporad, J. R. (1992). Psychoanalytically orientated psychotherapy. In E. S. Paykel (Ed.), *Handbook of affective disorders.* New York: Guilford Press.

Ben-Ezra, M., Leshem, E., & Goodwin, R. (2015). In the wake of national trauma: Psychological reactions following the Charlie Hebdo attack. *American Journal of Psychiatry, 172*(8), 795–796.

Ben-Natan, M., Sharon, I., Barbashov, P., Minasyan, Y., Hanukayev, I., Kajdan, D., & Klein-Kremer, A. (2014). Risk factors for child abuse: Quantitative correlational design. *Journal of Pediatric Nursing, 29*(3), 220–227.

Bennett, M. P. (1998). The effect of mirthful laughter on stress and natural killer cell cytotoxicity. *Dissertation Abstracts International: Section B: The Sciences and Engineering, 58*(7–B), 3553.

Bennett, S., & Walkup, J. T. (2018, June 5). Anxiety disorders in children and adolescents: Epidemiology, pathogenesis, clinical manifestations, and course. *UpToDate.* Retrieved from http://www.uptodate.com.

Ben-Shakhar, G., & Bar, M. (2019). *The lying machine: Mysticism and pseudo-science in personality assessment and prediction.* New York: Routledge.

Bergink, V., Bouvy, P. F., Vervoort, J. P., Koorengevel, K. M., Steegers, E. P., & Kushner, S. A. (2012). Prevention of postpartum psychosis and mania in women at high risk. *American Journal of Psychiatry, 169*(6), 609–615.

Bergman, H., Rathbone, J., Agarwal, V., & Soares-Weiser, K. (2018). Antipsychotic reduction and/or cessation and antipsychotics as specific treatments for tardive dyskinesia. *Cochrane Database of Systematic Reviews, 2,* CD000459.

Bergner, R. M., & Bunford, N. (2017). Mental disorder is a disability concept, not a behavioral one. *Philosophy, Psychiatry, & Psychology, 24*(1), 25–40.

Bergner, R. M., & Bunford, N. (2014). *Mental disorder is a disability concept, not a behavioral one: An empirical investigation.* Athens, OH: Ohio University.

Berk, S. N., & Efran, J. S. (1983). Some recent developments in the treatment of neurosis. In C. E. Walker (Ed.), *The handbook of clinical psychology: Theory, research, and practice* (Vol. 2). Homewood, IL: Dow Jones-Irwin.

Berman, A. L. (2018). Risk factors proximate to suicide and suicide risk assessment in the context of denied suicide ideation. *Suicide and Life-Threatening Behavior.* [Manuscript in press]

Berman, A. L. (1986). Helping suicidal adolescents: Needs and responses. In C. A. Corr & J. N. McNeil (Eds.), *Adolescence and death.* New York: Springer.

Berman, E. (2017). An inclusive psychoanalyst: Sidney Blatt's contribution in perspective. *Journal of the American Psychoanalytic Association, 65*(3), 525–533.

Bernecker, S. L., Coyne, A. E., Constantino, M. J., & Ravitz, P. (2017). For whom does interpersonal psychotherapy work?

A systematic review. *Clinical Psychology Review, 56*, 82–93.

Bernier, R., & Dawson, G. (2016). Autism spectrum disorders. In D. Cicchetti (Ed.), *Developmental psychopathology, Vol. 3: Maladaptation and psychopathology* (3rd ed.). New York: Wiley.

Bernstein, L. (2017, February 14). Poll: Mainstream media continues to lose the public's trust. *WJLA*.

Berry, M. D., & Berry, P. D. (2013). Contemporary treatment of sexual dysfunction: Reexamining the biopsychosocial model. *Journal of Sexual Medicine, 10*, 2627–2643.

Bertozzi, S., Londero, A. P., Fruscalzo, A., Driul, L., & Marchesoni, D. (2010). Prevalence and risk factors for dyspareunia and unsatisfying sexual relationships in a cohort of primiparous and secondiparous women after 12 months postpartum. *International Journal of Sexual Health, 22*(1), 47–53.

Best, D. (2017). Why the mechanisms of 12-step behaviour change should matter to clinicians. *Addiction, 112*(6), 938–939.

Beutler, L. E., Williams, R. E., Wakefield, P. J., & Entwistle, S. R. (1995). Bridging scientist and practitioner perspectives in clinical psychology. *American Psychologist, 50*(12), 984–994.

Bever, L. (2017, June 6). The disturbing trend of live-streamed suicides. *Chicago Tribune*.

BGS (British Geriatrics Society). (2016, February). Acute confusion/delirium. *BGS*. Retrieved from bgs.org.uk.

Bhatia, T., Gettig, E. A., Gottesman, I. I., Berliner, J., Mishra, N. N., Nimgaonkar, V. L., & Deshpande, S. N. (2016). Stratifying empiric risk of schizophrenia among first degree relatives using multiple predictors in two independent Indian samples. *Asian Journal of Psychiatry, 24*, 79–84.

Bhattacharya, R., Cross, S., & Bhugra, D. (Eds). (2010). *Clinical topics in cultural psychiatry*. London: Royal College of Psychiatrists.

Bigdeli, T. B., Maher, B. S., Zhao, Z., Sun, J., Medeiros, H., Akula, N., . . . Fanous, A. H. (2013). Association study of 83 candidate genes for bipolar disorder in chromosome 6q selected using an evidence-based prioritization algorithm. *American Journal of Medical Genetics. Part B, Neuropsychiatric Genetics, 162B*(8), 898–906.

Billard, T. J. (2018). Attitudes toward transgender men and women: Development and validation of a new measure. *Frontiers in Psychology, 9*, 387.

Bills, C. B., & Li, G. (2005). Correlating homicide and suicide. *International Journal of Epidemiology, 34*(4), 837–845.

Bina, R., & Glasser, S. (2017, December 27). Factors associated with attitudes toward seeking mental health treatment postpartum. *Women's Health*. [Epub ahead of print]

Binet, A., & Simon, T. (1916). *The development of intelligence in children (The Binet-Simon Scale)*. Baltimore: Williams & Wilkins.

Binswanger, I., & Elmore, J. G. (2018, April 23). Clinical care of incarcerated adults. *UpToDate*. Retrieved from http://www.uptodate.com.

BJS (Bureau of Justice Statistics). (2013, March 7). *Female victims of sexual violence, 1994–2010* (NCJ 240655). Retrieved from http://www.bjs.gov/index.cfm?tv=pbdetail&iid=4594.

BJS (Bureau of Justice Statistics). (2016). *Data collection: National Crime Victimization Survey (NCVS)*. Washington, DC: Author.

BJS (Bureau of Justice Statistics). (2016, April). *Assessing inmate cause of death: Deaths in Custody Reporting Program and National Death Index* (NCJ 249568). Retrieved from http://www.bjs.gov.

BJS (Bureau of Justice Statistics). (2016, October). *Criminal victimization, 2015* (NCJ 250180). Washington, DC: BJS.

BJS (Bureau of Justice Statistics). (2017). *Victims and offenders*. Washington, DC: Author.

BJS (Bureau of Justice Statistics). (2017, December 7). *Criminal victimization, 2016*. Retrieved from https://www.bjs.gov/index.

BJS (Bureau of Justice Statistics). (2017, December). *Criminal victimization, 2016*. Washington, DC: BJS.

BJS (Bureau of Justice Statistics). (2018, May). *Mortality in correctional institutes*. Retrieved from https://www.bjs.gov.

Black Youth Project. (2011). The attitudes and behavior of young Black Americans: Research summary. Retrieved from Black Youth Project website: www.blackyouthproject.com/survey/findings.

Black Youth Project. (2016). *About us*. Chicago, IL: Author.

Black Youth Project. (2018). *Discrimination archives*. Chicago, IL: Author.

Black, D. W. (2017, April 20). Treatment of antisocial personality disorder. *UpToDate*. Retrieved from http://www.uptodate.com.

Black, D. W. (2017, September 15). Antisocial personality disorder: Epidemiology, clinical manifestations, course and diagnosis. *UpToDate*. Retrieved from http://www.uptodate.com.

Black, M. C., Basile, K. C., Breiding, M. J., Smith, S. G., Walters, M. L., Merrick, M. T., . . . Stevens, M. R. (2011) *The National Intimate Partner and Sexual Violence Survey (NISVS): 2010 summary report*. Atlanta, GA: National Center for Injury Prevention and Control, CDC.

Blagov, P. S., Fowler K. A., & Lilienfeld, S. O. (2007). Histrionic personality disorder. In W. O'Donohue, K. A. Fowler, & S. O. Lilienfeld (Eds.). *Personality disorders: Toward the DSM-V*. Los Angeles: Sage Publications.

Blair, J., Mitchell, D., & Blair, K. (2005). *The psychopath: Emotion and the brain*. Malden, MA: Blackwell Publishing.

Blanchard, J. J., Bradshaw, K. R., Garcia, C. P., Nasrallah, H. A., Harvey, P. D., Casey, D., . . . O'Gorman, C. (2017). Examining the reliability and validity of the Clinical Assessment Interview for Negative Symptoms within the Management of Schizophrenia in Clinical Practice (MOSAIC) multisite national study. *Schizophrenia Research, 185*, 137–143.

Blashfield, R. K., Keele, J. W., Flanagan, E. H., & Miles, S. R. (2014). The cycle of classification: DSM-I through DSM-5. *Annual Review of Clinical Psychology, 10*, 25–51.

Blass, R.B. (2015). Conceptualizing splitting: On the different meanings of splitting and their implications for the understanding of the person and the analytic process. *International Journal of Psychoanalysis, 96*(1), 123–139.

Blaxton, J. M., & Bergeman, C. S. (2017). A process-oriented perspective examining the relationships among daily coping, stress, and affect. *Personality and Individual Differences, 104*, 357–361.

Blazer, D. G. (2018). Advancing our diagnostic tools and treatment options for delirium. *International Psychogeriatrics, 30*(4), 447–449.

Blennow, K., & Zetterberg, H. (2018). The past and the future of Alzheimer's disease fluid biomarkers. *Journal of Alzheimer's Disease, 62*(3), 1125–1140.

Bliss, E. L. (1980). *Multiple personality, allied disorders and hypnosis*. New York: Oxford University Press.

Block, J. (2015). Shortage of psychiatrists only getting worse. *Psychiatry Advisor*. Retrieved from http://www.psychiatryadvisor.com/shortage-of-psychiatrists-only-getting worse/printarticle/437233.

Bloom, B. L. (1984). *Community mental health: A general introduction* (2nd ed.). Monterey, CA: Brooks/Cole.

BLS (Bureau of Labor Statistics). (2015). *Economic News Release. Table A-3. Employment status of the Hispanic or Latino population by sex and age*. Retrieved from http://www.bls.gov/news.release.empsit.t03.htm.

BLS (Bureau of Labor Statistics). (2016). *Occupational employment statistics. Occupational employment and wages, May 2015: 21-1014 Mental health counselors*. Retrieved from https://data.bls.gov/cgi-bin/print.pl/oes/current/oes211014.htm.

BLS (Bureau of Labor Statistics). (2016). *Occupational employment statistics. Occupational employment and wages, May 2015. 29-1066 Psychiatrists*. Retrieved from https://www.bls.gov/oes/current/oes291066.htm.

BLS (Bureau of Labor Statistics). (2016). *Occupational outlook handbook, 2016–17 edition: Psychologists*. Washington, DC: U.S. Department of Labor. Retrieved from https://www.bls.gov/ooh/life-physical-and-social-science/psychologists.htm.

BLS (Bureau of Labor Statistics). (2016). *Occupational outlook handbook, 2016–17 edition: Social workers*. Washington, DC: U.S. Department of Labor. Retrieved from https://www.bls.gov/ooh/community-and-social-service/social-workers.htm.

BLS (Bureau of Labor Statistics). (2017, March 31). *Occupational employment statistics. Occupational employment and wages, May 2016 29-1066 psychiatrists*. Retrieved from https://www.bls.gov/oes/current/oes291066.htm.

BLS (Bureau of Labor Statistics). (2017, October 24). *Occupational outlook handbook. Woodworkers*. Retrieved from https://www.bls.gov/ooh/.

Blum, K., Chen, A. L. C., Thanos, P. K., Febo, M., Demetrovics, Z., Dushaj, K., . . . Badgaiyan, R. D. (2018). Genetic addiction risk score (GARS)™, a predictor of vulnerability to opioid dependence. *Frontiers in Bioscience* (Elite Edition), *10*, 175–196.

Blum, K., Febo, M., & Badgaiyan, R. D. (2016, October 12). Fifty years in the development of a glutaminergic-dopaminergic optimization complex (KB220) to balance brain reward circuitry in reward deficiency syndrome: A pictorial. *Austin Addiction Science, 1*(2).

Blum, K., Simpatico, T., Badgaiyan, R. D., Demetrovics, Z., Fratantonio, J., Agan, C., . . . Gold, M. S. (2015). Coupling neurogenetics (GARS) and a nutrigenomic-based dopaminergic agonist to treat Reward Deficiency Syndrome (RDS): Targeting polymorphic reward genes for carbohydrate addiction algorithms. *Journal of Reward Deficiency Syndrome, 1*(2), 75–80.

Blum, K., Braverman, E. R., Holder, J. M., Lubar, J. F., Monastra, V. J., Miller, D., & Comings, D. E. (2000). Reward deficiency syndrome: A biogenetic model for the diagnosis and treatment of impulsive, addictive, and compulsive behaviors. *Journal of Psychoactive Drugs, 32*(Suppl.), 1–68.

Blum, K., Noble, E. P., Sheridan, P. J., Montgomery, A., Ritchie, T., Jagadeeswaran, P., . . . Cohn, J. B. (1990). Allelic association of human dopamine D2 receptor gene in alcoholism. *Journal of the American Medical Association, 263*(15), 2055–2060.

Bock, C., Bukh, J. D., Vinberg, M., Gether, U., & Kessing, L. V. (2010). The influence of comorbid personality disorder and neuroticism on treatment outcome in first episode depression. *Psychopathology, 43*(3), 197–204.

Bodnar, A., Krzywotulski, M., Lewandowska, A., Chlopocka-Wozniak, M., Bartkowska-Sniatkowska, A., Michalak, M., & Rybakowski, J. K. (2016). Electroconvulsive therapy and cognitive functions in treatment-resistant depression. *17*(2), 159–164.

Boepple, L., & Thompson, J. K. (2016). A content analytic comparison of fitspiration and thinspiration websites. *International Journal of Eating Disorders, 49*(1), 98–101.

Boeve, B., McCormick, J., Smith, G., Ferman, T., Rummans, T., Carpenter, T., . . . Petersen, R. (2003). Mild cognitive impairment in the oldest old. *Neurology, 60*(3), 477–480.

Bogdan, R., & Taylor, S. (1976, January). The judged, not the judges: An insider's view of mental retardation. *American Psychologist, 31*(1), 47–52.

Bohnert, K. M., Ilgen, M. A., Louzon, S., McCarthy, J. F., & Katz, I. R. (2017). Substance use disorders and the risk of suicide mortality among men and women in the U.S. Veterans Health Administration. *Addiction, 112,* 1193–1201.

Boissoneault, L. (2017, March 6). How a soap opera virus felled hundreds of students in Portugal. *Smithsonian Magazine.*

Bole, C. B., Pislar, M., Sen, M., Tavcar, R., & Mrhar, A. (2017). Original research paper. Switching antipsychotics: Results of 16-month non-interventional, prospective, observational clinical research of inpatients with schizophrenia spectrum disorders. *Acta Pharmaceutica, 67*(1), 99–112.

Bond, B., Wright, J., & Bacon, A. (2017, August 31). What helps in self-help? A qualitative exploration of interactions within a borderline personality disorder self-help group. *Journal of Mental Health.* [Epub ahead of print]

Bonn, S. (2015, March 9). The history and rise of mass public shootings. *Psychology Today.*

Bonn, S. A. (2017, January 1). Why psychopaths are effective killers: Psychopaths are cold-blooded and calculating. *Psychology Today.*

Bonnet, M. H., & Arand, D. L. (2017, May 11). Treatment of insomnia in adults. *UpToDate.* Retrieved from www.uptodate.com.

Bonnet, M. H., & Arand, D. L. (2018, January 12). Clinical features and diagnosis of insomnia in adults. *UpToDate.* Retrieved from http://www.uptodate.com.

Bonnet, M. H., & Arand, L. D. (2017, November 1). Overview of insomnia in adults. *UpToDate.* Retrieved from http://www.uptodate.com.

Bonnet, S., Lacambre, M., Schandrin, A., Capdevielle, D., & Courtet, P. (2017). Insight and psychiatric dangerousness: A review of the literature. *Encephale, 43*(2), 146–153.

Bonsack, C., Golay, P., Gibellini Manetti, S., Gebel, S., Ferrari, P., Besse, C., . . . Morandi, S. (2016). Linking primary and secondary care after psychiatric hospitalization: Comparison between transitional case management setting and routine care for common mental disorders. *Frontiers in Psychiatry, 7,* 96.

Boos, S. C. (2017, August 7). Physical child abuse: Diagnostic evaluation and management. *UpToDate.* Retrieved from http://www.uptodate.com.

Boos, S. C. (2017, February 15). Physical child abuse: Recognition. *UpToDate.* Retrieved from http://www.uptodate.com.

Borden, K. A. (2017). Contemporary assessment practices. Part 1: General and diversity issues. *Professional Psychology: Research and Practice, 48*(2), 71–72.

Borge, F., Hoffart, A., Sexton, H., Martinsen, E., Gude, T., Hedley, L. M., & Abrahamsen, G. (2010). Pre-treatment predictors and in-treatment factors associated with change in avoidant and dependent personality disorder traits among patients with social phobia. *Clinical Psychology and Psychotherapy, 17*(2), 87–99.

Borkovec, T. D., Alcaine, O. M., & Behar, E. (2004). Avoidance theory of worry and generalized anxiety disorder. In R. G. Heimberg, C. L. Turk, & D. S. Mennin (Eds.), *Generalized anxiety disorder: Advances in research and practice* (pp. 77–108). New York: Guilford Press.

Bornstein, R. F. (2016). Toward a firmer foundation for ICD-11: On the conceptualization and assessment of personality pathology. *Personality and Mental Health, 10*(2), 123–126.

Bornstein, R. F. (2005). Psychodynamic theory and personality disorders. In S. Strack (Ed.), *Handbook of personality and psychopathology* (pp. 164–180). Hoboken, NJ: Wiley.

Bornstein, R. F. (2007). Dependent personality disorder. In W. O'Donohue, K. A. Fowler, S. O. Lilienfeld (Eds.). *Personality disorders: Toward the DSM-V.* Los Angeles: Sage Publications.

Bornstein, R. F. (2007). Might the Rorschach be a projective test after all: Social projection of an undesired trait alters Rorschach oral dependency scores. *Journal of Personality Assessment, 88*(3), 354–367.

Bornstein, R. F. (2012). Illuminating a neglected clinical issue: Societal costs of interpersonal dependency and dependent personality disorder. *Journal of Clinical Psychology, 68*(7), 766–781.

Both, S., Schultz, W. W., & Laan, E. (2017). Treating women's sexual desire and arousal problems. In Z. D. Peterson, *The Wiley-Blackwell handbook of sex therapy* (Chap. 2, pp. 11–31). Hoboken, NJ: Wiley-Blackwell.

Bott, E. (1928). Teaching of psychology in the medical course. *Bulletin of the Association of American Medical Colleges, 3,* 289–304.

Bouchard, S., Dumoulin, S., Robillard, G., Guitard, T., Klinger, E., Forget, H., . . . Roucaut, F. X. (2017). Virtual reality compared with *in vivo* exposure in the treatment of social anxiety disorder: A three-arm randomised controlled trial. *British Journal of Psychiatry, 210*(4), 276–283.

Bouck, E. C., & Park, J. (2016). Inclusion and students with an intellectual disability. In J. P. Bakken & F. E. Obiakor (Eds), *General and special education inclusion in an age of change: Impact on students with disabilities (Advances in special education, Vol. 31).* West Yorkshire, UK: Emerald Publishing Limited.

Boudewyn, M. A. (2017). Understanding working memory and attentional control impairments in schizophrenia. *Biological Psychiatry: Cognitive Neuroscience and Neuroimaging, 2*(3), 212–213.

Bouman, T. K., Mulkens, S., & van der Lei, B. (2017). Cosmetic professionals' awareness of body dysmorphic disorder. *Plastic and Reconstructive Surgery, 139*(2), 336–342.

Bouras, N., & Holt, G. (Eds.). (2010). *Mental health services for adults with intellectual disability: Strategies and solutions. The Maudsley Series.* New York, Psychology Press.

Bourin, M., Malinge, M., & Guitton, B. (1995). Provocative agents in panic disorder. *Therapie 50*(4), 301–306. [French].

Boutros, A., Kang, S. S., & Boutros, N. N. (2018). A cyclical path to recovery: Calling into question the wisdom of incarceration after restoration. *International Journal of Law and Psychiatry, 57,* 100–105.

Bowden, S. C., Saklofske, D. H., & Weiss, L. G. (2011). Invariance of the measurement model underlying the Wechsler Adult Intelligence Scale-IV in the United States and Canada. *Educational and Psychological Measurement, 71*(1), 186–199.

Bower, E. S., Wetherell, J. L., Mon, T., & Lenze, E. J. (2015). Treating anxiety disorders in older adults: Current treatments and future directions. *Harvard Review of Psychiatry, 23*(5), 329–342.

Bower, G. H. (1981). Mood and memory. *American Psychologist, 36*(2), 129–148.

Bowerman, M. (2016, October 12). Survey reveals what Americans fear the most. *USA Today.*

Bowers, A., Owen, R., & Heller, T. (2016). Care coordination experiences of people with disabilities enrolled in Medicaid managed care. *Disability and Rehabilitation.* Retrieved from http://www.tandfonline.com.

Bowers, A., Owen, R., & Heller, T. (2017). Care coordination experiences of people with disabilities enrolled in Medicaid managed care. *Disability and Rehabilitation, 39*(21), 2207–2214.

Bowler, R. M., Adams, S. W., Schwarzer, R., Gocheva, V. V., Roels, H. A., Kim, Y., . . . Lobdell, D. T. (2018). Validity of self-reported concentration and memory problems: Relationship with neuropsychological assessment and depression. *Journal of Clinical and Experimental Neuropsychology,* 1–11.

Bowring, D. L., Totsika, V., Hastings, R. P., Toogood, S., & McMahon, M. (2017).

Prevalence of psychotropic medication use and association with challenging behaviour in adults with an intellectual disability. A total population study. *Journal of Intellectual Disability Research, 61*, 604–617.

Boyer, E. W., Siefert, S. A., & Hernon, C. (2017, April 6). Methamphetamine: Acute intoxication. *UpToDate*. Retrieved from http://www.uptodate.com.

Boysen, G. A., & VanBergen, A. (2013). A review of published research on adult dissociative identity disorder: 2000–2010. *The Journal of Nervous and Mental Disease, 201*(1), 5–11.

Boysen, G. A., & VanBergen, A. (2014). Simulation of multiple personalities: A review of research comparing diagnosed and simulated dissociative identity disorder. *Clinical Psychology Review, 34*(1), 14–28.

Bradford, A. (2017, July 5). Female orgasmic disorder: Epidemiology, pathogenesis, clinical manifestations, course, assessment, and diagnosis. *UpToDate*. Retrieved from http://www.uptodate.com.

Bradford, A. (2017, July 6). Treatment of female orgasmic disorder. *UpToDate*. Retrieved from http://www.uptodate.com.

Brady, J. E., & Li, G. (2014). Trends in alcohol and other drugs detected in fatally injured drivers in the United States, 1999–2010. *American Journal of Epidemiology, 179*(6), 1093.

Braham, M. Y., Jedidi, M., Chkirbene, Y., Hmila, I., El Khai, M. C., Souguir, M. K., & Ben Dhiab, M. (2017). Caregiver-fabricated illness in a child: A case report of three siblings. *Journal of Forensic Nursing, 13*(1), 39–42.

Brakoulias, V., Starcevic, V., Belloch, A., Brown, C., Ferrao, Y. A., Fontenelle, L. F., . . . Viswasam, K. (2017). Comorbidity, age of onset and suicidality in obsessive-compulsive disorder (OCD): An international collaboration. *Comprehensive Psychiatry, 76*, 79–86.

Bram, A. D. (2017). Reviving and refining psychodynamic interpretation of the Wechsler Intelligence Tests: The verbal comprehension subtests. *Journal of Personality Assessment, 99*(3), 324–333.

Brand, B. L., Loewenstein, R. J., & Spiegel, D. (2014). Dispelling myths about dissociative identity disorder treatment: An empirically based approach. *Psychiatry, 77*(2), 169–189.

Branley, D. B., & Covey, J. (2017). Pro-ana versus Pro-recovery: A content analytic comparison of social media users' communication about eating disorders on Twitter and Tumblr. *Frontiers in Psychology, 8*, 1356.

Brannon, G. E. (2016). History and mental status examination. Retrieved from http://emedicine.medscape.com/article/293402–overview.

Bratek, A., Krysta, K., & Kucia, K. (2017). Psychiatric comorbidity in older adults with intellectual disability. *Psychiatria Danubina, 29*(Suppl. 3), 590–593.

Bratskeir, K. (2013, September 16). The habits of supremely happy people. *Huffington Post*.

Braun, D. L. (1996, July 28). Interview. In S. Gilbert, More men may seek eating-disorder help. *New York Times*.

Braverman, D. W., Marcus, B. S., Wakim, P. G., Mercurio, M. R., & Kopf, G. S. (2017). Healthcare professionals' attitudes about physician-assisted death: an analysis of their justifications and the role of terminology and patient competency. *Journal of Pain and Symptom Management, 54*, 538–545.

Braxton, L. E., Calhoun, P. S., Williams, J. E., & Boggs, C. D. (2007). Validity rates of the Personality Assessment Inventory and the Minnesota Multiphasic Personality Inventory-2 in a VA medical center setting. *Journal of Personality Assessment, 88*(1), 5–15.

Bremner, J. D. (2016). Traumatic stress from a multilevel developmental psychopathology perspective. In D. Cicchetti (Ed.), *Developmental psychopathology, maladaptation and psychopathology, Vol. 3: Maladaptation and psychopathology* (3rd ed., Chap. 9, pp. 1–39). New York: Wiley.

Bremner, J. D. (2002). *Does stress damage the brain? Understanding trauma-related disorders from a mind-body perspective.* New York: Norton.

Bremner, J. D., & Charney, D. S. (2010). Neural circuits in fear and anxiety. In D. J. Stein, E. Hollander & B. O. Rothbaum (Eds.), *Textbook of anxiety disorders* (2nd ed., pp. 55–71). Arlington, VA: American Psychiatric Publishing.

Brenner, I. (2018). Catching a wave: The hypnosis-sensitive transference-based treatment of dissociative identity disorder (DID). *American Journal of Clinical Hypnosis, 60*(3), 279–295.

Breslau, J., Gilman, S. E., Stein, B. D., Ruder, T., Gmelin, T., & Miller, E. (2017). Sex differences in recent first-onset depression in an epidemiological sample of adolescents. *Translational Psychiatry, 7*, e1139.

Bressert, S. (2016) Antisocial personality disorder treatment. *Psych Central*. Retrieved from https://psychcentral.com.

Bressert, S. (2016). Histrionic personality disorder treatment. *Psych Central*. Retrieved from https://psychcentral.com.

Bressert, S. (2016). Obsessive-compulsive personality disorder treatment. *Psych Central*. Retrieved from https://psychcentral.com.

Bressert, S. (2016). Schizotypal personality disorder. *Psych Central*. Retrieved from https://psychcentral.com.

Bressert, S. (2016, May 17). Facts about shyness. *Psych Central*. Retrieved from https://psychcentral.com.

Bressert, S. (2016, May 18). Dependent personality disorder treatment. *Psych Central*. Retrieved from https://psychcentral.com.

Bressert, S. (2017). Avoidant personality disorder symptoms. *Psych Central*. Retrieved from https://psychcentral.com.

Bressert, S. (2017). Dependent personality disorder treatment. *Psych Central*. Retrieved from https://psychcentral.com.

Bressert, S. (2017). Dissociative identity disorder treatment. *Psych Central*. Retrieved from https://psychcentral.com/disorders.

Bressert, S. (2017). Fetishistic disorder symptoms. *Psych Central*. Retrieved from https://psychcentral.com/disorders/fetishism-symptoms.

Bressert, S. (2018). Who gets bipolar disorder? *PsychCentral*. Retrieved on april 26, 2018, from https://psychcentral.com/lib/who-gets-bipolar disorder/.

Brewer, J. (2014). Mindfulness in the military. *American Journal of Psychiatry, 171*, 803–806.

Brewis, A., SturtzSreetharan, C., & Wutich, A. (2018, February 13). Obesity stigma as a globalizing health challenge. *Global Health Hub, 14*(1), 20.

Bridler, R., Häberle, A., Müller, S. T., Cattapan, K., Grohmann, R., Toto, S., . . . Greil, W. (2015). Psychopharmacological treatment of 2195 in-patients with borderline personality disorder: A comparison with other psychiatric disorders. *European Neuropsychopharmacology, 25*(6), 763–772.

Briggs, S., Slater, T., & Bowley, J. (2017). Practitioners' experiences of adolescent suicidal behaviour in peer groups. *Journal of Psychiatric and Mental Health Nursing, 24*, 293–301.

Britt, R. R. (2005, January 6). The odds of dying. *LiveScience.com*.

Brodeur, M. (2016, December 21). 10 negative body image thoughts you need to stop right now. *Verily Magazine*.

Bronskill, S. E., Anderson, G. M., Sykora, K., Wodchis, W. P., Gill, S., Shulman, K. I., & Rochon, P. A. (2004). Neuroleptic drug therapy in older adults newly admitted to nursing homes: Incidence, dose, and specialist contact. *Journal of the American Geriatrics Society, 52*(5), 749.

Brooks, A. C. (2013, December 14). A formula for happiness. *New York Times*.

Brooks, F., Michaelson, V., King, N., Inchley, J., & Pickett, W. (2018). Spirituality as a protective health asset for young people: An international comparative analysis from three countries. *International Journal of Public Health, 63*(3), 387–395.

Brooks, G. R., & Richardson, F. C. (1980). Emotional skills training: A treatment program for duodenal ulcer. *Behavior Therapist, 11*(2), 198–207.

Brosch, J. R., & Farlow, M. R. (2017, May 30). Early-onset dementia in adults. *UpToDate*. Retrieved from http://www.uptodate.com.

Brouwer, M. E., Williams, A. D., Forand, N. R., DeRubeis, R. J., & Bockting, C. L. H. (2019). Dysfunctional attitudes or extreme response style as predictors of depressive relapse and recurrence after mobile cognitive therapy for recurrent depression. *Journal of Affective Disorders, 243*, 48–54.

Brown, A. (2012, April 27). Chronic pain rates shoot up until Americans reach late 50s: Low-income and obese Americans more likely to have chronic pain. Retrieved from Gallup website: http://www.gallup.com/poll/154169.

Brown, C. A., & Weisman de Mamani, A. (2018). The mediating effect of family cohesion in reducing patient symptoms and family distress in a culturally informed family therapy for schizophrenia: A parallel-process latent-growth model. *Journal of Consulting and Clinical Psychology, 86*(1), 1–14.

Brown, E. M. (2018). François Leuret: The last moral therapist. *History of Psychiatry, 29*(1), 38–48.

Brown, G. R. (2017, September). Exhibitionistic disorder (exhibitionism). *Merck Manual*. Retrieved from https://www.merckmanuals.com/professional/psychiatric-disorders/sexuality,-gender-dysphoria,-and-paraphilias.

Brown, G. R. (2017, September). Pedophilic disorder (pedophilia). *Merck Manual*. Retrieved from https://www.merckmanuals.com/

professional/psychiatric-disorders/sexuality,-gender-dysphoria,-and-paraphilias.

Brown, G. R. (2017, September). Transvestism (transvestic disorder). *Merck Manual.* Retrieved from https://www.merckmanuals.com/home/mental-health-disorders/sexuality.

Brown, G. R. (2017, September). Voyeuristic disorder (voyeurism). *Merck Manual.* Retrieved from https://www.merckmanuals.com/professional/psychiatric-disorders/sexuality,-gender-dysphoria,-and-paraphilias.

Brown, G. W. (2002). Social roles, context and evolution in the origins of depression. *Journal of Health and Social Behavior, 43*(3), 255–276.

Brown, G. W., & Harris, T. O. (1978). *Social origins of depression: A study of psychiatric disorder in women.* London: Tavistock.

Brown, J. L. (2017). Physician exposure to direct-to-consumer pharmaceutical marketing: Potential for creating prescribing bias. *American Journal of Medicine, 130*(6), e247–e248.

Brown, K. P. (2018, April 20). Insanity defense typology. *Behavioral Sciences & the Law.* [Epub ahead of print]

Brown, L., Beutler, L. E., Patterson, J. H., Bongar, B., & Holleran, L. (2016). Psychotherapy with people exposed to mass casualty events: Theory and practice. In A. J. Consoli, L. E. Beutler, & B. Bongar, *Comprehensive textbook of psychotherapy: theory and practice: Part II: Psychotherapy by modalities and populations* (2nd ed., Chap. 27). New York: Oxford University Press.

Brown, N. W. (2017). *Group therapy.* CreateSpace Independent Publishing Platform.

Brown, R. C., & Plener, P. L. (2017). Non-suicidal self-injury in adolescence. *Current Psychiatry Reports, 19*(3), 20.

Brownley, K. A., Peat, C. M., La Via, M., & Bulik, C. M. (2015). Pharmacological approaches to the management of binge eating disorder. *Drugs, 75*(1), 9–32.

Bruch, H. (1962). Perceptual and conceptual disturbances in anorexia nervosa. *Psychosomatic Medicine, 24,* 187–194.

Bruch, H. (1973). *Eating disorders: Obesity, anorexia nervosa and the person within.* New York: Basic Books.

Bruch, H. (1978). *The golden cage: The enigma of anorexia nervosa.* Cambridge, MA: Harvard University Press.

Bruch, H. (1991). The sleeping beauty: Escape from change. In S. I. Greenspan & G. H. Pollock (Eds.), *The course of life, Vol. 4: Adolescence.* Madison, CT: International Universities Press.

Bruch, H. (2001). *The golden cage: The enigma of anorexia nervosa.* Cambridge, MA: Harvard University Press.

Brühl, A. B., Delsignore, A., Komossa, K., & Weidt, S. (2014). Neuroimaging in social anxiety disorder—A meta-analytic review resulting in a new neurofunctional model. *Neuroscience & Biobehavioral Reviews, 47,* 260–280.

Brunet, K., & Birchwood, M. (2010). Duration of untreated psychosis and pathways to care. In P. French, J. Smith, D. Shiers, M. Reed, & M. Rayne (Eds.), *Promoting recovery in early psychosis: A practice manual* (pp. 9–16). Hoboken, NJ: Wiley-Blackwell.

Bryant, R. (2017, February 17). Acute stress disorder in adults: Epidemiology, pathogenesis, clinical manifestations, course, and diagnosis. *UpToDate.* Retrieved from http://www.uptodate.com.

Bryant, R. (2018, February 27). Treatment of acute stress disorder in adults. *UpToDate.* Retrieved from http://www.uptodate.com.

Bryman, A. (2016). *Social research methods* (5th ed.). New York: Oxford University Press.

Bryner, J. (2011). Close friends less common today, study finds. *Live Science.* Retrieved from http://www.livescience.com/16879.

BSA (Boy Scouts of America). (2017). *Bullying awareness.* Retrieved from http://www.scouting.org/training/YouthProtection/bullying.aspx.

BSA (Bullying Statistics in America). (2014). A 2014 presentation of statistics and graphs on bullying.

BSA (Bullying Statistics in America). (2017). A 2017 presentation of statistics and graphs on bullying.

Buchman-Schmitt, J. M., Chu, C., Michaels, M. S., Hames, J. L., Silva, C., Hagan, C. R., . . . Joiner, T. E., Jr. (2017). The role of stressful life events preceding death by suicide: Evidence from two samples of suicide decedents. *Psychiatry Research, 256,* 345–352.

Buckley, L., Bonar, E. E., Walton, M. A., Carter, P. M., Voloshyna, D., Ehrlich, P. F., & Cunningham, R. M. (2017). Marijuana and other substance use among male and female underage drinkers who drive after drinking and ride with those who drive after drinking. *Addictive Behaviors, 71,* 7–11.

Buckner, J. D., Lemke, A. W., Jeffries, E. R., & Shah, S. M. (2017). Social anxiety and suicidal ideation: Test of the utility of the Interpersonal-Psychological Theory of Suicide. *Journal of Anxiety Disorders, 45,* 60–63.

Bucsek, M. J., Giridharan, T., MacDonald, C. R., Hylander, B. L., & Repasky, E. A. (2018). An overview of the role of sympathetic regulation of immune responses in infectious disease and autoimmunity. *International Journal of Hyperthermia, 34*(2), 135–143.

Budhwani, H., Hearld, K. R., & Chavez-Yenter, D. (2015). Generalized anxiety disorder in racial and ethnic minorities: A case of nativity and contextual factors. *Journal of Affective Disorders, 175,* 275–280.

Buehler, S. (2017). Treating sexual problems in clients with mental illness. In Z. D. Peterson, *The Wiley-Blackwell handbook of sex therapy* (Chap. 22, pp. 359–368). Hoboken, NJ: Wiley-Blackwell.

Bukalo, O., Pinard, C. R., & Holmes, A. (2014). Mechanisms to medicines: Elucidating neural and molecular substrates of fear extinction to identify novel treatments for anxiety disorders. *British Journal of Pharmacology, 171*(20), 4690–4718.

Bukstein, O. (2016, November 3). Attention deficit hyperactivity disorder in adults: Epidemiology, pathogenesis, clinical features, course, assessment, and diagnosis. *UpToDate.* Retrieved from http://www.uptodate.com.

Bukstein, O. (2018, April 23). Attention deficit hyperactivity disorder in adults: Epidemiology, pathogenesis, clinical features, course, assessment, and diagnosis. *UpToDate.* Retrieved from http://www.uptodate.com.

Bulik, B. S. (2017). *The top 10 most-advertised prescription drug brands.* FiercePharma.

Bulik, C. M., Kleiman, S. C., & Yilmaz, Z. (2016). Genetic epidemiology of eating disorders. *Current Opinion in Psychiatry, 29*(6), 383–388.

Burack, J. A., Russo, N., Green, C. G., Landry, O., & Iarocci, G. (2016). Developments in the developmental approach to intellectual disability. In D. Cicchetti (Ed.), *Developmental psychopathology, Vol. 3: Maladaptation and psychopathology* (3rd ed.). New York: Wiley.

Burch, R., Rizzoli, P., & Loder, E. (2018). The prevalence and impact of migraine and severe headache in the United States: Figures and trends from government health studies. *Headache: The Journal of Head and Face Pain, 58*(4), 496–505.

Burg, M. M. (2017, December 18). Psychological treatment of cardiac patients. *Clinical Health Psychology.* Washington, DC: APA.

Burke, K. (2016, May 24). 63 texting statistics that answer all your questions. *Text request.* Retrieved from https://www.textrequest.com.

Burke, S. M., Cohen-Kettenis, P. T., Veltman, D. J., Klink, D. T., & Bakker, J. (2014). Hypothalamic response to the chemo-signal androstadienone in gender dysphoric children and adolescents. *Frontiers in Endocrinology, 5,* 60.

Burke, S. M., Kreukels, B. P., Cohen-Kettenis, P. T., Veltman, D. J., Klink, D. T., & Bakker, J. (2016). Male-typical visuospatial functioning in gynephilic girls with gender dysphoria: Organizational and activational effects of testosterone. *Journal of Psychiatry & Neuroscience, 41*(6), 395–404.

Burke, S. M., Manzouri, A. H., Dheine, C., Bergström, K., Arver, S., Feusner, J. D., & Savic-Berglund, I. (2018). Testosterone effects on the brain in transgender men. *Cerebral Cortex, 28*(5), 1582–1596.

Burke, T. A., Jacobucci, R., Ammerman, B. A., Piccirillo, M., McCloskey, M. S., Heimberg, R. G., & Alloy, L. B. (2018). Identifying the relative importance of non-suicidal self-injury features in classifying suicide ideation, plans, and behavior using exploratory data mining. *Psychiatry Research, 262,* 175–183.

Burke, K., & Riley, J. (2010). Coronary artery disease. In C. Margereson & S. Trenoweth (Eds.), *Developing holistic care for long-term conditions* (pp. 255–273). New York: Routledge/Taylor & Francis Group.

Burns, T. (2010). Modern community care strategies for schizophrenia care: Impacts on outcome. In W. F. Gattaz & G. Busatto (Eds.), *Advances in schizophrenia research 2009* (pp. 417–427). New York: Springer Science + Business Media.

Burns, T., & Drake, B. (2011). Mental health services and patients with schizophrenia. In D. R. Weinberg & P. Harrison (Eds.), *Schizophrenia* (pp. 625–643). Hoboken, NJ: Wiley-Blackwell.

Burnsed, B. (2014, July 22). Rates of excessive drinking among student-athletes falling. *NCAA.* Retrieved from http://www.ncaa.org.

Burrell, L. V., Mehlum, L., & Qin, P. (2018). Sudden parental death from external causes and risk of suicide in the bereaved offspring: A national study. *Journal of Psychiatric Research, 96,* 49–56.

Burt, K. B., Coatsworth, J. D., & Masten, A. S. (2016). Competence and psychopathology in development. In D. Cicchetti (Ed.), *Developmental psychopathology, Vol. 4: Risk, resilience, and intervention* (3rd ed.). New York: Wiley.

Burtăverde, V., Chraif, M., Aniţei, M., & Mihăilă, T. (2016). The incremental validity of the Dark Triad in predicting driving aggression. *Accident Analysis and Prevention, 96,* 1–11.

Busch, A. C., Denduluri, M., Glass, J., Hetzel, S., Gugnani, S. P., Gassman, M., . . . Brown, R. (2017). Predischarge injectable versus oral Naltrexone to improve postdischarge treatment engagement among hospitalized veterans with alcohol use disorder: A randomized pilot proof-of-concept study. *Alcoholism: Clinical and Experimental Research, 41,* 1352–1360.

Busch, A. M., Ciccolo, J. T., Puspitasari, A. J., Nosrat, S., Whitworth, J. W., & Stults-Kolehmainen, M. (2017). Preferences for exercise as a treatment for depression. *Mental Health and Physical Activity, 10,* 68–72.

Busch, F. N., Milrod, B. L., & Shear, K. (2010). Psychodynamic concepts of anxiety. In D. J. Stein, E. Hollander, & B. O. Rothbaum (Eds.), *Textbook of anxiety disorders* (2nd ed., pp. 117–128). Arlington, VA: American Psychiatric Publishing.

Busch, F. N., Rudden, M. G., & Shapiro, T. (2004). *Psychodynamic treatment of depression.* Washington, DC: American Psychiatric Publishing.

Bushman, B. J., Baumeister, R. F., & Stack, A. D. (1999). Catharsis, aggression, and persuasive influence: Self-fulfilling or self-defeating prophecies? *Journal of Personality and Social Psychology, 76*(3), 367–376.

Bustillo, J., & Weil, E. (2018, August 11). Psychosocial interventions for schizophrenia. *UpToDate.* Retrieved from http://www.uptodate.com.

Bustillo, J., & Weil, E. (2018, June 3). Psychosocial interventions for severe mental illness. *UpToDate.* Retrieved from http://www.uptodate.com.

Buzzell, G. A., Troller-Renfree, S. V., Barker, T. V., Bowman, L. C., Chronis-Tuscano, A., Henderson, H. A., . . . Fox, N. A. (2017). A neurobehavioral mechanism linking behaviorally inhibited temperament and later adolescent social anxiety. *Journal of the American Academy of Child and Adolescent Psychiatry, 56*(12), 1097–1105.

Byers, A. L., Covinsky, K. E., Neylan, T. C., & Yaffe, K. (2014). Chronicity of posttraumatic stress disorder and risk of disability in older persons. *JAMA Psychiatry, 71*(5), 540–546.

Byrd, A. L., Manuck, S. B., Hawes, S. W., Vebares, T. J., Nimgaonkar, V., Chowdari, K. V., . . . Stepp, S. D. (2018, February 22). The interaction between monoamine oxidase A (MAOA) and childhood maltreatment as a predictor of personality pathology in females: Emotional reactivity as a potential mediating mechanism. *Development and Psychopathology.* [Epub ahead of print]

Byrne, K. A., Patrick, C. J., & Worthy, D. A. (2016). Striatal dopamine, externalizing proneness, and substance abuse: Effects on wanting and learning during reward-based decision making. *Clinical Psychological Science, 4*(5), 760–774.

Bystritsky, A. (2018, January 17). Pharmacotherapy for generalized anxiety disorder in adults. *UpToDate.* Retrieved from http://www.uptodate.com.

Cable, A. (2008, November 14). Divorced from reality: All three accounts of the Second Life love triangle that saw a woman separate from her husband for having a cyber-affair. *Daily Mail, UK.*

Cabrera, F. J. P., Herrera, A. R. C., Rubalcava, S. J. A., & Martinez, K. I. M. (2017, June 2). Behavior patterns of antisocial teenagers interacting with parents and peers: A longitudinal study. *Frontiers in Psychology, 8,* 757.

Cachelin, F. M., Phinney, J. S., Schug, R. A., & Striegel-Moore, R. M. (2006). Acculturation and eating disorders in a Mexican American community sample. *Psychology of Women Quarterly, 30*(4), 340–347.

Cacioppo, C. N., Conway, L. J., Mehta, D., Krantz, I. D., & Noon, S. E. (2016). Attitudes about the use of internet support groups and the impact among parents of children with Cornelia de Lange syndrome. *American Journal of Medical Genetics Part C: Seminars in Medical Genetics, 172*(2), 229–236.

Cacioppo, J., & Freberg, L. (2016). *Discovering pychology: The science of mind* (2nd edition). Boston: Cengage Learning.

Cagle, J. (2018, April 11). Mariah Carey on why she kept her bipolar disorder hidden for years: Lived in denial and isolation. *People.com.*

Calarco, M. (2017). Does depression turn self-medication into addiction? *Psych Central.* Retrieved from https://psychcentral.com/blog/archives/2016/10/15/does-depression-turn-self-medication-into-addiction/.

Caldwell, C. (2017, April). American carnage: The new landscape of opioid addiction. *First Things.*

Calhoun, B. H., Maggs, J. L., & Loken, E. (2018). Change in college students' perceived parental permissibility of alcohol use and its relation to college drinking. *Addictive Behaviors, 76,* 275–280.

Caligor, E., & Petrini, M. J. (2018, March 21). Narcissistic personality disorder: Epidemiology, pathogenesis, clinical manifestations, course, assessment, and diagnosis. *UpToDate.* Retrieved from http://www.uptodate.com.

Caligor, E., & Petrini, M. J. (2018, March 21). Treatment of narcissistic personality disorder. *UpToDate.* Retrieved from http://www.uptodate.com.

Caligor, E., Kernberg, O. F., Clarkin, J. F., & Yeomans, F. E. (Eds.). (2018). *Psychodynamic therapy for personality pathology: Treating self and interpersonal functioning* (1st ed.). Washington, DC: American Psychiatric Publishing.

Caligor, E., & Clarkin, J. F. (2010). An object relations model of personality and personality pathology. In J. F. Clarkin, P. Fonagy, & G. O. Gabbard (Eds.), *Psychodynamic psychotherapy for personality disorders: A clinical handbook* (pp. 3–36). Arlington, VA: American Psychiatric Publishing.

Call, N. A., Mevers, J. L., McElhanon, B. O., & Scheithauer, M. C. (2017). A multidisciplinary treatment for encopresis in children with developmental disabilities. *Journal of Applied Behavior Analysis, 50*(2), 332–344.

Callahan, L. A., Steadman, H. J., McGreevy, M. A., & Robbins, P. C. (1991). The volume and characteristics of insanity defense pleas: An eight-state study. *Bulletin of the American Academy of Psychiatry Law, 19*(4), 331–338.

Calzada, E., Barajas-Gonzalez, R. G., Huang, K. Y., & Brotman, L. (2017). Early childhood internalizing problems in Mexican- and Dominican-origin children: The role of cultural socialization and parenting practices. *Journal of Clinical Child & Adolescent Psychology, 46*(4), 551–562.

Cameron, E. E., Hunter, D., Sedov, I. D., & Tomfohr-Madsen, L. M. (2017). What do dads want? Treatment preferences for paternal postpartum depression. *Journal of Affective Disorders, 215,* 62–70.

Campbell, D., & Hale, R. (2017). *Working in the dark: Understanding the pre-suicide state of mind.* New York: Routledge.

Campbell, E. C., Caroff, S. N., & Mann, S. C. (2017, September 15). Co-occurring schizophrenia and substance use disorder: Epidemiology, pathogenesis, clinical manifestations, course, assessment and diagnosis. *UpToDate.* Retrieved from http://www.uptodate.com.

Campbell, E. C., Caroff, S. N., & Mann, S. C. (2018, February 5). Pharmacotherapy for co-occurring schizophrenia and substance use disorder. *UpToDate.* Retrieved from http://www.uptodate.com.

Campbell, E. C., Caroff, S. N., & Mann, S. C. (2018, February 5). Psychosocial interventions for co-occurring schizophrenia and substance use disorder.

Campbell, K. (2016, March 23). *The pitfalls of direct-to-consumer advertising in medicine. U.S. News & World Report. Health Care.*

Campos, R. C., Holden, R. R., & Santos, S. (2018). Exposure to suicide in the family: Suicide risk and psychache in individuals who have lost a family member by suicide. *Journal of Clinical Psychology, 74*(3), 407–417.

Canat, L., Degirmentepe, R. B., Atalay, H. A., Aikan, I., Özbir, S., Culha, M. G., & Ötünçtemur, A. (2018). The relationship between female sexual function index domains and premature ejaculation. *International Urology and Nephrology, 50*(4), 633–637.

Canetta, S., Sourander, A., Surcel, H., Hinkka-Yli-Salomäki, S., Leiviskä, J., Kellendonk, C., . . . Brown, A. S. (2014). Elevated maternal C-reactive protein and increased risk of schizophrenia in a national birth cohort. *American Journal of Psychiatry, 171*(9), 960–968.

Canner, J. K., Harfouch, O., Kodadek, L. M., Pelaez, D., Coon, D., Offodile, A. C., 2nd, . . . Lau, B. D. (2018, February 28). Temporal trends in gender-affirming surgery among transgender patients in the United States. *JAMA Surgery.* [Epub ahead of print]

Cao, H., Zhou, N., Fang, X., & Fine, M. (2017). Marital well-being and depression in Chinese marriage: Going beyond satisfaction and ruling out critical confounders. *Journal of Family Psychology, 31,* 775–784.

Capobianco, L., Morrison, A. P., & Wells, A. (2018). The effect of thought importance on stress responses: A test for the metacognitive model. *Stress, 21*(2), 128–135.

CareerBuilder. (2012, April 18). 37% of companies use social networks to research potential job candidates. *CareerBuilder.* Retrieved from http://www.careerbuilder.com/share/aboutus/pressreleasesdetail.

CareerBuilder. (2017). Number of employees using social media to screen candidates has increased 500 percent over the last decade. Chicago, IL: CareerBuilder. Retrieved from http://www.careerbuilder.com/share/aboutus/pressreleasedetail.

Carey, B. (2016, April 3). Investigating the minds of mass killers. *New York Times.*

Carey, B. (2017, August 30). The true story behind Sybil. Retrieved from http://www.cbc.ca/books/the-true-story-behind-sybil-and-her-multiple-personalities-1.4268459.

Carpenter, A. C., & Krendl, A. C. (2018). Are eyewitness accounts biased? Evaluating false memories for crimes involving in-group or out-group conflict. *Society for Neuroscience, 13*(1), 74–93.

Carpenter, A. L., Pincus, D. B., Furr, J. M., & Comer, J. S. (2018). Working from home: An initial pilot examination of videoconferencing-based cognitive-behavioral therapy for anxious youth delivered to the home setting. *Behavior Therapy, 49,* 917–930.

Carpenter, K. M., Williams, K., & Worly, B. (2017). Treating women's orgasmic difficulties. In Z. D. Peterson (Ed.), *The Wiley-Blackwell handbook of sex therapy* (Chap. 5, pp. 57–71). Hoboken, NJ: Wiley-Blackwell.

Carr, S. N., & Francis, A. J. P. (2010). Do early maladaptive schemas mediate the relationship between childhood experiences and avoidant personality disorder features? A preliminary investigation in a non-clinical sample. *Cognitive Therapy and Research, 34*(4), 343–358.

Carroll, R. A. (2007). Gender dysphoria and transgender experiences. In S. R. Leiblum (Ed.), *Principles and practice of sex therapy* (4th ed., pp. 477–508). New York: Guilford Press.

Carroll, T. D., Currier, J. M., McCormick, W. H., & Drescher, K. D. (2017). Adverse childhood experiences and risk for suicidal behavior in male Iraq and Afghanistan veterans seeking PTSD treatment. *Psychological Trauma. 9,* 583–586.

Caruso, R. J., Nanni, M. G., Riba, M., Sabato, S., Mitchell, A. J., Croce, E., & Grassi, L. (2017). Depressive spectrum disorders in cancer: Prevalence, risk factors and screening for depression: A critical review. *Acta Oncologica, 56*(2), 146–155. DOI:10.1080/0284186X.2016.1266090.

Cash, D. K., & Lane, S. M. (2017). Context influences interpretation of eyewitness confidence statements. *Law and Human Behavior, 41*(2), 180–190.

Cash, T. F., & Henry, P. E. (1995). Women's body images: The results of a national survey in the U. S. A. *Sex Roles, 33*(1/2), 19–28.

Cawley, R., Pontin, E. E., Touhey, J., Sheehy, K., & Taylor, P. J. (2019). What is the relationship between rejection and self-harm or suicidality in adulthood? *Journal of Affective Disorders, 242,* 123–134.

Cayman, S. (2014). *Sex facts: 369 facts to blow you away.* Chichester, UK: Summersdale.

CBC. (2008, May 13). The world's worst natural disasters: Calamities of the 20th and 21st centuries. *CBC News.*

CDC (Centers for Disease Control and Prevention). (2010). *Suicide rates among persons ages 10 years and older, by race/ethnicity and sex, United States, 2002–2006. National Suicide Statistics at a Glance.* Atlanta, GA: CDC.

CDC (Centers for Disease Control and Prevention). (2010, December 3). QuickStats: Percentage of adults who had migraines or severe headaches, pain in the neck, lower back, or face/jaw. by sex. National Health Interview Survey, 2009. *Morbidity and Mortality Weekly Report, 59*(47), 1557.

CDC (Centers for Disease Control and Prevention). (2011). *High blood pressure facts.* Retrieved from http://www.cdc.gov/bloodpressure/facts.htm.

CDC (Centers for Disease Control and Prevention). (2013). *Suicide and self-inflicted injury.* Atlanta, GA: CDC.

CDC (Centers for Disease Control and Prevention). (2014). *Data and statistics.* Washington, DC: CDC.

CDC (Centers for Disease Control and Prevention). (2014). *National suicide statistics at a glance.* Atlanta, GA: CDC.

CDC (Centers for Disease Control and Prevention). (2014). *Older persons' health.* Washington, DC: CDC.

CDC (Centers for Disease Control and Prevention). (2015). *Caloric intake from fast food among children and adolescents in the United States, 2011–2012.* Data Brief 213. Atlanta, GA: CDC.

CDC (Centers for Disease Control and Prevention). (2015). *Table 41 (page 1 of 3). Severe headache or migraine, low back, and neck pain among adults aged 18 and over, by selected characteristics: United States, selected years 1997–2014.* Retrieved from https://www.cdc.gov/nchs/data/hus/ 2015/041.pdf.

CDC (Centers for Disease Control and Prevention). (2015, March 17). *High cholesterol facts.* Retrieved from https://www.cdc.gov/cholesterol/facts.htm.

CDC (Centers for Disease Control and Prevention). (2016, April). *Suicide rates for females and males by race and ethnicity: United States, 1999 and 2014.* Hyattsville, MD: NCHS.

CDC (Centers for Disease Control and Prevention). (2016, January). *Mortality among centenarians in the United States, 2000–2014.* NCHS data brief No. 233. Hyattsville, MD: NCHS.

CDC (Centers for Disease Control and Prevention). (2016, June 16). *Heart disease fact sheet.* Retrieved from https://www.cdc.gov/dhdsp/data_statistics/fact_sheets/fs_heart_disease.htm.

CDC (Centers for Disease Control and Prevention). (2016, November 30). *High blood pressure facts.* Retrieved from https://www.cdc.gov/bloodpressurel/facts.htm.

CDC (Centers for Disease Control and Prevention). (2016, October 20). *Fact sheets–Underage drinking.* Atlanta, GA: CDC.

CDC (Centers for Disease Control and Prevention). (2017). *Data overview: Drug overdose.* Atlanta, GA: CDC.

CDC (Centers for Disease Control and Prevention). (2017). *Economic trends in tobacco.* Atlanta, GA: CDC.

CDC (Centers for Disease Control and Prevention). (2017). *Fact sheets—Binge drinking.* Atlanta, GA: CDC.

CDC (Centers for Disease Control and Prevention). (2017). *Heroin overdose data.* Atlanta, GA: CDC.

CDC (Centers for Disease Control and Prevention). (2017). *National Survey of Family Growth: Key statistics.* Atlanta, GA: CDC.

CDC (Centers for Disease Control and Prevention). (2017). Opioid data analysis. *CDC.* Retrieved from https://www.cdc.gov.

CDC (Centers for Disease Control and Prevention). (2017). *QuickStats: Age-adjusted rate for suicide, by sex—National Vital Statistics System, United States, 1975–2015.* Retrieved from https://www-cdc-gov.ezproxy.princeton.edu/mmwr/volumes/66/wr/mm6610a7.htm.

CDC (Centers for Disease Control and Prevention). (2017). *Quitting smoking.* Atlanta, GA: CDC.

CDC (Centers for Disease Control and Prevention). (2017). *Sexual risk behaviors: HIV, STD, & teen pregnancy prevention* Atlanta, GA: CDC.

CDC (Centers for Disease Control and Prevention). (2017, February 27). *Most recent asthma data.* Retrieved from https://www.cdc.gov/asthma/most_recent_data/htm.

CDC (Centers for Disease Control and Prevention). (2017, January 3). *Learning disorder.* Atlanta, GA: CDC.

CDC (Centers for Disease Control and Prevention). (2017, January 19). *Hypertension.* Retrieved from https://www.cdc.gov/nchs/fastats/hypertension.htm.

CDC (Centers for Disease Control and Prevention). (2017, June 1). *Adverse drug event monitoring.* Hyattsville, MD: NCHS.

CDC (Centers for Disease Control and Prevention). (2017, June 16). *Impaired driving: Get the facts.* Atlanta, GA: CDC.

CDC (Centers for Disease Control and Prevention). (2017, June 6). *Data and statistics: FASDs.* Atlanta, GA: CDC.

CDC (Centers for Disease Control and Prevention). (2017, June 7). *Binge drinking.* Atlanta, GA: CDC.

CDC (Centers for Disease Control and Prevention). (2017, March 17). *Leading causes of death.* Retrieved from https://www.cdc.gov/nchs/fastats/leading-causes-of-death.htm.

CDC (Centers for Disease Control and Prevention). (2017, March 17). *Suicide and self-inflicted injury.* Retrieved from https://www.cdc.gov/nchs/fastats/suicide.htm.

CDC (Centers for Disease Control and Prevention). (2017, March 6). America's opioid epidemic is worsening. *The Economist.*

CDC (Centers for Disease Control and Prevention). (2017, May 12). *Youth bullying: What does the research say?* Atlanta, GA: CDC.

CDC (Centers for Disease Control and Prevention). (2017, May 17). *Tobacco-related mortality.* Retrieved from https://www.cdc.gov/tobacco/data_statistics/fact_sheets/health_effects/tobacco_related_mortality/index.htm.

CDC (Centers for Disease Control and Prevention). (2017, May 3). *Data & statistics: Mental, behavioral, and developmental health of children aged 2–8 years.* Atlanta, GA: CDC.

CDC (Centers for Disease Control and Prevention). (2017, May 3). *Life expectancy: 78.8 years.* Retrieved from https://www.cdc.gov.

CDC (Centers for Disease Control and Prevention). (2017, November 28). *Heart disease facts.* Atlanta, GA: CDC.

CDC (Centers for Disease Control and Prevention). (2018, April 20). *Behavior or conduct problems*. Atlanta, GA: CDC.

CDC (Centers for Disease Control and Prevention). (2018, April 20). *Behavior or conduct problems*. Atlanta, GA: CDC.

CDC (Centers for Disease Control and Prevention). (2018, April 5). *High blood pressure facts*. Atlanta, GA: CDC.

CDC (Centers for Disease Control and Prevention). (2018, June 14). *Fewer U.S. high school students having sex, using drugs*. Retrieved from https://www.cdc.gov/media/releases/2018/p0614-yrbs.html.

CDC (Centers for Disease Control and Prevention). (2018, March 20). *Attention deficit/hyperactivity disorder: Data & statistics*. Atlanta, GA: CDC.

CDC (Centers for Disease Control and Prevention). (2018, March 27). *Binge drinking*. Atlanta, GA: CDC.

CDC (Centers for Disease Control and Prevention). (2018, May 10). *Fetal alcohol spectrum disorders: Basics about FASDs*. Atlanta, GA: CDC.

CDC (Centers for Disease Control and Prevention). (2018, May 4). *Economic trends in tobacco*. Atlanta, GA: CDC.

CDC (Centers for Disease Control). (2015, November 5). *Drowsy driving: Asleep at the wheel*. Atlanta, GA: Author.

CDPS (Colorado Department of Public Safety). (2018). *The use of polygraph in sex offender treatment*. Denver, CO: Author.

Cerdá, M., Nandi, V., Frye, V., Egan, J. E., Rundle, A., Quinn, J.W., . . . Koblin, B. (2017, April 5). Neighborhood determinants of mood and anxiety disorders among men who have sex with men in New York City. *Social Psychiatry and Psychiatric Epidemiology*. [Epub ahead of print]

Cerniglia, L., Cimino, S., Tafa, M., Marzilli, E., Ballarotto, G., & Bracaglia, F. (2017). Family profiles in eating disorders: Family functioning and psychopathology. *Psychology Research and Behavior Management, 10*, 305–312.

Cervesi, C., Park, S. Y., Galling, B., Molteni, S., Masi, G., Gerhard, T., Olfson, M., & Correll, C. U. (2017). Extent, time course, and moderators of antipsychotic treatment in youth and mood disorders: Results of a meta-analysis and meta-regression analyses. *Journal of Clinical Psychiatry, 78*, 347–357.

Chadwick, P. K. (2014). Peer-professional first-person account: Before psychosis—schizoid personality from the inside. *Schizophrenia Bulletin, 40*(3), 483–486.

Chamberlain, S. R., Redden, S. A., Leppink, E., & Grant, J. E. (2017). Problematic internet use in gamblers: Impact on clinical and cognitive measures. *CNS Spectrums, 22*(6), 495–503.

Chambers, J. (2017). The neurobiology of attachment: From infancy to clinical outcomes. *Psychodynamic Psychiatry, 45*(4), 542–563.

Chan, A. T., Sun, G. Y., Tam, W. W., Tsoi, K. K., & Wong, S. Y. (2017). The effectiveness of group-based behavioral activation in the treatment of depression: An updated meta-analysis of randomized controlled trial. *Journal of Affective Disorders, 208*, 345–354.

Chan, C. C., Szeszko, P. R., Wong, E., Tang, C. Y., Kelliher, C., Penner, J. D., . . . Hazlett, E. A. (2018, February 14). Frontal and temporal cortical volume, white matter tract integrity, and hemispheric asymmetry in schizotypal personality disorder. *Schizophrenia Research*. [Epub ahead of print]

Chandra, A., Mosher, W. D., & Copen, C. (2011). Sexual behavior, sexual attraction, and sexual identity in the United States: Data from the 2006–2008 national survey of family growth. *National Health Statistics Reports, 36*, March 3.

Chang, G. (2017, April 18). Substance misuse in pregnant women. *UpToDate*. Retrieved from http://www.uptodate.com.

Chang, G. (2018, February 15). Alcohol intake and pregnancy. *UpToDate*. Retrieved from http://www.uptodate.com.

Chang, J. S., Hsiao, J-R., & Chen, C-H. (2017). *ALDH2* polymorphism and alcohol-related cancers in Asians: A public health perspective. *Journal of Biomedical Science, 24*, 19.

Chang, L. Y., Chang, H. Y., Lin, L. N., Wu, C. C., & Yen, L. L. (2017). Disentangling the effects of depression on trajectories of sleep problems from adolescence through young adulthood. *Journal of Affective Disorders, 217*, 48–54.

Chapman, B. P., Benedict, R. H., Lin, F., Roy, S., Federoff, H. J., & Mapstone, M. (2017). Personality and performance in specific neurocognitive domains among older persons. *American Journal of Geriatric Psychiatry, 25*(8), 900–908.

Chaput, J-P., Weippert, M., LeBlanc, A. G., Hjorth, M. F., Michaelsen, K. F., Katzmarzyk, P. T., . . . Sjödin, A. M. (2016). Are children like werewolves? Full moon and its association with sleep and activity behaviors in an international sample of children. *Frontiers in Pediatrics, 4*, 24.

Charney, A. W., Ruderfer, D. M., Stahl, E. A., Moran, J. L., Chambert, K., Belliveau, R. A., . . . Sklar, P. (2017). Evidence for genetic heterogeneity between clinical subtypes of bipolar disorder. *Translational Psychiatry. 7*(1), e993.

Charney, D. S., Woods, S. W., Goodman, W. K., & Heninger, G. R. (1987). Neurobiological mechanisms of panic anxiety: Biochemical and behavioral correlates of yohimbine-induced anxiety. *American Journal of Psychiatry, 144*(8), 1030–1036.

Charney, D. S., Woods, S. W., Price, L. H., Goodman, W. K., Glazer, W. M., & Heninger, G. R. (1990). Noradrenergic dysregulation in panic disorder. In J. C. Ballenger (Ed.), *Neurobiology of panic disorder*. New York: Wiley-Liss.

Chassin, L., Colder, C. R., Hussong, A., & Sher, K. J. (2016). Substance use and substance use disorders. In D. Cicchetti (Ed.), *Developmental psychopathology, Vol. 3: Maladaptation and psychopathology* (3rd ed., Chap. 19, pp. 833–897). Hoboken, NJ: John Wiley.

Chavira, D. A., Grilo, C. M., Shea, M. T., Yen, S., Gunderson, J. G., Morey, L. C., . . . McGlashan, T. H. (2003). Ethnicity and four personality disorders. *Comprehensive Psychiatry, 44*(6), 483–491.

Che, X. Q., Song, N., Gao, Y., Ren, R. J., & Wang, G. (2018). Precision medicine of frontotemporal dementia: from genotype to phenotype. *Frontiers in Bioscience (Landmark Edition), 23*, 1144–1165.

Chefetz, R. A. (2017). Issues in consultation for treatments with distressed activated abuser/protector self-states in dissociative identity disorder. *Journal of Trauma and Dissociation. 18*(3): 465–475.

Chen, H., Wang, X., Huang, Y., Li, G., Liu, Z., Li, Y., & Geng, H. (2019). Prevalence, risk factors and multi-group latent class analysis of lifetime anxiety disorders comorbid depressive symptoms. *Journal of Affective Disorders, 243*, 360–365.

Chen, X., Jiang, Y., Chen, L., He, H., Dong, L., Hou, C., . . . Luo, C. (2017). Altered hippocampo-cerebello-cortical circuit in schizophrenia by a spatiotemporal consistency and causal connectivity analysis. *Frontiers in Neuroscience, 11*, 25.

Cheong, E. V., Sinnott, C., Dahly, D., & Kearney, P. M. (2017). Adverse childhood experiences (ACEs) and later-life depression: Perceived social support as a potential protective factor. *BMJ Open, 7*(9), e013228.

Cherry, K. (2017, April 25). 10 fascinating facts about personality. *Verywell*. Retrieved from https://www.verywell.com/facts-about-personality-2795436.

Cherry, K. (2018). 9 common dreams and what they supposedly mean: What do dreams really mean? *Verywellmind*. Retrieved from https://verywellmind.com/understanding-your-dreams.

Chesnes, M., & Jin, G. Z. (2016). *Direct-to-consumer advertising and online search*. Federal Trade Commission.

Cheung, G., & Sundram, F. (2017). Understanding the progression from physical illness to suicidal behavior: A case study based on a newly developed conceptual model. *Clinical Gerontologist, 40*(2), 124–129.

Chhabra, K. H., Adams, J. M., Jones, G. L., Yamashita, M., Schlapschy, M., Skerra, A., . . . Low, M. J. (2016). Reprogramming the body weight set point by a reciprocal interaction of hydrothalamic leptin sensitivity and *Pomc* gene expression reverts extreme obesity. *Molecular Metabolism, 5*(10), 869–881.

Chi, S., Yu, J., Tan, M., & Tan, L. (2014). Depression in Alzheimer's disease: Epidemiology, mechanisms, and management. *Journal of Alzheimer's Disease, 42*(3), 739–755.

Choca, J. P., & Rossini, E. D. (2018). *Assessment using the Rorschach inkblot test (Psychological Assessment Series)*. Washington, DC: American Psychological Association.

Choi, K. W., Na, E. J., Hong, J. P., Cho, M. J., Fava, M., Mischoulon, D., Cho, H., & Jeon, H. J. (2018). Alcohol-induced disinhibition is associated with impulsivity, depression, and suicide attempt: A nationwide community sample of Korean adults. *Journal of Affective Disorders, 227*, 323–329.

Choi, S. W., Shin, Y. C., Kim, D. J., Choi, J. S., Kim, S., Kim, S. H., & Youn, H. (2017). Treatment modalities for patients with gambling disorder. *Annals of General Psychiatry, 16*, 23.

Choi, Y. S., Lee, E. J., & Cho, Y. (2017). The effect of Korean-group cognitive behavioural therapy among patients with panic disorder in clinic settings. *Journal of Psychiatric and Mental Health Nursing, 24*(1), 28–40.

Chomet, N. (2018). *Coping with body shaming.* New York: Rosen Young Adult.

Chou, T., Carpenter, A., Kerns, C. E., Elkins, R. M., Green, J. G., & Comer, J. S. (2017). Disqualified qualifiers: Evaluating the utility of the revised DSM-5 definition of potentially traumatic events among area youth following the Boston Marathon bombing. *Depression and Anxiety, 34,* 367–373.

Chowdhary, N., Jotheeswaran, A. T., Nadkarni, A., Hollon, S. D., King, M., Jordans, M. J., . . . Patel, V. (2014). The methods and outcomes of cultural adaptations of psychological treatments for depressive disorders: A systematic review. *Psychological Medicine, 44*(6), 1131–1146.

Christensen, A. (2017, January 10). Most selfie takers aren't narcissists, study says. *PhysicsForums.* Retrieved from https://phys.org/news.

Christensen, A., & Doss, B. D. (2017). Integrative behavioral couple therapy. *Current Opinion in Psychology, 13,* 111–114.

Christensen, B. S., Gronbaek, M., Osler, M., Pedersen, B. V., Graugaard, C., & Frisch, M. (2011). Sexual dysfunctions and difficulties in Denmark: Prevalence and associated sociodemographic factors. *Archives of Sexual Behavior, 40*(1), 121–132.

Christensen, A., Atkins, D. C., Baucom, B., & Yi, J. (2010). Marital status and satisfaction five years following a randomized clinical trial comparing traditional versus integrative behavioral couple therapy. *Journal of Consulting and Clinical Psychology, 78*(2), 225–235.

Christensen, A., Doss, B. D., & Jacobson, N. S. (2014). *Reconcilable differences: Rebuild your relationship by rediscovering the partner you love—without losing yourself* (2nd ed.). New York: Guilford Press.

Christian, C. (2017, October 13). Child abuse: Epidemiology, mechanisms, and types of abusive head trauma in infants and children. *UpToDate.* Retrieved from http://www.uptodate.com.

Christiansen, E., Agerbo, E., Bilenberg, N., & Stenager, E. (2016). SSRIs and risk of suicide attempts in young people: A Danish observational register-based historical cohort study using propensity score. *Nordic Journal of Psychiatry, 70*(3), 167–175.

Chu, C. S., Stubbs, B., Chen, T. Y., Tang, C. H., Li, D. J., Yang, W. C., . . . Lin, P. Y. (2018). The effectiveness of adjunct mindfulness-based intervention in treatment of bipolar disorder: A systematic review and meta-analysis. *Journal of Affective Disorders, 225,* 234–245.

Chu, J., Leino, A., Pflum, S., & Sue, S. (2016). Psychotherapy with racial/ethnic minority groups: Theory and practice. In A. J. Consoli, L. E. Beutler, & B. Bongar (Eds.), *Comprehensive textbook of psychotherapy: Theory and practice* (2nd ed., pp. 346–362). New York: Oxford University Press.

Chudal, R., Gissler, M., Sucksdorff, D., Lehti, V., Suominen, A., Kinkka-Yli-Salomaki, S., . . . Sourander, A. (2014). Parental age and the risk of bipolar disorders. *Bipolar Disorders, 16,* 624–632.

Cicchetti, D. (2016). *Developmental psychopathology* (3rd ed., 4 vols.). New York: Wiley.

Cicchetti, D. (2016). *Developmental psychopathology, Vol. 1: Theory and method* (3rd ed.). New York: Wiley.

Cicchetti, D. (2018). A multilevel developmental approach to the prevention of psychopathology in children and adolescents. In J. Butcher (Ed.-in-Chief), *APA handbook of psychopathology, Vol. 2, Psychopathology in children and adolescents* (Chap. 3). Washington, DC: APA.

Cicchetti, D. (Ed.) (2016). *Developmental psychopathology, maladaptation and psychopathology, Vol. 3: Maladaptation and psychopathology* (3rd ed.). New York: Wiley.

Cicchetti, D., & Toth, S. L. (2016). Child maltreatment and developmental psychopathology: A multilevel perspective. In D. Cicchetti (Ed.), *Developmental psychopathology, Vol. 3: Maladaptation and psychopathology* (3rd ed., pp. 457–512). New York: Wiley.

Ciliberti, M. G., Albenzio, M., Inghese, C., Santillo, A., Marino, R., Sevi, A., & Caroprese, M. (2017). Peripheral blood mononuclear cell proliferation and cytokine production in sheep as affected by cortisol level and duration of stress. *Journal of Dairy Science, 100*(1), 750–756.

Cipolletta, S., Votadoro, R., & Faccio, E. (2017). Online support for transgender people: An analysis of forums and social networks. *Health & Social Care in the Community, 25,* 1542–1551.

Cipriano, A., Cella, S., & Cotrufo, P. (2017). Nonsuicidal self-injury: A systematic review. *Frontiers in Psychology, 8,* 1946.

Ciraulo, D. A., Shader, R. I., & Greenblatt, D. J. (2011). Clinical pharmacology and therapeutics of antidepressants. In D. A. Ciraulo & R. I. Shader (Eds.), *Pharmacotherapy of depression* (2nd ed., pp. 33–124). New York: Springer Science + Business Media.

Cirelli, C. (2016, December 8). Insufficient sleep: Definition, epidemiology, and adverse outcomes: *UpToDate.* Retrieved from http://www.uptodate.com.

CISCRP (Center for Information and Study on Clinical Research Participation). (2013). *Clinical trial facts and figures for health professionals.* Boston, MA: CISCRP.

Clark, D. A. (2018). *The anxious thoughts workbook: Skills to overcome the unwanted intrusive thoughts that drive anxiety, obsessions, and depression.* Oakland, CA: New Harbinger Publications.

Clark, D. A., & Beck, A. T. (2010). *Cognitive therapy of anxiety disorders: Science and practice.* New York: Guilford Press.

Clark, D. A., & Beck, A. T. (2012). *The anxiety and worry workbook: The cognitive behavioral solution.* New York: Guilford Press.

Clarke, J. C., & Saunders, J. B. (1988). *Alcoholism and problem drinking: Theories and treatment.* Sydney, Australia: Pergamon Press.

Clarkin, J. F., Cain, N., Lenzenweger, M. F., & Levy, K. N. (2018). Transference-focused psychotherapy. In W. J. Livesley & R. Larstone (Eds.), *Handbook of personality disorders: Theory, research, and treatment* (2nd ed., Ch. 32). New York: Guilford Press.

Clarkin, J. F., Livesley, W. J., & Meehan, K. B. (2018). Clinical assessment. In W. J. Livesley & R. Larstone (Eds.), *Handbook of personality disorders: Theory, research, and treatment* (2nd ed., Ch. 21). New York: Guilford Press.

Clausen, L., Rosenvinge J. H., Friborg, O., & Rokkedal, K. (2011). Validating the Eating Disorder Inventory-3 (EDI-3): A comparison between 561 female eating disorders patients and 878 females from the general population. *Journal of Psychopathology and Behavioral Assessment, 33*(1), 101–110.

CMSAC (Central MN Sexual Assault Center). (2017). *Facts and statistics: Facts about sexual assault.* St. Cloud, MN: CMSAC.

Coates, T. D. (2018, February 18). Drug-induced neutropenia and agranulocytosis. *UpToDate.* Retrieved from http://www.uptodate.com.

Coffey, M. J. (2017, November 22). Catatonia in adults: Epidemiology, clinical features, assessment, and diagnosis. *UpToDate.* Retrieved from http://www.uptodate.com.

Coffey, M. J. (2017, November 22). Catatonia: Treatment and prognosis. *UpToDate.* Retrieved from http://www.uptodate.com.

Coffin, P. (2017, April 10). Prevention of lethal opioid overdose in the community. *UpToDate.* Retrieved from http://www.uptodate.com.

Cohen, K. M., & Savin-Williams, R. C. (2017). Treating sexual problems in lesbian, gay, and bisexual clients. In Z. D. Peterson (Ed.), *The Wiley-Blackwell handbook of sex therapy* (Chap. 17, pp. 269–290). Hoboken, NJ: Wiley-Blackwell.

Cohen, N. (2009, July 28). "A Rorschach cheat sheet on Wikipedia?" *New York Times,* p. A1.

Coker, T. R., Elliott, M. N., Toomey, S. L., Schwebel, D. C., Cuccaro, P., Emery, S., . . . Schuster, M. A. (2016). Racial and ethnic disparities in ADHD diagnosis and treatment. *Pediatrics, 138*(3).

Colburn, D. (1996, November 19). Singer's suicide doesn't lead to "copycat" deaths. *Washington Post Health,* p. 5.

Cole, M. (2016, August 13). Aversion therapy and learning to overcome bad habits. *Today's Therapist.*

Coleman, K. J., Stewart, C., Waitzfelder, B. E., Zeber, J. E., Morales, L. S., Ahmed, A. T., . . . Simon, G. E. (2016). Racial-ethnic differences in psychiatric diagnoses and treatment across 11 health care systems in the mental health research network. *Psychiatry Services, 67*(7), 749–757.

Coleman, L. (1984). *The reign of error: Psychiatry, authority, and law.* Boston: Beacon.

Colen, C. G., Ramey, D. M., Cooksey, E. C., & Williams, D. R. (2018). Racial disparities in health among nonpoor African Americans and Hispanics: The role of acute and chronic discrimination. *Social Science & Medicine, 199,* 167–180.

Colletti, G., Lynn, S. J., & Laurence, J-R. (2010). Hypnosis and the treatment of dissociative identity disorder. In S. J. Lynn, J. W. Rhue, & I. Kirsch (Eds.), *Handbook of clinical hypnosis* (2nd ed., pp. 433–451). Washington, DC: American Psychological Association.

Colli, A., Tanzilli, A., Dimaggio, G., & Lingiardi, V. (2014). Patient personality and therapist response: An empirical investigation. *American Journal of Psychiatry, 171*(1), 102–108.

Collingwood, J. (2016). The link between bipolar disorder and creativity. *Psych Central.* Retrieved from https://psychcentral.com.

Collins, B. M., & Stam, H. J. (2015). Freeman's transorbital lobotomy as an anomaly: A material culture examination of surgical instruments and operational spaces. *History of Psychology, 18*(2), 119–131.

Collins, J. L., Thompson, K., Sherry, S. B., Glowacka, M., & Stewart, S. H. (2018). Drinking to cope with depression mediates the relationship between social avoidance and alcohol problems: A 3-wave, 18-month longitudinal study. *Addictive Behaviors, 76,* 182–187.

Coluccia, A., Gabbrielli, M., Gualtieri, G., Ferretti, F., Pozza, A., & Fagiolini, A. (2016). Sexual masochism disorder in asphyxiophilia: A deadly yet underrecognized disease. *Case Reports in Psychiatry, 2016,* ID 5474862.

Comas-Díaz, L. (2019). Multicultural theories of psychotherapy. In D. Wedding & R. J. Corsini (Eds.), *Current psychotherapies* (11th ed., Ch. 15). Independence, KY: Cengage Publications.

Comer, J. S., & Bry, L. J. (2018). Research methodology in clinical child and adolescent psychology. In T. H. Ollendick, S. W. White, & B. A. White (Eds.), *The Oxford handbook of clinical child and adolescent psychology* (Chap. 8). NY: Oxford University Press.

Comer, J. S., Bry, L., Poznanski, B., & Golik, A. M. (2016). Children's mental health in the context of terrorist attacks, ongoing threats, and possibilities of future terrorism. *Current Psychiatry Reports, 18,* 79.

Comer, J. S., Chow, C., Chan, P., Cooper-Vince, C., & Wilson, L. A. S. (2013). Psychosocial treatment efficacy for disruptive behavior problems in young children: A meta-analytic examination. *Journal of the American Academy of Child and Adolescent Psychiatry, 52,* 26–36.

Comer, J. S., Dantowitz, A., Chou, T., Edison, A. L., Elkins, R. M., Kerns, C., Brown, B., & Green, J. G. (2014). Adjustment among area youth after the Boston Marathon bombing and subsequent manhunt, *Pediatrics, 134*(1), 7–14.

Comer, J. S., Dantowitz, A., Chou, T., Edison, A. L., Elkins, R. M., Kerns, C., Brown, B., & Green, J. G. (2014). Adjustment among area youth after the Boston Marathon bombing and subsequent manhunt, *Pediatrics, 134*(1), 7–14.

Comer, J. S., Del Busto, C., Dick, A. S., Furr, J. M., & Puliafico, A. C. (2019). Adapting PCIT to treat anxiety problems in young children: The PCIT CALM Program. In L. Niec (Ed.), *Handbook of parent-child interaction therapy: Innovations and applications for research and practice.* New York: Springer Publishing.

Comer, J. S., Furr, J. M., & Gurwitch, R. (2018). Terrorism exposure and the family: Where we are, and where we go next. In B. Fiese (Ed.), *APA handbook of contemporary family psychology.* Washington, DC: APA.

Comer, J. S., Furr, J. M., Kerns, C. E., Miguel, E., Coxe, S., Elkins, R. M., . . . Freeman, J. B. (2017). Internet-delivered, family-based treatment for early-onset OCD: A pilot randomized trial. *Journal of Consulting and Clinical Psychology, 85,* 178–186.

Comer, J. S., Furr, J. M., Miguel, E., Cooper-Vince, C. E., Carpenter, A. L., Elkins, R. M., . . . Chase, R. (2017). Remotely delivering real-time parent training to the home: An initial randomized trial of Internet-delivered Parent-Child Interaction Therapy (I-PCIT). *Journal of Consulting and Clinical Psychology, 85,* 909–917.

Comer, J. S., Golik, A., & Martin, J. (2019). Learning from the past: Understanding children's mental health after 9/11 and after the Boston Marathon bombing. In S. Tyano, C. W. Hoven, & L. Amsel (Eds.), *Responses to children's mental health needs after major disasters: An international perspective.* New York: Springer.

Comer, J. S., Hong, N., Poznanski, B., Silva, K., & Wilson, M. (2019). Evidence base update on the treatment of early childhood anxiety and related problems. *Journal of Clinical Child and Adolescent Psychology.*

Comer, J. S., Mojtabai, R., & Olfson, M. (2011). National trends in the antipsychotic treatment of psychiatric outpatients with anxiety disorders. *American Journal of Psychiatry, 168*(10), 1057–1065.

Comer, J. S., Olfson, M., & Mojtabai, R. (2010). National trends in child and adolescent psychotropic polypharmacy in office-based practice, 1996–2007. *Journal of the American Academy of Child & Adolescent Psychiatry, 49*(10), 1001–1010.

Comer, R. (1973). *Therapy interviews with a schizophrenic patient.* Unpublished manuscript.

Compean, E., & Hamner, M. (2019). Posttraumatic stress disorders with secondary psychotic features (PTSD-SP): Diagnostic and treatment challenges. *Progress in Neuro-Psychopharmacology & Biological Psychiatry, 88,* 265–275.

Conrad, D., Wilker, S., Pfeiffer, A., Lingenfelder, B., Ebalu, T., Lanzinger, H., . . . Kolassa, S. (2017). Does trauma event type matter in the assessment of traumatic load? *European Journal of Psychotraumatology, 8*(1), 1344079.

Conradi, H. J., Kamphuis, J. H., & de Jonge, P. (2018). Adult attachment predicts the seven-year course of recurrent depression in primary care. *Journal of Affective Disorders, 225,* 160–166.

Conti, A. A. (2014). Western medical rehabilitation through time: A historical and epistemological review. *The Scientific World Journal, 2014,* 432506.

Conti, C., Mennitto, C., De Francesco, G., Fraticelli, F., Vitacolonna, E., & Fulcheri, M. (2017). Clinical characteristics of diabetes mellitus and suicide risk. *Frontiers in Psychiatry, 8,* 40.

Cook, N., Ayers, S., & Horsch, A. (2018). Maternal posttraumatic stress disorder during the perinatal period and child outcomes: A systematic review. *Journal of Affective Disorders, 225,* 18–31.

Cooney, P., Jackman, C., Tunney, C., Coyle, D., & O'Reilly, G. (2018, May 3). Computer-assisted cognitive behavioural therapy: The experiences of adults who have an intellectual disability and anxiety or depression. *Journal of Applied Research in Intellectual Disabilities.* [Epub ahead of print]

Coons, P. M., & Bowman, E. S. (2001). Ten-year follow-up study of patients with dissociative identity disorder. *Journal of Trauma and Dissociation, 2*(1), 73–89.

Cooper, A. A., Kline, A. C., Graham, B., Bedard-Gilligan, M., Mello, P. G., Feeny, N. C., & Zoellner, L. A. (2017). Homework "dose," type, and helpfulness as predictors of clinical outcomes in prolonged exposure for PTSD. *Behavior Therapy, 48*(2), 182–194.

Cooper, M. (2008). *Essential research findings in counselling and psychotherapy: The facts are friendly.* Los Angeles, CA: Sage Publications.

Cooper, M. (2016). *Existential therapies* (2nd ed.). Los Angeles: Sage Publications.

Cooper, R. (2014). On deciding to have a lobotomy: Either lobotomies were justified or decisions under risk should not always seek to maximize expected utility. *Medicine, Health Care, and Philosophy, 17*(1), 143–154.

Copen, C. (2017). *Condom use during sexual intercourse among women and men aged 15–44 in the United States: 2011–2015 National Survey of Family Growth.* Atlanta, GA: CDC, National Health Statistics Report, No. 105.

Copen, C. E., Chandra, A., & Febo-Vazquez, M. S. (2016, January 7). Sexual behavior, sexual attraction, and sexual orientation among adults aged 18–44 in the United States: Data from the 2011–2013 National Survey of Family Growth. Atlanta, GA: CDC, National Health Statistics Report, No. 88.

Corathers, S. D. (2018). Collaboration is key to developing effective hormonal treatment paradigms for transgender youth. *Journal of Adolescent Health, 62*(4), 361–362.

Corey, G. (2017). *Theory and practice of counseling and psychotherapy* (10th ed.). Independence, KY: Cengage Learning.

Cornacchio, D., Bry, L. J., Sanchez, A. L., Poznanski, B., & Comer, J. S. (2017). Psychosocial treatment and prevention of conduct problems in early childhood. In J. E. Lochman & W. Matthys (Eds.), *The Wiley handbook of disruptive and impulse-control disorders.* New York: Wiley.

Cornacchio, D., Crum, K. I., Coxe, S., Pincus, D. B., & Comer, J. S. (2016). Irritability and severity of anxious symptomatology among youth with anxiety disorders. *Journal of the American Academy of Child and Adolescent Psychiatry, 55,* 54–61.

Cornacchio, D., Sanchez, A. L., Chou, T., & Comer, J. S. (2017). Cognitive-behavioral therapy for children and adolescents. In S.G. Hofmann & G. Asmundson (Eds.), *The science of cognitive behavioral therapy: From theory to therapy.* New York: Elsevier.

Corral-Corral, I., & Corral-Corral, C. (2016). Tarantism in Spain in the eighteenth century: Latrodectism and suggestion. [Spanish] *Revista de Neurologia, 63*(8), 370–379.

Corrie, S., & Callanan, M. M. (2001). Therapists' beliefs about research and the scientist-practitioner model in an evidence-based health care climate? A qualitative study. *British Journal of Medical Psychology, 74*(2), 135–149.

Corrigan, P. W., Schomerus, G., Shuman, V., Kraus, D., Perlick, D., Harnish, A., . . . Smelson, D. (2017). Developing a research agenda for reducing the stigma of addictions, Part II: Lessons from the mental health stigma literature. *American Journal on Addictions, 26*(1), 67–74.

Corring, D., O'Reilly, R. L., Sommerdyk, C., & Russell, E. (2018, April 26). What clinicians say about the experience of working with individuals on community treatment orders. *Psychiatric Services.* [Epub ahead of print]

Coryell, W. (2018, April 1). Unipolar depression in adults: Course of illness. *UpToDate.* Retrieved from http://www.uptodate.com.

Coskun, M., & Ozturk, M. (2013). Sexual fetishism in adolescence: Report of two cases. *Journal of Psychiatry and Neurological Sciences, 26,* 199–205.

Costa, R. T. D., Carvalho, M. R., Ribeiro, P., & Nardi, A. E. (2018, February 15). Virtual reality exposure therapy for fear of driving: Analysis of clinical characteristics, psychological response, and sense of presence. *Revista Brasileira de Psiquiatria.* [Epub ahead of print]

Costantino, G., Litman, L., Waxman, R., Dupertuis, D., Pais, E., Rosenzweig, C., . . . Canales, M. M. F. (2014). Tell-me-a-story (TEMAS) assessment for culturally diverse children and adolescents. *Rorschachiana, 35*(2), 154–175.

Costantino, G., Dana, R. H., & Malgady, R. G. (2007). *TEMAS (Tell-Me-A-Story) assessment in multicultural societies.* Mahwah, NJ: Lawrence Erlbaum.

Costello, E. J., & Angold, A. (2016). Developmental epidemiology. In D. Cicchetti (Ed.), *Developmental psychology, Vol. 1: Theory and Method* (3rd ed.). New York: Wiley.

Cottle, J. (2016, March 15). Facebook and mental health: Is social media hurting or helping? *MentalHelp.net.*

Cottler, L. B., Hu, H., Smallwood, B. A., Anthony, J. C., Wu, L. T., & Eaton, W. W. (2016). Nonmedical opioid pain relievers and all-cause mortality: A 27-year follow-up from the Epidemiologic Catchment Area Study. *American Journal of Public Health, 106*(3), 509–516.

Cottrell, D. B., & Williams, J. (2016). Eating disorders in men. *Nurse Practitioner, 41*(9), 49–55.

Covey, R. D. (2017). The temporary insanity defense. In M. D. White (Ed.), *The insanity defense: Multidisciplinary views on its history, trends, and controversies* (Chap. 2, pp. 23–60). Westport, CT: Praeger.

Coyne, S. M., Padilla-Walker, L. M., & Holmgren, H. G. (2018). A six-year longitudinal study of texting trajectories during adolescence. *Child Development, 89*(1), 58–65.

Cozzi, G., Minute, M., Skabar, A., Pirrone, A., Jaber, M., Neri, E., . . . Barbi, E. (2017). Somatic symptom disorder was common in children and adolescents attending an emergency department complaining of pain. *Acta Paediatrica, 106*(4), 586–593.

Crabtree, S. (2011). *U.S. seniors maintain happiness highs with less social time* (Gallup poll 151457). *Gallup.* Retrieved from http://www.gallup.com/poll/151457.

Craig, T. K., Rus-Calafell, M., Ward, T., Leff, J. P., Huckvale, M., Howarth, E., . . . Garety, P. A. (2018). AVATAR therapy for auditory verbal hallucinations in people with psychosis: A single-blind, randomised controlled trial. *Lancet Psychiatry, 5*(1), 31–40.

Craig, T., Ward, T., & Rus-Calafell, M. (2016). AVATAR therapy for refractory auditory hallucinations. In B. Pradhan, N. Pinninti, & S. Rathod (Eds.), *Brief interventions for psychosis: A clinical compendium* (Chap. 4). London: Springer.

Craig, T., & Power, P. (2010). Inpatient provision in early psychosis. In P. French, J. Smith, D. Shiers, M. Reed, & M. Rayne (Eds.), *Promoting recovery in early psychosis: A practice manual* (pp. 17–26). Hoboken, NJ: Wiley-Blackwell.

Cramer, P. (2017), Defense mechanism card pull in TAT stories. *Journal of Personality Assessment, 99*(1), 15–24.

Crandall, M. (2018, February 28). Trends of gender-affirming surgery among transgender patients in the United States. *JAMA Surgery.* [Epub ahead of print]

Craske, C. M., & Barlow, D. H. (2014). Panic disorder and agoraphobia. In D. H. Barlow, *Clinical handbook of psychological disorders* (5th ed., pp. 1–61). New York: Guilford Press.

Craske, M. G. (2017). *Cognitive-behavioral therapy.* Washington, DC: American Psychological Association.

Craske, M. (2017, May 26). Psychotherapy for panic disorder with or without agoraphobia in adults. *UpToDate.* Retrieved from http://www.uptodate.com.

Craske, M. (2018, March 1). Psychotherapy for generalized anxiety disorder in adults. *UpToDate.* Retrieved from http://www.uptodate.com.

Craske, M., & Bystritsky, A. (2017, December 1). Approach to treating generalized anxiety disorder in adults. *UpToDate.* Retrieved from http://www.uptodate.com.

Crawford, C., Burns, J., & Fernie, B. A. (2015). Psychosocial impact of involvement in the Special Olympics. *Research in Developmental Disabilities, 45-46,* 93–102.

CRC (Cyberbullying Research Center). (2016, November 26). *2016 cyberbullying data.* Retrieved from https://cyberbullying.org.

CRC (Cyberbullying Research Center). (2017, January 3). *Millions of students skip school each year because of bullying.* Retrieved from https://cyberbullying.org.

CRC (Cyberbullying Research Center). (2017, June 2). *More on the link between bullying and suicide.* Retrieved from https://cyberbullying.org.

CRCC (Cleveland Rape Crisis Center). (2014). Sexual violence on college campuses. Retrieved from CRCC website: http://www.clevelandrapecrisis.org/resources/statistics/sexual-violence-on-college-campuses.

Creswell, J. D. (2017). Mindfulness interventions. *Annual Review of Psychology, 68,* 491–516.

Cristea, I. A., Gentili, C., Cotet, C. D., Palomba, D., Barbui, C., & Cuijpers, P. (2017). Efficacy of psychotherapies for borderline personality disorder: A systematic review and meta-analysis. *JAMA Psychiatry, 74*(4), 319–328.

Cronin, E., Brand, B. L., & Mattanah, J. F. (2014). The impact of the therapeutic alliance on treatment outcome in patients with dissociative disorders. *European Journal of Psychotraumatology, 5*d, 22676.

Crow, S. J. (2017, July 17). Bulimia nervosa in adults: Pharmacotherapy. *UpToDate.* Retrieved from http://www.uptodate.com.

Crow, T. J. (1980). Positive and negative schizophrenic symptoms and the role of dopamine: II. *British Journal of Psychiatry, 137,* 383–386.

Crow, T. J. (1985). The two-syndrome concept: Origins and current status. *Schizophrenia Bulletin, 11*(3), 471–486.

Crow, T. J. (1995). Brain changes and negative symptoms in schizophrenia. *Psychopathology, 28*(1), 18–21.

Crow, T. J. (2008). The "big bang" theory of the origin of psychosis and the faculty of language. *Schizophrenia Research, 102*(1–3), 31–52.

CRS (Congressional Research Service). (2016, March 3). Heroin production in Mexico and U.S. policy. *CRS.* Retrieved from https://fas.org/sgp/crs/row/IN10456.pdf.

Crystal, S., Kleinhaus, K., Perrin, M., & Malaspina, D. (2012). Advancing paternal age and the risk of schizophrenia. In A. S. Brown & P. H. Patterson (Eds.), *The origins of schizophrenia* (pp. 140–155). New York: Columbia University Press.

CSP Daily News. (2017, March 7). *E-cig sales to hit $27 billion by 2022: Study.* Retrieved from http://www.cspdailynews.com.

Cui, L. B., Liu, K., Li, C., Wang, L. X., Guo, F., Tian, P., . . . Yin, H. Putamen-related regional and network functional deficits in first-episode schizophrenia with auditory verbal hallucinations. *Schizophrenia Research, 173*(1-2), 13–22.

Cui, Y., Liu, B., Song, M., Lipnicki, D. M., Li, J., Xie, S., . . . Jiang, T. (2018). Auditory verbal hallucinations are related to cortical thinning in the left middle temporal gyrus of patients with schizophrenia. *Psychological Medicine, 48*(1), 115–122.

Cuijpers, P., Centili, C., Banos, R. M., Garcia-Campayo, J., Botella, C., & Cristea, I. A. (2016). Relative effects of cognitive and behavioral therapies on generalized anxiety disorder, social anxiety disorder and panic disorder: A meta-analysis. *Journal of Anxiety Disorders, 43,* 79–89.

Cuijpers, P., Karyotaki, E., Weitz, E., Andersson, G., Hollon, S. D., & van Straten, A. (2014). The effects of psychotherapies for major depression in adults on remission, recovery and improvement: A meta-analysis. *Journal of Affective Disorders, 159,* 118–126.

Culp, A. M., Clyman, M. M., & Culp, R. E. (1995). Adolescent depressed mood, reports of suicide attempts, and asking for help. *Adolescence, 30*(120), 827–837.

Culver, J. L., & Pratchett, L. C. (2010). Adjunctive psychosocial interventions in the management of bipolar disorders. In T. A. Ketter (Ed.), *Handbook of diagnosis and treatment of bipolar disorders* (pp. 661–676). Arlington, VA: American Psychiatric Publishing.

Cummings, J. R., Ji, X., Allen, L., Lally, C., & Druss, B. G. (2017). Racial and ethnic differences in ADHD treatment quality among Medicaid-enrolled youths. *Pediatrics, 139*(6), e20162444.

Cunningham, G. R., & Khera, M. (2018, January 31). Evaluation of male sexual dysfunction. *UpToDate.* Retrieved from http://www.uptodate.com.

Cunningham, G. R., & Rosen, R. C. (2018, April 18). Overview of male sexual dysfunction. *UpToDate.* Retrieved from http://www.uptodate.com.

Cunningham, K. C., LoSavio, S. T., Dennis, P. A., Farmer, C., Clancy, C. P., Hertzberg, M. A., . . . Beckham, J. C. (2019). Shame as a mediator between posttraumatic stress disorder symptoms and suicidal ideation among veterans. *Journal of Affective Disorders, 243,* 216–219.

Curtiss, J., Andrews, L., Davis, M., Smits, J., & Hofmann, S. G. (2017). A meta-analysis of pharmacotherapy for social anxiety disorder: An examination of efficacy, moderators, and mediators. *Expert Opinion on Pharmacotherapy, 18*(3), 243–251.

Cutler, D. M., Glaeser, E. L., & Norberg, K. E. (2001). Explaining the rise in youth suicide. In J. Gruber (Ed.), *Risky behavior among youths: An economic analysis* (pp. 219–269). Chicago: University of Chicago Press.

Cutrer, F. M., & Bajwa, Z. H. (2017, November 13). Pathophysiology, clinical manifestations, and diagnosis of migraine in adults. *UpToDate*. Retrieved from http://www.uptodate.com.

Cutright, P., & Fernquist, R. M. (2001). The relative gender gap in suicide: Societal integration, the culture of suicide and period effects in 20 developed countries, 1955–1994. *Social Science Research, 30*(1), 76–99.

Cutting, J. (2015). First rank symptoms of schizophrenia: Their nature and origin. *History of Psychiatry, 26*(2), 131–146.

Cuvelier, M. (2002). Victim, not villain. The mentally ill are six to seven times more likely to be murdered. *Psychology Today, 35*(3), 23.

Cynkar, A. (2007). The changing gender composition of psychology. *The Monitor, 38*(6), 46.

Da Paz, N. S., & Wallander, J. L. (2017). Interventions that target improvements in mental health for parents of children with autism spectrum disorders: A narrative review. *Clinical Psychology Review, 51*, 1–14.

da Rosa, G., Martin, P., Gondo, Y., Hirose, N., Ishioka, Y., & Poon, L. (2014). Examination of important life experiences of the oldest-old: Cross-cultural comparisons of U.S. and Japanese centenarians. *Journal of Cross-Cultural Gerontology, 29*(2), 109–130.

da Silva, A. P., Valente, A., Chaves, C., Matos, A., Gil, A., Santos, A. C., . . . Bicho, M. (2018, March 13). Characterization of Portuguese centenarian eating habits, nutritional biomarkers, and cardiovascular risk: A case control study. *Oxidative Medicine and Cellular Longevity, 2018:* 5296168.

Daalman, K., Boks, M. P., Diederen, K. M., de Weijer, A. D., Blom, J. D., Kahn, R. S., & Sommer, I. E. (2011). The same or different? A phenomenological comparison of auditory verbal hallucinations in healthy and psychotic individuals. *Journal of Clinical Psychiatry, 72*(3), 320–325.

Dahl, M. (2015, April 10). The more money you make, the more sleep you get. *NY Magazine*.

Dahlhaus, R. (2018). Of men and mice: Modeling the Fragile X Syndrome. *Frontiers in Molecular Neuroscience, 11*, 41.

Dahling, J. J., Whitaker, B. G., & Levy, P. E. (2008). The development and validation of a new Machiavellianism scale. *Journal of Management, 35*, 219–257.

Dahne, J., Lejuez, C. W., Kustanowitz, J., Felton, J. W., Diaz, V. A., Player, M. S., & Carpenter, M. J. (2017). Moodivate: A self-help behavioral activation mobile app for utilization in primary care: Development and clinical considerations. *International Journal of Psychiatry in Medicine, 52*(2), 160–175.

Dai, H. J., Su, E. C., Uddin, M., Jonnagaddala, J., Wu, C. S., & Syed-Abdul, S. (2017). Exploring associations of clinical and social parameters with violent behaviors among psychiatric patients. *Journal of Biomedical Informatics, 75S*, S149–S159.

Daigre, C., Rodríguez-Cintas, L., Tarifa, N., Rodríguez-Martos, L., Grau-Lopez, L., Berenguer, M., . . . Roncero, C. (2015). History of sexual, emotional or physical abuse and psychiatric comorbidity in substance-dependent patients. *Psychiatry Research, 229*(3), 743–749.

Dalsbø, T. K., Steiro, A., Strømme, H., & Reinar, L. M. (2017). Effectiveness of tapering from methadone or buprenorphine maintenance treatment compared to traditional maintenance treatment for people with opiate addiction: Systematic review. *Folkehelseinsuttet*. Retrieved from https://www.fhi.no/en.

Dana, R. H. (Ed.). (2015). *Handbook of cross-cultural and multicultural personality assessment*. New York: Routledge.

Dana, R. H. (2000). Culture and methodology in personality assessment. In I. Cuellar & F. A. Paniagua (Eds.), *Handbook of multicultural mental health* (pp. 97–120). San Diego, CA: Academic Press.

Dana, R. H. (2005). *Multicultural assessment: Principles, applications, and examples*. Mahwah, NJ: Lawrence Erlbaum.

Dando, C. (2017, January 26). I specialise in the psychology of torture, so I know the truth behind Trump's claims that waterboarding works. *The Independent Online*. Retrieved from http://www.independent.co.uk.

Danquah, M. N-A. (1998). *Willow weep for me: A black woman's journey through depression*. New York: W. W. Norton.

Dasgupta, P., Bhattacherjee, S., Dasgupta, S., Roy, J. K., Mukherjee, A., & Biswas, R. (2017). Nomophobic behaviors among smartphone using medical and engineering students in two colleges in West Bengal. *Indian Journal of Public Health, 61*(3), 199–204.

Daugherty, J. C., Puente, A. E., Fasfous, A. F., Hidalgo-Ruzzante, N., & Pérez-Garcia, M. (2017). Diagnostic mistakes of culturally diverse individuals when using North American neuropsychological tests. *Applied Neuropsychology: Adult, 24*(1), 16–33.

Daugherty, J., & Copen, C. (2016, March 17). Trends in attitudes about marriage, childbearing, and sexual behavior: United States, 2002, 2006–2010, and 2011–2013. Atlanta, GA: CDC, National Health Statistics Report, No. 92.

Davenport, L. (2017, August 30). Aerobic exercise improves cognition in depression. *Medscape*.

Davidson, K. M. (2018). Cognitive-behavioral therapy. In W. J. Livesley & R. Larstone (Eds.), *Handbook of personality disorders: Theory, research, and treatment* (2nd ed., Ch. 28). New York: Guilford Press.

Davidson, L., & Chan, K. K. S. (2014). Common factors: Evidence-based practice and recovery. *Psychiatric Services, 65*(5), 675–677.

Davis, M. (1992). Analysis of aversive memories using the fear potentiated startle paradigm. In M. Butters & L. R. Squire (Eds.), *The neuropaychology of memory* (2nd ed.). New York: Guilford Press.

Davis, E., Burden, R., & Manning, R. (2010). Early intervention and vocational opportunities. In P. French, J. Smith, D. Shiers, M. Reed, & M. Rayne (Eds.), *Promoting recovery in early psychosis: A practice manual* (pp. 140–146). Hoboken, NJ: Wiley-Blackwell.

Dayan, J., Rauchs, G., & Guillery-Girard, B. (2017, February 1). Rhythms dysregulation: A new perspective for understanding PTSD? *Journal of Physiology Paris*. [Epub ahead of print]

de Beurs, D. P., Bosmans, J. E., de Groot, M. H., de Keijser, J., van Duijn, E., de Winter, R. P., & Kerkhof, A. M. (2015). Training mental health professionals in suicide practice guideline adherence: Cost-effectiveness analysis alongside a randomized controlled trial. *Journal of Affective Disorders, 186*, 203–210.

de Castro, S. M., Ünlü, Ç., Tuynman, J. B., Honig, A., van Wagensveld, B. A., Steller, E. P., & Vrouenraets, B. C. (2014). Incidence and risk factors of delirium in the elderly general surgical patient. *American Journal of Surgery, 208*(1), 26–32.

De Cort, K., Schroijen, M., Hurlemann, R., Claassen, S., Hoogenhout, J., Van den Bergh, O., . . . Schruers, K. (2017). Modeling the development of panic disorder with interoceptive conditioning. *European Neuropsychopharmacology, 27*(1), 59–69.

De Genna, N. M., & Feske, U. (2013). Phenomenology of borderline personality disorder: The role of race and socioeconomic status. *The Journal of Nervous and Mental Disease, 201*(12), 1027–1034.

de Jonge, P., Roest, A. M., Lim, C. C., Florescu, S. E., Bromet, E. J., Stein, D. J., . . . Scott, K. M. (2016). Cross-national epidemiology of panic disorder and panic attacks in the world mental health surveys. *Depression and Anxiety, 33*(12), 1155–1177.

de Leede-Smith, S., & Barkus, E. (2013). A comprehensive review of auditory verbal hallucinations: Lifetime prevalence, correlates, and mechanisms in healthy and clinical individuals. *Frontiers in Human Neurosciences, 7*, 367.

De Leo, D., & Evans, R. (2004). *International suicide rates and prevention strategies*. Cambridge, MA: Hogrefe & Huber.

De Nadia. A. S., Karver, M. S., Murphy, T. K., Cavitt, M. A., Alvaro, J. L., Bengtson, M., . . . Storch, E. A. (2017). Common factors in pediatric psychiatry: A review of essential and adjunctive mechanisms of treatment outcome. *Journal of Child and Adolescent Psychopharmacology, 27*(1), 10–18.

De Neve, J. E., & Ward, G. (2017) Happiness at work. In J. Helliwell, R. Layard, & J. Sacks (Ed.), *World happiness report 2017*. New York: Sustainable Development Solutions Network.

de Vries, R. E. (2018). Three nightmare traits in leaders. *Frontiers in Psychology*, (9), 871.

Deacon, B. J., & Spielmans, G. I. (2017). Is the efficacy of "antidepressant" medications overrated? In S. O. Lilienfeld and I. D. Waldman (Eds.), *Psychological science under scrutiny: Recent challenges and proposed solutions* (Chap. 13). New Jersey: John Wiley.

Decker, H. S. (2016). Cyclical swings: The bête noire of psychiatry. *History of Psychology, 19*(1), 52–56.

Deeley, Q. (2017). Hypnosis as therapy for functional neurologic disorders. *Handbook of Clinical Neurology, 139*, 585–595.

Dein, S. (2017). Recent work on culture and schizophrenia: Epidemiological and anthropological approaches. *Global Journal of Archaeology & Anthropology, 1*(3), 1–5.

Deitz, S. M. (1977). An analysis of programming DRL schedules in educational settings. *Behavioral Research and Therapy, 15*(1), 103–111.

Delgadillo, J., Asaria, M., Ali, S., & Gilbody, S. (2016). On poverty, politics and psychology: The socioeconomic gradient of mental healthcare utilisation and outcomes. *British Journal of Psychiatry, 209*(5), 429–430.

Delgado, D. (2018, June 4). 5 reasons eating disorders may flare up in summer months. *Psychology Today.* Retrieved from https://www.psychologytoday.com/us/blog/eating-disorders/201806/5-reasons-eating-disorders-may-flare-in-summer-months.

Delgado, J. (2017, March 2). Intoxication from LSD and other common hallucinogens. *UpToDate.* Retrieved from http://www.uptodate.com.

Dell, P. F. (2010). Involuntariness in hypnotic responding and dissociative symptoms. *Journal of Trauma & Dissociation, 11*(1), 1–18.

Demory-Luce, D., & Motil, K. J. (2018, February 12). Adolescent eating habits. *UpToDate.* Retrieved from http://www.uptodate.com.

Dendy, C. A. Z. (2016, February 11). Impact of ADHD on school performance. *HealthyPlace.* Retrieved from https://www.healthyplace.com/adhd.

Deng, Y., Hung, K. S. Y., Lui, S. S. Y., Chui, W. W. H., Lee, J. C. W., Wang, Y., . . . Cheung, E. F. C. (2019). Tractography-based classification in distinguishing patients with first-episode schizophrenia from healthy individuals. *Progress in Neuro-Psychopharmacology & Biological Psychiatry, 88,* 66–73.

Dennhardt, A. A., Murphy, J. G., McDevitt-Murphy, M. E., & Williams, J. L. (2016). Drinking motives mediate the relationship between alcohol reward value and alcohol problems in military veterans. *Psychology of Addictive Behaviors, 30*(8), 819–826.

Dennis, J. P., & Brown, G. K. (2011). Suicidal older adults: Suicide risk assessments, safety planning, and cognitive behavioral therapy. In K. H. Sorocco & S. Lauderdale (Eds.), *Cognitive behavior therapy with older adults: Innovations across care settings* (pp. 95–123). New York: Springer Publishing.

Denno, D. W. (2017). Andrea Yates: A continuing story about insanity. In M. D. White (Ed.), *The insanity defense: Multidisciplinary views on its history, trends, and controversies* (Chap. 12). Westport, CT: Praeger Publishers.

DePaulo, B. M. (2013, April 5). On getting married and (not) getting happier: What we know. Retrieved from http://belladepaulo.com/2013/04/05/on-getting-married-and-not-getting-happpier.

DePaulo, B. M. (2013, March 15). Marriage and happiness: 18 long-term studies. *Psychology Today.*

DeVeaugh-Geiss, J., Moroz, G., Biederman, J., Cantwell, D. P., Fontaine, R., Griest, J. H., . . . Landau, P. (1992). Clomipramine hydrochloride in childhood and adolescent obsessive compulsive disorder. A multicenter trial. *Journal of the American Academy of Child and Adolescent Psychiatry, 31*(1), 45–49.

DeVos, S. L., Corjuc, B. T., Oakley, D. H., Nobuhara, C. K., Bannon, R. N., Chase, A., . . . Hyman, B. T. (2018). Synaptic tau seeding precedes tau pathology in human Alzheimer's disease brain. *Frontiers in Neuroscience, 12,* 267.

Dhejne, C., Lichtenstein, P., Boman, M., Johansson, A. L. V., Langström, N., & Landén, M. (2011). Long-term follow-up of transsexual persons undergoing sex reassignment surgery: Cohort study in Sweden. *PLoS ONE, 6*(2), e16885.

Di Florio, A., Jones, L., Forty, L., Gordon-Smith, K., Blackmore, E. R., Heron, J., . . . Jones, I. (2014). Mood disorders and parity: A clue to the aetiology of the postpartum trigger. *Journal of Affective Disorders, 152–154,* 334–339.

Di Rosa, M., Kofahl, C., McKee, K., Bien, B., Lamura, G., Prouskas, C., . . . Mnich, E. (2011). A typology of caregiving situations and service use in family careers of older people in six European countries: The EUROFAMCARE study. *GeroPsych: The Journal of Gerontopsychology and Geriatric Psychiatry, 24*(1), 5–18.

Diamond, D., & Meehan, K. B. (2013). Attachment and object relations in patients with narcissistic personality disorder: Implications for therapeutic process and outcome. *Journal of Clinical Psychology, 69*(11), 1148–1159.

Dickerson, C. (2017, November 13). After hurricane, signs of a mental health crisis haunt Puerto Rico. *New York Times.*

Dickerson, F., Schroeder, J., Stallings, C., Origoni, A., Katsafanas, E., Schwienfurth, L. A., . . . Yolken, R. (2014). A longitudinal study of cognitive functioning in schizophrenia: Clinical and biological predictors. *Schizophrenia Research, 156*(2/3), 248–253.

Diefenbach, S., & Christoforakos, L. (2017). The selfie paradox: Nobody seems to like them yet everyone has reasons to take them. An exploration of psychological functions of selfies in self-presentation. *Frontiers in Psychology, 87,* 7.

Dillard, D. A., Avey, J. P., Robinson, R. F., Smith, J. J., Beals, J., Manson, S. M., & Comtois, K. A. (2017). Demographic, clinical, and service utilization factors associated with suicide-related visits among Alaska native and American Indian adults. *Suicide and Life-Threatening Behavior, 47*(1), 27–37.

Dimidjian, S., Martell, C. R., Herman-Dunn, R., & Hubley, S. (2014). Behavioral activation for depression. In D. H. Barlow (Ed.), *Clinical handbook of psychological disorders* (5th ed., Chap. 9). New York: Guilford Press.

Dimsdale, J. E., Sharma, N., & Sharpe, M. (2011). What do physicians think of somatoform disorders? *Psychosomatics: Journal of Consultation Liaison Psychiatry, 52*(2), 154–159.

Ding, J. M., & Kanaan, R. A. (2017). Conversion disorder: A systematic review of current terminology. *General Hospital Psychiatry, 45,* 51–55.

Dinger, U., Ehrenthal, J. C., Nikendei, C., & Schauenburg, H. (2017). Change in self-esteem predicts depressive symptoms at follow-up after intensive multimodular psychotherapy for major depression. *Clinical Psychology & Psychotherapy, 24*(5), 1040–1046. Discrepancies between self- and adult-perceptions of social competence in children with neuropsychiatric disorders. *Child: Care, Health and Development, 43*(5),670–678.

Dishion, T. J., & Patterson, G. R. (2016). The development and ecology of antisocial behavior: Linking etiology, prevention, and treatment. In D. Cicchetti (Ed.), *Developmental psychopathology, Vol. 3: Maladaptation and psychopathology* (3rd ed.). New York: Wiley.

Dittrich, K., Fuchs, A., Bermpohl, F., Meyer, J., Führer, D., Reichl, C., . . . Resch, F. (2018). Effects of maternal history of depression and early life maltreatment on children's health-related quality of life. *Journal of Affective Disorders, 225,* 280–288.

Dixon, L. B., & Schwarz, E. C. (2014). Fifty years of progress in community mental health in US: The growth of evidence–based practices. *Epidemiology and Psychiatric Sciences, 23*(1), 5–9.

Dobson, D., & Dobson, K. S. (2017). *Evidence-based practice of cognitive-behavioral therapy* (2nd ed.). New York: Guilford Press.

Doctor, R. M., & Neff, B. (2001). Sexual disorders. In H. S. Friedman (Ed.), *Specialty articles from the encyclopedia of mental health.* San Diego: Academic Press.

Dodes, L. M., & Khantzian, E. J. (2016). Individual psychodynamic psychotherapy. In A. H. Mack, K. T. Brady, S. I. Miller, & R. J. Frances (Eds.). *Clinical textbook of addictive disorders* (4th ed., Ch. 26, pp. 548–562). New York: Guilford Press.

Doering, S., Hörz, S., Rentrop, M., Fischer-Kern, M., Schuster, P., Benecke, C., . . . Buchheim, P. (2010). Transference-focused psychotherapy v. treatment by community psychotherapists for borderline personality disorder: Randomised controlled trial. *British Journal of Psychiatry, 196*(5), 389–395.

Dohrmann, R. J., & Laskin, D. M. (1978). An evaluation of electromyographic feedback in the treatment of myofascial pain-dysfunction syndrome. *Journal of the American Medical Association, 96,* 656–666.

DOJ (U.S. Department of Justice). (2010). Arrests. *Crime in the United States 2009.* http://www.fbi.gov/ucr/cius2009/arrests/index.html.

DOJ (U.S. Department of Justice). (2014). *Crime in the United States 2013.* http://www.fbi.gov/about-us/cjis/ucr/crime-in-the-u.s./2013.

DOJ (U.S. Department of Justice). (2017, December 6). *Statistical briefing book. Law enforcement & juvenile crime: Juvenile arrests.* Washington, DC: OJJDP.

Dole, V. P., & Nyswander, M. (1965). A medical treatment for heroin addiction. *Journal of the American Medical Association, 193,* 646–650.

Dole, V. P., & Nyswander, M. (1967). Heroin addiction, a metabolic disease. *Archives of Internal Medicine, 120,* 19–24.

Dolezsar, C. M., McGrath, J. J., Herzig, A. M., & Miller, S. B. (2014). Perceived racial discrimination and hypertension: A comprehensive systematic review. *Health Psychology, 33*(1), 20–34.

Donnelly, B., Touyz, S., Hay, P., Burton, A., Russell, J., & Caterson, I. (2018). Neuroimaging in bulimia nervosa and binge eating disorder: a systematic review. *Journal of Eating Disorders, 6*(3).

Donohoue, P. A. (2017, December 6). Causes and clinical manifestations of primary adrenal insufficiency in children. *UpToDate.* Retrieved from http://www.uptodate.com.

Dorahy, M. J., Brand, B. L., Sar, V., Krüger, C., Stavropoulos, P., Martínez-Taboas, A., . . . Middleton, W. (2014).

Dissociative identity disorder: An empirical overview. *The Australian and New Zealand Journal of Psychiatry, 48*(5), 402–417.

Dossat, A. M., Bodell, L. P., Williams, D. L., Eckel, L. A., & Keel, P. K. (2014). Preliminary examination of glucagon-like peptide-1 levels in women with purging disorder and bulimia nervosa. *International Journal of Eating Disorders*.

Dove. (2016). *Dove global beauty and confidence report*. Englewood Cliffs, NJ: Author.

DPE (Department for Professional Employees). (2016). *Social service workers: An occupational overview. Fact sheet 2016*. Washington, DC: DPE, AFL-CIO.

Draper, B. M. (2014). Suicidal behaviour and suicide prevention in later life. *Maturitas, 79*(2), 179–183.

Dreisbach, S. (2011). Shocking body-image news: 97% of women will be cruel to their bodies today. *Glamour*. Retrieved from *Glamour* website: http://www.glamour.com/health-fitness/2011/02.

Drouin, M., Coupe, M., & Temple, J. R. (2017). Is sexting good for your relationship? It depends . . . *Computers in Human Behavior, 75*, 749–756.

Drouin, M., & Landgraff, C. (2012). Texting, sexting, attachment, and intimacy in college students' romantic relationships. *Computers in Human Behavior, 28*, 444–449.

Drutz, J. E. (2017, April 14). Autism spectrum disorder and chronic disease: No evidence for vaccines or thimerosal as a contributing factor. *UpToDate*. Retrieved from http://www.uptodate.com.

DTL (Ditch the Label). (2017). *The annual bullying survey 2017*. Los Angeles: Ditch the Label.

Duan, W., Fei, Y., Zhao, J., & Guo, X. (2018, January 1). Incremental validity of the comprehensive inventory of thriving in predicting self-reporting mental and physical health among community populations. *Journal of Health Psychology*. [Epub ahead of print]

Dube, A., Moffatt, M., Davison, C., & Bartels, S. (2018). Health outcomes for children in Haiti since the 2010 earthquake: A systematic review. *Prehospital and Disaster Medicine, 33*(1), 77–88.

Ducharme, J. (2018, March 6). Kevin Love opens up about his first panic attack: 'We're all carrying around things that hurt'. *Time*. Retrieved from http://time.com/5187641/kevin-love-panic-attacks/.

Duenwald, M. (2003, March 18). "Oldest old" still show alertness. *New York Times*.

Duffy, A., & Grof, P. (2018, February 28). Lithium treatment in children and adolescents. *Pharmacopsychiatry*. [Epub ahead of print]

Dugas, M. J., Brillon, P., Savard, P., Turcotte, J., Gaudet, A., Ladouceur, R., . . . Gervais, N. J. (2010). A randomized clinical trial of cognitive-behavioral therapy and applied relaxation for adults with generalized anxiety disorder. *Behavior Therapy, 41*(1), 46–58.

Dugas, M. J., Buhr, K., & Ladouceur, R. (2004). The role of intolerance of uncertainty in etiology and maintenance. In R. G. Heimberg, C. L. Turk, & D. S. Mennin (Eds.), *Generalized anxiety disorder: Advances in research and practice* (pp. 143–163). New York: Guilford Press.

Dugas, M. J., Laugesen, N., & Bukowski, W. M. (2012). Intolerance of uncertainty, fear of anxiety, and adolescent worry. *Journal of Abnormal Child Psychology, 40*(6), 863–870.

Dunbar, R. I. (2016). Do online social media cut through the constraints that limit the size of offline social networks? *Royal Society Open Science, 3*(1), 150292.

Dundas, I., Thorsheim, T., Hjeltnes, A., & Binder, P. E. (2016). Mindfulness-based stress reduction for academic evaluation anxiety: A naturalistic longitudinal study. *Journal of College Student Psychotherapy, 30*(2), 114–131.

Dunham, I. (2018, September 26). Human genes: Time to follow the roads less traveled? *PLoS Biology, 16*(9), e3000034.

Duperrouzel, J., Hawes, S., Lopez-Quintero, C., Pacheco-Colon, I., Comer, J. S., & Gonzalez, R. (2018). The association between adolescent cannabis use and anxiety: A parallel process analysis. *Addictive Behaviors, 78*, 107–113.

Durbin, A., Rudoler, D., Durbin, J., Laporte, A., & Callaghan, R. C. (2014). Examining patient race and area predictors of inpatient admission for schizophrenia among hospital users in California. *Journal of Immigrant and Minority Health, 16*(6), 1025–1034.

Durkheim, E. (1897). *Suicide*. New York: Free Press. [Work republished 1951]

Durkin, K. F., & Hundersmarck, S. (2008). Pedophiles and child molesters. In E. Goode & D. A. Vail (Eds.), *Extreme deviance*. Los Angeles: Pine Forge Press.

Dusi, N., De Carlo, V., Delvecchio, G., Bellani, M., Soares, J. C., & Brambilla, P. (2019). MRI features of clinical outcome in bipolar disorder: A selected review: Special section on "Translational and neuroscience studies in affective disorders." *Journal of Affective Disorders, 243*, 559–563.

Duval, E. R., Javanbakht, A., & Liberzon, I. (2015). Neural circuits in anxiety and stress disorders: A focused review. *Therapeutics and Clinical Risk Management, 11*, 115–126.

Duval-Harvey, J., & Rogers, K. M. (2010). Attention-deficit/hyperactivity disorder. In R. L. Hampton, T. P. Gullotta, & R. L. Crowel (Eds.), *Handbook of African American health* (pp. 375–418). New York: Guilford Press.

Dworkin, E. R., Wanklyn, S., Stasiewicz, P. R., & Coffey, S. F. (2018). PTSD symptom presentation among people with alcohol and drug use disorders: Comparisons by substance of abuse. *Addictive Behaviors, 76*, 188–194.

Dyl, J., Kittler, J., Phillips, K. A., & Hunt, J. I. (2006). Body dysmorphic disorder and other clinically significant body image concerns in adolescent psychiatric inpatients: Prevalence and clinical characteristics. *Child Psychiatry and Human Development, 36*(4), 369–382.

Eastman, M., Foshee, V., Ennett, S., Sotres-Alvarez, D., Reyes, H. L. M., Faris, R., & North, K. (2018). Profiles of internalizing and externalizing symptoms associated with bullying victimization. *Journal of Adolescence, 65*, 101–110.

EBSCO. (2018). *Mental measurements yearbook with tests in print internacional*. Ipswich, MA: Author. Retrieved from https://www.ebsco.com/products/research-databases.

Eckler, P., Kalyango, Y., & Paasch, E. (2017). Facebook use and negative body image among U.S. college women. *Women's Health, 57*(2), 249–267.

Economist, The. (2010, December 16). Age and happiness: The U-bend of life. *The Economist*. Retrieved from http://www.economist.com/node/17722567.

EIE (Enough Is Enough). (2017). *Cyberbullying statistics*. Retrieved from http://enough.org/stats_cyberbullying.

Eisner, P., Klasen, M., Wolf, D., Zerres, K., Eggermann, T., Eisert, A., . . . Mathiak, K. (2017). Cortico-limbic connectivity in MAOA-L carriers is vulnerable to acute tryptophan depletion. *Human Brain Mapping, 38*(3), 1622–1635.

Eisold, K. (2013, December 21). Hidden motives: A look at the hidden factors that really drive our social interactions. *Psychology Today*.

Eker, C., Simsek, F., Yılmazer, E. E., Kitis, O., Cinar, C., Eker, O. D., . . . Gonul, A. S. (2014). Brain regions associated with risk and resistance for bipolar I disorder: A voxel-based MRI study of patients with bipolar disorder and their healthy siblings. *Bipolar Disorders, 16*(3), 249–261.

Ekern, J. (2014, April 28). Eating disorder statistics and research. Retrieved from http:www.eatingdisorderhope.com.

Ekern, J. (2018, February 14). Anorexia nervosa: Causes, symptoms, signs & treatment help. Retrieved from https://www.eatingdisorderhope.com/information/anorexia.

Elhai, J. D., Dvorak, R. D., Levine, J. C., & Hall, B. J. (2017). Problematic smartphone use: A conceptual overview and systematic review of relations with anxiety and depression psychopathology. *Journal of Affective Disorders, 207*, 251–259.

Elkins, R. L., Richards, T. L., Nielsen, R., Repass, R., Stahlbrandt, H., & Hoffman, H. G. (2017). The neurobiological mechanism of chemical aversion (emetic) therapy for alcohol use disorder: An fMRI study. *Frontiers in Behavioral Neuroscience, 11*, 182.

Elkins, R. M., Mian, N. D., Comer, J. S., & Pincus, D. B. (2017). Parent-Child Interaction Therapy (PCIT) and its adaptations. In J. L. Luby (Ed.), *Handbook of preschool mental health: Development, disorders, and treatment* (2nd ed.). New York: Guilford Press.

Ellenberger, H. F. (1970). *The discovery of the unconscious*. New York: Basic Books.

Ellenberger, H. F. (1972). The story of "Anna O.": A critical review with new data. *Journal of the History of the Behavioral Sciences, 8*, 267–279.

Elliott, E., & Vollm, B. (2016, October 17). The utility of post-conviction polygraph testing among sexual offenders. *Sexual Abuse*. [Epub ahead of print]

Ellis, A. (1962). *Reason and emotion in psychotherapy*. Secaucus, NJ: Lyle Stuart.

Ellis, A. (2016). *How to stubbornly refuse to make yourself miserable about anything—Yes, anything!* New York: Citadel Press.

Ellis, A., & Ellis, D. J. (2019). Rational emotive behavior therapy. In D. Wedding & R. J. Corsini (Eds.), *Current psychotherapies* (11th ed., Ch. 5). Independence, KY: Cengage Publications.

Ellis, C. C., Peterson, M., Bufford, R., & Benson, J. (2014). The importance of group cohesion in inpatient treatment of combat-related PTSD. *International Journal of Group Psychotherapy, 64*(2), 208–226.

Ellis, H. (2015). Franz Mesmer: Pioneer in the treatment of functional disease or charlatan? *British Journal of Hospital Medicine, 76*(3), 170.

Elwood, C. E., Poythress, N. G., & Douglas, K. S. (2004). Evaluation of the Hare P-SCAN in a non-clinical population. *Personality and Individual Differences, 36*(4), 833–843.

Elzy, M., & Karver, M. (2018). Behaviour vs. perception: An investigation into the components of emotional invalidation. *Personality and Mental Health, 12*(1), 59–72.

Emanuel, E. (2017). Euthanasia and physician-assisted suicide: Focus on the data. *Medical Journal of Australia, 206*(8), 339–340.

Emanuel, E. J., Onwuteaka-Philipsen, B. D., Urwin, J. W., & Cohen, J. (2016). Attitudes and practices of euthanasia and physician-assisted suicide in the United States, Canada, and Europe. *JAMA, 316*(1), 79.

Eme, R. (2017). Developmental psychopathology: A primer for clinical pediatrics. *World Journal of Psychiatry, 7*(3), 159–162.

Emmelkamp, P. M. (1982). Exposure in vivo treatments. In A. Goldstein & D. Chambless (Eds.), *Agoraphobia: Multiple perspectives on theory and treatment.* New York: Wiley.

Enatescu, V., Enatescu, I., Craina, M., Gluhovschi, A., Papava, I., Romosan, R., . . . Bernad, E. (2014). State and trait anxiety as a psychopathological phenomenon correlated with postpartum depression in a Romanian sample: A pilot study. *Journal of Psychosomatic Obstetrics and Gynaecology, 35*(2), 55–61.

Endom, E. E. (2017, March 22). Child neglect and emotional maltreatment. *UpToDate.* Retrieved from http://www.uptodate.com.

Engel, S., Steffen, K., & Mitchell, J. E. (2017, March 6). Bulimia nervosa in adults: Clinical features, course of illness, assessment, and diagnosis. *UpToDate.* Retrieved from www.uptodate.com.

Englander, E., & McCoy, M. (2018). Sexting—Prevalence, age, sex, and outcomes. *JAMA Pediatrics, 172*(4), 317–318.

Englbrecht, M., Alten, R., Aringer, M., Baerwald, C. G., Burkhardt, H., Eby, N., . . . Wendler, J. (2017). Validation of standardized questionnaires evaluating symptoms of depression in rheumatoid arthritis patients: Approaches to screening for a frequent yet underrated challenge. *Arthritis Care & Research, 69*(1), 58–66.

Epstein, N. B., & Zheng, L. (2017). Cognitive-behavioral couple therapy. *Current Opinion in Psychology, 13,* 142–147.

Erikson, E. (1963). *Childhood and society.* New York: Norton.

Erkic, M., Bailer, J., Fenske, S. C., Schmidt, S. N. L., Trojan, J., Schröder, A., . . . Mier, D. (2018). Impaired emotion processing and a reduction in trust in patients with somatic symptom disorder. *Clinical Psychology & Psychotherapy, 25*(1), 163–172.

Erlangsen, A., Vach, W., & Jeune, B. (2005). The effect of hospitalization with medical illnesses on the suicide risk in the oldest old: A population-based register study. *Journal of the American Geriatrics Society, 53*(5), 771–776.

Ernst, E. (2017, August 13). Complementary and alternative therapies for cancer. *UpToDate.* Retrieved from http://www.uptodate.com.

Erving, C. L. (2017). Physical-psychiatric comorbidity: Implications for health measurement and the Hispanic epidemiological paradox. *Social Science Research, 64,* 197–213.

Espinoza, R. T., & Unützer, J. (2017, December 14). Diagnosis and management of late-life unipolar depression. *UpToDate.* Retrieved from http://www.uptodate.com.

Etgar, S., & Amichai-Hamburger, Y. (2017). Not all selfies took alike: Distinct selfie motivations are related to different personality characteristics. *Frontiers in Psychology, 8,* 842.

Etkin, A. (2010). Functional neuroanatomy of anxiety: A neural circuit perspective. In M. B. Stein & T. Steckler (Eds.), *Behavioral neurobiology of anxiety and its treatment. Current topics in behavioral neurosciences* (pp. 251–277). New York: Springer Science + Business Media.

Etxeberria, I., Etxebarria, I., & Irdaneta, E. (2017, February 17). Profiles in emotional aging: Does age matter? *Aging & Mental Health.* [Epub ahead of print]

Evans, S. W., Owens, J., & Bunford, N. (2014). Evidence-based psychosocial treatments for children and adolescents with attention-deficit/hyperactivity disorder. *Journal of Clinical Child and Adolescent Psychology, 43,* 527–551.

Fábrega, H., Jr. (2010). Understanding the evolution of medical traditions: Brain/behavior influences, enculturation, and the study of sickness and healing. *Neuropsychoanalysis, 12*(1), 21–27.

Fairburn, C. G., Bailey-Straebler, S., Basden, S., Doll, H. A., Jones, R., Murphy, R., . . . Cooper, Z. (2015). A transdiagnostic comparison of enhanced cognitive behavior therapy (CBT-E) and interpersonal psychotherapy in the treatment of eating disorders. *Behavior Research and Therapy, 70,* 64–71.

Fairburn, C. G., & Cooper, Z. (2014). Eating disorders: A transdiagnostic protocol. In D. H. Barlow, *Clinical handbook of psychological disorders* (5th ed., Chap. 17). New York: Guilford Press.

Fairburn, C. G., Cooper, Z., Shafran, R., & Wilson, G. T. (2008). Eating disorders: A transdiagnostic protocol. In D. H. Barlow (Ed.), *Clinical handbook of psychological disorders: A step-by-step treatment manual* (4th ed.). New York: Guilford Press.

Fakhoury, M. (2018). Imaging genetics in autism spectrum disorders: Linking genetics and brain imaging in the pursuit of the underlying neurobiological mechanisms. *Progress in Neuro-Psychopharmacology and Biological Psychiatry, 80*(Pt B), 101–114.

Falconer, C. J., Cutting, P., Bethan Davies, E., Hollis, C., Stallard, P., & Moran, P. (2017). Adjunctive avatar therapy for mentalization-based feasibility study. *Evidence-Based Mental Health, 20*(4), 123–127.

Fan, Q., Liao, L., & Pan, G. (2017). The application of cognitive remediation therapy in the treatment of mental disorders. *Shanghai Archives of Psychiatry, 29*(6), 373–375.

Fanelli, G., & Serretti, A. (2019). The influence of the serotonin transporter gene 5-HTTLPR polymorphism on suicidal behaviors: A meta-analysis. *Progress in Neuro-Psychopharmacology & Biological Psychiatry, 88,* 375–387.

Fanta, C. H. (2017, March 6). Diagnosis of asthma in adolescents and adults. *UpToDate.* Retrieved from http://www.uptodate.com.

Farber, B. A., Manevich, I., Metzger, J., & Saypol, E. (2005). Choosing psychotherapy as a career: Why did we cross that road? *Journal of Clinical Psychology, 61*(8), 1009–1031.

Farberow, N. L., & Litman, R. E. (1970). *A comprehensive suicide prevention program.* Unpublished final report, Suicide Prevention Center of Los Angeles, Los Angeles.

Farchione, T. J., Boswell, J. F., & Wilner, J. G. (2017). Behavioral activation strategies for major depression in transdiagnostic cognitive-behavioral therapy: An evidence-based case study. *Psychotherapy, 54*(3), 225–230.

Fardouly, J., Pinkus, R. T., & Vartanian, L. R. (2017). The impact of appearance comparisons made through social media, traditional media, and in person in women's everyday lives. *Body Image, 20,* 31–39.

Farkas, M. (2013). Pedophilia. *Psychiatria Hungarica: A Magyar Pszichiátriai Társaság Tudományos Folyóirata, 28*(2), 180–188.

Farlow, M. R. (2018, June 22). Epidemiology, pathology, and pathogenesis of dementia with Lewy bodies. *UpToDate.* Retrieved from http://www.uptodate.com.

Farmer, R. F., & Chapman, A. L. (2015). *Behavioral interventions in cognitive behavior therapy: Practical guidance for putting theory into action* (2nd ed.). Washington, DC: APA Books.

Farmer, R. F., & Nelson-Gray, R. O. (2005). Behavioral treatment of personality disorders. In R. F. Farmer & R. O. Nelson-Gray (Eds.), *Personality-guided behavior therapy* (pp. 203–243). Washington, DC: American Psychological Association.

Farokhnia, M., Sheskier, M. B., Lee, M. R., Le, A. N., Singley, E., Bouhlal, S., . . . Leggio, L. (2018, April 14). Neuroendocrine response to GABA-B receptor agonism in alcohol-dependent individuals: Results from a combined outpatient and human laboratory experiment. *Neuropharmacology.* [Epub ahead of print]

Farrell, J. M., & Shaw, I. A. (2018). *Experiencing schema therapy from the inside out: A self-practice/self-reflection workbook for therapists (Self-practice/self-reflection guides for psychotherapists).* New York: Guilford Press.

Faubion, M. D. (2016, September-October). Evaluating defendants for competency and sanity. Austin, TX: Texas District & County Attorneys Association.

Faugere, M., Micoulaud-Franchi, J. A., Faget-Agius, C., Lançon, C., Cermolacce, M., & Richieri, R. (2018). High C-reactive protein levels are associated with depressive symptoms in schizophrenia. *Journal of Affective Disorders, 225,* 671–675.

Fay, B. P. (1995). The individual versus society: The cultural dynamics of criminalizing suicide. *Hastings International and Comparative Law Review, 18,* 591–615.

Fazel, S., Hayes, A. J., Bartellas, K., Clerici, M., & Trestman, R. (2016). The mental health of prisoners: A review of prevalence, adverse outcomes and interventions. *Lancet Psychiatry, 3*(9), 871–881.

Fazel, S., Wolf, A., Larsson, H., Lichtenstein, P., Mallett, S., & Fanshawe, T. R. (2017).

Identification of low risk of violent crime in severe mental illness with a clinical prediction tool (Oxford Mental Illness and Violence tool [OxMIV]): A derivation and validation study. *Lancet Psychiatry, 4*(6), 461–468.

FBI (Federal Bureau of Investigation). (2014) Ten-year arrest trends. Totals, 2003–2012. Washington, DC: Department of Justice, Criminal Justice Information Services.

FBI (Federal Bureau of Investigation). (2016, November 14). Latest hate crime statistics released: Annual report sheds light on serious issue. *FBI*. Retrieved from https://www.fbi.gov/news/stories/2015.

FBI (Federal Bureau of Investigation). (2016, September 26). *Latest crime statistics released: Increase in violent crime, decrease in property crime*. Washington, DC: FBI.

FBI (Federal Bureau of Investigation). (2017). *2016 crime statistics released: Violent crime increases, property crime decreases*. Retrieved from https://www.fbi.gov/news/stories.

FBI (Federal Bureau of Investigation). (2017). *Active shooter resources*. Washington DC: FBI.

FBI (Federal Bureau of Investigation). (2017). *Resources: Reports and publications*. Washington, DC: FBI.

FDA (Food and Drug Administration). (2015). *The impact of direct-to-consumer advertising*. Retrieved from https://www.fda.gov/drugs/ResourcesForYou/consumers/ucm143562.htm.

FDA (U.S. Food and Drug Administration). (2016). *Keeping watch over direct-to-consumer ads*. (last updated 6/14/2016). Washington, DC: U.S. Department of Health and Human Services.

FDA (U.S. Food and Drug Administration). (2016). *The impact of direct-to-consumer advertising*. Washington, DC: U.S. Department of Health and Human Services.

FDA (U.S. Food & Drug Administration). (2018, January 16). *Development & approval process (drugs)*. Retrieved from https://www.fda.gov/Drugs/DevelopmentApproval Process/.

Federoff, J. P., & Marshall, W. L. (2010). Paraphilias. In D. McKay, J. S. Abramowitz, & S. Taylor (Eds.), *Cognitive-behavioral therapy for refractory cases: Turning failure into success* (pp. 369–384). Washington, DC: American Psychological Association.

Feki, I., Mdhaffar, K., Hentati, S., Sallemi, R., & Masmoudi, J. (2017). Depression in elderly patients with schizophrenia. *European Psychiatry, 41*(Suppl Apr), S654.

Feldman, N. (2017, January 4). Sex offender lockup should trouble court more. *Bloomberg View*.

Feldman, R., Bailey, R. A., Muller, J., Le, J., & Dirani, R. (2014). Cost of schizophrenia in the Medicare program. *Population Health Management, 17*(3), 190–196.

Fennig, S., Fennig, S., & Roe, D. (2002). Cognitive-behavioral therapy for bulimia nervosa: Time course and mechanisms of change. *General Hospital Psychiatry, 24*(2), 87–92.

Fernandez, S. (2017). Anxiety disorders in childhood and adolescence: A primary care approach. *Pediatric Annals, 46*(6), e213–e216.

Fernquist, R. M. (2007). How do Durkheimian variables impact variation in national suicide rates when proxies for depression and alcoholism are controlled? *Archives of Suicide Research, 11*(4), 361–374.

Ferrando, C. (U.), & Thomas, T. N. (2018, April 4). Transgender surgery: Male to female. *UpToDate*. Retrieved from http://www.uptodate.com.

Ferrara, P., Ianniello, F., Villani, A., & Corsello, G. (2018). Cyberbullying a modern form of bullying: Let's talk about this health and social problem. *Italian Journal of Pediatrics, 44*(1), 14.

Feuer, M. (2016, November 17). Interview. In C. Abate, Body shaming in an age of social media. *Healthline News*.

Fieve, R. R. (1975). *Moodswing*. New York: Morrow.

Figley, C. R. (1978). Symptoms of delayed combat stress among a college sample of Vietnam veterans. *Military Medicine, 143*(2), 107–110.

Fine, C. G., & Madden, N. E. (2000). Group psychotherapy in the treatment of dissociative identity disorder and allied dissociative disorders. In R. H. Klein & V. L. Schermer (Eds.), *Group psychotherapy for psychological trauma* (pp. 298–325). New York: Guilford Press.

Fingher, N., Dinstein, I., Ben-Shachar, M., Haar, S., Dale, A. M., Eyler, L., Pierce, K., & Courchesne, E. (2017). Toddlers later diagnosed with autism exhibit multiple structural abnormalities in temporal corpus callosum fibers. *Cortex*.

Fink, D. S., Santaella-Tenorio, J., & Keyes, K. M. (2018). Increase in suicides the months after the death of Robin Williams in the US. *PLoS ONE, 13*(2), e0191405.

Fink, S., & Risen, J. (2017, June 21). Psychologists open a window on brutal C.I.A. interrogations. *New York Times*.

Finley, E. P., Noël, P. H., Mader, M., Haro, E., Bernardy, N., Rosen, C. S., . . . Pugh, M. J. (2017). Community clinicians and the Veterans Choice Program for PTSD Care: Understanding provider interest during early implementation. *Medical Care, 55* Suppl 7, Suppl 1: S61–S70.

Firger, J. (2016, February 10). For runway models, high fashion means a dangerously low BMI. *Newsweek*.

Fischer, B. A., & Buchanan, R. W. (2018, January 16). Schizophrenia in adults: Epidemiology and pathogenesis. *UpToDate*. Retrieved from http://www.uptodate.com.

Fischer, B. A., & Buchanan, R. W. (2018, January 26). Schizophrenia in adults: Clinical manifestations, course, assessment, and diagnosis. *UpToDate*. Retrieved from http://www.uptodate.com.

Fischer, B. A. (2012). Maltreatment of people with serious mental illness in the early 20th century: A focus on Nazi Germany and eugenics in America. *The Journal of Nervous and Mental Disease, 200*(12), 1096–1100.

Fischer, S., Meyer, A. H., Dremmel, D., Schlup, B., & Munsch, S. (2014). Short-term cognitive-behavioral therapy for binge eating disorder: Long-term efficacy and predictors of long-term treatment success. *Behaviour Research and Therapy, 58*, 36–42.

Flavin, D. K., Franklin, J. E., & Frances, R. J. (1990). Substance abuse and suicidal behavior. In S. J. Blumenthal & D. J. Kupfer (Eds.), *Suicide over the life cycle: Risk factors, assessment, and treatment of suicidal patients*. Washington, DC: American Psychiatry Press.

Flick, C. (2016). Informed consent and the Facebook emotional manipulation study. *Research Ethics, 12*(1), 14–28.

Floros, G. D. (2018). Gambling disorder in adolescents: Prevalence, new developments, and treatment challenges. *Adolescent Health, Medicine and Therapeutics, 9*, 43–51.

Foa, E. B., McLean, C. P., Zang, Y., Rosenfield, D., Yadin, E., Yarvis, J. S., . . . Strong Star Consortium. (2018). Effect of prolonged exposure therapy delivered over 2 weeks vs 8 weeks vs present-centered therapy on PTSD symptom severity in military personnel: A randomized clinical trial. *JAMA, 319*(4), 354–364.

Foa, E., Hembree, E., & Rothbaum, B. O. (2017). *Prolonged exposure therapy for PTSD: Emotional processing of traumatic experiences (treatments that work)*. New York: Oxford University Press.

Foerde, K., Steinglass, J. E., Shohamy, D., & Walsh, B. T. (2015). Neural mechanisms supporting maladaptive food choices in anorexia nervosa. *Nature Neuroscience, 18*, 1571.

Foldvary-Schaefer, N. (2017, July 28). Disorders of arousal from non-rapid eye movement sleep in adults. *UpToDate*. Retrieved from http://www.uptodate.com.

Fonagy, P. (2015). The effectiveness of psychodynamic psychotherapies: An update. *World Psychiatry, 14*, 137–150.

Fonagy, P., & Luyten, P. (2016). A multilevel perspective on the development of borderline personality disorder. In D. Cicchetti (Ed.), *Developmental psychopathology, Vol. 3: Maladaptation and psychopathology* (3rd ed., pp. 726–792). New York: Wiley.

Fonagy, P., & Luyten, P. (2018). Attachment, mentalizing, and the self. In W. J. Livesley & R. Larstone (Eds.), *Handbook of personality disorders: Theory, research, and treatment* (2nd ed.). New York: Guilford Press.

Fonagy, P., & Luyten, P. (2018). Conduct problems in youth and the RDoC approach: A developmental, evolutionary-based view. *Clinical Psychology Review, 64*, 57–76.

Fonagy, P., Luyten, P., Allison, E., & Campbell, C. (2017). What we have changed our minds about: Part 1. Borderline personality disorder as a limitation of resilience. *Borderline Personality Disorder and Emotion Dysregulation, 4*, 11.

Fonagy, P., Luyten, P., Allison, E., & Campbell, C. (2017). What we have changed our minds about: Part 2. Borderline personality disorder, epistemic trust and the developmental significance of social communication. *Borderline Personality Disorder and Emotion Dysregulation, 4*, 9.

Fooducate. (2016, April 7). The weight loss industry by numbers. *Fooducate*. Retrieved from http://www.fooducate.com.

Foote, B. (2018, January 25). Dissociative identity disorder: Epidemiology, pathogenesis, clinical manifestations, course, assessment, and diagnosis. *UpToDate*. Retrieved from http://www.uptodate.com.

Forand, N. R., Barnett, J. G., Strunk, D. R., Hindiyeh, M. U., Feinberg, J. E., & Keefe, J. R. (2018). Efficacy of guided iCBT for depression and mediation of change by cognitive skill acquisition. *Behavior Therapy, 49*(2), 295–307.

Forcier, M., & Olson-Kennedy, J. (2018, March 28). Gender development and clinical presentation of gender nonconformity in children and adolescents. *UpToDate*. Retrieved from http://www.uptodate.com.

Ford, R., King, T., Priest, N., & Kavanagh, A. (2017). Bullying and mental health and suicidal behavior among 14- to 15-year-olds in a representative sample of Australian children. *Australian & New Zealand Journal of Psychiatry, 51,* 897–908.

Ford, T. (2000). The influence of womanist identity on the development of eating disorders and depression in African American female college students. *Dissertation Abstracts International: Section A: Humanities and Social Sciences, 61,* 2194.

Foreyt, J. P., Poston, W. S. C., & Goodrick, G. K. (1996). Future directions in obesity and eating disorders. *Addictive Behavior, 21*(6), 767–778.

Forgatch, M. S., & Patterson, G. R. (2010). Parent management training—Oregon model: An intervention for antisocial behavior in children and adolescents. In J. R. Weisz & A. E. Kazdin (Eds.), *Evidence-based psychotherapies for children and adolescents* (2nd ed., pp. 159–177). New York: Guilford Press.

Forman, S. F. (2017, October 25). Eating disorders: Overview of epidemiology, clinical features, and diagnosis. *UpToDate*. Retrieved from http://www.uptodate.com.

Forman, S. F. (2017, November 17). Eating disorders: Overview of prevention and treatment. *UpToDate*. Retrieved from http://www.uptodate.com.

Forsberg, M. M. (2017). Delirium update for postacute care and long-term care settings: A narrative review. *Journal of the American Osteopathic Association, 117*(1), 32–38.

Forster, M., Grigsby, T. J., Rogers, C. J., & Benjamin, S. M. (2018). The relationship between family-based adverse childhood experiences and substance use behaviors among a diverse sample of college students. *Addictive Behaviors, 76,* 298–304.

Fortune, S. A., & Hawton, K. (2007). Suicide and deliberate self-harm in children and adolescents. *Paediatrics and Child Health, 17*(11), 443–447.

Foster, J. D., Campbell, W. K., & Twenge, J. M. (2003). Individual differences in narcissicm: Inflated self-views across the lifespan and around the world. *Journal of Research in Personality, 37,* 469–486.

Fouet, T. (2017). Psychological support for people bereaved by suicide. *Soins, 62*(814), 47–48. [French]

Fournier, G. (2018). Projective personality test. *Psych Central*. Retrieved from https://psychcentral.com/encyclopedia.

Fox, J. A., Levin, J., & Fridel, E. E. (2018). *Extreme killing: Understanding serial and mass murder* (4th ed.). Los Angeles: SAGE Publications.

Frances, A. (2015). Don't throw out the baby with the bath water. *Australian & New Zealand Journal of Psychiatry, 49*(6), 577.

Frances, A. (2016). A report card on the utility of psychiatric diagnosis. *World Psychiatry, 15*(1), 32–33.

Frances, A., & Ruffalo, M. L. (2018, May 3). Mental illness, civil liberty, and common sense. *Psychiatric Times*.

Francis, J., Jr., & Young, G. B. (2014, August 22). Diagnosis of delirium and confusional states. *UpToDate*. Retrieved from http://www.uptodate.com.

Frank, G. K., Shott, M. E., Hagman, J. O., & Mittal, V. A. (2013). Alterations in brain structures related to taste reward circuitry in ill and recovered anorexia nervosa and in bulimia nervosa. *American Journal of Psychiatry, 170,* 1152.

Frank, J. D. (1973). *Persuasion and healing* (Rev. ed.). Baltimore: Johns Hopkins University Press.

Frankel, A. S., Bass, S. B., Patterson, F., Dai, T., & Brown, D. (2018). Sexting, risk behavior, and mental health in adolescents: An examination of 2015 Pennsylvania Youth Risk Behavior Survey data. *Journal of School Health, 88*(3), 190–199.

Franklin, M. E., & Foa, E. B. (2014). Obsessive compulsive disorder. In D. H. Barlow (Ed.), *Clinical handbook of psychological disorders: A step-by-step treatment manual* (5th ed., pp. 155–205). New York: Guilford Press.

Franklin, T. (2017). Best practices in multicultural assessment of cognition. In R. S. McCallum, *Handbook of nonverbal assessment* (Chap. 4, pp. 39–46). New York: Springer.

Fraser, J. (2016, April 28). Involuntary mental health commitment. *Pittsburgh Today.*

Frederick, D. A., John, H. K. S., Garcia, J. R., & Lloyd, E. A. (2018). Differences in orgasm frequency among gay, lesbian, bisexual, and heterosexual men and women in a U.S. national sample. *Archives of Sexual Behavior, 47*(1), 273–288.

Frederick, D. A., Sandhu, G., Morse, P. J., & Swami, V. (2016). Correlates of appearance and weight satisfaction in a U.S. National Sample: Personality, attachment style, television viewing, self-esteem, and life satisfaction. *Body Image, 17,* 191–203.

Freud, S. (1894). The neuropsychoses of defense. In J. Strachey (Ed.), *The standard edition of the complete psychological works of Sigmund Freud* (Vol. 3). London: Hogarth Press. [Work republished 1962.]

Freud, S. (1914). On narcissism. In *Complete psychological works* (Vol. 14). London: Hogarth Press. [Work republished 1957.]

Freud, S. (1915). A case of paranoia counter to psychoanalytic theory. In *Complete psychological works* (Vol. 14). London: Hogarth Press. [Work republished 1957.]

Freud, S. (1917). *A general introduction to psychoanalysis* (J. Riviere, Trans.). New York: Liveright. [Work republished 1963.]

Freud, S. (1917). Mourning and melancholia. In *Collected papers* (Vol. 4, pp. 152–172). London: Hogarth Press and the Institute of Psychoanalysis. [Work republished 1950.]

Freud, S. (1924). The loss of reality in neurosis and psychosis. In *Sigmund Freud's collected papers* (Vol. 2, pp. 272–282). London: Hogarth Press.

Freud, S. (1933). *New introductory lectures on psychoanalysis*. New York: W. W. Norton.

Freud, S. (1961). *The future of an illusion*. New York: W. W. Norton.

Frey, R. (2005). Hallucination. In S. L. Chamberlin & B. Narins (Eds.), *Gale encyclopedia of neurological disorders*. PA: Thomson Gale.

Frey, W. H. (2018, March 14). The U.S. will become "minority white" in 2045, Census projects. *Brookings*. Retrieved from https://www.brookings.edu/blog/the-avenue.

Freytes, I. M., LeLaurin, J. H., Zickmund, S. L., Resende, R. D., & Uphold, C. R. (2017). Exploring the post-deployment reintegration experiences of veterans with PTSD and their significant others. *American Journal of Orthopsychiatry, 87*(2), 149–156.

Frias, A., Gonzalez, L., Palma, C., & Farriols, N. (2017). Is there a relationship between borderline personality disorder and sexual masochism in women. *Archives of Sexual Behavior, 46*(3), 747–754.

Friedel, R. O. (2018). *Borderline personality disorder demystified: An essential guide for understanding and living with BPD* (Rev. ed.). New York: De Capo Lifelong Books/HBG.

Frieden, T. (2016, December 17). How to end America's growing opioid epidemic. *Fox News*.

Friedman, M., & Rosenman, R. (1959). Association of specific overt behavior pattern with blood and cardiovascular findings. *Journal of the American Medical Association, 169,* 1286.

Friedman, M., & Rosenman, R. (1974). *Type A behavior and your heart*. New York: Knopf.

Fries, G. R., Dimitrov, D. H., Lee, S., Braida, N., Yantis, J., Honaker, C., . . . Walss-Bass, C. (2018). Genome-wide expression in veterans with schizophrenia further validates the immune hypothesis for schizophrenia. *Schizophrenia Research, 192,* 255–261.

Fristad, M. A., & Black, S. R. (2018). Mood disorders in childhood and adolescence. In J. N. Butcher & J. M. Hooley (Eds.), *APA handbook of psychopathology.* Vol. 2. *Psychopathology in children and adolescents* (Ch. 13). Washington, DC: American Psychological Association.

Fromm-Reichmann, F. (1948). Notes on the development of treatment of schizophrenia by psychoanalytic psychotherapy. *Psychiatry, 11,* 263–273.

Frone, M. R. (2016). Work stress and alcohol use: Developing and testing a biphasic self-medication model. *Work Stress, 30*(4), 374–394.

Frosch, W. A., Robbins, E. S., & Stern, M. (1965). Untoward reactions to lysergic acid diethylamide (LSD) resulting in hospitalization. *New England Journal of Medicine, 273,* 1235–1239.

Frydman, I., de Sales Andrade, J. B., Vigne, P., & Fontenelle, L. F. (2016). Can neuroimaging provide reliable biomarkers for obsessive-compulsive disorder? A narrative review. *Current Psychiatry Reports, 18*(10), 90.

Fugl-Meyer, K. S., Bohm-Starke, N., Petersen, C. D., Fugl-Meyer, A., Parish, S., & Giraldi, A. (2013). Standard operating procedures for female genital sexual pain. *Journal of Sexual Medicine, 10,* 83–93.

Fujiwara, T., Yagi, J., Homma, H., Mashiko, H., Nagao, K., Okuyama, M., Great Japan Earthquake Follow-up for Children Study Team. (2017). Suicide risk among young children after the Great East Japan earthquake: A follow-up study. *Psychiatry Research, 253,* 318–324.

Fukumoto, M., Hashimoto, R., Ohi, K., Yasuda, Y., Yamamori, H., Umeda-Yano, S., . . . Takeda, M. (2014). Relation between remission status and attention in patients with schizophrenia. *Psychiatry and Clinical Neurosciences, 68*(3), 234–241.

Furnham, A., Richards, S. C., & Paulhus, D. L. (2013). The Dark Triad of personality: A 10-year review. *Social and Personality Psychology Compass, 7*, 199–216.

Furr, J. M., Comer, J. S., Villodas, M., Poznanski, B., & Gurwitch, R. (2018). Trauma and child psychopathology: From risk and resilience to evidence-based intervention. In P. C. Kendall & J. Butcher (Eds.), *APA handbook of child psychopathology*. Washington, DC: APA.

Furr, J. M., Sanchez, A. L., Hong, N., & Comer, J. S. (2019). Exposure therapy for childhood selective mutism: Principles, practices, and procedures. In T. Peris, E. Storch, & J. McGuire (Eds.), *A clinician's guide to exposure therapy for children and adolescents*. New York: Elsevier.

Fuss, J., Briken, P., & Klein, V. (2018). Gender bias in clinicians' pathologization of atypical sexuality: A randomized controlled trial with mental health professionals. *Scientific Reports, 8*(1), 3715.

Gabbard, G., & DeJean, V. (2018, February 20). Unipolar depression in adults: Psychodynamic psychotherapy. *UpToDate*. Retrieved from http://www.uptodate.com.

Gabbe, P. T., Reno, R., Clutter, C., Schottke, T. F., Price, T., Calhoun, K., . . . Lynch, C. D. (2017). Improving maternal and infant child health outcomes with community-based pregnancy support groups: Outcomes from Moms2B Ohio. *Maternal and Child Health, 21*(5), 1130–1138.

Galán, C. A., Choe, D. E., Forbes, E. E., & Shaw, D. S. (2018). Interactions between empathy and resting heart rate in early adolescence predict violent behavior in late adolescence and early adulthood. *Journal of Child Psychology and Psychiatry*. [Manuscript in press]

Gallegos, C. E., Baier, C. J., Bartos, M., Bras, C., Dominguez, S., Mónaco, N., . . . Minetti, A. (2018, April 2). Perinatal glyphosate-based herbicide exposure in rats alters brain antioxidant status, glutamate and acetylcholine metabolism and affects recognition memory. *Neurotoxicity Research*. [Epub ahead of print]

Gallup Poll. (2005). Three in four Americans believe in paranormal. *Gallup News Service*. http://www.gallup.com/poll/16915/three-four-americans-believe-paranormal.aspx.

Gallup Poll. (2013). Most Americans practice charitable giving, volunteerism. Retrieved from Gallup website: http://www.gallup.com/poll/166250.

Gallup Poll. (2015, September 18). Trust in U.S. judicial branch sinks to new low of 53%. *Gallup News*. Retrieved from http://www.gallup.com/poll/185528.

Gallup Poll. (2016, December 7-11). Honesty/ethics in professions. *Gallup News*. Retrieved from http://www.gallup.com/poll/1654.

Gallup Poll. (2017, June 12). Majority of Americans remain supportive of euthanasia. *Gallup*. Retrieved from http://www.gallup.com/poll/211928.

Gallup Poll. (2018, January 16). *American views: Trust, media, and democracy* [Survey]. Retrieved from https://news.gallup.com/poll/225470/media-seen-key-democracy-not-supporting.aspx.

Galvez, J. F., Thommi, S., & Ghaemi, S. N. (2011). Positive aspects of mental illness: A review in bipolar disorder. *Journal of Affective Disorders, 28*(3), 185–190.

Gamboa, C. (2017, February 4). Women face unique challenges in overcoming opioid dependence. *Drug Addiction Now*. Retrieved from https://www.drugaddictionnow.com.

Gamwell, L., & Tomes, N. (1995). *Madness in America: Cultural and medical perceptions of mental illness before 1914*. Ithaca, NY: Cornell University Press.

Gao, S., Guo, F., Sun, X., Zhang, N., Gong, Y., & Xu, L. (2017). The inhibitory effects of Nesfatin-1 in ventromedial hypothalamus on gastric function and its regulation by nucleus accumbens. *Frontiers in Physiology, 7*, 634.

Gao, T., Li, J., Zhang, H., Gao, J., Kong, Y., Hu, Y., & Mei, S. (2018). The influence of alexithymia on mobile phone addiction: The role of depression, anxiety and stress. *Journal of Affective Disorders, 225*, 761–766.

Gao, X., Cao, Q., Cheng, Y., Zhao, D., Wang, Z., Yang, H., . . . Yang, Y. (2018). Chronic stress promotes colitis by disturbing the gut microbiota and triggering immune system response. *Proceedings of the National Academy of Sciences USA, 115*(13), E2960–E2969.

Gao, K., Kemp, D. E., Wang, Z., Ganocy, S. J., Conroy, C., Serrano, M. B., . . . Calabrese, J. R. (2010). Predictors of nonstabilization during the combination therapy of lithium and divalproex in rapid cycling bipolar disorder: A post-hoc analysis of two studies. *Psychopharmacology Bulletin, 43*(1), 23–38.

Garb, H. N. (2006). The conjunction effect and clinical judgment. *Journal of Social and Clinical Psychology, 25*(9), 1048–1056.

Garb, H. N. (2010). Clinical judgment and the influence of screening on decision making. In A. J. Mitchell & J. C. Coyne (Eds.), *Screening for depression in clinical practice: An evidence-based guide* (pp. 113–121). New York: Oxford University Press.

Garcia, D., Persson, B. N., Al Nima, A., Brulin, J. G., Rapp-Ricciardi, M., & Kajonius P. J. (2018). IRT analyses of the Swedish Dark Triad Dirty Dozen. *Heliyon, 4*(3).

Garcia, J. R., Gesselman, A. N., Siliman, S. A., Perry, B. L., Coe, K., & Fisher, H. E. (2016, July 29). Sexting among singles in the USA: Prevalence of sending, receiving, and sharing sexual messages and images. *Sex Health*. [Epub ahead of print]

Gard, A. M., Waller, R., Shaw, D. S., Forbes, E. E., Hariri, A. R., & Hyde, L. W. (2017). The long reach of early adversity: Parenting, stress, and neural pathways to antisocial behavior in adulthood. *Biological Psychiatry: Cognitive Neuroscience and Neuroimaging, 2*(7), 582–590.

Gardner, B., Murrie, D., & Torres, A. (2018, May 2). Insanity findings and evaluation practices: A state-wide review of court-ordered reports. *Behavioral Sciences & the Law*. [Epub ahead of print]

Garner, D. M., Olmsted, M. P., & Polivy, J. (1991). *The EDI-2*. Odessa, FL: Psychological Assessment Resources.

Garner, D. M., Olmsted, M. P., & Polivy, J. (2004). *The EDI-3*. Odessa, FL: Psychological Assessment Resources.

Garner, D. M. (1997). The 1997 body image survey results. *Psychology Today, 30*(1), 30–44.

Garner, D. M. (2005). *Eating Disorder Inventory TM-3 (EDI TM-3)*. Lutz, Florida: Psychological Assessment Resources.

Garner, D. M., Garfinkel, P. E., Schwartz, D., & Thompson, M. (1980). Cultural expectations of thinness in women. *Psychological Reports*, 47, 483–491.

Garner, D. M., Olmsted, M. P., & Polivy, J. (1984). *The EDI*. Odessa, FL: Psychological Assessment Resources.

Garofalo, C., & Wright, A. G. C. (2017). Alcohol abuse, personality disorders, and aggression: The quest for a common underlying mechanism. *Aggression and Violent Behavior, 34*, 1–8.

Garza, I., & Schwedt, T. J. (2018, February 14). Chronic migraine. *UpToDate*. Retrieved from http://www.uptodate.com.

Gaudiano, B. A., Davis, C. H., Epstein-Lubow, G., Johnson, J. E., Mueser, K. T., & Miller, I. W. (2017). Acceptance and commitment therapy for inpatients with psychosis (the REACH Study): Protocol for treatment development and pilot testing. *Healthcare, 5*, 23.

Gaudiano, B. A. (2013, September 29). Psychotherapy's image problem. *New York Times*.

Gavric, D., Moscovitch, D. A., Rowa, K., & McCabe, R. E. (2017). Post-event processing in social anxiety disorder: Examining the mediating roles of positive metacognitive beliefs and perceptions of performance. *Behaviour Research and Therapy, 91*, 1–12.

Gay, P. (1999, March 29). Psychoanalyst Sigmund Freud. *Time*, pp. 66–69.

Gay, P. (2006). *Freud: A life for our time*. New York: W. W. Norton.

GCBH (Global Council on Brain Health). (2017). *The brain and social connectedness: GCBH recommendations on social engagement and brain health*. Retrieved from www.GlobalCouncilOnBrainHealth.org.

Gebhard, P. H. (1965). Situational factors affecting human sexual behavior. In F. Beach (Ed.), *Sex and behavior*. New York: Wiley.

Geerlings, M. I., & Gerritsen, L. (2017). Late-life depression, Hippocampal volumes, and hypothalamic-pituitary-adrenal axis regulation: A systematic review and meta-analysis. *Biological Psychiatry, 82*, 339–350.

Gehricke, J.-G., Kruggel, F., Thampipop, T., Alejo, S. D., Tatos, E., Fallon, J., & Muftuler, L. T. (2017). The brain anatomy of attention-deficit/hyperactivity disorder in young adults: a magnetic resonance imaging study. *PLoS ONE, 12*(4), e0175433.

Gelfand, D. M., Jenson, W. R., & Drew, C. J. (1982). *Understanding child behavior disorders*. New York: Holt, Rinehart & Winston.

Gellatly, J., Pedley, R., Molloy, C., Butler, J., Lovell, K., & Bee, P. (2017). Low intensity interventions for obsessive-compulsive disorder (OCD): A qualitative study of mental health practitioner experiences. *BMC Psychiatry, 17*(1), 77.

Gentile, J. P., Snyder, M., & Marie Gillig, P. (2014). Stress and trauma: Psychotherapy and pharmacotherapy for depersonalization/derealization disorder. *Innovations in Clinical Neuroscience, 11*(7–8), 37–41.

Gentile, J. P., Dillon, K. S., & Gillig, P. M. (2013). Psychotherapy and pharmacotherapy for patients with dissociative identity disorder. *Innovations in Clinical Neuroscience, 10*(2), 22–29.

Gentile, S., & Fusco, M. L. (2017). Untreated perinatal paternal depression: Effects on offspring. *Psychiatry Research, 252,* 325–332.

Geoffreys, C. (2015). *Paranoid personality disorder: The ultimate guide to symptoms, treatment, and prevention (personality disorders).* CreateSpace Independent Publishing Platform.

Geradt, M., Jahnke, S., Heinz, J., & Hoyer, J. (2018). Is contact with children related to legitimizing beliefs toward sex with children among men with pedophilia? *Archives of Sexual Behavior, 47*(2), 375–387.

Gerez, M., Suárez, E., Serrano, C., Castanedo, L., & Tello, A. (2016). The crossroads of anxiety: Distinct neurophysiological maps for different symptomatic groups. *Neuropsychiatric Disease and Treatment, 12,* 159–175.

Geriatric Mental Health Foundation. (2013, October 7). Causes and risk factors for senior mental illness. Retrieved from http://www.aplaceformom.com/blog.

Gerring, J. (2017). *Case study research: Principles and practices (strategies for social inquiry)* (2nd ed.). New York: Cambridge University Press.

Gesi, C., Carmassi, C., Shear, K. M., Schwartz, T., Ghesquiere, A., Khaler, J., & Dell'Osso, L. (2017). Adult separation anxiety disorder in complicated grief: an exploratory study on frequency and correlates. *Comprehensive Psychiatry, 72,* 6–12.

Ghafoori, B., Barragan, B., Tohidian, N., & Palinkas, L. (2013). Racial and ethnic differences in symptom severity of PTSD, GAD, and depression in trauma-exposed, urban, treatment-seeking adults. *Journal of Traumatic Stress, 25*(1), 106–110.

Gheorghiu, V. A., & Orleanu, P. (1982). Dental implant under hypnosis. *American Journal of Clinical Hypnosis, 25*(1), 68–70.

Giami, A. (2015). Between DSM and ICS: Paraphilias and the transformation of sexual norms. *Archives of Sexual Behavior, 44*(5), 1127–1138.

Gifford, M., Friedman, S., & Majerus, R. (2010). *Alcoholism.* Santa Barbara, CA: Greenwood Press/ABC-CLIO.

Gigante, A., Navarini, L., Margiotta, D., Barbano, B., Afeitra, A., & Rosato, E. (2018, April 23). Erectile dysfunction: Imbalance between pro-angiogenic and anti-angiogenic factors in systemic sclerosis. *European Journal of Internal Medicine.* [Epub ahead of print]

Gilbert, S. (2011). Eating disorders in women of African descent. In J. Alexander & J. Treasure (Eds.), *A collaborative approach to eating disorders* (pp. 249–261). New York: Taylor & Francis.

Gilbert, S. C., Keery, H., & Thompson, J. K. (2005). The media's role in body image and eating disorders. In J. H. Daniel & E. Cole (Eds.), *Featuring females: Feminist analyses of media* (pp. 41–56). Washington, DC: American Psychological Association.

Gill, D., & Warburton, W. (2014). An investigation of the biosocial model of borderline personality disorder. *Journal of Clinical Psychology, 70*(9), 866–873.

Gillam, R. B., & Petersen, D. B. (2011). Language disorders in school-age children. In R. B. Gillam, T. P. Marquardt, & F. N. Martin (Eds.), *Communication sciences and disorders: From science to clinical practice* (2nd ed., pp. 245–270). Boston, MA: Jones and Bartlett Publishers.

Gil-Llario, M. D., Morell-Mengual, V., Ballester-Amal, R., & Diaz-Rodriguez, I. (2018). The experience of sexuality in adults with intellectual disability. *Journal of Intellectual Disability Research, 62*(1), 72–80.

Ginn, N. C., Clionsky, L. N., Eyberg, S. M., Warner-Metzger, C., & Abner, J. P. (2017). Child-Directed Interaction Training for young children with autism spectrum disorders: Parent and child outcomes. *Journal of Clinical Child and Adolescent Psychology, 46,* 101–109.

Gipps, R. G. T. (2017). Does the cognitive therapy of depression rest on a mistake? *BJPsych Bulletin, 41*(5), 267–271.

Giraldi, A., Rellini, A. H., Pfaus, J., & Laan, E. (2013). Female sexual arousal disorders. *Journal of Sexual Medicine, 10,* 58–73.

Giraldo, D. L., Garcia-Arteaga, J. D., Cárdenas-Robledo, S., & Romero, E. (2018). Characterization of brain anatomical patterns by comparing region intensity distributions: Applications to the description of Alzheimer's disease. *Brain and Behavior, 8*(4), e00942.

Giuntella, O. (2016). The Hispanic health paradox: New evidence from longitudinal data on second and third-generation birth outcomes. *Science Direct, 2,* 84–89.

Glad, K. A., Hafstad, G. S., Jensen, T. K., & Dyb, G. (2017). A longitudinal study of psychological distress and exposure to trauma reminders after terrorism. *Psychological Trauma, 9*(Suppl. 1), 145–152.

Glasofer, D. R. (2017, June 30). Psychotherapy guide for generalized anxiety disorder: An overview of popular types of talk therapy. *Verywell/mind.* Retrieved from https://www.verywellmind.com.

Glenn, A. L., Han, H., Yang, Y., Raine, A., & Schug, R. A. (2017). Associations between psychopathic traits and brain activity during instructed false responding. *Psychiatry Research, 266,* 123–137.

Glenn, A. L., Remmel, R. J., Raine, A., Schug, R. A., Gao, Y., & Granger, D. A. (2015). Alpha-amylase reactivity in relation to psychopathic traits in adults. *Psychoneuroendocrinology, 54,* 14–23.

Glenn, J. J., Werntz, A. J., Slama, S. J., Steinman, S. A., Teachman, B. A., & Nock, M. K. (2017). Suicide and self-injury-related implicit cognition: A large-scale examination and replication. *Journal of Abnormal Psychology, 126*(2), 199–211.

Gloster, A. T., Klotsche, J., Ciarrochi, J., Eifert, G., Sonntag, R., Wittchen, H. U., & Hoyer, J. (2017). Increasing valued behaviors precedes reduction in suffering: Findings from a randomized controlled trial using ACT. *Behaviour Research and Therapy, 91,* 64–71.

Gloster, A. T., Sonntag, R., Hoyer, J., Meyer, A. H., Heinze, S., Ströhle, A., . . . Wittchen, H-U. (2015). Treating treatment-resistant patients with panic disorder and agoraphobia using psychotherapy: A randomized controlled switching trial. *Psychotherapy and Psychosomatics, 84*(2), 100–109.

Gloster, A. T., Klotsche, J., Gerlach, A. L., Hamm, A., Ströhle, A., Gauggel, S., . . . Wittchen, H. (2014). Timing matters: change depends on the stage of treatment in cognitive behavioral therapy for panic disorder with agoraphobia. *Journal of Consulting and Clinical Psychology, 82*(1), 141–153.

Glover, N. G., Crego, C., & Widiger, T. A. (2011). The clinical utility of the five factor model of personality disorder. *Personality Disorders, 3*(2), 176–184.

Glovin, D. (2014, September 9). Baseball caught looking as fouls injure 17,500 fans a year. *Bloomberg.*

Godlasky, A. (2018, February 16). How do you go back to school in a place of bloodshed? *USA Today.*

Godlewska, B. R., Pike, A., Sharpley, A. L., Ayton, A., Park, R. J., Cowen, P. J., & Emir, U. E. (2017). Brain glutamate in anorexia nervosa: A magnetic resonance spectroscopy case control study at 7 Tesla. *Psychopharmacology, 234*(3), 421–426.

Goetz, K., Kleine-Budde, K., Bramesfeld, A., & Stegbauer, C. (2018). Working atmosphere, job satisfaction and individual characteristics of community mental health professionals in integrated care. *Health & Social Care in the Community.* [Manuscript in press]

Gola, H., Engler, H., Schauer, M., Adenauer, H., Riether, C., Kolassa, S., . . . Kolassa, I. (2012). Victims of rape show increased cortisol responses to trauma reminders: A study in individuals with war- and torture-related PTSD. *Psychoneuroendocrinology, 37*(2), 213–220.

Golbeck, J. (2016, August 5). Social anxiety and Internet use: What we know. *Psychology Today.*

Gold, M. (2016). Children of alcoholics. *Psych Central.* Retrieved from https://psychcentral.com.

Goldenberg, I., & Stanton, M. (2019). Family therapy. In D. Wedding & R. J. Corsini (Eds.), *Current psychotherapies* (11th ed., Ch. 11). Independence, KY: Cengage Publications.

Golder, S., Ahmed, S., Norman, G., & Booth, A. (2017). Attitudes toward the ethics of research using social media: A systematic review. *Journal of Medical Internet Research, 19*(6), e195.

Goldstein, D. M., & Hall, K. (2015). Mass hysteria in Le Roy, New York: How brain experts materialized truth and outscienced environmental inquiry. *Journal of the American Ethnological Society, 42*(4), 640–657.

Goldstein, I. (2014). Unfair: Government-approved sexual medicine treatments only available for men. *Journal of Sexual Medicine, 11,* 317–320.

Goldstein, I., Chambers, R., Tang, W., Stecher, V., & Hassan, T. (2018, March 22). Real-world observational results from a database of 48 million men in the United States: Relationship of cardiovascular disease, diabetes mellitus and depression with age and erectile dysfunction. *International Journal of Clinical Practice.* [Epub ahead of print]

Goldstein, J. (2016). Geel, Belgium: A model of "community recovery." *Samford University Psychology Department.* Retrieved from http://www.geelmentalhealth.com.

Goldston, D. B., Molock, S. D., Whitbeck, L. B., Murakami, J. L., Zayas, L. H., & Hall, G. C. N. (2008). Cultural considerations in adolescent suicide prevention and psychosocial treatment. *American Psychologist, 63*(1), 14–31.

Goltseker, K., Bolotin, L., & Barak, S. (2017). Counterconditioning during reconsolidation prevents relapse of cocaine memories. *Neuropsychopharmacology, 42,* 716–726.

Gomez Penedo, J. M., Constantino, M. J., Coyne, A. E., Bernecker, S. L., & Smith-Hansen, L. (2018, January 19). Patient baseline interpersonal problems as moderators of outcome in two psychotherapies for bulimia nervosa. *Psychotherapy Research.* [Epub ahead of print]

Gomez, M. M. (2016, March 30). *Jury trials outside in* (Kindle edition). LexisNexis.

Gómez-Gil, E., Esteva, I., Almaraz, M. C., Pasaro, E., Segovia, S., & Guillamon, A. (2010). Familiarity of gender identity disorder in non-twin siblings. *Archives of Sexual Behavior, 39*(2), 546–552.

Gong, J., Chen, G., Jia, Y., Zhong, S., Zhao, L., Luo, X., . . . Wang, Y. (2019). Disrupted functional connectivity within the default mode network and salience network in unmedicated bipolar II disorder. *Progress in Neuro-Psychopharmacology & Biological Psychiatry, 88,* 11–18.

Gonidakis, F., Kravvariti, V., & Varsou, E. (2015). Sexual function of women suffering from anorexia nervosa and bulimia nervosa. *Journal of Sex and Marital Therapy, 41*(4), 368–378.

González, H. M., Tarraf, W., Whitfield, K. E., & Vega, W. A. (2010). The epidemiology of major depression and ethnicity in the United States. *Journal of Psychiatric Research, 44,* 1043–1051.

González-Fernández, S., Fernández-Rodríguez, C., Paz-Caballero, M. D., & Pérez-Álvarez, M. (2018). Treating anxiety and depression of cancer survivors: Behavioral activation versus acceptance and commitment therapy. *Psicothema, 30*(1), 14–20.

Goodman, M. (2013). Patient highlights: Female genital plastic/cosmetic surgery. *Journal of Sexual Medicine, 10*(8), 2125–2126.

Goodman, W. (2017). What causes obsessive-compulsive disorder (OCD)? *Psych Central.* Retrieved from https://psychcentral.com/disorders/ocd.

Goodnough, A., & Atkinson, S. (2016, April 30). A potent side effect to the Flint water crisis: Mental health problems. *The New York Times.*

Goodwin, H., Yiend, J., & Hirsch, C. R. (2017). Generalized anxiety disorder, worry and attention to threat: A systematic review. *Clinical Psychology Review, 54,* 107–122.

Goodwin, R., Kaniasty, K., Sun, S., & Ben-Ezra, M. (2017). Psychological distress and prejudice following terror attacks in France. *Journal of Psychiatric Research, 16*(91), 111–115.

Goodyer, I. M., Reynolds, S., Barrett, B., Byford, S., Dubicka, B., Hill, J., . . . Fonagy, P. (2017). Cognitive-behavioural therapy and short-term psychoanalytic psychotherapy versus brief psychosocial intervention in adolescents with unipolar major depression (IMPACT): A multicentre, pragmatic, observer-blind, randomised controlled trial. *Health Technology Assessment, 21*(12), 1–94.

Gordon, S. (2018, February 5). The impact of bullying on everyday life: The effects of bullying. *Very Well Family.* Retrieved from https://www.verywellfamily.com/bullying-impact-4157338.

Gore, W. L., & Widiger, T. A. (2015). Assessment of dependency by the FFDI: Comparisons to the PID-5 and maladaptive agreeableness. *Personality and Mental Health, 9*(4), 258–276.

Gore, W. L., & Widiger, T. A. (2016). Fluctuation between grandiose and vulnerable narcissism. *Personality Disorders, 7*(4), 363–371.

Gorelick, D. A. (2017, February 10). Cocaine use disorder in adults: Epidemiology, pharmacology, clinical manifestations, medical consequences, and diagnosis. *UpToDate.* Retrieved from http://www.uptodate.com.

Gorelick, D. A. (2018, February 15). Cannabis use and disorder: Epidemiology, comorbidity, health consequences, and medico-legal status. *UpToDate.* Retrieved from http://www.uptodate.com.

Gorelick, D. A. (2018, February 15). Treatment of cannabis use disorder. *UpToDate.* Retrieved from http://www.uptodate.com.

Gorenstein, D. (2013, May 17). *How much is the DSM-5 worth? Marketplace.org.*

Goshen, C. E. (1967). *Documentary history of psychiatry: A source book on historical principles.* New York: Philosophy Library.

Gosling, S. D., Sandy, C. J., & Potter, J. (2015, April 28). Personalities of self-identified "dog people" and "cat people." *Anthrozoös, 23*(3), 213–222.

Gottesman, I. I. (1991). *Schizophrenia genesis.* New York: Freeman.

Gottlieb, J. D., Gidugu, V., Maru, M., Tepper, M. C., Davis, M. J., Greenwold, J., . . . Mueser, K. T. (2017). Randomized controlled trial of an internet cognitive behavioral skills-based program for auditory hallucinations in persons with psychosis. *Psychiatric Rehabilitation Journal, 40*(3), 283–292.

Gottschalk, M. G., Leussis, M. P., Ruland, T., Gjeluci, K., Petryshen, T. L., & Bahn, S. (2017). Lithium reverses behavioral and axonal transport-related changes associated with ANK3 bipolar disorder gene disruption. *European Neuropsychopharmacology, 27*(3), 274–288.

Gouin, J-P, Glaser, R., Loving, T. J., Malarkey, W. B., Stowell, J., Houts, C., & Kiecolt-Glaser, J. K. (2009). Attachment avoidance predicts inflammatory responses to marital conflict. *Brain, Behavior, and Immunity, 23*(7), 898–904.

Gould, M. S., Kleinman, M. H., Lake, A. M., Forman, J., & Midle, J. B. (2014). Newspaper coverage of suicide and initiation of suicide clusters in teenagers in the USA, 1988–96: A retrospective, population-based case-control study. *Lancet Psychiatry, 1,* 34–43.

Gowensmith, W. N., Murrie, D. C., Boccaccini, M. T., & McNichols, B. J. (2017). Field reliability influences field validity: Risk assessment of individuals found not guilty by reason of insanity. *Psychological Assessment, 29*(6), 786–794.

Gowing, L., Ali, R., White, J. M., & Mbewe, D. (2017). Buprenorphine for managing opioid withdrawal. *Cochrane Database of Systematic Reviews, 2,* CD002025.

Gozlan, O. (2011). Transsexual surgery: A novel reminder and a navel remainder. *International Forum of Psychoanalysis, 20*(1), 45–52.

Gradus, J. L. (2017, March 30). *PTSD: National Center for PTSD: Epidemiology of PTSD.* Retrieved from https://www.ptsd.va.gov/professional/PTSD-overview.

Graham, J. R. (2006). *MMPI-2: Assessing personality and psychopathology* (4th ed.). New York: Oxford University Press.

Graham, J. R. (2011). *MMPI-2: Assessing personality and psychopathology.* New York: Oxford University Press.

Gramlich, L., Tandon, P., & Rahman, A. (2017, January 26). Nutritional status in patients with sustained heavy alcohol use. *UpToDate.* Retrieved from http://www.uptodate.com.

Granholm, E., Holden, J., Link, P. C., & McQuaid, J. R. (2014). Randomized clinical trial of cognitive behavioral social skills training for schizophrenia: Improvement in functioning and experiential negative symptoms. *Journal of Consulting and Clinical Psychology.* [Manuscript submitted for publication]

Grant, J. E., & Chamberlain, S. R. (2017). Clinical correlates of symptom severity in skin picking disorder. *Comprehensive Psychiatry, 78,* 25–30.

Grant, J. E., Odlaug, B. L., Chamberlain, S. R., Keuthen, N. J., Lochner, C., & Stein, D. (2012). Skin picking disorder. *The American Journal of Psychiatry, 169*(11), 1143–1149.

Grant, J. E., Redden, S. A., Leppink, E. W., & Chamberlain, S. R. (2017). Trichotillomania and co-occurring anxiety. *Comprehensive Psychiatry, 72,* 1–5.

Grant, J. E., Redden, S. A., Leppink, E. W., & Odlaug, B. L. (2015). Skin picking disorder with co-occurring body dysmorphic disorder. *Body Image, 15,* 44–48.

Gray, H. (1959). *Anatomy of the human body* (27th ed.). Philadelphia: Lea & Febiger.

Gray, J. A., & McNaughton, N. (1996). The neuropsychology of anxiety: Reprise. In D. A. Hope (Ed.), *The Nebraska symposium on motivation* (Vol. 43). Lincoln: University of Nebraska Press.

Gray, K. (2017, June 1). Here's why millennials are so dedicated to practicing mindfulness. *Brit+Co.* Retrieved from https://www.brit.co.

Gray, N. A., Zhou, R., Du, J., Moore, G. J., & Manji, H. K. (2003). The use of mood stabilizers as plasticity enhancers in the treatment of neuropsychiatric disorders. *Journal of Clinical Psychiatry, 64*(Suppl. 5), 3–17.

Gray, S. J., & Gallo, D. A. (2016). Paranormal psychic believers and skeptics: A large-scale test of the cognitive differences hypothesis. *Memory and Cognition, 44*(2): 242–261.

Green, E. (2016, June 22). Sleeping pills – Do the benefits outweigh the risks? *No Sleepless Nights.* Retrieved from http://www.nosleeplessnights.com.

Green, J., & Garg, S. (2018). Annual research review: The state of autism intervention science: Progress, target psychological and biological mechanisms and future prospects. *Journal of Child Psychology and Psychiatry, 59*(4), 424–443.

Green, M., & Lankford, R., Jr. (2017). *Body image and body shaming (hot topics).* Farmington Hills, MI: Lucent Books.

Green, S. A. (1985). *Mind and body: The psychology of physical illness.* Washington, DC: American Psychiatric Press.

Greenberg, B. (2018, April 24). The five biggest myths about crisis text line. *American Foundation for Suicide Prevention.* Retrieved from https://afsp.org/five- biggest-myths-crisis-text-line/.

Greenberg, D. B. (2016, January 27). Somatization, epidemiology, pathogenesis, clinical features, medical evaluation, and diagnosis. *UpToDate*. Retrieved from www.uptodate.com.

Greenberg, D. B. (2016, November 15). Somatization: Treatment and prognosis. *UpToDate*. Retrieved from www.uptodate.com.

Greenberg, G. (2011, December 27). Inside the battle to define mental illness. *Wired Magazine*.

Greene, K. M., & Maggs, J. L. (2017). Academic time during college: Associations with mood, tiredness, and binge drinking across days and semesters. *Journal of Adolescence, 56, 24–33.*

Greening, L., Stoppelbein, L., Fite, P., Dhossche, D., Erath, S., Brown, J., Cramer, R., & Young, L. (2008). Pathways to suicidal behaviors in childhood. *Suicide and Life-Threatening Behavior, 38*(1), 35–45.

Greer, S., Kramer, M. R., Cook-Smith, J. N., & Casper, M. L. (2014). Metropolitan racial residential segregation and cardiovascular mortality: Exploring pathways. *Journal of Urban Health, 91*(3), 499–509.

Greger, H. K., Myhre, A. K., Lydersen, S., & Jozefiak, T. (2016, May 10). Child maltreatment and quality of life: A study of adolescents in residential care. *Health and Quality of Life Outcomes, 14*:74.

Gregory, B., & Peters, L. (2017). Changes in the self during cognitive behavioural therapy for social anxiety disorder: A systematic review. *Clinical Psychology Review, 52,* 1–18.

Greist, J. H. (2018). Generalized anxiety disorder (GAD). *Merck Manual Professional Version*. Retrieved from https://www.mer ckmanuals.com.

Grella, C. E. (2018, March 25). What do women with substance use disorders want? *Addiction*. [Epub ahead of print]

Greller, H., & Gupta, A. (2017, August 22). Benzodiazepine poisoning and withdrawal. *UpToDate*. Retrieved from http://www.uptodate.com.

Gressier, F., Letranchant, A., & Hardy, P. (2015). Post-partum psychosis. *La Revue Du Praticien, 65*(2), 232–234. [Article in French]

Griffin, R. M. (2014). E-cigarettes 101. *WebMD*. Retrieved from http://www/webmd/com/smoking-cessation.

Griffiths, F., Dobermann, T., Cave, J. A. K., Thorogood, M., Johnson, S., Salamatian, K., . . . Goudge, J. (2015). The impact of online social networks on health and health systems: A scoping review and case studies. *Policy & Internet, 7*(4), 473–496.

Griffiths, S., Murray, S. B., Bentley, C., Gratwick-Sarll, K., Harrison, C., & Mond, J. M. (2017). Sex differences in quality of life impairment association with body dissatisfaction in adolescents. *Journal of Adolescent Health, 61*(1), 77–82.

Griffiths, S., Murray, S. B., Krug, I., & McLean, S. A. (2018, January 24). The contribution of social media to body dissatisfaction, eating disorder symptoms, and anabolic steroid use among sexual minority men. *Cyberpsychology, Behavior, and Social Networking, 21*(3), 149-156. [Epub ahead of print]

Grigg, J. R. (1988). Imitative suicides in an active duty military population. *Military Medicine, 153*(2), 79–81.

Grilo, C. M., Masheb, R. M., Brody, M., Toth, C., Burke-Martindale, C. H., & Rothschild, B. S. (2005). Childhood maltreatment in extremely obese male and female bariatric surgery candidates. *Obesity Research, 13,* 123–130.

Grilo, C. M., Masheb, R. M., White, M. A., Gueorguieva, R., Barnes, R. D., Walsh, B. T., . . . Garcia, R. (2014). Treatment of binge eating disorder in racially and ethnically diverse obese patients in primary care: Randomized placebo-controlled clinical trial of self-help and medication. *Behaviour Research and Therapy, 58,* 1–9.

Grob, G. N. (1966). *The state and the mentally ill: A history of Worcester State Hospital in Massachusetts, 1830–1920.* Chapel Hill: University of North Carolina Press.

Grodstein, F. (2018, April 3). Estrogen and cognitive function. *UpToDate*. Retrieved from http://www.uptodate.com.

Grohol, J. (2016). Types of therapies: Theoretical orientations and practices of therapists. *Psych Central*. Retrieved from https://psychcentral.com/lib.

Grohol, J. M. (2015). *6 surprising, bizarre facts you didn't know about Freud*. Retrieved from http://psychcentral.com/blog/archives/2015/07/09.

Groopman, J. (2017, January 9). The voices in our heads. *The New Yorker.*

Grossi, V., Forte, G., Sanese, P., Peserico, A., Tezil, T., Lepore Signorile, M., . . . Simone, C. (2018, May 4). The longevity SNP rs2802292 uncovered: HSF1 activates stress-dependent expression of FOXO3 through an intronic enhancer. *Nucleic Acids Research*. [Epub ahead of print]

Groth-Marnat, G., & Wright, A. J. (2016). *Handbook of psychological assessment* (6th ed.). Hoboken, NJ: Wiley.

Grover, S., & Avasthi, A. (2018). Clinical practice guidelines for management of delirium in elderly. *Indian Journal of Psychiatry, 60*(Suppl. 3), S329–S340.

Grover, S., Chakrabarti, S., Ghormode, D., Agarwal, M., Sharma, A., & Avasthi, A. (2015). Catatonia in inpatients with psychiatric disorders: A comparison of schizophrenia and mood disorders. *Psychiatry Research, 229*(3), 919–925.

Grubin, D. (2010). Polygraphy. In J. M. Brown & E. A. Campbell (Eds.), *The Cambridge handbook of forensic psychology* (pp. 276–282). New York: Cambridge University Press.

Gruebner, O., Rapp, M. A., Adli, M., Kluge, U., Galea, S., & Heinz, A. (2017). Cities and mental health. *Deutsches Ärzteblatt, 114*(8), 121–127.

Gruenewald, P. J., Treno, A. J., Holder, H. D., & LaScala, E. A. (2016) 18 community-based approaches to the prevention of substance use-related problems. In K. J. Sher (Ed.), *Oxford handbook of substance use and substance use disorders* (Vol. 1, Chap. 18, pp. 600–624). New York: Oxford University Press.

Grünblatt, E., Marinova, Z., Roth, A., Gardini, E., Ball, J., Geissler, J., . . . Walitza, S. (2018). Combining genetic and epigenetic parameters of the serotonin transporter gene in obsessive-compulsive disorder. *Journal of Psychiatric Research, 96,* 209–217.

Grzelak, T., Dutkiewicz, A., Paszynska, E., Dmitrzak-Weglarz, M., Slopien, A., & Tyszkiewicz-Nwafor, M. (2017). Neurobiochemical and psychological factors influencing the eating behaviors and attitudes in anorexia nervosa. *Journal of Physiology and Biochemistry, 73*(2), 297–305.

GSS (General Social Survey). (2016). General social survey. *NORC at the University of Chicago.*

Gu, Q., Hou, J. C., & Fang, X. M. (2018). Mindfulness meditation for primary headache pain: A meta-analysis. *Chinese Medical Journal, 131*(7), 829–838.

Guillamon, A., Junque, C., & Gómez-Gil, E. (2016). A review of the status of brain structure research in transsexualism. *Archives of Sexual Behavior, 45,* 1615–1648.

Guina, J., Nahhas, R. W., Sutton, P., & Farnsworth, S. (2018). The influence of trauma type and timing on PTSD symptoms. *Journal of Nervous and Mental Disease, 206*(1), 72–76.

Guo, L., Liu, Y., Wang, X., Yuan, M., Yu, Y., Zhang, X., & Zhao, S. (2017). Significance of penile hypersensitivity in premature ejaculation. *Scientific Reports, 7*(1), 10441.

Gurak, K., & Weisman de Mamani, A. (2016). Risk and protective factors, perceptions of family environment, ethnicity, and schizophrenia symptoms. *Journal of Nervous and Mental Disease, 204*(8), 570–577.

Gurak, K., & Weisman de Mamani, A. (2017). Caregiver expressed emotion and psychiatric symptoms in African Americans with schizophrenia: An attempt to understand the paradoxical relationship. *Family Process, 56*(2),476-486.

Guterman, J. T., Martin, C. V., & Rudes, J. (2011). A solution-focused approach to frotteurism. *Journal of Systemic Therapies, 30*(1), 59–72.

Gutman, D. A., & Nemeroff, C. B. (2011). Stress and depression. In R. J. Contrada & A. Baum (Eds.), *The handbook of stress science: Biology, psychology, and health* (pp. 345–357). New York: Springer Publishing.

Guttmacher Institute. (2017, September). *Adolescent sexual and reproductive health in the United States.* New York: Guttmacher Institute

Guttmacher Institute. (2018). Insurance coverage of contraceptives. Washington, DC: Guttmacher Institute. Retrieved from https://www.guttmacher.org/state-policy/explore.

Guynn, J. (2017, March 1). Facebook takes steps to stop suicides on Live. *USA Today.*

Gyani, A., Shafran, R., Rose, S., & Lee, M. J. (2015). A qualitative investigation of therapists' attitudes towards research: Horses for courses? *Behavioural and Cognitive Psychotherapy, 43*(4), 436–438.

Haagen, J. G., Smid, G. E., Knipscheer, J. W., & Kleber, R. J. (2015). The efficacy of recommended treatments for veterans with PTSD: A metaregression analysis. *Clinical Psychology Review, 40,* 184–194.

Haaken, J., & Reavey, P. (Eds.). (2010). *Memory matters: Contexts for understanding sexual abuse recollections.* New York: Routledge/Taylor & Francis Group.

Hackett, G., Kirby, M., Wylie, K., Heald, A., Ossei-Gerning, N., Edwards, D., & Muneer, A. (2018). British Society for Sexual Medicine guidelines on the management of erectile dysfunction in men: 2017. *Journal of Sexual Medicine, 15*(4), 430–457.

Hadar, R., Voget, M., Vengeliene, V., Haumesser, J. K., van Riesen, C., Avchalumov, Y., . . . Winter, C. (2017, January 1). Altered neural oscillations and elevated dopamine levels in the reward pathway during alcohol relapse. *Behavioural Brain Research, 316,* 131–135.

Häfner, H., & an der Heiden, W. (1988). The mental health care system in transition: A study in organization, effectiveness, and costs of complementary care for schizophrenic patients. In C. N. Stefanis & A. D. Rabavilis (Eds.), *Schizophrenia: Recent biosocial developments*. New York: Human Sciences Press.

Haggerty, J. (2017). Treatment of ADHD in children. *Psych Central*. Retrieved from https://psychcentral.com.

Haghighatfard, A., Andalib, S., Amini Faskhodi, M., Sadeghi, S., Ghaderi, A. H., Moiradkhani, S., . . . Ghadimi, Z. (2018). Gene expression study of mitochondrial complex I in schizophrenia and paranoid personality disorder. *World Journal of Biological Psychiatry*. [Manuscript in press]

Haile, C. N. (2012). History, use, and basic pharmacology of stimulants. In T. R. Kosten, T. F. Newton, De La Garza, R., II, & Haile, C. N. (Eds.), *Cocaine and methamphetamine dependence: Advances in treatment* (pp. 13–84). Arlington, VA: American Psychiatric Publishing.

Hall, K. (2007). Sexual dysfunction and childhood sexual abuse: Gender differences and treatment implications. In S. R. Leiblum (Ed.), *Principles and practice of sex therapy* (4th ed., pp. 350–370). New York: Guilford Press.

Hall, K. (2017). Treating sexual problems in survivors of sexual trauma. In Z. D. Peterson (Ed.), *The Wiley-Blackwell handbook of sex therapy* (Chap. 24, pp. 389–406). Hoboken, NJ: Wiley-Blackwell.

Hall, L., & Cohn, L. (2010). *Bulimia: A guide to recovery*. Carlsbad, CA: Gurze Books.

Hallberg, J., Kaldo, V., Arver, S., Dhejne, C., & Öberg, K. G. (2017). A cognitive-behavioral therapy group intervention for hypersexual disorder: A feasibility study. *Journal of Sexual Medicine, 14*(7), 950–958.

Hallevy, G. (2017). The shadows of normality: Legal insanity under modern criminal law. In M. D. White (Ed.), *The insanity defense: Multidisciplinary views on its history, trends, and controversies* (Chap. 4, pp. 97–132). Westport, CT: Praeger.

Hall-Flavin, D. K. (2016). What does it mean to have a nervous breakdown? *Mayo Clinic, Mayo Foundation for Medical Education and Research*.

Hallgren, M., Vancampfort, D., & Stubbs, B. (2017). Exercise is medicine for depression: Even when the "pill" is small. *Neuropsychiatric Disease and Treatment, 12,* 2715–2721.

Halperin, J. M. (2017). Developmental psychopathology in the post-genomics era: Substantial challenges but reasons for hope. *Journal of Child Psychology and Psychiatry, 58*(3), 219–221.

Hamadjida, A., Nuara, S. G., Gourdon, J. C., & Huot, P. (2018). Trazodone alleviates both dyskinesia and psychosis in the parkinsonian marmoset model of Parkinson's disease. *Journal of Neural Transmission (Vienna), 125*(9), 1355–1360.

Hameed, M. A., & Lewis, A. J. (2016). Offspring of parents with schizophrenia: A systematic review of developmental features across childhood. *Harvard Review of Psychiatry, 24*(2), 104–117.

Hamilton, L. D., & Meston, C. M. (2013). Chronic stress and sexual function in women. *Journal of Sexual Medicine, 10,* 2443–2454.

Hamilton, S. S. (2016, November 16). Reading difficulty in children: Intervention. *UpToDate*. Retrieved from http://www.uptodate.com.

Hamilton, S. S. (2017, July 3). Reading difficulty in children: Normal reading development and etiology of reading difficulty. *UpToDate*. Retrieved from http://www.uptodate.com.

Hamilton, S. S. (2017, June 26). Developmental coordination disorder: Clinical features and diagnosis. *UpToDate*. Retrieved from http://www.uptodate.com.

Hamilton, S. S. (2018, March 7). Reading difficulty in children: Clinical features and evaluation. *UpToDate*. Retrieved from http://www.uptodate.com.

Hamilton, S. S. (2018, March 8). Reading difficulty in children: Interventions. *UpToDate*. Retrieved from http://www.uptodate.com.

Hammen, C. (2016). Depression and stressful environments: Identifying gaps in conceptualization and measurement. *Anxiety, Stress & Coping, 29*(4), 335–351.

Hammond, T. E., Crowther, A., & Drummond, S. (2018). A thematic inquiry into the burnout experience of Australian solo-practicing clinical psychologists. *Frontiers in Psychology, 8,* 1996.

Hamo, N., Abramovitch, A., & Zohar, A. (2018). A computerized neuropsychological evaluation of cognitive functions in a subclinical obsessive-compulsive sample. *Journal of Behavior Therapy and Experimental Psychiatry, 59,* 142–149.

Han, S., Zong, X., Hu, M., Yu, Y., Wang, X., Long, Z., . . . Chen, H. (2018). Frequency-selective alteration in the resting-state corticostriatal-thalamo-cortical circuit correlates with symptoms' severity in first-episode drug-naive patients with schizophrenia. *Schizophrenia Research*. [Manuscript in press]

Handel, R. W. (2016). An introduction to the Minnesota Multiphasic Personality Inventory-Adolescent-Restructured Form (MMPI-A-RF). *BMC Psychology, 23*(4), 361–373.

Hankin, B. L., Snyder, H. R., & Gulley, L. D. (2016). Cognitive risks in developmental psychopathology. In D. Cicchetti (Ed.), *Developmental psychopathology, Vol. 3: Maladaptation and psychopathology* (3rd ed.). New York: Wiley.

Hanna, E., Ward, L. M., Seabrook, R. C., Jerald, M., Reed, L., Giaccardi, S., & Lippman, J. R. (2017). Contributions of social comparison and self-objectification in mediating associations between Facebook use and emergent adults' psychological well-being. *Cyberpsychology, Behavior, and Social Networking, 20*(3), 172–179.

Hanna, D., Kershaw, K., & Chaplin, R. (2009). How specialist ECT consultants inform patients about memory loss. *Psychiatric Bulletin, 33*(11), 412–415.

Hannesdottir, D. K., Sigurjonsdottir, S. B., Njardvik, U., & Ollendick, T. H. (2018, April 17). Do youth with separation anxiety disorder differ in anxiety sensitivity from youth with other anxiety disorders? *Child Psychiatry & Human Development*. [Epub ahead of print]

Hansen, M., Ross, J., & Armour, C. (2017). Evidence of the dissociative PTSD subtype: A systematic literature review of latent class and profile analytic studies of PTSD. *Journal of Affective Disorders, 213,* 59–69.

Hansson, L., Middelboe, T., Sorgaard, K. W., Bengtsson, T. A., Bjarnason, O., Merinder, L., . . . Vinding, H. R. (2002). Living situation, subjective quality of life and social network among individuals with schizophrenia living in community settings. *Acta Pyschiatrica Scandinavica, 106*(5), 343–350.

Hao, Q., Wang, U., Ding, X., Dong, B., Yang, M., Dong, B., & Wei, Y. (2018). G-395A polymorphism in the promoter region of the KLOTHO gene associates with frailty among the oldest-old. *Scientific Reports, 8*(1), 6735.

Harada, K., Kitaguchi, T., Kamiya, T., Aung, K. H., Nakamura, K., Ohta, K., & Tsuboi, T. (2017). Lysophosphatidylinositol-induced activation of the cation channel TRPV2 triggers glucagon-like peptide-1 secretion in enteroendocrine L cells. *Journal of Biological Chemistry, 292,* 10855–10864.

Hardin, S. B., Weinrich, S., Weinrich, M., Garrison, C., Addy, C., & Hardin, T. L. (2002). Effects of a long-term psychosocial nursing intervention on adolescents exposed to catastrophic stress. *Issues in Mental Health Nursing, 23*(6), 537–551.

Hare, R. D. (1993). *Without conscience: The disturbing world of the psychopaths among us*. New York: Pocket Books.

Harford, T. C., Yi, H. Y., Chen, C. M., & Grant, B. F. (2018). Substance use disorders and self- and other-directed violence among adults: Results from the National Survey on Drug Use and Health. *Journal of Affective Disorders, 225,* 365–373.

Harkness, K. L., & Monroe, S. M. (2016). The assessment and measurement of adult life stress: Basic premises, operational principles, and design requirements. *Journal of Abnormal Psychology, 125*(5), 727–745.

Haroules, B. (2007). Involuntary commitment is unconstitutional. In A. Quigley (Ed.), *Current controversies: Mental health*. Detroit: Greenhaven Press/Thomson Gale.

Harrington, A. (2012). The fall of the schizophrenogenic mother. *The Lancet, 379*(9823), 1292–1293.

Harris Interactive. (2011). *Large majorities support doctor assisted suicide for terminally ill patients in great pain*. (Harris Poll #9, January 25, 2011). New York: Harris Interactive.

Harris Interactive. (2013). *Are Americans still serving up family dinners?* (Harris Poll #82). New York: Harris Interactive.

Harris Interactive. (2014, February 19). *6 in 10 Americans say they or someone they know have been bullied*. (Harris Poll #17). New York: Harris Interactive.

Harris Poll. (2013, May 30). *Are you happy? It may depend on age, race/ethnicity and other factors (Harris Poll #30)*. New York: Harris Interactive.

Harris Poll. (2015, June 3). *Older Americans, those who are religious, and even political party members are happier* (Harris Poll #30). New York: Harris Interactive.

Harris Poll. (2016, July 8). *Latest happiness index reveals American happiness at all-time low* (Harris Poll #50). New York: Harris Interactive.

Harris, A. (2017, March 1). Facebook harnesses artificial intelligence to combat live suicide broadcasts. *Miami Herald*.

Harris, J. C. (2010). *Intellectual disability: A guide for families and professionals*. New York: Oxford University Press.

Harrison, N. A., Johnston, K., Corno, F., Casey, S. J., Friedner, K., Humphreys, K., . . . Kopelman, M. D. (2017). Psychogenic amnesia: Syndromes, outcome, and patterns of retrograde amnesia. *Brain, 140*(9), 2498–2510.

Hart, C. L., & Ksir, C. (2015). *Drugs, society, and human behavior* (16th ed.). New York: McGraw-Hill Publishing.

Hart, C. L., & Ksir, C. J. (2017, November 7). *Drugs, society, and human behavior* (17th ed.). Columbus, OH: McGraw-Hill Higher Education.

Hartmann, U., & Waldinger, M. D. (2007). Treatment of delayed ejaculation. In S. R. Leiblum (Ed.), *Principles and practice of sex therapy* (4th ed., pp. 241–276). New York: Guilford Press.

Hartney, E. (2014). Additions: Can marijuana cause infertility? Retrieved from http://addictions.about.com/od/legalissues/f/Can-Marijuana-Cause-Infertility.htm.

Hausman, A. (2008). Direct-to-consumer advertising and its effect on prescription requests. *Journal of Advertising Research, 48*(1), 42–56.

Havinga, P. J., Boschloo, L., Bloemen, A. J., Nauta, M. H., de Vries, S. O., Penninx, B. W., . . . Hartman, C. A. (2017). Doomed for disorder? High incidence of mood and anxiety disorders in offspring of depressed and anxious patients: A prospective cohort study. *Journal of Clinical Psychiatry, 78*(1), e8–e17.

Hawk, L. W., Jr., Fosco, W. D., Colder, C. R., Waxmonsky, J. G., Pelham, W. E., Jr., & Rosch, K. S. (2018, May 7). How do stimulant treatments for ADHD work? Evidence for mediation by improved cognition. *Journal of Child Psychology and Psychiatry*. [Epub ahead of print]

Hawks, E., Blumenthal, H., Feldner, M. T., Leen-Feldner, E. W., & Jones, R. (2011). An examination of the relation between traumatic event exposure and panic-relevant biological challenge responding among adolescents. *Behavior Therapy, 42*(3), 427–438.

Hayden, L. A. (1998). Gender discrimination within the reproductive health care system: Viagra v. birth control. *Journal of Law and Health, 13*, 171–198.

Hayes, S. C. (2016). Acceptance and commitment therapy, relational frame theory, and the third wave of behavioral and cognitive therapies (republished article). *Behavior Therapy, 47*(6), 869–885.

Haynes, S. G., Feinleib, M., & Kannel, W. B. (1980). The relationship of psychosocial factors to coronary heart disease in the Framingham study: III. Eight-year incidence of coronary heart disease. *American Journal of Epidemiology, 111*, 37–58.

He, M., Ma, J., Ren, Z., Zhou, G., Gong, P., Liu, M., . . . Zhang, X. (2019). Association between activities of daily living disability and depression symptoms of middle-aged and older Chinese adults and their spouses: A community based study. *Journal of Affective Disorders, 242*, 135–142.

He, Y., Gewirtz, A. H., Lee, S., & August, G. (2018, February 9). Do parent preferences for child conduct problem interventions impact parenting outcomes? A pilot study in community children's mental health settings. *Journal of Marital and Family Therapy*. [Epub ahead of print]

Healy, S., & Tyrrell, M. (2013). Importance of debriefing following critical incidents. *Emergency Nurse, 20*(10), 32–37.

Hébert, M., Langevin, R., & Oussaïd, E. (2018). Cumulative childhood trauma, emotion regulation, dissociation, and behavior problems in school-aged sexual abuse victims. *Journal of Affective Disorders, 225*, 306–312.

Hedaya, R. J. (2011). Health matters: Connecting you to the sources of health. Panic disorders: Part 2. *Psychology Today*. Retrieved from http://www.psychologytoday.com/blog/health-matters/201102.

Hedman, L. C., Petrila, J., Fisher, W. H., Swanson, J. W., Dingman, D. A., & Burris, S. (2016). State laws on emergency holds for mental health stabilization. *Psychiatry Services, 67*(5), 529–535.

Heflin, M. T. (2018, May 8). Geriatric health maintenance. *UpToDate*. Retrieved from http://www.uptodate.com.

Heilbrun, K., Goldstein, N. E. S., & Redding, R. E. (Eds.). (2005). *Juvenile delinquency: Prevention, assessment, and intervention* (pp. 85–110). New York: Oxford University Press.

Heiman, J. R. (2007). Orgasmic disorders in women. In S. R. Leiblum (Ed.), *Principles and practice of sex therapy* (4th ed., pp. 84–123). New York: Guilford Press.

Heimberg, R. G., & Magee, L. (2014). Social anxiety disorder. In D. H. Barlow (Ed.), *Clinical handbook of psychological disorders: A step-by-step treatment manual* (5th ed., pp. 114–154). New York: Guilford Press.

Heimberg, R. G., Brozovich, F. A., & Rapee, R. M. (2010). A cognitive-behavioral model of social anxiety disorder: Update and extension. In S. G. Hofmann & P. M. DiBartolo (Eds.), *Social anxiety: Clinical, developmental, and social perspectives*. New York: Academic Press.

Helander, M., Lochman, J., Högström, J., Ljotsson, B., Hellner, C., & Enebrink, P. (2018). The effect of adding Coping Power Program-Sweden to Parent Management Training-effects and moderators in a randomized controlled trial. *Behaviour Research and Therapy, 103*, 43–52.

Held-Poschardt, D., Sterzer, P., Schlagenhauf, F., Pehrs, C., Wittmann, A., Stoy, M., . . . Ströhle, A. (2018). Reward and loss anticipation in panic disorder: An fMRI study. *Psychiatry Research, 271*, 111–117.

Hellstrom, W. J. G., & DeLay, K. (2017, June 27). Male dyspareunia. *UpToDate*. Retrieved from http://www.uptodate.com.

Hembree-Kigin, T. L., & McNeil, C. B. (2013). *Parent-child interaction therapy (Clinical Child Psychology Library)*. New York: Springer Science + Business Media.

Henderson, V. (2010). Diminishing dissociative experiences for war veterans in group therapy. In S. S. Fehr (Ed.), *101 interventions in group therapy* (rev. ed., pp. 217–220). New York: Routledge/Taylor & Francis Group.

Henggeler, S. W., & Sheidow, A. J. (2012). Empirically supported family-based treatments for conduct disorder and delinquency in adolescents. *Journal of Marital and Family Therapy, 38*(1), 30–58.

Henn, F. (2013). Using brain imaging to understand the response to cognitive therapy in panic disorder. *American Journal of Psychiatry, 170*, 1235–1236.

Henrich, J., Heine, S. J., & Norenzayan, A. (2010, June). The weirdest people in the world? *Behavioral and Brain Sciences, 33*(2–3), 61–83; discussion, 83–135.

Henriksen, M. G., Nordgaard, J., & Jansson, L. B. (2017). Genetics of schizophrenia: Overview of methods, findings and limitations. *Frontiers in Human Neuroscience, 11*, 322.

Heppner, P. P., Wampold, B. E., Owen, J., Thompson, M. N., & Wang, K. T. (2016). *Research design in counseling* (4th ed.). Belmont, CA: Brooks Cole.

Herbenick, D., Fu, T. J., Arter, J., Sanders, S. A., & Dodge, B. (2018). Women's experiences with genital touching, sexual pleasure, and orgasm: Results from a U.S. probability sample of women ages 18 to 94. *Journal of Sex and Marital Therapy, 44*(2), 201–212.

Herbenick, D., Reece, M., Schick, V., Sanders, S. A., Dodge, B., & Fortenberry, J. D. (2010). Sexual behavior in the United States: Results from a national probability sample of men and women ages 14–94. *Journal of Sexual Medicine, 7*(5), 255–265.

Herbenick, D., Schick, V., Reece, M., Sanders, S. A., Smith, N., Dodge, B., & Fortenberry, J. D. (2013). Characteristics of condom and lubricant use among a nationally representative probability sample of adults ages 18–59 in the United States. *Journal of Sexual Medicine, 10*, 474–483.

Herbert, J. D. (2007). Avoidant personality disorder. In W. O'Donohue, K. A. Fowler, & S. O. Lilienfeld (Eds.). *Personality disorders: Toward the DSM-V*. Los Angeles: Sage Publications.

Herman, B. (2015, May 28). Fat-shaming and body-shaming, a history: Author talks thigh gaps, "Dad bods" and why we hate fat. *International Business Times*.

Hermes, E. A., Hoff, R., & Rosenheck, R. A. (2014). Sources of the increasing number of Vietnam era veterans with a diagnosis of PTSD using VHA services. *Psychiatric Services, 65*(6), 830–832.

Hermida, A. P., Glass, O. M., Shafi, H., & McDonald, W. M. (2018). Electroconvulsive therapy in depression: Current practice and future direction. *Psychiatric Clinics of North America, 41*(3), 341–353.

Hernandez, M., Marangoni, C., Grant, M. C., Estrada, J., & Faedda, G. L. (2017). Parental reports of prodromal psychopathology in pediatric bipolar disorder. *Current Neuropharmacology, 15*(3), 380–385.

Heron, M. (2016, June 30). Deaths: Leading causes for 2014. *National Vital Statistics Report, 65*(5).

Herper, M. (2018, April 19). Opioid prescriptions dropped in every state last year. *Forbes*. Retrieved from https://www.forbes.com/sites.

Hertz, M. F., & Donato, I. (2013). Bullying and suicide: A public health approach *Journal of Adolescent Health, 53,* S1–S3.

Hess, A. (2009 June 16). *Huffington Post:* Sometimes a cigar is just a nipple is just sexist. *Washington City Paper.*

Hess, A. (2016, January 26). How "-phobic" became a weapon in the identity wars. *New York Times.*

Heston, L. L. (1992). *Mending minds: A guide to the new psychiatry of depression, anxiety, and other serious mental disorders.* New York: W. H. Freeman.

Heylens, G., De Cuyper, G., Zucker, K. J., Schelfaut, C., Elaut, E., Vanden Bossche, H., De Baere, E., & T'Sjoen, G. (2012). Gender identity disorder in twins: A review of the case report literature. *Journal of Sexual Medicine, 9*(3), 751–757.

HHS (U.S. Department of Health and Human Services). (2009). *Mental health and African Americans.* Washington, DC: Office of Minority Health.

HHS (U.S. Department of Health and Human Services). (2017). *Mental health myths and facts.* Washington, DC: USDHHS.

Hicks, K. (2014). A biocultural perspective on fictive kinship in the Andes: Social support and women's immune function in El Alto, Bolivia. *Medical Anthropology Quarterly, 28*(3), 440–458.

Hill, C. E., Spiegel, S. B., Hoffman, M. A., Kivlighan, D. M., & Gelso, C. J. (2017, January 30). Therapist expertise in psychotherapy revisited. *The Counseling Psychologist, 45*(1), 99–112.

Hill, R. M., Del Busto, C. T., Buitron, V., & Pettit, J. W. (2018, February 2). Depressive symptoms and perceived burdensomeness mediate the association between anxiety and suicidal ideation in adolescents. *Archives of Suicide Research.* [Epub ahead of print]

Hille, R. B. (2017, January 6). *LexisNexis practice guide: New Jersey pleadings, 2017 edition.* LexisNexis.

Hillemeier, M. M., Foster, E. M., Heinrichs, B., & Heier, B. (2007). Racial differences in parental reports of attention-deficit/hyperactivity disorder behaviors. *Journal of Developmental and Behavioral Pediatrics, 28*(5), 353–361.

Hinrichsen, G. A. (1999). Interpersonal psychotherapy for late-life depression. In M. Duffy (Ed.), *Handbook of counseling and psychotherapy with older adults.* New York: Wiley.

Hiroeh, U., Appleby, L., Mortensen, P.-B., & Dunn, G. (2001). Death by homicide, suicide, and other unnatural causes in people with mental illness: A population-based study. *Lancet, 358*(9299), 2110–2112.

Hirsch, M., & Birnbaum, R. J. (2017, August 24). Sexual dysfunction caused by selective serotonin reuptake inhibitors (SSRIs): Management. *UpToDate.* Retrieved from http://www.uptodate.com.

Hirsch, M., & Birnbaum, R. J. (2017, July 10). Monoamine oxidase inhibitors (MAOIs) for treating depressed adults. *UpToDate.* Retrieved from http://www.uptodate.com.

Hirsch, M., & Birnbaum, R. J. (2017, November 16). Tricyclic and tetracyclic drugs: Pharmacology, administration, and side effects. *UpToDate.* Retrieved from http://www.uptodate.com.

Hirsch, M., & Birnbaum, R. J. (2018, January 31). Selective serotonin reuptake inhibitors: Pharmacology, administration, and side effects. *UpToDate.* Retrieved from http://www.uptodate.com.

Hisle-Gorman, E., Susi, A., Stokes, T., Gorman, G., Erdie-Lalena, C., & Nylund, C. M. (2018, April 18). Prenatal, perinatal, and neonatal risk factors of autism spectrum disorder. *Pediatric Research.* [Epub ahead of print]

Hithersay, R., Hamburg, S., Knight, B., & Strydom, A. (2017). Cognitive decline and dementia in Down syndrome. *Current Opinion in Psychiatry, 30*(2), 102–107.

HN (Hospital News). (2018). *Understanding delay in treatment for first episode psychosis.* Retrieved from https://hospitalnews.com/understanding-delay-in-treatment-for-first-episode-psychosis/#.

Ho, E. (2012, July 23). Almost everyone doesn't trust the Internet. *Time.*

Hodgetts, S., Gallagher, P., Stow, D., Ferrier, I. N., & O'Brien, J. T. (2017). The impact and measurement of social dysfunction in late-life depression: An evaluation of current methods with a focus on wearable technology. *International Journal of Geriatric Psychiatry, 32*(3), 247–255.

Hofer, H., Frigerio, S., Frischknecht, E., Gassmann, D., Gutbrod, K., & Müri, R. M. (2013). Diagnosis and treatment of an obsessive-compulsive disorder following traumatic brain injury: A single case and review of the literature. *Neurocase, 19*(4), 390–400.

Hoff, P. (2015). The Kraepelinian tradition. *Dialogues in Clinical Neuroscience, 17*(1), 31–41.

Hofmann, S. G. (2018, January 26). Psychotherapy for social anxiety disorder in adults. *UpToDate.* Retrieved from http://www.uptodate.com.

Hofmann, S. G., & Hinton, D. E. (2014). Cross-cultural aspects of anxiety disorders. *Current Psychiatry Reports, 16*(6), 450.

Hogarty, G. E., Goldberg, S. C., Schooler, N. R., & Ulrich, R. F. (1974). Drug and sociotherapy in the aftercare of schizophrenic patients: II. Two-year relapse rates. *Archives of General Psychiatry, 31*(5), 603–608.

Hogarty, G. E., Greenwald, D. P., & Eack, S. M. (2006). Durability and mechanism of effects of cognitive enhancement therapy. *Psychiatric Services, 57*(12), 1751–1757.

Hoge, E. A., Bui, E., Palitz, S. A., Schwarz, N. R., Owens, M. E., Johnston, J. M., . . . Simon, N. M. (2018). The effect of mindfulness meditation training on biological acute stress responses in generalized anxiety disorder. *Psychiatry Research.* [Article in press]

Hoge, E. A., Guidos, B. M., Mete, M., Bui, E., Pollack, M. H., Simon, N. M., & Dutton, M. A. (2017). Effects of mindfulness meditation on occupational functioning and health care utilization in individuals with anxiety. *Journal of Psychosomatic Research, 95,* 7–11.

Holinger, P. C., & Offer, D. (1982). Prediction of adolescent suicide: A population model. *American Journal of Psychiatry, 139,* 302–307.

Holinger, P. C., & Offer, D. (1991). Sociodemographic, epidemiologic, and individual attributes. In L. Davidson & M. Linnoila (Eds.), *Risk factors for youth suicide.* New York: Hemisphere.

Holinger, P. C., & Offer, D. (1993). *Adolescent suicide.* New York: Guilford Press.

Hollander, I. (2006). Viagra's rise above women's health issues: An analysis of the social and political influences on drug approvals in the United States and Japan. *Social Science & Medicine, 62*(3), 683–693.

Holliday, R. P., Holder, N. D., Williamson, M. L. C., & Suris, A. (2017). Therapeutic response to cognitive processing therapy in white and black female veterans with military sexual trauma-related PTSD. *Cognitive Behavior Therapy, 46,* 432–444.

Holmes, L. (2018, January 4). Suicide rates in the U.S. *Verywellmind.* Retrieved from https://www.verywellmind.com.

Holmes, T. H., & Rahe, R. H. (1967). The Social Readjustment Rating Scale. *Journal of Psychosomatic Research, 11,* 213–218.

Holmes, T. H., & Rahe, R. H. (1989). The Social Readjustment Rating Scale. In T. H. Holmes & E. M. David (Eds.), *Life change, life events, and illness: Selected papers.* New York: Praeger.

Holt, H., Beutler, L. E., Kimpara, S., Macias, S., Haug, N. A., Shiloff, N., . . . Stein, M. (2015). Evidence-based supervision: Tracking outcome and teaching principles of change in clinical supervision to bring science to integrative practice. *Psychotherapy (Chicago), 52*(2), 185–189.

Holtom-Viesel, A., & Allan, S. (2014). A systematic review of the literature on family functioning across all eating disorder diagnoses in comparison to control families. *Clinical Psychology Review, 34*(1), 29–43.

Holtzheimer, P. E. (2017, August 11). Unipolar depression in adults: Treatment with surgical approaches. *UpToDate.* Retrieved from http://www.uptodate.com.

Holtzheimer, P. E. (2017, January 24). Depression in adults: Overview of neuromodulation procedures. *UpToDate.* Retrieved from www.uptodate.com.

Holtzheimer, P. E. (2017, September 24). Unipolar depression in adults: Indications, efficacy, and safety of transcranial stimulation (TMS). *UpToDate.* Retrieved from http://www.uptodate.com.

Holtzheimer, P. E. (2018, February 20). Depression in adults: Overview of neuromodulation procedures. *UpToDate.* Retrieved from http://www.uptodate.com.

Holz, N. E., Zohsel, K., Laucht, M., Banaschewski, T., Hohmann, S., & Brandeis, D. (2018). Gene X environment interactions in conduct disorder: Implications for future treatments. *Neuroscience and Biobehavioral Reviews.* [Manuscript in press]

Holzer, K. J., & Vaughn, M. G. (2017). Antisocial personality disorder in older adults: A critical review. *Journal of Geriatric Psychiatry and Neurology, 30*(6), 291–302.

Hong, V. (2016). Borderline personality disorder in the emergency department. *Harvard Review of Psychiatry, 24*(5), 357.

Hopkins, D. (2014, June). Benjamin Rush (1746–1813). *Journal of Mississippi State Medical Association, 55*(7), 245.

Hopko, D. R., Robertson, S. M. C., Widman, L., & Lejuez, C. W. (2008). Specific phobias. In M. Hersen & J. Rosqvist (Eds.), *Handbook of psychological assessment, case*

conceptualization, and treatment, Vol. 1: Adults* (pp. 139–170). Hoboken, NJ: John Wiley & Sons.

Hopwood, C. J., & Waugh, M. (Eds.). (2018). *The DSM-5 alternative model of personality disorders: Integrating multiple paradigms of personality assessment.* (1st ed.). New York: Routledge.

Horney, K. (1937). *The neurotic personality of our time.* New York: Norton.

Hornor, G. (2017). Resilience. *Journal of Pediatric Health Care, 31*(3), 384–390.

Horowitz, J. A., Damato, E. G., Duffy, M. E., & Solon, L. (2005). The relationship of maternal attributes, resources, and perceptions of postpartum experiences to depression. *Research in Nursing and Health, 28*(2), 159–171.

Horowitz, J. A., Damato, E., Solon, L., Metzsch, G., & Gill, V. (1995). Postpartum depression: Issues in clinical assessment. *Journal of Perinatal Medicine, 15*(4), 268–278.

Horton, S. E., Hughes, J. L., King, J. D., Kennard, B. D., Westers, N. J., Mayers, T. L., & Stewart, S. M. (2016). Preliminary examination of the Interpersonal Psychological Theory of Suicide in an adolescent clinical sample. *Journal of Abnormal Child Psychology, 44*(6), 1133–1144.

Horwitz, A. G., Czyz, E. K., & King, C. A. (2014). Predicting future suicide attempts among adolescent and emerging adult psychiatric emergency patients. *Journal of Clinical Child and Adolescent Psychology, 53,* 1–11.

Hoshi, A., Tsunoda, A., Yamamoto, T., Tada, M., Kakita, A., & Ugawa, Y. (2018, February 6). Altered expression of glutamate transporter-1 and water channel protein aquaporin-4 in human temporal cortex with Alzheimer's disease. *Neuropathology and Applied Neurobiology.* [Epub ahead of print]

Hough, S., DenBoer, J. W., Crehan, E. T., Stone, M. T., & Hicks, T. (2017). Treating sexual problems in clients with cognitive and intellectual disabilities. In Z. D. Peterson (Ed.), *The Wiley-Blackwell handbook of sex therapy* (Chap. 21, pp. 345–358). Hoboken, NJ: Wiley-Blackwell.

Houghton, D. (2013, August 12). Cited in T. Miller, Too many selfies on Facebook can damage relationships: Study. *New York Daily News.*

Houston, G. (2016). *Counsel Heal: Mental Health: 5 negative effects of social media on your mental health.* Retrieved from http://www.counselheal.com/articles/24341/20160518.

Howard, M., Muris, P., Loxton, H., & Wege, A. (2016). Anxiety-proneness, anxiety symptoms, and the role of parental overprotection in young South African children. *Journal of Child and Family Studies, 26*(1), 262–270.

Howard, S., Myers, L. B., & Hughes, B. M. (2017, January 20). Repressive coping and cardiovascular reactivity to novel and recurrent stress. *Anxiety, Stress & Coping,* 1–13. [Epub ahead of print]

Howell, E. F. (2011). *Understanding and treating dissociative identity disorder: A rational approach.* New York: Routledge/Taylor & Francis Group.

Howland, R. H. (2014). Vagus nerve stimulation. *Current Behavioral Neuroscience Reports, 1*(2), 64–73.

Howland, R. H. (2012). Dietary supplement drug therapies for depression. *Journal of Psychosocial Nursing and Mental Health Services, 50*(6), 13–16.

Hoyer, M., & Heath, B. (2012, December 19). A mass killing in U.S. occurs every 2 weeks. *USA Today.*

HRW (Human Rights Watch). (2018, February 5). "They want docile": How nursing homes in the United States overmedicate people with dementia. Retrieved from https://www.hrw.org/report.

Hshieh, T. T., Inouye, S. K., & Oh, E. S. (2018). Delirium in the elderly. *Psychiatric Clinics of North America, 41*(1), 1–17.

Hsiao, Y. H., Chang, C. H., & Gean, P. W. (2018). Impact of social relationships on Alzheimer's memory impairment: Mechanistic studies. *Journal of Biomedical Science, 25*(1), 3.

Hsieh, N. (2017). A global perspective on religious participation and suicide. *Journal of Health and Social Behavior, 58*(3), 322–339.

HSPH (Harvard School of Public Health). (2016, July). *The workplace and health.* Boston, MA: Harvard.

Hu, X., Kim, A., Siwek, N., & Wilder, D. (2017). The Facebook paradox: Effects of facebooking on individuals' social relationships and psychological well-being. *Frontiers in Psychology, 8,* 87.

Hua, A., & Major, N. (2016). Selective mutism. *Current Opinion in Pediatrics, 28,* 114–120.

Huang, J-J., Yang, Y-P., & Wu, J. (2010). Relationships of borderline personality disorder and childhood trauma. *Chinese Journal of Clinical Psychology, 18*(6), 769–771.

Hucker, S. J. (2008). Sexual masochism: Psychopathology and theory. In D. R. Laws & W. T. O'Donohue (Eds.), *Sexual deviance: Theory, assessment, and treatment* (2nd ed., pp. 250–263). New York: Guilford Press.

Hugdahl, K., & Sommer, I. E. (2018). Auditory verbal hallucinations in schizophrenia from a levels of explanation perspective. *Schizophrenia Bulletin, 44*(2), 234–241.

Hughes, S. (2011). Untangling Alzheimer's. *The Pennsylvania Gazette, 109*(4), 30–41.

Huguet, A., Rao, S., McGrath, P. J., Wozney, L., Wheaton, M., Conrod, J., & Rozario, S. (2016, May 2). A systematic review of cognitive behavioral therapy and behavioral activation apps for depression. *PLoS ONE, 11*(5), e0154248.

Huh, J., Le, T., Reeder, B., Thompson, H. J., & Demiris, G. (2013). Perspectives on wellness self-monitoring tools for older adults. *International Journal of Medical Informatics, 82*(11), 1092–1103.

Hui, C., & Zhihui, Y. (2017). Group cognitive behavioral therapy targeting intolerance of uncertainty: A randomized trial for older Chinese adults with generalized anxiety disorder. *Aging & Mental Health, 21*(12), 1294–1302.

Hulett, J. M., Armer, J. M., Stewart, B. R., & Wanchai, A. (2015). Perspectives of the breast cancer survivorship continuum: Diagnosis through 30 months post-treatment. *Journal of Personalized Medicine, 5*(2), 174–190.

Humphrey, J. A. (2006). *Deviant behavior.* Upper Saddle River, NJ: Pearson/Prentice Hall.

Huo, Y., Chu, Y., Guo, L. Liu, L., Xia, X., & Wang, T. (2017). Cortisol is associated with low frequency of interleukin 10-producing B cells in patients with atherosclerosis. *Cell Biochemistry and Function, 35*(3), 178–183.

Huprich, S. K., Nelson, S. M., Paggeot, A., Lengu, K., & Albright, J. (2017). Object relations predicts borderline personality disorder symptoms beyond emotional dysregulation, negative affect, and impulsivity. *Personality Disorders, 8*(1), 46–53.

Hurlbert, D. F. (1993) A comparative study using orgasm consistency training in the treatment of women reporting hypoactive sexual desire. *Journal of Sex & Marital Therapy, 19,* 41–55.

Hussain, A., Nygaard, E., Sigveland, J., & Heir, T. (2016). The relationship between psychiatric morbidity and quality of life: Interview study of Norwegian tsunami survivors 2 and 6 years post-disaster. *BMC Psychiatry, 16,* 173.

Hyde, J. S. (1990). *Understanding human sexuality* (4th ed.). New York: McGraw-Hill.

Hyde, J. S. (2005). The genetics of sexual orientation. In J. S. Hyde (Ed.), *Biological substrates of human sexuality.* Washington, DC: American Psychological Association.

Hyland, P., Murphy, J., Shevlin, M., Vallières, F., McElroy, E., Elkit, A., . . . Cloitre, M. (2017). Variation in post-traumatic response: The role of trauma type in predicting ICD-11 PTSD and CPTSD symptoms. *Social Psychiatry and Psychiatric Epidemiology, 52,* 727–736.

Hymel, S., & Swearer, S. M. (2015). Four decades of research on school bullying: An introduction. *American Psychologist, 70,* 293–299.

Iadarola, S., Hetherington, S., Clinton, C., Dean, M., Reisinger, E., Huynh, L., & Kasari, C. (2015). Services for children with autism spectrum disorder in three, large urban school districts: Perspectives of parents and educators. *Autism; The International Journal of Research and Practice, 19*(6), 694–703.

Ibrahim, H., & Hassan, C. Q. (2017). Posttraumatic stress disorder symptoms resulting from torture and other traumatic events among Syrian Kurdish refugees in Kurdistan region, Iraq. *Frontiers in Psychology, 8,* 241.

Iglehart, J. K. (2016). Future of long-term care and the expanding role of Medicaid managed care. *New England Journal of Medicine, 374*(2), 182–187.

Igoumenou, A., Harmer, C. J., Yang, M., Coid, J. W., & Rogers, R. D. (2017). Faces and facets: The variability of emotion recognition in psychopathy reflects its affective and antisocial features. *Journal of Abnormal Psychology, 126*(8), 1066–1076.

Igwe, M. N. (2013). Dissociative fugue symptoms in a 28-year-old male Nigerian medical student: A case report. *Journal of Medical Case Reports, 7,* 143.

Ihle, W., Jahnke, D., Heerwagen, A., & Neuperdt, C. (2005). Depression, anxiety, and eating disorders and recalled parental rearing behavior. *Kindheit Entwicklung, 14*(1), 30–38.

Iimori, T., Nakajima, S., Miyazaki, T., Tarumi, R., Ogyu, K., Wada, M., . . . Noda, Y. (2019). Effectiveness of the prefrontal repetitive transcranial magnetic stimulation on cognitive profiles in depression, schizophrenia, and Alzheimer's disease: A systematic review. *Progress in Neuro-Psychopharmacology & Biological Psychiatry, 88,* 31–40.

Imm, K. R., Williams, F., Housten, A. J., Colditz, G. A., Drake, B. F., Gilbert, K. L., & Yang, L. (2017). African American prostate

cancer survivorship: Exploring the role of social support in quality of life after radical prostatectomy. *Journal of Psychosocial Oncology, 35*(4), 409–423.

Infogalactic. (2016, January 11). *List of natural disasters by death toll.* Retrieved from http://infogalactic.com/info/List_of_natural_disasters_by_death_toll.

Ingersoll, K. (2017, March 2). Motivational interviewing for substance use disorders. *UpToDate.* Retrieved from http://www.uptodate.com.

Innocence Project. (2017). *Eyewitness misidentification.* New York: Author.

Insel, T. (2017). Interview. In A. Rogers, Star neuroscientist Tom Insel leaves the Google-spawned Verily for . . . a startup? *Wired.* Retrieved from https://www.wired.com.

Irwin, M. R., & Bursch, B. (2018, January 25). Factitious disorder imposed on self (Munchausen syndrome). *UpToDate.* Retrieved from http://www.uptodate.com.

Isacsson, G., & Rich, C. L. (2014). Antidepressant drugs and the risk of suicide in children and adolescents. *Pediatric Drugs, 16*(2), 115–122.

Islam, M. M., Conigrave, K. M., Day, C. A., Nguyen, Y., & Haber, P. S. (2014). Twenty-year trends in benzodiazepine dispensing in the Australian population. *Internal Medicine Journal, 44*(1), 57–64.

Isomaa, R., and Isomaa, A-L. (2014). And then what happened? A 5-year follow-up of eating disorder patients. *Nordic Journal of Psychiatry,* 68(8), 567–572.

Ivleva, E. I., Clementz, B. A., Dutcher, A. M., Arnold, S. J. M., Jeon-Slaughter, H., Aslan, S., . . . Tamminga, C. A. (2017). Brain structure biomarkers in the psychosis biotypes: Findings from the bipolar-schizophrenia network for intermediate phenotypes. *Biological Psychiatry, 82*(1), 26–39.

Ivy, J. W., Meindl, J. N., Overley, E., & Robson, K. M. (2017). Token economy: A systematic review of procedural descriptions. *Behavior Modification, 41,* 708–737.

IWS (Internet World Stats). (2011). Top 20 countries with the highest number of Internet users. Retrieved from http://www.internetworldstats.com/top20.htm.

Jablensky, A. (2000). Epidemiology of schizophrenia: The global burden of disease and disability. *European Archives of Psychiatry and Clinical Neuroscience, 250,* 274–285.

Jabr, F. (2017, January 1). Why exercise may be the best fix for depression. *Scientific American.*

Jacob, M., Larson, M., & Storch, E. (2014). Insight in adults with obsessive-compulsive disorder. *Comprehensive Psychiatry, 55*(4), 896–903.

Jacobs, D. (2011). *Analyzing criminal minds: Forensic investigative science for the 21st century. Brain, behavior, and evolution.* Santa Barbara, CA: Praeger/ABC-CLIO.

Jacobs, J. R., & Bovasso, G. B. (2009). Re-examining the long-term effects of experiencing parental death in childhood on adult psychopathology. *Journal of Nervous and Mental Disease, 197*(1), 24–27.

Jacobsen, K. H. (2016). *Introduction to health research methods* (2nd ed.). Burlington, MA: Jones & Bartlett Learning.

Jacobson, G. (1999). The inpatient management of suicidality. In D. G. Jacobs (Ed.), *The Harvard Medical School guide to suicide assessment and intervention.* San Francisco: Jossey-Bass.

Jacobson, R. (2018). Eating disorders and college. *Child Mind Institute.* Retrieved from http://childmind.org/article/eating-disorders-and-college/.

Jacoby, N., Overfeld, J., Binder, E. B., & Heimb, C. M. (2016). Stress neurobiology and developmental psychopathology. In D. Cicchetti (Ed.), *Developmental psychopathology: Vol. 2, Developmental neuroscience* (3rd ed., Chap. 21, pp. 787–831). New York: Wiley.

Jacques, N., de Mola, C. L., Joseph, G., Mesenburg, M. A., & de Silveira, M. F. (2019). Prenatal and postnatal maternal depression and infant hospitalization and mortality in the first year of life: A systematic review and meta-analysis. *Journal of Affective Disorders, 243,* 201–208.

Jafferany, M., Khalid, Z., McDonald, K. A., & Shelley, A. J. (2018). Psychological aspects of factitious disorder. *Primary Care Companion for CNS Disorders, 20*(1).

Jäger, P. (2018, May 15). Stress and health of internally displaced female Yezidis in Northern Iraq. *Journal of Immigrant and Minority Health.* [Epub ahead of print]

Jagsch, C., Dietmaier, G., Jagsch, M., & Roller, R. E. (2018). [Schizophrenia spectrum disorders in elderly patients: Analysis of reasons for admission to a department of geriatric psychiatry]. *Zeitschrift für Gerontologie und Geriatrie, 51*(2), 206–212. [German]

Jain, A., Christopher, P., & Appelbaum, P. S. (2018). Civil commitment for opioid and other substance use disorders: Does it work? *Psychiatric Services, 69*(4), 374–376.

Jain, S. (2017, April 4). How to use exercise to manage depression. *WebMD.*

Jakob, J. M., Lamp, K., Rauch, S. A., Smith, E. R., & Buchholz, K. R. (2017). The impact of trauma type or number of traumatic events on PTSD diagnosis and symptom severity in treatment seeking veterans. *Journal of Nervous and Mental Disease, 205*(2), 83–86.

Jakobsen, K. D., Skyum, E., Hashemi, N., Schjerning, O., Fink-Jensen, A., & Nielsen, J. (2017). Antipsychotic treatment of schizotypy and schizotypal personality disorder: A systematic review. *Journal of Psychopharmacology, 31*(4), 397–405.

James, G. M., Baldinger-Melich, P., Philippe, C., Kranz, G. S., Vanicek, T., Hahn, A., . . . Lanzenberger, R. (2017, February 6). Effects of selective serotonin reuptake inhibitors on interregional relation of serotonin transporter availability in major depression. *Frontiers in Human Neuroscience, 11,* 48.

James, S., Reddy, S. P., Ellahebokus, A., Sewpaul, R., & Naidoo, P. (2017). The association between adolescent risk behaviours and feelings of sadness or hopelessness: A cross-sectional survey of South African secondary school learners. *Psychology, Health & Medicine, 22*(7), 778–789.

James, W. (1890). *Principles of psychology* (Vol. 1). New York: Holt, Rinehart & Winston.

Jamison, K. R. (1995). *An unquiet mind.* New York: Vintage Books.

Jamison, K. R. (1995, February). Manic-depressive illness and creativity. *Scientific American,* pp. 63–67.

Janicak, P. G. (2017, August 31). Bipolar disorder in adults and lithium: Pharmacology, administration, and side effects. *UpToDate.* Retrieved from http://www.uptodate.com.

Janssens, S., Moens, H., Coppens, V., Vandendriessche, F., Hulstijn, W., Sabbe, B., & Morrens, M. (2018). Psychomotor assessment as a tool to differentiate schizophrenia from other psychotic disorders. *Schizophrenia Research, 200,* 92–96.

Jansson, L. M. (2017, August 8). Infants of mothers with substance use disorder. *UpToDate.* Retrieved from http://www.uptodate.com.

Janus, S. S., & Janus, C. L. (1993). *The Janus report on sexual behavior.* New York: Wiley.

Jaremka, L. M., Fagundes, C. P., Peng, J., Bennett, J. M., Glaser, R., Malarkey, W. B., & Kiecolt-Glaser, J. K. (2013). Loneliness promotes inflammation during acute stress. *Psychological Science, 24*(7), 1089–1097.

Jarlenski, M., Barry, C. L., Gollust, S., Graves, A. J., Kennedy-Hendricks, A., & Kozhimannil, K. (2017). Polysubstance use among U.S. women of reproductive age who use opioid for nonmedical reasons. *American Journal of Public Health, 107,* 1308–1310.

Jarrett, R. B., & Vittengl, J. (2016, October 21). Unipolar depression in adults: Continuation and maintenance treatment. *UpToDate.* Retrieved from www.uptodate.com.

Javier, S. J., Moore, M. P., & Belgrave, F. Z. (2016). Racial comparisons in perceptions of maternal and peer attitudes, body dissatisfaction, and eating disorders among African American and White women. *Women's Health, 56*(6), 615–633.

Jennings, J. R., Pardini, D. A., & Matthews, K. A. (2017). Heart rate, health, and hurtful behavior. *Psychophysiology, 54*(3), 399–408.

Jensen, L., & Padilla, R. (2017). Effectiveness of environment-based interventions that address behavior, perception, and falls in people with Alzheimer's disease and related major neurocognitive disorders: A systematic review. *American Journal of Occupational Therapy, 71*(5), 7105180030p1-7105180030p10.

Jernigan, T. L., & Stiles, J. (2017, January). Construction of the human forebrain. *Wiley Interdisciplinary Reviews: Cognitive Science, 8*(1-2).

Ji, X., Druss, B. G., Lally, C., & Cummings, J. R. (2018). Racial-ethnic differences in patterns of discontinuous medication treatment among Medicaid-insured youths with ADHD. *Psychiatry Services, 69*(3), 322–331.

Jiann, B-P., Su, C-C., & Tsai, J-Y. (2013). Is female sexual function related to the male partners' erectile function? *Journal of Sexual Medicine, 10,* 420–429.

Jibson, M. D. (2017, March 6). First-generation antipsychotic medications: Pharmacology, administration, and comprehensive side effects. *UpToDate.* Retrieved from http://www.uptodate.com.

Jibson, M. D. (2017, May 15). Second-generation antipsychotic medications: Pharmacology, administration, and side effects. *UpToDate.* Retrieved from http://www.uptodate.com.

Jibson, M. D. (2018, March 23). First-generation antipsychotic medications: Pharmacology, administration, and comparative side effects. *UpToDate.* Retrieved from http://www.uptodate.com.

John, A. P., Yeak, K., Ayres, H., Dragovic, M. (2017). Successful implementation of a cognitive remediation program in everyday clinical practice for individuals living with schizophrenia. *Psychiatric Rehabilitation Journal, 40*(1), 87–93.

Johns, M. M., Beltran, O., Armstrong, H. L., Jayne, P. E., & Barrios, L. C. (2018, April 26). Protective factors among transgender and gender variant youth: A systematic review by socioecological level. *Journal of Primary Prevention*. [Epub ahead of print]

Johnson, B. A. (2017, October 17). Pharmacotherapy for alcohol use disorder. *UpToDate*. Retrieved from http://www.uptodate.com.

Johnson, J. (2018, January 10). Overcoming sexual performance anxiety. *Medical News Today*. Retrieved from https://www.medicalnewstoday/com/articles.

Johnson, L. A. (2005, July 21). Lobotomy back in spotlight after 30 years. *Netscape News*.

Johnson, S. (2017). An emotionally focused approach to sex therapy. In Z. D. Peterson (Ed.), *The Wiley-Blackwell handbook of sex therapy* (Chap. 16, pp. 250–266). Hoboken, NJ: Wiley-Blackwell.

Johnson, T. D. (2011, December). Online-only: Report: Teens who often eat dinner with family less likely to drink, smoke, or use drugs. *The Nation's Health, 41*(9), E46.

Johnston, J. E. (2017, January 19). Serial killers in 2016. *Psychology Today*.

Johnston, L. D., O'Malley, P. M., Miech, R. A., Bachman, J. G., & Schulenberg, J. E. (2017). *Monitoring the Future national survey results on drug use, 1975–2016: Overview, key findings on adolescent drug use*. Ann Arbor: Institute for Social Research, The University of Michigan.

Joiner, T. E. (2005). *Why people die by suicide*. Cambridge, MA: Harvard University Press.

Joiner, T. E. (2009). The interpersonal-psychological theory of suicidal behavior: Current empirical status. *American Psychological Association*. Retrieved from http://www.apa.org/science/about/psa/2009/06/sci-brief.aspx.

Joiner, T. E., Buchman-Schmitt, J. M., Chu, C., & Horn, M. A. (2017). A sociobiological extension of the interpersonal theory of suicide. *Crisis, 38*(2), 69–72.

Jonason, P. K., Foster, J. D., Egorova, M. S., Parshikova, O., Csathó, Á., Oshio, A., & Gouveia, V. V. (2017). The Dark Triad traits from a life history perspective in six countries. *Frontiers in Psychology, 8*, 1476.

Jonason, P. K., Girgis, M., & Milne-Home, J. (2017). The exploitive mating strategy of the Dark Triad traits: Tests of rape-enabling attitudes. *Archives of Sexual Behavior, 46*(3), 697–706.

Jonason, P. K., Li, N. P., & Buss, D. M. (2010). The costs and benefits of the Dark Triad: Implications for mate poaching and mate retention tactics. *Personality and Individual Differences, 48*(4), 373–378.

Jonason, P. K., Li, N. P., Webster, G. D., & Schmitt, D. P. (2009). The Dark Triad: Facilitating a short-term mating strategy in men. *European Journal of Personality, 23*, 5–18.

Jonason, P. K., Valentine, K. A., Li, N. P., & Harbeson, C. L. (2011). Mate-selection and the Dark Triad: Facilitating a short-term mating strategy and creating a volatile environment. *Personality and Individual Differences, 51*, 759–763.

Jones, C. R. G., Simonoff, E., Baird, G., Pickles, A., Marsden, A. J. S., Tregay, J., . . . Charman, T. (2018). The association between theory of mind, executive function, and the symptoms of autism spectrum disorder. *Autism Research, 11*(1), 95–109.

Jones, D. N., & Paulhus, D. L. (2017). Duplicity among the Dark Triad: Three faces of deceit. *Journal of Personality and Social Psychology, 113*(2), 329–342.

Jones, D. W. (2017). Moral insanity and psychological disorder: The hybrid roots of psychiatry. *History of Psychiatry, 28*, 263–279.

Jones, I., Chandra, P. S., Dazzan, P., & Howard, L. M. (2014). Bipolar disorder, affective psychosis, and schizophrenia in pregnancy and the post-partum period. *Lancet, 384*(9956), 1789.

Jones, M. C. (1968). Personality correlates and antecedents of drinking patterns in males. *Journal of Consulting and Clinical Psychology, 32*, 2–12.

Jones, M. C. (1971). Personality antecedents and correlates of drinking patterns in women. *Journal of Consulting and Clinical Psychology, 36*, 61–69.

Joseph, B. (2018). Primary caregivers perceived stress, social support and expressed emotion while caring for persons with first episode psychosis. *Asian Journal of Psychiatry, 31*, 1.

Joshi, K., Mao, L., Biondi, D. M., & Millet, R. (2018). The Research and Evaluation of Antipsychotic Treatment in Community Behavioral Health Organizations, Outcomes (REACH-OUT) study: Real-world clinical practice in schizophrenia. *BMC Psychiatry, 18*(1), 24.

Joshi, S. V., Hartley, S. N., Kessler, M., & Barstead, M. (2015). School-based suicide prevention: Content, process, and the role of trusted adults and peers. *Child and Adolescent Psychiatric Clinics of North America, 24*(2), 353–370.

Joshi, S., Mooney, S. J., Rundle, A. G., Quinn, J. W., Beard, J. R., & Cerdá, M. (2016). Pathways from neighborhood poverty to depression among older adults. *Health & Place, 43*, 138–143.

Jovanovic, T., Nylocks, K. M., Gamwell, K. L., Smith, A., Davis, T. A., Norrholm, S. D., & Bradley, B. (2014). Development of fear acquisition and extinction in children: Effects of age and anxiety. *Neurobiology of Learning and Memory, 113*, 135–142.

Joyal, C. C. (2015). Defining "normophilic" and "paraphilic" sexual fantasies in a population-based sample: On the importance of considering subgroups. *Sexual Medicine, 3*(4), 321–330.

Joyal, C. C. (2017). Linking crime to paraphilia: Be careful with label. *Archives of Sexual Behavior, 46*(4), 865–866.

Juckel, G. (2014). Serotonin: From sensory processing to schizophrenia using an electrophysiological method. *Behavioural Brain Research*. [Advance electronic publication]

Judd, S., & Parker, G. F. (2018). Court-ordered evaluations from a mental health court. *Journal of the American Academy of Psychiatry and the Law, 46*(1), 52–62.

Juvonen, J., & Ho, A. Y. (2008). Social motives underlying antisocial behavior across middle school grades. *Journal of Youth and Adolescence, 37*, 747.

Kaess, M. (2018). Bullying: Peer-to-peer maltreatment with severe consequences for child and adolescent mental health. *European Child & Adolescent Psychiatry*. [Epub ahead of print]

Kagan, J. (2007). The limitations of concepts in developmental psychology. In G. W. Ladd (Ed.), *Appraising the human developmental sciences: Essays in honor of Merrill-Palmer Quarterly* (pp. 30–37). Detroit, MI: Wayne State University Press.

Kahn, A. P., & Fawcett, J. (1993). *The encyclopedia of mental health*. New York: Facts on File.

Kamenov, K., Twomey, C., Cabello, M., Prina, A. M., & Ayuso-Mateos, J. L. (2017). The efficacy of psychotherapy, pharmacotherapy and their combination on functioning and quality of life in depression: A meta-analysis. *Psychological Medicine, 47*(3), 414–425.

Kaminski, J. W., & Claussen, A. H. (2017). Evidence-base update for psychosocial treatments for disruptive behaviors in children. *Journal of Clinical Child and Adolescent Psychology, 46*, 477–499.

Kampman, K. (2018, March 23). Pharmacotherapy for stimulant use disorders in adults. *UpToDate*. Retrieved from http://www.uptodate.com.

Kampman, K. (2018, March 23). Psychosocial interventions for stimulant use disorder in adults. *UpToDate*. Retrieved from http://www.uptodate.com.

Kampmann, I. L., Emmelkamp, P. M., Hartanto, D., Brinkman, W. P., Zijlstra, B. J., & Morina, N. (2016). Exposure to virtual social interactions in the treatment of social anxiety disorder: A randomized controlled trial. *Behaviour Research and Therapy, 77*, 147–156.

Kane, J. M., Robinson, D. G., Schooler, N. R., Mueser, K. T., Penn, D. L., Rosenheck, R. A., . . . Heinssen, R. K. (2016). Comprehensive versus usual community care for first-episode psychosis: 2-year outcomes from the NIMH RAISE Early Treatment Program. *American Journal of Psychiatry, 173*(4), 362.

Kanehisa, M., Kawashima, C., Nakanishi, M., Okamoto, K., Oshita, H., Masuda, K., . . . Akiyoshi, J. (2017). Gender differences in automatic thoughts and cortisol and alpha-amylase responses to acute psychosocial stress in patients with obsessive-compulsive personality disorder. *Journal of Affective Disorders, 217*, 1–7.

Kaneya, R. (2017, December 5). Why the number of criminal defendants sent to the state hospital is soaring. *Honolulu Civil Beat*.

Kang, H. S., Myung, W., Na, D. L., Kim, S. Y., Lee, J., Han, S., . . . Kim, D. K. (2014). Factors associated with caregiver burden in patients with Alzheimer's disease. *Psychiatry Investigation, 11*(2), 152–159.

Kangelaris, K. N., Vittinghoff, E., Otte, C., Na, B., Auerbach, A. D., & Whooley, M. A. (2010). Association between a serotonin transporter gene variant and hopelessness among men in the Heart and Soul Study. *Journal of General Internal Medicine, 25*(10), 1030–1037.

Kanner, B. (1995). *Are you normal? Do you behave like everyone else?* New York: St. Martin's Press.

Kanner, B. (1998, February). Are you normal? Turning the other cheek. *American Demographics.*

Kanner, B. (2005). *Are you normal about sex, love, and relationships?* New York: St. Martin's Press.

Kanner, L. (1943). Autistic disturbances of affective contact. *Nervous Child, 2,* 217.

Kanner, L. (1954). To what extent is early infantile autism determined by constitutional inadequacies? In *Genetics and the inheritance of integrated neurological and psychiatric patterns.* Baltimore: Williams and Wilkins.

Kantor, E. D., Rehm, C. D., Haas, J. S., Chan, A. T., & Giovannucci, E. L. (2015). Trends in prescription drug use among adults in the United States from 1999–2012. *Journal of the American Medical Association, 314*(17), 1818–1831.

Kantor, M. (2010). *The essential guide to overcoming avoidant personality disorder.* Santa Barbara, CA: Praeger/ABC-CLIO.

Kantrowitz, B., & Springen, K. (2004, August 9). What dreams are made of. *Newsweek, 144*(6), 40–47.

Kapardis, A. (2017). Offender-profiling today: An overview. In C. D. Spinellis, N. Theodorakis, E. Billis, & G. Papadimitrakopoulos (Eds.), *Europe in crisis: Crime, criminal justice, and the way forward* (pp. 739–754). Greece: Ant. N. Sakkoulas Publishers. Retrieved from http://www.crime-in-crisis.com.

Kapfhammer, H. P. (2017). Factitious disorders. *Nervenarzt, 88*(5), 549–570. [German]

Kapitanyan, R., & Su, M. (2018, January 3). Second generation (atypical) antipsychotic medication poisoning. *UpToDate.* Retrieved from http://www.uptodate.com.

Kaplan, H. S. (1974). *The new sex therapy: Active treatment of sexual dysfunction.* New York: Brunner/Mazel.

Kaplan, M. (2016). Clinical considerations regarding regression in psychotherapy with patients with conversion disorder. *Psychodynamic Psychiatry, 44*(3), 367–384.

Katz, J. (2017, June 5). Drug deaths in America are rising faster than ever. *New York Times,* Section: The Upshot.

Kaufman, S. B. (2013, October 3). The real link between creativity and mental illness. *Scientific American.*

Kaya, C., Tansey, T. N., Melekoglu, M., Cakiroglu, O., & Chan, F. (2017, December 20). Psychometric evaluation of Turkish version of the Perceived Stress Scale with Turkish college students. *Journal of Mental Health.* [Epub ahead of print]

Kayhan, F., Küçük, A., Satan, Y., Ilgün, E., Arslan, S., & Ilik, F. (2016). Sexual dysfunction, mood, anxiety, and personality disorders in female patients with fibromyalgia. *Neuropsychiatric Disease and Treatment, 12,* 349–355.

Kazano, H. (2012). Asylum: The huge psychiatric hospital in the 19th century U.S. *Seishin Shinkeigaku Zasshi = Psychiatria Et Neurologia Japonica, 114*(10), 1194–1200.

Kazdin, A. E. (2015). Clinical dysfunction and psychosocial interventions: The interplay of research, methods, and conceptualization of challenges. *Annual Review of Clinical Psychology, 11,* 25–52.

Kazdin, A. E. (2017). *Research design in clinical psychology* (4th ed.). New York: Pearson.

Kazdin, A. E. (2002). Psychosocial treatments for conduct disorder in children and adolescents. In P. E. Nathan & J. M. Gorman (Eds.), *A guide to treatments that work* (2nd ed., pp. 57–85). London: Oxford University Press.

Kazdin, A. E. (2005). *Parent management training: Treatment for oppositional, aggressive, and antisocial behavior in children and adolescents.* New York: Oxford University Press.

Kazdin, A. E. (2010). Problem-solving skills training and parent management training for oppositional defiant disorder and conduct disorder. In J. R. Weisz, & A. E. Kazdin (Eds.), *Evidence-based psychotherapies for children and adolescents* (2nd ed., pp. 211–226) New York: Guilford Press.

Kazdin, A. E. (2012). *Behavior modification in applied settings* (7th ed.). Long Grove, IL: Waveland Press.

Kearney, C. A. (2013). *Casebook in child behavior disorders* (5th ed.). Independence, KY: Cengage Publications.

Keatley, D. A., Golightly, H., Shephard, R., Yaksic, E., & Reid, S. (2018, March 1). Using behavior sequence analysis to map serial killers' life histories. *Journal of Interpersonal Violence.* [Epub ahead of print]

Kedmey, D. (2013, June 5). Avatar therapy may silence schizophrenia sufferers' demons. *Time.*

Keefer, A. (2015, January 28). Elderly living with family. *Livestrong.com.* Retrieved from Live Strong website: http://www.livestrong.com/article/95828.

Keel, P. K. (2018). Eating disorders. In J. N. Butcher (Ed.-in-chief), *APA handbook of psychopathology* (Vol. 1, Ch. 21). Washington, DC: APA.

Keen, E. (1970). *Three faces of being: Toward an existential clinical psychology.* New York: Appleton-Century-Crofts.

Keene, C. D., Montine, T. J., & Kuller, L. H. (2018, January 19). Epidemiology, pathology, and pathogenesis of Alzheimer disease. *UpToDate.* Retrieved from http://www.uptodate.com.

Keeshin, B. R., Strawn, J. R., Luebbe, A. M., Saddaña, S. N., Wehry, A. M., DelBello, M. P., & Putnam, F. W. (2014). Hospitalized youth and child abuse: A systematic examination of psychiatric morbidity and clinical severity. *Child Abuse and Neglect, 38*(1), 76–83.

Keitner, G. (2017, March 30). Family and couples therapy for treating depressed adults. *UpToDate.* Retrieved from https://uptodate.com.

Kellett, S., & Hardy, G. (2014). Treatment of paranoid personality disorder with cognitive analytic therapy: A mixed methods single case experimental design. *Clinical Psychology and Psychotherapy, 21*(5), 452–464.

Kellner, C. (2018, January 11). Unipolar major depression in adults: Indications for and efficacy of electroconvulsive therapy (ECT). *UpToDate.* Retrieved from http://www.uptodate.com.

Kelly, J. F. (2017). Is Alcoholics Anonymous religious, spiritual, neither? Findings from 25 years of mechanisms of behavior change research. *Addiction, 112*(6), 929–936.

Kelly, K. M., & Mezuk, B. (2017). Predictors of remission from generalized anxiety disorder and major depressive disorder. *Journal of Affective Disorders, 208,* 467–474.

Kemper, A. R., Maslow, G. R., Hill, S., Namdari, B., Allen LaPointe, N. M., Goode, A. P., . . . Sanders, G. D. (2018, January). Attention deficit hyperactivity disorder: Diagnosis and treatment in children and adolescents [Internet]. Rockville, MD: Agency for Healthcare Research and Quality. Report No. 18-EHC005-EF. *AHRQ Comparative Effectiveness Reviews.*

Kendall, P. C., Swan, A. J., Carper, M. M., & Hoff, A. L. (2018). Anxiety disorders among children and adolescents. In J. N. Butcher & J. M. Hooley (Eds.), *APA handbook of psychopathology. Vol. 2. Psychopathology in children and adolescents* (Ch. 11). Washington, DC: American Psychological Association.

Kendall, J., & Hatton, D. (2002). Racism as a source of health disparity in families with children with attention deficit hyperactivity disorder. *Advances in Nursing Science, 25*(2), 22–39.

Kendall-Tackett, K. A. (2010). *Depression in new mothers: Causes, consequences, and treatment alternatives* (2nd ed.). New York: Routledge/Taylor & Francis Group.

Kendig, S., Keats, J. P., Hoffman, M. C., Kay, L. B., Miller, E. S., Simas, T. A., . . . Lemieux, L. A. (2017). Consensus bundle on maternal mental health: Perinatal depression and anxiety. *Journal of Midwifery & Women's Health, 129,* 422–430.

Kendler, K. S., & Engstrom, E. J. (2018). Criticisms of Kraepelin's psychiatric nosology: 1896–1927. *American Journal of Psychiatry, 175*(4), 316–326.

Kendler, K. S., Heath, A., & Martin, N. G. (1987). A genetic epidemiologic study of self-report suspiciousness. *Comprehensive Psychiatry, 28*(3), 187–196.

Kendler, K. S., Neale, M. C., Kessler, R. C., Heath, A. C., & Eaves, L. J. (1993). Panic disorder in women: A population-based twin study. *Psychological Medicine, 23,* 397–406.

Kendler, K. S., Ochs, A. L., Gorman, A. M., Hewitt, J. K., Ross, D. E., & Mirsky, A. F. (1991). The structure of schizotypy: A pilot multitrait twin study. *Psychiatry Research, 36*(1), 19–36.

Kendler, K. S., Ohlsson, H., Keefe, R. S. E., Sundquist, K., & Sundquist, J. (2018). The joint impact of cognitive performance in adolescence and familial cognitive aptitude on risk for major psychiatric disorders: A delineation of four potential pathways to illness. *Molecular Psychiatry.* [Manuscript in press]

Kendler, K. S., Walters, E. E., Neale, M. C., Kessler, R. C., Heath, A. C., & Eaves, L. J. (1995). The structure of the genetic and environmental risk factors for six major psychiatric disorders in women: Phobia, generalized anxiety disorder, panic disorder, bulimia, major depression, and alcoholism. *Archives of General Psychiatry, 52*(5), 374–383.

Kenneback, S., & Bonin, L. (2016, October 4). Suicidal behavior in children and adolescents: Epidemiology and risk factors. *UpToDate.* Retrieved from www.uptodate.com.

Kennebeck, S., & Bonin, L. (2017, April 7). Suicidal ideation and behavior in children and adolescents: Evaluation and management. *UpToDate.* Retrieved from www.uptodate.com.

Kennebeck, S., & Bonin, L. (2017, November 21). Suicidal behavior in children and adolescents:

Epidemiology and risk factors. *UpToDate*. Retrieved from http://www.uptodate.com.

Kerber, K., Taylor, K., & Riba, M. B. (2011). Treatment resistant depression and comorbid medical problems: Cardiovascular disease and cancer. In J. F. Greden, M. B. Riba, & M. G. McInnis (Eds.), *Treatment resistant depression: A roadmap for effective care* (pp. 137–156). Arlington, VA: American Psychiatric Publishing.

Kernberg, O. F. (2018). *Treatment of severe personality disorders: Resolution of aggression and recovery of eroticism* (1st ed.). Washington, DC: American Psychiatric Publishing.

Kernberg, O. F. (1997). Convergences and divergences in contemporary psychoanalytic technique and psychoanalytic psychotherapy. In J. K. Zeig (Ed.), *The evolution of psychotherapy: The third conference*. New York: Brunner/Mazel.

Kernberg, O. F. (2005). Object relations theories and technique. In E. S. Person, A. M. Cooper, & G. O. Gabbard (Eds.), *The American Psychiatric Publishing textbook of psychoanalysis* (pp. 57–75). Washington, DC: American Psychiatric Publishing.

Kerns, C. E., Elkins, R. M., Carpenter, A. L., Chou, T., Green, J. G., & Comer, J. S. (2014). Caregiver distress, shared traumatic exposure, and child adjustment among area youth following the 2013 Boston Marathon bombing. *Journal of Affective Disorders, 167*, 50–55.

Kerns, C. E., Pincus, D. B., McLaughlin, K., & Comer, J. S. (2017). Maternal emotion regulation during child distress, child anxiety accommodation, and links between maternal and child anxiety. *Journal of Anxiety Disorders, 50*, 52–59.

Kerr, W. C., Kaplan, M. S., Huguet, N., Caetano, R., Giesbrecht, N., & McFarland, B. H. (2017). Economic recession, alcohol, and suicide rates: Comparative effects of poverty, foreclosure, and job loss. *American Journal of Preventive Medicine, 52*(4), 469–475.

Kerridge, B. T., Pickering, R., Chou, P., Saha, T. D., & Hasin, D. S. (2018). DSM-5 cannabis use disorder in the National Epidemiologic Survey on Alcohol and Related Conditions-III: Gender-specific profiles. *Addictive Behaviors, 76*, 52–60.

Kessler, R. C., Adler, L. A., Berglund, P., Green, J. G., McLaughlin, K. A., Fayyad, J., Russo, L. J., Sampson, N. A., Shahly, V., & Zaslavsky, A. M. (2014). The effects of temporally secondary co-morbid mental disorders on the associations of DSM-IV ADHD with adverse outcomes in the U.S. National Comorbidity Survey Replication Adolescent Supplement (NCS-A). *Psychological Medicine, 44*(8), 1779–1792.

Kessler, R. C., Sampson, N. A., Berglund, P., Gruber, M. J., Al-Hamzawi, A., Andrade, L., . . . Wilcox, M. A. (2015). Anxious and non-anxious major depressive disorder in the World Health Organization Mental Health Surveys. *Epidemiology and Psychiatry Sciences, 24*(3), 210–226.

Kessler, R. C., Adler, L. A., Barkley, R., Biederman, J., Conners, C. K., Faraone, S. V., . . . Zaslavsky, A. M. (2005). Patterns and predictors of attention-deficit/hyperactivity disorder persistence into adulthood: Results from the National Comorbidity Survey Replication. *Biological Psychiatry, 57*(11), 1442–1451.

Kessler, R. C., Avenevoli, S., Green, J., Gruber, M. J., Guyer, M., He, Y., . . . Merikangas, K. R. (2009). National comorbidity survey replication adolescent supplement (NCS-A): III. Concordance of DSM-IV/CIDI diagnoses with clinical reassessments. *Journal of the American Academy of Child and Adolescent Psychiatry, 48*(4), 386–399.

Kessler, R. C., Demier, O., Frank, R. G., Olfson, M., Pincus, H. A., Walters, E. E., . . . Zaslavsky, A. M. (2005). Prevalence and treatment of mental disorders, 1990 to 2003. *The New England Journal of Medicine, 352*(24), 2515–2523.

Kessler, R. C., DuPont, R. L., Berglund, P., & Wittchen, H. U. (1999). Impairment in pure and comorbid generalized anxiety disorder and major depression at 12 months in two national surveys. *American Journal of Psychiatry, 156*(12), 1915–1923.

Kessler, R. C., Gruber, M., Hettema, J. M., Hwang, I., Sampson, N., & Yonkers, K. A. (2010). Major depression and generalized anxiety disorder in the National Comorbidity Survey follow-up survey. In D. Goldberg, K. S. Kendler, P. J. Sirovatka, & D. A. Regier (Eds.), *Diagnostic issues in depression and generalized anxiety disorder: Refining the research agenda for DSM-V* (pp. 139–170). Washington, DC: American Psychiatric Association.

Kessler, R. C., McGonagle, K. A., Zhao, S., Nelson, C. B., Hughes, M., Eshleman, S., . . . Kendler, K. S. (1994). Lifetime and 12-month prevalence of DSM-III-R psychiatric disorders among persons aged 15–54 in the United States: Results from the National Comorbidity Survey. *Archives of General Psychiatry, 51*(1), 8–19.

Kessler, R. C., Petukhova, M., Sampson, N. A., Zaslavsky, A. M., & Wittchen, H. (2012). Twelve-month and lifetime prevalence and lifetime morbid risk of anxiety and mood disorders in the United States. *International Journal of Methods In Psychiatric Research, 21*(3), 169–184.

Kessler, R. C., Ruscio, A. M., Shear, K., & Wittchen, H-U. (2010). Epidemiology of anxiety disorders. In M. B. Stein & T. Steckler (Eds.), *Behavioral neurobiology of anxiety and its treatment. Current topics in behavioral neurosciences* (pp. 21–35). New York: Springer Science + Business Media.

Keyes, K. M., Platt, J., Kaufman, A. S., & McLaughlin, K. A. (2017). Association of fluid intelligence and psychiatric disorders in a population-representative sample of US adolescents. *JAMA Psychiatry, 74*(2), 179–188.

Keys, A., Brozek, J., Henschel, A., Mickelson, O., & Taylor, H. L. (1950). *The biology of human starvation*. Minneapolis: University of Minnesota Press.

KFF (Kaiser Family Foundation). (2016). *Population distribution by race/ethnicity*. Retrieved from http://kff.org/other/state-indicator/distribution-by-race/ethnicity.

Khandaker, G., Jung, J., Britton, P. N., King, C., Yin, J. K., & Jones, C. A. (2016). Long-term outcomes of infective encephalitis in children: A systematic review and meta-analysis. *Developmental Medicine and Child Neurology, 58*, 1108–1115.

Kharasch, E. D. (2017). Current concepts in methadone metabolism and transport. *Clinical Pharmacology in Drug Development, 6*(2), 125–134.

Khazan, O. (2017, April 18). The link between opioids and unemployment. *The Atlantic*.

Khera, M., & Cunningham, G. R. (2018, February 5). Treatment of male sexual dysfunction. *UpToDate*. Retrieved from http://www.uptodate.com.

Kibria, A. A., & Metcalfe, N. H. (2016). A biography of William Tuke (1732–1822): Founder of the modern mental asylum. *Journal of Medical Biography, 24*(3), 384–388.

Kiecolt-Glaser, J. K., Garner, W., Speicher, C., Penn, G. M., Holliday, J., & Glaser, R. (1984). Psychosocial modifiers of immunocompetence in medical students. *Psychosomatic Medicine, 46*, 7–14.

Kiecolt-Glaser, J. K., Glaser, R., Gravenstein, S., Malarkey, W. B., & Sheridan, J. (1996). Chronic stress alters the immune response to influenza virus vaccine in older adults. *Proceedings of the National Academy of Science, 93*, 3043–3047.

Kienast, T., Stoffers, J., Bermpohl, F., & Lieb, K. (2014). Borderline personality disorder and comorbid addiction: Epidemiology and treatment. *Deutsches Ärzteblatt International, 111*(16), 280–286.

Kiernicki, K., & Helme, D. W. (2017). Effects of image congruency on persuasiveness and recall in direct-to-consumer prescription drug advertising. *Health Mark Quarterly, 34*(4), 284–301.

Kiesler, D. J. (1966). Some myths of psychotherapy research and the search for a paradigm. *Psychological Bulletin, 65*, 110–136.

Kiesler, D. J. (1995). Research classic: Some myths of psychotherapy research and the search for a paradigm: Revisited. *Psychotherapy Research, 5*(2), 91–101.

Kiger, P. J. (2017, September 27). 10 types of study bias. *HowStuffWorks*. Retrieved from https://science.howstuffworks.com/life/.

Kikkert, M. J., Driessen, E., Peen, J., Barber, J. P., Bockting, C., Schalkwijk, F., . . . Dekker, J. J. (2016). The role of avoidant and obsessive-compulsive personality disorder traits in matching patients with major depression to cognitive behavioral and psychodynamic therapy: A replication study. *Journal of Affective Disorders, 205*, 400–405.

Kikuchi, H., Fujii, T., Abe, N., Suzuki, M., Takagi, M., Mugikura, S., Takahashi, S., & Mori, E. (2010). Memory repression: Brain mechanisms underlying dissociative amnesia. *Journal of Cognitive Neuroscience, 22*(3), 602–613.

Killingsworth, M. (2013, July 16). Does mind-wandering make you unhappy? *Greater Good*. Retrieved from http://greatergood.berkeley.edu.

Killingsworth, M. A., & Gilbert, D. T. (2010). A wandering mind is an unhappy mind. *Science, 330*(6006), 932.

Kim, C., & Cho, Y. (2017). Does unstable employment have an association with suicide rates among the young? *International Journal of Environmental Research and Public Health, 14*(5).

Kim, D. R., Epperson, C. N., Weiss, A. R., & Wisner, K. L. (2014). Pharmacotherapy of postpartum depression: An update. *Expert Opinion on Pharmacotherapy, 15*(9), 1223–1234.

Kim, E., Lee, J-A., Sung, Y., & Choi, S. M. (2016). Predicting self-posting behavior on social networking sites: An extension of theory of planned behavior. *Computers in Human Behavior, 62,* 116–123.

Kim, H., Lim, C-S., & Kaang, B-K. (2016). Neuronal mechanisms and circuits underlying repetitive behaviors in mouse models of autism spectrum disorder. *Behavioral and Brain Functions, 12,* 3.

Kim, I., Kim, D., & Jung, H. (2016). Dissociative identity disorders in Korea: Two recent cases. *Psychiatry Investigation, 13*(2), 250–252.

Kim, J. S., Lee, E. J., Chang, D. I., Park, J. H., Ahn, S. H., Cha, J. K., . . . Choi-Kwon, S. (2017). Efficacy of early administration of escitalopram on depressive and emotional symptoms and neurological dysfunction after stroke: A multicentre, double-blind, randomised, placebo-controlled study. *Lancet Psychiatry, 4*(1), 33–41.

Kim, J. W., & Chock, T. M. (2015, July). Body image 2.0: Associations between social grooming on Facebook and body image concerns. *Computers in Human Behavior, 48*(2015), 331–339.

Kim, J. Y., Yang, S. H., Kwon, J., Lee, H. W., & Kim, H. (2017). Mice subjected to uncontrollable electric shocks show depression-like behaviors irrespective of their state of helplessness. *Behavioural Brain Research, 322*(Pt. A), 138–144.

Kim, J. M., Park, J. W., & Lee, C. S. (2014). Evaluation of nocturnal bladder capacity and nocturnal urine volume in nocturnal enuresis. *Journal of Pediatric Urology, 10*(3), 559–563.

Kim, M. K., Lee, K. S., Kim, B., Choi, T. K., & Lee, S. H. (2016). Impact of mindfulness-based cognitive therapy on intolerance of uncertainty in patients with panic disorder. *Psychiatry Investigation, 13*(2), 196–202.

Kim, S. R., Nho, J. H., & Nam, J. H. (2017, September 11). Relationships among Type-D personality, symptoms and quality of life in patients with ovarian cancer receiving chemotherapy. *Journal of Psychosomatic Obstetrics & Gynecology.* [Epub ahead of print]

Kim, S., Colwell, S. R., Kata, A., Boyle, M. H., Georgiades, K. (2018). Cyberbullying victimization and adolescent mental health: Evidence of differential effects by sex and mental health problem type. *Journal of Youth and Adolescence.* [Manuscript in press]

Kim, S., Ha, J. H., Yu, J., Park, D., & Ryu, S. (2014). Path analysis of suicide ideation in older people. *International Psychogeriatrics/IPA, 26*(3), 509–515.

Kimball, A. (1993). Nipping and tucking. In Skin deep: Our national obsession with looks. *Psychology Today, 26*(3), 96.

King, M., Lodwick, R., Jones, R., Whitaker, H., & Petersen, I. (2017). Death following partner bereavement: A self-controlled case series analysis. *PLoS ONE, 12*(3), e0173870.

Kingsberg, S. A., Althof, S., Simon, J. A., Bradford, A., Bitzer, J., Carvalho, J., . . . Shifrin, J. L. (2017). Female sexual dysfunction: Medical and psychological treatments, Committee 14. *Journal of Sexual Medicine, 14*(12), 1463–1491.

Kingsberg, S. A., Tkachenko, N., Lucas, J., Burbrink, A., Kreppner, W., & Dickstein, J. B. (2013). Characterization of orgasmic difficulties by women: Focus group evaluation. *Journal of Sexual Medicine, 10,* 2242–2250.

Kingsberg, S., & Spadt, S. K. (2018, January 23). Approach to the woman with sexual pain. *UpToDate.* Retrieved from http://www.uptodate.com.

Kingsberg, S., & Spadt, S. K. (2018, January 23). Approach to the woman with sexual pain. *UpToDate.* Retrieved from http://www.uptodate.com.

Kiosses, D. N., Gross, J. J., Banerjee, S., Duberstein, P. R., Putrino, D., & Alexopoulos, G. S. (2017). Negative emotions and suicidal ideation during psychosocial treatments in older adults with major depression and cognitive impairment. *American Journal of Geriatric Psychiatry, 25,* 620–629.

Kirkham, F. J. (2017). Neurocognitive outcomes for acute global acquired brain injury in children. *Current Opinion in Neurology, 30,* 148–155.

Kirmayer, L. J. (2001). Cultural variations in the clinical presentation of depression and anxiety: Implications for diagnosis and treatment. *Journal of Clinical Psychiatry, 62*(Suppl. 13), 22–28.

Kisely, S., & Xiao, J. (2017, December 14). Cultural and linguistic diversity increases the likelihood of compulsory community treatment. *Schizophrenia Research.* [Epub ahead of print]

Kishita, N., & Laidlaw, K. (2017). Cognitive behaviour therapy for generalized anxiety disorder: Is CBT equally efficacious in adults of working age and older adults? *Clinical Psychology Review, 52,* 124–136.

Klan, T., Jasper, F., & Hiller, W. (2017). Predictors of the application of exposure in vivo in the treatment of agoraphobia in an outpatient clinic: An exploratory approach. *Psychotherapy Research, 27*(1), 64–73.

Klein, D. F. (1964). Delineation of two drug-responsive anxiety syndromes. *Psychopharmacologia, 5,* 397–408.

Klein, D. F., & Fink, M. (1962). Psychiatric reaction patterns to imipramine. *American Journal of Psychiatry, 119,* 432–438.

Klein, D., & Attia, E. (2017, February 15). Anorexia nervosa in adults: Clinical features, course of illness, assessment, and diagnosis. *UpToDate.* Retrieved from www.uptodate.com.

Kleinplatz, P. J. (2010). "Desire disorders" or opportunities for optimal erotic intimacy? In S. R. Leiblum (Ed.), *Treating sexual desire disorders: A clinical casebook* (pp. 92–113). New York: Guilford Press.

Kline, N. S. (1958). Clinical experience with iproniazid (Marsilid). *Journal of Clinical and Experimental Psychopathology, 19*(1, Suppl.), 72–78.

Kluft, R. P. (1988). The dissociative disorders. In J. Talbott, R. Hales, & S. Yudofsky (Eds.), *Textbook of psychiatry.* Washington, DC: American Psychiatric Press.

Kluft, R. P. (1991). Multiple personality disorder. In A. Tasman & S. M. Goldfinger (Eds.), *American Psychiatric Press review of psychiatry* (Vol. 10). Washington, DC: American Psychiatric Press.

Kluft, R. P. (2000). The psychoanalytic psychotherapy of dissociative identity disorder in the context of trauma therapy. *Psychoanalytical Inquiry, 20*(2), 259–286.

Kluft, R. P. (2001). Dissociative disorders. In H. S. Friedman (Ed.), *Specialty articles from the encyclopedia of mental health.* San Diego: Academic Press.

Knatz, S., Murray, S. B., Matheson, B., Boutelle, K. N., Rockwell, R., Eisler, I., & Kaye, W. H. (2015) A brief, intensive application of multi-family-based treatment for eating disorders. *Eating Disorders, 23*(4), 315–324.

Knezevic, D., & Mizrahi, R. (2018). Molecular imaging of neuroinflammation in Alzheimer's disease and mild cognitive impairment. *Progress in Neuro-Psychopharmacology and Biological Psychiatry, 80*(Pt. B), 123–131.

Knoll, J. L. (2010). The "pseudocommando" mass murderer: Part I, the psychology of revenge and obliteration. *Journal of the American Academy of Psychiatry and the Law. 38,* 87–94.

Knott, L. (2011). Delusions and hallucinations. *Patient.co.uk.* Retrieved from http://www.patient.co.uk/print/1715.

Knowthenet. (2013). Nineteen-year-old males revealed as top trolling target. Retrieved from http://www.knowthenet.org.uk/articles/nineteen-year-old-males.

Ko, J. Y., Rockhill, K. M., Tong, V. T., Morrow, B., & Farr, S. L. (2017 February 17). Trends in postpartum depressive symptoms—27 states, 2004, 2008, and 2012. *Morbidity and Mortality Weekly Report/CDC, 66*(6), 153–158.

Ko, K., Byun, M. S., Yi, D., Lee, J. H., Kim, C. H., & Lee, D. Y. (2018). Early-life cognitive activity is related to reduced neurodegeneration in Alzheimer signature regions in late life. *Frontiers in Aging Neuroscience, 20,* 70.

Kocsis, R. N. (2008). *Serial murder and the psychology of violent crimes.* Totowa, NJ: Humana Press.

Kodal, A., Fjermestad, K., Bjelland, I., Gjestad, R, Öst, L. G., Bjaastad, J. F., . . . Wergeland, G. J. (2018). Long-term effectiveness of cognitive behavioral therapy for youth with anxiety disorders. *Journal of Anxiety Disorders, 53,* 58–67.

Koenen, K. C., Lyons, M. J., Goldberg, J., Simpson, J., Williams, W. M., Toomey, R., . . . Tsuang, M. T. (2003). Co-twin control study of relationships among combat exposure, combat-related PTSD, and other mental disorders. *Journal of Traumatic Stress, 16*(5), 433–438.

Koenigsberg, H. W., Harvey, P., Mitropoulou, V., New, A. Goodman, M., Silverman, J., . . . Siever, L. J. (2001). Are the interpersonal and identity disturbances in the borderline personality disorder criteria linked to the traits of affectivity and impulsivity? *Journal of Personality Disorders, 15,* 358–370.

Koerner, N., Mejia, T., & Kusec, A. (2017). What's in a name? Intolerance of uncertainty, other uncertainty-relevant constructs, and their differential relations to worry and generalized anxiety disorder. *Journal of Clinical Psychiatry, 46*(2), 141–161.

Koetting, C. (2015). Caregiver-fabricated illness in a child. *Journal of Forensic Nursing, 11*(2), 114–117.

Koh, H. K. (2017). Community-based prevention and strategies for the opioid crisis. *JAMA, 318*(11), 993–994.

Koh, Y. W., Chui, C. Y., Tang, C. K., & Lee, A. M. (2014). The prevalence and risk factors of paternal depression from the antenatal to the postpartum period and the relationships between antenatal and postpartum depression among fathers in Hong Kong. *Depression Research and Treatment, 2014,* 127632.

Kohen, D. P., & Olness, K. (2011). *Hypnosis and hypnotherapy with children* (4th ed.). New York: Routledge/Taylor & Francis Group.

Kohut, H. (1977). *The restoration of the self.* New York: International Universities Press.

Kohut, H. (2001). On empathy. *European Journal for Psychoanalytic Therapy and Research, 2*(2), 139–146.

Kok, R., Avendano, M., Bago d'Uva, T., & Mackenbach, J. (2012). Can reporting heterogeneity explain differences in depressive symptoms across Europe? *Social Indicators Research, 105*(2), 191–210.

Kolar, D. (2017). Current status of electroconvulsive therapy for mood disorders: A clinical review. *Evidence-Based Mental Health, 20,* 12–14.

Kolata, G. (2016, October 1). The shame of fat shaming. *New York Times.*

Kolko, D. J., & Berkout, O. V. (2017, April). Child physical abuse. In S. N. Gold (Ed.), *APA handbook of trauma psychology* (Vol. 1, Chap. 17, pp. 99–115). Washington, DC: APA.

Kolodny, A., & Frieden, T. R. (2018). Government actions to curb the opioid epidemic: Reply. *JAMA, 319*(15), 1620–1621.

Kooyman, I., & Walsh, E. (2011). Societal outcomes in schizophrenia. In D. R. Weinberg & P. Harrison (Eds.), *Schizophrenia* (pp. 644–665). Hoboken, NJ: Wiley-Blackwell.

Korda, J. B., Goldstein, S. W., & Goldstein, I. (2010). The role of androgens in the treatment of hypoactive sexual desire disorder in women. In S. R. Leiblum (Ed.), *Treating sexual desire disorders: A clinical casebook* (pp. 201–218). New York: Guilford Press.

Kornack, J., Herscovitch, B., & Williams, A. L. (2017). A response to Papatola and Lustig's paper on navigating a managed care peer review: Guidance for clinicians using applied behavior analysis in the treatment of children on the autism spectrum. *Behavior Analysis in Practice, 10*(4), 386–394.

Korte, K. J., Bountress, K. E., Tomko, R. L., Killeen, T., Moran-Santa Maria, M., & Back, S. E. (2017). Integrated treatment of PTSD and substance use disorders: The mediating role of PTSD improvement in the reduction of depression. *Journal of Clinical Medicine, 6*(1), 9.

Kosilov, K. V., Geltser, B. I., Loparev, S. A., Kuzina, I. G., Shakirova, O. V., Zhuravskaya, N. S., & Lobodenko, A. (2018, May 5). The optimal duration of alarm therapy use in children with primary monosymptomatic nocturnal enuresis. *Journal of Pediatric Urology.* [Epub ahead of print]

Kosinski, M., Matz, S. C., Gosling, S. D., Popov, V., & Stillwell, D. (2016). Facebook as a research tool. *Monitor on Psychology, 47*(3), 70.

Kosinski, M., Stillwell, D., & Graepel, T. (2013). Private traits and attributes are predictable from digital records of human behavior. *Proceedings of the National Academy of Sciences of the United States of America, 110*(15), 5802–5805.

Koss, M. P., Swartout, K. M., White, J. W., Thompson, M. P., Abbey, A., & Bellis, A. L. (2015). Trajectory analysis of the campus serial rapist assumption. *JAMA Pediatrics, 169,* 1148–1154.

Koss, M. P., & Heslet, L. (1992). Somatic consequences of violence against women. *Archives of Family Medicine, 1*(1), 53–59.

Koss, M. P., Abbey, A., Campbell, R., Cook, S., Norris, J., Testa, M., . . . White, J. (2008). Revising the SES: A collaborative process to improve assessment of sexual aggression and victimization: Erratum. *Psychology of Women Quarterly, 32*(4), 493.

Koss, M. P., White, J. W., & Kazdin, A. E. (2011). Violence against women and children: Perspectives and next steps. In M. P. Koss, J. W. White, & A. E. Kazdin (Eds.), *Violence against women and children, Vol. 2: Navigating solutions* (pp. 261–305). Washington, DC: American Psychological Association.

Koss, M. P., White, J. W., & Kazdin, A. E. (Eds.). (2011). *Violence against women and children, Vol. 2: Navigating solutions.* Washington, DC: American Psychological Association.

Kosten, T. R., George, T. P., & Kleber, H. D. (2005). The neurobiology of substance dependence: Implications for treatment. In R. J. Frances, A. H. Mack, & S. I. Miller (Eds.), *Clinical textbook of addictive disorders* (3rd ed., Chap. 1, pp. 3–15). New York: Guilford Press.

Kosten, T. R., George, T. P., & Kleber, H. D. (2011). The neurobiology of substance dependence: Implications for treatment. In R. J. Frances, S. I. Miller, & A. H. Mack (Eds.), *Clinical textbook of addictive disorders* (3rd ed., Chap. 1, pp. 3–21). New York: Guilford Press. [Paperback edition]

Kovera, M. B. (2017, March 13). *The psychology of juries* (1st ed.). Washington, DC: American Psychological Association.

Kposowa, A. J., McElvain, J. P., & Breault, K. D. (2008). Immigration and suicide: The role of marital status, duration of residence, and social integration. *Archives of Suicide Research, 12*(1), 82–92.

Kraan, T. C., Velthorst, E., Themmen, M., Valmaggia, L., Kempton, M. J., McGire, P., . . . EGEI High Risk Study. (2018). Child maltreatment and clinical outcome in individuals at ultra-high risk for psychosis in the EU-GEI High Risk Study. *Schizophrenia Bulletin.* [Manuscript in press]

Krack, P., Hariz, M. I., Baunez, C., Guridi, J., & Obeso, J. A. (2010). Deep brain stimulation: From neurology to psychiatry? *Trends in Neurosciences, 33*(10), 474–484.

Kragh, J. V. (2017). Neurosyphilis. Historical perspectives on general paresis of the insane. *JSM Schizophrenia, 2*(2), 1013.

Kralovec, K., Kunrath, S., Fartacek, C., Pichler, E. M., & Plöderl, M. (2018). The gender-specific associations between religion/spirituality and suicide risk in a sample of Austrian psychiatric inpatients. *Suicide and Life-Threatening Behavior.* [Manuscript in press]

Kramer, A. D. I., Guillory, J. E., & Hancock, J. T. (2014). Experimental evidence of massive-scale emotional contagion through social networks. *PNAS, 111*(24), 8788–8790.

Krasnova, H., Wenninger, H., Widjaja, T., & Buxmann, P. (2013). Envy on Facebook: A hidden threat to users' life satisfaction? *Internationale Tagung Wirtschaftsinformatik, 27.02.* Retrieved from http://www.AISEL.SIDNRT.ORG/WI2013.

Krause, M., Zhu, Y., Huhn, M., Schneider-Thoma, J., Bighelli, I., Nikolakopoulou, A., & Leucht, S. (2018, January 24). Antipsychotic drugs for patients with schizophrenia and predominant or prominent negative symptoms: A systematic review and meta-analysis. *European Archives of Psychiatry and Clinical Neuroscience.* [Epub ahead of print]

Krause-Utz, A., Frost, R., Winter, D., & Elzinga, B. M. (2017). Dissociation and alterations in brain function and structure: Implications for borderline personality disorder. *Current Psychiatry Reports, 19*(1), 6.

Krauss, D. A., Gongola, J., Scurich, N., & Busch, B. (2018, April 24). Mental state at time of offense in the hot tub: An empirical examination of concurrent expert testimony in an insanity case. *Behavioral Sciences & the Law.* [Epub ahead of print]

Krebs, G., de la Cruz, L. F., Monzani, B., Bowyer, L., Anson, M., Cadman, J., . . . Mataix-Cols, D. (2017). Long-term outcomes of cognitive-behavior therapy for adolescent body dysmorphic disorder. *Behavior Therapy.*

Kring, A. M., & Neale, J. M. (1996). Do schizophrenic patients show a disjunctive relationship among expressive, experiential, and psychophysiological components of emotion? *Journal of Abnormal Psychology, 105*(2), 249–257.

Krippner, S., & Paulson, C. M. (2006). Posttraumatic stress disorder among U.S. combat veterans. In T. G. Plante (Ed.), *Mental disorders of the new millennium, Vol. 2: Public and social problems.* Westport, CT: Praeger Publishers.

Krisberg, B. A. (2018). *Juvenile justice and delinquency.* Thousand Oaks, CA: Sage Publications.

Krishnan, R. (2017, March 7). Unipolar depression in adults: Epidemiology, pathogenesis, and neurobiology. *UpToDate.* Retrieved from http://www.uptodate.com.

Kritikos, T. K., Comer, J. S., He, M., Curren, L., & Tompson, M. C. (2019). Combat experiences and PTSD among military-serving parents: A meta-analytic examination of associated offspring and family outcomes. *Journal of Abnormal Child Psychology.*

Krueger, R. B. (2010). The DSM diagnostic criteria for sexual masochism. *Archives of Sexual Behavior, 39*(2), 346–356.

Krull, K. R. (2018, February 27). Attention deficit hyperactivity disorder in children and adolescents: Clinical features and diagnosis. *UpToDate.* Retrieved from http://www.uptodate.com.

Krull, K. R. (2018, January 31). Attention deficit hyperactivity disorder in children and adolescents: Overview of treatment and prognosis. *UpToDate.* Retrieved from http://www.uptodate.com.

Krull, K. R. (2018, January 31). Attention deficit hyperactivity disorder in children and adolescents: Overview of treatment and prognosis. *UpToDate.* Retrieved from http://www.uptodate.com.

Krull, K. R. (2018, March 20). Attention deficit hyperactivity disorder in children and adolescents: Treatment with medications. *UpToDate.* Retrieved from http://www.uptodate.com.

Krull, K. R. (2018, May 17). Attention deficit hyperactivity disorder in children and adolescents: Epidemiology and pathogenesis. *UpToDate.* Retrieved from http://www.uptodate.com.

Krupić, F., Custovic, S., Jasarevic, M., Sadic, S., Fazlic, M., Grbic, K., & Samuelsson, K. (2019). Ethnic differences in the perception of pain: A systematic review of qualitative and quantitative research. *Medicinski Glasnik (Zenica)16*(1). [Epub ahead of print]

Krupnick, J. L., Green, B. L., Amdur, R., Alaoui, A. Belouali, A., Roberge, E., . . . Dutton, M. A. (2017). An internet-based writing intervention for PTSD in veterans: A feasibility and pilot effectiveness trial. *Psychological Trauma, 9*(4), 461–470.

Kube, T., Siebers, V. H. A., Herzog, P., Glombiewski, J. A., Doering, B. K., & Rief, W. (2018). Integrating situation-specific dysfunctional expectations and dispositional optimism into the cognitive model of depression: A path-analytic approach. *Journal of Affective Disorders, 229,* 199–205.

Kucharska, J. (2017, November 10). Religiosity and the concept of god moderate the relationship between the type of trauma, posttraumatic cognitions, and mental health. *Journal of Trauma & Dissociation.* [Epub ahead of print]

Kuhn, R. (1958). The treatment of depressive states with G-22355 (imipramine hydrochloride). *American Journal of Psychiatry, 115,* 459–464.

Kuhn, T. S. (1962). *The structure of scientific revolutions.* Chicago: University of Chicago Press.

Kulkarni, J. (2017). Complex PTSD — A better description for borderline personality disorder? *Australasian Psychiatry, 25*(4), 333–335.

Kunst, M. J. J. (2011). Affective personality type, post-traumatic stress disorder symptom severity and post-traumatic growth in victims of violence. *Stress and Health: Journal of the International Society for the Investigation of Stress, 27*(1), 42–51.

Kurlansik, S. L., & Maffei, M. S. (2016). Somatic symptom disorder. *American Family Physician, 93*(1), 49–54.

Kuzucan, A., Doshi, P., & Zito, J. M. (2017). Pharmacists can help to end direct-to-consumer advertising. *American Journal of Health-System Pharmacy, 74*(10), 640–642.

Kyaga, S., Landén, M., Boman, M., Hultman, C. M., Långström, N., & Lichtenstein, P. (2013). Mental illness, suicide and creativity: 40-year prospective total population study. *Journal of Psychiatric Research, 47*(1), 83–90.

Kyaga, S., Lichtenstein, P., Boman, M., Hultman, C., Långström, N., & Landén, M. (2011). Creativity and mental disorder: Family study of 300,000 people with severe mental disorder. *British Journal of Psychiatry, 199*(5), 373–379.

La Greca, A. M., Comer, J. S., & Lai, B. (2016). Trauma and child health: An introduction to the Special Issue. *Journal of Pediatric Psychology, 41,* 1–4.

La Greca, A. M., Danzi, B. A., & Chan, S. F. (2017). DSM-5 and ICD-11 as competing models of PTSD in preadolescent children exposed to a natural disaster: Assessing validity and co-occurring symptomatology. *European Journal of Psychotraumatology, 8*(1), 1310591.

Laan, E., Rellini, A. H., & Barnes, T. (2013). Standard operating procedures for female orgasmic disorder: Consensus of the International Society for Sexual Medicine. *Journal of Sexual Medicine, 10,* 74–82.

Lahey, B. B. (2008). Oppositional defiant disorder, conduct disorder, and juvenile delinquency. In S. P. Hinshaw & T. P. Beauchaine (Eds.), *Child and adolescent psychopathology* (pp. 335–369). Hoboken, NJ: Wiley.

Lahmann, C., Henningsen, P., & Noll-Hussong, M. (2010). Somatoform pain disorder—Overview. *Psychiatria Danubina, 22*(3), 453–458.

Lakhan, S. E., & Vieira, K. F. (2008). Nutritional therapies for mental disorders. *Nutrition Journal, 7,* 2.

Lambert, M. J. (2015). Progress feedback and the OQ-system: The past and the future. *Psychotherapy (Chicago), 52*(4), 381–390.

Lambert, M. J. (2010). Using outcome data to improve the effects of psychotherapy: Some illustrations. In M. J. Lambert, *Prevention of treatment failure: The use of measuring, monitoring, and feedback in clinical practice* (pp. 203–242). Washington, DC: American Psychological Association.

Lambert, M. J., Shapiro, D. A., & Bergin, A. E. (1986). The effectiveness of psychotherapy. In S. L. Garfield & A. E. Bergin (Eds.), *Handbook of psychotherapy and behavioral change* (3rd ed.). New York: Wiley.

Lampe, L. (2015). Social anxiety disorders in clinical practice: Differentiating social phobia from avoidant personality disorder. *Australasian Psychiatry, 23*(4), 343–346.

Lampe, L., & Malhi, G. S. (2018). Avoidant personality disorder: Current insights. *Psychology Research and Behavior Management, 11,* 55–66.

Lamprecht, F., Kohnke, C., Lempa, W., Sack, M., Matzke, M., & Munte, T. F. (2004). Event-related potentials and EMDR treatment of posttraumatic stress disorder. *Neuroscience Research, 49*(2), 267–272.

Lanas, A., & Chan, F. K. L. (2017, February 24). Peptic ulcer disease. *The Lancet.* Retrieved from http://dx.doi.org/10.1016/S0140-6736(16)32404-7.

Lancet, The. (2010, February 2). Retraction—Ileal-lymphoid-nodular hyperplasia, non-specific colitis, and pervasive developmental disorder in children. *The Lancet.*

Lancioni, G. E., Singh, N. N., O'Reilly, M. F., Sigafoos, J., Bosco, A., Zonno, N., & Badagliacca, F. (2011). Persons with mild or moderate Alzheimer's disease learn to use urine alarms and prompts to avoid large urinary accidents. *Research in Developmental Disabilities, 32*(5), 1998–2004.

Landa, R. J. (2018). Efficacy of early interventions for infants and young children with, and at risk for, autism spectrum disorders. *International Review of Psychiatry, 30*(1), 25–39.

Lane, H., Rose, L. E., Woodbrey, M., Arghavani, D., Lawrence, M., & Cavanaugh, J. T. (2017). Exploring the effects of using an oral appliance to reduce movement dysfunction in an individual with Parkinson disease: A single-subject design study. *Journal of Neurologic Physical Therapy, 41*(1), 52–58.

Lang, J. (1999, April 16). Local jails dumping grounds for mentally ill. *Detroit News.*

Lange, C., Deutschenbaur, L., Borgwardt, S., Lang, U. E., Walter, M., & Huber, C. G. (2017). Experimentally induced psychosocial stress in schizophrenia spectrum disorders: A systematic review. *Schizophrenia Research, 182,* 4–12.

Langleben, D. D., Hakun, J. G., Seelig, D., Wang, A. L., Ruparel, K., Bilker, W. B., & Gur, R. C. (2016). Polygraphy and functional magnetic resonance imaging in lie detection: A controlled blind comparison using the concealed information test. *Journal of Clinical Psychiatry. 77*(10), 1372–1380.

Långström, N., & Seto, M. C. (2006). Exhibitionist and voyeuristic behavior in a Swedish national population survey. *Archives of Sexual Behavior, 35,* 427–435.

Lanier, C. (2010). Structure, culture, and lethality: An integrated model approach to American Indian suicide and homicide. *Homicide Studies: An Interdisciplinary & International Journal, 14*(1), 72–78.

Lankford, A. (2013). *The myth of martyrdom.* New York: St. Martin's Press.

Lankford, A., & Tomek, S. (2018). Mass killings in the United States from 2006 to 2013: Social contagion or random clusters? *Suicide and Life-Threatening Behavior.* [Manuscript in press]

Lanska, D. J. (2018). The dancing manias: Psychogenic illness as a social phenomenon. *Frontiers in Neurology and Neuroscience, 42,* 132–141.

Lapidus, K. B., Kopell, B. H., Ben-Haim, S., Rezai, A. R., & Goodman, W. K. (2013). History of psychosurgery: A psychiatrist's perspective. *World Neurosurgery, 80*(3-4), S27.e1–16.

LaRosa, J. (2018, January 2). Top 6 trends for the weight loss industry in 2018. *Market Research.com.* Retrieved from https://blog.marketresearch.com/top-6-trends-for-the-weight-loss-market-in-2018.

Larson, E. B. (2018, March 27). Evaluation of cognitive impairment and dementia. *UpToDate.* Retrieved from http://www.uptodate.com.

Latzer, Y., Katz, R., & Spivak, Z. (2011). *Facebook users more prone to eating disorders.* University of Haifa, Israel. [Unpublished manuscript]

Lau, J. Y., Belli, S. R., Gregory, A. M., & Eley, T. C. (2014). Interpersonal cognitive biases as genetic markers for pediatric depressive symptoms: Twin data from the Emotions, Cognitions, Heredity and Outcome (ECHO) study. *Development and Psychopathology, 26,* 1267–1276.

Laumann, E. O., Gagnon, J. H., Michael, R. T., & Michaels, S. (1994). *The social organization of sexuality.* Chicago: University of Chicago Press.

Laumann, E. O., Nicolosi, A., Glasser, D. B., Paik, A., Gingell, C., Moreira, E., & Wang, T. (2005). Sexual problems among women and men aged 40–80 years: Prevalence and correlates identified in the Global Study of Sexual Attitudes and Behaviors. *International Journal of Impotence Research, 17,* 39–57.

Laumann, E. O., Paik, A., & Rosen, R. C. (1999). Sexual dysfunction in the United States: Prevalence and predictors. *Journal of the American Medical Association, 281*(13), 1174.

Lavender, J. M., Brown, T. A., & Murray, S. B. (2017). Men, muscles, and eating disorders: An overview of traditional and muscularity-oriented disordered eating. *Current Psychiatry Reports, 19*(6), 32.

Lavin, M. (2008). Voyeurism: Psychopathology and theory. In D. R. Laws & W. T. O'Donohue (Eds.), *Sexual deviance: Theory, assessment, and treatment* (2nd ed., pp. 305–319). New York: Guilford Press.

Law, E., Yang, J. H., Coit, M. H., & Chan, E. (2016). Toilet school for children with failure to toilet train: Comparing a group therapy model with individual treatment. *Journal of Developmental & Behavioral Pediatric, 37*(3), 223–230.

Laws, R. (2016). The rise and fall of relapse prevention: An update. In D. P. Boer, *The Wiley handbook on the theories, assessment and treatment of sexual offending* (Vol. 3, Chap. 60, pp. 1299–1312). Hoboken, NJ: Wiley-Blackwell.

Lawson, E. A., & Miller, K. K. (2017, December 19). Anorexia nervosa: Endocrine complications and their management. *UpToDate*. Retrieved from http://www.uptodate.com.

Lazarou, S. (2017, December 13). Surgical treatment of erectile dysfunction. *UpToDate*. Retrieved from http://www.uptodate.com.

Lazarov, O., Robinson, J., Tang, Y. P., Hairston, I. S., Korade-Mirnics, Z., Lee, V. M., . . . Sisodia, S. S. (2005). Environmental enrichment reduces A-beta levels and amyloid deposition in transgenic mice. *Cell, 120*(5), 572–574.

Lazarus, D. (2017, February 15). Direct-to-consumer drug ads: A bad idea that's about to get worse. *Los Angeles Times*.

Lazarus, R. S., & Folkman, S. (1984). *Stress, appraisal, and coping*. New York: Springer Publishing.

Lazzari, C., Shoka, A., & Kulkarni, K. (2017, March). Are psychiatric hospitals and psychopharmacology the ultimate remedies for social problems? A narrative approach to aid socio-psychopharmacological assessment and treatment. *International Journal of Medical Research and Pharmaceutical Sciences, 4*(3).

Leavy, P. (2017). *Research design: Quantitative, qualitative, mixed methods, arts-based, and community-based participatory research approaches*. New York: Guilford Press.

LeBlanc, S. (2017, April 25). Baker proposal targets revenge porn, teenagers' sexting. *US News*.

Lebow, J. L. (2017). Editorial: The multidisciplinary world of couple and family therapy and family science. *Family Process, 56*(4), 795–798.

Lebow, J. L., & Uliaszek, A. A. (2010). Couples and family therapy for personality disorders. In J. J. Magnavita (Ed.), *Evidence-based treatment of personality dysfunction: Principles, methods, and processes*. (pp. 193–221). Washington, DC: American Psychological Association.

Lebow, J. L., Chambers, A. L., Christensen, A., & Johnson, S. M. (2012). Research on the treatment of couple distress. *Journal of Marital and Family Therapy, 38*(1), 145–168.

LeCroy, C. W., & Holschuh, J. (Eds.). (2012). *First person accounts of mental illness and recovery*. Hoboken, NJ: Wiley.

LeDoux, J. E. (2000). Emotion circuits in the brain. *Annual Review of Neuroscience, 23*, 155–184.

LeDoux, J. E., & Pine, D. S. (2016). Using neuroscience to help understand fear and anxiety: A two-system framework. *American Journal of Psychiatry, 173*(11), 1083–1093.

Ledoux, S., Miller, P., Choquet, M., & Plant, M. (2002). Family structure, parent-child relationships, and alcohol and other drug use among teenagers in France and the United Kingdom. *Alcohol and Alcoholism, 37*(1), 52–60.

Lee, B., Leavitt, M., Bernick, C., Leger, G., Rabinovici, G., & Banks, S. (2018, April 2). A systematic review of positron emission tomography of tau, amyloid beta, and neuroinflammation in chronic traumatic encephalopathy: The evidence to-date. *Journal of Neurotrauma*. [Epub ahead of print]

Lee, C., Coe, C. L., & Ryff, C. D. (2017). Social disadvantage, severe child abuse, and biological profiles in adulthood. *Journal of Health and Social Behavior, 58*(3), 371–386.

Lee, D. J., Weathers, F. W., Sloan, D. M., Davis, M. T., & Domino, J. L. (2017). Development and initial psychometric evaluation of the Semi-Structured Emotion Regulation Interview. *Journal of Personality Assessment, 99*(1), 56–66.

Lee, G., & Bae, H. (2017). Therapeutic effects of phytochemicals and medicinal herbs on depression. *BioMed Research International, 207*, article 6596241.

Lee, J., & Freeman, J. L. (2016). Embryonic exposure to 10 ug L(-1) lead results in female-specific expression changes in genes associated with nervous system development and function and Alzheimer's disease in aged adult zebrafish brain. *Metallomics, 8*(6), 589–596.

Lee, J., Peterson, S. M., & Freeman, J. L. (2017). Sex-specific characterization and evaluation of the Alzheimer's disease genetic risk factor sorl1 in zebrafish during aging and in the adult brain following a 100 ppb embryonic lead exposure. *Journal of Applied Toxicology, 37*(4), 400–407.

Lee, M. C., Yu, W. C., Shih, Y. H., Chen, C. Y., Guo, Z. H., Huang, S. J., . . . Chen, Y. R. (2018). Zinc ion rapidly induces toxic, off-pathway amyloid-b derived diffusible ligands in Alzheimer's disease. *Scientific Reports, 8*(1), 4772.

Lee, R. (2017). Mistrustful and misunderstood: A review of paranoid personality disorder. *Current Behavioral Neuroscience Reports, 4*(2), 151–165.

Lee, S. E., & Miller, B. L. (2016, January 6). Frontotemporal dementia: Clinical features and diagnosis. *UpToDate*. Retrieved from http://www.uptodate.com.

Lee, S. J., Kim, K. R., Lee, S. Y., & An, S. K. (2017). Impaired social and role function in ultra-high risk for psychosis and first-episode schizophrenia: Its relations with negative symptoms. *Psychiatry Investigation, 14*(5), 539–545.

Lee, J., & Freeman, J. L. (2014). Zebrafish as a model for investigating developmental lead (Pb) neurotoxicity as a risk factor in adult neurodegenerative disease: A mini-review. *Neurotoxicology, 43*, 57–64.

Leem, J., & Deane, C. M. (2019). High-throughput antibody structure modeling and design using ABodyBuilder. *Methods in Molecular Biology, 1851*, 367–380.

Leemans, C., & Loas, S. (2016). On the relationship between emotional dependency and abuse. [French] *Revue Médicale de Bruxelles, 37*(2), 79–86.

Leenaars, A. A. (2004). Altruistic suicide: A few reflections. *Archives of Suicide Research, 8*(1), 1–7.

Leff, J., Williams, G., Huckvale, M., Arbuthnot, M., & Leff, A. P. (2014). Avatar therapy for persecutory auditory hallucinations: What is it and how does it work? *Psychosis, 6*(2), 166–176.

Leff, J., Williams, G., Huckvale, M., Arbuthnot, M., & Leff, A. (2013). Computer-assisted therapy for medication-resistant auditory hallucinations: Proof-of-concept study. *British Journal of Psychiatry, 202*, 428–433.

Lehman, S. (2016, March 8). Kids who skip lunch are missing out on essential nutrients. *Health News*.

Lehrner, A., & Yehuda, R. (2018). Trauma across generations and paths to adaptation and resilience. *Psychological Trauma, 10*(1), 22–29.

Leibold, N. K., van den Hove, D., Viechtbauer, W., Kenis, G., Goossens, L., Lange, I., . . . Schruers, K. R. (2017). Amiloride-sensitive cation channel 2 genotype affects the response to a carbon dioxide panic challenge. *Journal of Psychopharmacology, 31*, 1294–1301.

Leichsenring, F., & Salzer, S. (2014). A unified protocol for the transdiagnostic psychodynamic treatment of anxiety disorders: An evidence-based approach. *Psychotherapy, 51*(2), 224–245.

Lembke, A., & Humphreys, K. (2016). Self-help organizations for substance use disorders. In K. J. Sher (Ed.), *Oxford handbook of substance use and substance use disorders* (Vol. 2, Chap. 20, pp. 582–593). New York: Oxford University Press.

Lenhard, F., Andersson, E., Mataix-Cols, D., Ruck, C., Vigerland, S., Högström, J., . . . Serlachius, E. (2017). Therapist-guided, Internet-delivered cognitive-behavioral therapy for adolescents with obsessive-compulsive disorder: A randomized controlled trial. *Journal of the American Academy of Child and Adolescent Psychiatry, 56*(1), 10–19.

Lenzenweger, M. F. (2018). Schizotypy, schizotypic psychopathology, and schizophrenia: Understanding the nature, basis, and manifestation of the schizophrenia spectrum. In J. N. Butcher (Ed.-in-chief), *APA handbook of psychopathology* (Vol. 1, Ch. 15). Washington, DC: APA.

Lenzenweger, M. F., & Depue, R. A. (2016). Toward a developmental psychopathology of personality disturbance: A neurobehavioral dimensional model incorporating genetic, environmental, and epigenetic factors. In D. Cicchetti (Ed.), *Developmental psychopathology* (3rd ed., Vol. 3, Chap. 24, pp. 1079–1110). New York: Wiley.

Lepage, C., Muehlmann, M., Tripodis, Y., Hufschmidt, J., Stamm, J., Green, K., . . . Koerte, I. K. (2018, May 19). Limbic system structure volumes and associated neurocognitive functioning in former NFL players. *Brain Imaging and Behavior*. [Epub ahead of print]

Lepp, A., Barkley, J. E., & Karpinski, A. C. (2014). The relationship between cell phone use, academic performance, anxiety, and satisfaction with life in college students. *Computers in Human Behavior, 31,* 343–350.

Lerner, M. D., Mazefsky, C. A., White, S. W., & McPartland, J. C. (2018). Autism spectrum disorder. In J. N. Butcher & J. M. Hooley (Eds.), *APA handbook of psychopathology. Vol. 2. Psychopathology in children and adolescents* (Ch. 20). Washington, DC: American Psychological Association.

Levenson, H. (2017, June 19). *Brief dynamic therapy (Theories of Psychotherapy Series),* 2nd ed. Washington, DC: American Psychological Association.

Levenson, J. L. (2018, January 17). Somatic symptom disorder: Epidemiology and clinical presentation. *UpToDate.* Retrieved from http://www.uptodate.com.

Levenson, J. L. (2018, January 18). Somatic symptom disorder: Assessment and diagnosis. *UpToDate.* Retrieved from http://www.uptodate.com.

Levenson, J. L. (2018, January 18). Somatic symptom disorder: Treatment. *UpToDate.* Retrieved from http://www.uptodate.com.

Levenson, J. L. (2018, January 25). Illness anxiety disorder: Epidemiology, clinical presentation, assessment, and diagnosis. *UpToDate.* Retrieved from http://www.uptodate.com.

Levenson, J. L. (2018, January 25). Illness anxiety disorder: Treatment and prognosis. *UpToDate.* Retrieved from http://www.uptodate.com.

Levenson, J. L. (2018, January 26). Psychological factors affecting other medical conditions: Clinical features, assessment, and diagnosis. *UpToDate.* Retrieved from http://www.uptodate.com.

Levi, O., Shoval-Zuckerman, Y., Fruchter, E., Bibi, A., Bar-Haim, Y., & Wald, I. (2017). Benefits of a psychodynamic group therapy (PGT) model for treating veterans with PTSD. *Journal of Clinical Psychology, 73,* 1247–1258.

Levine, D. (2017, June 6). The many ways exercise fights depression. *U.S. News & World Report.*

Levine, S. B. (2017). Ethical concerns about emerging treatment paradigms for gender dysphoria. *Journal of Sex & Marital Therapy, 23,* 1–16.

Levinson, D. F., & Nichols, W. E. (2014). *Major depression and genetics.* Stanford, CA: Stanford, School of Medicine.

Levinson, H. (2011, November 8). The strange and curious history of lobotomy. *BBC News Magazine.*

Levula, A., Harré, M., & Wilson, A. (2018). The association between social network factors with depression and anxiety at different life stages. *Community Mental Health Journal, 54*(6), 842–854.

Levy, T. B., Barak, Y., Sigler, M., & Aizenberg, D. (2011). Suicide attempts and burden of physical illness among depressed elderly inpatients. *Archives of Gerontology and Geriatrics, 52*(1), 115–117.

Lewinsohn, P. M., Antonuccio, D. O., Steinmetz, J. L., & Teri, L. (1984). *The coping with depression course.* Eugene, OR: Castalia.

Lewinsohn, P. M., Clarke, G. N., Hops, H., & Andrews, J. (1990). Cognitive-behavioral treatment for depressed adolescents. *Behavior Therapist, 21,* 385–401.

Lewis, B. A., Gjerdingen, D., Schuver, K., Avery, M., & Marcus, B. H. (2018). The effect of sleep pattern changes on postpartum depressive symptoms. *BMC Women's Health, 18*(1), 12.

Lewis, E. T., 3rd, & Dwyer, R. G. (2018). Psychosis and sexual offending: A review of current literature. *International Journal of Offender Therapy and Comparative Criminology, 62*(11), 3372–3384.

Lewis, R. W., Fugl-Meyer, K. S., Corona, G., Hayes, R. D., Laumann, E. O., Moreira, E. D., Jr., . . . Segraves, T. (2010). Definitions/epidemiology/risk factors for sexual dysfunction. *Journal of Sexual Medicine, 7,* 1598–1607.

Li, B. Y., Wang, Y., Tang, H. D., & Chen, S. D. (2017). The role of cognitive activity in cognition protection: From bedside to bench. *Translational Neurodegeneration, 6,* 7.

Li, C-Y., Larsen, S., & Yap, T. (2017). Nocturnal penile tumescence study. In S. Minhas & J. Mulhall (Eds.), *Male sexual dysfunction: A clinical guide* (Chap. 15, pp. 129–132). UK: John Wiley & Sons.

Li, J., Alper, H. E., Gargano, L. M., Maslow, C. B., & Brackbill, R. M. (2018). Re-experiencing 9/11-related PTSD symptoms following exposure to Hurricane Sandy. *International Journal of Emergency Mental Health, 20*(3).

Li, L., Xue, Z., Chen, L., Chen, X., Wang, H., & Wang, X. (2017). Puerarin suppression of Ab_{1-42}-induced primary cortical neuron death is largely dependent on ERb. *Brain Research, 1657,* 87–94.

Li, W., & Caltabiano, N. (2017). Prevalence of substance abuse and socio-economic differences in substance abuse in an Australian community-dwelling elderly sample. *Health Psychology Open, 4*(1). doi:10.1177/2055102917708136

Li, L., Wu, M., Liao, Y., Ouyang, L., Du, M., Lei, D., . . . Gong, Q. (2014). Grey matter reduction associated with posttraumatic stress disorder and traumatic stress. *Neuroscience and Biobehavioral Reviews, 43,* 163–172.

Liang, L. A., Berger, U., & Brand, C. (2019). Psychosocial factors associated with symptoms of depression, anxiety and stress among single mothers with young children: A population-based study. *Journal of Affective Disorders, 242,* 255–264.

Libman, H., Melin, J. A., Sullivan, D. J., & Sokol, H. N. (2017, July 7). What's new in geriatrics. *UpToDate.* Retrieved from http://www.uptodate.com.

Lieberman, A. (2018). Counseling issues: Addressing behavioral and emotional considerations in the treatment of communication disorders. *American Journal of Speech-Language Pathology, 27*(1), 13–23.

Lieberman, A. F., & Chu, A. T. (2016). Childhood exposure to interpersonal trauma. In D. Cicchetti, *Developmental psychopathology, Vol. 3: Maladaptation and psychopathology* (3rd ed., Chap. 10). New York: Wiley.

Lieberman, J. A., Girgis, R. R., Brucato, G., Moore, H., Provenzano, F., Kegeles, L., . . . Small, S. A. (2018, January 9). Hippocampal dysfunction in pathophysiology of schizophrenia: A selective review and hypothesis for early detection and intervention. *Molecular Psychiatry.* [Epub ahead of print]

Lieberman, L., Gorka, S. M., Shankman, S. A., & Phan, K. L. (2017). Impact of panic on psychophysiological and neural reactivity to unpredictable threat in depression and anxiety. *Clinical Psychological Science, 5*(1), 52–63.

Liebman, J. I., McKinley-Pace, M. J., Leonard, A. M., Sheesley, L. A., Gallant, C. L., Renkey, M. E., & Lehman, E. B. (2002). Cognitive and psychosocial correlates of adults' eyewitness accuracy and suggestibility. *Personality and Individual Differences, 33*(1), 49–66.

Liese, B. S., & Reis, D. J. (2016). Failing to diagnose and failing to treat an addicted client: Two potentially life-threatening clinical errors. *Psychotherapy (Chicago), 53*(3), 342–346.

Lilienfeld, S. O., & Latzmann R. D. (2018). Personality disorders: Current scientific status and ongoing controversies. In J. N. Butcher (Ed.-in-chief), *APA handbook of psychopathology* (Vol. 1, Ch. 23). Washington, DC: APA.

Lilienfeld, S. O., Watts, A. L., & Smith, S. F. (2015). Successful psychopathy: A scientific status report. *Current Directions in Psychological Science, 24,* 298–303.

Lim, A., Hoek, H. W., Deen, M. L., Blom, J. D., & GROUP Investigators. (2016). Prevalence and classification of hallucinations in multiple sensory modalities in schizophrenia spectrum disorders. *Schizophrenia Research, 176,* 493–499.

Lincoln, T. M., & Peters, E. (2018, January 16). A systematic review and discussion of symptom-specific cognitive behavioural approaches to delusions and hallucinations. *Schizophrenia Research.* [Epub ahead of print]

Lindau, S. T., Schumm, L. P., Lamann, E. O., Levinson, W., O'Muircheartaigh, C. A., & Waite, L. J. (2007). A study of sexuality and health among older adults in the United States. *New England Journal of Medicine, 357,* 762–774.

Lindblom, J., Vänskä, M., Flykt, M., Tolvanen, A., Tiitinen, A., Tulppala, M., & Punamäki, R. L. (2017). From early family systems to internalizing symptoms: The role of emotion regulation and peer relations. *Journal of Family Psychology, 31*(3), 316–326.

Lindenberg, K., Halasy, K., Szász-Janocha, C., & Wartberg, L. (2018). A phenotype classification of internet use disorder in a large-scale high-school study. *International Journal of Environmental Research and Public Health, 15*(4).

Lindenmayer, J. P., & Khan, A. (2012). Psychopathology. In J.A. Lieberman, T. S. Stroup, & D. O. Perkins (Eds.), *Essentials of schizophrenia* (pp. 11–54). Arlington, VA: American Psychiatric Publishing.

Lindqvist, E. K., Sigurjonsson, H., Möllermark, C., Rinder, J., Farnebo, F., & Lundgren, T. K. (2017). Quality of life improves early after gender reassignment surgery in transgender women. *European Journal of Plastic Surgery, 40*(3), 223–226.

Lindsley, C. W. (2017). Chronic traumatic encephalopathy (CTE): A brief historical overview and recent focus on NFL players. *ACS Chemical Neuroscience, 8*(8), 1629–1631.

Linehan, M. M., Korslund, K. E., Harned, M. S., Gallop, R. J., Lungu, A., Neacsiu, A. D., . . . Murray-Gregory, A. M. (2015). Dialectical behavior therapy for high suicide risk in individuals with borderline personality disorder: A randomized clinical trial and component analysis. *JAMA Psychiatry, 72*(5), 475–482.

Linehan, M. M., Cochran, B. N., & Kehrer, C. A. (2001). Dialectical behavior therapy for borderline personality disorder. In D. H. Barlow (Ed.), *Clinical handbook of psychological disorders* (3rd ed., pp. 470–522). New York: Guilford Press.

Linehan, M. M., Dimeff, L. A., Reynolds, S. K., Comtois, K. A., Welch, S. S., Heagerty, P., & Kivlahan, D. R. (2002). Dialectical behavior therapy versus comprehensive validation therapy plus 12-step for the treatment of opioid dependent women meeting criteria for borderline personality disorder. *Drug and Alcohol Dependence, 67*(1), 13–26.

Lines, L. M., & Wiener, J. M. (2014, February). *Racial and ethnic disparities in Alzheimer's disease: A literature review.* Research Triangle Park, NC: RTI International. Retrieved from https//aspe.hhs.gov.

Ling, H. (2018). Untangling the tauopathies: Current concepts of tau pathology and neurodegeneration. *Parkinsonism & Related Disorders.* [Manuscript in press]

Linszen, M. M. J., van Zanten, G. A., Teunisse, R. J., Brouwer, R. M., Scheltens, P., & Sommer, I. E. (2018). Auditory hallucinations in adults with hearing impairment: A large prevalence study. *Psychological Medicine*, 1–8.

Lippy, C., & DeGue, S. (2016). Exploring alcohol policy approaches to prevent sexual violence perpetration. *Trauma, Violence, & Abuse, 17*(1), 26–42.

Littlefield, A. K., & Sher, J. K. (2010). The multiple, distinct ways that personality contributes to alcohol use disorders. *Social and Personality Psychology Compass, 4*(9), 767–782.

Liu, A. (2007). *Gaining: The truth about life after eating disorders.* New York: Warner Books.

Liu, R. T., Kleiman, E. M., Nestor, B. A., & Cheek, S. M. (2015). The hopelessness theory of depression: A quarter century in review. *Clinical Psychology, 22*(4), 345–365.

Liu, T., Zhong, S., Wang, B., Liao, X., Lai, S., & Jia, Y. (2019). Similar profiles of cognitive domain deficits between medication-naïve patients with bipolar II depression and those with major depressive disorder. *Journal of Affective Disorders, 243,* 55–61.

Liu, W., Fang, F., Zhang, C., & Storch, E. A. (2017). Cognitive behavioral therapy practices in the treatment of obsessive-compulsive disorder in China. *Annals of Translational Medicine, 5*(1), 8.

Liu, Y., Yu, X., Yang, B., Zhang, F., Zou, W., Na, A., . . . Yin, G. (2017). Rumination mediates the relationship between overgeneral autobiographical memory and depression in patients with major depressive disorder. *BMC Psychiatry, 17*(1), 103.

Livesley, W. J. (2017). *Integrated modular treatment for borderline personality disorder: A practical guide to combining effective treatment methods.* New York: Cambridge University Press.

Lloyd, J., Lloyd, H., Fitzpatrick, R., & Peters, M. (2017). Treatment outcomes in schizophrenia: Qualitative study of the views of family carers. *BMC Psychiatry, 17*(1), 266.

Loewenstein, R. J. (2018, May 18). Dissociative amnesia: Epidemiology, pathogenesis, clinical manifestations, course, and diagnosis. *UpToDate.* Retrieved from http://www.uptodate.com.

Loftus, E. F. (2017). Eavesdropping on memory. *Annual Review of Psychology, 68,* 1–18.

Loftus, E. F., & Greenspan, R. L. (2017). If I'm certain, is it true? Accuracy and confidence in eyewitness memory. *Psychological Science in the Public Interest, 18*(1), 1–2.

Loftus, E. F. (1993). The reality of repressed memories. *American Psychologist, 48,* 518–537.

Loftus, E. F. (2001). Imagining the past. *Psychologist, 14*(11), 584–587.

Loftus, E. F. (2003). Make-believe memories. *American Psychologist, 58*(11), 867–873.

Logrip, M. L., Walker, J. R., Ayanwuyi, L. O., Sabino, V., Ciccocioppo, R., Koob, G. F., & Zorrilla, E. P. (2018). Evaluation of alcohol preference and drinking in msP rats bearing a *Crhr1* promoter polymorphism. *Frontiers in Psychiatry, 9,* 28.

Lohani, S., Poplawsky, A. J., Kim, S. G., & Moghaddam, B. (2017). Unexpected global impact of VTA dopamine neuron activation as measured by opto-fMRI. *Molecular Psychiatry, 22*(4), 585–594.

Loharikar, A., Suragh, T. A., MacDonald, N. E., Balakrishnan, M. R., Benes, O., Lamprianou, S., . . . McNeil, M. M. (2018). Anxiety-related adverse events following immunization (AEFI): A systematic review of published clusters of illness. *Vaccine, 36*(2), 299–305.

Lombardo, P. A. (2017). A child's right to be well born: Venereal disease and the eugenic marriage laws, 1913–1935. *Perspectives in Biology and Medicine, 60*(2), 211–232.

Longpré, N., Guay, J. P., & Knight, R. A. (2017, October 1). MTC Sadism Scale: Toward a dimensional assessment of severe sexual sadism with behavioral markers. *Assessment.*

Longpré, N., Guay, J. P., Knight, R. A., & Benbouriche, M. (2018). Sadistic offender or sexual sadism? Taxometric evidence for a dimensional structure of sexual sadism. *Archives of Sexual Behavior, 47*(2), 403–416.

Loomer, H. P., Saunders, J. C., & Kline, N. S. (1957). A clinical and pharmacodynamic evaluation of iproniazid as a psychic energizer. *America Psychiatric Association Research Report, 8,* 129.

Lopes, B., & Yu, Y. (2017). Who do you troll and why: An investigation into the relationship between the Dark Triad personalities and online trolling behaviours towards popular and less popular Facebook profiles. *Computers in Human Behavior, 77,* 69–76.

López, S. R., & Guarnaccia, P. J. (2000). Cultural psychopathology: Uncovering the social world of mental illness. *Annual Review of Psychology, 51,* 571–598.

López, S. R., & Guarnaccia, P. J. (2005). Cultural dimensions of psychopathology: The social world's impact on mental illness. In B. A. Winstead & J. E. Maddux, *Psychopathology: Foundations for a contemporary understanding* (pp. 19–37). Mahwah, NJ: Lawrence Erlbaum.

LoPiccolo, J. (1991). Post-modern sex therapy for erectile failure. In R. C. Rosen & S. R. Leiblum (Eds.), *Erectile failure: Diagnosis and treatment.* New York: Guilford Press.

LoPiccolo, J. (2002). Postmodern sex therapy. In F. W. Kaslow (Ed.), *Comprehensive handbook of psychotherapy: Integrative/eclectic* (Vol. 4, pp. 411–435). New York: Wiley.

LoPiccolo, J. (2004). Sexual disorders affecting men. In L. J. Haas (Ed.), *Handbook of primary care psychology* (pp. 485–494). New York: Oxford University Press.

Lorand, S. (1968). Dynamics and therapy of depressive states. In W. Gaylin (Ed.), *The meaning of despair.* New York: Jason Aronson.

Lovaas, O. I. (1987). Behavioral treatment and normal educational/intellectual functioning in young autistic children. *Journal of Consulting and Clinical Psychology, 55,* 3–9.

Lovaas, O. I. (2003). *Teaching individuals with developmental delays: Basic intervention techniques.* Austin, TX: Pro-Ed.

Lovejoy, M. (2001). Disturbances in the social body: Differences in body image and eating problems among African-American and white women. *Gender and Society, 15*(2), 239–261.

Löwe, B., & Gerloff, C. (2018, April 19). Functional somatic symptoms across cultures: Perceptual and health care issues. *Psychosomatic Medicine.* [Epub ahead of print]

Lowes, R. (2016, December 29). Assisted death: Physician support continues to grow. *Medscape.*

Luber, B. M., Davis, S., Bernhardt, E., Neacsiu, A., Kwapil, L., Lisanby, S. H., & Strauman, T. J. (2017). Using neuroimaging to individualize TMS treatment for depression: Toward a new paradigm for imaging-guided intervention. *Neuroimage, 148,* 1–7.

Lublin, N. (2014, February 4). Cited in L. Kaufman, In texting era, crisis hotlines put help at youths' fingertips. *New York Times.*

Luborsky, L. (1973). Forgetting and remembering (momentary forgetting) during psychotherapy. In M. Mayman (Ed.), *Psychoanalytic research and psychological issues* (Monograph 30). New York: International Universities Press.

Luborsky, L. B., Barrett, M. S., Antonuccio, D. O., Shoenberger, D., & Stricker, G. (2006). What else materially influences what is represented and published as evidence? In J. C. Norcross, L. E. Beutler, & R. F. Levant (Eds.), *Evidence-based practices in mental health: Debate and dialogue on the fundamental questions* (pp. 257–298). Washington, DC: American Psychological Association.

Luborsky, L., Rosenthal, R., Diguer, L., Andrusyna, T. P., Berman, J. S., Levitt, J. T., . . . Krause, E. D. (2002). The dodo bird verdict is alive and well—mostly. *Clinical Psychology: Science and Practice, 9*(1), 2–12.

Luborsky, L., Singer, B., & Luborsky, L. (1975). Comparative studies of psychotherapies. *Biological Psychiatry, 32,* 995–1008.

Lucas, L. (2016, September 28). Changing the way police respond to mental illness. *CNN.*

Luders, E., Sánchez, F. J., Tosun, D., Shattuck, D. W., Gaser, C., Vilain, E., & Toga, A. W. (2012). Increased cortical thickness in male-to-female transsexualism. *Journal of Behavioral and Brain Science, 2*(3), 357–362.

Ludwig, A. M. (1995). *The price of greatness: Resolving the creativity and madness controversy.* New York: Guilford Press.

Luftman, K., Aydelotte, J., Rix, K., Ali, S., Houck, K., Coopwood T. B., . . . Davis, M. (2017). PTSD in those who care for the injured. *Injury, 48*(2), 293–296.

Lundberg, U. (2011). Neuroendocrine measures. In R. J. Contrada & A. Baum (Eds.), *The handbook of stress science: Biology, psychology, and health* (pp. 531–542). New York: Springer Publishing.

Luo, S., Zhu, Y., Xu, Y., & Kong, Q. (2017). The oxytocinergic system modulates sadistic context-dependent empathy in humans. *Scientific Reports, 7*(1), 12463.

Lusk, J., Brenner, L. A., Betthauser, L. M., Terrio, H., Scher, A. I., Schwab, K., & Poczwardowski, A. (2015). A qualitative study of potential suicide risk factors among Operation Iraqi Freedom/Operation Enduring Freedom soldiers returning to the Continental United States (CONUS). *Journal of Clinical Psychology, 71*(9), 843–855.

Lyness, J. M. (2016, September 13). Unipolar depression in adults: Assessment and diagnosis. *UpToDate*. Retrieved from https://uptodate.com.

Lyons, L. (2015). *Using hypnosis with children: Creating and delivering effective interventions.* New York: Norton.

Ma, J., Batterham, P. J., Calear, A. L., & Han, J. (2016). A systematic review of the predictions of the Interpersonal-Psychological Theory of Suicide behavior. *Clinical Psychology Review, 46,* 34–45.

MacIntosh, H. B., Fletcher, K., & Collin-Vézina, D. (2016) "As time went on, I just forgot about it": Thematic analysis of spontaneous disclosures of recovered memories of childhood sexual abuse. *Journal of Child Sexual Abuse, 25*(1), 56–72.

MacIsaac, T. (2014, January 30). Life beyond Earth: Space aliens live quietly among us, say some scientists and officials. *Epoch Times*. Retrieved from http://www.theepochtimes.com.

MacLaren, V. V. (2001). A qualitative review of the Guilty Knowledge Test. *Journal of Applied Psychology, 86*(4), 674–683.

MacNeill, L. P., & Best, L. A. (2015). Perceived current and ideal body size in female undergraduates. *Eating Behaviors, 18,* 71–75.

Mader, J. (2017, March 1). How teacher training hinders special-needs students. *The Atlantic.*

Madigan, S., Ly, A., Rash, C. L., Van Ouytsel, J., & Temple, J. R. (2018). Prevalence of multiple forms of sexting behavior among youth: A systematic review and meta-analysis. *JAMA Pediatrics, 172*(4), 327–335.

Magny, E., Le Petitcorps, H., Pociumban, M., Bouksani-Kacher, Z., Pautas, E., Belmin, J., . . . Lafuente-Lafuente, C. (2018). Predisposing and precipitating factors for delirium in community-dwelling older adults admitted to hospital with this condition: A prospective case series. *PLoS ONE, 13*(2), e0193034.

Mahboubi, S., Salimi, Y., Jorjoran Shushtari, Z., Rafiey, H., & Sajjadi, H. (2017, December 15). Sibling cigarette smoking and peer network influences on substance use potential among adolescents. A population-based study. *International Journal of Adolescent Medicine and Health*. [Epub ahead of print]

Mahoney, A., Karatzias, T., & Hutton, P. (2019). A systematic review and meta-analysis of group treatments for adults with symptoms associated with complex post-traumatic stress disorder. *Journal of Affective Disorders, 243,* 305–321.

Mahtani, K., Spencer, E. A., Brassey, J., & Heneghan, C. (2018). Catalogue of bias: Observer bias. *BMJ Evidence-Based Medicine, 23*(1), 23–24.

Maier, S. F., & Seligman, M. E. (2016). Learned helplessness at fifty: Insights from neuroscience. *Psychological Review, 123*(4), 349–367.

Mainwaring, D. (2017, May 25). More people are getting "sex change" surgeries than ever before . . . but it's not what you think. *LifeSite News.*

Majumder, A., & Sanyal, D. (2016). Outcome and preferences in female-to-male subjects with gender dysphoria: Experience from Eastern India. *Indian Journal of Endocrinology and Metabolism, 20*(3), 3308–3311.

Majumder, A., & Sanyal, D. (2017). Outcome and preferences in male-to-female subjects with gender dysphoria: Experience from Eastern India. *Indian Journal of Endocrinology and Metabolism, 21*(1), 21–25.

Mäkinen, M., Lindberg, N., Komulainen, E., Puukko-Viertomies, L. R., Aalberg, V., & Marttunen, M. (2015). Psychological well-being in adolescents with excess weight. *Nordic Journal of Psychiatry, 69*(5), 354–363.

Mäkinen, M., Marttunen, M., Komulainen, E., Terevnikov, V., Puukko-Birtyomird, L-R., Aalberg, V., & Lindberg, N. (2015). Development of self-image and its components during a one-year follow-up in non-referred adolescents with excess and normal weight. *Child and Adolescent Psychiatry and Mental Health, 9,* 5.

Mäkinen, M., Puukko-Viertomies, L-R., Lindberg, N., Siirnes, M. A., & Aalberg, V. (2012). Body dissatisfaction and body mass in girls and boys transitioning from early to mid-adolescence: Additional role of self-esteem and eating habits. *BMC Psychiatry, 12,* 35.

Makovac, E., Meeten, F., Watson, D. R., Herman, A., Garfinkel, S. N., Critchley, H. D., & Ottaviani, C. (2016). Alterations in amygdala-prefrontal functional connectivity account for excessive worry and autonomic dysregulation in generalized anxiety disorder. *Biological Psychiatry, 80,* 786–795.

Makwana, B., Lee, Y., Parkin, S., & Farmer, L. (2018). Selfie-esteem: The relationship between body dissatisfaction and social media in adolescent and young women. *The Inquisitive Mind.* Retrieved from http://www.in-mind.org/article/selfie-esteem-the-relationship-between-body-dissatisfaction-and-social-media-in-adolescent.

Malhi, G. S., Tanious, M., Das, P., Coulston, C. M., & Berk, M. (2013). Potential mechanisms of action of lithium in bipolar disorder. Current understanding. *CNS Drugs, 27*(2), 135–153.

Malki, S., & Einat, T. (2017, May 24). To include or not to include—This is the question: Attitudes of inclusive teachers toward the inclusion of pupils with intellectual disabilities in elementary schools. *Education, Citizenship and Social Justice.*

Maller, R. G., & Reiss, S. (1992). Anxiety sensitivity in 1984 and panic attacks in 1987. *Journal of Anxiety Disorders, 6*(3), 241–247.

Maloney, J., & Chaudhuri, S. (2017, April 23). Against all odds, the U.S. tobacco industry is rolling in money. *The Wall Street Journal.*

Mandal, A. (2014). Hallucination types. *News-Medical*. Retrieved from http://www.news-medical.net/health/hallucination-types.aspx.

Mandolesi, L., Polverino, A., Montuori, S., Foti, F., Ferraioli, G., Sorrentino, P., & Sorrentino, G. (2018). Effects of physical exercise on cognitive functioning and wellbeing: Biological and psychological benefits. *Frontiers in Psychology, 9,* 509.

Manfredi, C., Caselli, G., Rovetto, F., Rebecchi, D., Ruggiero, G. M., Sassaroli, S., & Spada, M. M. (2011). Temperament and parental styles as predictors of ruminative brooding and worry. *Personality and Individual Differences, 50*(2), 186–191.

Mann, J. J., & Currier, D. (2007). Neurobiology of suicidal behavior. In R. Tatarelli, M. Pompili, & P. Girardi (Eds.), *Suicide in psychiatric disorders.* New York: Nova Science Publishers.

Mann, M. (2009). The secrets behind the ten happiest jobs. *Excelle.* Retrieved from http://www.excelle.monster.com/benefits/articles/4033.

Manschreck, T. (2017, September 29). Delusional disorder. *UpToDate.* Retrieved from http://www.uptodate.com.

Maples-Keller, J. L., Price, M., Rauch, S., Gerardi, M., & Rothbaum, B. O. (2017). Investigating relationships between PTSD symptom clusters within virtual reality exposure therapy for OEF/OIF Veterans, *Behavior Therapy, 48*(2), 147–155.

Marchand, W. R. (2014). Neural mechanisms of mindfulness and meditation: Evidence from neuroimaging studies. *World Journal of Radiology, 6*(7), 471–479.

Marcoux, L., Michon, P., Lemelin, S., Voisin, J. A., Vachon-Presseau, E., & Jackson, P. L. (2014). Feeling but not caring: Empathic alteration in narcissistic men with high psychopathic traits. *Psychiatry Research, 224*(3), 341–348.

Marden, J. R., Walter, S., Kaufman, J. S., & Glymour, M. M. (2016). African ancestry, social factors, and hypertension among non-Hispanic blacks in the health and retirement study. *Biodemography and Social Biology, 62*(1), 19–35.

Marder, S., & Davis, M. (2017, August 6). Clinical manifestations, differential diagnosis, and initial management of psychosis in adults. *UpToDate.* Retrieved from http://www.uptodate.com.

Margo, J. L. (1985). Anorexia nervosa in adolescents. *British Journal of Medical Psychology, 58*(2), 193–195.

Maris, R. W. (2001). Suicide. In H. S. Friedman (Ed.), *Specialty articles from the encyclopedia of mental health.* San Diego: Academic Press.

MarketWatch. (2014). Packaging for an aging population. *MarketWatch* press release, July 10, 2014.

Markovitz, P. (2018). Pharmacotherapy. In W. J. Livesley & R. Larstone (Eds.), *Handbook of personality disorders: Theory, research, and treatment* (2nd ed., Ch. 35). New York: Guilford Press.

Marks, I. M. (1977). Phobias and obsessions: Clinical phenomena in search of a laboratory model. In J. Maser and M. Seligman (Eds.), *Psychopathology: Experimental models.* San Francisco: Freeman.

Marks, I. M. (1987). *Fears, phobias and rituals: Panic, anxiety and their disorders.* New York: Oxford University Press.

Marmar, C. R., Schlenger, W., Henn-Haase, C., Qian, M., Purchia, E., Li, M., . . . Kulka, R. A. (2015). Course of posttraumatic stress disorder 40 years after the Vietnam War: Findings from the National Vietnam Veterans Longitudinal Study. *JAMA Psychiatry, 72*(9), 875–881.

Marques, F. de A., Legal, E-J., & Hofelmann, D. A. (2012). Body dissatisfaction and common mental disorders in adolescents. *Revista Paulista de Pediatria, 30*(4), 553–561.

Mars, B., Heron, J., Biddle, L., Donovan, J. L., Holley, R., Piper, M., . . . Gunnell, D. (2015). Exposure to, and searching for, information about suicide and self-harm on the Internet: Prevalence and predictors in a population-based cohort of young adults. *Journal of Affective Disorders, 185,* 239–245.

Marshall, W. L., & Marshall, L. E. (2015). Psychological treatment of the paraphilias: A review and an appraisal of effectiveness. *Current Psychiatry Reports, 17,* 47.

Marshall, W. L., & Marshall, L. E. (2016). The treatment of adult male sexual offenders. In D. P. Boer, *The Wiley handbook on the theories, assessment and treatment of sexual offending* (Vol. 3, Chap. 1). Hoboken, NJ: Wiley-Blackwell.

Marshall, W. L., Marshall, L. E., Serran, G. A., & O'Brien, M. D. (2011). *Rehabilitating sexual offenders: A strength-based approach.* Washington, DC: American Psychological Association.

Marshall, W. L., Serran, G. A., Marshall, L. E., & O'Brien, M. D. (2008). Sexual deviation. In M. Hersen & J. Rosqvist (Eds.), *Handbook of psychological assessment, case conceptualization and treatment, Vol. 1: Adults.* Hoboken, NJ: John Wiley & Sons.

Marshall, T., Jones, D. P. H., Ramchandani, P. G., Stein, A., & Bass, C. (2007). Intergenerational transmission of health benefits in somatoform disorders. *British Journal of Psychiatry, 191*(4), 449–450.

Marsiglia, F. F., & Smith, S. J. (2010). An exploration of ethnicity and race in the etiology of substance use: A health disparities approach. In L. Scheier (Ed.), *Handbook of drug use etiology: Theory, methods, and empirical findings* (pp. 289–304). Washington, DC: American Psychological Association.

Marston, W. M. (1917). Systolic blood pressure changes in deception. *Journal of Experimental Psychology, 2,* 117–163.

Martell, C. R., Dimidjian, S., & Herman-Dunn, R. (2010). *Behavioral activation for depression: A clinician's guide.* New York: Guilford Press.

Martell, C. R., Dimidjian, S., & Herman-Dunn, R. (2013). *Behavioral activation for depression: A clinician's guide.* New York: Guilford Press.

Martin, D. M., Gálvez, V., & Loo, C. K. (2015). Predicting retrograde autobiographical memory changes following electroconvulsive therapy: Relationships between individual, treatment, and early clinical factors. *The International Journal of Neuropsychopharmacology* 1–8. [Advance publication]

Martin, F., & Oliver, T. (2018, February 23). Behavioral activation for children and adolescents: A systematic review of progress and promise. *European Child & Adolescent Psychiatry.* [Epub ahead of print]

Martin, L., Kidd, M., & Seedat, S. (2019). The effects of childhood maltreatment and anxiety proneness on neuropsychological test performance in non-clinical older adolescents. *Journal of Affective Disorders, 243,* 133–144.

Martin, R. J. (2018, January 12). Complementary, alternative, and integrative therapies for asthma. *UpToDate.* Retrieved from http://www.uptodate.com.

Martin, R. J., & Chaney, B. H. (2018, September 5). Exploration of the relationship between concussions and depression symptoms, anxiety symptoms, and hazardous drinking among a sample of college students. *Journal of Dual Diagnosis.* [Epub ahead of print]

Martin, S. A., Atlantis, E., Lange, K., Taylor, A. W., O'Loughlin, P., Wittert, G. A., and members of the Florey Adelaide Male Ageing Study (FAMAS). (2014). Predictors of sexual dysfunction incidence and remission in men. *Journal of Sexual Medicine, 11,* 1136–1147.

Martin, S. F., & Levine, S. B. (2018, July 17). Fetishistic disorder. *UpToDate.* Retrieved from http://www.uptodate.com.

Martino, F., Spada, M. M., Menchetti, M., Lo Sterzo, E., Sanza, M., Tedesco, P., . . . Berardi, D. (2017, February 14). Substance-related and addictive disorders as mediators between borderline personality disorder and aggressive behavior. *Clinical Psychologist.* [Epub ahead of print]

Martino, M., Magioncalda, P., Yu, H., Li, X., Wang, Q., Meng, Y., . . . Li, T. (2018). Abnormal resting-state connectivity in a substantia nigra-related striato-thalamo-cortical network in a large sample of first-episode drug-naïve patients with schizophrenia. *Schizophrenia Bulletin, 44*(2), 419–431.

Martins, M. V., Peterson, B. D., Almeida, V., Mesquita-Guimarães, J., & Costa, M. E. (2014). Dyadic dynamics of perceived social support in couples facing infertility. *Human Reproduction* (Oxford, England), *29*(1), 83–89.

Martire, L.M., Hemphill, R.C., Zhaoyang, R., Stephens, M.A.P., Franks, M.M., & Stanford, A.M. (2018). Daily marital tension and symptom severity in older adults with diabetes or osteoarthritis. *Annals of Behavioral Medicine, 52*(10), 842–853.

Mary, L., Piton, A., Schaefer, E., Mattioli, F., Nourisson, E., Feger, C., . . . Giurgea, I. (2018, April 26). Disease-causing variants in *TCF4* are a frequent cause of intellectual disability: Lessons from large-scale sequencing approaches in diagnosis. *European Journal of Human Genetics.* [Epub ahead of print]

Mash, E. J., & Wolfe, D. A. (2015). *Abnormal Child Psychology* (6th ed). New York: Wadsworth.

Mash, E. J., & Wolfe, D. A. (2018). *Abnormal Child Psychology* (7th ed). Boston, MA: Cengage Learning.

Maslow, A. H. (1970). *Motivation and personality* (2nd ed.). New York: Harper & Row.

Massau, C., Kärgel, C., Weiß, S., Walter, M., Ponseti, J., Hc Krueger, T., . . . Schiffer, B. (2017). Neural correlates of moral judgment in pedophilia. *Social Cognitive and Affective Neuroscience, 12*(9), 1490–1499.

Massau, C., Tenbergen, G., Kärgel, C., Weiß, S., Gerwinn, H., Pohl, A., . . . Schiffer, B. (2017). Executive functioning in pedophilia and child sexual offending. *Journal of the International Neuropsychological Society, 23*(6), 460–470.

Masters, W. H., & Johnson, V. E. (1966). *Human sexual response.* Boston: Little, Brown.

Masters, W. H., & Johnson, V. E. (1970). *Human sexual inadequacy.* Boston: Little, Brown.

Mataix-Cols, D., & de la Cruz, L. F. (2017, November 14). Hoarding disorder in adults: Epidemiology, pathogenesis, clinical manifestations, course, assessment, and diagnosis. *UpToDate.* Retrieved from http://www.uptodate.com.

Mather, M. (2016). *Fact sheet: Aging in the United States.* Washington, DC: PRB.

Mather, M., Jacobsen, L. A., & Pollard, K. M. (2015, December). Aging in the United States. Washington, DC: PRB.

Mathes, B. M., Oglesby, M. E., Short, N. A., Portero, A. K., Raines, A. M., & Schmidt, N. B. (2017). An examination of the role of intolerance of distress and uncertainty in hoarding symptoms. *Comprehensive Psychiatry, 72,* 121–129.

Mathew, J., & McGrath, J. (2002). Readability of consent forms in schizophrenia research. *Australian & New Zealand Journal of Psychiatry, 36*(4), 564–565.

Matsumoto, D., & Juang, L. (2016). *Culture and psychology* (6th ed.). Stamford, CT: Wadsworth Publishing.

Matthys, W., & Lochman, J. E. (2017). *Oppositional defiant disorder and conduct disorder in childhood* (2nd ed.). New York: Wiley.

Mattingly, G. W., Wilson, J., & Rostain, A. L. (2017). A clinician's guide to ADHD treatment options. *Postgraduate Medicine, 129*(7), 657–666.

Mayberg, H. S., Lozano, A. M., Voon, V., McNeely, H. E., Seminowicz, D., Hamani, C., . . . Kennedy, S. H. (2005). Deep brain stimulation for treatment-resistant depression. *Neuron, 45,* 651–660.

Mayhew, A. J., Pigeyre, M., Couturier, J., & Meyre, D. (2018). An evolutionary genetic perspective of eating disorders. *Neuroendocrinology, 106*(3), 292–306.

Mayo, D., Corey, S., Kelly, L. H., Yohannes, S., Youngquist, A. L., Stuart, B. K., . . . Loewy, R. L. (2017). The role of trauma and stressful life events among individuals at clinical high risk for psychosis: A review. *Frontiers in Psychiatry, 8,* 55.

Mayo, C., & George, V. (2014). Eating disorder risk and body dissatisfaction based on muscularity and body fat in male university students. *Journal of American College Health, 62*(6), 407–415.

Mazulla, S. L., & LiVecchi, P. (2018). *Ethics for counselors: Integrating counseling and psychology standards.* New York: Springer Publishing.

Mazza, M., Mariano, M., Peretti, S., Masedu, F., Pino, M. C., & Valenti, M. (2017). The role of theory of mind on social information processing in children with autism spectrum disorders: A mediation analysis. *Journal of Autism and Developmental Disorders, 47,* 1369–1379.

Mazzilli, R., Angeletti, G., Olana, S., Delfino, M., Zamponi, V., Rapinesi, C., . . . Mazzilli, F. (2018). Erectile dysfunction in patients taking psychotropic drugs and treated with phosphodiesterase-5 inhibitors. *Archivio Italiano di Urologia e Andrologia, 90*(1), 44–48.

McAfee. (2014). *Study reveals majority of adults share intimate details via unsecured digital devices.* Santa Clara, CA: Author.

McCabe, R. E. (2018, January 25). Specific phobia in adults: Epidemiology, clinical manifestations, course and diagnosis. *UpToDate*. Retrieved from http://www.uptodate.com.

McCabe, R. E., & Swinson, R. (2017, December 14). Cognitive-behavioral therapies for specific phobia in adults. *UpToDate*. Retrieved from http://www.uptodate.com.

McCarthy, B., & Wald, L. M. (2017). A psychobiosocial approach to sex therapy. In Z. D. Peterson (Ed.), *The Wiley-Blackwell handbook of sex therapy* (Chap. 12, pp. 190–202). Hoboken, NJ: Wiley-Blackwell.

McClintock, A. S., Perlman, M. R., McCarrick, S. M., Anderson, T., & Himawan, L. (2017). Enhancing psychotherapy process with common factors feedback: A randomized, clinical trial. *Journal of Counseling Psychology, 64*(3), 247–260.

McClintock, C. H., Lau, E., & Miller, L. (2016). Phenotypic dimensions of spirituality: Implications for mental health in China, India, and the United States. *Frontiers in Psychology, 7,* 1600.

McCloskey, M. S., & Drabick, D. A. G. (2018). Understanding the development and management of antisocial disorders in adolescents. In J. N. Butcher & J. M. Hooley (Eds.), *APA handbook of psychopathology. Vol. 2. Psychopathology in children and adolescents* (Ch. 18). Washington, DC: American Psychological Association.

McCloud, A., Barnaby, B., Omu, N., Drummond, C., & Aboud, A. (2004). Relationship between alcohol use disorders and suicidality in a psychiatric population: In-patient prevalence study. *British Journal of Psychiatry, 184*(5), 439–445.

McConnaughey, J. (2014, May 17). Alcohol use may worsen in nursing homes. *ABC News*. Retrieved from ABC News website: http://abcnews.go.com/health.

McConnell, D., Feldman, M., & Aunos, M. (2017). Parents and parenting with intellectual disabilities: An expanding field of research. *Journal of Applied Research in Intellectual Disabilities, 30,* 419–422.

McCord, D. M. (2018, January 23). *Assessment using the MMPI-2-RF (Psychological Assessment Series).* Washington, DC: American Psychological Association.

McCrady, B. S., Owens, M. D., Borders, A. Z., & Brovko, J. M. (2014). Psychosocial approaches to alcohol use disorders since 1940: A review. *Journal of Studies on Alcohol and Drugs, 75*(Suppl. 75), 68–78.

McCrady, B. S. (2014). Alcohol use disorders. In D. H. Barlow, *Clinical handbook of psychological disorders* (5th ed., Chap. 13). New York: Guilford Press.

McDade, E. M., & Petersen, R. C. (2018, February 5). Mild cognitive impairment: Prognosis and treatment. *UpToDate*. Retrieved from http://www.uptodate.com.

McDaniel, B. T., & Drouin, M. (2015). Sexting among married couples: Who is doing it, and are they more satisfied? *Cyberpsychology, Behavior, and Social Networking, 18*(11), 826–834.

McDermott, B. E., Leamon, M. H., Feldman, M. D., & Scott, C. L. (2012). Factitious disorder and malingering. In J. A. Bourgeois, U. Parthasarathi, & A. Hategan (Eds.), *Psychiatry review and Canadian certification exam preparation guide* (pp. 267–276). Arlington, VA: American Psychiatric Publishing.

McEachin, J. J., Smith, T., & Lovaas, O. I. (1993). Long-term outcome for children with autism who received early intensive behavioral treatment. *American Journal of Mental Retardation, 97*(4), 359–372.

McEvoy, K., Osborne, L. M., Nanavati, J., & Payne, J. L. (2017). Reproductive affective disorders: A review of the genetic evidence for premenstrual dysphoric disorder and postpartum depression. *Current Psychiatry Reports, 19*(12), 94.

McFeeters, D., Boyda, D., & O'Neill, S. (2015). Patterns of stressful life events: Distinguishing suicide ideators from suicide attempters. *Journal of Affective Disorders, 175,* 192–198.

McGauran, D. (2016, January 7). The 10 most common fear motivators. *Active Beat*.

McGoldrick, M., Loonan, R., & Wohlsifer, D. (2007). Sexuality and culture. In S. R. Leiblum (Ed.), *Principles and practice of sex therapy* (4th ed., pp. 416–441). New York: Guilford Press.

McGuffin, P., Katz, R., Watkins, S., & Rutherford, J. (1996). A hospital-based twin register of the heritability of DSM-IV unipolar depression. *Archives of General Psychiatry, 53,* 129–136.

McGuire, P. K., Silbersweig, D. A., Wright, I., Murray, R. M., Frackowiak, R. S., & Frith, C. D. (1996). The neural correlates of inner speech and auditory verbal imagery in schizophrenia: Relationship to auditory verbal hallucinations. *British Journal of Psychiatry, 169*(2), 148–159.

McGuire, T. G. (2016). Achieving mental health care parity might require changes in payments and competition. *Health Affairs,* 35(6), 1029–1377.

McGurk, S. R., Mueser, K. T., Mischel, R., Adams, R., Harvey, P. D., McClure, M. M., . . . Siever, L. J. (2013). Vocational functioning in schizotypal and paranoid personality disorders. *Psychiatry Research, 210*(2), 498–504.

McIlvaine, R. (2011, January 25). 3-D software becoming safeware to returning soldiers with PTSD. *Army News Service*.

McIngvale, E., Rufino, K., Ehlers, M., & Hart, J. (2017, March 1). An in-depth look at the scrupulosity dimension of obsessive-compulsive disorder. *Journal of Spirituality in Mental Health.* [Published online]

McKeown, S., & Taylor, L. K. (2018, April 16). Perceived peer and school norm effects on youth antisocial and prosocial behaviours through intergroup contact in Northern Ireland. *British Journal of Social Psychology.* [Epub ahead of print]

McKetin, R. (2018, March 8). Methamphetamine psychosis: Insights from the past. *Addiction*. [Epub ahead of print]

Mckew, M. (2017). Study finds risk of suicide higher for female nurses. *Nursing Standard, 31*(30), 10.

McKinney, C., & Caetano, R. (2016). Substance use and race and ethnicity. In K. J. Sher (Ed.), *Oxford handbook of substance use and substance use disorders* (Vol. 1, Chap. 14, pp. 483–525). New York: Oxford University Press.

McLay, R. N., Daylo, A. A., & Hammer, P. S. (2006). No effect of lunar cycle on psychiatric admissions or emergency evaluations. *Military Medicine, 17*(12), 1239–1242.

McLean, D., Thara, R., John, S., Barrett, R., Loa, P., McGrath, J., & Mowry, B. (2014). DSM-IV "Criterion A" schizophrenia symptoms across ethnically different populations: Evidence for differing psychotic symptom content or structural organization? *Culture, Medicine and Psychiatry, 38*(3), 408–426.

McMahon, C. G., Jannini, E., Waldinger, M., & Rowland, D. (2013). Standard operating procedures in the disorders of orgasm and ejaculation. *Journal of Sexual Medicine, 1,* 204–229.

McMahon, R. J., & Frick, P. J. (2005). Evidence-based assessment of conduct problems in children and adolescents. *Journal of Clinical Child and Adolescent Psychology, 34,* 477–505.

McMahon, R. J., & Frick, P. J. (2007). Conduct and oppositional disorders. In E. J. Mash & R. A. Barkley (Eds.), *Assessment of childhood disorders* (4th ed., pp. 132–183) New York: Guilford Press.

McNally, R. J. (2016). The legacy of Seligman's "Phobias and Preparedness" (1971). *Behavior Therapy, 47*(5), 585–594.

McNally, R. J. (2017) False memories in the laboratory and in life: Commentary on Brewin and Andrews, 2016. *Wiley Online Library*. Retrieved from http://wileyonlinelibrary.com.

McNally, R. J. (2004, April 1). Psychological debriefing does not prevent posttraumatic stress disorder. *Psychiatric Times*, p. 71.

McNally, R. J., & Geraerts, E. (2009). A new solution to the recovered memory debate. *Perspectives on Psychological Science, 4*(2), 126–134.

McNally, R. J., Clancy, S. A., Barrett, H. M., & Parker, H. A. (2005). Reality monitoring in adults reporting repressed, recovered, or continuous memories of childhood sexual abuse. *Journal of Abnormal Psychology, 114*(1), 147–152.

McNeil, E. B. (1967). *The quiet furies*. Englewood Cliffs, NJ: Prentice Hall.

McNicol, M. L., & Thorsteinsson, E. B. (2017). Internet addiction, psychological distress, and coping responses among adolescents and adults. *Cyberpsychology, Behavior, and Social Networking, 20*(5), 296–304.

McPherson, M., Smith-Lovin, L., & Brashears, M. (2006). Social isolation in America: Changes in core discussion networks over two decades. *American Sociological Review, 71,* 353–375.

McRee, J. (2017). How perceptions of mental illness impact EAP utilization. *Benefits Quarterly, 33*(1), 37–42.

Meana, M. (2012). *Sexual dysfunction in women. Advances in psychotherapy—Evidence-based practice*. Cambridge, MA: Hogrefe Publishing.

Meana, M., Fertel, E., & Maykut, C. (2017). Treating genital pain associated with sexual intercourse. In Z. D. Peterson (Ed.), *The Wiley-Blackwell handbook of sex therapy* (Chap. 7, pp. 98–114). Hoboken, NJ: Wiley-Blackwell.

Meaney, R., Hasking, P., & Reupert, A. (2016.) Prevalence of borderline personality disorder in university samples: Systematic review, meta-analysis and meta-regression. *PLoS ONE, 11*(5): e0155439.

Meersand, P. (2011). Psychological testing and the analytically trained child psychologist. *Psychoanalytic Psychology, 28*(1), 117–131.

Meganck, R. (2017). Beyond the impasse—Reflections on dissociative identity disorder from a Freudian–Lacanian perspective. *Frontiers in Psychology, 8*, 789.

Mehler, P. (2016, August 2). Anorexia nervosa in adults and adolescents: Medical complications and their management. *UpToDate*. Retrieved from www.uptodate.com.

Mehler, P. (2017, April 29). Anorexia nervosa in adults and adolescents: The refeeding syndrome. *UpToDate*. Retrieved from www.uptodate.com.

Mehler, P. (2017, April 5). Anorexia nervosa in adults: Evaluation for medical complications and criteria for hospitalization to manage these complications. *UpToDate*. Retrieved from www.uptodate.com.

Mehta, D., Newport, D. J., Frishman, G., Kraus, L., Rex-Haffner, M., Ritchie, J. C., . . . Binder, E. B. (2014). Early predictive biomarkers for postpartum depression point to a role for estrogen receptor signaling. *Psychological Medicine*, 1–14.

Meichenbaum, D. (2017). *The evolution of CBT: A personal and professional journey with Don Meichenbaum*. New York: Routledge.

Meichenbaum, D. H. (1975). A self-instructional approach to stress management: A proposal for stress inoculation training. In I. Sarason & C. D. Spielberger (Eds.), *Stress and anxiety* (Vol. 2). New York: Wiley.

Meichenbaum, D. H. (1993). Stress inoculation training: A 20-year update. In P. M. Lehrer & R. L. Woolfolk (Eds.), *Principles and practice of stress management* (2nd ed.). New York: Guilford Press.

Meijer, E. H., & Verschuere, B. (2010). The polygraph and the detection of deception. *Journal of Forensic Psychology Practice, 10*(4), 325–338.

Meinhard, N., Kessing, L. V., & Vinberg, M. (2014). The role of estrogen in bipolar disorder, a review. *Nordic Journal of Psychiatry, 68*(2), 81–87.

Melechi, A. (2016, September 29). Bodies of evidence: Psychologists and the CIA torture scandal. *Times Higher Education*.

Meloy, J. R., & Yakeley, J. (2010). Psychodynamic treatment of antisocial personality disorder. In J. F. Clarkin, P. Fonagy, & G. O. Gabbard (Eds.), *Psychodynamic psychotherapy for personality disorders: A clinical handbook* (pp. 311–336). Arlington, VA: American Psychiatric Publishing.

Melton, G. B., Petrila, J., Poythress, N. G., & Slobogin, C. (2007). *Psychological evaluations for the courts: A handbook for mental health professionals and lawyers* (3rd ed.). New York: Guilford Press.

Melton, G. B., Petrila, J., Poythress, N. G., Slobogin, C., Otto, R. K., Mossman, D., & Condie, L. O. (2017). *Psychological evaluations for the courts: A handbook for mental health professionals and lawyers* (4th ed.). New York: Guilford Press.

Melville, J. (1978). *Phobias and obsessions*. New York: Penguin.

Menary, K. R., Corbin, W. R., & Chassin, L. (2017). Associations between early internalizing symptoms and speed of transition through stages of alcohol involvement. *Development and Psychopathology, 29*(4), 1455–1467.

Mendelson, T., & Eaton, W. W. (2018). Recent advances in the prevention of mental disorders. *Social Psychiatry and Psychiatric Epidemiology, 53*(4), 325–339.

Meng, L., Chen, Y., Xu, X., Chen, T., Lui, S., Huang, X., Sweeney, J. A., Li, K., & Gong, Q. (2018). *The neurobiology of brain recovery from traumatic stress: A longitudinal DTI study. Journal of Affective Disorders, 225*, 577–584.

Meng, X., Fleury, M. J., Xiang, Y. T., Li, M., & D'Arcy, C. (2018, January 18). Resilience and protective factors among people with a history of child maltreatment: A systematic review. *Social Psychiatry and Psychiatric Epidemiology*. [Epub ahead of print]

Menon, J., & Kandasamy, A. (2018). Relapse prevention. *Indian Journal of Psychiatry, 60*(Suppl. 4), S473–S478.

Merenda, R. R. (2008). The posttraumatic and sociocognitive etiologies of dissociative identity disorder: A survey of clinical psychologists. *Dissertation Abstracts International: Section B: The Sciences and Engineering, 68*(8-B), 55–84.

Mergl, R., Allgaier, A. K., Hautzinger, M., Coyne, J. C., Hegerl, U., & Henkel, V. (2018). One-year follow-up of a randomized controlled trial of sertraline and cognitive behavior group therapy in depressed primary care patients (MIND study). *Journal of Affective Disorders, 230*, 15–21.

Merikangas, K. R., He, J., Rapoport, J., Vitiello, B., & Olfson, M. (2013). Medication use in U.S. youth with mental disorders. *JAMA Pediatrics, 167*(2), 141–148.

Merlo, P., Devita, M., Mandelli, A., Rusconi, M. L., Taddeucci, R., Terzi, A., . . . Mondini, S. (2018). Alzheimer Café: An approach focused on Alzheimer's patients but with remarkable values on the quality of life of their caregivers. *Aging Clinical and Experimental Research, 30*(7), 767–774.

Merten, E. C., Cwik, J. C., Margraf, J., & Schneider, S. (2017). Overdiagnosis of mental disorders in children and adolescents (in developed countries). *Child and Adolescent Psychiatry and Mental Health, 11*, 5.

Mesri, B., Niles, A. N., Pittig, A., LeBeau, R. T., Haik, E., & Craske, M. G. (2017). Public speaking avoidance as a treatment moderator for social anxiety disorder. *Journal of Behavior Therapy and Experimental Psychiatry, 55*, 66–72.

Mewton, L., & Andrews, G. (2016). Cognitive behavioral therapy for suicidal behaviors: Improving patient outcomes. *Psychology Research and Behavior Management, 9*, 21–29.

Mewton, L., Visontay, E., Chapman, C., Newton, N., Slade, T., Kay-Lambkin, F., & Teesson, M. (2018, March 26). Universal prevention of alcohol and drug use: An overview of reviews in an Australian context. *Drug and Alcohol Review*. [Epub ahead of print]

Meyer, A., Danielson, C. K., Danzig, A. P., Bhatia, V., Black, S. R., Bromet, E., . . . Klein, D. N. (2017). Neural biomarker and early temperament predict increased internalizing symptoms after a natural disaster. *Journal of the American Academy of Child and Adolescent Psychiatry, 56*(5), 410–416.

Meyer, J. D., Koltyn, K. F., Stegner, A. J., Kim, J. S., & Cook, D. B. (2016). Influence of exercise intensity for improving depressed mood in depression: A dose-response study. *Behavior Therapy, 47*(4), 527–537.

Mez, J., Daneshvar, D. H., Kiernan, P. T., Abdolmohammadi, B., Alvarez, V. E., Huber, B. R., . . . McKee, A. C. (2017). Clinicopathological evaluation of chronic traumatic encephalopathy in players of American football. *JAMA, 318*(4), 360–370.

MHA (Mental Health America). (2008). *Americans reveal top stressors, how they cope*. Alexandria, VA: Author.

MHA (Mental Health America). (2017). *Housing*. Alexandria, VA: MHA.

MHA (Mental Health America). (2017). *Position Statement 55: Confining sexual predators in the mental health system*. Alexandria, VA: MHA.

MHA (Mental Health America). (2017). *Self-injury (cutting, self-harm or self-mutilation)*. Alexandria, VA: MHA.

MHA (Mental Health America). (2018). *Depression in women*. Alexandria, VA: Author.

MHA (Mental Health America). (2018). *Position Statement 55: Confining sexual predators in the mental health system*. Alexandria, VA: MHA.

MHA (Mental Health America). (2018). *Position Statement 57: In support of the insanity defense*. Alexandria, VA: MHA.

Miano, A., Grosselli, L., Roepke, S., & Dziobek, I. (2017). Emotional dysregulation in borderline personality disorder and its influence on communication behavior and feelings in romantic relationships. *Behaviour Research and Therapy, 95*, 148–157.

Michal, M. (2011). Review of depersonalization: A new look at a neglected syndrome. *Journal of Psychosomatic Research, 70*(2), 199.

Middleman, A. B., & Olson, K. A. (2017, March 16). Confidentiality in adolescent health care. *UpToDate*. Retrieved from http://www.uptodate.com.

Miguel, E. M., Chou, T., Golik, A., Cornacchio, D., Sanchez, A. L., DeSerisy, M., & Comer, J. S. (2017). Examining the scope and patterns of deliberate self-injurious cutting content in popular social media. *Depression and Anxiety, 34*, 786–793.

Mihura, J. L., Meyer, G. J., Dumitrascu, N., & Bombel, G. (2016). On conducting construct validity meta-analyses for the Rorschach: A reply to Tibon Czopp and Zeligman (2016). *Journal of Personality Assessment, 98*(4), 343–350.

Mike, A., King, H., Oltmanns, T. F., & Jackson, J. J. (2017, December 22). Obsessive, compulsive, and conscientious? The relationship between OCPD and personality traits. *Journal of Personality*. [Epub ahead of print]

Miller, A. (2015). The purpose of a clinical interview in a psychological assessment. *Chron.com*. Retrieved from http://work.chron.com/purpose-clinical-interview-psychological.

Miller, A. (2017). Dissociation in families experiencing intimate partner violence. *Journal of Trauma & Dissociation*. February 16, 1–14. [Epub ahead of print]

Miller, A. (2017, July 5). Examples of why you want to be a counselor. *Career Trend*. Retrieved from https://careertrend.com.

Miller, C. M., & Burch, A. D. S. (2017, March 15). Before suicide by hanging, girl pleaded in vain for mom's acceptance. *Miami Herald*. Retrieved from http://www.miamiherald.com.

Miller, D., & Hanson, A. (2016, October 16). *Committed: The battle over involuntary psychiatric care*. Baltimore, MD: JHU Press.

Miller, J. D., Lynam, D. R., Hyatt, C. S., & Campbell, W. K. (2017). Controversies in narcissism. *Annual Review of Clinical Psychology, 13,* 291–315.

Miller, K. (2016, January 4). The shocking results of Yahoo Health's body-positivity survey. *Yahoo.com*.

Miller, K. L., Dove, M. K., & Miller, S. M. (2007). *A counselor's guide to child sexual abuse: Prevention, reporting and treatment strategies*. Paper based on a program presented at the Association for Counselor Education and Supervision Conference, Columbus, OH.

Miller, N. E. (1948). Studies of fear as an acquirable drive: I. Fear as motivation and fear-reduction as reinforcement in the learning of new responses. *Journal of Experimental Psychology, 38,* 89–101.

Miller, P. M., Ingham, J. G., & Davidson, S. (1976). Life events, symptoms, and social support. *Journal of Psychiatric Research, 20*(6), 514–522.

Miller, T. (2013, August 12). Too many selfies on Facebook can damage relationships: Study. *New York Daily News*.

Millichap, J. G. (2010). *Attention deficit hyperactivity disorder handbook: A physician's guide to ADHD* (2nd ed.). New York: Springer Science + Business Media.

Millon, T. (1969). *Modern psychopathology: A biosocial approach to maladaptive learning and functioning*. Philadelphia: Saunders.

Millon, T. (2011). *Disorders of personality: Introducing a DSM/ICD spectrum from normal to abnormal* (3rd ed.). Hoboken, NJ: John Wiley Sons.

Mills, C. P., Hill, H. M., & Johnson, J. A. D. (2018). Mediated effects of coping on mental health outcomes of African American women exposed to physical and psychological abuse. *Violence Against Women, 24*(2), 186–206.

Minkkinen, J., Oksanen, A., Kaakinen, M., Keipi, T., & Räsänen, P. (2017). Victimization and exposure to pro-self-harm and pro-suicide websites: A cross-national study. *Suicide and Life-Threatening Behavior, 47*(1), 14–26.

Minuchin, S. (1974). *Families and family therapy*. Cambridge, MA: Harvard University Press.

Minuchin, S. (1987). My many voices. In J. K. Zeig (Ed.), *The evolution of psychotherapy*. New York: Brunner/Mazel.

Minuchin, S. (2007). Jay Haley: My teacher. *Family Process, 46*(3), 413–414.

Minuchin, S., Zeig, J., & Johnson, S. (2017). *A dialogue with Salvador Minuchin*. Presented at the 2017 Psychotherapy Networker Symposium in Washington, D.C.

Minuchin, S., Lee, W-Y., & Simon, G. M. (2006). *Mastering family therapy: Journeys of growth and transformation* (2nd ed.). Hoboken, NJ: John Wiley & Sons.

MIP (Mental Illness Policy). (2017). 250,000 mentally ill are homeless. 150,000 seriously mentally ill are homeless. New York: MIP. Retrieved from https://www.mentalillnesspolicy.org.

MIP (Mental Illness Policy). (2017). *Victimization of people with mental illness* (two articles). New York: MIP. Retrieved from https://www.mentalillnesspolicy.org.

Miranda, J., Siddique, J., Belin, T. R., & Kohn-Wood, L. P. (2005). Depression prevalence in disadvantaged young black women: African and Caribbean immigrants compared to U.S.-born African Americans. *Social Psychiatry and Psychiatric Epidemiology 40*(4), 253–258.

Miret, M., Nuevo, R., Morant, C., Sainz-Cortón, E., Jiménez-Arriero, M. A., López-Ibor, J. J., . . . Ayuso-Mateos, J. L. (2011). The role of suicide risk in the decision for psychiatric hospitalization after a suicide attempt. *Crisis: Journal of Crisis Intervention and Suicide Prevention, 32*(2), 65–73.

Mitchell, A. J., Rao, S., & Vaze, A. (2011). Can general practitioners identify people with distress and mild depression? A meta-analysis of clinical accuracy. *Journal of Affective Disorders, 130*(1-2), 26–36.

Mitchell, J. E. (2018, February 20). Bulimia nervosa in adults: Cognitive-behavioral therapy (CBT). *UpToDate*. Retrieved from http://www.uptodate.com.

Mitchell, J. E., & Zunker, C. (2017, November 16). Bulimia nervosa and binge eating disorder in adults: Medical complications and their management. *UpToDate*. Retrieved from http://www.uptodate.com.

Mitchell, J. T. (1983). When disaster strikes. . . the critical incident stress debriefing process. *Journal of Emergency Medical Services, 8,* 36–39.

Mitchell, J. T. (2003). Crisis intervention & CISM: A research summary. Retrieved from http://www.icisf.org/articles/cism_research_summary.pdf.

Mitchell, S. I. (2018, January 23). Palliative care of patients with advanced dementia. *UpToDate*. Retrieved from http://www.uptodate.com.

Moberg, K. (2018). The role of managed care professionals and pharmacists in combating opioid abuse. *American Journal of Managed Care, 24*(Suppl. 10), S215–S223.

Moeller, S. J., & Paulus, M. P. (2018). Toward biomarkers of the addicted human brain: Using neuroimaging to predict relapse and sustained abstinence in substance use disorder. *Progress in Neuro-Psychopharmacology and Biological Psychiatry, 80*(Pt. B), 143–154.

Moens, M. A., Weeland, J., Van der Giessen, D., Chhangur, R. R., & Overbeek. G. (2018, January 2). In the eye of the beholder? Parent-observer discrepancies in parenting and child disruptive behavior assessments. *Journal of Abnormal Child Psychology*. [Epub ahead of print]

Mohler, H., & Okada, T. (1977). Benzodiazepine receptor: Demonstration in the central nervous system. *Science, 198*(4319), 849–851.

Mohlman, J., Eldreth, D. A., Price, R. B., Staples, A. M., & Hanson, C. (2017). Prefrontal—limbic connectivity during worry in older adults with generalized anxiety disorder. *Aging & Mental Health, 21*(4), 426–438.

Moldavsky, D. (2004, June 1). Transcultural psychiatry for clinical practice. *Psychiatric Times, XXI*(7), p. 36.

Mongilio, H. (2017, October 17). Could brain scans determine guilt or innocence in court? *NOVA Next, PBS*.

Monteith, L. L., Bahraini, N. H., & Menefee, D. S. (2018). Perceived burdensomeness: Thwarted belongingness, and fearlessness about death: Associations with suicidal ideation among female veterans exposed to military sexual trauma. *Journal of Clinical Psychology*. [Manuscript in press]

Montejo, A-L., Perahia, D. G. S., Spann, M. E., Wang, F., Walker, D. J., Yang, C. R., & Detke, M. J. (2011). Sexual function during long-term duloxetine treatment in patients with recurrent major depressive disorder. *Journal of Sexual Medicine, 8*(3), 773–782.

Monteleone, A. M., Castellini, G., Volpe, U., Ricca, V., Lelli, L., Monteleone, P., & Maj, M. (2018). Neuroendocrinology and brain imaging of reward in eating disorders: A possible key to the treatment of anorexia nervosa and bulimia nervosa. *Progress in Neuro-Psychopharmacology and Biological Psychiatry, 80*(Pt. B), 132–142.

Montes, K. S., Witkiewitz, K., Andersson, C., Fossos-Wong, N., Pace, T., Berglund, M., & Marimer, M. E. (2017). Trajectories of positive alcohol expectancies and drinking: An examination of young adults in the U.S. and Sweden. *Addictive Behaviors, 73,* 74–80.

Moore, G., & Pfaff, J. A. (2017, May 23). Assessment and emergency management of the acutely agitated or violent adult. *UpToDate*. Retrieved from http://www.uptodate.com.

More, J. Y., Bruna, B. A., Lobos, P. E., Galaz, J. L., Figueroa, P. L., Namias, S., . . . Adasme, T. (2018, March 1). Calcium release mediated by redox-sensitive RyR2 channels has a central role in hippocampal structural plasticity and spatial memory. *Antioxidants & Redox Signaling*. [Epub ahead of print]

Moreno, C. (2018). Towards understanding and acting on risk factors for developmental psychopathology. *European Child & Adolescent Psychiatry, 27*(1), 1–3.

Moreno, M. A. (2018). What parents need to know about sexting. *JAMA Pediatrics, 172*(4), 400.

Moreno, C., Laje, G., Blanco, C., Jiang, H., Schmidt, A. B., & Olfson, M. (2007). National trends in the outpatient diagnosis and treatment of bipolar disorder in youth. *Archives of General Psychiatry, 64*(9), 1032–1039.

Morgan, C. D., & Murray, H. A. (1935). A method of investigating fantasies: The Thematic Apperception Test. *Archives of Neurological Psychiatry, 34,* 289–306.

Morgan, J. P. (2017, December 27). Clinical manifestations, diagnosis, and management of the cardiovascular complications of cocaine abuse.

UpToDate. Retrieved from http://www.uptodate.com.

Morgan, P. L., & Farkas, G. (2016). Evidence and implications of racial and ethnic disparities in emotional and behavioral disorders identification and treatment. *Behavioral Disorders, 41,* 122–131.

Morgan, T. A., & Zimmerman, M. (2018). Epidemiology of personality disorders. In W. J. Livesley & R. Larstone (Eds.), *Handbook of personality disorders: Theory, research, and treatment* (2nd ed., Ch. 10). New York: Guilford Press.

Morgentaler, A., Polzer, P., Althof, S., Bolyakov, A., Donatucci, C., Ni, X., . . . Basaria, S. (2017). Delayed ejaculation and associated complaints: Relationship to ejaculation times and serum testosterone levels. *Journal of Sexual Medicine, 14*(9), 1116–1124.

Morkem, R., Williamson, T., Patten, S., Queenan, J. A., Wong, S. T., Manca, D., & Barber, D. (2017). Trends in antidepressant prescribing to children and adolescents in Canadian primary care: A time-series analysis. *Pharmacoepidemiology and Drug Safety, 26*(9), 1093–1099.

Moroni, F., Procacci, M., Pellecchina, G., Semerari, A., Nicolo, G., Carcione, A., . . . Colle, L. (2016). Mindreading dysfunction in avoidant personality disorder compared with other personality disorders. *Journal of Nervous and Mental Disease, 204*(10), 752–757.

Morris, A. (2017, March 6). NH struggling to solve psychiatric problem. *U.S. News & World Report.*

Morris, M. C., Kouros, C. D., Hellman, N., Rao, U., & Garber, J. (2014). Two prospective studies of changes in stress generation across depressive episodes in adolescents and emerging adults. *Development and Psychopathology, 26,* 1385–1400.

Morrison, A. P., Law, H., Carter, L., Sellers, R., Emsley, R., Pyle, M., . . . Haddad, P. M. (2018). Antipsychotic drugs versus cognitive behavioural therapy versus a combination of both in people with psychosis: A randomized controlled pilot and feasibility study. *Lancet Psychiatry, 5*(5), 411–423.

Morton, J. (2017). Interidentity amnesias in dissociative identity disorder. *Cognitive Neuropsychiatry, 22*(4), 315–330.

Morton, J. (2018). Autonoesis and dissociative identity disorder. *Behavioral and Brain Sciences, 41,* e23.

Mosconi, L., Murray, J., Davies, M., Williams, S., Pirraglia, E., Spector, N., . . . de Leon, M. J. (2014). Nutrient intake and brain biomarkers of Alzheimer's disease in at-risk cognitively normal individuals: A cross-sectional neuroimaging pilot study. *BMJ Open, 4*(6), E004850.

Mosconi, L., Walters, M., Sterling, J., Quinn, C., McHugh, P., Andrews, R. E., . . . Convit, A. (2018). Lifestyle and vascular risk effects on MRI-based biomarkers of Alzheimer's disease: A cross-sectional study of middle-aged adults from the broader New York City area. *BMJ Open, 8*(3), e019362.

Mosconi, L., Berti, V., Glodzik, L., Pupi, A., De Santi, S., & de Leon, M. J. (2010). Pre-clinical detection of Alzheimer's disease using FDG-PET, with or without amyloid imaging. *Journal of Alzheimer's Disease, 20*(3), 843–854.

Mosconi, L., De Santi, S., Li, J., Tsui, W. H., Li, Y., Boppana, M., . . . de Leon, M. J. (2008). Hippocampal hypometabolism predicts cognitive decline from normal aging. *Neurobiology of Aging, 29*(5), 676–692.

Moscovitch, D. A., Rowa, K., Paulitzki, J. R., Ierullo, M. D., Chiang, B., Antony, M. M., & McCabe, R. E. (2013). Self-portrayal concerns and their relation to safety behaviors and negative affect in social anxiety disorder. *Behaviour Research and Therapy, 51*(8), 476–486.

Moshier, S. J., & Otto, M. W. (2017). Behavioral activation treatment for major depression: A randomized trial of the efficacy of augmentation with cognitive control training. *Journal of Affective Disorders, 210,* 265–268.

Moultrie, J. K., & Engel, R. R. (2017). Empirical correlates for the Minnesota Multiphasic Personality Inventory-2-Restructured form in a German inpatient sample. *Psychological Assessment, 29*(10), 1273–1289.

Mowrer, O. H. (1939). A stimulus-response analysis of anxiety and its role as a reinforcing agent. *Psychological Review, 46,* 553–566.

Mowrer, O. H. (1947). On the dual nature of learning: A reinterpretation of "conditioning" and "problem-solving." *Harvard Education Review, 17,* 102–148.

Mowrer, O. H., & Mowrer, W. M. (1938). Enuresis: A method for its study and treatment. *American Journal of Orthopsychiatry, 8,* 436–459.

Mu, S. H., Xu, M., Duan, J. X., Zhang, J., & Tan, L. H. (2017). Localizing age-related changes in brain structure using voxel-based morphometry. *Neural Plasticity, 2017,* 6303512.

Mueller, S. C., De Cuypere, G., & T'Sjoen, G. (2017). Transgender research in the 21st century: A selective critical review from a neurocognitive perspective. *American Journal of Psychiatry, 174*(12), 1155–1162.

Muhle, R. A., Reed, H. E., Stratigos, K. A., & Veenstra-VanderWeele, J. (2018, March 28). The emerging clinical neuroscience in autism spectrum disorder: A review. *JAMA Psychiatry.* [Epub ahead of print]

Mukamal, K. J. (2018, January 29). Overview of the risks and benefits of alcohol consumption. *UpToDate*. Retrieved from http://www.uptodate.com.

Mulder, R. T. (2018). Cultural aspects of personality disorder. In W. J. Livesley & R. Larstone (Eds.), *Handbook of personality disorders: Theory, research, and treatment* (2nd ed., Ch. 5). New York: Guilford Press.

Müller, H. A., Benke, D., Ralvenius, W. T., Mu, L., Schibli, R., Zeilhofer, H. U., & Krämer, S. D. (2017). $GABA_A$ receptor subtypes in the mouse brain: Regional mapping and diazepam receptor occupancy by in vivo [^{18}F] flumazenil PET. *Neuroimage, 150,* 279–291.

Müller, N., Weidinger, E., Leitner, B., & Schwarz, M. J. (2015). The role of inflammation in schizophrenia. *Frontiers in Neuroscience, 9,* 372.

Mullin, A. S., Hilsenroth, M. J., Gold, J., & Farber, B. A. (2017). Changes in object relations over the course of psychodynamic psychotherapy. *Clinical Psychology & Psychotherapy, 24*(2), 501–511.

Mullins, N., Power, R. A., Fisher, H. L., Hanscombe, K. B., Euesden, J., Iniesta, R., . . . Lewis, C. M. (2016). Polygenic interactions with environmental adversity in the aetiology of major depressive disorder. *Psychological Medicine, 46*(4), 759–770.

Mundy, P. (2018). A review of joint attention and social-cognitive brain systems in typical development and autism spectrum disorder. *European Journal of Neuroscience, 47*(6), 497–514.

Munsey, C. (2010). The kids aren't all right. *Monitor on Psychology, 41*(1), 22–25.

Muntner, P., Adballa, M., Correa, A., Griswold, M., Hall, J. E., Jones, D. W., . . . Appel, L. J. (2017). Hypertension in blacks: Unanswered questions and future directions for the JHS (Jackson Heart Study). *Hypertension, 69*(5), 761–769.

Murad, M. H., Elamin, M. B., Garcia, M. Z., Mullan, R. J., Murad, A., Erwin, P. J., & Montori, V. M. (2010). Hormonal therapy and sex reassignment: A systematic review and meta-analysis of quality of life and psychosocial outcomes. *Clinical Endocrinology, 72*(2), 214.

Murdock, K. K. (2013). Texting while stressed: Implications for students' burnout, sleep, and well-being. *Psychology of Popular Media Culture, 2,* 207–221.

Muris, P., Merckelbach, H., Otgaar, H., & Meijer, E. (2017). The malevolent side of human nature: A meta-analysis and critical review of the literature on the Dark Triad (narcissism, Machiavellianism, and psychopathy). *Perspectives on Psychological Science, 12,* 183–204.

Murphy, W. D., & Page, I. J. (2006). Exhibitionism. In R. D. McAnulty & M. M. Burnette (Eds.), *Sex and sexuality, Vol. 3: Sexual deviation and sexual offenses.* Westport, CT: Praeger Publishers.

Murray, L. K., Nguyen, A., & Cohen, J. A. (2014). Child sexual abuse. *Child and Adolescent Psychiatric Clinics of North America, 23*(2), 321–337.

Murray-Close, D., Nelson, D. A., Ostrov, J. M., Casas, J. F., & Crick, N. R. (2016). Relational aggression: A developmental psychopathology perspective. In D. Cicchetti (Ed.), *Developmental psychopathology, Vol. 4: Risk, resilience, and intervention* (3rd ed.). New York: Wiley.

Musser, E. D., & Nigg, J. T. (2018). Emotion dysregulation across emotion systems in attention deficit/hyperactivity disorder. *Journal of Clinical Child and Adolescent Psychology.* [Manuscript in press]

Myers, C. E., Radell, M. L., Shind, C., Ebanks-Williams, Y., Beck, K. D., & Gilbertson, M. W. (2016). Beyond symptom self-report: Use of a computer "avatar" to assess post-traumatic stress disorder (PTSD) symptoms. *Stress, 19*(6), 593–598.

MyPlan.com. (2016). Top ten lists/Highest job satisfaction. Retrieved from www.myplan.com/careers/top_ten/highest-job-satisfaction.php.

Mysko, C. (2016, November 17). Interview. In C. Abate, Body shaming in an age of social media. *Healthline News.*

Nace, E. P. (2011). Alcohol. In R. J. Frances, S. I. Miller, & A. H. Mack (Eds.), *Clinical textbook of addictive disorders* (3rd ed., Chap. 5, pp. 73–90). New York: Guilford Press. [Paperback edition]

Nace, E. P. (2005). Alcohol. In R. J. Frances, A. H. Mack, & S. I. Miller (Eds.), *Clinical textbook of addictive disorders* (3rd ed., Chap. 5, pp. 75–104). New York: Guilford Press.

NAELA (National Academy of Elder Law Attorneys). (2014). Aging and special needs statistics. Retrieved from http://www.naela.org/public/about_NAELA/Media/.

NAELA (National Academy of Elder Law Attorneys). (2016). *Aging and special needs statistics.* Vienna, VA: NAELA.

Nahata, L., Chelvakumar, G., & Leibowitz, S. (2017). Gender-affirming pharmacological interventions for youth with gender dysphoria: When treatment guidelines are not enough. *Annals of Pharmacotherapy, 51,* 1023–1032.

Nair, G., Evans, A., Bear, R. E., Velakoulis, D., & Bittar, R. G. (2014). The anteromedial GPi as a new target for deep brain stimulation in obsessive compulsive disorder. *Journal of Clinical Neuroscience, 21*(5), 815–821.

NAMI (National Alliance on Mental Illness). (2016). *Mental health by the numbers.* Arlington, VA: NAMI.

NAMI (National Alliance on Mental Illness). (2017). *Mental health by the numbers.* Arlington, VA: NAMI. Retrieved from https://www.nami.org.

NAMI (National Alliance on Mental Illness). (2018). *Family members and caregivers.* Arlington, VA: NAMI. Retrieved from https://www.charitynavigator.org.

NAMI (National Alliance on Mental Illness). (2018). *Mental health by the numbers.* Arlington, VA: NAMI. Retrieved from https://www.nami.org.

NAMI (National Alliance on Mental Illness). (2018). *Crisis Intervention Team (CIT) Programs.* Arlington, VA: NAMI.

NAN (National Autism Network). (2017). *Autism facts and statistics.* Retrieved from http://nationalautismnetwork.com.

Naoi, M., Maruyama, W., & Shamoto-Nagai, M. (2018). Type A monoamine oxidase and serotonin are coordinately involved in depressive disorders: From neurotransmitter imbalance to impaired neurogenesis. *Journal of Neural Transmission (Vienna),* [Manuscript in press]

Narayanan, G., & Naaz, S. (2018). A transdiagnostic approach to interventions in addictive disorders: Third wave therapies and other current interventions. *Indian Journal of Psychiatry, 60*(Suppl. 4), S522–S528.

NARPA (National Association for Rights Protection and Advocacy). (2018). *The RDA's regulation of ECT (shock treatment): A beginner (or refresher) course.* Portland, ME: NARPA.

Nathan, D. (2011). *Sybil exposed: The extraordinary story behind the famous multiple personality case.* New York: Free Press.

National Center for PTSD. (2008). Appendix A. Case examples from Operation Iraqi Freedom. *Iraq War Clinician Guide.* Washington, DC: Department of Veterans Affairs.

Nauert, R. (2016, July 14). Suicide prevention hotlines can be improved. *Psych Central News.*

Nautiyal, K. M., Okuda, M., Hen, R., & Blanco, C. (2017). Gambling disorder: An integrative review of animal and human studies. *Annals of the New York Academy of Sciences, 1394*(1), 106–127.

Nayak, A., Sangoi, B., & Nachane, H. (2018, February 1). School refusal behavior in Indian children: Analysis of clinical profile, psychopathology and development of a best-fit risk assessment model. *Indian Journal of Pediatrics.* [Epub ahead of print]

NB (No Bullying). (2016, September 30). *How many kids get bullied a year.* (In Bullying Facts, Bullying Resources). Retrieved from https://nobullying.com.

NB (No Bullying). (2017, April 10). *Bullying statistics: The ultimate guide!* Retrieved from https://nobullying.com.

NBC (National Broadcasting Company). (2012, February 2). *Mystery teen illness grows in upstate New York. NBC Nightly News.*

NBPC (National Bullying Prevention Center). (2016, December 8). *Bullying statistics.* Retrieved from http://www.pacer.org/bullying/resources.

NCASA (National Center on Addiction and Substance Abuse at Columbia University). (2007, March). *Wasting the best and brightest: Substance abuse at America's colleges and universities.* Washington DC: Author.

NCBH (National Council for Behavioral Health). (2017, March 28). *The psychiatric shortage: Causes and solutions.* Washington, DC: Author.

NCBH (National Council for Behavoral Health). (2015, August 31). *Is the problem cultural incompetence or racism?* Washington, DC: Author.

NCCIH (National Center for Complementary and Integrative Health). (2016). Use of complementary health approaches in the U.S.: Most-used mind & body practices. *NCCIH.* Retrieved from https://nccih.nih.gov.

NCD (National Council on Disability). (2018). *Deinstitutionalization: Unfinished business.* Washington, DC: NCD.

NCES (National Center for Education Statistics). (2016). *Table 322.50. Bachelor's degrees conferred to females by postsecondary institutions, by race/ethnicity and field of study: 2012–13 and 2013–14.* Washington, DC: National Center for Education Statistics.

NCES (National Center for Education Statistics). (2016). *Table 322.40. Bachelor's degrees conferred to males by postsecondary institutions, by race/ethnicity and field of study: 2012–13 and 2013–14.* Washington, DC: National Center for Education Statistics.

NCHS (National Center for Health Statistics). (2014). *Health, United States, 2013, with special feature on prescription drugs.* Hyattsville, MD: NCHS.

NCHS (National Center for Health Statistics). (2014). *Older persons' health.* Hyattsville, MD: NCHS.

NCHS (National Center for Health Statistics). (2016). *Health, United States, 2016, with chartbook on long-term trends in health.* Hyattsville, MD: NCHS.

NCI (National Cancer Institute). (2017, November 2). *Depression (PDQ®)—Health Professional Version.* Retrieved from https://www.cancer.gov/about-cancer/coping/feelings/depression-hp-pdq.

NCPTSD (National Center for PTSD). (2016, July 17). Facts about PTSD. *PsychCentral.*

NCSL (National Conference of State Legislatures). (2018, March 28). *State medical marijuana laws.* Washington, DC: NCSL.

NCVS (National Crime Victimization Survey). (2014). *National Crime Victimization Survey, 2013.* Washington, DC: Bureau of Justice Statistics.

NCVS (National Crime Victimization Survey). (2014). *Rape trauma syndrome.* Washington, DC: Bureau of Justice Statistics.

NCVS (National Crime Victimization Survey). (2017). *Data collection.* Retrieved from http://bjs.ojp.usdoj.gov/index.

Neacsiu, A. D., & Linehan, M. M. (2014). Dialectical behavior therapy for borderline personality disorder. In D. H. Barlow (Ed.), *Clinical handbook of psychological disorders* (5th ed., pp. 394–461). New York: Guilford Press.

Neal, T. M. S. (2018, February 12). Forensic psychology and correctional psychology: Distinct but related subfields of psychological science and practice. *American Psychologist.* [Epub ahead of print]

NEDA (National Eating Disorders Association). (2018). *Statistics & research on eating disorders.* New York: NEDA.

NEDA (National Eating Disorders Association). (2018). Statistics & research on eating disorders. Retrieved from https://www.nationaleatingdisorders.org/statistics-research-eating-disorders.

Neikrug, A. B., & Ancoli-Israel, S. (2017, September 19). Sleep-wake disturbances and sleep disorders in patients with dementia. *UpToDate.* Retrieved from http://www.uptodate.com.

Nelson, L., & Odujebe, O. (2017, June 21). Cocaine: Acute intoxication. *UpToDate.* Retrieved from http://www.uptodate.com.

Netz, Y. (2017). Is the comparison between exercise and pharmacologic treatment of depression in the clinical practice guideline of the American College of Physicians evidence-based? *Frontiers in Pharmacology, 8,* 257.

Neumaier, F., Paterno, M., Alpdogan, S., Tevoufouet, E. E., Schneider, T., Hescheler, J., & Albanna, W. (2017). Surgical approaches in psychiatry: A survey of the world literature on psychosurgery. *World Neurosurgery, 97,* 603–634.

Neumark-Sztainer, D. R., Wall, M. M., Haines, J. I., Story, M. T., Sherwood, N. E., & van den Berg, P. A. (2007). Shared risk and protective factors for overweight and disordered eating in adolescents. *American Journal of Preventative Medicine, 33*(5), 359–369.

Newby, J. M., Smith, J., Mason, E., Mahoney, A. E. J., & Andrews, G. (2018). Internet-based cognitive behavioral therapy versus psychoeducation control for illness anxiety disorder and somatic symptom disorder: A randomized controlled trial. *Journal of Consulting and Clinical Psychology,* 86(1), 89–98.

Newman, B. M., Bauer, I. E., Soares, J. C., & Sheline, Y. I. (2017). Neural structure and organization of mood pathology. In R. J. DeRubeis & D. R. Strunk (Eds.), *The Oxford handbook of mood disorders* (Chap. 19). New York: Oxford University Press.

Newman, F. (2013, May 1). Determining what is normal behavior and what is not. *Psychology Today.*

Neziroglu, F., McKay, D., Todaro, J., & Yaryura-Tobias, J. A. (1996). Effect of cognitive behavior therapy on persons with body dysmorphic disorder and comorbid Axis II diagnoses. *Behavior Therapist, 27,* 67–77.

Neziroglu, F., Roberts, M., & Yaryura-Tobias, J. A. (2004). A behavioral model for body dysmorphic disorder. *Psychiatric Annals, 34*(12), 915–920.

NFER (National Foundation for Educational Research). (2010). Tellus4 national report (DCSF Research Report 218). Retrieved from http://www.nfer.ac.uk/publications/TEL01/.

Ng, Q. X., Yong, B. Z. J., Ho, C. Y. X., Lim, D. Y., & Yeo, W. S. (2018). Early life sexual abuse is associated with increased suicide attempts: An update meta-analysis. *Journal of Psychiatric Research, 99,* 129–141.

Ng, T. S., Lin, A. P., Koerte, I. K., Pasternak, O., Liao, H., Merugumala, S., . . . Shenton, M. E. (2014). Neuroimaging in repetitive brain trauma. *Alzheimer's Research and Therapy, 6*(1), 10.

NIAAA (National Institute of Alcohol Abuse and Alcoholism). (2018, January). NIAAA—Understanding alcohol's impact on health. Retrieved from http://pubs.niaaa.nih.gov/publications/impactsfactsheet/impactsfactsheet.htm.

NIAAA (National Institute on Alcohol Abuse and Alcoholism). (2017). *College drinking.* NIAAA. Retrieved from http://www.niaaa.nih.gov.

NIDA (National Institute on Drug Abuse). (2014). America's addiction to opioids: Heroin and prescription drug abuse. *NIDA.* (Retrieved from https://www.drugabuse.gov.

NIDA (National Institute on Drug Abuse). (2016). *Misuse of prescription drugs: Older adults.* Bethesda, MD: NIH.

NIDA (National Institute on Drug Abuse). (2018). *Club drugs.* Bethesda, MD: NIDA. Retrieved from https://www.drugabuse.gov/drugs-abuse/club-drugs.

Nigg, J. T. (2016). Attention and impulsivity. In D. Cicchetti (Ed.), *Developmental psychology, Vol. 3: Maladaptation and psychopathology* (3rd ed.). New York: Wiley.

Nigg, J. T. (2017). Annual research review: On the relations among self-regulation, self-control, executive functioning, effortful control, cognitive control, impulsivity, risk-taking, and inhibition for developmental psychopathology. *Journal of Child Psychology and Psychiatry, 58*(4), 361–383.

Nijinsky, V. (1936). *The diary of Vaslav Nijinsky.* New York: Simon & Schuster.

Nikolaus, S., Müller, H. W., & Hautzel, H. (2017). Different patterns of dopaminergic and serotonergic dysfunction in manic, depressive and euthymic phases of bipolar disorder. *Nuklearmedizin, 56*(5), 191–200.

Nimbi, F. M., Tripodi, F., Rossi, R., & Simonelli, C. (2018). Expanding the analysis of psychosocial factors of sexual desire in men. *Journal of Sexual Medicine, 15*(2), 230–244.

NIMH (National Institute of Mental Health). (2016). *Major depression with severe impairment among adolescents.* Bethesda, MD: Author.

NIMH (National Institute of Mental Health). (2017). *Agoraphobia among adults.* Bethesda, MD: Author.

NIMH (National Institute of Mental Health). (2017). *Any anxiety disorder among adults.* Bethesda, MD: Author.

NIMH (National Institute of Mental Health). (2017). *Any personality disorder.* Bethesda, MD: Author.

NIMH (National Institute of Mental Health). (2017). *Attention-deficit/hyperactivity disorder among adults.* Bethesda, MD: Author.

NIMH (National Institute of Mental Health). (2017). *Avoidant personality disorder.* Bethesda, MD: Author.

NIMH (National Institute of Mental Health). (2017). *Bipolar disorder among adults.* Bethesda, MD: Author.

NIMH (National Institute of Mental Health). (2017). *Eating disorders among adults–Anorexia nervosa.* Bethesda, MD: NIMH.

NIMH (National Institute of Mental Health). (2017). *Eating disorders among adults–Bulimia nervosa.* Bethesda, MD: NIMH.

NIMH (National Institute of Mental Health). (2017). *Generalized anxiety disorder among adults.* Bethesda, MD: Author.

NIMH (National Institute of Mental Health). (2017). *Panic disorder among adults.* Bethesda, MD: Author.

NIMH (National Institute of Mental Health). (2017). *Post-traumatic stress disorder among adults.* Bethesda, MD: Author.

NIMH (National Institute of Mental Health). (2017). *Schizophrenia.* Bethesda, MD: Author.

NIMH (National Institute of Mental Health). (2017). *Social phobia among adults.* Bethesda, MD: Author.

NIMH (National Institute of Mental Health). (2017). *Specific phobia among adults.* Bethesda, MD: Author.

NIMH (National Institute of Mental Health). (2017). *Use of mental health services and treatment among adults.* Bethesda, MD: Author.

NIMH (National Institute of Mental Health). (2017, November). *Major depression.* Bethesda, MD: Author.

NIMH (National Institute of Mental Health). (2017, November). *Social anxiety disorder.* Bethesda, MD: Author.

NIMH (National Institute of Mental Health). (2018). *Research domain criteria (RDoC).* Bethesda, MD: Author.

Ning, L., Guan, S., & Liu, J. (2017). Impact of personality and social support on posttraumatic stress disorder after traffic accidents. *Medicine (Baltimore), 96*(34), e7815.

Nishikawa, S., Fujisawa, T. X., Kojima, M., & Tomoda, A. (2018). Type and timing of negative life events are associated with adolescent depression. *Frontiers in Psychiatry, 9,* 41.

Nivard, M. G., Gage, S. H., Hottenga, J. J., van Beijsterveldt, C. E., Abdellaoui, A., Bartels, M., . . . Middeldorp, C. M. (2018). Genetic overlap between schizophrenia and developmental psychopathology: Longitudinal and multivariate polygenic risk predictions of common psychiatric traits during development. *Schizophrenia Bulletin.* [Manuscript in press]

NLM (National Library of Medicine). (2015). *Encopresis.* Retrieved from MedlinePlus website: https://www.nlm.nih.gov/medlineplus/ency/article/001570.htm.

NMHA (National Mental Health Association). (1999, June 5). Poll. *U.S. Newswire.*

Nobles, C. J., Valentine, S. E., Borba, C. P., Gerber, M. W., Shtasel, D. L., & Marques, L. (2016). Black-white disparities in the association between posttraumatic stress disorder and chronic illness. *Journal of Psychosomatic Research, 85,* 19–25.

Nobre, P. J. (2017). Treating men's erectile problems. In Z. D. Peterson (Ed.), *The Wiley-Blackwell handbook of sex therapy* (Chap. 4, pp. 40–56). Hoboken, NJ: Wiley-Blackwell.

Nock, M. K., Deming, C. A., Fullerton, C. S., Gilman, S. E., Goldenberg, M., Kessler, R. C., . . . Ursano, R. J. (2013). Suicide among soldiers: A review of psychosocial risk and protective factors. *Psychiatry: Interpersonal and Biological Processes, 76,* 97–125.

Nock, M. K., Dempsey, C. L., Aliaga, P. A., Brent, D. A., Heeringa, S. G., Kessler, R. C., . . . Benedek, D. (2017, May 15). Psychological autopsy study comparing suicide decedents, suicide ideators, and propensity score matched controls: Results from the study to assess risk and resilience in service members (Army STARRS). *Psychological Medicine, 47,* 2663–2674.

Nock, M. K., Millner, A. J., Joiner, T. E., Gutierrez, P. M., Han, G., Hwang, I., . . . Kessler, R. C. (2018). Risk factors for the transition from suicide ideation to suicide attempt: Results from the Army Study to Assess Risk and Resilience in Servicemembers (Army STARRS). *Journal of Abnormal Psychology, 127*(2), 139–149.

Nock, M. K., Green, J. G., Hwang, I., McLaughlin, K. A., Sampson, N. A., Zaslavsky, A. M., & Kessler, R. C. (2013). Prevalence, correlates, and treatment of lifetime suicidal behavior among adolescents: Results from the National Comorbidity Survey Replication Adolescent Supplement. *JAMA Psychiatry, 70*(3), 300–310.

Nock, M. K., Stein, M. B., Heeringa, S. G., Ursano, R. J., Colpe, L. J., Fullerton, C. S., . . . Kessler, R. C. (2014). Prevalence and correlates of suicidal behavior among soldiers: Results from the Army Study to Assess Risk and Resilience in Servicemembers (Army STARRS). *JAMA Psychiatry, 71*(5), 514–522.

Nock, N. L., Minnes, S., & Alberts, J. L. (2017). Neurobiology of substance use in adolescents and potential therapeutic effects of exercise for prevention and treatment of substance use disorders. *Birth Defects Research, 109*(20), 1711–1729.

Nolan, D., & Amico, C. (2016, February 23). How bad is the opioid epidemic? *Frontline.* Retrieved from http://www.pbs.org/WGBH/frontline.

Nolen-Hoeksema, S. (1990). *Sex differences in depression.* Stanford, CA: Stanford University Press.

Nolen-Hoeksema, S. (2002). Gender differences in depression. In I. H. Gotlib & C. L. Hammen (Eds.), *Handbook of depression* (pp. 492–509). New York: Guilford Press.

Nolen-Hoeksema, S. (2012). Emotion regulation and psychopathology: The role of gender. *Annual Review of Clinical Psychology, 8,* 161–187.

Noll-Hussong, M., Herberger, S., Grauer, M., Otti, A., & Gündel, H. (2013). Aspects of post-traumatic stress disorder after a traffic accident. *Versicherungsmedizin/Herausgegeben*

Von Verband Der Lebensversicherung-Unternehmen, 65(3), 132–135.

Nomi, J. S., Bolt, T. S., Ezie, C. E. C., Uddin, L. Q., & Heller, A. S. (2017). Moment-to-moment BOLD signal variability reflects regional changes in neural flexibility across the lifespan. *Journal of Neuroscience, 37*(22), 5539–5548.

Noonan, D. (2003, June 16). A healthy heart. *Newsweek, 141*(24), 48–52.

Noonan, S. (2014). Veterinary wellness: Mindfulness-based stress reduction. *Canadian Veterinary Journal, 55,* 134–135.

Norcross, J. C., & Beutler, L. E. (2019). Integrative psychotherapies. In D. Wedding & R. J. Corsini (Eds.), *Current psychotherapies* (11th ed., Ch. 14). Independence, KY: Cengage Publications.

Norcross, J. C., Hogan, T. P., Koocher, G. P., & Maggio, L. A. (2017). *Clinician's guide to evidence-based practices: Behavioral health and addictions* (2nd ed.). New York: Oxford University Press.

Norcross, J. C., & Beutler, L. E. (2014). Integrative psychotherapies. In D. Wedding & R. J. Corsini (Eds.), *Current psychotherapies* (10th ed., pp. 499–532). Independence, KY: Cengage Publications.

Norcross, J. C., & Farber, B. A. (2005). Choosing psychotherapy as a career: Beyond "I want to help people." *Journal of Clinical Psychology, 61*(8), 939–943.

Norcross, J. C., & Lambert, M. J. (2011). Psychotherapy relationships that work II. *Psychotherapy, 48*(1), 4–8.

Norcross, J. C., Karpiak, C. P., & Santoro, S. O. (2005). Clinical psychologists across the years: The division of clinical psychology from 1960 to 2003. *Journal of Clinical Psychology, 61*(12), 1467–1483.

Norman, G. R., Monteiro, S. D., Sherbino, J., Ilgen, J. S., Schmidt, H. G., & Mamede, S. (2017). The causes of errors in clinical reasoning: Cognitive biases, knowledge deficits, and dual process thinking. *Academic Medicine, 92*(1), 23–30.

Norman, R., Lecomte, T., Addington, D., & Anderson, E. (2017). Canadian treatment guidelines on psychosocial treatment of schizophrenia in adults. *Canadian Journal of Psychiatry, 62*(9), 617–623.

Norman, S. B., Haller, M., Kim, H. M., Allard, C. B., Porter, K. E., Stein, M. B., . . . Progress Team. (2018, February 16). Trauma related guilt cognitions partially mediate the relationship between PTSD symptom severity and functioning among returning combat veterans. *Journal of Psychiatric Research, 100,* 56–62.

Norton, A. (2011). Imagined smells can precede migraines. Retrieved from http://www.reuters.com/article/us-smells-migraines/imagined-smells-can-precede-migraines-idUSTRE79D4L120111014.

Nourse, R., Adamshick, P., & Stoltzfus, J. (2017). College binge drinking and its association with depression and anxiety: A prospective observational study. *East Asian Archives of Psychiatry, 24*(1), 18–25.

Novais, F., Araujo, A., & Godinho, P. (2015). Historical roots of histrionic personality disorder. *Frontiers in Psychology, 6,* 1463.

Nowak, D. E., & Aloe, A. M. (2014). The prevalence of pathological gambling among college students: A meta-analytic synthesis, 2005–2013. *Journal of Gambling Studies, 30*(4), 819–843.

NPD Group. (2008). Entertainment Trends Report. Cited by Mike Antonucci in *San Jose Mercury News,* April 3, 2008.

NPT (Network of Philanthropic Trust). (2017). *Charitable giving statistics.* Retrieved from https://www.nptrust.org/philanthropic-resources/charitable-giving-statistics/.

NSDUH (National Survey on Drug Use and Health). (2013). Results from the 2012 National Survey on Drug Use and Health: Mental health findings, NSDUH Series H-47, HHS Publication No. (SMA) 13-4805. Rockville, MD: Substance Abuse and Mental Health Services Administration.

NSDUH (National Survey on Drug Use and Health). (2016, September 8). *Results from the 2015 National Survey on Drug Use and Health: Detailed tables. Prevalence estimates, standard errors, P values, and sample sizes.* Rockville, MD: SAMHSA.

NSDUH (National Survey on Drug Use and Health). (2017). *Results from the 2016 National Survey on Drug Use and Health: Detailed tables.* Rockville, MD: Substance Abuse and Mental Health Services Administration.

NSOPW (National Sex Offender Public Website). (2018). Facts and statistics. Washington, DC: U.S. Department of Justice.

NSPCC (National Society for the Prevention of Cruelty to Children). (2013). Reported in *BBC News.* One in five children bullied online, says NSPCC survey (August 11, 2013).

Nugent, A. C., Bain, E. E., Carlson, P. J., Neumeister, A., Bonne, O., Carson, R. E., . . . Drevets, W. C. (2013). Reduced post-synaptic serotonin type 1A receptor binding in bipolar depression. *European Neuropsychopharmacology, 23*(8), 822–829.

NVSR (National Vital Statistics Reports). (2010, August 9). *Births: Final data for 2007. National vital statistics reports, 58(24).* Hyattsville, MD: National Center for Health Statistics.

NVSR (National Vital Statistics Reports). (2016, June 2). *Births: Preliminary data for 2015.* Volume *65*(3). Hyattsville, MD: National Center for Health Statistics.

NVSR (National Vital Statistics Reports). (2016, June 30). *Deaths: Final data for 2014. Volume 65*(4). Hyattsville, MD: National Center for Health Statistics.

Nyström, M. B., Stenling, A., Sjöström, E., Neely, G., Lindner, P., Hassmén, P., . . . Carlbring, P. (2017). Behavioral activation versus physical activity via the Internet: A randomized controlled trial. *Journal of Affective Disorders, 215,* 85–93.

O Ciardha, C., Gannon, T. A., & Ward, T. (2016). The cognitive distortions of child sexual abusers: Evaluating key theories. In D. P. Boer, *The Wiley handbook on the theories, assessment and treatment of sexual offending* (Vol. 1, Chap. 10, pp. 207–222). Hoboken, NJ: Wiley-Blackwell.

O'Brien, C. P. (2013). Cited in NPR Staff. With addiction, breaking a habit means resisting a reflex. *Weekend Edition Sunday.* Retrieved from http://www.npr.org/2013/10/20/238297311/with-addiction-breaking.

O'Brien, S. A. (2017, March 1). Facebook wants to get smarter about suicide prevention. *CNN Money.* Retrieved from http://money.cnn.com.

O'Dea, B., Larsen, M. E., Batterham, P. J., Calear, A. L., & Christensen, H. (2018). A linguistic analysis of suicide-related Twitter posts. *Crisis.* [Manuscript in press]

O'Hara, M. W., & Wisner, K. L. (2014). Perinatal mental illness: Definition, description and aetiology. *Best Practice & Research. Clinical Obstetrics and Gynaecology, 28*(1), 3–12.

O'Sullivan, D. J., O'Sullivan, M. E., O'Connell, B. D., O'Reilly, K., & Sarma, K. M. (2018). Attributional style and depressive symptoms in a male prison sample. *PLoS ONE, 13*(1), e0190394.

O'Sullivan, L. F., Brotto, L. A., Byers, S., Majerovich, J. A., & Wuest, J. A. (2014). Prevalence and characteristics of sexual functioning among sexually experienced middle to late adolescents. *Journal of Sexual Medicine, 11,* 630–641.

OA (Opportunity Agenda). (2017). *A review of public opinion research related to black male achievement.* New York: OA.

Oates, G. L. (2016). Effects of religiosity dimensions on physical health across non-elderly Black and White American panels. *Review of Religious Research, 58*(2), 249–270.

Odagaki, Y. (2017). A case of persistent generalized retrograde autobiographical amnesia subsequent to the Great East Japan Earthquake in 2011. *Case Reports in Psychiatry,* article 5173605.

Oerbeck, B., Overgaard, K. R., Stein, M. B., Pripp, A. H., & Kristensen, H. (2018, January 22). Treatment for selective mutism: A 5-year follow-up study. *European Child & Adolescent Psychiatry.* [Epub ahead of print]

Ohman, A., & Mineka, S. (2003). The malicious serpent: Snakes as a prototypical stimulus for an evolved module of fear. *Current Directions in Psychological Science, 12*(1), 5–9.

Ohring, R., Graber, J. A., & Brooks-Gunn, J. (2002). Girls' recurrent and concurrent body dissatisfaction: Correlates and consequences over 8 years. *International Journal of Eating Disorders, 31*(4), 404–415.

Oinas-Kukkonen, H., & Mantila, L. (2010). Lisa, Lisa the machine says I have performed an illegal action. Should I tell the police? A survey and observations of inexperienced elderly Internet users. In *Proceedings of the 12th annual conference of the Southern Association for Information Systems.* Charleston, South Carolina, March 12–14, 2009. Pp. 145–151.

Okawa, J. B., & Hauss, R. B. (2007). The trauma of politically motivated torture. In E. K. Carll (Ed.), *Trauma psychology: Issues in violence, disaster, health, and illness* (Vol. 1). Westport, CT: Praeger Publishers.

Oldehinkel, A. J., Ormel, J., Verhulst, F. C., & Nederhof, E. (2014). Childhood adversities and adolescent depression: A matter of both risk and resilience. *Development and Psychopathology, 26*(4, Pt. 1), 1067–1075.

Olfson, M., King, M., & Schoenbaum, M. (2016). Stimulant treatment of young people in the United States. *Journal of Child and Adolescent Psychopharmacology, 26,* 520–526.

Oliver, C., Licence, L., & Richards, C. (2017). Self-injurious behavior in people with intellectual disability and autism spectrum disorder. *Current Opinion in Psychiatry, 30,* 97–101.

Oliver, J. M., Anzalone, A. J., Stone, J. D., Turner, S. M., Blueitt, D., Garrison, J. C., . . . Jagim, A. R. (2018, May 29). Fluctuations in blood biomarkers of head trauma in NCAA football athletes over the course of a season. *Journal of Neurosurgery.* [Epub ahead of print]

Ollove, M. (2017). Getting the mentally ill out of jails. *Pew Charitable Trusts.* Retrieved from http://www.pewtrusts.org.

Olmsted, M. P., MacDonald, D. E., McFarlane, T., Trottier, K., & Colton, P. (2015). Predictors of rapid relapse in bulimia nervosa. *International Journal of Eating Disorders, 48*(3), 337–340.

Olson, L. A., & Patrick, C. J. (2018). Clinical aspects of antisocial personality disorder and psychopathy. In W. J. Livesley & R. Larstone (Eds.), *Handbook of personality disorders: Theory, research, and treatment* (2nd ed.). New York: Guilford Press.

Olson-Kennedy, J., & Forcier, M. (2018, March 28). Management of gender nonconformity in children and adolescents. *UpToDate.* Retrieved from http://www.uptodate.com.

Oltean, H. R., Hyland, P., Vallières, F., & David, D. O. (2018). An empirical assessment of REBT models of psychopathology and psychological health in the prediction of anxiety and depression symptoms. *Behavioural and Cognitive Psychotherapy, 45,* 600–615.

Olten, B., & Bloch, M. H. (2018). Meta regression: Relationship between antipsychotic receptor binding profiles and side-effects. *Progress in Neuro-Psychopharmacology & Biological Psychiatry, 84*(Pt. A), 272–281.

Onwuteaka-Philipsen, B. D., Brinkman-Stoppelenburg, A., Penning, C., de Jong-Krul, G. J. F., van Delden, J. J. M., & van der Heide, A. (2012, July 11). Trends in end-of-life practices before and after the enactment of the euthanasia law in the Netherlands from 1990 to 2010: A repeated cross-sectional survey. *The Lancet.* Retrieved from http://dx/doi.org/10.1016/S0140-6736(12)61034-4.

OPA (Office of Protection and Advocacy for Persons with Disabilities). (2016). *"Your rights in a psychiatric facility," A P&A self-help publication.* CT: Author.

Opinion Research Corporation Poll/CNN. (2011, March 18-20). Disaster preparedness and relief. *PollingReport.com.*

Opinion Research Corporation. (2004). National Survey Press Release. May 17, 2004.

Oquendo, M. A., Lizardi, D., Greenwald. S., Weissman, M. M., & Mann, J. J. (2004). Rates of lifetime suicide attempt and rates of lifetime major depression in different ethnic groups in the United States. *Acta Psychiatrica Scandinavica, 110*(6), 446–451.

Oquendo, M. A., Russo, S. A., Underwood, M. D., Kassir, S. A., Ellis, S. P., Mann, J. J., & Arango, V. (2006). Higher post-mortem prefrontal 5-HT2A receptor binding correlates with lifetime aggression in suicide. *Biological Psychiatry, 59,* 235–243.

Orwelius, L., Kristenson, M., Fredrikson, M., Walther, S., & Sjöberg, F. (2017). Hopelessness: Independent associations with health-related quality of life and short-term mortality after critical illness: A prospective, multicentre trial. *Journal of Critical Care, 41,* 58–63.

Osman, M., & Parnell, A. C. (2015). Effect of the First World War on suicide rates in Ireland: An investigation of the 1864–1921 suicide trends. *British Journal of Psychiatry Open, 1*(2), 164–165.

Osmanağaoğlu, N., Creswell, C., & Dodd, H. F. (2018). Intolerance of uncertainty, anxiety, and worry in children and adolescents: A meta-analysis. *Journal of Affective Disorders, 225,* 80–90.

Ostermaier, K. K. (2018, January 5). Down syndrome: Clinical features and diagnosis. *UpToDate.* Retrieved from http://www.uptodate.com.

Oudgenoeg-Paz, O., Mulder, H., Jongmans, M. J., van der Ham, J. M., & Van der Stigchel, S. (2017). The link between motor and cognitive development in children born preterm and/or with low birth weight: A review of current evidence. *Neuroscience and Biobehavioral Reviews, 80,* 382–393.

Overdorf, V., Kollia, B., Makarec, K., & Alleva Szeles, C. (2016). The relationship between physical activity and depressive symptoms in healthy older women. *Gerontology and Geriatric Medicine, 2,* 2333721415626859.

Overton, D. (1964). State-dependent or "dissociated" learning produced with pentobarbital. *Journal of Comparative Physiology and Psychology, 57,* 3–12.

Overton, D. (1966). State-dependent learning produced by depressant and atropine-like drugs. *Psychopharmacologia, 10,* 6–31.

Owen, R., Dempsey, R., Jones, S., & Gooding, P. (2018). Defeat and entrapment in bipolar disorder: Exploring the relationship with suicidal ideation from a psychological theoretical perspective. *Suicide and Life-Threatening Behavior.* [Manuscript in press]

Owens, A. P., Low, D. A., Iodice, V., Critchley, H. D., & Mathias, C. J. (2017). The genesis and presentation of anxiety in disorders of autonomic overexcitement. *Autonomic Neuroscience, 203,* 81–87.

Özdel, K., Taymur, I., Guriz, S. O., Tulaci, R. G., Kuru, E., Turkcapar, M. H. (2014, August 29). Measuring cognitive errors using the Cognitive Distortions Scale (CDS): Psychometric properties in clinical and non-clinical samples. *PLOS One.* Retrieved from https://doi.org/10.137/journal.pone.0105956.

PA (Parents Anonymous). (2017). Website. Claremont, CA: Parents Anonymous. Retrieved from http://parentsanonymous.org.

Paast, N., Khosravi, Z., Memari, A. H., Shayestehfar, M., & Arbabi, M. (2016). Comparison of cognitive flexibility and planning ability in patients with obsessive compulsive disorder, patients with obsessive compulsive personality disorder, and healthy controls. *Shanghai Archives of Psychiatry, 28*(1), 28–34.

Pace, C. (2017, July 20). Alcohol withdrawal: Epidemiology, clinical manifestations, course, assessment, and diagnosis. *UpToDate.* Retrieved from http://www.uptodate.com.

Padwa, L. (1996). *Everything you pretend to know and are afraid someone will ask.* New York: Penguin.

Page, T. F., Pelham, W. E., Fabiano, G. A., Greiner, A. R., Gnagy, E. M., Hart, K. C., . . . Pelham, W. E. (2016). Comparative cost analysis of sequential, adaptive, behavioral, pharmacological, and combined treatments for childhood ADHD. *Journal of Clinical Child and Adolescent Psychology, 45,* 416–427.

Palagini, L., Domschke, K., Benedetti, F., Foster, R. G., Wulff, K., & Riemann, D. (2019). Developmental pathways towards mood disorders in adult life: Is there a role for sleep disturbances? *Journal of Affective Disorders, 243,* 121–132.

Pallardy, C. (2015, February 15). Male & female active physicians: 70 statistics by specialty. *Becker's GI & Endoscopy.* Retrieved from http://www.beckersasc.com/gastroenterology-and-endoscopy/male-female.html.

Palley, W. (2014). Data point: Digital distractions help drive Millennials to mindfulness. *JWT Intelligence,* February 7, 2014.

Palsetia, D., Rao, G. P., Tiwari, S. C., Lodha, P., & De Sousa, A. (2018). The clock drawing test versus mini-mental status examination as a screening tool for dementia: A clinical comparison. *Indian Journal of Psychological Medicine, 40*(1), 1–10.

Pandey, D., & Shrivastava, P. (2017). Mediation effect of social support on the association between hardiness and immune response. *Asian Journal of Psychiatry, 26,* 52–55.

Pankevich, D. E., Teegarden, S. L., Hedin, A. D., Jensen, C. L., & Bale, T. L. (2010). Caloric restriction experience reprograms stress and orexigenic pathways and promotes binge eating. *Journal of Neuroscience, 30*(48), 16399–16407.

Paris, J. (2010). Estimating the prevalence of personality disorders in the community. *Journal of Personality Disorders, 24*(4), 405–411.

Paris, J. (2012). The rise and fall of dissociative identity disorder. *Journal of Nervous and Mental Disease, 200*(12), 1076–1079.

Paris, J. (2014). Modernity and narcissistic personality disorder. *Personality Disorders, 5*(2), 220–226.

Paris, J. (2018). Childhood adversities and personality disorders. In W. J. Livesley & R. Larstone (Eds.), *Handbook of personality disorders: Theory, research, and treatment* (2nd ed., Ch. 17). New York: Guilford Press.

Parisette-Sparks, A., & Kreitler, C. M. (2017). Retrospective reports of childhood relationships and associations with adult anxiety and depression. *Journal of Basic and Applied Research, 3*(2), 59–70.

Park, C. H. K., Yoo, S. H., Lee, J., Cho, S. J., Shin, M. S., Kim, E. Y., . . . Ahn, Y. M. (2017). Impact of acute alcohol consumption on lethality of suicide methods. *Comprehensive Psychiatry, 75,* 27–34.

Park, E. R. (2018, January 5). Behavioral approaches to smoking cessation. *UpToDate.* Retrieved from http://www.uptodate.com.

Park, J., & Bouck, E. (2018). In-school service predictors of employment for individuals with intellectual disability. *Research in Developmental Disabilities, 77,* 68–75.

Park, K. K., & Koo, J. (2017, November 1). Skin picking (excoriation) disorder and related disorders. *UpToDate.* Retrieved from http://www.uptodate.com.

Park, S. H., & Han, K. S. (2017, April 6). Blood pressure response to meditation and yoga: A systematic review and meta-analysis. *Journal* of Alternative and Complementary Medicine*. [Epub ahead of print]

Park, T. W. (2017, September 26). Benzodiazepine use disorder: Epidemiology, pathogenesis, clinical manifestations, course, and diagnosis. *UpToDate*. Retrieved from http://www.uptodate.com.

Parker, G. E. (2016). A framework for navigating Institutional Review Board (IRB) oversight in the complicated zone of research. *Cureus, 8*(10), e844.

Parker, G., McCraw, S., & Bayes, A. (2018, March 1). Borderline personality disorder: Does its clinical features show specificity to differing developmental risk factors? *Australasian Psychiatry*. [Epub ahead of print]

Parker, S., Nichter, M., Vuckovic, N., Sims, C., & Ritenbaugh, C. (1995). Body image and weight concerns among African American and white adolescent females: Differences that make a difference. *Human Organization, 54*(2), 103–114.

Parmar, A., & Sarkar, S. (2016). Neuroimaging studies in obsessive compulsive disorder: A narrative review. *Indian Journal of Psychological Medicine, 38*(5), 386–394.

Parsons, E. M., Straub, K. T., Smith, A. R., & Clerkin, E. M. (2017). Body dysmorphic, obsessive-compulsive, and social anxiety disorder beliefs as predictors of in vivo stressor responding. *Journal of Nervous and Mental Disease, 205,* 471–479.

Patel, N. A., & Elkin, G. D. (2015). Professionalism and conflicting interests: The American Psychological Association's involvement in torture. *AMA Journal of Ethics, 17*(10), 924–930.

Patel, S. R., Humensky, J. L., Olfson, M., Simpson, H. B., Myers, R., & Dixon, L. B. (2014). Treatment of obsessive-compulsive disorder in a nationwide survey of office-based physician practice. *Psychiatric Services (Washington, D.C.), 65*(5), 681–684.

Paterniti, S., Sterner, I., Caldwell, C., & Bisserbe, J. C. (2017). Childhood neglect predicts the course of major depression in a tertiary care sample: A follow-up study. *BMC Psychiatry, 17*(1), 113.

Patrick, C. J. (2007). Antisocial personality disorder and psychopathy. In W. O'Donohue, K. A. Fowler, & S. O. Lilienfeld (Eds.). *Personality disorders: Toward the DSM-V.* Los Angeles: Sage Publications.

Patrick, M. E., Fairlie, A. M., & Lee, C. M. (2018). Motives for simultaneous alcohol and marijuana use among young adults. *Addictive Behaviors, 76,* 363–369.

Patriquin, M. A., Hamon, S. C., Harding, M. J., Nielsen, E. M., Newton, T. F., De La Garza, R., 2nd, & Nielsen, D. A. (2017). Genetic moderation of cocaine subjective effects by variation in the TPH1, TPH2, and SLC6A4 serotonin genes. *Psychiatric Genetics, 27,* 178–186.

Patterson, D. (2011). The linkage between secondary victimization by law enforcement and rape case outcomes. *Journal of Interpersonal Violence, 26*(2), 328–347.

Patterson, P. H. (2012). Animal models of the maternal infection risk factor for schizophrenia. In A. S. Brown & P. H. Patterson (Eds.), *The origins of schizophrenia* (pp. 255–281). New York: Columbia University Press.

Paul, G. L. (1967). The strategy of outcome research in psychotherapy. *Journal of Counseling Psychology, 31,* 109–118.

Paul, G. L. (2000). Milieu therapy. In A. E. Kazdin (Ed.), *Encyclopedia of psychology* (Vol. 5, pp. 250–252). New York: Oxford University Press.

Paulk, A., Dowd, D. A., Zayac, R., Eklund, A., & Kildare, C. (2014). The relationship between culture, geographic region, and gender on body image: A comparison of college students in the Southeast and Pacific Northwest regions of the United States. *Sociological Spectrum, 34*(5), 442–452.

Paulo, M., Scruth, E. A., & Jacoby, S. R. (2017). Dementia and delirium in the elderly hospitalized patient: Delirium is a medical emergency. *Clinical Nurse Specialist, 31*(2), 66–69.

Paulus, F. W., Ohmann, S., von Gontard, A., & Popow, C. (2018, April 6). Internet gaming disorder in children and adolescents: A systematic review. *Developmental Medicine & Child Neurology*. [Epub ahead of print]

Paulus, M. (2017, January 15). Methamphetamine use disorder: Epidemiology, clinical manifestations, course, assessment, and diagnosis. *UpToDate*. Retrieved from http://www.uptodate.com.

Payne, A. F. (1928). *Sentence completion.* New York: New York Guidance Clinics.

Payne, J. (2017, September 14). Treatment of postpartum psychosis. *UpToDate*. Retrieved from http://www.uptodate.com.

Payne, J. (2018, February 27). Postpartum psychosis: Epidemiology, pathogenesis, clinical manifestations, course, assessment, and diagnosis. *UpToDate*. Retrieved from http://www.uptodate.com.

Pear, R. (2013, December 11). Fewer psychiatrists seen taking health insurance. *New York Times*.

Peavy, M. (2017, May 26). Psychosocial interventions for opioid use disorder. *UpToDate*. Retrieved from http://www.uptodate.com.

Pedersen, T. (2016, October 31). Childhood PTSD may alter structure of brain networks. *Psych Central News*. Retrieved from http://psychcentral.com.

Peebles, R., Lesser, A., Park, C. C., Heckert, K., Timko, C. A., Lantzouni, E., . . . Weaver, L. (2017). Outcomes of an inpatient medical nutritional rehabilitation protocol in children and adolescents with eating disorders. *Journal of Eating Disorders, 5,* 7.

Pelham, W. E., Fabiano, G. A., Waxmonsky, J. G., Greiner, A. R., Gnagy, E. M., Pelham, W. E., . . . Murphy, S. A. (2016). Treatment sequencing for childhood ADHD: A multiple-randomization study of adaptive medication and behavioral interventions. *Journal of Clinical Child and Adolescent Psychology, 45,* 396–415.

Pellecchia, G., Moroni, F., Colle, L., Semerari, A., Carcione, A., Fera, T., . . . Procacci, M. (2018). Avoidant personality disorder and social phobia: Does mindreading make the difference? *Comprehensive Psychiatry, 80,* 163–169.

Pelletier, J. F., & Davidson, L. (2015). At the very roots of psychiatry as a new medical specialty: The Pinel–Pussin partnership. [French] *Santé Mentale au Québec, 40*(1), 19–33.

Pendery, M. L., Maltzman, I. M., & West, L. J. (1982). Controlled drinking by alcoholics? New findings and a reevaluation of a major affirmative study. *Science, 217*(4555), 169–175.

Perdeci, Z., Gulsun, M., Celik, C., Erdem, M., Ozdemir, B., Ozdag, F., & Kilic, S. (2010). Aggression and the event-related potentials in antisocial personality disorder. *Bulletin of Clinical Psychopharmacology, 20*(4), 300–306.

Perez, M., Ohrt, T. K., & Hoek, H. W. (2016). Prevalence and treatment of eating disorders among Hispanics/Latino Americans in the United States. *Current Opinion in Psychiatry, 29*(6), 378–382.

Perlin, M. L. (2017). The insanity defense: Nine myths that will not go away. In M. D. White (Ed.), *The insanity defense: Multidisciplinary views on its history, trends, and controversies* (Chap. 1, pp. 3–22). Westport, CT: Praeger.

Perna, G., Alciati, A., Riva, A., Micieli, W., & Caldirola, D. (2016). Long-term pharmacological treatments of anxiety disorders: An updated systematic review. *Current Psychiatry Reports, 18*(3), 23.

Perpetuini, D., Bucco, R., Zito, M., & Merla, A. (2018). Study of memory deficit in Alzheimer's disease by means of complexity analysis of fNIRS signal. *Neurophotonics, 5*(1), 011010.

Perrault, E. K., & Nazione, S. A. (2016). Informed consent–uninformed participants: Shortcomings of online social science consent forms and recommendations for improvement. *Journal of Empirical Research on Human Research Ethics, 11*(3), 274–280.

Perrin, M., Vandeleur, C. L., Castelao, E., Rothen, S., Glaus, J., Vollenweider, P., & Preisig, M. (2014). Determinants of the development of post-traumatic stress disorder, in the general population. *Social Psychiatry and Psychiatric Epidemiology, 49*(3), 447–457.

Perry, K. (2017, March 8). Franklin County coroner spars with politicians over heroin fight. *The Columbus Dispatch*.

Perry, K. J., & Ostrov, J. M. (2018). Testing a higher order model of internalizing and externalizing behavior: The role of aggression subtypes. *Child Psychiatry and Human Development*. [Manuscript in press]

Perugi, G., Medda, P., Zanello, S., Toni, C., & Cassano, G. B. (2011, March 21). Episode length and mixed features as predictors of ECT nonresponse in patients with medication-resistant major depression. *Brain Stimulation, 5*(1), 18–24.

Peters, E. M. J., Müller, Y., Snaga, W., Fliege, H., Reisshauer, A., Schmidt-Rose, T., . . . Kruse, J. (2017). Hair and stress: A pilot study of hair and cytokine balance alteration in healthy young women under major exam stress. *PLoS ONE, 12*(4), e0175904.

Petersen, J. L., & Hyde, J. S. (2011). Gender differences in sexual attitudes and behaviors: A review of meta-analytic results and large datasets. *Journal of Sex Research, 48*(2-3), 149–165.

Peterson, Z. D. (Ed.). (2017). *The Wiley-Blackwell handbook of sex therapy.* Hoboken, NJ: Wiley-Blackwell.

Pettypiece, S. (2015, April 10). How psychiatrists are failing the patients who need them most. *Bloomberg.com*.

Pew Research Center. (2010). *8% of online Americans use Twitter.* Washington, DC: Author.

Pew Research Center. (2011). Twitter, launched five years ago, delivers 350 billion tweets a day. *Media Mentions.* Washington, DC: Pew Internet & American Life Project.

Pew Research Center. (2013). Modern parenthood. *Pew Social Trends.* Retrieved from http://www.pewsocialtrends.org/2013/03/14.

Pew Research Center. (2013). *Social networking fact sheet.* Washington, DC: Pew Internet & American Life Project.

Pew Research Center. (2014). *Social media update 2013: Main findings.* Washington, DC: Pew. Retrieved from Pew Internet website: http://www.pewinternet.org/2013/12/30/social-media-update-2013.

Pew Research Center. (2014, November 14). *Chapter 2: The demographics of remarriage.* Washington, DC: Author. Retrieved from http://www.pewsocialtrends.org.

Pew Research Center. (2015). *Raising kids and running a household: How working parents share the load.* Washington, DC: Pew Research Center.

Pew Research Center. (2015, August 4). *Texting is most common way teens get in touch with closest friend.* Washington, DC: Author. Retrieved from Pew Internet website: http://www.pewinternet.org.

Pew Research Center. (2015, October 5). California legalizes assisted suicide amid growing support for such laws. *Pew Research.* Retrieved from http://www.pewresearch.org/fact-tank/2015/10/05.

Pew Research Center. (2016, July 6). Few have a lot of confidence in information from professional news outlets or friends and family, though majorities show at least some trust in both, but social media garners less trust than either. *Pew Research Center Journalism & Media.* Retrieved from http://www.pewinternet.org.

Pew Research Center. (2016, November 11). *Social media update 2016.* Washington, DC: Author.

Pew Research Center. (2016, October 12). Support for marijuana legalization continues to rise.

Pew Research Center. (2017). *2. Living arrangements of older Americans by gender.* Washington, DC: Author.

Pew Research Center. (2017, July 11). Online harassment 2017. *Pew Research Center: Internet & Technology.* Retrieved from http://www.pewinternet.org.

Pew Research Center. (2017, June 27). U.S. public trust in science and scientists. *Pew Research Center: Internet & Technology.* Retrieved from http://www.pewinternet.org.

Pew Research Center. (2017, May 17). *1. Technology use among seniors.* Washington, DC: Author. Retrieved from http://www.pewinternet.org.

Pfeffer, C. R. (2003). Assessing suicidal behavior in children and adolescents. In R. A. King & A. Apter (Eds.), *Suicide in children and adolescents* (pp. 211–226). Cambridge, England: Cambridge University Press.

Pfefferbaum, B., Newman, E., & Nelson, S. D. (2014). Mental health interventions for children exposed to disasters and terrorism. *Journal of Child and Adolescent Psychopharmacology, 24*(1), 24–31.

Phalen, P., Ray, B., Watson, D. P., Huynh, P., & Greene, M. S. (2018, March 20). Fentanyl related overdose in Indianapolis: Estimating trends using multilevel Bayesian models. *Addictive Behaviors.* [Epub ahead of print]

Pham, A. V., Carlson, J. S., & Koschiulek, J. F. (2010). Ethnic differences in parental beliefs of attention-deficit/hyperactivity disorder and treatment. *Journal of Attention Disorders, 13*(6), 584–591.

Phillips, D. P. (1974). The influence of suggestion on suicide: Substantive and theoretical implications of the *Werther* effect. *American Sociological Review, 39,* 340–354.

Phillips, D. P., & Ruth, T. E. (1993). Adequacy of official suicide statistics for scientific research and public policy. *Suicide and Life-Threatening Behavior, 23*(4), 307–319.

Phillips, K. (2015). Obsessive-compulsive and related disorders. In A. Tasman, J. Kay, J. A. Lieberman, M. B. First, & M. Riba (Eds.). *Psychiatry* (2 vols., 4th ed., pp. 1093–1128). Hoboken, NJ: Wiley-Blackwell.

Phillips, K. A. (2016, May 24). Body dysmorphic disorder: Epidemiology, pathogenesis, and clinical features. *UpToDate.* Retrieved from http://www.uptodate.com.

Phillips, K. A. (2017, January 15). Body dysmorphic disorder: Treatment and prognosis. *UpToDate.* Retrieved from http://www.uptodate.com.

Philo, C., & Andrews, J. (2016). Introduction: Histories of asylums, insanity and psychiatry in Scotland. *History of Psychiatry.* [Advance online publication, PMID: 27956649]

Piacentini, J., Bennett, S., Compton, S. N., Kendall, P. C., Birmaher, B., Albano, A. M., . . . & Walkup, J. (2014). 24- and 36-week outcomes for the Child/Adolescent Anxiety Multimodal Study (CAMS). *Journal of the American Academy of Child and Adolescent Psychiatry, 53,* 297–310.

Pianta, R. C. (2016). Classroom processes and teacher-student interaction: Integrations with a developmental psychopathology perspective. In D. Cicchetti (Ed.), *Developmental psychopathology, Vol. 4: Risk, resilience, and intervention* (3rd ed.). New York: Wiley.

Piatt, A. (2013). Facebook may improve working memory, cognition in elderly. *Neuropsychology.* Retrieved from http://www.neuropsychology.co/2013/03/03/working-memory.

Pickert, K. (2014, February 3). The art of being mindful, *Time.*

Piersol, C. V., Canton, K., Connor, S. E., Giller, I., Lipman, S., & Sager, S. (2017). Effectiveness of interventions for caregivers of people with Alzheimer's disease and related major neurocognitive disorders: A systematic review. *American Journal of Occupational Therapy, 71*(5), 7105180020p1-7105180020p10.

Pieters, J. (2018, March 30). Pedophilia manual spread in Netherlands; Minister considers ban. *NL Times.*

Pike, K. (2017, March 17). Anorexia nervosa in adults: Cognitive-behavioral therapy (CBT). *UpToDate.* Retrieved from www.uptodate.com.

Pike, K. M., Dunne, P. E., & Addai, E. (2013). Expanding the boundaries: Reconfiguring the demographics of the "typical" eating disordered patient. *Current Psychiatry Reports, 15*(11), 411.

Pillay, B., Lee, S. J., Katona, L., Burney, S., & Avery, S. (2014). Psychosocial factors predicting survival after allogeneic stem cell transplant. *Supportive Care in Cancer, 22*(9), 2547–2555.

Pinals, D. A., Packer, I., Fisher, B., & Roy, K. (2004). Relationship between race and ethnicity and forensic clinical triage dispositions. *Psychiatric Services 55,* 873–878.

Pinkham, A. E. (2014). Social cognition in schizophrenia. *Journal of Clinical Psychiatry, 75*(Suppl. 2), 14–19.

Pinto, A., Ansell, E., Wheaton, M. G., Krueger, R. F., Morey, L., Skodol, A. E., & Clark, L. A. (2018). Obsessive-compulsive personality disorder and component personality traits. In W. J. Livesley & R. Larstone (Eds.), *Handbook of personality disorders: Theory, research, and treatment* (2nd ed., Ch. 26). New York: Guilford Press.

Pinto, A., Eisen, J. L., Mancebo, M. C., & Rasmussen, S. A. (2008). Obsessive-compulsive personality disorder. In J. S. Abramowitz, D. McKay, & S. Taylor (Eds.), *Obsessive-compulsive disorder: Subtypes and spectrum conditions.* Oxford, England: Elsevier.

Piper, B. J., Shah, D. T., Simoyan, O. M., McCall, K. L., & Nichols, S. D. (2018). Trends in medical use of opioids in the U.S., 2006–2016. *American Journal of Preventive Medicine, 54*(5), 652–660.

Pivalizza, P. (2017, October 26). Intellectual disability in children: Management, outcomes, and prevention. *UpToDate.* Retrieved from http://www.uptodate.com.

Pivalizza, P., *& Lalani, S. R.* (2018, January 8). Intellectual disability in children: Definition, diagnosis, and assessment of needs. *UpToDate.* Retrieved from http://www.uptodate.com.

Pizzagalli, D. A. (2017). Frontocingulate dysfunction in depression: Toward biomarkers of treatment response. *Nature.* Retrieved from http://www.nature.com.

Pizzorno, J. E., Murray, M. T., & Joiner-Bey, H. (2016). Peptic ulcers. In J. E. Pizzorno, M. T. Murray, & H. Joiner-Bey (Eds.), *The Clinician's Handbook of Natural Medicine* (3rd ed., pp. 779–786). UK: Elsevier Health Sciences.

Plante, T. G. (2016). Is Facebook the new Rorschach? *Psychology Today.*

Planty, M., Hussar, W., Snyder, T., Provasnik, S., Kena, G., Dinkes, R., . . . Kemp, J. (2008). *The condition of education 2008.* Washington, DC: National Center for Education Statistics.

Plaud, J. J. (2007). Sexual disorders. In P. Sturmey (Ed.), *Functional analysis in clinical treatment. Practical resources for the mental health professional* (pp. 357–377). San Diego, CA: Elsevier Academic Press.

Poletti, M., Carretta, E., Bonvicini, L., & Giorgi-Rossi, P. (2018). Cognitive clusters in specific learning disorder. *Journal of Learning Disabilities, 51*(1), 32–42.

Polo, A. J., Alegria, M., Chen, C.-N., & Blanco, C. (2011). The prevalence and comorbidity of social anxiety disorder among United States Latinos: A retrospective analysis of data from 2 national surveys. *Journal of Clinical Psychiatry, 72*(8), 1096–1105.

Ponseti, J., Bruhn, D., Nolting, J., Gerwinn, H., Pohl, A., Stirn, A., . . . Kruger, T. H. C. (2018). Decoding pedophilia: Increased anterior insula response to infant animal pictures. *Frontiers in Human Neuroscience, 11*, 645.

Pontes, N. M. H., Ayres, C. G., Lewandowski, C., & Pontes, M. C. F. (2018). Trends in bullying victimization by gender among U.S. high school students. *Research in Nursing & Health, 41*(3), 243–251.

Pop, C. (2016). Self-esteem and body image perception in a sample of university students. *Eurasian Journal of Educational Research, 64*, 31–44.

Pope, K. S., & Vasquez, M. J. T. (2016). *Ethics in psychotherapy and counseling: A practical guide* (5th ed.). New York: Wiley.

Pope, K. S., & Wedding, D. (2019). Contemporary challenges and controversies. In D. Wedding & R. J. Corsini (Eds.), *Current psychotherapies* (11th ed., Ch. 16). Independence, KY: Cengage Publications.

Pope, K. S., & Tabachnick, B. G. (1993). Therapists' anger, hate, fear and sexual feelings: National survey of therapists' responses, client characteristics, critical events, formal complaints and training. *Professional Psychology: Research and Practice, 24*, 142–152.

Pope, K. S., & Vasquez, M. J. T. (2011). *Ethics in psychotherapy and counseling: A practical guide* (4th ed.). Hoboken, NJ: John Wiley & Sons.

Pope, K. S., Tabachnick, B. G., & Keith-Spiegel, P. (1987). Ethics of practice: The beliefs and behaviors of psychologists as therapists. *American Psychologist, 42*, 993–1006.

Popova, S., Lange, S., Probst, C., Gmel, G., & Rehm, J. (2017, March). Estimation of national, regional, and global prevalence of alcohol use during pregnancy and fetal alcohol syndrome: A systematic review and meta-analysis. *Lancet Global Health, 5*, e290–e299.

Poretz, M., & Sinrod, B. (1991). *Do you do it with the lights on?* New York: Ballantine Books.

Posmontier, B. (2010). The role of midwives in facilitating recovery in postpartum psychosis. *Journal of Midwifery & Women's Health, 55*(5), 430–437.

Post, R. M. (2017, February 16). Bipolar disorder in adults: Choosing maintenance treatment. *UpToDate*. Retrieved from http://www.uptodate.com.

Post, R. M., Ballenger, J. C., & Goodwin, F. K. (1980). Cerebrospinal fluid studies of neurotransmitter function in manic and depressive illness. In J. H. Wood (Ed.), *The neurobiology of cerebrospinal fluid* (Vol. 1). New York: Plenum Press.

Post, R. M., Lake, C. R., Jimerson, D. C., Bunney, J. H., Ziegler, M. G., & Goodwin, F. K. (1978). Cerebrospinal fluid norepinephrine in affective illness. *American Journal of Psychiatry, 135*(8), 907–912.

Poulsen, S., Lunn, S., Daniel, S. F., Folke, S., Mathiesen, B. B., Katznelson, H., & Fairburn, C. G. (2014). A randomized controlled trial of psychoanalytic psychotherapy or cognitive-behavioral therapy for bulimia nervosa. *American Journal of Psychiatry, 171*(1), 109–116.

Powell, M. P., Lochman, J. E., Boxmeyer, C. L., Barry, T. D., & Pardini, D. A. (2017). The Coping Power Program for aggressive behavior in children. In J. R. Weisz & A. E. Kazdin (Eds.), *Evidence-based psychotherapies for children and adolescents* (3rd ed.). New York: Guilford Press.

Pozzi, M., Radice, S., Clementi, E., Molteni, M., & Nobile, M. (2016). Antidepressants and suicide and self-injury: Causal or casual association? *International Journal of Psychiatry in Clinical Practice, 20*(1), 47–51.

PRB (Population Reference Bureau). (2015, December). Population bulletin: Aging in the United States. *PRB, 70*(2).

Predmore, Z., Ramchand, R., Ayer, L., Kotzias, V., Engel, C., Ebener, P., . . . Haas, G. L. (2017). Expanding suicide crisis services to text and chat. *Crisis, 38*, 255–260.

Press, D., & Alexander, M. (2017, October 23). Management of neuropsychiatric symptoms of dementia. *UpToDate*. Retrieved from http://www.uptodate.com.

Press, D., & Alexander, M. (2018, January 16). Treatment of dementia. *UpToDate*. Retrieved from http://www.uptodate.com.

Press, D., & Alexander, M. (2018, January 23). Prevention of dementia. *UpToDate*. Retrieved from http://www.uptodate.com.

Press, D., & Alexander, M. (2018, March 26). Cholinesterase inhibitors in the treatment of dementia. *UpToDate*. Retrieved from http://www.uptodate.com.

Price, M. (2011). Upfront: Marijuana addiction a growing risk as society grows more tolerant. *Monitor on Psychology, 42*(5), 13.

Price, R. W. (2017, February 14). HIV-associated neurocognitive disorders: Epidemiology, clinical manifestations, and diagnosis. *UpToDate*. Retrieved from http://www.uptodate.com.

Price, R. W. (2018, January 8). HIV-associated neurocognitive disorders: Management. *UpToDate*. Retrieved from http://www.uptodate.com.

Priday, L. J., Byrne, C., & Totsika, V. (2017). Behavioural interventions for sleep problems in people with an intellectual disability: A systematic review and meta-analysis of single case and group studies. *Journal of Intellectual Disability Research, 61*(1), 1–15.

Probst, T., Geib, C., Güroff, E., & Mühlberger, A. (2017). Training the social skill "being able to demand" vs. training the social skill "being able to say no": A randomized controlled trial with healthy individuals. *Journal of Behavior Therapy and Experimental Psychiatry, 57*, 1–5.

Prochaska, J. O., & Norcross, J. C. (2018). *Systems of psychotherapy: A transtheoretical analysis* (9th ed.). New York: Oxford University Press.

Prochaska, J. O., & Norcross, J. C. (2013). *Systems of psychotherapy: Transtheoretical analysis* (8th ed.). Independence, KY: Cengage Learning.

ProCon. (2016). *Should prescription drugs be advertised directly to consumers?* Santa Monica, CA: ProCon.

Pruchno, R. (2014). All in the family: Prison or treatment for people with mental illness? *Psychology Today*. Retrieved from *Psychology Today* website: http://www.psychologytoday.com/blog/all-in-the-family/201402/prison-or-treatment-people-mental-illness.

Pruessner, M., Cullen, A. E., Aas, M., & Walker, E. F. (2017). The neural diathesis-stress model of schizophrenia revisited: An update on recent findings considering illness stage and neurobiological and methodological complexities. *Neuroscience & Biobehavioral Reviews, 73*, 191–218.

Pu, J., Zhou, X., Liu, L., Zhang, Y., Yang, L., Yuan, S., . . . Xie, P. (2017). Efficacy and acceptability of interpersonal psychotherapy for depression in adolescents: A meta-analysis of randomized controlled trials. *Psychiatry Research, 253*, 226–232.

Puppo, V., & Sharif, H. (2017). Premature ejaculation is not a disease. *International Journal of Urology, 24*(8), 641.

Putnam, F. W. (1984). The psychophysiologic investigation of multiple personality disorder. *Psychiatric Clinics of North America, 7*, 31–40.

Putnam, F. W. (2000). Dissociative disorders. In A. J. Sameroff, M. Lewis et al. (Eds.), *Handbook of developmental psychopathology* (2nd ed., pp. 739–754). New York: Kluwer Academic/Plenum Press.

Putnam, F. W. (2006). Dissociative disorders. In D. Cicchetti & D. J. Cohen (Eds.), *Developmental psychopathology, Vol. 3: Risk, disorder, and adaptation* (2nd ed., pp. 657–695). Hoboken, NJ: John Wiley & Sons.

Putnam, F. W., Zahn, T. P., & Post, R. M. (1990). Differential autonomic nervous system activity in multiple personality disorder. *Journal of Psychiatric Research, 31*(3), 251–260.

Quas, J. A., Malloy, L. C., Melinder, A., Goodman, G. S., D'Mello, M., & Schaaf, J. (2007). Developmental differences in the effects of repeated interviews and interviewer bias on young children's event memory and false reports. *Developmental Psychology, 43*(4), 823–837.

Quek, J., Newman, L. K., Bennett, C., Gordon, M. S., Saeedi, N., & Melvin, G. A. (2017). Reflective function mediates the relationship between emotional maltreatment and borderline pathology in adolescents: A preliminary investigation. *Child Abuse & Neglect, 72*, 215–226.

Quill, T. E., & Battin, M. P. (2018, January 12). Physician-assisted dying: Understanding, evaluating, and responding to requests for medical aid in dying. *UpToDate*. Retrieved from http://www.uptodate.com.

Quillian, L., & Pager, D. (2010). Estimating risk: Stereotype amplification and the perceived risk of criminal victimization. *Social Psychology Quarterly, 73*(1), 79–104.

Quirk, S. E., Berk, M., Chanen, A. M., Koivumaa-Honkanen, H., Brennan-Olsen, S. L., Pasco, J. A., & Williams, L. J. (2016). Population prevalence of personality disorder and associations with physical health comorbidities and health care service utilization: A review. *Personality Disorders, 7*(2), 136–146.

Quirk, S. E., Berk, M., Pasco, J. A., Brennan-Olsen, S. L., Chanen, A. M., Koivumaa-Honkanen, H., . . . Williams, L. J. (2017). The prevalence, age distribution and comorbidity of personality disorders in Australian women. *Australian & New Zealand Journal of Psychiatry, 51*(2), 141–150.

Qureshi, N. A., & Al-Bedah, A. M. (2013). Mood disorders and complementary and alternative medicine: A literature review. *Neuropsychiatric Disease and Treatment, 9*, 639–658.

Rabella, M., Grasa, E., Corripio, I., Romero, S., Mananas, M. A., Antonijoan, R. M., . . . Riba, J. (2016). Neurophysiological evidence impaired self-monitoring in schizotypal personality disorder and its reversal by dopaminergic antagonism. *NeuroImage: Clinical, 11,* 770–779.

Rabinovici, G. D. (2017). Advances and gaps in understanding chronic traumatic encephalopathy: From pugilists to American football players. *JAMA, 318*(4), 338–340.

Rachman, S. (1966). Sexual fetishism: An experimental analog. *Psychological Record, 18,* 25–27.

Radcliff, N. (2017, May 12). Laugh, giggle, be joyful—for lol. *Washington Times.* Retrieved from http://www.washingtontimes.com.

Radulovic, J., Jovasevic, V., & Meyer, M. A. (2017). Neurobiological mechanisms of state-dependent learning. *Current Opinion in Neurobiology, 45,* 92–98.

Rahim, Z. (2017, March 20). Norway is happiest country in the world. What's the secret? *Time.com.*

Raine, A. (2018). Antisocial personality as a neurodevelopmental disorder. *Annual Review of Clinical Psychology, 14,* 259–289.

RAINN (Rape, Abuse & Incest National Network). (2009). *Campus safety.* Retrieved from RAINN website: https://www.rainn.org/public-policy/campus-safety.

RAINN (Rape, Abuse & Incest National Network). (2016). *Perpetrators of sexual violence: Statistics.* Retrieved from https://www.rainn.org/statistics.

RAINN (Rape, Abuse & Incest National Network). (2016). *Victims of sexual violence: Statistics.* Retrieved from https://www.rainn.org/statistics.

Raj, V., Rowe, A. A., Fleisch, S. B., Paranjape, S. Y., Arain, A. M., & Nicolson, S. E. (2014). Psychogenic pseudosyncope: Diagnosis and management. *Autonomic Neuroscience: Basic and Clinical, 184,* 66–72.

Rajeh, A., Amanullah, S., Shivakumar, K., & Cole, J. (2017). Interventions in ADHD: A comparative review of stimulant medications and behavioral therapies. *Asian Journal of Psychiatry, 25,* 131–135.

Ram, Y., Liberman, U., & Feldman, M. W. (2018, January 23). Evolution of vertical and oblique transmission under fluctuating selection. *Proceedings of the National Academy of Sciences USA.* [Epub ahead of print]

Ramesh, T., Igoumenou, A., Vazquez Montes, M., & Fazel, S. (2018, April 4). Use of risk assessment instruments to predict violence in forensic psychiatric hospitals: A systematic review and meta-analysis. *European Psychiatry, 52,* 47–53.

Ramey, C. T. (2018, April 11). The Abecedarian Approach to Social, Educational, and Health Disparities. *Clinical Child and Family Psychology Review.* [Epub ahead of print]

Ramey, C. T., & Ramey, S. L. (2004). Early learning and school readiness: Can early intervention make a difference? *Merrill-Palmer Quarterly, 50*(4), 471–491.

Ramey, C. T., & Ramey, S. L. (2007). Early learning and school readiness: Can early intervention make a difference? In G. W. Ladd, (Ed.), *Appraising the human developmental sciences: Essays in honor of Merrill-Palmer Quarterly, Landscapes of childhood* (pp. 329–350). Detroit, MI: Wayne State University Press.

Ramsey, C. M., Spira, A. P., Mojtabai, R., Eaton, W. W., Roth, K., & Lee, H. B. (2013). Lifetime manic spectrum episodes and all-cause mortality: 26-year follow-up of the NIMH Epidemiologic Catchment Area Study. *Journal of Affective Disorders, 151*(1), 337–342.

Rankin, E. D. (2017). Developmental considerations in the origins of object relations: Implications for normative development and clinical practice. *Psychoanalytic Review, 104*(1), 87–109.

Rapport, M. D., Kofler, M. J., Alderson, R. M., & Raiker, J. S. (2008). Attention-deficit/hyperactivity disorder. In D. Reitman (Ed.), *Handbook of psychological assessment, case conceptualization, and treatment, Vol. 2: Children and adolescents.* Hoboken, NJ: John Wiley & Sons.

Rash, C. J., Stitzer, M., & Weinstock, J. (2017). Contingency management: New directions and remaining challenges for an evidence-based intervention. *Journal of Substance Abuse Treatment, 72,* 10–18.

Rashid, T., & Seligman, M. (2019). Positive psychotherapy. In D. Wedding & R. J. Corsini (Eds.), *Current psychotherapies* (11th ed., Ch. 13). Independence, KY: Cengage Publications.

Rasic, D., Hajek, T., Alda, M., & Uher, R. (2014). Risk of mental illness in offspring of parents with schizophrenia, bipolar disorder, and major depressive disorder: A meta-analysis of family high-risk studies. *Schizophrenia Bulletin, 40*(1), 28–38.

Raskin, N. J., Rogers, C. R., & Witty, M. C. (2019). Client-centered therapy. In D. Wedding & R. J. Corsini (Eds.), *Current psychotherapies* (11th ed., Ch. 4). Independence, KY: Cengage Publications.

Rasmusson, A. M., & Shalev, A. Y. (2014). Integrating the neuroendocrinology, neurochemistry, and neuroimmunology of PTSD to date and the challenges ahead. In M. J. Friedman, T. M. Keane, & P. A. Resick (Eds.). *Handbook of PTSD: Science and practice* (2nd ed., pp. 275–299). New York: Guilford Press.

Ratcliffe, R. (2014). How do other countries tackle bullying? *The Guardian.* Retrieved from http://www.theguardian/teacher-network/teacher-blog/2013.

Rathbone, C. J., Ellis, J. A., Baker, I., & Butler, C. R. (2014). Self, memory, and imagining the future in a case of psychogenic amnesia. *Neurocase, 21*(6), 727–737.

Rauscher, L., & Wilson, B. D. (2017). Super heroes and lucky duckies: Racialized stressors among teachers. *Cultural Diversity & Ethnic Minority Psychology, 23*(2), 220–229.

Ravitz, P., Watson, P., & Grigoriadis, S. (2013). *Psychotherapy essentials to-go: Interpersonal therapy for depression.* New York: W. W. Norton.

Raviv, S. (2010). *Being Ana.* Bloomington, IN: iUniverse.

Raz, M. (2013). *The lobotomy letters: The making of American psychosurgery (Rochester studies in medical history).* New York: University of Rochester Press.

Rea, I. M. (2017, June 17). Towards ageing well: Use it or lose it: Exercise, epigenetics and cognition. *Biogerontology.* [Epub ahead of print]

Read, J. (2016, October 24). Why auditory hallucinations are commonplace and have meaning. *Newsweek.*

Reamer, F. G. (2013). Social work in a digital age: Ethical and risk management challenges. *Social Work, 58*(2), 163–172.

Reavell, J., Hopkinson, M., Clarkesmith, D., & Lane, D. A. (2018). Effectiveness of cognitive behavioral therapy for depression and anxiety in patients with cardiovascular disease: A systematic review and meta-analysis. *Psychosomatic Medicine, 80*(8), 742–753.

Redinger, M. J., Crutchfield, P., Gibb, T. S., Longstreet, P., & Strung, R. (2018). Conversion disorder diagnosis and medically unexplained symptoms. *American Journal of Bioethics, 18*(5), 31–33.

Redmond, D. E. (1977). Alterations in the function of the nucleus locus coeruleus: A possible model for studies of anxiety. In I. Hanin & E. Usdin (Eds.), *Animal models in psychiatry and neurology.* New York: Pergamon Press.

Redmond, D. E. (1979). New and old evidence for the involvement of a brain norepinephrine system in anxiety. In W. E. Fann, I. Karacan, A. D. Pokorny, & R. L. Williams (Eds.), *Phenomenology and treatment of anxiety.* New York: Spectrum.

Redmond, D. E. (1981). Clonidine and the primate locus coeruleus: Evidence suggesting anxiolytic and anti-withdrawal effects. In H. Lal & S. Fielding (Eds.), *Psychopharmacology of clonidine.* New York: Alan R. Liss.

Regier, P. (2016). Drug epidemics: Now and then. *Addiction Unscripted.*

Rehm, I. C., Foenander, E., Wallace, K., Abbott, J. M., Kyrios, M., & Thomas, N. (2016). What role can avatars play in e-mental health interventions? Exploring new models of client-therapist interaction. *Frontiers in Psychiatry, 7,* 186.

Reichenberg, A., Cederlof, M., McMillan, A., Trzaskowski, M., Kapara, O., Fruchter, E., . . . Lichtenstein, P. (2016). Discontinuity in the genetic and environmental causes of the intellectual disability spectrum. *Proceedings of the National Academy of Sciences, 113,* 1098–1103.

Reidenberg, D. (2017). Facebook takes steps to stop suicides on Live. Interviewed in Guynn, J. (2017, March 1). *USA Today.*

Reinfjell, T., Karstad, S. B., Berg-Nielsen, T. S., Luby, J. L., & Wichstrøm, L. (2016). Predictors of change in depressive symptoms from preschool to first grade. *Development and Psychopathology, 28,* 1517–1530.

Reisch, T., Seifritz, E., Esposito, F., Wiest, R., Valach, L., & Michel, K. (2010). An fMRI study on mental pain and suicidal behavior. *Journal of Affective Disorders, 126*(1–2), 321–325.

Reisner, A. D., & Piel, J. L. (2018). Mental condition requirement in competency to stand trial assessments. *Journal of the American Academy of Psychiatry and the Law, 46,* 86–92.

Reitan, R. M., & Wolfson, D. (1996). Theoretical, methodological, and validational bases of the Halstead-Reitan neuropsychological test battery. In I. Grant & K. M. Adams (Eds.), *Neuropsychological assessment of neuropsychiatric disorders* (2nd ed., pp. 3–42). New York: Oxford University Press.

Reitan, R. M., & Wolfson, D. (2005). The effect of age and education transformations on neuropsychological test scores of persons with diffuse or bilateral brain damage. *Applied Neuropsychology, 12*(4), 181–189.

Remberk, B., Bażyńska, A. K., Bronowska, Z., Potocki, P., Krempa-Kowalewska, A., Niwiński, P., & Rybakowski, F. (2015). Which aspects of long-term outcome are predicted by positive and negative symptoms in early-onset psychosis? An exploratory eight-year follow-up study. *Psychopathology, 48*(1), 47–55.

Remes, O., Brayne, C., van der Linde, R., & Lafortune, L. (2016). A systematic review of reviews on the prevalence of anxiety disorders in adult populations. *Brain and Behavior, 6*(7), e00497.

Remick, R. A., Evans, A., & Bates, A. T. (2017). Exercise as medicine: An evidence-based treatment for depression. *BC Medical Journal, 59*(2), 83–84.

Remington, G., Foussias, G., Fervaha, G., & Agid, O. (2014). Schizophrenia, cognition, and psychosis. *JAMA Psychiatry, 71*(3), 336–337.

Renk, K., Stephenson, J'N., Khan, M., & Cunningham, A. (2017). Evidence-based methods of dealing with social difficulties in conduct disorder. In J. L. Matson (Ed.), *Handbook of social behavior and skills in children* (pp. 323–361). New York: Springer International Publishing.

Reuters. (2010, April 8). *They walk among us: 1 in 5 believe in aliens?* Retrieved from http://www.reuters.com/assets/print?aid.

Reuveni, I., Pelov, I., Reuveni, H., Bonne, O., & Canetti, L. (2017). Cross-sectional survey on defensive practices and defensive behaviours among Israeli psychiatrists. *BMJ Open, 7*(3), e014153.

Reynolds, G., Field, A. P., & Askew, C. (2017). Reductions in children's vicariously learnt avoidance and heart rate responses using positive modeling. *Journal of Clinical Child and Adolescent Psychology.* DOI: 10.1080/15374416.2016.1138410.

Rezaei, M., Khalighinasab, M. R., & Saadat, M. (2017). Association between genetic polymorphisms at promoter region of the catalase gene and risk of dependency to heroin. *Psychiatry Research, 251,* 235–236.

Rhéaume, C., Arsenault, B. J., Després, J., Faha, Boekholdt, S. M., Wareham, N. J., . . . Chir, M. (2014). Impact of abdominal obesity and systemic hypertension on risk of coronary heart disease in men and women: The EPIC Norfolk Population Study. *Journal of Hypertension, 32*(11), 2224–2230.

Ribeiro, A., Ribeiro, J. P., & von Doellinger, O. (2018). Depression and psychodynamic psychotherapy. *Revista Brasileira de Psiquiatria, 40*(1), 105–109.

Ribeiro, J. D., & Joiner, T. E. (2009). The interpersonal-psychological theory of suicidal behavior: Current status and future directions. *Journal of Clinical Psychology. 65*(12), 1291–1299.

Riblet, N., Shiner, B., Watts, B. V., Mills, P., Rusch, B., & Hemphill, R. R. (2017). Death by suicide within 1 week of hospital discharge: A retrospective study of root cause analysis reports. *Journal of Nervous and Mental Disease, 205*(6), 436–442.

Rice, F., Riglin, L., Lomax, T., Souter, E., Potter, R., Smith, D. J., . . . Thapar, A. (2019). Adolescent and adult differences in major depression symptom profiles. *Journal of Affective Disorders, 243,* 175–181.

Richards, I. L., Subar, A., Touyz, S., & Rhodes, P. (2018). Augmentative approaches in family-based treatment for adolescents with restrictive eating disorders: A systematic review. *European Eating Disorders Review, 26*(2), 92–111.

Richardson, J. R., Roy, A., Shalat, S. L., von Stein, R. T., Hossain, M. M., Buckley, B., . . . German, D. C. (2014). Elevated serum pesticide levels and risk for Alzheimer disease. *JAMA Neurology, 71*(3), 284–290.

Richardson, M., Hussain, Z., & Griffiths, M. D. (2018, February 8). Problematic smartphone use, nature connectedness, and anxiety. *Journal of Behavioral Addictions.* [Epub ahead of print]

Richmond, M. K., Pampel, F. C., Wood, R. C., & Nunes, A. P. (2017). The impact of employee assistance services on workplace outcomes: Results of a prospective, quasi-experimental study. *Journal of Occupational Health Psychology, 22*(2), 170–179.

Rickard, N., Arjmand, H. A., Bakker, D., & Seabrook, E. (2016). Development of a mobile phone app to support self-monitoring of emotional well-being: A mental health digital innovation. *JMIR Mental Health, 3*(4), e49.

Riddle, M. A., Maher, B. S., Wang, Y., Grados, M., Bienvenu, O. J., Goes, F. S., . . . Samuels, J. (2016). Obsessive-compulsive personality disorder: Evidence for two dimensions. *Depression and Anxiety, 33*(2), 128–135.

Rieber, R. W. (1999, March). Hypnosis, false memory, and multiple personality: A trinity of affinity. *History of Psychiatry, 10*(37), 3–11.

Rieber, R. W. (2002). The duality of the brain and the multiplicity of minds: Can you have it both ways? *History of Psychiatry 13*(49, Pt. 1), 3–18.

Rieber, R. W. (2006). *The bifurcation of the self: The history and theory of dissociation and its disorders.* New York: Springer Science + Business Media.

Riesch, S. K., Jacobson, G., Sawdey, L., Anderson, J., & Henriques, J. (2008). Suicide ideation among later elementary school-aged youth. *Journal of Psychiatric and Mental Health Nursing, 15*(4), 263–277.

Rigotti, N. A. (2018, February 17). Overview of smoking cessation management in adults. *UpToDate.* Retrieved from http://www.uptodate.com.

Rigotti, N. A., & Kalkhoran, S. (2017, August 22). E-cigarettes. *UpToDate.* Retrieved from http://www.uptodate.com.

Rigotti, N. A., & Kalkhoran, S. (2018, April 5). E-cigarettes. *UpToDate.* Retrieved from http://www.uptodate.com.

Riley, K. E., Lee, J. S., & Safren, S. A. (2017). The relationship between automatic thoughts and depression in a cognitive-behavioral treatment for people living with HIV/AIDS: Exploring temporality and causality. *Cognitive Therapy and Research, 41*(5), 712–719.

Rindal, E. J., Chrobak, Q. M., Zaragoza, M. S., & Weihing, C. A. (2017, February 7). Mechanisms of eyewitness suggestibility: Tests of the explanatory role hypothesis. *Psychonomic Bulletin and Review.* [Epub ahead of print]

Rittenhouse, M. (2016, May 7). Identifying eating disorder issues in the African American community. *Eating Disorder Hope.* Retrieved from https://www.eatingdisorderhope.com/blog.

Ritter, M. R., Blackmore, M. A., & Heimberg, R. G. (2010). Generalized anxiety disorder. In D. McKay, J. S. Abramowitz, & S. Taylor (Eds.), *Cognitive-behavioral therapy for refractory cases: Turning failure into success* (pp. 111–137). Washington, DC: American Psychological Association.

Riva-Posse, P., Choi, K. S., Holtzheimer, P. E., Crowell, A. L., Garlow, S. J., Rajendra, J. K., . . . Mayberg, H. S. (2018). A connectomic approach for subcallosal cingulate deep brain stimulation surgery: Prospective targeting in treatment-resistant depression. *Molecular Psychiatry.* [Manuscript in press]

Rivard, M., Morin, M., Mello, C., Terroux, A., & Mercier, C. (2018, May 1). Follow-up of children with autism spectrum disorder 1 year after early behavioral intervention. *Behavior Modification.* [Epub ahead of print]

Rivenbark, J. G., Odgers, C. L., Caspi, A., Harrington, H., Hogan, S., Houts, R. M., . . . Moffitt, T. E. (2018). The high societal costs of childhood conduct problems: Evidence from administrative records up to age 38 in a longitudinal birth cohort. *Journal of Child Psychology and Psychiatry, 59*(6), 703–710.

Rizzi, M., & Marras, C. E. (2017). Deep brain stimulation for the treatment of aggressive behaviour: Considerations on pathophysiology and target choice. *Stereotactic and Functional Neurosurgery, 95*(2), 114–116.

Roaiah, M. F., Elkhayat, Y. I., Rashed, L. A., Gamal El Din, S. F., El Guindi, A. M., & Abd El Salam, M. A. (2018). Study of the prevalence of 5 HT-2C receptor gene polymorphisms in Egyptian patients with lifelong premature ejaculation. *Andrologia, 50*(2).

Robert, G., & Zadra, A. (2014). Thematic and content analysis of idiopathic nightmares and bad dreams. *Sleep, 37*(2), 409–417.

Roberts, R., Neasham, A., Lambrinudi, C., & Khan, A. (2018). A quantitative analysis of antipsychotic prescribing trends for the treatment of schizophrenia in England and Wales. *JRSM Open, 9*(4), 2054270418758570.

Robertson, C. A., & Knight, R. A. (2014). Relating sexual sadism and psychopathy to one another, non-sexual violence, and sexual crime behaviors. *Aggressive Behavior, 40*(1), 12–23.

Robins, C. J., Zerubavel, N., Ivanoff, A. M., & Linehan, M. M. (2018). Dialectical behavior therapy. In W. J. Livesley & R. Larstone (Eds.), *Handbook of personality disorders: Theory, research, and treatment* (2nd ed.). New York: Guilford Press.

Robinson, M. (2017, January 8). It's 2017: Here's where you can legally smoke weed now. *Business Insider.*

Robinson-Papp, J., Sharma, S. K., George, M. C., & Simpson, D. M. (2017). Assessment of autonomic symptoms in a medically complex, urban patient population. *Clinical Autonomic Research, 27*(1), 25–29.

Robitaille, M. P., Checknita, D., Vitaro, F., Tremblay, R. E., Paris, J., & Hodgins, S. (2017). A prospective, longitudinal, study of men with borderline personality disorder with and without comorbid antisocial personality disorder. *Borderline Personality Disorder and Emotion Dysregulation, 4,* 25.

Robles, R., Fresán, A., Vega-Ramirez, H., Cruz-Islas, J., Rodriguez-Pérez, V., Dominguez-Martinez, T., & Reed, G. M. (2016). Removing transgender identity from the classification of mental disorders: A Mexican field study for ICD-11. *Lancet Psychiatry, 3*(9), 850–859.

Robson, D. (2017, January 19). How East and West think in profoundly different ways. *BBC-Future*. Retrieved from http://www.bbc.com/future/story/20170118-how-east-and-west-think-in-profoundly-different-ways.

Rocca, P., Montemagni, C., Zappia, S., Piterà, R., Sigaudo, M., & Bogetto, F. (2014). Negative symptoms and everyday functioning in schizophrenia: A cross-sectional study in a real world-setting. *Psychiatry Research, 218*(3), 284–289.

Roche, T. (2002, January 20). The Yates odyssey. *TIME.com: Nation*.

Rochon, P. A. (2018, June 26). Drug prescribing for older adults. *UpToDate*. Retrieved from http://www.uptodate.com.

Rocks, T., Pelly, F., & Wilkinson, P. (2014). Nutrition therapy during initiation of refeeding in underweight children and adolescent inpatients with anorexia nervosa: A systematic review of the evidence. *Journal of the Academy of Nutrition and Dietetics, 114*(6), 897–907.

Rodav, O., Levy, S., & Hamdan, S. (2014). Clinical characteristics and functions of non-suicide self-injury in youth. *European Psychiatry, 29*(8), 503–508.

Rodebaugh, T. L., Levinson, C. A., Langer, J. K., Weeks, J. W., Heimberg, R. G., Brown, P. J., . . . Liebowitz, M. R. (2017). The structure of vulnerabilities for social anxiety disorder. *Psychiatry Research, 250,* 297–301.

Rodgers, R. F., Lowy, A. S., Halperin, D. M., & Franko, D. L. (2016). A meta-analysis examining the influence of pro-eating disorder websites on body image and eating pathology. *European Eating Disorders Review, 24*(1), 3–8.

Rodgers, R. F., Peterson, K. E., Hunt, A. T., Spadano-Gasbarro, J. L., Richmond, T. K., Greaney, M. L., & Bryn Austin, S. (2017). Racial/ethnic and weight status disparities in dieting and disordered weight control behaviors among early adolescents. *Eating Behaviors, 26,* 104–107.

Rodnitzky, R. (2018, July 10). Cognitive impairment and dementia in Parkinson disease. *UpToDate*. Retrieved from http://www.uptodate.com.

Roepke, S., & Vater, A. (2014). Narcissistic personality disorder: An integrative review of recent empirical data and current definitions. *Current Psychiatry Reports, 16,* 445.

Roesch, R. (1991). *The encyclopedia of depression*. New York: Facts on File.

Roesch, R. (2016, December). Competency to stand trial in the American legal system. *Oxford Research Encyclopedia of Psychology*. Retrieved from http://psychology.oxfordre.com.

Roesler, T. A., & Jenny, C. (2018, January 25). Medical child abuse (Munchausen syndrome by proxy). *UpToDate*. Retrieved from http://www.uptodate.com.

Rogers, C. R. (1951). *Client-centered therapy*. Boston: Houghton Mifflin.

Rogers, C. R. (1954). The case of Mrs. Oak: A research analysis. In C. R. Rogers & R. F. Dymond (Eds.), *Psychotherapy and personality change* (pp. 259–269). Chicago: University of Chicago Press.

Rogers, C. R. (1987). Rogers, Kohut, and Erickson: A personal perspective on some similarities and differences. In J. K. Zeig (Ed.), *The evolution of psychotherapy*. New York: Brunner/Mazel.

Rogers, M. L., Kelliher-Rabon, J., Hagen, C. R., Hirsch, J. K., & Joiner, T. E. (2017). Negative emotions in veterans relate to suicide risk through feelings of perceived burdensomeness and thwarted belongingness. *Journal of Affective Disorders, 208,* 15–21.

Rogler, L. H., Malgady, R. G., & Rodriguez, O. (1989). *Hispanics and mental health: A framework for research*. Malabar, FL: Krieger Publishing.

Rogoll, J., Petzold, M., & Ströhle, A. (2018). [Selective mutism]. *Nervenarzt, 89*(5), 591–602. [German].

Rojas, A. (2017, August 2). New survey shows nearly half of Americans believe in aliens. *Huffington Post*.

Rojas, S. L., & Widiger, T. A. (2017). Coverage of the DSM-IV-TR/DSM-5 Section II personality disorders with the DSM-5 dimensional trait model. *Journal of Personality Disorders, 31(4), 462–482.*

Rolin, H., Fossion, P., Kotsou, I., & Leys, C. (2018). Perspectives on resilience: Trait or aptitude? *Revue Médicale de Bruxelles, 39*(1), 22–28. [French]

Rollin, H. R., & Reynolds, E. H. (2018). Yorkshire's influence on the understanding and treatment of mental diseases in Victorian Britain: The golden triad of York, Wakefield, and Leeds. *Journal of the History of the Neurosciences, 27*(1), 72–84.

Rolls, E. T. (2017). The roles of the orbitofrontal cortex via the habenula in non-reward and depression, and in the responses of serotonin and dopamine neurons. *Neuroscience & Biobehavioral Reviews, 75,* 331–334.

Romero-Martínez, A., Figueiredo, B., & Moya-Albiol, L. (2014). Childhood history of abuse and child abuse potential: The role of parent's gender and timing of childhood abuse. *Child Abuse and Neglect, 38*(3), 510–516.

Ronningstam, E. (2011). Narcissistic personality disorder: A clinical perspective. *Journal of Psychiatric Practice, 17*(2), 89–99.

Ronningstam, E. (2017). Intersect between self-esteem and emotion regulation in narcissistic personality disorder: Implications for alliance building and treatment. *Borderline Personality Disorder and Emotion Dysregulation, 4,* 3.

Roper. (2017). *Public attitudes about mental health*. Ithaca, NY: Roper Center for Public Opinion Research, Cornell University.

Ros, R., & Graziano, P. (2018). Social functioning in children with or at risk for attention deficit/hyperactivity disorder. *Journal of Clinical Child and Adolescent Psychology*. [Manuscript in press]

Rose, S. W., Mayo, A., Ganz, O., Perreras, L., D'Silva, J., & Cohn, A. (2018, February 9). Perceived racial/ethnic discrimination, marketing, and substance use among young adults. *Journal of Ethnicity in Substance Abuse*. [Epub ahead of print]

Rose, T., Joe, S., & Lindsey, M. (2011). Perceived stigma and depression among black adolescents in outpatient treatment. *Children and Youth Services Review, 33*(1), 161–166.

Rosell, D. R. (2017, June 14). Schizotypal personality disorder: Epidemiology, pathogenesis, clinical manifestations, course, and diagnosis. *UpToDate*. Retrieved from http://www.uptodate.com.

Rosell, D. R. (2018, May 24). Schizotypal personality disorder: Epidemiology, pathogenesis, clinical manifestations, course, and diagnosis. *UpToDate*. Retrieved from http://www.uptodate.com.

Rosen, E. F., Anthony, D. L., Booker, K. M., Brown, T. L., Christian, E., Crews, R. C., . . . Petty, L. C. (1991). A comparison of eating disorder scores among African American and white college females. *Bulletin of Psychosomatic Society, 29*(1), 65–66.

Rosen, R. C. (2007). Erectile dysfunction: Integration of medical and psychological approaches. In S. R. Leiblum (Ed.), *Principles and practice of sex therapy* (4th ed., pp. 277–310). New York: Guilford Press.

Rosen, R. C., & Rosen, L. R. (1981). *Human sexuality*. New York: Knopf.

Rosenblum, G. D., & Lewis, M. (1999). The relations among body image, physical attractiveness, and body mass in adolescence. *Child Development, 70*(1), 50–64.

Rosenhan, D. L. (1973). On being sane in insane places. *Science, 179*(4070), 250–258.

Rosenström, T., Ystrom, E., Torvik, F. A., Czajkowski, N. O., Gillespie, N. A., Aggen, S. H., . . . Reichborn-Kjennerud, T. (2017). Genetic and environmental structure of DSM-IV criteria for antisocial personality disorder: A twin study. *Behavior Genetics, 47*(3), 265–277.

Rosenthal, R. (1966). *Experimenter effects in behavioral research*. New York: Appleton-Century-Crofts.

Rosenthal, R. N., Levounis, P., & Herron, A. J. (2016). Polysubstance use, abuse, and dependence. In A. H. Mack, K. T. Brady, S. I. Miller, & R. J. Frances (Eds.). *Clinical textbook of addictive disorders* (4th ed., Ch. 14, pp. 267–291). New York: Guilford Press.

Rosenthal, R. N. (2011). Alcohol abstinence management. In J. H. Lowinson & P. Ruiz (Eds.), *Substance abuse: A comprehensive textbook* (5th ed.). Philadelphia, PA: Lippincott Williams & Wilkins.

Rosky, J. W. (2016). More polygraph futility: A comment on Jensen, Shafer, Roby, and Roby (2015). *Journal of Interpersonal Violence, 31*(10), 1956–1970.

Rosky, J. W. (2013). The (f)utility of post-conviction polygraph testing. *Sexual Abuse: A Journal of Research and Treatment, 25*(3), 259–281.

Roslan, N. S., Jaafar, N. R. N., Sidi, H., Baharuddin, N., Kumar, J., Das, S., & Hussein, N. H. N. (2017, June 21). The bio-psycho-social dimension in women's sexual desire: "Argumentum ad novitatem." *Current Drug Targets*. [Epub ahead of print]

Ross, C. (2018). *Treatment of dissociative identity disorder: Techniques and strategies for stabilization*. Richardson, TX: Manitou Communications.

Ross, C. (2018). Why do women hate their bodies? *Psych Central*. Retrieved from https://psychcentral.com.

Ross, C. A., & Ness, L. (2010). Symptom patterns in dissociative identity disorder patients and the general population. *Journal of Trauma & Dissociation, 11*(4), 458–468.

Ross, D. A., Arbuckle, M. R., Travis, M. J., Dwyer, J. B., van Schalkwyk, G. I., & Ressler, K. J. (2017). An integrated neuroscience perspective on formulation and treatment planning for posttraumatic stress disorder: An educational review. *JAMA Psychiatry, 74*, 407–415.

Rotenberg, K. J., Costa, P., Trueman, M., & Lattimore, P. (2012). An interactional test of the reformulated helplessness theory of depression in women receiving clinical treatment for eating disorders. *Eating Behaviors, 13*(3), 264–266.

Roth, D. L., Usher, T., Clark, E. M., & Holt, C. L. (2016). Religious involvement and health over time: Predictive effects in a national sample of African Americans. *Journal for the Scientific Study of Religion, 55*(2), 417–424.

Rothbaum, B. O. (2017, February 3). Psychotherapy for posttraumatic stress disorder in adults. *UpToDate*. Retrieved from https://www.uptodate.com.

Rothbaum, B. O., Foa, E. B., Riggs, D. S., Murdock, T., & Walsh, W. (1992). A prospective examination of posttraumatic stress disorder in rape victims. *Journal of Traumatic Stress, 5*(3), 455–475.

Rothenberg, A. (2015, March 8). Creativity and mental illness. Creativity is highly adaptive and the actual processes involved are all healthy. *Psychology Today*. Retrieved from https://www.psychologytoday.com/blog/creativity-explorations-in-art-literature-science-and-the-everyday/201503/creativity-and-mental.

Rothschild, A. J. (2017, September 25). Unipolar major depression with psychotic features: Acute treatment. *UpToDate*. Retrieved from http://www.uptodate.com.

Rowland, D. I., & Cooper, S. E. (2017). Treating men's orgasmic difficulties. In Z. D. Peterson, *The Wiley-Blackwell handbook of sex therapy* (Chap. 6, pp. 72–97). Hoboken, NJ: Wiley-Blackwell.

Roy-Byrne, P. P. (2016, May 26). Panic disorder in adults: Epidemiology, pathogenesis, clinical manifestations, course, assessment, and diagnosis. *UpToDate*. Retrieved from http://www.uptodate.com.

Roy-Byrne, P. P. (2017, May 15). Pharmacotherapy for panic disorder with or without agoraphobia in adults. *UpToDate*. Retrieved from http://www.uptodate.com.

Roy-Byrne, P. P. (2018, January 25). Panic disorder in adults: Epidemiology, pathogenesis, clinical manifestations, course, assessment, and diagnosis. *UpToDate*. Retrieved from http://www.uptodate.com.

Roy-Byrne, P. P., & Craske, M. (2017, August 1). Approach to treating panic disorder with or without agoraphobia in adults. *UpToDate*. Retrieved from http://www.uptodate.com.

Rubens, S. L., Gudiño, O. G., Fite, P. J., & Grande, J. M. (2018). Individual and neighborhood stressors, sleep problems, and symptoms of anxiety and depression among Latino youth. *American Journal of Orthopsychiatry, 88*(2), 161–168.

Rubenstein, L. M., Freed, R. D., Shapero, B. G., Fauber, R. L., & Alloy, L. B. (2016). Cognitive attributions in depression: Bridging the gap between research and clinical practice. *Journal of Psychotherapy Integration, 26*(2), 103–115.

Rubin, D. M., Curtis, M. L., & Matone, M. (2014). Child abuse prevention and child home visitation: Making sure we get it right. *JAMA Pediatrics, 168*(1), 5–6.

Rubio-Aurioloes, E., & Bivalacqua, T. J. (2013). Standard operational procedures for low sexual desire in men. *Journal of Sexual Medicine, 10*, 94–107.

Rudge, S., Feigenbaum, J. D., & Fonagy, P. (2018). Mechanisms of change in dialectical behaviour therapy and cognitive behaviour therapy for borderline personality disorder: A critical review of the literature. *Journal of Mental Health*. [Manuscript in press]

Ruggero, C. J., Kotov, R., Callahan, J. L., Kilmer, J. N., Luft, B. J., & Bromet, E. J. (2013). PTSD symptom dimensions and their relationship to functioning in World Trade Center responders. *Psychiatry Research, 210*(3), 1049–1055.

Rupert, P. A., Miller, A. O., Tuminello Hartman, E. R., & Bryant, F. B. (2012). Predictors of career satisfaction among practicing psychologists. *Professional Psychology: Research and Practice, 43*(5), 495–502.

Rus-Calafell, M., Garety, P., Ward, T., Williams, G., Huckvale, M., Leff, J., & Craig, T. K. (2015). Confronting auditory hallucinations using virtual reality: The avatar therapy. *Studies in Health Technology and Informatics, 219*, 192–196.

Ruscio, J. (2015). Labeling theory. In R. L. Cautin & S. O. Lilienfeld, *The encyclopedia of clinical psychology*. Hoboken, NJ: John Wiley & Sons.

Rush, J. A. (2018, January 24). Unipolar depression in adults: Treatment with antidepressant combinations. *UpToDate*. Retrieved from http://www.uptodate.com.

Russell, J. E. A. (2014, July 10). Practice mindfulness for better, and quite possibly longer, life. *Tampa Bay Times*.

Russo, F. (2016, January 1). Is there something unique about the transgender brain? *Scientific American*.

Russo, F. (2016, January 1). Transgender kids: What does it take to help them thrive? *Scientific American*.

Russo, F. (2017, January 6). Where transgender is no longer a diagnosis. *Scientific American*.

Russo, F. (2018, January). Loneliness can be toxic. *Scientific American*.

Russo, N. F., & Tartaro, J. (2008). Women and mental health. In F. L. Denmark & M. A. Paludi (Eds.), *Psychology of women: A handbook of issues and theories* (2nd ed., pp. 440–483). Westport, CT: Praeger Publishers.

Rutledge, P. (2013, October 20). Positively media: How we connect and thrive through emerging technologies. *Psychology Today*.

Ruys, J. F. (2017). *Demons in the Middle Ages (past imperfect)*. Leeds, UK: Arc Humanities Press.

Ruzek, J. I., Schnurr, P. P., Vasterling, J. J., & Friedman, J. (Eds.). (2011). *Caring for veterans with deployment-related stress disorders*. Washington, DC: American Psychological Association.

Ryan, S. M., Strege, M. V., Oar, E. L., & Ollendick, T. H. (2017). One session therapy for specific phobias in children: Comorbid anxiety disorders and treatment outcome. *Journal of Behavior Therapy and Experimental Psychiatry, 54*, 128–134.

Rydell, M., Lundström, S., Gillberg, C., Lichtenstein, P., & Larsson, H. (2018, February 27). Has the attention deficit hyperactivity disorder phenotype become more common in children between 2004 and 2014? Trends over 10 years from a Swedish general population sample. *Journal of Child Psychology and Psychiatry*. [Epub ahead of print]

Ryles, F., Meyer, T. D., Adan-Manes, J., MacMillan, I., & Scott, J. (2017). A systematic review of the frequency and severity of manic symptoms reported in studies that compare phenomenology across children, adolescents and adults with bipolar disorders. *International Journal of Bipolar Disorders, 5*(1), 4.

Sabouri, S., Gerber, M., Sadeghi Bahmani, D., Lemola, S., Clough, P. J., Kalak, N., . . . Brand, S. (2016). Examining Dark Triad traits in relation to mental toughness and physical activity in young adults. *Neuropsychiatric Disease and Treatment, 27*(12), 229–235.

Sabri, O., Meyer, P. M., Gräf, S., Hesse, S., Wilke, S., Becker, G. A., . . . Brust, P. (2018). Cognitive correlates of a4b2 nicotine acetylcholine receptors in mild Alzheimer's dementia. *Brain, 141*(6), 1840–1854.

Sacks, O. (2012). *Hallucinations*. New York: Vintage Books.

Sacks, O. (2012, November 3). Seeing things? Hearing things? Many of us do. *New York Times*.

Sacks, O. (2017). *The river of consciousness*. New York: Knopf.

Sadeghi, K., Ahmadi, S. M., Moghadam, A. P., & Parvizifard, A. (2017). The study of cognitive change process on depression during aerobic exercises. *Journal of Clinical and Diagnostic Research, 11*(4), IC01–IC05.

Sadeghi, K., Ahmadi, S. M., Rezaei, M., Miri, J., Abdi, A., Khamoushi, F., . . . Jamshidi, K. (2016). A comparative study of the efficacy of cognitive group therapy and aerobic exercise in the treatment of depression among the students. *Global Journal of Health Science, 8*(10), 54171.

Sadeh, N., Londahl-Shaller, E. A., Piatigorsky, A., Fordwood, S., Stuart, B. K., McNiel, D. E., . . . Yaeger, A. M. (2014). Functions of non-suicidal self-injury in adolescents and young adults with borderline personality disorder symptoms. *Psychiatry Research, 216*(2), 217–222.

Sadiq, S., Suhail, K., Gleeson, J., & Alvarez-Jimenez, M. (2017). Expressed emotion and the course of schizophrenia in Pakistan. *Social Psychiatry and Psychiatric Epidemiology, 52*(5), 587–593.

Safer, D. J. (2016). Recent trends in stimulant usage. *Journal of Attention Disorders, 20*, 471–477.

Safran, J. D., Kriss, A., & Foley, V. (2019). Psychoanalytic psychotherapies. In D. Wedding & R. J. Corsini (Eds.), *Current psychotherapies* (11th ed., Ch. 2). Independence, KY: Cengage Publications.

Sajatovic, M., & Chen, P. (2017, November 22). Geriatric bipolar disorder: Acute treatment. *UpToDate*. Retrieved from http://www.uptodate.com.

Sajatovic, M., & Chen, P. (2017, October 6). Geriatric bipolar disorder: Epidemiology, clinical features, assessment, and diagnosis. *UpToDate*. Retrieved from http://www.uptodate.com.

Salari, A., Bakhtiari, A., & Homberg, J. R. (2015). Activation of GABA-A receptors during postnatal brain development increases anxiety- and depression-related behaviors in a time- and dose-dependent manner in adult mice. *European Neuropsychopharmacy: The Journal of the European College of Neuropsychopharmacology, 25*(8), 1260–1274.

Salary.com. (2016). Psychologist salaries. Retrieved from www.salary.com/psychologist-salary.html.

Salcedo, B. (2018, January 19). The comorbidity of anxiety and depression. *National Alliance on Mental Illness*. Retrieved from https://www.nami.org/blogs/NAMI-Blog/January-2018.

Salkind, N. J. (2017). *Research design: Quantitative, qualitative, mixed methods, arts-based, and community-based participatory research approaches*. New York: Guilford Press.

Salkovskis, P. M., Millar, J., Gregory, J. D., & Wahl, K. (2017). The termination of checking and the role of just right feelings: A study of obsessional checkers compared with anxious and non-clinical controls. *Behavioural and Cognitive Psychotherapy, 45*(2), 139–155.

Salkovskis, P. M. (1985). Obsessional-compulsive problems: A cognitive-behavioural analysis. *Behavioral Research and Therapy, 23*, 571–584.

Salkovskis, P. M. (1999). Understanding and treating obsessive-compulsive disorder. *Behavioral Research and Therapy, 37*(Suppl. 1), S29–S52.

Salkovskis, P. M., Thorpe, S. J., Wahl, K., Wroe, A. L., & Forrester, E. (2003). Neutralizing increases discomfort associated with obsessional thoughts: An experimental study with obsessional patients. *Journal of Abnormal Psychology, 112*(4), 709–715.

Saltzman, J. A., & Liechty, J. M. (2016, August 22). Family correlates of childhood binge eating: A systematic review. *Eating Behaviors*. [Epub ahead of print]

Sam, F. E. (2016, October 8). Reasons why fear is actually a good thing. *The Blog*. Retrieved from http://www.huffingtonpost.com.

Samek, D. R., Keyes, M. A., Hicks, B. M., Bailey, J., McGue, M., & Iacono, W. G. (2014). General and specific predictors of nicotine and alcohol dependence in early adulthood: Genetic and environmental influences. *Journal of Studies on Alcohol and Drugs, 75*(4), 623–634.

SAMHSA (Substance Abuse and Mental Health Services Administration). (2014). *Projections of national expenditures for treatment of mental and substance use disorders. 2010–2020*. Rockville, MD: SAMHSA.

SAMHSA (Substance Abuse and Mental Health Services Administration). (2016, November 15). *The CBHSQ Report: Serious mental illness among adults below the poverty line*. Rockville, MD: SAMHSA

SAMHSA (Substance Abuse and Mental Health Services Administration). (2017, January 20). *Publications and resources on suicide prevention*. Rockville, MD: SAMHSA. Retrieved from https://www.samhsa.gov.

SAMHSA (Substance Abuse and Mental Health Services Administration). (2017, February). *Suicide clusters within American Indian and Alaska Native communities: A review of the literature and recommendations*. Rockville, MD: SAMHSA. Retrieved from https://www.samhsa.gov.

SAMHSA (Substance Abuse and Mental Health Services Administration). (2017). *Buprenorphine*. Retrieved from https://www.samhsa.gov/medication-assisted-treatment/treatment/buprenorphine.

SAMHSA (Substance Abuse and Mental Health Services Administration). (2017). *Data, outcomes, and quality*. Rockville, MD: SAMHSA.

SAMHSA (Substance Abuse and Mental Health Services Administration). (2018). *Schizophrenia*. SAMHSA. Retrieved from https://www.samhsa.gov/treatment/mental-health-disorders/schizophrenia.

SAMHSA (Substance Abuse and Mental Health Services Administration). (2018, January 17). *American Indian and Alaska Native: Tribal affairs*. Rockville, MD: SAMHSA. Retrieved from https://www.samhsa.gov.

SAMHSA (Substance Abuse and Mental Health Services). (2017, September 20). *Evidence-based practices web guide: Substance abuse prevention evidence-based practices (EBP)*. Rockville, MD: SAMHSA. Retrieved from https://www.samhsa.gov/ebp-web-guide.

SAMHSA (Substance Abuse and Mental Health Services). (2018, March 21). *Reports and detailed tables from the 2015 National Survey on Drug Use and Health (NSDUH)*. Rockville, MD: SAMHSA.

Samorodnitzky-Naveh, G., Geiger, S. B., & Levin, L. (2007). Patients' satisfaction with dental esthetics. *Journal of the American Dental Association, 138*(6), 805–808.

Sanburn, J. (2013, September 13). Inside the National Suicide Hotline: Preventing the next tragedy. *Time.com*.

Sanchez, A. L., Cornacchio, D., Chou, T., Leyfer, O., Coxe, S., Pincus, D. B., & Comer, J. S. (2017). Development of a scale to evaluate young children's responses to uncertainty and low environmental structure. *Journal of Anxiety Disorders, 45*, 17–23.

Sanchez, A. L., Cornacchio, D., Poznanski, B., Golik, A., Chou, T., & Comer, J. S. (2018). The effectiveness of school-based mental health services for elementary-aged children: A meta-analysis. *Journal of the American Academy of Child and Adolescent Psychiatry, 57*, 153–165.

Sanchez, A. L., Kendall, P. C., & Comer, J. S. (2016). Evaluating the intergenerational link between maternal and child intolerance of uncertainty: A preliminary cross-sectional examination. *Cognitive Therapy and Research, 40*, 532–539.

Sanders, T. (2016, December 1). *The Oxford handbook of sex offences and sex offenders*. New York: Oxford University Press.

Sandler, C. X., Goldstein, D., Horsfield, S., Bennett, B. K., Friedlander, M., Bastick, P. A., . . . Lloyd, A. R. (2017, May 11). Randomized evaluation of cognitive-behavioral therapy and graded exercise therapy for post-cancer fatigue. *Journal of Pain and Symptom Management*. [Epub ahead of print]

Sandler, I. N., Wolchik, S. A., & Ayers, T. S. (2008). Resilience rather than recovery: A contextual framework on adaptation following bereavement. *Death Studies, 32*, 59–73.

Sandler, M. (1990). Monoamine oxidase inhibitors in depression: History and mythology. *Journal of Psychopharmacology, 4*(3), 136–139.

Sareen, J. (2018, January 25). Posttraumatic stress disorder in adults: Epidemiology, pathophysiology, clinical manifestations, course, assessment and diagnosis. *UpToDate*. Retrieved from http://www.uptodate.com.

Sareen, J., Afifi, T. O., McMillan, K. A., & Asmundson, G. J. G. (2011). Relationship between household income and mental disorders: Findings from a population-based longitudinal study. *Archives of General Psychiatry, 68*(4), 419–426.

Savino, A. C., & Fordtran, J. S. (2006). Factitious disease: Clinical lessons from case studies at Baylor University Medical Center. *Proceedings (Baylor University Medical Center), 19*(3), 195–208.

Sawni, A., & Breuner, C. C. (2017, March 24). Clinical hypnosis, an effective mind-body modality for adolescents with behavioral and physical complaints. *Children (Basel), 4*(4).

Schadenberg, A. (2012, September 25). Euthanasia is out of control in the Netherlands: New Dutch statistics. *LifeSite*. Retrieved from LifeSite website: http://www.lifesitenews.com/blogs/.

Schat, A., van Noorden, M. S., Giltay, E. J., Noom, M. J., Vermeiren, R. R. J. M., & Zitman, F. G. (2017). Concordance between self-reported and observer-rated anxiety severity in outpatients with anxiety disorders: The Leiden routine outcome monitoring study. *Psychology and Psychotherapy, 90*(4), 705–719.

Scheffers, M., van Duijin, M. A. J., Beldman, M., Bosscher, R. J., van Busschbach, J. T., & Schoevers, R. A. (2019). Body attitude, body satisfaction and body awareness in a clinical group of depressed patients: An observational study on the associations with depression severity and the influence of treatment. *Journal of Affective Disorders, 242*, 22–28.

Schienle, A., Hettema, J. M., Cáceda, R., & Nemeroff, C. B. (2011). Neurobiology and genetics of generalized anxiety disorder. *Psychiatric Annals, 41*(2), 111–123.

Schiffer, B., Pawliczek, C., Müller, B. W., Wiltfang, J., Brüne, M., Forsting, M., . . . Hodgins, S. (2017). Neural mechanisms underlying affective theory of mind in violent antisocial personality disorder and/or schizophrenia. *Schizophrenia Bulletin, 43*(6), 1229–1239.

Schildkraut, J. J. (1965). The catecholamine hypothesis of affective disorders: A review of supporting evidence. *American Journal of Psychiatry, 122*(5), 509–522.

Schildkrout, B. (2016). 5 Mental health diagnostic challenges: Update on "To err is human." *Psychiatric Times, 33*(2), 3.

Schmidt, H. M., Munder, T., Gerger, H., Frühauf, S., & Barth, J. (2014). Combination of psychological interventions and phosphodiesterase-5 inhibitors for erectile dysfunction: A narrative review and meta-analysis. *Journal of Sexual Medicine, 11,* 1376–1391.

Schmidtman, E. A., Hurley, R. A., & Taber, K. H. (2017). Secular mindfulness-based interventions: Efficacy and neurobiology. *Journal of Neuropsychiatry and Clinical Neurosciences, 29*(2), A6–A83.

Schmitgen, M. M., Depping, M. S., Bach, C., Wolf, N. D., Kubera, K. M., Vasic, N., . . . Wolf, R. C. (2019). Aberrant cortical neurodevelopment in major depressive disorder. *Journal of Affective Disorders, 243,* 340–347.

Schneeberger, A. R., Huber, C. G., Lang, U. E., Muenzenmaier, K. H., Castille, D., Jaeger, M., . . . Link, B. G. (2017). Effects of assisted outpatient treatment and health care services on psychotic symptoms. *Social Science & Medicine, 175,* 152–160.

Schneider, K. J., & Krug, O. T. (2017). *Existential-humanistic therapy (Theories of Psychotherapy Series),* 2nd ed. Washington, DC: American Psychological Association.

Schneider, K. L., & Shenassa, E. (2008). Correlates of suicide ideation in a population-based sample of cancer patients. *Journal of Psychosocial Oncology, 26*(2) 49–62.

Schneier, F. R. (2017, May 3). Social anxiety disorder in adults: Epidemiology, clinical manifestations, and diagnosis. *UpToDate.* Retrieved from http://www.uptodate.com.

Schneier, F. R., Moskow, D. M., Choo, T. H., Galfalvy, H., Campeas, R., & Sanchez-Lacay, A. (2017). A randomized controlled pilot trial of vilazodone for adult separation anxiety disorder. *Depression and Anxiety, 34*(12), 1085–1095.

Schöttle, D., Schimmelmann, B. G., Ruppelt, F., Bussopulos, A., Friedling, M., Nika, E., . . . Lambert, M. (2018). Effectiveness of integrated care including therapeutic assertive community treatment in severe schizophrenia: Spectrum and bipolar I disorders: Four-year follow-up of the ACCESS II study. *PLoS ONE, 13*(2), e0192929.

Schreiber, F. R. (1973). *Sybil.* Chicago: Regnery.

Schreiber, J., & Culpepper, L. (2018, February 19). Suicidal ideation and behavior in adults. *UpToDate.* Retrieved from http://www.uptodate.com.

Schroeder, R. A. (2018, January 25). Unique practice, unique place: Exploring two assertive community treatment teams in Maine. *Issues in Mental Health Nursing,* 1–7. [Epub ahead of print]

Schuch, F. B., Morres, I. D., Ekkekakis, P., & Rosenbaum, S. (2017, April). Exercise works for depression: Bridging the implementation gap and making exercise a core component of treatment. *Acta Neuropsychiatrica, 29*(2), 124–126.

Schulman, J. K., & Erickson-Schroth, L. (2017). Mental health in sexual minority and transgender women. *Psychiatric Clinics of North America, 40*(2), 309–319.

Schultz, D. S., & Brabender, V. M. (2012). More challenges since Wikipedia: The effects of exposure to internet information about the Rorschach on selected comprehensive system variables. *Journal of Personality Assessment, 95*(2), 149–158.

Schultz, L. T., Heimberg, R. G., & Rodebaugh, T. L. (2008). Social anxiety disorder. In M. Hersen & J. Rosqvist (Eds.), *Handbook of psychological assessment, case conceptualization, and treatment, Vol. 1: Adults* (pp. 204–236). Hoboken, NJ: John Wiley & Sons.

Schumm, J. A., Koucky, E. M., & Bartel, A. (2014). Associations between perceived social reactions to trauma-related experiences with PTSD and depression among veterans seeking PTSD treatment. *Journal of Traumatic Stress, 27*(1), 50–57.

Schuster, S. (2016, April 6). Facebook creates new support tool to help people who are suicidal. *The Mighty.* Retrieved from http://www.themighty.com.

Schwartz, S. (1993). *Classic studies in abnormal psychology.* Mountain View, CA: Mayfield Publishing.

Schwartzman, C. M., Boisseau, C. L., Sibrava, N. J., Mancebo, M. C., Eisen, J. L., & Rasmussen, S. A. (2017). Symptom subtype and quality of life in obsessive-compulsive disorder. *Psychiatry Research, 249,* 307–310.

Scott, K. M., Koenen, K. C., King, A., Petukhova, M. V., Alonso, J., Bromet, E. J., . . . Kessler, R. C. (2018). Post-traumatic stress disorder associated with sexual assault among women in the WHO World Mental Health Surveys. *Psychological Medicine, 48*(1), 155–167.

Sebastian, R. S., Goldman, J. D., & Enns, C. W. (2010, September). *Snacking patterns of U.S. adolescents. Food Surveys Research Group, Dietary Data Brief No. 2.* Retrieved from www.ars.usda.gov/ba/bhnrc/fsrg.

Sebert, K. R. (2014, July 17). Kesha reborn. *Elle Magazine* (UK edition).

Sedghi, A. (2013). 10 years of bullying data: What does it tell us? *The Guardian.* Retrieved from http://www.theguardian.com/news/datablog/2013/may/23/.

Seelman, K. L, Miller, J. F., Fawcett, Z. E. R., & Cline, L. (2018, April 30). Do transgender men have equal access to health care and engagement in preventing health behaviors compared to cisgender adults? *Social Work in Health Care.* [Epub ahead of print]

Seeman, M. V. (2016). Schizophrenogenic mother. In J. Lebow, A. Chambers, & D. C. Breunlin (Eds.). *Encyclopedia of couple and family therapy.* New York: Springer.

Seeman, P. (2011). Schizophrenia diagnosis and treatment. *CNS Neuroscience & Therapeutics, 17*(2), 81–82.

Seery, M. D., Holman, E. A., & Silver, R. C. (2010). Whatever does not kill us: Cumulative lifetime adversity, vulnerability, and resilience. *Journal of Personality and Social Psychology, 99,* 1025–1041.

Segal, Z. (2017, January 10). Mindfulness based cognitive therapy as maintenance treatment for unipolar major depression. *UpToDate.* Retrieved from http://www.uptodate.com.

Seibel, B. L., de Brito Silva, B., Fontanari, A. M. V., Catelan, R. F., Bercht, A. M., Stucky, J. L., . . . Costa, A. B. (2018). The impact of parental support on risk factors in the process of gender affirmation of transgender and gender diverse people. *Frontiers in Psychology, 9,* 399.

Seiden, R. H. (1981). Mellowing with age: Factors influencing the nonwhite suicide rate. *International Journal of Aging and Human Development, 13,* 265–284.

Seidman, L. J., & Nordentoft, M. (2015). New targets for prevention of schizophrenia: Is it time for interventions in the premorbid phase? *Schizophrenia Bulletin, 41*(4), 795–800.

Seitz, D., Purandare, N., & Conn, D. (2010). Prevalence of psychiatric disorders among older adults in long-term care homes: A systematic review. *International Psychogeriatrics, 22*(7), 1025–1039.

Seligman, M. E. P. (2012,). *Flourish: A visionary new understanding of happiness and well-being.* New York: Atria Books.

Seligman, M. E. P. (1975). *Helplessness.* San Francisco: Freeman.

Seligman, M. E. P. (2002). *Authentic happiness: Using the new positive psychology to realize your potential for lasting fulfillment.* New York: Free Press.

Seligman, M. E. P., & Fowler, R. D. (2011). Comprehensive soldier fitness and the future of psychology. *American Psychologist, 66*(1), 82–86.

Selkoe, D. J. (1992). Alzheimer's disease: New insights into an emerging epidemic. *Journal of Geriatric Psychiatry, 25*(2), 211–227.

Selkoe, D. J. (2011). Alzheimer's disease. *Cold Spring Harbor Perspectives in Biology, 3*(7).

Selling, L. S. (1940). *Men against madness.* New York: Greenberg.

Sendler, D. J. (2018). Lethal asphyxiation due to sadomasochistic sex training: How some sex partners avoid criminal responsibility even though their actions lead to someone's death. *Journal of Forensic and Legal Medicine, 56,* 59–65.

Sergeant, S., & Mongrain, M. (2014). An online optimism intervention reduces depression in pessimistic individuals. *Journal of Consulting and Clinical Psychology, 82*(2), 263–274.

Seto, M. C. (2008). *Pedophilia and sexual offending against children: Theory, assessment, and intervention.* Washington, DC: American Psychological Association.

Sevarino, K. (2017, April 10). Opioid withdrawal: Clinical manifestations, course, assessment, and diagnosis. *UpToDate.* Retrieved from http://www.uptodate.com.

Sevarino, K. (2018, April 11). Medically supervised opioid withdrawal during treatment for addiction. *UpToDate.* Retrieved from http://www.uptodate.com.

Shafi, A. M. A., & Shafi, R. M. A. (2014). Cultural influences on the presentation of depression. *Open Journal of Psychiatry, 4,* 390–395.

Shain, M., & AAP Committee on Adolescence. (2016). Suicide and suicide attempts in adolescents. *Pediatrics, 138*(1).

Shapiro, F., & Forrest, M. S. (2016). *EMDR: The breakthrough therapy for overcoming anxiety, stress, and trauma.* New York: Hachette Book Group.

Shapiro, J. R., Bauer, S., Andrews, E., Pisetsky, E., Bulik-Sullivan, B., Hamer, R. M.,

& **Bulik, C. M.** (2010). Text messaging in the treatment of bulimia nervosa. *Clinician's Research Digest, 28*(12).

Sharf, R. S. (2015). *Theories of psychotherapy & counseling: Concepts and cases* (6th ed.) Belmont, CA: Brooks Cole.

Sharma, A., Madaan, V., & Petty, F. D. (2006). Exercise for mental health. *Primary Care Companion, Journal of Clinical Psychiatry.* (2), 106.

Shaw, K. (2004). *Oddballs and eccentrics.* Edison, NJ: Castle Books.

Shaw, R. J., Spratt, E. G., Bernard, R. S., & DeMaso, D. R. (2010). Somatoform disorders. In R. J. Shaw & D. R. DeMaso (Eds.), *Textbook of pediatric psychosomatic medicine* (pp. 121–139). Arlington, VA: American Psychiatric Publishing.

Sheerin, C. M., Lind, M. J., Bountress, K., Nugent, N. R., & Amstadter, A. B. (2017). The genetics and epigenetics of PTSD: Overview, recent advances, and future directions. *Current Opinion in Psychology, 14,* 5–11.

Sheikh, K. (2017, August 10). Do you hear what I hear? Auditory hallucinations yield clues to perception. *Scientific American.*

Sheldon, P. (2008). The relationship between unwillingness-to-communicate and students' Facebook use. *Journal of Media Psychology, 20*(2), 67–75.

Sheng, C., Huang, Y., & Han, Y. (2018). Dissection of prodromal Alzheimer's disease. *Frontiers in Bioscience (Landmark Edition), 23,* 1272–1291.

Shenk, D. (2001). *The forgetting: Alzheimer's: Portrait of an epidemic.* New York: Doubleday.

Shepherd, J. (2016). "I am very glad and cheered when I hear the flute": The treatment of criminal lunatics in late Victorian Broadmoor. *Medical History, 60*(4), 473–491.

Sheras, P., & Worchel, S. (1979). *Clinical psychology: A social psychological approach.* New York: Van Nostrand.

Shergill, S. S., Brammer, M. J., Williams, S. R., Murray, R. M., & McGuire, P. K. (2000). Mapping auditory hallucinations in schizophrenia using functional magnetic resonance imaging. *Archives of General Psychiatry, 57*(11), 1033–1038.

Sherry, A., & Whilde, M. R. (2008). Borderline personality disorder. In M. Hersen & J. Rosqvist (Eds.), *Handbook of psychological assessment, case conceptualization and treatment, Vol. 1: Adults* (pp. 403–437). Hoboken, NJ: John Wiley & Sons.

Sherva, R., & Kowall, N. W. (2018, June 6). Genetics of Alzheimer disease. *UpToDate.* Retrieved from http://www.uptodate.com.

Sheynin, J., & Liberzon, I. (2017). Circuit dysregulation and circuit-based treatments in posttraumatic stress disorder. *Neuroscience Letters, 649,* 133–138.

Shi, P., Ren, H., Li, H., & Dai, Q. (2018). Maternal depression and suicide at immediate prenatal and early postpartum periods and psychosocial risk factors. *Psychiatry Research, 261,* 298–306.

Shifren, J. L. (2018, May 25). Overview of sexual dysfunction in women: Epidemiology, risk factors, and evaluation. *UpToDate.* Retrieved from http://www.uptodate.com.

Shin, Y. C., Lee, D., Seol, J., & Lim, S. W. (2017). What kind of stress is associated with depression, anxiety and suicidal ideation in Korean employees? *Journal of Korean Medical Science, 32*(5), 843–849.

Shinba, T. (2017). Major depressive disorder and generalized anxiety disorder show different autonomic dysregulations revealed by heart-rate variability analysis in first-onset drug-naive patients without comorbidity. *Psychiatry and Clinical Neurosciences, 71*(2), 135–145.

Shiner, R. L., & Allen, T. A. (2018). Developmental psychopathology of personality disorders. In W. J. Livesley & R. Larstone (Eds.), *Handbook of personality disorders: Theory, research, and treatment* (2nd ed., Ch. 18). New York: Guilford Press.

Shire, S. Y., Shih, W., Chang, Y. C., & Kasari, C. (2018). Short play and communication evaluation: Teachers' assessment of core social communication and play skills with young children with autism. *Autism,* 22(3), 299–310.

Shneidman, E. S. (1963). Orientations toward death: Subintentioned death and indirect suicide. In R. W. White (Ed.), *The study of lives.* New York: Atherton.

Shneidman, E. S. (1981). Suicide. *Suicide and Life-Threatening Behavior, 11*(4), 198–220.

Shneidman, E. S. (1987, March). At the point of no return. *Psychology Today.*

Shneidman, E. S. (1993). *Suicide as psychache: A clinical approach to self-destructive behavior.* Northvale, NJ: Jason Aronson.

Shneidman, E. S. (2001). *Comprehending suicide: Landmarks in 20th-century suicidology.* Washington, DC: American Psychological Association.

Shneidman, E. S. (2005). Anodyne psychotherapy for suicide: A psychological view of suicide. *Clinical Neuropsychiatry, 2*(1), 7–12.

Shulman, S., & Scharf, M. (2018). Adolescent psychopathology in times of change: The need for integrating a developmental psychopathology perspective. *Journal of Adolescence, 65,* 95–100.

Shuttleworth-Edwards, A. B. (2016). Generally representative is representative of none: Commentary on the pitfalls of IQ test standardization in multicultural settings. *Clinical Neuropsychologist, 30*(7), 975–998.

Sibley, M. H., Campez, M., & Raiker, J. S. (2018). Reexamining ADHD-related self-reporting problems using polynomial regression. *Assessment.* [Manuscript in press]

Sibley, M. H., Coxe, S. J., Campez, M., Morley, C., Olson, S., Hidalgo-Gato, N., . . . Pelham, W. E. (2018). High versus low intensity summer treatment for ADHD delivered at secondary school transitions. *Journal of Clinical Child & Adolescent Psychology, 47*(2), 248–265.

Sicile-Kira, C. (2014). *Autism spectrum disorder: The complete guide to understanding autism* (Rev. ed.). New York: Perigee Trade.

Sidran Institute. (2016). *Post traumatic stress disorder fact sheet.* Retrieved from https://www.sidran.org.

Silbersweig, D. A., Stern, E., Frith, C., Cahill, C., Holmes, A., Grootoonk, S, . . . Frackowiak, R. S. J. (1995). A functional neuroanatomy of hallucinations in schizophrenia. *Nature, 378,* 176–179.

Silk, J. S., Tan, P. Z., Ladouceur, C. D., Meller, S., Siegle, G. J., McMakin, D. L., . . . Ryan, N. D. (2018). A randomized clinical trial comparing individual cognitive behavioral therapy and child-centered therapy for child anxiety disorders. *Journal of Clinical Child and Adolescent Psychology.* [Manuscript in press]

Silva, C., Hagan, C. R., Rogers, M. L., Chiurliza, B., Podlogar, M. C., Horn, M. A., . . . Joiner, T. E. (2017). Evidence for the propositions of the interpersonal theory of suicide among a military sample. *Journal of Clinical Psychology, 73*(6), 669–680.

Silverman, M., & Krueger, R. F. (2018). Taking stock of relationships among personality disorders and other forms of psychopathology. In W. J. Livesley & R. Larstone (Eds.), *Handbook of personality disorders: Theory, research, and treatment* (2nd ed., Ch. 9). New York: Guilford Press.

Simeon, D. (2017, April 4). Psychotherapy of depersonalization/derealization disorder. *UpToDate.* Retrieved from http://www.uptodate.com.

Simeon, D. (2017, July 6). Pharmacotherapy of depersonalization/derealization disorder. *UpToDate.* Retrieved from http://www.uptodate.com.

Simkin, P., & Klein, M. C. (2018, February 16). Nonpharmacologic approaches to management of labor pain. *UpToDate.* Retrieved from http://www.uptodate.com.

Simmon, J. (1990). Media and market study. In skin deep: Our national obsession with looks. *Psychology Today, 26*(3), 96.

Simon, G. (2017, March 17). Unipolar depression in adults and initial treatment: General principles and prognosis. *UpToDate.* Retrieved from http://www.uptodate.com.

Simon, G. (2017, November 15). Effect of antidepressants on suicide risk in adults. *UpToDate.* Retrieved from http://www.uptodate.com.

Simon, G., & Ciechanowski, P. (2017, March 17). Unipolar depression in adults and initial treatment: General principles and prognosis. *UpToDate.* Retrieved from http://www.uptodate.com.

Simon, H. (2013, August 29). In-depth report: Complications of peptic ulcer. *New York Times.*

Simonton, D. K. (2010). So you want to become a creative genius? You must be crazy! In D. H. Cropley, A. J. Cropley, J. C. Kaufman, & M. A. Runco (Eds.), *The dark side of creativity* (pp. 218–234). New York: Cambridge University Press.

Simpson, H. B. (2016, March 6). Obsessive-compulsive disorder in adults: Epidemiology, pathogenesis, clinical manifestations, course, and diagnosis. *UpToDate.* Retrieved from http://www.uptodate.com.

Simpson, H. B. (2017, June 22). Pharmacotherapy for obsessive-compulsive disorder in adults. *UpToDate.* Retrieved from http://www.uptodate.com.

Simpson, H. B. (2017, October 17). Obsessive-compulsive disorder in adults: Epidemiology, pathogenesis, clinical manifestations, course, and diagnosis. *UpToDate.* Retrieved from http://www.uptodate.com.

Sinclair, I., Parry, E., Biehal, N., Fresen, J., Kay, C., Scott, S., & Green, J. (2016). Multi-dimensional treatment foster care in England: Differential effects by level of initial antisocial behavior. *European Child & Adolescent Psychiatry, 25*(8), 843–852.

Singal, J. (2017, May 12). Psychologists: Stop blaming mass shootings on video games. *New York Magazine*.

Singh, G. K., & Siahpush, M. (2014). Widening rural-urban disparities in all-cause mortality and mortality from major causes of death in the USA, 1969–2009. *Journal of Urban Health, 91*(2), 272–292.

Singh, S., Kumar, A., Agarwal, S., Phadke, S. R., & Jaiswal, Y. (2014). Genetic insight of schizophrenia: Past and future perspectives. *Gene, 535*(2), 97–100.

Sinyor, M., Williams, M., Vincent, M., Schaffer, A., Yip, P. S. F., & Gunnell, D. (2019). Suicide deaths by gas inhalation in Toronto: An observational study of emerging methods of suicide. *Journal of Affective Disorders, 243*, 226–231.

Sipe, T. A., Finnie, R. C., Knopf, J. A., Qu, S., Reynolds, J. A., Thota, A. B., . . . Nease, D. J. (2015). Effects of mental health benefits legislation: A community guide systematic review. *American Journal of Preventive Medicine, 48*(6), 755–766.

Sirey, J. A., Franklin, A. J., McKenzie, S. E., Ghosh, S., & Raue, P. J. (2014). Race, stigma, and mental health referrals among clients of aging services who screened positive for depression. *Psychiatric Services, 65*(4), 537–540.

Siris, S. G., & Braga, R. J. (2017, March 13). Anxiety in schizophrenia. *UpToDate*. Retrieved from http://www.uptodate.com.

Siris, S. G., & Braga, R. J. (2018, April 11). Depression in schizophrenia. *UpToDate*. Retrieved from http://www.uptodate.com.

Sizemore, C. C. (1991). *A mind of my own: The woman who was known as "Eve" tells the story of her triumph over multiple personality disorder*. New York: William Morrow.

Sizemore, C. C., & Pitillo, E. S. (1977). *I'm Eve*. Garden City, NY: Doubleday.

Skinner, B. F. (1957). *Verbal behavior*. Englewood Cliffs, NJ: Prentice-Hall.

Skinner, B. F. (1958). Diagramming schedules of reinforcement. *Journal of the Experimental Analysis of Behavior, 1*, 67–68.

Skodol, A. (2017, April 27). Borderline personality disorder: Epidemiology, clinical features, course, assessment, and diagnosis. *UpToDate*. Retrieved from http://www.uptodate.com.

Skodol, A. (2017, December 1). Overview of personality disorders. *UpToDate*. Retrieved from http://www.uptodate.com.

Skodol, A. (2018, April 11). Treatment of borderline personality disorder. *UpToDate*. Retrieved from http://www.uptodate.com.

Skodol, A. (2018, March 2). Dimensional-categorical approach to assessing personality disorder pathology. *UpToDate*. Retrieved from http://www.uptodate.com.

Skodol, A., & Bender, D. (2016, September 2). Approaches to the therapeutic relationship in patients with personality disorders. *UpToDate*. Retrieved from http://www.uptodate.com.

Skodol, A., & Bender, D. (2016, September 26). Establishing and maintaining a therapeutic relationship in psychiatric practice. *UpToDate*. Retrieved from http://www.uptodate.com.

Skodol, A., & Bender, D. (2018, March 21). Establishing and maintaining a therapeutic relationship in psychiatric practice. *UpToDate*. Retrieved from http://www.uptodate.com.

Slater, M. E., Godette, D., Huang, B., Ruan, W. J., & Kerridge, B. T. (2017). Sexual orientation-based discrimination, excessive alcohol use, and substance use disorders among sexual minority adults. *LGBT Health, 4*(5), 337–344.

Sleboda, P., & Sokolowska, J. (2017). Measurements of rationality: Individual differences in information processing, the transitivity of preferences and decision strategies. *Frontiers in Psychology, 8*, 1844.

Sloan, D. M. (2002). Does warm weather climate affect eating disorder pathology? *International Journal of Eating Disorders, 32*, 240–244.

Slovenko, R. (2011). Psychotherapy testimonial privilege in criminal cases. Presentation at American College of Forensic Psychiatry conference, San Diego, CA. March 23, 2011.

Sluhovsky, M. (2011). Spirit possession and other alterations of consciousness in the Christian Western tradition. In E. Cardeña & M. Winkelman (Eds.), *Altering consciousness: Multidisciplinary perspectives, Vols. 1, 2: History, culture, and the humanities: Biological and psychological perspectives* (pp. 73–88). Santa Barbara, CA: Praeger/ABC-CLIO.

Sluhovsky, M. (2017). *Becoming a new self: Practices of belief in early modern Catholicism*. Chicago, IL: University of Chicago Press.

SMA (Selective Mutism Association). (2018). FAQ: Selective mutism. Retrieved from https://www.selectivemutism.org/learn/faq/.

SMA (SurveyMonkey Audience). (2017, June 21). Study: Feeling selfie-ish? You're not alone. *SurveyMonkey*. Retrieved from https://www.surveymonkey.com/blog.

Smallwood, R. F., Potter, J. S., & Robin, D. A. (2016). Neurophysiological mechanisms in acceptance and commitment therapy in opioid-addicted patients with chronic pain. *Psychiatry Research, 250*, 12–14.

Smietana, B. (2016, December 6). Most Americans say assisted suicide is morally acceptable. *Lifeway Research*.

Smith, A. (2014). *6 new facts about Facebook*. Washington, DC: Pew Research Center.

Smith, A. J., & Smith, L. A. (2016). Viral carcinogenesis. *Progress in Molecular Biology and Translational Science, 144*, 121–168.

Smith, A. M., Wells, G. L., Lindsay, R. C. L., & Myerson, T. (2018). Eyewitness identification performance on showups improves with an additional-opportunities instruction: Evidence for present-absent criteria discrepancy. *Law and Human Behavior, 42*(3), 215–226.

Smith, B. L., Lyons, C. E., Correa, F. G., Benoit, S. C., Myers, B., Solomon, M. B., & Herman, J. P. (2017). Behavioral and physiological consequences of enrichment loss in rats. *Psychoneuroendocrinology, 77*, 37–46.

Smith, K., & Milazzo-Sayre, L. (2014, August 7). *Highlights of the National Mental Health Services Survey, 2010*. Rockville, MD: NCBI Bookshelf, The CBHSQ Report.

Smith, M. L., & Glass, G. V. (1977). Meta-analysis of psychotherapy outcome studies. *American Psychologist, 32*(9), 752–760.

Smith, M. L., Glass, G. V., & Miller, T. I. (1980). *The benefits of psychotherapy*. Baltimore: Johns Hopkins University Press.

Smith, R., Shepard, C., Wiltgen, A., Rufino, K., & Fowler, J. C. (2017). Treatment outcomes for inpatients with obsessive-compulsive personality disorder: An open comparison trial. *Journal of Affective Disorders, 209*, 273–278.

Smith, T. (2008, January 29). Real-life fears faced in online world: Helping alter-egos in "second life" helps people cope. *CBS News*. Retrieved from http:www.cbsnews.com/video/watch/?id=3764862.

Smith, T. W. (2007). *Job satisfaction in the United States*. Chicago, IL: University of Chicago.

Smith, T., Iadarola, S., Mandell, D. S., Harwood, R., & Kasari, C. (2017). Community-partnered research with urban school districts that serve children with autism spectrum disorder. *Academic Pediatrics, 17*(6), 614–619.

Smith, Y., & Spitzmueller, M. C. (2016). Worker perspectives on contemporary milieu therapy: A cross-site ethnographic study. *Social Work Research, 40*(2), 105–116.

Smolek, T., Jadhav, S., Brezovakova, V., Cubinkova, V., Valachova, B., Novak, P., & Zilka, N. (2018, May 16). First-in-rat study of human Alzheimer's disease tau propagation. *Molecular Neurobiology*. [Epub ahead of print]

Smyth, J. M., & Pennebaker, J. W. (2001). What are the health effects of disclosure? In A. Baum, T. A. Revenson, & J. E. Singer (Eds.), *Handbook of health psychology* (pp. 339–348). Mahwah, NJ: Lawrence Erlbaum.

Snyder, B. L. (2018, February 15). Women with dissociative identity disorder who experience intimate partner violence. *Journal of Psychosocial Nursing and Mental Health Services*. [Epub ahead of print]

Snyder, W. V. (1947). *Casebook of non-directive counseling*. Boston: Houghton Mifflin.

Soares, W. B., Dos Santos, E. B., Bottino, C. M. C., & Elkis, H. (2017). Psychotic symptoms in older people without dementia from a Brazilian community-based sample: A seven years' follow-up. *PLoS ONE, 12*(6), e0178471.

Soares-Weiser, K., Rathbone, J., Ogawa, Y., Shinohara, K., & Bergman, H. (2018). Miscellaneous treatments for antipsychotic-induced tardive dyskinesia. *Cochrane Database of Systematic Reviews, 3*, CD000208.

Sobell, M. B., & Sobell, L. C. (1973). Individualized behavior therapy for alcoholics. *Behavior Therapist, 4*(1), 49–72.

Sobell, M. B., & Sobell, L. C. (1984). The aftermath of heresy: A response to Pendery et al.'s (1982) critique of "Individualized Behavior Therapy for Alcoholics." *Behavioral Research and Therapy, 22*(4), 413–440.

Soffer-Dudek, N. (2017). Arousal in nocturnal consciousness: How dream- and sleep-experiences may inform us of poor sleep quality, stress, and psychopathology. *Frontiers in Psychology, 8*:733.

Sofin, Y., Danker-Hopfe, H., Gooren, T., & Neu, P. (2017). Predicting inpatient detoxification outcome of alcohol and drug dependent patients: The influence of sociodemographic environment, motivation, impulsivity, and medical comorbidities. *Journal of Addiction*, ID 6415831. Retrieved from https://www.hindawi.com.

Solar, A. (2014). A supported employment linkage intervention for people with schizophrenia who want a chance to work. *Australasian Psychiatry, 22*(3), 245–247.

Soler, J., Elices, M., Pascual, J. C., Martin-Blanco, A., Feliu-Soler, A., Carmona, C., & Portelia, M. J. (2016, January 11). Effects of mindfulness training on different components of impulsivity in borderline personality disorder: Results from a pilot randomized study. *Borderline Personality Disorder and Emotion Dysregulation, 3,* 1.

Soliman, M., Santos, A. M., & Lohr, J. B. (2008). Emergency, inpatient, and residential treatment. In K. T. Mueser & D. V. Jeste (Eds.), *Clinical handbook of schizophrenia* (pp. 339–353). New York: Guilford Press.

Soloff, P. H., & Chiappetta, L. (2018). Suicidal behavior and psychosocial outcome in borderline personality disorder at 8-year follow-up. *Journal of Personality Disorders.* [Manuscript in press]

Soloff, P. H., & Chiappetta, L. (2018, February 22). 10-year outcome of suicidal behavior in borderline personality disorder. *Journal of Personality Disorders.* [Epub ahead of print]

Soloff, P. H., Abraham, K., Burgess, A., Ramaseshan, K., Chowdury, A., & Diwadkar, V. A. (2017). Impulsivity and aggression mediate regional brain responses in borderline personality disorder: An fMRI study. *Psychiatry Research: Neuroimaging, 260,* 76–85.

Soloff, P. H., Chiappetta, L., Mason, N. S., Becker, C., & Price, J. C. (2014). Effects of serotonin-2A receptor binding and gender on personality traits and suicidal behavior in borderline personality disorder. *Psychiatry Research, 222*(3), 140–148.

Solomon, G. (2018). Chronic traumatic encephalopathy in sports: A historical and narrative review. *Developmental Neuropsychology, 43*(4), 279–311.

Sommers-Flanagan, J., & Sommers-Flanagan, R. (2017). *Clinical interviewing* (6th edition). Hoboken, NJ: Wiley.

Song, Y., & Shi, M. (2017). Associations between empathy and big five personality traits among Chinese undergraduate medical students. *PLoS ONE, 12*(2), e0171665.

Sood, M. R. (2018, March 28). Functional fecal incontinence in infants and children: Definition, clinical manifestations and evaluation. *UpToDate.* Retrieved from http://www.uptodate.com.

Sood, M. R. (2018, May 8). Chronic functional constipation and fecal incontinence in infants and children: Treatment. *UpToDate.* Retrieved from http://www.uptodate.com.

Soole, R., Kölves, K., & De Leo, D. (2015). Suicide in children: A systematic review. *Archives of Suicide Research, 19*(3), 285–304.

Sotgiu, I. (2016). How do we remember happy life events? A comparison between eudaimonic and hedonic autobiographical memories. *Journal of Psychology, 150*(6), 685–703.

Southwick, S. M., & Charney, D. S. (2012). *Resilience: The science of mastering life's greatest challenges.* New York: Cambridge University Press.

Soyka, M. (2017). Treatment of benzodiazepine dependence. *New England Journal of Medicine, 376*(24), 2399–2400.

Spagna, A., He, G., Jin, S., Gao, L., Mackie, M. A., Tian, Y., . . . Fan, J. (2018). Deficit of supramodal executive control of attention in schizophrenia. *Journal of Psychiatric Research, 97,* 22–29.

Spanton, T. (2008, July 28). UFOs: We believe. *The Sun.* Retrieved from http://www.thesun.co.uk/sol/homepage/news/ufos/article1477122.ece.

Sperry, L. (2016). *Handbook of diagnosis and treatment of DSM-5 personality disorders: Assessment, case conceptualization, and treatment* (3rd ed.). New York: Routledge.

Sperry, S. H., & Kwapil, T. R. (2017). What can daily life assessment tell us about the bipolar spectrum? *Psychiatry Research, 252,* 51–56.

Spiegel, D. (2009). Coming apart: Trauma and the fragmentation of the self. In D. Gordon (Ed.), *Cerebrum 2009: Emerging ideas in brain science* (pp. 1–11). Washington, DC: Dana Press.

Spiegler, M. D., & Guevremont, D. C. (2015). *Contemporary behavior therapy* (6th edition). Independence, KY: Cengage Learning.

Spirito, A., Simon, V., Cancilliere, M. K., Stein, R., Norcott, C., Loranger, K., & Prinstein, M. J. (2011). Outpatient psychotherapy practice with adolescents following psychiatric hospitalization for suicide ideation or a suicide attempt. *Clinical Child Psychology and Psychiatry, 16*(1), 53–64.

Spitzer, R. L., Gibbon, M., Skodol, A. E., Williams, J. B. W., & First, M. B. (Eds.). (1994). *DSM-IV casebook: A learning companion to the diagnostic and statistical manual of mental disorders* (4th ed.). Washington, DC: American Psychiatric Press.

Spitzer, R. L., Skodol, A., Gibbon, M., & Williams, J. B. W. (1981). *DSM-III case book.* Washington, DC: American Psychiatric Press.

Spitzer, R. L., Skodol, A., Gibbon, M., & Williams, J. B. W. (1983). *Psychopathology: A case book.* New York: McGraw-Hill.

Spizzirri, G., Duran, F. L. S., Chaim-Avancini, T. M., Serpa, M. H., Cavallet, M., Pereira, C. M. A., . . . Abdo, C. H. N. (2018). Grey and white matter volumes either in treatment-naïve or hormone-treated transgender women: A voxel-based morphometry study. *Scientific Reports, 8*(1), 736.

Spoelder, M., Dourojeanni, J. P. F., de Git, K. C. G., Baars, A. M., Lesscher, H. M. B., & Vanderschuren, L. J. M. J. (2017). Individual differences in voluntary alcohol intake in rats: Relationship with impulsivity, decision making and Pavlovian conditioned approach. *Psychopharmacology, 234*(14), 2177–2196.

SPRC (Suicide Prevention Resource Center). (2013). *Suicide among racial/ethnic populations in the U.S.: American Indians/Alaska Natives.* Waltham, MA: Education Development Center, Inc.

Spurk, D., Keller, A. C., & Hirschi, A. (2015). Do bad guys get ahead or fall behind? Relationships of the dark triad of personality with objective and subjective career success. *Social Psychological and Personality Science, 7*(2), 113–121.

Stack, S., & Rockett, I. R. H. (2018). Are suicide note writers representative of all suicides? Analysis of the National Violent Death Reporting System. *Suicide and Life-Threatening Behavior, 48*(1), 12–20.

Stahlberg, O., Anckarsater, H., & Nilsson, T. (2010). Mental health problems in youths committed to juvenile institutions: Prevalences and treatment needs. *European Child & Adolescent Psychiatry, 19*(12), 893–903.

Stamberg, S. (2017, July 6). "Architecture of an asylum" tracks history of U.S. treatment of mental illness. *NPR 24-Hour Program Stream.*

Stamm, T. J., Sondergeld, L. M., Juckel, G., & Bauer, M. (2018, January 30). Psychotherapy for people with bipolar disorders: An overview of evidence-based procedures and new developments. *Nervenarst.* [Epub ahead of print] [German]

Stanley, I. H., Horn, M. A., & Joiner, T. E. (2015). Mental health service use among adults with suicide ideation, plans, or attempts: Results from a national survey. *Psychiatric Services* (Washington, D.C.), app.ips 201400593. [Electronic publication]

Stanton, K., & Zimmerman, M. (2018). Clinician ratings of vulnerable and grandiose narcissistic features: Implications for an expanded narcissistic personality disorder diagnosis. *Personality Disorders, 9*(3), 263–272.

Starcevic, V. (2015). Trichotillomania: Impulsive, compulsive or both? *Australian & New Zealand Journal of Psychiatry, 49*(7), 660–661.

Starcevic, V., & Brakoulias, V. (2017). Current understanding of the relationships between obsessive-compulsive disorder and personality disturbance. *Current Opinion in Psychiatry, 30*(1), 50–55.

Starcevic, V., & Brakoulias, V. (2014). New diagnostic perspectives on obsessive-compulsive personality disorder and its links with other conditions. *Current Opinion in Psychiatry, 27*(1), 62–67.

Starr, T. B., & Kreipe, R. E. (2014). Anorexia nervosa and bulimia nervosa: Brains, bones and breeding. *Current Psychiatry Reports, 16*(5), 441.

STAT. (2016, April 5). "Truly terrifying": Chinese suppliers flood US and Canada with deadly fentanyl. *STAT.* Retrieved from https://www.statnews.com.

Statista. (2017). *Number of reported forcible rape cases in the United States from 1990 to 2015.* Retrieved from https://www.statista.com/statistics.

Statista. (2018). *Number of resident patients in psychiatric inpatient settings in the U.S. as of 2014, by type of organization.* New York: Statista. Retrieved from https://www.statista.com/statistics/81816.

Statista. (2018). *The 10 most significant natural disasters worldwide by death toll from 1980 to 2017.* Retrieved from https://www.statista.com/statistics/268029/natural-disasters-by-death-toll-since-1980/.

Statistic Brain. (2018). *Bipolar disorder statistics.* Retrieved from www.statisticbrain.com/bipolar-disorder-statistics.

Steadman, H. J., Monahan, J., Robbins, P. C., Appelbaum, P., Grisso, T., Klassen, D., . . . Roth, L. (1993). From dangerousness to risk assessment: Implications for appropriate research strategies. In S. Hodgins (Ed.), *Mental disorder and crime.* New York: Sage Publications.

Steele, I. H., Thrower, N., Noroian, P., & Saleh, F. M. (2018). Understanding suicide across the lifespan: A United States perspective of suicide risk factors, assessment & management. *Journal of Forensic Science, 63*(1), 162–171.

Steffen, P. R., Masters, K. S., & Baldwin, S. (2017). What mediates the relationship between religious service attendance and aspects of well-being? *Journal of Religion & Health, 56*(1), 158–170.

Stein, C. H., Leith, J. E., Osborn, L. A., Greenberg, S., Petrowski, C. E., Jesse, S., . . . May, M. C. (2015). Mental health system historians: Adults with schizophrenia describe changes in community mental health care over time. *The Psychiatric Quarterly, 86*(1), 33–48.

Stein, M. B. (2017, February 3). Pharmacotherapy for posttraumatic stress disorder in adults. *UpToDate*. Retrieved from http://www.uptodate.com.

Stein, M. B. (2018, January 26). Pharmacotherapy for social anxiety disorder in adults. *UpToDate*. Retrieved from http://www.uptodate.com.

Steinglass, J. (2016, September 28). Anorexia nervosa in adults and adolescents: Nutritional rehabilitation (nutritional support). *UpToDate*. Retrieved from www.uptodate.com.

Steinmetz, K. (2014, June 9). America's transition. *Time Magazine*.

Stekel, W. (2010). *Sadism and masochism: The psychopathology of sexual cruelty*. Chicago, IL: Solar Books/Solar Asylum.

Stephens, S., Leroux, E., Skilling, T., Cantor, J. M., & Seto, M. C. (2017). Taxometric analyses of pedophilia utilizing self-report, behavioral, and sexual arousal indicators. *Journal of Abnormal Psychology, 126*(8), 1114–1119.

Stern, A. (1938). Psychoanalytic investigation and therapy in the borderline group of neuroses. *Psychoanalytical Quarterly, 7*, 467–489.

Stern, A. M. (2016). Eugenics, sterilization, and historical memory in the United States. *História, Ciências, Saúde-Manguinhos, 23*(Suppl1), 195–212.

Sternberg, R. J., Grigorenko, E. L., & Bundy, D. A. (2001). The predictive value of IQ. *Merrill-Palmer Quarterly, 47*(1), 1–41.

Stevelink, S., Jones, M., Hull, L., Pernet, D., MacCrimmon, S., Goodwin, L., . . . Wessely, S. (2018, October 8). Mental health outcomes at the end of the British involvement in the Iraq and Afghanistan conflicts: A cohort study. *British Journal of Psychiatry*. [Epub ahead of print]

Stevens, J. P., Wall, M. J., Novack, L., Hsu, D. J., & Howell, M. D. (2018). The critical care crisis of opioid overdoses in the United States. *Annals of the American Thoracic Society*. [Manuscript in press]

Stewart, J. G., Valeri, L., Esposito, E. C., & Auerbach, R. P. (2018). Peer victimization and suicidal thoughts and behaviors in depressed adolescents. *Journal of Abnormal Child Psychology, 46*(3), 581–596.

Stewart, R. E., & Chambless, D. L. (2007). Does psychotherapy research inform treatment decisions in private practice? *Journal of Clinical Psychology, 63*(3), 267–281.

Stewart, T. M., & Williamson, D. A. (2008). Bulimia nervosa. In M. Hersen & J. Rosqvist (Eds.), *Handbook of psychological assessment, case conceptualization and treatment, Vol. 1: Adults*. Hoboken, NJ: John Wiley & Sons.

Stibich, M. (2017, March 16). Sexual activity among older populations. *Verywell*.

Stice, E., & Desjardins, C. D. (2018, March 17). Interactions between risk factors in the prediction of onset of eating disorders: Exploratory hypothesis generating analyses. *Behaviour Research and Therapy*. [Epub ahead of print]

Stice, E., Gau, J. M., Rohde, P., & Shaw, H. (2017). Risk factors that predict future onset of each DSM-5 eating disorder: Predictive specificity in high-risk adolescent females. *Journal of Abnormal Psychology, 126*(1), 38–51.

Stice, E., Rohde, P., Shaw, H., & Gau, J. M. (2017). Clinical-led, peer-led, and internet-delivered dissonance-based eating disorder prevention programs: Acute effectiveness of these delivery modalities. *Journal of Consulting and Clinical Psychology, 85*, 883–895.

Stice, E., Yokum, S., & Waters, A. (2015, December 7). Dissonance-based eating disorder prevention program reduces reward region response to thin models: How actions shape valuation. *PLoS ONE*. Retrieved from https://doi.org/10.1371/journal.pone.0144530.

Stice, E., Marti, C. N., & Rohde, P. (2013). Prevalence, incidence, impairment, and course of the proposed DSM-5 eating disorder diagnoses in an 8-year prospective community study of young women. *Journal of Abnormal Psychology, 122*(2), 445–457.

Stickel, F., Moreno, C., Hampe, J., & Morgan, M. Y. (2017). The genetics of alcohol dependence and alcohol-related liver disease. *Journal of Hepatology, 66*, 195–211.

Stickley, A., Ng, C. F. S., Inoue, Y., Yazawa, A., Koyanagi, A., Kodaka, M., . . . Watanabe, C. (2016). Birthdays are associated with an increased risk of suicide in Japan: Evidence from 27,007 deaths in Tokyo in 2001–2010. *Journal of Affective Disorders, 200*, 259–265.

Stinchfield, R., McCready, J., Turner, N. E., Jimenez-Murcia, S., Petry, N. M., Grant, J., . . . Chapman, H. (2016). Reliability, validity, and classification accuracy of the DSM-5 diagnostic criteria for gambling disorder and comparison to DSM-IV. *Journal of Gambling Studies, 32*(3), 905–922.

Stitzer, M., Cunningham, C. S., & Sweeney, M. M. (2017, November 7). Contingency management for substance use disorders: Efficacy, implementation, and training. *UpToDate*. Retrieved from http://www.uptodate.com.

Stock, A. K., Rädle, M., & Beste, C. (2019). Methamphetamine-associated difficulties in cognitive control allocation may normalize after prolonged abstinence. *Progress in Neuro-Psychopharmacology & Biological Psychiatry, 88*, 41–52.

Stolbach, A., & Hoffman, R. S. (2018, April 19). Acute opioid intoxication in adults. *UpToDate*. Retrieved from http://www.uptodate.com.

Stone, J., & Sharpe, M. (2017, June 20). Conversion disorder in adults: Epidemiology, pathogenesis, and prognosis. *UpToDate*. Retrieved from http://www.uptodate.com.

Stone, J., & Sharpe, M. (2018, February 14). Conversion disorder in adults: Treatment. *UpToDate*. Retrieved from http://www.uptodate.com.

Stone, J., & Sharpe, M. (2018, January 25). Conversion disorder in adults: Clinical features, assessment, and comorbidity. *UpToDate*. Retrieved from http://www.uptodate.com.

Stone, J., & Sharpe, M. (2018, January 25). Conversion disorder in adults: Terminology, diagnosis, and differential diagnosis. *UpToDate*. Retrieved from http://www.uptodate.com.

Stone, M. H. (2010). Sexual sadism: A portrait of evil. *Journal of the American Academy of Psychoanalysis and Dynamic Psychiatry, 38*(1), 133–157.

Stovall, J. (2016, May 17). Bipolar disorder in adults: Pharmacotherapy for acute mania and hypomania. *UpToDate*. Retrieved from www.uptodate.com.

Stovall, J. (2018, February 6). Bipolar disorder in adults: Choosing pharmacotherapy for acute mania and hypomania. *UpToDate*. Retrieved from http://www.uptodate.com.

Stovall, J. (2018, February 6). Bipolar disorder in adults: Epidemiology and pathogenesis. *UpToDate*. Retrieved from http://www.uptodate.com.

Strada, E. A., & Portenoy, R. K. (2018, January 12). Psychological, rehabilitative, and integrative therapies for cancer pain. *UpToDate*. Retrieved from http://www.uptodate.com.

Strain, E. (2017, April 10). Opioid use disorder: Epidemiology, pharmacology, clinical manifestations, course, screening, assessment, and diagnosis. *UpToDate*. Retrieved from http://www.uptodate.com.

Strain, E. (2017, January 13). Pharmacotherapy for opioid use disorder. *UpToDate*. Retrieved from http://www.uptodate.com.

Strain, E. (2018, April 17). Pharmacotherapy for opioid use disorder. *UpToDate*. Retrieved from http://www.uptodate.com.

Strassberg, D. S., Cann, D., & Velarde, V. (2017). Sexting by high school students. *Archives of Sexual Behavior, 46*, 1667–1672.

Strassberg, D. S., McKinnon, R. K., Sustaíta, M. A., & Rullo, J. (2013). Sexting by high school students: An exploratory and descriptive study. *Archives of Sexual Behavior, 42*(1), 15–21.

Street, A. E., Bell, M. E., & Ready, C. B. (2011). Sexual assault. In D. M. Benedek, & G. H. Wynn (Eds.), *Clinical manual for management of PTSD* (pp. 325–348). Arlington, VA: American Psychiatric Publishing.

Strickland, B. R., Hale, W. D., & Anderson, L. K. (1975). Effect of induced mood states on activity and self-reported affect. *Journal of Consulting and Clinical Psychology, 43*(4), 587.

Strober, M., & Yager, J. (1985). A developmental perspective on the treatment of anorexia nervosa in adolescents. In D. M. Garner & P. E. Garfinkel (Eds.), *Handbook of psychotherapy for anorexia nervosa and bulimia*. New York: Guilford Press.

Strohl, K. P. (2016, June 24). Overview of obstructive sleep apnea in adults. *UpToDate*. Retrieved from http://www.uptodate.com.

Stroup, T. S., & Marder, S. (2017, May 23). Pharmacotherapy for schizophrenia: Acute and maintenance phase treatment. *UpToDate*. Retrieved from http://www.uptodate.com.

Stubbs, B., Vancampfort, D., Rosenbaum, S., Ward, P. B., Richards, J., Soundy, A., . . . Schuch, F. B. (2016). Dropout from exercise randomized controlled trials among people with depression: A meta-analysis and meta regression. *Journal of Affective Disorders, 190*, 457–466.

Stunkard, A. J. (1959). Eating patterns and obesity. *Psychiatric Quarterly, 33*, 284–295.

Sturmey, P., & Didden, R. (2014). *Evidence-based practice and intellectual disabilities.* Hoboken, NJ: Wiley.

Stürup-Toft, S., O'Moore, E. J., & Plugge, E. H. (2018). Looking behind the bars: Emerging health issues for people in prison. *British Medical Bulletin, 125*(1), 15–23.

Suchowersky, O. (2018, January 18). Huntington disease: Management. *UpToDate.* Retrieved from http://www.uptodate.com.

Sullivan, E. M., Annest, J. L., Simon, T. R., Luo, F., & Dahlberg, L. L. (2015). Suicide trends among persons aged 10–24 years—United States, 1994–2012. *Morbidity and Mortality Weekly Report, 64*(8), 201–205.

Sullivan, H. S. (1953). *The interpersonal theory of psychiatry.* New York: Norton.

Sun, F. K., Lu, C. Y., Tseng, Y. S., & Chiang, C. Y. (2018). Factors predicting recovery from suicide in attempted suicide patients. *Journal of Clinical Nursing.* [In press]

Sun, Y. R., Herrmann, N., Scott, C. J. M., Black, S. E., Khan, M. M., & Lanctôt, K. L. (2018). Global grey matter volume in adult bipolar patients with and without lithium treatment: A meta-analysis. *Journal of Affective Disorders, 225,* 599–606.

Suppes, T. (2018, February 12). Bipolar disorder in adults: Clinical features. *UpToDate.* Retrieved from http://www.uptodate.com.

Suppes, T., Baldessarini, R. J., Faedda, G. L., & Tohen, M. (1991). Risk of recurrence following discontinuation of lithium treatment in bipolar disorder. *Archives of General Psychiatry, 48*(12), 1082–1088.

Surawy, C., McManus, F., Muse, K., & Williams, J. M. (2015). Mindfulness-based cognitive therapy (MBCT) for health anxiety (hypochondriasis): Rationale, implementation and case illustration. *Mindfulness, 6*(2), 382–392.

Sushma, C., & Tavaragi, M. S. (2016). Moral treatment: Philippe Pinel. *International Journal of Indian Psychology, 3*(2), no. 8.

Sutton, P., & Gates, B. (2019). Giving voice to adults with intellectual disabilities and experience of mental ill-health: Validity of a psychosocial approach. *Nurse Researcher, 26*(2), 19–26.

Svartberg, M., & McCullough, L. (2010). Cluster C personality disorders: Prevalence, phenomenology, treatment effects, and principles of treatment. In J. F. Clarkin, P. Fonagy, & G. O. Gabbard (Eds.), *Psychodynamic psychotherapy for personality disorders: A clinical handbook* (pp. 337–367). Arlington, VA: American Psychiatric Publishing.

Swain, S. P., Behura, S. S., Dash, M. K., Nayak, A. K., & Pati, S. S. (2017). The influence of psychosocial dysfunctions in chronic schizophrenia patients in remission: A hospital-based study. *Indian Journal of Psychological Medicine, 39*(2), 157–163.

Swami, V., Barron, D., Weis, L., & Furnham, A. (2016). Bodies in nature: Associations between exposure to nature, connectedness to nature, and body image in U.S. adults. *Body Image, 18,* 153–161.

Swanson, J., Swartz, M., Van Dorn, R. A., Monahan, J., McGuire, T. G., Steadman, H. J., & Robbins, P. C. (2009). Racial disparities in involuntary outpatient commitment: Are they real? *Health Affairs, 28*(3), 816–826.

Swanson, S. A., & Colman, I. (2013). Association between exposure to suicide and suicidality outcomes in youth. *Canadian Medical Association Journal, 185*(10), 870–877.

Swartz, H. A. (2017, June 27). Interpersonal psychotherapy (IPT) for depressed adults: Specific interventions and techniques. *UpToDate.* Retrieved from http://www.uptodate.com.

Swartz, H. A. (2018, April 1). Interpersonal psychotherapy (IPT) for depressed adults: Indications, theoretical foundation, general concepts, and efficacy. *UpToDate.* Retrieved from http://www.uptodate.com.

Swartz, M. S., Frohberg, N. R., Drake, R. E., & Lauriello, J. (2012). Psychosocial therapies. In J. A. Lieberman, T. S. Stroup, & D. O Perkins (Eds.), *Essentials of schizophrenia* (pp. 207–224). Arlington, VA: American Psychiatric Publishing.

Sweeney, M. D., Zhao, Z., Montagne, A., Nelson, A. R., & Zlokovic, B. V. (2019). Blood-brain barrier: From physiology to disease and back. *Physiological Reviews, 99*(1), 21–78.

Swift, A. (2016, September 14). Americans' trust in mass media sinks to new low. *Gallup.* Retrieved from http://www.gallup.com/poll/195542.

Sysko, R., & Devlin, M. (2017, November 14). Binge eating disorder in adults: Overview of treatment. *UpToDate.* Retrieved from http://www.uptodate.com.

Sysko, R., & Devlin, M. (2017, November 14). Binge eating disorder: Cognitive-behavioral therapy (CBT). *UpToDate.* Retrieved from http://www.uptodate.com.

Szalavitz, M. (2013, July 18). Apps for mastering your mood. *Time.*

Tabas, L. J., Warren, R., Waters, B., & Lusardi, A. (2017, October 24). *Pennsylvania legislature exploring court-ordered outpatient treatment.* Philadelphia, PA: Obermayer Rebmann Maxwell & Hippel.

TAC (Treatment Advocacy Center). (2017). *Assisted outpatient treatment: Frequently asked questions.* Arlington, VA: Author.

TACA (Talking About Curing Autism). (2017, January 29). *Latest autism statistics.* Retrieved from https://www.tacanow.org.

Tackett, J. L., Herzhoff, K., Balsis, S., & Cooper, L. (2016). Toward a unifying perspective on personality pathology across the lifespan. In D. Cicchetti (Ed.), *Developmental psychopathology Vol. 3: Developmental neuroscience* (3rd ed., pp. 1039–1078). New York: Wiley.

Takeda, A. (2015, April 13). Zoe Kravitz gets real about past struggles with eating disorders: New film The Road Within "triggered some old stuff." *Us Weekly.*

Takenaka, M. C., Araujo, L. P., Maricato, J. T., Nascimento, V. M., Guereschi, M. G., Rezende, R. M., . . . Basso, A. S. (2016). Norepinephrine controls effector T cell differentiation through b2-adrenergic receptor-mediated inhibition of NF-kB and AP-1 in dendritic cells. *Journal of Immunology, 196*(2), 637–644.

Tallis, F. (2014, January 23). *How to stop worrying: New edition (Overcoming common problems).* Sheldon Press. [Kindle]

Tallis, F. (2015, October 22). *The Sheldon short guide to worry and anxiety.* Sheldon Press. [Kindle]

Tallis, F., Davey, G., & Capuzzo, N. (1994). The phenomenology of non-pathological worry: A preliminary investigation. In G. Davey & F. Tallis (Eds.), *Worrying: Perspectives on theory, assessment and treatment* (pp. 61–89). Chichester, England: John Wiley.

Tan, J. X., & Fajardo, M. L. R. (2017). Efficacy of multisystemic therapy in youths aged 10–17 with severe antisocial behaviour and emotional disorders: A systematic review. *London Journal of Primary Care, 9*(6), 95–103.

Tandon, S., Keefe, K. A., & Taha, S. A. (2017). Mu opioid receptor signaling in the nucleus accumbens shell increases responsiveness of satiety-modulated lateral hypothalamus neurons. *European Journal of Neuroscience, 45,* 1418–1430.

Tang, W., Zhu, Q., Gong, X., Zhu, C., Wang, Y., & Chen, S. (2016). Cortico-striato-thalamo-cortical circuit abnormalities in obsessive-compulsive disorder: A voxel-based morphometric and fMRI study of the whole brain. *Behavioural Brain Research, 313,* 17–22.

Tang, Y. Y., & Bruya, B. (2017, May 9). Mechanisms of mind-body interaction and optimal performance. *Frontiers in Psychology, 8,* 647.

Tangpricha, V., & Safer, J. D. (2018, August 22). Transgender men: Evaluation and management. *UpToDate.* Retrieved from http://www.uptodate.com.

Tanzilli, A., Muzi, L., Ronningstam, E., & Lingiardi, V. (2017). Countertransference when working with narcissistic personality disorder: An empirical investigation. *Psychotherapy, 54*(2), 184–194.

Tarquinio, C., Rotonda, C., Houllé, W. A., Montel, S. D., Rydberg, J. A., Minary, L., . . . Alla, F. (2016). Early psychological preventive intervention for workplace violence: A randomized controlled explorative and comparative study between EMDR-Recent Event and Critical Incident Stress Debriefing. *Issues in Mental Health Nursing, 37*(11), 787–799.

Tarsy, D. (2016, December 14). Tardive dyskinesia: Clinical features and diagnosis. *UpToDate.* Retrieved from http://www.uptodate.com.

Tarsy, D. (2016, December 14). Tardive dyskinesia: Etiology and epidemiology. *UpToDate.* Retrieved from http://www.uptodate.com.

Tarsy, D. (2017, May 4). Tardive dyskinesia: Prevention and treatment. *UpToDate.* Retrieved from http://www.uptodate.com.

Tarsy, D. (2018, April 19). Tardive dyskinesia: Prevention and treatment. *UpToDate.* Retrieved from http://www.uptodate.com.

Tartakovsky, M. (2016). Schizophrenia and genetics: Research update. *Psych Central.* Retrieved from https://psychcentral.com.

Tasca, G. A., Hilsenroth, M., & Thompson-Brenner, H. (2014). Psychoanalytic psychotherapy or cognitive-behavioral therapy for bulimia nervosa. *American Journal of Psychiatry, 171*(5), 503–584.

Tashakova, O. (2011, March 25). Am I too fat? *Khaleej Times.*

Taubert, J., van Golde, C., & Verstraten, F. A. (2017). Who is the usual suspect? Evidence of a selection bias toward faces that make direct eye contact in a lineup task. *iperceptions, 8*(1), 2041669517690411.

Tavares, I. M., Laan, E. T. M., & Nobre, P. J. (2018). Sexual inhibition is a vulnerability factor for orgasm problems in women. *Journal of Sexual Medicine, 15*(3), 361–372.

Taycan, O., Özdemir, A., & Erdogan, T. S. (2017). Alexithymia and somatization in depressed patients: The role of the type of somatic symptom attribution. *Noro Psikiyatri Arsivi, 54*(2), 99–104.

Taylor, A., & Kim-Cohen, J. (2007). Meta-analysis of gene-environment interactions in developmental psychopathology. *Development and Psychopathology, 19,* 1029–1037.

Taylor, E. A., Ward, R. M., & Hardin, R. (2017, Spring). Examination of drinking habits and motives of collegiate student-athletes. *Journal of Applied Sport Management, 9*(1), 56.

Taylor, F. R. (2017, November 2). Tension-type headache in adults: Pathophysiology, clinical features, and diagnosis. *UpToDate*. Retrieved from http://www.uptodate.com.

Taylor, L. E., Swerdfeger, A. L., & Eslick, G. D. (2014). Vaccines are not associated with autism: An evidence-based meta-analysis of case-control and cohort studies. *Vaccine, 32*(29), 3623–3629.

Taylor, M. A. (2018). A comprehensive study of mass murder precipitants and motivations of offenders. *International Journal of Offender Therapy and Comparative Criminology, 62*(2), 427–449.

Taylor, W. D. (2014). Depression in the elderly. *New England Journal of Medicine, 371,* 1228–1236.

Taylor, B., Carswell, K., & Williams, A. C. (2013). The interaction of persistent pain and post-traumatic re-experiencing: A qualitative study in torture survivors. *Journal of Pain and Symptom Management, 46*(4), 546–555.

Ten Have, M., Nuyen, J., Beekman, A., & de Graaf, R. (2013). Common mental disorder severity and its association with treatment contact and treatment intensity for mental health problems. *Psychological Medicine, 43*(10), 2203–2213.

Tenke, C. E., Kayser, J., Pechtel, P., Webb, C. A., Dillon, D. G., Goer, F., . . . Bruder, G. E. (2017). Demonstrating test-retest reliability of electrophysiological measures for healthy adults in a multisite study of biomarkers of antidepressant treatment response. *Psychophysiology, 54*(1), 34–50.

Teo, A. R., Chan, B. K., Saha, S., & Nicolaidis, C. (2019). Frequency of social contact in-person vs. on Facebook: An examination of associations with psychiatric symptoms in military veterans. *Journal of Affective Disorders, 243,* 375–380.

Tetrault, J. M., & O'Connor, P. G. (2017, May). Risky drinking and alcohol use disorder: Epidemiology, pathogenesis, clinical manifestations, course, assessment, and diagnosis. *UpToDate*. Retrieved from http://www.uptodate.com.

Thackray, A. E., Deighton, K., King, J. A., & Stensel, D. J. (2016, September 21). Exercise, appetite and weight control: Are there differences between men and women? *Nutrients, 8*(9), 583.

Thalmayer, A. G., Harwood, J. M., Friedman, S., Azocar, F., Watson, L. A., Xu, H., & Ettner, S. L. (2018, May 8). The Mental Health Parity and Addiction Equity Act evaluation study: Impact on nonquantitative treatment limits for specialty behavioral health care. *Health Services Research*. [Epub ahead of print]

Thapa, S., Selya, A. S., & Jonk, Y. (2017). Time-varying effects of parental alcoholism on depression. *Preventing Chronic Disease, 14,* E136.

Thibaut, F., Bradford, J. M., Briken, P., De La Barra, F., Hassler, F., Cosyns, P., & WFSBP Task Force on Sexual Disorders. (2016). The World Federation of Societies of Biological Psychiatry (WFSBP) guidelines for the treatment of adolescent sexual offenders with paraphilic disorders. *World Journal of Biological Psychiatry, 17*(1), 2–38.

Thibaut, F., De La Barra, F., Gordon, H., Cosyns, P., & Bradford, J. M. W. (2010). The World Federation of Societies of Biological Psychiatry (WRSBP) guidelines for the biological treatment of paraphilias. *World Journal of Biological Psychiatry, 11*(3-4), 604–655.

Thigpen, C. H., & Cleckley, H. M. (1957). *The three faces of Eve*. New York: McGraw-Hill.

Thomas, J. (2014, January/February). Most psychologists misinformed on "duty to warn." *The National Psychologist,* pp. 3–4.

Thomas, J. J., Lee, S. D., & Becker, A. E. (2016). Updates in the epidemiology of eating disorders in Asia and the Pacific. *Current Opinion in Psychiatry, 29*(6), 354–362.

Thomasson, E. (2012, June 12). Right-to-die movement sees gain as world ages. *Reuters*.

Thompson, N. J., Fiorillo, D., Rothbaum, B. O., Ressler, K. J., & Michopoulos, V. (2018). Coping strategies as mediators in relation to resilience and posttraumatic stress disorder. *Journal of Affective Disorders, 225,* 153–159.

Thompson, S. (2016, October 27). The 13 highest-grossing horror film franchises of all time at the U.S. box office. *Forbes*. Retrieved from http://www.forbes.com.

Thompson, S. (2017, August). 3 exercise tips to prevent and treat depression. *FastTwitchGrandma*. Retrieved from https://fasttwitchgrandma.com.

Thompson-Brenner, H. (2016). Relationship-focused therapy for bulimia and binge eating: Introduction to the special section. *Psychotherapy, 53*(2), 185–187.

Thompson-Hollands, J., Kerns, C. E., Pincus, D. B., & Comer, J. S. (2014). Parental accommodation of child anxiety and related symptoms: Range, impact, and correlates. *Journal of Anxiety Disorders, 28,* 765–773.

Thornton, L. M., Mazzeo, S. E., & Bulik, C. M. (2011). The heritability of eating disorders: Methods and current findings. In R. A. H. Adan & W. H. Kaye (Eds.), *Behavioral neurobiology of eating disorders. Current topics in behavioral neurosciences* (pp. 141–156). New York: Springer-Verlag Publishing.

Thornton, L., Handley, T., Kay-Lambkin, F., & Baker, A. (2017). Is a person thinking about suicide likely to find help on the internet? An evaluation of Google search results. *Suicide and Life-Threatening Behavior, 47*(1), 48–53.

Thurston, M. D., Goldin, P., Heimberg, R., & Gross, J. J. (2017). Self-views in social anxiety disorder: The impact of CBT versus MBSR. *Journal of Anxiety Disorders, 47,* 83–90.

Tietze, K. J., & Fuchs, B. (2017, June 15). Sedative-analgesic medications in critically ill adults: Properties, dosage regimens, and adverse effects. *UpToDate*. Retrieved from http://www.uptodate.com.

Tight, M. (2017). *Understanding case study research: Small-scale research with meaning.* Los Angeles: Sage Publications.

Tiihonen, J., Tanskanen, A., & Taipale, H. (2018, April 6). 20-year nationwide follow-up study on discontinuation of antipsychotic treatment in first-episode schizophrenia. *American Journal of Psychiatry.* [Epub ahead of print]

Tingle, J. (2018). Monitoring the Mental Health Act: A need to protect patients' rights. *British Journal of Nursing, 27*(6), 344–345.

Tint, A., Thomson, K., & Weiss, J. A. (2017). A systematic literature review of the physical and psychosocial correlates of Special Olympics participation among individuals with intellectual disability. *Journal of Intellectual Disability Research, 61*(4), 301–324.

Tofler, G. H. (2018, February 21). Psychosocial factors in acute myocardial infarction. *UpToDate*. Retrieved from http://www.uptodate.com.

Tompson, M. C., Sugar, C. A., Langer, D. A., & Asarnow, J. R. (2017). A randomized clinical trial comparing family-focused treatment and individual supportive therapy for depression in childhood and early adolescence. *Journal of the American Academy of Child and Adolescent Psychiatry, 56,* 515–523.

Tondo, L., Vázquez, G. H., Baethge, C., Baronessa, C., Bolzani, L., Koukopoulos, A., . . . Baldessarini, R. J. (2015). Comparison of psychotic bipolar disorder, schizoaffective disorder, and schizophrenia: An international, multisite study. *Acta Psychiatrica Scandinavica.* [Electronic publication]

Tone, E. B., Garn, C. L., & Pine, D. S. (2016). Anxiety regulation: A developmental psychopathology perspective. In D. Cicchetti (Ed.), *Developmental psychopathology, Vol. 2: Developmental neuroscience* (3rd ed.). New York: Wiley.

Tone, E. B., Garn, C. L., & Pine, D. S. (2016). Anxiety regulation: A developmental psychopathology perspective. In D. Cicchetti (Ed.), *Developmental psychopathology, Vol. 3: Developmental neuroscience* (3rd ed.). New York: Wiley.

Topper, M., Emmelkamp, P. M., Watkins, E., & Ehring, T. (2017). Prevention of anxiety disorders and depression by targeting excessive worry and rumination in adolescents and young adults: A randomized controlled trial. *Behaviour Research and Therapy, 90,* 123–136.

Torales, J., Barrios, I., & Villalba, J. (2017). Alternative therapies for excoriation (skin picking) disorder: A brief update. *Advances in Mind/Body Medicine, 31*(1), 10–13.

Torrey, E. F. (2014). *Surviving schizophrenia: A family manual* (6th ed.). New York: Harper Paperbacks.

Torrey, E. F. (2001). *Surviving schizophrenia: A manual for families, consumers, and providers* (4th ed.). New York: HarperCollins.

Toth, S. L., Petrenko, C. L. M., Gravener-Davis, J. A., & Handley, E. D. (2016). Advances in prevention science: A developmental psychopathology perspective. In D. Cicchetti (Ed.), *Developmental psychopathology,*

Vol. 4: Risk, resilience, and intervention (3rd ed.). New York: Wiley.

Town, J. M., Abbass, A., Driessen, E., Luyten, P., & Weerasekera, P. (2017). Updating the evidence and recommendations for short-term psychodynamic psychotherapy in the treatment of major depressive disorder in adults. *The Canadian Journal of Psychiatry, 62*(1), 73–74.

Treasure, J., & Cardi, V. (2017). Anorexia nervosa, theory and treatment: Where are we 35 years on from Hilde Bruch's foundation lecture? *European Eating Disorders Review, 25*(3), 139–147.

Trotter Davis, M., Bateman, B., & Avorn, J. (2017). Educational outreach to opioid prescribers: The case for academic detailing. *Pain Physician, 20*(2S), S147–S151.

Trucco, E. M., Villafuerte, S., Hussong, A., Burmeister, M., & Zucker, R. A. (2018). Biological underpinnings of an internalizing pathway to alcohol, cigarette, and marijuana use. *Journal of Abnormal Psychology, 127*(1), 79–91.

True, W. R., & Lyons, M. J. (1999). Genetic risk factors for PTSD: A twin study. In R. Yehuda (Ed.), *Risk factors for posttraumatic stress disorder.* Washington, DC: American Psychiatric Press.

Trull, T. J., Jahng, S., Tomko, R. L., Wood, P. K., & Sher, K. J. (2010). Revised NESARC personality disorder diagnoses: Gender, prevalence, and comorbidity with substance dependence disorders. *Journal of Personality Disorders, 24*(4), 412–426.

Trull, T. J., & Widiger, T. A. (2003). Personality disorders. In G. Stricker, T. A. Widiger, & I. B. Wiener (Eds.), *Handbook of psychology: Clinical psychology.* New York: Wiley.

Tsai, T. H., Chang, H. T., Chen, Y. J., & Chang, Y. S. (2017). Determinants of user acceptance of a specific social platform for older adults: An empirical examination of user interface characteristics and behavioral intention. *PLoS ONE, 12*(8), e0180102.

Tse, P. S., González, D. A., & Jenkins, S. R. (2018). Validating the structure of the depression and somatic symptoms scale. *Psychosomatics, 59*(3), 277–282.

Tsoukas, A., & March E. (2018, January 26). Predicting short- and long-term mating orientations: The role of sex and the dark tetrad. *Journal of Sex Research,* 1–13.

Tsuang, M., Domschke, K., Jerkey, B. A., & Lyons, M. J. (2004). Agoraphobic behavior and panic attack: A study of male twins. *Journal of Anxiety Disorders, 18*(6), 799–807.

Tsui, P., Deptula, A., & Yuan, D. Y. (2017). Conversion disorder, functional neurological symptom disorder, and chronic pain: Comorbidity, assessment, and treatment. *Current Pain and Headache Reports, 21*(6), 29.

Tu, N. D., & Baskin, L. S. (2018, March 2). Nocturnal enuresis in children: Management. *UpToDate.* Retrieved from http://www.uptodate.com.

Tu, N. D., Baskin, L. S., & Arnhym, A. M. (2017, July 12). Nocturnal enuresis in children: Etiology and evaluation. *UpToDate.* Retrieved from http://www.uptodate.com.

Tucker, P., Pfefferbaum, B., Nitiéma, P., Wendling, T. L., & Brown, S. (2018). Do direct survivors of terrorism remaining in the disaster community show better long-term outcome than survivors who relocate? *Community Mental Health Journal, 54*(4), 429–437.

Tull, M. (2017, February 15). Are some racial groups more likely to develop PTSD? *Verywell.* Retrieved from https://www.verywell.com.

Tull, M. T., Berghoff, C. R., Wheeless, L. E., Cohen, R. T., & Gratz, K. L. (2018). PTSD symptom severity and emotion regulation strategy use during trauma cue exposure among patients with substance use disorders: Associations with negative affect, craving, and cortisol reactivity. *Behavior Therapy, 49*(1), 57–70.

Tune, L. E., & DeWitt, M. A. (2011). Delirium. In E. Coffey, J. L. Cummings, M. S. George, & D. Weintraub (Eds.), *The American Psychiatric Publishing textbook of geriatric neuropsychiatry.* Arlington, VA: American Psychiatric Publishing, Inc.

Turkle, S. (2013, December 21). Cited in K. Eisold, Hidden motives: A look at the hidden factors that really drive our social interactions. *Psychology Today.*

Turkle, S. (2013, October 10). "We need to talk": Missed connections with hyperconnectivity. Cited in *NPR.* Retrieved from http://www.npr.org/2013/02/10/171490660.

Turkle, S. (2015). *Reclaiming conversation: The power of talk in a digital age.* New York: Penguin Press.

Turkle, S. (2017). *Alone together: Why we expect more from technology and less from each other* (Rev. ed.). New York: Basic Books.

Turner, D. S. (2017). Crack epidemic: United States history (1980s). *Encyclopaedia Britannica.* Retrieved from https://www.britannica.com.

Turner, D., Petermann, J., Harrison, K., Krueger, R., & Briken, P. (2017, November 17). Pharmacological treatment of patients with paraphilic disorders and risk of sexual offending: An international perspective. *World Journal of Biological Psychiatry.* [Epub ahead of print]

Turner, E. H., Matthews, A. M., Linardatos, E., Tell, R. A., & Rosenthal, R. (2008). Selective publication of antidepressant trials and its influence on apparent efficacy. *New England Journal of Medicine, 358,* 252–260.

Twenge, J. M., & Foster, J. D. (2008). Mapping the scale of the narcissism epidemic: Increases in narcissism 2002–2007 within ethnic groups. *Journal of Research in Personality, 42,* 1619–1622.

Twining, R. C., Vantrease, J. E., Love, S., Padival, M., & Rosenkranz, J. A. (2017). An intra-amygdala circuit specifically regulates social fear learning. *Nature Neuroscience, 20,* 459–469.

Twohig, M. P., & Levin, M. E. (2017). Acceptance and commitment therapy as a treatment for anxiety and depression: A review. *Psychiatric Clinics of North America, 40*(4), 751–770.

U.S. Census Bureau. (2010). Race and ethnicity. *American FactFinder.* Retrieved from http://factfinder.census.gov/serviet/ACSSAFFPeople?.

U.S. Census Bureau. (2015, March 3). *New Census Bureau report analyzes U.S. population projections.* Retrieved from http://www.census.gov/newsroom/press-release/CB15-TPS.16.html.

U.S. Census Bureau. (2016). International populations reports, P95/16-1, *An Aging World: 2015.* Washington, DC: U.S. Government Publishing Office.

U.S. Census Bureau. (2016, April 15). *FFF: Older Americans Month: May 2016.* Release no. CB16-FF.08. Washington, DC: U.S. Census Bureau.

U.S. Census Bureau. (2016, March). *An aging world: 2015: International population reports.* Retrieved from https://www.census.gov/.

U.S. Census Bureau. (2016, November 17). *The majority of children live with two parents, Census Bureau reports.* Retrieved from http://www.census.gov/newsroom/press-releases/2016/CB16-192.html.

U.S. Census Bureau. (2016, September 13). *Income and poverty in the United States: 2015.* Report #P60-256. Washington, DC: U.S. Government Publishing Office.

U.S. Census Bureau. (2017, April 10). *Facts for features: Older Americans Month: May 2017.* Release no. CB17-FF.08. Washington, DC: U.S. Census Bureau.

U.S. Census Bureau. (2018). Population projections. Retrieved from https://www.census.gov/programs-surveys/popproj.html.

Udesky, L. (2014). Stroke and depression. *HealthDay.* Retrieved from http://consumer.healthday.com/encyclopedia.

Uher, R., & Zwicker, A. (2017). Etiology in psychiatry: Embracing the reality of poly-gene-environmental causation of mental illness. *World Psychiatry, 16*(2), 121–129.

Ulrich, R. S. (1984). View from a window may influence recovery from surgery. *Science, 224,* 420–421.

UNESCO (United Nations Educational, Scientific and Cultural Organization). (2017). *School violence and bullying: Global status Report.* Paris: UNESCO.

United Nations. (2013). *World population ageing 2013.* Geneva: UN, Department of Economic and Social Affairs, Population Division.

United Nations. (2016). *Human Development Reports: Table I: Human Development Index and its components.* New York: UN Development Programme.

United Nations. (2017). *World population aging 1950–2050: III. Changing balance between age groups.* New York: UN, DESA, Population Division.

Upshur, C. C., Jenkins, D., Weinreb, L., Gelberg, L., & Orvek, E. A. (2018). Homeless women's service use, barriers, and motivation for participating in substance use treatment. *American Journal of Drug and Alcohol Abuse. 44*(2), 252–262.

Urcuyo, K. R., Boyers, A. E., Carver, C. S., & Antoni, M. H. (2005). Finding benefit in breast cancer: Relations with personality, coping, and concurrent well-being. *Psychology and Health, 20*(2), 175–192.

Ursano, R. J., Boydstun, J. A., & Wheatley, R. D. (1981). Psychiatric illness in U.S. Air Force Vietnam prisoners of war: A five-year follow-up. *American Journal of Psychiatry, 138*(3), 310–314.

Ursano, R. J., McCarroll, J. E., & Fullerton, C. S. (2003). Traumatic death in terrorism and disasters: The effects of posttraumatic stress and behavior. In R. J. Ursano, C. S. Fullerton, & A. E. Norwood (Eds.), *Terrorism and disaster: Individual and community mental health* *interventions* (pp. 308–332). New York: Cambridge University Press.

Usami, M., Iwadare, Y., Watanabe, K., Kodaira, M., Ushijima, H., Tanaka, T., & Saito, K. (2016). Long-term fluctuations in traumatic symptoms of high school girls who survived from the 2011 Japan tsunami: Series of questionnaire-based cross-sectional surveys. *Child Psychiatry & Human Development, 47*(6), 1002–1008.

USDHHS (U.S. Department of Health and Human Services). (2017). *Facts about bullying.* Retrieved from https://www.stopbullying.gov/media/facts.

USDVA (U.S. Department of Veteran Affairs). (2015, August 13). *PTSD: National Center for PTSD: Women, trauma, and PTSD*. Retrieved from https://www.ptsd.va.gov.

USDVA (U.S. Department of Veteran Affairs). (2016, February 23). *PTSD: National Center for PTSD: Types of debriefing following disasters.* Retrieved from https://www.ptsd.va.gov.

USGS (U.S. Geological Survey). (2011, April 14). Earthquakes with 1000 or more deaths since 1900. Retrieved from http://earthquake/usgs/gov/earthquakes/world/world_deaths.php.

Vadini, F., Calella, G., Pieri, A., Ricci, E., Fulcheri, M., Verrocchio, M. C., . . . Parruti, G. (2018). Neurocognitive impairment and suicide risk among prison inmates. *Journal of Affective Disorders, 225,* 273–277.

Vahia, V. N., & Vahia, I. V. (2008). Schizophrenia in developing countries. In K. T. Mueser & D. V. Jeste (Eds.), *Clinical handbook of schizophrenia* (pp. 549–555). New York: Guilford Press.

Vakil, N. B. (2015, March 11). Overview of the complications of peptic ulcer disease. *UpToDate*. Retrieved from http://www.uptodate.com.

Vakil, N. B. (2015, March 12). Peptic ulcer disease: Genetic, environmental, and psychological risk factors and pathogenesis. *UpToDate*. Retrieved from http://www.uptodate.com.

Vakil, N. B. (2017, July 5). Peptic ulcer disease: Genetic, environmental, and psychological risk factors and pathogenesis. *UpToDate*. Retrieved from http://www.uptodate.com.

Vaknin S. (2015, June 30). *Malignant self-love: Narcissism revisited* (10th ed.). *Amazon Digital Services*.

Vaknin, S. (2016). The borderline patient: A case study. *HealthyPlace*. Retrieved from https://www.healthyplace.com/personality-disorders.

Valbak, K. (2001). Good outcome for bulimic patients in long-term group analysis: A single-group study. *European Eating Disorders Review, 9*(1), 19–32.

Valenstein, E. S. (1986). *Great and desperate cures.* New York: Basic Books.

Valentine, S. E., & Shipherd, J. C. (2018, March 28). A systematic review of social stress and mental health among transgender and gender non-conforming people in the United States. *Clinical Psychology Review.* [Epub ahead of print]

Vall, E., & Wade, T. D. (2015). Predictors of treatment outcome in individuals with eating disorders: A systematic review and meta-analysis. *International Journal of Eating Disorders.* [Electronic publication]

Vallarino, M., Henry, C., Etain, B., Gehue, L. J., Macneil, C., Scott, E. M., . . . Scott, J. (2015). An evidence map of psychosocial interventions for the earliest stages of bipolar disorder. *Lancet Psychiatry, 2,* 548–563.

Vallejos, M., Cesoni, O. M., Farinola, R., & Prokopez, C. R. (2017, March 17). Childhood adversities in men with schizophrenia: Dose-response vs. trauma specific hypothesis. *Archives of Paediatrics and Developmental Pathology, 1*(1), 1002.

van den Noort, M., Lim, S., Litscher, G., & Bosch, P. (2018). Transcranial magnetic stimulation for treating older patients with treatment-resistant depression. *Journal of Affective Disorders, 225,* 278–279.

van der Kruijs, S. M., Bodde, N. G., Carrette, E., Lazeron, R. C., Vonck, K. J., Boon, P. M., . . . Aldenkamp, A. P. (2014). Neurophysiological correlates of dissociative symptoms. *Journal of Neurology, Neurosurgery, and Psychiatry, 85*(2), 174–179.

van Diermen, L., van den Ameele, S., Kamperman, A. M., Sabbe, B. C. G., Vermeulen, T., Schrijvers, D., & Birkenhäger, T. K. (2018). Prediction of electroconvulsive therapy response and remission in major depression: Meta-analysis. *British Journal of Psychiatry, 212*(2), 71–80.

van Duijl, M., Nijenhuis, E., Komproe, I. H., Gernaat, H. B. P. E., & de Jong, J. T. (2010). Dissociative symptoms and reported trauma among patients with spirit possession and matched healthy controls in Uganda. *Culture, Medicine and Psychiatry, 34*(2), 380–400.

Van Durme, K., Goossens, L., & Braet, C. (2012). Adolescent aesthetic athletes: A group at risk for eating pathology? *Eating Behaviors, 13*(2), 119–122.

van Geel, M., Vedder, P., & Tanilon, J. (2014). Relationship between peer victimization, cyberbullying, and suicide in children and adolescents: A meta-analysis. *JAMA Pediatrics, 168*(5), 435–442.

Van Hecke, A. V., Oswald, T., & Mundy, P. (2016). Joint attention and the social phenotype of autism spectrum disorder: A perspective from developmental psychopathology. In D. Cicchetti (Ed.), *Developmental psychopathology, Vol. 3: Maladaptation and psychopathology* (3rd ed.). New York: Wiley.

van Lankveld, J. J. D. M. (2017). Self-help and biblio-sex therapy. In Z. D. Peterson (Ed.), *The Wiley handbook of sex therapy* (Part IV, Chap. 29, pp. 468–482). Chichester, UK: John Wiley & Sons.

Van Meter, A. R., Burke, C., Kowatch, R. A., Findling, R. L., & Youngstrom, E. A. (2016). Ten-year updated meta-analysis of the clinical characteristics of pediatric mania and hypomania. *Bipolar Disorder, 18,* 19–32.

van Spronsen, F. J., van Wegberg, A. M. J., Ahring, K., Belanger-Quintana, A., Blau, N., Bosch, A. M., . . . MacDonald, A. (2017). Key European guidelines for the diagnosis and management of patients with phenylketonuria. *Lancet: Diabetes and Epidemiology, 5,* 743–756.

van Vonderen, K. E., & Kinnally, W. (2012). Media effects on body image: Examining media exposure in the broader context of internal and other social factors. *American Communication Journal, 14*(2), 41–57.

Vance, S. R. Jr., Lasofsky, B., Ozer, E., & Buckelew, S. M. (2018, March 24). Teaching paediatric transgender care. *Clinical Teacher.* [Epub ahead of print]

Vaquero, L., Cámara, E., Sampedro, F., Pérez de Los Cobos, J., Batlle, F., Fabregas, J. M., . . . Riba, J. (2017). Cocaine addiction is associated with abnormal prefrontal function, increased striatal connectivity and sensitivity to monetary incentives, and decreased connectivity outside the human reward circuit. *Addiction Biology, 22*(3), 844–856.

Vasterling, J. J., Asian, M., Proctor, S. P., Ko, J., Marx, B. P., Jakupcak, M., . . . Concato, J. (2016). Longitudinal examination of posttraumatic stress disorder as a long-term outcome of Iraq War deployment. *American Journal of Epidemiology, 184,* 796–805.

Vazquez, K., Sandler, J., Interian, A., & Feldman, J. M. (2017). Emotionally triggered asthma and its relationship to panic disorder, *ataques de nervois,* and asthma-related death of a loved one in Latino adults. *Journal of Psychosomatic Research, 93,* 76–82.

Vedel, A., & Thomsen, D. K. (2017). The Dark Triad across academic majors. *Personality and Individual Differences, 116,* 86–91.

Vellante, F., Sarchione, F., Ebisch, S. J. H., Salone, A., Orsolini, L., Marini, S., . . . Di Giannantonio, M. (2018). Creativity and psychiatric illness: A functional perspective beyond chaos. *Progress in Neuro-Psychopharmacology & Biological Psychiatry, 80*(Pt. B), 91–100.

Verano, J. W. (2017). Reprint of differential diagnosis: Trepanation. *International Journal of Paleopathology, 19,* 111–118.

Vetter, H. J. (1969). *Language behavior and psychopathology.* Chicago: Rand McNally.

Vicianova, M. (2015). Historical techniques in lie detection. *European Journal of Psychology, 11*(3): 522–534.

Vieta, E., & Colom, F. (2017, March 22). Bipolar disorder in adults: Managing poor adherence to maintenance pharmacotherapy. *UpToDate*. Retrieved from http://www.uptodate.com.

Viguera, A. (2016, November 9). Postpartum unipolar major depression: Epidemiology, clinical features, assessment, and diagnosis. *UpToDate*. Retrieved from http://www.uptodate.com.

Viguera, A. (2017, January 12). Severe postpartum unipolar major depression: Treatment. *UpToDate*. Retrieved from http://www.uptodate.com.

Virdi, S., & Weiss, K. J. (2017). Involuntary administration of medication in mental health facilities. *Journal of the American Academy of Psychiatry and the Law Online, 45*(2), 265–267.

Vitelli, R. (2013). Can social media spread epidemics? *Psychology Today*. Retrieved from http://www.psychologytoday.com/blog/media-spotlight/201309/can-social-media-spread-epidemics.

Vitelli, R. (2016, May 4). Can celebrity suicides lead to copycat deaths? *Psychology Today.*

Vittana. (2018). *26 poverty and crime statistics*. Seattle, WA: Vittana. Retrieved from https://vittana.org.

Vogel, J., & Baran, M. (2016). Inconclusive: The truth about lie detector tests. *APM (American Public Media) Reports.*

Vogt, D. S., Dutra, L., Reardon, A., Zisserson, R., & Miller, M. W. (2011). Assessment of trauma, posttraumatic stress disorder, and related mental health outcomes. In J. I. Ruzek, P. P. Schnurr, J. J. Vasterling, & M. J. Friedman (Eds.), *Caring for veterans with deployment-related stress disorders* (pp. 59–83). Washington, DC: American Psychological Association.

Vogt, D., Smith, B. N., Fox, A. B., Amoroso, T., Taverna, E., & Schnurr, P. P. (2017). Consequences of PTSD for the work and family quality of life of female and male U.S. Afghanistan and Iraq War veterans. *Social Psychiatry and Psychiatric Epidemiology, 52*(3), 341–352.

Volkow, N. D., Koob, G. F., & McLellan, T. (2016). Neurobiologic advances from the brain disease model of addiction. *New England Journal of Medicine, 374,* 363–371.

Volkow, N. D., Woodcock, J., Compton, W. M., Throckmorton, D. C., Skolnick, P., Hertz, S., & Wargo, E. M. (2018, March 28). Medication development in opioid addiction: Meaningful clinical end points. *Science Translational Medicine, 10*(434).

Volkow, N. D., Fowler, J. S., & Wang, G. J. (2002). Role of dopamine in drug reinforcement and addiction in humans: Results from imaging studies. *Behavioral Pharmacology, 13,* 355–366.

Volkow, N. D., Fowler, J. S., & Wang, G. J. (2004). The addicted human brain viewed in the light of imaging studies: Brain circuits and treatment strategies. *Neuropharmacology, 47*(Suppl. 1), 3–13.

Volmer, J., Koch, I. K., & Göritz, A. S. (2016). The bright and dark sides of leaders' Dark Triad traits: Effects on subordinates' career success and well-being. *Personality and Individual Differences, 101,* 413–418.

Volz, K., Leonhart, R., Stark, R., Vaitl, D., & Ambach, W. (2017). Psychophysiological correlates of the misinformation effect. *International Journal of Psychophysiology,* April 8, *117,* 1–9. [Epub ahead of print]

von Hahn, L. E. (2016, November 9). Specific learning disabilities in children: Evaluation. *UpToDate.* Retrieved from http://www.uptodate.com.

von Hahn, L. E. (2016, September 29). Specific learning disabilities in children: Clinical features. *UpToDate.* Retrieved from http://www.uptodate.com.

von Hahn, L. E. (2017, April 28). Specific learning disabilities in children: Role of the primary care provider. *UpToDate.* Retrieved from http://www.uptodate.com.

von Hahn, L. E. (2017, May 22). Specific learning disabilities in children: Educational management. *UpToDate.* Retrieved from http://www.uptodate.com.

von Hahn, L. E. (2018, May 10). Specific learning disabilities in children: Role of the primary care provider. *UpToDate.* Retrieved from http://www.uptodate.com.

Voon, P., Karamouzian, M., & Kerr, T. (2017). Chronic pain and opioid misuse: A review of reviews. *Substance Abuse Treatment, Prevention, and Policy, 12*(1), 36.

Vos, J., & Vitali, D. (2018, September 24). The effects of psychological meaning-centered therapies on quality of life and psychological stress: A meta-analysis. *Palliative & Supportive Care.* [Epub ahead of print]

Vuori, M., Autti-Rämö, I., Junttila, N., Vauras, M., & Tuulio-Henriksson, A. (2017). Discrepancies between self- and adult-perceptions of social competence in children with neuropsychiatric disorders. *Child: Care, Health and Development, 43*(5), 670–678.

Vuori, M., Tuulio-Henriksson, A., Nissinen, H., & Autti-Rämö, I. (2015). [Family-based psychosocial interventions for children with attention deficit hyperactivity disorder (ADHD), oppositional defiant disorder, and conduct disorder]. *Duodecim, 131*(17), 1561–1568. [Finnish].

Wade, K. A., Nash, R, A., & Lindsay, D. S. (2018). Reasons to doubt the reliability of eyewitness memory: Commentary on Wixted, Mickes, and Fisher (2018). *Perspectives on Psychological Science, 13*(3), 339–342.

Wakefield, A. J., Murch, S. H., Anthony, A., Linnell, J., Casson, D. M., Malik, M., . . . Walker-Smith, J. A. (1998). Retracted: Ileal-lymphoid-nodular hyperplasia, non-specific colitis, and pervasive developmental disorder in children. *The Lancet, 351*(9103), 637–641.

Walentynowicz, M., Raes, F., Van Diest, I., & Van den Bergh, O. (2017). The specificity of health-related autobiographical memories in patients with somatic symptom disorder. *Psychological Medicine, 79*(1), 43–49.

Walker, D. M., & Nestler, E. J. (2018). Neuroepigenetics and addiction. *Handbook of Clinical Neurology, 148,* 747–765.

Walker, E. F., Ryan, A. T., Bridgman Goines, K. C., Novacek, D. M., Goulding, S. M., . . . Trotman, H. D. (2016). Multilevel approaches to schizophrenia and other psychotic disorders: The biobehavioral interface. In D. Cicchetti (Ed.), *Developmental psychopathology, Vol. 3, Maladaptation and psychopathology* (Chap. 22, pp. 997–1038). Hoboken, NJ: John Wiley & Sons.

Walkup, J. T., Albano, A. M., Piacentini, J., Boris, B., Compton, S. N., Sherrill, J., . . . Kendall, P.C. (2008). Cognitive behavioral therapy, sertraline, or a combination in childhood anxiety. *New England Journal of Medicine, 359,* 2753–2766.

Walsh, B. T. (2018, April 4). Anorexia nervosa in adults: Pharmacotherapy. *UpToDate.* Retrieved from http://www.uptodate.com.

Walsh, E. C., Eisenlohr-Moul, T. A., Minkel, J., Bizzell, J., Petty, C., Crowther, A., . . . Dichter, G. S. (2019). Pretreatment brain connectivity during positive emotion upregulation predicts decreased anhedonia following behavioral activation therapy for depression. *Journal of Affective Disorders, 243,* 188–192.

Walsh, R. (2019). Meditation and psychotherapy. In D. Wedding & R. J. Corsini (Eds.), *Current psychotherapies* (11th ed., Ch. 12). Independence, KY: Cengage Publications.

Walton, E. L. (2018). For better or worse: Immune system involvement in Alzheimer's disease. *Biomedical Journal, 41*(1), 1–4.

Walton, J. L., Cuccurullo, L. J., Raines, A. M., Vidaurri, D. N., Allan, N. P., Maieritsch, K. P., & Franklin, C. L. (2017). Sometimes less is more: Establishing the core symptoms of PTSD. *Journal of Traumatic Stress, 30*(3), 254–258.

Wang, C., Liu, B., Zhang, X., Cui, Y., Yu, C., & Jiang, T. (2018). Multilocus genetic profile in dopaminergic pathway modulates the stratum and working memory. *Scientific Reports, 8*(1), 5372.

Wang, G. S. (2018, February 12). Cannabis (marijuana): Acute intoxication. *UpToDate.* Retrieved from http://www.uptodate.com.

Wang, J., Wei, Q., Yuan, X., Jiang, X., Xu, J., Zhou, X., . . . Wang, K. (2018). Local functional connectivity density is closely associated with the response of electroconvulsive therapy in major depressive disorder. *Journal of Affective Disorders, 225,* 658–664.

Wang, M., Wang, X., & Liu, L. (2016). Paternal and maternal psychological and physical aggression and children's anxiety in China. *Child Abuse & Neglect, 51,* 12–20.

Wang, P. S., Berglund, P., Olfson, M., Pincus, H. A., Wells, K. B., & Kessler, R. C. (2005). Failure and delay in initial treatment contact after first onset of mental disorders in the National Comorbidity Survey Replication. *Archives of General Psychiatry, 62,* 603–613.

Wang, P. S., Lane, M., Olfson, M., Pincus, H. A., Wells, K. B., & Kessler, R. C. (2005). Twelve-month use of mental health services in the United States. *Archives of General Psychiatry, 62,* 629–640.

Wang, Q., Shelton, R. C., & Dwivedi, Y. (2018). Interaction between early-life stress and FKBP5 gene variants in major depressive disorder and post-traumatic stress disorder: A systematic review and meta-analysis. *Journal of Affective Disorders, 225,* 422–428.

Wang, S. W., & Repetti, R. L. (2016). Who gives to whom? Testing the support gap hypothesis with naturalistic observations of couple interactions. *Journal of Family Psychology, 30*(4), 492–502.

Wang, S. S. (2007, December 4). The graying of shock therapy. *Wall Street Journal. Online.* Retrieved from http://online.wsg.com/public/article_print/SB119673737406312767.html.

Wang, S., Che, T., Levit, A., Shoichet, B. K., Wacker, D., & Roth, B. L. (2018). Structure of the D2 dopamine receptor bound to the atypical antipsychotic drug risperidone. *Nature, 555*(7695), 269–273.

Wang, X. (2017). History of world neurosurgery. *Zhonghua Yi Shi Za Zhi, 47*(3), 160–164. [Chinese]

Wang, X., Chen, Q., & Yang, M. (2017). Effect of caregivers' expressed emotion on the care burden and rehospitalization rate of schizophrenia. *Patient Preference and Adherence, 11,* 1505–1511.

Wang, Y. G., Chen, S., Xu, Z. M., Shen, Z. H., Wang, Y. Q., He, X. Y., . . . Wang, Y. Q. (2017). Family history of suicide and high motor impulsivity distinguish suicide attempters from suicide ideators among college students. *Journal of Psychiatric Research, 90,* 21–25.

Wang, Y., Tang, J., Zhou, F., Yang, L. & Wu, J. (2017). Comprehensive geriatric care reduces acute perioperative delirium in elderly patients with hip fractures: A meta-analysis. *Medicine, 96*(26), e7361.

Wang, Z., Whiteside, S., Sim, L., Farah, W., Morrow, A., Alsawas, M., . . . Murad, M. H. (2017, August). *Anxiety in children* [Internet]. Rockville, MD: Agency for Healthcare Research and Quality.

Waters, B. (2015, June 24). 23 mental health professionals interviewed about their jobs. *Psychology Today.*

Waters, F., & Fernyhough, C. (2017). Hallucinations: A systematic review of points of similarity and difference across diagnostic classes. *Schizophrenia Bulletin, 43*(1), 32–43.

Watkins, E. R., & Nolen-Hoeksema, S. (2014). A habit-goal framework of depressive rumination. *Journal of Abnormal Psychology, 123*(1), 24–34.

Watson, J. B., & Rayner, R. (1920). Conditioned emotional reaction. *Journal of Experimental Psychology, 3,* 1–14.

Watson, P. J., & Shalev, A. Y. (2005). Assessment and treatment of adult acute responses to traumatic stress following mass traumatic events. *CNS Spectrums, 10*(2), 123–131.

Watterson, R. A., Williams, J. V., Lavorato, D. H., & Patten, S. B. (2017). Descriptive epidemiology of generalized anxiety disorder in Canada. *Canadian Journal of Psychiatry, 62*(1), 24–29.

Way, M. J., Ali, M. A., McQuillin, A., & Morgan, M. Y. (2017). Genetic variants in ALDH1B1 and alcohol dependence risk in a British and Irish population: A bioinformatic and genetic study. *PLoS ONE, 12*(6), e0177009.

Wayne, T. (2017, May 5). Social insecurity: Internet turns boomers into twits. *New York Times.*

WCSAP (Washington Coalition of Sexual Assault Programs). (2016, December 6). *The effects of sexual assault.* Olympia, WA: WCSAP.

Webb, J. B., Fiery, M. F., & Jafari, N. (2016). "You better not leave me shaming!": Conditional indirect effect analyses of anti-fat attitudes, body shame, and fat talk as a function of self-compassion in college women. *Body Image, 18,* 5–13.

Weber, B. (2016, August 5). Chris Costner Sizemore, patient behind "The Three Faces of Eve," dies at 90. *New York Times.*

Weber-Goericke, F., & Muehlhan, M. (2019). A quantitative meta-analysis of fMRI studies investigating emotional processing in excessive worriers: Application of activation likelihood estimation analysis. *Journal of Affective Disorders, 243,* 348–359.

Webster-Stratton, C. (2016). The incredible years: Use of play interventions and coaching for children with externalizing difficulties. In T. M. Reddy, T. Files-Hall, & C. E. Schaefer (Eds.), *Empirically based play interventions for children* (2nd ed.). Washington, D.C.: American Psychological Association.

Wechsler, H., Lee, J. E., Kuo, M., Seibring, M., Nelson, T. F., & Lee, H. (2002). Trends in alcohol use, related problems and experience of prevention efforts among US college students 1993 to 2001: Results from the 2001 Harvard School of Public Health College Alcohol Study. *Journal of American College Health, 50,* 203–217.

Weck, F., Neng, J. B., Richtberg, S., Jakob, M., & Stangier, U. (2015). Cognitive therapy versus exposure therapy for hypochondriasis (health anxiety): A randomized controlled trial. *Journal of Consulting and Clinical Psychology, 83*(4), 665–676.

Wedding, D., & Corsini, R. J. (Eds.). (2019). *Current psychotherapies* (11th ed.). Independence, KY: Cengage Publications.

Weeks, D. J. (2015). *The gifts of eccentrics: Imagination in reality.* CreateSpace Publishing Platform.

Weeks, D., & James, J. (1995). *Eccentrics: A study of sanity and strangeness.* New York: Villard.

Weersing, V. R., Jeffreys, M., Do, M. T., Schwartz, K. T., & Bolanco, C. (2017). Evidence base update of psychosocial treatments for child and adolescent depression. *Journal of Clinical Child and Adolescent Psychology, 46,* 11–43.

Weigold, M. (2018, May 9). Selfie psychology: Would you risk your life for a photo? *The Philadelphia Inquirer.* Retrieved from http://www.philly.com/philly/health/selfie-psychology-would-you-risk-your-life-for-a-photo-20180509.html#loaded.

Weiner, I. B., & Greene, R. L. (2017). *Handbook of personality assessment* (2nd ed.). Hoboken, NJ: Wiley.

Weiner, R. (2014, September 13). Colleges ramp up efforts to prevent sex assaults. *USA Today.* Retrieved from http://www.usatoday.com/story/news/nation/2014/09/13/.

Weinshenker, N. (2014). *Teenagers and body image: What's typical and what's not?* New York: NYU Child Study Center. Retrieved from http://www.education.com.

Weis, J., Gully, J., & Marks, S. (2016). The interplay of factitious disorder and palliative care encounters: A case series. *Journal of Palliative Medicine, 19*(2), 238–243.

Weishaar, M. E., & Beck, A. T. (2006). Cognitive theory of personality and personality disorders. In S. Strack (Ed.), *Differentiating normal and abnormal personality* (2nd ed., pp. 113–135). New York: Springer Publishing Co.

Weiss, D. E. (1991). *The great divide.* New York: Poseidon Press/Simon & Schuster.

Weiss, F. (2011). Alcohol self-administration. In M. C. Olmstead (Ed.), *Animal models of drug addiction. Springer protocols: Neuromethods* (pp. 133–165). Totowa, NJ: Humana Press.

Weisskirch, R. S., Drouin, M., & Delevi, R. (2017). Relational anxiety and sexting. *Journal of Sex Research, 54*(6), 685–693.

Weissman, L., & Bridgemohan, C. (2017, July 12). Autism spectrum disorder in children and adolescents: Pharmacologic interventions. *UpToDate.* Retrieved from http://www.uptodate.com.

Weissman, L., & Bridgemohan, C. (2017, June 14). Autism spectrum disorder in children and adolescents: Behavioral and educational interventions. *UpToDate.* Retrieved from http://www.uptodate.com.

Weissman, L., & Bridgemohan, C. (2018, April 16). Autism spectrum disorder in children and adolescents: Pharmacologic interventions. *UpToDate.* Retrieved from http://www.uptodate.com.

Weissman, L., & Bridgemohan, C. (2018, May 9). Autism spectrum disorder in children and adolescents: Overview of management. *UpToDate.* Retrieved from http://www.uptodate.com.

Weissman, M. M. (2018). Postpartum depression and its long-term impact on children: Many new questions. *JAMA Psychiatry, 75*(3), 227–228.

Weissman, M. M., Berry, O. O., Warner, V., Gameroff, M. J., Skipper, J., Talati, A., . . . Wickramaratne, P. (2016). A 30-year study of 3 generations at high risk and low risk for depression. *JAMA Psychiatry, 73*(9), 970–977.

Weissman, M. M., Wickramaratne, P., Gameroff, M. J., Warner, V., Pilowsky, D., Kohad, R. G., . . . Talati, A. (2016). Offspring of depressed parents: 30 years later. *American Journal of Psychiatry, 173,* 1024–1032.

Weitzman, C., & Rojmahamongkol, P. (2018, February 20). Fetal alcohol spectrum disorder: Clinical features and diagnosis. *UpToDate.* Retrieved from http://www.uptodate.com.

Wells, A. (2005). The metacognitive model of GAD: Assessment of meta-worry and relationship with DSM-IV generalized anxiety disorder. *Cognitive Therapy and Research, 29*(1), 107–121.

Wells, A. (2011). Metacognitive therapy. In J. D. Herbert & E. M. Forman (Eds.), *Acceptance and mindfulness in cognitive behavior therapy: Understanding and applying the new therapies* (pp. 83–108). Hoboken, NJ: John Wiley & Sons Inc.

Wells, A. (2014). *Cognitive therapy of anxiety disorders: A practical guide* (2nd ed.). Hoboken, NJ: Wiley-Blackwell.

Wells, G. L., Steblay, N. K., & Dysart, J. E. (2015). Double-blind photo lineups using actual eyewitnesses: An experimental test of a sequential versus simultaneous lineup procedure. *Law and Human Behavior, 39*(1), 1–14.

Wells, G. L., Steblay, N. K., & Dysart, J. E. (2011). *A test of the simultaneous vs. sequential lineup methods: An initial report of the AJS National Eyewitness Identification Field Studies.* Des Moines, Iowa: American Judicature Society.

Wen, T. (2016). Can you beat a lie detector test? *BBC Future.*

Werbart, A., Missios, P., Waldenström, F., & Lilliengren, P. (2017, July 17). "It was hard work every session": Therapists' view of successful psychoanalytic treatments. *Psychotherapy Research.* [Epub ahead of print]

Weremowicz, S. (2018, February 1). Congenital cytogenetic abnormalities. *UpToDate.* Retrieved from http://www.uptodate.com.

Werner-Seidler, A., Afzali, M. H., Chapman, C., Sunderland, M., & Slade, T. (2017). The relationship between social support networks and depression in the 2007 National Survey of Mental Health and Well-being. *Social Psychiatry and Psychiatric Epidemiology, 52*(12), 1463–1473.

Wertheimer, A. (2001). *A special scar: The experiences of people bereaved by suicide* (2nd ed.). East Sussex, England: Brunner-Routledge.

Wesselhoeft, R., Heiervang, E. R., Kragh-Sorensen, P., Sorensen, M. J., & Bilenberg, N. (2016). Major depressive disorder and subthreshold depression in prepubertal children from the Danish National Birth Cohort. *Comprehensive Psychiatry, 70,* 65–76.

West, R. (2016, April 14). *Yes, America can afford to dramatically reduce poverty and increase opportunity.* Washington, DC: Center for American Progress.

Westermeyer, J. (2001). Alcoholism and comorbid psychiatric disorders among American Indians. *American Indian and Alaska Native Mental Health Research, 10,* 27–51.

Westermeyer, J. (2004). Acculturation: Advances in theory, measurement, and applied research. *Journal of Nervous and Mental Disease, 192*(5), 391–392.

Whalen, D. J., Sylvester, C. M., & Luby, J. (2017). Depression and anxiety in preschoolers: A review of the past 7 years. *Child and Adolescent Psychiatric Clinics of North America, 26,* 503–522.

Wheaton, M. G., & Pinto, A. (2017). The role of experimental avoidance in obsessive-compulsive personality disorder traits. *Personality Disorders, 8,* 383–388.

Wherry, J. N. (2018). Assessment of abused youth. In J. N. Butcher & J. M. Hooley (Eds.), *APA handbook of psychopathology. Vol. 2. Psychopathology in children and adolescents* (Ch. 9). Washington, DC: American Psychological Association.

Whisman, M. A., & Beach, S. H. (2012). Couple therapy for depression. *Journal of Clinical Psychology, 68*(5), 526–535.

Whitaker, R. (2002). *Mad in America: Bad science, bad medicine, and the enduring mistreatment of the mentally ill.* Cambridge, MA: Perseus.

Whitaker, R. (2010). *Anatomy of an epidemic: Magic bullets, psychiatric drugs, and the astonishing rise of mental illness in America.* Norwalk, CT: Crown House Publishing Limited.

Whitbourne, S. K. (2013). Shedding light on psychology's Dark Triad. *Psychology Today, 1,* 1–7.

Whitbourne, S. K. (2016, August 27). Are selfie-takers really narcissists? *Psychology Today.*

White, P. (2017, March 26). Rorschach and Wikipedia: The battle of the inkblots. *The Globe and Mail.* Retrieved from https://www.theglobeandmail.com/news/national.

WHO (World Health Organization). (2012). *10 facts on ageing and the life course.* Retrieved from http://www.who.int/features/factfiles/.

WHO (World Health Organization). (2012). *About ageing and life course.* Retrieved from http://www.who.int/ageing/about/ageing_life_course/en/.

WHO (World Health Organization). (2014). *7. Addiction to nicotine.* Retrieved from http://www.who.int/tobacco/publications/gender/women_tob_epidemic/en/.

WHO (World Health Organization). (2017). *Chronic respiratory diseases.* Retrieved from http://www.who.int/respiratory/asthma/en.

WHO (World Health Organization). (2017). *Depression.* Retrieved from http://www.who.int/mediacentre/factsheets/fs369/en/.

WHO (World Health Organization). (2017). *Gender and women's mental health.* Retrieved from http://www.who.int/mental_health/prevention/genderwomen/en/.

WHO (World Health Organization). (2017). *Tobacco Free Initiative (TFI): WHO report on the global tobacco epidemic 2017.* Retrieved from http://www.who.int/tobacco/global_report/2017/en/.

WHO (World Health Organization). (2017, April 4). *Age-standardized suicide rates (per 100,000 population).* Retrieved from WHO/Global Health Observer data repository, http://apps.who.int/gho.

WHO (World Health Organization). (2017, February). *Depression.* Retrieved from http://www.who.int/mediacentre/factsheets/fs369/en/.

WHO (World Health Organization). (2017, May). *Tobacco.* Retrieved from http://www.who.int/mediacentre/factsheets/fs339/en/.

WHO (World Health Organization). (2018). *Chronic respiratory diseases: Asthma.* Retrieved from http://www.who.int./respiratory/asthma/en/.

WHO (World Health Organization). (2018). *Mental health: Schizophrenia.* Retrieved from http://www.who.int/mental_health/management/schizophrenia/en/.

WHO (World Health Organization). (2018, March 16). *Classifications. The 11th Revision of the International Classification of Diseases (ICD-11) is due by 2018!* Retrieved from http://www.who.int//classifications/icd/revision/en/.

Wichstrom, L., Belsky, J., & Steinsbekk, S. (2017). Homotypic and heterotypic continuity of symptoms of psychiatric disorders from age 4 to 10 years: A dynamic panel model. *Journal of Child Psychology and Psychiatry.*

Wieczner, J. (2016). Meditation has become a billion-dollar business. *Fortune.* Retrieved from http://fortune.com.

Wiederhold, B. K. (2015). Does sexting improve adult sexual relationships? *Cyberpsychology, Behavior, and Social Networking, 18*(11), 627.

Wilens, T. E., Yule, A., Martelon, M., Zulauf, C., & Faraone, S. V. (2014). Parental history of substance use disorders (SUD) and SUD in offspring: A controlled family study of bipolar disorder. *American Journal on Addictions, 23*(5), 440–446.

Williams, J., & Nieuwsma, J. (2018, May 10). Screening for depression in adults. *UpToDate.* Retrieved from http://www.uptodate.com.

Williams, L. M. (2017). Defining biotypes for depression and anxiety based on large-scale circuit dysfunction: A theoretical review of the evidence and future directions for clinical translation. *Depress Anxiety, 34*(1), 9–24.

Williams, N. J., Scott, L., & Aarons, G. A. (2018). Prevalence of serious emotional disturbance among U.S. children: A meta-analysis. *Psychiatric Services, 69*(1), 32–40.

Williams, P. (2010). Psychotherapeutic treatment of Cluster A personality disorders. In J. F. Clarkin, P. Fonagy, & G. O. Gabbard (Eds.), *Psychodynamic psychotherapy for personality disorders: A clinical handbook.* Arlington, VA: American Psychiatric Publishing, Inc.

Williams, T. M. (2008). *Black pain: It just looks like we're not hurting.* New York: Scribner.

Wilson, J. (2017). Biological, genetic and environmental causes of oppositional defiant disorder. *News-Medical.* Retrieved from https://www.news-medical.net.

Wilson, K. R., Jordan, J. A., Kras, A. M., Tavkar, P., Bruhn, S., Asawa, L. E., . . . Trask, E. (2010). Adolescent measures: Practitioner's guide to empirically based measure of social skills. In D. W. Nangle, D. J. Hansen, C. A. Erdley, & P. J. Norton (Eds.), *Practitioner's guide to empirically based measures of social skills* (pp. 327–381). New York: Springer Publishing.

Wilson, L. C. (2016). *The Wiley handbook of the psychology of mass shootings.* Hoboken, NJ: Wiley-Blackwell.

Wilson, P. W. F., & Douglas, P. S. (2017, April 6). Epidemiology of coronary heart disease. *UpToDate.* Retrieved from http://www.uptodate.com.

Wilson, R. S., Scherr, P. A., Schneider, J. A., Tang, Y., & Bennett, D. A. (2007). Relation of cognitive activity to risk of developing Alzheimer disease. *Neurology, 69*(20), 1911–1920.

Wilson, R. S., Segawa, E., Boyle, P. A., & Bennett, D. A. (2012). Influence of late-life cognitive activity on cognitive health. *Neurology, 78*(15), 1123–1129.

Wilt, J., & Revelle, W. (2019). The Big Five, everyday contexts and activities, and affective experience. *Personality and Individual Differences, 136,* 140–147.

Wiltsey-Stirman, S., & Comer, J. S. (2019). What are we even trying to implement? Considering the relative merits of promoting evidence-based practices, protocols, principles, or policy. *Clinical Psychology: Science and Practice.*

Wincze, J. P., Bach, A. K., & Barlow, D. H. (2008). Sexual dysfunction. In D. H. Barlow (Ed.), *Clinical handbook of psychological disorders: A step-by-step treatment manual* (4th ed.). New York: Guilford Press.

Winegard, B., & Ferguson, C. J. (2016). The development of rampage shooters: Myths and uncertainty in the search for causes. In L. C. Wilson (Ed.), *The Wiley handbook of the psychology of mass shootings* (Chap. 4, pp. 59–76). Hoboken, NJ: Wiley-Blackwell.

Winkelman, J. W. (2018, May 2). Overview of the treatment of insomnia in adults. *UpToDate.* Retrieved from http://www.uptodate.com.

Winston, D. (2016, February 26). A 5-minute breathing meditation to cultivate mindfulness. *Mindful.* Retrieved from https://www.mindful.org.

Winter, S., Diamond, M., Green, J., Karasic, D., Reed, T., Whittle, S., & Wylie, K. (2016). Transgender people: Health at the margins of society. *Lancet, 23,* 388, 390–400.

Wirtz, A. L., Poteat, T. C., Malik, M., & Glass, N. (2018, January 1). Gender-based violence against transgender people in the United States: A call for research and programming. *Trauma, Violence, & Abuse.* [Epub ahead of print]

Wise, E. H. (2018). Torture scandal prompts broader look at ethics. *The National Psychologist,* January/February, 21.

Wisehart, D. (2015, March 9). 9 fundamental fears that motivate your characters. *Characterchange.*

Witcomb, G. L., Bouman, W. P., Claes, L., Brewin, N., Crawford, J. R., & Arcelus, J. (2018). Levels of depression in transgender people and its predictors: Results of a large matched control study with transgender people accessing clinical services. *Journal of Affective Disorders, 235,* 308–315.

Witt, K., Milner, A., Allisey, A., Davenport, L., & LaMontagne, A. D. (2017). Effectiveness of suicide prevention programs for emergency and protective services employees: A systematic review and meta-analysis. *American Journal of Industrial Medicine, 60*(4), 394–407.

Witthöft, M., Gropalis, M., & Weck, F. (2018). Somatic symptom and related disorders. In J. N. Butcher (Ed.-in-chief), *APA handbook of psychopathology,* (Vol. 1, Ch. 22). Washington, DC: APA.

Wittkowski, H., Hinze, C., Häfner-Harms, S., Oji, V., Masjosthusmann, K., Mooninger, M., . . . Foell, D. (2017). Munchausen by proxy syndrome mimicking systemic autoinflammatory disease: Case report and review of the literature. *Pediatric Rheumatology Online Journal, 15*(1), 19.

Wixted, J. T., & Wells, G. L. (2017). The relationship between eyewitness confidence and identification accuracy: A new synthesis. *Psychological Science in the Public Interest, 18*(1), 10–65.

Wohltmann, J. (2013). *Should grandma join Facebook?* Presentation at International Neuropsychological Society Annual Meeting. Hawaii.

Wolberg, L. R. (1967). *The technique of psychotherapy.* New York: Grune & Stratton.

Wolberg, L. R. (2005). *The technique of psychotherapy.* Lanham, MD: Jason Aronson.

Wolk, D. A., & Dickerson, B. C. (2017, May 12). Clinical features and diagnosis of Alzheimer disease. *UpToDate.* Retrieved from http://www.uptodate.com.

Wolniewicz, C. A., Tiamiyu, Weeks, J. W., & Elhai, J. D. (2018). Problematic smartphone use and relations with negative affect, fear of missing out, and fear of negative and positive evaluation. *Psychiatry Research, 262,* 618–623.

Wolpe, J. (1969). *The practice of behavior therapy.* Oxford, England: Pergamon Press.

Wolpe, J. (1987). The promotion of scientific psychotherapy: A long voyage. In J. K. Zeig (Ed.), *The evolution of psychotherapy.* New York: Brunner/Mazel.

Wong, J. P. S., Stewart, S. M., Claassen, C., Lee, P. W. H., Rao, U., & Lam, T. H. (2008). Repeat suicide attempts in Hong Kong community adolescents. *Social Science and Medicine, 66*(2), 232–241.

Wong, M. M., Brower, K. J., & Zucker, R. A. (2011). Sleep problems, suicidal ideation, and self-harm behaviors in adolescence. *Journal of Psychiatric Research, 45*(4), 505–511.

Wood, J. (2016, May 27). Multiple personality disorder rooted in traumatic experiences. *Psych Central.* Retrieved from http://psychcentral.com.

Wood, J. (2016, November 5). Brain scan can beat polygraph at detecting lies. *Psych Central News.*

Wood, J. (2017, February 12). Poverty, violent neighborhoods can up depression in older adults. *Psych Central.* Retrieved from https://psychcentral.com/news/2017/02/12.

Woodside, D. B., Bulik, C. M., Halmi, K. A., Fichter, M. M., Kaplan, A., Berrettini, W. H., . . . Kaye, W. H. (2002). Personality, perfectionism, and attitudes towards eating in parents of individuals with eating disorders. *International Journal of Eating Disorders, 31*(3), 290–299.

Wright, C. B. (2017, May 11). Treatment and prevention of vascular dementia. *UpToDate.* Retrieved from http://www.uptodate.com.

Wright, C. B. (2017, May 2). Etiology, clinical manifestations, and diagnosis of vascular dementia. *UpToDate.* Retrieved from http://www.uptodate.com.

Wright, J. (2017, February 7). *Get well soon: History's worst plagues and the heroes who fought them.* New York: Harry Holt & Co.

Wylie, R. A., & Wylie, K. R. (2016). Sexual masochism disorder. In R. Balon (Ed.), *Practical guide to paraphilia and paraphilic disorders* (Ch. 8, pp. 107–122). Switzerland: Spring International.

Wymbs, B. T., McCarthy, C. A., Mason, W. A., King, K. M., Baer, J. S., Vander Stoep, A., & McCauley, E. (2014). Early adolescent substance use as a risk factor for developing conduct disorder and depression symptoms. *Journal of Studies on Alcohol and Drugs, 75*(2), 279–289.

Xiang, X., Owen, R., Langi, F. L. F. G., Yamaki, K., Mitchell, D., Heller, T., . . . Jordan, N. (2018, August 31). Impacts of an integrated Medicaid managed care program for adults with behavioral health conditions: The experience of Illinois. *Administration and Policy in Mental Health.* [Epub ahead of print]

Xie, W., & Zhang, W. (2018). Mood-dependent retrieval in visual long-term memory: Dissociable effects on retrieval probability and mnemonic precision. *Cognition & Emotion, 32*(4), 674–690.

Xu, J., Wang, H., Zhang, L., Xu, Z., Li, T., Zhou, Z., . . . Hu, Q. (2018). Both hypo-connectivity and hyper-connectivity of the insular subregions associated with severity in children with autism spectrum disorders. *Frontiers in Neuroscience, 12,* 234.

Xu, W., Liu, Y., Chen, J., Guo, Q., Liu, K., Wen, Z., . . . Shi, Y. (2017). Genetic risk between the CACNA1I gene and schizophrenia in Chinese Uygur population. *Hereditas, 155,* 5.

Yaden, D. B., Eichstaedt, J. C., & Medaglia, J. D. (2018). The future of technology in positive psychology: Methodological advances in the science of well-being. *Frontiers in Psychology, 9,* 962.

Yalom, I. D., & Josselson, R. (2019). Existential psychotherapy. In D. Wedding & R. J. Corsini (Eds.), *Current psychotherapies* (11th ed., Ch. 8). Independence, KY: Cengage Publications.

Yang, H., Brand, J. S., Fang, F., Chiesa, F., Johansson, A. L., Hall, P., & Czene, K. (2017). Time-dependent risk of depression, anxiety, and stress-related disorders in patients with invasive and in situ breast cancer. *International Journal of Cancer, 140*(4), 841–852.

Yang, W., & Zhang, X. (2017, January 17). Common factors vs. specific ingredients in psychotherapy: Controversy and integration. *Advances in Psychological Science, 25*(2), 253–264.

Yao, Z., Liao, M., Hu, T., Zhang, Z., Zhao, Y., Zhang, F., . . . Li, L. (2017). An effective method to identify adolescent generalized anxiety disorder by temporal features of dynamic functional connectivity. *Frontiers in Human Neuroscience, 11,* 492.

Yaser, A., Slewa-Younan, S., Smith, C. A., Olson, R. E., Guajardo, M. G. U., & Mond, J. (2016). Beliefs and knowledge about post-traumatic stress disorder amongst resettled Afghan refugees in Australia. *International Journal of Mental Health Systems, 10,* 31.

Yates, G. P., & Feldman, M. D. (2017). Factitious disorder: A systematic review of 455 cases in the professional literature. *General Hospital Psychiatry, 41,* 20–28.

Yates, G., & Bass, C. (2017). The perpetrators of medical child abuse (Munchausen syndrome by proxy): A systematic review of 796 cases. *Child Abuse & Neglect, 72,* 45–53.

Yazdi, K., Rumetshofer, T., Gnauer, M., Csillag, D., Rosenleitner, J., & Kleiser, R. (2019). Neurobiological processes during the Cambridge gambling task. *Behavioural Brain Research, 356,* 295–304.

Yazdi, M., Roohafza, H., Feizi, A., & Sarafzadegan, N. (2018). Association of stressful life events and psychological problems profile: Results from a large-scale cross-sectional study among Iranian industrial employees using Bayesian quantile structural equation model. *EXCLI, 17,* 620–633.

Yehuda, R., Flory, J. D., Bierer, L. M., Henn-Haase, C., Lehrner, A., Desarnaud, F., . . . Meaney, M. J. (2015). Lower methylation of glucocorticoid receptor gene promoter 1F in peripheral blood of veterans with posttraumatic stress disorder. *Biological Psychiatry, 77*(4), 356–364.

Yehuda, R., & Bierer, L. M. (2007). Transgenerational transmission of cortisol and PTSD risk. *Progress in Brain Research, 167,* 121–135.

Yom-Tov, E., Brunstein-Klomek, A., Hadas, A., Tamir, O., & Fennig, S. (2016). Differences in physical status, mental state and online behavior of people in pro-anorexia web communities. *Eating Behaviors, 22,* 109–112.

Yom-Tov, E., Brunstein-Klomek, A., Mandel, O., Hadas, A., & Fennig, S. (2018, February 22). Inducing behavioral change in seekers of pro-anorexia content using internet advertisements: Randomized controlled trial. *JMIR Mental Health, 5*(1), e6.

Yontef, G., & Jacobs, L. (2019). Gestalt therapy. In D. Wedding & R. J. Corsini (Eds.), *Current psychotherapies* (11th ed., Ch. 9). Independence, KY: Cengage Publications.

Yoon, E., Coburn, C., & Spence, S. A. (2018, January 15). Perceived discrimination and mental health among older African Americans: The role of psychological well-being. *Aging & Mental Health.* [Epub ahead of print]

You, J., Wang, C., Rodriguez, L., Wang, X., & Lu, Q. (2018, January). Personality, coping strategies and emotional adjustment among Chinese cancer patients of different ages. *European Journal of Cancer Care, 27*(1).

Young, G. (2017). PTSD in court II: Risk factors, endophenotypes, and biological underpinnings in PTSD. *International Journal of Law and Psychiatry, 51,* 1–21.

Young, J. E., Rygh, J. L., Weinberger, A. D., & Beck, A. T. (2014). Cognitive therapy for depression. In D. H. Barlow, *Clinical handbook of psychological disorders* (5th ed., Chap. 7). New York: Guilford Press.

Young, K. S. (2017). The evolution of internet addiction. *Addictive Behaviors, 64,* 229–230.

Young, K. S., LeBeau, R. T., Niles, A. N., Hsu, K. J., Burklund, L. J., Mesri, B., . . . Craske, M. G. (2019). Neural connectivity during affect labeling predicts treatment response to psychological therapies for social anxiety disorder. *Journal of Affective Disorders, 242,* 105–110.

Young, M. E., Bell, Z. E., & Fristad, M. A. (2016). Validation of a brief structured interview: The Children's Interview for Psychiatric Syndromes (ChIPS). *Journal of Clinical Psychology in Medical Settings, 23*(4), 327–340.

Young, L., & Kemper, K. J. (2013). Integrative care for pediatric patients with pain. *Journal of Alternative and Complementary Medicine, 19*(7), 627–632.

Ystrom, E., Reichborn-Kjennerud, T., Neale, M. C., & Kendler, K. S. (2014). Genetic and environmental risk factors for illicit substance use and use disorders: Joint analysis of self and co-twin ratings. *Behavior Genetics, 44*(1), 1–13.

Yu, W., Chen, J., Hu, J., & Hu, J. (2018, January 24). Relationship between mental health and burden among primary caregivers of outpatients with schizophrenia. *Family Process.* [Epub ahead of print]

Yu, Y. H. (2017). Making sense of metabolic obesity and hedonic obesity. *Journal of Diabetes, 9,* 656–666.

Yu, Y., Liu, Z. W., Tang, B. W., Zhao, M., Liu, X. G., & Xiao, S. Y. (2017). Reported family burden of schizophrenia patients in rural China. *PLoS ONE, 12*(6), e0179425.

Yuenyongchaiwat, K. (2017). Cardiovascular response to mental stress tests and the prediction of blood pressure. *Indian Journal of Psychological Medicine, 39*(4), 413–417.

Yusko, D. (2008). At home, but locked in war. Retrieved from *Times-Union (Albany) Online.*

Zaejian, J. (2014, February 18). Current research on outpatient commitment laws ("Laura's Law" in California). *Mad in America.* Retrieved from https://www.madinamerica.com.

Zafar, S., Shafiq, M., Younas, N., Schmitz, M., Ferrer, I., & Zerr, I. (2017). Prion protein interactome: Identifying novel targets in slowly and rapidly progressive forms of Alzheimer's disease. *Journal of Alzheimer's Disease, 59*(1), 265–275.

Zalsman, G., Hawton, K., Wasserman, D., van Heeringen, K., Arensman, E., Sarchiapone, M., . . . Zohar, J. (2016). Suicide prevention strategies revisited: 10-year systematic review. *Lancet Psychiatry, 3*(7), 646–659.

Zanarini, M. C., Temes, C. M., Ivey, A. M., Cohn, D. M., Conkey, L. C., Frankenburg, F. R., & Fitzmaurice, G. M. (2017). The 10-year course of adult aggression toward others in patients with borderline personality disorder and axis II comparison subjects. *Psychiatry Research, 252,* 134–138.

Zandersen, M., & Pamas, J. (2018, January 24). Identity disturbance, feelings of emptiness, and the boundaries of the schizophrenia spectrum. *Schizophrenia Bulletin.* [Epub ahead of print]

Zannas, A. (2014, October 18). Why depression and aging are linked to increased disease risk. *European College of Neuropsychopharmacology.*

Zannas, A. S., & West, A. E. (2014). Epigenetics and the regulation of stress vulnerability and resilience. *Neuroscience, 264,* 157–170.

Zarbo, C., Tasca, G. A., Cattafi, F., & Compare, A. (2015). Integrative psychotherapy works. *Frontiers in Psychology, 6,* 2021.

Zarzar, T., Sheitman, B., Cook, A., & Robbins, B. (2018). Reducing length of acute inpatient hospitalization using a residential stepdown model for patients with serious mental illness. *Community Mental Health Journal.* [Manuscript in press]

Zeigler-Hill, V., Besser, A., Morag, J., & Campbell, W. K. (2016). The Dark Triad and sexual harassment proclivity. *Personality and Individual Differences, 89,* 47–54.

Zemore, S. E. (2017). Implications for future research on drivers of change and alternatives to Alcoholics Anonymous. *Addiction, 112*(6), 940–942.

Zerbe, K. J. (2017). Feminist psychodynamic psychotherapy, Part 2: A perspective from practice. *Eating Disorders Review, 28*(1). Retrieved from eatingdisordersreview.com.

Zerbe, K. J. (2008). *Integrated treatment of eating disorders beyond the body betrayed.* New York: W. W. Norton.

Zerbe, K. J. (2010). Psychodynamic therapy for eating disorders. In C. M. Grilo & J. E. Mitchell (Eds.), *The treatment of eating disorders: A clinical handbook* (pp. 339–358). New York: Guilford Press.

Zerwas, S., Lund, B C., Von Holle, A., Thornton, L. M., Berrettini, W. H., Brandt, H., . . . Bulik. C. M. (2013). Factors associated with recovery from anorexia nervosa. *Journal of Psychiatric Research, 47*(7), 972–979.

Zeschel, E., Bingmann, T., Bechdolf, A., Krüger-Oezguerdal, S., Correll, C. U., Leopold, K., . . . Juckel, G. (2015). Temperament and prodromal symptoms prior to first manic/hypomanic episodes: Results from a pilot study. *Journal of Affective Disorders, 173,* 339–344.

Zhang, X., Norton, J., Carriere, I., Ritchie, K., Chaudieu, I., & Ancelin, M. L. (2015). Generalized anxiety in community-dwelling elderly: Prevalence and clinical characteristics. *Journal of Affective Disorders, 172,* 24–29.

Zhang, X., Zhang, J., Procter, N., Chen, X., Su, Y., Lou, F., & Cao, F. (2017). Suicidal ideation and psychological strain among patients diagnosed with stomach cancer: The mediation of psychopathological factors. *Journal of Nervous and Mental Disease, 205,* 550–557.

Zhao, Y., He, A., Zhu, F., Ding, M., Hao, J., Fan, Q., . . . Ma, X. (2018). Integrating genome-wide association study and expression quantitative trait locus study identifies multiple genes and gene sets associated with schizophrenia. *Progress in Neuro-Psychopharmacology and Biological Psychiatry, 81,* 50–54.

Zheng, F., Liu, Y., Yuan, Z., Gao, X., He, Y., Liu, X., . . . Qiu, J. (2018, April 20). Age-related changes in cortical and subcortical structures of healthy adult brains: A surface-based morphometry study. *Journal of Magnetic Resonance Imaging.* [Epub ahead of print]

Zhou, E. S., & Bober, S. L. (2017). Treating sexual problems in cancer patients and survivors. In Z. D. Peterson, *The Wiley-Blackwell handbook of sex therapy* (Chap. 23, pp. 369–388). Hoboken, NJ: Wiley-Blackwell.

Zhou, S. G., Hou, Y. F., Liu, D., & Zhang, X. Y. (2017). Effect of cognitive behavioral therapy versus interpersonal psychotherapy in patients with major depressive disorder: A meta-analysis of randomized controlled trials. *Chinese Medical Journal, 130*(23), 2844–2851.

Zhu, Q., Yu, X., Wu, Z., Lu, F., & Yuan, Y. (2018). Antipsychotic drug poisoning monitoring of clozapine in urine by using coffee ring effect based surface-enhanced Raman spectroscopy. *Analytica Chimica Acta, 1014,* 64–70.

Zimbardo, P. (1976). *Rational paths to madness.* Presentation at Princeton University, Princeton, NJ.

Zucker, K. J. (2010). Gender identity and sexual orientation. In M. K. Dulcan (Ed.), *Dulcan's textbook of child and adolescent psychiatry* (pp. 543–552). Arlington, VA: American Psychiatric Publishing.

Zucker, K. J., & Bradley, S. J. (1995). *Gender identity disorder and psychosexual problems in children and adolescents.* New York: Guilford Press.

Zucker, R. A., Ellis, D. A., Bingham, C. R., & Fitzgerald, H. E. (1996). The development of alcoholic subtypes: Risk variation among alcoholic families during early childhood. *Alcohol Health and Research World, 20,* 46–54.

Zucker, R. A., Hicks, B. M., & Heitzeg, M. M. (2016). Alcohol use and the alcohol use disorders over the life course: A cross-level developmental review. In D. Cicchetti (Ed.), *Developmental psychopathology, Vol. 3, Maladaptation and psychopathology* (Chap. 18, pp. 793–832). Hoboken, NJ: John Wiley Sons.

Credits

Permission has been given to republish excerpts on the pages listed from the following sources (**bold** page numbers indicate the locations of the excerpts in this text).

Chapter 1

page 6: Frank, Jerome D., M.D., Ph.D. *Persuasion and Healing: A Comparative Study of Psychotherapy.* pp. 2–3. © 1961, 1973 The Johns Hopkins University Press.

Chapter 2

page 36: Spitzer, R. L., Skodol, A., Gibbon, M., & Williams, J. B. W. (1983). *Psychopathology: A case book.* New York: McGraw-Hill; **page 46:** Wolberg, L. R. (1967). *The technique of psychotherapy.* WB Saunders Co. Elsevier Health Science Books, p. 662; **page 51:** Republished with permission of Guilford Publications from Beck, A. T., Rush, A. J., Shaw, B. F., & Emery, G., *Cognitive therapy of depression* (1979). Copyright © 1979 Guilford Publications; permission conveyed through Copyright Clearance Center, Inc.; **page 57:** Snyder, W. V. (1947). *Casebook of non-directive counseling.* Boston: Houghton Mifflin, pp. 2–24; **page 59:** Keen, E. (1970). *Three faces of being: Toward an existential clinical psychology.* New York: Meredith Corp., p. 200. (Reprinted by permission of Irvington Publishers); **page 64:** Sheras, P. & Worchel, S. (1979). *Clinical psychology: A social psychological approach.* New York: Van Nostrand, pp. 108–110.

Chapter 3

page 79: Aiken, L. R. (1985). *Psychological testing and assessment* (5th ed.). Boston: Allyn & Bacon, p. 372.

Chapter 4

pages 107 and 110: Ellis, Albert. (1962). *Reason and emotion in psychotherapy.* Secaucus, NJ: Lyle Stuart. Copyright © 1962. All rights reserved. Reprinted by arrangement with Kensington Publishing Corp., www.kensingtonbooks.com; **page 110:** Ellis, A. (1962). *Reason and emotion in psychotherapy.* Secaucus, NJ: Lyle Stuart; **page 113:** Melville, 1978, p. 59; **page 117:** Marks, I. M. (1977). Phobias and obsessions: Clinical phenomena in search of a laboratory model. In J. Maser & M. Seligman (Eds.), *Psychopathology: Experimental models.* New York: Worth Publishers, p. 192; **page 118:** Hogan, R. A. "The implosive technique." *Behaviour Research and Therapy* 6 (1968), pp. 423–31. Copyright © 1968. Republished with permission of Elsevier Science and Technology Journals; permission conveyed through Copyright Clearance Center, Inc.; **page 119:** Agras, W. S. (1985). *Panic: Facing fears, phobias, and anxiety.* New York: Worth Publishers. Reprinted with permission; **page 124:** LeCroy, C. W., & Holschuch, J. (2012). *First person accounts of mental illness and recovery.* Hoboken, NJ: Wiley; **page 129:** Spitzer, R. L., Skodol, A., Gibbon, M., & Williams, J. B. W. (1981). *DSM-III case book* (1st ed.). Washington, DC: American Psychiatric Press; **page 131:** Emmelkamp, P. M. (1982). Exposure in vivo treatments. In A. Goldstein & D. Chambless (Eds.), *Agoraphobia: Multiple perspectives on theory and treatment.* New York: Wiley. **page 134:** Marks, I. M. (1987). *Fears, phobias and rituals: Panic, anxiety and their disorders.* New York: Oxford University Press, p. 371.

Chapter 5

page 139: National Center for PTSD 2008 Appendix A. Case examples from Operation Iraqi Freedom. *Iraq War Clinician Guide.* Washington, DC: Department of Veteran Affairs, http://www.ptsd.va.gov/professional/materials/manuals/iraq-war-clinician-guide.asp; **page 160:** James 1890, pp. 391–393; *Principles of psychology* (Vol. 1). New York: Holt, Rinehart & Winston; **page 168:** Kluft, 1988, p. 580; The dissociative disorders. In J. Talbott, R. Hales, & S. Yudofsky (Eds.), *Textbook of psychiatry.* Washington, DC: American Psychiatric Press.

Chapter 6

page 173: From *Willow Weep for Me: A Black Woman's Journey Through Depression* by Meri Nana-Ama Danquah. Copyright © 1998 by Meri Nana-Ama Danquah. Used by permission of W. W. Norton & Company, Inc., and by permission of Anne Edelstein Literary Agency. All rights reserved; **page 175:** Williams, T. M. (2008) p. 9; *Black pain: It just looks like we're not hurting.* New York: Scribner; **page 184:** Excerpt from "An Episodic Illness Turns Chronic" in *Anatomy of an Epidemic: Magic Bullets, Psychiatric Drugs, and the Astonishing Rise of Mental Illness in America* by Robert Whitaker, copyright © 2010 by Robert Whitaker. Used by permission of Crown Books, an imprint of the Crown Publishing Group, a division of Random House LLC. All rights reserved. Any third party use of this material, outside of this publication, is prohibited. Interested parties must apply directly to Penguin Random House LLC for permission; **page 188:** Arieti & Bemporad, 1978, pp. 275–284. *Severe and mild depression: The psychotherapeutic approach.* New York: Basic Books; **page 191:** Fieve 1975; *Moodswing.* New York: Morrow; **page 191:** Spitzer, R. L., Skodol, A., Gibbon, M., & Williams, J. B. W. (1983). *Psychopathology: A case book.* New York: McGraw-Hill; **page 194:** Republished with permission of Guilford Publications from Beck, A. T., Rush, A. J., Shaw, B. F., & Emery, G., *Cognitive therapy of depression* (1979). Copyright © 1979 Guilford Publications; permission conveyed through Copyright Clearance Center, Inc.; **page 197:** Republished with permission of Transaction Aldine, from *The silent language of psychotherapy: Social reinforcement of unconscious processes,* Beier & Young, second edition, 1984; permission conveyed through Copyright Clearance Center, Inc.; **page 203:** *British Journal of General Practice.* Sep 1, 2006; 56(530): 726–728. On madness: a personal account of rapid cycling bipolar disorder. By Anonymous; **page 207:** Excerpt from *An Unquiet Mind* by Kay Redfield Jamison, copyright © 1995 by Kay Redfield Jamison. Used by permission of Alfred A. Knopf, an imprint of the Knopf Doubleday Publishing Group, a division of Random House LLC. All rights reserved.

Chapter 7

page 211: Yusko, D. (2008). *At home, but locked in war.* Retrieved from: Times Union (Albany) Online. Copyright © 2008. Reprinted by permission of the Times Union; **page 219:** Shneidman, E. S. (1987, March). At the point of no return. *Psychology Today,* p. 56; **page 226:** Berman, A. L. (1986). Helping suicidal adolescents: Needs and responses. In C. A. Corr & J. N. McNeil (Eds.), *Adolescence and death.* New York: Springer; **page 234:** Shneidman, E. S. (1985). *Definition of suicide.* New York: Wiley.

Chapter 8

page 239: Excerpt from Savino, Adria C., and Fordtran, John S., "Factitious Disease: Clinical Lessons from Case Studies at Baylor University Medical Center," *Baylor University Medical Center Proceedings* 19.3 (July 2006). Copyright © 2006, Baylor University Medical Center. Reprinted by permission; **page 243:** Spitzer, R. L., Skodol, A., Gibbon, M., & Williams, J. B. W. (1981). *DSM-III case book: A learning companion to the diagnostic and statistical manual of mental disorders* (1st ed.). Washington, DC: American Psychiatric Press; **page 244:** Green, S. A. (1985). *Mind and body: The psychology of physical illness.* Washington, DC: American Psychiatric Press.

Chapter 9

page 266: Raviv, S. (2010). *Being Ana: a memoir of anorexia nervosa.* Bloomington: iUniverse; **page 267:** Bruch, H. (1973). *Eating disorders: Obesity, anorexia nervosa and the person within.* New York: Basic Books; **page 269:** Hall, L., with Cohn, L. (1980). *Eat without fear.* Santa Barbara, CA: Gürze; **page 275:** Bruch, H. (1978). *The golden cage: The enigma of anorexia nervosa.* Cambridge, MA: Harvard University Press; **page 279:** Zerbe, K. J. (2008). *Integrated treatment of eating disorders beyond the body betrayed.* New York: W. W. Norton; **pages 284, 285:** Republished with permission of Guilford Publications, from Strober, M., & Yager, J., A developmental perspective on the treatment of anorexia nervosa in adolescents. In D. M. Garner & P. E. Garfinkel (Eds.), *Handbook of Psychotherapy for anorexia nervosa and bulimia* (1985). Copyright © 1985

Guilford Publications; permission conveyed through Copyright Clearance Center, Inc.

Chapter 10

page 294: Spitzer, R. L., Skodol, A., Gibbon, M., & Williams, J. B. W. (1983). *Psychopathology: A case book.* New York: McGraw-Hill; **page 304:** Hart, C. & Ksir, C. (2013). *Drugs, society, and human behavior.* New York: McGraw-Hill Education.

Chapter 11

Pages 334, 342: Spitzer, R. L., Skodol, A., Gibbon, M., & Williams, J. B. W. (1983). *Psychopathology: A case book.* New York: McGraw-Hill; **page 337:** Rosen, R. C., & Rosen, L. R. (1981). *Human sexuality.* New York: Knopf; **page 350:** Coskun, M., & Ozturk, M. (2013). Excerpt from p. 200 in "Sexual Fetishism in Adolescence: Report of Two Cases." *Düsünen Adam: The Journal of Psychiatry and Neurological Sciences* 26.2, pp. 199–205. Copyright © 2013. Reprinted by permission; **page 354:** Janus, S. S., & Janus, C. L. (1993). *The Janus report on sexual behavior.* New York: Wiley. Reprinted with permission of the Janus estate.

Chapter 12

pages 363, 364: Arieti, S. (1974). *Interpretation of schizophrenia.* New York: Basic Books; **page 368:** Anonymous, "First person account: Social, economic, and medical effects of schizophrenia." Republished with permission of Oxford University Press from *Schizophrenia Bulletin* 22.1 (1996), pp. 183–85; permission conveyed through Copyright Clearance Center, Inc.; **page 380:** Excerpt from "Anecdotal Thoughts" in *Anatomy of an Epidemic: Magic Bullets, Psychiatric Drugs, and the Astonishing Rise of Mental Illness in America* by Robert Whitaker, copyright © 2010 by Robert Whitaker. Used by permission of Crown Books, an imprint of the Crown Publishing Group, a division of Random House LLC. All rights reserved. Any third party use of this material, outside of this publication, is prohibited. Interested parties must apply directly to Penguin Random House LLC for permission; **page 383:** Comer, R. (1973). Therapy interviews with a schizophrenic patient. Unpublished manuscript.

Chapter 13

pages 403, 418, 421, 425: Millon, T. (2011). *Disorders of personality: Introducing a DSM/ICD spectrum from normal to abnormal* (3rd ed.). Hoboken, NJ: John Wiley & Sons. Copyright © 2011. Reproduced with permission of John Wiley & Sons, Inc. [ISBN: 9780470040935]; **page 406:** Hare, R. D. (1993). *Without conscience: The disturbing world of the psychopaths among us.* New York: Pocket Books. Copyright Guilford Press. Reprinted with permission of The Guilford Press; **page 410:** Sam Vaknin, *Malignant Self-Love* (Narcissus Publications, 2015). Copyright © 1999–2013 by Lidija Rangelovska.

Chapter 14

pages 435, 444, 455: Republished with permission of South-Western College Publishing, a division of Cengage Learning, from *Casebook in child behavior disorders,* Kearney, C. A., 5th ed. (2013); permission conveyed through Copyright Clearance Center, Inc.; **page 450:** Gelfand, D. M., Jenson, W. R., & Drew, C. J. (1982). *Understanding child behavior disorders.* New York: Holt, Rinehart & Winston; **page 460:** Bogdan, R., & Taylor, S. (1976, January). The judged, not the judges: An insider's view of mental retardation. *American Psychologist, 31*(91), 47–52.

Chapter 15

page 471: Heston, Leonard L. (1992). Excerpts from the book *Mending Minds: A Guide to the New Psychiatry of Depression, Anxiety, and Other Serious Mental Disorders* by Leonard L. Heston. Copyright © 1991 by Leonard L. Heston. Used by permission of Henry Holt and Company. All rights reserved; **page 474:** Hinrichsen, G. A. (1999). Interpersonal psychotherapy for late-life depression. In M. Duffy (Ed.), *Handbook of counseling and psychotherapy with older adults.* New York: Wiley; **page 482:** Excerpt from *The Forgetting: Alzheimer's: Portrait of an Epidemic* by David Shenk, copyright © 2001, 2002 by David Shenk. Used by permission of ICM Partners and by permission of Doubleday, an imprint of the Knopf Doubleday Publishing Group, a division of Penguin Random House LLC. All rights reserved. Any third party use of this material, outside of this publication, is prohibited. Interested parties must apply directly to Penguin Random House LLC for permission.

Chapter 16

page 501: Coleman, L. (1984). *The reign of error: Psychiatry, authority, and law.* Boston: Beacon. Copyright 1984, Lee Coleman. Used by permission.

Name Index

Subject Index

Note: Page numbers followed by f and t indicate figures and tables, respectively.